A DICTIONARY OF
MODERN
ENGLISH USAGE

H. W. FOWLER

A DICTIONARY OF
MODERN
ENGLISH USAGE

Edited with an Introduction and Notes by
DAVID CRYSTAL

OXFORD
UNIVERSITY PRESS

OXFORD

UNIVERSITY PRESS

Great Clarendon Street, Oxford OX2 6DP

Oxford University Press is a department of the University of Oxford.
It furthers the University's objective of excellence in research, scholarship,
and education by publishing worldwide in

Oxford New York

Auckland Cape Town Dar es Salaam Hong Kong Karachi
Kuala Lumpur Madrid Melbourne Mexico City Nairobi
New Delhi Shanghai Taipei Toronto

With offices in

Argentina Austria Brazil Chile Czech Republic France Greece
Guatemala Hungary Italy Japan Poland Portugal Singapore
South Korea Switzerland Thailand Turkey Ukraine Vietnam

Oxford is a registered trade mark of Oxford University Press
in the UK and in certain other countries

Published in the United States
by Oxford University Press Inc., New York

A Dictionary of Modern English Usage first published 1926
This edition first published 2009

British Library Cataloguing in Publication Data

Data available

Library of Congress Cataloging-in-Publication Data

Library of Congress Control Number: 2009921241

Typeset by Cepha Imaging Private Ltd., Bangalore, India
Printed in Great Britain by
Clays Ltd., St Ives plc

ISBN 978-0-19-953534-7

3

CONTENTS

INTRODUCTION

No book had more influence on twentieth-century attitudes to the English language in Britain than Henry Fowler's *Dictionary of Modern English Usage*. Within a few years, people no longer felt it necessary even to mention the title and talked simply of 'Fowler'. Adjectives soon followed—*Fowlerian, Fowlerish, Fowleresque*—and he eventually received the ultimate linguistic accolade, of being turned into a common noun. The practice continues. In February 2008 William F. Buckley wrote a piece for the United Press Syndicate on the verbal traps used by Obama and Clinton in the race for the democratic nomination: it was entitled 'A Fowler's of Politics'.

How did the *Dictionary* come to be written? The memorial note at the front of the book tells us that Henry and his brother Frank began to plan the book together in 1911. It was a curious arrangement. They were committed to working on *The Pocket Oxford Dictionary*, the successor to the *Concise Oxford Dictionary*, which they had completed that year. But Henry was horrified at the thought of the drudgery involved in compiling another dictionary, and wanted to devote his linguistic energies to something more creative. The brothers therefore agreed that Frank would work on the *Pocket* and Henry on a different kind of book, and they would exchange roles after each had completed a quarter or so of their respective texts—that is, if Henry could bring himself to being a lexicographer again. Henry would often comment on his 'misolexicography', as he put it: 'I am no true lexicographer', he wrote in a letter to his Oxford publisher in his seventies, saying that the only parts of the science of language he cared about were 'grammar & idiom'.

In fact, the idea for the book had first come up in 1907, following the warm reception given to *The King's English* the year before. The publishers were interested in a follow-up companion, and Henry responded with the suggestion that they write something in which 'approval & condemnation [would be] less stingily dealt out than has been possible in the official atmosphere of a complete dictionary'. They first proposed a large idioms dictionary, but this was turned down. They then suggested a shorter book which would warn 'against the unidiomatic', and this was welcomed. Oxford University Press referred to it as the 'Reduced Idioms Dictionary', and later as 'the Perfect Englishspeaker's Companion'. Following lengthy discussions with the Press over the kind of information to be included, the scope was widened to include observations on spelling and pronunciation.

Henry had completed only about a quarter of the book when the First World War began, and he and Frank—despite their ages—enlisted. When the War ended, he tried to work on it again, but, following Frank's death in 1918, he found his time totally taken up with the need to complete the *Pocket Dictionary*, which he eventually sent to the Press in 1922. He was relieved then to be able to return to what he called his 'general vade-mecum of English writing'. The Society for Pure English had been established in 1913, but was forced to abandon its plans until what it called the 'national distraction' of the War was over. When it began publishing its Tracts after the War, the series contained several of the longer articles Fowler was preparing for his book. He eventually sent it to press at the end of 1923. A move from Guernsey to Somerset led to a considerable delay in processing the proofs, and it took another three years before the *Dictionary* saw the light of day. It was published on 22 April 1926.

The Climate of the Time

Fowler's life coincided with a remarkable period in British linguistic history. The growth of comparative philology in the early nineteenth century had led to an explosion of interest in the history of language and languages, and one of the consequences was the increased study of English and its regional varieties. The Early English Text Society was founded in 1864. The English Dialect Society began publishing its regional volumes in 1873. The International Phonetic Association was formed in France in 1886 and presented its first phonetic alphabet two years later. Daniel Jones, who would become Britain's best-known phonetician, published the first edition of his *English Pronouncing Dictionary* in 1917. Most importantly, the Philological Society (established in the year Fowler was born) was planning its first major project in lexicography. It was eventually entrusted to James Murray, who in 1879 began the gargantuan task of compiling the *New English Dictionary*—which would appear, over fifty years later, as the *Oxford English Dictionary*. Fascicles of different letters were to be published from 1884, and Fowler kept abreast of them.

It was also a great age of individualists. In 1873 Isaac Pitman founded his Phonetic Institute in Bath, advocating the importance of short-hand and spelling reform. In 1878 the Dorset writer William Barnes made his case for maintaining the Anglo-Saxon character of English in his *Outline of English Speech-Craft*. And a few years later George Bernard Shaw took up the cudgels on behalf of spelling reform, sim-plified punctuation, and other language projects, one of which—the application of phonetics in elocution—received a dramatic interpret-ation in the form of *Pygmalion* in 1914 (with Daniel Jones providing the inspiration for Henry Higgins). In a literary context, several nov-elists, such as Dickens and Hardy, painted word-pictures full of the realities of everyday speech. As a lexicographical individualist, Fowler was in good company.

The focus on everyday speech in all its bewildering diversity was in sharp contrast to the educational ethos of the period, with its concen-tration on written texts, Classical languages, formal grammar, and the combination of prescriptive ('do') and proscriptive ('do not') rules governing 'correct' usage. There was a concern to maintain the lin-guistic values that had been established by the language scholars of the late eighteenth century, such as Bishop Lowth, John Walker, and Samuel Johnson, as part of a trend to give linguistic identity to an educated class within Britain. The Society for Pure English (SPE) made this very clear in its opening Tract (October 1919):

The ideal of the Society is that our language in its future development should be controlled by the forces and processes which have formed it in the past; that it should keep its English character, and that the new elements added to it should be in harmony with the old.

The concern was real. Several other European countries, the SPE members observed, had men of letters to guide the development of language, whereas 'the English language, which is now rapidly spread-ing over the world, is subject to no such guidance, and to very little intelligent criticism'. Moreover, the old methods of training were under threat. In 1890, grammar had been dropped as a compulsory subject in the school curriculum, and in 1921 the Newbolt Report on the teaching of English went so far as to say that uncertainty about the facts of usage made it 'impossible to teach English grammar in the schools'. The SPE nailed its flag to the mast: 'The Society, therefore, will place itself in opposition to certain tendencies of modern taste;

which taste it hopes gradually to modify and improve.' Both Henry and Frank are listed as members.

Fowler was thus writing at a time when the prescriptive approach to language was beginning to lose its pedagogical dominance and yet was attracting fresh levels of support from the literary elite. Revising his *Dictionary* for final publication in the early 1920s, he plainly felt the tension between the traditional focus on a small set of words, pronunciations, and grammatical usages, as indicators of 'correct' linguistic behaviour, and the diverse and changing realities of the way educated people actually used language in their everyday lives. Many of his entries comment upon it, and, as we shall see, he was not entirely sure how to deal with it. His solid educational background in English grammar, Latin, and Greek was pulling him in one direction; his considerable observational linguistic alertness was pulling him in another, urging him to recognize the huge changes in usage that were taking place in an age which, inter alia, had seen several wars, a scientific revolution (Charles Darwin's *On the Origin of Species* was published the year after he was born), the suffragette movement, and the growth of a new kind of popular press (*Daily Mail* 1896, *Daily Mirror* 1903, *Daily Sketch* 1909). Fowler was not alone in his uncertainty. The BBC, founded in 1923, debated at length the kind of English that should be used in broadcasting, and a few years later concluded that they needed to establish a committee in order to make linguistic decisions. Fowler, by contrast, decided to go it alone, though he frequently defers to the growing files of the *OED*, to which his earlier lexicographical work for the Press granted him privileged access.

The tension Fowler reflects in the *Dictionary* became a major issue in the later decades of the century. Following the emergence of linguistics as a science, attitudes polarized into an opposition between descriptive and prescriptive approaches to language study—an opposition which coloured all popular work on language after the 1950s. With the eventual demise of the prescriptive approach in British schools, the polarity is less prominent today, but it is still present, and prescriptive works do continue to appear alongside the descriptive treatments of language which characterize modern grammars and dictionaries. Any appraisal of Fowler thus has to be viewed from the perspective of this polarity.

Fowler is usually hailed as the supreme arbiter of usage, and his *Dictionary* as the apotheosis of the prescriptive approach. But anyone who reads the whole work soon finds that this is a considerable over-simplification. He turns out to be far more sophisticated in his analysis of language than most people realize. Several of his entries display a concern for descriptive accuracy which would do any modern linguist proud. And although the book is full of his personal likes and dislikes, his prescriptivism—unlike that practised by many of his disciples—is usually intelligent and reasoned. He readily condemns rules which he considers to be absurdly artificial—something which later pedants tend to ignore. I have encountered people who inveigh against the split infinitive, prepositions at the end of sentences, and opening a sentence with *but*—to take just three topics—and who cite *Modern English Usage* in their support, evidently unaware of Fowler's strong condemnation of their pedantry.

The Importance of Idiom

If there is one principle on which Fowler places particular reliance, it is the notion of 'idiom'. Repeatedly he justifies a usage by referring to 'English idiom', by which he seems to have in mind a mixture of cultural and linguistic factors. Idiom, he says (at **idiom**), is

any form of expression that, as compared with other forms in which the principles of abstract grammar, if there is such a thing, would have allowed the idea in question to be clothed, has established itself as the particular way preferred by Englishmen & therefore presumably characteristic of them. . . . [It is] the same as natural or racy or unaffected English.

How is this notion to be operationalized? As the quotation illustrates, not by referring to prescriptive ('abstract') grammars. It is possible, he says, to be 'idiomatic but ungrammatical', and whenever there is a conflict, idiom should take precedence. For example, in discussing usages like *such a small matter* (at **such, 5**), he comments 'the objectors have grammar on their side', but adds: 'Shall we then be meek & mend our ways at their bidding?' And he answers: 'Why, no, not wholesale,' for our response should depend on our sense of idiom.

Idiom for Fowler is not a matter of grammar, but of frequency of use. Here are three examples of his reasoning, in relation to syntax, pronunciation, and spelling. Discussing the usage *not unconnected* (at **not, 2**), he observes: 'the very popularity of the idiom in English is proof enough that there is something in it congenial to the

English temperament'. At **PRONUNCIATION** he says 'we deserve not praise but censure if we decline to accept the popular pronunciation of popular words'. And he defends the spelling of *halyard* 'not on etymological grounds, but as established by usage', adding the wry comment, 'tilting against established perversions . . . is vanity in more than one sense' (at **halyard**).

This sounds as if Fowler is nailing his flag firmly to the usage mast, and indeed several entries reinforce this view. At **domestic**, 'usage is irresistible'; at **EM**-, 'the usage of most writers' is said to be 'sensible & democratic'; at **hotchpot** he chooses a usage because it is 'the prevailing form'. And he is aware that 'usage, also, changes in such matters with time' (at **than, 6**). There is a fuller statement at **able, 4**:

The words & usages to which exception is taken should be tested not by the original Latin practice, nor by the subsequent French practice, nor by the English practice of any particular past period . . . but by what inquiry may reveal as the now current conception of how words in -*ble* are to be formed & what they may mean.

But, as the word 'perversions' in the previous paragraph suggests, along with phrases elsewhere such as 'the despotism of usage' (at -**EN VERBS FROM ADJECTIVES,** p. 142), all is not as it seems. When Fowler encounters a usage he does not like, his language alters, and we find negative phrasing alongside a recognition of widespread usage. Thus we find at **ELEGANT VARIATION** (p. 131), 'There are few literary faults so widely prevalent'; and at **entertain** the use of *entertain to* (instead of *at*) is said to have become 'stock reporters' English', observing that 'the reporters themselves are beyond cure'.

It is possible to sense the tension between Fowler's instinct as a linguistic observer and his urge to reflect the canons of a prescriptive age. This is what he has to say on the choice between *that* and *which* (at **that (rel. pron.), 1**, p. 634):

What grammarians say should be has perhaps less influence on what shall be than even the more modest of them realize; usage evolves itself little disturbed by their likes & dislikes. And yet the temptation to show how better use might have been made of the material to hand is sometimes irresistible.

He often does not resist, as with a particular usage of **super**-:

[it] is so evidently convenient that it is vain to protest when others indulge in it, & so evidently barbarous that it is worth while to circumvent it oneself when one can do so without becoming unintelligible.

And, in relation to one of Fowler's pet hates, the use of *their* with a singular, he says (at **they, 1**):

the grammarians are likely, nevertheless, to have their way on the point . . . few good modern writers would flout the grammarians so conspicuously.

The circularity is noteworthy: because only 'good' writers never use *their* with a singular, the use of *their* with a singular will be found only in 'bad' writers.

The problem in reading Fowler is that one never knows which way he is going to vote. Is he going to allow a usage because it is widespread, or is he going to condemn it for the same reason? The same kind of circularity can be sensed at **claim**, where a usage 'now of daily currency' is nonetheless said to be 'contrary to British idiom'. And at **SLIPSHOD EXTENSION** the usages listed are all widely used, but that does not save them:

he is injuring the language, however unconsciously, both by helping to break down a serviceable distinction, & by giving currency to a mere token word in the place of one that is alive.

How does Fowler know what is idiomatic? Writing in an age where there were no corpora of examples, he inevitably relies on his own intuition and on serendipitous encounters, as in his entry at **Mahomet**, which begins with 'I asked a middle-aged lady'. We are not usually told who his informants are. Preferences in usage are vaguely identified: 'most of us' prefer the word *meal* (at **collation**); the objection to *determinedly* is 'very general' (at **determinately**). The impression the entries give is that Fowler considers to be idiomatic what he himself uses. Usages he does not like are given such labels as 'ugly' (e.g. at **historicity**) or even 'evil' (e.g. at **respectively**). If asked to defend this, he would doubtless say 'Tenacious clinging to the right of private judgement is an English trait that a mere grammarian may not presume to deprecate' (at **EM-**).

The Problem of Consistency

Private judgement is certainly what we find throughout this book. But the trouble with private judgement, as opposed to a judgement based on sound linguistic principles, is that it leads inevitably to a lack of consistency. We can see this especially in the way Fowler handles semantic change. It is a fact of language that words change their meaning over time, developing new senses and blurring older senses. The historical listings in the *OED* show that the vast majority of the non-technical words in the language have developed in this way. If usage is really an arbiter, then it is not a case of such changes being either good or bad: they merely reflect the way in which people want to talk about things. There would be no change at all if people did not think it useful. But many people dislike such change, fearing that the language is losing an important focus or a valuable distinction. Which view does Fowler adopt?

Different entries give different answers. At **proposition** he asserts 'that there is nothing unsound in principle about the development of sense', but at **phenomenal** he condemns a sense development which has had 'unreasonable vogue' and recommends that 'believers in sound English may deliver their attack upon such usages with hope of success'. **Oblivious** is a word 'badly misused' because of its semantic shift, but the new meaning of **obnoxious** should be recognized because it is so comprehensible. At **forceful**, he is hotly against the coming together of *forceful* and *forcible* ('Such writers injure the language'); but at **circumstance**, people who object to *under the circumstances*, on the grounds that it should be *in the circumstances*, are said to be 'puerile'. Or again: it is impossible to discern a coherent principle in his treatment of the *-ence|-ancy* variants. The distinction between *permanence* and *permanency* is praised (at **permanence**), but that between *pertinence* and *pertinency* is not (at **pertinence**). He allows the distinction between *radiance* and *radiancy* (at **radiance**) on the grounds that, though the latter is rare, it is 'metrically useful or rhetorically effective'; but he does not allow this criterion in such cases as *pertinency*.

It is this unpredictability of opinion which makes it difficult to generalize about Fowler. He is strongly against longer forms of words (at **LONG VARIANTS**) but he nonetheless supports *pacificist* against *pacifist*. At **NOVELESE**, he asserts that writers 'must be varied' and avoid clichés, then in the next entry, **NOVELTY-HUNTING**, says that it is 'a confession of weakness' to say 'something new' when a tested word exists. In his discussion of **SAXONISM**, his conclusion is sound ('conscious deliberate Saxonism is folly') and his list of criteria admirable: the choice or rejection of particular words should depend not on their descent but on considerations of expressiveness, intelligibility, brevity, euphony, or ease of handling. But repeatedly we find him relying on the very notion he is here rejecting: descent (i.e. etymology). For example, at **forlorn hope**, we read 'it is well to keep the original meaning in mind', and at **miocene** scientists are condemned for 'the monstrosities with which scientific men . . . defile the language' because of their unawareness of Greek origins. Many other entries express strong support for the maintenance of earlier meanings of a word, such as at **aggravate**, **transpire**, and **meticulous** (a 'wicked word'). The use of *aggravate* and *aggravation* in the sense of 'annoy, vex' he says 'should be left to the uneducated. It is for the most part a feminine or childish colloquialism'. This sort of language sits uncomfortably alongside 'etymological knowledge is of less importance to writers than might be supposed' (at **TRUE & FALSE ETYMOLOGY,** p. 665). And when we see him criticizing the views of Latin scholars about English usage (at **infringe**) on the grounds that 'Latin is not English', it is difficult to know where he stands on the matter.

This last reference suggests that Fowler is against the use of a Latinate perspective in English grammar teaching. Certainly he was writing at a time when he could assume a great deal of knowledge of Latin, and many of his entries make routine reference to the quantities of Latin vowels, the Latin case system, and suchlike. He is well aware, as he says at **CASES, 2**, that 'We know that grammarians are often accused, & indeed often guilty, of fogging the minds of English children with terms & notions that are essential to the understanding of Greek & Latin syntax, but have no bearing on English'. And yet we see repeatedly a Latinate mindset at work in the *Dictionary*, as these next examples illustrate: at **exit**, he insists that with a plural subject the verb must be *exeunt*; at **I**, the usage *it is me* is called a 'lapse'; and at **us, 1** he marks the *us* of *it becomes us* as ungrammatical, preferring *we* (though admitting that this might be thought pedantic). He can be as purist as anyone when it comes to classical origins. At **a-, an-**, he insists that these prefixes should be used only with Greek stems; Latin roots are banned: '*amoral* . . . being literary, is inexcusable, & *non-moral* should be used instead'. So it remains unclear what Fowler's views really are.

There is a similar uncertainty over his approach to the relationship between spelling and pronunciation. Sometimes he is insistent on having all the letters sounded. At **fifthly** he wants to hear a separate *f* and *th*, at **foully** he tells us to 'pronounce both *ls*', and at **pneumatic**, he looks forward to the day when the *p* will be sounded: 'It is to be hoped that these silent letters may recover their voices.' On the other hand, at **often** he talks about 'uneasy half-literates who like to prove that they can spell' by pronouncing *medicine* with an *i*; at **recogni-zance** he tells us to 'pronounce rĭcŏ´n-'; and at **postscript** he recommends a pronunciation without the medial *t*. A pronunciation which follows the spelling at **turbine** is said to be 'misguided'.

Such inconsistency is typical of pedants with no formal linguistic training, but it is surprising to see it in someone who knows so much about the organizing principles of language. There are entries where Fowler displays an awareness of the way language works which is as balanced and objective as anything produced by later practitioners of linguistics. For example, he is aware of one of the fundamental principles of modern descriptive linguistics—the way speech and writing have to be judged by different criteria. At **kind**, we see him distinguishing the use of *kind of* in 'print' and 'hasty talk'; at **number, 7**, we see him identifying the issue of speech processing in subject/verb concord, and at **who & whom, 1**, we see him avoiding the kind of blanket judgement which characterizes naive prescriptivism:

The interrogative *who* is often used in talk where grammar demands *whom* . . . No further defence than 'colloquial' is needed for this.

He is also aware of the importance of stylistic level, as at **that (conj.), 2**:

the use or omission of the *t[hat]* of a substantival clause depends partly on whether the tone is elevated or colloquial.

And he regularly recognizes the relevance of formality vs informality as a factor influencing usage. But—to take this last example—he nonetheless has his doubts about some of the formality distinctions which have developed in the language. He lists several examples at **FORMAL WORDS** (e.g. *cease* vs *stop*), remarking that 'the less of such change there is the better'. From comments such as these, I conclude that, although Fowler is a brilliant observer of usage and a master-analyst, he is unable to detach himself completely from his own language upbringing. I sense a linguist inside him crying to get out, but being held back by a prescriptive conscience.

Modern thinking

The modernity of his thinking can be seen in some of his grammatical terms (at **TECHNICAL TERMS**), such as *frequentative*, and in some of his definitions. He was writing at a time before the term *morpheme* had arrived in linguistics, but that notion is clearly anticipated in his definition of *root* as 'the ultimate elements of language not admitting of analysis'. His distinction between wide and narrow senses of *complement* also looks forward to present-day accounts of complementation. His discussion of how to analyse *few* (p. 178), systematically examining the syntactic contexts in which the word appears, shows he can reason like any modern structuralist grammarian. His four syntactic criteria for the use of *very* could have come from any modern descriptive grammar (at **very**), e.g. '2. Is it used attributively (*a —— damaged reputation*) or predicatively (*the car is —— damaged*)?'

At times he is surprisingly modern. For example, those who think a notion of sentence weight is a recent innovation must think again. In his very thorough essay on **INVERSION** he observes that 'the difference must lie in the length of the subject' (p. 288), and at **POSITION OF ADVERBS, 6** he points out that '[t]he longer the adverb in proportion to the object, the more marked is the offence of interpolating it'. Another example is his explanation of the reasons for the lack of synonymy in English: at **SYNONYMS** he anticipates the discussion found in linguistically motivated work on semantics in the 1960s, referring to differences of frequency, geography, and society. His criterion of substitution ('words either of which in one or other of its acceptations can sometimes be substituted for the other without affecting the meaning of a sentence') could have been written by any structuralist linguist, as could his illustrations:

it does not matter . . . whether I say a word has 'two senses' or 'two meanings', & *sense* & *meaning* are therefore loose synonyms; but if 'He is a man of sense' is rewritten as 'He is a man of meaning', it becomes plain that *sense* & *meaning* are far from perfect synonyms.

He also knows when to stop, realizing that a linguistic state of affairs is too complicated to be handled in a book of this kind. The entry at **gerund, 3** is a good example of Fowler throwing in the towel: 'it is better not to state them [the rules]'. So is the entry at **big, great, large**: 'The differences in meaning & usage cannot be exhaustively set forth'.

There is a great deal of real wisdom in the *Dictionary*. His heart is clearly in the right place when at **LITERARY CRITICS' WORDS** he criticizes unnecessary jargon and at **TAUTOLOGY** points out the dangers to the reader ('if his author writes loosely he probably thinks loosely also'). He gives sound advice against displaying superior knowledge (at **FRENCH WORDS**). And his essay at **QUOTATION** on appropriate and inappropriate usage is one of the best in the book.

But alongside these passages of real insight we encounter entries which seem to inhabit a different linguistic planet, such as at **SUPERFLUOUS WORDS**. 'That there are such things in the language is likely to be admitted', he begins. But the notion of superfluous words needs a much more sophisticated treatment than Fowler is prepared to give it. For, it might be asked, how can a word in frequent everyday use possibly be superfluous? By definition, it must be of use to the people who use it. The notion does make some sense when it is used to describe alternative forms of a word that is coming into the language—such as the various forms of *discordant* which were being used in English in Shakespeare's time (*discordful, discordic, discordive*, etc.); but people themselves acted to control the superfluity, for within a short time the only form in use was the one we use today. Some of Fowler's examples might be considered superfluous if we ignore regional variation (as in the case of *elevator* vs *lift*), but of course we cannot ignore it, for regional linguistic identity is an important fact of life. And even within one dialect, the arrival of an alternative form may turn out to have unexpected uses: *elevator*, for example, offers a different set of phonological properties compared with *lift*; and it is easy to see how British users might want to exploit those properties, such as finding the rhythm or rhyme offered by *elevator* an appropriate choice on occasion, notwithstanding its American background. Fowler's examples teach us one thing: that it is impossible to predict, from a set of alternatives, which items are destined for a permanent place in the language and which are not. If Fowler had his way, we would no longer be able to use such words as *asset, brochure, meticulous, emotive*, and *mentality* ('a truly superfluous word'). While recognizing that some sets of words may exist in a temporary state of superfluity, therefore, it is unwise to choose between them, as Fowler does.

Back on my own linguistic planet, Fowler is often brilliant at explaining the semantic distinction between sets of lexical items. Among his best entries from the first part of the alphabet are at **ceremonial, ceremonious**; **cheerful, cheery** ('The cheerful feels & perhaps shows contentment, the cheery shows & probably feels it'); **comedy, farce, burlesque**; **commence(ment)**; **definite, definitive**; **disposal, disposition**; and **essential, necessary, requisite**. At the same time, his selection of lexical entries shows that he is not entirely living on the same planet as most of us. He includes many words that are learned or arcane to the point of obscurity: a selection from the first third of the book is **chibouk, chouse, cothurnus, curule, deuteragonist, disseise, duumvir, farouche, felloe**, and **foulard**. These are included without their rarity being raised as an issue. Nor does he stint himself: **idola fori** receives nearly two columns of discussion.

There is a strong encyclopedic bias in the book's coverage, with several sets of entries going beyond definitional necessity and giving us information about 'the world' (in Fowler's time). Some entries are purely encyclopedic (as at **MUSES**) and he sometimes actually quotes from encyclopedias (as at **fir, pine**). On the whole, he focuses on definitions, often using the *OED* as a source (as at **hart**). The result is that several of his entries resemble the synonym essays found in modern dictionaries—another instance of his being ahead of his time: there are good examples at **humour, jargon, jocose, tax, time, transparent**, and **wind**. He also occasionally provides thesaurus-type listings, such as at **sign**. At times it is possible to sense the tension that all lexicographers feel when they find themselves having to cope with concepts of a highly specialized or sensitive kind. He bravely tries to distinguish *molecule, atom, electron*, and *corpuscle* (at **molecule**), and after dealing with *socialism, communism*, and *anarchism* (at **socialism**), he adds an anxious endnote pointing out that he has only been talking about the meaning of these politically contentious terms, not their respective merits.

One of the fascinating things about the *Dictionary* is the way the encyclopedic perspective draws our attention to the time during which Fowler was writing. In his entry at **fascist** he reflects whether the words 'are to be temporary or permanent in England'; at **cinema** he thinks the forms beginning with *c-* (as opposed to *k-*) are 'destined to constant popular use'; at **federation**, he reflects on the 'proposed League of Nations' (he was writing this entry in 1918); at **INVERSION** (p. 285) he draws an (unfavourable) analogy with 'the fashionable high heels placed somewhere below the middle of the foot'. Just occasionally, the contemporary allusions let us (almost a century on) down, as in the obscure opening of **HACKNEYED PHRASES**, with its references to articles in *Punch*. The occasional references to contemporary slang (e.g. at **immense**) allow us to hear the linguistic echoes of an earlier age. And the gender differences of the time regularly raise their head: at **clever**, we read that the word 'is much misused, especially in feminine conversation'; at **irrelevant**, 'it is not difficult, with a little fishing, to extract it from ladies' and at so, **3**, he warns against 'the danger of yielding to this weakness [saying such things as *so uncertain*] ("feminine" it would have been called before the ladies had learnt to write)'.

Style and Pedantry

Fowler's own style is well worthy of study in its own right, and it is perhaps the main reason so many people have made such use of the *Dictionary*. He writes with an attractive frankness, passion, and sincerity, so that even when we disagree with him we recognize that here is someone who has the best of intentions towards the wellbeing of the language. The impression he gives is of an endearingly eccentric, schoolmasterly character, driven at times to exasperation by the infelicities of his wayward pupils, but always wanting the best for them and hoping to provide the best guidance for them in a world where society and language are undergoing rapid change. He may shake his stick at us, but we never feel we are actually going to be beaten.

Humour is not something we readily associate with the *Dictionary of Modern English Usage*, but it is difficult not to smile when we encounter entries which display a vivid and imaginative turn of phrase, especially to express his mock-suffering in the face of bad usage. Take his tintack analogy at **not, 6** (p. 384):

Not only out of its place is like a tintack loose on the floor; it might have been most serviceable somewhere else, & is capable of giving acute & undeserved pain where it is.

Or the religious analogy at the beginning of **nor**:

nor is a word that should come into our minds as we repeat the General Confession. Most of us in our time have left undone those things which we ought to have done (i.e. failed to put in *nor* when it was wanted) & done those things which we ought not to have done (i.e. thrust it in when there was no room for it).

Or the gardening analogy in the middle of **COMPOUND PREPOSITIONS**:

they are almost the worst element in modern English, stuffing up the newspaper columns with a compost of nouny abstractions.

He displays an appealing dry humour, seen for example at **DIDACTICISM** or at **FOREIGN DANGER** ('Two or three specimens follow, for those who do not like cross references'). We can sense the thin smile. And he is not averse to adopting a parodic style when he wants to (e.g. the use of 'you know' at **humanist** or of 'gentlemen' at **metaphor**). Indeed, if there is any single feature which characterizes the bulk of his writing it is his ability to blend linguistic precision with ironic commentary.

On the other hand, it has to be admitted that his own writing does not always live up to the high standard he sets himself. At **LOVE OF THE LONG WORD**, he states categorically that 'Good English does consist in the main of short words'. This is a well-recognized and desirable principle, but it is often ignored by Fowler himself. A few lines later we have, for example, 'what is here deprecated is the tendency among the ignorant to choose'; or, to take an example at random from elsewhere: 'a few of the grosser & more recurrent incongruities, connected with particular words, must suffice by way of illustration' (p. 266). He cites two examples of good usage: in one there are only four polysyllabic words out of 56 (7 per cent) and in the other twelve out of 101 (12 per cent). This suggests the goal towards which writers should strive. The percentage for Fowler (excluding the words and phrases used as examples) is usually between 30 and 40 per cent.

It is a hard life, being a prescriptive writer, for you must always be watching your back. You know that, at the first opportunity, a critic (usually another pedant) will condemn you for failing to live up to the rules you adumbrate. Fowler does his best to adopt his own stylistic principles. For example, he places prepositions at the ends of clauses whenever he can (an example: the bottom of the first column at **DOUBLE PASSIVES**, p. 121). But it is not difficult to find instances of sentences whose length or complexity make them hard to process, such as the 56-word opening sentence at **NOVELTY-HUNTING**, with its long and unwieldy subject construction, or the accumulation of negatives and qualifications at **forward(s)**: 'it is quite doubtful whether *forward* is not possible'. At **literally**, we read that we ought 'to be at pains to repudiate' the emphatic use of this word, but then we encounter it at **negotiate**, where Fowler condemns a usage which, he says, 'stamps a writer as literarily [*sic*] a barbarian'. His definition of **pleonasm** is 'the using of more words than are required to give the sense intended'; but a few lines into the entry we read 'repeated with less & less of impressiveness', where the *of* is pleonastic, by his own account.

In his entry at **PEDANTRY**, Fowler shows he is well aware of the slippery nature of this term:

my pedantry is your scholarship, his reasonable accuracy, her irreducible minimum of education, & someone else's ignorance. It is therefore not very profitable to dogmatize here on the subject; an essay would establish not what pedantry is, but only the place in the scale occupied by the author

He goes on to list a sample of pedantries, from which 'the reader who has views of his own will be able to place the book in the pedantry scale & judge what may be expected of it'. This task turns out not to be so easy, because of the inconsistencies mentioned earlier in this essay. It is never clear why some usages are dismissed in such terms as 'mere pedantry' (e.g. at **egregious**, **confidant**, **obstetric**), and yet other usages of a very similar kind are praised.

I have to confess that I remain puzzled by Fowler. How can someone assert so many sensible principles about usage and then break them so often? I applaud such statements as we read at **first, 5**, where he recognizes that some people prefer *first* to *firstly*. This is

one of the harmless pedantries in which those who like oddities because they are odd are free to indulge, provided that they abstain from censuring those who do not share the liking.

But censure, albeit often expressed in an ironic or kindly way, is what we find in most of the entries in the book. Or again, at **PURISM** we see this notion defined as 'a needless & irritating insistence on purity or correctness of speech'. But at **shall & will** he asserts: 'no formal grammar or dictionary can be held to have done its duty if it has not laid down the necessary rules'; and at **our**, he talks about 'the repulsive *their*' as an alternative to *his or her*. Or again, at **SUPERSTITIONS** we find another excellent principle. In relation to such rules as not beginning a sentence with *but*, ending a sentence with a preposition, or splitting an infinitive, he comments: 'how misleading their sweet simplicity is', and continues:

to let oneself be so far possessed by conventions whose grounds one has not examined as to take a hand in enforcing them on other people is to lose the independence of judgement that, if not so smothered, would enable one to solve the numerous problems for which there are no rules of thumb.

But if this principle were applied consistently, we would lose half the entries in the *Dictionary*.

The Status of Fowler

Despite Fowler's acknowledged status as *the* usage pundit of the twentieth century, the difficulty of using his book in a principled and systematic way led to his influence on subsequent usage and attitudes being very mixed. People bought the book in their thousands, but they did not always follow his recommendations. Judging by the references made to his *Dictionary*, he was certainly influential in focusing attention on a number of usage issues, such as *all right* vs *alright*, *different to* vs *different from*, *due to* vs *owing to*, *whatever* vs *what ever*, etc. (at **ever**), *nice* (at **VOGUE-WORDS**), *will* vs *shall*, and the need to distinguish confusible words (at **PAIRS & SNARES**). On the other hand, people largely disregarded his fierce condemnation of such issues as the position of *only* (at **only**), subject/verb concord (at **majority**), split infinitives (at **POSITION OF ADVERBS, SPLIT INFINITIVE**), end-placed prepositions (at **PREPOSITION AT END**), the use of *first* vs *firstly* (at **first**), conjunctions at the beginning of sentences (at **SUPERSTITIONS**), and the subjunctive (at **SUBJUNCTIVES**). He provides a convenient list at **FETISHES**. About half of his specific lexical recommendations were ignored, such as the use of *collocutor* instead of *interlocutor*, or *contradictious* instead of *contradictory*, or *flutist* instead of *flautist*. And in several cases of disputed usage, Fowler could not have had any influence simply because he does not deal with them: he has no separate essay on clichés, for example, nor does he express an opinion on such issues as *the reason why*, *between you and I*, *disinterested* vs *uninterested*, or the use of an apostrophe before a plural ending (*potato's*), all of which loomed large in later usage books.

It is impossible to be anything other than hugely impressed by Fowler's enthusiasm and skill as a lexicographer. The *Dictionary* is unprecedented in the range of alternative usages it presents, though we need to note that it is by no means comprehensive in its coverage. To take just three examples from the beginning of the book, he deals with *adhere* and *adhesion* but not *adherence*, and there are no entries on the distinction between *adviser* and *advisor*, or between *adapter* and *adaptor* (though *adapter* is mentioned at **-OR**). We also need to be aware that the headword-list often lacks desirable cross-references: the book contains entries which deal with issues of clarity and sentence-length, for example, but there are no headwords pointing to them.

For the entries he does include, he proves to be an excellent organizer of information, extremely thorough in his collation of relevant items (such as the way he brings together the different kinds of spelling problems in one place, pp. 555–6).

He is also an amazing collector of examples, especially from the press. He gives the impression of having extracted citations from virtually every available quality newspaper during his compiling years. But in his very thoroughness there lies a difficulty which has often been noticed. It is impossible to know just how many items from his collection he did *not* include in the *Dictionary*, but there are many entries where one feels he has tried to use the lot, resulting in entries that are overlong and overpowering. At ELEGANT VARIATION, for example, we find over five columns of instances. Fowler is perfectly well aware of his practice, for he observes that the main objective of this entry is 'to nauseate by accumulation of instances, as sweet-shop assistants are cured of larceny by cloying' (p. 132). But the result, all too often, is not what he intended. One loses sight of the wood because of the proliferation of trees.

Fowler continues to exercise a fascination on those who are interested in the English language, whether as analysts or stylists. The irony is that few people, editors aside, have read the *Dictionary* in its entirety. A dictionary is not meant to be read in that way, of course; it is there to respond serendipitously to our needs. But if we want to arrive at a balanced assessment of Fowler's contribution to the linguistic history of ideas, we need to retrace his method and his practice as fully as we can. Reading every word of Fowler is an enthralling, if often exhausting experience, but it enables us to go beyond the popular mythology and get a better sense of the intriguing personality and linguistic genius of this remarkable lexicographer.

NOTE ON THE TEXT

A Dictionary of Modern English Usage was published in 1926. It was an immediate success, selling 60,000 in its first year, and quickly establishing itself as a standard work of reference. A second edition, edited by Sir Ernest Gowers, appeared in 1965: apart from updating, Gowers pruned some of the illustrative quotations, eliminated some duplication, cut out the eight pages on French words and their pronunciation, and removed the long article on technical terms, redistributing some of its contents around the book. He also replaced the 'list of general articles' at the front of the book with a 'classified guide'. A third edition, edited by the *Oxford English Dictionary*'s editor Robert Burchfield, appeared in 1996, and was more controversially received, due to the editor's policy of introducing a more descriptive dimension into the entries. While acknowledging the greater range and scholarly depth of the new edition, critics felt that much of the spirit of the original Fowler had been lost. The Burchfield edition, however, continued to sell well in an age more interested in linguistic explanations than prescriptions, and a pocket version, edited by Robert Allen, appeared in 2003, with a second edition in 2008.

SELECT BIBLIOGRAPHY

Books by Henry Watson Fowler

More Popular Fallacies (London: Elliot Stock, 1904).

Sentence Analysis (Oxford: Clarendon Press, 1906).

Si Mihi! (London: Brown, Langham, 1907); reissued as *If Wishes Were Horses* (London: Allen & Unwin, 1929).

Between Boy and Man (London: Watts, 1908).

A Dictionary of Modern English Usage (Oxford: Clarendon Press, 1926).

Some Comparative Values (Oxford: Blackwell, 1929).

Rhymes of Darby to Joan (London: Dent, 1931).

Collaboration with Francis George Fowler

The Works of Lucian, trans. (Oxford: Clarendon Press, 1905).

The King's English (Oxford: Clarendon Press, 1906; abridged edn., 1908).

Concise Oxford Dictionary (Oxford: Clarendon Press, 1911; 2nd edn., 1929).

Pocket Oxford Dictionary (Oxford: Clarendon Press, 1924).

Collaboration with Others

Little, W., Fowler, H. W., and Coulson, J., *Shorter Oxford English Dictionary* (Oxford: Clarendon Press, 1933).

Biographies and Personal Background

McMorris, J., *The Warden of English: The Life of H. W. Fowler* (Oxford: Oxford University Press, 2001).

Murray, K. M. E., *Caught in the Web of Words: James Murray and the Oxford English Dictionary* (New Haven: Yale University Press, 1977; Oxford: Oxford University Press, 1979).

Sutcliffe, P., *The Oxford University Press: An Informal History* (Oxford: Clarendon Press, 1978).

Lexicography

Bailey, R. W. (ed.), *Dictionaries of English* (Ann Arbor: University of Michigan Press, 1987; Cambridge: Cambridge University Press, 1989).

Brewer, Charlotte, *Treasure-House of the Language: The Living OED* (New Haven: Yale University Press, 2007).

Burchfield, R. (ed.), *Studies in Lexicography* (Oxford: Clarendon Press, 1987).

Creswell, T. J., *Usage in Dictionaries and Dictionaries of Usage* (Tennessee: University of Alabama, 1975).

Hartmann, R. R. K., *Lexicography: Principles and Practice* (London: Academic Press, 1983).

—— and James, G., *Dictionary of Lexicography* (London: Routledge, 1998).

Hitchings, H., *Dr Johnson's Dictionary* (London: John Murray, 2005).

Ilson, R. (ed.), *Lexicography: An Emerging International Profession* (Manchester: Manchester University Press, 1986).

Landau, S., *Dictionaries: The Art and Craft of Lexicography* (New York: Scribner, 1984; Cambridge: Cambridge University Press, 1989).

McArthur, T., *Worlds of Reference* (Cambridge: Cambridge University Press, 1986).

Other Usage Guides

Gowers, E., *The Complete Plain Words* (London: HMSO, 1954; rev. edn. by S. Greenbaum & J. Whitcut, 1986).

Johnson, E. D., *Handbook of Good English* (New York: Washington Square Press, 1982).

Jones, Daniel, *English Pronouncing Dictionary* (1917), 16th edn. ed. P. Roach, J. Hartman, and J. Setter (Cambridge: Cambridge University Press, 2003).

Partridge, E., *Usage and Abusage* (London: Hamish Hamilton, 1947).

Peters, P., *The Cambridge Guide to English Usage* (Cambridge: Cambridge University Press, 2004).

History of English

Crystal, D., *The Cambridge Encyclopedia of the English Language* (Cambridge: Cambridge University Press, 2nd edn., 2003).

—— *The Stories of English* (London: Penguin, 2004).

—— *The Fight for English: How Language Pundits Ate, Shot and Left* (Oxford: Oxford University Press, 2006).

Hogg, R., and Denison, D. (eds.), *A History of the English Language* (Cambridge: Cambridge University Press, 2006).

Mugglestone, L. (ed.), *The Oxford History of English* (Oxford: Oxford University Press, 2006).

A CHRONOLOGY OF H. W. FOWLER

Life	*Historical and Cultural Background*
1858 Born on 10 March at Tonbridge, Kent, to father Robert and mother Caroline (née Watson); the eldest of a family of eight (seven sons, one daughter).	Founding of the Philological Society of Great Britain.
1859	Charles Darwin, *On the Origin of Species*
1861	American Civil War begins (to 1865).
*c.*1869 Attends a private boarding school in Germany.	
1870 Henry's brother, Francis George, born 3 September.	Brewer's *Dictionary of Phrase and Fable*
1871 Enters Rugby school; studies Latin and Greek as his main subjects, also French and German; becomes secretary of school debating society; acts in school theatre productions; in his final year, wins a prize for a translation of Shelley into Greek verse; becomes head of his house, School House.	
1877 Wins scholarship to Balliol College, Oxford.	
1879 Death of his father; appointed an executor of his father's will; as eldest son, takes responsibility for looking after the family; mother moves to Kensington, London, in early 1880s.	
1881 Leaves Oxford with a second-class grade in Moderations and Literae Humaniores; failure to pass the obligatory Divinity exam meant his degree was not finally awarded until 1886. Takes a temporary teaching post at Fettes school in Edinburgh.	
1882 Takes a permanent post at Sedbergh school in Yorkshire, teaching Latin, Greek, and English; devises a card system to help pupils with their syntax learning.	
1884	First fascicle of the *New English Dictionary*
1888	International Phonetic Alphabet published.

Life	*Historical and Cultural Background*
*c.*1890 Mother moves to Eastbourne.	Grammar dropped as a compulsory subject in British primary schools.
1895 Death of his mother.	
1896	Invention of wireless telegraphy.
1898	Second Boer War begins (to 1902).
1899 Leaves Sedbergh, dissatisfied with teaching as a profession, and finding that his lack of religious belief made it impossible to prepare boys for confirmation. Arrives in Chelsea, London, 14 Paulton's Square; begins writing articles on newspapers and journals; writes several unpublished essays (now lost); a frequent winner of verse translation competitions in newspapers; joins the Inns of Court Volunteers.	
1901	Death of Queen Victoria.
1903 Moves to Guernsey, where his brother Frank had settled as a tomato-grower in 1899.	First flight by the Wright brothers in the USA.
1904 Elliot Stock publishes his first book, a collection of essays, *More Popular Fallacies*, under the pseudonym of Quillet; not a success.	
1905 Clarendon Press publishes the first collaboration between Henry and Frank, a 4-volume translation of *Lucian* in the Oxford Library of Translations; enthusiastically received.	
1906 Clarendon Press publishes the second collaboration between Henry and Frank, *The King's English*, the authors identified only by their initials in the Preface; a great though controversial success, a second edition quickly follows. Clarendon Press publishes his short book, *Sentence Analysis*, anonymously, but with little success. Begins work with Frank on Oxford dictionaries.	
1907 Publishes privately a book of autobiographical essays *Si Mihi!* (If I Had) under the pseudonym Egomet (reissued under his name in 1929 with the title *If Wishes Were Horses*).	

Life	*Historical and Cultural Background*
1908 Publishes privately a book of schoolmasterly essays *Between Boy and Man*. Marries Jessie Marian Wills, 10 March, on his fiftieth birthday. Clarendon Press publishes an abridged edition of *The King's English*, which stays in print for sixty years.	
1909	Ford produces Model T cars.
1910	Death of King Edward VII.
1911 Publication of the first edition of the *Concise Oxford Dictionary*, edited with Frank, to great acclaim. Proposes a book on usage to Oxford, eventually to become *Modern English Usage*.	
1913	Society for Pure English established; first crossword puzzle introduced.
1914	First World War begins; Shaw's *Pygmalion* opens in London.
1915 Having lied about his age, enlists with Frank in the 23rd Battalion Royal Fusiliers, a special unit established for older recruits; arrives in France in December.	
1916 Sent back to England, then given a medical discharge from the army (gout); teaches at Sedbergh for a term; engages in munitions work.	
1917	Daniel Jones, *English Pronouncing Dictionary*
1918 Frank dies of tuberculosis in a military hospital in Dover.	First World War ends.
1919 Henry resumes work on the *Pocket Dictionary*, begun by Frank before the War, and also on *Modern English Usage*, but leaves the latter to concentrate on the former.	
1921 Publishes his first Tract for the Society of Pure English, 'On hyphens, shall & will, should & would in the newspapers of today'.	
1922 Recommences work on *Modern English Usage*.	Partition of Northern Ireland and Eire.
1923 At the end of the year, sends in text of *Modern English Usage*.	BBC begins radio broadcasts.
1924 *Pocket Oxford Dictionary* is published to great acclaim. Begins work on a section of the *Shorter Oxford Dictionary*.	

Life

1925 Moves to Hinton St George, Somerset.

1926 *Modern English Usage* published, 22 April. Begins revision of the *Concise*; completed by the end of 1927. Has an operation to remove an eye.

General Strike in Britain; BBC establishes its Advisory Committee on Spoken English.

1927

First talking film, Al Jolson in *The Jazz Singer*

1928 Finishes work on his section of the *Shorter Oxford* (though the book is not published until 1933).

Publication of the *Oxford English Dictionary.*

1929 Second edition of the *Concise Oxford Dictionary.* Blackwell publishes a book of essays, *Some Comparative Values*; Allen and Unwin publishes the reissued *If Wishes Were Horses.*

Stock market crash in USA.

1930 Begins work on a proposed *Oxford Dictionary of Modern English*, but stops as his wife's health deteriorates; resumes again in 1931, but his own poor health makes progress slow; despite later involving collaborators, the work is never completed. Death of Jessie from cancer, 1 October.

1931 J. M. Dent publishes his verses to his wife, written over twenty-two years, as *Rhymes of Darby to Joan.* H. G. Le Mesurier joins Henry as a collaborator.

1932 His brother Arthur joins Henry as a collaborator.

1933 Publication of the *Shorter Oxford Dictionary*; dies 26 December from pneumonia following influenza.

A DICTIONARY OF
MODERN
ENGLISH USAGE

I think of it as it should have been, with its prolixities docked, its dullnesses enlivened, its fads eliminated, its truths multiplied. He had a nimbler wit, a better sense of proportion, and a more open mind, than his twelve-year-older partner; and it is matter of regret that we had not, at a certain point, arranged our undertakings otherwise than we did.

In 1911 we started work simultaneously on The Pocket Oxford Dictionary and this book; living close together, we could, and did, compare notes; but each was to get one book into shape by writing its first quarter or half; and so much only had been done before the war. The one in which, as the less mechanical, his ideas and contributions would have had much the greater value had been assigned, by ill chance, to me. In 1918 he died, aged 47, of tuberculosis contracted during service with the B.E.F. in 1915–16.

The present book accordingly contains none of his actual writing; but, having been designed in consultation with him, it is the last fruit of a partnership that began in 1903 with our translation of Lucian.

H. W. F.

ACKNOWLEDGEMENTS

I cannot deny myself the pleasure of publicly thanking Lt-Col.
H. G. Le Mesurier, C.I.E., who not only read and criticized in detail
the whole MS. of this book, but devised, at my request, a scheme
for considerably reducing its bulk. That it was not necessary to
adopt this scheme is due to the generosity of the Clarendon Press
in consenting to publish, at no high price, an amount much greater
than that originally sanctioned.

On behalf of the Press, Mr. Frederick Page and Mr. C. T. Onions have
made valuable corrections and comments.

The article on *morale* has appeared previously in the *Times Literary
Supplement*, that on *only* in the *Westminster Gazette*, and those on
Hyphens, Inversion, Metaphor, Split infinitive, Subjunctives, and
other matters, in *S.P.E.*

H. W. F.

KEY TO PRONUNCIATION

VOWELS

ā ē ī ō ū o͞o (*mate, mete, mite, mote, mute, moot*)
ă ĕ ĭ ŏ ŭ o͝o (*rack, reck, rick, rock, ruck, rook*)
ä ë ï ö ü o͝o = ā, o͞o or o͝o, &c.
a e i o u ar er or   These italic letters stand for light vague
                              sounds (stigm*a*, sil*e*nt, cous*i*n, cont*a*in,
                              s*u*bmit, begg*ar*, p*er*tain, mot*or*).
ār ēr īr ōr ūr (*mare, mere, mire, more, mure*)
ar er or (*part, pert, port*)
ah aw oi oor ow owr (*bah, bawl, boil, boor, brow, bower*)

CONSONANTS

of which the value needs defining

ch (*child, each* : not as in *chaos, champagne, loch*)
dh (dhăt, mŭ′dher, = *that, mother*)
g (*gag, get* : not as in *gentle*)
j (jŭj = *judge*)
ng (*singer* : not as in *finger, ginger*)
ngg (fĭ′ngger = *finger*)
s (saws = *sauce* : not as in *laws*)
th (*thinketh* : not as in *this, smooth*)
zh (ro͞ozh, vĭ′zhn, = *rouge, vision*)
For h, r, w, in ah, ar &c., ow, owr, see Vowels

LIST OF
GENERAL ARTICLES

as distinguished from those on individual words. In the dictionary, the titles of most such articles are printed in small capitals. Those of which the titles are bracketed in this list contain only cross references to others in which their subjects are dealt with. A few individual words such as *and, do, each, that,* important rather as framework than for themselves, are also included ; the articles upon these, dealing with points of grammar or idiom that arise every day, are in effect of the general kind ; but they are here distinguished from the others by italics (*as,* not As).

-ex, -ix
-ey & -y in adjectives
-ey, -ie, -y, in diminutives
Facetious formations
fact
fail
False emphasis
False quantity
False scent
far
fellow
Feminine designations
Fetishes
few
-fied
first
follow
for
Foreign danger
For-, fore-
Formal words
French words
Friday
-ful
(Full stop)
Fused participle
Gallicisms
Generic names &c.
Genteelism
Gerund
-g-, -gg-
Grand compounds
Greek g
Hackneyed phrases
had
half
Hanging-up
hardly
have
Haziness
he
help
his
hon.
hope
however
Hybrid derivatives
Hyphens
-i
(-ible)
(-ic)
-ic(al)
-ics
i. e.

if & when
Illiteracies
Illogicalities
Im-
-in & -ine
In- & un-
inasmuch as
Incompatibles
Incongruous vocabulary
Indirect question
(-ine)
(Infinitive)
-ing
in order that
in so far
in that
into
Intransitive p. p.
Inversion
(Inverted commas)
-ion & -ment
-ion & -ness
Irrelevant allusion
is
-ise) (-ize
-ism & -ity
-ist, -alist, &c.
it
Italian sounds
Italics
its
-ize, -ise
jargon
Jingles
judg(e)ment &c.
just
kind
lady
last
Latin plurals
-latry
latter
lay & lie
Legerdemain with two senses
less
-less
lest
Letter forms
(-lier)
like
-like
-lily
Literary critics' words

Literary words
-lived
-ll-, -l-
Long variants
lord
Love of the long word
lu
-ly
Malaprops
Mannerisms
me
means
-ment
Metaphor
(-meter)
million
Misapprehensions
Misprints
Misquotation
-m-, -mm-
moral(e)
more
-most
much
mulatto
Muses
Mute e
need
Needless variants
Negative & affirmative in parallel clauses
Negatives
neither
(-ness)
never so
next
-n-, -nn-
no
nor
not
Noun & adjective accent
Noun & verb accent
Novelese
Novelty-hunting
Number
-o-
Object-shuffling
(Oe, œ, e)
-o(e)s
of
(Omission of *it*)
-on
once
one

LIST OF GENERAL ARTICLES

ABBREVIATIONS, SYMBOLS, ETC.

a., adjective
aa., adjectives
adj., adjective
adv., adverb
advl, adverbial
arch., archaic
A.V., Authorized Version
c., century
cc., centuries
cf. (=*confer*), compare
conj., conjunction
dim., diminutive
Dipl., Diplomacy
D.N.B., Dictionary of National Biography
e. g. (=*exempli gratia*), for instance
ellipt., elliptical
Enc. Brit., Encyclopaedia Britannica
F, French
Gk, Greek
Gram., Grammar
i. e. (=*id est*), that is
indic., indicative
ind. obj., indirect object

int., interjection
L, Latin
Lit., Literature
lit., literally
Log., Logic
MS., manuscript
MSS., manuscripts
n., noun
nn., nouns
obj., object
OED, Oxford English Dictionary
Palaeogr., Palaeography
part., participle present
pers., person
pl., plural
p.p., past or passive participle
pr., pronounce
pref., prefix
prep., preposition
pron., pronoun
pron., pronounce
Pros., Prosody
refl., reflexive
rel., relative
Rhet., Rhetoric

R.V., Revised Version
s.f. (=*sub finem*), near the end
sing., singular
S.P.E., (Tracts of the) Society for Pure English
subj., subjunctive
suf., suffix
U.K., United Kingdom
U.S., United States of America
v., verb
var., variant
vb, verb
vol., volume

&, and
&c., et cetera
)(, placed between words to be compared
/, placed between separate quotations
[], containing words that are not part of the quotation

Small capitals refer the reader to the article so indicated, for further information.

A Dictionary of

ENGLISH USAGE

a, an. 1. *A* is used before all consonants except silent h (*a history, an hour*) ; *an* was formerly usual before an unaccented syllable beginning with h (*an historical work*), but now that the h in such words is pronounced the distinction has become pedantic, & *a historical* should be said & written ; similarly *an humble* is now meaningless & undesirable. *A* is now usual also before vowels preceded in fact though not in appearance by the sound of y or w (*a unit, a eulogy, a one*).

2. The combinations of *a* with *few* & *many* are a matter of arbitrary but established usage : *a few, a great many, a good many*, are idiomatic, but *a many, a good few*, are now illiterate or facetious or colloquial ; *a very few* is permissible (in the sense some-though-not-at-all-many,whereas *very few* means not-at-all-many-though-some), but *an extremely few* is not ; see FEW.

3. *A, an*, follow instead of preceding the adjectives *many, such*, & *what* (*many an artist, such a task, what an infernal bore !*) ; they also follow any adjective preceded by *as* or *how* (*I am as good a man as he ; knew how great a labour he had undertaken*), usually any adjective preceded by *so* (*so resolute an attempt deserved success ; a so resolute attempt* is also English, but suggests affectation), & often any adjective preceded by *too* (*too exact an*, or *a too exact, adherence to instructions*). The late position should not be adopted with other words than *as, how, so, too* ; e.g., in *Which was quite sufficient an indication/Can anyone choose more glorious an exit ?/Have before them far more brilliant a future/*, the normal order (*a quite* or *quite a sufficient, a more glorious, a far more brilliant*) is also the right one.

4. *A, an*, are sometimes ungrammatically inserted, especially after *no* adj., to do over again work that has already been done ; so in *No more signal a defeat was ever inflicted* (*no* = not a ; with this ungrammatical use cf. the merely ill-advised arrangement in *Suffered no less signal a defeat*, where *no* is an adverb & *a* should precede it as laid down in 3 above).*/The defendant was no other a person than Mr Benjamin Disraeli* (*no other* = not another).*/Glimmerings of such a royally suggested even when not royally edited an institution are to be traced* (*even . . . edited* being parenthetic, we get *such a royally suggested an institution*).

a-, an-, not or without, should be prefixed only to Greek stems ; of such compounds there are some hundreds, whereas Latin-stemmed words having any currency even in scientific use do not perhaps exceed four. There are the botanical *acapsular* & *acaulous*, the biological *asexual*, & the literary *amoral*. The last, being literary, is inexcusable, & *non-moral* should be used instead. The other three should not be treated as precedents for future word-making.

abandon, n., abattoir. See FRENCH WORDS.

abbreviate, abdicate, make *abbreviable, abdicable* : see -ABLE 1.

abdomen. Pronounce ăbdō′měn.

abetter, -or. See -OR.
Abigail. See SOBRIQUETS.
abjection, abjectness. See -ION &
-NESS.

ablatively, ablativally, &c. Adverbs
from the names of grammatical cases
are best formed in -ively. There is
no doubt about the names used in
modern English grammar ; everyone would say *subjectively, objectively,* & *possessively.* And, though
the Latin case-names have adjectives in -ival, as *datival,* it will be
admitted that ' used vocatively '
at any rate is hardly tolerable, that
none of the forms in -ively is very
objectionable, & that it is worth
while to secure consistency. The
adjectives, then, should be *nomina-
tival, vocatival, accusatival, genitival,
datival, ablatival, subjective, objective,*
& *possessive* (though the attributive
use of the noun, as in *the genitive
termination,* must still be common),
& the adverbs *nominatively &c.,
subjectively* &c.

-ABLE, -IBLE, &c. 1. Normal use
of *-able* as living suffix. 2. *-able* &
other *-ble* forms. 3. Negative forms
of adjectives in *-ble.* 4. *-ble* words of
exceptional form or sense.
1. Normal use of -able as living
suffix. The suffix *-able* is a living
one, & may be appended to any
transitive verb to make an adjective
with the sense *able,* or *liable,* or
allowed, or *worthy,* or *requiring,* or
bound, to be ——ed. If the verb ends
in mute -e, this is dropped except
after soft c or g (*usable, likable,
dyable, pronounceable, manageable,
bridgeable*). Verbs ending in -y preceded by a consonant change y into i
(*justifiable, triable* ; but *buyable*).
Verbs with the Latin-derived ending
-ate that have established adjectives
drop the *-ate* (*demonstrable, abominable, alienable, appreciable, calculable,
expiable, execrable,* &c.) ; & nonce-
adjectives from such verbs should
be similarly formed (*accumulable,
adulterable, educable, confiscable, sat-
urable,* &c.) except when the verb is
disyllabic (*dictatable, creatable, cas-*

tratable, crematable, locatable ; not
dictable &c. on the analogy of *placable* or *probable*) ; but see also
-ATABLE ; *administer & register*
form similarly *administrable & regis-
trable.* No verbs in *-ble, -cle, -dle,
-fle, -gle, -kle, -ple, -sle, -tle, -zle,* have
established adjectives in *-able* ; but
adjectives made for the nonce from
them should drop the -e (*bafflable,
hustlable, muzzlable,* &c.).
Nonce-adjectives in *-able* may be
formed even from those verbs whose
established representatives are in the
list of words in *-ible &c.* given in 2,
especially when the established word
has to some extent lost the verbal or
contracted a special sense. Thus a
mistake may be called *uncorrectable,*
because *incorrigible* has become
ethical in sense ; *solvable* may be
preferred because *soluble* has entered
into an alliance with *dissolve* ; &
destroyable by dynamite may seem
less pedantic than *destructible by*
because *destructible* tends to be
purely adjectival.
2. -able & other -ble forms. The
following list (to which are to be
added the negative or positive forms
made by adding or omitting *in-, un-,
non-,* is intended to include all the
existing *-ble* adjectives other than
those in *-able* ; words not found in
it should be spelt with *-able* ; & for
the italicized words, though they
exist, it is recommended to substitute the accompanying form in
-able. It may be observed that there
is only one word in the list, *gullible,*
of which the stem is not ultimately
Latin ; but the form, which should
have been *gullable,* may perhaps be
thought too firmly established to be
meddled with ; & the same plea may
prevent the rejection of such words
as *conductible, distensible,* & *refrangible,* which, though it is a pity they
were not originally made of the more
easily understood & equally legitimate *-able* type (*refrangible,* which
should be *refringible,* is actually less
correct than *refractable*), have at
least a technical, though hardly a
general currency.

List of -*ble* words not in -*able* : accessible ; adducible ; admissible ; apprehensible ; audible ; avertible ; coercible ; *collapsible*, collapsable ; *collectible*, collectable ; combustible ; comestible ; compatible ; comprehensible; compressible ; *conductible*, conductable ; *connectible*, connectable; contemptible; *contractible*, contractable; convertible ; convincible ; corrigible; corruptible; credible; deducible; defeasible ; defensible ; depressible ; *descendible*, descendable ; destructible ; *diffusible*, diffusable ; digestible; dirigible; *discernible*, discernable ; discerptible ; *discussible*, discussable ; dismissible ; dissoluble ; *distensible*, distendable ; divertible ; divisible; edible; educible; eligible; excerptible; exhaustible; exigible; *expansible*, expandable; expressible; *extendible*, *extensible*, extendable ; fallible ; feasible ; feeble ; fencible ; flexible ; forcible; fungible; fusible ; *gullible*, gullable ; horrible ; *immiscible*, unmixable ; impartible (not from *impart*) ; impassible (not from *pass*) ; imperscriptible ; imprescriptible; impressible; incontrovertible; indefeasible ; indefectible; indelible; inducible ; intelligible ; invincible ; irascible; irresistible; legible; negligible ; noble ; omissible ; oppressible ; ostensible ; perceptible ; *perfectible*, perfectable ; permissible ; *persuasible*, persuadable ; pervertible ; plausible ; possible ; *preventible*, preventable ; producible ; *protrusible*, protrudable ; reducible ; *reflexible*, reflectable; *refrangible*, refractable ; remissible ; reprehensible ; repressible ; resoluble ; responsible ; *reversible*, reversable ; revertible ; risible ; seducible ; sensible ; soluble ; submersible ; suggestible ; susceptible ; *suspensible*, suspendable ; suppressible ; tangible ; terrible ; traducible ; vendible ; visible ; voluble.

The principle is that the normal form -*able* should be used when there is no objection to it ; there is an objection when a word is itself well established with -*ible* &c. in general use, & therefore *digestable*, *perceivable*, are not to be substituted for *digestible* & *perceptible* ; there is also an objection, though a less forcible one, when, though the word itself is not established in the -*ible* form, it is one of a set that includes an established word in -*ible* ; thus *incontrovertible* & *convertible* should decide the form of *avertible*, *divertible*, *pervertible*, & *revertible* ; *digestible*, that of *suggestible* ; in favour of *adducible*, *educible*, *inducible*, *producible*, *seducible*, & *traducible*, there is added to the influence of (*ir*)*reducible* & *deducible* a legitimate dislike to the ugly forms in -*eable*. The existence of a single established -*ible* word of a more or less technical kind need not be allowed much weight ; e.g., *fusible* does not suffice to condemn *confusable*, *diffusable*, *refusable*, & *suffusable*.

3. Negative forms of adjectives in -ble. The adjectives in -*ble* being required with especial frequency in negative contexts, the question often arises whether the negative form of any particular word should be made with *in*- or *un*- ; the following rules will perhaps be found satisfactory :

(*a*) Negatives from -*ble* words other than those in -*able* have *in*- (or *ig*-, *il*-, *im*-, *ir*-) ; the only exceptions are words already beginning with the prefix *im*- or *in*- (*impressible*, *intelligible*), & *feasible*, *feeble*, *plausible*, *voluble*, all of which take, or would take if required in the negative, *un*-.

(*b*) Negatives from words in -*able* have *un*- unless they are in the following list ; and the *un*- form is recommended for the italicized words, though the *in*- (*im*-, *ir*-, &c.) form exists.

Negatives in -*able* not having *un*- : illimitable ; immeasurable ; immitigable ; immovable ; immutable ; impalpable ; impassable ; impayable (the French word; cf. *unpayable* from English *pay*) ; impeccable ; impenetrable; imperishable; impermeable; imperturbable ; implacable ; imponderable ; impracticable ; impregnable ; improbable ; inalienable ; *in-*

alterable; *inappeasable*; inappellable; inapplicable ; inappreciable ; *inapproachable*; incalculable ; incapable; *incognizable* ; incommensurable ; *incommunicable* ; *incommutable* ; incomparable ; *incomputable* ; inconceivable ; *incondensable* ; inconsiderable ; inconsolable ; *inconsumable*; incontestable ; incurable ; *indecipherable*; indeclinable ; *indecomposable*; indefatigable; indefinable; *indemonstrable* ; indescribable ; *indeterminable*; indispensable; indisputable ; indistinguishable ; *indistributable*; indomitable; indubitable; ineffable; ineffaceable ; ineluctable ; inequitable; ineradicable; inerrable; *inescapable* ; inestimable ; inevitable; inexcusable; *inexecutable* ; inexorable; inexpiable; inexplicable; inexpugnable; inextinguishable; inextricable ; inhospitable ; inimitable ; *innavigable* ; innumerable ; insatiable ; inscrutable ; inseparable ; insufferable ; insupportable ; insurmountable ; interminable ; intolerable ; intractable ; invaluable ; invariable ; inviolable ; invulnerable ; irreclaimable ; *irrecognizable*; irreconcilable ; irrecoverable ; irrecusable ; irredeemable ; irrefragable ; *irrefrangible* (unrefractable); irrefutable ; irremediable ; irremovable; irreparable; *irreplaceable*; irreproachable ; *irresolvable* ; irretrievable ; irrevocable.

4. -ble words of exceptional form or sense. The normal formation & sense of adjectives in *-able* has been explained in 1 ; & adjectives in *-ible* have the same ordinary range of sense. There are however large numbers of words, & certain usages, that do not conform to this simple type, & to some of them (*a reliable man, perishable articles, dutiable goods, feedable pasture, an unplayable wicket, a carriageable road, an actionable offence, a payable mine, unwritable paper,* & others) exception is often taken. The advocatus diaboli who opposes their recognition has the advantage of an instantly plausible case that can be put clearly & concisely : we do not

rely a man, nor perish articles, nor play a wicket ; therefore we have no right to call a man unreliable, & so with the rest. An answer on the same pattern would be that neither do we dispense a man, yet our right to call him indispensable is not questioned. But it is better to go on broader lines, sacrificing the appearance of precision & cogency, & point out that the termination *-ble* has too wide a range in regard both to formation & to sense, & the analogies offered by the *-ble* words are too various & debatable, to allow of the application of cut-&-dried rules. The words & usages to which exception is taken should be tested not by the original Latin practice, nor by the subsequent French practice, nor by the English practice of any particular past period, even if any of these were as precise as is sometimes supposed, but by what inquiry may reveal as the now current conception of how words in *-ble* are to be formed & what they may mean. In determining that conception we cannot help allowing the incriminated words themselves to count for something ; it may seem unfair that *reliable* should itself have a voice in deciding its own fate ; but it is no more unfair than that possession should be nine points of the law ; the existence of the still more modern *payable mine, playable wicket, unwritable paper,* has in the same way its value as evidence; the witness-box is open to the prisoner. Apart, however, from this special proof that the current conception of *-ble* is elastic, it is easy to show that at the present stage of its long history & varied development it could not be rigid. In the first place the original formation & meaning of many common words containing it are obscured by the nonexistence in English of verbs to which they can be neatly referred (*affable, amenable, amicable, arable, audible, capable, credible, culpable, delectable, durable, edible, equable, fallible, feasible, feeble, formidable,* *horrible, hospitable, impeccable, impregnable, legible, liable, miserable, mutable, palpable, plausible, possible, probable, terrible, visible,* & many others). Secondly, there are many common words in which the sense of *-ble* either is (as sometimes in Latin), or (which is as much to the point) seems to be, not passive but active (*affable, agreeable, amiable, amicable, available, capable, changeable, comfortable, conformable, conversable, delectable, durable, fallible, favourable, hospitable, impeccable, irascible, mutable, passable, perishable, pleasurable, profitable, sociable, stable, suitable, susceptible, terrible, variable, vegetable, visible, voluble,* &c.). Thirdly, *-ble* is often appended, or (which is as much to the point) seems to be appended, to nouns instead of to verbs (*accessible, actionable, available, carriageable, changeable, chargeable, charitable, clubbable, comfortable, companionable, creditable, dutiable, equitable, fashionable, favourable, forcible, impressionable, knowledgeable, laughable, marriageable, miserable, objectionable, peaceable, personable, pleasurable, profitable, proportionable, reasonable, reputable, responsible, salable, seasonable, sensible, serviceable, sizable, sociable, treasonable, unexceptionable, valuable, veritable,* &c.). To take a single example in detail, no-one but a competent philologist can tell whether *reasonable* comes from the verb or the noun *reason,* nor whether its original sense was that can be reasoned out, or that can reason, or that can be reasoned with, or that has reason, or that listens to reason, or that is consistent with reason; the ordinary man knows only that it can now mean any of these, & justifiably bases on these & similar facts a generous view of the termination's capabilities; *credible* meaning for him worthy of credence, why should not *reliable* & *dependable* mean worthy of reliance & dependence? *durable* meaning likely to endure, why should not *payable* & *perishable* mean likely to pay & perish?

In conclusion, a selection follows of words in *-ble,* some of them established & some questionable, that illustrate the looser uses of the termination; the paraphrases are offered merely by way of accommodating each word to what is taken to be the current conception of *-ble* :—*accountable,* liable to account; *actionable,* liable to an action; *answerable,* bound to answer, answering (*a. to expectation*); *appealable,* subject to appeal; *available,* that may avail; *bailable,* admitting of bail; *carriageable,* fit for carriages; *chargeable,* involving charge; *clubbable,* fit for a club; *companionable,* fit for a companion; *conformable,* that conforms; *conversable,* fit for conversing; *customable,* liable to customs; *demurrable,* open to demur; *dependable,* worthy of dependence; *descendable,* subject to laws of descent; *dutiable,* liable to duty; *feedable,* that will serve for feed; *impressionable,* open to impressions; *indispensable,* not admitting of dispensation; *knowledgeable,* having or capable of knowledge; *laughable,* providing a laugh; *marriageable,* fit for marriage; *merchantable,* fit for the merchant; *objectionable,* open to objection; *payable,* likely to pay; *peaceable,* inclined to peace; *perishable,* apt to perish; *personable,* having person or presence; *perspirable,* permitting perspiration; *playable,* fit for play; *pleasurable,* affording pleasure; *practicable,* adapted for practice; *profitable,* affording profit; *proportionable,* showing proportion; *reliable,* worthy of reliance; *revertible,* liable to reversion; *risible,* adapted for laughing; *salable,* fit for sale; *seasonable,* fit for the season; *sizable,* having size; *skatable,* fit for skating; *statutable,* according to statute; *tollable,* subject to tolls; *unconscionable,* not according to conscience; *unexceptionable,* not open to exception; *unwritable,* not fit for writing.

ablutions. See PEDANTIC HUMOUR.

abolishment, abolition. See -ION & -MENT.

aborigines. The word being still usually pronounced with a consciousness that it is Latin (i.e. with -ēz), the sing. *aborigine* (-nĭ) is felt to be anomalous & avoided or disliked ; the adj. *aboriginal* used as a noun is the best singular.

abridg(e)ment. For spelling see JUDGEMENT.

abrogate makes *-gable* ; see -ABLE 1.

absence. For *conspicuous by a.* see HACKNEYED PHRASES.

absolute. See LU ; &, for the sense in grammar, TECHNICAL TERMS.

ABSOLUTE CONSTRUCTION. 1. The insertion of a comma between noun & participle in the absolute use is indisputably wrong ; it arises from the writer's or the compositor's taking the noun, because it happens to stand first, for the subject of the main verb ; & it puts the reader to the trouble of readjusting, after he has formed it, his notion of the sentence's structure. *The King having read his speech from the throne, their Majesties retired* is the right form ; but newspaper writing or printing is so faulty on the point that it would appear nine times out of ten as *The King, having read his* &c. **2.** The case in this construction is the subjective ; e.g. *There being no clear evidence against him, & he* (not *him*) *denying the charge, we could do nothing.* There is little danger of the rule's being broken except where a pronoun stands as complement ; though no-one would write *me being the person responsible*, the form *the person responsible being I* is likely to be shrunk from ; *me* is ungrammatical & should not be used except colloquially ; *myself* is usually possible, but not always. The formula *whom failing* (= or in default of him) should be either *who failing* or *failing whom* ; the justification of *failing whom* is that *failing* has, like *during* &c., passed into a preposition, & *whom failing* is a confusion between the two right forms.

3. The following example of one absolute construction enclosed in another is a pretty puzzle for those who like such things : *To the new Greek Note Bulgaria replied by a Note which was returned to the Bulgarian Foreign Minister*, Greece, it being declared, not wishing *to enter into any bargaining.* It is clear enough that that will not do, & that it must be changed into (*a*) *it being declared that Greece did not wish*, or (*b*) *Greece not wishing, it was declared, to . . .* ; but why will it not do ? Because the absolute construction ' it being declared ' cannot, like the ' it was declared ' of *b*, be parenthetic, but must be in adverbial relation to the sentence ; knowing that, we ask what ' it ' is, & find that it can only be an anticipatory *it* (see IT) equivalent to ' that Greece did not wish ' ; but the consequent expansion ' Greece, that Greece did not wish being declared, not wishing ' makes nonsense.

ABSOLUTE POSSESSIVES. Under this term are included the words *hers, ours, theirs, & yours*, & (except in the archaic attributive-adjective use, as *thine eyes*) *mine & thine*. The ordinary uses of these need not be set forth here. But a mistake is often made when two or more possessives are to be referred to a single noun that follows the last of them : the absolute word in -s or -ne is wrongly used in the earlier place(s) instead of the simple possessive. The correct forms are : *your & our & his efforts* (not *yours & ours*) ; *either my or your informant must have lied* (not *mine*) ; *her & his mutual dislike* (not *hers*) ; *our without your help will not avail* (not *ours*). There is no doubt a natural temptation to substitute the wrong word ; the simple possessive seems to pine at separation from its property. The true remedy is a change of order :—*your efforts & ours & his* ; *my informant or yours* ; *our help without yours.* It is not always available, however ; *her &*

his mutual dislike must be left as it is.

absorbedly. Four syllables ; see -EDLY.

abstraction, abstractness. See -ION & -NESS.

abysmal, abyssal. The first is the rhetorical word (*abysmal ignorance, degradation, bathos*) ; *abyssal*, formerly used in the same way, has now been appropriated as a technical term meaning of the bottom of the ocean or of a depth greater than 300 fathoms.

Academe properly means *Academus* (a Greek hero) ; & its use as a poetic variant for *academy*, though sanctioned by Shakspere, Tennyson, & Lowell, is a mistake; *the grove of A.*, however, (Milton) means rightly The Academy.

Academy. *The A., the Garden, the Lyceum, the Porch, the Tub,* are names used for five chief schools of Greek philosophy, their founders, adherents, & doctrines : *the A.*, Plato, the Platonists, & Platonism ; *the Garden*, Epicurus, the Epicureans, & Epicureanism ; *the Lyceum*, Aristotle, the Aristotelians, & Aristotelianism ; *the Porch*, Zeno, the Stoics, & Stoicism ; *the Tub*, Antisthenes, the Cynics, & Cynicism.

acapsular. See A-, AN-.
acatalectic. See TECHNICAL TERMS.
acaulous. See A-, AN-.
accelerate makes *-rable* ; see -ABLE 1.
accent. Pronounce the noun ă′ksnt, the verb aksĕ′nt ; see NOUN & VERB ACCENT.

accent(uate). In figurative senses (draw attention to, emphasize, make conspicuous, &c.) the long form is now much the commoner ; in literal senses (sound or write with an accent), though either will pass, the short prevails ; & the DIFFERENTIATION is worth encouraging.

acceptance, acceptation. The words, once used indifferently in several senses, are now fully differentiated. *Acceptation* means only the interpretation put on something (*the*

word in its proper acceptation means love ; the various acceptations of the doctrine of the Trinity), while *acceptance* does the ordinary work of a verbal noun for *accept* (*find acceptance*, be well received ; *beg* or *ask* one's *acceptance of*, ask him to accept ; cf. *ask his acceptation of*, ask how he understands ; *cards of acceptance*, accepting an invitation ; *acceptance of persons*, partiality ; *acceptance of a bill*, drawee's accepting of responsibility ; *endorses my acceptance of the terms*, agrees with me in accepting them ; cf. *endorses my acceptation of them*, agrees with my view of their drift).

accepter, -or. See -OR.
accept of. This, formerly used almost as widely as the simple verb, is now restricted to the meaning *consent to receive as a gift or benefit or possession*. We can still *accept of* a gift or favour, *of* a person's love or hand or company, *of* a brace of grouse, & the like, though even these phrases tend to become archaic. But a theory, an emendation, advice, an apology, a ruling, a challenge, we only *accept*.

access, accession. There are probably, in modern usage, no contexts in which one of these can be substituted for the other without the meaning's being modified. But, perhaps owing to the fact that, with such modification, similar collocations for both are not uncommon, the wrong one is sometimes carelessly or ignorantly chosen. With regard to arriving, *accession* means arrival, *access* opportunity of arriving ; accordingly *accession to the throne* means becoming sovereign, *access to the throne* opportunity of petitioning the sovereign ; we can say *His access to fortune was barred*, or *His accession to fortune had not yet taken place*, but not the converse. The idea of increase, often present in *accession*, is foreign to *access* ; *an access of fury, fever, joy, despair, &c.*, is a fit or sudden attack of it, which may occur whatever the previous state of mind may have been, whereas *an accession of* any of them can only mean a heightened degree of the one that already existed; *our forces have had no accession,* have not been augmented in numbers, *have had no access,* have not been able to enter.

accessary, accessory. The words, though they have separate histories, are often confused; but a fairly clear line of distinction can be made out. *Accessary* involves the notion of complicity or intentional aid or consent, & is accordingly used only where that notion is applicable, i.e. chiefly (as a noun) of persons & (as an adjective) of persons or their actions (*he was an accessary, if not the principal*; *the accessaries also were punished*; *this course has made us accessary to the crime*; *was guilty of accessary action*). *Accessory* has no such implication of consent, &, though it includes the notion of contributing to a result, emphasizes especially the subordinate nature of the contribution; it is applied chiefly to things (*the accessory details of the picture*; *that is only an accessory,* an unessential feature; *the accessories,* the not indispensable accompaniments).

accidence. See TECHNICAL TERMS.
acclimatize, -imate, -imatization, -imatation, -imation. *Acclimatize, acclimatization,* are the forms for which general usage seems to have decided. Some writers wish to retain the others with reference to the process when brought about by natural as opposed to human agency; but it is doubtful whether the words are in common enough use for the differentiation to gain currency; &, failing differentiation, it is better that the by-forms should perish.

accommodate makes *-dable*; see -ABLE 1.
accompany. For inflexions see VERBS IN -IE &c., 6.
accompan(y)ist. See -IST.
accomplice, accomplish. The OED

gives the pronunciation with -ŏm-, not -ŭm-, as the established one for both words, though 'the historical pronunciation' of *accomplish* was with -ŭm-.

accord, account. The phrases are *of* one's *own accord, on* one's *own account*; *of* one's *own account* is a confusion. See CAST-IRON IDIOM.

according as. There is a tendency to repeat the phrase (like BETWEEN), with a mistaken idea of making the construction clearer, in contexts where the repetition is not merely needless, but wrong. For instance, the second *according as it* should be omitted in
The big production will be harmful or the reverse, according as it can command the Government to insure it a monopoly in all circumstances, or according as it works with the knowledge that, if it abuses its trust, the door is freely open to the competing products of other countries.
The error is at once apparent if the clause (for it is a single clause, in fact) is reduced to its simplest expression—(will be harmful or the reverse) according as it is irresponsible or responsible; no-one would write *or according as it is responsible*; the temptation comes in long sentences only, & must be resisted. *Or according as* is legitimate only when what is to be introduced is not, as in the quotation, the necessarily implied alternative or the other extreme of the same scale, but another scale or pair of alternatives. Man attains happiness or not *according as he deserves it or not* (right), *according as he deserves it or does not deserve it* (right), *according as he deserves it or according as he does not deserve it* (wrong), *according as he deserves it or according as he can digest his food* (right).

accouchement &c. See FRENCH WORDS.
account. Unlike *regard,* & like *consider,* this verb does not in good modern usage admit of *as* before its complement; *I account it a piece of*

good fortune ; *you are accounted wise* or *a wise man.*

accoutre. Part. *-tring* ; see -RE & -ER.

accumulate makes *-lable* ; see -ABLE 1.

accumulative. The word, formerly common in various senses, has now given place to *cumulative* in most of them, retaining in ordinary use only the sense *given to accumulating property, acquisitive.*

accusal. See -AL NOUNS.

accusatival(ly), accusative(ly). See ABLATIVELY.

acharnement. See FRENCH WORDS.

ache, the letter. See AITCH.

acid test. See POPULARIZED TECHNICALITIES.

acknowledge(ment). For pronunciation see KNOWLEDGE. For -dg(e)ment see JUDGEMENT.

acoustic. Pronunciation varies between -ow- & -ōō-. In favour of -ōō- is the adoption from French, the sound of Greek *ov* in the more recent English pronunciation of Greek, & the general impression that the value of *ou* in outlandish words is ōō ; in favour of -ow- is the older & still common English pronunciation of Greek, & the normal value of *ou* in English. If the word came into popular use, it would probably be with -ow-, which even now perhaps tends to prevail.

acquaintanceship is a NEEDLESS VARIANT for *acquaintance.*

act vb. In the sense *behave like,* the word, once used as freely as *play,* has contracted a slangy or vulgarly colloquial tone, & is now more appropriate in such expressions as *act the giddy goat* than in *act the philosopher, lover, child,* or even *fool,* in all of which *play* is better.

act, action. The distinction between the two words is not always clear. The natural idea that *act* should mean the thing done, & *action* the doing of it, is not even historically quite true, since *act*

represents the Latin noun *actus* (which is very close to *actio* in sense) as well as the Latin participle *actum* ; but, if not true, it has influence enough to prevent *act* from being commonly used in the more abstract senses ; we can speak only of the *action,* not the *act,* of a machine, when we mean the way it acts ; & *action* alone has the collective sense, as in *his action throughout* (i.e. his acts or actions as a whole) *was correct* ; there are also other senses in which there is obviously no choice open. In contexts that do admit of doubt, it may be said generally that *action* tends to displace *act.* If we were making the phrases for the first time now, we should probably prefer *action* in *Through God will we do great acts, The Acts of the Apostles, By the act of God, Be great in act as you have been in thought, I deliver this as my act & deed.* This tendency, however, is by no means always effective ; it is indifferent, for instance, whether we say *we are judged by our acts* or *by our actions* ; there is no appreciable difference between *it was an act,* & *it was an action, that he was to regret bitterly.* And in certain contexts *act* more than holds its ground : (1) in the sense deed of the nature *of* ; *it would be an act* (never *action*) *of folly, cruelty, madness, kindness, mercy,* &c. ; similarly in the sense deed characteristic *of* ; *it was the act* (rarely *action*) *of a fool* (cf. *the actions of a fool cannot be foreseen,* where the sense is not *characteristic deed,* but simply *deed*). On the other hand, when for *of folly* or *of a fool* &c. *foolish* &c. is substituted, *action* is commoner than *act*—*a cruel, kind, foolish, noble, base, action* or *act.* (2) In the sense instant of doing : *caught in the act, was in the very act of jumping.* (3) In antithesis with *word, thought, plan,* &c., when these mean rather every word, each thought, a particular plan, than speech, thinking, planning : *faithful in word & act* (but *in speech & action*) ; *innocent in thought & act* (but *supreme in thought & action*) ; *the act was mine, the plan yours* (but *a strategy convincing in plan, but disappointing in action*).

actuality. See LITERARY CRITICS' WORDS.

acuity, acuteness. See -TY & -NESS.

adagio. Pl. *-os* ; see -O(E)S 4.

ad captandum. See TECHNICAL TERMS.

addicted to. This should be followed by an ordinary noun or a verbal noun in -ing—*is addicted to whisky, is addicted to reading the jokes in Punch aloud*—& never by an infinitive, as in *is addicted to read the jokes aloud*. The wrong construction, which occasionally occurs, is probably suggested by the commonest phrase—*addicted to drink*, in which *drink* is the noun.

addle, addled. The adjectival use of *addle* as in *an addle egg, his brain is addle*, is correct, & was formerly common ; but to prefer it now to the usual *addled* is a DIDACTICISM. It still prevails, however, in compounds, as *addle-pate, addle-brained.*

adducible, -eable. Use -ible ; see -ABLE 2.

adhere, adhesion. The established phrase *give in* one's *adhesion to* a policy, party, leader, &c., means to declare one's acceptance of, & describes a single non-continuous act ; it is to be observed, however, that *adhere to* is not used, by good writers at least, in the corresponding sense *accept* or *declare acceptance of*, but only in that of remaining constant to.

adieu. See -X, & FRENCH WORDS.

adipose. See PEDANTIC HUMOUR.

adjectivally, adjectively, &c. *Adjectivally & substantivally* are preferable to *adjectively & substantively* (cf. ABLATIVELY) because (1) the words *adjective* & (in the grammatical sense) *substantive* are now regarded as nouns ; so far as they are still used as adjectives, they are felt to be nouns used attributively ; adverbs formed directly from them

therefore cause uneasiness ; (2) the adjectives *adjectival & substantival* are of such frequent occurrence in modern grammar that it is natural to form the adverbs from them ; (3) adverbs from the other part-of-speech names correspond to *adjectivally*, not to *adjectively—adverbially, pronominally, verbally*, &c., not *adverbly* &c.

adjudicate makes *-cable* ; see -ABLE 1.

administratrix. For pl. see -TRIX.

admirable. See POSITIVE WORDS.

admiredly. A bad form ; see -EDLY.

admission, -ittance, -issible, -ittable. Of the nouns, *admission* is used in all senses (*No admittance except on business* is perhaps the only phrase in which the substitution of *admission* would be noticed), while *admittance* is confined to the primary sense of *letting in*, & even in that sense tends to disappear. *You have to pay for admission* is now commoner than *for admittance*, & so with *What is needed is the admission of outside air* ; *admission 6d.* is now the regular form ; on the other hand *Such an admittance* (instead of *admission*) *would give away the case* is now impossible.

The difference between the adjectives is that *admissible* is the established word, & *admittable*, though formerly current, is now regarded as merely made for the occasion, & used only when the connexion with *admit* is to be clear ; this is chiefly in the predicate, as *Defeat is admittable by anyone without dishonour*.

admit of. This combination, formerly used indifferently with *admit* in several senses, is now restricted to the sense *present an opening* or *leave room for*, & to impersonal nouns usually of an abstract kind as subject : *His veracity admits of no question* (but not *I can admit of no question*) ; *A hypothesis admits by its nature of being disputed* (but not *he admits of being argued with*) ; *A modern battleship does not admit of careless handling*.

admonishment, admonition. See -ION & -MENT.

ado. Pl. -os ; see -O(E)S 3.

adopted, adoptive. The incorrect use of *adopted* with *parents, father, mother,* &c., is to a certain extent excused by such allowed attributive uses as *the condemned cell* ; that is the cell of the condemned, & the adopted father is the father of the adopted. But, while *condemned* saves a clumsy periphrasis, *adopted* saves only the trouble of remembering *adoptive.*

adulterate makes -*rable* ; see -ABLE 1.

adumbrate. See -ATABLE.

advancedly. Four syllables if used ; see -EDLY.

advance(ment). There are no contexts in which *advancement* can be substituted for *advance* without damage to or change in the sense ; in the following sentence *advance* should have been written :—*It will not be by the setting of class against class that advancement will be made.* It is true that both words can be used as verbal nouns of *to advance* ; but *advance* represents its intransitive & *advancement* its transitive sense ; *the advance of knowledge* is the way knowledge is advancing, whereas *the advancement of knowledge* is action taken to advance knowledge. Apart from this verbal-noun use with *of* following, & from a technical sense in law, *advancement* has only the sense of preferment or promotion, never the more general one of progress.

adventurous, venturesome, adventuresome, venturous. Usage has decisively declared for the first two & against the last two. *Adventuresome* & *venturous,* when used, are due to either ignorance or avoidance of the normal.

ADVERBS. See POSITION OF ADVERBS.

adverse. Unlike *averse,* this can be followed only by *to* ; *Politicians who had been very adverse from the Suez-Canal scheme* is wrong.

advertise. Not -*ize* ; see -ISE)(-IZE.

advisedly. Four syllables ; see -EDLY.

advocate. Unlike *recommend, propose, urge,* & other verbs, this is not idiomatically followed by a *that*-clause, but only by an ordinary or a verbal noun. In *Dr Felix Adler advocates that close attention shall be paid to any experiments,* either *urges* should be substituted for *advocates,* or *that* & *shall be paid* should be omitted or give place to *the paying of.*

Æ, Œ. These ligatures, of which the pronunciation is identical (ē), are also in some founts of type so much alike that compositors often use one for the other & unlearned readers have their difficulties with spelling increased. It seems desirable that in the first place all words in common enough use to have begun to waver between the double letter & the simple e (as *phenomenon* now rarely *phae-* or *phæ-, pedagogy* now rarely *pae-* or *pæ-, medieval* still usually -*aeval* or -*æval, ecumenical* still usually *oe-* or *œ-, penology* now rarely *poe-* or *pœ-, Phebe* still usually *Phoe-* or *Phœ-*) should be written with the e alone ; & secondly, in words that have not yet reached or can for special reasons never reach the stage in which the simple e is acceptable, ae & oe should be preferred to æ & œ (*Caesar, gynaecocracy, paedobaptism, homoeopathy, diarrhoea, Boeotian, Oedipus* ; the plurals & genitives of classical first-declension nouns, as *sequelae, Heraclidae, aqua vitae*). It is sometimes argued that if *Cæsar* & *Æneas* are to be written *Caesar* & *Aeneas* it will become necessary to use the diaeresis (*aërial*) wherever the a & e are pronounced separately, since the present distinction will be lost ; that the present distinction, however, is of little use is shown by the frequency with which *ærated* is printed for *aerated* ; it is not held necessary to write *oreäd* because *read* is pronounced rēd, & the case for *aërial* is no stronger. In French words like *chef-d'œuvre* the ligature œ must obviously be kept ; whether it is kept or not in *manoeuvre*, where the pronunciation is anomalous, is of no great importance.

-AE, -AS, in plurals of nouns in -a. Most English nouns in -a are from Latin (or latinized Greek) nominative feminine singular nouns, which have in Latin the plural ending *-ae*; but not all ; e. g., *sofa* is from Arabic ; *stanza & vista* are from Italian ; *subpoena* is not nominative ; *drama & comma* are neuter ; *stamina & prolegomena* are plural ; & with all such words -ae is impossible. Of the majority, again, some retain the Latin -ae in English either as the only or as an alternative plural ending (*antennae* only, *formulae* or *-las*), & some have always *-as* (*ideas, areas, villas*). The use of plurals in -ae therefore presents some difficulty to non-latinists. For most words with which -ae is possible or desirable, the information is given in their dictionary places ; for the principle of choice when both -ae & -as are current, see LATIN PLURALS 1, 3.

aeon, æon, eon. The first form is recommended ; see Æ, Œ.

aerate, aërate. The first form is recommended ; see Æ, Œ. The form *ærated* is a mere blunder, but very common.

aerial, aërial. The first form is recommended ; see Æ, Œ.

aery, aerie, eyry, eyrie. The first two forms are preferable to the others, which according to the OED & Professor Skeat are due to a theory of the derivation (from *egg* ; *eyry* = eggery) that is known (though the ultimate origin of *aery* is doubtful) to be wrong.

aesthetic. The word, which means etymologically *concerned with sensuous perception*, was introduced into English to supply *sense of beauty* with an adjective. It is in place in such contexts as *a. principles, from an a. point of view, an a. revival occurred, a. considerations do*

not appeal to him. It is less so in the meanings *professing* or *gifted with this sense* (*I am not a.* ; *a. people*), *dictated by* or *approved by* or *evidencing this sense* (*a very a. combination* ; *aesthetically dressed* ; *a. chintzes & wallpapers* ; *flowers on a table are not so a. a decoration as a well-filled bookcase*) ; & still less so when it is little more than a pretentious substitute for *beautiful* (*that green is so a.* ; *a not very a. little town*).

aetat., aet. The words, being abbreviations of *aetatis suae* (of his, her, their, age) must be written with the period, & not as in : *The Die-Hards had as their leader Lord Halsbury,* aetat 86. / *It was Mr. Chaplin,* aetat 70, *who.* / *A manifesto from Lord Roberts,* aetat 79. For *aet-, æt-,* see Æ, Œ.

affaire de cœur. See FRENCH WORDS.

affect, effect. These verbs are not synonyms requiring differentiation, but words of totally different meaning, neither of which can ever be substituted for the other. *Affect* (apart from other senses in which it is not liable to confusion with *effect*) means have an influence on, produce an effect on, concern, effect a change in : *effect* means bring about, cause, produce, result in, have as result. *These measures chiefly a. the great landowners. It does not a. me. It may seriously a.* (i. e. injure) *his health. A single glass of brandy may a.* (alter for better or worse the prospects of) *his recovery. A single glass of brandy may e.* (bring about) *his recovery. This will not a.* (change) *his purpose. This will not e.* (secure) *his purpose. We hope to e. an improvement. I effected my escape.*

affectionately. See LETTER FORMS.

affiliate makes *-liable* ; see -ABLE 1.

affinity. The prepositions normally used after this are, according to context, *between & with.* When the sense is less *relationship* or *likeness* than *attraction* or *liking, to* or *for* are sometimes used instead of *with* ; this should not be done ; in places where *with* is felt to be inappropriate, the truth is that *affinity*, which properly describes a reciprocal relationship only, has been used of a one-sided one, & should itself be replaced by another word. Cf. *sympathy with* & *for*.

affix, n. See TECHNICAL TERMS.
à fond. See FRENCH WORDS. It should be remembered that *à fond* & *au fond* mean different things, *à fond* to the bottom, i.e. thoroughly, & *au fond* at bottom, i.e. when one penetrates below the surface.

aforesaid. See PEDANTIC HUMOUR.
a fortiori. See TECHNICAL TERMS.
afterward(s). *Afterward*, once the prevalent form, is now obsolete in British use, but survives in U.S.
age. For synonymy see TIME.
aged. *A. 54* &c., ājd ; *an a. man* &c., ā′jĭd.
agenda. If a singular is required (=one item of the agenda) it is now *agendum*, the former singular *agend* being obsolete.

agent provocateur. See FRENCH WORDS.
aggrandize(ment). The accent of the verb is on the first & of the noun on the second syllable. See RECESSIVE ACCENT.

aggravate, aggravation. 1. The use of these in the sense *annoy, vex, annoyance, vexation*, should be left to the uneducated. It is for the most part a feminine or childish colloquialism, but intrudes occasionally into the newspapers. *To aggravate* has properly only one meaning—to make (an evil) worse or more serious. The right & the wrong use are shown in : (right) *A premature initiative would be calculated rather to a. than to simplify the situation* ; (wrong) *The reopening of the contest by fresh measures that would a. their opponents is the last thing that is desired in Ministerial circles.* It is in the participle (*and*

a very stupid, tiresome, aggravating man he is) that the vulgarism is commonest.

2. *Aggravate* makes *aggravable* ; see -ABLE 1.

aggrievedly. Four syllables if used ; see -EDLY.
agio. Pl. *-os* ; see -O(E)s 4.
agitate makes *agitable* ; see -ABLE 1.
ago. If *ago* is used, & the event to be dated is given by a clause, it must be by one beginning with *that* & not *since*. The right forms are :— *He died 20 years ago* (no clause) ; *It is 20 years since he died* (no *ago*) ; *It was 20 years ago that he died.* The following examples are wrong ; the tautology *ago since* is naturally commoner, but is equally wrong, in sentences like the second, where a parenthesis intervenes :—*It is barely 150 years ago since it was introduced./ Yet it is only just over sixty years ago, as an article in the new edition of the ' Encyclopaedia Britannica ' reminds us, since facilities for cheap travel were first introduced.* For similar mistakes, see HAZINESS.

agréments. See FRENCH WORDS.
agricultur(al)ist. See -IST.
aide-de-camp. See FRENCH WORDS.
aiguille. See FRENCH WORDS.
aim. The verb in the metaphorical sense of purpose or design or endeavour is idiomatically followed by *at* with the gerund & not by *to* with the infinitive. Probably no-one will doubt this who sees the two constructions side by side :—*he aimed at being, he aimed to be, the power behind the throne* ; *arguments are aimed to produce, arguments are aimed at producing, conviction* ; *what do you aim at doing ? what do you aim to do ?* But the analogy of *purpose* &c., which take the infinitive & not the gerund, leads unobservant writers wrong. And the infinitive construction, though not good British, appears to be good American, since it is certainly a favourite with Emerson, & is given in Webster's & the Century & Standard Dictionaries as the normal verb-construc-

tion (*at* with the gerund not being even mentioned) after *aim*.

aîné. See FRENCH WORDS.

aitch, ache. The original spelling is *ache*, but *aitch* (*drop* one's *aitches*) is now universal.

aitch-bone. *H-bone, edge-bone, ash-bone*, & other forms, are due to random shots at the etymology. *Aitch-bone*, though it does not reveal the true origin of the word (L *natis* buttock, with loss of n- as in *adder* &c.), suggests no false one & corresponds to the pronunciation.

-AL NOUNS. When a noun in *-al* is given in its alphabetical place with a simple reference to this article, the meaning is that its use is deprecated. There is a tendency to invent or revive unnecessary verbal nouns of this form. The many that have passed into common use (as *trial, arrival, refusal, acquittal, proposal*) have thereby established their right to exist. But when words of some age (as *revisal, refutal, appraisal, accusal*) have failed to become really familiar & remained in the stage in which the average man cannot say with confidence off-hand that they exist, the natural conclusion is that there is no work for them that cannot be adequately done by the more ordinary verbal nouns in -ion (*revision*), -ation (*refutation, accusation*), & -ment (*appraisement*). When there is need on an isolated occasion for a verbal noun that shall have a different shade of meaning from those that are current (e. g. *accusal* may suggest itself as fitter to be followed by an objective genitive than *accusation* ; cf. *the accusal of a murderer, the accusation of murder*), or that shall serve when none already exists (there is e. g. no noun *beheadment*), it is better to make shift with the gerund (*the accusing, the beheading*) than to revive an unfamiliar *accusal* or invent *beheadal*. The use of rare or new -al nouns, however, is due only in part to a legitimate desire for the exactly appropriate form ; to some writers the out-of-

the-way word is dear for its own sake, or rather is welcome as giving an air of originality to a sentence that if ordinarily expressed would be detected as commonplace ; they are capable of writing *bequeathal* for *bequest, agreeal* for *agreement, allowal* for *allowance*, or *arisal* for *arising* ; except for this dislike of the normal word, we should have had *account* instead of *recountal* in *Of more dramatic interest is the recountal of the mission imposed upon Sir James Lacaita*, & to *recount* these in *But this is not the place for a recountal of these thrilling occurrences* ; cf. *retiral* in *There were many retirals at the dissolution. Carousal, surprisal, supposal, decrial*, may be mentioned among the hundreds of needless -al words that have been actually used.

à la. The sex of the person whose name is introduced by this does not affect the form, *la* agreeing not with it but with an omitted *mode : à la reine* ; *à la* (not *au*) *maître-d'hôtel* ; *a Home-rule Bill à la* (not *au*) *Gladstone. Au* with adjectives, as in *au naturel, au grand sérieux*, (cf. *à la française* &c.) is not used in English except in phrases borrowed entire from French.

alarm, alarum. *Alarum* is by origin merely a variant of *alarm*, & the two nouns were formerly used without distinction in all senses. In poetry *alarum* may still bear any of the senses except that of fear or apprehension ; but in ordinary use it is restricted to the senses of alarm-signal, warning-signal, or clock or other apparatus that gives these. This being a clear & useful differentiation, it is to be regretted that *alarm-clock*, & *alarm* in the same sense, should (owing to the trade in alarums from America, where the differentiation has not been made) be reviving.

alarmedly. Four syllables if used ; see -EDLY.

albeit. See ARCHAISM.

albino. Pl. *-os* ; see -O(E)S 6. Fem. *albiness*.

Albion. See SOBRIQUETS.

alcaics. See TECHNICAL TERMS.

ale, beer. In the trade, & in statistics & the like, the two words are distinguished in meaning. But in ordinary use, as at table, both denote the same thing, including the pale & excluding the dark varieties of malt liquor ; the difference is that *beer* is the natural current word, & *ale* is a GENTEELISM.

alexandrine. See TECHNICAL TERMS.

alien. The prepositions after the adjective are *from* & *to*. *From* is the earlier usage, & represents the commoner Latin construction, though *alienus* with the dative is also good Latin. There is perhaps a slight preference for *from* where mere difference or separation is meant (*We are entangling ourselves in matters a. from our subject*), & for *to* when repugnance is suggested (*cruelty is a. to his nature*). But this distinction is usually difficult to apply, & the truth seems rather that *to* is getting the upper hand of *from* in all senses (cf. DIFFERENT, A-VERSE).

alienate makes *-nable* ; see -ABLE 1.

alight. The past tense & p.p. are *alighted* in ordinary use ; but in poetry *alit* has been written by Byron, Shelley, & Poe.

align(ment), aline(ment). The OED pronounces for the spelling with ne & against that with gn. On the verb it says ' As *line* is the Eng. spelling of Fr. *ligne* & *ligner*, there is no good reason for retaining the unetymological *g* in the derivative ' ; & on the noun ' The Eng. form *alinement* is preferable to *alignment*, a bad spelling of the Fr.' Usage as clearly pronounces for the -gn- forms ; in the OED quotations gn is just four times as numerous as ne. The claims of usage & etymology are often hard to decide between (cf. RHYME). No-one would propose to correct *admiral*, *aisle*, or *cretin*, back into conformity with Arabic *amir*, Latin *ala*, or Greek *khristianos*, though the insertion of d & s, & the

omission of h, are 'unetymological ' ; & on the other hand unnoticed corrections of words taken from French (as *scholastic*, respelt on Greek *skhole* after being taken directly from *scolastique*) are innumerable. But *align* is not only the established form ; it is also more correct than *aline* ; correction on Latin analogies (*adlineare, allineare*) could only give *alline* ; & *aline* regarded as a purely English formation would have no meaning, a- in the sense *to* not being a recognized formative element. *Alline(ment)* seems defensible but inexpedient, *aline(ment)* indefensible, & *align-(ment)* unobjectionable.

-(al)ist. For such alternative forms as *agriculturist & agriculturalist*, see -IST.

alit. 1. See ALIGHT. 2. *Alit* for *alight* or *lit*, as in *the lamps are alit*, is a blunder.

alkali. The pronunciation is usually -lï, but sometimes -lī. The plural should be & usually is *alkalis* ; but the -lï pronunciation, suggesting *alkaly* as the singular, has produced a by-form *alkalies*.

allay. For inflexions see VERBS IN -IE &c., 1.

allegedly. Four syllables if used ; see -EDLY.

allegory. See TECHNICAL TERMS. For *a.* & *parable*, see SIMILE & METAPHOR.

allegro. Pl. *-os* ; see -O(E)S 3.

alleluia. The spelling now usual is *hallelujah*.

alleviate makes *-viable* ; see -ABLE 1.

alley. The plural is *alleys*.

alliteration. See TECHNICAL TERMS.

allocate. See -ATABLE.

allowedly. Four syllables if used ; see -EDLY.

allow of. This is undergoing the same limitation as ADMIT OF, but the process has not gone so far ; *Jortin is willing to allow of other miracles, A girl who allows of no impertinent flattery*, are hardly felt to be archaic, though *of* would now usually be omitted. The normal use, & sense, however, are the same as those of *admit of*.

almighty. So spelt ; see -LL-, -L-, 4.

all right. The words should always be written separate ; there are no such forms as *all-right, allright*, or *alright*, though even the last, if seldom allowed by the compositors to appear in print, is often seen (through confusion with *already* & ALTOGETHER) in MS. This rule holds not only when the two words are completely independent, as in *The three answers, though different, are all right*, but also where they may be regarded as forming a more or less fixed phrase. So: *The scout's report was ' All right '* (i. e. all is right)./ *Is he all right? / ' Will you come for a walk ? ' ' All right './ All right, you shall hear of this again./ Oh, I know them apart all right*.

all the time. The phrase is idiomatic English only when the time in question is a definite period fixed by the context, as in :—*I did not see you because I was looking at her a. t. t.* (that you were present) ; *Well, I knew that a. t. t.* (that you were supposing I did not) ; *He pretends friendship, & a. t. t.* (that he pretends it) *he is plotting against one* ; *I have been a free-trader a. t. t.* (that others have been wavering). Used generally without such implied definition, in the sense *all day & every day* (*Actors act while they are on the stage, but he acts a. t. t.* ; *We hold that a Tariff Reformer must be a Tariff Reformer all the time, & not an opportunist*), it is slang.

allusion, allude. 1. For pronunciation see LU.

2. The words are much misused by journalists & others. An allusion is a covert or indirect reference, in which the application of a generality to the person or thing it is really aimed at, or the identification of something that the speaker or writer appears by his words to have in mind but does not name, is left for the hearer or reader to make ; it is never an outright or explicit mention. *Allude to* has the same limitations. Examples of the legitimate use are :—*We looked at each other wondering which of us he was alluding to* ; *Though he never uses your name, the allusion to you is obvious* ; *He is obscure only because he so often alludes* (or *only owing to his frequent allusions*) *to contemporary events now forgotten*.

The misuse is seen in :—*When the speaker happened to name Mr. Gladstone, the allusion was received with loud cheers./ The lecturer then alluded at some length to the question of strikes*.

It may be added that *allude to* is often chosen, out of foolish verbosity, when the direct *mean* would do better ; so *When you said ' some people cannot tell the truth ', were you alluding to* (did you mean) *me ?* ; but this is rather an abuse than a misuse.

ally, vb. For inflexions see VERBS IN -IE &c., 6.

alma mater. See BATTERED ORNAMENTS, & SOBRIQUETS.

almanac. The OED recognizes this spelling only.

almoner. The OED gives the pronunciation ǎ'lmoner. But as the word, though existing as (part of) the title of certain functionaries, is better known in transferred & general uses, it is perhaps safe to prophesy that the pronunciation ah'moner, already common owing to *alms*, will prevail.

almost. For *a. quite* see INCOMPATIBLES.

alone. The adverbial use of *alone* with *not* in place of the usual *only* (*more might be done, & not alone by the authorities, but . . .*) is a survival, & like other archaisms is to be avoided except in poetry or in prose of a really poetic type. In ordinary writing it is one of the thousand little mechanical devices by which ' distinction of style ' is vainly sought ; the following passage shows it in characteristic surroundings :— *Recourse to porters, whose limited* loads are carried on the head, savours more of operations in the West African bush than on the Indian frontier, so that not alone in the region passed through, but in its transport will our latest little war wear an interesting & unusual aspect.

This censure does not apply to the adjectival use (*It is not youth alone that needs . . .*), in which *not* & *alone* are usually separated.

à l'outrance. The French phrase is *à outrance* or *à toute outrance*, never *à l'outrance*. Those who use French phrases to suggest that they are at home with French should accordingly be careful to write *à outrance*. For those who use them merely as the handiest way of expressing themselves the form that is commoner in English is as good as the other, & does not lay them open to the charge of pedantry. So with *double entendre* for French *double entente*, *nom de plume* for *nom de guerre*, *morale* for *moral*, *locale* for *local*, *chorale* for German *Choral*, & others.

already. The adverb is so spelt ; see -LL-, -L-, 4 ; this does not affect the use of the two separate words, as in *Tell me when it is all ready* ; cf. ALTOGETHER.

alright. See ALL RIGHT.

also. The word is an adverb, & not a conjunction ; nevertheless, it is often used in the latter capacity where *and* (*also*), *but also*, or *as well as*, would be in place. In talk, where the informal stringing on of after-thoughts is legitimate, there is often no objection to this (*Remember your watch & money ; also the tickets*) ; & the deliberate afterthought may appear similarly in print (*The chief products are hemp & cigars ; also fevers*). But it is the writer's ordinary duty to settle up with his after-thoughts before he writes his sentence, & consequently the unassisted *also* that is proper to the after-thought gives a slovenly air to its sentence.

Great attention has been paid to the

history of legislation, also [& also] to that of religion. / We are giving these explanations gently as friends, also [and] patiently as becomes neighbours. / ' Special ' is a much overworked word, it being used to mean great in degree, also [but also] peculiar in kind. / Mr. Sonnenschein's volume will show . . . Shakespeare's obligations to the ancients, also [as well as] the obligations of modern writers to Shakespeare.

alternative. 1. *Alternative(ly)* had formerly, besides their present senses, those now belonging only to *alternate(ly)* ; now that the differentiation is complete, confusion between the two (*Frenchmen have become accustomed to these changes of front in German policy, singular methods which consist in blowing alternatively hot & cold*) is still less excusable, because less common, than between DEFINITE & DEFINITIVE.

2. There are also difficulties about the correct use of the noun *alternative*, for dealing with which it is necessary to realize clearly its different senses. These are now distinguished, with illustrations that may serve to show what is idiomatic & what is not :—

a. Set, especially pair, of possibilities from which one only can be selected ; this is often practically equivalent to *choice*. *The only a. is success or* (not *&*) *death. We have no a. in the matter.*

b. Either of such pair or any one of such set. *Either a. is, any of the aa. is, both aa. are, all the aa. are, intolerable. The aa., the only aa., are success &* (not *or*) *death.*

c. Second of such pair, the first being in mind. *We need not do it ; but what is the a. ? We must do it ; there is no* (not *no other*) *a. The* (not *the other*) *a. is to die.*

d. Other of such a set, one at least being in mind. *If we decline, what are the aa. ? The only a. is to die. You may say* lighted *or* lit *or* alight ; *there is no other a. The only aa. to it are gas &* (not *or*) *candles.*

although. See THOUGH.

alto. Pl. -*os* ; see -O(E)S 6.

altogether. Confusion between this & *all together* is not uncommon (*Until at last, gathered altogether again, they find their way down to the turf./A long pull, a strong pull, & a pull altogether./Great efforts have been made . . . to bring the troops out altogether in brigades, & even in divisions. All together* should have been used in each). *Altogether* is right only in the senses *entirely* or *on the whole*.

alto-relievo. Pl. -*os* ; see -O(E)S 6. Preferable forms are the English *high relief* & the Italian *alto rilievo*.

aluminium. See LU.

amalgamate. See -ATABLE.

amateur. The best pronunciation is ă'mătūr, the next best ămătūr' ; it is high time that vain attempts at giving the French -*eur* should cease, since the word is in everyday use among the uneducated. Cf. LIQUEUR, & see FRENCH PRONUNCIATION.

amazedly. Four syllables ; see -EDLY.

ambidext(e)rous. Spell without the -*e*- ; see DEXT(E)ROUS.

âme damnée. See FRENCH WORDS.

ameliorate makes -*rable*; see -ABLE 1.

amende honorable. See FRENCH WORDS.

amenity. Pronounce -měn- ; the restoration of -mēn- (Latin *amoenus*) is pedantic ; see FALSE QUANTITY.

America(n). The use of *America* for *the United States* & *American* for (*citizen*) *of the U. S.* is open to as much & as little objection as that of *England* & *English*(*man*) for *Great Britain* (& *Ireland*), *British*, & *Briton*. It will continue to be protested against by purists & patriots, & will doubtless survive the protests.

à merveille. See FRENCH WORDS.

amid, amidst. 1. Both are LITERARY WORDS, subject to the limitations of their kind.

2. As to the alternative forms, the OED states that ' There is a ten-

dency to use *amidst* more distributively, e.g. of things scattered about, or a thing moving, in the midst of others '. This may be true, though it is difficult to establish ; to take a phrase quoted from Thackeray, *amidst the fumes of tobacco* would, by the OED tendency, be changed to *amid*, which is not in fact more natural. Another distinction that may be hazarded is that *amid* has dropped out of ordinary use still more completely than *amidst*, & is therefore felt to be inappropriate in many contexts that can still bear *amidst*. When we find *amid* in a passage of no exalted or poetical kind (*A certain part of his work . . . must be done amid books*), our feeling is that *amidst* would have been less out of place, though *among* would have been still better.

among, amongst. There is certainly no broad distinction either in meaning or in use between the two. The OED illustrates under *amongst* each of the separate senses assigned to *among* ; it does, however, describe *amongst* as ' less usual in the primary local sense than *among*, &, when so used, generally implying dispersion, intermixture, or shifting position '. Such a distinction may be accepted on authority, but can hardly be made convincing by quotations even on the liberal scale of the OED. It is remarkable, at any rate, that one of the forms should not by this time have driven out the other (cf. *on* & *upon*, *although* & *though*, *while* & *whilst*, *amid* & *amidst*). The survival of both without apparent differentiation may possibly be due to the unconscious desire for euphony or ease ; few perhaps would say *amongst strangers* with *among* to hand, *amongst us* is easier to say than *among us*. Some confirmation of this is found by comparing the ratio borne by initial vowels to initial consonants after *amongst* with the corresponding ratio after *among* ; reckoned upon the nineteenth-century quotations in the OED, this ratio is four times as high for *amongst* as for *among*; though the total number of quotations is too small to justify the belief that this proportion prevails generally, it probably indicates a tendency. It may be said with some confidence that (1) *among* is the normal word, (2) *amongst* is more usual before vowels, but (3) before *the*, which so commonly follows as easily to outnumber all other initials, the two forms are used quite indifferently.

amoral, non-moral. See A-, AN-.

amour. Being established in English, & not likely ever to be expelled, it is better pronounced with the normal English accent (ă'moor). Retention of a foreign accent undoubtedly discourages the popular use of a word, & if the word is worth having at all this is very undesirable. See FRENCH PRONUNCIATION.

amour-propre. See FRENCH WORDS. *Vanity* usually gives the meaning as well, &, if as well, then better.

amphibol(ol)ogy. See TECHNICAL TERMS.

ample, used as an attributive adjective in the sense *plenty of* (*he has a. courage*; *there is a. time*; *a. opportunities were given*) is legitimate only with nouns denoting immaterial or abstract things. It is often wrongly attached to nouns that, like *butter, oil, water, coal,* denote substances of indefinite quantity; *We have a. water for drinking*, *There is a. coal to carry us through the winter,* are wrong. The misuse is perhaps traceable to four lines of false analogy : (1) *a.* is common, & correct, with such nouns as *stabling, cellarage, accommodation, ammunition, cattle, money, plant, rolling-stock,* which, though used concretely as collectives for the real concretes *stable, cellar, apartment &c., powder &c., beast, coin &c., machine &c., waggon &c.,* are strictly abstract words = supply of; (2) though *There is a. coal* is wrong, *The coal,* or *Our coal, is a.* is not wrong; the explanation is that *the coal, our coal,* denotes

a quantity, & is an abstract phrase, though *coal* is a concrete word; this is only possible when *a.* is predicative & not attributive, but it naturally misleads; (3) there are many words that belong sometimes to the *butter* class, & sometimes to the *stabling* class; *linen* may mean either the material (*a.* is then wrong; so *We have a. linen for half-a-dozen shirts*), or supply of linen articles (*a.* is then right; so *They will start housekeeping with a. linen, plate, & crockery*); (4) other words with which in their concrete sense *a.* is wrong may in some figurative or abstract sense take it; a ship may have *a.* water (i.e. space) to turn in, though the crew cannot have *a.* water to drink; & *a. butter* may mean plenty of flattery though not plenty of butter.

amplify. For inflexions see VERBS IN -IE &c., 6.

amputate makes *amputable*; see -ABLE 1.

amuck, the familiar spelling, due to popular etymology, but going back to the seventeenth century & well established, should be maintained against the DIDACTICISM *amok*.

amusedly. Four syllables if used; see -EDLY.

amusive is best avoided. It serves in fact (though differentiation might have taken place) no purpose not better served by *amusing*; & in spite of its actual age it always suggests either ignorance or NOVELTY-HUNTING.

an. See A, AN.

anachronic, anachronistic. The long form is better (1) because owing to the places of its accents (ănakrŏ'nĭk, ană'kronĭ'stĭk; cf. ănă'kronĭzm) its connexion with its noun is more instantly apparent, & (2) because it is therefore commoner.

anacoluthon, anacrusis. See TECHNICAL TERMS.

anagoge. See GREEK G.

anagram. See TECHNICAL TERMS.

ANALOGY. 1. As a logical re-source. 2. As an influence in word-formation. 3. As a corrupter of idiom.

1. As a logical resource. The meaning of analogy in logic is given under TECHNICAL TERMS ; we are here little concerned with it ; it is perhaps the basis of most human conclusions, its liability to error being compensated for by the fre-quency with which it is the only form of reasoning available ; but its literary, not its logical, value is what we have now to do with. Its literary merits need not be pointed out to anyone who knows the Parables, or who has read the essays of Bacon or Montaigne, full of analogies that flash out for the length of a line or so & are gone : *Money is like muck, not good unless it be spread.* What does need pointing out is unfortunately its demerit—the deadly dullness of the elaborate artificial analogy favoured by journ-alists who think it necessary to write down to their audience & make their point plain to the meanest capacity. The journalist has a view upon the reorganization of the War Office & the right relations between Parliament, the Secretary of State, the Commander-in-Chief, & the minor officials. He says what he can, directly, in favour of his view ; & then, lest ' our people ' should miss the point, he goes on to trans-port them into a great household or estate, & explain what confusion would result if the owner did not arrange on a particular plan the re-lations of majordomo, butler, cook, & footmen, or of land-agent, tenants, grooms, & gardeners. ' Our people ' is no more familiar with majordomos & land-agents than with Commanders-in-Chief, & so he finds it well to repeat with emphasized dullness about the type what he has argued dully enough about the antitype. Specimens fully bearing out this generalized descrip-tion are too long to quote ; but the following gives a fair idea of the essential stupidity of these fabricated

analogies, against which no warning can be too strong ; they are on a level with talking to a schoolboy about the puff-puff ; let it be read & compared with the money that is like muck : *The Government are playing the part of a man entrusted with the work of guarding a door beset by enemies. He refuses to let them in at once, but pro-vides them with a large bag of gold, & at the same time hands them out a crowbar amply strong enough to break down the door. That is the Government's idea of preserving the Union & safeguarding the integrity of the United Kingdom.*

2. As an influence in word-forma-tion. In the making of words, & in the shape that they take, analogy is the chief agent. Wanting a word to express about some idea a relation that we know by experience to be expressible about other ideas, we apply to the root or stem associated with it what strikes us as the same treatment that has been applied to those others. That is, we make the new word on the analogy of the old ; & in ninety-nine cases we make it right, being all old hands at the job ; for each of us, in the course of a day, makes large numbers of words that he has never seen in a dictionary or grammar, & for which his only warrant is merely an unconscious conviction that they are analogical ; nearly every inflexion is an instance ; we are taught, perhaps, that the past of *will* is *would*, or the plural of *ox* is *oxen*, but not that the past of *inflate* is *inflated* or the plural of *book* is *books* ; those forms we make when we want them by analogy, & generally make them right. Occa-sionally, however, we go wrong : *The total poll midway in December was 16,244 so that upwards of half the electors were abstentients.* The writer wanted a single word for persons guilty of abstention, & one too that would not, like *abstainer*, make us think of alcohol ; *dissension* came into his head as rhyming with *abstention* ; if that yields, said he, *dissentients*, why should *abstention*

not yield *abstentients* ? Because the correspondence between *abstention* & *dissension* is not quite so close as he assumed ; if he had remembered *dissentire* & *abstinere*, analogy would have led him to *abstinents* instead of to *abstentients*. That is a live newspaper instance of the fallibility of analogy, & dead specimens may be found in any etymological dictionary —dead in the sense that the unsoundness of their analogical basis excites no attention as we hear the words. Who thinks of *chaotic, operatic, dilation, dandiacal,* & *direful,* as malformations ? yet none of them has any right to exist except that the men who made them thought of *eros* as a pattern for *chaos, drama* for *opera, relate* for *dilate, maniac* for *dandy,* & *dread* for *dire,* though each pattern differed in some essential point from the material to be dealt with ; the objection to some of the words is explained in the separate articles. These malformations, it is true, have now all the rights of words regularly made ; they have prospered, & none dare call them treason ; but those who try their luck with *abstentients* & the like must be prepared to pass for ignoramuses. See also HYBRID DERIVATIVES, & (talking of *ignoramuses,* for which false analogy has been known to substitute *ignorami*) LATIN PLURALS.

3. As a corrupter of idiom. That is the capacity in which analogy chiefly requires notice in this book. Understanding by *idiom* the way in which it comes natural to an Englishman to word what he wishes to express, as opposed to the ways that might occur to an imaginary being presented with the bare vocabulary of English to make himself intelligible with, & by *an idiom* any particular combination of words, or pattern of phrase, or construction, that has become habitual with us to the exclusion of other possibilities, the pranks played by analogy upon idiom & idioms are innumerable. Of the following extracts each ex-

hibits an outrage upon idiom, & each is due to the assumption that some word or phrase may be treated in a way that would be legitimate if another of roughly the same meaning had been used instead ; that other is given in a bracket, sometimes with alternative forms :—
They are capable of braving this consequence, but we do not think the public need fear that they will do it for anything less than what they are honestly convinced to be a *real necessity* (they honestly believe to be)./ *The double task was performed only* at the expenditure *of laborious days & nights* (cost)./*The feature mostly remarked upon in his style when contesting individual games was the complete* absorption *which the great expert* bestowed *upon the board* (attention)./*Those regulations about good husbandry so* unpopular *to farmers & landlords* (unpalatable)./ *Roumania indicated her* reluctance to any step *compromising her future good relations with Germany* (repugnance ; *or* reluctance to take)./ *Several English papers* attribute a desire on the part of Canada *to do a little coquetting with the United States* (detect, *or* conjecture ; *or* attribute to Canada)./*Whether such a scheme would come under the category of ' public utility ' is* ambiguous (doubtful)./*We should be sorry to see the slightest* obstacle placed *by Free Traders* to *an honest & dignified withdrawal on the part of their opponents* (opposed ; *or* placed in the way of withdrawal)./*Questions of international law, in which an intimate* acquaintance *of Scottish jurisprudence was particularly useful* (knowledge ; *or* acquaintance with)./ *Mr. H. Belloc, who has not often* admitted to ignorance *on any subject, has owned . . .* (confessed to ignorance ; *or* admitted ignorance)./ *The Government of this South American Republic are naturally* alert to *the fact that . . .* (alive, *or* awake)./ *The newspaper reader who was scared by placards which* alleged *to give authentic news of the naval crisis*

(purported, *or* professed)./*It is more probable that the forecast is imperfect than that the German Government has withdrawn its previous* compliance to *the whole demand* (consent ; *or* compliance with)./

These are all casual lapses, each revealing that the writer is not a master of idiomatic English, but not caused by any widespread misapprehension of the meaning of particular words. There are, however, words whose sufferings under analogy are more serious, so that the unidiomatic substitute tends to supplant the true English ; some of these, dealt with in separate articles, are : *as well as* (=besides ; see WELL) ; ANTICIPATE (= expect) ; ADVOCATE (= recommend) ; AIM (=purpose) ; CLAIM (= assert) ; DUE TO (=owing to) ; EQUAL 2 ; FOIST (=fob) ; FEASIBLE (=possible) ; HOPE (=expect) ; HARDLY 2 (=no sooner) ; IN ORDER THAT (=so that) ; INSTIL (=inspire) ; OBLIVIOUS (=insensible) ; POSSIBLE (=able) ; PREFER (=wish rather) ; REGARD 3 (=consider) ; SUPERIOR 3 (=better) ; VARIOUS (=several). See also the general articles OBJECT-SHUFFLING, SLIPSHOD EXTENSION, & CAST-IRON IDIOM ; & examples of wrong analogy, of less importance, will be found also under *forbid, intimidate, lethargy, measure, motive, opportunity, prejudice, privilege, propensity, resentment, stigmatize, sufficient, tend, the more* (THE 5, 6), *tinker,* & *value.*

analyse is better than *analyze*, but merely as being the one of two equally indefensible forms that has won. The correct but now impossible form would be *analysize* (or *analysise*), with *analysist* for the existing *analyst* ; see also -IST.

anapaest, anaphora. See TECHNICAL TERMS.

anarchism. See SOCIALISM for distinction.

anastrophe. See TECHNICAL TERMS.

anchoret, anchorite. The OED states that the two forms are now equally common. The first has the two advantages of representing the Greek original (*anakhōrētēs*) more closely, & corresponding better with the surviving feminine *anchoress* (*anchoritess* being now archaic).

anchovy. Usually ănchō'vĭ ; rarely, by RECESSIVE ACCENT, ă'nchovĭ.

anchylose, ankylose. The right form would be *ancylose*. The established one is *anchylose*, with h inserted to preserve the hard sound ; these irregular devices are regrettable, since it is a matter of absolute indifference whether the hard sound is preserved or not, while the inserted h puts the Greek scholar off the track. The form with k, which is occasionally used, would have secured the sound more certainly & not deceived the scholar.

ancien régime. See FRENCH WORDS.

and. 1. *And which.* 2. Bastard enumeration. 3. Commas in enumeration.

1. For *and which* see WHICH.

2. Bastard Enumeration. There is perhaps no blunder by which journalists & other hasty writing is so commonly defaced at present as the one exemplified in *He plays good cricket, likes golf & a rubber of whist.* The forms of enumeration with which we need concern ourselves in dealing with this are

He is Y & Z (1)
He is (A,) X, Y, & Z (2)
He is (A &) X & Y & Z (3)
He is (A,) Y, Z (4)

Nos 1 & 2 are the ordinary idiomatic forms ; 3 is unusual but unobjectionable ; 4 is exceptional, & used only as a sometimes justifiable stylistic device. The writer of *He plays* &c. (who surely is not, & certainly ought not to be, indulging in stylistic devices) thinks he is using No 2, but is in fact using No 4, with a No 1 as one of its members ; he thinks the items of his enumeration are three (as they would have been if he had said *& loves a rubber*), but they are in fact two ; he thinks he is avoiding the unusual No 3 (which would require *& likes golf &*

loves a rubber), but is in fact avoiding the normal N⁰ 1.

The test for this now prevalent slovenliness is fortunately very simple : in a N⁰ 2 (i.e. in the form we all habitually use for enumerations of more than two items) there must be nothing common to two or more of the items without being common to all. In the *He plays* example the word *likes* is common to the golf & whist items, but has no relation to the cricket item. In the following examples, numerous because the temptation presents itself in different forms of greater or less insidiousness, what is common to some but not all items is in roman type ; corrections are added in brackets ; but it may be said in general that insertion of the missing *and*, from which ignorant writers shrink consciously or unconsciously, is usually attended with no more damage to euphony than that repetition of essential words by the fear of which ELEGANT VARIATION, in all its distressing manifestations, is produced ; there is nothing to offend the ear in *He plays good cricket, & likes golf & a rubber of whist.*

Hence loss of *time, of money, & sore trial of patience* (reduce to a N⁰ 1 with a N⁰ 1 in its first item :—*time & money, &*)./*Penn's letters are courtly in tone,* full of *friendly advice, & affectionate wishes* (reduce to 1, with a 1 in second item :—*& full* ; *advice &*)./It was *terse, pointed, & a tone of good humour made it enjoyable* (reduce to 1, with a 1 in first item :—*terse & pointed*)./ *He has his ideals,* is *well read, a lover of poetry, & a student* (reduce to 1 with a 2 in second item :—*& is*)./*His workmen* are *better housed, better fed, & get a third more in wages* (reduce to 1 with a 1 in first item :—*housed & fed*)./ *He has not advanced with the rapidity of Sir A. B., who was ' called ' at the Middle Temple in* 1894, became *a Q.C. in* 1895, *& a Bencher in* 1900 (reduce to 1 :—*who, after being called*)./*Moltke* had *recruited, trained,*

& knew by heart all the men under him (reduce to 1 with a 1 in first item :—*had recruited & trained & knew*)./ *Unemployed workmen gathered before the buildings,* hooted the prince *when he entered them, & on his departure* (reduce to 1 by placing a comma before *gathered* or removing that after *buildings*)./. . . *Neipperg, who* countermanœuvred with *vigilance, good judgment, & would not come to action* (reduce to 1 with a 1 in first item :—*vigilance & good*)./ *Make some sacrifice in order to* pass *the Appropriation Bill, the Finance Bill, the Expiring Laws Continuance Act, & make progress with . . .* (reduce to 1 with a 2 in first item :— *Bill, & the Expiring*)./*For* it *fails to include many popular superstitions, does not evidence any great care in its composition, & its arrangement is amateurish* (correct into 2 :—*& is amateurish* in arrangement)./*The Protectionist method* is *extremely wasteful, quickly exhausted,* inflicts the maximum of injury *on consumers, & on the great majority of producers* (the blunder is double ; make two 1 s :—*wasteful & quickly exhausted* ; *it*)./In 1889 *he rode in Australia, Africa, & two years ago he rode over the Pyrenees* (reduce to 1 with a 1 in first item :—*Australia & Africa*)./*Light is thrown upon* Herrick's *friendships, travelling,* his life *as a Cavalier, & as Vicar of Dean Prior* (double blunder ; reduce to 1 with a 1 in each item :— *Herrick's friendships & travels, & his life both as*).

A few bad enumerations are added for which carelessness rather than a wrong theory seems responsible. *The centuries during which the white man kidnapped, enslaved, ill-treated, & made of the black a beast of burden* (*& made a beast of burden of* ; or *& ill-treated the black & made him a*)./ *He has been successively Governor of the Gold Coast, has done good work in Hong Kong, & has governed Natal* (*has successively been* ; *Coast, done* ; *& governed*)./*Many of these authoresses are rich, influential, & are*

*surrounded by sycophants who . . .
(& surrounded)./It is true he has
worked upon old material, has indulged in no more serious research
than a perusal of the English &
French chronicles of the age & most
of the modern works dealing with the
subject (material & indulged).*

3. *And* & commas in enumerations
of the (A,) X, Y, & Z form (i.e., such
as :—Every *man woman & child*
was killed ; *Blue brown & grey*
eyes ; Blue *eyes skies & ties* ; An
honest sober & industrious man ;
Some *French Latin & other* words
have been borrowed).

There is no agreement at present
on the punctuation ; we may see :—
*Every man, woman, & child, was
killed* ; *Every man, woman, & child
was killed* ; *Every man, woman &
child, was killed* ; *Every man, woman
& child was killed.*

This licence, however, often leaves
readers helpless against ambiguity ;
e.g., if the comma after the last item
is a matter of indifference, the reader
faced with *A party formidable, intelligent, & numerous outside the
House* cannot possibly tell whether
the limitation *outside* &c. applies to
all three adjectives or only to the
last ; & if the comma before the
and is indifferent, he cannot tell
whether, in *All the most important
documents, declarations & resolutions,
which comprise the American constitution,* he has three separate items
(documents, declarations, resolutions), or whether the second &
third are the two items that make
up the first.

The only rule that will obviate such
uncertainties is that after every
item, including the last unless a
heavier stop is needed for independent reasons, the comma should be
used (*Every man, woman, & child,
was killed* ; *They killed every man,
woman, & child.*).

Accordingly, in the ambiguous examples above, a comma should be
inserted after *numerous,* & one after
declarations. Those examples are
actual extracts from newspapers, &

more such extracts follow, with
corrections :—*The only plan is . . .
to bring all the resources of the Poor
Law, the local authorities, &* charity
to *bear on the rest (charity, to)./Little
more than reading, writing, arithmetic,
drawing, &* singing is *taught (singing,
is)./This humourist, sentimentalist, &
not too reverent* agnostic must *find
life packed with entertainment (agnostic, must)./*The *cost of renting,* repairing & improving transferred *school
buildings (repairing, &* improving,
*transferred)./The modes in which I
now feel, desire, &* think arise *out
of the modes in which I have previously done so (think, arise)./The
design & scope of it do credit to the
organizers & planners, the artists &
architects, & the men of* business who
*have worked together in preparing it
(business, who.* Misinterpretation is
obviated ; for the relative clause
probably belongs to all the items)./
*The smooth grey of the beech stem,
the silky texture of the* birch & *the
rugged pine & oak (birch, &.* Without this, pine & oak have silky
texture).

One concession, however, must be
made. Among the examples corrected above there are none of the
type in which several adjectives
enumerated as (A,) X, Y, & Z are
attached to a following noun. The
rule would require us to write *They
have blue, brown, & grey, eyes* ; *Some
French, Latin, & other, words have
been borrowed.* These being intolerable, it is clear that a loophole must
be made ; & an analogy that will
serve is offered by the invariable
form of the corresponding enumeration without *and.* Logic would
require *A sober, honest, industrious,
man* ; but we write *A sober, honest,
industrious man* ; & the same licence
must be recognized for *Some French,
Latin, & other words.*

andantino. Pl. *-os* ; see -O(E)S 3.

anemone. Puzzling to pronounce ;
an emine(nce), not *an enemy,* gives
the order of consonants.

anent, apart from its use in Scotch

law-courts, where it is in place, is chiefly met with in letters to the press ; that is, it is a favourite with unpractised writers who, on their holiday excursions into print, like to show that they possess gala attire. See ARCHAISM. *Anent* is often found in the company of dubious syntax & sense, as in :—*Sir,*—*Your* remarks *today on the result of the Canadian election anent the paragraph in the Philadelphia Record* is, *I am glad to see, the first* sign *of real appreciation of* . . . (*is* should be *are* ; & he is not glad that it is the *first* sign).

aneurysm, not *aneurism.* The y is due to Greek *eurus* wide ; the false form suggests the totally different sense *nervelessness* ; cf. MESEMBRIAN-THEMUM.

angel. *Talk of an a.* is a GENTEEL-ISM.

angina. To say ă'njĭna was long regarded as a sad lapse from Latinity, & ănjī'na was expected of all educated persons. Progress in Plautine prosody has revealed that the i was short in Latin, & OED gives precedence to ă'njĭna. See FALSE QUANTITY.

angle n., **angle** v., **angler.** The noun *angle* (fish-hook) is now hardly used except in the BATTERED ORNA-MENT *brother of the a.* The verb is chiefly a stylish synonym (see WORKING & STYLISH WORDS) for *fish. Angler,* on the other hand, has a real use, since *fisher* is archaic, & *fisherman* is assumed, unless context forbids, to mean one who makes his living by fishing with nets.

anglice, -cè. See LATINE.
Anglo-Indian. For ambiguous meaning, see MULATTO 4.
ankle, ancle. The -k- is usual.
annihilate makes -*lable* ; see -ABLE 1.
announce. See FORMAL WORDS.
annoyedly. A bad form ; see -EDLY.
annul. So spelt, but -*lled* &c. ; see -LL-, -L-.
annunciation. Pronounce -sĭă- ; see -CIATION.
another. For *one a.* see EACH 2

for *But that is a. story* see HACK-NEYED PHRASES.
ant is usually pronounced ănt, without the north-&-south variation between ă & ah (as in can't, grass, path), by way of differentiation from *aunt.*

antagonize. As a synonym for *oppose, resist, neutralize, counteract,* the word is recognized in diction-aries ; but the OED quotations for it are far from impressive, & it may safely be said that the occasions are rare indeed when one of those words would not be preferable to it. It does appear in those senses in modern journalism, but perhaps never without producing an effect of vulgar display ; see WORKING & STYLISH WORDS. One or two quota-tions may be given in which there can be no doubt of the meaning :— *Socrates ends by saying that we should antagonize gambling on the ground of its being bad business & not as being bad morals./Every attempt to sub-stitute coercion for persuasion is a reversion to the very ideals which Labour collectively professes to an-tagonize./The Democrats have given notice of a determination to antagonize this & all other Bills for* . . . The last is from the OED, which states that this use (person opposing thing) is American English only ; the first two examples show that it has since appeared in England ; it is to be hoped than it may not last on either side of the Atlantic.

But *a.* has another sense in which it does good service, & should certainly not be banned. That is to *rouse* or *incur the hostility of,* to *expose* one-*self by* one's *action to the enmity of.* This sense probably comes also from America, where it is commoner than in England ; but its usefulness is so obvious that we should welcome it. As the OED has only one example, a few quotations may be worth giving to enable readers to judge of its merits ; it should be observed that the idea is not *oppose,* though opposing is implied, but something

more complicated & perhaps not otherwise expressible in one word :—
But the President was afraid to antagonize Senator Aldrich & the other leaders of the Stand-pat Republicans./Rather than antagonize the two New England Senators on whom the woollen manufacturers were leaning, he signed a re-enactment of the notorious Schedule K./The Reciprocity Bill was passed; but by pressing it through Congress President Taft antagonized both the Standpatters & the Insurgent Republicans./ Hulme, with his militarist impulse in thought, had a rare gift for forcing people to dissent from him; no one could more successfully antagonize from a lecture-platform an audience assembled with the most docile intentions./We are heartily in favour of doing nothing to antagonize the princes & chiefs of India./Tenderness to Germany would not have conciliated that country & would have antagonized our Allies./The Government will seek to employ its majority to carry out a home programme that will antagonize the electors./It assumes infallibility & warns off critics in a tone of determination sufficient to antagonize the man who approaches its findings with an open mind. In some of these *estrange* would pass, but in most it would be unsuitable.

antenna. Pl. *-nae.*

antepenult. See TECHNICAL TERMS.

Anthony is spelt with & pronounced without h.

anthropoid. Either ănthrŏ′poid or ă′nthropoid is legitimate ; see FALSE QUANTITY.

anthropophagi. See GREEK G.

anticipate. 1. *A.* makes *-pable* ; see -ABLE 1.

2. Unidiomatic use. *Exhibitions of feeling were, of course,* anticipated *to take place on Monday./This book, which, we repeat, might have been* anticipated *to contain a manifesto of the aims of the young intellectuals of America, proves to be .../A noteworthy act, which may be* anticipated *to have far-reaching effects in the*

future of the Balkan situation. The OED has nine separately numbered definitions, & 35 quotations, for *anticipate.* None of the definitions, & none of the quotations, suggest the possibility of such a use as is seen in all the above newspaper extracts ; the writers have thought their sentences with the homely *expect,* which would have served perfectly, & then written them with the FORMAL WORD *anticipate* ; ANALOGY has duped them into supposing that since it vaguely resembles *expect* in sense it must be capable of the same construction.

anticlimax. See TECHNICAL TERMS.

antiphlogistine &c. See GREEK G.

antipodes. Pronounce ăntĭ′podēz. Though *antipode* is said still to exist as a singular (*Selfishness is the very antipode of self-love*), the modern idiom is to use the plural form only, treating it as a singular when it means thing diametrically opposite (*The antipodes of selfishness is self-love*).

antiquarian. Both this & *antiquary* were formerly used as adjectives & nouns. Now that *antiquary* has been restricted to the noun use, & *antiquarian* has become chiefly adjectival, the absolute restriction of the latter to the adjective use seems very desirable.

ANTI-SAXONISM. There are, indeed, no anti-Saxonists, properly speaking ; that is to say, anti-Saxonism is not, like its verbal counterpart Saxonism, a creed ; but, if it is not a creed, it is a propensity & a practice that goes far to account for the follies of Saxonism, & is here named on that ground. *Happenings & forewords & forebears & birdlore & wheelman & betterment* are almost justified as a revulsion from the turgid taste that finds satisfaction in *transpire & materialize & eventuate, optimism & mentality, idiosyncrasy & psychological moment, proposition & protagonist, in connexion with & with reference to.* All of these are now in constant use, & often misuse ; that the meaning of many of them is vague is a recommendation to one kind of writer as saving him the trouble of choosing between more precise synonyms, & to one kind of reader as a guarantee that clear thought is not going to be required of him ; a further account of the attraction of such words will be found in LOVE OF THE LONG WORD. Others are chosen not because they are, like these, in constant use, but because they are not ; to say *nomenclature* instead of *name, replica* for *copy, premier* for *first, major* for *greater, evince* for *show, malnutrition* for *underfeeding, prior to* for *before,* is AVOIDANCE OF THE OBVIOUS ; & PEDANTIC HUMOUR suggests *gulosity, cacophonous, osculatory, sartorial,* & *cachinnation.*

Anti-Saxonism, then, is here used as a name for the frame of mind that turns away not so much from the etymologically English vocabulary as from the homely or the simple or the clear ; it may perhaps have been observed that the word given above as preferable to *replica* was *copy,* which is no more Saxon than *replica* ; it is more English, for all that, just as *ridiculous* is more English than *risible.* Readers who would like to study the effect of yielding to the practice will find quotations under nearly all the words that have been given as specimens, in their separate articles ; & for others half a dozen are here collected, most of them containing rather a misuse than a mere use of the word concerned :— *But he had the most tremendous* optimism in *the future triumph of his cause./Pleasing & original also are the landscapes in which vegetation is given* the meticulous significance *reminiscent of the* douanier *Rousseau./In the Small Rodent House, the Echidna was busy sucking up his milk supper through his long bill,* oblivious to *the eavesdroppers./Neither France nor Great Britain could* indulge in such an eventuality *at the present juncture./The 6s. increase*

in the price of coal may not materialize *after all.*

antistrophe, antithesis. See TECHNICAL TERMS.

antitype. See TYPE.

anxious. The objections made to it in the sense *eager* (*to* hear, improve, go, &c.) as a modernism, & in the sense *calculated to cause anxiety* (*It is a very a. business* ; *You will find her an a. charge*) as an archaism, are negligible ; both are natural developments, the first is almost universally current, & the second is still not infrequent.

any. 1. Compounds. *Anybody, anything, anyhow, anywhere, anywhen, anywhither,* are always single words ; so also the adverb *anywise* (but *in any wise*) ; for *anyone, any one,* see ONE ; *any way* is best written as two words (*I cannot manage it any way*) except perhaps when it means *at all events, however that may be, at any rate* (*Any way,* or *Anyway, I can endure it no longer*) ; *at any rate,* not *at anyrate.*

2. *He is the most generous man of anyone I know.* This common idiom, which looks illogical (*of all I know* being the logical form) is no doubt defensible as a development or survival of the archaic type *Caesar, the greatest traveller, of a prince, that had ever been. Of* there means *in the way of,* & we should now write *for* instead of it. But that sense of *of* being preserved in this idiom alone, the idiom itself is not likely long to resist the modern dislike of the illogical. It therefore seems desirable to avoid such things as :— *Edward Prince of Wales is the eighteenth who has borne that title, the most illustrious, perhaps, of any heir-apparent in the world* (more *illustrious than that of any).* /The Standard Oil Company *is credited with having the largest Eastern trade of any American enterprise* (of all *American enterprises* ; or *a larger trade than any other*).

aorist. See TECHNICAL TERMS.

à outrance. See À L'OUTRANCE, & FRENCH WORDS.

aperçu. See FRENCH WORDS.

apex. For plural see -EX₁ -IX, 4.

aphaeresis, aphetic. See TECHNICAL TERMS.

aplomb. See FRENCH WORDS.

apocope, apodosis. See TECHNICAL TERMS.

apophthegm should be so spelt, & pronounced ă'pŏfthĕm. The word is not a popular one ; to drop the ph in spelling conceals the derivation ; & there is no more reason for dropping it in sound than for that conversion of it into p in *diphthong* & *diphtheria* which is a notorious vulgarism.

aposiopesis, a posteriori. See TECHNICAL TERMS.

apostle. See PRONUNCIATION, Silent t.

APOSTROPHE. See POSSESSIVE PUZZLES, & -ED & 'D, for some points concerning its use ; &, for the sense in rhetoric, TECHNICAL TERMS.

appal(l). The double l is better ; see -LL-, -L-, 3. In any case -*lled* &c., see -LL-, -L-, 1.

a(p)panage. Either form will do ; *appa-* is perhaps commoner in general, & *apa-* in learned, use.

apparent(ly). 1. Either pronunciation (-ārent, -ărent) is legitimate ; see FALSE QUANTITY. 2. For commas before & after *apparently*, see THEREFORE.

appeared is liable to the same misuse as *seemed* with the PERFECT INFINITIVE.

appendix. Pl. -*dices* (-sēz) or -*dixes* (-ĭz) ; see -EX, -IX, 4.

applicable. See RECESSIVE ACCENT.

apply. For inflexions see VERBS IN -IE &c., 6.

apposition. See TECHNICAL TERMS.

appraisal. See -AL NOUNS.

appreciate makes -*ciable* ; see -ABLE 1.

appreciation. See -CIATION.

apprehend -**ension, comprehend** -**ension.** So far as the words are liable to confusion, i.e. as synonyms of *understand(ing)*, the *ap-* forms denote the getting hold or grasping, & the *com-* forms the having hold or full possession, of what is understood. What is *beyond my apprehension* I have no cognizance of ; what is *beyond my comprehension* I am merely incapable of fully understanding. To *apprehend* a thing *imperfectly* is to have not reached a clear notion of it ; to *comprehend* it *imperfectly* is almost a contradiction in terms. *I apprehend that A is B* advances an admittedly fallible view; *I comprehend that A is B* states a presumably indisputable fact.

apprise, not -*ize* ; see -ISE)(-IZE.

appropriate, v., makes -*priable* ; see -ABLE 1.

a priori. See TECHNICAL TERMS.

apropos is so clearly marked by its pronunciation as French, & the French construction is, owing to *à propos de bottes*, so familiar, that it is better always to use *of* rather than *to* after it ; probably *to* is partly accounted for by some confusion with *appropriate* (*His interpolation of stories that were not always strictly apropos to the country through which we were passing*). See FRENCH WORDS.

apt, liable. Followed by *to* with the infinitive in the senses *having an unfortunate tendency* (apt), *exposed to a risk* (liable), the words are so near in meaning that one of them (*liable*) is often wrongly used for the other. It may perhaps be laid down that *apt* is the right word except when the infinitive expresses not merely an evil, but an evil that is one to the subject. This is so, & therefore *liable* is right, in :—*We are l. to be overheard* (being overheard is an evil to us) ; *Matinée-hat wearers are l. to be insulted* ; *The goods are l. to suffer.* It is not so, & therefore *apt* is the only word, in :—*Curses are a. to come home to roost* (the evil is not to the curses, but to the curser) ; *Damage is a. to be done* ; *Matinée hats are a. to cause ill-*

temper ; *Difficulties are a. to occur* ; *Lovers' vows are a. to be broken.* It is usually not so, & therefore *apt* is usually the right word, in :—*He is a. to promise more than he can perform* (but *liable*, if the evil suggested is the shame he feels) ; *Cast iron is a. to break* (but *liable*, if we are sorry for the iron & not for its owner).

Since *liable* is apt to encroach, & *apt* is liable to suffer neglect, the best advice is never to use *l.* till *a.* has been considered & rejected.

aquarium. Pl. *-ums, -a* ; see -UM.

Arab, Arabian, Arabic. With exceptions for a phrase or two, such as *gum arabic*, the three adjectives are now differentiated, *Arab* meaning of the Arabs, *Arabian* of Arabia, & *Arabic* of the language or writing or literature of the Arabs. So we have *an Arab horse, child, girl, chief, sheikh* ; *Arab courage, fanatics, fatalism, traditions, philosophy* ; *the Arabian gulf, desert, fauna & flora* ; *Arabian gales* ; *the Arabic numerals* ; *an Arabic word* ; *Arabic writing, literature.* *Arab* & *Arabian* can sometimes be used indifferently ; thus *an Arab village* is one inhabited by Arabs ; if it happens to be in Arabia it is also *an Arabian village*, & may be called by either name ; *the Arab war* is one with Arabs ; *the Arabian war* is one in Arabia ; & the two may be one. Also *Arabian* may still be used instead of *Arab* of what belongs to or goes back to the past, as *Arabian records, monuments, philosophy, conquests.*

arbitrate makes *-trable* ; see -ABLE 1.

arbo(u)r. Keep the -u- ; but see -OUR & -OR.

arch, adj. For meaning see JOCOSE.

arch-, arche-, archi-. Though the prefix *arch-* (chief &c.) is pronounced arch in all words except *archangel* & its derivatives, the longer forms are always pronounced arkī : so *archbishop* (-ch-), but *archiepiscopal* (-k-) ; *archdeacon* (-ch-), but *archidiaconal* (-k-). The ch is hard in *archetype, archimandrite, Archimedes, architectonic, architrave.*

ARCHAISM. A certain number of words through the book are referred to this article, & such reference, where nothing more is said, is intended to give warning that the word is dangerous except in the hands of an experienced writer who can trust his sense of congruity ; archaic words thrust into a commonplace context to redeem its ordinariness are an abomination. More detailed remarks will be found in the general articles INCONGRUOUS VOCABULARY, REVIVALS, SUBJUNCTIVES, & WARDOUR STREET. Particular words under which the question of archaism is discussed are *anent, arride, aught, bounden, breakfast, burthen, chide, choler(ic), confident* (n.), *derringdo, except* (conj.), *fall* (autumn), *forebears, forenoon, gotten, howbeit, parlous, perchance, sandblind, save* (prep.), *subtile, surcease* ; & a few specimens of those for which the mere reference described above has been thought sufficient are *albeit, bashaw, belike, betwixt, broider(y), certes, damsel, fortune* (vb), *peradventure, quoth(a), & whit.*

archipelago. Pl. *-os* ; see -O(E)S 7.

ardo(u)r. Keep the -u- ; but see -OUR & -OR.

area. For synonyms see FIELD.

are, is. When one of these is required between a subject & a complement that differ in number (*these things . . . a scandal*), the verb must follow the number of the subject (*are*, not *is*, *a scandal*). *The wages of sin is death* is an archaism ; we do not now say *his wages is*, but *are, a pound a week* ; & we do not say *a pound are*, but *is, his wages* ; when, as here, subject & complement can change places without alteration of sense, so that it may be doubted which is which, the verb must agree with what precedes, & not with what follows ; when, however, the undoubted subject happens, as in a question, to follow, the verb agrees with it, as *But what proof are*, not *is, these facts of your theory ?*. In accordance with these rules, *are* & *is* should replace the roman-type *is* & *are* in :—*Apparently what that school desires to see* are *pipe-clayed & brass-buttoned companies of boys./But the moral inconsistencies of our contemporaries* is *no proof thereof./The pages which describe how* . . . is *a typical piece of description./The only difficulty in Finnish* are *the changes undergone by the stem./What is really practical about soldiering in the field* are *long marches, continuous operations* . . ./*What we want* are 300,000 *or more Territorials.*

argot. See FRENCH WORDS, &, for meaning & use, JARGON.

arguing in a circle. See TECHNICAL TERMS.

argumentum ad—. See TECHNICAL TERMS.

arise, in the literal senses of getting up & mounting, has given place except in poetic or archaic use to *rise.* In ordinary speech & writing it means merely to come into existence or notice or to originate *from,* & that usually (but cf. *new prophets a. from time to time*) of such abstract subjects as *question, difficulties, doubt, occasion, thoughts, result, effects.*

Aristotele′an, Aristote′lian. ' The latter more common '—OED. Cf. MEPHISTOPHELIAN, HERCULEAN.

arithmetical. See PROGRESSION.

armadillo. Pl. *-os* ; see -O(E)S 7.

arme blanche. See FRENCH WORDS.

armistice. Pronounce ar′mĭstĭs, not armĭ′stĭs ; see RECESSIVE ACCENT.

armo(u)r. Keep the u ; but see -OUR & -OR.

arms (weapons). The singular is late, rare, & best avoided. Instead of describing a particular pattern of rifle or sword as ' a beautifully balanced arm ', it is worth while to take the trouble of remembering *weapon.* We do well to sacrifice the exhaustive brevity of *The report of a fire-arm was heard* & risk ambiguity with *gun,* inaccuracy with *pistol,* or extravagance with *pistol, rifle, or gun,*—unless, of course, we have the luck to hit upon *shot.* The

only sense in which the singular is idiomatic (*either arm* =cavalry or infantry ; *each arm* =cavalry, infantry, & artillery) is made tolerable, perhaps, by suggesting the other *arm* & being interpreted as branch of the service (cf. *the secular arm*).

army & navy. This, the familiar order, is rightly corrected in toasts, public speeches, & the like, into *Navy & Army* ; but where precedence is not in question it is both needless & impossible to get the correction accepted.

around is, in British use, a disappearing variant of *round.* It is still the normal form in certain combinations, as *a. & about,* (*the air*) *a. & above* (*us*), *all a.* (*are signs of decay*) ; & it can be used without being noticeable in a few of the senses of *round,* as *seated a. the table, diffuses cheerfulness a. her, spread destruction a.* But it is hardly possible to say *winter comes a., all the year a., win one a., send the hat a., a room hung a. with pictures, travel a. the world, show one a.* American usage is quite different ; among the examples in an American dictionary are the following impossibilities for an Englishman :—*He went through, but I ran a.* ; *He turned a.* ; *The earth turns a. on its axis* ; *Go a. to the post office* ; *The church a. the corner* ; *Loaf a. the city.*

arouse. The relation of this to *rouse* is much like that of *arise* to *rise* ; that is, *rouse* is almost always preferred to it in the literal sense & with a person or animal as object. *A.* is chiefly used with the senses *call into existence, occasion,* & with such abstracts as *suspicion, fears, cupidity, passions,* as object of the active or subject of the passive :—*This at once aroused my suspicions* ; *Cupidity is easily aroused.* Not *I shook his arm, but failed to a. him.*

arpeggio. Pl. *-os* ; see -O(E)S 4.

arrant makes *-est* ; see -ER & -EST, 4.

arride. See ARCHAISM. Its modern vogue is no doubt attributable to Charles Lamb.

arrière-pensée. See FRENCH WORDS.
arrive. For the absolute sense *reach* *success* or *recognition* see GALLICISMS.
arsis. See TECHNICAL TERMS.
art. For the broad distinction between *a.* & *science*, see SCIENCE.
articulate, vb, makes *-lable*; see -ABLE 1.
artiste. 1. The word is applicable to either sex; *artists & artistes* as a phrase for male & female performers is a mere blunder.
2. In the sense *professional singer, dancer,* or *other public performer, artiste* serves a useful purpose; it is best restricted to this use, in which it conveys no judgement that the performance is in fact artistic; if it is desired to intimate that a cook, tailor, hairdresser, &c., or an artiste, makes his occupation into a fine art, *artist,* & not *artiste,* is the right word :—*He is quite an artist*; *What an artist!*

Arty, -ie. See -EY, -IE, -Y.
as. 1. *Equally as.* 2. Causal *as* placed late. 3. *As to.* 4. *As if, as though.* 5. *As,* relative pronoun. 6. Omission of *as.* 7. *As* = in the capacity of. 8. Case after *as.* 9. *As a fact.* 10. *As well as.* 11. *As follow(s)* &c.
1. For the illiterate *equally as* (*good* &c.), see EQUALLY.
2. Causal *as* placed late, *as* meaning since, because, seeing that, for, &c. To causal or explanatory *as-*clauses, if they are placed before the main sentence (*As he only laughed at my arguments, I gave it up*) there is no objection. The reverse order (*I gave it up, as he only laughed at my arguments*) is, except when the fact adduced is one necessarily known to the hearer or reader & present to his mind (*I need not translate, as you know German*), intolerable to anyone with a literary ear. All good writers instinctively avoid it; but, being common in talk, it is much used in print also by those who have not yet learnt that composition is an art & that sentences require arrangement. The first passage quoted suggests the kind of writer most liable to this mainly illiterate weakness; the second & third, with their successive *as-*clauses, exhibit the total lack of ear that accompanies it; & a few other gross offences are added :—
One is pleased to find that Mr P. Gannon still maintains his form, as he won the Open Challenge cup in face of such opponents as . . ./The Sunningdale man, indeed, put up a most strenuous fight, as his 154 equalled the total of . . . Mr Carlisle's golf, however, was much more consistent than Mr Gannon's, as to his two 77's Mr Gannon opposed an 82 & a 72./They strongly advocate a diminution on the petroleum duty, as it would lead to a great increase of work, it being largely used for industrial purposes, as coal is scarce here. / The reduction of the interest on Italian Consols represents a very great event for the young kingdom. as it shows what a large credit it enjoys, especially abroad, as that operation could not be carried out without the assistance of French & German bankers./Frivolous applications are fully guarded against, as there must accompany the application a statutory declaration./The Government have been induced to take this course as they are much impressed by the great value of the discoveries made./ The sketch of Milton's life is inserted in this volume as it illustrates some points that occur in the Sonnets.
3. *As to.* This has a legitimate use—to bring into prominence at the beginning of a sentence something that without it would have to stand later (*As to Smith, it is impossible to guess what line he will take*); it has, for instance, been wrongly omitted in : *Whether the publishers will respond to Sir Charles Stanford's appeal or not it is too early to speak with any confidence.* A spurious imitation of legitimacy occurs when *as to* introduces what would even without it stand at the head of the sentence, as in : *As to how far such*

reinforcements are available this is quite another matter ; omit ' as to ' & ' this ', & the order is unaffected ; the writer has chosen to get out of the room by a fire-escape when the door was open.

Apart from this, it is usually either a slovenly substitute for some simple preposition (*Proper notions as to* [of] *a woman's duty.*/*She had been sarcastic as to* [about] *his hunting.*/*Piece of business as to* [upon] *which Dr. Thorne had been summoned.*/*Bantered himself as to* [on] *his own want of skill.*/*The manufacturer complains that everything as to* [concerning] *the future is left to the whim of the Board of Trade.*/*A singular degree of rarity prevails as to* [among] *the earlier editions of this romance*) ; or entirely otiose (*The only points on which the Government found fault were* [as to] *the Permanent Settlement and* [as to] *the system on which . . .*/*You ask the pertinent question* [as to] *how many of the doctors who signed the pledge were practising.*/*It appeared to be somewhat uncertain* [as to] *whether the new docks scheme would be commenced at the Tilbury or the Albert Dock end.*/*Asked* [as to] *what effect the arrest of the players would have on the American tour, Mr. Yeats said . . .*/*With the idea of endeavouring to ascertain* [as to] *this.*/*Doubt is expressed* [as to] *whether this will affect the situation.*/*The question* [as to] *how far the Sultan will . . .*).

As might be expected, those who put their trust in a phrase that is usually either vague or otiose are constantly betrayed by it into positive bad grammar : *Unless it has some evidence as to whom the various ideas belong* (i.e. as to to whom).*/A different dance according as to whether the child is a male or a female* (i.e. according as the child is).*/It is open to doubt as to what extent individual saving prevails*, and *No two people seem to agree as to what extent it is one country and one race* (i.e. as to to what extent).*/It is not quite clear as to what happened* (This implies the ungrammatical *As

to what happened is not clear* instead of the normal *What happened is not clear*).*/The question does not relate solely to the possibility of Mr. Whitaker accepting appointment, but also as to whether any more suitable candidate can be suggested* (' relate as to ' ?—relativity would seem to be as upsetting to Priscian as to Euclid). The popular favourites : *The question as to whether, The doubt as to whether*, may almost be included among the ungrammatical developments, since *the* doubt or question demands an indirect question in simple apposition ; in such forms as *Doubts are expressed as to whether*, the ' as to ' is not incorrect, but merely repulsive ; *An interesting question therefore remains as to how far science will provide us with the power* may lawfully be written ; *The interesting* &c. may not.

4. As if, as though. These should invariably be followed by a past conditional, & not by a present form (*would*, not *will* ; *could*, not *can* ; *did*, not *does* ; *was* or *were*, not *is* ; *had gone*, not *has gone* ; *knew*, not *knows*). The full form of the incorrect *It is scanned curiously, as if mere scanning* will *resolve its nature* is *It is scanned curiously, as* it would be scanned *if mere scanning* would *resolve its nature* ; & the omission of *it would be scanned* leaves *would resolve* unchanged. *As though*, about which the same demonstration is not possible, is precisely equivalent to *as if*, & is subject to the same rule ; & the rule applies to the still more elliptical use of either form in exclamations (*As if*, or *As though, you didn't* [not *don't*] *know that!*) as well as to the use with an expressed main sentence. The mistake of putting the verb in a present tense is especially common after *it looks* or *seems*, where there is the insufficient excuse that the clause gives a supposed actual fact ; but it is spreading so fast that sometimes the supposition is admittedly false :—*But it looks for the moment as if these will* [*would*] *have *to be abandoned./It looks as if a new lot of men have [had] sprung up who will [would] require their share of the public plunder./ To the observer from without it seems as if there has [had] been some lack of stage-management./ Tariff Reformers have received the result of the Canadian elections as though they now expect[ed] Canada to give a greater preference to British goods./It is not as though a sound liquor is [was or were] supplied.*

5. *As,* relative pronoun. The distinction between *as* the relative pronoun, capable of serving as subject or object of a verb, & *as* the relative adverb, not capable of so serving, must be grasped if a well-marked type of blunder is to be avoided. Examples of the blunder are :— *The ratepayers have no direct voice in fixing the amount of the levy,* as is possessed *by the unions./ The visit to Reval would be an official visit paid by the King to the Emperor,* as had been paid *previously to other sovereigns./Some nasty things were said about him,* as have been said *about others./ The decision to send a special mission is not intended as anything more than a mere act of international courtesy,* as is customary *on such occasions./ The best substitute is not another specialist, but the man trained to act for himself in all circumstances,* as it has been the glory of our nation to produce./*With a speed of eight knots,* as has been found practicable, *the passage would occupy five days./ There were not two dragon sentries keeping ward,* as *in magic legend* are usually found *on duty.* If these sentences, the faultiness of which will probably be admitted at sight, are examined, it will be seen that for each two cures are possible : one is to substitute for *as* an undoubted relative pronoun, *such as* or *which* (*such as is possessed*; *which has been found practicable*) ; the other is to insert a missing subject or object (*as* one *is possessed*; *as* official visits *had been paid* ; *as* such things *have been said* ; *as* such courtesy *is customary* ; *as it has*

been our glory to produce him ; *as* it *has been found practicable* to steam ; *as* dragons *are usually found*). Either method of correction suggests the same truth, that *as* in these sentences is not a relative pronoun, & has been wrongly treated as one, though an adverb. The fact is that when *as* is used as a relative pronoun the antecedent is never a simple noun that has already been expressed (which must be represented by an ordinary relative—*such as, which, who, that*), but a verb or verbal notion, or a previously unexpressed noun, that has to be gathered from the main sentence. Thus we cannot say *To affect poverty, as is now often affected* (i.e. which poverty is affected) ; but we can say *To affect poverty, as is now often done* (i.e. which affecting is done). If this test is applied to the incorrect sentences above, it will be found that each antecedent of the supposed relative pronoun is of the illegitimate kind, a simple expressed noun—*voice, visit, things, courtesy, man, speed, sentries.* It may perhaps occur to the reader that a legitimate substitute for *as is possessed by the unions* in the first example would be *as the unions have,* & that *as* then represents *which voice* & consequently invalidates our rule ; that it seems to do so, however, is owing to a peculiarity of the verb *have. The ratepayers possess no voice, as the unions* do ; *the ratepayers exercise no voice, as the unions do* ; *the ratepayers have no voice, as the unions* (not *do,* but) *have* ; *have* (in the sense *possess*), being never represented like other verbs by DO, is allowed when used where *do* would be substituted for any other verb to take the construction proper to *do* ; *as the unions possess it* or *do* ; *as the unions exercise one* or *do* ; but *as the unions have* simply.

On the other hand, failure to recognize that *as* is a relative pronoun sometimes produces mistakes of a different kind :—*Epeiros, as it is well known, was anciently in-*

habited by . . . (*as* =which fact, & *it* is therefore impossible unless *as* is omitted)./*I do not think, as apparently does Mr Thorne*, that . . . (*as* = which thinking, & the inversion is impossible* ; read *as Mr Thorne apparently does*).

6. Omission of *as*. *As* is commonly but wrongly omitted after the verb REGARD, especially when complications arise with another *as* similar to that in *But it is not so much as a picture of the time as a study of humanity that Starvecrow Farm claims attention* (*as as a study* has been too much for even a literary critic's virtue) ; cf. the omissions of *to* in the *as to* quotations (3 above).

7. *As* = in the capacity of. When this is used, care must be taken to avoid the mistake corresponding to what is called the unattached participle ; we can say *He gave this advice as leader of the opposition*, or *This advice was given by him as leader, he* & *him* supplying the point of attachment ; but we cannot say *The advice which he tendered to the Peers was given as leader of the opposition*.

8. Case after *as*. It is a matter of no great practical importance, case being distinguishable only in a few pronouns, & these pronouns occurring so seldom after *as* that most of the examples given in illustration will have an artificial air ; but some points may be noticed :—*a*. Sometimes a verb is to be supplied ; the right case must then be used, or the sense may be spoilt ; *You hate her as much as I* implies as I hate her ; *You hate her as much as me* implies as you hate me. *b*. *As* is never to be regarded as a preposition ; the objective case after it, when right, is due either to the filling up of an elliptic sentence as in *a* or to causes explained in *c* & *d* ; *When such as her die, She is not so tall as me*, are wrong. *c*. The phrases *such—as he* &c., *so—as he* &c., may be treated as declinable compound adjectives (cf. German *was für ein*), which gives *Such men as* he *are intolerable*

but *I cannot tolerate such men as him, Never was so active a man as he* but *I never knew so active a man as him* ; to ban this construction & insist on writing *he* always, according to the *a* method, seems pedantic, though *he* is always admissible. *d*. In many sentences the supplying of a verb supposed to have been omitted instead of repeated, as in *a*, is impossible or difficult, & the case after *as* simply follows that of the corresponding noun before *as* ; *as* is then equivalent to *as being* (cf. Greek ὡς ἄν, ὡς ὄντα, &c.) ; so *I recognized this man as him who had stared at me* ; *You dressed up as she, You dressed yourself up as her, I dressed you up as her, You were dressed up as she* ; *The entity known to me as I, The entity that I know as me*.

9. *As a fact* ; see FACT.

10. *As well as* ; see WELL.

11. For *as concern(s), regard(s), follow(s)*, see CONCERN, FOLLOW.

ascendancy, ascendant. 1. Spelling. Though *-ancy* is not much commoner than *-ency*, it is better as corresponding to *ascendant*, which is much commoner than *ascendent*. 2. Usage & meaning. *The ascendancy of, Have an* or *the ascendancy over, be in the ascendant*, are the normal phrases; in the first two *ascendant* is archaic for *ascendancy*, & is better avoided ; in the third, which is less detached than the others from its astrological origin, *ascendancy* is wrong, & when used (*It is not recorded what stars were in the ascendency when Winston Churchill was born./Jimmie's better angel was in the ascendency*) is attributable to ignorance. Both words mean domination or prevailing influence, & not upward tendency or rising prosperity or progress.

ascension used of climbing, instead of *ascent* (*she had begun her ascension of the hill*), is a GALLICISM.

ascertainedly. Five syllables ; see -EDLY.

asexual. See A-, AN-.

ashamedly. Four syllables if used ; see -EDLY.

ashen. See -EN ADJECTIVES.

aside does not mean on each side (*We sat five aside in the suburban train*; *They were playing three aside*); *a side* must be written; cf. £500 *a year* (not *ayear*).

askance, askant. See NEEDLESS VARIANTS. *Askance* is the usual form, & the OED account of *askant* is : Apparently a later variant of *askance*.

aspirate. See TECHNICAL TERMS.

assassinate makes *-nable*; see -ABLE 1.

assay, essay, vbs. A differentiation tends to prevail by which *assay* is confined to the sense *test*, & *essay* to the sense *attempt*; the OED says : 'Except as applied to the testing of metals, *assay* is now an archaic form of *essay*.' *Essay* itself has by this time the dignity attaching to incipient archaism; but the distinction should be observed.

asset is a false form; the great popularity, due chiefly to the sporting reporter, that it now enjoys as a saver of trouble to those who have not time to choose between *possession, gain, advantage, resource,* & other synonyms, or to recast their sentences into conformity with established idiom, is of recent date ; & an effort should be made to do without it. Most of those who use it are probably unaware that, though now treated as plural, *assets* is itself (cf. *riches*) a singular ; the *-s* is not a plural termination ; French *assez* (enough) being its source, *-ts* represents the French *-z*; & the right sense of the word is that which it has had till lately—what suffices or should suffice to meet liabilities. The false singular originates in incorrect uses like *The chances of a dividend depend upon the realization of two assets, one a large debt, & the other* . . . See POPULARIZED TECHNICALITIES. A number of quotations are added to show how common the abuse is, the kind of writer that indulges in it, & how easily it may be avoided :—*Hearne is bowling*

splendidly, & though veteran in years he is [*an*] *indispensable* [*a.*] *to Middlesex./Her forehand drive—her most trenchant* [*a.*] (*stroke*)./*In man-lifting kites hauled by 25-knot destroyers, resonant lungs are* [*something of an a.*] (*serviceable*)./*It was Mr. John Ball who showed us that the experience of years is* [*an incalculable a.*] *when it comes to the strain of a championship* (*invaluable*)./*Nor is it every doctor who despises club practice ; many find it a very handy* [*a.*] *which they do not like to lose* (source of income)./*I do not regret that the Unionist Party has made the subject its own ; it is its best* [*a.*] (*card*)./*As sound a head as that of his Reverence is* [*a distinct a.*] *to society* (of value)./*A local reputation for their lavender production has been established, which is no doubt* [*a*] *valuable* [*a.*]./[*The value of cheerful service is an a.*] *which the directors do not seem to have taken into consideration* (Cheerful service has a value)./*These examples are one of the greatest* [*assets which the people can possess*] (possessions the people can have)./*The net result of my reading & meditation is the conviction that Mr. Chesterton is a valuable* [*a.*] *of the orthodox faith* (pillar).

assign. Derivatives & allied words are pronounced as follows :— *assignable* (-īna-), *assignation* (-ĭg-), *assignat* (ă'sĭgnăt), *assignor* (ăsĭnor'), *assignee* (ăsĭnē').

assimilate makes *-lable*; see -ABLE 1.

assimilation. See TECHNICAL TERMS.

assist, in the sense *be present* (*at* a performance &c.), is now a GALLICISM ; in the sense *help* (*to* potatoes &c.), it is a GENTEELISM. For *a.* & *help*, see WORKING & STYLISH WORDS.

association. See -CIATION.

assonance. See REPETITION s.f.

assume, presume. Where the words are roughly synonymous, i.e. in the sense *suppose*, the object-clause after *presume* expresses what the presumer really believes, till it is disproved, to be true ; that after *assume*, what the assumer postulates, often as a confessed hypothesis. It may be owing to this distinction that the *that* of the object-clause is usually expressed after *assume* (the omission is at once felt to be wrong in *I assume Turkey would require such a cash payment of at least £500,000*), & usually omitted after *presume* (*I presume you know*; *I assume that you know*).

assure, assurance. 1. These words have never found general acceptance in the sense of paying premiums to secure contingent payments, though they are used by insurance offices & agents, & so occasionally by their customers, especially when death is the event insured against (*life assurance*; *assure one's life*); apart from such technical use, *insure & insurance* hold the field.
2. *Assure* for *ensure* (make certain the occurrence &c. of) is now rare (*That will ensure, rarely assure, your success*).

assuredly. Four syllables; see -EDLY.

asylum. Pl. *-ms*; see -UM.

asyndeton. See TECHNICAL TERMS. Pl. *-ta, -ns*; see -ON 1.

-ATABLE. In spite of the general rule given under -ABLE for the formation of adjectives in -able from verbs in -ate, the short form with -at- omitted would be disagreeably pedantic in many cases where either the verb itself is little used in literature, or the dropping of -at- amounts to disguising the word (as in disyllables, *create, vacate*, &c.), or the -able adjective is likely to be very seldom used, or confusion with another word might result. Thus *incubate*, at least in the sense in which its -able adjective is likely to be wanted, is a technical rather than a literary word; *inculcable* is not instantly recognized as from *inculcate*; *inculpable* is both likely to be understood as not culpable, & unlikely to be often wanted; & accordingly *incubatable, inculcatable, inculpatable*, are less impossible than *incubable, inculcable*, & *inculpable*.

The practice should be to use -atable where the shorter form is felt to be out of the question. Simple reference to this article under any word means that -atable is better.

atelier. See FRENCH WORDS.
attempt. For *was attempted to be done* &c. see DOUBLE PASSIVES.
attic. See GARRET.
attorney. Pl. *-eys.*
attraction. For the sense in grammar see TECHNICAL TERMS.
au. See À LA.
au fait. See FRENCH WORDS.
au fond. See À FOND, & FRENCH WORDS.
aught. See ARCHAISM; *for a. I know* is the only phrase in which the word is still current in ordinary speech, & even there *all* is displacing it.
au grand sérieux. See FRENCH WORDS.
aunt. Pronounce ahnt; see ANT. For *aunty, -ie*, see -EY, -IE, -Y.
au pied de la lettre, au revoir. See FRENCH WORDS.
authentic, genuine. The distinction commonly drawn between the words is by no means universally observed, especially when either is used without special reference to the other; but, when it is present to the mind, *authentic* implies that the contents of a book, picture, account, or the like, correspond to facts & are not fictitious, & *genuine* implies that its reputed is its real author :—*a genuine Hobbema*; *An authentic description*; *The Holbein Henry VIII is both authentic & genuine* (represents Henry as he was, or is really a portrait of him, & is by Holbein). The artificial character of the distinction, however, is illustrated by the fact that *authenticate* serves for to establish either as authentic or as genuine.

authenticate makes *-cable*; see -ABLE 1.

authoress is a word regarded with dislike in literary circles, on the grounds, perhaps, that sex is irrelevant to art, & that the common unliterary public has no concern with its superiors' personality. The public thinks otherwise, & may be trusted to keep a useful word in existence, even though it has so far failed to bring into existence what it needs much more, a handy feminine for *doctor*. See FEMININE DESIGNATIONS.

autocar, automobile. Now that *motor(-car)* has fully established its supremacy, it would be well if these rivals could be cleared away.

avail, vb. The constructions *be availed of, avail of,* illustrated in the following quotations are wrong :— *If economical means of transport are availed of* (made use of)./ *No salvage appliances could have been availed of in time* (utilized)./*Watt & Fulton bethought themselves that power must be availed of, & not let off & wasted* (used)./*A desire to avail of the quieter phase of national emotion* (take advantage of).

The normal construction is *avail* one*self* of (*I shall a. myself of your kind offer*). From this are wrongly evolved (' with indirect passive, esp. in U.S.' says the OED) such forms as *The offer was availed of* ; the absurdity of this is patent as soon as the method is applied to similar reflexive verbs ; because we can say *They busy themselves in politics, You should rid yourself of cant, Many devote themselves to religion,* we do not infer that *Politics are busied in, Cant should be ridded of, Religion is often devoted to,* are English ; as little does *avail* one*self of the offer* justify *the offer was availed of.* It is from the last incorrect form that the non-reflexive active is logically enough deduced, so that *avail of the offer* takes the place of the original *avail* one*self of the offer. Available,* which perhaps encourages the use of these bad constructions, lends them no real support ; its original sense was *that can avail,* &, apart from the great looseness of usage characterizing these adjectives (see -ABLE), what it would suggest is rather *avail the offer* than *avail of the offer.*

avenge, revenge, vengeance. *Avenge & vengeance* are one pair, *revenge* verb & noun another. The distinction between the two pairs is neither very clear nor consistently observed. This is natural, since the same act done under the same conditions may be described either as *vengeance* or as *revenge* according to the point of view from which it is regarded. It may be said, roughly, that *vengeance* is the making things even by an offender's being made to suffer something more or less equivalent to his offence, while *revenge* is the satisfying of the offended party's resentment by the same means ; one act may effect both, but it will be spoken of by one name or the other according to context. It is in harmony with this that the subject of the active verb *revenge* is ordinarily the wronged party, & its object either himself or a wrong done at least indirectly to him, while the subject of *avenge* is ordinarily a disinterested party, & its object another person or a wrong done to another. Exceptions are numerous, & too complicated in their nature to be set forth here ; but the general principle that personal feeling is the thing thought of when *revenge* is used, & the equalization of wrongs when *avenge* or *vengeance* is used, may assist choice.

Misuses of the verbs other than confusion between them are not frequent enough to require much notice ; but it may be worth mention that the wrongdoer is never rightly the object of either, as in : *The Russian . . . will avenge as has been his custom to avenge the birds of prey who swooped down upon him in his helplessness.*

averse, aversion. To insist on *from* as the only right preposition after these, in spite of the more general use of *to* (*What cat 's averse to fish ?*— Gray. *He had been averse to extreme courses.*—Macaulay. *Nature has put into man an aversion to misery.*— Locke) is one of the pedantries that spring of a little knowledge. If *averse* meant originally turned away, & *a* is Latin for away, this did not prevent even the writers of classical Latin from using the dative after *aversus*; nor, if it had, need it prevent us, to whom the original & physical sense is not usually present, from using after *averse* & *aversion* the preposition that best fits their true sense of (harbouring) dislike.

avocation, originally a calling away, an interruption, a distraction, was for some time commonly used as a synonym for *vocation* or *calling*, with which it is properly in antithesis. This misuse is now less common, & the word is generally used in the plural, a person's avocations being the things he devotes time to, his pursuits or engagements in general, the affairs he has to see to; his vocation as such is neither excluded from, nor necessarily included in, his avocations.

AVOIDANCE OF THE OBVIOUS is very well, provided that it is not itself obvious; but, if it is, all is spoilt. Expel *eager* or *greedy* from your sentence in favour of *avid*, & your reader wants to know why you have done it; if he can find no better answer than that you are attitudinizing as an epicure of words for whom nothing but the rare is good enough, or, yet worse, that you are painfully endeavouring to impart some much needed unfamiliarity to a platitude, his feeling towards you will be something that is not admiration. The obvious is better than obvious avoidance of it. *Nobody could have written ' Clown ' who had not been (as Mr. Disher is known to be) an* avid *collector of pantomime traditions & relics./Everything is just in a state of suspended animation, & the House, instead of being in its usual bustle on account day, is* devoid./*Lord Lansdowne has done the Liberal Party a good turn by putting Tariff Reform to the front; about this there can be no* dubiety./ *If John never ' finishes ' anything else, he can at least claim by sheer* labour to have completed over five-score *etchings*. There are some who would rather see *eager & empty & doubt & a hundred* in those sentences than *avid, devoid, dubiety, & fivescore*; & there are some who would not; the examples are typical enough to sort tastes. *Avid & dubiety* are not yet hackneyed in the function of escapes from the obvious; they will be so one day if their qualifications in this kind are appreciated, & then their virtue will be gone.

Several words can be thought of that have been through this course. Starting as variants for the business word, they have been so seized upon by those who scorn to talk like other people as to become a badge by which we may know them; after which they pass into general use by the side of the words to which they were preferred, giving the language pairs of useless synonyms that have lost whatever distinction there may once have been between them. Such words are *cryptic, dual, facile, forceful, foreword, & Gallic*, as used without the justification of special meanings instead of *obscure, double, easy, forcible, preface, & French*; on all of these except *cryptic* (a word whose *sole* function seems to be that which is our subject) comment will be found in their separate articles; a few examples of the uses deprecated are:—' *A sensible young man, of rough but mild manners, & very seditious ' ; this description, excepting the first clause, is somewhat cryptic./ The combination of cricket & rowing ' blues ' is very rare ; the late J. W. Dale was the last Cambridge man to earn the dual distinction.* The ' dual event ' is perhaps already, & will surely soon be, upon us. / *The reunion of a Labour & Socialist World Conference has not proved to be so facile to arrange as it appeared./' I blame the working of the Trade Board ' said Mr. Newey, forcefully, ' for keeping wages at an artificial figure './The theme is a big one, covering, we are told in a fore-*

*word, those comprehensive acts &
aspects of policy which . . .*
Other articles containing relevant
matter are ADVENTURESOME, FOOT-
ING, FORENOON, MAYBE, NOMEN-
CLATURE, REITERANT, SAID 2, 3, &
SENSE vb.

avoirdupois. Pronounce ǎ'verde-
poiz.

avouch, avow, vouch. The living
senses of the three words are distinct ; but, as a good deal of confusion has formerly prevailed between
them, the dictionaries are not very
helpful to inquirers, providing quotations under each for senses that
now belong only to one of the
others ; it is therefore worth while
to state roughly the modern usage.
Avouch, which is no longer in common use, means guarantee, solemnly
aver, prove by assertion, maintain
the truth or existence of, vouch for,
(*A miracle avouched by the testimony
of . . .* ; *Millions were ready to avouch
the exact contrary* ; *Offered to avouch
his innocence with his sword*). *Avow*
means own publicly to, make no
secret of, not shrink from admitting,
acknowledge one's responsibility for,
(*Think what one is ashamed to avow* ;
Avowed himself my enemy ; *Avowed
his determination to be revenged*; *Always avows,* & cf. in the contrary sense
disavows, his agents). *Vouch* is now
common only in the phrase *vouch for,*
which has taken the place of *avouch*
in ordinary use, & means pledge one's
word for (*Will you vouch for the truth
of it ?* ; *I can vouch for his respectability*).

avowedly. Four syllables ; see
-EDLY.

await, wait. *Await* is always transitive, but wait is not always intransitive. *I am awaiting to hear your
decision* is not English; *I await,* & *I
wait, your decision* are equally good.

awake, awaken, wake, waken.
Awake has past *awoke* rarely
awaked, & p.p. *awaked* rarely *awoke* ;
wake has past *woke* rarely (& that
usually in transitive sense) *waked,*

& p.p. *waked* rarely *woke* or *woken* ;
awaken & *waken* have -ed.
Distinction between the forms is
difficult, but with regard to modern
usage certain points may be made :—
(1) *Wake* is the ordinary working
verb (*You will wake the baby* ; *Something woke me up* ; *I should like to be
waked at* 7.30 ; *Wake the echoes*),
for which the others are substituted
to add dignity or formality, or to
suit metre, or as in 3 or 5 below.
(2) *Wake* alone has (& that chiefly in
waking) the sense *be* or *remain
awake* (*Sleeping or waking* ; *In our
waking hours* ; *This kept me waking*). (3) *Awake* & *awaken* are
usually preferred to the others in
figurative senses (*When they awoke,*
or *were awakened,* to *their danger* ;
This at once awakened suspicion ;
The national spirit awoke, or *was
awakened* ; *A rude awakening*).
(4) *Waken* & *awaken* tend to be restricted to the transitive sense ;
when he wakens is rarer for *when he
wakes* than *that will waken him* for
that will wake him. (5) In the passive, *awaken* & *waken* are often
preferred to *awake* & *wake,* perhaps
owing to uncertainty about the p.p.
forms of the latter pair ; *it wakened
me* is rare for *it woke* or *waked me,*
but *I was wakened by it* is common
for *I was waked* or *woke* or *woken by
it* ; see also the alternative forms in
3 above. (6) *Up* is very commonly
appended to *wake,* rarely to *waken,*
& hardly at all to *awake* & *awaken.*

away. For *once & away* see ONCE.
For *cannot away with* see ARCHAISM.

awkward. See -ER & -EST, 2.

axe. The spelling *ax,* though
' better on every ground, of etymology, phonology, & analogy ' (OED),
is so strange to 20th-c. eyes that it
suggests pedantry & is unlikely to
be restored.

axis. Pl. *axes* (-ēz, not -ĭz).

ay, aye. The word meaning *yes* is
pronounced ī, & the word meaning
ever is pronounced ā ; but which
spelling corresponds to which pronunciation is disputed ; the nautical

Ay, ay, sir is usually written thus ; & *aye* is probably the commoner spelling now for *ever* ; on the other hand *the ayes have it* is usual, though *-es* may there be intended for the plural termination. *Ay* (ī) yes, *aye* (ā) ever, seems likely to prevail ; but the authority of the OED is on the other side.

B

babe, baby. In the primary sense *baby* is now the regular form, & *babe* archaic, poetic, or rhetorical. In figurative use, *babe* implies guilelessness, innocence, or ignorance, & *baby* unmanliness.

baboo. Pronounce bah'bōō. Pl. *-oos* ; see -O(E)S 4.

baccara(t). Pronounce băˈkarah. The spelling with -t is commoner in English, & that without -t in French.

bacchanal, bacchant(e). *Bacchanal* & *bacchant* are both used of males or females, or males & females, but with a tendency to be restricted to males ; *bacchante* is used of females only. *Bacchant* is always pronounced băˈkant ; *bacchante* bakăˈnt, băˈkant, or bakăˈntī. *Bacchant* has *bacchants* or *bacchantes* ; *bacchante* has *bacchantes* (-ts or -tīz).

bacillus. Pl. *bacillī* ; see -US, & LATIN PLURALS. For the meaning, see SCHIZOMYCETES.

BACK-FORMATION. A dictionary definition of the term is : Making from a supposed derivative (as *lazy, banting*) of the non-existent word (*laze, bant*) from which it might have come. It is natural to guess that the words *scavenger, darkling,* & *gridiron,* are formed from verbs *scavenge* & *darkle* & a noun *grid,* & consequently to use those verbs & noun if occasion arises ; those who first used them, however, were mistaken, & were themselves making the words out of what they wrongly took for their derivatives ; similarly *banting* is not formed from *bant,* but is the name first of a man. & then of

his system, out of which the verb to *bant* was made by back-formation. This will perhaps sufficiently explain the references made here & there to this article. Some back-formations are not generally recognized as such, & have the full status of ordinary words, e.g. *diagnose* (from *diagnosis*), *drowse* (from *drowsy*), *sidle* (from *sideling = sidelong*), *grovel* (from *grovelling,* an adverb). But more often they are felt to be irregular, & used only as slang or jocosely ; so BURGLE, CHINEE, DONATE, *enthuse, locomote, maffick,* ORATE, *proce'ss* (go in procession), *resurrect, revolute.* Other articles that may be looked at are BRINDLE, COSE, DARKLE, FILTRATE, GRID, GUERILLA, & SALVE.

back of as a preposition is an American, not a British, idiom.

backsheesh. See BAKSHEESH.

bacterium. Pl. *bacteria* ; see -UM. For the meaning, see SCHIZOMYCETES.

badge. For synonymy, see SIGN.

badinage. Pronounce băˈdĭnahzh.

baggage. As applied to the belongings that a person travels with on land, the word is an Americanism for *luggage.*

bagnio. Pl. *-os* ; see -O(E)S 4.

baignoire. See FRENCH WORDS.

bail is right, & *bale* wrong, in the sense throw water out ; the derivation is from French *baille* bucket.

bailable. For the sense, admitting of bail, see -ABLE 4.

baksheesh is the form recommended.

balance, in the sense *rest* or *remainder,* is, except where the difference between two amounts that have to be compared is present to the mind, a SLIPSHOD EXTENSION. We may fairly say ' you may keep the balance ', because the amount due & the amount that more than covers it suggest comparison ; but in ' the b. of the day is given to amusement ' such a comparison between amounts is, though not impossible, farfetched, & the plain word (*rest,* or *remainder*) is called for.

ballad. See TECHNICAL TERMS.

ballade. Pronounce balah'd ; for meaning, see TECHNICAL TERMS.

ballon d'essai. See FRENCH WORDS.

ballyrag, bullyrag. The etymology is unknown ; the second form is probably due to a supposed connexion, described by the OED as 'unlikely', with *bully* ; the first form is still common, & seems preferable.

balm. For *b. in Gilead* see BATTERED ORNAMENTS & HACKNEYED PHRASES.

baluster, ban(n)ister. *Banisters* (better with single n) is now, though originally a corruption only of *balusters*, the established form for the commonest sense in which the words are used, i.e. the uprights supporting a staircase handrail with or without the rail itself. *Baluster* is best applied only to the vase-shaped supports of a balustrade.

bambino. Pl. *-os* ; see -O(E)S 6.

bamboo. Pl. *-oos* ; see -O(E)S 4.

banal, banality. These are LITERARY CRITICS' WORDS, imported from France by a class of writers whose jaded taste relishes novel or imposing jargon. In French they have had a continuous history & a natural development from their original to their present sense ; in English they have not, & we accordingly remain conscious that they are exotics. With *common, commonplace, trite, trivial, mean, vulgar, truism, platitude,* & other English words, to choose among, we certainly do not need them.

bandit. Of the two plurals, *bandits* tends to prevail over *banditti*, especially when the reference is to more or less clearly realized individuals :—*The mountains are infested with banditti* ; *The cost of suppressing the banditti* ; *Two of the bandits conducted me to the appointed place* ; *You are all bandits.*

banister. See BALUSTER.

banjo. Pl. *-oes* ; see -O(E)S 1.

bank. A river's right bank is that on the right of the river regarded as a person going down to his destination.

baptist(e)ry. The -tery form is best.

bar. *B. sinister,* used by novelists as a symbol of illegitimacy, is strictly incorrect, *bend* or *baton sinister* being the true term ; it is, however, so familiar that to correct it, except where there is real need for technical accuracy, is pedantic ; see DIDACTICISM.

barbarian, barbaric, barbarous. The difference in usage among the three adjectives is roughly, & setting aside special senses of the first, as follows. *Barbarian,* as an adjective, is now regarded as an attributive use of the noun *barbarian* ; i.e., it is used only in such contexts as would be admissible for nouns like *soldier* or *German* (*a soldier king* or *people* ; *German ancestry* or *thoroughness*), & means consisting of barbarians, being a barbarian, belonging to or usual with barbarians. So we have *barbarian tribes, hosts, frankness, courage* ; *a barbarian king, home, empire* ; *barbarian man* (the human race as barbarians) ; *the barbarian world.*

The other two words are ordinary adjectives, but differ in their implications. *Barbaric* is used with indulgence, indifference, or even admiration, & means of the simple, unsophisticated, uncultured, unchastened, tasteless, or excessive kind that prevails among barbarians. We speak of *barbaric taste, finery, splendour, costume, gold, hospitality, simplicity, strength, health.*

Barbarous, on the other hand, always implies at least contempt, & often moral condemnation ; it means that is unfit for or unworthy of or revolts or disgraces or would disgrace the civilized : *barbarous ignorance, speech, customs, style, words, cruelty, treatment, tyranny.*

It should be observed that the same noun may be qualified by all three words according to the sense wanted: *barbarian gold* is money supplied by barbarians ; *barbaric gold* is the metal used over lavishly in decoration ; & *barbarous gold* is the material prosperity that blinds to higher things ; *a barbarian king* is a king of barbarians ; *a barbaric king* one throned in rude splendour ; *a barbarous king* a cruel despot.

barbarism, barbarity, barbarousness. The three nouns all belong to the adjective *barbarous*, but the first two are now (putting aside intentional archaism & metaphor) clearly distinguished. *Barbarism* means uncivilized condition, grossly uncultivated taste, or an illiterate expression ; *barbarity* means grossly cruel conduct or treatment, or a grossly cruel act ; *barbarousness* may be substituted for either of the others where the sense *quality* or *degree* is to be given unmistakably :— *They live in barbarism* ; *The barbarism,* or *barbarousness, of his style* ; ' *Thou asketh* ' *is a barbarism* ; *He treats prisoners with barbarity* ; *The barbarity,* or *barbarousness, of the decree is irrelevant* ; *Unheard-of barbarities.*

BARBARISMS is a hard word to fling about, apt to wound feelings, though it may break no bones ; perhaps it would be better abstained from ; but so too would the barbarisms themselves. What after all is a barbarism ? It is for the most part some word that, like its name, is apt to wound feelings—the feelings, however, of much fewer persons, those who have about Greek & Latin not merely, like the Eton boys of a former generation, ' a profound conviction that there are such languages ', but a sufficient acquaintance with & love of them to be pained by outrages upon their methods of word-formation. In this era of democracy it can hardly be expected that the susceptibilities of so small a minority should be preferred to the comfort of the millions, & it is easier for the former to dissemble their dislike of barbarisms than for the latter to first find out what they are & then avoid them.

These are unfortunately two separate difficulties, both serious. One may lack the information that would enable one to decide whether *bureaucrat* & *cablegram* & *electrocute* & *pleistocene* are or are not barbarisms ; it is indeed obtainable for any particular word from a competent philologist ; but life is not long enough to consult a competent philologist every time one of the hundreds of dubious words confronts one ; nor yet is it long enough for an *ad hoc* course of Latin & Greek grammar. And then, even if the philologist has been consulted, or the course gone through, what next ? are we to talk geology or electricity & abstain from *pleistocene* & *impedance* ? No ; a barbarism is like a lie ; it has got the start of us before we have found it out, & we cannot catch it ; it is in possession, & our offers of other versions come too late.

That barbarisms should exist is a pity ; to expend much energy on denouncing those that do exist is a waste ; to create them is a grave misdemeanour ; & the greater the need of the word that is made, the greater its maker's guilt if he miscreates it. A man of science might be expected to do on his great occasion what the ordinary man cannot do every day, ask the philologist's help ; that the famous *eocene-pleistocene* names were made by ' a good classical scholar ' (see Lyell in D.N.B.) shows that word-formation is a matter for the specialist.

It will have been gathered that in this book barbarisms have not been thought of the practical importance that would demand elaborate discussion. What there is on the subject is chiefly in the general articles HYBRID DERIVATIVES & -O-, & under the words *Briticism, bureaucrat, cablegram, calmative, climactic, coastal, electrocute, impedance, nounal,* & *pleistocene.*

baresark, for *berserker,* is a corrupt modern form owing its existence to a probably false etymology.

baritone. See BARYTONE.

bark, barque. The two forms are now usually differentiated, *bark* being a poetic synonym for ship or boat, & *barque* the technical term for a ship of special rig.

baronage, barony, baronetage, baronetcy. The forms in -*age* are collectives, meaning all the barons (or peers), all the baronets, list or book of barons &c. Those in -*y* are abstracts, meaning rank or position or title of a baron or baronet.

baroque. See TECHNICAL TERMS.

barricado. Pl. -*os* ; see -O(E)S 6.

barytone, -ritone. The first is the best spelling. The -y- is the normal English transliteration of the original Greek *v*, which has been changed to -i- in the derivative Italian *baritono*. The prevailing though not invariable English practice in adopting words at second hand is to undo such intermediate changes & transliterate the originals consistently. It would be justifiable to take the Italian *baritono* whole ; but if we anglicize the ending we should follow the ordinary English method of transliteration. It is probably true that writers on music usually prefer *bari-* ; but they are not yet irrevocably committed ; of two OED quotations from Grove one has *bary-* & one *bari-*. French spells *baryton* ; & in the grammatical sense concerned with accentuation *barytone* is the only form.

basal, basic. These unEnglish-looking adjectives, neither of which existed before the nineteenth century, were manufactured merely as adjuncts to certain technical uses of the noun *base* in botany, chemistry, & architecture, where *fundamental* would have been misleading. But a tendency has lately arisen to allow these upstarts to supplant *fundamental*, with its 500-years tradition, in those general & figurative contexts in which they are unnecessary & incongruous. The native element of *basal* & *basic* is seen in :—*The*

elytra have a basal gibbosity ; *The basal portion of the main petiole* ; *Its capital resting on its basic plinth* ; *Basic salts, phosphates, oxides*. On the other hand *fundamental* should be substituted in :—*Classification should rest on the most basal characteristics.*/*This is our basic principle.*/ *The happy thought which is the basic idea of* Truth's *Christmas number.*/ *The great basic industry is agriculture*. Many of those who use the words are no doubt sensible of the incongruity, but hope that what they have to say will be more convincing if seasoned with a pinch of the up-to-date & scientific.

bas bleu. See FRENCH WORDS.

bashaw is now only an ornamental ARCHAISM, the correct *pasha* having taken its place.

basin, bason. The first spelling is both commoner & better ; the second is probably due to the established pronunciation (bā′sn) ; but cf. *cousin*.

basis. Pl. *basēs* ; see LATIN PLURALS.

bas-relief, bass-relief, basso-relievo, basso-rilievo. The first form is French, the last Italian, & the other two are corruptions ; the plural of the third is *basso-relievos*, & of the fourth *bassi-rilievi*. It is recommended to use the first & pronounce it bä′srĭlēf.

bassinet. This, & not *bassinette* or *berceaunette*, is the right spelling ; the wrong forms are pseudo-French.

bastinado. Pl. -*os* ; see -O(E)S 3.

Batavian. For *B.* = Dutch, in *B. grace* &c., see POLYSYLLABIC HUMOUR.

bath. Pl. pron. bahdhz ; see -TH & -DH.

bathetic, bathotic. These are made in imitation of *pathetic, chaotic* ; but *pathetic* is not analogous, & *chaotic* is itself irregular. An adjective for *bathos* is, however, almost a necessity to the literary critic, & the OED states that *bathetic* is ' A favourite word with reviewers ' ; it is the better of the two.

baton should be written without the circumflex & pronounced bă'tn.

battalion has plural *battalions*, & not even in poetic style *battalia* ; *battalia* is a singular word (It. *battaglia*) meaning battle array ; but being archaic, & often following *in* (*Friedrich draws out in battalia.—* Carlyle), it is taken as meaning battalions.

BATTERED ORNAMENTS. On this rubbish-heap are thrown, usually by a bare cross-reference, such synonyms of the ELEGANT-VARIATION kind as *alma mater, daughter of Eve, sleep of the just, & brother of the* ANGLE ; such metonymies as *the buskin* or *cothurnus & the sock* for tragedy & comedy ; such jocular archaisms as *consumedly* & VASTLY ; such foreign scraps as *dolce far niente, gang agley,* & CUI BONO ? ; such old phrases as *in* DURANCE *vile* & *who was* DESTINED *to be* ; such adaptable frames as *where* ——*s most do congregate* & *on* —— INTENT ; & such quotations customarily said with a wink or written instead of one as *Tell it not in Gath* or *balm in Gilead.* The title of the article, & their present company, are as much comment as is needed for most of them ; but a few words will be found elsewhere on those that contain a word in small capitals ; & other articles from which the list may be enlarged are : FACETIOUS FORMATIONS ; GALLIC-ISMS 5 ; HACKNEYED PHRASES ; INCONGRUOUS VOCABULARY ; IRRE-LEVANT ALLUSION ; MANNERISMS ; MISQUOTATION ; NOVELESE ; OUT-HEROD ; POPULARIZED TECHNICALI-TIES ; SAID 3 ; SOBRIQUETS ; STOCK PATHOS ; SUBJUNCTIVES ; SUPER-LATIVES ; VOGUE-WORDS 3 ; WAR-DOUR STREET ; WORKING & STYLISH WORDS ; WORN-OUT HUMOUR ; & ZEUGMA.

battue. Pronounce batōō', or as French.

bay. For *b.* & *gulf*, see GULF.

bay, bow, -window. A *bay-w.,* named as making a bay in the room, is one that projects outwards from the wall in a rectangular, polygonal, or semicircular form ; *bow-w.,* though often loosely applied to any of these shapes, is properly restricted to the curved one.

-B-, -BB-. Monosyllables ending in b double it before suffixes beginning with vowels if the sound preceding it is a single vowel (a, e, i, o, u, or y), but not if it is a diphthong or a vowel & r : *cabby, webbed, glibbest, bobbed, shrubbery* ; but *dauber, barbed.* Words of more syllables (e.g. *rhubarb, sillabub, hubbub, Beelzebub, cherub*) are few, & it will suffice to mention *cherubic* (so spelt), & *hobnob* (*-bbed, -bbing*).

be. 1. Number of the copula. 2. *Be & were*, subjunctives. 3. *Be* +adverb+participle. 4. Elliptical omissions. 5. Auxiliary)(copulative. 6. Case of the complement. 7. Forms.

1. For the number of the verb between a subject & a complement of different numbers (*The wages of sin is death* ; *The only obstacle are the wide ditches*), see ARE, IS.

2. For use & abuse of *be & were* as subjunctives (*If an injunction be obtained & he* defies it ; *It were to be wished*), see SUBJUNCTIVES.

3. For mistaken fear of separating *be* from its participle &c. (*If his counsel still is followed* ; *The right wholly to be maintained*), see POSI-TION OF ADVERBS.

4. *He is dead, & I alive* ; *I shall dismiss him, as he ought to be.* For such forms see ELLIPSIS 1, 3.

5. Confusion of auxiliary & copulative uses. In *The visit was made* we have *was* auxiliary ; in *The impression was favourable* we have *was* copulative. It is slovenly to make one *was* serve in both capacities, as in *The first visit* was *made & returned, & the first impression of the new neighbours on the Falconet family highly favourable* ; *was* should be repeated after *family*—though, if *created* had stood instead of *highly favourable,* the repetition would have been unnecessary.

6. Case of the complement. The rule that the complement must be in the same case as the subject of the copula (*You believed that* it *was* he ; *You believed* it *to be* him) is often broken in talk (*It wasn't me*), but should be observed in print, except when the solecism is preserved in dialogue as characteristic. The temptation in its simplest forms is rare, but may occur ; Meredith, for instance, writes *I am she, she* me, *till death & beyond it*, where the ungrammatical *me* is not satirically intended ; & this should not be imitated. Two special types of sentence, however, call for mention. One is that illustrated by *We feed children* whom *we think are hungry* ; for this gross but common blunder see WHOM. The other is seen in *He has been, & not only passed for, our leader*, where it pains the grammarian to find that *leader* is subjective after *has been*, but objective after *for*. We might be tempted to disregard his pain as due merely to a pedantic familiarity with Latin, in which the cases are not so often indistinguishable in form ; but if we pass the *leader* sentence as good enough for English, we are committed also to *This plan, which I have often tried & has never failed me* ; & from that every well-regulated mind will shrink, if only because the step from *A man that hates me & I hate* to *Jones, who hates me & I hate* is so fatally easy. Whether resistance is desirable may be better judged from a genuine production of the ill-regulated mind :— *It gave a cachet of extreme clericalism to the Irish Party which it does not deserve, but must prejudice it not a little in the eyes of English Radicalism.*

7. Forms. Those that require notice are (a) *an't, ain't*, (b) the singular subjunctives, & (c) *wast, wert*. (a) *A(i)n't* is merely colloquial, & as used for *isn't* is an uneducated blunder & serves no useful purpose. But it is a pity that *a(i)n't* for *am not*, being a natural

contraction & supplying a real want, should shock us as though tarred with the same brush. Though *I'm not* serves well enough in statements, there is no abbreviation but *a(i)n't I?* for *am I not?* or *am not I?* ; & the shamefaced reluctance with which these full forms are often brought out betrays the speaker's sneaking affection for the *ain't I* that he (or still more she) fears will convict him of low breeding (*Well, I'm doing it already, ain't I?* ; *Yes, ain't I a lucky man?* ; *I'm next, ain't I?*). (b) The present subjunctive has *be* throughout (*Be I fair or foul* ; *If thou be true* ; *Be it so*), the form *beest*, originally indicative but used for a time as second singular subjunctive, being obsolete. The singular of the past subjunctive is *were, wert, were* (*If I were you* ; *Wert thou mine* ; *It were wise*), *were* for the second person being obsolete. (c) *Wert*, originally indicative, was adopted like *beest* as a subjunctive form, & though it is still sometimes used alternatively with *wast* as indicative, the modern tendency is to differentiate the two & make *wert* subjunctive only (*When thou wast true* ; *If thou wert true*)—a natural development that should be encouraged.

beano. Pl. *-os* ; see -O(E)S 6.

bear, vb. See FORMAL WORDS. For p.p. see BORN(E).

beat. The old p.p. *beat*, still the only form in *dead-beat*, lingers colloquially also in the sense *worsted, baffled* (*I won't be beat* ; *Has never been beat*), but now suggests ignorance rather than archaism.

beau has pl. *beaux* (or *beaus* ; see -X).

beau geste. See FRENCH WORDS, & GESTURE.

beau-ideal. If the word is to be used it should be pronounced bō-īdē'al, & written without accent. But neither in its only French sense of ideal beauty, nor in its current English sense of perfect type or highest possible embodiment *of* something, is there any occasion to use it, unless as a shoddy ornament. The English sense is based on the error of supposing *idéal* to be the noun (instead of the adjective) in the French phrase ; & the English noun *ideal*, without *beau*, is accordingly the right word to use, unless *flower, perfection, very type, pattern, pink,* or some other word, is more suitable.

beau monde. See FRENCH WORDS.

beauteous. See POETICISMS, & PLENTEOUS.

beautiful. *But the home b. needs other growing greenery when the festive season arrives./THE BED BEAUTIFUL. To see the English bed of supreme beauty you must take train to* . . . Such vulgarizing adaptations of Bunyan, now common, have upon readers the effect described in IRRELEVANT ALLUSION.

beautify. For inflexions see VERBS IN -IE &c., 6.

beaux yeux. See FRENCH WORDS.

because. After such openings as *The reason is, The reason why . . . is,* the clause containing the reason must not begin with *because,* but with *that.* Correct accordingly :— *The reason was because they had joined societies which became bankrupt./The chief reason why he welcomed this bill was b. he regarded it as . . ./The reason why he had always avoided the honour of the Garter was because he knew that it cost £1000. Their joining, his belief, his knowledge,* are the reasons ; & these can be paraphrased into the noun-clauses *that they had joined* &c., but not into the adverbial clauses *because they had joined* &c. For similar mistakes, see HAZINESS.

beccafico. Pl. *-os* ; see -O(E)S 6.

bedizen. The OED allows both ī & ĭ, but prefers the ī, & states that ' all English orthoepists ' do so.

bedouin (bĕ′dŏoē′n) serves as noun singular or plural (*bedouins* being now comparatively rare), or as adjective. The forms *bedawy* or *bedawee* (sing.), & *bedawin* or *bedaween*

(pl.), are also now used as nearer to the Arabic ; see DIDACTICISM.

beef. For plural see -VE(D).

befal(l), befel(l). The second l should be kept ; see -LL-, -L-, 4.

begging the question. See TECHNICAL TERMS.

begin. 1. Past tense *began,* formerly also (& still rarely) *begun.* 2. For *It was begun to be built* &c., see DOUBLE PASSIVES.

behalf & behoof are often confused both in construction & in sense. Modern usage is settling down to a clear differentiation ; & those who are not fully conversant with the history of the words would do well to confine themselves to the really current types here given. *On his* &c. *behalf,* or *on behalf of all* &c., means *as representing him, all,* &c. (*I can speak only on my own behalf ; Application was made on behalf of the prosecutor*) ; *on* is the normal preposition ; the phrase does not mean, except additionally & by chance, for the advantage of ; it is still in common use. *For* or *to his* &c. *behoof,* or *for* or *to the behoof of all* &c., means *for* or *to the advantage of him, all,* &c. (*For the behoof of the unlearned ; To the use & behoof of him & his heirs ; Taking towns for his own behoof*) ; *for* & *to* are the prepositions ; *the* is normally used ; the meaning of *behoof* is simply advantage ; the phrases are more or less archaic.

behemoth. Bĭhē′mŏth is the correct pronunciation, though bē′ĭmŏth is perhaps commoner.

beholden, beholding. As p.p. of *behold, beholden* is now obsolete except in poetry. In the sense bound by gratitude (in which it got when *bchold* could still mean hold fast) it is still in use, though archaic by the side of *obliged ; beholding* in that sense is an ancient error due to ignorance of how *beholden* got its meaning, & should be allowed to perish.

behoof. See BEHALF.

behove, behoove. The first spelling is the better. As to pronunciation, the OED says ' Historically it rimes with *move, prove*, but being now mainly a literary word, it is generally made to rime with *rove, grove*, by those who know it only in books '.

belay, belie. For inflexions see VERBS IN -IE &c., 1, 3.

belike. See ARCHAISM.

belittle has one meaning that may pass uncensured, viz, to dwarf by contrast (*A tower not so tall as to b. the main building*). The OED says ' The word appears to have originated in U.S. ; whence in recent English use in sense 3 ', which is ' depreciate, decry the importance of '. It cannot be denied that since 1881, the date of the earliest British quotation, it has gained considerable currency in this sense ; but it is still felt by many to be an undesirable alien that should not be allowed to supplant the old-established words, of which we have a large supply suitable for various contexts & shades of meaning—*disparage, decry, depreciate, make light of, slight, run down, cry down, poohpooh, deride, ridicule, slight, minimize, lower*.

belles-lettres survives chiefly in publishers' circulars, library catalogues, & book reviews, its place having been taken elsewhere by *literature* (sometimes *mere* or *pure literature*) used in a special sense ; that sense is, as defined by the OED, ' Writing which has claim to consideration on the ground of beauty of form or emotional effect '. Like other words that require a speaker to attempt alien sounds (such as the ending -ĕtr is), *belles-lettres* can never become really current ; & its right to live at all, by the side of *literature*, depends on the value of a differentiation thus expressed by the OED :—' But it is now generally applied (when used at all) to the lighter branches of literature or the aesthetics of literary study ' ; i.e., *Paradise Lost* is rather literature than belles-lettres, though *The*

Essays of Elia is both. This restricted application, however, itself needs defence, *b*. properly including the epic as much as the toy essay, just as *literature* does. We could in fact do very well without *b*., & still better without its offshoots *belletrist* & *belletristic*.

belly is a good word now almost done to death by GENTEELISM. It lingers in proverbs & phrases, but even they are being amended into up-to-date delicacy, & the road to the heart lies less often through the b. than through the stomach or the tummy. The slaying of the slayer now in course of performance by *tummy* illustrates the vanity of genteel efforts ; a perpetual succession of names, often ending in nursery ineptitudes (*smock, shift, chemise, shimmy*), must be contrived. *Stomach* for *belly* is a specially bad case, because the meaning of *stomach* has to be changed before it can take the place of *b*. in many contexts. The tendency, however, is perhaps irresistible.

beloved is, when used as a p.p. (*b. by all ; was much b.*), disyllabic (-ŭvd) ; as a mere adjective (*dearly b. brethren ; the b. wife of*), or as a noun (*my b.*), it is trisyllabic (-ŭvĭd) ; the first of these rules is sometimes broken in ignorance of usage, & the second with a view to the emphasis attaching to what is unusual. Cf. *blessed, cursed*.

below, under. There is a fairly clear distinction between the prepositions, worth preserving at the cost of some trouble ; but the present tendency is to obscure it by allowing *under* to encroach ; & if this continues *b*. will seem more & more stilted, till it is finally abandoned to the archaists. The distinction is that *b*., like its contrary *above* (cf. also the Latin *infra* & *supra*), is concerned with difference of level & suggests comparison of independent things, whereas *under*, like its contrary *over* (cf. also **the**

Latin *sub* & *super*) is concerned with superposition & subjection, & suggests some interrelation. The classes b. us are merely those not up to our level ; those u. us are those that we rule. *B. the bridge* means with it higher up the stream ; *u. the bridge*, with it overhead. Contexts in which *b.* is both right & usual are *b. par, b. the salt*. Contexts in which *u.* is encroaching are *men b.* 45, *b.* one's *breath, no-one b. a bishop, incomes b.* £160. Contexts in which *u.* is both right & usual are *u. the sun, the sod, the table, the circumstances, the Stuarts, tyranny, protection*, one's *wing*, one's *thumb, a cloud*. Cf. also BENEATH.

beneath has still one generally current sense—too mean(ly) or low for (*He married b. him* ; *It is b. contempt* ; *It would be b. me to notice it*). Apart from this it is now a poetic, rhetorical, or emotional substitute for *under* or *below*.

Benedick, not *Benedict*, is the spelling in *Much Ado*, & should always be the spelling when the name is used generically for a confirmed or captured bachelor ; but *Benedict* is often used (*Penalize the recalcitrant Benedicts by putting a heavy tax upon them*) either (& probably) in ignorance, or on the irrelevant ground that Shakspere might have done well to use the more etymological form in -ct.

Bengalee, -ali. Pronounce běng-gaw'lĭ. The form in -ee is perhaps still the commoner.

benign, benignant, malign, malignant. The distinction between the long & short forms is not very clear, nor is it consistently observed. But it may be said generally that *benign* & *malign* refer rather to effect, & *benignant* & *malignant* to intention or disposition :—*Exercises a benign* or *malign influence* ; *A benignant* or *malignant deity*. An unconscious possessor of the evil eye has *a malign* but not *a malignant look* ; discipline is benign rather than benignant, indulgence benignant

rather than benign. The difference is the same in kind, though less in degree, as that between *beneficent, maleficent*, & *benevolent, malevolent*. It is to be noticed, however, (1) that the impulse of personification often substitutes the *-ant* forms for the others, e.g. as epithets of *destiny, chance*, &c. ; (2) that the distinction is less generally maintained between *benign* & *benignant* than between the other two (e.g., *of benign appearance* is common, where *benignant* would be better) ; (3) that nevertheless in medical use as epithets of diseases, morbid growths, &c., the forms are *benign* (as would be expected) & *malignant* (contrary to the rule) ; this use of *malignant* is perhaps a stereotyped example of the personifying tendency, which *benign* escaped because *benignant*, a recent formation, did not exist when the words were acquiring their medical sense. See also MALIGNANCY.

bereaved, bereft. The essential principle is perhaps that *bereaved* is resorted to in the more emotional contexts, *bereft* being regarded as the everyday form (cf. BELOVED). The result in practice is that (1) *bereft* is used when the loss is specified by an *of*-phrase, & *bereaved* when it is not, the latter naturally suggesting that it is the greatest possible (*Are you bereft of your senses ?* ; *The blow bereft him of consciousness* ; *A bereaved mother* ; *Weeping because she is bereaved*) ; but (2) *bereaved* is sometimes used even before *of* when the loss is that of a beloved person (*A mother bereft*, or *bereaved, of her children* ; *Death bereft*, or *bereaved, her of him*). See -T & -ED.

beseech. *Besought* is the established past & p.p., though *beseeched*, on which the OED comment is merely ' now regarded as incorrect ', still occurs, probably by inadvertence, & Milton has *beseecht*.

beside(s). The forms have been fully differentiated in ordinary modern use, though they are often confused again in poetry, & by those who prefer the abnormal or are unobservant of the normal. (1) *Beside* is now only a preposition, *besides* having all the adverbial uses ; *besides* would have been normal in *And what is more, she may keep her lover beside.*/*We talked of thee & none beside.* (2) *Beside* alone has the primary prepositional senses *by the side of* (*Sat down beside her* ; *She is an angel beside you*), *out of contact with* (*beside* one-*self*, *the question, the mark, the purpose*). (3) *Besides* alone has the secondary prepositional senses *in addition to, except* ; it would have been normal in *Other men beside ourselves.* / *I have no adviser beside you.*

besom. Pronounce bē'zm. It has two uses only, (1) as the name for a gardener's twig broom, (2) as a poetic expression for some purifying or destroying agency.

bespeak. The p.p. form *bespoke* perhaps lingers only, beside the now usual *bespoken*, as an attributive adjective meaning made to order (*bespoke goods, boots, &c.*) in contrast with *ready-made*.

bestir is now always used reflexively (*must b. myself*), & never, idiomatically, as an ordinary transitive verb ; *stirred* should have been used in *The example of the French in Morocco has bestirred Italy into activity in Africa*.

bête noire. See FRENCH WORDS. Those who wish to use the phrase in writing must not suppose, like the male writer quoted below, that the gender can be varied : *From the very first, & for some reason that has always been a mystery to me, I was his* bête noir.

bethink has constructions & meanings of its own, & can never serve as a mere ornamental substitute for *think*, as in *They will bethink themselves the only unhappy on the earth.*

bêtise. See FRENCH WORDS.

bet. Both *bet* & *betted* are in idiomatic use as past tense & p.p. *He bet me £5 I could not* ; *They betted a good deal in those days* ; *I have bet £500 against it* ; *How much has been bet on him ?* ; *The money was all betted away.* These examples, in which it will probably be admitted that the form used is better than the other, suggest that *bet* is preferred in the more usual connexion, i.e. with reference to a definite transaction or specified sum, & *betted* when the sense is more general.

better. The idiomatic phrase *had better* requires care ; the following, for instance, contains a violation of usage :—*The fact that many moderate men on both sides were disquieted by the incident of the Prince's presence in the House was enough to satisfy him that he* had better been *away.* Correct forms are *He had better be away, He had better have been away.* *He had better been away*, which is not English, is perhaps due, when it occurs, to confusion with the totally different construction, correct though tending to the archaic, *He had been better away.* In this last, *better* belongs to *he*, & the full form is *He would have been better* (*if he had been*) *away*, so that *better* necessarily follows, & does not precede *been.* But in *He had better have been away*, the full form is *He would have* (i.e. find) (*it*) *better* (*to*) *have been away*, & *better* belongs to *it*, i.e. to *to have been away* (not, of course, *to been*).

better, bettor. See -OR.

betterment. For the use of the word in general contexts, & apart from its technical application to property, see SAXONISM. *The late Lady Victoria devoted her entire life to the b. of the crofters & fishermen* ; if the writer had been satisfied with the English for *betterment*, which is *improvement*, he would not have been blinded by the unusual word to the fact that he was writing nonsense ; the lady's effort was not to better or improve the crofters, but their lot. *He would reform our methods all round, beginning with increased attention to the milk supply & the consequent b. of infant feeding.*

between is a sadly ill-treated word ; the point on which care is most necessary is that numbered 5.
1. *B. you & I.* 2. *B. each, every.* 3. *B. . . . & b.* 4. *Difference b.* 5. *B. . . . or &c.*

1. *B. you & I*, which is often said, perhaps results from a hazy remembrance of hearing *you & me* corrected in the subjective.

2. *B.* may be followed by a single plural (*b. two perils*) as well as by two separate expressions with *and* (*b. the devil & the deep sea*) ; but it must not be followed by a single expression in which a distributive such as *each* or *every* is supposed to represent a plural. The following must be corrected :— *A batsman who tried to gain time by blowing his nose b. every ball* (after every ball, b. the balls, *or* b. every ball & the next). *The absence of professional jealousy that must exist in future b. each member of our profession* (b. the members, *or if emphasis is indispensable*, b. each member ... & the rest).

3. *B. . . . & b.* The temptation to repeat *b.* with the second term, which comes in long sentences, must be resisted ; *B. you & b. me* is at once seen to be absurdly wrong ; the following is as ungrammatical:— *The claim yesterday was for the difference b. the old rate, which was a rate by agreement, & b. the new, of which the Water Board simply sent round a notice.* See OVER-ZEAL.

4. *B.*, used after words like *difference*, seems to tempt people to put down for one of the terms the exact opposite of what they mean :—*My friend Mr. Bounderby would never see any difference b. leaving the Coketown ' hands ' exactly as they were & requiring them to be fed with turtle soup & venison out of gold spoons* (for *leaving* read *refusing to leave*)./ *There is a very great distinction between a craven truckling to foreign nations & adopting the attitude of the proverbial Irishman at a fair, who goes about asking if anybody would like to tread on the tail of his coat* (Read *avoiding* for *adopting*).

5. *B. . . . or &c.* In the commonest use of *b.*, i.e. where two terms are separately specified, the one & only right connexion between those terms is *and*. But writers indulge in all sorts of freaks ; the more exceptional & absurd of these, in which *against, whereas, & to*, are experimented with, are illustrated in :— *It is the old contest b. Justice & Charity, b. the right to carry a weapon oneself against the power to shelter behind someone else's shield* (Here ELEGANT VARIATION has been at work ; to avoid repeating *between* . . . *and* is more desirable than to please the grammarian)./ *He distinguishes b. certain functions for which full & rigorous training is necessary, whereas others can very well be discharged by men who have had only the limited training* (Read *& others that can*)./ *Societies with a membership b. one thousand* to *five thousand*. These are freaks or accidents ; the real temptation, strong under certain circumstances, is to use *or* for *and* ; *They may pay in money* or *in kind* is wrongly but naturally converted into *The choice is b. payment in money* or *in kind*. So *We have in that substance the link b. organic* or *inorganic matter*./*Forced to choose b. the sacrifice of important interests on the one hand* or *the expansion of the Estimates on the other*./ *He must choose b. coming to an agreement which is being widely denounced as anti-patriotic*, or *insisting on a solution which would probably create fresh dangerous friction*. These again are simple, requiring no further correction than the change of *or* to *and*. Extenuating circumstances can be pleaded only when one or each of the terms is compound & has its parts connected by *and*, as in :—*The question lies b. a God & a creed*, or *a God in such an abstract sense that does not signify* (Read *b. a God & a creed on the one hand*, & *on the other a God in such* &c.)./*The conflict, which was previously b. the mob & the Autocracy, is now b. the Parliament & the King* or *the Parliament*

& the Bureaucracy (This means that the question now is whether Parliament & King, or Parliament & Bureaucracy, shall rule, & this way of putting it should be substituted : *The conflict was previously b. mob & Autocracy ; but the question* &c.).

betwixt. See ARCHAISM.

beverage. See PEDANTIC HUMOUR, & WORKING & STYLISH WORDS.

beware is now used only where *be* would be the part required with *ware* regarded as = cautious, i.e. in the imperative (*B. of the dog !*), infinitive (*He had better b.*), & pres. subjunctive (*Unless they b.*) ; *bewaring, I beware* or *bewared, was bewared of,* &c., are obsolete.

bewilderedly. See -EDLY.

bi- prefixed to English words of time (*bi-hourly, bi-weekly, bi-monthly, bi-quarterly, bi-yearly*) gives words that have no merits & two faults : they are unsightly hybrids, & they are ambiguous. To judge from the OED, the first means only two-hourly ; the second & third mean both two-weekly, two-monthly, & half-weekly, half-monthly ; & the last two mean only half-quarterly, half-yearly. Under these desperate circumstances we can never know where we are. There is no reason why the *bi-* hybrids should not be allowed to perish, & the natural & unambiguous *two-hourly & half-hourly, fortnightly & half-weekly, two-monthly & half-monthly, half-yearly & half-quarterly, two-yearly & half-yearly,* of which several are already common, be used regularly in place of them & the words (*bien-nial, bimestrial*) on which they were fashioned ; these latter have now almost become ambiguous themselves from the ambiguity of the mis-shapen brood sprung of them.

biannual, probably invented to stand to *biennial* as *half-yearly* to *two-yearly,* is sometimes confused with & sometimes distinguished from it. *Half-yearly* is the right word ; see BI-.

bias. For inflexions see -S-, -SS-.

bias(s)edly. A bad form ; see -EDLY.

bicentenary, bicentennial. See CENTENARY.

biceps, triceps. If plurals are wanted, it is best to say *-cepses,* the regular English formation ; not *-cipites* (the true Latin), both because it is too cumbrous, & because Latin scholars do not know the words as names of muscles ; nor *-ceps,* which is a mere blunder ; cf. FORCEPS, & see LATIN PLURALS 4.

bid. 1. In the auction sense the past & p.p. are both *bid* (*He bid up to £10 ; Nothing was bid*). **2.** In other senses, the past is usually spelt *bade* & pronounced băd (cf. *ate*) ; the p.p. is *bidden,* but *bid* is preferred in some phrases, esp. *Do as you are bid.* **3.** *Bid* one *go* &c. has been displaced in speech by *tell* one *to go* &c., but lingers in literary use. **4.** In the sense *command,* the active is usually followed by infinitive without *to* (*I bade him go*), but the passive by *to* (*He was bidden to go*).

bide. Apart from archaism & poetic use, the word is now idiomatic only in *b.* one's *time,* & its past in this phrase is *bided.*

bien entendu. See FRENCH WORDS.
biennial. See BI-.
bienséance. See FRENCH WORDS.

big, great, large. The differences in meaning & usage cannot be exhaustively set forth ; but a few points may be made clear. Roughly, the notions of mere size & quantity have been transferred from *great* to *large* & *big ; great* is reserved for less simple meanings, as will be explained below ; *large* & *big* differ, first, in that the latter is more familiar & colloquial, & secondly, in that each has additional senses— *large* its own Latin sense of generous, & *big* certain of the senses proper to *great,* in which it tends to be used sometimes as a colloquial & sometimes as a half-slang substitute. It will be best to classify the chief uses of *great* as the central word, with incidental comments on the other two.

1. With abstracts expressing things that vary in degree, *great* means *a high degree of* (*g. care, ignorance, happiness, tolerance, charity, joy, sorrow, learning, facility, generosity, comfort*) ; *big* is not idiomatic with any of these ; & though *large* is used with *tolerance, charity, & generosity*, it is in a special sense—broad-minded or prodigal. With words of this kind that happen themselves to mean size or quantity (*size, quantity, bulk, magnitude, amount, tonnage*) *large & big* are sometimes used, though neither is as idiomatic as *great*, & *big* is slangy.

2. With words denoting persons or things such that one specimen of the class deserves the name more fully than another (e. g., one fool is more a fool, but one boot is not more a boot, than another), *great* does not imply size, but indicates that the specimen has the essential quality in a high degree ; so *a g. opportunity, occasion, friend, landowner, majority, schoolmaster, shot* (shooter), *nuisance, stranger, brute, fool, haul, race* (contest), *undertaking, success, linguist, age*. Here *large* could be substituted with *landowner, majority, haul, & undertaking*, but merely because a large quantity of land, votes, fish, or money, is involved ; *big* could stand with the same four on the same ground ; it is slangily used also with most of the others ; this is bad ; *a great fool* should mean a very foolish fool, & *a big fool* one whose stature belies his wits.

3. *A great* has the meaning *eminent, of distinction*, & *the g.* the meaning *chief, principal, especial* (*a g. man* ; *g. houses* ; *a g. family* ; *the g. advantage*, or *thing, is*) ; & from these comes the use of *great* as a distinctive epithet (*the g. auk* ; *G. Britain* ; *Alexander the G.* ; *the g. toe* ; *go out by the g. gate*), with the idea of size either absent or quite subordinate. In these senses *large* cannot be used, though it would

stand with many of the same words in a different sense (*a g. family* has distinguished, but *a l. family* numerous, members) ; *big* is here again slangily & ambiguously substituted for *great* ; *a big man* should refer to the man's size, or be extended only (as in *the big men of the trade* ; cf. *large* with *landowner* &c. in 2) to express the quantity of his stock or transactions. *The b. toe*, however, & such examples as *the b. gate*, show that *big* may serve as a distinctive epithet instead of *great* without slangy effect when difference of size is the salient point of distinction ; & in such contexts it is now idiomatic.

4. Finally, *great* does sometimes mean of remarkable size—the sense that it has for the most part resigned to *large & big*— ; but it is so used only where size is to be represented as causing emotion ; *large & big* give the cold fact ; *great* gives the fact coloured with feeling ; e. g., *He hit me with a great stick* is better than *with a large* or *big stick*, if I am angry about its size ; but in *Perhaps a big* or *large stick might do* it would be impossible to substitute *great* ; similarly *Big dogs are better out of doors*, but *I am not going to have that great dog in here* ; *His feet are large* or *big*, but *Take your great feet off the sofa* ; *What a great head he has !* suggests admiration of the vast brain or fear of the formidable teeth it probably contains, whereas *What a large head he has !* suggests dispassionate observation.

bi-hourly. See BI-.
bike. See CURTAILED WORDS.
bilbo. Pl. *-oes* ; see -O(E)S 1.
billet doux. Pronounce bĭ′lĭdōō′. The plural is *billets doux*, but should be pronounced bĭ′lĭdōō′z. See FRENCH WORDS.

billion, trillion, quadrillion, &c. It should be remembered that these words do not mean in American (which follows the French) use what they mean in British English. For us they mean the 2nd, 3rd, 4th, &c.,

power of a million ; i.e., a billion is a million millions, a trillion a million million millions, &c. For Americans they mean a thousand multiplied by itself twice, three times, four times, &c. ; i.e., a billion is a thousand thousand thousands or a thousand millions, a trillion is a thousand thousand thousand thousands or a million millions, &c.

bi-monthly, bi-quarterly. See BI-.

bird's nest, bird('s)-nest(ing). The noun should always have the 's, & is better without the hyphen as two words (pl. *birds' nests*) than with it (pl. *bird's-nests*). In the verb & gerund the 's is also usual, but is often omitted.

bise. See WIND, n.

bishopric. See SEE.

bistre, -ter. See -RE & -ER.

bivalve. For *succulent b.* see PEDANTIC HUMOUR.

bivouac. Participles *-cked, -cking* ; see -C-, -CK-.

bi-weekly, bi-yearly. See BI-.

black(en). The short form is used when the intentional laying on of colouring-matter is meant, & otherwise the long ; we black boots with blacking, grates with black lead, & faces with burnt cork ; we blacken a reputation, oak blackens with age, & the ceiling is blackened with smoke ; an exception is that we black, rather than blacken, a person's eye for him. See -EN VERBS.

blague. See FRENCH WORDS.

blam(e)able. Spell without the -e- ; see MUTE E.

blank verse. See TECHNICAL TERMS.

blarney, vb. For inflexions see VERBS IN -IE &c., 2.

blasé. See FRENCH WORDS.

-ble. See -ABLE.

blended, blent. *Blended* is now the everyday form (*carefully blended teas* ; *he successfully blended amusement with instruction*) ; but *blent* survives in poetic, rhetorical, & dignified contexts (*pity & anger blent*).

blessed, blest. The accent used below (*blessèd*) is for the purpose of the article only. The attributive adjective is regularly disyllabic (*blessèd innocence* ; *what a blessèd thing is sleep !* ; *the blessèd dead* ; *every blessèd night* ; *not a blessèd one*), & the plural noun with *the*, which is an absolute use of the adjective, is so also ; but the monosyllabic pronunciation is sometimes used in verse, or to secure emphasis by the unusual, or in archaic phrases ; the spelling is then *blest* :—*our blest Redeemer* ; *that blest abode* ; *the Isles, the mansions, of the Blest.* The past tense, p.p., & predicative adjective, are regularly monosyllabic ; the spelling is usually *blessed* in the past tense, *blest* in clearly adjectival contexts, & variable in the p.p. (*He blessed himself* ; *God has blessed me with riches* ; *He is blessed, or blest, with good health, in his lot*, &c. ; *Blessed, or blest, if I know* ; *Those who win heaven, blest are they* ; *It is twice blest*) ; in the beatitudes & similar contexts, however, *blessèd* is usual. *Blessèd* makes sometimes *-est* ; see -ER & -EST 4.

blessedness. For *single b.*, see WORN-OUT HUMOUR.

blithesome is a NEEDLESS VARIANT of *blithe* ; see -SOME.

blizzard. For synonymy see WIND, n.

blond(e). The *-e* should be dropped ; the practice now usual is to retain it when the word is used either as noun or as adjective of a woman & drop it otherwise (*the blonde girl* ; *she is a blonde* ; *she has a blond complexion* ; *the blond races*) ; but this is by no means universal, & the doubt between *blond women* & *blonde women* (with *blondes women* in the background) at once shows its absurdity.

bloody, vb. For inflexions see VERBS IN -IE &c., 6.

bloom, blossom. Strictly, *bloom* n. & v. refers to the flower as itself the ultimate achievement of the plant, & *blossom* n. & v. to the flower as promising fruit ; the distinction, as regards literal flowers, is perhaps rather horticultural than literary or general ; at any rate it is often neglected ; but *The roses are in bloom, The apple-trees are in blossom,* & other uses, confirm it ; and in figurative contexts, the *blooming-time* or *bloom* of a period of art is its moment of fullest development, when its *blossoming-time* or *blossom* is already long past.

blouse. Pronounce blowz.

blowzed, -sed, blowzy, -sy. The OED spells with z.

bluebell. In the south this is the wild hyacinth, *Scilla nutans* ; in the north, & esp. in Scotland, it is the flower called in the south *harebell, Campanula rotundifolia,* with fewer, larger, & thinner-textured flowers than the other.

blu(e)ish. Spell without e. See MUTE E.

bluey. See -EY & -Y.

boatswain. The nautical pronunciation (bō'sn) has become so general that to avoid it is more affected than to use it. See PRONUNCIATION.

bodeful is a modern stylish substitute for *ominous* ; see WORKING & STYLISH WORDS, & SAXONISM.

body, vb. For inflexions see VERBS IN -IE &c., 6.

bog(e)y, bogie. The OED prefers *bogy* for the bugbear, & *bogie* in coachbuilding ; the golf word is usually spelt *Bogey.*

bohea. Pronounce bōhē'.

bolt, boult. The word of which the spelling varies is that meaning to sift. Of this the OED says :—'The historical spelling of the word is *boult* : unfortunately the dictionaries have confounded it with ' [the other verb *bolt*] ' & authorized the spelling *bolt* '. It is perhaps, however, not too late to restore the better spelling *boult* in literary use at least.

bombasine. The OED puts first the pronunciation bŏmbazē'n.

bona fide(s). *Bona fide* is a Latin

ablative meaning *in good faith* ; its original use is accordingly adverbial (*Was the contract made* bona fide *?*) ; but it is also & more commonly used attributively like an adjective (*Was it a* bona fide, or bona-fide, *contract ?*) ; in this attributive use the hyphen is correct, but not usual ; in the adverbial use it is wrong. *Bona fides* is the noun (*His* bona fides *was questioned*) ; the mistake is sometimes made by those who know no Latin of using *fide* instead of *fides* : *The fact that Branting accepted the chairmanship of the Committee should be sufficient evidence of its* bona-fide.

bonbon. See FRENCH WORDS.

bond(s)man. The two forms are properly distinct, *bondsman* meaning a surety & being connected with the ordinary *bond* & *bind,* & *bondman* meaning a villein, serf, or man in bondage, & having (like *bondage*) nothing to do with *bond* & *bind* ; but *bondsman* is now rare in its true sense, & on the other hand is much more used than *bondman* in the sense proper to the latter. The confusion is not likely to be corrected, & is of no importance.

Bon(e)y. See -EY, -IE, -Y.

bonhomie. See FRENCH WORDS.

bon mot. See FRENCH WORDS. The plural is *bons mots.*

bonne. See FRENCH WORDS.

bonne bouche. The meaning of the phrase in French is not that which we have given it ; but variation of meaning or form is no valid objection to the use of a phrase once definitely established ; see À L'OUTRANCE.

bonnes fortunes, bon ton, bon vivant. See FRENCH WORDS.

bookcase. Pronounce bŏŏ'k-kās, not bŏŏ'kās.

bookie, -y. See -EY, -IE, -Y.

bookman. See NOVELTY-HUNTING, SAXONISM.

booze, -zy, bouse, -sy, bowse, -sy. The *booz-* forms are now established, & the others should be abandoned.

born(e). The p.p. of *bear* in all senses except that of birth is *borne*

(*I have borne with you till now*; *Was borne along helpless*) ; *borne* is also used, when the reference is to birth, (a) in the active (*Has borne no children*), & (b) in the passive when *by* follows (*Of all the children borne by her one survives*) ; the p.p. in the sense of birth, when used passively without *by*, is *born* (*Was born blind*; *A born fool* ; *Of all the children born to them* ; *The melancholy born of solitude* ; *Born in* 1898).

borné. See FRENCH WORDS.

botanic(al). The -ic form is ' now mostly superseded by *botanical*, except in names of institutions founded long ago, as " The Royal Botanic Society " ' —OED. See -IC(AL).

both. 1. *Both ... as well as.* 2. Redundant *both.* 3. Common parts in *both ... and* phrases.

1. *Both ... as well as.* To follow *b.* by *as well as* instead of *and*, as is often done either by inadvertence or in pursuit of the unusual, is absurd ; how absurd is realized only when it is remembered that the *as well* of *as well as* is itself the demonstrative to which the second *as* is relative, & can stand in the place occupied by *both* instead of next door to *as*. In the following examples, either omit *both* or read *and* for *as well as* ; *as well*, it will be seen, can be shifted into the place of *both*, if the object is to give timely notice that the carters' strike, the composer, or the adjective, is not the whole of the matter :—*He has figured prominently b. in the carters' strike, in which many of his members were involved, as well as in the more recent railway strike.*/ *The metrostyle will always be of exceeding interest, b. to the composer as well as to the public.*/Which *differs from who in being used b. as an adjective as well as a noun.*

2. Redundant *both.* The addition of *both* to *equal(ly)*, *alike*, *at once*, *between*, or any other word that makes it needless, is at least a fault of style, & at worst (e.g. with *between*) an illogicality. In the ex-

amples, *both* should be omitted, unless the omission of the other word(s) in roman type is preferable or possible :—*If any great advance is to be* at once b. *intelligible & interesting.*/ *The currents shifted the mines, to the* equal *danger* both *of friend & foe.*/*We find* b. *Lord Morley & Lord Lansdowne* equally *anxious for a workable understanding.*/ *To the ordinary Protestant* b. *Latitudinarian & High-Churchman were* equally *hateful.*/ *The International Society is not afraid to invite comparisons* between *masters* b. *old & new.*

3. Common parts in *both ... and* phrases. Words placed between the *both* & the *and* are thereby declared not to be common to both members ; accordingly, *B. in India & Australia* is wrong ; the right arrangements are (a) *B. in India & in Australia,* (b) *In b. India & Australia* ; of these b sounds formal, & is often shrunk from as a remedy worse than the disease ; but there is no objection to a, which should be used. Similarly, *B. the Indians & the Australians* is right & unobjectionable ; *B. the Indians & Australians* is common but wrong ; *The b. Indians & Australians* is theoretically right but practically impossible.

boulevard. See FRENCH WORDS.

boult. See BOLT.

bounden is still used, & *bound* is not, with *duty.* It is also used alternatively with *bound* as the p.p. of *bind* in the sense *oblige* (*I am much bounden*, or *bound, to you*) ; but the whole verb, including the p.p., is a mere ARCHAISM in this sense.

bounteous, -iful. See PLENTEOUS.

bourgeois. See FRENCH WORDS. As the name of a printing TYPE, in which sense the word is English, it is pronounced berjoi's.

bourn(e). There are two words, which were originally *burn* & *borne*, but are now not distinguished, consistently at any rate, either in spelling or in pronunciation. The first (which retains in Scotland & the north its original form *burn*) means a stream, but is now applied as a current word only to the torrents of the chalk downs, full in winter & dry in summer ; it serves in poetry as an ornamental synonym for *brook*. The second means properly a boundary (from French *borne*) as in *The undiscovered country from whose borne No traveller returns*, but is used almost solely, with a distorted memory of that passage, in the sense of destination or goal. The OED prefers *bourn* stream, & *bourne* goal, & the differentiation would be useful.

bowdlerize. Pronounce bow-.

bowsprit. Pronounce bō-.

brace, n. (= two). See COLLECTIVES 3.

brachycephalic, -lous. See -CEPHALIC.

brachylogy. See TECHNICAL TERMS.

braggadocio. Pl. *-os* ; see -O(E)S 4.

brain(s), in the sense of wits, may often be either singular or plural, the latter being perhaps, as the OED suggests, the familiar, & the former the dignified use. In *suck* or *pick* a person's *brain(s)*, the number is indifferent ; *Has no bb.* is commoner than *Has no b.*, but either is English. Some phrases, however, admit only one number or the other, e.g. *cudgel* one's *bb.*, *have* a thing *on the b.*, *have* one's *b. turned.*

brainy, meaning acute, ingenious, &c., is, & may as well remain, an Americanism.

brake, break, nn. The words meaning (1) bracken, (2) thicket, (3) lever, (4) crushing or kneading or peeling or harrowing instrument, (5) steadying-frame, though perhaps all of different origins, are spelt *brake* always. The word that means checking-appliance is usually *brake*, but *break* sometimes occurs owing to a probably false derivation from *to break* (the OED refers it to N⁰ 3 above, which it derives from OF *brac* = F *bras* arm). The word meaning horsebreaker's carriage-frame, & applied also to a large wagonette, is

usually, & probably should be, *break* ; but *brake* is not uncommon. The word meaning fracture &c. is always *break*.

Bramah (*B. lock* &c.) is pronounced bră-, not brah-.

branch. For synonymy see FIELD.

bran(d)-new. The spelling with -d̄ is the right (fresh as from the furnace) ; but the d is seldom heard, & often not written.

bravado. Pl. *-os* ; see -O(E)S 3.

brave in the sense of fine or showy is an ARCHAISM, & in the sense of worthy a GALLICISM ; *make a b. show*, however, is fully current.

bravo, brava, bravi. In applauding operatic performers &c., the first form is used to a man, the second to a woman, & the third to the company.

bravo. Pl. *-oes* in sense bullies, *-os* in sense cries of applause ; see -O(E)S 1, 3.

brazen. See -EN ADJECTIVES, & -ER & -EST 2.

breadthways, -wise. See -WAYS, -WISE.

break. 1. For p.p. see BROKE(N). 2. For spelling of nouns see BRAKE, BREAK.

breakfast, break one's **fast.** The divided form is now a mere ARCHAISM. Pronounce brě'kfast.

breeches &c. The singular noun & its derivatives (*breechloader, breeching*, &c.) have usually -ēch- in pronunciation ; *breeches* the garment has always -ĭch-, & the verb *breech* (put child into bb.) usually follows this.

breese, breeze, brize, are all existent spellings of the word meaning gadfly. A difference from the other *breeze* being useful, the first is recommended.

brevet, n. & v. Pronounce brě'vĭt, not brĭvě't ; the past & p.p. are accordingly *breveted*, see -T-, -TT-.

breviary. Pronounce brē- ; see FALSE QUANTITY.

bricken. See -EN ADJECTIVES.

brier, briar. 1. For the word meaning thorny bush, the spelling *brier*, & the monosyllabic pronunciation briī̆r, are nearer the original & preferable ; *brere* is still nearer, but now a poetic archaism only. 2. The name of the pipe-wood is an entirely different word, but also best spelt *brier*.

brilliance, -cy. See -CE, -CY.

brindle(d), brinded. The original form *brinded* is archaic, & should be used only in poetry. *Brindled*, a variant of it, is now the ordinary adjective, & *brindle*, a BACK-FORMATION from this, & convenient as a name for the colour, should be used only as a noun.

brisken. See -EN VERBS.

Britain, British, Briton. For the relation of these to *England, English(man)*, see ENGLAND.

Briticism, the name for an idiom used in Great Britain & not in America, is a BARBARISM, & should be either *Britannicism* or *Britishism*, just as *Hibernicism* or *Irishism* will do, but not *Iricism*. *Gallicism* & *Scot(t)icism* cannot be pleaded, since *Gaulish* & *Scotch* are in Latin *Gallicus* & *Scot(t)icus*, but *British* is *Britannicus*. The verbal critic, who alone uses such words, should at least see to it that they are above criticism.

Britisher is a word made in America, but now discountenanced in American dictionaries as ' in jocose use only ' or as ' almost disused ' ; if these phrases give the actual & not merely the desirable American usage, on which point there are doubts, it is time that British writers reconciled themselves to relinquishing the word in its convenient function of announcing that the user of it is American. If, on the other hand, the word is still current in America, Englishmen have both as little right to object to outsiders' applying it to them & as little occasion to use it themselves, as the Germans have to quarrel with us for calling them *Germans* & not *Dutch* or to change their name to please us.

broad, wide. Both words have general currency ; their existence side by side is not accounted for by one's being more appropriate to any special style ; what difference there is must be in meaning ; yet how close they are in this respect is shown by their both having *narrow* as their usual opposite, & both standing in the same relation, if in any at all, to *long*. Nevertheless, though they may often be used indifferently (*a b.* or *a w. road* ; *three feet w.* or *b.*), there are (1) many words with which one may be used & not the other, (2) many with which one is more idiomatic than the other though the sense is the same, (3) many with which either can be used, but not with precisely the same sense as the other ; these numbered points are illustrated below.

The explanation seems to be that *wide* refers to the distance that separates the limits, & *broad* to the amplitude of what connects them. When it does not matter which of these is in our minds, either word does equally well ; if the hedges are far apart, we have a w. road ; if there is an ample surface, we have a b. road ; it is all one. But (1) backs, shoulders, chests, bosoms, are b., not w., whereas eyes & mouths are w., not b. ; *at w. intervals, give a w. berth, a w. ball, w. open*, in all of which b. is impossible, have the idea of separation strongly ; & *w. trousers, w. sleeves, w. range, w. influence, w. favour, w. distribution, the w. world*, where b. is again impossible, suggest the remoteness of the limit. Of the words that admit b. but refuse w. some are of the simple kind (*b. blades, spearheads, leaves* ; *the b. arrow*), but with many some secondary notion such as generosity or downrightness or neglect of the petty is the representative of the simple idea of amplitude (*b. daylight, B. Church, b. jests, b. farce, b. hint, b. Scotch, b. facts, b. outline*).
(2) Some words with which one of the two is idiomatic, but the other

not impossible, are :—(preferring *broad*) *expanse, brow, forehead, lands, estates, acres, brim, mind, gauge* ; (preferring *wide*) *opening, gap, gulf, culture*.

(3) Some illustrations of the difference in meaning between *broad* & *wide* with the same word ; the first two may be thought fanciful, but hardly the others : *A w. door* is one that gives entrance to several abreast, *a b. door* one of imposing dimensions ; *a w. river* takes long to cross, *a b. river* shows a fine expanse of water ; *a w. generalization* covers many particulars, *a b. generalization* disregards unimportant exceptions ; a page has *a b. margin*, i.e. a fine expanse of white, but we allow *a w. margin* for extras, i.e. a great interval between the certain & the possible costs ; *a w. distinction* or *difference* implies that the things are very far from identical, but *a b. distinction* or *difference* is merely one that requires no subtlety for its appreciation.

broadness is now used instead of the usual *breadth* only when the meaning is coarseness or indelicacy of expression.

Brobdingnag (not *-ignag*) is the spelling.

broccoli (not *-oco-*, nor *-lo*) is the best spelling. The word is an Italian plural, & is generally used collectively like *spinach* &c. ; but if *a* or the plural is wanted, *a broccoli, two broccolis*, are the forms.

brochure, pamphlet. See FRENCH WORDS. *B.* has no right to exist in English, since it is not needed by the side of *p.* Its introduction in the 19th c. was probably due to misconception of the French uses. In French *b.* is used where the French *p.* (chiefly applied to scurrilous or libellous or violently controversial pamphlets) is inappropriate. The sense ' a few leaves of printed matter stitched together ' has always belonged in English to *p.*, though it has by the side of this general sense the special one (different from the French) ' *p.* bearing on some question

of current interest (esp. in politics or theology) '. ' Dans sa brochure appelée en anglais *pamphlet* ', quoted in French dictionaries from Voltaire, gives us the useful hint that the English for *b.* is *p.*

broider(y). See ARCHAISM, POETICISMS.

broke(n). The form *broke*, now obsolete or a blunder in most senses, is still idiomatic (1) as p.p. of *break* = dismiss the service (*he was broke for cowardice*) except in the attributive use (*a broken officer*), and (2) in the slang phrase *stony-broke*.

bromine. For pronunciation see IODINE.

bronco. Pl. *-os* ; see -O(E)S 6.

brow. *In the sweat of thy brow* is a MISQUOTATION.

Bruin. See SOBRIQUETS.

brusque, though formerly so far naturalized as to be spelt *brusk* & pronounced brŭsk, is now usually pronounced broŏsk.

brutal, brute, brutish. *Brutal* differs from *brute* in its adjectival or attributive use, & from *brutish*, in having lost its simplest sense *of the brutes as opposed to man* & being never used without implying moral condemnation. Thus, while *brute* force is contrasted with skill, *brutal* force is contrasted with humanity. In torturing a mouse, a cat is *brutish*, & a person *brutal*. For comparison of *brutal*, see -ER & -EST, 4.

Brythonic. See GAELIC.

bubo, buffalo. Pl. *-oes* ; see -O(E)S 1.

buck. See HART.

buffet. The OED pronounces this bŭ′fĭt in the sense *sideboard* or *cupboard*, & as French in the sense *refreshment bar*. See also FRENCH WORDS.

buffo. Pl. *-os* ; see -O(E)S 6.

bugaboo. Pl. *-oos* ; see -O(E)S 4.

bulbul. Pronounce boo′lbool.

bulletin. See FRENCH WORDS.

bully, vb. For inflexions see VERBS IN -IE &c., 6.

bullyrag. See BALLYRAG.

bumble-bee, humble-bee. See

NEEDLESS VARIANTS. Neither form, however, though there is no difference of meaning, is a mere variant of the other ; they are independent formations, one allied with *boom*, & the other with *hum*. The first form is preferable, because its imitative origin is more apparent.

bummalo. Pl. -*os* ; see -O(E)S 6.

bunkum, buncombe. The first spelling is recommended, as decidedly the prevalent one. The second, from an American place-name, is the original ; but the word is equally significant with either spelling, & no purpose is served by trying to re-establish the less usual.

buoy is now pronounced boi, & attempts to restore bwoi, the pronunciation ' recognized by all orthoepists British & American ', are doomed to fail ; the OED, in spite of the statement quoted, puts boi first.

bur, burr. The word meaning prickly seed-vessel &c. is usually, & might conveniently be always, *bur* ; the word describing northern pronunciation is always *burr* ; in all the other words, which are less common, *burr* is usual & might well be made universal.

burden, burthen. The second form is, even with reference to a ship's carrying capacity, for which *burden* is now often used, a NEEDLESS VARIANT ; & in other uses it is an ARCHAISM.

bureaucrat, &c. The formation is so barbarous that all attempt at self-respect in pronunciation may perhaps as well be abandoned. It might be possible to insist on būrō'krăt & būrō'krăsĭ as against būr'okrăt & būrŏ'krăsĭ ; but būrō'-kră'tĭk must inevitably be vanquished by būr'okră'tĭk ; &, that being so, it is better to give the whole thing up, & pretend that *-eau-* is the formative *-o-* that ordinarily precedes *-crat* &c. ; all is then plain sailing ; it is only to be desired that

the spelling could also be changed to *burocrat* &c.

burgh, burgher. *Burgh*, still in English use with reference to Scotch elections, is pronounced like the English form *borough*. *Burgher*, an archaism, is pronounced ber'ger.

burgle. See BACK-FORMATION. A verb being undoubtedly wanted, & words on the pattern of *burglarize* being acceptable only when there is no other possibility, it is to be hoped that *burgle* may outgrow its present facetiousness & become generally current.

burlesque, caricature, parody, travesty. In wider applications the words are often interchangeable ; a badly conducted trial, for instance, may be called *a b.*, *a c.*, *a p.*, or *a t.*, *of justice* ; a perverted institution may be said, without change of sense, to *b.*, *c.*, *p.*, or *t.*, *its founder's intentions* ; &, the others having no adjectives of their own, the adjective *burlesque* can serve them, as well as its own noun, in that capacity (*a b. portrait, poem,* &c.). Two distinctions, however, are worth notice :— (1) *b.*, *c.*, & *p.*, have, besides their wider uses, each a special province ; action or acting is burlesqued, form & features are caricatured, & verbal expression is parodied, (2) *travesty* differs from the others both in having no special province, & in being more used than they (though all four may be used either way) when the imitation is intended to be or pass for an exact one but fails, & not to amuse by its mixture of likeness & unlikeness to the original.

burnt, burned. *Burnt* is the usual form, esp. in the p.p. ; *burned* tends to disappear, & is chiefly used with a view to securing whatever impressiveness or beauty attaches to the unusual ; see -T & -ED.

burr. See BUR.
burst, bust. In the slang expressions *b. up*, *b.-up*, go *a b.*, *on the b.*, &c., the spelling *bust* is established,

& should be used by those who use the phrases.

bury. For inflexions see VERBS IN -IE &c., 6.

bus is sufficiently established to require no apostrophe; for the plural, see -S-, -SS-.

business, busyness. The second form, pronounced bĭ'zĭnĭs, is used as the simple abstract noun of *busy* (the state &c. of being busy) for distinction from the regular *business* with its special developments of meaning.

buskin. For *the b.* meaning the tragic stage &c. see BATTERED ORNAMENTS.

bustle. See PRONUNCIATION, Silent t.

busy, vb. For inflexions see VERBS IN -IE &c., 6.

but. 1. Case after *b.* = except. 2. Redundant negative after *b.* 3. Illogical *b.* 4. Wheels within wheels. 5. *B. . . . however.* 6. *But which.*

1. Case after *but* = except. The question is whether *b.* in this sense is a preposition, & should therefore always take an objective case (*No-one saw him but me*, as well as *I saw no-one but him*), or whether it is a conjunction, & the case after it is therefore variable (*I saw no-one but him*, i.e. but I did see *him*; *No-one saw him but I*, i.e. but *I* did see him). The answer is that *but* was originally a preposition meaning outside, but is now usually made a conjunction, the subjective case being preferred after it when admissible. A correspondent who has collected a large number of examples in which an inflected pronoun follows *but* informs me that 95% of them show the conjunctional use; *Whence all b. he* (not *him*) *had fled* exemplifies, in fact, the normal modern literary use. *All but him* is used (a) by those who either do not know or do not care whether it is right or not—& accordingly it is still good colloquial—, & (b) by the few who, being aware that *b.* is originally prepositional, are also proud of the knowledge & willing to air it—& accordingly it is still

pedantic-literary. It is true that the conjunctional use has prevailed owing partly to the mistaken notion that *No-one knows it b. me* is the same sort of blunder as *It is me*; but it has prevailed, in literary use, & it is in itself legitimate; it would therefore be well for it to be universally accepted.

2. Redundant negative after *but.* *But* (now rare), *but that* (literary), & *but what* (colloq.), have often in negative & interrogative sentences the meaning *that . . . not.* But just as *I shouldn't wonder if he didn't fall in* is often heard in vulgar speech where *didn't fall* should be *fell*, so careless writers insert after *but* the negative already implied in it. Examples (all wrong) :—*Who knows b. that the whole history of the Conference might* not *have been changed?* / *Who knows but what agreeing to differ may* not *be a form of agreement rather than a form of difference?* / *How can Mr. Balfour tell b. that two years hence he may* not *be tired of official life?*

For similar mistakes, see HAZINESS.

3. Illogical *but.* A very common & exasperating use of *but* as the ordinary adversative conjunction is that illustrated below. A writer having in his mind two facts of opposite tendency, & deciding to give them in two separate & complete sentences connected by *but*, forgets that the mere presence of the opposed facts is not enough to justify *but*; the sentences must be so expressed that the total effect of one is opposed to that of the other; he must not be seduced into throwing in an additional circumstance in one (usually the second) of his sentences that will have the unintended effect of neutralizing the contrast :—*In vain the horse kicked & reared, b. he could not unseat his rider* (if the kicking was in vain, the failure to unseat involves no contrast; either *in vain* or *but* must be dropped)./*Pole was averse to burning Cranmer, b. it was Mary who decided that his recantation was not genuine & that he must die* (The fact in

contrast with Pole's averseness is Cranmer's having to die ; this may be given simply—*but Cranmer was burnt*, or with additional details— *it was decided &c.*, or even *Mary decided &c.*—, as long as the opposition between the sentences remains ; but *it was Mary who decided* at once makes the second sentence harmonious instead of contrasted with the first ; *And it was Mary who decided*, or *But Mary decided*./*So far as Mr. Haldane's scheme tends towards the encouragement of local patriotism, it can do nothing but good ; but the only point about the scheme which seems to me to be doubtful concerns the question of the divided responsibility* (There being only one doubtful point is in harmony, not contrast, with the goodness admitted in the first sentence. Omit *but*, or else write *But there is a doubtful point &c.*)./*Our correspondent is singularly well informed, but the one thing he apparently does not know is the arguments of his fellow Tariff-reformers* (Omit either *but* or *the one thing . . . is*)./*It is in no spirit of hostility to the Committee of Union & Progress that these lines are written ; but it is a sincere appeal to the men of courage & goodwill at Salonica to strive to set their house in order* (Either omit *but*, or convert the two sentences into one by writing *but in sincere appeal* ; we then have the correct form *It is not black, but white* instead of the incorrect *It is not black, but it is white*)./ *To the revealed objects of that Club he takes no exception, b. what alarms him is the fact that the new Club has been apparently formed behind the back of Mr. Balfour* (Either omit *but*, or write *b. he is alarmed by*).

Since less excusable blunders than these, due to gross carelessness, occasionally occur (e.g. *It is not an evergreen, as is often represented ; b. its leaves fall in the autumn, & are renewed in the spring*), it may be well to put down the right & wrong types in the simplest form :—(right) *It is not black, but white* : *It is not*

black *; it is white* : *It is not black ; but it is nearly black* : (wrong) *It is not black, but it is white* : *It is not black, b. it is nearly white*.

4. Wheels within wheels. A few examples will show the disagreeable effect produced when inside one of the contrasted sentences connected by *but* an internal contrast, also indicated by *but*, is added :—(a) *B. he did not follow up his threats by any prompt action against the young king, b. went off to Germany to conclude the campaign against his brother Lewis of Bavaria. B. on arriving in Bavaria he did not strike down his enemy, b. made a six months' truce with him.* (b) *You have come not to a scattered organization, b. to an organization which is in its infancy, b. which is yet real.* (c) *I gazed upon him for some time, expecting that he might awake ; b. he did not, b. kept on snoring.* (d) *The reformers affirm the inward life, b. they do not trust it, b. use outward & vulgar means.* (e) *There was a time when golf was a Scottish speciality, b. it has followed Scottish precedents in spreading over the whole country south of the Tweed. B. we are glad that it is a Scot who has ventured to blame golf.*

5. *But . . . however* is perhaps always due to mere carelessness :— (a) *If any real remedy is to be found, we must first diagnose the true nature of the disease ; b. that, however, is not hard.* (b) *B. one thing, however, had not changed, & that was . . .* (c) *The enemy's cavalry withdrew with losses, b. they returned, however, reinforced by . . .*

6. For *but which* see WHICH.

buxom. See -ER & -EST, 2.

buz(z). See -Z-, -ZZ-.

by, prep., owing to the variety of its senses, is apt to be unintentionally used several times in the same sentence ; when the uses are parallel & the repetition intentional (*We can now travel by land, by sea, or by air*), monotony is better than the ELEGANT VARIATION (*by land, on the sea, or through the air*) often affected ; but

such accidental recurrences of *by* as
are here shown are slovenly (cf. OF):—
*The author's attempt to round off the
play by causing Maggie to conquer by
making John laugh by her poor joke
about Eve was not worthy of him./Pal-
merston wasted the strength derived by
England by the great war by his brag.*

by, bye, by-. The spelling, & usage
in regard to separating the two
parts, hyphening them, or writing
them as one word, are variable. As
the noun & adjective are merely
developments of the adverb or preposition, it would have been reasonable to spell always *by* ; but *bye* is
now too firmly established in some
uses to be abolished ; & the question
of hyphening, separating, or combining, is difficult. The following
scheme might secure consistency
without violating any usage that
deserves respect.
1. The noun is *bye* (*leg-bye* ; *Jones
a bye* ; *by the bye*).
2. The adjective (collateral, subordinate, incidental, additional, &c.)
should be written *by-* (*by-road,
by-election*, &c.) ; the spelling *bye*
is due to the desire to distinguish
from the preposition, but is only
needed for this purpose if the hyphen
(unobjectionable even in words made
for the nonce ; *the by-effects* is no
worse than *the bye effects*) is omitted.
3. The adverb should be spelt *by* &
joined on without hyphen (*bygone,
bystander*, &c.).
4. Some special words :—*by & by*
has the adverb or preposition twice,
& should follow their spelling ;
bye-bye sleep, & *bye-bye* good-bye,
are unconnected with *by*, & have
usually the *e* ; *by-law* is perhaps
also unconnected, & is often spelt
bye-, but may well be assimilated to
words under rule 2.
A list is added for convenience :
by & by, by-blow, bye (n.), bye-bye,
by-election, by-end, bygone, by-lane,
by-law, by-name, by-pass, bypast,
by-path, by-play, by-product,
by-road, bystander, by-street, by
the bye, by-way, by-word, by-work.

C

cabbalist(ic), cabbala, &c. These
are the right spellings, not *caba-*.
cable(gram). The verb *cable* (transmit, inform, &c., by cable) is both
convenient & unobjectionable; *cablegram* is not only a BARBARISM, but
a needless one, since *cable* (cf. *wire* vb
& n.) serves perfectly as a noun also
in the sense submarine telegram.

cacao. Pronounce kakā'ō, & see
COCOA. Pl. *-os* ; see -O(E)S 3.
cache. See FRENCH WORDS.
cachet is mainly a LITERARY
CRITICS' WORD (*bears the c. of genius*
&c.), & should be expelled as an
alien ; *stamp, seal, sign manual*, are
good enough for English readers.
See FRENCH WORDS ; &, for synonymy, SIGN.

cachinnate, -ation, -atory. See
POLYSYLLABIC HUMOUR.
cacoethes scribendi. See BATTERED
ORNAMENTS.
cacophonous, cacophony. See
ANTI-SAXONISM.
cactus. Pl. usually *-uses* ; see -US.
caddie, caddy. The golf-attendant
has *-ie*, see -EY, -IE, -Y ; the tea-box
has *-y*.
caddis is preferable to *caddice*.
cadet. For this pronounced as
French & appended to a name see
FRENCH WORDS.
cadi. Pronounce kah'dĭ ; pl. *cadis*.
cadre, being an established military
technicality, should be anglicized in
sound & pronounced kah'der, in pl.
kah'derz ; the French pronunciation
is especially inconvenient in words
much used in the plural.

caduceus. Pl. *-ceī* ; see -US.
caecum, Caesar, caesious, caesura,
&c. See Æ, Œ.
caesura. See TECHNICAL TERMS.
café is naturalized in the sense
coffee-house or restaurant ; in the
sense coffee it is a FRENCH WORD.
café chantant, café noir. See
FRENCH WORDS.
caffeine. Pronounce kă'flīn.
Caffre. See KAFIR.

caiman. See CAYMAN.

caique. Pronounce kaē′k.

caisson. Pronounce kä′sn.

caky, not *cakey*. See -EY & -Y.

calcareous, -rious. The first form is definitely wrong, the ending *-ceous* from Latin *-arius*, which gives *-arious* or *-ary* in English ; but it is so firmly established that perhaps a return to the correct but now obsolete second form is out of the question.

calculate. 1. *C.* makes *calculable* ; see -ABLE 1. 2. The Americanism is an example of SLIPSHOD EXTENSION ; the sense I consider-as-the-result-of-a-calculation passes into the simple sense I consider. *We shall win, I c., by a narrow majority* shows the normal use, the assumption at least being that the numbers have been reckoned & compared. *We shall be in time, I c.* is (according to British usage) correct if the time wanted & the time at disposal have been worked out in detail, but wrong if it is a mere general expression of sanguineness. *You don't know everything, I c.* is the full-fledged Americanism.

calculus. The medical word has pl. *-lī* ; the mathematical, *-luses*. See -US.

caldron. See CAULDRON.

Caledonian. Putting aside its special sense (*inhabitant*) *of ancient Scotland*, & its ornamental use in names of clubs, companies, &c., the word serves chiefly as material for POLYSYLLABIC HUMOUR.

calembour. See FRENCH WORDS.

calendar, Calends, not k-, is usual.

calf. For plural &c. see -VE(D).

calibre. The OED prefers this spelling (not *-ber*) & the pronunciation kă′lĭber. See -RE & -ER.

calico. Pl. *-os* ; see -O(E)S 3.

caliph is the spelling, & kā′lĭf the pronunciation, put first by the OED, which states, however, that ' orientalists now favour *Khalif* ' ; see DIDACTICISM.

calligraphy &c. should not be altered to *calig-*. Greek compounds are made either with καλλι- from κάλλος beauty, or with καλο- from καλός beautiful. Choice is therefore between *calligraphy* & *calography* ; & as the actual Greek compounds were καλλιγραφία &c., *calligraphy* is obviously right.

callus. Pl. *-uses* ; see -US. The word is often wrongly spelt *callous*, from confusion with the adjective.

calmative, being queer both in pronunciation (kă′lmatĭv, not kah′matĭv) & in formation (there is no Latin word for *-ative* to be attached to), should be left to the doctors, if even they have a use for it beside *sedative*, as a technical term.

caloric, a word now no longer in scientific use, is preserved as a synonym for *heat* only by PEDANTIC HUMOUR.

calumniate makes *-niable* ; see -ABLE 1.

camaraderie. See FRENCH WORDS.

cambric. Pronounce kā-.

camellia. The spelling with -ll- is quite fixed, & the mispronunciation -mē-, now so prevalent as to be almost justified by usage, will no doubt give way to -mĕ- as the spelling becomes familiar.

camelopard does not contain the word *leopard*, & should be neither spelt nor pronounced as if it did. Pronounce kamĕ′lopard. But *giraffe* is now the usual word.

camembert. See FRENCH WORDS.

cameo. Pronounce kă′mĭŏ. Pl. *cameos*, see -O(E)s 4. For *c.*, *intaglio*, & *relief*, see INTAGLIO.

camomile, cha-. *Ca-* is the literary & popular form ; *cha-*, which represents the Latin & Greek spelling but has no chance of general acceptance, would be better abandoned in pharmacy also.

campanile. Pronounce kămpanē′lĭ. Pl. *-les*.

Canaan(ite). The prevalent pronunciation is undoubtedly kā′nyan-(ĭt), & this is a quite justifiable escape from the difficult & unEnglish kā′na-an ; kā′na-an passes into kā′nayan, & that into kā′nyan ; the pronunciation kā′nan, alone recognized by the OED, but chiefly in clerical use, is a worse evasion of the same difficulty.

canaille. See FRENCH WORDS.

canard should be anglicized, & have the d of the sing. & the ds of the pl. sounded.

cancel makes -*lled* &c.; see -LL-, -L-.

candelabrum. The pl. -*bra* is still preferred to -*brums* ; the false sing. -*bra* with pl. -*bras* should not be used.

candid. See -ER & -EST 4.

cando(u)r. Keep the u ; but see -OUR & -OR.

cane makes *cany* ; see -EY & -Y.

canine. The pronunciation kā′nīn (not kanī′n, nor kă′nīn), though little recognized in dictionaries, is both the commonest & the best. *Feline, bovine, asinine, leonine*, are enough to show that RECESSIVE ACCENT is natural ; &, if kă- is due to dread of FALSE QUANTITY, it is certainly not worth fighting for on that ground.

CANNIBALISM. That words should devour their own kind is a sad fact, but the guilt is perhaps less theirs than their employers' ; at any rate the thing happens :—*The true facts should be made known in regard to whom is actually due the credit of first proving the existence of petroleum in this country. To* has swallowed a *to./It is more or less—& certainly* more *than less—a standardized product. More* has swallowed a *more./ Although the latter were overwhelmingly superior in numbers, the former had the advantage of being under one control, &* that *of Napoleon himself. That* has swallowed a *that* ; the full form would be ' & that control the control of ', which gives ' & that that of ' ; but this cannibal may perhaps be thought to have consumed rather himself than another of his kind./The less said about the method the insurgents were being dealt with in *all too many cases the better. In* has swallowed an *in*,

since ' to deal with the insurgents this method ' is not English, though ' this way ' is./*The Council of the League shall direct the Members of the League as to which combatant is to be applied the Decree of Non-intercourse. To* has swallowed a *to*, as its way is when employed by AS-*to* writers.

cannon. 1. For plural see COLLECTIVES 2. 2. As the natural name for the thing, *c.* is passing out of use & giving place to *gun*, which is now the regular word except when context makes it ambiguous.

cañon, canyon. The second is recommended. Pron. kă′nyon.

canorous. See POETICISMS.

cant. For meaning & use, see JARGON.

cantatrice is usually pronounced as Italian (-ēchā), sometimes as French (-ēs) ; *singer* should be preferred when it is not misleading ; other English substitutes, as *songstress, female singer*, are seldom tolerable ; but see FEMININE DESIGNATIONS.

canto. Pl. -*os* ; see -O(E)S 6.

canton(ment). The noun *canton* is usually kăntŏ′n, sometimes kă′nton. The verb is in civil use kăntŏ′n, but in military use generally kantōō′n. The noun *cantonment*, which is military only, is generally kantōō′nment.

canvas(s). The material is best spelt -*as* ; so also the verb meaning to line &c. with c. ; for the plural of the noun, & for *canvas(s)ed* &c. in this sense, see -S-, -SS-. The verb meaning to discuss, ask votes, &c., has always -*ss* ; so also the noun meaning the process &c. of canvassing in this sense.

caoutchouc. Pronounce kow′chōōk.

capercailye, -lzie. The best spelling is the first, with pronunciation kăperkā′lyĭ.

capitalize, -ization, -ist. Accent the first, not the second syllables ; see RECESSIVE ACCENT.

capsizal. See -AL ; *capsize* is noun as well as verb.

caption, in the sense title or heading (' chiefly used in U.S.'—OED), is rare in British use, & might well be rarer.

carabineer, carbine. Though *carbine* has displaced *carabine*, the -a- remains in *The Carabineers* as the name of a regiment ; cf. WELCH.

carafe is, apart from its use in Scotland, chiefly a GENTEELISM for *water-bottle*.

caravanserai, -sera, -sary. The first spelling (pronounce -rī) is the best.

carbolic, carbonic. The first is the spelling for the disinfectant, the second for the poisonous gas.

carcass, -ase. The -ss form stands first in the OED.

careful. See -ER & -EST 4.

CARELESS REPETITION. See REPETITION OF WORDS & SOUNDS.

caret. Pronounce kă′rĕt.

cargo. Pl. *-oes* ; see -O(E)S 1.

caricature. See BURLESQUE.

caries is a Latin singular meaning decay ; pronounce kār′ĭēz.

carillon. Pronounce kă′rĭlyon, or as in FRENCH WORDS.

cark(ing). The verb is practically obsolete, & the adjective, surviving only as a meaningless epithet of *care*, should be let die too.

carnelian. See CORNELIAN.

carol makes *-ller*, *-lling*, &c. ; see -LL-, -L-.

carotid. Pronounce kărŏ′tĭd ; see FALSE QUANTITY.

carousal. See -AL ; *carouse* is itself a noun.

carpet. For *on the c.* (under discussion) see GALLICISMS ; a disadvantage peculiar to the phrase is that the sense required for *c.*, viz tablecloth, is obsolete.

carriageable. For such formations see -ABLE 4.

carry. For inflexions see VERBS IN -IE &c., 6.

Carry, -ie. See -EY, -IE, -Y.

carte, quart(e), in fencing. The first spelling, still the commonest except in technical books following

1351

French authorities, should be preferred if only as keeping the pronunciation right.

carte blanche, carte-de-visite. See FRENCH WORDS.

cartel, in the old senses, is pronounced kar′tl ; in the new sense of manufacturers' combination it represents German *Kartell*, & is often so spelt; it may therefore be expected to accent the last syllable for some time at least. The manufacturers' c. is a contract between independent establishments regulating the amount of output for each, & in certain cases also the prices (*Enc. Brit.*) ; cf. TRUST.

carven is a REVIVAL, not having been used between the 16th & 18th cc.

caryatid. Pronounce kărĭă′tĭd.

case. There is perhaps no single word so freely resorted to as a trouble-saver, & consequently responsible for so much flabby writing. The following extract from a legal treatise, in which the individual uses are comparatively justifiable, shows how the word now slips off the pen even of an educated writer :—*In the majority of cc. where reprisals have been the object, the blockade has been instituted by a single State, while in cc. of intervention several powers have taken part ; this is not, however, necessarily the c.*
To obviate the suspicion of an intolerant desire to banish it from the language, let it be admitted that *case* has plenty of legitimate uses, as in :—*If I were in your c. ; A bad c. of blackmailing ; I am only putting a c. ; Circumstances alter cc. ; In c. of fire, give the alarm ; Take brandy with you in c. of need ; The plaintiff has no c. ; What succeeds in one c. may fail in another ; Never overstate your c. ; Tariff-reform is in bad c. ; In no c. are you to leave your post ; It would be excusable for a starving man, but that was not your c. ; There are seven cc. of cholera.*

D

The bad uses are due sometimes to the lazy impulse to get the beginning of a sentence down & to let the rest work itself out as it may, & sometimes to a perverted taste for long-windedness, PERIPHRASIS, or ELEGANT VARIATION. It will be seen that *in the case of*, the worst offender, can often be simply struck out (brackets are used to show this), & often avoided by the most trifling change, such as the omission of another word (also bracketed). Many examples are given, in the hope that any writer who has inspected the mis-shapen brood may refuse to bring more of them into the world :—
Older readers will, at least (in the c. of) those who abhor all Jingoist tendencies, regret that the authors have . . ./He has used this underplot before in (the c. of) ' *The Fighting Chance* '.*/ That he could be careful in correcting the press he showed in (the c. of) the* ' *Epistle to John Driden* '.*/In the cc. above noted, when two or more handlings of the same subject by the author exist, the comparison of the two usually suffices to show how little vamping there is in (the c. of) the latter./(In the c. of) Pericles (, the play) is omitted./(In the c. of) cigars sold singly (they) were made smaller./ (In the c. of Purvey his) name was first mentioned in connexion with Bible translation in 1729* (Purvey's). *In the latter c. lines were laid down, but (in the c. of) the ponderous motor-'bus machine (it) runs . . ./(In) Mr Baring Gould('s c. he) was, like Miss Hesba Stretton, mistaken for a relative./In every c. except that of France the increase has been more rapid than in the c. of the United Kingdom* (every country except F. ; in the U.K.).*/Though this sort of thing proceeds from a genuine sentiment in (the c. of) Burns./In the c. of no poet is there less difference between the poetry of his youth & that of his later years* (No poet exhibits less).*/Of sympathy Mr Baring has a full measure, which, in his c., is more valuable an asset than familiarity with military text-books* (which is more valuable

to him than).*/All those tears which inundated Lord Hugh Cecil's head were dry in the c. of Mr Harold Cox* (dry for Mr).*/In the instances under notice, except in the c. of Braddell, there was no disposition to treat the bowling lightly./In no c. does the writer of any one of the four Gospels give his own name* (None of the four evangelists gives).*/(In) many (cc. the) answers lacked care./He has large interests in various joint-stock enterprises, &, in cc., possesses a seat on the board* (& sits on the board of some of these).*/In no one c. did the Liberals win a seat./Even in the purely Celtic areas only in two or three cc. do the first bishops bear Celtic names* (only two or three of the first bishops bear).*/That in all public examinations acting teachers in every c. be associated with the Universities* (teachers are always associated). *ced/In many (cc. of) largely frequented buildings, as much dust as this may be extracted every week./His historical pictures were (in many cc.) masterly* (Many of his).*/In this & other cc., such as coal, the world is living on its capital* (What, coal a case ? we cry it mercy; we took it for a fuel).

The ELEGANT VARIATIONist, as was implied above, is in clover with *case* ; it is provided, in *instance*, with one of those doubles that he loves to juggle with, & *be the case* enables him to show his superiority to the common mortal who would tamely repeat a verb ; we conclude with a few of his vagaries :—*Although in eight cc. the tenure of office of members had expired, in every instance the outgoing member had been re-elected./ Thunderstorms have in several cc. occurred, & in most instances they have occurred at night./In thirty-two cc. there are Liberal candidates in the field, & in eleven instances Socialists supply the third candidate./There are four cc. in which old screen-work is still to be found in Middlesex churches, & not one of these instances is so much as named./We gather that he remained what his previous record had led us to anticipate would be the c.*

(anticipate that he would remain)./ *This Conference will lay a foundation broader & safer than has hitherto been the c.* (been laid)./*It is not often worth while harking back to a single performance a fortnight old ; but this is not the c. with the Literary Theatre Club's production of Salome* (but it is worth while).

casein. Pronounce kā′sĭĭn.

CASES. 1. General. 2. The status of case. 3. Specimens of case mistakes. 4. Temptations.

1. General. The sense of case is not very lively among English-speakers because, very few words having retained distinguishable case-forms, it is much more often than not needless to make up one's mind what case one is using for the purpose of avoiding solecisms. Mistakes occur chiefly, though not only, with (a) the few words having case-forms, mostly personal pronouns, & (b) the relative pronouns. Accordingly, necessary warnings, with illustrations & discussion, are given in the articles I, ME, HE, SHE, WE, US, THEY, WHO 1, 2, THAT REL. PRON. 5, & WHAT 3 ; & to these may be added BE 6, LET, & THAN, which words are apt to deceive weak grammarians. To those warnings the reader is referred for practical purposes, & the present article can be devoted to a confession of faith in case as an enduring fact, a miscellaneous collection of quotations showing that it cannot quite be trusted to take care of itself, & a glance at the conditions that make mistakes most likely.

2. The status of case. Is case, then, a notion permanently valuable & inevitably present, or can we, & may we as well, rid our minds of it ? We know that grammarians are often accused, & indeed often guilty, of fogging the minds of English children with terms & notions that are essential to the understanding of Greek & Latin syntax, but have no bearing on English. We know that the work done by the classical case-endings has been in large part transferred in English to two substitutes : the difference between the nominative & the accusative (or subject & object) English indicates mainly by the order in which it arranges its words ; & the dative, ablative, locative, & such cases, it replaces by various prepositions. We know that English had once case-forms for nouns as well as pronouns, & that nevertheless it found them of so little use that it has let them all disappear. We know that, if the novelists are to be trusted, the uneducated find the case-endings even of pronouns superfluous ; ' Me & my mate likes ends ' said the ruffian who divided the rolypoly between himself & his ally & left their guest the hiatus ; he had no use for *I*, even when the place to be filled was that which belongs to the subject, & the instinct of case, if it exists untaught, might have been expected to act. We know, lastly, that not everyone who has learnt grammar enough to qualify as journalist or novelist is quite safe on his cases when the test is a little more severe than in *Me & my mate*.

Is the upshot that case is moribund, that our remaining case-forms are doomed to extinction, that there is behind them no essential notion or instinct of case itself, that no fuss whatever need be made about the matter, that the articles of which a list was given above are much ado about nothing, & that the right policy is to let the memory of case fade away as soon as we can agree whether *I* or *me*, *she* or *her*, *who* or *whom*, is to be the survivor of its pair ? Possibly it is ; SUBJUNCTIVES are nearly dead ; case too may be mortal ; but that fight to a finish between *I* & *me* & the other pairs will be a lengthy affair, & for as long as it lasts the invisible cases will have their visible champions to muster round. Meanwhile let me confess my faith that case visible & invisible is an essential of the English language, & that the right policy is not to welcome neglect of its rules, but to demand that in the novels & the newspapers, from which most of us imbibe our standards of language, they should be observed.

3. Specimens of case mistakes.

A. *Three years of dining are a preliminary for* he *who would defend his fellows./Should not a Christian community receive with open arms* he *who comes out into the world with clean hands & a clean heart?/They came to fight in order to pick up the challenge of* he *who had said ' Our future lies on the water './But it is the whimsical perplexity of Americans contemplating the appearance of London that provides* he *who guides with most amusement.*

B. *I saw a young girl gazing about, somewhat open-mouthed & confused,* whom *I guessed (correctly) to be* she *whom I had come to meet./It is not likely that other & inferior works were done at the same time by an impostor pretending to be* he*./*

C. *One comes round again to the problem of Kant—*he*, too, a cosmopolitan like Goethe./It is sad to look in vain for a perambulator in Nursemaids' Walk, & to discover only one solitary person, &* he *a sentry, on the steps of the Albert Memorial.*

D. *Eye hath not seen, nor ear heard, neither have entered into the heart of man,* the things *which God hath prepared for them that love him./Yet the coal is there in abundant quantities, & there is nothing the world wants so much or* can *be dispensed with such handsome profit to those who produce it.*

E. *By that time Mr Macdonald will be in possession of the decision of the Conservative Party, & it will then be for* he *& his advisers to take a decision.*

F. *Let Gilbert's future wife be* whom *she might.*

4. Temptations. The groups in the last section exemplify the conditions that put one off one's guard & suggest a wrong case. First in frequency & deadliness comes the personal pronoun in a place requiring the objective case followed by a relative that must be subjective, when there is a temptation to regard *he-who* or *they-who* as a single word that surely cannot need to have the question of case settled twice over for it ; & hazy notions of something one has heard of in classical grammar called relative attraction perhaps induce a comfortable feeling that one will be safe whether one writes *he* or *him*. That is a delusion ; neither relative attraction nor inverse attraction (the right term here) is a name to conjure with in modern English grammar, though the textbooks can muster a Shaksperian & Miltonic example or two ; in modern grammar they are only polite names for elementary blunders. All the A examples should have *him* instead of *he.*

The next temptation is to assume, perhaps from often hearing *It is me* corrected to *It is I*, that a subjective case cannot be wrong after the verb to *be*. But in the B examples it is not *to be* that decides the case of *he & she* ; it is *whom & impostor*, & *her & him* must be substituted.

It is hard not to sympathize with the victims of the next trap—appositions such as those of the C examples. ' Him, too, a cosmopolitan ', ' & him a sentry ', do sound as if one was airing one's knowledge of the concords. Well, perhaps it is better to air one's knowledge than one's ignorance of them ; but the escape from both is to be found in evading the pronoun (*another cosmopolitan,* or *also a cosmopolitan*) or sacrificing the apposition (*& he was a sentry*).

The invisibility of case in nouns tempts us to try sometimes whether they may not be made to serve two masters. In the verse from *Corinthians* that stands first in D, *things* has to serve *seen-&-heard* as object, & *have entered* as subject. 1 Cor. ii. 9 is the reference, & a glance at the R.V. shows, with its *which* in italics, that the Revisers did not regard its grammar as passable. The second D example has the peculiarity that the word whose case is in question, viz *that*, not only has no distinguishable cases, but is not on show at all ; but the sentence is ungrammatical unless it is inserted twice— *nothing* that *the world wants so much*, or that *can be dispensed.*

Another trap is the compound subject or object ; when instead of a single pronoun there are a pronoun & a noun to be handled, the case often goes wrong where if the pronoun had been alone there would have been no danger. Even the divider of the rolypoly, who can easily be believed to have said *Me & my mate likes*, would never have said *Me likes* ; still less could we have had in the E example *It will be for he to take.*

The F example is a little more complicated, but of a kind that not infrequently presents itself. The temptation is to look before & after, & doubt in which direction the governing factor is to be found. We first, perhaps, put aside the error of supposing that *be* requires a subjective, i.e. *who*, & remember that *let* puts *wife* in the objective, which raises a presumption that the same case will follow, i.e. *whom* ; but then it perhaps occurs to us that the part to be played by *who*(m) is that of complement to *may* (*be*), which ought to be in the same case as *she.* In this difficulty the last resource is to write the sentence in full, *Let Gilbert's wife be her who she may be* ; & the insertion of the omitted *her* having provided the first *be* with the objective complement that it requires, we find ourselves able to write *who* as the subjective complement required by the second *be* ; *who* is in fact the grammatical English ; cf. WHOEVER.

casino. Pl. *-os* ; see -O(E)S 6.

cast, vb. See FORMAL WORDS.

cast(e). *Caste* is sometimes wrongly written for *cast* in certain senses less obviously connected with the verb *cast*—mould, type, tendency, hue, &c. The confusion is the more

natural since *cast* was formerly the prevalent spelling for the hereditary class also ; but the words are now differentiated, & *cast* is the right form in such contexts as :—*reflections of a moral c., heroines of such a c., a man of the c. of Hooker & Butler, my mind has a melancholy c., his countenance was of the true Scottish c., a strongly individual c. of character, their teeth have a yellowish c.*

caster, -or. The word meaning pepperbox &c., & swivelled chair-wheel, should be *caster*, meaning literally thrower, & veerer, from the ordinary & an obsolete sense of *cast* ; but *-or*, probably due to confusion with other *castors*, is now usual.

cast iron used as a noun (*c. i. is more brittle*) should be written as two separate words ; *cast-iron* is the attributive or adjectival form (*a c.-i. bracket*) ; see HYPHENS.

CAST-IRON IDIOM. Between Idiom & ANALOGY a secular conflict is waged. Idiom is conservative, standing in the ancient ways, insisting that its property is sacrosanct, permitting no jot or tittle of alteration in the shape of its phrases. Analogy is progressive, bent on extending liberty, demanding better reasons than use & wont for respecting the established, maintaining that the matter is what matters & the form can go hang. Analogy perpetually wins, is for ever successful in recasting some piece of the cast iron ; Idiom as perpetually renews the fight, & turns to defend some other object of assault. ' We aim to prove it ', 'This is claimed to be the best', 'They are oblivious to hardship ', ' I doubt that it ever happened ', ' In order that the work can proceed ', ' He is regarded an honest man ', 'A hardly won victory ', ' With a view of establishing himself '—all these, says Idiom, are outrages on English ; correct them, please, to : We aim *at* prov*ing* it, They claim *that* this is the best, They are *insensible* to hardship, I doubt *whether* it ever happened, In order that the work *may* (*be able to*) proceed, He is regarded *as* an honest man, A *hard* won victory, With a view *to* establishing himself. But why? retorts Analogy; is not to *aim* the same as to *design*? is not to *claim* to *represent*? does not *oblivious* mean *insensible*? is not to *doubt* to *be unconvinced*? would not *so that* convey the same as *in order that*? is not *regarding considering*? is not -ly the adverbial ending, & is not *won* to be modified by an adverb? &, if *in view of* is English, why should *with a view of* be unEnglish? Away with such hair-splittings & pedantries! when one word is near enough to another to allow me to use either, I propose to neglect your small regulations for the appurtenances proper to each.

Not that Analogy, & those whom it influences, are offenders so deliberate & conscious as that account might seem to imply; they treat *regard* like *consider* not because they choose to flout the difference that Idiom observes, but because it comes natural to them to disregard distinctions that they have not noticed. In ANALOGY 2 it has been pointed out that it has very important functions to perform apart from waging its war upon Idiom; & therefore the admission that this book is wholly partisan in that war need not be interpreted as a condemnation of analogy always & everywhere; the Analogy that wars against Idiom is unsound or hasty or incomplete analogy.

The cast-iron nature of idiom may now be illustrated by a few phrases, shortened down to the utmost, in which some change that to the eye of reason seems of slight importance has converted English into something else :—He did it on his own *accord*; *Contented* himself by saying; Spain was materially *enhanced*; We *entertained* him to dinner; Tried to *father* it on to me; Follow events at close *hand*; *Lest* the last state becomes worse than the first; Is to a great *measure* true; Had every *motive* in doing it; A fact of which

he took every *opportunity*; Am not *privileged* with his friendship; Has been *promoted* to captain; The *resentment* I feel to this Bill; We must *rise* equal to the occasion; Fell *sheerly* down; I cannot *state* he was present; Stood me in splendid *stead*; Guests came by *the* hundreds; It was not long *until* he called. Discussion or actual quotations for these lapses will be found under the words italicized; & a few articles that have special bearing on the present subject are : AIM; CLAIM; DOUBT(FUL); FACT; FRIDAY; IN ORDER THAT; OBLIVIOUS; PLEASURE; PREFER 3; REGARD 2; RESORT; SUCH 1; THAT CONJ. 2; UNIDIOMATIC -LY; & VIEW.

castle. See PRONUNCIATION, Silent t. *C. in the air* is English; *c. in Spain* is a GALLICISM.

castrate. See -ATABLE.

casuistic(al). The OED has four quotations for each form; of the -ic four, three are later than the 18th c., of the -ical four only one; from which it would seem that -ic is the modern choice; see -IC(AL).

catachresis. See TECHNICAL TERMS.

catacomb. Pronounce -ōm.

catalectic. See TECHNICAL TERMS.

catamaran. OED puts first kăta-mară'n.

catarrh should not be used for *cold* without good reason; see WORKING & STYLISH WORDS.

catchpole, -oll. The OED puts -ole first.

catchup. See KETCHUP.

category should be used by no-one who is not prepared to state (1) that he does not mean *class*, & (2) that he knows the difference between the two; see WORKING & STYLISH WORDS, & POPULARIZED TECHNICALITIES.

cater, quatre, in dice &c. Spell *cater* & pronounce kā'ter; for the other names see CINQUE.

Catholic It is open to Roman-Catholics to use *C.* by itself in a sense that excludes all but themselves; but it is not open to a Protestant to use it instead of *Roman-Catholic* without implying that his own Church has no right to the name of *C.* Neither the desire of brevity (as in *the C. countries*) nor the instinct of courtesy (as in *I am not forgetting that you are a C.*) should induce anyone who is not Roman-C. to omit the *Roman-*.

catholic(al)ly. Both forms are rare, & consequently no differentiation has been established ; *a catholicly & a catholically minded person* may mean either one of wide sympathies &c. or one inclined to Catholicism.

catsup. See KETCHUP.

cattle. See COLLECTIVES 5.

ca(u)ldron. Spell with the u.

cause. *The main cause of the higher price of meat in France is due to the exclusion of foreign cattle.* The main cause is the exclusion ; the price is due to the exclusion ; out of two rights is made a wrong. See HAZINESS for this type of blunder ; with *reason* it is still commoner than with *cause.*

cause célèbre, causerie, causeuse. See FRENCH WORDS.

causerie. See TECHNICAL TERMS.

causeway, causey. Either form is correct, the first being not a false spelling of the second, but a shortening of *causey-way.* *Causeway,* however, has so far ousted *causey* (except in some local names) that those who use the latter are naturally taken for pedants protesting against an error that is, after all, not an error ; see DIDACTICISM.

caveat. Pronounce kā'vĭăt, & see FALSE QUANTITY.

caviar(e). Spelling & sound have varied greatly ; the pronunciation kăvĭar', & the corresponding spelling *caviar,* are recommended.

cavil makes *-ller, -lling,* &c. ; see -LL-, -L-.

cayman, cai-. Spell with *y.*

-C-, -CK-. When a word ending in c has a suffix beginning with a vowel added to it, the hard c is preserved before the native suffixes -ed, -er, -ing, & -y, by the addition of k (*mimicked, bivouacker, trafficking, panicky*), but not before the classical suffixes -ian, -ism, -ist, -ity, -ize (*musician, criticism, publicist, electricity, catholicize*).

cease is rapidly giving way to *stop,* as *cast* has given way to *throw* ; it is no longer the word that presents itself first ; we substitute it for *stop* when we want our language to be dignified ; it is now poetic, rhetorical, formal, or old-fashioned, though not sufficiently so to have such labels attached to it in dictionaries. No effort should be made to keep words of this kind at work ; they should be allowed to go into honourable retirement, from which the poets & the rhetoricians can summon them at need ; the man who says he is going to *c. work* is, unless the statement has a rhetorical importance, merely pompous. See FORMAL WORDS.

-ce, -cy. Among the hundreds of words corresponding to actual or possible adjectives or nouns in -ant or -ent, large numbers now present no choice of form : no-one hesitates between *avoidance, forbearance, admittance, magnificence, coincidence,* or *intelligence,* & a form in -cy ; nor between *buoyancy, constancy, vacancy, agency, decency,* or *cogency,* & a form in -ce. But about large numbers also it may easily happen that one has doubts which is the right form, or whether one is as good as the other, or whether both exist but in different senses : *persistence* or *persistency? frequency* or *frequence? emergency* or *emergence?* When there is doubt about a word not given in its place in this book, & again when one is given without further comment than *See* -CE, -CY, it is to be presumed that either -ce or -cy may be used ; but three generalities may be added. First, that short words favour -cy, & longer ones -ce ; it was not by design, but by a significant accident, that all the -cy words given above as having no -ce alternatives were metrical matches for *buoyancy*. Secondly, that many words tend to use the -ce form in the singular, but -*cies* rather than -*ces* in the plural, e.g. *irrelevance*, but *irrelevancies*. And thirdly, that euphony often decides, in a particular context, for one or the other ending. Of the first point a good illustration is provided by *frequency* & *innocence* ; formerly both endings were common for each, but now from the shorter adjective *frequent* -ce is almost obsolete, & from the longer *innocent* -cy is an archaism preserved by Bible texts. On the second it may be added that words used concretely in the plural meaning specimens of the quality &c. (*truculencies* = truculent phrases, *irrelevancies* = irrelevant points, *inadvertencies* = acts of inadvertence) partly account for the peculiarity, since when there is differentiation it is -cy, not -ce, that tends to the concrete, as in *emergency* = event that emerges compared with *emergence* = the emerging. And on the third point convincing examples will be found under *transparence*.

Articles in which differentiation between the two forms is recorded as existing or recommended are *consistence, dependence, effervescence, emergence, independence, indifference, permanence, persistence* ; *residency* & *excellency* are forms chiefly used in special senses while the -ce forms do the general work ; & under *complacency* the -cy form is recommended for differentiation not from *complacence*, but from *complaisance*.

cedarn. See -EN ADJECTIVES.

cee-spring, C-spring. The second form is perhaps better ; cf. D-trap, L-joint, Collar of SS, T-square, U-tube, V-joint, Y-cartilage.

Celestial = *Chinese*. Except in *the C. Empire*, which translates a native name for China & may be used seriously, the word is facetious only,

& ranks with POLYSYLLABIC HUMOUR.

'cello. Pl. -*os* ; see -O(E)S 6. Being now much commoner than *violoncello*, it might well do without its apostrophe. Pr. chĕ'lō, see ITALIAN.

Celt(ic), K-. The spelling *C*-, & the pronunciation s-, are the established ones, & no useful purpose seems to be served by the substitution of k-.

celtice, -cè. See LATINE.
cenobite &c. See COENOBITE.
centenary, centennial, nn. meaning hundredth anniversary. *Centenary*, the usual British form, has the disadvantage that the notion of years is not, except by modern development, contained in it ; this, however, is true also of *century*, & need not count for much. *Centennial*, chiefly used (as a noun) in America, has the disadvantage that it gives a less convenient pattern for forming the names of higher anniversaries on. As these are sometimes wanted, it is worth while to maintain *centenary*.
The shots made at these higher names often resulting in monstrosities, a list of not intolerable forms is here offered. *Bicentenary*, which might have been *ducenary*, & *tercentenary* (*trecenary*), must be taken as established ; but *quatercentenary* & *quincentenary* need not. The pronunciations sĕntē'narĭ (not sĕ'ntĭ-) & mĭlē'narĭ (desirable in itself for distinction from *millinery*) would suit the others best. Centē'nary, bicentē'nary, tercentē'nary, quadringē'nary, quingē'nary, sescē'nary, septingē'nary, octingē'nary, nongē'nary, millē'nary.

centi-, hecto- In the metric system *centi-* denotes division, & *hecto-* multiplication, by a hundred ; cf. DECA-, DECI-, & KILO-, MILLI-.

centime. See FRENCH WORDS.
cento. Pl. -*os*, see -O(E)S 6. The pronunciation is sĕ- ; the word is Latin, but is often mispronounced chĕ- as if Italian ; the Italian is *centone*, & the French *centon*.

centre, center. See -RE & -ER ; &, for *cent(e)ring*, SPELLING POINTS 4.

century. Each c. as ordinally named (*the 5th, 16th, c.*) contains only one year (500, 1600) beginning with the number that names it, & ninety-nine (401–499, 1501–1599) beginning with a number lower by one. Accordingly 763, 1111, 1300, 1912, belong to the 8th, 12th, 13th, & 20th, cc. For the curiously different Italian reckoning, see TRECENTO.

-cephalic, -cephalous. Compounds (*brachy-, dolicho-, hydro-,* &c.) accent the -ceph- of *-cephalous*, but the -al- of *-cephalic*. As there is no difference of meaning, however, & -ic is the commoner, *-cephalous* should be abandoned as a NEEDLESS VARIANT.

cerement is disyllabic (sērm-).

ceremonial, ceremonious, aa. *Ceremonial* means connected with or constituting or consisting of or fit for a ceremony (i.e. a piece of ritual or formality) or ceremonies (*the -al law ; a -al occasion ; for -al reasons ; -al costume*). *Ceremonious* means full of or resulting from ceremony i.e. attention to forms (*why be so -ous ? ; -ous people ; -ous politeness*). In these examples the termination not used could hardly be substituted, even with change of meaning. But with some words -al & -ous are both possible, though not indifferent : *a -ous court* is a sovereign's court in which ceremony is much observed ; *a -al court* would be a judicial court set up to regulate ceremonies ; A visitor may make *a -ous entry* into a room, but an army *a -al entry* into a town that has capitulated.

ceriph. See SERIF.

certes. Pronounce ser'tĕz. See ARCHAISM.

certify. For inflexions see VERBS IN -IE &c., 6.

certitude is now restricted to the single sense of absolute conviction or feeling quite sure ; *certainty* can, but often does not, mean this also, & the use of c. may therefore obviate ambiguity.

cerulean. See Æ, Œ.

cervical is pronounced servī'kl by purists, but ser'vĭkl is commoner ; see on *doctrinal* in FALSE QUANTITY ; the Latin for neck is *cerviæ, -ĭcis*.

Cesarevitch or **-witch, Cesarevna,** are the right forms for the Czar's eldest son & that son's wife. Pronounce sĭză'rĭwĭch. *Czarevitch* is an obsolete title superseded by *Grand Duke*.

cess. For synonymy see TAX.

ceterach. Pronounce sĕ'terăk.

ceteris paribus. Pronounce sē'terĭs pă'rĭbus.

chagrin. Pronounce shagrē'n. The pronunciation shagrĭ'n, used to avoid improbable confusion with *shagreen*, would commit us to *chagrinned* instead of *chagrined* ; see -N-, -NN-.

chagrinedly. Four syllables ; see -EDLY.

chairwoman. See FEMININE DESIGNATIONS.

chaldron. Pronounce chawl-.

chalet. See FRENCH WORDS.

chalybeate. Pronounce kalī'bĭat.

cham. Pronounce kăm.

chamade. See FRENCH WORDS.

chamois, in or used for c.-leather, is best pronounced shă'mĭ.

chamomile. See CAMOMILE.

champaign. The OED pronounces chă'mpān, & rejects shămpā'n & shă'mpān.

chance, n., makes *chancy* ; see -EY & -Y.

chance, vb, as a synonym for *happen* (*it chanced that* . . . ; *I chanced to meet him*) stands in the same relation to it as CEASE to *stop*.

chancellery, -ory, -erie. The first form (accented on the first syllable) is that preferred by the OED.

Change, in *on Change*, is not an abbreviation of *Exchange*, & should have no apostrophe.

chantage. See FRENCH WORDS ; *blackmail* is generally preferable.

Chanticleer. See SOBRIQUETS.

chanty, sh-, sailors' hauling-song. Spell c-, but pronounce shă- ; the anomaly is accounted for by the supposed derivation from French *chantez* sing ye.

chap, chop, jaw or cheek. In *lick* one's *cc.*, *fat-cc.*, *c.-fallen*, both spellings are common ; in *Bath c.*, *chap* only is used, &, in *the cc. of the Channel*, *chops* only.

chaperon. The addition of a final e is wrong. Pronounce shă′peron.

char-à-banc is a word in popular use, & the popular pronunciation (shă′rabăng) should be accepted ; if the spelling *sharabang*, or at the least *charabanc*, could be introduced too, so much the better. See FRENCH WORDS ; the French spelling in the singular is *char-à-bancs*.

character is a valuable & important word with several well-marked senses. The worst thing that can happen to such a word is that it should be set to do inferior & common work, which, while it could be more suitably done by meaner words, has to be done so often that the nobler word is cheapened by familiarity. *Character*, like *case* & other good words, now occurs a hundred times as a mere element in PERIPHRASIS for once that it bears any of its independent senses. The average writer can perhaps not be expected to abstain from the word for the word's sake ; but, if he realizes that at the same moment that he degrades the word he is making his sentence feeble and turgid, he will abstain from it for his own sake. A few slightly classified examples of the abuse are therefore added.

(a) *C.* is used with adjectives as a substitute for an abstract-noun termination, *-ness*, *-ty*, &c. :—*The very full c. of the stage-directions indicates* . . . (great fullness)./*On account of its light C., Purity & Age Usher's whisky is a whisky that will agree with you* (lightness. But this is the kind of literature in which such idioms are most excusable)./ *Unmoved by any consideration of the unique & ancient c. of the fabric* (uniqueness & antiquity).

(b) A simple adjective *x* is watered into *of a* x *character* ; the right water for such solutions, which are bad in themselves when not necessary, is *kind* ; but the simple adjective is usually possible :—*Employment of a patriotic c.* (patriotic employment)./*There is no unemployment of a chronic c. in Germany.*/ *The attention which they receive is of a greatly improved c.*/*His influence must have been of a very strong c. to persuade her.*/*The number of misprints is inconsiderable ; we have noticed only one of a disconcerting c.* (kind ; *or* one that need be disconcerting)./*Payments of the c. in question* (of this kind ; *or* such payments).

character, characteristic. For synonymy see SIGN.

char(e). The form *chare* (part. *charing*, pron. -ā̆r-) is said by the OED to be the usual one. This is doubtful even now, & the invariable & commoner *charwoman* is at any rate sure to establish *char, charring*, before long.

chargé d'affaires. See FRENCH WORDS.

charivari. Pronounce shar′ĭvar′ĭ.

charlatan &c. Pronounce sh-.

Charles's wain. For -s's see POSSESSIVE PUZZLES 1.

charm. For the noun in literary criticism see LITERARY CRITICS' WORDS.

chartreuse. See FRENCH WORDS.

chasse, chassé, chassis. See FRENCH WORDS.

chasten. See PRONUNCIATION, Silent t.

chastise is never spelt with z ; see -ISE)(-IZE.

château, chauffeur, chaussure. See FRENCH WORDS ; &, for *châteaux* or *chateaus*, -x.

cheap(ly). See UNIDIOMATIC -LY.

check (draft on bank). See CHEQUE.

checker. See CHEQUER.

(check)mate. *Mate* is the usual form in chess, & *checkmate* in figurative use.

cheerful, cheery. The latter has reference chiefly to externals—

voice, appearance, manner, &c. Resignation may be cheerful without being cheery ; & a person may have a cheerful, but hardly a cheery, spirit without his neighbours' discovering it. The cheerful feels & perhaps shows contentment, the cheery shows & probably feels it. For *cheerful* see -ER & -EST, 4.

chef, chef-d'œuvre. See FRENCH WORDS.

chemist &c., **chy-.** *Che-* is now established, though *chymist* is still sometimes seen over drug-shop windows.

cheque, though merely a variant of *check*, is in British usage clearly & usefully differentiated from it with the sense bank-draft, *check* being chiefly American in this sense.

chequer, checker. The first spelling is very much commoner for both the noun & the verb.

cherub, cherubic. *Cherub* has pl. *cherubim* chiefly when *the Cherubim* are spoken of as a celestial order ; *cherubims* is wrong ; in figurative use *cherubs* is usual. *Cherubic* (see -B-, -BB-) is pronounced -ōōb-.

ches(t)nut. Spell with & pronounce without the *t*.

chevalier d'industrie. See FRENCH WORDS.

chevaux de frise. See FRENCH WORDS. *Cheval de frise* is now rare ; *chevaux de frise* is treated either as sing. or as pl. (*a wall with a c.d.f.*, or *a wall with c.d.f.*).

chevelure. See FRENCH WORDS.

chevy. See CHIVY.

chiaroscuro. Pronounce kyar'-oskoor'ō.

chiasmus. See TECHNICAL TERMS.

chibouk, -ouque. Pronounce ch- ; spell -*k*.

chic. See FRENCH WORDS.

chicane. Pronounce sh-.

chick(en). *Chicken* is the original & still the ordinary form, *chick* serving as a diminutive & being used chiefly of an unhatched or unfledged bird, the young of small birds, or (endearingly, in pl.) children. For pl. of *chicken* see COLLECTIVES 4.

chide stands to *scold* as CEASE to *stop*. Past *chid*, p.p. *chid*(*den*).

chiefest, formerly common, is now felt to be an unnatural form, & used only as an ornament.

chiffon. See FRENCH WORDS.

chilblain. So spelt ; see -LL-, -L-, 4.

childish, childlike. The distinction drawn is so familiar that *childish* is in some danger of being restricted to the depreciatory use that is only one of its functions, while *childlike* is applied outside its sphere ; the face, for instance, that we like a child to have should be called not a childlike, but a childish face ; the rule that *childish* has a bad sense is too sweeping, & misleads. *Childish* used of adults or their qualities, & *childlike* (which should always be so used), have the opposite implications of blame & approval ; *childish* means 'that ought to have outgrown something or to have been outgrown', & *childlike* 'that has fortunately not outgrown something or been outgrown' ; *childish simplicity* in an adult is a fault ; *childlike simplicity* is a merit ; but *childish simplicity* may mean also simplicity in (& not as of) a child, & convey no blame ; *childish enthusiasm* may be either a child's enthusiasm or a man's silly enthusiasm ; *childlike enthusiasm* is only that of a man who has not let his heart grow hard.

childly. See REVIVALS.

chilli is the right spelling for the capsicum pod (unconnected with *Chili*) ; pl. *chillies*.

chill(y). The form *chill* (as adj.) is only a LITERARY WORD, *chilly* being that in general use.

chimera, -aera, -æra. See Æ, Œ. Pronounce kǐmēr'a.

Chinaman &c. The normal uses are :—*A Chinaman* (rarely *Chinese*) ; *three Chinamen* (sometimes *Chinese*) ; *50,000 Chinese* (sometimes *Chinamen*) ; *the Chinese* (rarely *Chinamen*). *Chinee* for *Chinaman* is a BACK-FORMATION from *Chinese* pl., &, being still felt to be irregular, is rare except as conscious slang, but common in such use.

chiropodist is a BARBARISM & a GENTEELISM.

chirrup(p)ing &c. See -P-, -PP-.

chisel makes *-lled* &c. ; see -LL-, -L-.

chivalry &c. The pronunciation sh-, instead of ch-, though based on a mistake, is now established, & the OED places it first. Of the adjectives *chivalrous* & *chivalric* the second should be either let die as a NEEDLESS VARIANT or restricted to the merely grammatical function of representing the phrase *of chivalry*, as in *the chivalric ages*.

c(h)ive. Spell with the h.

chivy, che-. The -i- certainly gives the prevailing sound, &, being now written also more often than it was, will doubtless become the accepted spelling before long.

chlorine. For pronunciation see IODINE.

chloroform. The OED pronounces klōr'o-, not klŏ'ro-. The latter, however, which is also common, is (see FALSE QUANTITY) not illegitimate.

chock-full is the spelling, not *choke-full.*

choir, quire. Though the first spelling, which goes back little further than the 18th c., neither bears its pronunciation on its face nor represents the French or the Latin forms well, & is therefore inferior, attempts to restore *quire* are not likely to succeed, & are best avoided.

choler(ic). *Choler*, except when used historically with reference to the four humours, is now a mere ARCHAISM ; *choleric*, however, has survived it, & is preferable in some contexts to *irascible, quick-tempered,* &c.; pron. kŏ'lerĭk.

choliambic. See TECHNICAL TERMS.

chop, cutlet. A chop is cut from the loin & includes a rib ; a cutlet is cut from the neck, or may be a small piece of meat from any part & include no bone.

chorale. Pronounce korah'l. As to spelling, the -e is strictly incorrect, but both usual & convenient, obviating confusion with the adj. *choral* ; cf. LOCALE & MORALE, & see À L'OUTRANCE.

c(h)ord. There are two words *chord*, one of which, that used in Harmony, has no connexion with *cord* ; the other (*touch the right chord* ; *the chord of an arc* ; *the vocal chords* ; *the spinal chord*) is the same as *cord*, but has had its spelling corrected after the Greek original. It is well to remember that in the four phrases mentioned *chord* means simply string ; but the spelling *cord*, which would have been legitimate & avoided confusion in any of them, is ruled out by custom except in the last & possibly the last but one.

chose jugée. See FRENCH WORDS.

chouse, having been current for 300 years (Ben Jonson 1610), need not be avoided as slang by those who have occasion to use it.

christen. See PRONUNCIATION, Silent t.

Christmas. Pronounce krĭ'smas ; see PRONUNCIATION, Silent t.

chromo. See CURTAILED WORDS. Pl. *-os*, see -O(E)S 5.

chronic in the illiterate use for bad, intense, severe, (*the weather has been c.* ; *that was a c. fight last night*), is a SLIPSHOD EXTENSION. See POPULARIZED TECHNICALITIES.

chronique scandaleuse. See FRENCH WORDS.

chrysalis has pl. *chrysalises, chrysalids*, or *chrysalides* (krĭsǎ'lĭdēz) ; the first should be made the only form.

chute. See SHOOT.

chutney, -nee. Spell *-ney.*

chymist &c. See CHEMIST.

-ciation. Nouns in *-ation* from verbs in *-ciate* have, if they follow their verbs, the very unpleasant combination of two neighbouring syllables with the -sh- sound (ĭmǎshĭā'shn from *emaciate*). The alternative pronunciation -siāshn, sometimes recognized by the OED (e.g. in *association*), avoids the bad sound, & is legitimate on the analogy of *denunciation, pronunciation, annunciation*, of which all might have had, & the last has in *annunciate*, a verb in *-ciate* as well as that in *-ounce*. Words in *-tiation* (as *initiation*) can perhaps hardly be treated in the same way, except those that, like *negotiation*, have alternative forms with *-c-* for *-t-*; nĭgōsĭā'shn seems possible, but not propĭsĭā'shn.

cicada, cicala, cigala. The first is the original Latin word taken into English (pronounce -kā-); the second is Italian (-kah-); the third is the French *cigale* with termination assimilated in English to the others (-gah-). The first is recommended.

cicatrice, cicatrix. The first, pronounced sĭ'katrĭs & in pl. sĭ'katrĭsĭz, is the English word. The second, pronounced sĭkā'trĭks & in pl. sĭkatrĭ'sēz, is the Latin in surgical & other scientific use.

cicerone. Pronounce chĭcherō'nĭ; pl. *ciceroni*, pron. -nē.

ci-devant. See FRENCH WORDS.

Cincinnatus. So spelt.

cinema, cinematograph, kin-. The cin- forms are obviously more handy for words destined to constant popular use, & should be accepted heartily. There is indeed very little in any of the objections made to them. The points are: (1) c or k?; (2) the syllable accented; & (3) the curtailed form of *cinema*. 1. English c for Greek k, far from being wrong, is normal; cf. *catholic, cenotaph, Circe, colon, cubic, cycle*. It may be regrettable that, since *kinetic* & *kinematic* are abnormally spelt, the connexion of *cinematograph* with them is obscured; but that is their fault, not its. 2. The vowel sounds & the syllable accents will be found justified in the article FALSE QUANTITY. The chief objection—to misplacing in sĭ'nĭma the stress of the Greek kĭnē'ma—falls to the ground when it is remembered that *cinema* is not the Greek word *kinema* at all,

but a curtailed form of *cinematograph*, whose second syllable is bound to be -nĭ- in popular speech. 3. Curtailing is an established habit, no worse in *cinema* than in the schoolboy's *rep*, our ancestors' *mob*, or our own *dynamo* & *bike* & *phone*; see CURTAILED WORDS.

Cingalese. See SINHALESE.

cinq(ue). The five on dice &c. is pronounced sĭngk, & best spelt *cinque*. *Ace, deuce, trey* (-ā), *cater* (kā-), & *sice* (sīs), are the others of the series.

cinquecento. Pronounce chĭngkwĭchĕ'ntō; for meaning see TRECENTO.

cinq(ue)foil. Pronounce sĭ'ngkfoil. The OED puts the longer form first.

cipher. So spelt; see Y & I.

Circe. Pronounce ser'sĭ.

circuit(ous). Pronounce ser"kĭt, but serkū'ĭtus (not ser'kĭtus).

circulate makes *-lable*; see -ABLE 1.

circumbendibus. See FACETIOUS FORMATIONS.

circumcise, not *-ize*; see -ISE)(-IZE.

circumlocutional, -nary, -utory. Though an adjective is often wanted for *circumlocution*, none of these three has won any favour; it is better to make shift with *periphrastic*.

circumstance. The objection to *under the cc.*, & insistence that *in the cc.* is the only right form, because what is round us is not over us, is puerile. To point out that *round* applies as much to vertical as to horizontal relations, & that a threatening sky is a c. no less than a threatening bulldog (*Under the circumstances I decided not to venture*), might lay one open to the suspicion of answering fools according to their folly. A more polite reply is that 'the cc.' means the state of affairs, & may naturally be conceived as exercising the pressure under which one acts. *U. t. cc.* is neither illogical nor of recent invention (1665 in OED), & is far more often heard than *i. t. cc.* The OED, far from hinting that either form is incorrect, assigns them different functions :—' Mere situation is expressed by " *in* the circumstances ", action affected is performed " *under* the circumstances " '.

cirque. Pronounce serk.
cirrus has pl. *cirri* ; see -US.
Cissy, -ie. See -EY, -IE, -Y.
cit(e)able. Spell *-ta-* ; see MUTE E.
cither(n), cittern, gittern, zither(n). When the forms are distinguished, *cither* is the general word including the ancient cithara & its more modern representatives, *zither(n)* is appropriated to the Tyrolese instrument, & *cithern, cittern, gittern*, all mean that common in the 16th & 17th cc. ; *cittern & gittern* might well be dropped as NEEDLESS VARIANTS.

cityless. So spelt ; cf. *pitiless*.
civil. See -ER & -EST, 4.
clad. See CLOTHE.
claim. 1. A vulgarism that has made its way, probably through the advertisement column, into journalism, & is now of daily currency, is the use of *claim* in the senses of *assert, maintain*, or *represent*, with the infinitive construction admissible after them, but not after it (see ANALOGY). The only legitimate infinitive after *c.* occurs when *c.* is in the active & also has the same subject as the infinitive (*he claims to have proved his case, to be the heir, to be rewarded*). Examples of the false idiom are :—*This new product, which Mr Sandow claims to be absolutely pure* (asserts)./*An automatic self-starter, which is claimed to be very reliable* (represented)./*The gun is claimed to be the most serviceable weapon of its kind* (asserted)./ *Failure to live up to what we c. to be our most serious convictions* (represent)./*Usage is not, as it is often claimed to be, the absolute law of language* (asserted)./*A play by Tolstoy, which is claimed to take the first place among . . .* (represented)./ *A problem which is claimed to be among the most pressing* (maintained).
2. The use of *claim* n. or vb follow-

ed by (or implying) a *that*-clause, when *c.* means not *demand* but *assert(ion)*, is also, though less grossly, contrary to British idiom ; *I c.* (demand) *that it should be postponed* is English, but hardly *I c.* (assert) *that it is false* :—*The c. is made that there are a certain class of men out of work who . . ./The Prussian franchise, the reform of which, it is claimed by Liberals, the Reichstag will have to take in hand.*

clamant in the senses clamorous, shouting, insistent, (*a c. crowd, c. appetites*) is a POETICISM ; in the sense flagrant or crying (*a c. injustice, scandal*) it is due to NOVELTY-HUNTING.

clamour, clamorous. See -OUR- & -OR-.
clandestine. Pronounce klăndĕ'stĭn.
clangour, clangorous. See -OUR- & -OR-.
claque. See FRENCH WORDS.
Clarenc(i)eux. The OED puts the spelling *-ceux* first, & pronounces klă'rensū.
clarify, clarity. The OED pronounces klărĭ- ; klā̆rĭ- is also legitimate, but not (see FALSE QUANTITY) obligatory. For inflexions of *-fy*, see VERBS IN -IE &c., 6.
clari(o)net. The two forms denote the same instrument, but the *-onet* form is in more general use (& therefore preferable in literature), while musicians & musical connoisseurs affect the other.
classic(al). The adjectives are distinguished rather by suitability to different contexts than by difference of meaning. *Classical* is the usual word, & it would perhaps never be noticeably the wrong one, even where *classic* is more idiomatic (e. g., we can say, if we choose, *This is classical ground*) ; on the other hand, there are many combinations in which *classic* would sound ridiculous ; *classic education, classic allusions*, are impossible. *Classic*, however, is often preferred (1) where the language is of an ornate kind

(compare *steeped in classic lore* with *learned in classical mythology*) ; (2) where the speaker's emotion of admiration or respect is to be conveyed (compare *Do you prefer the classical or the romantic style?* with *A style classic in its perfect self-restraint*; *I did not ask for classical regularity of features* with *The classic regularity of his features*; *St Andrews, the classic home of golf* with R. v. *Hobbes was cited as the classical case*).

classify. For inflexions see VERBS IN -IE &c., 6.

clause. It conduces both to clearness & to brevity if the word in its grammatical sense is applied only to what is sometimes called a *subordinate c.*, & never either to a complete sentence or to the framework of the sentence, which is often called the *main* or *principal c.*, but may equally well be called *main sentence*. The definition of a c., then, should be ' subordinate words including a subject & predicate, but syntactically equivalent to a noun or adjective or adverb ' ; in this book the word is always to be understood thus.

clayey. See -EY & -Y.

clear(ly). See UNIDIOMATIC -LY.

cleave, split, has past tense *clove* or *cleft* or *cleaved*, p.p. *cloven* or *cleft* or *cleaved*.

cleave, stick, has past tense *cleaved* or (arch.) *clave*, p.p. *cleaved*.

clematis. Pronounce klĕ'matĭs ; see FALSE QUANTITY.

clench, -inch. The spellings are so far differentiated as to be generally applied thus : we *clench* a nail, a rivet, our hands, jaws, & teeth, an object held, a rope ; we *clinch* an argument & a bargain, & the fact or statement that settles an argument is a *clincher*.

clerestory. Pronounce klēr'storĭ.

clerk. The pronunciation -erk, now sometimes heard instead of the long-established -ark, is due to excessive respect for spelling ; cf. OFTEN.

clever is much misused, especially

in feminine conversation, where it is constantly heard in the sense of learned, well read, bookish, or studious ; a woman whose cleverness is apparent in all she does will tell you that she wishes she was c., that she cannot read c. books (meaning those of the graver kind), & that Mr Jones must be a very c. man, for he has written a dictionary. But in fact ignorance & knowledge have no relation to cleverness, which implies ingenuity, adroitness, readiness, mental or manual quickness, wit, & other qualities incompatible with dullness, but not with ignorance or dislike of books.

clew, clue. The words are the same, but the more recent *clue* is now established in the usual sense of idea or fact that may lead to a discovery, while *clew* is retained in the nautical sense, & in the old-fashioned sense *skein* or *ball of wool* from which the usual sense of *clue* has been developed.

cliché. See FRENCH WORDS, &, for the meaning, TECHNICAL TERMS. *Clothing among them was* a minus quantity./*Engine troubles were* the order of the day. The roman-type phrases are cc.

clientele should be written without italics or accent, & pronounced klĭentē'l ; see FRENCH WORDS.

climacteric. The old pronunciation was klĭmăktĕ'rĭk, which stands first in the OED ; but klĭmă'kterĭk (see RECESSIVE ACCENT) is probably now commoner & is likely to prevail.

climactic is falsely formed from *climax*, & it may fairly be demanded of the literary critics who alone have occasion for the adjective that they should mend or end it.

climax. See TECHNICAL TERMS.

clime is distinguished from *climate* (1) in being more suited for poetic & rhetorical use ; it occurs, however in ordinary prose also, with the limitation that (2) it means always region (often with reference to its characteristic weather), &

never, like climate, the weather conditions themselves ; we say *strangers from every c.*, but never *the country has a delightful c.*

cling has past *clung*, not *clang*.

cliqu(e)y. Spell *-quy* ; see -EY & -Y.

close *C. the door, the window, your mouth*, used in the literal sense & in everyday speech instead of *shut*, expose the speaker to grave suspicion of GENTEELISM, though *The door is closed for ever upon that possibility*, & similar figurative uses, are innocent. See also FORMAL WORDS.

close(ly). See UNIDIOMATIC -LY.

closure, gag, guillotine, kangaroo. The first is the name given to a provision by which debate in the House of Commons can be cut short in spite of the wish of a minority to continue it ; the closure is brought into operation by a motion That the Question be now put.

Gag is the word used chiefly by the closured party to describe the ordinary closure or its developments, the guillotine & the kangaroo.

The *guillotine*, or closure by compartments, is thus defined in the *Ency. Brit.* :—' The guillotine means that the House decides how much time shall be devoted to certain stages of a measure, definite dates being laid down at which the closure shall be enforced & division taken '.

The *kangaroo*, or kangaroo closure, is a further development. The guillotine having the disadvantage that the limited time may be wasted on minor matters & none be left for important ones, the Chairman of Committees is empowered to select the amendments that shall be debated, the unselected ones being voted on without debate.

cloth may be pronounced either -awth or -ŏth ; the plural of the first is -awdhz, but of the second -ŏths. See also -TH & -DH.

clothe has *clad* beside *clothed* both as past & p.p. While *clothed*, however, is suitable to all contexts (except where *dressed* is preferable as less formal), *clad* is (1) always

slightly, & often intolerably, archaic in effect, & (2) never used absolutely, but always with some specification of the kind of clothing. Accordingly, *clad* cannot be substituted in *You were fed & clothed at my expense, He clothed himself hurriedly, When he was clothed he admitted us.* But *clothed* can be substituted in any of the following phrases, which are selected as favourable for the use of clad :—*Lightly, well, insufficiently, clad* ; *He clad himself in shining armour* ; *Clad with righteousness* ; *Hills clad with olives* ; *Clad in blue.*

clothes. The usual pronunciation is klōz, though this is often deliberately abstained from in the mistaken belief (confirmed by the OED) that it is ' vulgar or careless '. See PRONUNCIATION.

cloud-burst. See WIND, n.

clubbable. See -ABLE 4.

clue. See CLEW.

co-. There are three ways of writing *cooperate* (coop-, co-op-, coöp-), & two of writing *copartner* (cop-, co-p-). The diaeresis should at once be rejected as possible only in some words (those in which *co-* is followed by a vowel), whereas the hyphen is possible in all. Next it should be recognized that hyphens in the middle of words are no ornament, & admittance should be refused to all that cannot prove their usefulness. In the alphabetical list given below of the commoner words beginning with *co-* together or *co-*complementary, the spelling printed is to be taken as recommended, & the number affixed to each word refers the reader to the following classification :—

1. In some words the hyphen is never used.

2. Many are either so common or so analysable at a glance that the hyphen, though sometimes used, is entirely superfluous.

3. Some are used & seen only by the learned, who may be expected to know them at a glance without hyphens.

4. Some always have the hyphen apparently by way of a (*sic*), or announcement that the spelling is intentional.

5. Some, if no hyphen is used, tend to fall at the first glance into wrong syllables & so perplex.

6. When a writer believes himself to be making a new word, he naturally uses the hyphen—*my co-secretary, their co-authorship*, &c.

ESTABLISHED WORDS IN CO-.

coacervation 3. coadjutor 1. coadunate 3. coagulate 1. coalesce 1. coalition 1. coaxial 3. co-declination 5. coeducation 2. coefficient 2. coequal 2. coerce 1. coessential 2. co-etaneous 5. coeternal 2. coeval 2. coexecutor 2. coexist 2. coextensive 2. cognate 1. cohabit 1. coheir 2. cohere 1. coincide 1. coinstantaneous 2. coition 1. co-latitude 5. cooperate 2. coopt 2. coordinate 2. coparcenary 2. copartner 2. co-relation 4. co-religionist 4. co-respondent 4. cosecant 3. coseismal 3. cosignatory 2. cosine 2. cotangent 2. cotemporary 2. co-tenant 5. co-tidal 5.

coal. 1. *Haul, & call, over the cc.* are both in use, though the former is perhaps commoner. 2. *Coal-vase* for -*scuttle* is chiefly a shop term, but appears sometimes as a GENTEELISM. 3. *Coal-mouse, coal-tit(mouse)*, are better spelling than *cole-*, since the latter obscures the connexion with *c*.

coastal is a BARBARISM, the -*oa*-showing at once that -*al* has been added to an English & not a Latin word. If an adjective had been really needed, it should have been *costal*; but the attributive function can be performed by *coast* (*the coast trade, towns*, &c.; *a coast voyage*), & the predicative by *coastwise* or *on, along*, &c., *the coast. Coastal* should be abandoned.

coat-card, court-. *Coat-* is the original form, but it has been ousted by the corruption *court-*, & is marked as obsolete in the OED.

cobalt. Pronounce kō′bawlt.

cobra de capello. Spell *de*, & pronounce dĭ.

cocaine. The pronunciation kokā′n, stigmatized by the OED (in 1893) as vulgar, is now so general that attempts to maintain kō′kaĭn are useless.

coccyx. Pronounce kŏ′ksĭks.

Cockaigne is properly the name of a luxurious Utopia ; the use of it for London as the home of Cockneys is a mistake or a pun.

cockle. *The cc. of the heart* is of some age (quoted from 1671) but of disputed origin ; such phrases are best not experimented with, but kept to their customary form & context (*rejoice, warm, the cc. of the heart*).

cockneyfied. So spelt ; see -FIED.

cock's-comb, cockscomb, coxcomb. The first for the comb of a cock, the second for the fool's cap & the plants, & the third for the fop.

cocky, cocksy, coxy. The first is the form in general colloquial use, the last a schoolboy variant established in particular schools, & the second the fuller but less used spelling for the third.

coco(a), coker. *Cacao & coco*, independent words, have corrupted each other till the resulting *cocoa* is used always for the drink & often for the coco(a)-nut palm ; *coker(nut* &c.) is a shop spelling devised to obviate the confusion. *Coco-nut, coco fibre*, &c., are still used, though the -*a* more often appears ; they should be kept in existence if possible, & *cocoa* be restricted to the drink & the powder from which it is made ; the uncrushed seeds & the plant are still usually spelt *cacao*.

codify. Pronounce kŏ-, not kō-. The tendency to prefer ă, ĕ, ĭ, ŏ, to ā, ē, ī, ō, in such forms is seen in *gratify, pacify, ratify, edify, specify, verify, vilify, vivify, modify* ; whether a similar list on the other side could be made is very doubtful.

codex has pl. *codicēs* ; see -EX, -IX.

codlin(g). Spell with the g.

c(o)enobite. Spell coe- ; see Æ, Œ.

coercible, -eable. Spell *-ible* ; see -ABLE 2.

coffee. Pronounce kŏ-, not kaw-.

cog. The phrase *cogged dice* is due to a misunderstanding of the old *to cog dice*, which meant not to load them, but to cheat in throwing them ; *loaded* should be used.

cogent. See -ER & -EST, 4.

cogitate makes *-itable*; see -ABLE 1.

cognate. For the sense in grammar see TECHNICAL TERMS.

cognizance, cognizant, cognizable, cognize. *Cognize* alone has the *-g-* always sounded. Of the four, *cognizance* is the word from which the others have sprung, & it had for some time no *-g-* to be sounded ; the introduction of the *-g-* has affected pronunciation, but kŏn- is still common in the first three, & should be maintained at least in *cognizance* & *cognizant* ; *cognizable* should be either kŏ'nĭzabl or, if it is to be assimilated to *cognize*, kŏgnī'zabl. For synonyms of *-nce*, see SIGN.

coiffeur, coiffure. See FRENCH WORDS.

coincidence. *The long arm of c.* is a HACKNEYED PHRASE. Varying its form, endowing it with muscles, making it throw people about, & similar attempts at renovation, only make matters worse :—*The author does not strain the muscles of coincidence's arm to bring them into relation./Nor does Mrs Moberly shrink from a use of ' the long arm' quite unnecessarily./The long arm of c. throws the Slifers into Mercedes's Cornish garden a little too heavily.*

colander, cullender. Both are pronounced kŭ'lender ; the first spelling, which is nearer the Latin stem (cf. *percolate*), is also more frequent in the 19th-c. quotations in the OED.

col-, com-, con-. There is a tendency among the more or less illiterate, on whom spelling exercises an excessive influence, to pronounce words beginning with these syllables & having the word-accent on the second syllable (such as *collective, colloquial, combustible, commandment, commercial, concomitant, condition, confederate*) with a distinct short o (kŏndĭ'shn, kŏmah'ndment, instead of the correct kndĭ'shn, komah'ndmnt).

colicky. Spell the adj. with *-cky* ; cf. *bivouac(ked)*, & -C-, -CK-.

collapsable, -ible. The first is better; see -ABLE 2.

collate. See -ATABLE.

collation. The reporter who can be content with *repast* instead wins the moderate gratitude, & he who says *meal* the fervent admiration, of most of us ; see WORKING & STYLISH WORDS.

collectable, -ible. The first is better ; see -ABLE 2.

COLLECTIVES. The word is applied to many different things, & in TECHNICAL TERMS an attempt is made to disentangle them. *Flock* [1] (a number of sheep or parishioners) is a collective of one kind, & *flock* [2] (woollen waste) is of another ; *flock* [1] may be treated as singular or plural (*His f. was attacked by wolves* ; *His f. was without a pastor* or *were unanimous in disapproval*), & can itself be used in the plural with the ordinary difference in meaning from the singular (*shepherds tending their flocks*) ; *flock* [2] can be used either in the singular or in the plural, the meaning being the same, a material, & *flock* being treated always as singular & *flocks* as plural (*A flock mattress* ; *A mattress of flock* or *flocks* ; *the flock has, the flocks have, not been disinfected*). But the word *collective* is applied to both, as well as to mány equally dissimilar kinds of noun, for which see TECHNICAL TERMS.

Reference of a word to this article means that it has the peculiarity indicated by the number of the following table that is given in the reference.

1. Words that have no separate plural form, but are the same in both numbers, e.g. *counsel, deer, grouse, reindeer, salmon, sheep, trout,* (*Many counsel were briefed* ; *The grouse were shy* ; *We saw no deer*).

2. Words having a plural, but whose singular used in a collective sense, & treated as either singular or plural, is generally preferred to it, e.g. *shot, cannon,* (*The shot scatters too much* ; *Three shot were extracted from his head*).

3. Words of number or amount that when used after definite or indefinite numerals have often or usually the singular instead of the plural form, e.g. *brace, dozen, hundred, fathom, pound, hundredweight,* (*We shot 20 brace* ; *Six fathom deep* ; *A few hundredweight of coal* ; *Six pound of lard*).

4. Names of an animal or vegetable that can have *a* & mean an individual, or be used in the singular without *a* & mean the things as food or as objects of sport, e.g. *salmon, lamb, pig, grouse, potato, cabbage,* (*Went out sticking pig* ; *Have some potato* ; *Cabbage is a blood-purifier*).

5. Words having no plural, but able, being nouns of multitude, to take either a singular or a plural verb, e.g. *cattle* (*The c. is sold* ; *The c. are in the hay*). For the many blunders occasioned by these words (*The German Government acknowledge him as its official courier*) see PERSONIFICATION.

college. The indiscriminate assumption of the name by schools that are no more colleges than others contented with the ordinary title is a sad degradation & obscuring of the word's meaning. Mothers (not yet, perhaps, fathers) are now heard to speak of sending their boys to college when they mean merely to school ; this at least should be resisted ; it is too late to ask the self-styled 'colleges' to consider whether it is for their real dignity to use *c.* in the same way as our grandfathers are laughed at for using *academy*. See WORKING & STYLISH WORDS.

collie, colly. See -EY, -IE, -Y.

collocutor, colloquist, interlocutor, are rival candidates for a post that undoubtedly ought to be filled ; we all need occasionally a single word to stand for *the other speaker, the person who was talking to & being talked to by* me, you, him, or her. None of the three is very satisfactory, but if two could be rejected the third would have a better chance, & *collocutor* (kŏ'lokūter) seems the best.

collusion &c. 1. Pronounce -lōō- ; see LU. 2. The notion of fraud or underhandedness is essential to collusion, & the following is a misuse :—*The two authors, both professors at Innsbruck, appear to be working in c.* ; the supposed arrangement is merely that their periods shall not overlap ; *in collaboration* will therefore not do ; if *in concert* will not, the thing must be given at length.

COLON. See STOPS.

colossal in the sense not of enormous (as in *c. folly* &c.), but of indescribably entertaining or delightful or ridiculous, is a Germanism not deserving adoption ; the similar use of *immense*, though we do not name it *honoris causâ*, is at least of native development.

colo(u)r. Keep the -u- ; but see -OUR & -OR. For synonymy see TINT.

colour makes *colourable, colourist,* but *coloration, decolorize* ; see -OR & -OUR, -OR- & -OUR-, HYBRID DERIVATIVES.

com-. For pronunciation in *commandment* &c., see COL-.

combat. Pronounce kŭ-. Part. & p.p. *-ating, -ated* ; see -T-, -TT-.

combe. See COOMB.

combinedly. Four syllables if used ; see -EDLY.

come. For *c. into* one's *life,* see HACKNEYED PHRASES.

come-at-able, get-at-able. Write with the hyphens. *C.* was made as long ago as the 17th c., but, except in *g.*, the experiment has not been successfully repeated, & probably will not be.

comedian, tragedian, have, in the sense *actor*, the feminines *comedienne, tragedienne,* perhaps best pronounced kŏmē'dĭĕ'n, trăjē'dĭĕ'n, & written without accents ; see FRENCH PRO-NUNCIATION. It is unfortunate that *c.* & *t.* also mean writer, which leads to ambiguity ; but the introduction of *comedist* & *tragedist* for the writers is a remedy worse than the disease ; we cannot begin now to talk of *the Greek comedists & tragedists,* for instance.

comedy, farce, burlesque. As species of drama, the three are distinguished in that *comedy* aims at entertaining by the fidelity with which it presents life as we all know it, *farce* at raising laughter by the outrageous absurdity of the situations or characters exhibited, & *burlesque* at tickling the fancy of the audience by caricaturing plays or actors with whose style it is familiar.

comestibles. See WORKING & STYLISH WORDS, & FORMAL WORDS.

comic(al). The broad distinction, sometimes obscured by being neglected, is that that is *comic* of which the aim or origin is comedy, & that is *comical* of which the effect, whether intended or not, is comedy. A *comic actor* is merely one who acts comedy ; a *comical actor,* one who makes the audience laugh. *Comic hesitation* is that in which the hesitator is playing the comedian ; *comical hesitation,* that in which observers find comedy, whether the hesitator meant them to or was unconscious of them. Accordingly, *comic* is the normal epithet (though *comical* may be used, in a different sense) with *actor, opera, scene, relief, song, singer, history, paper* ; *comical* is normal (subject to the converse reserve) with *face, effect, expression, deformity, earnestness, attempt, terror, hesitation, fiasco.* There is some tendency (*the attempt was comic in the extreme* ; *The disaster had its*

comic side) to use *comic* where *comical* is the right word. This may possibly be a sign that *comical* is on the way to become archaic & obsolete ; but, the difference of meaning being fairly definite & of real use, this would be regrettable.

comity, from Latin *cōmis* courteous, means courtesy, & *the c. of nations* is the obligation recognized by civilized nations to respect each other's laws & usages as far as their separate interests allow. It has nothing to do with Latin *cōmes* companion, & phrases based on this false derivation (*obtain admittance to the c. of states* ; *entered into the c. of nations* ; *a useful member of the civilized c.*), & implying the sense *company, association, league, federation,* &c., are wrong.

COMMA. See STOPS.
commando. Pl. *-os* ; see -O(E)S 6.
comme il faut. See FRENCH WORDS.
commemorate makes *-rable* ; see -ABLE 1.

commence(ment). The writers who prefer *ere* & *save* to *before* & *except* may be expected to prefer *c.* to *begin(ning)* in all contexts. *Begin* is the word always thought & usually said, but it is translated sometimes before it is said, & often before it is written, into *c.,* which is described by the OED as ' precisely equivalent to the native *begin* '. It is a good rule never to do this translation except when *begin* or *beginning* is felt to be definitely incongruous ; see WORKING & STYLISH WORDS. In official announcements *c.* is appropriate ; the play-bill tells us when the performance will *c.,* though we ask each other when it *begins.* The grave historical style also justifies *c.,* & historians' phrases, such as *c. hostilities,* keep their form when transferred to other uses, though we *begin,* & do not *c.,* a quarrel ; similarly we *c. operations,* but merely *begin dinner.* As against the precise equivalence mentioned above, it should be observed that *begin* has, owing to its greater commonness, more nearly passed into a mere auxiliary than *c.* ; & from this it results (1) that *begin*, not *c.*, is even in formal style the right word before an infinitive ; in *The landholders commenced to plunder indiscriminately*, any one can perceive that *began* would be better ; (2) that *c.* retains more than *begin* the positive sense of initiative or intention, & is especially out of place with an infinitive when this sense is absent, as in *Even the warmest supporters of the Chancellor of the Exchequer must be commencing to feel that he should give some slight consideration to . . .*

commiserate. *The late Emperor Francis Joseph, who commiserated* with *the imperial bird for that it had but a single head.* The orthodox use of *c.* is transitive, & the OED gives no quotation showing *with*.

commission(n)aire is best anglicized both in spelling (*-onaire*) & in pronunciation (komĭshonār').

commissure. Pronounce kŏ'mĭsūr.

commitment, committal. In nearly all senses the two forms are interchangeable, but *-tal* gains ground while *-ment* loses it. The sense engagement, however, i. e. the being committed to doing something, belongs almost only to *-ment*, & the sense perpetration, i. e. the committing *of* some offence, almost only to *-tal*.

committee, in the original sense of person to whom something is committed (esp. now the care of a lunatic), is pronounced kŏmĭtē'.

common makes *-er*, *-est* ; see -ER & -EST.

common, epicene, neuter, in their grammatical application, though often confused, have distinct senses. A *common* noun is one that can take a masculine or a feminine epithet according to the sex of the individual (*canis niger* a black dog, *canis nigra* a black bitch) ; an *epicene* word is one that, though its epithets are always masculine or always feminine, can be applied to an individual of either sex (*aquila nigra* a black male

eagle or a black female eagle) ; a *neuter* word is one of which the epithets are neither masculine nor feminine (*animal nigrum*).

commonplace, platitude, triviality, truism. The words are all often used as terms of reproach in describing the statements made by a speaker or writer ; but none of them is identical in sense with any other, & if they are not to be misused a rough idea at least of the distinctions is necessary. It is something to remember that no-one should welcome *platitude, triviality*, or *truism* in the strict sense, as a description of a statement of his own, whereas it may be a merit in a statement to be a *commonplace* or a *truism* in its loose sense.

A *commonplace* is a thing that, whether true or false, is so regularly said on certain occasions that the repeater of it can expect no credit for originality ; but the commonplace may be useful.

A *platitude* is a thing the stating of which as though it were enlightening or needing to be stated convicts the speaker of dullness ; a platitude is never valuable. The word is misused in :—*It is a p. that the lack of cottages is one of the chief of the motive forces which drive the peasantry to the towns.*

A *triviality* is a thing the saying of which as though it were adequate to the occasion convicts the speaker of silliness ; a triviality is never to the purpose.

A *truism* in the strict sense (to which it might be well, but is perhaps now impossible, to confine it) is a statement in which the predicate gives no information about the subject that is not implicit in the definition of the subject itself. *What is right ought to be done* ; since the *right* is definable as *that which ought to be done*, this means *What ought to be done ought to be done*, i. e., it is a disguised identical proposition, or a truism. *It is not well to act with too great haste* ; *too great haste* being haste greater than it is well to act with, the sentence tells us no more, though it pretends to, than anyone who can define *too great haste* knew before the predicate *is not well* was added. But *What is right pays*, or in other words *Honesty is the best policy*, is not a truism either in the strict sense (since it makes a real statement & not a sham one) or in the loose sense (since its truth is disputable) ; nor is *It is not well to act in haste* a truism of either kind. Both statements, however, are commonplaces, & often platitudes.

A *truism* in the loose sense is a thing that, whether in point or not, is so indisputably true that the speaker is under no obligation to prove it, & need not fear contradiction. This sense is a SLIPSHOD EXTENSION ; the writer who describes his principle as a *t.* in order to justify his drawing conclusions from it would do better to call it an *axiom* ; & the critic who depreciates some one else's statements as *tt.*, not in the strict sense, but meaning merely that they are too familiar to be of value, should call them *platitudes* or *commonplaces*.

common sense should be written as two separate words except when it is used attributively, & should then be hyphened :—*The philosophy of common sense* ; *The common-sense philosophy* ; cf. *bona fide*.

communal. The OED gives ko-mū′nal preference over kŏ′mūnal, but RECESSIVE ACCENT is likely to prevail, & the latter is recommended. See FALSE QUANTITY (on *doctrinal*).

commune. Both nouns (corporation &c. & converse &c.) are pronounced kŏ′mŭn. In the verb, komū′n will probably prevail in the end (see NOUN & VERB ACCENT), but kŏ′mŭn is perhaps oftener heard at present.

communicate makes *-cable* ; see -ABLE 1.

communism. See SOCIALISM for distinction.

communiqué. See FRENCH PRONUNCIATION. Certain newspapers, or writers, have taken lately to printing the word with no accent, presumably to be called kŏmūnē′k. This seems ill-advised, the literal sense ' communicated thing ', & the difference from words like *critique* & *physique*, being at present exhibited by the accent & surely worth preserving.

companionable. For such formations see -ABLE 4.

comparative(ly). For *a comparatively few, the comparative few*, &c., see FEW.

COMPARATIVES. For misuses, see -ER & -EST, MORE, & THAN.

compare, in the sense *suggest or state a similarity*, is regularly followed by *to*, not *with* ; in the sense *examine or set forth the details of a supposed similarity or estimate its degree*, it is regularly followed by *with*, not *to*. *He compared me to Demosthenes* means that he suggested that I was comparable to him or put me in the same class ; *He compared me with Demosthenes* means that he instituted a detailed comparison or pointed out where & how far I resembled or failed to resemble him. Accordingly, the preposition in each of the following is the one required by idiom :—*Witness compared the noise to thunder* ; *The lecturer compared the British field-gun with the French* ; *The effect of a trumpet-blast on the ear is comparable to that of scarlet on the eye* ; *Shakspere is hardly comparable with Milton* ; *Compared with*, or *to*, *him I am a bungler* (this is a common type in which either sense is applicable).

After the intransitive verb (*a boiled mullet cannot c. with a baked one*), *with* alone is possible.

compass. For synonymy see FIELD.

compendium. Pl. *-ums*, *-a* ; see -UM.

compensate. 1. Formerly kom-pĕ′nsāt, but now kŏ′mpensāt ; see RECESSIVE ACCENT ; *compensatory*

&c. will probably conform & accent the first before long, but usually accent the second still. 2. *C.* makes *-sable* ; see -ABLE 1.

competence, -cy. Neither has any sense in which the other cannot be used ; the first form is gaining on the second ; & it would be well if *competency* could be abandoned as a NEEDLESS VARIANT ; see -CE, -CY.

complacence, -cy. There is no distinction that can be called established ; the second form is the commoner, & is less liable to confusion with *complaisance* (see foll.) ; *complacence* might be dropped as a NEEDLESS VARIANT ; see -CE, -CY.

complacent, -ency, complaisant, -ance. 1. The two sets have clearly differentiated meanings, but are often confused (see below) ; it would help to obviate this confusion if the more easily distinguished & better established pronunciation of the second set (kŏmplĭză'nt, -ă'ns, not komplā'znt, -ā'zns) were made invariable, & if *complacency* were always preferred to *-acence* (see prec.).

2. He is *complacent* who is pleased with himself or his state, or with other persons or things as they affect him ; the word is loosely synonymous with *contented.* He is *complaisant* who is anxious to please by compliance, service, indulgence, or flattery ; the word is loosely synonymous with *obliging.* The wrong choice has been made in each of these sentences :—*He owed such funds as he possessed to French* complacency./*He has nothing more to expect from the* complacency *of the authorities.*/*The display of the diamonds usually stopped the tears, & she would remain in a* complaisant *state until . . .*

Note, 1924. I wrote the above in 1913, fortified by the OED descriptions (dated 1893) of *complacence, -acency,* & *-acent,* in the senses proper to *complaisance, -aisant,* as respectively ' *Obs.*', ' *?Obs.*', & ' *?Obs.*' It is a curious illustration of the

changing fashions in words that I have since collected a dozen newspaper examples of *complac-* words wrongly used for *complais-,* & none of the contrary mistake. It looks as if some journalists had forgotten the existence of *complais-* & the proper meaning of *complac-.*

complement. For the sense in grammar, see TECHNICAL TERMS. In the verb *-ent* is clearly sounded (-ĕnt) if not given the main accent ; in the noun it is neither accented nor clearly sounded (-ent) ; see NOUN & VERB ACCENT.

complete, vb. See FORMAL WORDS.

complicacy, by the side of the established *complexity,* has no claim to favour, & is perhaps due to mere NOVELTY-HUNTING.

compliment. The pronunciation varies as with COMPLEMENT.

complin(e). ' The final *e* is modern & unhistorical '—OED.

compo has pl. *-os* ; see -O(E)S 5.

composedly. Four syllables ; see -EDLY.

compost. Pronounce -ŏst.

compound, n. & v. See NOUN & VERB ACCENT.

COMPOUND PREPOSITIONS, CON-JUNCTIONS, &c. A selection of these is :—*as to* (AS 3) ; *for the purpose of* ; INASMUCH AS ; *in* CON-NEXION 2 *with* ; *in favour of* ; *in order that, to* ; *in reference to* ; *in relation to* ; IN SO FAR *as, that* ; *in so much that* ; IN THAT ; *in the absence of* ; *in the* CASE *of* ; *in the* INSTANCE *of* ; *in the matter of* ; *in the* NEIGHBOURHOOD *of* ; *in the region of* ; *of the character of* ; *of the nature of* ; *with a* VIEW *to* ; *with reference to* ; *with* REGARD *to* ; *with relation to* ; *with respect to.* And one or two specimens of their work are :—*At least* 500,000 *houses are required, & the aggregate cost is* in the region of £400,000,000./*Sir Robert Peel used to tell an amusing story of one of these banquets,* in the case of *which he & Canning were seated on opposite sides of Alderman Flower.*/*If I have a complaint to proffer against Mr Bedford,* *it certainly is, except perhaps* in the case of ' *Monna Vanna* ', *not* in the matter of *the plays to which he has refused a licence, but* in regard to *a few of the plays which he sanctioned./France is now going through a similar experience* with regard to *Morocco to that which England had to undergo* with reference to *Egypt after the occupation.*

But so much has been said on the subject, & so many illustrations given, elsewhere (see PERIPHRASIS, & the words in small capitals in the list above) that nothing but a very short general statement need be made here. Of such phrases some are much worse in their effects upon English style than others, *in order that* being perhaps at one end of the scale, & *in the case of* or *as to* at the other ; but, taken as a whole, they are almost the worst element in modern English, stuffing up the newspaper columns with a compost of nouny abstractions. To young writers the discovery of these forms of speech, which are used very little in talk & very much in print, brings an expansive sense of increased power ; they think they have acquired with far less trouble than they anticipated the trick of dressing up what they may have to say in the right costume for public exhibition. Later, they know better, & realize that it is feebleness, instead of power, that they have been developing ; but by that time the fatal ease that the compound-preposition style gives (to the writer, that is) has become too dear to be sacrificed.

comprehend. See APPREHEND.
compress, n. & v. See NOUN & VERB ACCENT.
comptroller, cont-. The first spelling is not merely archaic, but erroneous, being due to false association with *count* (F *conter* f. L *computare*).
computable, -ative. The accent now varies, but will probably settle on the first syllables ; see RECESSIVE ACCENT.

comrade. Pronounce kŏ-, not kŭ-.
con-. For pronunciation in *continue* &c., see COL-.
concavity. Pronounce -kăv-.
conceal. See FORMAL WORDS.
concentrate &c. 1. Accents as in COMPENSATE &c., 2. See -ATABLE.
concept is a philosophical term, & should be left to the philosophers ; the substituting of it for the ordinary word *conception* as below is due to NOVELTY-HUNTING :—[a caricature has been described] *Now this point of view constantly expressed must have had its influence on popular concepts.* See POPULARIZED TECHNICALITIES.

concern. In (*so far*) *as concerns* or *regards*, the number of the verb (which is impersonal, or has for its unexpressed subject ' our inquiry ' or some similar phrase) is invariable ; the change to plural, as in the quotation that follows, is due, like *as* FOLLOW, to misapprehension :— *Many of these stalks were failures, so far as* concern *the objective success.*

concernedly. Four syllables ; see -EDLY.
concernment has no senses that are not as well, & now more naturally & frequently, expressed by the noun *concern* ; the substitution of the latter was censured as affectation in the 17th c., but the boot is now on the other leg, & *c.* should be dropped as a NEEDLESS VARIANT.

concert, n. & v. See NOUN & VERB ACCENT.
concerto. Pronounce konchār'tō ; pl. *-os*, see -O(E)S 6.
concession(n)aire Omit the -n-, & pronounce -sĕsh- ; cf. COMMISSIONAIRE.
concessive. See TECHNICAL TERMS.
concettism. Pronounce -chĕt-.
conch. Pronounce -k.
concierge. See FRENCH WORDS.
conciliate makes *-liable*; see -ABLE 1.
conciseness, concision. The first is the English word familiar to the ordinary man ; *concision* is the LITERARY CRITICS' WORD, more recent in English, used by writers

under French influence, & often requiring the reader to stop & think whether he knows its meaning :— *The writing of verse exacts concision, clear outline, a damming of the waters at the well-spring.* See -ION & -NESS.

concolo(u)rous. See HYBRID DE-RIVATIVES.

concomitance, -cy. The second is now a NEEDLESS VARIANT ; see -CE, -CY.

concord. For the sense in grammar, see TECHNICAL TERMS.

concordat. Pronounce konkor'dăt.

concupiscence, -ent. Accent second, not third, syllables.

concur makes concur'ring, but concu'rrent &c. ; see PRONUNCIA-TION, s.f.

condemning. Pronounce -ĕmĭng.

condign meant originally *deserved*, & could be used in many contexts, with *praise* for instance as well as with *punishment*. It is now used only with words equivalent to *punishment*, & means deservedly severe, the severity being the important point, & the desert merely a condition of the appropriateness of the word ; that it is an indispensable condition, however, is shown by the absurd effect of :— *Count Zeppelin's marvellous voyage through the air has ended in c. disaster.*

condolence. Pronounce kondō'lens.

condottiere. Pronounce -tyārĭ. Pl. -ri, pron. -rē.

conduct, n. & v. See NOUN & VERB ACCENT.

conductress. See FEMININE DE-SIGNATIONS.

conduit. Pronounce kŭ'ndĭt.

coney. See CONY.

confection. The French dress-making term properly means no more than a piece of attire not made to measure ; but, being applied chiefly to fashionable wraps &c., it is sometimes misunderstood as expressing in itself (like *creation*) the speaker's exclamatory admiration.

confederacy, -eration. See FEDERA-TION.

confer(r)able. Of the verbs in *-fer*

accented on the last syllable, two form adjectives in *-ble* of which the spelling & accent are fixed (*pre'ferable & tra'nsferable*). The others, for which various forms have been tried (*confer, confe'rrable ; defer,* none ; *infer, i'nferable & infe'rible & infe'rrable & infe'rrible ; refer, re'ferable & refe'rrable & refe'rrible*), should be made to follow these two, & the forms should be *co'nferable, i'nferable,pre'ferable,re'ferable,tra'nsferable.*

confessedly. Four syllables ; see -EDLY.

confidant, -ante, -ent, nn. *Co'nfident* was in use as a noun meaning confidential friend or person to whom one entrusted secrets long before the other forms were introduced ; but it is now an ARCHAISM, & to revive it is pedantry. *Confidant* is masculine & *confidante* feminine ; they are indistinguishable in pronunciation, & accent the last syllable.

configuration, configure. For pronunciation, see FIGURE.

confines, n. Accent the first syllable ; see NOUN & VERB ACCENT.

confiscate &c. 1. Accents as in COMPENSATE &c. 2. *C.* makes *confiscable* ; see -ABLE 1.

conflict, n. & v. See NOUN & VERB ACCENT.

conformable. For such formations see -ABLE 4.

confrère. See FRENCH WORDS.

confusedly. Four syllables ; see -EDLY.

congé, congee. The second, formerly established, is now obsolete or archaic ; for the first, see FRENCH WORDS.

congeries. Pronounce konjĕ'rĭēz.

congratulate makes *-lable* ; see -ABLE 1.

congregate. *Where* ——*s most do c.* is a BATTERED ORNAMENT.

conjugate makes *-gable* ; see -ABLE 1.

conjugation, conjunction. See TECHNICAL TERMS.

conjunctive (mood) is a term that had much better be dropped. The forms denoted by *c.* & *subjunctive* are the same, & *subjunctive* is the much better known name. *C.* might have been useful in distinguishing uses if it had been consistently applied ; but it means sometimes the forms however used (*subjunctive* then being a division under it restricted to the subordinate uses), sometimes the forms when used as main verbs (*subjunctive* then being a division parallel to it restricted as before), & sometimes merely the forms when used as main verbs of conditional sentences (*subjunctive* then being, very unreasonably, the name for all uses, dependent or independent, & *c.* a division under it). This is hopeless confusion ; *c.* should be given up, *subjunctive* be used as the name of the forms whatever their use, & the differences of function be conveyed by other words (*dependent, conditional, optative,* &c.).

conjure in the sense *bcsccch* is pronounced konjoor', in other senses kŭ'njɐr.

conjuror, -er. In the OED 19th-c. quotations, *-or* is five times as common as *-er*, & it might well be accepted as the only form.

connectable, -ible. The first is recommended ; see -ABLE 2.

connexion, -ction. 1. The first is the right spelling ; see -XION.

2. *In c. with* is a formula that every one who prefers vigorous to flabby English will have as little to do with as he can ; see PERIPHRASIS. It should be clearly admitted, however, that there is sometimes no objection to the words ; this is when they are least of a formula & *c.* has a real meaning (*Buses run i.c.w. the trains; The isolated phrase may sound offensive, but taken i.c.w. its context it was not so*). In the prevalent modern use, however, it is worn down into a mere compound preposition, with vagueness & pliability as its only merits. The worst writers use it, from sheer love of verbiage, in preference to a single word that would be more appropriate (*The three outstanding features*

i.c.w. [i.e., of] *our ' Batchworth Tinted ', as sample set enclosed, are as follows*). The average writer is not so degraded as to choose it for its own sake, but he has not realized that when *i.c.w.* presents itself to him it is a sign that laziness is mastering his style, or haziness his ideas. Of the examples that follow, the first two are characteristic specimens of compound-prepositional periphrasis :—*The special difficulty* in *Professor Minocelsi's* case *arose* i. c. w. *the view he holds* relative to *the historical value of* . . . (Prof. M. was specially hampered by his views on)./*Regulations* with regard to *the provision of free places* i.c.w. *secondary education* (Regulations for providing free places in secondary schools)./*Canvey Island, which is again coming into prominence* i. c. w. *the proposal to establish a great wharf there* (to which attention has been called by)./*Mr J. M. is having a hard time* i.c.w. *his desire for reelection.*/*Sir S. P. will shortly retire from the secretaryship* i.c.w. *the age limit.*

connoisseur. Pronounce kŏnaser' ; the modern French spelling (*-nai-*) should not be used.

connote, denote. This article is concerned only with the correlated senses of the two words. *C.*, not being really in popular use, has no senses except the correlated ones ; but *d.* has popular uses out of relation to *c.*, as *A high pulse denotes* (is a symptom of) *fever* ; *Let* f *d.* (be the appointed symbol for) *the force exerted* ; *This surely denotes* (shows) *that the question is decided.*

When *c.* & *d.* are in expressed or implied antithesis, the difference is twofold, sense 1 of each corresponding to sense 1 only of the other, & sense 2 to sense 2 only.

1. A word denotes all the objects having the attributes that it connotes (or implies the joint presence of). *Father* denotes the first Person of the Trinity, Adam, Edward VII, Eclipse, & all others to whom the connotation or connotative meaning of *father* applies. *Ugly* denotes Socrates, Wilkes, the black country, cowardice, & all other things to which the connotation of *ugly* applies. The whole of the objects taken together are the word's *denotation* or denotative meaning.

A word connotes all the attributes common to the objects that it denotes (or is predicable of). *Father* connotes fatherhood or having begotten, male sex, prior existence, & all other attributes common to the objects included in the denotation of *father*. *Ugly* connotes ugliness or violation of standards of beauty, repellent effect on an observer, &c. The sum of the common attributes is the word's *connotation* or connotative meaning.

2. A word denotes the contents of its barest adequate definition. *Father* denotes one that has begotten. *Ugly* denotes violating standards of beauty. The word's *denotation* is this barest definition alone.

A word connotes all or any of the attributes that, without being denoted by it, are associated with it either as deducible from its denotation or as observed to be common to all normal specimens answering to its denotation. *Father* connotes male sex, prior existence, greater experience, affection, guidance, &c. *Ugly* connotes repellent effect, immunity from dangers peculiar to beauty, disadvantage in the marriage market, &c. The whole of these are the connotation, & any of them is part of the connotation, of the word.

conquer(or), conquest. Pronounce kŏ'ngker(er), kŏ'ngkwĕst.

conscience. Write *for conscience'* sake; see SAKE.

conscientious. Pronounce kŏnsĭ- or kŏnshĭ- ; see -CIATION.

consecutive. For the sense in syntax see TECHNICAL TERMS.

consensus means unanimity, or unanimous body, of opinion or testimony. The following, in which it is confused with *census*, is nonsense : *Who doubts that if a consensus were taken, in which the interrogated had the honesty to give a genuine reply, we should have an overwhelming majority ?*

consequential is a word severely restricted in its application by modern idiom ; it is unidiomatic in several of the senses that it might have or has formerly borne.

1. Where doubt can arise between it & *consequent*, the latter should always be used when the sense is the simple & common one of *resulting*, & *-ial* be reserved for that of *required for consistency with something else*. Thus *In the consequent confusion he vanished*, but *The consequential amendments were passed*. *Consequential confusion* is not English ; *the consequent amendments* is, but means not (as with *-ial*) those necessitated by one previously accepted, but those that resulted from (e.g.) the opposition's hostility or the discovery of a flaw. The right use is seen in *A good many of these undiscussed changes were only consequential alterations* : but the following sentence (in which *consequent* would be better, but either is possible) shows that the line is sometimes hard to draw :—*Yet whilst he washes his hands of the methods of the Albert Hall, with its consequential campaign of resistance & its cry of ' no servant tax ', he declares that the Bill must not be passed.*

2. *C.* does not mean of consequence ; a c. person may or may not be important ; all we know is that he is self-important ; *Mr C. bustled about, feeling himself the most c. man in the town* would not now be English.

3. *C.* does not now mean having great consequences. For *so desperate & so c. a war as this* there should be substituted *a war so desperate & so pregnant with consequences*.

4. *A c. crime* &c. is an act that was not criminal &c. in its own nature, but amounts to a crime &c. in virtue

of its consequences :—*There is a difference between direct contradiction & merely c. inconsistency.*

conservative. Perhaps the most ridiculous of SLIPSHOD EXTENSIONS is the rapidly spreading use of this word as an epithet, in the sense of moderate, safe, or low, with *estimates, figure,* &c. :—*8,000 killed is considered a c. estimate./The damage is placed on a c. estimate at 20,000,000 dollars./Seas that even the c. ship's logs called ' mountainous './The figure is probably an over-estimation, & a more c. estimate is that of Kohler./ At least 6,000,000 dollars an hour ; this is a most c. estimate ; probably it is too low./Based upon the price of 4½d. per ft, & with reasonable care this should be a c. figure./The distributing side of the market takes a more c. & certainly more hopeful view.*

conservatoire, conservatory. The French, German, & Italian musical institutions are best called by their native names—*conservatoire, conservatorium, conservatorio. Academy* or *School of Music* is better than *Conservatory* for corresponding English institutions.

considerable, in the sense *a good deal of,* is applied in British use only to immaterial things (*I have given it c. attention*). The use with material things is an Americanism ; the following are from definitions in two American dictionaries :—*Silk fabric containing c. gold or silver thread./ Certain pharmaceutical preparations similar to cerates, but containing c. tallow.*

considerateness, consideration. *Consideration,* so far as it is comparable with *-ateness,* means thought for others, while *-ateness* means the characteristic of taking (or implying) such thought ; see -ION & -NESS. It is therefore sometimes indifferent which is used (*He showed the greatest -ateness* or *-ation* ; *Thanks for your -ateness* or *-ation*). But more often one is preferable :—*His -ateness is beyond all praise* ; *I was treated with -ation* ; *He was struck by the -ateness of the offer.*

consist. *C. of* introduces a material, & *c. in* a definition or a statement of identity ; we must not say *the moon consists in green cheese* (no-one would), nor *virtue consists of being good* (many do). ELEGANT VARIATION between the two is absurd :—*The external world consisted, according to Berkeley, in ideas* ; *according to Mr Mill it consists of sensations & permanent possibilities of sensation. Of* is wrong in *The most exceptional feature of Dr Ward's book undoubtedly consists of the reproduction of photographs.*

consistence, -cy. See -CE, -CY. The *-cy* form is now invariable in the noun that means being consistent, i.e. not inconsistent (*-cy is an overrated virtue*). In the noun meaning degree of thickness in liquids usage varies ; *A -ce something like that of treacle,* & *Mud varying in -cy & temperature,* are both from Huxley ; it would be well if *-ce* could be made the only form in this sense, as *-cy* in the other. It is sometimes doubtful now whether freedom from inconsistency is meant or metaphorical solidity ; among the OED quotations are :—*Reports begin to acquire strength & -ce* ; *A vague rumour daily acquiring -cy & strength.* The removal of such doubt would be one of the advantages of the limitation proposed above for *-ce.*

consistory. Accent the first syllable ; see RECESSIVE ACCENT.

consociation. Pronounce -sŏsĭ- ; see -CIATION.

consolatory Pronounce -sŏl-.

console, bracket, table, &c. Accent the first (kŏ′nsōl).

consols. Accent the last (konsŏ′lz).

consommé. See FRENCH WORDS.

consort. Pronounce the noun kŏ′nsort, the verb konsor′t ; see NOUN & VERB ACCENT.

conspectus. Pl. *-uses* ; see -US.

conspicuity, -ousness. See -TY & -NESS.

conspicuous. For *c. by absence* see HACKNEYED PHRASES (*Even in the examination for the M.D., literary quality & finish is often c. by its absence*).

constable. Pronounce kŭn-.

constitution(al)ist. See -IST.

constrainedly. Four syllables ; see -EDLY.

construct, construe, translate, with reference to language. To *translate* is to reproduce the meaning of (a passage &c.) in another language, or sometimes in another & usually a more intelligible style. To *construe* is to exhibit the grammatical structure of (a passage &c.), either by translating closely (& so it is often tantamount to *translate*) or by analysis. A sense of *construe* formerly common, but now disappearing & better abandoned, is that in which *construct* is taking its place (Aim *should not be constructed*, or *construed, with an infinitive*). The right pronunciation of *construe* (for which *conster* was long the prevalent form) is kŏ'nstrōō ; the konstrōō' now often heard by the side of the noun (kŏ'nstrōō) is no doubt due to the NOUN-&-VERB-ACCENT tendency.

constructive, in legal & quasi-legal use, is applied to an act that, while it does not answer to the statutory or formal definition of the offence &c. under which (qualified by *c.*) it is classed (*c. treason, rebellion, blasphemy, obligation,* &c.), is seen, when the true construction is put upon its motive or tendency, to amount to such an offence &c. (*It was at most c. blasphemy*). Cf. the analogous use of CONSEQUENTIAL.

consubstantiation. For pronunciation see -CIATION.

consuetude. Pronounce -swĭ-.

consumedly. Four syllables ; see -EDLY. But the word is a BATTERED ORNAMENT.

consummate. 1. Pronounce the adj. konsŭ'mĭt, the verb kŏ'nsŭmāt ; see PARTICIPLES 5A. 2. See -ATABLE.

consummation. For *a c. devoutly to be wished* see HACKNEYED PHRASES.

consumption, consumptive, should be kept alive, if possible, as better words for ordinary non-scientific use than *tuberculosis & tuberculous.*

contaminate makes *-nable* ; see -ABLE 1.

contango. Pl. *-os* ; see -O(E)S 3.

contemn. Pronounce part. -ĕmĭng, but agent-noun -ĕmner.

contemplate &c. 1. Accents as in COMPENSATE &c. 2. See -ATABLE.

co(n)temporary, -oraneous, &c. The OED shows conclusively that *con-* is the only right spelling.

contemptible) (contemptuous. *Mr Sherman, speaking in the Senate, called the President a demagogue who contemptibly disregarded the Government, because President Wilson, speaking at Columbia yesterday, said an International Labour Conference would be held at Washington, whether the Treaty was ratified or not.* Mr Sherman probably meant, & not improbably said, *contemptuously.* See PAIRS & SNARES.

content, v. *C.* one*self with* (not *by*) is the right form of the phrase that means not go beyond some course ; the following are wrong :—*We must c. ourselves for the moment by observing that from the juridical stand-point the question is a doubtful one./The petition contents itself by begging that the isolation laws may be carried out.*

content(ment). The two forms now mean practically the same, *contentment* having almost lost its verbal use (*The contentment of his wishes left him unhappy*) & meaning, like *content,* contented state. *Contentment* is the usual word, *content* surviving chiefly in *to heart's content* & as a poetic or rhetorical variant.

content(s), what is contained. The OED says ' The stress *conte'nt* is historical, & still common among the educated '. The stress *co'ntent* is due partly to NOUN & ADJECTIVE ACCENT & partly to the wish to differentiate from *content* = contentment. But *contents* is still almost always accented on the last, & that accent is recommended for *content* also.

contest. 1. Pronounce the noun kŏ′ntĕst, the verb kontĕ′st ; see NOUN & VERB ACCENT.
2. The intransitive use of the verb (*Troops capable of contesting success-fully against the forces of other na-tions* ; cf. the normal *contesting the victory with*) is much rarer than it was, & is better left to *contend*.

continual, continuous. That is *-al* which either is always going on or recurs at short intervals & never comes (or is regarded as never coming) to an end. That is *-ous* in which no break occurs between the beginning & the (not necessarily or even presumably long-deferred) end.

continuance, continuation, continu-ity. *Continuance* has reference to *continue* in its intransitive senses of *last, go on* ; *continuation* to *continue* in its transitive senses of *prolong, go on with,* & (in the passive) *be gone on with*. Choice between the two is therefore open when the same sense can be got at from two directions ; *We hope for a -ance of your favours* means that we hope they will con-tinue ; *We hope for a -ation of them* means that we hope you will con-tinue them ; & these amount to the same thing. But the addition that continues a tale or a house is its *-ation*, not its *-ance*, & the time for which the pyramids have lasted is their *-ance*, not their *-ation* ; we can wait for a *-ation*, but not for a *-ance*, *of hostilities* ; we like a thing *for a -ance*, but not *for a -ation* ; &, generally speaking, the distinction has to be borne in mind. *Con-tinuity*, though occasionally confused with *continuance*, is less liable to misuse, & it is enough to say that its reference is not to *continue*, but to *continuous*. For *solution of con-tinuity* see POLYSYLLABIC HUMOUR.

continuant. See TECHNICAL TERMS.
contract, n. & v. See NOUN & VERB ACCENT.
contractable, -ible. The first is better ; see -ABLE 2.

contradictious, -tory. The mean-ings *given to contradicting, captious, cavilling, cantankerous, quarrelsome,* do not belong to *contradictory* ; if either word is to be used, it must be *-tious* ; but this, though not in fact a new word, is always used with an uneasy suspicion that it has been made as a temporary stopgap, & it is better to choose one of the many synonyms.

contralto. Pl. *-os* ; see -O(E)S 6.
contrary. 1. The original accent (kontrār′i) lingers (1) with the un-educated in all ordinary uses of the adjective (not, perhaps, in *the c.*) ; (2) with most speakers in the jocose or childish *c.* for *perverse* or *peevish*, & in *contrariness, -ly*, used similarly ; (3) with many speakers in *contrari-wise*, especially when it either repre-sents *on the c.* rather than *in the c.* manner, or is used playfully.
2. *On the c., on the other hand.* The idiomatic sense of *o. t. o. h.* is quite clear ; except by misuse (see below) it never means *far from that*, i.e., it never introduces something that conflicts with the truth of what has preceded, but always something reconcilable, though in contrast, with it. The following two examples should have *o. t. c.* instead of *o. t. o. h.* :—*It cannot be pleaded that the detail is negligible ; it is, o. t. o. h., of the greatest importance./The object is not to nourish 10,000 cats by public charity ; it is, o. t. o. h., to put them to sleep in the lethal chamber.* An example of the right use is :—*Food was abundant ; water, o. t. o. h.,* (or *o. t. o. h., water*) *was running short.*
The use of *o. t. c.* is less simple ; it may have either of the senses of which *o. t. o. h.* has only one ; i.e., it may mean either *on the other hand* or *far from that* ; but if it stands first in its sentence it can only mean *far from that.* Thus *Food was abun-dant ; o. t. c., water was running short* is impossible ; but *Food was abundant ; water, o. t. c., was running short* is correct, though *o. t. o. h.* is commoner &, with a view to future

differentiation, preferable. If *o. t. c.* is to stand first, it must be in such forms as *Food was not abundant ; o. t. c., it was running short.*

contrary, converse, opposite. These are sometimes confused, & occasionally precision is important. If we take the statement *All men are mortal*, its contrary is *Not all men are mortal*, its converse is *All mortal beings are men*, & its opposite is *No men are mortal*. The contrary, however, does not exclude the opposite, but includes it as its most extreme form. Thus *This is white* has only one opposite, *This is black*, but many contraries, as *This is not white*, *This is coloured*, *This is dirty*, *This is black* ; & whether the last form is called the *contrary*, or more emphatically the *opposite*, is usually indifferent. But to apply *the opposite* to a mere contrary (e.g. to *I did not hit him* in relation to *I hit him*, which has no opposite), or to the converse (e.g. to *He hit me* in relation to *I hit him*, to which it is neither contrary nor opposite), is a looseness that may easily result in misunderstanding ; the temptation to go wrong is intelligible when it is remembered that with certain types of sentence (*A exceeds B*) the converse & the opposite are identical (*B exceeds A*).

contrast. 1. Pronounce the noun kŏ'ntrăst, the verb kontră'st ; see NOUN & VERB ACCENT. 2. The transitive use of the verb with one of the contrasted things as subject, in the sense *be a c. to* or *set off by c.*, was formerly common, but in modern writing is either an archaism or a blunder ; *with* should always be inserted. The use meant is seen in :—*The sun-tinged hermit & the pale elder c. each other.*/*Monks whose dark garments contrasted the snow.*/*The smooth slopes are contrasted by the aspect of the country on the opposite bank.*

control makes *-lled*, *-llable*, &c. ; see -LL-, -L-.

contumac(it)y. See LONG VARIANTS.
contumacy. Accent the first syllable ; see RECESSIVE ACCENT.
contumely. The possible pronunciations, given here in order of merit, are no less than five :— kŏ'ntūmlĭ, kŏ'ntūmē'lĭ, kŏ'ntūmĭlĭ, kontū'mĭlĭ, kontū'mlĭ. The well-known line *The oppressor's wrong, the proud man's c.* does much to kill the last two, which are irreconcilable with it, & to encourage the first, which seems to those whose knowledge of metre is limited to fit blank verse better than the second & third. The second is kept in being by *contumelious*. The OED gives only the third ; but that has less chance than any other of surviving ; a stressed syllable followed by three unstressed ones is very unpopular except with professors & the like if there is an alternative handy, which is the reason why *despi'cable*, *hospi'table*, &c., still maintain their ground even against the RECESSIVE ACCENT.

convenance, convenience. For *mariage de c.*, & *the convenances*, see FRENCH WORDS. For *marriage of convenience* see GALLICISMS.

conversable. For such formations see -ABLE 4.
conversance, -cy. See -CE, -CY.
conversation(al)ist. See -IST.
conversazione. Pronounce -ătsĭŏ'nĭ. Pl. *-nes* (-nĭz), *-ni* (-nē) ; the first is better.
converse, talk &c. Pronounce the noun kŏ'nvers, the verb konver's ; see NOUN & VERB ACCENT.
converse(ly). 1. Pronounce the adj. kŏ'nvers, but the adv. konver'slĭ. 2. For the sense of *the converse*, see CONTRARY, CONVERSE.
convert. Pronounce the noun kŏ'nvert, the verb konver't ; see NOUN & VERB ACCENT.
convertible, -able. The first is usually better ; see -ABLE 2.
convey. For inflexions see VERBS IN -IE &c., 2.
conveyance. See FORMAL WORDS.
convict. Pronounce the noun

kŏ'nvĭkt, the verb konvĭ'kt ; see
NOUN & VERB ACCENT.

convincedly. Four syllables if
used ; see -EDLY.

convolvulus. Pl. -*uses* ; see -US.

convoy. Pronounce the noun
kŏ'nvoi, the verb konvoi' ; see NOUN
& VERB ACCENT. For verb inflexions
see VERBS IN -IE &c., 4.

cony, coney. The first, with pl.
conies, is better.

cooee, cooey, signal-cry. The OED
puts *cooee* first.

cooky, -ie, -ey. See -EY, -IE, -Y.

coolie, -ly, -lee. The first is the
usual modern form ; see -EY, -IE, -Y.

coomb, combe. The OED prefers
the first.

cooperate, coopt, coordinate. For
co-o-, coŏ-, coo-, see CO-.

coordinate makes -*nable* ; see
-ABLE 1.

coot. For pl. see COLLECTIVES 4.

copra. Pronounce kŏ'pra.

copulative. See TECHNICAL TERMS.

copy, vb. For inflexions see VERBS
IN -IE &c., 6.

coquet(te) &c. The noun is now
always -*ette*, & is applied to females
only. The verb, formerly *coquet*
only, is often now, & will no doubt
before long be only, -*ette* ; the
accent, & the influence of -*etting*,
-*etted*, -*ettish*, will ensure that. The
noun *coquetry*, for which the OED
gives kŏ'kĭtrĭ as the only pronunciation, may be expected to change
similarly to the already common
kŏkĕ'trĭ.

corbel gives *corbelled* ; see -LL-, -L-.

cord, chord. For uses in which the
spelling is doubtful, see C(H)ORD.

cordelier. Pronounce kordīlēr'.

cordillera. Pronounce kordĭlyār'a.

cordon. Pronounce kor'dn.

core. ' Rotten at the core ' is a
MISQUOTATION.

co-respondent &c. See CO-.

cornelian, car-. The first is right
(from French *corneline*), & the
second due to mistaken etymology.

cornucopia. Pl. -*as*, not -*ae*.

corolla. Pl. -*as* ; see -AE, -AS.

corona Pl. -*ae* ; see -AE, -AS.

coronal. Pronounce the noun
(circlet) kŏ'ronal, the adj. (of the
skull, of a corona) korō'nal.

coronet(t)ed. Omit the second t ;
see -T-, -TT-.

corporal, corporeal, aa. Neither is
now a common word except in particular phrases. *Corporal* means *of
the human body*, & is common in
-*al punishment* ; it is also rarely used
with *deformity*, *beauty*, *defects*, &
such words, instead of the usual
personal or *bodily*. *Corporeal* means
of the nature of body, *material*,
tangible ; so our -*eal habitation* (the
body), *the -eal presence of Christ in
the Sacrament*.

corposant. Pronounce kor'pozant.

corps. Pronounce in sing. kōr, but
in pl. (though the spelling is the
same) kōrz ; see FRENCH WORDS.

corpulence, -cy. There is no difference ; -*ce* is recommended ; -*cy*
should be dropped as a NEEDLESS
VARIANT.

corpus. Pl. *corpora* ; see LATIN
PLURALS.

corpuscle. Pronounce kor'pusl ;
see PRONUNCIATION.

corral. Pronounce koră'l.

correctitude, a recent formation
(not given in OED vol. dated 1893),
is a NEEDLESS VARIANT for *correctness*.

correlate. See -ATABLE.

correlatives. See TECHNICAL TERMS.

corrigendum. Pl. (much commoner
than the sing.) -*da* ; see -UM.

corroborate makes -*rable* ; see
-ABLE 1.

corsage. See FRENCH WORDS.

corset. Pronounce kor'sĭt ; the
spelling -*ette*, the pronunciation
korsĕ't, & the use of the plural for a
single specimen, are mere blunders.

cors(e)let. Omit the -*e*-.

cortège. See FRENCH WORDS ;
procession is usually adequate.

Cortes. Pronounce kor'tĕs.

cortex. Pl. -*ices* (-ĭsēz) ; see -EX,
-IX.

Corybant. Pronounce kŏ'rĭbănt.
Pl. -*ts* or -*tes* (kŏrĭbă'ntēz).

Corydon. Pronounce kŏ'rĭdn.

coryphaeus. Spell *-ae-* ; see Æ, Œ. Pl. *-aeī* ; see -US.

cosaque. See FRENCH WORDS.

cose, coze, cosy, cozy. The established spelling for the adjective (a Scotch word of doubtful origin) is *cosy*. The verb (& noun) meaning *sit* (*sitting*) *by the fire* &c. is a BACK-FORMATION from this, & therefore best spelt *cose*. The verb (& noun) meaning *gossip* or *chat* is referred to French *causer* talk, & the spelling *coze*, which is the usual one, is also desirable, since the senses of the two verbs are very liable to confusion, by way of distinction. The noun *cosy* or *cozy* meaning a kind of seat is probably from the adjective, though helped to become a noun by the French *causeuse*. The spellings recommended, then, are :—*cosy*, comfortable, seat, teapot-warmer; *cose*, sit at ease, spell of sitting so; *coze*, chat (n. & v.).

cosset makes *-eting*, *-eted* ; see -T-, -TT-.

coster(monger). See CURTAILED WORDS.

costume. The verb is kŏstū′m. This pronunciation is probably commoner, & is preferred by the OED, for the noun also ; but kŏ′stŭm (see NOUN & VERB ACCENT) is often heard.

cosy -zy. See COSE.

cot(e). The word for *bed* is or was Anglo-Indian, is unconnected with the other words, & is always *cot*. The poetic word for *cottage*, & the word for *shelter* (usually seen in compounds, as *sheep-c.*), represent allied but separate old-English words ; *cot* is now invariable in the sense *cottage*, & *cote* usual in the sense *shelter* ; the latter, however, whether spelt *cote* or *cot*, is usually pronounced kŏt, especially in the commonest word *dovecote*.

cotemporary. See CONTEMPORARY.

co-tenant. See CO-.

cothurnus. Pl. *-nī* ; see -US. As a word for *tragedy*, *c.* is a BATTERED ORNAMENT.

co-tidal. See CO-.

cotill(i)on. Spell with the -i-.

cottar, cotter, cottier. The words are clearly distinguished from *cottager* by being applicable not to any one who lives in a cottage, but to peasants doing so under certain conditions of tenure. As compared with each other, however, there is no differentiation between them that is of value ; it is merely that the *-tar*, *-ter*, forms are more used of the Scotch variety, & *-tier* of the Irish. It would be well if *cottar* were made the sole form, *cotter* left to the pin or bolt, & *cottier* abandoned.

cotyledon. Pl. *-ns* ; see -ON 3.

couch, bed, sofa, &c. As a general word for anything that is lain on, bed, lair, &c., the word is poetic only. As a mere synonym for the ordinary word *sofa* in conversation, it is a GENTEELISM. As the name for a particular shape of sofa, it is a trade word.

couch, the weed. The OED prefers the pronunciation kowch, & describes kōōch as that of the southern counties only.

couchant. Pronounce kow′chant.

could. For such forms as *Could he see you now*, see SUBJUNCTIVES.

couleur de rose, coulisses, couloir. See FRENCH WORDS.

coulomb. Pronounce kōōlŏ′m.

co(u)lter. Spell with -u-.

council, -sel, -cillor, -sellor. A board or assembly, & the meeting of such a body, has always *-cil*, & a member of it is *-cillor*. The abstract senses *consultation*, *advice*, *secret* (*keep* one's *c.*), belong to *-sel*, & one who gives advice is, as such, a *-sellor*, though he may be a *-cillor* also ; *my -cillors* are the members of my (e.g., the king's) council ; *my counsellors*, those who advise me officially or otherwise. *Counsel*, however, has also the semi-concrete sense of the person or persons (never *counsels*) pleading for a party to a law-suit (*The second of our three counsel was the best*) ; the use is originally abstract, as when *All the wealth & fashion stands for all the* *rich &c. people*, or as though *advice* were said for *adviser(s)*.

countenance, face, physiognomy, visage. *Face* is the proper name for the part ; *countenance* is the face with reference to its expression ; *physiognomy*, to the cast or type of features. *Visage* is now a LITERARY WORD, used ornamentally for *face* without special significance.

counterpart means thing exactly similar to, not opposite to or contrasted with, another ; the following is nonsense : *All this is utterly false, the truth is its very counterpart.*

country dance. The form *contredance* or *-se* (i.e. counter-dance) is wrong ; the words mean native dance or dance of our country.
countryfied, -ified. The first is recommended ; see -FIED.

coup. Pronounce kōō ; pl. *coups*, pron. kōōz. For *c. d'état, de grâce, de main, de théâtre, d'œil*, see FRENCH WORDS.

couple. See COLLECTIVES 3.
couplet. See TECHNICAL TERMS.
coupon. Pronounce kōō'pŏn ; see FRENCH WORDS.
course. *Of c.*, as the herald of an out-of-the-way fact that one has just unearthed from a book of reference, is a sad temptation to journalists :—*From this marriage came Charles James Fox ; his father was, o. c., created Baron Holland in 1763./Milton o. c. had the idea of his line from Tacitus./He is, o. c., a son of the famous E. A. Sothern, of ' Lord Dundreary ' fame./The House being in Committee, the Speaker would not, o. c., under ordinary circumstances, have been present./Much speculation . . . as to the precise degree of pageant which will attend Sir Edward Grey's admission ; the full pageant, o. c., is that which is associated with a Chapter of the Order.*

court-card is now the established form ; see COAT-CARD.
court martial. Write as two words for the noun, & hyphen only for the verb ; see HYPHENS, group **Court Martial*. Pl. *courts martial*.

courteous, courtesy, are variously pronounced ker-, kōr-, & koor- ; the first is recommended.
courtesan, -zan. Spell *-san*, & pronounce kōrtizǎ'n.
courtier. Pronounce kōr-.
coûte que coûte. See FRENCH WORDS.
Coventry. The OED prefers kŏ- to kŭ-.
coverlet, -lid. Both forms are old ; the first is better, the ending almost certainly representing French *lit* bed, & not English *lid*.

covert, n. The *-t* is now so seldom sounded, & is so often omitted even in writing, that what distinction remains between *covert* & *cover* may be said to be valueless. The only sense in which *covert*, otherwise a NEEDLESS VARIANT, is worth preserving is the ornithological one (*wing-coverts* &c.), in which the *-t* is invariable.

covetous is often, even when read in church, mispronounced -chus on the supposed analogy of *righteous*, & sometimes mis-spelt *-teous*.

coward(ly). The identification of coward & bully has gone so far in the popular consciousness that persons & acts in which no trace of fear is to be found are often called *coward(ly)* merely because advantage has been taken of superior strength or position ; such action may be unchivalrous, unsportsmanlike, mean, tyrannical, & many other bad things, but not cowardly ; cf. the similar misuse of DASTARDLY.

cowl-like. For the hyphen see -LIKE.
cowrie, -y. Spell *-ie*.
cowslip. The true division is cow & slip, not cow's & lip ; & the usual pronunciation with s, not z, is accordingly right.

coxcomb, cocks-. See COCKSCOMB.
coxswain. Pronounce kŏ'ksn.

coxy. See COCKY.
coyote. Pronounce koyō'tǐ.
coze, cozy. See COSE.
crabbed. See -ER & -EST, 4.
cramp, as an adjective meaning crabbed or hard to understand (*c. words, terms, style*), narrow (*a c. corner*), niggling (*writes a c. hand*), has now had its senses divided between *crabbed* & *cramped*, & the use of it is an affectation.

cran(e)age. Spell without *-e-* ; see MUTE E.
cranesbill, crane's-bill. The apostrophe & hyphen are better dispensed with in established words of this type ; cf. COCKSCOMB.

cranium. Pl. *-ia, -ms* ; see -UM.
crape, crêpe. The first is the English word, the second the shop French.
crasis. See TECHNICAL TERMS. Pl. *crases* (krā'sēz).
crayfish, craw-. The first is the British form, the second ' now used chiefly in U.S.' (OED).
crayon. Pronounce krā'on, & not as French.
create. See -ATABLE.
crèche. See FRENCH WORDS.
credence, credit. Apart from the isolated phrase *letter of credence* & the concrete ecclesiastical sense *table* or *shelf, credence* has only one meaning—belief or trustful acceptance ; the use seen in *Two results stand out clearly from this investigation . . . ; neither of these gives any credence to the assertions of Lord Ridley that Protectionist countries had fared better than Great Britain* is a mere blunder ; *give credence to* means believe, simply ; *support* or *credibility* is the word wanted. *Credit*, on the other hand, is rich in meanings, & it is a pity that it should be allowed to deprive *credence* of its ewe-lamb ; *credence* would be better in *Charges like these may seem to deserve some degree of credit*, & in *To give entire credit to whatever he shall state*. Even *give credit (to)* has senses of its own (*I give him credit for knowing better than that* ; *No credit given on small orders*), which are all the better

for not being confused with the only sense of *give credence to* (*One can give no credence to his word*).

credo. Pl. *-os* ; see -O(E)S 6.
creese, crease, kris, Malay dagger. The first spelling is recommended as neither too outlandish (& see DIDACTICISM) nor liable to confusion.

cremate. See -ATABLE.
cremona. See CROMORNE.
crenel(le), crenellated. Spell *crenel* & pronounce krĕ'nl. **Crenellated** has -ll- ; see -LL-, -L-.
creole. See MULATTO 3.
crêpe, crépon. See FRENCH WORDS.
crescendo. Pronounce krĕsh-. Pl. *-os*, see -O(E)S 3.
cretic. See TECHNICAL TERMS.
cretin. Pronounce krĕ'tǐn.
crétonne. Pronounce krĕ'tŏn.
crick, rick, wrick, whether identical in origin or not, are so in sense ; the third spelling is recommended ; cf. *wrinkle & crinkle, wrack & rack*.

cringe makes *-ging* ; see MUTE E.
crisis. Pl. *crises* (krī'sēz).
criterion. Pl. *-ia* ; see -ON 1. For synonymy see SIGN.
critique is in less common use than it was, &, with *review, criticism, & notice*, ready at need, there is some hope of its dying out.

crochet, croquet, make *-eting, -eted*, pronounced krō'shǐng, krō'klǐng, krō'shǐd, krō'kǐd.
Croesus. Spell so ; see Æ, Œ.
cromorne, krummhorn, cremona. Either the first or the second should be used, the second being the original (German), the first the French pronunciation of the second, & the third a misleading confusion with *Cremona* (*violin* &c.).

crooked. See -ER & -EST, 2. A stick that is not straight is a krŏō'kǐd stick ; one provided with a crook is a krŏōkt stick.

croquet. For *-ed, -ing*, see CROCHET.
crosier, -zier. The OED prefers -s-.
croup(e). The throat trouble is always *croup*. The rump varies, but

the *-e*, due to the French original, might well be insisted on.

croupier. Pronounce krōō′pĭer.

crow. The past is now usually crowed (*They crowed over us*; *The baby crowed loudly*; *Three cocks crowed*, or *crew, at the same moment*); *crew* is used always in *the cock crew* when there is reference to the N.T. passage, & alternatively with *crowed* when *cock* is the subject in other connexions.

crown. *The C.* is often used as a phrase for the king or queen regarded not as a person, but as a part of the constitution. It does not follow that pronouns appropriate to *king* can be used after it, as in these absurdities :—*The incontestable fact that the C. nowadays acts, & can only act, on the advice of* his *Ministers.*/*The people of this country are little likely to wish to substitute for this* [rule by Cabinet] *rule by the C., for whom the experiment would be most fraught with peril.*

crucify. For inflexions see Verbs in -ie &c., 6.

cruel makes *-ller, -llest.*

crumby, -my. Where the reference is to actual crumb(s), as in *a c. loaf* or *tablecloth*, use *-by*; in the secondary senses *fat, comfortable, rich*, &c., use *-my.* The right spelling for noun & adjective would be *crum(my)*, *b* being due to false Analogy merely; but, failing a general reform of spelling, usage is fixed.

cruse, jar. The OED prefers krōōs to krōōz.

cryptic. For this as compared with *mysterious, obscure, hidden,* & other synonyms, see Working & stylish words.

crystalline. In ordinary use, pronounce krĭ′stalĭn, see Recessive accent; but in poetic & rhetorical use krĭstă′lĭn is common, cf. *wĭnd.*

cubic(al). *Cubic* is the form in all senses except that of shaped like a cube. So *-ic measure, contents, foot, equation*; but *a -ical box* or

stone. *Cubic*, however, is used of minerals crystallizing in cubes, as *-ic alum, saltpetre.* See -ic(al).

cuckold. Pronounce kŭ′kld.

cudgel makes *-lled, -lling*; see -ll-, -l-.

cue, queue. Both are pronounced kū. In billiards, & in the theatrical use (with the transferred applications, as in *take* one's *c. from*), *cue* is invariable. In the sense *string of people &c. waiting their turn*, *queue* is invariable. In the sense *pigtail*, *queue*, which is usual, is recommended.

cui bono ? As generally used, i.e. as a pretentious substitute for *To what end ?* or *What is the good ?*, the phrase is at once a Battered ornament & a blunder. The words mean *To whom was it for a good ?*, i.e. *Who profited by it* or *had something to make out of it ?*, i.e. *If you want to know who brought it about ask yourself whose interest it was that it should happen.* Those who do not want it in this sense should leave it alone. The following is an amusing attempt to press the correct translation of the Latin into the service of the ordinary pointless use :—*We have had repeated occasion of late to press the question ' Cui bono ? ' in relation to the proposal to force the Government to a creation of peers. We must ask it again, in reference to the scandal of yesterday. What is the good of it ? Who stands to gain ?* See Misapprehensions.

cuirass(ier). Pronounce kwĭră′s, kwĭrasēr′ or kūrasēr′.

cuisine, cul-de-sac. See French words.

culinary. Pronounce kū′lĭnarĭ. The word is a favourite with the Polysyllabic-humourist, who often pronounces it kŭl-.

cullender. See colander.

cult, as now used, dates only from the middle of last century; its proper place is in books on archaeology, comparative religion, & the like; that it should be ousting *worship* in general use is regrettable ; see ANTI-SAXONISM.

cultivate makes *-vable* ; see -ABLE 1.

culture. For the effect on the word of the German *Kultur*, cf. FRIGHTFULNESS.

cum(m)in. The OED prefers *cumin* ; but, besides the service done by the second *m* in keeping the pronunciation of a not very common word steady, the spelling of *Matt.* xxiii. 23 (*cummin* in AV & RV) is sure to prevail in a word chiefly used with reference to that passage.

cumulative. See ACCUMULATIVE.

cumulus. Pl. *-lī* ; see -US.

cuneiform. The slovenly pronunciation kū'nĭform, not uncommon, should be avoided, & to this end kūnē'ĭform is preferable to the more difficult kū'nĭiform ; cf. CONTUMELY.

cunning. See -ER & -EST, 4.

cup. For ' cups that cheer ' see HACKNEYED PHRASES.

cupola. Pronounce kū'pŏla.

curaçao, -çoa. Spell *-çao* ; pronounce kūr'asō.

curare, -ra, wourali. Spell *curare*, & pronounce kūrar'ĭ.

curate. For ' the curate's egg ' see HACKNEYED PHRASES, & WORN-OUT HUMOUR.

curator. Pronounce kūrā'tor except in the Scotch-law use (ward's guardian), in which it is kūr'ator.

curb, kerb. The second is a variant merely, but is now much commoner than *curb* in the sense *footpath-edging*, & seems likely to prevail in the closely allied senses *fender*, *border*, *base*, *framework*, *mould*. For the bit-chain, & in the sense *check* n. or v., *curb* is invariable.

curé. See FRENCH WORDS.

curio. Pl. *-os*, see -O(E)S 4, 5. It is a CURTAILED WORD.

curriculum. Pl. *-la* ; see -UM.

currish. See PRONUNCIATION s.f.

curse. For ' curses not loud but deep ' see HACKNEYED PHRASES.

cursed, curst. The adjective *cursed*

is disyllabic except sometimes in verse ; the form *curst* is chiefly used either to show that the rare monosyllabic pronunciation is meant (esp. in verse), or to differentiate the archaic sense *ill-tempered*. See -ER & -EST, 4.

cursedly. Three syllables ; see -EDLY.

cursive. See TECHNICAL TERMS.

CURTAILED WORDS. Some of these establish themselves so fully as to take the place of their originals or to make them seem pedantic ; others remain slangy or adapted only to particular audiences. A small proportion of them, including specimens of various dates & status, has here been collected as possibly useful to those who have, or wish to have, views on the legitimacy of curtailment : *aero*(plane) ; *bike* (bicycle) ; *brig*(antine) ; (omni)*bus* ; *cab*(riolet) ; *cad*(et) ; *cent*(um) ; *chromo*(lithograph) ; *cinema*(tograph) ; *cons* (contras) ; (ra)*coon* ; *consols* (consolidated funds) ; *coster*(monger) ; *cover*(point) ; *cox*(swain) ; *curio*(sity) ; *cycle* (tricycle or bicycle) ; *dynamo*(-electric machine) ; (in)*flu*(enza) ; *gym*(nasium) ; *magneto* (-electric machine) ; *mob*(ile vulgus) ; *mods* (moderations) ; *pants* (pantaloons) ; *par*(agraph) ; *phiz* (physiognomy) ; (tele)*phone* ; *photo*(graph) ; *pi*(ous) ; *pop*(ular concert) ; *pram* (perambulator) ; *prep*(aration) ; *pro*(fessional) ; *props* (properties) ; *pub*(lic house) ; *quad*(rangle) ; *quotes* (quotation marks) ; *radio*(activity) ; *rep*(robate) ; *rep*(etition) ; *rhino*(ceros) ; *spats* (spatterdashes) ; *spec*(ulation) ; *specs* (spectacles) ; *stereo*(type) ; *Strad*(ivarius) ; *stylo*(graph) ; *sub*(altern) ; *sub*(stitute) ; *super*(ior) ; *super*(numerary) ; *tan*(gent) ; (de)*tec*(tive) ; *turps* (turpentine) ; *vert* (convert or pervert) ; *vet*(erinary) ; *vice*(-chairman) ; *vice*(-chancellor) ; *vice*(-president) ; *viva* (voce) ; *Zoo*(logical gardens).

curtain-raiser. See GALLICISMS.

curts(e)y, courtesy. *Courtesy* is

archaic & affected for *curtsy*; *curtsy* n. & v. (*curtsied*, *curtsying*) is better than *curtsey*, which involves *curt-seyed*; see VERBS IN -IE &c., 2, 6.

curule. Pronounce kūr′ōōl.

curvet. Pronounce kervĕ′t in noun & verb, & spell the verb parts *-tted*, *-tting*, see -T-, -TT-.

cushat. Pronounce kŭ′shat.

customs. For synonymy see TAX.

cuticle. See PEDANTIC HUMOUR.

cutlet. See CHOP.

cycle. For the noun & verb as an abbreviation for 'bicycle or tri-cycle', see CURTAILED WORDS. For *c.* as a time-word, see TIME.

cyclone. See WIND, n.

cyclopaedia, -dic. For *-pae-*, *-pæ-*, *-pe-*, see Æ, Œ. The longer forms *encyclo-* are in themselves better, & *encyclopaedia*, being common in titles, is also the prevalent form; but *cyclopaedic* is becoming the more usual form for the adjective; cf. *accumulate* & *cumulative*.

cyclopean, -pian. The first (sĭklo-pē′an) is more usual than the second (sĭklō′pĭan); but neither is wrong.

cyclop(s). The forms recommended are: for the singular *cyclops*; & for the plural the classical *cyclopes* (sĭklō′pēz) except in jocular or familiar use, for which the English formation *cyclopses* is suitable. The sing. *cyclop* with pl. *cyclops* results in confusion.

cymbalo. Pl. *-os*; see -O(E)S 6.

cymbocephalic, -ous. See -CE-PHALIC.

Cymric. Pronounce kĭ-.

cynic(al). As an adjective, *cynic* is used only in the sense *of the ancient philosophers called Cynics* (except in the technical terms *cynic year*, *cynic spasm*), & the word that describes temperament &c. is *cynical*; see -IC(AL).

cypher. See CIPHER.

Czar. See TSAR.

Czarewitch. See CESAREWITCH.

Czech, -ck. Spell *Czech*, & pro-nounce chĕk.

D

dactyl. See TECHNICAL TERMS.

dado. Pl. *-oes*; see -O(E)S 1.

daedal, dæ-. See Æ, Œ.

daemon, dæ- Write *dae-*; see Æ, Œ. This spelling, instead of *demon*, is used to distinguish the Greek-mythology senses of supernatural being, indwelling spirit, &c., from the modern sense of devil.

daguerreotype. The OED pro-nounces -gĕro-.

dahlia. Pronounce dā′lya.

dais. Pronounce dās; 'always a monosyllable in Fr., & in Eng. where retained as a living word; the disyllabic pronunciation is a "shot" at the word from the spelling'— OED.

damnable. See -ER & -EST, 4.

damning, in the sense *cursing*, is pronounced without the *n*; in the sense *fatally conclusive* it usually has the *n* sounded.

damp(en). See -EN VERBS.

damsel. See ARCHAISM.

danceress. See FEMININE DE-SIGNATIONS.

dandiacal, dandyfied. The amuse-ment provided by incorrect forma-tions like *dandiacal* (as though there were a *dandiac* corresponding to *maniac* &c.) is evanescent, & the words should be allowed to vanish with it, especially when an alterna-tive word exists, as here. For spelling of *dandyfied* see -FIED.

dandruff, -iff. The OED places the -*uff* form first.

dare. 1. *Dare* & *dares*. 2. *Durst*. 3. *Dare say*. 1. *Dare* as 3rd pers. sing. pres. indic. is the idiomatic form instead of *dares* when the infinitive depending on it either has no *to* or is understood; this occurs chiefly, but not only, in interroga-tive & negative sentences. Thus *dares*, though sometimes used in mistaken striving after correctness, would be contrary to idiom in *Dare he do it?*; *He dare not!—Yes, he* *dare*; *He dare do anything*; *No-one dare oppose him.*

2. *Durst*, which is a past indicative & past subjunctive beside *dared*, is obsolescent, & nowhere now required, like *dare* above, by idiom; the contexts in which it is still sometimes preferred to *dared* are negative sentences & conditional clauses where there is an infinitive either understood or having no *to* (*But none durst*, or *dared to*, or *dared*, *answer him*; *I would do it if I durst*, or *dared*).

3. *Dare say* as a specialized phrase with the weakened sense incline to think, not deny, admit as likely (cf. the unweakened sense in *I dare say what I think*, *Who dare say it?*, *He dared to say he*, or *that he*, *would not do it*) has certain peculiarities : (*a*) even when not parenthetic (*You*, *I d. s., think otherwise*), it is never followed by the conjunction *that* (*I d. s. it*, not *that it, is a mere lie*); (*b*) it is never *dare to say* in direct speech, & the *to* is rare & better avoided in indirect speech also (*He dared say the difficulty would disappear*; *I told him I dared say he would change his mind*; *He dares say it does not matter*); (*c*) to avoid ambiguity, it is sometimes written as one word (*I dare say she is innocent*, I am sure of it; *I daresay she is innocent*, I can believe it); but this device is useless as long as it is not universally accepted, & it cannot be applied to the indirect *dares* & *dared*; it is simpler to avoid *I dare say* in the unspecialized sense wherever it can be ambiguous.

dark(e)y. See -EY, -IE, -Y.

darkle. Being a recent formation (19th cent.) based on a mistake (see foll.), & not having, like the analogous *grovel*, won any real currency, the verb has little to recommend it, & should be let die; its only use is ornamental, & as an ornament it is pinchbeck. See BACK-FORMATION.

darkling is an adverb formed with the now forgotten adverbial termination *-ling*, & means in the dark (*Our lamps go out & leave us d.*; *The wakeful bird sings d.*); by a natural extension it is also used as an attributive adjective (*Like d. nightingales they sit*; *They hurried on their d. journey*). But having nothing to do with the participial *-ing* it does not mean growing dark &c.; from the mistaken notion that it is a participle spring both the misuses of the word itself & the spurious verb DARKLE.

darling. See -ER & -EST, 4.

dartle is too new to deserve respect, & too old, being still rare, to have prospects; it should be let die.

DASH. For double dashes as a form of parenthesis, see STOPS.

dashing. See -ER & -EST, 4.

dastard(ly). The essential & original meaning of the words is the same as that of *coward(ly)*, so far at least that both pairs properly connote want of courage; but so strong is the false belief that every bully must be a coward that acts requiring great courage are constantly described as cowardly or dastardly if they are so carried out as not to give the victim a sporting chance; the throwing of a bomb at a king's carriage is much less dastardly than shooting a partridge, because the thrower takes a very real risk; but even when he recklessly exposes himself to being torn to pieces, the absurd headline 'Dastardly Outrage' is inevitable. The true meaning is seen in 'A laggard in love & a dastard in war'. The words should at least be reserved for those who do avoid all personal risk.

data is plural only (*The d. are*, not *is, insufficient.*/*What are the d.?*/*We have no d.*); the singular, comparatively rare, is *datum*; *one of the data* is commoner than *a datum*; but *datum-line*, line taken as a basis, is common. *My Intelligence Department has furnished me with so much valuable data* illustrates the mistake of taking the plural for a singular.

date. For *d.*, *epoch*, &c., see TIME.

dat(e)able. Spell *-ta-*; see MUTE E.

datival(ly), dative(ly). See ABLA-TIVE.

daughter. For *d. of joy* see GAL-LICISMS.

daughter-in-law formerly included *step-daughter*; now, *my d.-in-law* has become my daughter by her marriage, & *my step-d.* has done so by my marriage, & the two are confused only in ignorance.

davits. The OED prefers dă- to dā-.

-D-, -DD-. Monosyllables ending in d double it before suffixes beginning with vowels if the sound preceding it is a single vowel (a, e, i, o, u, or y), but not if it is a diphthong or a doubled vowel or a vowel & r : *caddish, redden, bidding, trodden, tubby*; but *deaden, breeder, goodish, plaided, lardy*. Words of more than one syllable follow the rule for monosyllables if their last syllable is accented or is itself a word in combination (*forbidding, bedridden*), but otherwise do not double the d (*nomadic, nakedest, rigidity, periodical*).

dead letter, apart from its theological & post-office uses, is a phrase for a regulation that has still a nominal existence, but is no longer observed or enforced; the application of it to what was never a regulation but has gone or is going out of use, as quill pens, horse-traction, amateur football, &c., or to a regulation that loses its force only by actual abolition (*the one-sex franchise will soon be a d. l.*), is a SLIPSHOD EXTENSION.

deal, n. 1. The use of *a d.* instead of *a great* or *good d.*, though as old as Richardson & Johnson (the Shaksperian *what a deal!* can hardly be adduced), has still only the status of a colloquialism, & should be avoided in writing even when the phrase stands as a noun (*saved him a d. of trouble*), & still more when it is adverbial (*this was a d. better*). 2. *A d.* in the sense of a piece of bargaining or give-&-take is still slang.

dean, doyen. The FRENCH WORD *doyen*, a bad stumbling-block to the mere English-speaker, & the unfamiliar GALLICISM *dean*, are equally objectionable; as there is nothing complicated about the idea to be expressed, *senior*, with the assistance if necessary of whatever noun may be appropriate, should be made to do the work.

dearie, -y. See -EY, -IE, -Y.

dear(ly), advv. With the verb *love*, *dearly* is now the regular form, & *dear* merely poetic; but with *buy, sell, pay, cost,* &c., *dear* is still idiomatic, & the tendency born of mistaken grammatical zeal to attach an UNIDIOMATIC -LY should be resisted.

dearth. *I think it of interest to point out* what a singular d. of information exists *on several important points*; for this favourite journalistic device see PERIPHRASIS; read *how little we know*.

débâcle. See FRENCH WORDS.

debark(ation) are NEEDLESS VARIANTS for the better established *disemb-*.

debat(e)able. Spell *-ta-*; see MUTE E.

debauchee. Pronounce dĕboshē'.

debouch(ment). Pronounce dĭboōsh-.

debris, dé-. Write without accent, & pronounce dĕ'brē.

début, débutant(e). *Début* can only be pronounced as French, & should not be used by any one who shrinks from the necessary effort. There is no reason why *debutant* should not be written without accent, pronounced dĕ'būtant, & treated like *applicant* &c. as of common gender. See FRENCH WORDS.

deca-, deci-. In the metric system, *deca-* means multiplied, & *deci-* divided, by ten; *decametre*, 10 m., *decimetre*, $\frac{1}{10}$ m.; so with *gramme, litre,* &c.

decad(e). The *-e* is now usual. Pronounce dĕ'kad.

decapitate makes *decapitable*; see -ABLE 1.

decent makes *-er, -est* ; see -ER & -EST.

decided, decisive. *Decisive* is often used loosely where *decided* is the right word, just as DEFINITIVE is a common blunder for *definite*, & *distinctive* an occasional one for *distinct*. A *decided* victory or superiority is one the reality of which is unquestionable ; a *decisive* one is one that decides or goes far towards deciding some issue ; a *decided* person is one who knows his own mind, & a *decided* manner that which comes of such knowledge ; a *decisive* person, so far as the phrase is correctly possible at all, is one who has a way of getting his policy or purpose carried through. The two meanings are quite separate ; but, as the *decided* tends to be *decisive* also, it gets called so even when decisiveness is irrelevant. Examples of the wrong use are :— *The serjeant, a decisive man, ordered . . ./A decisive leaning towards what is most simple./It was not an age of decisive thought./Poe is decisively the first of American poets.* The following suggests a further confusion with *incisive* :—*The* Neue Freie Presse *makes some very decisive remarks about the Italian operations at Preveza.*

decimate means originally to kill every tenth man among as a punishment for cowardice or mutiny. Its application is naturally extended to the destruction in any way of a large proportion of anything reckoned by number, e.g. a population is decimated by the plague ; but naturally also anything that is directly inconsistent with the proper sense (*A single frosty night decimated the currants by as much as 80 %*) must be avoided. See SLIPSHOD EXTENSION.

decimo sexto. See FOLIO. Pl. *-os* ; see -O(E)S 6.

declarant, declaredly, declarative, declaratory. Pronounce -ā̆rant, -ā̆rĕdlĭ, -ă̆ratĭv, -ă̆ratorĭ ; for the second see -EDLY.

déclassé. See FRENCH WORDS.

declension (gram.). See TECHNICAL TERMS.

declinal, declination, declinature, in the sense *courteous refusal* (*The declinals were grounded upon reasons neither unkind nor uncomplimentary./ Yuan persists in his declination of the Premiership./The reported declinature of office by the Marquis of Salisbury*), are three unsatisfactory attempts to provide *decline* with a noun. It is better to be content with *refusal*, modified, if really necessary, by an adjective. See -AL NOUNS, & PRESUMPTUOUS WORD-FORMATION.

declin(e)able. Omit the *-e-* ; see MUTE E.

décolleté(e). See FRENCH WORDS.

decolo(u)rize &c. See HYBRID DERIVATIVES.

decorate makes *-rable* ; see -ABLE 1.

decorous. Pronounce dĭkōr′us, not dĕ′korus.

decrease. See NOUN & VERB ACCENT.

decry. For inflexions see VERBS IN -IE &c., 6.

dedicate makes *-cable* ; see -ABLE 1.

deducible, -eable. See -ABLE 2.

deduction. See TECHNICAL TERMS.

deem. See WORKING & STYLISH WORDS.

deep(ly). See UNIDIOMATIC -LY.

deer. See COLLECTIVES 1.

defamatory. Pronounce dĭfă′matorĭ.

defect. For ' the defects of his qualities ' see HACKNEYED PHRASES.

defective, deficient. The differentiation tends to become complete, *defective* being associated more & more exclusively with *defect*, & *deficient* with *deficit*. That is deficient of which there is either not enough or none, that is defective which has something faulty about it ; so *deficient quantity, revenue, warmth, means* ; *defective quality, condition, sight, pronunciation, boots* ; *a defective chimney, valve, manuscript, hat.* With some words quantity & quality come to the same thing ; for instance, *much* or *great insight* is the same as *deep* or *penetrating insight*; consequently a person's insight may be described indifferently as *defective* or *deficient*. Again, deficiency in or of a part constitutes a defect in the whole, & consequently a person may be called either *deficient* or *defective in courage* or *knowledge* or *sympathy*, & milk may be *defective* (though *deficient* is commoner) *in fatty matter*; compare *The dialogue is not defective* (or *deficient*) *in ease & grace* with *Ease & grace are not deficient* (never *defective*) *in the dialogue*; the following wrongly neglects this distinction :—*I wish you had a Fortunatus hat; it is the only thing defective in your outfit*; here *deficient* is required, though there would have been no objection to *It is the only thing in which your outfit is defective*; a verb or noun of which some part is deficient or wanting is called *defective*, where *deficient* would also be possible if the combination had not been stereotyped. Lastly, either word may sometimes be used, but with a difference of meaning from the other; *deficient water* or *light* is too little water or light; but *defective water* is impure &c.; & *defective light* is uncertain &c.; similarly, *a defective supply* in being irregular or unreliable rather than insufficient in the aggregate.

deficit. The pronunciation dĭfĭ'sĭt is wrong; the OED prefers dĕ'fĭsĭt 'to dē'fĭsĭt, which is however perhaps as common; the Latin quantity (see FALSE QUANTITY) is no guide.

defile (pass n. & v.). See NOUN & VERB ACCENT.

defin(e)able. Omit the *-e-*; see MUTE E.

definite, definitive. Confusion between the two, & especially the use of *definitive* for *definite*, is very common; many writers seem to think the words mean the same, but the longer & less usual will be more imposing; & mistakes are made easy by the fact that many nouns can be qualified by either, though

with different effects. Putting aside exceptional senses that have nothing to do with the confusion (as when *definitive* means of the defining kind), *definite* means defined, clear, precise, unmistakable, &c., & *definitive* means having the character of finality; or, to distinguish them by their opposites, that is *definite* which is not dubious, vague, loose, inexact, uncertain, undefined, or questionable; & that is *definitive* which is not temporary, provisional, debatable, or alterable. *A definite offer* is one of which the terms are clear; *a definitive offer* is one that must be taken or left without chaffering; *definite jurisdiction* is that of which the application or the powers are precisely laid down, & *definitive jurisdiction* is that from which there is no appeal; either word can be applied with similar distinctions, to *answer, terms, treaty, renunciation, statement, result*, &c. But with many words to which *definite* is rightly & commonly applied (*a definite pain, accusation, structure, outline, forecast*) *definitive* either is not used except by mistake for *definite*, or gives a meaning rarely required (e.g. *a definitive forecast* means, if anything, one that its maker announces his intention of abiding by). The following examples show wrong uses, mostly of *definitive* :—*We should be glad to see more definitive teaching./The fact that Sunday must be altogether omitted from the day-boy's life, as part of his definitively school career, would alone convince me that . . ./The Bill has not yet been drawn up, & the Government are not responsible for 'forecasts', however definitively they may be written./The definitive qualities of jurisprudence have not often found so agreeable an exponent as the author of these essays./If Turkey desires peace, she must definitely renounce what she has already lost* (here, however, if the sense *explicitly* suffices, & the stronger sense *unreservedly* is not intended, no change is necessary).

deflexion, -ction. See -XION.

defrayal. See -AL NOUNS.

defy. For inflexions see VERBS IN -IE &c., 6.

dégagé. See FRENCH WORDS.

degree. The phrase *to a d.*, however illogical it seems as a substitute for *to the last degree*, is at least as old as *The Rivals* (*Your father, sir, is wrath to a d.*), & objection to it is futile.

de haut en bas. See FRENCH WORDS.

deify. For inflexions see VERBS IN -IE &c., 6.

deism, theism. Though the original meaning is the same, the words have been so far differentiated that *deism* is understood to exclude, & *theism* (though less decidedly) to include, belief in supernatural revelation, in providence, & in the maintenance of a personal relation between Creator & creature.

déjeuner. See FRENCH WORDS.

delectable. In ordinary use (except in *d. lozenges*, which are meant to be recommended by their name) the word is now ironical only ; i.e., it is to be taken always, as *precious* is sometimes, to mean the opposite of what it says ; in poetry, sometimes in fanciful prose, & in *the d. mountains*, it retains its original sense ; so in *Of all the fleeting visions which I have stored up in my mind I shall always remember the view across the plain as one of the most d.*

delegate, v., makes *-gable* ; see -ABLE 1.

deliberative. For the sense in grammar, see TECHNICAL TERMS. The sense *not hasty in decision or inference*, which was formerly among those belonging to the word, has been assigned to *deliberate* by modern differentiation ; the use of *d.* in that sense now (*All three volumes are marked by a cautious & d. tone, that commends them to thoughtful men*) instead of *deliberate* is to be classed with the confusions between AL-TERNATIVE, DEFINITIVE, & *alternate, definite.*

delightful. See -ER & -EST, 4.

delightsome. See POETICISMS, & -SOME.

delineate makes *-neable* ; see -ABLE 1.

delude &c. For pronunciation see LU.

delusion, illusion. It cannot be said that the words are never interchangeable ; it is significant of their nearness in meaning that *illusion* has no verb corresponding to *delude* (*illude* having died out), & *delusion* has none corresponding to *disillusion* (*undeceive* & *disillusion* being used according as the delusion has been due to others' machinations or to the victim's own error). Nevertheless, in any given context one is usually better than the other ; two distinctions are here offered :—

1. *A d.* is a belief that, though false, has been surrendered to & accepted by the whole mind as the truth, & may be expected to influence action ; *d.* is being possessed by *a d. An i.* is an impression that, though false, is entertained provisionally on the recommendation of the senses or the imagination, but awaits full acceptance & may be expected not to influence action ; *i.* is the entertaining of *an i.* We labour under dd., but indulge in ii. The dd. of lunacy, the ii. of childhood or of enthusiasm. A dangerous d., a pleasant i. Delusive hopes result in misguided action, illusive hopes merely in disappointment. That the sun moves round the earth was once a d., & is still an i. The theatre spectator, the looker at a picture or a mirror, experience i. ; if they lose consciousness of the actual facts entirely, the i. is complete ; if the spectator throws his stick at the villain, or the dog flies at his image, i. has passed into d.

2. The existing thing that deludes is a d. ; the thing falsely supposed to exist, or the sum of the qualities with which an existing thing is falsely invested, is an i. Optimism (if unjustified) is a d. ; Heaven is (if non-existent) an i. If a bachelor

dreams that he is married, his marriage is an i. ; if he marries in the belief that marriage must bring happiness, he may find that marriage is a d. A mirage, or the taking of it for a lake, is a d. ; the lake is an i. What a conjuror actually does—his real action—is a d. ; what he seems to do is an i. ; the belief that he does what he seems to do is a d. The world as I conceive it may for all I know be an i. ; &, if so, the world as it exists is a d.

demagogic &c. For pronunciation see GREEK G.

demean. There are two verbs. One, which is always reflexive, means to conduct oneself or behave, & is connected with *demeanour* & derived from old French *demener* (*He demeans himself like a king*). The other, which is usually but not always reflexive (*I would not d. myself to speak to him* ; *A chair which it would not d. his dignity to fill*), means to lower or debase. This seems to be the product of a confusion between the first verb & the adjective *mean*, &, though it is occasionally found as a normal word in good authors, it is commonest on the lips of the uneducated or in imitations of them, & is best avoided except in such contexts.

démenti. See FRENCH WORDS.

demesne. 1. ' The prevailing pronunciation in the dictionaries & in the modern poets is dĭmē'n, but dĭmā'n is also in good legal & general use, & is historically preferable.'—OED.
2. *Demesne, domain.* The two words are by origin the same, but in technical use there are several distinctions between them that cannot be set forth here. In the wide general sense of *sphere, region, province*, the established form is *domain*, & the use of *demesne* is due to NOVELTY-HUNTING.

demi-monde, demi-mondaine. See FRENCH WORDS.

demise, not *-ize* ; see -ISE)(-IZE.

demonetize. For -mŏn- or -mŭn- see PRONUNCIATION.

demoniac(al). The adjectives are not clearly differentiated ; but there is a tendency to regard *-acal* as the adjective of *demon*, so that it is the form chosen when wickedness is implied, & *-ac* as the adjective of the noun *demoniac*, so that it is chosen to convey the notion of the intensity of action produced by possession (*demoniacal cruelty, demoniac energy*). Pron. -ō'nĭăk, -ī'akl.

de'monstrate, de'monstrator, demo'nstrable, demo'nstrative. 1. The accents are those shown. 2. For *demonstrable* see -ABLE 1.

demur. In pronunciation the nouns are always *demŭ'rrer, demŭ'r-rage*, but the participle is either *demur'ring* or *demŭ'rring* ; see PRONUNCIATION s.f.

dengue. Pronounce dĕ'nggā.

denier. Pronounce dĭnēr'.

Denmark. For ' something rotten in the state of D.' see IRRELEVANT ALLUSION.

denote. See CONNOTE.

dénouement. See FRENCH WORDS, & TECHNICAL TERMS.

de nouveau. See FRENCH WORDS.

dental. For the phonetic sense, see TECHNICAL TERMS.

dentifrice is a shop word, occasionally heard also as a GENTEELISM.

denunciation. Pronounce -sĭa-, & see -CIATION.

deny. For inflexions see VERBS IN -IE &c., 6.

departed. For *the d., the dear d.,* &c., see STOCK PATHOS.

department. For synonymy see FIELD.

depend. The slovenly construction illustrated below, in which *it depends* is followed by an indirect question without *upon*, is growing common, but is indefensible :—' *Critics ought to be artists who have failed* '. *Ought they ?* *It all* depends who *is going to read the criticism, & what he expects to learn from it.*

dependable. For such formations

(that can be depended *upon*), see -ABLE 4.

dependant, -ent. The noun has *-ant*, rarely *-ent*; the adj. *-ent*, rarely *-ant*.

dependence, -ency. The first is now usual, though not invariable, in all the abstract senses (*a life of -ce*; *no -ce can be put upon his word*; *the -ce of the harvest on weather*; *the gospel is our -ce*; *during the -ce of the negotiations*), & *-cy* is almost confined to the concrete sense of a thing that depends upon or is subordinate to another, esp. a dependent territory (*the cotton trade & its -cies*; *India is a British -cy*). See -CE, -CY.

depicture, though in fact an old verb, has never established itself in general currency, & perhaps always sets a reader wondering whether it is a blunder due to hesitation between *depict* & *picture*; it might well be abandoned as a NEEDLESS VARIANT.

deponent (in grammar). See TECHNICAL TERMS.

depopulate makes *-lable*; see -ABLE 1.

depositary, -tory, are properly applied, *-tary* to the person or authority to whom something is entrusted, & *-tory* to the place or receptacle in which something is stored; & the distinction is worth preserving, though in some contexts (*a diary as the d. of one's secrets*; *the Church as the d. of moral principles*) either may be used indifferently.

depot. Write without accents or italics, & pronounce dĕ′pō.

deprecate (do the reverse of *pray for*) & its derivatives *-cation, -catory*, often appear in print, whether by the writer's or the compositor's blunder, in place of *depreciate* (do the reverse of *praise*) & its derivatives *-ciation, -ciatory*:—*Mr Birrell's amusing deprecation of the capacity of Mr Ginnell to produce a social revolution in Ireland.*/*The self-deprecatory mood in which the English people find themselves.*

deprecate, depreciate, make *-cable, -ciable*; see -ABLE 1.

depreciation. Pronounce -ēsǐ- ; see -CIATION.

depressedly. Four syllables ; see -EDLY.

deprival. See -AL NOUNS.

deprivation. Pronounce either dēprǐ- or dĕprǐ-, not dĕprī- nor dēprī-.

Derby(shire). Pronounce dar-.

de règle, de rigueur. See FRENCH WORDS.

derisory. The OED definitions (dated 1894) make no distinction between this & *derisive*, being almost in the same words for both. About the meaning of *derisive* (conveying derision, deriding) there is no doubt ; & if *derisory* means precisely the same it may well be regarded as a NEEDLESS VARIANT, so clearly is *derisive* now in possession. But, by the sort of differentiation seen in MASTERFUL & *masterly*, a distinct sense has lately been given to *derisory*, & is now common in the newspapers ; as *derisive* means conveying derision, so *derisory* means inviting or worthy only of derision, too insignificant or futile for serious consideration ; it is applied to offers, plans, suggestions, &c. As Larousse illustrates the use of *dérisoire* by ' proposition dérisoire ', the new sense may be a Gallicism, but it would be a natural enough development in English, the word being no longer needed in the sense now nearly monopolized by *derisive*, even without French influence. If the differentiation is to be satisfactory, *derisory* should, like *masterful*, be no longer recognized in its former sense. See also RISIBLE. The following quotation gives the passive meaning unambiguously : *They will not cover the absence of those supplies from the Ukraine & Roumania which were promised to the people & have only been forthcoming in derisory quantities.*

deriv(e)able. Omit the *-e-* ; see MUTE E.

dernier ressort. See FRENCH WORDS.

derring-do. This curious word, now established as an archaic noun meaning desperate courage, is traced to a misinterpreted passage of Chaucer, in which Troilus is described as second to none ' In dorryng don that longeth to a knyght ', *i.e.* ' in daring (to) do what belongs to a knight '. Spenser, a lover of old phrases, apparently taking it for a noun, as if the line meant ' in bold achievement, which is a knightly duty ', made *derring doe* in this sense a part of his regular vocabulary. The derivation is a surprise ; but, if Spenser did make a mistake, it does not follow that modern poetical writers should abstain from saying ' deeds of derring-do ' ; the phrase is part & parcel of an English that is suited to some occasions.

derringer. Pronounce -j*er*.

descant. Pronounce the noun dě'-skant, & the verb dĭskă'nt ; see NOUN & VERB ACCENT.

descendable, -ible. Use the first ; see -ABLE 2.

describ(e)able. Omit the *-e-* ; see MUTE E.

describeless. See -LESS.

description. The less this is used as a mere substitute for *kind* or *sort* (*no food of any d.* ; *crimes of this d.* ; *every d. of head-covering*), the better ; see WORKING & STYLISH WORDS.

descry. For inflexions see VERBS IN -IE &c., 6.

desecrate makes -*crable*; see -ABLE 1.

deservedly. Four syllables ; see -EDLY.

déshabillé. See *dishabille* (the anglicized form), & FRENCH WORDS.

desiccate. See -ATABLE.

desiderate is a word that we should be better without. Readers, outside the small class that keeps up its Latin, do not know the meaning of it, taking it for the scholar's pedantic or facetious form of *desire*. Writers are often in the same case (see the sentence quoted below ; we do not d. what we cannot be prevented from preserving), &, if they are not,

are ill-advised in using the word unless they are writing for readers as learned as themselves :—*In this she acts prudently, probably feeling that there is nothing in the Bill that could prevent her, & those like-minded, acting as benevolently towards their servants as before, & so preserving the ' sense of family unity ' she so much desiderates.*

desiderative. See TECHNICAL TERMS.

desideratum. Pl. -*ta* ; see -UM. Pron. dĭsĭderā'tm.

designate, vb. See -ATABLE.

designedly. Four syllables ; see -EDLY.

desist(ance). The OED pronounces -zĭ-, not -sĭ-, & prefers -*ance* to -*ence*.

desolate, vb, makes -*lable* ; see -ABLE 1.

desolated, as polite exaggeration for *very sorry* &c., is a GALLICISM.

despatch. See DISPATCH.

desperado. Pronounce -ādō. Pl. -*oes*, see -O(E)S 1.

desperation never now means, as formerly, mere despair or abandonment or loss of hope, but always the reckless readiness to take the first course that presents itself because every course seems hopeless.

despicable. Pronounce dě'spĭkabl, not dĭspĭ'kabl ; see RECESSIVE ACCENT.

despise, not -*ize* ; see -ISE)(-IZE.

destine. (*Who was*) *destined to be* &c., when it means no more than *who has since become* or *afterwards became*, is a BATTERED ORNAMENT.

detachedly. A bad form ; see -EDLY.

detail. Pronounce the noun dē'tāl, the verb dĭtā'l ; see NOUN & VERB ACCENT.

détente. See FRENCH WORDS.

deter. Pronounce the participle dĭter'ing, but the adj. dĭtě'rent ; see PRONUNCIATION s.f.

determinately, determinedly. The sense *with determination, in a resolute way*, does not belong to the first at all, though some writers use it (*Thurlow applied himself -ately to the business of life*) as an escape from the second. A better escape is to use *resolutely, firmly, with determination,* or some other substitute. The objection to *determinedly,* which is very general, is perhaps based on reluctance to give it the five syllables that are nevertheless felt to be its due (see -EDLY). An example or two will illustrate the ugliness of the word :—*In causes in which he was heart & soul convinced no-one has fought more -edly & courageously* (with greater determination & courage)./*Cobbett opposed -edly the proposed grant of £16,000./However, I -edly smothered all premonitions./He is -edly opposed to limited enfranchisement.*

detestable. Accent the second syllable.

detestation. The OED gives dē-, not dĕ-.

detour, dé-. Write without accent & italics, & pronounce ditoor'.

de trop. See FRENCH WORDS.

deuteragonist. The pronunciation recommended is dūteragō'nĭst ; see PROTAGONIST.

Deuteronomy. The accentuation dūterŏ'nomĭ is better than dū'teronomĭ, which is impossible for the ordinary speaker ; cf. CONTUMELY.

devastate. See -ATABLE.

device. For synonymy see SIGN.

devil, n. *Devil's advocate* is very dangerous to those who like a picturesque phrase but dislike the trouble of ascertaining its sense. In the following example, for instance, the not unnatural blunder is made of supposing that it means a whitewasher, or one who pleads for a person who either is or is supposed to be wicked :—*Because the d.'s a. always starts with the advantage of possessing a bad case, Talleyrand's defender calls forth all our chivalrous sympathy.* The real *d.'s a.,* on the contrary, is one who, when the right of a person to canonization as a saint is being examined, puts the devil's claim to the ownership of him by collecting & presenting all the sins that he has ever committed ; far from being the

whitewasher of the wicked, the d.'s a. is the blackener of the good. And in this other the writer referred to is in fact devil's advocate in ' the rest of his book ', & something quite different (' God's advocate ', say) in ' an early chapter ' : *He tries in an early chapter to act as ' devil's advocate ' for the Soviet Government, and succeeds in putting up a plausible case for the present* régime. *But the rest of his book is devoted to showing that this Bolshevist case is based on hypocrisy, inaccuracy, and downright lying.* See MISAPPREHENSIONS.

devil, vb, makes *-lled, -lling* ; see -LL-, -L-.

devilish. The adjective has three syllables (*d. cruelty* &c.), but the adverb only two (*a d. fine girl* ; pronounce dĕ'vlĭsh).

devil(t)ry. The *-try* form is a mere corruption.

devise, not *-ize* ; see -ISE)(-IZE.

deviser, -sor. *Devisor* is the person who devises property, & is in legal use only ; *-er* is the agent-noun of *devise* in other senses ; see OR.

devolute, though an old verb in fact, has been dormant for three centuries, & is to be regarded rather as a BACK-FORMATION from *devolution* than as a REVIVAL ; it is unnecessary by the side of *devolve,* which should have been used in (with *on* for *to*) :—*The House will devise means of devoluting some of its work to more leisured bodies.*

dexter. See SINISTER.

dext(e)rous. The shorter form is recommended.

d(h)ow is included by the OED among ' words erroneously spelt with dh ' ; *dow* was common down to 1860, & should be restored.

diabolic(al). Roughly, *-ic* means of, & *-ical* as of, the devil :—*Horns, tail, & other -ic attributes* ; *He behaved with -ical cruelty.* See -IC(AL).

diaeresis. Spell *-ae-,* not *-æ-* ; see Æ, Œ. Pl. *-reses* (-sēz).

DIAERESIS. See TECHNICAL TERMS.

The mark, when used, should be placed over the second of the vowels that are to be kept unmixed (aërated). It should not be regarded, however, as a permanent part of any word's spelling, but kept in reserve for occasions on which special need of it is felt ; cf. Æ, Œ, & CO-.

diadem makes *diademed* ; see -M-, -MM-.

diagnosis. Pl. *-oses* (-ōsēz).

diagram makes *diagrammatic* ; see -M-, -MM-.

dialect. For *d.*, *patois*, *vernacular*, &c., see JARGON.

dialectal, -ic, -ical. The natural adjective for *dialect* would be *-ic* or *-ical*, & both forms were formerly used as such, besides serving as adjectives to the noun *dialectic* ; but to avoid confusion *dialectal* has recently been formed & found acceptance, so that we now speak of *dialectic(al) skill*, but *dialectal words* or *forms*.

dialogist. See GREEK G.

dialogue is neither necessarily, nor necessarily not, the talk of two persons ; see TECHNICAL TERMS ; for the want of a word confined to two, see DUOLOGUE.

diapason. Pronounce dīapā´zn.

diarchy, dy-. Spell *di-*. *D.* is to *monarchy* as *dibasic, dicotyledon, digraph, dimeter, dioecious, dioxide, distich,* & *disyllable*, are to *monocotyledon, monoxide, monosyllable,* & the other *mono-* words. *Monologue* & *dialogue* are not a relevant pair, *dialogue* having nothing to do with Gk *di-* two-.

diarrhoea, -œa. See Æ, Œ.

diastole. Pronounce dĭă´stolĭ.

dictate. Accent the noun (usu. pl.) dī´ktāt(s), the verb dĭktā´t ; see NOUN & VERB ACCENT.

dictatress, -trix. The *-ess* form is preferable in such words of the kind as are for ordinary & not merely legal use ; & the OED quotes Byron, Scott, & Helps, for *dictatress*.

dictionary, encyclopaedia, lexicon. A *d.*, properly so called, is concerned merely with words regarded as materials for speech ; an *e.* is concerned with the things for which the words are names. But since some information about the thing is necessary to enable the words to be used rightly, & opinions differ upon the how much of this, most dictionaries contain some matter that is strictly of the cyclopaedic kind ; & in loose use *d.* comes to be applied to any encyclopaedia that is alphabetically arranged. *Lexicon* means the same as *d.*, but is usually kept to the restricted sense, & is moreover rarely used except of Greek, Hebrew, Syriac, or Arabic dd.

dictum. Pl. *-ta* ; see -UM.

DIDACTICISM. ' No mortal but is narrow enough to delight in educating others into counterparts of himself ' ; the statement is from *Wilhelm Meister*. Men, especially, are as much possessed by the didactic impulse as women by the maternal instinct. Some of them work it off *ex officio* upon their children or pupils or parishioners or legislative colleagues, if they are blest with any of these ; others are reduced to seizing casual opportunities, & practise upon their associates in speech or upon the world in print. The Anglo-Indian who has discovered that the suttee he read of as a boy is called *sati* by those who know it best is not content to keep so important a piece of knowledge to himself ; he must have the rest of us call it *sati*, like the Hindoos (ah, no—Hindus) & himself ; at any rate, he will give us the chance of mending our ignorant ways by printing nothing but *sati* & forcing us to guess what word known to us it may stand for. The orientalist whom histories have made familiar with the *Khalif* is determined to cure us of the delusion, implanted in our childish minds by hours with some bowdlerized *Arabian Nights*, that there was ever such a being as our old friend the Caliph. Literary critics saddened by our hazy notions of French do their best to lead us by example from *nom de plume* & *morale* to *nom de guerre* & *moral*. Dictionary devotees whose devotion extends to the etymologies think it bad for the rest of us to be connecting *amuck* with *muck*, & come to our rescue with *amok*. These & many more, in each of their teachings, teach us one truth that we could do as well without, & two falsehoods that are of some importance. The one truth is, for instance, that *Khalíf* has a greater resemblance to Arabic than *Caliph* ; is that of use to anyone who does not know it already ? The two falsehoods are, the first that English is not entitled to give what form it chooses to foreign words that it has occasion to use ; & the second, that it is better to have two or more forms coexistent than to talk of one thing by one name that all can understand. If the first is not false, why do we say *Germany* & *Athens* & *Lyons* & *Constantinople* instead of *Deutschland* & the rest ? or allow the French to insult us with *Londres* & *Angleterre* ? That the second is false not even our teachers would deny ; they would explain instead that their aim is to drive out the old wrong form with the new right one. That they are most unlikely to accomplish, while they are quite sure to produce confusion temporary or permanent ; see MAHOMET for a typical case.

Seriously, our learned persons & possessors of special information should not, when they are writing for the general public, presume to improve the accepted vocabulary ; when they are addressing audiences of their likes, they may naturally use, to their hearts' content, the forms that are most familiar to writer & readers alike ; but otherwise they should be at the pains to translate technical terms into English. And, what is of far greater importance, when they do forget this duty, we others who are unlearned, & naturally speak not in technical terms but in English,

should refuse to be either cowed by the fear of seeming ignorant, or tempted by the hope of passing for specialists, into following their bad example without their real though insufficient excuse.

Among articles bearing on the question are addle, amuck, bar (sinister), causeway, harem, Hindu, Caliph, creese, Mahomet, moral(e), moujik, mussulman, & nom de guerre.

differ, in the sense *be different*, *exhibit a difference*, is followed only by *from*, not by *with*. In the sense *have a difference of opinion*, *express dissent*, *dispute*, it is followed usually by *with*, but sometimes by *from*.

difference. *There is all the d. in the world between deceiving the public by secret diplomacy & carrying on the day-to-day business of negotiation from the housetops.* Why, certainly ; but was it worth while to tell us so obvious a fact ? If the writer had put in a *not* before either *deceiving* or *carrying*, he would have told us both something of value & what he meant. See ILLOGICALITIES. *Difference* so often tempts to this particular illogicality as to deserve special mention.

different. That *d.* can only be followed by *from* & not by *to* is a SUPERSTITION. Not only is *to* 'found in writers of all ages ' (OED) ; the principle on which it is rejected (You do not say *differ to* ; therefore you cannot say *d. to*) involves a hasty & ill-defined generalization. Is it all derivatives, or derivative adjectives, or adjectives that were once participles, or actual participles, that must conform to the construction of their parent verbs ? It is true of the last only ; we cannot say *differing to* ; but that leaves *d.* out in the cold. If it is all derivatives, why do we say *according, agreeably, & pursuant, to instructions*, when we have to say *this accords with, agrees with*, or *pursues, instructions ?* If derivative adjectives, why *derogatory to, inconceivable* *to,* in contrast with *derogates from, not to be conceived by?* If ex-participle adjectives, why do *pleases, suffices, defies, me* go each its own way, & yield *pleasant to, sufficient for,* & *defiant of, me?* The fact is that the objections to *d. to,* like those to AVERSE *to,* SYMPATHY *for,* & COMPARE *to,* are mere pedantries. This does not imply that *d. from* is wrong ; on the contrary, it is ' now usual ' (OED) ; but it is only so owing to the dead set made against *d. to* by mistaken critics.

differentia. Pl. *-iae* ; see -AE, -AS. For synonymy see SIGN.

differentiate makes *-entiable* ; see -ABLE 1.

differentiation. See -CIATION.

DIFFERENTIATION. In dealing with words, the term is applied to the process by which two words that can be used indifferently in two meanings become appropriated one to one of the meanings & one to the other. Among the OED's 18th-c. quotations for *spiritual & spirituous* are these two :—*It may not here be improper to take notice of a* wise & spiritual *saying of this young prince./ The Greeks, who are a* spirituous & wise *people.* The association of each with *wise* assures us rather startlingly that a change has taken place in the meaning of *spirituous*; it & *spiritual* have now been appropriated to different senses, & it would be difficult to invent a sentence in which one would mean the same as the other ; that is, differentiation is complete. In a living language such differentiation is perpetually acting upon thousands of words ; to take a modern example, *airship,* when first used, meant any locomotive aircraft, whether lighter or heavier than air ; now, by differentiation from *aeroplane,* it has been confined to the former kind. Most differentiations are, when fully established, savers of confusion & aids to brevity & lucidity, though in the incomplete stage there is a danger of their

actually misleading readers who have not become aware of them when writers are already assuming their acceptance. Differentiations become complete not by authoritative pronouncements or dictionary fiats, but by being gradually adopted in speaking & writing ; it is the business of all who care for the language to do their part towards helping serviceable ones through the dangerous incomplete stage to that in which they are of real value. There are many references through the book to this article. The matter is, however, simple in principle, the difficulty being in the details ; & all that need be done is to collect here, with some classification, a few differentiated words, those about which information is given in their places being printed in small capitals.

A. Words completely & securely differentiated :—*adulteration & adultery* ; *apologue & apology* ; *can & con* ; *catch & chase* ; *cloths & clothes* ; *coffer & coffin* ; *coign & coin* ; *conduct & conduit* ; *convey & convoy* ; *costume & custom* ; *courtesy &* CURTSY ; *cud & quid* ; *dam & dame* ; *defer & differ* ; PRONOUNCEMENT & *pronunciation*; *vice-queen & vicereine.*

B. Words fully differentiated, but sometimes confounded by ignorant or too learned writers :—ACCEPTANCE & *acceptation* ; *alternate &* ALTERNATIVE; CONJURE' & *con'jure*; CONTINUANCE & *continuation* ; DEFINITE & *definitive* ; *distinct &* DISTINCTIVE ; ESPECIAL(LY) & *special-(ly)* ; EXCEEDING(*ly*) & *excessive(ly)* ; *historic &* HISTORICAL ; IMMOVABLE & *irremovable* ; *intense &* INTENSIVE ; LEGISLATION & *legislature* ; *loose &* loosen (-EN VERBS) ; LUXURIANT & *luxurious* ; MASTERFUL & *masterly* ; OLYMPIAN & *Olympic* ; PRECIOSITY & *preciousness* ; *proposal &* PROPOSITION ; *rough &* ROUGHEN ; *slack &* SLACKEN ; *transcendent &* TRANSCENDENTAL ; TRIUMPHAL & *triumphant* ; VILLAIN & *villein.*

C. Words in which an incipient or neglected differentiation should be encouraged :—ASSAY & *essay* (vbs) ; COMPLACENT & *complaisant* ; DEFECTIVE & *deficient* ; *derisive* & DERISORY ; FALSEHOOD, *falseness*, & *falsity* ; FEVERISH & *feverous* ; OBLIQUENESS & *obliquity* ; OPACITY & *opaqueness* ; PROFESSORATE & *professoriate* ; SPRINT & *spurt* ; TRICKSY & *tricky*.

D. Words in which a desirable but little recognized differentiation is here advocated :—APT & *liable* ; CONSISTENCE & *consistency* ; INCLUDE & *comprise* ; INDIFFERENCE & *indifferency* ; INFANTILE & *infantine* ; PENDANT, *pennant*, & *pennon* ; SPIRT & *spurt* ; STOREY & *story* ; THAT & *which*.

E. Words vainly asking for differentiation :—SPECIALITY & *specialty*.

F. Differentiated forms needlessly made :—SPIRITISM for *spiritualism* ; *stye* for STY ; *tyre* for TIRE.

difficile. See FRENCH WORDS.

diffusable, -ible. The first is recommended ; see -ABLE 2.

dig. *Digged* is archaic ; *dug* should be used except when reference is intended to some biblical or other known passage.

digest. Pronounce the noun dī'jĕst, the verb dījĕ'st ; see NOUN & VERB ACCENT.

digit has technical uses in anatomy &c. ; as a mere substitute for *finger*, it ranks with PEDANTIC HUMOUR.

dignify. For inflexions see VERBS IN -IE &c., 6.

digraph. See TECHNICAL TERMS.

dike, dyke. The first is the right form.

dilatation, -lation, -latator, -lator, -later. The forms *dilation*, *dilator*, are wrongly formed on the false ANALOGY of *calculation*, *-lator*, &c., in which *-at-* represents the Latin 1st-conj. p.p. stem ; in *dilate*, unlike *calculate*, the *-at-* is common to the whole Latin verb, of which the adj. *latus* (wide) is a component. In surgical use the correct *-latation* & the incorrect *-lator* prevail. The simplest remedy is to keep *-latation*, but change *-lator* to *-later*, this

(though not *-lation*) being a legitimate English formation.

dilate makes *-table* ; see MUTE E.

dilatory. Pronounce dĭ'latorĭ.

dilemma. The use of *d.* as a mere finer word for *difficulty* when the question of alternatives does not definitely arise is a SLIPSHOD EXTENSION ; it should be used only when there is a pair, or at least a definite number, of lines that might be taken in argument or action, & each is unsatisfactory. See POPULARIZED TECHNICALITIES.

dilettante. Pl. *-ti* (pron. *-tē*).

dilute. Pronounce the adj. dī'lūt, the verb dīlōō't ; see PARTICIPLES 5 A, & LU.

dim. For ' dim religious light ' see IRRELEVANT ALLUSION.

dimeter. See TECHNICAL TERMS.

diminishment is a NEEDLESS VARIANT beside *diminution* ; it was dormant for two centuries, but is now occasionally used (*Ireland is perhaps the only other European country that has shown a d. in its inhabitants*), perhaps inadvertently. See -ION & -MENT.

diminuendo. Pl. *-os* ; see -O(E)S 3.

diminutive has a valuable technical sense in grammar ; in general use (*a d. child, pony, apple, house, nose*) it is preferred to the ordinary words *tiny, small, stunted*, &c., chiefly by the POLYSYLLABIC HUMOURIST.

dinghy, dingey. The first is best.

dingo. Pl. *-oes* ; see -O(E)S 1.

diocese, -cess. The right spelling is *-ese*, but the pronunciation is usually weakened to *-ĕs* or *-ĭs*. For *d.*, *bishopric*, & *see*, see SEE.

diphth-. *Diphtheria, diphthong,* & their derivatives, are sometimes misspelt, & very often mispronounced, the first *-h-* being neglected ; dĭfth- is the right sound, & dĭpth- a vulgarism.

diploma. The pl. is always *-mas* in the ordinary senses (certificate of degree &c.), though *-mata* lingers in unusual senses (State paper &c.) as an alternative.

diplomat(ist). The longer English formation is preferable to the un-English -*mat*, the pronunciation of which, though in fact simple (dĭ'-plomăt), seems doubtful to those who are not familiar with the word.

diptych. Pronounce -ĭk.

direct(ly). 1. The right adverb in some contexts (e.g. *You should go d. to Paris, to the fountain-head*) is *direct*, not *directly*; see UNIDIOMATIC -LY.

2. The conjunctional use of *directly* (*I came d. I knew*) is quite defensible, but is chiefly colloquial.

directress, -trix. See FEMININE DESIGNATIONS. As fem. of *director*, -*tress* is better, cf. DICTATRESS; but -*trix* has a use in geometry (pl. -*trices*, see -TRIX).

direful is a NEEDLESS VARIANT for *dire* in sense, & in formation is based on a false analogy (*dreadful*).

dirigible, -geable. Write -*gible*; see -ABLE 2.

dirty, vb. For inflexions see VERBS IN -IE &c., 6.

disc. See DISK.

discernable, -ible. The first is better; see -ABLE 2.

disciplinary. The pronunciation dĭsĭplĭ'narĭ is recommended in preference to dĭ'sĭplĭnarĭ, which is suited only for academic articulation; cf. CONTUMELY.

discobolus. Pl. -*lī*; see -US.

discolo(u)ration. See HYBRID DERIVATIVES.

discomfit. There is a tendency to use this in too weak or indefinite a sense (*Bell, conscious of past backslidings, seemed rather discomfited*). It is perhaps mistaken sometimes for the verb belonging to the noun *discomfort*. It has nothing to do with that, & means overwhelm or utterly defeat.

discomposedly. Five syllables; see -EDLY.

disconnexion, -ction. Spell -*xion*; see -XION.

discontent. For ' the winter of our d.' see IRRELEVANT ALLUSION.

discord, discount, discourse. Accent the nouns on the first, the verbs on the second syllables; see NOUN & VERB ACCENT.

discrete (separate, abstract, &c.) should be accented dĭ'skrēt, not dĭskrē't; the first is both natural in English accentuation (cf. the opposed adj. *concrete*), & useful as distinguishing the word from the familiar *discreet*.

discriminate, v., makes -*nable*; see -ABLE 1.

discuss, used with wine, food, &c., as object, may be classed with WORN-OUT HUMOUR.

discussable, -ible. The first is recommended; see -ABLE 2.

disenthral(l), -alment. See ENTHRALL, & -LL-, -L-, 3.

disfranchise, not -*ize*; see -ISE)(-IZE.

disgraceful. See POSITIVE WORDS.

disgruntle(d). ' Now chiefly U.S.' (OED); resort to words of this kind amounts usually to an admission that one's matter is dull & needs enlivening.

disguise, not -*ize*; see -ISE)(-IZE.

disguisedly. Four syllables; see -EDLY.

disgustful was formerly common in the sense *disgusting*, but has now been so far displaced by that word as to be a NEEDLESS VARIANT in that sense. In the sense *inspired by disgust* (*a d. curiosity*) it is unobjectionable.

dishabille. Pronounce dĭ'sabē'l.

disillusion(ize). It is a pity that there should be two forms of the verb. The first is recommended; *disbud, discredit, discrown, disfigure, dismast,* give sufficient support for the use of *dis-* before a noun in the sense *deprive* or *rid of*; -*ize* is the refuge of the destitute & should be resorted to only in real destitution; & the verbal noun is undoubtedly *disillusionment*.

disinterested &c. For the accent see INTEREST.

disjunctive. See TECHNICAL TERMS.

disk, disc. ' The earlier & better spelling is disk ' (OED).

dislocate. See -ATABLE.

dislodg(e)ment. Keep the *-e-* ; see JUDGEMENT.

dismal. For ' the d. science ' see SOBRIQUETS. For comparison, see -ER & -EST, 4.

dismission, the predecessor of *dismissal*, has been completely dispossessed by it, & must now be regarded as a NEEDLESS VARIANT.

dispatch, des-. The OED gives good reasons for preferring *dis-*. See also FORMAL WORDS.

dispel means to drive away in different directions, & must have for object a word to which that sense is applicable (*darkness, fear, cloud, suspicions*), & not, as in the following sentence, a single indivisible thing:— *Lord Carrington effectually dispelled yesterday the suggestion that he resigned the Presidency because he feared . . .* He might dispel the suspicion, or repel the suggestion, suspicion being comparable to a cloud, but suggestion to a missile.

dispensable. For the sense *that can be dispensed with*, see -ABLE 4.

dispersedly. Four syllables ; see -EDLY.

dispiteous. See REVIVALS.

displeasedly. A bad form ; see -EDLY.

disposable. For the sense *that can be disposed of*, see -ABLE 4.

disposal, disposition. In some contexts there is no choice (*His -ition is merciful* ; *The -al of the empty bottles is a difficulty*) ; in some either word may be used indifferently (*The money is at your -al or -ition*) ; & in some the choice depends upon the sense required (*The -ition of the troops* is the way they are stationed for action &c., & is general's work ; *The -al of the troops* is the way they are lodged &c. when not being used, & is quartermaster's work). When doubt arises, it is worth while to remember that *-ition* corresponds to *dispose*, & *-al* to *dispose of*. So *The -ition of the books is excellent* (they are excellently disposed, i.e. arranged), but *The -al of the books*

was soon managed (they were soon disposed of, i.e. either sold or got out of the way) ; *The -ition of the body is stiff* (it is stiffly disposed, i.e. arranged), but *The -al of the body proved impossible* (it could not be disposed of, i.e. destroyed or concealed). *The testamentary -ition of property*, i.e. the way it is disposed or arranged by will, & *The testamentary -al of property*, i.e. the way it is disposed of or transferred by will, describing the same act from different points of view, are naturally used without much discrimination. The same is true of *at* one's *-al* or *-ition* ; but in this formula *-al* is now much commoner, just as *You may dispose of the money as you please* is now commoner than *You may dispose it*.

disproved, -en. The first is recommended ; see PROVE.

disputable. Accent dĭ'spūtabl, not dĭspū'tabl ; see RECESSIVE ACCENT.

dissatisfiedly. A bad form ; see -EDLY.

disseise, -ze, disseisin, -zin. Spell *-se, -sin* ; see SEIZE.

dissemble, dissimulate. There is no clear line of distinction between the two. *Dissemble* is the word in ordinary use, & the other might have perished as a NEEDLESS VARIANT, but has perhaps been kept in being because it is, unlike *dissemble*, provided with a noun (*dissimulation*), & a contrasted verb (*simulate*), & is more convenient for use in connexion with these.

disseminate makes *-nable, -tor* ; see -ABLE 1, -OR.

dissimilation. See TECHNICAL TERMS.

dissimulate, dissipate, dissociate, make *-lable, -pable, -ciable* ; see -ABLE 1.

dissociation. See -CIATION.

dissoluble, dissolvable. 1. Pronounce dĭ'solŏobl, dĭzŏ'lvabl.
2. *Dissoluble* is the established word, & may be used in all senses ; but *dissolvable* often represents *dissolve* when it means make a solution

of in liquid (*sugar is -vable* or *-uble in water*), & sometimes in other senses (*a Chamber -uble* or *-vable at the Minister's will*) ; see -ABLE 2.

dissolute, -ution. For pronunciation see LU.

dissolve. Pronounce dĭzŏ′lv.

di(s)syllable. Omit one *s* ; see DISYLLABLE.

distendable, -dible, -sible. The first is recommended ; see -ABLE 2.

distich. Pronounce -ĭk ; for meaning see -STICH.

distil(l). The modern form is *-il* ; see -LL-, -L-.

distinction, as a LITERARY CRITICS' WORD, is, like *charm*, one of those on which they fall back when they wish to convey that a style is meritorious, but have not time to make up their minds upon the precise nature of its merit. They might perhaps defend it as an elusive name for an elusive thing ; but it is rather an ambiguous name for any of several things, & it is often doubtful whether it is the noun representing *distinctive* (markedly individual), *distinguished* (nobly impressive), *distingué* (noticeably wellbred), or even *distinct* (concisely lucid). A few quotations follow ; but the vagueness of the word cannot be brought out without longer extracts than are admissible, & the reader of reviews must be left to observe for himself :—*His character & that of his wife are sketched with a certain d./She avoids any commonplace method of narration, but if she achieves a certain d. of treatment in the process, she detracts enormously from the interest of her story./The book is written with a d. (save in the matter of split infinitives) unusual in such works./Not only is distinctness from others not in itself d., but distinctness from others may often be the very opposite of d., indeed a kind of vulgarity./Despite its length, an inclination to excessive generalization, & an occasional lack of stylistic d. verging upon obscurity, this book is a remarkable piece of literary criticism.*

distinctive means *serving* or *used to*

discriminate, characteristic, so called by way of distinction. But it is often misused (cf. DEFINITIVE, ALTERNATIVE) for *distinct* (*The refugees at length ceased to exist as a d. people./ Distinctively able & valuable.* On the other hand *distinctively* would have been the appropriate word in *The Swiss name of* Edelweiss *will be given to the village, the houses having the high-pitched roofs & other features of* distinctly *Swiss architecture*) ; & sometimes for *distinguished* (*During a long public life he served the interests of his class well in many d. positions./ Mr Klitguard, Mr Richard Blondel, Miss Jean Sterling Mackinlay, . . . & a number of other d. people*).

distinctly, in the sense *really quite,* is the badge of the superior person indulgently recognizing unexpected merit in something that we are to understand is not quite worthy of his notice :—*The effect as the procession careers through the streets of Berlin is described as d. interesting./ Quite apart from its instructive endeavours, the volume is d. absorbing in its dealing with the romance of banking.*

distingué. See FRENCH WORDS.

distrait, -te. See FRENCH WORDS. Use *-ait* of males (*-ā*), *-aite* of females (*-āt*) ; of things (*expression, air, mood, answer,* &c.), *-ait* always.

distributive (in grammar). See TECHNICAL TERMS.

disyllable, diss-. The first is better ; the double *s* is due to French, in which it served the purpose of preserving the hard sound (s, not z) ; in English the prefix is *di-*, not *dis-*.

ditto. Pl. *-os* ; see -O(E)S 3.

diurnal should not now be used in the sense of *daily*, i.e. recurring every day, though that was formerly one of its possible meanings ; in modern use, (1) when opposed to *nocturnal* it means *by day*, (2) when opposed to *annual* &c. it means occupying a day.

divers(e). The two words are the same, but differentiated in spelling, pronunciation, & sense, *divers* (dī′-verz) implying number, & *diverse* (dĭver's) difference ; cf. *several* & *various*, each of which has both senses without differentiation.

diversify. For inflexions see VERBS IN -IE &c., 6.

dizen. For dĭ-, dī-, see BEDIZEN.

do. 1. *Did* subjunctive. 2. *Do have.* 3. *Do* as substitute.

1. For *did* as in *Did I believe it, it would kill me* see SUBJUNCTIVES.

2. *Do have.* Protests are common against the use of *do* as an auxiliary to *have.* It is, however, often legitimate, as in *Did the Roman women have votes ?* ; *Do you have coffee for breakfast ?* ; *Savages do not have toothache* ; *We did not have to pay* ; *I did not have my hair cut.* In most of these the simple *had* or *have* is disagreeably formal, & in the *coffee* example *Have you coffee ?* could only mean Is there any to make the drink with ?. The objection should be limited to sentences in which the reference is to a single occasion or instance & also the sense of *have* is *possess* or something near it ; this rule allows the examples given above (the first three escaping by one loophole, & the last two by the other), & condemns the following :—*In Lanarkshire, although I do not have any statistics, thousands of foreigners are settled.*/*Mr Birrell was dining with some friends, one of whom did not have all his wits about him.*/ *Counsel said the appellant took steps to have herself arrested, therefore she did not have any malicious intent.*/ *They didn't even have the grace to cover their refusal with an excuse.* The admissibility of *does have* in the following will depend on whether *a turbot* & *the fish* mean a particular turbot the man was watching, or any turbot :—*He had been struck with the detailed resemblance obtaining between the markings of a turbot's skin & those of the gravel on which it lay ; & he asked himself the question —Was this a mere coincidence, or does the fish have the power of controlling the colour pattern ?*

3. *Do* as substitute. The use of *do,*

whether by itself or in conjunction with *as, so, it, which,* &c., instead of a verb of which some part has occurred previously, is a convenient & established idiom ; but it has often bad results.

a. *They do not wish to see the Act of 1903 break down, as break down it is bound to do* ; omit either *break down* or *do.*

b. *Great Britain is faithful to her agreements when she finds an advantage in doing so.*/*It ought to have been satisfying to the young man, & so, in a manner of speaking, it did. Do* &c. must not be substituted for a copulative *be* & its complement.

c. *As to the question whether sufficient is known as to the food of birds, the author feels bound to reply that we do not.*/*Although nothing is said as to Cabinet rank being associated with the two offices, it may be assumed that both do so.*/*The title of ' Don ' is now applied promiscuously throughout Spain very much as we do the meaningless designation of ' Esquire '.*/*It may justly be said, as Mr Paul does, that . . .*/*Some of them wrote asking to be reinstated, which we did.*/*Reference to it was also made by Lord Crewe ; in doing so he said . . .*/*The Speaker said it ought to be withdrawn, & Mr King did so at once.*/*It seems reasonable that some kind of guarantee should be given ; at all events it would be politic to do so.*/*A large number had been grudgingly supported by relatives who would now cease to do so.*/*Why was it not pushed to a victorious conclusion in the House of Lords, where the party had the power to do so ?* Unless the subject & the voice of *do* will be the same as those of the previous verb, it should not be used ; but transgression of this rule results sometimes in flagrant blunders, as in the first two or three examples, & sometimes merely in what, though it offends against idiom, is (since *do so* means strictly *act thus*) grammatically defensible.

d. *The dissolution which was forced upon the country was deliberately done so as to avoid giving an advantage to the Unionists./The ambassador gave them all the assistance which the Imperial nature of his office made it obligatory upon him to do./We have got to make a commission in the Territorial Force fashionable, the right thing for every gentleman to do./ To inflict upon themselves a disability which one day they will find the mistake & folly of doing.* In these examples *do* is in grammatical relation to a noun (*dissolution, assistance, commission, disability*) that is only a subordinate part of the implied whole (*the forcing of a dissolution, the giving of assistance, the holding of a commission, the inflicting of a disability*) to which alone it is in logical relation ; we do not *do* a dissolution, a commission, &c. These sentences, however, in which *do* is a transitive verb meaning *perform*, are not properly examples of the substitute *do* ; but the mistakes in them are due to the influence of that idiom.

do (the musical note). Pl. *dos* ; see -O(E)S 3.

doat. See DOTE.

docile. The OED pronounces dō'sil or dŏ'sĭl, with preference to the first.

doctor. See PHYSICIAN.

doct(o)ress. It is a serious inconvenience that neither form (-*tress* would be the better) has been brought into any but facetious use as a prefixed title ; the device of inserting a Christian name after *Doctor* (*Dr Mary Jones*) is clumsy, & sometimes (*Dr Evelyn Jones*) ineffectual. See FEMININE DESIGNATIONS.

doctrinal. The accentuation dŏ'k-trīnal is recommended ; see FALSE QUANTITY.

document. It is sometimes forgotten that the word includes more than the parchments or separate papers to which it is usually applied ; a coin, picture, monument, passage in a book &c., that serves as evidence, may be a d., & the following remark on ' Dd. illustrative of the Continental Reformation ' is ab-

surd :—*It is a collection not only (as the title implies) of dd., but also of passages from books & letters.* The phrase *human d.* is more than a mere metaphor.

dodo. Pl. -*oes* ; see -O(E)S 1.

doe. See HART.

do(e)st. In modern, though not in older, use the auxiliary has *dost* only, & the independent verb *doest* only.

dogged. See -ER & -EST, 4.

doggy, -ie. See -EY, -IE, -Y.

dogma. Pl. -*mas*, formerly -*mata* ; see LATIN PLURALS.

doily, doiley, doyly. The first is the OED spelling.

dolce far niente. See BATTERED ORNAMENTS.

dole, grief. See REVIVALS.

dolichocephalic, -ous. See -CEPHALIC.

domain. For synonymy see FIELD. See also DEMESNE.

Domesday, dooms-. *D. Book* is spelt *Domes-* but pronounced dōōmz-; elsewhere the spelling is *dooms-*.

domestic, n., though it survives in legal & other formal use, in PEDANTIC HUMOUR, & as a GENTEELISM, has been superseded for ordinary purposes by *servant* taken in a limited sense. Such losses of differentiation may be regretted, but usage is irresistible.

domesticate makes -*cable* ; see -ABLE 1.

domesticity. The OED pronounces dō-; see FALSE QUANTITY.

dominate makes -*nable* ; see -ABLE 1.

domino. Pl. -*os* ; see -O(E)S 1.

don, vb. See FORMAL WORDS.

donate is ' chiefly U.S.'—OED. It is a BACK-FORMATION from *donation* :—*He recently donated a site for the proposed Hindu University.*

donation. See FORMAL WORDS.

dossier. Pronounce dŏ'syer. See FRENCH WORDS.

dost. See DO(E)ST.

dot (dowry). See FRENCH WORDS.

dote, doat. Spell *dote.*

double. The common quotation (*Macbeth*, IV. i. 83) is ' make assurance double sure ' (not *doubly*).

DOUBLE CASE. *An ex-pupil of Verrall's . . . cannot but recall the successive states of mind that he possessed—or, more truly, possessed him—in attending Verrall's lectures.* Here *that* is first objective & then subjective; see CASES 3 D 4, THAT rel. pr., & WHICH.

DOUBLE CONSTRUCTION. *They are also entitled to* prevent *the smuggling of alcohol into the States,* & to reasonable assistance *from other countries to that end.* 'Entitled to prevent [infin.] . . . & to assistance [noun]' is a change of a kind discussed in SWAPPING HORSES.

double entendre is the established English form, & has been in common use from the seventeenth century; the modern attempt to correct it into *double entente* suggests ignorance of English rather than knowledge of French; cf. À L'OUTRANCE. See FRENCH WORDS.

DOUBLE PASSIVES. *The point is sought to be evaded*: monstrosities of this kind, which are as repulsive to the grammarian as to the stylist, perhaps spring by false analogy from the superficially similar type seen in *The man was ordered to be shot.* But the simple forms from which they are developed are dissimilar :—They ordered the man *to be shot,* but They seek *to evade* the point; whereas *man* is one member of the double-barrelled object of *ordered, point* is the object not of *seek* at all, but of *evade*; therefore, whereas *man* can be made subject of the passive *was ordered* while its fellow-member is deferred, *point* cannot be made subject of the passive *is sought,* never having been in any sense the object of *seek.*

To use this clumsy & incorrect construction in print amounts to telling the reader that he is not worth writing readable English for; a speaker may find himself compelled to resort to it because he must not stop to recast the sentence he has started on; but writers have no such excuse. Some of the verbs most maltreated in this way are *attempt, begin, desire, endeavour, hope, intend, propose, purpose, seek,* & *threaten*; a few examples follow :—*Now that the whole is attempted to be systematized./The mystery was assiduously, though vainly, endeavoured to be discovered./The darkness of the house (forgotten to be opened, though it was long since day) yielded to the glare./No greater thrill can be hoped to be enjoyed./Considerable support was managed to be raised for Waldemar./The commissioners proposed to be appointed will give their whole time./Such questions as Prayerbook Revision & the Mass Vestments, now threatened to be authoritatively revived, have to be decided.*

doubt(ful). It is contrary to idiom to begin the clause that depends on these with *that* instead of the usual *whether,* except when the sentence is negative (*I do not doubt . . .* ; *There is no doubt . . .* ; *It was never doubtful . . .*) or interrogative (*Do you doubt . . . ?* ; *Is there any doubt . . . ?* ; *Can it be doubtful . . . ?*). Even in such sentences *whether* is sometimes better (*I do not doubt whether I have a head on my shoulders*), but rules on that point are needless; the mistake against which warning is required is the use of *that* in affirmative statements. It is especially common (probably from failure to decide in time between *doubt & deny* or *disbelieve, doubtful & false*), but equally wrong, when the clause is placed before *doubt(ful)* instead of in the normal order. *Whether* should have been used in :—*It was generally doubted that France would permit the use of her port./I must be allowed to doubt that there is any class who deliberately omit . . ./That the movement is as purely industrial as the leaders claim may be doubted./So afraid of men's motives as to doubt that anyone can be honest./That I have been so misled is extremely doubtful./That Mr Bennett would, or even could, write an uncompromisingly sad story we are inclined to doubt./It is very doubtful* *whether it was ever at Dunstaffnage, & still more doubtful that it came from Ireland./That his army, if it retreats, will carry with it all its guns we are inclined to doubt.*

doubtless, no doubt, undoubtedly, &c. *Doubtless & no doubt* have been weakened in sense till they no longer convey certainty, but either probability (*You have doubtless* or *no doubt heard the news*) or concession (*No doubt he meant well enough ; It is doubtless very unpleasant*). When real conviction or actual knowledge on the speaker's part is to be expressed, it must be by *undoubtedly, without* (*a*) *doubt,* or *beyond a doubt* (*He was undoubtedly guilty*).

douceur. See FRENCH WORDS.

dour. Pronounce door, not dowr.

douse, dowse. The OED gives *-wse* for the verb concerned with the divining-rod (so *dowser, dowsing-rod,* &c.), & *-use* for the other verb or verbs.

dow. See DHOW.

dower, dowry. The two words, originally the same, are differentiated in ordinary literal use, *dower* being the widow's life share of her husband's property, & *dowry* the portion brought by a bride to her husband ; but in poetic or other ornamental use *dower* has often the sense of *dowry* ; & either is applied figuratively to talents &c.

doyen. See DEAN.

dozen. See COLLECTIVES 2.

drachm, drachma, dram. *Drachm* was the prevalent form in all senses ; but now the coin is almost always *drachma,* the indefinite small quantity is always *dram,* & *dram* is not uncommon even where *drachm* is still usual, in apothecaries' & avoirdupois weight. Pron. *drachm* drăm, *drachma* dră'kma.

draft, draught, &c. *Draft* is merely a phonetic spelling of *draught,* but some differentiation has taken place. *Draft* has ousted *draught* in banking, & to a great extent in the military sense *detach*(*ment*) ; it is also usual

in the sense (*make*) *rough copy* or *plan* (a good *draftsman* is one who drafts Bills well, a good *draughtsman* one who draws well). In all the other common senses (game of *dd.,* air-current, ship's displacement, *beer on d., beast of d.,* haul of fish, dose, liquor), *draught* is still the only recognized British form ; in U.S. *draft* is much more widely used.

dragoman. The pl. is correctly *-mans,* & usually *-men* ; for choice between them see DIDACTICISM.

draughtswoman. See FEMININE DESIGNATIONS.

draw. See FORMAL WORDS.

dreadful. See -ER & -EST, 4.

dream. The ordinary past & p.p. is *dreamt* (-ĕmt) ; *dreamed* (-ēmd) is preferred in poetry & in impressive contexts. See also -T & -ED.

drib(b)let. *Driblet* is both the usual & (f. obs. vb *drib*+-*let*) the more correct form.

drink has past tense *drank,* p.p. *drunk* ; the reverse uses (*they drunk, have drank*) were formerly not unusual, but are now blunders or conspicuous archaisms.

droll. For synonymy see JOCOSE.

dromedary. Pronounce drŏm- ; the abnormal drŭm-, though put first in the OED, is not likely to resist the influence of the spelling.

drunk(en). The difference, as now established, is complex. *Drunk* is in predicative use only, or at least is unidiomatic as an attribute ; *Trodden into the kennels as a drunk mortal* (Carlyle ; cf. the normal *I met a drunken man*) is either affectation or an emphasizing, which should have been otherwise effected, of the distinction between mortal now the worse for drink (*drunk*) & one often the worse for it (*drunken*). *Drunken* is the attributive word, whether the meaning is *now in drink* or *given to drink* or *symptomatic* &c. *of drunkenness* (*I saw a -en man ; A lazy -en lying ne'er-do-weel ; His -en habits*) ; it may be used predicatively also, but only in the sense given to drink (cf. *He was -en & dissolute* with *He was drunk & incapable*) ; *He was -en yesterday* is contrary to modern idiom.

drunken. See -ER & -EST, 4.

dry &c. The spelling in some derivatives of *dry* & other adjectives & verbs of similar form (monosyllables with *y* as the only vowel) is disputable. The prevalent forms for *dry* are, from the adjective *drier, driest, drily, dryness, dryish,* & from the verb *dryer.* 1. The other adjectives are four only—*shy, sly, spry,* & *wry.* Much the most usual spelling for these is with *y* throughout—*shyer, shyest, shyly, shyness, shyish*; this should be made invariable for them ; & it would be well if *dryer, dryest,* & *dryly,* could be written also ; but since *dry* is the commonest word, & its preference for the *i* is undoubted, the inconsistency will probably continue. 2. With the agent-nouns in *-er* consistency might more easily be attained ; *dryer*, prevalent in technical use (oil-painting, pottery, &c.), should be corrected to *drier.* The other verbs are eleven—*cry, fly, fry, ply* use, *ply* bend, *pry, shy* start, *shy* throw, *sky, spy, try.* An agent-noun may be wanted for any of these ; three of them form such nouns in which the *i* is invariable—*crier, pliers,* & *trier* (legal)— ; those in which spelling varies—*drier, flier, frier* (frying-pan), *shier* (shying horse)—as well as those of which the existence is doubtful (*priers* or *spiers upon others* ; *a skier of cricket-balls* ; *a plier of the oar*) should be assimilated to *crier,* & the *y* forms should be dropped. See also VERBS IN -IE &c., 6.

dual(istic). Both words are of the learned kind, & better avoided when such ordinary words as *two, twofold, twin, double, connected, divided, half-&-half, ambiguous,* will do the work :—*The skirt was dual* (divided), *& rather short./Dual* (double) *ownership./The dual* (connected) *questions of ' abnormal places ' & a minimum wage would bring about a deadlock./*

The Government is pleased with the agitation for electoral reasons, but does not desire it to be too successful ; the reason for this dualistic (half-&-half) *attitude is that . . .* See POPULARIZED TECHNICALITIES.

dubbin(g). Spell with *-g* ; it is from *dub* smear with grease, & parallel to *binding, seasoning,* &c.

dubiety. Pronounce dūbī′itĭ ; see FALSE QUANTITY. For *d.* & *doubt,* see WORKING & STYLISH WORDS.

ducat. Pronounce dŭ′kat.

duck. For pl. see COLLECTIVES 4.

due. Under the influence of ANALOGY, *due to* is often used by the illiterate as though it had passed, like *owing to,* into a mere compound preposition. In all the examples below *owing* would stand, but *due,* which must like ordinary participles & adjectives be attached to a noun, & not to a notion extracted from a sentence, is impossible ; it is not the horse, the rooks, he, the articles, or Lostwithiel, that are due, but the failure of the movement, the distrust of the rooks, & so on :—*The old trade union movement is a dead horse, largely d. to the incompetency of the leaders./Rooks, probably d. to the fact that they are so often shot at, have a profound distrust of man./D. largely to his costume, he suggested a respectable organist./Some articles have increased in price, d. to the increasing demand./As an example I take the name of Lostwithiel, surely a beautiful sound, & in my case not d. to pleasant memories, as I have never been there.*

duet(t), quartet(te), &c. The forms recommended are (*solo*), *duet,* (*trio*), *quartet, quintet, sextet, septet, octet, nonet.*

Dulcinea. The right accentuation is dŭlsĭnē′a (see verses in *Don Quixote*).

dul(l)ness, ful(l)ness. Use *-ll-,* as in all other words in which *-ness* follows *-ll* (*chillness, drollness, illness, nullness, shrillness, smallness, stillness, wellness,* &c.) ; see -LL-, -L-, 4.

dum(b)found(er). Write *dumbfound*; it is probably *dumb+confound*.

duodecimo. See FOLIO. Pl. *-os*; see *-o(E)s* 6.

duologue is a bad formation, but there are difficulties in the way of making a good one ; *dyologue*, which is better only in one respect, is indistinguishable in sound from *dialogue*; *dilogy* conflicts with *trilogy* & *tetralogy*; *dittologue* suggests *ditto*; *biloquy* after *soliloquy* is less bad than *duologue* after *monologue*. The best course is to get along as well as may be with *dialogue*, *duet*, & periphrasis ; barbarous formation is peculiarly bad in words that are designed only for the use of the educated.

duplex. For plural see *-EX, -IX*, 2.

durance, duress(e). 1. *Durance* now means only the state of being in confinement, is a purely decorative word, & is rare except in the phrases *in durance, in durance vile*— the latter a BATTERED ORNAMENT. *Duress* means the application of constraint, which may or may not take the form of confinement, to a person ; it is chiefly in legal use, with reference to acts done under illegal compulsion, & is commonest in the phrase *under duress*. 2. The OED prefers the spelling *duress* & the accentuation dūrĕ's.

durst. See DARE.

duteous, dutiful. The second is the ordinary word ; *duteous* (a rare formation, exactly paralleled only in *beauteous*) is kept in being beside it by its metrical convenience (six of the seven OED quotations are from verse), & when used in prose has consequently the air of a POETICISM ; see also PLENTEOUS.

dutiable. For such forms see *-ABLE* 4.

duty. For synonymy see TAX.

duumvir. Pl. *-virs*, rarely *-virī*.

dwarf. For pl. see *-VE(D)*.

dwarfen. See *-EN VERBS*.

dwell, in the sense *have* one's *abode*, has been ousted in ordinary use by *live*, but survives in poetic, rhetorical, & dignified use ; see WORKING & STYLISH WORDS.

dyarchy. See DIARCHY.

dye makes *dyeing* as a precaution against confusion with *dying* from *die*; cf. *singeing*)(*impinging*. See VERBS IN *-IE* &c., 7.

dynamic(al). Both words date from the 19th c. only, & *-ic* tends to become more & *-ical* less common ; the only use in which *-ical* seems preferable is as the adjective of *dynamics* (*-ical principles*; *an abstract -ical proposition*). See *-IC(AL)*.

·dynamiter, -tard. Use *-er*.

dynamo. Pl. *-os*; see *-o(E)s* 5. It is a CURTAILED WORD (*dynamo-electric machine*).

dysentery. Pronounce dĭ's'entrĭ.

dyspepsia, -sy. The word was formerly anglicized, but *-sia* is now usual.

E

each. 1. Number of, & with, *e*. 2. *Each other*. 3. *Between e*.

1. Number. *E*. as subject is invariably singular, even when followed by *of them* &c.: *E. of the wheels has 12 spokes* (not *have*). When *e*. is not the subject, but in apposition with a plural noun or pronoun as subject, the verb (& complement) is invariably plural: *The wheels have 12 spokes e.*; *the wheels e. have 12 spokes* (this latter order is better avoided) ; *the wheels are e. 12-spokers*. But the number of a later noun or pronoun, & the corresponding choice of a possessive adjective, depend upon whether *e*. stands before or after the verb, & this again depends on the distributive emphasis required. If the distribution is not to be formally emphasized, *e*. stands before the verb (or its complement, or some part of the phrase composing it), & the plural number & corresponding possessive are used : *We e. have our own nostrums* (not *his own nostrum*, nor *our own nostrum*) ; *They are e. of them masters in their own homes.* If the distribution is to be formally insisted on, *e*. stands after the verb

(& complement) & is followed by singular nouns & the corresponding possessives : *we are responsible e. for his own vote* (also sometimes, by confusion, *e. for our own votes*, & sometimes, by double confusion, *e. for our own vote*). The following forms are incorrect in various degrees :—*Brown, Jones, & Robinson e. has a different plan./You will go e. your own way./They have e. something to say for himself./E. of these verses have five feet./They e. of them contain a complete story./We are master e. in his own house./Guizot & Gneist, e. in their generation, went to school to the history of England to discover . . ./The People's Idols mount, e. his little tub, &, brazenthroated, advertises his nostrum, the one infallible panacea.* A correspondent informs me that in the hymn-lines (*A. & M.* 289) ' Soon will you & I be lying *E.* within our narrow bed ' *our* has been substituted for the original *his* ; the corrector has been offended by HIS of the common gender, & failed to observe that he has restricted the application to married couples.

2. *Each other* is now treated as a compound word, the verb or preposition that governs *other* standing before *e*, instead of in its normal place, *& they hate e. o., they sent presents to e. o.*, being usually preferred to *e. hates the other*(*s*), *they sent presents e. to the other*(*s*) ; but the phrase is so far true to its origin that its possessive is *e. other's* (not *others*'), & that it cannot be used when the case of *other* would be subjective :—*a lot of old cats ready to tear out e. other's* (not *others*') *eyes* ; *we know e. what the other wants* (not *what e. o. wants*). *E. o.* is by some writers used only when no more than two things are referred to, *one another* being similarly appropriated to larger numbers ; the differentiation is neither of present utility nor based on historical usage ; the old distributive of two as opposed to several was not *e.*, but *either* ; & *either other*, which formerly existed

beside *e. o.* & *one another*, would doubtless have survived if its special meaning had been required.

3. *Between e.* For such expressions as ' *three minutes b. e. scene* ' see BETWEEN.

ear. Pronounce ēr (not yēr). Public readers of the Litany (*we have heard with our ears*), please note ; the modern loss of the r trill in *our* makes *our ears* a difficulty for readers who do not remember to restore it *pro hac vice*.

earthen, earthly, earthy. *Earthen* is still in ordinary use (see -EN ADJECTIVES) in the sole sense *made of earth* (either soil or potting clay). *Earthly* has two senses only :—(1) *belonging to this transitory world* as opposed to heaven or the future life, & (2, in negative context) *practically existent or discoverable by mortal man. Earthy* means *of the nature, or having an admixture, of earth* (soil, dross, gross materialism). *An earthen mound, rampart, pot. Earthly joys, grandeur ; the earthly paradise ; their earthly pilgrimage ; is there any earthly use, reason, &c.? ; for no earthly consideration ;* cf. the slang *he hasn't an earthly* (i. e. chance). *An earthy precipitate formed in a few minutes ; the ore is very earthy ; an upright man, but incurably earthy in his views & desires.*

earwig. A *yearwig* (see EAR) is a pronunciation sometimes heard.

easterly, northerly, southerly, westerly. Chiefly used of wind, & then meaning *east &c. or thereabouts, rather from the eastern &c. than from the other half of the horizon* ; else only of words implying either motion, or position conceived as attained by previous motion :—*an easterly wind* ; *took a southerly course ; the most easterly outposts of western civilization.* Not *southerly* (but *south*) *aspect* ; not *the easterly* (but *eastward*) *position* ; not *the westerly* (but *west*) *end of the church* ; not *westerly* (but *western*) *ways of thought.*

eat. The past is spelt *ate* (rarely *eat*) & pronounced ĕt (wrongly āt).

ebullition. Pronounce ĕbŭl-, not ĕbū-.

echo. Pl. *echoes* ; see -O(E)S 1.

éclaircissement, éclat. See FRENCH WORDS.

economic(al). The nouns *economics* & *economy* having nearly parted company (though Political Economy, like the King's Proctor, impedes full divorce), it is convenient that each should have its own adjective. Accordingly, *-ic* is now associated only with economics, & *-ical* only with economy ; an *economic rent* is one in the fixing of which the laws of supply & demand have had free play ; an *economical rent* is one that is not extravagant ; in practice the first generally means a rent not too low (for the landlord), & the second one not too high (for the tenant). In ' the question of economical help for Russia by sending her goods from this country ', the wrong word has been chosen.

ecumenical. See Æ, Œ.

-ED & 'D. When occasion arises to append the *-ed* that means *having* or *provided with* so-&-so to words with unEnglish vowel terminations (-a, -i, -o, &c.), it is best to avoid the bizarre appearance of *-aed* &c. & to write 'd : *one-idea'd, ennui'd, mustachio'd* ; *a camera'd bystander* ; *the wistaria'd walls* ; *a rich-fauna'd region* ; *long-pedigree'd families* ; *the campanile'd piazza* ; *a many-sea'd empire* ; *uncinema'd villages* ; *full-aroma'd coffee* ; *a shanghai'd sailor* ; *ski'd mountaineers.* Even with familiar words in *-o*, as *halo* & *dado*, the apostrophe is perhaps better ; & *ideaed, aromaed, ennuied*, & such words, are deliberately avoided because they look absurd.

eddy, vb. For inflexions see VERBS IN -IE &c., 6.

edge. For *e.-bone* see AITCH-BONE ; for *edgeways, -wise*, see -WAYS, -WISE.

edifice. See POMPOSITIES.

edify. For inflexions see VERBS IN -IE &c., 6.

editress. See FEMININE DESIGNATIONS.

-EDLY. An apology is perhaps due for ' setting out a stramineous subject ' at the length this article must run to ; but some writers certainly need advice upon it (*Women & girls stayed their needles while the Liberal leader's wife & daughter chatted informedly with them*), & few have time for the inductive process required, in default of perfect literary instinct, to establish sound rules.

Experiments in unfamiliar adverbs of this type (as *embarrassedly, boredly, mystifiedly, determinedly, biassedly, painedly, awedly*) lay the maker open to a double suspicion : he may be NOVELTY-HUNTING (conscious, that is, of a dullness that must be artificially relieved) or he may be putting down the abnormal in the belief that it is normal (betraying, that is, that his literary ear is at fault).

The following is offered as a fairly complete list of the standard words ; there are some hundreds of others to which there is no objection, but these will suffice to test doubtful forms by. The list is in three parts, first adverbs from adjectives in *-ed*, secondly adverbs from adjective-noun compounds in *-ed*, & lastly adverbs from true past participles. 1. *belatedly, benightedly, conceitedly, crabbedly*, crookedly*, dementedly, deucedly*, doggedly*, jaggedly*, learnedly*, nakedly, raggedly*, ruggedly*, sacredly, stiltedly, wickedly, wretchedly**. 2. *-bloodedly* (*cold-b.* &c.), *-fashionedly*** (*old-f.* &c.), *-handedly* (*open-h.* &c.), *-headedly* (*wrong-h.* &c.), *-heartedly* (*warm-h.* &c.), *-humouredly*** (*good-h.* &c.), *-mindedly* (*absent-m.*), *-naturedly*** (*ill-n.* &c.), *-sidedly* (*lop-s.* &c.), *-sightedly* (*short-s.* &c.), *-spiritedly* (*low-s.* &c.), *-temperedly*** (*ill-t.* &c.), *-windedly* (*long-w.* &c.), *-wittedly* (*slow-w.* &c.). 3 (including some with corresponding negative or positive forms in equally or less common use, which need not be mentioned). *abstractedly, admittedly, advisedly*, assuredly*, avowedly*, collectedly, confessedly*, confoundedly, connectedly, constrain-*

edly*, consumedly*, contentedly, curs-edly*, decidedly, dejectedly, delight-edly, deservedly*, designedly*, de-votedly, disappointedly, disinterest-edly, disjointedly, dispiritedly, dis-tractedly, excitedly, fixedly*, guard-edly, heatedly, hurriedly**, jadedly, markedly*, misguidedly, perplexedly*, pointedly, professedly*, repeatedly, reputedly, resignedly*, restrainedly*, rootedly, statedly, unabatedly, un-affectedly, unconcernedly*, undaunt-edly, undisguisedly*, undisputedly, undoubtedly, unexpectedly, unfeign-edly*, unfoundedly, uninterruptedly, unitedly, unreservedly*, unwontedly.

It will probably be admitted by everyone that the list is made up wholly of words known to be in the language already & not having to be manufactured, with doubts about their right to exist, for some special occasion. Most readers will admit also that, while it is physically possible to say any of those starred without allowing a separate syllable to the *-ed-*, the only ones actually so pronounced by educated persons are those with two stars ; *fixedly*, for instance, demands its three syllables, & *unconcernedly* its five. It will further be observed that all but one (*hurriedly*) of the (two-starred) words that drop the extra syllable are in the part of the list containing what are called parasynthetic compounds, i.e. words of the type *good-humour-edly*.

The upshot is that, among the hundreds of adverbs in *-edly* that may suggest themselves as con-venient novelties, (1) those that *must* sound the e are unobjection-able, e.g. *animatedly, offendedly, unstintedly* ; (2) of those in which the e can (physically) be either sounded or silent none (with the exception of the classes in Nᵒˢ 3 & 4 below) are tolerable unless the writer is prepared to have the e sounded ; thus the user of *com-posedly, confusedly, dispersedly, ab-sorbedly, & declaredly*, will not resent their being given four syllables each, & they pass the test ; but no-one

will write *experiencedly, accomplish-edly, boredly, skilledly*, or *discour-agedly*, & consent to the *ed*'s being a distinct syllable ; they are there-fore ruled out ; (3) *hurriedly* sug-gests that such forms as *palsiedly, worriedly, variedly, frenziedly, & studiedly* (from verbs in unaccented *-ȳ*) are legitimate ; (4) words in unaccented *-ure, -our*, or *-er*, seem to form passable adverbs in *-edly* without the extra syllable, as *mea-suredly, injuredly, perjuredly, labour-edly, pamperedly, bewilderedly, che-queredly* ; most two-starred words in the second part of the standard list answer to this description ; (5) none from verbs in *-ȳ*, or from those in *-ble, -cle*, &c., as *triedly, satisfiedly, troubledly, puzzledly*, are endurable.

These conclusions may be con-firmed by comparing many couples of possible words. Take *dementedly & derangedly, degradedly & deprav-edly, dejectedly & depressedly, open-handedly & open-armedly, admittedly & ownedly, dispiritedly & dismayedly, delightedly & charmedly, disgustedly & displeasedly*. The reason why the first of each couple is possible & the second (except to novelty-hunters) impossible is that we instinctively shrink from the *ed* syllable (archaic when phonetics allow the e to be silent) except in established words ; *charmedly* as a disyllable is felt to flout analogy, & as a trisyllable is a bizarre mixture of the archaic & the newfangled.

educate makes *educable* (see -ABLE 1).
education(al)ist. See -IST.
educe. *Educible* is better than *educeable* ; see -ABLE 2.
Edy, -ie. See -EY, -IE, -Y.
eel-like. For the hyphen, see -LIKE.
effect, vb. See AFFECT.
effective, effectual, efficacious, effi-cient. The words all mean having effect, but with different applica-tions & certain often disregarded shades of meaning. *Efficacious* applies only to things (especially now to medicines) used for a pur-pose, & means *sure to have*, or

usually having, the desired effect.
Efficient applies to agents or their action regarded as theirs or (with more or less of personification) to instruments &c., & means *capable of producing the desired effect, not incompetent or unequal to a task.* *Effectual* applies to action apart from the agent, & means not falling short of the complete effect aimed at. *Effective* applies to the thing done or to its doer as such, & means *having a high degree of effect.*

An efficacious remedy, (now rare) *cement ; a drug of known efficacy.*

An efficient general, cook ; efficient work, organization ; an efficient bicycle ; efficient cause is a special use preserving the original etymological sense ' doing the work '.

Effectual measures ; an effectual stopper on conversation ; effectual demand in Political Economy is demand that actually causes the supply to be brought to market.

An effective speech, speaker, contrast, cross-fire ; effective assistance, cooperation. An effective blockade, effective capital, effective membership, preserve a now less common sense ' not merely nominal but carried into action '.

effervescence, -cy. The *-ce* form means the act or process, or the product (bubbles &c.), of effervescing ; the *-cy* form (now rare) means the tendency or capacity to effervesce (*has lost its -cy*), though in this sense too *-ce* is now more frequent. See -CE, -CY.

e. g. is short for *exempli gratiâ,* & means only ' for instance '. Nonlatinists are apt to think that it does not matter whether *e. g.* or I.E. is used ; so *Mr —— took as the theme of his address the existence of what he called a psychic attribute, e. g., a kind of memory, in plants.* Italics, & a following comma, are unnecessary, but not wrong.

ego(t)ism. The two words are modern formations of about the same date. Etymologically, there is no difference between them to affect the sense, but *egoism* is correctly & *egotism* incorrectly formed —a fact that is now, since both are established, of no importance. *Egotism* is, or was till recently, the more popular form, & is (perhaps consequently) restricted to the more popular senses—excessive use of *I* in speech or writing, & self-importance or self-centredness in character. *Egoism* shows signs of ousting *egotism* even in these senses, but is also used in metaphysics & ethics as a name for the theory that a person has no proof that anything exists outside his own mind, & for the theory that self-interest is the foundation of morality. However arbitrary the differentiation may be, it serves a useful purpose if it can yet be maintained.

egregious. The etymological sense is simply *eminent* or *of exceptional degree* (*e grege,* out of the flock). The use of the word has been narrowed in English till it is applied only to nouns expressing contempt, & especially to a few of these, as *ass, coxcomb, liar, impostor, folly, blunder, waste. The e. Jones* &c. is occasionally used in the sense *that notorious ass Jones ;* & with neutral words like *example e.* is the natural antithesis to *shining*—*a shining example of fortitude, an e. example of incapacity.* Reversion to the original sense, as in the following, is mere pedantry : *There is indeed little aforethought in most of our daily doings, whether gregarious or egregious.*

eighteenmo. See FOLIO. Pl. *-os ;* see -O(E)S 6.

eighth. Spell thus, but pronounce ātth, not āth.

eighties, 'ei-. See TWENTIES.

eirenicon, ir-. Usually spelt *eir-,* & pronounced īrē′nĭkŏn. As it is chiefly in learned use, it is odd that the spelling should be anomalous. *Irenicum* would be the Latinized & normally transliterated form ; *irenicon* the normally transliterated Greek form ; *eirenikon* the Greek written in English letters. All these have been rejected for the now established mixture *eirenicon*.

either. 1. The pronunciation ī-, though not more correct, is displacing ē- in educated speech, & will probably prevail.
2. The sense *each of the two*, as in *the room has a fireplace at e. end*, is archaic, & should be avoided except in verse or in special contexts.
3. The sense *any one of a number (above two)*, as in *e. of the angles of a triangle*, is loose ; *any* or *any one* should be preferred.
4. The use of a plural verb after *e.*, as in *if e. of these methods are successful*, is a very common grammatical blunder.
5. *Either . . . or*. In this alternative formula *e.* is frequently misplaced. The misplacement should be avoided in careful writing, but is often permissible colloquially. There are two correct substitutes for *You are e. joking or have forgotten* ; some writers refuse one of these, *You e. are joking or have forgotten*, on the ground that it looks pedantic ; but there is no such objection to the other, *E. you are joking or you have forgotten* ; in conversation, however, the incorrect form is defensible because a speaker who originally meant *(are) forgetting* to answer to *are joking* cannot, when he discovers that he prefers *have forgotten*, go back without being detected (as a writer can) & put things in order. See UNEQUAL YOKEFELLOWS ; some examples follow of the slovenliness that should not be allowed to survive proof-correction.

. . . unless it sees its way to do something effective e. towards keeping the peace or limiting the area of conflict.
Their hair is usually worn e. plaited in knots or is festooned with cocks' feathers.
It is not too much to say that trade unions e. should not exist, or that all workers should join compulsorily.
The choice before the nations will be e. that of finding a totally different &

far better method of regulating their affairs, or of passing rapidly from bad to worse.
Either . . . or is sometimes not disjunctive, but equivalent to *both . . . and* or *alike . . . and* : *The continuance of atrocities, the sinking of the* Leinster, *the destruction of French & Belgian towns & villages, are a fatal obstacle* either *to the granting of an armistice* or *to the discussion of terms.* In such cases, *alike* (or *both*) . . . *and* should be preferred, or else proper care should be taken with *either* ; ' an obstacle to either granting an armistice or discussing terms ' would do it.

eke, adv. See PEDANTIC HUMOUR.
eke out. The meaning is to make something, by adding to it, go further or last longer or do more than it would without such addition. The proper object is accordingly a word expressing not the result attained, but the original supply. You can eke out your income or (whence the SLIPSHOD EXTENSION) a scanty subsistence with odd jobs or by fishing, but you cannot eke out a living or a miserable existence. You can e. o. your facts, but not your article, with quotations. You can e. o. ink with water or words with gestures, but not a rabbit-hutch with or out of wire-netting. The first quotation below illustrates the right use, & the others the wrong ones.
Mr Weyman first took to writing in order to e. o. an insufficient income at the Bar./These disconsolate young widows would perforce relapse into conditions of life at once pitiful & sordid, eking out in dismal boarding-houses or humble lodgings a life which may have known comfort./Dr Mitford eked out a period of comparative freedom from expense by assisting the notorious quack, Dr Graham./A man the very thought of whom has ruined more men than any other influence in the nineteenth century, & who is trying to e. o. at last a spoonful of atonement for it all.

1351

F

*

elaborate, v., makes *-rable* ; see -ABLE 1.

elaborateness, elaboration. See -ION & -NESS.

élan. See FRENCH WORDS.

elapse. The noun corresponding to the verb *e.* is not now *e.*, but *lapse.* ' Hearing nothing about it after the e. of a month Mr Cowen wrote to Mr Redford ' may be the words of a writer who knows that *e.* was formerly a noun, but there is nothing in the context to call for archaism.

elder, -est. These forms are now almost confined to the indication of mere seniority among the members of a family ; for this purpose the *old-* forms are not used except when the age has other than a comparative importance or when comparison is not the obvious point. Thus we say *I have an elder* (not *older*) *brother* in the simple sense a brother older than myself ; but *I have an older brother* is possible in the sense a brother older than the one you know of ; & *Is there no older son ?* means Is there none more competent by age than this one ? *My elder* (*-est*) *cousin* would now be usually understood to mean the senior of a family of two (more than two) who are my cousins ; & *my older cousin* would be preferred in either of the senses my cousin who is older than I or the senior of the two cousins of different families that I have. Outside this restricted use of family seniority, *elder* & *eldest* linger in a few contexts, but are giving place to *older* & *oldest.* Thus *Who is the eldest man here ?, The elder men were less enthusiastic, An elder contemporary of mine, There was more character in the elder man, A tradition that has come down from elder times.*

electric(al). See -IC(AL). The longer form, once much the commoner (the OED quotes *electrical shock, battery, eel,* & *spark,* never now heard), survives only in the sense *of* or *concerning electricity,* & is not necessarily preferred even in that sense except where there is danger that *electric* might mislead ; e.g. *had no electrical effect* might be resorted to as a warning that ' did not alter the state of the atmosphere as regards electricity ' is meant, & not ' failed to startle ' ; on the other hand the difference between the ' electric book ' that gives one shocks & the ' electrical book ' that improves one's knowledge of science is obvious.

electrify. For inflexions see VERBS IN -IE &c., 6.

electrocute, -cution. This BARBARISM jars the unhappy latinist's nerves much more cruelly than the operation denoted jars those of its victim. He first realizes that the words must be designed on the pattern of *execution.* It then strikes him that the design itself was ill-advised, since the desideratum was a parallel not to *execution* (which includes electrocution) but to *hang(ing)* & *behead(ing).* He is next horrified by the dawning suspicion that the word-maker took *-cut-* (from *quatere*) instead of the indivisible *secut-* (from *sequi*) for the stem of *execution,* & derived it from *excutere.* The best that can be made of a bad business is to pretend that *electrocute* comes from *electrocutere* (to strike electrically) & change *electrocution* (impossible on that assumption) into *electrocussion.* Though the recognized verbs of *concussion, discussion,* & *percussion,* are *concuss, discuss,* & *percuss, concute* & *discute* are possible & formerly existent forms of the first two, so that *electrocute* & *electrocussion* might pass, failing English parallels (it is a pity that *shock* is not available) for *hang* & *behead.*

electron. Pl. *-ns* ; see -ON 2.

eleemosynary. Seven syllables : ĕlĭē-mŏ'zĭnarĭ.

ELEGANT VARIATION. It is the second-rate writers, those intent rather on expressing themselves prettily than on conveying their meaning clearly, & still more those whose notions of style are based on a few misleading rules of thumb, that are chiefly open to the allurements of elegant variation. Thackeray may be seduced into an occasional lapse (*careering during the season from one great dinner of twenty* covers *to another of eighteen guests*—where however the variation in words may be defended as setting off the sameness of circumstance) ; but the real victims, first terrorized by a misunderstood taboo, next fascinated by a newly discovered ingenuity, & finally addicted to an incurable vice, are the minor novelists & the reporters. There are few literary faults so widely prevalent, & this book will not have been written in vain if the present article should heal any sufferer of his infirmity.

The fatal influence (see SUPERSTITIONS) is the advice given to young writers never to use the same word twice in a sentence—or within 20 lines or other limit. The advice has its uses ; it reminds any who may be in danger of forgetting it that there are such things as pronouns, the substitution of which relieves monotony ; the reporter would have done well to remember it who writes : *Unfortunately* Lord Dudley *has never fully recovered from the malady which necessitated an operation in Dublin some four years since, during* Lord Dudley's *Lord-Lieutenancy.* It also gives a useful warning that a noticeable word used once should not be used again in the neighbourhood with a different application. This point will be found fully illustrated in REPETITION ; but it may be shortly set out here, a kind providence having sent a neatly contrasted pair of quotations :—(A) *Dr Labbé* seriously *maintains that in the near future opium-smoking will be as* serious *as the absinthe scourge in France* ; (B) *The return of the Nationalists to Parliament means that they are prepared to treat* seriously *any* serious *attempt to get Home Rule into working order.* Here A would be much improved by changing *serious* to *fatal,* & B would be as much weakened by changing *serious* to *real* ; the reason is that

the application of *seriously* & *serious* is in A different, the two being out of all relation to each other, & in B similar ; *I am serious in calling it* serious suggests only a vapid play on words ; *we will be serious if you are* serious is good sense ; but the rule of thumb, as usual, omits all qualifications, & would forbid B as well as A. Half a dozen examples are added of the kind of repetition against which warning is needed, to bring out the vast difference between the cases for which the rule is intended & those to which it is mistakenly applied :—*Meetings at which they* passed *their time* passing *resolutions pledging them to resist./A debate which took wider ground than that* actually *covered by the* actual *amendment itself./The observations made yesterday by the Recorder in charging the Grand Jury in the case of the men* charged *with inciting soldiers not to do their duty./We much* regret *to say that there were very* regrettable *incidents at both the mills./The figures I have* obtained *put a very different complexion on the subject than that generally* obtaining./*Doyle drew the original of the outer sheet of Punch as we still know it ; the* original *intention was that there should be a fresh illustrated cover every week.*

These, however, are mere pieces of gross carelessness, which would be disavowed by their authors. Diametrically opposed to them are sentences in which the writer, far from carelessly repeating a word in a different application, has carefully not repeated it in a similar application ; the effect is to set readers wondering what the significance of the change is, only to conclude disappointedly that it has none :—*The Bohemian Diet will be the second Parliament to elect* women *deputies, for Sweden already has several* lady *deputies./There are a not inconsiderable number of* employers *who appear to hold the same opinion, but certain* owners—*notably those of South Wales —hold a contrary view to this./Mr John Redmond has just now a path* to tread *even more thorny than that which Mr Asquith has to* walk. What has Bohemia done that its females should be mere women ? Are owners subject to influences that do not affect employers ? of course they might be, & that is just the reason why, as no such suggestion is meant, the word should not be changed. And can Mr Asquith really have taught himself to walk without treading ? All this is not to say that *women & employers & tread* should necessarily be repeated—only that satisfactory variation is not to be so cheaply secured as by the mechanical replacing of a word by a synonym ; the true corrections are here simple, (1) *several* alone instead of *several women* (or *lady) deputies,* (2) *some* alone instead of *certain employers* (or *owners*), (3) *Mr Asquith's* instead of *that which Mr Asquith has to tread* (or *walk*) ; but the writers are confirmed variationists—nail-biters, say, who no longer have the power to abstain from the unseemly trick.

Before making our attempt (the main object of this article) to nauseate by accumulation of instances, as sweet-shop assistants are cured of larceny by cloying, let us give special warning against two temptations. The first occurs when there are successive phrases each containing one constant & one variable ; the variationist fails to see that the varying of the variable is enough, & the varying of the constant also is a great deal too much ; he may contrive to omit his constant if he likes, but he must not vary it :— *There are 466 cases ; they consist of 366 matrimonial* suits, *56 Admiralty* actions, *& 44 Probate* cases (strike out *suits & actions* ; but even to write *cases* every time is better than the variation)./*The total number of farming properties is 250,000 ; of these only 800 have more than 600 acres ; 1,600 possess between 300 & 600 acres, while 116,600 own less than eight acres apiece* (if *while* is changed to *and, possess & own,* which anyhow require not *properties* but *proprietors,*

can be dropped ; or *have* can be repeated)./*At a higher* rate *or lower* figure, *according to the special circumstances of the district* (omit *rate*)./ *It was Tower's third* victory, *& Buxton's second* win (drop either *victory* or *win*).

The second temptation is to regard *that & which* as two words that are simply equivalent & (the variationist would say *& which*) exist only to relieve each other when either is tired. This equivalence is a delusion, but one that need not be discussed here, & the point to be observed in the following quotations is that, even if the words meant exactly the same, it would be better to keep the first selected on duty than to change guard :—*He provides a philosophy* which *disparages the intellect & that forms a handy background for all kinds of irrational beliefs* (omit *that*)./*A scheme for unification* that *is definite & which will serve as a firm basis for future reform* (omit *which*)./*A pride that at times seemed like a petty punctilio, a self-discipline* which *seemed at times almost inhuman in its severity* (repeat *that*).

And now the reader may at length be turned loose among dainties of every kind ; his gorge will surely rise before the feast is finished. *In every case the fish copied on its back the pattern on which it lay, though not with equal success in every* instance./*There are four cases in which old screen-work is still to be found in Middlesex churches, & not one of these* instances *is so much as named.*/ *In 32* cases *there are Liberal candidates in the field, & in all* instances *so-called Socialists supply the third candidate.*/*Dr Tulloch was for a time* Dr Boyd's *assistant, & knew the* popular preacher *very intimately, & the* picture *he gives* of the genial essayist *is a very engaging one.*/ *Rarely does the ' Little Summer ' linger until* November, *but at times its stay has been prolonged until quite late in* the year's penultimate month./ *Several who have never given formal* adherence to the Unionist Party, although their votes have frequently been given to that section./The addressee of many epistles in the volumes of ' Letters of Charles Dickens './ GERMAN EMPEROR'S VISIT TO AUSTRIAN MONARCH./The export trade of the U.S. with the Philippines has increased by nearly 50%, while that of the U.K. has decreased by one-half./Curiously enough, women played the male parts, whilst men were entrusted with the female characters./France is now going through a similar experience with regard to Morocco to that which England had to undergo with reference to Egypt./There was once a famous statesman of whom his great rival said that he was inebriated with the exuberance of his own verbosity ; Ruskin was never thus intoxicated./If there is no material cause of quarrel between Russia & Germany, still less is there any material ground for quarrel between Britain & Germany./While I feel quite equal to the rôle of friendly & considerate employer, I do not feel adequate to the part of a special Providence./If I have a complaint to proffer against Mr Redford, it certainly is, except perhaps in the case of ' Monna Vanna ', not in the matter of the plays to which he has refused a licence, but in regard to a few of the plays which he sanctioned./ Were I an artist, I could paint the Golf Links at Gaya & call it ' A Yorkshire Moor ' ; I could depict a water-way in Eastern Bengal & call it ' The Bure near Wroxham ' ; I could portray a piece of the Punjab & call it ' A Stretch of Essex './ In the Punjab, in Calcutta, & in the Hills the former school predominates ; in the rest of India the latter school prevails./We have a section which cries out at all times that Germany is the enemy, & we have another section which insists that Russia is the peril./ Not only should an agreement be come to, but it has always been certain that it will be arrived at./Just as nothing is sacred to the sapper, so nought is romantic to the scientific explorer./ They spend a few weeks longer in

their winter home than in their summer habitat./It is interesting & satisfactory that a Wykehamist & an Oxonian should be succeeded by an Oxonian & Wykehamist. It will also be interesting & satisfactory to anyone who has lasted out to this point to observe that this skilled performer, who has brought off a double variation (reversing the order of the titles, & stripping the second Wykehamist of his article), has been trapped into implying by the latter change that the successor is one man & the predecessor(s) two.

elegiacs, elegy. See TECHNICAL TERMS.

elemental, elementary. The two words are now pretty clearly differentiated, the reference of -al being to ' the elements ' either in the old sense of earth, water, air, & fire, or as representing the great forces of nature conceived as their manifestations (or metaphorically the human instincts comparable in power to those forces) ; & that of -ary being to elements in the more general sense of simplest component parts or rudiments. Elemental fire, strife, spirits, passion, power : elementary substances, constituents, facts, books, knowledge, schools. The -al form is often wrongly chosen by those who have not observed the differentiation, & think that an occasional out-of-the-way word lends distinction to their style; so: The evergrowing power of the State, the constant extension of its activities, threaten the most elemental liberties of the individual./Responsible government in Canada was still in its most elemental stage.

elevator, by the side of the established English lift, is a cumbrous & needless Americanism ; it should at least be restricted to its hardly avoidable commercial sense of grain-hoist. See SUPERFLUOUS WORDS.

elfish. See ELVISH.
eliminate, -ation. 1. The essential meaning (etymologically ' turn out of doors ') is the expulsion, putting

away, getting rid, or ignoring, of elements that for some reason are not wanted ; the verb does not mean to extract or isolate for special consideration or treatment the elements that *are* wanted, as in *He would e. the main fact from all confusing circumstantials,* & in *hypotheses of the utmost value in the elimination of truth.* See POPULARIZED TECHNICALITIES.

2. The verb makes *eliminable* (see -ABLE 1).

ELLIPSIS. 1. *Be & have.* 2. Second part of compound verb. 3. With change of voice. 4. *That* (conj.). 5. After *than.* 6. With inversion. 7. *That* (rel. pron.). That the reader may at once realize the scope of the inquiry, a few ellipses of miscellaneous types are first exhibited :—

The ringleader was hanged & his followers∧*imprisoned.*/*The evil consequences of excess of these beverages is much greater than*∧*alcohol.*/*Mr Balfour blurted out that his own view was*∧*the House of Lords was not strong enough.*/*No State ever has*∧ *or can adopt the non-ethical idea of property.*/*The House of Lords would have really revised the Bill, as no doubt it could be*∧*with advantage.*/ *Not only may such a love have deepened & exalted, &*∧*may*∧*still deepen & exalt, the life of any man, but* . . .

When a passage would, if fully set out, contain two compound members corresponding to each other, how far may the whole be shortened by omitting in one of these members (' understanding ', in grammatical phrase) a part that is either expressed in the other or easily inferable from what is there expressed ? Possible varieties are so many that it will be better not to hazard a general rule, but to say that the expressed can generally, & the inferable can in specially favourable circumstances, be ' understood ', & then proceed to some types in which mistakes are common.

1. Ellipsis of parts of *be* & *have.*

Not only the expressed part can be understood, but also the corresponding part with change of number or person :—*The ringleader was hanged & his followers imprisoned* ; *He is dead, & I alive* ; *The years have passed & the appointed time come.* These are permissible ; not all that is lawful, however, is expedient, & the licence is not to be recommended outside sentences of this simple pattern ; with the intervening clause in the following quotation it is clearly ill-advised : *A number of stumbling-blocks have been removed, & the road along which the measure will have to travel straightened out* ; it should be observed that it is the distance of *straightened* from *have been,* & not the change of number in the verbs, that demands the insertion of *has been.*

2. Ellipsis of second part of compound verb. Only the expressed part can be understood ; *No State can or will adopt* would be regular, but *No State has or can adopt* is (however common) an elementary blunder. The understanding of an infinitive with *to* out of one without *to* (*A standard of public opinion which ought & we believe will strengthen the sense of parental responsibility*) is equally common & equally wrong ; insert after *ought* either *to strengthen* or *to.*

3. Ellipsis with change of voice. Even if the form required is identical with that elsewhere expressed, it cannot be understood if the voice is different ; to omit *revised* is out of the question in *Though we do not believe that the House of Lords would have really revised the Bill, as no doubt it could be*∧*with advantage.* Still less can the passive *managed* be supplied from the active *manage* in *Mr Dennett foresees a bright future for Benin if our officials will manage matters conformably with its ' customs ', as they ought to have been*∧*.* And with these may be classed the leaving us to get *to be* out of the preceding *to* in *If the two lines are to cross, the rate of loss*∧*reduced to zero,*

*& a definite increase in the world's
shipping to be brought about . . .*

4. Omission of *that* (conjunction).
Though this is strictly speaking not
an ellipsis, but rather an exercise of
the ancient right to abstain from
subordinating a substantival clause
(*And I seyde his opinioun was good—*
Chaucer), it may conveniently be
mentioned here. Three examples
will suffice to show the unpleasantness of ill-advised omission, & to
suggest some cautions :—*Sir,—I am
abashed to see*∧*in my notice of Mr
Bradley Birt's* " ' *Sylhet* ' *Thackeray* "
∧ *I have credited the elder W. M.
Thackeray with sixteen children.*/
*Mr Balfour blurted out that his own
view was*∧*the House of Lords was
not strong enough.*/*I assert*∧*the feeling in Canada today is such against
annexation that* . . . The first illustrates the principle that if there is
the least room for doubt where
the *that* would come, it should be
expressed & not understood. The
second leads us to the rule that when
the contents of a clause are attached
by part of *be* to such words as
opinion, decision, view, or *declaration*
(a very common type), *that* must be
inserted ; it at the same time illustrates the motive that most frequently causes wrong omissions—
the sensible reluctance to make one
that-clause depend on another— ;
but this is always avoidable by
other, though often less simple,
means. The third involves a matter
of idiom, & reminds us that while
some verbs of saying & thinking can
take or drop *that* indifferently, many
have a strong preference for one or the
other use (see THAT CONJ.) ; *assert* is
among those that habitually take *that*.

5. Ellipsis after *than* is extremely
common, & so various in detail as
to make the laying down of any
general rule impossible. The comparative claims of brevity on the one
hand, & on the other of the comfort
that springs from feeling that all is
shipshape, must in each case be
weighed with judgement. It will be
best to put together a few examples,

ranging from the more to the less
obvious, in which doubts whether
all is right with the sentence obtrude
themselves. *The evil consequences of
excess of these beverages is much
greater than* ∧ *alcohol* ; i.e., than the
evil consequences of excess of alcohol
are great ; shall we (a) omit *are
great* ? yes, everyone does it ; (b)
omit *the evil consequences of excess
of* ? no, no-one could do it but one
who could also write, like this author,
consequences is ; (c) retain all this ?
no—waste of words ; (d) shorten to
those of excess of ? yes, unless the
knot is cut by writing *than with
alcohol.*/*This was due to the feeling
that the Bill went further than public
opinion warranted or was justified* ;
i.e., than what opinion warranted
or what was justified ; either *what*
could be omitted if its clause stood
alone ; but since the two *whats* are
in different cases, one being subject
& the other object, there is felt to
be a grammatical blunder lurking
under cover of *than.*/*That export
trade is advancing with greater rapidity than our trade has ever increased* ;
i.e., than any rapidity with which
ours has increased ; shorten to *than
our trade has ever increased with* ; or,
better, substitute *more rapidly* for
with greater rapidity./*The proceedings
were more humiliating to ourselves
than I can recollect in the course of
my political experience* ; i.e., than
I can recollect any proceedings being
humiliating ; shorten to *any that I
can recollect.*/*The interpretations are
more uniformly admirable than could,
perhaps, have been produced by any
other person* ; i.e., than any would
have been admirable that . . . ;
shorten to *than what could,* though
the misplacing of *perhaps,* which
belongs to the main sentence, will
cry all the louder for correction.

6. Ellipsis complicated by inversion. In questions, & in sentences
beginning with *nor* & certain other
words, inversion is normal, the subject standing after the verb or its
auxiliary instead of before it (*Never
heard I* or *Never did I hear,* not

Never I heard). When a sentence or clause thus inverted has to be enlarged by a parallel member of the kind in which ellipsis would naturally be resorted to, difficulties arise. *Why is a man in civil life perpetually slandering & backbiting his fellow men, & is unable to see good even in his friends ?* The repetition of *is* without that of *why* & the subject is impossible ; in this particular sentence the removal of the second *is* solves the problem as well as the re-insertion of (at the least) *why is such a man* ; but often full repetition is the only course possible./ *Not only may such a love have deepened & exalted, & may still deepen & exalt, the life of any man of any age, but* . . . The inversion has to be carried on ; that is, *not only*, & the subject placed after *may*, must be repeated if *may* is repeated ; &, *may* being here indispensable, nothing less will do than *not only* (with *and* omitted) *may it still deepen.*

7. For ellipsis of *that* (rel. pron.), & of prepositions governing *that* (rel. pron.), see THAT REL. PRON.

elongate. See -ATABLE.

else. The adverb *e.* has come so near to being compounded with certain indefinite pronouns & words of similar character (*anybody, everyone, little, all,* &c.) that separation is habitually avoided, & e.g. *Nobody is ignorant of it e.* is unidiomatic ; correspondingly, the usual possessive form is not *everyone's* &c. *e.,* which is felt to be pedantic though correct, but *everyone else's.* With interrogative pronouns the process has not gone so far ; though *What e. did he say ?* is the normal form, *What did he say e. ?* (with which compare the very unusual *Nothing was said e.*) is unobjectionable ; correspondingly, *who else's* may be used colloquially, but *whose else* (cf. *anybody's e.*) has maintained its ground ; & of the forms *Who else's should it be ?, Whose e. should it be ?, Whose should it be e. ?,* the last is perhaps the best.

elucidate makes *-dable* ; see -ABLE 1.

elusive, elusory. That is elusive which we fail, in spite of efforts, to grasp physically or mentally ; *the elusive ball, half-back, submarine* ; *elusive rhythm, perfume, fame* ; *an elusive image, echo, pleasure.* That is elusory which turns out when attained to be unsatisfying, or which is designed to pass as of more solid or permanent value than it is ; *elusory fulfilment, success, victory, possession, promises.*
The elusive mocks its pursuer, the elusory its possessor ; *elusive* is synonymous with *evasive, elusory* with *illusive.*

elvish, elfish. ' The older form *elvish* is still the more usual '—OED. See -VE(D).

Elysium. Pl. *-ms* ; see -UM.

emaciation. Pronounce *-ăsĭ-* ; see -CIATION.

emancipate makes *-pable* ; see -ABLE 1.

EM- & IM-, EN- & IN-. The words in which hesitation between e- & i- is possible are given in the form recommended ; readers who wish for more than an unsupported recommendation will find notes below.
embed, empanel, encage, encase, enclose &c., *encrust*, encrustment, endorse*, endorsement, endue, enfold, engraft, enmesh, ensure* (in general senses), *entrench, entrust, entwine, entwist, enwrap* ; *incrustation, indorsation, ingrain, ingrained, inquire, inquiry, insure* (in financial sense), *insurance, inure, inweave.*
*but cf. *incrustation, indorsation.*
Tenacious clinging to the right of private judgement is an English trait that a mere grammarian may not presume to deprecate, & such statements as the OED's *The half-latinized* enquire *still subsists beside* inquire will no doubt long remain true. Spelling, however, is not one of the domains in which private judgement shows to most advantage, & the general acceptance of the above forms on the authority of the OED (from which the remarks in

inverted commas below are taken, & which recognizes as the criterion not any pedantic canon, but the usage of most writers) would be a sensible & democratic concession to uniformity.

embed : ' *e.* is now the more common form '.

empanel : the OED gives *e.* precedence.

encage : ' *i.*, the obs. var. of *e.*'.

encase : ' *i.*, var. of *e.*'.

enclose : ' The preponderance of usage (in England at least), as well as etymological propriety, is in favour of *e.*'.

encrust : ' The dictionaries mostly favour *i.*, but *e.* appears to be the more frequent in actual use '.

endorse : ' *E.* is more frequent in commercial & general literary use, but *i.* is more usual in law books '; conformity on the part of the lawyers would be a graceful proceeding.

endue : ' The form *e.* is now the more common in all the living senses '.

enfold : ' *i.*, obs. var. of *e.*'.

engraft : ' *i.*, obs. var. of *e.*'.

enmesh : *immesh* & *emmesh* are less used than *enmesh*.

ensure : ' In general usage *i.* is now limited to the financial sense, in which the form *e.* is wholly obs.'.

entrench : ' The form *i.* is that favoured by modern dictionaries, but in recent use *e.* seems to be more frequent '.

entrust : ' The form *i.*, though preferred in many recent dictionaries, is now rare in actual use '.

entwine, entwist, enwrap : ' *i.*, var. of *e.*'.

incrustation, indorsation : The *i-* of these (cf. *endorse, encrust*) is due to the preference for completely latinizing words with a conspicuously Latin ending.

ingrain(ed) : ' In the participial adjective used attributively, though not in the verb, the form with *in-* is more common than that with *en-* '; the adjective being perhaps a hundred times as common as the verb, & being often so accented (on the

first) that there can be no doubt about its beginning with i & not e, the rare verb will surely conform before long.

inquire, inquiry : The OED gives *i.* the precedence, but says ' The half-latinized *e.*' (the unlatinized form being *enquere*) ' still subsists beside *i.*'.

insure : See *ensure* above.

inure : ' *E.*, an earlier form of *i.*, by which it is now superseded except in the legal sense '; see INURE.

inweave : The OED gives precedence to *i.*

embarkation. The OED gives this as the standard form ; &, where all three forms are justifiable—*embarcation* as the French original. *imbarcation* as properly latinized. & *embarkation* as agreeing with *embark*— it is well to accept the OED ruling.

embargo. Pl. *-os* ; see -O(E)S 6.

embarrassedly. A bad form ; see -EDLY.

embed, im-. See -EM & -IM-.

emblem. For synonymy see SIGN.

embody. For inflexions see VERBS IN -IE &c., 6.

embonpoint. See FRENCH WORDS.

embrasure. Pronunciation : OED ĕmbrā'zhyer ; Nav. & Mil., also ĕmbrazhoor'.

embryo. Pl. *-os* ; see -O(E)S 4.

emend(ation). The words are now confined strictly to the conjectural correction of errors in MS. or printed matter, or to changes deliberately compared to this by metaphor ; they are not used, like *amend(ment)*, of improvement or correction in general.

Emerald Isle. See SOBRIQUETS.

emergence, emergency. The two are now completely differentiated, *-ce* meaning emerging or coming into notice, & *-cy* meaning a juncture that has arisen, esp. one that calls for prompt measures, & also (more recently) the presence of such a juncture (*in case of -cy*). See -CE, -CY.

émeute. See FRENCH WORDS.

emmesh. See EM- & IM-.

emolument. See FORMAL WORDS.

emotion. The tendency to restrict the word to the display of feeling as opposed to the feeling itself, or at least to manifested as opposed to unmanifested feeling, is illustrated in *The total absence of e., combined with an intensity of feeling & simplicity, left an impression upon all attendants.* The restriction is unwarranted ; *e.* includes ' a mental " feeling " or " affection " (e.g. of pleasure or pain, desire or aversion, surprise, hope or fear, &c.) '—OED.

emotive, by the side of *emotional*, which means *of the emotions* as well as *given to emotion*, is a SUPERFLUOUS WORD.

empanel, impanel. See EM- & IM-. Either makes *-lled* &c. ; see -LL-, -L-.

Empire City. See SOBRIQUETS.

employee, employé. The case for the English form is stronger than with most such pairs. One of them is needed, not for literary but for purely business purposes ; & a good plain word with no questions of spelling & pronunciation & accents & italics & genders about it is therefore best. Moreover the *-ee* termination is becoming more & more a living suffix in English. The OED twenty-seven years ago labelled *employee* ' rare exc. U.S.' ; but it is high time it was naturalized. The native words *men, hands, workmen, staff,* &c., are still, however, preferable where they give the meaning equally well.

emporium. For this as a synonym for *shop*, see POMPOSITIES. Pl. *-ms, -a* ; see -UM.

empressement. See FRENCH WORDS.

empty, vb. For inflexions see VERBS IN -IE &c., 6.

emulate makes *-lable* ; see -ABLE 1.

-EN ADJECTIVES. The only adjectives of this type still in ordinary natural use with the sense made of so-&-so are *earthen, flaxen, hempen, wheaten, wooden,* & *woollen* ; we actually prefer *earthen vessels, flaxen*

thread, hempen rope, wheaten bread, wooden ships, & *woollen socks,* to *earth vessels, flax thread, hemp rope, wheat bread, wood ships,* & *wool socks.* Several others (*brazen, golden, leaden, leathern, oaken, oaten, silken, waxen*) can still be used in the original sense (made of brass &c.) with a touch of archaism or for poetic effect, but not in everyday contexts :—*the brazen hinges of Hellgate,* but *brass hinges do not rust* ; *a golden crown* in hymns & fairy-stories, but *a gold crown* in an inventory of regalia ; *a lead pipe,* but *leaden limbs* ; *a leathern jerkin,* but *a leather portmanteau* ; *silken hose,* but *silk pyjamas* ; *an oaken staff,* but *an oak umbrella-stand* ; *an oaten pipe,* but *oat bread* ; *the comb's waxen trellis,* but *wax candles.* Their chief use, however, is in secondary & metaphorical senses—*brazen impudence, golden prospects, leathern lungs, silken ease, waxen skin,* & the like. When well-meaning persons, thinking to do the language a service by restoring good old words to their rights, thrust them upon us in their literal sense where they are out of keeping, such patrons merely draw attention to their clients' apparent decrepitude—apparent only, for the words are hale & hearty, & will last long enough if only they are allowed to confine themselves to the jobs that they have chosen.

There are other words of the same formation (*ashen, bricken, cedarn, silvern,* &c.) that are solely archaic (or pseudo-archaic) & ornamental. The exceptional OLDEN will be found in its place.

en- & in-. See EM- & IM-.

encage, incage. See EM- & IM-.

encase, incase. See EM- & IM-.

enclitic. See TECHNICAL TERMS.

enclose, inclose. See EM- & IM-.

encomium. Pl. *-ms, -a* ; see -UM.

encrust, incrustation. See EM- & IM-.

endeavour. *A somewhat ponderous jibe has been endeavoured to be levelled at the First Lord of the Admiralty because he* ... For this use of *endeavour,* with which *somewhat* is in perfect harmony, see DOUBLE PASSIVES. See also FORMAL WORDS.

endemic, epidemic. An endemic disease is one habitually prevalent in a particular place; an epidemic disease is one that breaks out in a place & lasts for a time only.

endorse, indorsation. See EM- & IM-. The use of *endorse* in advertisements (*Paderewski endorses the pianola*) is an example of unsustained metaphor (METAPHOR 2 A) worth mention because advertisements play a considerable part in forming the language of those who read little else. You can endorse, literally, a cheque or other paper, &, metaphorically, a claim or argument; but to talk of endorsing material things other than papers is a solecism.

endue, indue. See EM- & IM-.

endways, -wise. See -WAYS, -WISE.

enema. ' The normal pronunciation is ĕ′nĭma but the incorrect form [ĭnē′ma] is in very general use '— OED. See FALSE QUANTITY.

enervate. See -ATABLE.

enfold, infold. See EM- & IM-.

enforce. *They were prepared to take action with a view to enforcing this country into a premature & vanquished peace.* This use of *e.* for *force* or *compel* or *drive*, with a person or agent as object, though common two or three centuries ago, is obsolete; today we force a person into peace, or enforce peace. See NOVELTY-HUNTING, OBJECT-SHUFFLING.

enforceable. So spelt; see MUTE E.

enfranchise, not -*ize*; see -ISE)(-IZE.

England, English(man). The incorrect use of these words as equivalents of *Great Britain, United Kingdom, British Empire, British, Briton,* is often resented by the Scotch, Irish, & Welsh; their susceptibilities are natural, but are not necessarily always to be deferred to. It must be remembered that no Englishman, & perhaps no Scot even, calls himself a Briton without

a sneaking sense of the ludicrous. How should an Englishman utter the words *Great Britain* with the glow of emotion that for him goes with *England* ? he talks the *English* language; he has been taught *English* history as one tale from Alfred to George V; he has known in his youth how many Frenchmen are a match for one *Englishman*; he has heard of the word of an *Englishman* & of *English* fair play, scorns certain things as *unEnglish*, & aspires to be an *English* gentleman; he knows that *England* expects every man to do his duty, & that to the foreigner his nation is the *Anglais* & *Engländer* & *Inglesi*; in the word *England,* not in *Britain,* all these things are implicit. The case is not so strong against *British,* since we can speak of the British Empire, the British army or navy or constitution, & British trade, without feeling the word inadequate; yet even it is unfit for many contexts; who speaks of a British gentleman, British home life, British tailoring, or British writers, or condemns with an ' unBritish ' ? on the other hand the British matron, the British parent, & the British public, have an unenviable notoriety. The attempt to forbid thirty millions of people the use of the only names that for them are in tune with patriotic emotion, or to compel them to stop & think whether they mean their country in a narrower or a wider sense each time they name it, is doomed to failure. The most that can be expected is that the provocative words should be abstained from on the more provocative occasions, & that when Scots & others are likely to be within earshot *Britain* & *British* should be inserted as tokens, but no more, of what is really meant.

english, vb. See REVIVALS, SAXONISM.

engraft, in-. See EM- & IM-.

enhance. *Spain felt that the war could not touch her, but that, on the contrary, while the rest of Europe was* *engaged in mutual destruction, she would be materially enhanced.* A dangerous word for the unwary. Her *material prosperity* may *be enhanced*, but *she* cannot *be enhanced* even *in material prosperity*, though a book may *be enhanced in value* as well as have *its value enhanced*. E. (& *be enhanced*) with a personal object (or subject) has long been obsolete. See CAST-IRON IDIOM.

enjambment. See TECHNICAL TERMS.
enjoin. The construction with a personal object & an infinitive (*The advocates of compulsory service e. us to add a great army for home defence to* . . .) is not recommended. The OED quotes Steele, *They injoined me to bring them something from London*, & Froude, *The Pope advised & even enjoined him to return to his duties*; but the archaic sound of the first will be admitted, & in the other 'advised' takes most of the responsibility. The ordinary modern use is *e. caution* &c. *upon* one, not *e.* one *to* do or be.

en masse. See FRENCH WORDS.
enmesh. See EM- & IM-.
ennui. Pronounce ŏnwē'; see FRENCH WORDS.
ennuied, ennui'd. See -ED & 'D.
enormous, enormity. The two words have drifted so far apart that the use of either in connexion with the limited sense of the other is unadvisable. *Enormous sin* & *The impression of enormity produced by the building* are both etymologically possible expressions; but to use the first lays one open to suspicion of pedantry, & to use the second to suspicion of ignorance.

enough & sufficient(ly). 1. In the noun use (= adequate amount), the preference of *s.* to *e.* (*have you had s. ?*, *s. remains to fill another*) may almost be dismissed as a GENTEELISM; besides being shorter, *e.* has the grammatical advantage of being a real noun.
2. In the adjective use (*is there e.*, or *s.*, *butter ?*) *s.* has the advantage of being a true adjective, while *e.* is

only a quasi-adjective; for *e. evidence* is an abbreviation (as with *a hundred men, much difficulty*, &c.) for *e. of evidence*; the consequence is that *a s. supply* is possible, & *an e. supply* is not. In spite of the fact, however, that *s.* is always & *e.* only sometimes available, *e.* is to be preferred as the more natural & vigorous word wherever mere amount can be regarded as the only question : *is there e. butter*, or *butter e., for the week ?* ; *he has courage e. for anything.* But where considerations of quality or kind are essential, *s.* is better; compare *for want of s. investigation* with *there has been investigation e.* ; the first implies that it has not been thorough or skilful, the second that the time given to it has been excessive.
3. In the adverbial use, neither word suffers from a grammatical handicap, *e.* being as true an adverb as *sufficiently.* Choice is dictated (often without the chooser's knowledge) in part by the feeling that a plain homely word, or a formal polysyllable, is appropriate (*he does not idle e.* ; *he does not indulge s. in recreation*), & in part by the limitation of *e.* pointed out above to mere amount or degree (*the meat is not boiled e.* ; *he does not s. realize the consequences*) ; often, however, *e.* is so undeniably more vigorous that it is worth while to help it out with *clearly, fully, far, deeply*, &c., rather than accept the single word *s.* ; compare *he has proved his point clearly e.* with *he has s. proved his point.*

en passant. See FRENCH WORDS.
enquire, enquiry, in-. See EM- & IM-.
en règle. See FRENCH WORDS.
enrol(l). Spell *enrol*, but *-lling* &c. ; see -LL-, -L-.
en route, ensemble. See FRENCH WORDS.
ensure, insure, assure. For *e.* & *i.*, see EM- & IM- ; for *e.* & *a.*, see ASSURE 2.
entail. In spite of the increasing

tendency to differentiate (see NOUN & VERB ACCENT) the noun keeps the accent on the last syllable.

entente. See FRENCH WORDS.

enteric (fever). Newspaper readers who have noticed the disappearance of typhoid & the increase of *e.* may be glad to learn the relation between them. ' *Typhoid fever* : a specific eruptive fever (formerly supposed to be a variety of typhus), character- ized by intestinal inflammation & ulceration : more distinctively, & now more usually, called *enteric fever* '—OED.

enterprise, not *-ize* ; see -ISE)(-IZE.

entertain. A guest is entertained *at* a meal, not *to* it. The OED quotes for the right form, & gives no example of the other ; that, how- ever, is because letter E was pub- lished in the 19th century ; since then *e. to* has become stock re- porters' English ; Dr Page was entertained *to* a banquet, Mr Lloyd George *to* a supper, & the members of the French Free Trade League *to* luncheon & *to* dinner. The question is whether the complaint can be con- fined, like phossy jaw & such things, to the trade; that the reporters them- selves are beyond cure is plain when one of them states that *The Chair- man suggested that the missing M.P. had been trapped by suffragists, & followed this up by entertaining the waiting audience to a song.*

enthral(l). Spell *enthrall* ; see -LL-, -L-.

enthuse. See BACK-FORMATION.

entire. *There is not a single county in the e. of Ireland in which. . .* This, which sounds like a foolish modern use comparable with that of VARIOUS, is in fact an old one, become ' some- what rare ' (OED). It may as well become rarer, for all that.

entitled means having a right (*to* do something) or a just claim (*to* some advantage) ; it does not mean bound (*to* do) or liable (*to* a penalty) ; but it is now being badly misused :— *Germany has suffered bitterly, is*

suffering bitterly, & Germany is entitled to suffer *for what she has* done./*If these people choose to come here* [into court] *& will not learn our heathen language, but prefer their gibberish or jargon, I consider they are* entitled to pay *for it.*

entity. The word is one of those regarded by plain people, whether readers or writers, with some alarm & distrust as smacking of philosophy. Its meaning, however, is neither more nor less recondite than that of the corresponding native word, which no one shies at ; *e.* is *being,* & *an e.* is *a being.* The first or abstract sense is comparatively rare ; *e. is better than nonentity* means the same as *it is better to be than not to be.* In the second or concrete sense, *an e.* differs only so far from *a being* that the latter as used by others than philosophers has come to exclude, while *e.* includes, any non-sentient or impersonal but actually existing thing ; a plant or a stone or a State may be called an e., but is not, outside of philosophy, called a being; *e.* therefore has a right to its place even in the popular vocabulary.

entourage, entr'acte. See FRENCH WORDS.

entrench, in-. See EM- & IM-.

entre nous, entrepôt. See FRENCH WORDS.

entresol. See FLOOR.

entrust. Modern idiom allows only two constructions : to e. (a task, a charge, a secret) *to* someone ; to e. (someone) *with* a task &c. The verb no longer means to put trust in simply (that is to *trust,* not e.), nor to commission or employ or charge *to* do (for which those verbs, or again to *trust,* will serve). The obsolete uses are seen in : *King Edward* entrusted him *implicitly, & invariably acted upon his advice.*/*By victory the fighting men have achieved what their country has* entrusted *them to do.* See CAST-IRON IDIOM.

entrust, entwine, entwist, in-. See EM- & IM-.

ENUMERATION FORMS. One of the first requisites for the writing of good clean sentences is to have acquired the art of enumeration, that is, of stringing together three or four words or phrases of identical grammatical value without going wrong. This cannot be done by blind observance of the rule of thumb that *and* & *or* should be used only once in a list. It will suffice here to illustrate very shortly the commonest type of error :—*The introductory paragraph is sure, firm, & arouses expectancy at once./If he raises fruit, vegetables, or keeps a large number of fowls./A matter in which the hopes & fears of so many of My subjects are keenly concerned, & which, unless handled with fore-sight, judgment, & in the spirit of mutual concession, threatens to . . .* (Prime Minister's English, presumably ; certainly not King's English). The matter will be found fully dis-cussed under AND 2 ; OR is liable to corresponding ill treatment ; & a particular form of bad enumeration is set forth in the article WALLED-UP OBJECT.

enunciate makes -*ciable* ; see -ABLE 1.

enunciation. See -CIATION.

enure. See INURE, & EM- & IM-.

envelop. See -P-, -PP-. The obso-lete spellings *envelope, envelopes,* in the verb, are now to be regarded as mere mistakes.

envelope. The French spelling (-*ppe*) has long gone, & the French pronunciation should no longer be allowed to embarrass us, but give way to ĕ′nvelōp ; all the more now that the verb *envelop,* from its fre-quency in military bulletins, has become popular instead of merely literary.

-EN VERBS FROM ADJECTIVES. It being no part of most people's busi-ness to inquire into such matters, the average writer would probably say, if asked for an offhand opinion, that from any adjective of one syllable an -*en* verb could be formed

meaning to make or become so-&-so. That, at any rate, was roughly the position taken up by one party to a newspaper controversy some years ago on the merits of *quieten.* A very slight examination shows it to be remote from the facts ; -*en* cannot be called a living suffix. There are on the one hand some 50 verbs whose currency is beyond question ; on the other hand as many adjec-tives may be found that, though they look as fit for turning into verbs by addition of -*en* as the 50, no-one would dream of treating in that way ; some of them are allowed to become verbs without the -*en* (*lame, wet, blind, foul*) ; others have to go without a cognate verb (*harsh, grand, wise, sore*) ; others have their beginning operated on instead of their end (*large* & *enlarge, fine* & *refine, new* & *renew, plain* & *explain, strange* & *estrange, dense* & *condense*) ; & the despotism of usage is still clearer when it is noticed that we can say *moisten* but not *wetten, quicken* but not *slowen, thicken* & *fatten* but not *thinnen* or *leanen, deafen* but not *blinden, sweeten* but not *souren, sharpen* but not *blunten, cheapen* but not *dearen, greaten* but not *largen, freshen* but not *stalen, coarsen* but not *finen.* Between the two sets of adjectives, whose mind is made up, some taking & some re-fusing -*en*, there are a few about which questions may arise ; with some the right of the -*en* verb to exist is disputable, & with others the undoubted existence of two verbs (e.g. *loose* & *loosen*), one having -*en,* & one identical with the adjective, raises the question of differentiated senses ; & some remarks may be offered on each. The following is the list, thought to be fairly complete, of the ordinary -*en* verbs, not including anomalous ones like *strengthen,* nor any whose right to exist is dubious :—*blacken, brighten, broaden, cheapen, coarsen, darken, deaden, deafen, deepen, fasten, fatten, flatten, freshen, gladden, greaten, harden, lessen, liken, lighten, loosen, louden, madden, moisten, quicken, redden, ripen, roughen, sadden, sharpen, shorten, sicken, slacken, smarten, soften, steepen, stiffen, straighten, straiten, sweeten, tauten, thicken, tighten, toughen, weaken, whiten, widen, worsen.*

The debatable words are :

black & *blacken* : the second is the wider word used for most purposes, *black* being confined to the sense put black colour upon, besides being only transitive ; you black boots, glass, or your face, & black out a passage as censor ; you blacken a character ; stone blackens or is blackened with age.

brisken : not in OED.

dampen : old in English, but ' now chiefly U.S.' (OED) & a SUPER-FLUOUS WORD.

dwarfen : not in OED.

fat & *fatten* : the first is chiefly archaic, kept alive by *the fatted calf*, but also survives as a business word in cattle-breeding circles ; *fatten* is the ordinary word.

glad & *gladden* : *gladden* is now the ordinary word, but *to glad* is still in poetical use, & is familiar in Moore's *dear gazelle* lines.

greaten : ' now archaic ' (OED) ; but a word formerly much used, & not likely to perish.

loose & *loosen* : the broad distinction is that *loose* means undo or set free (opposite to bind), & *loosen* means make looser (opposite to tighten).

liven : a modern & merely colloquial word, but useful as the intransitive of *enliven*.

mad & *madden* : *mad* was formerly much used, especially as intransitive in the sense act madly ; this is now obsolete, so that ' far from the madding crowd', which is an example of it, is perhaps generally taken to mean from the distracting crowd ; & the only present function of *to mad* is to supply a poetical synonym for *madden*, which has suffered from wear & tear as a trivial exaggeration for annoy.

olden : this had a vogue during the 19th century in the sense *make* or

become older in looks or habits, & was an especial favourite of Thackeray's ; but, with *to age* well established, it is a SUPERFLUOUS WORD.

palen : in OED, with one quotation only ; *to pale* is the right word.

plump & *plumpen* : *plump* is fairly common in the sense *make plump* ; *plumpen* is rare, & a SUPERFLUOUS WORD.

quiet & *quieten* : *quiet* as a verb dates from 1440 at least, & appears in the Prayer Book, Shakspere, Burke, & Macaulay, besides many good minor writers ; it is both transitive & intransitive ; for *quieten*, perhaps the only -*en* verb from an adjective of more than one syllable, the most authoritative name quoted by the OED is Mrs Gaskell ; its inflexions (*quietened, quietening*, &c.) are ugly, & it must be classed as a SUPERFLUOUS WORD.

right & *righten* : *to right* is established, & *righten* (called ' rare ' by the OED, though used occasionally from the 14th century on) is a SUPERFLUOUS WORD.

rough & *roughen* : both are in full use, with some idiomatic differentiation, though often either will do ; see ROUGH(EN).

ruden : in OED, with one quotation ; to be regarded as a freak.

slack & *slacken* : as *rough(en)* ; see SLACK(EN).

smooth & *smoothen* : the OED gives numerous examples of *smoothen*, each of which, however, makes one wonder afresh why on earth (except sometimes metri gratia) the writer did not content himself with *smooth* ; *smoothen* had clearly a vogue in the early 19th century, but is now a SUPERFLUOUS WORD.

steep & *steepen* : *steep* is rare, & *steepen* the normal form.

stout & *stouten* : *stout* occurs only in special senses, & is archaic ; *stouten* is fairly common.

white & *whiten* : *to white* is perhaps only used in echoes of ' whited sepulchres ' & of ' as no fuller on earth can white them '.

worsen, though many writers perhaps shy at it & reluctantly prefer *deteriorate* in the intransitive sense, is quoted from Milton, George Eliot, & others.

environs. The OED recognizes the two pronunciations ĕnvīr'onz, ĕ'nvĭronz, in that order.

envisage. A 19th-century word only, & a surely undesirable GALLICISM. *Face, confront, contemplate, recognize, realize, view, & regard,* seem equal between them to all requirements. See WORKING & STYLISH WORDS.

envoy (in prosody). See TECHNICAL TERMS.

envy, vb. For inflexions see VERBS IN -IE &c., 6.

enwrap, in-. See EM- & IM-.

epaulet(te). ' The anglicized spelling *epaulet* is preferable, on the ground that the word is fully naturalized in use; but the form in -*ette* is at present more common '— OED.

epergne. This odd word, which seems to challenge one to show that one can pronounce French, but will be vainly sought in the French dictionary, is pronounced ĭper'n by the OED.

epexegetic. See TECHNICAL TERMS.

epic, adj. An increasingly popular use is *e. laughter, combat, contest, struggle, siege,* &c.; being barely recognized in the OED, it is probably new; as the meaning is mainly *such as we read of in Homer,* the word HOMERIC is perhaps better.

epicene. For the grammatical sense, see COMMON. Having no real function in English grammar, the word is kept alive chiefly as a more contemptuous synonym for *effeminate,* implying physical as well as moral sexlessness; for this purpose it is better suited than *common* or *neuter* owing to their familiarity in other senses.

epid(e)ictic. See GREEK G.
epidemic. See ENDEMIC.
epidermis. See POLYSYLLABIC HUMOUR.

epigram. See TECHNICAL TERMS.
epigrammatic. So spelt; see -M-, -MM-. Pron. ĕpĭgramă'tĭk.
epigraphy. See TECHNICAL TERMS.
epistle. See PRONUNCIATION, Silent t.
epoch, epoch-making. Under TIME, the meaning of the word *epoch* is explained. If an epoch were made every time we are told that a discovery or other event is epochmaking, our bewildered state of ceaseless transition from the thousands of eras we were in yesterday to the different thousands we were in today would be pitiful indeed. But luckily the word is blank cartridge, meant only to startle, & not to carry even so imponderable a bullet as conviction. Cf. UNIQUE, & UNTHINKABLE.

epode. See TECHNICAL TERMS.
epopee. The OED states that the word is ' now somewhat rare ', summarizes its meaning as ' = *epic* B ', i.e. the noun *epic,* & shows no reason why it should still exist. That it was formerly commoner than now was due to the fact that the competition between the Greek *epos,* the French *épopée,* & the naturalized adjective *epic,* for the post of English noun was not yet decided in favour of the last. Today *e.*'s only function is to enable learned writers to puzzle unlearned readers who know an epic but never heard of *epopee.* A SUPERFLUOUS WORD.

e pur si muove. See HACKNEYED PHRASES.

equable. The quality indicated is complex—not merely freedom from great changes, but that as well as remoteness from either extreme, a compound of uniformity & moderation. A continuously cold climate or a consistently violent temper is not *e.*; nor on the other hand is a moderate but changeable climate or a pulse that varies frequently though within narrow limits.

equal. 1. The verb makes *equalling* &c.; see -LL-, -L-.

2. *The navy is not e. in numbers or*

in strength to perform *the task it will be called upon to undertake* ; *perform* should be *performing* ; see GERUND 3, & ANALOGY.

3. *This work is* the e., if not better than anything *its author has yet done* ; *e.* lends itself particularly to this blunder ; see UNEQUAL YOKE-FELLOWS, & read *is e. to, if not better than, anything* . . .

4. For *equaller,* see -ER & -EST 2.

equally as. 1. The use of *as* instead of *with* in correlation with *equally* (*Hermes is patron of poets equally as Apollo*) is a relic of the time when *equally with* had not been established & writers were free (as with many other correlative pairs) to invent their own formulae.

2. The use of *equally as* instead of either *equally* or *as* by itself is an illiterate tautology, but one of which it is necessary to demonstrate the frequency, & therefore the danger, by abundant quotation : ' *Stokehold* ' *is equally as correct as* ' *stokehole* ' ; *our correspondent should consult a dictionary.*/*The Opposition are equally as guilty as the Government.*/*The round seeded sort is equally as hardy & much pleasanter to handle.*/*The labour crisis has furnished evidence equally as striking.*/*There was certainly no tuft, but equally as surely no wound.*/*A practice in some respects equally as inequitable as that which existed in former years.*/*He was outplayed by a man with a game more original in tactics & equally as severe as his own.*/*The forwards should be fast, but then they will be meeting men equally as speedy.*/*Unless retail prices are equally as satisfactory.*

equate. See -ATABLE.
equation. For *personal e.* see PERSONAL.

equerry. The established pronunciation is ĕ′kwerĭ, & the OED gives it precedence, though it explains that, as against ĭkwĕ′rĭ, it probably owes its victory to *e.*'s being popularly connected with *equus* horse, *equine,* &c. ; see TRUE & FALSE ETYMOLOGY. The RECESSIVE AC-

CENT tendency, however, would perhaps in any case have prevailed.

equitation. Chiefly serviceable to the POLYSYLLABIC HUMOURist.

equivalence, -cy. There appears to be no sort of differentiation ; the four-syllabled word is now much commoner, & the five-syllabled might well be let die. See -CE, -CY.

equivocation (in logic). See TECHNICAL TERMS.

era. For synonymy see TIME.
eradicate makes -*cable* ; see -ABLE 1.

-ER & -EST, MORE & MOST. Neglect or violation of established usage with comparatives & superlatives sometimes betrays ignorance, but more often reveals the repellent assumption that the writer is superior to conventions binding on the common herd. The remarks that follow, however, are not offered as precise rules, but as advice that, though generally sound, may on occasion be set aside.

1. The normal -*er* & -*est* adjectives. 2. Other common -*er* & -*est* adjectives. 3. -*er* & -*est* in adverbs. 4. Adjectives tolerating -*est* but not -*er.* 5. Stylistic extension of -*er* & -*est.* 6. Emotional -*est* without *the.* 7. Comparatives misused. 8. Superlatives misused.

1. The adjectives regularly compared with -*er* & -*est* in preference to *more* & *most* are (a) all monosyllables (*hard, sage, shy,* &c.) ; (b) disyllables in -y (*holy, lazy, likely,* &c.), in -le (*noble, subtile,* &c.), in -er (*tender, clever,* &c.), in -ow (*narrow, sallow,* &c.) ; (c) many disyllables with accent on the last (*polite, profound,* &c. ; but cf. *antique, bizarre, burlesque,* & the predicative adjectives *afraid, alive, alone, aware*) ; (d) trisyllabic negative forms of b & c words (*unholy, ignoble, insecure,* &c.).

2. Some other disyllables in everyday use not classifiable under terminations, as *common, cruel, pleasant,* & *quiet* (cf. *constant, sudden,* &c.) prefer -*er* & -*est* ; these are registered in their dictionary places. And many others, e. g. *awkward,* *brazen, buxom, crooked, equal,* can take *-er* & *-est* without disagreeably challenging attention.

3. Adverbs not formed with *-ly* from adjectives, but identical in form with them, use *-er* & *-est* naturally (*runs faster, sleeps sounder, hits hardest, hold it tighter*) ; some independent adverbs, as *soon, often, seldom,* do the same ; *-ly* adverbs, though comparatives in *-lier* are possible in archaic & poetic style (*wiselier said, softlier nurtured*), now prefer *more wisely* &c. ; but there is some freedom in the way of treating the comparative adjective, even where the positive is not so used, as an adverb (*easier said than done* ; *he writes cleverer than he talks* ; *try to state your case clearer*) ; this, however, is chiefly colloquial.

4. Many adjectives besides those described in 1 & 2 are capable in ordinary use, i. e. without the stylistic taint illustrated in 5 & 6, of forming a superlative in *-est*, used with *the* & serving as an emphatic form simply, while no-one would think of making a comparative in *-er* from them : *in the brutalest, civilest, timidest, winningest, cogentest, cheerfullest, cunningest, doggedest, drunkenest, candidest, damnablest, manner.* The terminations that most invite this treatment are *-ful, -ing, -able, -ed,* & *-id* ; on the other hand the very common adjective terminations *-ive, -ic,* & *-ous,* reject it altogether (*curiouser & curiouser* is a product of Wonderland). Though it is hard to draw a clear line between this use & the next, the intent is different ; the words are felt to be little less normal, & yet appreciably more forcible, than the forms with *most* ; they are superlatives only, & emphasis is their object ; an attempt is made to register them in their dictionary places.

5. As a stylistic device, based on NOVELTY-HUNTING, & developing into disagreeable MANNERISM, the use of *-er* & *-est* is extended to many adjectives normally taking *more* &

most, & the reader gets pulled up at intervals by *beautifuller, delicater, ancientest, diligentest, delectablest, dolefuller, devotedest, admirablest,* & the like. The trick served Carlyle's purpose, & has grown tiresome in his imitators. The extreme form of it is that which next follows.

6. The emotional *-est* without *the. Mlle Nau, an actress of considerable technical skill & a valuable power of exhibiting deepest emotion* ; this sentence is so obviously critical & unemotional that it shows fully the VULGARIZATION of a use that is appropriate only to high-poetic contexts. In so analytic a mood the critic should have been content with *deep emotion* ; if he had been talking descriptively, he might have gone as far as ' she exhibited the deepest emotion ' ; not unless he had been apostrophizing her in verse as ' deepest emotion's Queen ', or by whatever lyric phrase emotion (& not analysis) might have inspired, should he have dared to cut out his *the* & degrade the idiom sacred to the poets. Not that he is a solitary or original sinner ; half the second-rate writers on art & literature seem to think they have found in this now hackneyed device a facile way of exhibiting intense but restrained feeling.

7. Certain illogicalities to which the comparative lends itself may be touched upon. *Don't do it more than you* can *help,* meaning not what it says but the opposite (*than you cannot help*), is worth changing into *than you need* or *must* or *are obliged to,* unless it is to rank as a STURDY INDEFENSIBLE. *Better known than popular* is cured by resolving *better* into *more well. It is more or less—& certainly* more than less—*a standardized product* is a case of CANNIBALISM, one of the necessary two *mores* having swallowed the other. Unwise striving after double emphasis accounts for *He excelled as a lecturer more than as a preacher, because he felt* freer to bring more of *his personality into play,* & for *Were* *ever* finer *lines perverted to a* meaner *use ?*. In the first (a mixture of *freer to bring his & free to bring more of his*) the writer has done nothing worse than give himself away as a waster of words ; but in the second (a confusion of *were ever fine lines more spoilt ?* & *were ever finer lines spoilt ?*—the former alone being the sense meant) we have the force actually diminished, if a reader chooses to work it out, by the addition designed to strengthen it.

8. In superlatives, *the fairest of her daughters Eve* is still with us : *Sir E. Cassel's Christmas gift to the hospitals of £50,000 is only the latest of many acts of splendid munificence by which he has benefited his fellows before now* ; this gift is no more one (latest or not) of those ' before now ' than Eve is her own daughter.

And here is a well contrasted pair of mistakes ; the first is of a notorious type (for examples see ONE), & the second looks almost as if it was due to avoidance of the misunderstood danger ; read *have* for *has* in the first, & *has* for *have* in the other :— *In which case one of the greatest & most serious strikes which* has *occurred in modern times will take place./ Houdin was a wonderful conjuror, & is often reckoned the greatest of his craft who* have *ever lived.*

-ER & -OR. 1. The agent termination -*er* can be added to any existing English verb ; but with many verbs the regular agent-noun ends in -*or* & that in -*er* is an occasional one only, & with others both forms are established with or without differentiation of sense ; see also -OR.

2. When -*er* is added to verbs in -*y* following a consonant, *y* is changed to *i* (*occupier, carrier, flier*) ; but *y* is retained between a vowel & -*er* (*player, employer, buyer*).

Erastianism. See JANSENISM.

ere. See INCONGRUOUS VOCABULARY, & VULGARIZATION. *Before* should in all ordinary prose be preferred ; the following quotations show the fish out of water at its

unhappiest : *The iniquitous anomaly of the plural voter will be swept away ere we are much older./There is reason to suppose that he will have arrived at the South Pole long ere this & at the season best fitted for accurate observation./As many people may be aware, Christmas books are put in hand long ere the season with which they are associated comes round./In the opinion of high officials it is only a matter of time ere the city is cleared of the objectionable smoke pollution evil./ Ere the declaration of a general strike is made by the Trade Unions sincere efforts are being made by . . ./The firm manufactured 14½ million shells ere the Armistice.*

ergo (Latin for *therefore*) is archaic or obsolete in serious use, but still serves the purpose of drawing attention facetiously to the illogical nature of a conclusion : *He says it is too hot for anything ; ergo, a bottle of Bass.* See PEDANTIC HUMOUR.

Erin. See SOBRIQUETS.

Eros. We talk erotics more than we did, & there is an Eros that most Londoners have seen ; so the name has a future before it, & its pronunciation matters. The Greek word, in English mouths, is ĕ'rŏz ; but dictionaries that give it (the OED does not) seem to call it ēr'ŏs. As these false quantities have not, like e.g. that in *Sŏcrates*, the sanction of long familiarity, an effort might be made to establish ĕ'rŏz, or at the least ĕ'rŏs.

err. For *erring* see PRONUNCIATION s.f.

errand. Unconnected with *err* & *errant* ; see TRUE & FALSE ETYMOLOGY.

erratum. Pl. -*ta* ; see -UM.

erst, erstwhile. See PEDANTIC HUMOUR, & VULGARIZATION. *Incidentally, it may be mentioned that amongst Smithfield men ' boneless bag meat' has completely ousted the sausage from its erstwhile monopoly of jest & gibe.*

erupt. There is a natural tendency

to shrink from the word as if it were a newfangled derivative of *eruption* like the clipped words in BACK-FORMATION ; it has in fact been in good use for some centuries.

eschatology &c. Pronounce ĕska-.
eschscholtzia. So spelt ; pronounce ĭshŏ′ltsĭa (not ĕskŏl-).
escort, n. & v. See NOUN & VERB ACCENT.

Eskimo(s), Esquimaux. The former seems to be now the established English spelling ; the pronunciation is the same either way.

especial(ly). 1. (*E*)*special*(*ly*). 2. *Especially* with inversion. 3. *Especially as.* 1. (*E*)*special*(*ly*). The characteristic sense of the longer adjective & adverb is pre-eminence or the particular as opposed to the ordinary, that of the others being limitation or the particular as opposed to the general. There is however a marked tendency in the adjectives for *especial* to disappear & for *special* to take its place ; it may be said that *special* is now possible in all senses, though *especial* is still also possible or preferable in the senses (a) exceptional in degree, as *My especial friend is Jones, He handles the matter with especial dexterity, Oxford architecture receives especial attention,* (b) of, for, a particular person or thing specified by possessive adjective or case, as *For my* or *Smith's especial benefit, For the especial benefit of wounded soldiers.* In the adverbs the encroachments of the shorter form are more limited ; a writer may sometimes fall into saying *The reinforcements arrived at a* specially *critical moment,* where *an especially* would be better ; but it is as little allowable to say *The candidates,* specially *those from Scotland, showed ability* as *Candidates must be* especially *prepared* or *An arbitrator was* especially *appointed.* Two examples follow of *especially* used where *specially* is clearly meant ; in both the sense is not to an exceptional degree, but for one purpose & no other : *Only*

Mohammedans were permitted to work within the sacred zones, & Turkish engineers were especially trained by the Germans for this purpose./Agreeable features of the book will be the illustrations, including a number of reproductions of prints especially lent by Lord Rosebery & Mr Lewis Harcourt.
2. *Especially* with inversion. The word is a favourite with victims of this modern craze (see INVERSION) : *Springs of mineralized water, famous from Roman times onwards,* especially *did they come into renown during the nineteenth century./Mr Campbell does not recognize a change of opinion, but frankly admits a change of emphasis ;* especially *is he anxious at the present time to advance the cause of Liberal Evangelism.*
3. *Especially as.* It is worth notice that of the causal *as*-clauses discussed in AS 2 some types intolerable in themselves are made possible by the insertion of *especially* before *as* : *I shall have to ask for heavy damages, as my client's circumstances are not such as to allow of Quixotic magnanimity ; as by itself is, as usual, insufficient to give the remainder of the sentence the fresh push-off that, introducing an unforeseen consideration, it requires ; but* especially *inserted before* as, *by bespeaking attention, prevents the tailing off into insignificance that would otherwise ruin the balance.*

espièglerie. See FRENCH WORDS.
espionage. Pronounce ĕ′spyonĭj.
espy. For inflexions see VERBS IN -IE &c., 6.
essay. 1. For *e.* & *assay,* vv., see ASSAY.
2. The verb is accented on the last ; the noun, in its now commonest sense of a kind of literary piece, on the first. But in the wider & now less usual sense of *an attempt* the old accent on the last is still often heard ; that it was formerly so accented is evident from lines like *Whose first essay was in a tyrant's praise./This is th' essay of my*

unpractis'd pen./And calls his finish'd poem an Essay. See NOUN & VERB ACCENT.

essence & substance, essential(ly) & substantial(ly). The words started in life as Latin philosophical terms translating the Greek *ousia* (lit. being) & *hupostasis* (lit. underneathness) ; the meaning of the Greek words was practically the same, ' true inwardness ' being perhaps the nearest equivalent in native English, but the second was substituted by later Greek philosophers for the first as used by earlier ones ; similarly in Latin *substantia* was a post-Augustan synonym for Cicero's *essentia.* It is therefore natural that *essence & substance, essential(ly) & substantial(ly),* should on the one hand be sometimes interchangeable, & on the other hand develop, like most synonyms, on diverging lines with differentiations gradually becoming fixed. It may be said roughly that *s.* has moved in the direction of material & quantity, *e.* in that of spirit & quality. The strictly philosophical or metaphysical uses are beyond the scope of this book ; but some examples of the words in popular contexts may serve to show how they agree & disagree.

1. Examples in which either is possible, sometimes with & sometimes without change of sense, or with degrees of idiomatic appropriateness :
God is an essence (or less often *a s.*), i.e. a self-existent being./*I can give you the substance of what he said* (or less often *the e.*, implying the cutting out of all superfluous details)./*But he took care to retain the substance of power* (or less usually *the essence,* or archaically *the substantials,* or quite well *the essentials*)./*The essence of morality is right intention, the substance of it is right action* (the words could not be exchanged in this antithesis, but in either part by itself either word would do ; *the e. is that without which morality*

would not be what it is, *the s.* is that of which it is made up)./*Distinguish between the mere words of Revelation & its substance* (or *e.,* indifferently)./ *They give in substance the same account* (or *in essence* rarely, or *substantially* or *essentially*)./*The treaty underwent substantial modifications* (or *e.,* but *s.* means merely that they amounted to a good deal, *e.* that they changed the whole effect)./*Desire of praise is an essential part of human nature* (or *s.* ; if *e.,* human nature without it is inconceivable ; if *s.,* human nature is appreciably actuated by it)./*There is an essential difference* (or *s.* ; the latter much less emphatic)./*He remains the same in essentials* (or archaically *in substantials*)./*All parties received substantial justice* (or rarely *e.,* which implies much less, if any, ground for dissatisfaction).

2. Examples admitting of *essen-* only :
The essence of a triangle is three straight lines meeting at three angles./ What is the essence of snobbery ?/ Such talk is the essence of nonsense./ Time is of the essence of the contract./ Kubla Khan may be called essential poetry./The qualities essential to success./It is essential to know all the facts./This point is essential to the argument./An essentially vulgar person.

3. Examples admitting of *substan-* only :
Butter is a substance./Parting with the substance for the shadow./There is no substance in his argument./ A man of substance./A cloth with some substance in it./His failure to bring any substantial evidence./A substantial meal./A substantially built house.

essential, necessary, requisite. The words so far agree in the sense in which they are all commonest, i. e. *needed,* that in perhaps most sentences containing one of them either of the others could be substituted without serious change of meaning. It often matters nothing whether we say ' the e.' or ' the n.', or ' the r., qualities are courage & intelligence only '. They have reached the meeting-point, however, from different directions, bringing each its native equipment, of varying suitability for various tasks. For instance, in *We can hardly say that capital is as r. to production as land & labour* the least suitable of the three has been chosen, the word wanted to class the relation of land & labour to production being the strongest of all, whereas r. is the weakest.

If we call something e. we have in mind a whole that would not be what it is to be or is or was if the part in question were wanting ; the e. thing is such that the other thing is inconceivable without it. *E.* is the strongest word of the three.

When we call something n., we have in mind the irresistible action of causality or logic ; the n. thing is such that the other cannot but owe its existence to it or result in it. *N.* doubles the parts of *indispensable & inevitable.*

When we call something r., we have in mind merely an end for which means are to be found ; the r. thing is that demanded by the conditions, but need not be the only thing that could satisfy their demands, though it is usually understood in that sense. The fact that r. has no negative form corresponding to *une.* & *unn.* is significant of its less exclusive meaning.

For a trivial illustration or two :— Bails are r., but neither e. nor n., for cricket ; not e., for it is cricket without them ; not n., for their want need not stop the game. In the taking of an oath, religious belief is e., but neither n. nor r. ; the unbeliever's oath is no oath, but the want of belief need not prevent him from swearing, nor will belief help him to swear. Death is the n., but neither the e. nor the r. result of breaking one's neck ; that chain of cause & effect is for the present *

established ; but the discovery of a remedy is not inconceivable, & the result that has never been e. may some day not be even n. ; r. in this connexion can speak for itself. The alphabetical arrangement is unessential, but not unnecessary, & very requisite, in this book ; the dictionary without it would be a dictionary all the same, but the laws of causality make the publishers demand & the writer supply alphabetical order, & without it the purpose would be very badly served.

-est in superlatives. See -ER & -EST.

estate. *The three estates,* i. e. the Lords Spiritual, the Lords Temporal, & the Commons, is often wrongly applied to Sovereign, Lords, & Commons. The use of the phrase being now purely decorative, & the reader being often uncertain whether the user of it may mean Sovereign & Parliament, or Parliament, or all bishops & all peers & all electors, it is perhaps better left alone. *The third e.* is a phrase often used for the French bourgeoisie before the Revolution ; *& the fourth e.* is a jocular description of the newspaper press as one of the powers that have to be reckoned with in politics.

esteem. For *success of e.,* see GALLICISMS.

estimate, v. See -ATABLE.

estimate, estimation. The sense a judgement formed by calculation or consideration belongs to *estimate* & not to *estimation,* which means not the judgement itself, but the forming of it. The tendency described in LONG VARIANTS often leads writers astray, as in : *Norwegians can only wish that the optimistic estimation of Mr Ponting of the British minefields at Spitzbergen will come true.*

estimation. The use of *in my* &c. *e.* as a mere substitute for *in my* &c. *opinion* where there is no question of calculating amounts or degrees, as in *The thing is absurd in my e.,* is illiterate. *Tories love discussion :*

* i.e. in 1913 ; 1925 has disproved it, we read.

they cannot have too much of it. But they think it is going too far to translate words into action. That is not, in their e., playing the Parliamentary game.

estop is a useful word so long as it is restricted to the special sense that has secured its revival ; but to revive its wider sense convicts one of pedantry. The special legal sense is (in the passive) ' to be precluded by one's own previous act or declaration from alleging or doing something '. Two quotations will show the right & the wrong use :— (a) *No one defended more joyously the silencing of Mr Asquith last July, & Mr Maxse is estopped from complaining, now that his own method has been applied to himself* ; (b) *The road winds along the side of a barren mountain till it appears to be estopped by a high cliff.*

esurient. See POLYSYLLABIC HUMOUR.

etacism. See TECHNICAL TERMS.

etc. To resort to *&c.* in sentences of a literary character (*His faults of temper &c. are indeed easily accounted for*) is amateurish, slovenly, & incongruous :—*A compliment of this kind is calculated to increase their enthusiasm, courage, &c., to do their utmost./The Covenanted Civil Service with its old traditions & its hereditary hatred of interlopers, be they merchants, journalists, doctors, etc.* On the other hand, in the contexts to which it is appropriate, it is needless PURISM to restrict its sense to what the words could mean in Latin, i.e. (a) & *the rest* as opposed to & *other things,* (b) *and* the like as opposed to *or* the like, (c) & other *things* as opposed to *persons* ; the first restriction would exclude *His pockets contained an apple, a piece of string, &c.* ; the second would exclude ' Good ', ' fair ', ' excellent ', *&c., is appended to each name* ; the third would exclude *The Duke of A, Lord B, Mr C, &c., are patrons.* The reasonable punctuation with *&c.* is to put a comma before it when

more than one term has preceded, but not when one term only has preceded : *toads, frogs, &c.* ; but *toads &c.*

eternal. For ' the E. City ' see SOBRIQUETS.

ethic(al), ethics. 1. *ethic*)(*ethical.* 2. *ethic dative.* 3. *ethic*)(*ethics.* 4. *ethics,* number. 5. *ethics*)(*morals.* 6. *ethical*)(*moral.*

1. *ethic*)(*ethical.* The short form has now been almost displaced as an adjective by the long ; it is occasionally still used, but is noticeably archaic ; the only exception to this is in

2. The *ethic dative.* This, in which the word means emotional or expressive, is the name for a common Greek & Latin use in which a person no more than indirectly interested in the fact described in the sentence is introduced into it, usually by himself as the speaker, in the dative, which is accordingly most often that of the first personal pronoun. As the construction was formerly English also (*Come knock me at that door* = knock at the door, I tell you ; *Kills me some six or seven dozen of Scots* = Kills, they tell me, &c.), the grammatical name for it is still heard on occasion ; but its place has been taken by various modern colloquialisms, as *Knock, can't you ?, Kills, if you please.* See also under TECHNICAL TERMS.

3. *ethic*)(*ethics.* Of the two nouns the second is the one for ordinary use. It means the science of morals or study of the principles defining man's duty to his neighbours, a treatise on this, or a prevailing code of morality (*Ethics is,* or *are, not to be treated as an exact science* ; *That is surely from the Ethics,* i. e. Aristotle's ; *Our modern ethics are not outraged by this type of mendacity).* *Ethic* in any of these senses has a pedantic air ; it is chiefly in technical philosophic use, & its special meaning is a scheme of moral science (*The attempt to construct an ethic apart from theology).*

4. For the grammatical number of *ethics* see -ICS.

5. *ethics*)(*morals.* The two words, once fully synonymous, & existing together only because English scholars knew both Greek & Latin, have so far divided functions that neither is superfluous; they are not rivals for one job, but holders of complementary jobs; *ethics* is the science of morals, & *morals* are the practice of ethics; *His ethics may be sound, but his morals are abandoned.* That is the broad distinction; the points where confusion arises are three: (a) sometimes those who are talking about morals choose to call them ethics because the less familiar word strikes them as more imposing; (b) there is an unfounded impression that ethics is somehow more definitely than morals disconnected from religion; (c) the distinction is rather fine between the sense of *ethics* last given & illustrated in 3, i.e. prevailing code of morals, & morals themselves; but, though fine, it is clear enough.

6. *ethical*) (*moral.* It is in the nature of things that the dividing line between the adjectives should be less clear than with the nouns. For, if ethics is the science of morals, whatever concerns morals evidently concerns ethics too, & is as much ethical as moral; & vice versâ. Nevertheless, we talk of *a moral*, but not *an ethical*, man, when practice is in question, &, in the region of theory, we perhaps tend more & more to talk of *the ethical* rather than *the moral basis of* society, education, & so forth.

et hoc genus omne. A phrase on which the literary man who finds himself sorely tempted to ' end with a lazy *&c.*', but knows he mustn't, sometimes rides off not very creditably.

ethos. Pronounce ē′thŏs. It means the characteristic spirit informing a nation, an age, a literature, an institution, or any similar unit. In reference to a nation or State, it is

the sum of the intellectual & moral tendencies of which what the Germans call the nation's Kultur is the manifestation; like Kultur, it is not in itself a word of praise or blame, any more than *quality*.

euchre, -er. See -RE & -ER.

eulogy. For *a* or *an e.*, see A, AN.

euphemism, -mistic, -mize. The noun (cf. EUPHUISM) means (the use of a) mild or vague or periphrastic expression as a substitute for blunt precision or disagreeable truth: *Euphemism is more demoralizing than coarseness./Mistress is a euphemism for concubine./Protectionists have euphemized themselves into tariff-reformers.*

euphuism. The word is often ignorantly used for *euphemism*, with which it is entirely unconnected. It is named from Lyly's *Euphues* (i.e., The Man of Parts), fashionable in & after the 16th century as a literary model, & means affected artificiality of style, indulgence in antithesis & simile & conceits, subtly refined choice of words, preciosity. It is, unlike *euphemism*, a word with which no-one but the literary critic has any concern. A single example of the common misuse will suffice :— *While a financial euphuism christened railway construction a ' transformation of capital ', & not an expenditure.* See POPULARIZED TECHNICALITIES.

Eurasian. See MULATTO 1, 4.

European. For *a* or *an E.*, see A, AN.

evacuate makes -*cuable*; see -ABLE 1.

evadable. So spelt ; see MUTE E.

evaluate makes -*uable* ; see -ABLE 1.

evanish. The word is effective in poetry & poetic contexts ; for its use in such phrases as *the rapidly evanishing phantom of a Home-Rule majority*, see VULGARIZATION.

evaporate makes -*rable*; see -ABLE 1.

evasion, evasiveness. The latter is a quality only ; in places where quality, & not practice or action, is the clear meaning, *evasion* should not be used instead of it : *his evasion of the issue is obvious ; he is guilty of* *perpetual evasion* ; but *the evasiveness* (not *evasion*) *of his answers is enough to condemn him.* See -ION & -NESS.

eve. *On Christmas E., on the E. of St Agnes, on the e. of the battle, on the e. of departure, on the e. of great developments.* The strict sense of *e.* being the evening or day before, the first two phrases are literal, the last is metaphorical, & the two others may be either, i.e., they may mean *before* either with an interval of days or weeks, or with a night intervening, or actually on the same day. Nevertheless, in spite even of the chance of ambiguity, they are all legitimate ; what is not legitimate is to use the word in its metaphorical sense & yet remind the reader of the literal sense by some turn of words that involves it, as in *The most irreconcilable of Irish landlords are beginning to recognize that we are on the e. of the dawn of a new day in Ireland.* See METAPHOR.

Eve. For *daughter of Eve* see BATTERED ORNAMENTS, ELEGANT VARIATION, HACKNEYED PHRASES, PERIPHRASIS.

even. 1. Placing of *e.* 2. *E. so.*
1. Placing of *e.* It will be seen in POSITION OF ADVERBS that their placing is a matter partly of idiom & partly of sense ; *e.* is one of those whose placing is important to the sense. *The time to see them is just after breakfast, when they emerge from every other door, Pugs, Poodles, Pekinese, Dachshunds, Dandies, & ever so many more* whose names I do not e. know, *all chattering at the top of their voices as they walk, run, trot, waddle or pitter-patter along according to their kind.* The effect of putting *e.* there is to contrast *know* with some other verb ; what other verb ? if it had run *I cannot e. guess,* it would have been obvious to supply *much less know* ; but *know* leaves no room for a much less. The word that ought to have been marked out for contrast with another is not *know*, but *names. Whose e. names* is not possible ; *whose names even* is always

uncomfortable, & here would need commas before & after *e.* to prevent *e.* from gravitating to *I* ; so the writer has been content with *e.* in the wrong place. The true solution was to write *whose very names I do not know* (i.e. much less their looks &c.).
2. *Even so.* This is a phrase that has its uses ; it often serves as a conveniently short reminder to the reader that the contention before him is not the strongest that could be advanced, that deductions have been made, that the total is net & not gross. But some writers become so attached to this convenience that they resort to it (a) when it is a convenience to them & an inconvenience to their readers, i.e. when it takes a reader some time to discover what exactly the writer meant by it, & (b) when nothing, or one of the everyday conjunctions, would do as well. The following passages are none of them indefensible, but all exemplify the ill-judged *e. so,* used (when it conveys too much) to save the writer trouble, or (when it conveys too little) to gratify his fondness for the phrase :—*Quite the most striking contrast between votes polled & seats gained in the German elections may be found in the following figures :* [figures showing disproportion]. *That is on the first ballot,* but e. so *we can imagine the Radicals & National Liberals wondering whether the world can be so ill-contrived that nearly three million & a quarter voters returned only four members, whereas two millions return 81* (but, though the second may mend matters,)./ *Just at present the Act is the subject of misconceptions & misrepresentations, some of which can only be dissipated by actual experience of its working. It may be that,* e. so, *the people will dislike the Act* (even after experience)./*We do not for a moment expect that we shall be able to retain in these islands all our population ; we have Dominions over the seas in which many of them will find new homes still under the British flag. But,* even so, *we have to make our*

own countryside more attractive (though our population will be less ? or though emigrants will still be British ? Correct accordingly)./*I hope it won't come to this ; but,* e. so, *bridge-players will continue to take their finesses & call it just the luck when they go down* (if it does)./ *Yesterday Mr Bonar Law actually had the boldness to repeat in the House of Commons a charge he made at the Albert Hall.* E. so, *in the formula suggested by the single lady who was reputed to have had twins, we shall do well never to believe more than a half of what Mr Bonar Law says* (And yet)./*It is natural that France should be anxious not to lose on the swings what she gains on the roundabouts, & she has some reason for nervousness as to the interaction of commerce & politics.* E. so, *she will do well not to be over-nervous* (But)./*If the absent are always wrong, statesmen who have passed away are always gentlemen. But,* e. so, *we were not prepared for this tribute to those statesmen who fought for Home Rule in 1886 & 1893* (omit *e. so*).

evenness. So spelt.
evensong &c. See MORNING.
eventuality, eventuate. See ANTI-SAXONISM. The words are chiefly used in flabby journalese ; some characteristic specimens are :—*It is therefore not as a substitute for local veto that disinterested management is advocated, but as a second string to the bow of temperance reformers, a provision for the eventuality of the people refusing to avail themselves of the option of veto./We shall of course be told before long that the Territorial Force is on the eve of a complete breakdown . . . ; that, as Lord Haldane reminded us last week at Tranent, is very far from the case, however dear such an eventuality might be to the enemies of the Voluntary System./The Consular Body at Shanghai have determined upon the defence of the settlements in case of eventuality./The bogeys that were raised about the ruin did not eventuate,*

yet employers still want the assistants to work for long hours./May we be so impertinent as to inquire what policy Mr Lloyd George foreshadowed in his letter to Sir Horace Plunkett ? And why did not that policy eventuate ?

ever is often used in uneducated or ultra-colloquial talk as an emphasizer of *who, what, when,* & other interrogative words, corresponding to such phrases in educated talk as *who in the world, what on earth, where* (can he) *possibly* (be ?). When such talk is reproduced in print, *ever* should be a separate word—*what ever* &c., not *whatever* &c. For *e.* in letters see LETTER FORMS.

ever so (*though it were ever so bad* &c.). See NEVER SO.

every one. 1. *Every one*) (*everyone.* 2. Number of pronoun after *e.*

1. *Every one*) (*everyone. The . . . drawings are academical in the worst sense of the word ; almost everyone of them deserves a gold medal.* In this, the making of the two words into one is undoubtedly wrong ; it should only be done where *everybody* might be substituted ; that is never true when, as here, things & not persons are meant, nor yet when, as here, a partitive *of* follows ; in either of those cases it is agreed that the words should be kept separate. Unfortunately there is not the same agreement on the corresponding rule that when *everybody* can be substituted *everyone* should be used. The question cannot be decided for *everyone* by itself ; the parallel *anyone, no one,* & *someone* must be taken into account ; of these *no one* alone is fixed, & that is always two words, owing to the natural tendency to pronounce *noone* noon. On the side of one word we have (a) the fact that all the four words, when they mean anybody &c., have only one accent instead of the two that are heard when they mean any single &c., (b) the general usage of printers, based on this accentuation, with all except *no one.* On the side of two words we have (a) consistency, since

the others thus fall into line with *no one*, Mahomet-&-the-mountain-fashion, (b) escape from the mute e before a vowel inside a single word in *someone*, which is undesirable though not unexampled, (c) the authority of the OED, which gives precedence in all four to the separation. A very pretty quarrel. This dictionary's opinion is that the accent is far the most important point, that *anyone* & *everyone* & *someone* should be established, & that *no-one* is the right compromise between the misleading *noone* & the inconsistent *no one ; no-one* is as consistent with *everyone* as *co-ordinate* is with *subordinate*. The rules would then be these :—(1) *Anyone, everyone, no-one,* & *someone,* in the sense anybody, everybody, &c.; (2) *any one, every one, no one, some one,* each with two accents, in other uses.

2. Number of pronoun after *everyone* (*E. had made up their minds ; E. then looked about them silently*) ; on this question see NUMBER, 11.

evidence) (*exhibit* or *show*. To evidence something is to be the proof, or serve as evidence, of its existence or truth or occurrence. *You* do not e. care, i.e. that you are careful, but your state of instruction may e. care, i.e. that either you or your instructors have been careful, & *you* may by being obviously well instructed e. *your instructors'* care. It will be seen that *show* or *exhibit* could take the place of *e.* in the places that have been said to allow of it, but also that they would stand where it has been said that *e.* could not. Writers with a preference for the less common or the more technical-looking word are sometimes trapped by the partial equivalence into thinking that they may indulge their preference by using *e.* instead of *show*. A right & a wrong sentence will make the limitation of meaning clearer, & another wrong sentence will illustrate the importance of the exact words used in the definition given above of the meaning ; it

must be borne in mind, however, that that definition does not pretend to cover all senses of *e.*, but only those in which it is in danger of misuse.

Right use : *This work of Mr Phillipps, while it bears all the marks of scholarship, bears also the far rarer impress of original thought, & evidences the power of considering with an unusual detachment a subject which* . . .

Wrong use : *Mr Thayer evidences a remarkable grasp of his material, & a real gift for the writing of history.*

Negative use : *We regret that his work should be so unambitious in scope, for it fails to include many of the popular superstitions of today, does not evidence any great care or research in its composition, & its arrangement is amateurish.* If the definition above is correct, & to e. means to be *the* proof of, or to *serve* as the e. of, it is clear that it is one of those words that are in place only in affirmative sentences, & not in negative or neutral ones. Just as we say *This brandy is excellent,* but not *Bring me some excellent brandy,* or *The brandy is not excellent* (*good* is the word), so we say that work evidences care, but not that it does not e. care (*suggest* or *show* is the word); see POSITIVE WORDS.

evince has lost most of its meanings by lapse of time ; the OED's 1, 2, 3, & 4, are marked obsolete, & only 5 & 6 remain. An example of each surviving sense may be useful :— *The contrivances of nature decidedly e. intention*—Paley (i.e., are an evidence of) ; *The knees & upper part of the leg evincing muscular strength*—Scott (i.e., giving tokens of possessing, or revealing the presence of).

But it may almost be said that its ANTI-SAXONISM is the word's only claim to be used any longer ; those who like a full-dress word better than a plain one continue to use & sometimes to misuse it. The writer of one of the quotations below, in putting it next-door to *evident*, surely evinces a fondness for it that borders on foolishness ; & the other must have been unaware that, though either a person or an attitude can e. an emotion, neither a person nor an emotion can e. an attitude ; an attitude is nothing if not visible, & what is evinced is inferable but not visible. *Both the Tories & the Labour Party evinced an evident anxiety to stir up trouble on the Labour unrest in the railway world./The Opposition welcomed the Bill on first reading, did not divide against it on second reading, & have, on the whole, only evinced a legitimately critical attitude in Committee.*

evolution. See LU.

ex-. For such patent yet prevalent absurdities as *ex-Lord Mayor*, *ex-Chief Whip*, *ex-Tory Solicitor-General* (except in another sense than its writer means), see HYPHENS ; & for alternatives, LATE.

exactly, just. *E. what has happened or what is about to happen is not yet clear* ; *Just how the words are to be divided.* This now familiar idiom, in which *e.* or *j.* is prefixed to an indirect question, is a modern development. The *e.* or *j.* sometimes adds point, but is more often otiose, & the use of it becomes with many writers a disagreeable MANNERISM.

exaggerate. So spelt (L *agger* a heap). *E.* makes *exaggerable* ; see -ABLE 1.

exasperate makes *-rable* ; see -ABLE 1.

exceeding(ly) & excessive(ly). The difference is the same as that between *very great* or *very much* & *too great* or *too much*. It is not inherent in the words, nor very old, *excessive(ly)* having formerly had both meanings ; but it is now recognized by most of those who use words carefully, & is a useful DIFFERENTIATION. *excessively obliged to you* is not now standard English, & that *I was excessively annoyed* should be said

in repentant & not, as it usually is, in self-satisfied tones. A passage in which a good modern writer allows himself to disregard the now usual distinction may be worth giving : *I have said that in early life Henry James was not ' impressive '* ; *as time went on his appearance became, on the contrary,* excessively *noticeable & arresting. He removed the beard which had long disguised his face, & so revealed the strong lines of mouth & chin, which responded to the majesty of the skull.*

excellence, -cy. See -CE, -CY.

excellent. See POSITIVE WORDS.

except, as a conjunction governing a clause, i.e. as a substitute for the *unless* or *if . . . not* of ordinary educated speech, is either an ARCHAISM resorted to for one or other of the usual reasons, or else an illustration of the fact that old constructions often survive in uneducated talk when otherwise obsolete. In the quotation, archaism for one of the less defensible reasons is the explanation :—*But, e. the matter is argued as a mere matter of amour propre—&, for ourselves, we think it would be unjust & unfair to Mr Bonar Law to argue it in any such way—how is it possible to use such high-flown language about a mere ' change of method ' ?.*

excepting as a preposition has one normal use. When a possible exception is to be mentioned as not made, the form used is, instead of *not except*, either *not excepting* before the noun or *not excepted* after it : *All men are fallible except the Pope* ; *All men are fallible, not excepting the Pope* or *the Pope not excepted*. Other prepositional uses of *excepting* are unidiomatic ; but the word as a true participle or a gerund does not fall under this condemnation :—*He would treble the tax on brandy excepting only*, or *without even excepting, that destined for medicine.* An example of the use deprecated is : *The cost of living throughout the world, excepting in countries where special* *causes operate, shows a tendency to keep level.*

exception. *The e. proves the rule,* & phrases implying it, are so constantly introduced in argument, & so much more often with obscuring than with illuminating effect, that it is necessary to set out its different possible meanings, viz (1) the original simple legal sense, (2) the secondary rather complicated scientific sense, (3) the loose rhetorical sense, (4) the jocular nonsense, (5) the serious nonsense. The last of these is the only one that need be objected to directly, though 3 & 4 must bear the blame of bringing 5 into existence by popularizing an easily misunderstood phrase ; unfortunately 5 is much the commonest use. See POPULARIZED TECHNICALITIES.

1. ' Special leave is given for men to be out of barracks tonight till 11.0 p.m.' ; ' The exception proves the rule ' means that this special leave implies a rule requiring men, except when an exception is made, to be in earlier. The value of this in interpreting statutes is plain.

2. We have concluded by induction that Jones the critic, who never writes a kindly notice, lacks the faculty of appreciation ; one day a warm eulogy of an anonymous novel appears over his signature ; we see that this exception destroys our induction ; later it comes out that the anonymous novelist is Jones himself ; our conviction that he lacks the faculty of appreciation is all the stronger for the apparent exception when once we have found out that, being *self*-appreciation, it is outside the scope of the rule— which, however, we now modify to exclude it, saying that he lacks the faculty of appreciating *others*. Or again, it turns out that the writer of the notice is another Jones ; then our opinion of Jones the first is only strengthened by having been momentarily shaken. These kinds of exception are of great value in

scientific inquiry, but they prove the rule not when they are seen to be exceptions, but when they have been shown to be either outside of or reconcilable with the principle they seem to contradict.

3. *We may legitimately take satisfaction in the fact that peace prevails under the Union Jack, the Abor expedition being the exception that goes to prove the rule.* On the contrary, it goes to disprove it ; but no more is meant than that it calls our attention to & heightens by contrast what might otherwise pass unnoticed, the remarkable prevalence of peace.

4. ' If there is one virtue I can claim, it is punctuality.' ' Were you in time for breakfast this morning ? ' ' Well, well, the exception that proves the rule.' It is by the joint effect of this use & 3 that the proverb comes to oscillate between the two senses Exceptions can always be neglected, & A truth is all the truer if it is sometimes false.

5. It rained on St Swithin, it will rain for forty days ; July 31 is fine & dry, but our certainty of a wet August is not shaken, since today is an exception that (instead of at one blow destroying) proves the rule. This frame of mind is encouraged whenever a writer, aware or unaware himself of the limitations, appeals to the 2 use without clearly showing that his exception is of the right kind :—*That the incidence of import duties will be affected by varying conditions, & that in some exceptional cases the exporter will bear a large share of it, has never been denied ; but exceptions prove the rules & do not destroy them./The general principle of Disestablishing & Disendowing the Church in Wales will be supported by the full strength of Liberalism, with the small exceptions that may be taken as proving the rule.*

exceptionable, exceptional, unex-. The *-able* & *-al* forms, especially the negatives, are often confused by writers or compositors. *Exceptional* has to do with the ordinary sense of *exception*, & means out of the common ; *exceptionable* involves the sense of *exception* rarely seen except in *take exception to* & *open to exception* ; it means the same as the latter phrase, & its negative form means offering no handle to criticism. The usual mistake is that shown in :— *The picture is in unexceptional condition, & shows this master's qualities to a marked degree.*

excerpt. See NOUN & VERB ACCENT.
excessive(ly). See EXCEEDING(LY).
exchangeable. So spelt ; see MUTE E.
excisable. So spelt ; see MUTE E.
excise, not *-ize* ; see -ISE)(-IZE. For synonymy of *e.*, n., see TAX.
excitable. So spelt ; see MUTE E.

EXCLAMATION MARK. See STOPS.
excommunicate makes *-cable* ; see -ABLE 1.
exculpate. See -ATABLE.
excusable. So spelt ; see MUTE E.
execrate makes *-crable* ; see -ABLE 1.
executor. See -OR. In the special sense (testator's posthumous agent) pronounce ĭkzĕ′kūtor, in other senses ĕ′kzĭkūtor. The feminine is *executrix* (ĭkzĕ′k-), pl. *-trices* (for pronunciation of which see -TRIX).

exercisable. So spelt ; see MUTE E.
exercise, not *-ize* ; see -ISE)(-IZE.
exhalation, exhale. The h is pronounced in the verb, but usually not in the noun ; *exhale* makes *-lable*, see MUTE E.

exigence, -cy. *-cy* is now the commoner form ; *-ce* has no senses in which *-cy* would be unsuitable, while *-ce* sounds archaic in some ; it would be well to make *-cy* universal ; see -CE & -CY. The sense exactingness belongs to the French word *exigence*, which should be italicized & pronounced as French, at least until *exigence* is no longer used as synonymous with *exigency*.

exit, vb. Those who neither know Latin nor read plays are apt to forget or not know that this is a singular verb with plural *exeunt*, &

to write *exit the tariff-reformers* as complacently as *exit tariff-reform*. All the following are actual newspaper headings :—EXIT THE DAGOS./Exit the McKenna Duties./ EXIT BLACK LISTS./EXIT HERTLING & VON HINTZE./ EXIT THE COAL AND DUMPING MEASURES./EXIT THE MONITORS.

-ex, -ix. Naturalized Latin nouns in *-ex* & *-ix*, genit. *-icis*, vary in the form of the plural. The Latin plural is *-ices* (-ĭsēz), the English *-exes* (-ĕksĭz) ; some words use only one of these, & some both. See LATIN PLURALS.

1. Words in purely scientific or technical use (*codex, cortex, murex, silex,* &c.) are best allowed their Latinity ; to talk of *cortexes, codexes, murexes,* & *silexes,* is to take indecent liberties with physiology, palaeography, ichthyology, & geology, the real professors of which, moreover, usually prefer *-ices*.

2. Latin words borrowed as trade names (*simplex, duplex,* &c.) are for the period of their lives English ; if in talking of lamps you say you *find duplices better than central-draughts,* you are scarcely intelligible.

3. Words that have become the established English for an object (*ilex*) use *-exes* ; *under the shade of the ilices* shows ignorance of English more conspicuously than knowledge of Latin ; cf. -US & -UM. The question whether the ousting of the native names (e.g. of *holm-oak* by *ilex*) should have been or should be prevented is a separate one, to be decided for the individual word.

4. There are some words, however, whose use is partly scientific & partly popular, e.g. *apex, appendix, index, matrix, vertex, vortex* ; of these both plurals are used, with some tendency, but no more, to keep *-xes* for popular or colloquial & *-ices* for scientific or formal contexts :—*The line just avoids the apexes of the hills,* but *The shells have their apices eroded. Six patients had* *their appendixes removed, & I hate books with appendixes, but The evidence is digested in five appendices. A dial like a clock face with two indexes*, but *Integral, fractional, & negative indices. A heap of old stereotype matrixes*, but *Some of the species of whinstone are the common matrices* [for pronunciation see -TRIX] *of agate & chalcedony. Arrange the trestles with their vertexes alternately high & low*, but *In the vertices of curves where they cut the abscissa at right angles. Whirlpools or vortexes or eddies*, but *The vortices of modern atomists.* There is thus considerable liberty of choice; but with most words of this class the scientific use, & consequently the Latin plural, is much commoner than the other.

ex officio. When used as an adjective, the words should be hyphened : *I was there* ex officio, but *the* ex-officio *members of the committee.* See HYPHENS.

exonerate makes -*rable*; see -ABLE 1.
exordium. Pl. -*ms* or -*ia*; see -UM.
exoteric & exotic, of the same ultimate derivation, have entirely diverse applications. That is exoteric which is communicable to the outer circle of disciples (opp. *esoteric*) ; that is exotic which comes from outside the country (opp. *indigenous*); *exoteric doctrines*; *exotic plants.*

expandable, -ansible. See -ABLE, -IBLE, 2.

ex parte, when used as an adj., should be hyphened : *speaking ex parte*, but *an ex-parte statement*; see HYPHENS (Group *sub judice*).

expatiation. See -CIATION.
expect. Exception is often taken to the sense suppose, be inclined to think, consider probable. This extension of meaning is, however, so natural that it seems needless PURISM to resist it. *E.* by itself is used as short for *e. to find, e. that it will turn out that*, that is all :—*I e. he will be in time* ; *I e. he is there by this time* ; *I e. he was there* ; *I e.*

you have all heard all this before ; *Mr* ——'s *study is scholarly & thorough, & has had a good deal of expansion, we e., since it took the* —— *Essay Prize*, i.e., if the facts ever happen to come to our knowledge, we shall be surprised if they are not to that effect. The OED remarks that the idiom is 'now rare in literary use'; that is owing to the dead set that has been made at it ; but it is so firmly established in colloquial use that if, as is suggested above, there is no sound objection to it, the period of exile is not likely to be long.

expectorate, -ation, seem to be now the established American for *spit(ting) & spit(ting) out.* In British use they have as yet only the currency of medical terms & GENTEELISMS. This difference of status, which it is to be hoped will not be diminished from our side at least, is an object-lesson on the vanity of genteelism. The mealy-mouthed American must be by this time harder put to it with *expectorate* than the mealy-mouthed Englishman with *spit*; his genteelism has outgrown its gentility & become itself the plain rude word for the rude thing ; it must be discouraging to have to begin the search for decent obscurity all over again—with so promising a failure behind one, too. See POPULARIZED TECHNICALITIES.

expediency, -ce. The form first given is now much commoner in all surviving senses ; there is no incipient differentiation, & it is desirable that the now rare -*ce* should be abandoned. See -CE, -CY.

expedite. See FORMAL WORDS.
experiment, n. & v. See NOUN & VERB ACCENT.
experimentalize. See LONG VARIANTS.
expert. See NOUN & ADJ. ACCENT.
expiate makes *expiable, expiator* ; see -ABLE 1, -OR.
expiry. Pronounce -īrǐ.
expletive. The OED gives the pro-

nunciations ĕ'ksplĭtĭv, ĕksplē'tĭv, in that order. The noun use (oath or other interjection) being frequent & popular, & the adjective use (serving to fill out) literary & especially grammatical, the two pronunciations might well be made use of for DIFFERENTIATION ; cf. *expert*, & see NOUN & ADJECTIVE ACCENT ; the noun would be ĕ'ksplĭtĭv.

explicit & express. With a certain class of nouns (e.g. *declaration, testimony, promise, contract, understanding, incitement, prohibition*), either adjective can be used in the general sense of definite as opposed to virtual or tacit or vague or general or inferable or implied or constructive. One may nevertheless be more appropriate than the other. That is explicit which is set forth in sufficient detail ; that is express which is worded with intention. What is meant by calling a promise explicit is first that it has been put into words & secondly that its import is plain ; what is meant by calling it express is first, as before, that it has been put into words, & secondly that the maker meant it to bind him in the case contemplated. This second element in the meaning of *express* is now generally present in it where it is roughly synonymous with *explicit*, but has come into it by accident. An express promise was by origin simply an expressed promise, i. e. one put into words, *express* being a Latin participle of the kind seen in *suspect* = suspected, *subject* = subjected, & many others. When its participial sense ceased to be appreciated, it was natural that the familiar adjectival sense (*for the express purpose of* ; *express malice is when one with a sedate deliberate mind & formed design doth . . .*) should influence its meaning ; the idea of special intention is now almost invariably distinctive of *express* when it is preferred to *explicit*.

exploit. See NOUN & VERB ACCENT.
explosive (in phonetics). See TECHNICAL TERMS.

export, n. & v. See NOUN & VERB ACCENT.
exposé. See FRENCH WORDS.
exposition in the sense *public show of goods* &c. is a GALLICISM (or Americanism) for *exhibition*.
ex post facto. This is the established spelling ; but the person who knows the Latin words is worse off with it in this disguise than one who does not ; it should be *ex postfacto* (*ex* on the footing of *postfacto* later enactment). The ordinary rule of HYPHENS would then be applied, & we should say *It is undesirable to legislate ex postfacto*, but *ex-postfacto legislation is undesirable*. E. legislation is, for instance, the making of an act illegal after it has been committed ; but what is referred to in *facto* is not the 'doing' of the action but the 'enacting' of the law.

express, adj. See EXPLICIT.
express, vb. *Mr Justice Sankey expressed himself much troubled by the views expressed in Lord Wrenbury's letter.*/*Both men afterwards expressed themselves perfectly satisfied.* Insert *as* after *himself* & *themselves*. There is no authority for to express oneself satisfied &c. ; at any rate the OED has no acquaintance with it ; & it certainly requires the support of authority, whereas no such support is needed for the use with *as*. The fact is that ANALOGY is being allowed to confuse *express* with *declare* just as *regard* is wrongly given the construction of *consider*.

expressive. For 'to use an e. word' see SUPERIORITY.
expurgate. See -ATABLE.
extant had formerly the same sense as *existent* or *existing*, & was as widely applicable. Its sense & its application have been narrowed till it means only 'still in existence or not having perished at the present or the given past or future time', & is applied almost exclusively to documents, buildings or monuments, & customs. *E. memory, the e. generation, the e. crisis, e. States,* are unlikely or impossible phrases, &

the e. laws would be understood only of such as were on record but not in operation, of laws as documents & not as forces. The pronunciation recommended is ĕ′kstănt, but ĭk-stă′nt is not uncommon.

extemporaneous(ly) & extemporary, -ily, are cumbersome words ; *extempore* is seldom unequal to the need. See LONG VARIANTS.

extend. 1. For *extendable, extendible, extensible,* see -ABLE, 2.

2. *E.* for *give* or *accord* is, in its present vogue, a piece of turgid journalese. It might have been natural English ; you e. your hand literally, & from that through extending the hand of welcome to the metaphorical extending of a welcome is a simple enough passage. But native English did not go that way, perhaps because *give* & *accord* were already in constant use, one for everyday & the other for more formal contexts. *E.* in this sense has done its development in America, & come to us full-grown viâ the newspapers—a bad record. To e. a welcome is just tolerable because of its obviousness as a metaphor ; but the extending of a hearty reception, sympathy, congratulations, a hearing, a magnificent send-off, & the like, should if possible be barred (in America a congregation ' extends a call ' to the reverend gentleman of its choice) ; we have still *give* & *accord* to choose between, with *offer* & *proffer* to meet the demand for other shades of meaning. The following quotation shows an application in which even the notion of friendliness inherent in the metaphor has disappeared : *Being promptly deported by the German police, he appealed to the Foreign Office for redress, but Lord Salisbury informed him in a characteristically pointed official dispatch that he could see no grounds whatever for taking exception to the treatment which had been extended to him.*

Two points are to be observed in regard to the above advice : (a)

The condemnation does not touch such sentences as *You should e. to me the same indulgence,* where the metaphor may be different, & the meaning ' widen it so as to include me as well as someone else ' ; (2) it is not maintained that *e.* has never had the sense of give or accord in native English—it had in the 16th–18th centuries—, but only that the modernism does not descend direct from the native use ; having been reimported after export to America, it is now ill at ease in the old country.

extent. In the phrase *to . . . extent, e.* should not be qualified by adjectives introducing any idea beyond that of quantity ; *to what, to any, to some, to a great* or *vast* or *enormous* or *unknown* or *surprising, e.,* but not *Some of the girls even go* to the manlike e. of *holding meetings in the Park to discuss their grievances.*

extenuate. 1. *E.* makes *-uable* ; see -ABLE 1. 2. The root meaning being to thin down or whittle away, the proper object of the verb in its sense of make excuses for is a word expressing something bad in itself, as *guilt, cowardice, cruelty,* & not a neutral word such as *conduct* or *behaviour.* But since these latter, though neutral in themselves, are often converted by context into unmistakable words of blame, & are then legitimate objects of *e.,* the misapprehension arises that it can always govern them, & consequently that the meaning of excuse belongs to the verb, instead of to the combination between the verb & an object expressing something blamable. From this comes the further error of supposing that you can e., i.e. make excuses for, a person. In such cases etymology is of value.

exterior, external, extraneous, extrinsic. Etymologically the four differ only in the formative suffixes used, & there is no reason why any of them might not have acquired the senses of all ; *outside* is the fundamental meaning. It will be best to take them in pairs.

1. *exterior* & *external*. That is exterior which encloses or is outermost, the enclosed or innermost being interior. These opposites are chiefly applied to things of which there is a pair, & with conscious reference, when one is spoken of, to the other : the exterior court is one within which is an interior court ; the exterior door has another inside it ; exterior & interior lines in strategy are concentric curves one enclosing the other ; the exterior ear covers & leads to the interior ear ; & the exterior surface of a hollow ball, but not of a solid one, is a legitimate phrase.

That is external which is without & apart or whose relations are with what is without & apart, that which is within being internal. *The external world, external things, external evidence*, illustrate the first part of the definition ; *external appearances, worship,* & *action* (those that affect other persons or things somehow) illustrate the second part ; external debt & relations are those a country has to or with other countries.

In many phrases either *exterior* or *external* may be used, but usually with some difference of underlying meaning ; e. g., the exterior ear is thought of as the porch of the interior ear, but the external ear is the ear as seen by the outsider. Again, a building's exterior features & external features are different things, the former being those of its outside only, & the latter all, whether of outside or inside, that are visible as opposed to the structure that can only be guessed at. Similarly, with the nouns, *exterior* has the definite narrow material meaning of the outside, as opposed to the inside of a building or the inner nature of a person, while *externals* includes all about a person that reveals him to us, his acts & habits & manner of speech as well as his features & clothes.

2. *extraneous* & *extrinsic*. That is extraneous which is brought in, or comes or has come in, from without. A fly in amber, a bullet in one's chest, are extraneous bodies ; *extraneous aid, interference, light, sounds* ; extraneous points are questions imported into a discussion from which they do not naturally arise.

That is extrinsic which is not an essential & inherent part of something but is attached to it as a separable belonging, essential properties being intrinsic. A florin's intrinsic value is what the metal in it would have fetched before it was coined ; its extrinsic value is what is added by the stamp. A person's extrinsic advantages are such things as wealth & family interest, while his courage & talent are intrinsic advantages.

It is worth notice that *extrinsic* is now rare, being little used except when a formal contrary is wanted for the still common *intrinsic*. *Extraneous* on the other hand exists on its own account ; it has no formal contrary, *intraneous* being for practical purposes non-existent, & must make shift with *internal, intrinsic, indigenous, domestic, native,* or whatever else suits the particular context.

exterminate makes *-nable* ; see -ABLE 1.

exterritorial. See EXTRATERRITORIAL.

extract, n. & v. See NOUN & VERB ACCENT.

extraneous. See EXTERIOR.

extraordinary. Pronounce as five syllables (-tror-) not six (-trɑor-) ; the OED gives precedence to the shorter ; for the effect of spelling on sound, see PRONUNCIATION.

ex(tra)territorial(ity). The forms seem to be used quite indifferently. To the classical latinist, that is to say to 99% of those who are acquainted with Latin at all, the longer seems the only reasonable one, since *extra,* & not *ex,* is the classical Latin for outside of ; & this is perhaps a stronger consideration than the saving of a syllable. It would certainly be better to have one spelling only, & *extra-* is recommended.

extricate makes *-cable* ; see -ABLE 1.
extrinsic. See EXTERIOR.

-EY & -Y IN ADJECTIVES. The adjectival suffix is *-y*, not *-ey*. Weak spellers are often in doubt whether, when *-y* is appended to nouns in MUTE E (as *mite*), the *e* is to be dropped or kept. With the very few exceptions given below, it should be dropped (*mity*, not *mitey*). A selection of the commonest *-y* adjectives from nouns in mute *-e* will suffice to show the normal formation, & another list follows this, containing words of the kind in which the bad speller goes wrong ; he often does so because he conceives himself to be making a new, or at least hitherto unprinted, word, & is afraid of obscuring its connexion with the noun if he drops the *e*—a needless fear. The safe *-y* adjectives are : *bony, breezy, briny, crazy, easy, fleecy, fluky, gory, greasy, grimy, hasty, icy, lacy, mazy, miry, noisy, oozy, prosy, racy, rosy, scaly, shady, shaky, slimy, smoky, snaky, spicy, spiky, spongy, stony, wiry.* The shaky *-y* adjectives are : *caky, cany, chancy, fluty, gamy, homy, horsy, liny, mity, mousy, nervy, nosy, pursy, sidy, stagy, tuny, wavy, whity.*
The exceptions referred to above are :—

1. When an adjective in *-y* is made from a noun in *-y*, *e* is inserted to part *y* from *-y* : *clayey & skyey*, not *clayy* or *skyy*.
2. *Hole* makes *holey*, to prevent confusion with *holy* = hallowed.
3. Adjectives from nouns in *-ue* (ŏŏ) retain the *e* : *gluey & bluey*, not *gluy* or *bluy.*

eye, vb, makes *eying* ; see VERBS IN -IE &c., 7.

-EY, -IE, -Y, IN DIMINUTIVES. The most established type of all (*baby, daddy, granny*) has *-y* ; most proper names (*Tommy, Polly*) have *-y* ; it would be a simplification if *-y* could be made universal : but *-ie* & *-ey*

are the only forms in some proper names (*Charlie* or *Charley*, never *Charly* ; *Minnie* ; *Sukey*) ; *-ie* is preferred in Scotland, the native land of some diminutives (*laddie, lassie, caddie*) ; the retention of mute *-e*, giving *-ey* (*dovey, lovey, Nosey*, &c.) is more defensible than in the adjectives made with *-y* (see -EY & -Y IN ADJECTIVES) ; & generally variety seems unavoidable.
In the list the recommended form stands first or alone ; the principle has been to recommend plain *-y* wherever usage is not thought to be overwhelmingly against it ; the addition of another ending in brackets means that that form is perhaps commoner, but not so much so as to make the recommended one impossible. Some of the words included (*booby, caddy, looby, Mary, Marie, puppy, rooty, toddy,* & perhaps others) are not in fact diminutive forms, but being mistakable for such are liable to the same doubts. There is some tendency when a word is much used in the plural (*frillies, goodies, Johnnies, kiddies, kilties, sweeties*) to think that *-ie* must be the singular termination. Adjectives like *comfy* are given here because the *-y* is the diminutive ending, & not the adjective suffix.

Amy ; *Annie* ; *Arty*=Arthur (*-ie*) ; *aunty* (*-ie*) ; *baby* ; *Betty* ; *Billy* ; *billy* = cooking-pot ; *blacky* ; *Bobby* ; *bobby* = policeman ; *Bony* = Bonaparte (*-ey*) ; *booby* ; *bookie*=bookmaker ; *bubby*=brother or breast ; *bunny* ; *caddie*=golf-attendant ; *caddy*=tea-box ; *Carry* (*-ie*) ; *Charlie* (*-ey*) ; *Cissy* = Cecilia (*-ie*) ; *comfy* ; *cooky*=cook dear (*-ie*) ; *cookie*=cake ; *coolie* ; *corbie*=crow ; *daddy* ; *darky* (*-ey*) ; *deary* (*-ie*) ; *Dicky* ; *doggy* (*-ie*) ; *Dolly, d.* ; *dovey* ; *ducky* ; *Eddy*=Edward ; *Edy*=Edith (*-ie*) ; *Effie* ; *Emmy* ; *Fanny* ; *fatty* ; *Florrie* ; *Freddy* ; *frilly* ; *Froggy* ; *Georgy* = George ; *Georgie*=Georgina ; *girly* (*-ie*) ; *goody* = goodwife or sweetmeat ; *goosy* ; *granny* ; *Hetty* ; *hoodie* = crow : *hubby* ; *Jacky* ; *Jamy* (*-ie*) ;

Jeanie ; *Jemmy* ; *Jenny* ; *Jerry* ; *Jessie* ; *Johnny* ; *Katy* (*-ie*); *kiddy* ; *kilty* = Highlander (*-ie*); *Kitty* ; *laddie* ; *lassie* ; *looby* ; *lovey* = my love ; *mammy* ; *Marie*, French name ; *Mary*, English name ; *maty* = mate (*-ey*) ; *Milly* (*-ie*) ; *Minnie* ; *Missy* ; *Molly* ; *mummy* = mother ; *Neddy* ; *Nelly* (*-ie*) ; *nicy* ; *nighty* ; *Nosy* = big-nosed one (*-ey*) ; *nunky* = uncle ; *nursy* (*-ie*) ; *Paddy* ; *Patsy* ; *Patty* ; *Peggy* ; *piggy* (*-ie*) ; *pinny* ; *Polly* ; *puppy* ; *Reggy* (*-ie*) ; *Robby* (*-ie*) ; *rooty* = bread ; *Sammy* ; *Sandy* ; *Sawney* ; *shimmy* ; *sissy* = sister ; *slavey* ; *sonny* ; *Sophy* (*-ie*) ; *spooky* (*-ey*) ; *Sukey* ; *Susy* (*-ie*) ; *sweety* ; *Teddy* ; *toddy* ; *Tommy* ; *tommy* = bread ; *tummy* ; *Watty* = Walter ; *wifie* ; *Willy* (*-ie*) ; *Winnie*.

eyot. Pronounce āt ; the OED calls it ' a more usual variant of *ait* ', & ' an artificial spelling '.

eyrie. See AERY.

F

fabricate makes *-cable*, *-tor* ; see -ABLE 1, -OR.

facetiae, in booksellers' catalogues, is a euphemism for obscenities ; the following extract from such a catalogue is vouched for by the *Westminster Gazette* :—FACETIAE. 340 —Kingsley (C.) Phaethon ; or Loose Thoughts for Loose Thinkers, 2nd ed., 8vo, boards, 1s., 1854.

facetious. For synonymy see JOCOSE.

FACETIOUS FORMATIONS. A few specimens may be collected in groups illustrating more or less distinct types.

Pun or parody : anecdotage (anecdote, dotage) ; gigmanity (gigman, humanity) ; correctitude (correct, rectitude) ; judgematical (judge, dogmatic) ; goloptious (voluptuous) ; sacerdotage.

Mock mistakes : underconstumble, mischevious, splendiferous, Eyetalian.

*Popular etymology, real or sup-*posed : highstrikes (hysterics) ; jawbation (jobation).

Mock Latin : bonus, bogus, hocuspocus, hi-cocalorum (hic, hoc, horum ?).

Portmanteau words : galumph (gallop, triumph) ; chortle (snort, chuckle).

Incongruity of Latin trimmings to common English words : absquatulate ; circumbendibus ; omnium gatherum ; fistical ; babyolatry ; disgruntled ; contraption ; squandermania.

Irreverent familiarity : blimy (God blind me) ; crikey (Christ).

Onomatopoeia, obvious or obscure : bubblyjock ; collywobbles ; ramshackle ; pernickety ; rumbustious.

Long & ludicrous : galligaskins ; antigropelos ; cantankerous ; skedaddle ; panjandrum ; spiflicate.

facile. Its value as a synonym for *easy* or *fluent* or *dextrous* lies chiefly in its depreciatory implication. A f. speaker or writer is one who needs to expend little pains (& whose product is of correspondingly little import) ; a f. triumph or victory is easily won (& comes to little). Unless the implication in brackets is intended, the use of *f.* instead of its commoner synonyms (*a more economical & f. mode* ; *with a f. turn of the wrist*) is ill-judged & usually due to AVOIDANCE OF THE OBVIOUS.

facile princeps. Pronounce fă′sĭlĭ ; Latin adv. = easily (first).

facilitate. *The officer was facilitated in his search by the occupants.* We f. an operation, not the operator. A SLIPSHOD EXTENSION.

facsimile. Pronounce făksĭ′mĭlĭ.

fact is well equipped with idiomatic phrases. There are unquestionably established *in f.*, *in point of f.*, *as a matter of f.*, *the f. is*, & *the f. of the matter is*. It is a pity that the recent invention *as a f.* (of which no example is recorded in the OED) should be thrust upon us in addition to all these. It will be seen that in each of the few quotations that must suffice on so trifling a matter one or other of the familiar forms would have been more at home than this parvenu. *He says that a ' considerable part ' of the 25 millions is spent on new officials like locusts devouring the land ; as a f., barely one-thirtieth of that figure is due to new officials* (as a matter of f.)./*The Foreign Office has more than once been severely criticized for similar mistakes in the Reichstag & in the Press ; as a f., it is no more above serious blunders than are many other German institutions* (the f. is)./*It is quite arguable that the time given might have been better allocated, but as a f. nearly all the important points raised have been discussed* (in point of f.)./*The Pan-Germans & Nationalists can afford to be more independent than the Conservatives ; & as a f. they are so* (in f.).

That others besides journalists like the sound of the phrase appears from the following business letter :— *Dear Sirs . . . I accept your statement that the casks returned in March were steel not wood barrels. As a f.* [i.e., as a matter of f.] *the ledger clerk who was in our employ at the time is not now with us & he is entirely to blame . . . When your man returns sacks, casks, or as a f.* [i.e. in f.] *any other goods, a credit note is handed to him at the time.*

factious,factitious,fictitious. Though the words are not synonyms even of the looser kind, there is a certain danger of confusion between them because there are nouns with which two or all of them can be used, with meanings sometimes more & sometimes less wide apart. Thus *factious rancour* is the rancour that lets party spirit prevail over patriotism ; *factitious rancour* is a rancour that is not of natural growth, but has been deliberately created to serve someone's ends ; & *fictitious rancour* is a rancour represented as existing but imaginary. A party cry has a *factious value*, a silver coin a *factitious value* (cf. EXTRINSIC), &

a bogus company's shares a *fictitious value.*

factitive. See TECHNICAL TERMS.
factotum. Pl. *-ms* ; see -UM.
fadeless. See -LESS.
faerie, faery. Pronounce fā'erĭ. ' A variant of *fairy.* In present usage, it is practically a distinct word, adopted either to express Spenser's peculiar modification of the sense, or to exclude various unpoetical or undignified associations connected with the current form *fairy* '—OED. The distinction should be respected by all who care for the interests of the language & not only for their own momentary requirements. To say Faerie when one merely means Fairyland in trivial contexts is VULGARIZATION.

fag(g)ot. Spell with two *g*s.
faience. The use in English of a foreign ' general term comprising all the various kinds of glazed earthenware & porcelain '—the whole definition given in the OED—is hard to divine. Most of those who read the word are disappointed to find, on appeal to a dictionary, that it means nothing more specific. A SUPERFLUOUS WORD.

fail. 1. For *a failed harvest, coup, stockbroker,* &c., see INTRANSITIVE PAST PARTICIPLES.
2. *Failing* = in default of is a participle developed through the absolute construction into a preposition ; *if* or *since so-&-so fails* means the same as *in case of* or *on the failure of so-&-so.* Either the absolute or the prepositional use is accordingly legitimate, but not a mixture of the two ; the form *whom failing* familiar in companies' proxy notices is such a mixture ; it should be either ' failing whom ' (preposition & objective) or ' who failing ' (absolute & subjective).
3. *Fail* is one of the words apt to cause the sort of lapse noticed in NEGATIVES GONE WRONG : *New Year's Day is a milestone which the least observant of us can hardly fail to pass unnoticed.*

fainéant. See FRENCH WORDS.

faint. 1. For *fainted girls* &c. (cf. *fallen angels*) see INTRANSITIVE P.P.

2. *F.* or *feint lines, ruled f.* or *feint,* &c. *Feint* in these expressions means neither more nor less than *f.,* of which it is an older spelling (the origin being F *feindre* feign) preserved only by trade conservatism. As it is a needless puzzle to the uninformed customer, it should be spelt in the intelligible way.

fair(ly). 1. For *bid f., fight* or *hit* or *play f., f. between the eyes* &c., *speak* one *f.,* see UNIDIOMATIC -LY.

2. For the avoidance of ambiguity it should be remembered that *fairly* has the two oddly different senses of *utterly* (*I was f. beside myself*) & *moderately* (*a f. good translation*), & that context does not always make it clear which is meant.

fairy. 1. For *Fairyland & Faerie,* see FAERIE.

2. *F.* & *fay.* The difference is not in meaning, but merely in appropriateness to different contexts ; *f.* being now the everyday form, *fay* should be reserved for occasions demanding the unusual.

fait accompli. See FRENCH WORDS.

faithfully. 1. For *yours f.* see LETTER FORMULAE.

2. In *promise f., f.* is an ultra-colloquial or uneducated substitute for *definitely, explicitly, expressly, emphatically,* or *solemnly.*

3. *Deal f. with* is a phrase of biblical sound & doubtless of puritan origin, now used for the most part jocularly in the sense not treat with tenderness, punish or rebuke—one of the idioms that should not be spoilt by over-frequent use.

fakir, fakeer, faquir. The OED treats the first as the established form. Pronounce fakēr'.

fall. 1. For *is fallen, fallen angel,* &c., see INTRANSITIVE P.P.

2. The noun *f.* as a synonym for the ordinary *autumn* is either an Americanism, a provincialism, or an ARCHAISM ; as the last, it has its

right & its wrong uses ; as either of the others, it is out of place except in dialogue.

fallacy (in logic), **false analogy.** See TECHNICAL TERMS.

FALSE EMPHASIS. 1. *That being so, we say that it would be shameful if domestic servants were the only class of employed persons left outside the scheme of State Insurance.* What the writer means is It would be shameful for servants to be left out when all other employees are included. What he says means It would be shameful for nobody except servants to be excluded— which is plainly neither true nor his contention. The disaster is due to his giving too emphatic a place to a subordinate, though important, point ; what is shameful is the servants' exclusion, not the inclusion of anyone or everyone else. Care must be taken that, an two men ride of a horse, the groom & not the master rides behind.

2. An especially common form of false emphasis is the use of the emphatic word *both* (which means one as well as the other, or in one case as well as in the other) in places where that full sense is either unnecessary or impossible, instead of *the two, they,* or nothing at all. The point is clear if the two sentences (*a*) *Both fought well,* & (*b*) *To settle the matter both fought,* are compared. In *a,* emphasis is wanted ; not only one fought well, the other did too ; but, in *b,* of course one did not fight without the other's fighting, since it takes two to make a fight ; the needless *both* makes the reader wonder whom else they both fought. Obvious as the mistake is, it is surprising how often it occurs in sentences little more abstruse than *b* :—*Both men had something in common* (with whom ? with each other ; then why not *the two,* or *the men,* or *the two men,* or simply *they* ?)./*At present there is a complete divergence in the proposals of both Governments* (*the two,* or *the*)./*Lord*

Milner had fixed these prices because the Food Controller & the Board of Agriculture both *disagreed as to what they should be, & he had at least the wisdom to fix a price that they both disliked* (the first *both* is needless & misleading; the second is right). An instance at once more excusable & more fatal, both for the same reason, that hard thinking is necessary to get the thing disentangled, is : *This company has found that the men they employ in America can be depended on to produce a minimum of 40% more output than the men they employ abroad, & yet these men both in America & elsewhere may be of the same race & nationality at birth.* The point is not that in America, & just as much in (say) Italy, these men may be (say) Czechs, but that of any two men or any two sets of which one is employed in America & the other in Italy both may be (say) Italians ; it is not that America & Italy are in some matter alike, but that the difference between the employee in one & the employee in the other is constant ; *both,* inserted where it is, hopelessly disguises this ; read *these men of whom one is employed in America & one elsewhere.*

falsehood, falseness, falsity. Differentiation has been busy with the three, but has perhaps not yet done with them. At present *A falsehood* is a lie ; *falsehood* is lying regarded as an action, but it is also a statement or statements contrary to fact or the truth. *Falseness* is contrariness to fact regarded as a quality of a statement, but it is also lying & deception regarded as an element in character. *Falsity* is interchangeable with *falseness* in its first but not in its second sense. In the following examples the word used is, except where an alternative is shown, the only one of the three consistent with modern usage :— *That is a falsehood ; You told a falsehood ; He was convicted of falsehood ; Truth would be suppressed together with falsehood ; Truth exaggerated may become falsehood ; The falseness,* or *falsity, of this conclusion is obvious ; A falseness that even his plausibility could not quite conceal.*

FALSE QUANTITY. The phrase should be banished from the discussion of how to pronounce English words. The use of it betrays the user's ignorance that standard English teems with what are in one sense or another false quantities. Its implication is that, with some limitations or other, the sound of vowels in English words derived from Greek & Latin is decided by the sound in the words from which they come ; but these limitations are so variously conceived, when their existence is not ignored, that mere mention of false quantity is valueless. Take a score of words about the pronunciation of which opinions differ, & on which classical quantities might be expected to throw light ; the classical quantities are marked where they matter, & accents are added when acceptance of the classical quantity would naturally result in a particular stress :—amēnity, appărent, cănī′ne, cīnē′ma, commŭ′nal, dēficit, doctrī′nal, glă′dĭŏlŭs, ĭdyl, inter′nĕcine, pătriot, prō′tăgō′nist, rătion, salī′vary, Salonī′ca, sēmaphore, sīmian, Sŏcrates, trībunal, vertī′go. It will be clear from this list that the following of classical quantity may operate singly or doubly, i.e. on the sound of a vowel only, or through it on the word's balance, & that the secondary is much more noticeable than the primary effect ; the difference between pătriot & pātriot, appărent & appărent, is slight, but that between doctrī′nal & dŏ′ctrĭnal, vertī′go & ver′tĭgo, prō′tagō′nist & protă′gonist, is very great. How little weight is to be attached to classical quantity as an argument merely for one vowel sound against another will be plain from another score of examples, some of them actual Latin words, in which the unquestioned

pronunciation is a false quantity :—
ăgent, ălien, bŏnă fĭde, cŏmic, cor-
rŏborate, dĕcent, ēcho, ēthics, et
cētera, fastĭdious, ĭdĕa, jocŏsity (&
all in -osity), mĭlitary, mĭnor, mĭti-
gate, ŏdour, pathĕtic (& most in
-etic), sĕnile, sōlitary, varĭety (& all
in -iety). It is useless to call out
' false quantity ' to someone who
says rātion or ĭdyl or trĭbu′nal or
amĕnity when he can answer you
with ăgent, fastĭdious, mĭnor, or
ēcho. The simple fact is that in
determining the quality of a vowel
sound in English classical quantity
is of no value whatever ; to flout
usage & say Sōcrates is the merest
pedantry.

With regard to its secondary effect,
as an influence in selecting the
syllable in English words that shall
bear the stress, classical quantity is
not so negligible. A variation of
stress being a much more marked
thing than a vowel difference, the
non-latinist's attention is arrested
when a neighbour whom he credits
with superior knowledge springs
doctrī′nal upon him, & doctrī′nal
gets its chance. Whether doctrī′nal
is right is another question ; the
superior-knowledged one knows that
doctrina has a long i ; but has he
satisfied himself that a long i, not in
doctrina but in *doctrinalis*, i.e. with
no stress on it, has any right to
affect the stress of *doctrinal* ? Or
again, has the Grecian who knows
kĭnēma & objects to cĭ′nema reflected that *cinema* does not represent *kinema* itself, but is a shortening
of *cĭ′nemă′tograph*, which again has
passed through French & indeed
been there ' assembled ' on its way
from Greek to English ? if he had,
he would probably have held his
peace. In many words, such as
canine & *saline*, *vertigo*, the latinist's
first thoughts (kanī′n, salī′n, ver-
tī′gō) do not need modification on
his own part as *doctrī′nal* & *cinē′ma*
do ; but he has still to reckon with
the recessive-accent tendency, which
has as good a right to a voice in the
matter as his erudition, & will fight

hard & perhaps victoriously for
kā′nĭn, sā′lĭn, & ver′tĭgo.

After all deductions, however, a
small province is left in which the
false-quantity principle may fairly
reign ; if *clematis* is pronounced
klĭmā′tĭs, *enema* ĭnē′ma, & *gladiolus*
glădĭō′lus, what has been done is
this : in Greek & Latin words
adopted without modification, a
syllable that in the original is
neither long in quantity nor stressed
has been made the stressed syllable
in English ; they should be klĕ′matĭs,
ĕ′nĭma, & glă′dyolus (with indulgence to gladī′olus on the analogy
of *variety*). But on such disputes as
those between protă′gonist & prō′-
tagō′nist, cŏ′mmunal & commū′nal,
i′nternē′cine & inter′nĕcine, să′lĭvary
& salī′vary, mă′rĭtal & marī′tal,
cer′vĭcal & cervī′cal, ă′nthropoid &
anthrō′poid, its decision is not final ;
it is not judge, but a mere party to
the suit. Let the scholar plead his
case ; but since the ailment that he
long insisted on our calling ăngī′na
pectoris was discovered to be ă′ngĭna
after all, his pleadings are suspect.

FALSE SCENT. The laying of false
scent, i.e., the causing of a reader to
suppose that a sentence or part of
one is taking a certain course, which
he afterwards finds to his confusion
that it does not take, is an obvious
folly—so obvious that no-one commits it wittingly except when surprise is designed to amuse. But
writers are apt to forget that, if the
false scent is there, it is no excuse
to say they did not intend to lay it ;
it is their business to see that it is
not there, & this requires more care
than might be supposed. The
reader comes to a sentence not
knowing what it is going to contain ;
the writer knows ; consequently
what seems to the latter, owing to
his private information, to bear
unquestionably one sense & no
other may present to the former,
with his open mind, either a choice
of meanings or even a different one
only. Nor has the writer even the

satisfaction of calling his reader a fool for misunderstanding him, since he seldom hears of it ; it is the reader who calls the writer a fool for not being able to express himself.

The possibilities of false scent are too miscellaneous to be exhaustively tabulated ; the image of the reader with the open mind, ready to seize every chance of going wrong, should be always present to the inexperienced writer. A few examples, however, may suggest certain constructions in which special care is necessary :—*It was only after Mr Buckmaster, Lord Wodehouse, & Mr Freake, finding that they were unable to go, that the England team as now constituted, but with Major Hunter in the place of Captain Cheape, was decided on.* The writer knew that *after* was to be a preposition governing *Mr B.* &c. *finding* ; but the reader takes it for a conjunction with a verb yet to come, & is angry at having to reconsider. Such things happen with the FUSED PARTICIPLE./*Four years, the years that followed her marriage, suffice Lady Younghusband for her somewhat elaborate study, ' Marie Antoinette : Her Early Youth, 1770–1774 ' (Macmillan & Co., 15s. net).* The reader does not dream of jumping over Lady Y. to get at the owner of *her* (marriage) till *1770–1774* at the end throws a new light on the four years. See PRONOUNS for more such false scent./*The official announcement at Rome that the Ottoman Government, having failed to meet Italy's demands, Italy & Turkey were in a state of war from 2.30 yesterday afternoon, was promptly followed by hostilities.* The punctuation (see ABSOLUTE CONSTRUCTION) deludes us into expecting a verb for *the Ottoman Government*, instead of which comes a new subject./*The influences of that age, his open, kind, susceptible nature, to say nothing of his highly untoward situation, made it more than usually difficult for him to cast aside or rightly subordinate.*

Only the end of the sentence reveals that we were wrong in guessing the influences & his nature to be parts of a compound subject.

falsetto. Pl. *-os* ; see -O(E)s 6.

falsify. For inflexions see VERBS IN -IE &c., 6.

fanatic. Pronounce fană′tĭk. The word tends to lose its fully adjectival use. We say *I call a man fanatical* (or *a f.*, but not simply *f.*) *who . . .* See -IC(AL).

fancy, vb. For inflexions see VERBS IN -IE &c., 6.

fandango. Pl. *-os* ; see -O(E)s 6.

fanfare. It is perhaps better to pronounce the noun as a FRENCH WORD, since neither noun nor verb has become familiar English ; but the verb, if used, can hardly be treated as foreign, & should be fănfā̆r′. *fanfaronade*, however, is common enough to be fully anglicized (fănfărŏnă′d).

fantasia. fahntahzē′ah, făntah′zĭa —OED. The first is the Italian pronunciation, advisable at least for the technical musical term. In transferred senses the second is no doubt commoner, but perhaps due to ignorance rather than to choice.

fantasy, phantasy. ' In modern use *f.* & *p.*, in spite of their identity in sound & in ultimate etymology, tend to be apprehended as separate words, the predominant sense of the former being " caprice, whim, fanciful invention ", while that of the latter is " imagination, visionary notion " '—OED.

fantoccini. Pronounce făntochē′nĭ.

faquir. See FAKIR.

far. 1. *Farther*)(*further*. 2. (*So*) *f. from*. 3. *F.-flung*. 4. *As & so f. as*. 5. *So f. as*)(*so f. that*.

1. For *farther*)(*further*, see FARTHER.

2. (*So*) *f. from*. *So far from ' running '* the Conciliation Bill, the Suffragettes only reluctantly consented to it. This idiom is a curious, but established, mixture between Far from running it they consented to it reluctantly & They were so far from

running it that they consented to it reluctantly. It is always open, however to those who dislike illogicality to drop the *so* in the short form—Far from running it they consented to it reluctantly. But it is waste labour to tilt against STURDY INDEFENSIBLES.

3. *Far-flung*. *The f.-f. battle-line, our f.-f. empire*, &c. The present emotional value of this as a VOGUE-WORD is reckoned so high as often to outweigh such trifling matters as appropriateness :—*Set against all its* [the war's] *burden of sorrow & suffering & waste that millions of men from f.-f. lands have been taught to know each other better*. The lands are distant ; they are not far-flung ; but what matter ? *f.-f.* is a signal that our blood is to be stirred ; & so it is, if we do not stop to think./ *He is already popular, even in the remotest parts of this f.-f. constituency.*

4. *As & so f. as*. *As* or *so f. as x* cannot be used as short for *as far as x goes* or *so far as concerns x* ; in the following examples *concerns, regards, is concerned, goes*, &c., should have been inserted where omission is indicated :—*As far as getting the money he asked for* ∧, *Mr Churchill had little difficulty./The result was that the men practically met with a defeat so far as* ∧ *obtaining a definite pledge in regard to their demands./There is no case for the decision of the Law Lords, so far as* ∧ ' *Parliamentary representation* ' *being a recognized method by which unions could fulfil their legal function of* ' *regulating the relations between masters & workmen* './*They seem to treat the Chancellor of the Exchequer's Budget proposals as something which the moment they are made ought to be considered as unalterable in any respect, at all events so far as* ∧ *what is proposed by way of taxation.*

As or *so far as*, regarded as a compound preposition, is followed primarily by a word of place (*went as far as York*) ; secondarily it may have a noun (which may be an infinitive or gerund) that expresses

a limit of advance or progress (*He knows algebra as far as quadratics* ; *I have gone so far as to collect*, or *so far as collecting, statistics*). But when the purpose is to say not how far an action proceeds, but within what limits a statement is to be applied, as in all the examples at the beginning of this section, *as* & *so far as* are not prepositions, but conjunctions requiring a verb. The genesis of the misuse may be guessed at thus :—*I have gone as far as collecting statistics* (right). *As far as collecting statistics you have my leave to proceed* (correct, but unnatural order). *As far as collecting statistics he is competent enough* (cf. *knows algebra as far as quadratics* ; defensible, but better insert *goes* ; the Churchill sentence quoted is just below this level). *As far as collecting statistics, only industry is necessary* (impossible).

5. *So far as*)(*so far that*. *His efforts were so far successful* (*a*) *as they reduced*, or (*b*) *as to reduce*, or (*c*) *that they reduced, the percentage of deaths*. The *b* & *c* forms mean the same, & their interpretation is not in doubt : he reduced the percentage, & had that success. The meaning of *a* is different : if you want to know whether & how far he succeeded, find out whether & how far he reduced the percentage ; perhaps he did not reduce it, & therefore failed. But the *a* form is not infrequently used wrongly instead of *b* or *c* :—*The previous appeal made by M. Delcassé was so far successful as the Tsar himself sent orders to comply* (read *that* for *as* ; the sending of orders clearly took place, & such sending is not a variable by the degree of which success could be measured).

farce. See TECHNICAL TERMS, & COMEDY.

farceur. See FRENCH WORDS.

faro. Pronounce fār'ō.

farouche. The meaning, simply sullen-mannered from shyness (*cheval f., cheval qui craint la présence de* *l'homme*—Littré), is obscured by association ('the connexion is untenable'—OED) with *ferocious* ; see TRUE & FALSE ETYMOLOGY.

farrow, litter. *F*. is used of swine only, *l.* of any quadruped producing several young at a birth.

farther, further. The history of the two words appears to be that *further* is a comparative of *fore* & *should*, if it were to be held to its etymology, mean more advanced, & that *farther* is a newer variant of *further*, no more connected with *far* than *further* is, but affected in its form by the fact that *further*, having come to be used instead of the obsolete comparative of *far* (*farrer*), seemed to need a respelling that should assimilate it to *far*. This is intended for a popular but roughly correct summary of the OED's etymological account. As to the present use of the two forms, the OED says :—' In standard English the form *farther* is usually preferred where the word is intended to be the comparative of *far*, while *further* is used where the notion of *far* is altogether absent ; there is a large intermediate class of instances in which the choice between the two forms is arbitrary '.

This seems to be too strong a statement, or a statement of what might be a useful differentiation rather than of one actually developed or even developing. The fact is surely that hardly anyone uses the two words for different occasions ; most people prefer one or the other for all purposes, & the preference of the majority is for *further* ; the most that should be said is perhaps that *farther* is not common except where distance is in question. The three pairs of quotations following are selected for comparison from the OED stores.

1. Comparative of *far* :—*If you can bear your load no farther, say so.*— Ht Martineau. *It was not thought safe for the ships to proceed further in the darkness.*—Macaulay.

2. No notion of *far* :—*Down he sat without farther bidding.*—Dickens. *I now proceed to some further instances.* —De Morgan.

3. Intermediate:—*Punishment cannot act any farther than in as far as the idea of it is present in the mind.*—Bentham. *Men who pretend to believe no further than they can see.*—Berkeley.

On the whole, though differentiations are good in themselves, it is less likely that one will be established for *farther* & *further* than that the latter will become universal. In the verb, *further* is very much more common.

fascinate makes *-nable, -tor* ; see -ABLE 1, -OR.

fascine. Pronounce *fasē'n*.

fascist &c. The Italian words— *fascista* pl. *-ti, fascismo*—are pronounced (roughly) fahshē'stah -tē, -ē'smō. In English they should be fashi'sta,-tē,-ĭ'zmō, or else anglicized to *fascist* pl. *-s, -ism*, pronounced fă'sĭ-. Whether this full anglicization of the words is worth while cannot be decided till we know whether the things are to be temporary or permanent in England.

fasten. Pronounce fah'sn ; see PRONUNCIATION, Silent t.

fasti. Pronounce fă'stĭ.

fatalism)(determinism. The philosophical distinction between the words cannot here be more than roughly suggested, & is itself more or less arbitrary. *F.* says : Every event is pre-ordained ; you cannot act as you will, but only in the pre-ordained way. *D.* says : You can act (barring obstacles) as you will ; but then you cannot will as you will ; your will is determined by a complex of antecedents the interaction of which makes you unable to choose any but the one course. That is, *f.* assumes an external power decreeing irresistibly every event from the greatest to the least, while *d.* assumes the dependence of all things, including the wills of living beings, upon sequences of cause & effect that would be ascertainable if we were omniscient. The difference between the two views as practical guides to life is not great; one assures us that what is to be will be, the other that whatever is cannot but be; & either assurance relieves us of responsibility; but those are called determinists who decline to make assumptions (involving the ancient notion of Fate) about an external directing will.

Such, very roughly, is the difference between the two theories; but the popular distinction today is not between the names of two contrasted theories, but between the name of an abstract philosophy & that of a practical rule of life. *D.* is the merely intellectual opinion that the determinist or fatalist account of all that happens is true; *f.* is the frame of mind that disposes one at once to abandon the hope of influencing events & to repudiate responsibility for one's actions; *d.* is regarded as a philosophy, & *f.* as a faith.

fateful. *Will the Irish question, which has been fateful to so many Governments, prove one of the explosive forces which will drive the Coalition asunder?* Correct to *fatal*. Novelty-hunting, the desire to avoid so trite a word as *fatal*, is responsible for many *fatefuls*; cf. forceful. There was a reason good enough for inventing *fateful*, in the restriction of the older *fatal* to a bad sense; *fateful* could mean big with happy fate as well as with unhappy. But to use *fateful*, as in the quotation, where *fatal* would do as well as to renounce the advantage gained by its invention, & to sacrifice the interests of the language to one's own momentary desire for a gewgaw. See Pairs & snares.

father, n. For *the f. of History, lies,* see Sobriquets.

father, vb, in the sense fix the paternity of, is followed only by *on* or *upon* the father or author. *He was able also to say that the First Sea* *Lord repudiated the idea, which the advocates of compulsory service have attempted to f. on to him, that . . .* Impossible English; see Cast-iron idiom.

fathom. *Six &c. fathom,* rather than *fathoms*; see Collectives 3.

fat(ten). See -en verbs.

fault. *I am at f.*=I am puzzled; *I am in f.*=I am to blame. See Cast-iron idiom. *Mr* [Publisher] *recently published a work entitled ' Fifty Years of Golf : My Memories, by " Andra " Kirkaldy '. Mr Horace Hutchinson published in 1919, through Messrs Newnes, a work entitled ' Fifty Years of Golf '. Mr* [Publisher], *therefore, is at fault, & he expresses his regret that the mistake has been made.*

faun, satyr, yahoo. The first two are the Latin & the Greek name for woodland creatures, half beast & half man in form, half beast & half god in nature. Horse's tail & ears, goat's tail & horns, goat's ears & tail & legs, budding horns, are various symbols marking not the difference between the two, but that between either of them & man. The faun is now regarded rather as the type of unsophisticated & the satyr of unpurified man; the first is man still in intimate communion with Nature, the second is man still swayed by bestial passions. *S.* has probably had its implications fixed by association with *yahoo*, the type of man at his most despicable, for which see *Gulliver* Pt IV ; *f.* has not been affected by this.

fauna, flora, are singular nouns used as collectives, not plurals like *carnivora* &c. Their plurals, rarely needed, are *faunas & floras*, or *faunae & florae*. They are Latin goddess names made to stand for the realm of flowers, of animals, especially as represented in any given district.

fauteuil, faux pas. See French words.

favo(u)r. Keep the *-u-* ; but see -our & -or.

fay. See FAIRY 2.

feasible. With those who feel that the use of an ordinary word for an ordinary notion does not do justice to their vocabulary or sufficiently exhibit their cultivation (see WORK-ING & STYLISH WORDS), *f.* is now a prime favourite. Its proper sense is ' capable of being done, accomplished, or carried out ' (OED). That is, it means the same as *possible* in one of the latter's senses, & its true function is to be used instead of *possible* where that might be ambiguous. *A thunderstorm is possible* (but not *f.*). *Irrigation is possible* (or, indifferently, *f.*). *A counter-revolution is possible* ; i. e. (*a*) one may for all we know happen, or (*b*) we can if we choose bring one about ; but, if *b* is the meaning, *f.* is better than *possible* because it cannot properly bear sense *a* & therefore obviates ambiguity.

The wrong use of *f.* is that in which, by SLIPSHOD EXTENSION, it is allowed to have also the other sense of *possible*, & that of *probable*. This is described by the OED as ' hardly a justifiable sense etymologically, & . . . recognized by no dictionary '. It is however becoming very common ; in all the quotations, it will be seen that the natural word would be either *probable* or *possible*, one of which should have been chosen :— *Continuing, Mr Wood said :* ' *I think it is very f. that the strike may be brought to an end this week, & it is a significant coincidence that . . .*'./ *Witness said it was quite f. that if he had had night binoculars he would have seen the iceberg earlier.*/*We ourselves believe that this is the most f. explanation of the tradition.*/*This would appear to offer a f. explanation of the scaffold puzzle.*/*The reason given for the refusal was quite different & more f.*/*It is f. that the airship was struck by lightning & totally destroyed.*

feast. For ' f. of reason ' see HACK-NEYED PHRASES.

feature, vb. The use of this in cinema announcements instead of *represent* or *exhibit* is perhaps from America ; at any rate, while British dictionaries give no meanings that support it, the American ' Standard ' gives as normal ' The newspapers feature aviation '. Wherever it comes from, it is to be feared that from the cinema bills it will make its way into popular use, which would be a pity. (Yes ! 1924: *Boys' school & college outfits, men's footwear & under-garments, as well as . . ., are also featured.*)

fecund. The OED gives precedence to fĕ'- over fē'-.

federate makes -*rable*, -*tor* ; see -ABLE 1, -OR.

federation, confederation, confederacy. Writing in 1918, one may say that the Entente Powers are now a confederacy, that the proposed League of Nations would be a confederation, & that if that were further developed into a United States of Europe, that would be a federation. The following extracts from the OED bear this out :—
' *Confederacy* now usually implies a looser or more temporary association than *confederation*, which is applied to a union of States organized on an intentionally permanent basis.'/' In modern political use, *confederation* is usually limited to a permanent union of sovereign States for common action in relation to externals . . . The United States of America are commonly described as a *Confederation* (or confederacy) from 1777 to 1789 ; but from 1789 their closer union has been considered a " federation " or federal republic.'/[On *federation*] ' Now chiefly *spec.* the formation of a political unity out of a number of separate States, so that each retains the management of its internal affairs '.

fee, n. For synonymy see TAX.

fee, vb. The past & p.p. are best written *fee'd* ; see -ED & 'D.

feint, adj. See FAINT.

feldspar, not *felspar*. The first part is German *Feld* field, not *Fels* rock.

felicide. A PEDANTIC-HUMOUR word.
felicitate. See FORMAL WORDS.
fellah. Pl. *fellaheen* now more usual than *fellahs*.
felloe, felly. 'In England the forms seem to be equally in good use' (OED, which pronounces each as it is spelt). Perhaps the prevailing usage is to spell *-oe*, & say fĕ'lĭ.

fellow & hyphens. See HYPHENS for the principles that should decide between e.g. *fellow man, fellow-man,* & *fellowman.* Usage, however, is far from observing those principles with *f.*; they would require that *f. man,* if *man* is to bear the accent, as it does, should be written either *f. man* or *fellowman,* & that if *f.-man* is written it should be accented on *fellow* only; but *f.-man* is almost universal. All the combinations of *f.* with a noun (except *f.-feeling,* for which see below) would be best written as two separate words without hyphen, & they all are sometimes so written; but owing to the mistaken notion that words often used in juxtaposition must be hyphened even though their accent remains that which is proper to them when unhyphened, the more familiar combinations are so often seen with the hyphen that they now look queer & old-fashioned without it. *F.-feeling,* which is more of a true compound than the rest (*f.* not being another name for *feeling,* as it is for *soldier* in *f. soldier*), would be better written *fellowfeeling,* but this also has usually the hyphen.
A phrase or two may be given parallel to the *f.* phrases; sensible people abstain from hyphening these, because they either realize or feel instinctively that the effect of the hyphen would be to throw all the accent upon the first of the two words:—*Lord Mayor, lady help, Lady Superior, deputy Speaker, soldier statesman, mastiff puppy.*
Those who are not afraid of seeming old-fashioned can follow these analogies & write all the items of the following list except *fellowship* &

f.-feeling as two separate words; & no-one need shrink from writing so any of those in which a hyphen is not here inserted or any still less familiar combination; but where a hyphen is inserted, it is usual :— *f. author, f. Christian, f.-citizen, f.-commoner, f.-countryman, f. craftsman, f.-creature, f. executor, f.-feeling* or *fellowfeeling, f. heir, f. lodger, f.-man, f. passenger, fellowship, f. sinner, f.-soldier, f. subject, f. sufferer, f. traveller, f. worker.*

felo(-)de(-)se. Pronounce fēlōdĭsē'; it is better written as three words without hyphens except when used attributively as in *such* felo-de-se *conduct*; pl. (rare) *felones de se* or (wrongly) *felos de se* or (colloq.) *felo-de-ses.*

felspar. See FELDSPAR.
female, feminine, womanly. The fundamental difference between *female* & *feminine* is that the first is wider, referring things to the sex, human or not, while the other is limited to the human part of the sex. This would leave it indifferent in many contexts which word should be used; & yet we all know that, even in such contexts, nearly always one & not the other is idiomatic : *female ruler* & *cook,* but *feminine rule* & *cookery* ; *female attire, children, organs,* but *feminine gender, curiosity, arguments* ; & *female* & *feminine education* mean different things. It is clearly not true that *feminine* is always to be preferred when the reference is to human females only, since *female attire, female servant,* are better than *feminine attire* & *servant.*
A female is, shortly put, a she, or, put more at length, a woman-or-girl-or-cow-or-hen-or-the-like. The noun use is the original ; but, like all nouns, the word can be used attributively, & through the attributive use this noun has passed into an adjective. The female sex is the sex of which all members are shes ; that is the attributive use ; passing to, or rather towards, the full adjec-

tival use, we say so-&-so is female, meaning that it is of or for the female sex. Beyond that point as an adjective *female* has not gone ; *feminine*, on the other hand, is not a noun that has gone part way to complete adjectivehood ; it has been an adjective all its life, & means not merely of or for women, but of the kind that characterizes or may be expected from or is associated with women. That is, there are two factors in choosing between *female* & *feminine*, (a) that of the difference between all sex & human sex, & (b) that of the difference between the noun-adjective & the true adjective. The result is this : when the information wanted is the answer to the question *Of* (or *for*) *which sex ?*, use *female*, provided that the context sufficiently indicates the limitation to humankind ; when the question is *Of what sort ?*, use *feminine*. So we get *female ruler, cook, companion, Paul Pry*, but *feminine rule, cookery, companionship, curiosity* ; *female attire, organs, children, servants, screws* ; *the female ward* of a prison ; *female education* is the education provided for (of course, human) females, while *feminine education* is that which tends to cultivate the qualities characteristic of women. *Feminine* is the epithet for beauty, features, arguments, pursuits, sympathy, weakness, spite, & the like. The feminine gender is the one that includes nouns resembling women's names ; a man may be called feminine, but not female, if he is like women. For *female* or *feminine rhyme* &c., see MALE 2.

Womanly is used only to describe qualities peculiar to (a) good women as opposed to men (*w. compassion, sympathy, intuition*, &c.) or (b) developed women as opposed to girls (*w. beauty, figure, experience*).

female)(woman. *F.* in its noun use is sometimes convenient as a word that includes girls as well as women, & sometimes as including non-human as well as human f.

creatures. Where such inclusion is not specially desired, to call a woman a female is exactly as impolite as to call a lady a woman, without any of the sentimental implications that often make *woman* preferable to *lady* ; it is reasonably resented. It is not reasonable to extend this resentment to the adjective use of *female* ; but it is the mistaken extension that probably accounts for the apparent avoidance of the natural phrase *f. suffrage* & the use of the clumsy *woman suffrage* instead. As with *f. education* (for which see the previous article), *f. suffrage* is the short for the suffrage of (of course, human) f. creatures, i.e. women. It is to be hoped that when the way the women are going to vote comes, as it now will, to be a common theme of discussion, it will be called *the female vote* & not *the woman vote*, just as its counterpart will certainly be *the male vote* & not *the man vote* ; to turn *woman* into an adjective with *female* ready made is mere perversity.

FEMININE DESIGNATIONS. This article is intended as a counterprotest. The authoress, poetess, & paintress, & sometimes the patroness & the inspectress, take exception to the indication of sex in these designations. They regard the distinction as derogatory to them & as implying inequality between the sexes ; an author is an author, that is all that concerns any reader, & it is impertinent curiosity to want to know whether the author is male or female.

These ladies neither are nor pretend to be making their objection in the interests of the language or of people in general ; they object in their own interests only ; this they are entitled to do, but still it is lower ground, & general convenience & the needs of the King's English, if these are against them, must be reckoned of more importance than their sectional claims. Are these against them ? Undoubtedly. First, any word that does the work of two or more by packing several notions into one is a gain (the more civilized a language the more such words it possesses), if certain conditions are observed : it must not be cumbersome ; it should for choice be correctly formed ; & it must express a compound notion that is familiar enough to need a name.

Secondly, with the coming extension of women's vocations, feminines for vocation-words are a special need of the future ; everyone knows the inconvenience of being uncertain whether a doctor is a man or a woman ; hesitation in establishing the word *doctress* is amazing in a people regarded as nothing if not practical. Far from needing to reduce the number of our sex-words, we should do well to indulge in real neologisms such as *teacheress, singeress,* & *danceress,* the want of which drives us to *cantatrice, danseuse,* & the like ; *authoress* & *poetess* & *paintress* are not neologisms.

But are not the objectors, besides putting their own interests above those of the public, actually misjudging their own ? Their view is that the female author is to raise herself to the level of the male author by asserting her right to his name ; but if there is one profession in which more than in others the woman is the man's equal it is acting ; & the actress is not known to resent the indication of her sex ; the proof of real equality will be not the banishment of *authoress* as a degrading title, but its establishment on a level with *author*. Nor, after all, does an authoress, a doctress, a lioness, a votaress, a prophetess, or a Jewess, cease to be an author, a doctor, a lion, a votary, a prophet, or a Jew, because she ends in *-ess* ; she should call herself, & still more allow us without protest to call her, by the common or the feminine title according to the requirements of the occasion ; but *George Eliot the authoress* would then be as much more frequent than

G. E. the author as *the prophetess Deborah* than *the prophet D.*

It may perhaps aid consideration of the subject if short selections are given, A, of established feminine titles, B, of recent or impugned ones, &, C, of words unfortunately not provided with feminines.

A

Abbess, actress, administratrix, adultress, adventuress, ambassadress, deaconess, duchess, enchantress, executrix, giantess, goddess, governess, horsewoman, hostess, huntress, Jewess, lioness, mother, murderess, priestess, princess, procuress, prophetess, quakeress, queen, shepherdess, songstress, sorceress, stewardess, votaress, waitress, wardress.

B

Authoress, chairwoman, conductress, directress, doctress, draughtswoman, editress, inspectress, jurywoman, manageress, paintress, patroness, poetess, policewoman, protectress, tailoress.

C

Artist, aurist, clerk, cook, councillor, cyclist, lecturer, legatee, martyr, motorist, oculist, palmist, president, pupil, singer, teacher, typist.

Artist, in list C, illustrates well the need of feminines, since ignorant writers are often guilty of *artists & artistes*, meaning male & female performers.

feminineness, feminism, &c. The words on record in the OED are : *feminacy, feminality, femineity, feminicity, feminility, feminineness, femininism, femininity, feminism, feminity.* Of these *feminacy, feminality, feminicity,* & *feminility,* may be put out of court as mere failed experiments. *Femineity, -ineness, -inity,* & *-ity,* remain as competitors for the sense of woman's nature & qualities, none of them perceptibly differentiated in meaning. *Feminineness* is a word that does not depend on usage or dictionary-makers for its right to exist ; it can of course be used ; *-inity* & *-ity* are both as old as the 14th century & have been in use ever since ; of the two, *-inity* is the more correct form, but *-ity* is more euphonious & manageable, & is as justifiable as e. g. *virginity* ; *-eity* is a 19th-century formation, needless beside the others. It would be well if *feminity* could be appointed to the post, with *feminineness* as deputy, & *-inity* & *-eity* dismissed as SUPER-FLUOUS WORDS.

Femininism & *feminism* should have meanings different both from the above & from each other. *Femininism* should mean (a) an expression or idiom peculiar to women, & (b) the tendency in a man to feminine habits. *Feminism* (with *feminist* attached) should mean faith in woman, advocacy of the rights of women, the prevalence of female influence ; it may be worth mention that it, as compared with *femininism*, is not open to the well-known objections urged against *pacifism* & *pacifist* as compared with *pacificism* ; but the proposed sense, now pretty well established, is novel enough not to be recorded in the OED (1901).

femme-de-chambre. See FRENCH WORDS.

femoral. For *f. habiliments* see PEDANTIC HUMOUR.

femur. Pl. *femurs* or *femora* ; see LATIN PLURALS.

feoff, feoffee, feoffer or **feoffor, feoffment.** Pronounce fĕf-.

ferae naturae. *The law applies only to animals f. n.* ; *Rabbits are f. n.* ; *Rabbits are among the f. n.* The first two sentences show the correct, & the third the wrong use of the phrase, & the three together reveal the genesis of the misuse. *F. n.* is not a nominative plural, but a genitive singular, & means not ' wild kinds ', but ' of wild kind ', & it must be used only as equivalent to a predicative adjective, & not as a plural noun. See FOREIGN DANGER, & POPULARIZED TECHNICALITIES.

Feringhee. Pronounce ferĭ'nggĭ.

ferment, n. & vb. See NOUN & VERB ACCENT.

ferret, vb, makes *-eted* &c ; see -T-, -TT-.

fer(r)ule. The cap or ring for a stick has two *r*s, & is also spelt *ferrel* ; the teacher's implement (now in allusive use only) has one *r*, & is also spelt *ferula*. The two words are of separate origins.

ferry, vb. For inflexions see VERBS IN -IE &c., 6.

fertile. The OED gives precedence to -ĭl ; but -ĭl is now usual.

fervour. Keep the *-u-* ; but see -OUR & -OR.

festal, festive. Both words point to feast or festival, but the reference in *-al* is more direct ; a person is in festal mood if there is a festival & he is in tune with it, but he may be in festive mood even if he is merely feeling as he might if it were a festival. *A festal day* ; *in festal costume* ; *a festive scene* ; *the festive board*. The distinction is not regularly observed, but, such as it is, it accounts for the continued existence of the two words. There is something of the same difference between *festival* & *festivity* or *festivities*.

fetid, foetid. The OED prefers fĕ'tĭd as spelling & pronunciation. The Latin original is, correctly spelt, *fĕtidus* ; for ĕ see FALSE QUANTITY.

FETISHES, or current literary rules misapplied or unduly revered. Among the more notable or harmful are : SPLIT INFINITIVE ; FALSE QUANTITY ; avoidance of repetition (see ELEGANT VARIATION) ; the rule of thumb for *and* WHICH ; a craze for native English words (see SAXON-ISM) ; pedantry on the foreign spelling of foreign words (see MORALE) ; the notion that RELIABLE, AVERSE *to*, & DIFFERENT *to*, are marks of the uneducated ; the rule of thumb for *and* & *or* in ENUMERA-TION FORMS ; the dread of a PRE-POSITION AT END ; the idea that successive metaphors are mixed METAPHOR ; the belief that common words lack dignity (see FORMAL WORDS).

fetish, fetiche. The modern *-ish* seems to have superseded the older *-iche*. The OED gives fĕt- precedence over fēt-. Though it has the air of a mysterious barbarian word, it is in reality the same as *factitious*, & means (like an idol, the work of men's hands) a made thing.

fetus. See FOETUS.

feuilleton. See FRENCH WORDS.

feverish, feverous. The differentiation is incomplete. What can be done to help it on is to abstain from *feverish* in the one sense apt to cause fever (of places, conditions, &c.), & from *feverous* both in the literal senses suffering from fever, feeling or showing symptoms of fever, & in the metaphorical sense excited or eager or restless. This would be in conformity with the present tendency, which, though often disregarded, is plainly observable

few. 1. *Comparatively f.* 2. *Fewer number.* 1. As will be seen from the newspaper extracts below, ugly combinations of *comparative(ly)* with *a few & few* are now common. There is no possible objection to putting the adverb *comparatively* before the adjective *few*, as in *Comparatively few people are in the secret*; that is a normal construction not requiring comment; but *a comparatively few* is quite another matter, & so is *the comparative few*. The extracts now follow :—*The one beneficial treatment for such men could not be obtained excepting for* a comparatively few./*Its climate is such as to limit the residence of officials to* a comparatively few months *in the year./The whole area has been drained, levelled, & planned out in* a comparatively few weeks./*Those who do not marry, you may conclude, are used up by the work in* a comparatively few years./*Discussion in & out of the House has reduced these to* a comparatively few points./The comparative few *who take season tickets seldom travel every day.*

It is remarkable in the first place that of an idiom now enjoying such a vogue no trace whatever should appear in the OED's quotations either for *few* or for *comparative(ly)*; the explanation is doubtless that people of literary discernment, & even the writers of books in general, recoil from such a monstrosity, or did twenty years ago. It is, indeed, easier to call or feel it a monstrosity than to prove it one, because *a few* is itself an anomalous phrase, & therefore analogies for its treatment are not abundant; we must make the best of the few available; the main question is whether the *few* in *a few* is a noun or an adjective, & therefore to be qualified by an adjective or an adverb. There is first the familiar *a good few*, still current though colloquial; next, there are *a good many & a great many*, extant modifications of the now dialectal *a many*; thirdly, we know that *quite a few & not a few* are English, while *a quite few & a not few* are impossible. These show sufficiently that while *a few* taken together may be modified by an adverb, a modifying word placed between *a & few* can only be an adjective; in fact, the *few* of *a few* is itself a noun meaning small number. That it can be followed by a plural noun without an intervening *of* (*there are a few exceptions*) is nothing against this; it is parallel to *dozen, score, & hundred*: *a dozen eggs, a score years, a hundred men*, where, whether *of* is inserted or not, any modifying word is an adjective after, or an adverb before, the *a* (*a round dozen eggs, a full score of years, a good hundred men*, but *roughly* or *fully* or *quite a dozen* &c.). Consequently, if *comparative(ly)* is to be sandwiched it must be *a comparative few*, but if it is to precede the whole, or if it is to qualify *few* without *a*, it must be *comparatively*. On this showing all the above examples are wrong, the last as well as the others.

The objection will probably occur

to some readers : What, then, about *a very few*? may we not say *In a very few years all will be changed*? The answer is, first, that *a very few* is no doubt the origin of the mistaken constructions, & secondly that *very* is here not an adverb, but an adjective, as in *She is a very woman* or *devil*, or in *Living on a very minimum of food*; just as we can say *a poor* or *a wretched few*, so we can say *a mere* or *a very few*, with *very* an adjective ; but because *very* is now more familiar as an adverb, it is wrongly concluded that words that can only be adverbs will do.

It may be added that *Very few people were there* is better than *A very few people were there*, because *few* means some & not many, while *a few* means some & not none, so that *few* is better fitted than *a few* for combination with words expressing degree like *very*.

2. *Fewer number(s)* is a solecism, obvious as soon as one thinks, but becoming common ; correct to *smaller* in :—*Fortunately the number of persons on board was fewer than usual./The fewer number of days or hours we are . . ., the better it will be./The bird seems to have reached us in fewer numbers this year.*

fez. Pl. *fezzes*, adj. *fezzed*.

fiancé, -ée. See FRENCH WORDS, & INTENDED.

fiasco. Pl. *-os* ; see -O(E)S 6.

fibre, -ber. See -RE & -ER.

fibroma. Pl. *-omata* (-ō'-).

fibula. Pl. *-lae* or *-las*. Pron. fī'-.

fictitious. See FACTIOUS.

fiddle. If the word is, as the OED says, ' now only in familiar or contemptuous use ', it is matter for regret, & those who defy this canon deserve well of the language. We all learn the word *fiddle* as babies, & at a later age when we find ourselves expected to understand & use another word for it we explain *violin* to ourselves as ' the same as fiddle ' ; it is a case of WORKING & STYLISH WORDS in which, unfortunately, the majority has yielded to the seductions of stylishness. Even now, *She fiddles divinely* (as compared with *playing the violin* in that manner) surely supplies a felt need ; & as to the noun, a violin is a fiddle & a fiddle a violin, &, when an alternative is to hand, exotics like *violin* with accents on their last syllables should not be allowed to upset the natural run of English sentences.

fidget, vb, makes *-eting* &c. ; see -T-, -TT-.

fiducial, fiduciary. The second is the ordinary form, *fiducial* being used only in some technical terms in surveying, astronomy, &c.

fidus Achates. Pronounce fī'dus akā'tēz.

-FIED. The spelling of the jocular compounds in which a verb in *-fy* hardly exists is unsettled (*countrified* or *countryfied* &c.). It seems best to use *-i-* when the noun or adjective does not provide a convenient connecting syllable, but, when it does, not to alter it ; so *cockneyfied, countryfied, dandyfied, Frenchified, ladyfied, townified, yankeefied*.

field, in the sense of space proper to something (*f. of action, each in his own f.*, &c.). The synonyms for this are remarkably numerous ; the distinctions & points of agreement between these are fortunately obvious enough not to need elaborate setting forth ; but a list not pretending to completeness, & a characteristic phrase or so for each word, may be useful.

Area, branch, compass, department, domain, field, gamut, last, limit, line, locale, point, province, purview, question, radius, range, realm, record, reference, region, register, scale, scene, scope, sphere, subject, tether, theme.

A debate covering a wide area. *Unsurpassed in his own* branch. *Expenses beyond my* compass. *In every* department *of human activity. Belongs to the* domain *of philosophy. Distinguished in many* fields ; *is beyond the* field *of vision. In the whole* gamut *of crime. Stick to your* last. *Unconscious of his* limits. *Casuistry is not in my* line. *A very unsuitable* locale. *Talking beside the* point. *It is not our* province *to inquire. Comes within the* purview *of the Act. Constantly straying from the* question. *Outside the* range *of practical politics. Operating within a narrow* radius. *In the whole* realm *of Medicine. Don't travel outside the* record. *Such evidence is precluded by our* reference. *In the* region *of metaphysics. Any note in the lower* register. *Whatever the* scale *of effort required. A* scene *of confusion. Find* scope *for one's powers; limit the* scope *of the inquiry. Useful in his own* sphere. *Wanders from the* subject. *Get to the end of one's* tether. *Has chosen an ill defined theme.*

field officer. See OFFICER.
fiery. Two syllables (fīr′ĭ).
fifteen. ' The '15 ', ' the '45 '. The Jacobite risings of 1715 & 1745 are so remote that there is now some affectation in speaking of them by these names except in historical novels.

fifth(ly). Both the -f- & the -th should be, but are often not, clearly sounded; cf. *apophthegm, diphtheria, diphthong, sixth.*

fifties, 'fif-. See TWENTIES.
figure, figurant, figurative, &c. While it is pedantic to pronounce *figure* otherwise than as fĭ′ger, it is slovenly to let the natural English laxity go to this extreme with the less familiar *figuration, figurative, figurant, figurine,* &c. (fĭgūrā′shn &c.) ; see PRONUNCIATION.

filial. The OED recognizes only fĭl- ; fīl- is however often heard, but possibly only from latinists obsessed by the fear of FALSE QUANTITY.

filigree, -agree. The OED gives precedence to the first spelling.
fille de chambre, de joie. See FRENCH WORDS.

fillip, vb, makes *-iped* &c.; see -P-, -PP-.
fils. See FRENCH WORDS.
filthy lucre. See HACKNEYED PHRASES, & IRRELEVANT ALLUSION.
filtrate, vb, by the side of *filter,* vb, is a SUPERFLUOUS WORD suggesting BACK-FORMATION from *filtration* ; see LONG VARIANTS.

finable, not *fineable* ; see MUTE E.
final (in syntax). See TECHNICAL TERMS.
finale. Three syllables (fĭnah′lĭ).
financier, n. & v. See NOUN & VERB ACCENT.
fine, adj. *Not to put too f. a point upon it* is an apology for a downright expression, & means ' to put it bluntly '.

fine, n. *In fine,* a phrase now seldom used except in writing of a rather formal kind, has entirely lost the sense, which it once had, of *at last.* It is still sometimes used for *finally* or *lastly,* i.e. to introduce the last of a series of parallel considerations ; but in the interests of clearness it is better that it should be confined to its predominant modern use, = *in short* or *in fact* or *to sum up,* introducing a single general statement that wraps up in itself several preceding particular ones.

finger. The fingers are now usually numbered exclusively of the thumb—*first* (or *index*), *second* (or *middle*), *third* (or *ring*), & *fourth* (or *little*) ; but in the marriage service the third is called the fourth.

fingering, as a name for stockingwool, is not from *finger,* but represents French *fin grain* fine grain ; see TRUE & FALSE ETYMOLOGY.

finical, finicking, finikin. All that can be said with certainty about the derivation of the words & their mutual relations seems to be that *-al* is recorded 70 years earlier than the others. As to choice between them, the English termination *-cking* is best calculated to express a hearty British contempt for the tenuity naturally symbolized by the three short *i*s ; cf. *niggling & fiddling* ; *-cal* is now chiefly in literary & not colloquial use.

finish, = rather fine, should be spelt so, not *fineish* ; see MUTE E.

fiord, fjord. The OED gives precedence to fi-. The other spelling is apparently used in English only to help the ignorant to call it fyord ; as, instead of helping, it only puzzles them, it should be abandoned.

fire-arms. ' The singular is late & rare in use '—OED (which, however, quotes ' the report of a fire-arm ' from Thackeray).

fire out, in the sense *expel* or *dismiss* (a person), is still an Americanism.

fir, pine. Most of us have wished vaguely & vainly at times that they knew a fir from a pine. As the Scotch fir is not a fir, strictly speaking, but a pine, & as we shall continue to ignore this fact, it is plain that the matter concerns the botanist more than the man in the street. The following from the *Encyclopaedia Britannica* may, however, be useful :—' The firs are distinguished from the pines & larches by having their needle-like leaves placed singly on the shoots instead of growing in clusters from a sheath on a dwarf branch. Their cones are composed of thin, rounded, closely imbricated scales '. Pines differ ' from the firs in their hard woody cone-scales being thickened at the apex, & in their slender needle-shaped leaves growing from a membranous sheath either in pairs or from three to five together '.

first. 1. For *first &c. floor,* see FLOOR. 2. For *first &c. form,* see FORM. 3. *First thing* is equally idiomatic with *the first thing* (*shall do it f. t. when I get there*). 4. *The first two &c.*)(*the two &c. first.* When the meaning is not the possible but uncommon one of ' the two of which each alike is first ', modern logic has decided that *the first two* is right &

the two first, though the older idiom, wrong. Since many find themselves unable to remember which is logical without working it out, & disinclined to do that afresh every time, the simplest way is to suit the treatment of 2, 3, & 4 (beyond which the doubt hardly arises) to that of larger numbers ; no-one would say *the 23 first* instead of *the first 23,* & neither should one say *the two first* instead of *the first two.*

5. *First(ly), secondly, lastly.* The preference for *first* over *firstly* in formal enumerations is one of the harmless pedantries in which those who like oddities because they are odd are free to indulge, provided that they abstain from censuring those who do not share the liking. It is true that *firstly* is not in Johnson ; it is true that De Quincey labels it ' your ridiculous & most pedantic neologism of *firstly* ' ; the boot is on the other leg now ; it is the pedant that begins his list with *first* ; no-one does so by the light of nature ; it is an artificialism. Idioms grow old like other things, & the idiom-book of a century hence will probably not even mention *first, secondly.*

firth, frith. *Firth* is both the older form & the prevailing one.

fisc, fisk. ' The current spelling in Scots Law is *fisk,* in other uses *fisc* ' —OED.

fish. For pl. see COLLECTIVES 4.

fisher(man). See ANGLE(R).

fistic(al). See HYBRID DERIVATIVES, & FACETIOUS FORMATIONS.

fistula. Pl. *-as.*

fit. For ' fit audience though few ' see HACKNEYED PHRASES.

fivepenny, fivepence. The pronunciations fi′penī, fi′pns, will no doubt become universal if decimal coinage is introduced.

fix. 1. *Fixedly.* Three syllables ; see -EDLY. 2. *Fixedness*)(*fixity. Fixedness* is preferable in the sense intentness, perhaps from the connexion with *fixedly* ; in other senses the doubt about its pronunciation (it should have three syllables) has caused it to give place to *fixity* ; compare *Looking at her with mild fixedness* with *The unbending fixity of a law of nature.* 3. *Fix up* (arrange or organize), and *fixings* (apparatus or trimmings), are both Americanisms not yet naturalized in England.

4. Fixation. Most literary men know some Latin ; that Latin is chiefly of the classical kind, & a little of it is enough to make them aware that *figere*, & not *fixare*, is the classical Latin for fix. Consequently they feel an instinctive repugnance to the word *fixation*, &, perhaps unreasonably, prefer to say *fixing* instead of it whenever they can ; it is mostly left to those who need it in technical contexts. If a comparison could be made between *fixing* & *fixation* on the one hand, & (say) *liberating* & *liberation* on the other, it would be found that avoidance of *fixation* was far the more frequent.

fiz(z). See -z-, -zz-.
flaccid. Pronounce -ks-.
flageolet. Pronounce flăjŏlĕ't.
flail-like. For the hyphen see -LIKE.
flair means keen scent, capacity for getting on the scent of something desired, a good nose *for* something. The following quotations illustrate the risks taken (see FOREIGN DANGER) by writers who pick up their French at second hand :—*And I was eager to burst upon a civilian world with all the* flaire [sic] *of a newly discovered prima donna./Mrs —— has homely accomplishments ; a f. for cooking goes with her f. for writing* (a taste & a scent are different metaphorically as well as literally).

flambeau. Pl. *-s*, or *-x* (pron. -z) ; see -X.
flamboyant is a word borrowed from writers on architecture, who apply it to the French style (contemporary with English perpendicular) characterized by tracery whose wavy lines suggest the shape or motion of tongues of flame. It

is now fashionable in transferred senses ; but whereas it should be synonymous with *flowing* or *flexible* or *sinuous* or *free*, it is more often made to mean florid or showy or vividly coloured or courting publicity. A word of which the true & the usual meanings are at odds is ambiguous, & could well be spared. See POPULARIZED TECHNICALITIES.

flamingo. Pl. *-os* ; see -O(E)S 1.
flânerie, flâneur. See FRENCH WORDS.
flannel. Spell *flannelled, flannelly*, but *flannelette.* See -LL-, -L-.
flatulence, -cy. The prevailing form is *-ce* ; *-cy* might well be disused, unless it were worth while to assign it to the figurative sense of verbosity, & that sense is hardly common enough to need a special form. See -CE, CY.

flatways, -wise. See -WAYS, -WISE.
flautist, flutist. It is a comfort to learn from the OED that *flutist* (1603) is a much older-established word than *flautist* (1860). With three centuries behind us we can face it out against PRIDE OF KNOWLEDGE.

flavour makes *flavorous*, but *flavoursome* ; see -OUR- & -OR-.
flaxen. See -EN ADJECTIVES.
flèche. See FRENCH WORDS.
fledg(e)ling. Of the eight quotations in the OED, not one has the *-e-* ; but see JUDGEMENT.
flee. The verb is now little used except in the form *fled, fly & flying* having taken the place of *f. & fleeing.* For *is fled* &c., see INTRANSITIVE P.P.

fleece makes *fleeceable* (see -ABLE 1) & *fleecy* (see -EY & -Y).
fleshly, fleshy. The distinction is much the same as between *earthly* & *earthy.* *Fleshy* has the primary senses consisting of flesh (*fleshy tablets of the heart*), having a large proportion of flesh (*fleshy hands, fruit,* &c.), & like flesh (*fleshy softness, pink,* &c.) ; while *fleshly* has the secondary senses of proper to the

flesh or mortal body, sensual, un-spiritual, worldly, (*fleshly pleasures, perception, inclinations, affairs*, &c.).

fleur-de-lis. Pl. *fleurs-de-lis* ; pro-nunciation, alike in sing. & pl., flerdelē'. ' The form *flower de luce* survives as a poetical archaism & in U.S.'—OED.

flier, flyer. The first is better ; see VERBS IN -IE &c., 6.

flippant. For synonymy see JOCOSE.

flirtation, -atious, floatation. See HYBRID DERIVATIVES.

flock, = tuft of wool &c. *Flocks* or *flock* (see COLLECTIVES) is used as the name for the material.

flock, flood, vbs. See INTRANSI-TIVE P.P.

floor, storey. The numbering of floors & storeys is peculiar, the second floor, e.g., being the third storey. The ground-floor & the ground storey are the same, but the first floor & first storey are different, *first storey* being another name for ground storey, but the first floor being above it. In houses other than the one-storeyed there are : (1) Sometimes cellars (underground, & not used for habitation) ; (2) Sometimes a basement (partly or all underground, & used for habitation); (3) The first or ground storey, or ground floor ; (4) Sometimes a mez-zanine or entresol (low, & not reckoned in numbering) ; (5) The second storey or first floor ; (6) Sometimes other storeys or floors numbered onwards from the pre-ceding ; (7) Sometimes garrets or attics or lofts (with part of the upper room-space cut off by the roof).

flora. See FAUNA.

florilegium. Pl. *-ia*.

floruit (-or'ōoĭt) is a Latin verb meaning *he flourished* used with a date to give the period to which a person's activity may be assigned ; it is also used as a noun—*his f.* &c., i.e. the date at which he was active.

flotation. See HYBRID DERIVATIVES.

flotsam & jetsam. The distinction is between goods found afloat in the sea & goods found on land after being cast ashore. The original sense of *jetsam* was what had been jettisoned or thrown overboard.

flour, meal. Flour is bolted meal, i.e. meal from which the husks have been sifted out after grinding. Meal is the ground product of any cereal or pulse. *Flour* used by itself means wheat-flour ; applied to other kinds it is qualified (*rye-flour, corn-flour* i.e. flour of maize, &c.), *Meal* when used of wheat has *wheat* prefixed.

flow, in such phrases as *flown with insolence*, is said by the OED to be an obsolete past participle of *flow*, meaning flooded or swollen.

flow. For ' f. of soul ' see HACK-NEYED PHRASES.

flower-de-luce. See FLEUR-DE-LIS.

flu(e), for *influenza*. See CUR-TAILED WORDS ; *flu* is better than *flue*.

fluid, gas, liquid. *Fluid* is the wide term including the two others ; it denotes a substance that on the slightest pressure changes shape by rearrangement of its particles ; water, steam, oil, air, oxygen, elec-tricity, ether, are all fluids. Liquids & gases differ in that the first are incompressible, & the second elastic ; water & oil are liquid & fluid, but not gaseous ; steam & air & oxygen are gases & fluids, but not liquids.

flunkey. Pl. *-eys*.

fluorine. For pronunciation see IODINE.

flurried, flustered, fluttered. There is often a doubt which is the most appropriate word ; the following distinctions are tentative :— A person is flurried who, with several things to attend to, lets each interfere with the others ; a person is flustered in whom different im-pulses or emotions contend for ex-pression ; a person is fluttered who, being of a timid or apprehensive disposition, is confronted with a sudden emergency.

flute. 1. *Fluty*, not *flutey*; see -EY & -Y. 2. For *flutist* see FLAUTIST.

fluvial, fluviatile. There is no difference in meaning, & no reason why both should exist; *fluvial* is recommended, even if the longer form is slightly commoner. See LONG VARIANTS.

fly. 1. The noun is used as a COLLECTIVE in the sense plant-disease due to kinds of f. (*there is a good deal of f.*).
2. The verb makes *is flown* as well as *has flown*; see INTRANSITIVE P.P.
3. *Fly a kite* means (a) raise money by bill, (b) make an announcement or take a step with a view to finding out whether a plan has a chance of success.
4. *Fly-leaf* is a blank leaf forming part of something printed, especially one between the cover & the title-page of a book, or at the end of a circular or leaflet; it is not another name for a leaflet, which is, however, sometimes called a *fly-sheet*.
5. A *fly-wheel* is one whose sole function is by its inertia & momentum to make the movement of the shaft that works it continuous & regular; hence its metaphorical use.
6. For *flyer* see FLIER.

foal, colt, filly. *Foal* is of either sex, c. male, & *filly* female.

foam, froth. The natural definition of foam would be the froth of the sea, & that of froth the foam of beer. That is to say, foam suggests the sea, froth suggests beer, & while one word is appropriate to the grand or the beautiful or the violent, the other is appropriate to the homely or the ordinary or the dirty. One demands of foam that it be white; froth may be of what colour it pleases. Froth may *be* scum, but foam, though it may *become* scum, ceases to be foam in the process. It is perhaps also true that froth is thought of mainly as part of a liquid that has sent it to the top, & foam as a separate substance often detached in the act of making from its source. But the difference is much less in the meanings than in the suitable contexts.

focus. 1. The noun has pl. *-cuses* or

-ci (pron. -sī); the verb makes *focused, -cusing* ('in England commonly, but irregularly, written *focussed, -ing*'—OED); see -S-, -SS-.
2. The verb is liable to loose application, as in: *At one moment it seemed to be quite near, & at the next far away; for the ears, unaided by the eyes, can but imperfectly focus sound or measure its distance.* The f. of a sound being 'the point or space towards which the sound-waves converge' (OED), ears cannot f. sound except by taking their owner to the right point; the eyes do measure distance by focusing, having an apparatus for the purpose; the ears do not.

foetid. See FETID.

foetus, fetus. 'The etymologically preferable spelling with *e* in this word & its cognates is adopted as the standard form in some recent dictionaries, but in actual use is almost unknown.'—OED.

fogy, -gey. The OED gives precedence to *-gy*.

föhn. See WIND, n.

foist. *The general public is much too easily* foisted off *with the old cry of the shopman that ' there's no demand for that kind of thing '.* The public can be *fobbed* off with something, or the something can be fobbed off on the public; but *foist* has only the second construction; see ANALOGY & OBJECT-SHUFFLING.

folio. Pl. *-os*; see -O(E)S 4. The following account from a dictionary may be useful:—Leaf of paper &c. numbered only on front; two opposite pages, or single page, of ledger used for the two sides of account; number of words (72 or 90) as unit of length in document; (Bookbinding) once-folded sheet of printing-paper giving two leaves or four pages (*in f.*, made of ff.), (also *f. volume* &c.) a book or volume in f., (similarly of smaller sheets & books resulting from various foldings & named after the number of leaves to the sheet: *quarto* or *4to*, folded twice into four leaves; *sexto* or *6to*, thrice into 6 (rare) ; *octavo* or *8vo*, thrice into 8 ; *duodecimo* or *12mo*, 4 times into 12 ; *16mo* or *sextodecimo* or *decimo sexto* ; *18mo* or *octodecimo* ; *20mo*, *24mo*, *32mo*, *64mo* ; the last seven are or may be spoken *twelvemo* &c.).

folk has passed out of the language of the ordinary educated person, so far as he talks unaffectedly. It is still in provincial use, & is besides a favourite SAXONISM, whether in the singular or in the plural form (*folk*, a people, or people ; *folks*, people) ; there is also its use, imitated from German, in which the word is not archaic as in English, in such learned compounds as *folklore, folksong, & folk-etymology.* Neither Saxonism nor Germanism is a recommendation.

follow. *As follows. The main regulations of Mr Gladstone's new Order are* as follow :—*First . . ./ The principal items of reductions made since 1904–5 stand* as follow :

In all such contexts, *as follows* should be written. The OED ruling is : ' The construction in *as follows* is impersonal, & the verb should always be used in the singular '. And among its quotations is one from a *Rhetoric* of 1776 : ' A few late writers have inconsiderately adopted this last form ' [*as follow*] ' through a mistake of the construction '. However, persons who are pluming themselves on having detected a vulgar error that they can amend are not likely to admit that it is a mare's-nest on the unreasoned *ipse dixit* of an eighteenth-century rhetorician, or even of a twentieth-century OED ; & some discussion will be necessary. Unfortunately, full demonstration is hardly possible; but several considerations raise separate presumptions in favour of *follows* :—

1. It is certain that we all say *as follows* by the light of nature ; it is only to the sophisticated intelligence that *as follow* occurs (or would the reformers prefer *occur* ?).

2. Similar but more obvious mal-

treatment of other phrases suggests that the correctors of this too may be, though it does not prove that they are, mistaken :—(id est or i.e.) *Section* 15 (4), *which deals with persons* (ea sunt, *all present & future members of societies*) *entitled to receive medical attendance* ; the author of this (why, by the way, does he stop short of *ii sunt* or *eae sunt* ?) would presumably like Byron to have said *Arcades ambo, ea sunt blackguards both* ; but *id* does not mean that Arcadian or those Arcadians, it means that phrase. (Concerns) *Many of these stalks were failures, so far as* concern *the objective success* ; what the writer means is not so far as the stalks or the failures concern success, but so far as our discussion concerns it ; the familiar *as regards* is liable to the same mutilation.

3. The phrase *as follows*, which is very old, no doubt originated in sentences where there was no plural in the neighbourhood to raise awkward questions. The OED quotes (1426) *Was done als her fast folowys* (= as here directly follows), & (1548) *He openly sayde as foloweth. He spoke as follows* may be taken as the type ; that is obviously not a piece of normal grammar ; what would be the normal way of putting it ? *He spoke thus*, which is, at full length, *He spoke so as I shall tell you*, or *He spoke so as it shall be told*, or *He spoke so as the tale follows*, whence, by ellipse, *He spoke as follows.* This progress is surely natural ; but it is equally natural in *His words were so as I shall tell you*, or *His words were so as it shall be told*, or *His words were so as the tale follows*, whence *His words were as follows.* It is true that, when the idiom was being evolved, it was open to its makers to say, instead of *were so as the tale follows, were so as words follow* ; but they chose otherwise, hundreds of years ago, & the idiom is now fixed ; no-one would want to change it except under the impression that it was ungram-

matical ; to show that it is no more ungrammatical than the innovation is enough to condemn the latter.

fool's-cap, foolscap. The name of the paper size is usually written *foolscap*.

foot, n. For *at the foot of the letter* see GALLICISMS. *Footgear & footwear* are words little used except in advertisements.

foot, vb. *The bill*, or *the cost, foots up to £50* means that £50 is the amount at the foot of the paper on which the addition is done. The origin of *Who will foot* (i.e. pay) *the bill?* is not so clear ; perhaps pay the sum to which it foots up. Both phrases are good colloquial English.

footing. *We have not the smallest doubt that this is what will actually happen, & . . . we may discuss the situation* on the footing that *the respective fates of these two bills will be as predicted*. To give *f.* the sense of *assumption* or *hypothesis* is a SLIPSHOD EXTENSION ; the writer, in fact, on however intimate a f. he may be with lobby prophets, is on a slippery f. with the English vocabulary.

for, conj. Two questions of punctuation arise. *F.* is a coordinating conjunction, i.e. one that connects two independent sentences ; it is neither, like *therefore & nevertheless*, strictly speaking an adverb though serving the purpose of a connexion ; nor, like *since & because*, a subordinating conjunction that joins a mere clause to a sentence ; hence the two points.

1. Whereas, in *Therefore A is Equal to B*, & in *Nevertheless he did it*, it is a mere matter of rhetoric, depending on the emphasis desired, whether a comma shall or shall not follow *therefore & nevertheless*, it is with *for* a matter of grammatical correctness that there should be no comma ; *For, within it is a house of refinement & luxury* is wrong ; this naturally does not apply to places where a comma is needed for independent

reasons, as in *For, other things being equal, success is a fair test*.

2. Whereas *since & because*, connecting a clause to a preceding sentence, are rightly preceded by a comma only, the presumption with *for*, which connects two sentences, is that a semicolon should be written ; this does not rule out the comma, which will often pass when the *for* sentence is a short one ; but in such passages as the following the comma is clearly inadequate, & in general the semicolon should be regarded as normal, & the comma as the licence :—*This is no party question, for it touches us not as Liberals or Conservatives, but as citizens*.

foramen. Pl. *-mina*.

forasmuch as. Write thus.

forbears, n. See FOREBEARS.

forbid. 1. *forbad(e)*. The pronunciation is -ăd, not -ād, & the spelling *-ad* is, to judge by the OED quotations, nearly twice as common as *-ade*. 2. To *forbid* one *from* doing (*You may f. him, if you like, from toiling ten hours a day*) is an unidiomatic construction on the ANALOGY of *prohibit* or *prevent*.

forcedly. Three syllables, if used ; see -EDLY.

forceful, forcible. The main distinction in sense is that, while *forcible* conveys that force rather than something else is present, *forceful* conveys that much as opposed to little force is used or shown ; compare *forcible ejection* with a *forceful personality*. This leaves it often indifferent, so far as sense goes, which word is used ; a forcible style is a style with force in it, a forceful style one of great force. The sense distinction, however, is the less important part of the matter. By usage, *forcible* is the ordinary word, & *forceful* the word reserved for poetical or other abnormal use, where its special value depends partly on its infrequency & partly on the more picturesque suggestion of its suffix. Unluckily recent writers have taken to exploiting, & in the process destroying, this special value, by making a VOGUE-WORD of *forceful* & always using it in place of *forcible*. If this continues, we shall shortly find ourselves with a pair of exact synonyms either of which could well be spared instead of a pair serving different purposes. Such writers injure the language, which perhaps leaves them cool ; but they also, as regards their own interests, lose more in the opinion of the educated than they gain in that of the ignorant by avoiding the obvious word. In the following extracts there is, except in the first, no need whatever to say *forceful* instead of the natural *forcible* :— *Certainly he was a* forceful & impressive personality *at a time when the stature of international statesmen was not particularly great.*/*M. Briand had rightly calculated that he would have the people of France behind him in* his forceful endeavour *to restore order.*/*This may seem a trivial & inconsiderable argument to Major Morrison-Bell, but it seems to us that it is* as impressive & forceful today *as it was a quarter of a century ago.*/*It is his programme to urge upon the Throne peaceful abdication as the only alternative to* forceful expulsion./The forcefulness of the utterances *was in complete accord with the gravity of the evil which these representatives of the civilized world had met to grapple with.*

force majeure. See FRENCH WORDS.
forceps. Pl. the same ; but see SINGULAR -S.
fordo. See FOR-, FORE-.
fore. *To the fore* appears to mean properly (see OED) at hand, available, surviving, extant. In being borrowed by English from Scotch & Irish writers as a picturesque phrase, it has suffered a change of meaning, & is now established journalese for conspicuous. No great harm is done except that ambiguity may arise between the true & the new senses.

for(e)bears. As to the form, the prevalent but not sole modern spelling is without the *e* (the newspaper extracts below are exact) ; but the *e* seems better both as separating the noun from the verb *forbear* & as not disguising the derivation (*forebeers*, those who have *been before*) ; see FOR-, FORE-.
As to the use of the word by English writers, its only recommendation is that, being Scotch & not English, it appeals to the usually misguided instinct of NOVELTY-HUNTING. *Ancestors, forefathers, & progenitors*, supplemented when the tie is not of blood by *forerunners & predecessors*, are the English words. *By his* forebears *Lord Tankerville is connected with the* ancien régime *of France. His great grandfather, the Duc de Grammont* . . . (read *ancestors*)./*Birmingham is now being afforded an opportunity for offering some kind of posthumous reparation for the great wrong its forbears inflicted, close upon 120 years ago, on the illustrious Dr Priestley* (For *its forbears* read *it*. Birmingham's forbears would be not an earlier generation of Birmingham people, but any villages that may have stood where Birmingham now stands. If the writer had been content with an English word, he would hardly have fallen into that trap).

forecast. *So far as the operation of the guillotine resolution on the Insurance Bill can be* forecasted, *it seems probable that* . . . Whether we are to say *forecast* or *forecasted* in the past tense & participle depends on whether we regard the verb or the noun as the original from which the other is formed ; if the verb is original (= to guess beforehand) the past & p.p. will of course be *cast*; if the verb is derived (= to make a forecast) they will as certainly be *forecasted*. The verb is in fact recorded 150 years earlier than the noun, & we may therefore thankfully rid ourselves of the ugly *forecasted*; it may be hoped that we should do so even if history were against us, but this time it is kind.

foregather. See FORGATHER.

forego. See FOR-, FORE-.

foregone conclusion. The phrase is used when an issue supposed to be still open has really been settled beforehand, e.g. when a judge has made up his mind before hearing the evidence ; or again, when an event is so little doubtful that the doubt is negligible.

forehead. Pronounce fŏ'rĕd ; see PRONUNCIATION.

FOREIGN DANGER. Those who use words or phrases belonging to languages with which they have little or no acquaintance do so at their peril. Even in *e.g.*, *i.e.*, & *et cetera*, there lurk unsuspected possibilities of exhibiting ignorance ; with *toto caelo, bête noire, cui bono ?, bonâ fide, qua*, & *pacè*, the risk is greater ; & such words as *protagonist* & *phantasmagoria*, which one hesitates whether to call English or foreign, require equal caution. See all or any of the words & phrases mentioned, & FLAIR. Two or three specimens follow, for those who do not like cross references :—*I suggest that a Compulsory Loan be made* pro ratio *upon all capital* (pro ratâ)./ *Ricasoli, another of his* bêtes noirs (noires)./ *A man who claimed to be a Glasgow delegate, but whose* bona fides *were disputed, rose to propose the motion* (was)./ *We are calmly told that Cambridge was neither worse nor better than the rest of the world ; in fact, it was, we are assured,* in petto *the reflex of the corrupt world without* (in petto is not in little, but in one's heart, i.e. secretly)./ *THE TRAMP AS CENSOR* MORES (A headline ; morum).

foremost. See -MOST.

forenoon. *The Church Congress sat in two sections this forenoon . . . The afternoon programme was divided into three sections.* Even in contexts that, by the occurrence as here of *afternoon* in contrast, most suggest the use of *f.*, the natural English (though perhaps not the natural Scotch) is *morning. Forenoon*, having fallen out of use as *the* name for the first half of daylight, is now used by writers who dislike saying a plain thing in the plain way. See FORMAL WORDS, & WORKING & STYLISH WORDS.

foretaste, foretoken. See NOUN & VERB ACCENT.

foreword, preface. *F.* is a word invented fifty years ago as a SAXONISM by anti-latinists, & caught up as a VOGUE-WORD by the people who love a new name for an old thing. *P.* has a 500-year history behind it in English, &, far from being antiquated, is still *the* name for the thing. It is to be hoped that the vogue may pass, & the taste of the general public prevail again over that of publishers & authors. A decent retirement might be found for *f.* if it were confined to the particular kind of preface that is supplied by some distinguished person for a book written by someone else who feels the need of a sponsor.

But how one vogue-word drives out another ! Here in 1924 comes a book on whose title-page is mention of neither preface nor foreword ; instead, it is ' With a Prefatory Gesture by —— '. Poor old foreword ! your vogue is past, your freshness faded ; you are antiquated, vieux jeu, passé, démodé ; your nose is out of joint. And, when *gesture* shall have followed you to limbo, we may hope to get back to *preface*.

FOR-, FORE-. The prefix of the words *forbear* (vb), *forbid, forby* (Sc. for besides &c.), *fordo* (exhaust), *forfend, forgather* (assemble), *forget, forgive, forgo* (relinquish), *forlorn, forpined, forsake, forspent, forswear, forwearied*, & *forworn*, is unconnected with the English words *for* & *fore*, & means away, out, completely, &c. All these should be spelt with *for-*, not *fore-*, & the pronunciation should be, as it invariably is in the commoner ones such as *forbid*, fer- &

not for-. On the other hand the noun *for(e)bears*, & *foregoing* & *foregone* in *the foregoing list, a foregone conclusion*, contain the ordinary *fore*, & should be spelt with the *e*, & pronounced fōr- or for-, not *fer-*. *Foreclose* & *forfeit* contain another prefix again (L *foris* outside), though *foreclose* has had its spelling affected by natural confusion with English *fore*. All the words, whether established or made for the occasion, compounded with *fore*, as *forebode, forewarn, foreman, fore-ordained*, are spelt with the *e* & should have the fōr or for sound distinct.

forgather. 1. For the spelling see FOR-, FORE-. 2. The word is a Scotticism not quite at home in English, as appears in *Many interesting people he met at Lady St Helier's, where Mr Chamberlain, among others, foregathered*. It may perhaps be said that whenever the verb is not, as it usually is, in the plural, it is followed by *with*.

forge makes *-geable* ; see MUTE E.

forget makes *-ttable* ; see -T-, -TT-.

forgive makes *-vable* ; see MUTE E.

forgo. See FOR-, FORE-.

forgot, as a past participle for the current *forgotten*, is now, except in uneducated speech, a deliberate archaism.

forlorn hope is not an abstract phrase transferred by metaphor to a storming party, but has that concrete sense in its own right, & only gets the abstract sense of desperate chance &c. by misunderstanding. *Hope* is not the English word, but is a mis-spelling of the Dutch *hoop* = English *heap* ; the forlorn hope is the devoted or lost band, those who sacrifice themselves in leading the attack. The spelling of *hope* once fixed, the mistake was inevitable ; but it is well to keep the original meaning in mind ; see TRUE & FALSE ETYMOLOGY.

form. School 'forms' are usually numbered upwards from the first or lowest to the sixth or highest.

formalism, formality. It is only from the more abstract sense of *formality*, from *formality* as the name of a quality & not of an action, that *formalism* requires to be distinguished ; & there, while *formality* means the observance of forms, *formalism* is the disposition to use them & belief in their importance ; formality is the outward sign of formalism ; see -ISM & -ITY.

FORMAL WORDS. There are large numbers of words differing from each other in almost all respects, but having this point in common, that they are not the plain English for what is meant, not the form that the mind uses in its private debates to convey to itself what it is talking about, but translations of these into language that is held more suitable for public exhibition. We tell our thoughts, like our children, to put on their hats & coats before they go out ; we want the window *shut*, but we ask if our fellow passenger would mind its being *closed* ; we think of our soldiers as *plucky fellows*, but call them in the bulletins *valiant troops*. These outdoor costumes are often needed ; not only may decency be outraged sometimes by over-plain speech ; dignity may be compromised if the person who thinks in slang writes also in slang ; to the airman it comes natural to think & talk of his *bus*, but he does well to call it in print by another name. What is intended in this article is not to protest against *all* change of the indoor into the outdoor word, but to point out that the less of such change there is the better. A short haphazard selection of what are to be taken as formal words will put the reader in possession of the point ; but a full list would run into thousands ; it must be observed that no general attack is being made on these words as words ; it is only on the prevalent notion that the commoner synonyms given after each in brackets ought to be translated into these :—*accommodation* (room) ; *announce* (give out) ; *bear* (carry) ; *cast* (throw) ; *cease* (stop) ; *close* (shut) ; *collation* (meal) ; *comestibles* (food) ; *commence* (begin) ; *complete* (finish) ; *conceal* (hide) ; *conveyance* (carriage) ; *dispatch* (send off) ; *don* (put on) ; *donation* (gift) ; *draw* (pull) ; *emoluments* (pay) ; *endeavour* (try) ; *evince* (show) ; *expedite* (hasten) ; *extend* (give) ; *felicitate* (wish joy) ; *forenoon* (morning) ; *imbibe* (drink) ; *inquire* (ask) ; *luncheon* (lunch) ; *mucilage* (gum) ; *obtain* (get) ; *peruse* (read) ; *physic* (medicine) ; *preserve* (jam) ; *proceed* (go) ; *purchase* (buy) ; *remark* (say) ; *remove* (take away) ; *seek* (try, look for) ; *suborn* (bribe) ; *summon* (send for) ; *sustain* (suffer) ; *valiant* (brave) ; *veritable* (real or positive) ; *vessel* (ship).

There are very few of our notions that cannot be called by different names ; but among these names there is usually one that may be regarded as the thing's proper name, its *kurion onoma* or dominant name as the Greeks called it, for which another may be substituted to add precision or for many other reasons, but which is present to the mind even behind the substitute. A destroyer is a ship, &, though we never forget its shiphood, the reader is often helped if we call it a destroyer ; a vessel also is a ship, but the reader is not helped by our calling it a vessel, for the most part ; &, though to evince is to show, it does not help him to call showing evincing ; what happens is first the translation of *show* into *evince* by the writer, & then the retranslation of *evince* into *show* by the reader ; mind communicates with mind through a veil, & the result is at best dullness, & at worst misunderstanding. The proper name for a notion should not be rejected for another unless the rejector can give some better account to himself of his preference for the other than that he thinks it will look better in print. If his mental name for a thing is not the proper name, or if, being the proper name, it is also *im*proper, or essentially undignified, let him translate it ; but there is nothing to be ashamed of in

buy or *jam* or *say* that they should need translating into *purchase* & *preserve* & *remark* ; where they give the sense equally well, they are fit for any company & need not be shut up at home. Few things contribute more to vigour of style than a practical realization that the *kuria onomata*, the sovereign or dominant or proper or vernacular or current names, are better than the formal words.

format. See FRENCH WORDS.

former. For *the f.* as a pronoun, see LATTER. When the reference is to one of three or more individuals, *the first*, not *the f.*, should be used : *Among the* three *representatives of neutral States, Dr Castberg & Dr Nansen stand for Norway & M. Heringa for Holland* ; the former *is so convinced of . . .*

formula. The plurals *-lae, -las* are equally common ; see LATIN PLURALS.

formulate makes *-lable, -tor* ; see -ABLE 1, -OR.

fornicate. *Fornication*, as distinguished from *adultery*, implies that the woman is not a wife ; it is sometimes but not always understood to imply further that neither party is married. Agent-noun, *fornicator*, see -OR.

forrader, owing its existence entirely to the well-known anecdote, should not be corrected into *forwarder*, which hardly has an independent existence ; see also HACKNEYED PHRASES.

forswear. For *a forsworn lover, witness*, &c., see INTRANSITIVE P.P.

forte, person's strong point. For the spelling, which should have been (but should not be) *fort*, cf. MORALE.

forte (mus.). Two syllables.

forth. 1. *And so forth* is (cf. *& the* LIKE) a convenience to the writer who does not wish to rehearse his list at length, but shrinks from the suggestion, now so firmly attached to *&c.* as to disqualify it for literary use, that he breaks off because it is

too much trouble to proceed ; the slightly antique turn of the phrase acquits him of unceremoniousness ; *& so on* is in this respect midway between *& so forth* & *&c.*
2. *So far forth* has occasionally the advantage over *so far* of limiting the sense to extent & excluding the literal idea of distance ; more often its only claim to preference is what is always the only claim of *so far forth as* against *so far as*—its superior pomposity.

forties, 'for-. See TWENTIES.

fortieth. So spelt.

fortify. For inflexions see VERBS IN -IE &c., 6.

fortuitous means accidental, undesigned, &c. That it is sometimes confused with *fortunate*, perhaps through mere sound, perhaps by the help of *lucky*, is plain from :—*All's well that ends well, & his divorced wives, whom the autobiographer naïvely calls Divorcées Nos 1, 2, & 3, seem to have borne no kind of ill-will to their more fortunate successor. Reviewing my own Algerian experiences, I must say that I should not have expected so fortuitous a termination of a somewhat daring experiment./When first produced, its popularity was limited. Nevertheless it may now sail into a more fortuitous harbour on the strength of its author's later reputation.* For such mistakes see MALAPROPS.

fortune. 1. For the question between -tūn & -chōon, see PRONUNCIATION.
2. The verb (*it fortuned that, I fortuned upon*) is an ARCHAISM.

forty. For ' the Forty-five ' see FIFTEEN.

forward(s), adv. The OED says :— ' The present distinction in usage between *forward* & *forwards* is that the latter expresses a definite direction viewed in contrast with other directions. In some contexts either form may be used without perceptible difference of meaning ; the following are examples in which only one of them can now be used :

" The ratchet-wheel can move only *forwards* " ; " the right side of the paper has the maker's name reading *forwards* " ; " if you move at all it must be *forwards* " ; " my companion has gone *forward*" ; " to bring a matter *forward* " ; " from this time *forward*".' To this it must be added that there is a tendency, not yet exhausted, for *forward* to displace *forwards*, & that even in the less than twenty years since the publication of that statement there has been change. The reader will notice that, while he can heartily accept the banishment of *forwards* from the last three examples, it is quite doubtful whether *forward* is not possible in some or all of the first three.

fossil. Pronounce fŏ'sl ; see PRONUNCIATION.

fostress. So spelt.

foul, adv. See UNIDIOMATIC -LY.

foulard. The OED gives precedence to fŏolahr over fŏolar'd.

foully. Pronounce both *ls*. See UNIDIOMATIC -LY.

foundress. See FEMININE DESIGNATIONS.

fount(ain). *Fount* (apart from the sense in typography, which is another word, connected with *found*) is the poetical & rhetorical form of *fountain* ; to use it in ordinary contexts (e. g. in *fount-pen* for *fountain-pen*) is VULGARIZATION.

four. *On* or *upon all fours*, apart from its literal application to a person crawling, has now for its chief use the meaning of correspondence at all & not merely some points between two things (*The cases are not o. a. f.* ; *The analogy suggested is not o. a. f. with the actual facts*). This seems due to a misunderstanding of the earlier but now less familiar metaphorical use by which a theory, tale, plan, &c., was said to run or be o. a. f. when it was consistent with itself or proof against objections or without weak points— in fact did not limp like a dog on three legs or rock like a table with one leg too short. The step is easy, though illegitimate, from *The comparison is o. a. f.* (i.e. complete at all points) to *The things compared are o. a. f.* (i.e. alike at all points), & thence to *o. a. f. with*. Whether this is or is not its origin, *o. a. f. with* is now an established idiom.

fowl. The collective use of the singular (see COLLECTIVES 4 ; *all the fish & f. in the world*) still exists, but is not common.

fox. Fem. *vixen, bitch-fox, she-fox.*
foyer. See FRENCH WORDS.
fracas. Pronounce frä'kah ; pl. spelt *fracas*, & pronounced frä'kahz.
fraenum, frenum. The second is recommended ; see Æ, Œ. Pl. *-na.*
fragile. 1. Only -ĭl is recognized by the OED, but -īl is perhaps as common, & the choice rests entirely (see FALSE QUANTITY) with usage.
2. *fragile*)(*frail*. *Frail* is wider both in application & in sense. Whatever is fragile is also frail, but a woman may be frail (i.e. weaker than others in moral strength) who cannot be called fragile (i.e. weaker in physical strength). Where, as in most cases, either word is applicable, there is a certain difference of sense between (*fragile*) liable to snap or break or be broken & so perish & (*frail*) not to be reckoned on to resist breakage or pressure or to last long ; that is to say, the root idea of break is more consciously present in *fragile* owing to its unobscured connexion with *fragment & fracture.*

fragmentary. Accent on the first.
framboesia. For spelling see Æ, Œ.
frame, vb, makes *-mable* ; see MUTE E.
franc-tireur. See FRENCH WORDS.
Frankenstein. *I tell you this country may have to pay a long price for Carsonism, & if Toryism returned to power tomorrow the Frankenstein of its own creating will dog its steps from the first hour of its existence as a Government.* A sentence written by the creatrix of the creator of the creature may save some of those whose acquaintance with all three is

indirect from betraying the fact :— ' Sometimes I endeavoured to gain from Frankenstein the particulars of his creature's formation ; but on this point he was impenetrable '. *Frankenstein* is the creator-victim ; the creature-despot & fatal creation is *Frankenstein's monster*. The blunder is very common indeed— almost, but surely not quite, sanctioned by custom :—*If they went on strengthening this power they would create a F. they could not resist./In his belief they were in the miserable position of having created a F. which they could not control./Thus the Prime Minister has created a F. in his new forces in Ireland, which may in the end destroy the Government.*

frantic. 1. *Frantically*)(*franticly*. The first is recommended ; *-ically* is almost universal as the adverbial form of adjectives in *-ic*, & there is no gain (as with *politicly & politically*, where two meanings have to be distinguished) in keeping up two forms.
2. Synonyms are *frenzied, furious, mad, passionate, rabid, raging, raving, wild*. Of these : *frantic & frenzied* both mean beside oneself or driven into temporary madness by a cause specified or apparent from context (*frantic with pain, excitement*, &c. ; *the frenzied populace refused him a hearing*) ; in mere exaggerations, e. g. when joy is the cause, *frantic* is the word. *Furious* implies no more than anger that has got out of hand—or, of inanimate things, a degree of force comparable to this. *Passionate* applies primarily to persons capable of strong emotions, especially if they are also incapable of controlling them, & secondarily to the sort of action that results. *Rabid* now usually implies the carrying to great excess of some particular belief or doctrine, religious, political, social, medical, or the like (*a rabid dissenter, tory, teetotaller, faddist* ; *rabid virulence*). *Raging* chiefly describes the violence in inanimate things that seems to correspond to madness in man (cf. *furious* ; *a*

raging storm, pestilence, toothache).
Raving is an intensifying epithet for
madness or a madman. The uses of
mad & wild hardly need setting forth.

frappant. See FRENCH WORDS.
*No doubt the old British belief arose
from the peculiar white glare of the
sunlight reflected from the hawthorn
blossoms, which must have been far
more frappant when South Britain
was one vast forest.* ' Clear, please '
says John Bull when invited to
choose between crême or purée de
something & consommé de something else ; &, if he must decide
whether he will take his contrasts
frappant or otherwise, he can but
say ' striking, please '.

frate. Pronounce -ah′tā ; pl. *frati*
pron. -ah′tē.
frau, fräulein. Pronounce frow,
froi′lĭn.
free. 1. *Freeman)(free man.* The
single word has two senses, (a) person who has the ' freedom ' of a city
&c., & (b) person who is not a slave
or serf, citizen of a free State ; in
other senses (*at last I am a free man*,
i.e. have retired from business, lost
my wife, &c.) the words should be
separate.
2. *Free will, free-will, freewill.* The
hyphened form should be restricted
to the attributive use as in *a free-will
offering, the free-will theory.* In non-
philosophical use *free will* should be
written, & the OED prefers it even
for the philosophical term ; many
writers hyphen it in that sense, but
this transgresses the general principle of connexion between hyphen
& accent (for which see HYPHENS),
since the accent remains on *will* ;
&, if a separate form for the philosophical term is required, it should
be *freewill.*

Frenchify. For inflexions see
VERBS IN -IE &c., 6.

FRENCH WORDS. 1. Use. 2. Pronunciation. Display of superior
knowledge is as great a vulgarity as
display of superior wealth—greater,

indeed, inasmuch as knowledge
should tend more definitely than
wealth towards discretion & good
manners. That is the guiding principle alike in the using & in the
pronouncing of French words in
English writing & talk. To use
French words that your reader or
hearer does not know or does not
fully understand, to pronounce them
as if you were one of the select few
to whom French is second nature
when he is not of those few (& it is
ten thousand to one that neither
you nor he will be so), is inconsiderate & rude.
1. USE OF FRENCH WORDS. It
would be a satisfaction to have a
table divided into permissible words,
forbidden words, & words needing
caution ; but anyone who starts
sanguinely on the making of it is
likely to come, after much shifting
of words from class to class, to the
same conclusion as the writer of this
article—that of the thousand or so
French words having some sort of
currency in English none can be
prohibited, & almost none can be
given unconditional licences ; it is
all a matter of the audience & the
occasion. Only faddists will engage
in alien-hunting & insist on finding
native substitutes for *tête-à-tête,
agent provocateur, esprit de corps,
cadre, chaperon, chassis, chose jugée,
débris, force majeure, grand seigneur,
habitué, laissez-faire,* & a hundred
other words that save circumlocution. Only fools will think it commends them to the English reader
to decorate incongruously with such
bower-birds' treasures as *au pied de
la lettre, à merveille, bien entendu, les
convenances, coûte que coûte, quand
même, dernier ressort, impayable, jeu
de mots, par exemple, robe-de-chambre, sans doute, tracasseries,* & *sauter
aux yeux ;* yet even these, even the
abominations beginning & ending
that list, are in place as supplying
local colour or for other special
reasons on perhaps five per cent. of
the occasions on which they actually
appear. It would be easy to make

a set of pigeon-holes to contain the French words ; let us say :

A. The standard word for the thing (*aide-de-camp, ballet, chauffeur*).

B. Words accepted as practically English, though not indispensable (*beau, billet-doux, char-à-bancs*).

C. Circumlocution-savers (*blasé, au revoir, fait accompli*).

D. Diplomacy & politics (*pourparlers, communiqué, bloc*).

E. Dress & cookery (*moire antique, entrée, hors-d'œuvre*).

F. Local colour & travel (*concierge, trottoir, lycée*).

G. Sport & theatre (*savate, couloir, entr'acte*).

H. Art (*atelier, tache, genre*).

I. Literature (*causerie, cliché, jeu d'esprit*).

K. Euphemism (*abattoir, accouchement, souteneur*).

L. Pretentious decoration (*agréments, coûte que coûte, frappant*).

M. Needless substitutes for English words (*cul-de-sac, en route, brochure*).

N. Puzzles for the plain man (*acharnement, flâneur, impayable*).

But to distribute into such pigeon-holes when made is a less simple affair, owing to the disturbing effects of audience & occasion. Every writer, however, who suspects himself of the bower-bird instinct should make & use some such classification system, & remember that acquisitiveness & indiscriminate display are pleasing to contemplate only in birds & savages & children. The list below, given primarily for pronunciation, will afford also material for practice in selection &, above all, abstention.

2. PRONUNCIATION. To say a French word in the middle of an English sentence exactly as it would be said by a Frenchman in a French sentence is a feat demanding an acrobatic mouth ; the muscles have to be suddenly adjusted to a performance of a different nature, & after it as suddenly recalled to the normal state ; it is a feat that should not be attempted ; the greater its success as a *tour de force*,

the greater its failure as a step in the conversational progress ; for your collocutor, aware that he could not have done it himself, has his attention distracted whether he admires or is humiliated. All that is necessary is a polite acknowledgement of indebtedness to the French language indicated by some approach in some part of the word to the foreign sound, & even this only when the difference between the foreign & the corresponding natural English sound is too marked to escape a dull ear. For instance, in *tête-à-tête* no attempt need or should be made to distinguish French ê from English ā, but the calling it tā′tahtā′t instead of the natural English tātatā′t rightly stamps it as foreign ; again, *tour de force* is better with no un-English sound at all ; neither r need be trilled, & *tour* & *force* should both be exactly like the English words so spelt. On the other hand, there are some French sounds so obviously alien to the English mouth that words containing them (except such as are, like *coupon*, in daily use by all sorts & conditions of men) should either be eschewed by English speakers or have these sounds adumbrated ; they are especially the nasalized vowels (*an, en, in, on, un, am,* &c.), the diphthong *eu*, the unaccented *e*, & *u* ; to say bŏng for *bon* is as insulting to the French language as to pronounce *bulletin* in correct French is insulting to the man in the English street ; & kōōldesă′k for *cul-de-sac* is nearly as bad. In consulting the pronunciations given below, the reader will bear in mind that it is no business of this dictionary to tell him how French words are pronounced in French ; it has only to advise him how to pronounce them in English if he would neither exhibit a conscious superiority of education nor be suspected of boorish ignorance. The list is intended, then, to mitigate the precision of those who know French at least as much as to enlighten those who do not ; but, for the latter, a slight attempt must be made to indicate intelligibly the nature of the un-English sounds. They are all represented in the second or phonetic column of the list below by capital letters ; words in which no capitals are used need have no terrors for non-French-speakers ; & the values of all phonetics other than capital letters are the same as in other parts of the dictionary.

UN-ENGLISH SOUNDS

A, a sound that is neither ă nor ah nor ŭ, but approximates to all of these.

O, a sound between English aw & ŏ.

U, a sound between ōō, ū, & ē, the same as German ü, & as the u & eu & ui (*fule* for *fool*, *neuk* for *nook*, *buik* for *book*) used by reproducers of Scotch vernacular.

R, a roll or trill produced farther back in the mouth than the English r, & never (like that) allowed to go unsounded ; this R is, however, chiefly inserted after the usual symbols containing r (ar, er, ār, or, &c.), as a reminder that the trill is to be given.

Y, an elusive sound occurring chiefly in final syllables & suggesting that the speaker starts saying an additional syllable -ye but stops short before the vowel e is reached.

AN, a sound (strictly, several sounds between which the distinctions are too fine for representation here) that is neither ŏn, ŏng, ŏm, awn, awm, aw, nor ah, but partakes of them all, & approximates to one or other of them according to its position in a word.

IN, a sound (or sounds, as with AN) that is neither ăn, ahn, ăng, ăm, ahm, nor ahng, but bears to them the relation described under AN.

UN, a sound of the same nature as AN & IN, but with the vowel part of it resembling English untrilled er or ŭ.

EU, a sound roughly resembling English untrilled er, but with a u

element slightly perceptible ; the same as German ö.

UR, a sound differing from English trilled oor as U from English ōō & ŏŏ, or as Scotch dialect *puir* from English *poor*.

EUR, the R sound following EU.

(*e*), not an un-English sound ; the English *e*, but so lightly sounded at the end of a word after cl, br, &c., as not to be a separate syllable.

[s], [x], in the French-word column are inserted, often in the middle of compounds, to show the spelling of the French plural.

[s], [z], [ĭz], in the phonetic column show the pronunciation in English, but not in French, of the plural forms ; where such insertions are not made, it is better to pronounce the plural like the singular.

e, é, è, ê ; a special warning is necessary against the assumption that the normal sound of the plain or unaccented French e is ĕ or ā, e.g. that pĕ'tē (instead of petē') is the way to pronounce *petit* ; it has that sound only in exceptional positions, & wherever e is used in the phonetics care must be taken not to say ĕ or ā.

abandon, abă'ndon
abattoir[s], ă'batwar[z]
abbé[s], ă'bā[z]
accouchement[s], akōō'shmAN[z]
accoucheur[s], ăkōōshEUR'[z]
accoucheuse[s], ăkōōshEU'z [ ]
acharnement, AsharR'nemAN
à deux, ahdEU'
adieu[x], adyEU'[z]
affaire[s] *de cœur*, afăr'dekEUR'[ ]
à fond, ahfAN'
agent[s] *provocateur*[s],
   AzhAN' prOvOkAtEUR'[ ]
agréments, AgrămAN'
à huis clos, ahwēklō'
aide[s]*-de-camp*,
   ā'dekAN[z] (*or* -ŏng)
aide-mémoire, ādmĕmwarR'[z]
aiguille[s], ā'gwĕl[z]
aiguillette[s], āgwĭlĕ't[s]
aîné, ā'nā
à la, ah'lah
à la carte, ahlahkar't
à la mode, ahlahmO'd

à la Russe, ahlahrU's
âme[s] damnée[s], ahmdAnä'[ ]
amende[s] honorable[s],
    AmAN'dOnOrah'bl[ ]
à merveille, ahmärRvä'Y
amour[s], ä'moor[z]
amour-propre, amoorR'prO'pr(e)
ancien régime, AN'syAN rēzhē'm
annexe[s], ä'něks[ïz]
à outrance, ah ōotrAN's
apache[s], apah'sh[ïz]
aperçu[s], ApärRsU'[ ]
apéritif[s], apě'rïtěf[s]
aplomb, A'plAN
appui, Apwē'
après, Aprä'
à propos, ahpropō'
are[s], arR[ ]
arête[s], arä't[s]
argot, arRgō'
arme blanche, arm blANsh
arrière-pensée, arRyärR'pANsä'
arrondissement[s], ArANdē'smAN[]
artiste[s], artē'st[s]
assignat[s], ä'sïgnät[s]
atelier[s], A'tlyä[ ]
attaché[s], atä'shä[z]
auberge[s], ōbär'zh[ ]
au courant, ōkōorAN'
au fait, ōfä'
au fond, ōfAN'
au grand sérieux, ōgrAN'sěrēEU
au gratin, ōgrAtIN'
au naturel, ōnätürě'l
au pied de la lettre, ōpyä'dlahlě'tr(c)
au revoir, ōrevwarR'
automobile[s], awtomobē'l[z]
baccara(t), bä'karah
baignoire[s], běnwarR'[ ]
ballade[s], balah'd[z]
ballet[s], bä'lä[z]
ballon[s] d'essai, balAN'děsä'[ ]
bandeau[s], bändō'[z]
banquette[s], bANkě't[s]
barége, barä'zh
baroque, barō'k
barrage[s], bar'ïj[ïz]
bas bleu[s], bahblEU'[ ]
basque[s], bAsk[s]
bas relief[s], bä'srïlěf[s]
bastille[s], bästē'l[z]
batiste, batē'st
baton[s], bä'tn[z]
battue[s], batōo'[z]
beau[x], bō[z]

beau[x] geste[s], bōzhě'st[ ]
beau[x] idéal[s], bō ïdě'al[z]
beau monde, bōmaw'nd
beaux esprits, bōzěsprē'
beaux yeux, bōzyEU'
bêche-de-mer, bäshdemär'
béguinage[s], bě'gēnahzh[ïz]
béguine[s], běgē'n[z]
beige, bäzh
bel esprit, bělěsprē'
belle[s], běl[z]
belles-lettres, bělě'tr(e)
bête[s] noire[s], bätnwarR'[ ]
bétise[s], bätē'z[ ]
bezique, bïzē'k (F *bésique*)
bien entendu, byIN'ANtANdU'
bienséance, byIN'säAN's
bijou, bē'zhōō
bijouterie, bē'zhōōtrē'
billet[s]-doux, bïlïdōō'[z]
bise, bēz
bisque, bïsk
bizarrerie, bïzar'erē'
blague, blahg
blancmange[s], blamAN'zh[ïz]
blasé[s], blah'zä[ ]
bloc, blŏk
bonbon[s], bAN'bAN[z]
bonhomie, bŏnomē'
bonjour, bANzhoor'
bon[s] mot[s], bANmō'[z]
bonne[s], bŏn[z]
bonne bouche, bŏnbōō'sh
bonnes fortunes, bŏnforRtU'n
bonsoir, bANswarR'
bon ton, bANtAN'
bon[s] vivant[s], bANvē'vAN[ ]
borné[s], borR'nä[ ]
boudoir[s], bōō'dwar[z]
bougie[s], bōō'zhē[z]
bouillabaisse, bōōlyahbä's
bouilli, bōō'lyē
bouillon, bōō'lyAN
boulevard[s], bōō'lvarR[ ]
bouleversement, bōōlvärRsmAN'
bouquet[s], bōōkä'[z]
bourdon[s], boor'dŏn[z]
bourgeois, boor'zhwah
bourgeoisie, boorzhwahzē'
bourse[s], boors[ïz]
brassard[s], brasar'd[z]
brevet[s], brě'vït[s]
bric-à-brac, brï'kabräk
bricole, brï'kl
briquette[s], brïkě't[s]

brochure[s], brOshUR'[ ]
brunette[s], brōōně't[s]
brusque, brŏŏsk
buffet[s], bU'fā[z]
bulletin[s], bŏŏ'lĭtĭn[z]
bureau[x], būrō'[z]
bureau[x] *de change*,
   būrō'deshAN'zh[ ]
burnous, bernŏŏ's[ĭz]
cabaret[s], kA'barā[z]
cabinet[s], kă'bĭnā[z]
cachalot[s], kă'shalō[z]
cache[s], kAsh[ĭz]
cachet, kA'shā
cachou, kă'shŏŏ
cadet, kA'dā
cadre[s], kah'der[z]
café[s], kă'fā[z]
café[s] *au lait*, kă'fāōlā'[ ]
café[s] *chantant*[s],
   kă'fā shAN'tAN[ ]
café[s] *noir*[s], kăfānwarR'[ ]
caïque[s], kah-ē'k[s]
caisson[s], kā'sn[z]
calembour[s], kA'lANboor[ ]
calibre[s], kă'lĭber[z]
calorie[s], kă'lorĭ[z]
camaraderie, kAmarahderē'
camembert, kă'mANbārR
camisole[s], kă'misōl[z]
camouflage, kă'mŏŏflahzh
canaille, kanah'Y
canapé[s], kă'napā[ ]
canard[s], kanar'd[z]
cancan, kAN'kAN
cangue, kăngg
cantatrice[s], kANtahtrē's[ ]
caoutchouc, kow'chŏŏk
cap-à-pie, kăpapē'
caporal, kă'porahl
capote[s], kapō't[s]
carafe[s], karah'f[s]
carillon[s], kA'rēlyAN[ ]
Carmagnole, kar'manyŏl
carte blanche, kartblAN'sh
carte[s]-*de-visite*, kart devĭzē't[ ]
cartouche[s], kartŏŏ'sh[ĭz]
caserne[s], kazer'n[z]
casque[s], kăsk[s]
casserole[s], kă'serōl[z]
catafalque[s], kă'tăfălk[s]
cause[s] *célèbre*[s], kōz sělā'br(e)[ ]
causerie[s], kōzerē'[ ]
causeuse[s], kōzEU'z[ ]
céleste, sĭlě'st

centime[s], sANtē'm[z]
cerise, serē'z
chalet[s], shA'lā[z]
chamade[s], shamah'd[z]
chamois[ ], shă'mwah[ ]
champagne, shămpā'n
Champs Élysées, shANzĕlēzā'
chancre[s], shANkr(e)[ ]
chantage, shAN'tahzh
chanterelle[s], shANterĕ'l[z]
chapeau-bras, shapō'brah'
chaperon[s], shă'peron[z]
char[s]-*à-bancs*, shă'răbăng[z]
charade[s], sharah'd[z]
chargé[s]-*d' affaires*, sharzhādAfār'[ ]
charivari, shar'ĭvarĭ
charlatan[s], shar'latan[z]
charlotte russe, sharlotrU's
chartreuse, shartrEU'z
chasse, shAs
chassé[s], shă'sā[z]
chassepot[s], shă'spō[z]
châssis[ ], shă'sē[ ]
château[x], shAtō'[z]
châtelaine[s], shă'telăn[z]
chauffeur[s], shōfer'[z]
chaussure, shōsUR'
chef[s], shĕf[s]
chef[s]-*d' œuvre*, shĕdEU'vr(e)[ ]
chemisette[s], shĕmĭzĕ't[s]
chenille, shĭnē'l
chevalier[s]-*d'industrie*,
   shevA'lyădINdUstrē'[ ]
chevaux-de-frise, shevō'defrē'z
chevelure, shevelUR'
chevron[s], shĕ'vron[z]
chic, shēk
chiffon, shē'fAN
chignon[s], shē'nyAN[z]
chose[s] *jugée*[s], shōz zhUzhā'[ ]
chou[x], shŏŏ[ ]
chronique scandaleuse,
   krOnē'k skANdahlEU'z
chute[s], shŏŏt[s]
ci-devant, sēdvAN'
cirque, serk
clairvoyance, klārvoi'ans
clairvoyant[s], klārvoi'ant[s]
claque[s], klahk[s]
claqueur[s], klAkEUR'[ ]
cliché[s], klē'shā[z]
clientèle, klĭentē'l
clique[s], klēk[s]
cloisonné, klwah'zonā
cognac, kō'nyăk

coiffeur[s], kwahfEUR′[z]
coiffure[s], kwahfUR′
colporteur[s], kŏlportEUR′[z]
comédienne[s], kŏmēdĭě′n[z]
commandant[s], kŏmandă′nt[s]
comme il faut, kŏmělfō′
commissionnaire[s], kŏmĭshŏnār′[z]
commode[s], kŏmō′d[z]
communiqué[s], kŏmŪ′nĭkā[z]
compote, kŏ′mpōt
concessionnaire[s], konsěshŏnār[z]
concierge[s], kĂNsyār̄R′zh[ ]
concordat[s], konkor′dăt[s]
confrère[s], kĂN′frār̄[z]
congé[s], kĂN′zhā[z]
connoisseur[s], kŏnaser′[z]
conservatoire[s], konser′vatwar[z]
consommé, kĂNsOmā′
contour[s], kŏ′ntoor[z]
contretemps[ ], kĂN′tretAN[z]
convenances, kĂN′venANs
cordelier[s], kordelēr̄′[z]
cordon[s], kor′don[z]
cordon[s] *bleu*[s], korR′dAN blEU[ ]
corps[ ], kōr̄[z]
corsage, kor′sahzh
corset[s], kor′sĭt[s]
cortège[s], korRtă′zh[ ]
corvée, kor′vā
cosaque[s], kosah′k[s]
costumier[s], kOstŪmyā′[ ]
cotillon[s], kotĭ′lyon[z]
couleur de rose, kŏŏler′derŏ′z
coulisses, kŏŏlě′s
couloir[s], kŏŏ′lwar[z]
coulomb[s], kŏŏ′lŏm[z]
coup[s], kŏŏ[z]
coup[s]-*d'état*, kŏŏdětah′[z]
coup-de-grâce, kŏŏdegrah′s
coup[s]-*de-main*, kŏŏdemIN′[ ]
coup[s]-*de-théâtre*, kŏŏdetāah′tr(e)[ ]
coup-d'œil, kŏŏdEU′Y
coupé[s], kŏŏ′pā[z]
coupon[s], kŏŏ′pŏn[z]
coûte que coûte, kŏŏtkekŏŏ′t
crampon[s], kră′mpŏn[z]
crayon[s], krāon[z]
crèche[s], krāsh[ĭz]
crème, krăm
crème de la crème, krăm dlah krā′m
crème de menthe, krămdemAN′t
crêpe, krăp
crêpe de Chine, krăpdeshē′n
crépon, krě′pŏn
crétin[s], krě′tĭn[z]

cretonne, kretŏ′n
critique[s], krĭtē′k[s]
croquette[s], krokě′t[s]
crosse[s], krŏs[ĭz]
croupier[s], krŏŏ′pĭer[z]
cuirassier[s], kūrasēr̄′[z]
cuisine, kwĭzē′n
cul[s]-*de-sac*, kUdesA′k[ ]
curé[s], kU′rā[z]
daguerréotype[s], dagě′rotīp[s]
dais[ ], dās[ĭz]
dartre, dar′ter
débâcle[s], dĭbah′kl[z]
débris, dě′brē
début[s], dě′bU[z]
débutant[s], dě′bŭtant[s]
débutante[s], děbUtAN′t[ ]
décigramme[s], dě′sĭgrăm[z]
décilitre[s], dě′sĭlēter[z]
décimètre[s], dě′sĭmēter[z]
déclassé(e)[s], děklAsā′[ ]
décolleté(e)[s], děkŏ′ltā
dégagé(e)[s], dě′gAzhā
de haut en bas, deŏ′ANbah′
déjeuner[s], dě′zhEUnā[z]
delaine, dĭlā′n
démarche[s], děmarR′sh[ ]
démenti[s], děmANtē′[ ]
demi-monde, dě′mĭmŏnd
demi-mondaine[s], dmēmANdā′n[ ]
demoiselle[s], děmwahzě′l[z]
dénouement[s], dě′nŏŏmAN[z]
de nouveau, de nŏŏvō′
dépôt[s], dě′pŏ[z]
de règle, derā′gl
de rigueur, derēgEUR′
dernier ressort, dār̄R′nyā rěsorR′
déshabillé, dězA′bēyā′
détente[s], dětAN′t[ ]
détour[s], dĭtoor′[z]
de trop, detrŏ′
devoir[s], dě′vwar[z]
diablerie, dyahblerē′
difficile, dĭfĭsē′l
diplomat[s], dĭ′plomăt[s]
dishabille, dĭsabē′l
distingué(e)[s], dĭstIN′gā[ ]
distrait[s], distrā′[ ]
distraite[s], dĭstrā′t[ ]
dormeuse[s], dorRmEU′z[ ]
dossier[s], dŏ′syer[z]
dot, dOt
douane[s], dŏŏ′ahn[z]
double entendre, dŏŏblANtAN′dr(e)
double entente, dŏŏblANtAN′t

doublure[s], dōōblUR'[z]
douceur[s], dōōsEUR'[z]
douche[s], dōōsh[ĭz]
doyen[s], dwah'yAN[ ]
droit[s], droit[s]
duvet[s], dU'vā[z]
eau sucrée, ō'sŪkrā'
éclair[s], ĕ'klār[z]
éclaircissement[s], ĕklār̄sē'smAN[ ]
éclat, ĕklah'
élan, ĕ'lAN
élite, ĕlē't
Élysée, ĕlēzā'
embarras de choix,
    ANbArah' de shwah'
embarras de richesse,
    ANbArah' de rēshĕ's
embonpoint, AN'bANpwIN
émeute[s], ĕmEU't[ ]
employé(e)[s], ĕ'mploiē'[z]
empressement, ANprĕsmAN'
en casserole, ANkAscrO'l
en famille, ANfAmē'Y
en fête, ANfā't
en garçon, ANgarRsAN'
ennui, ŏnwē'
en masse, ANmA's
en passant, ANpAsAN'
en rapport, ANrAporR'
en route, ANrōō't
ensemble, ANsAN'bl(e)
entente[s], ANtAN't[ ]
entourage, ANtōōrah'zh
entr'acte[s], ANtrA'kt[ ]
entrée[s], AN'trā[z]
entremets, AN'tremā
entre nous, ANtrenōō'
entrepôt[s], AN'trepō[z]
espièglerie, ĕspyä'glerē'
esprit de corps, ĕsprē'dekōr
esprit d'escalier, ĕsprē'dĕscAlyā'
estaminet[s], ĕstä'mĭnä[z]
exposé[s], ĕkspō'sā[z]
fainéant[s], fänäAN'[ ]
fait accompli, fĕtAcANplē'
farceur[s], farsEUR'[ ]
fauteuil[s], fōtEU'Y[ ]
faux pas, fōpah'
femme de chambre,
    fA'mdeshAN'br(e)
feuilleton[s], fEUY'tAN[ ]
fiancé(e)[s], fyAN'sā[ ]
fille de chambre, fēY'deshAN'br(e)
fille[s] *de joie*, fēY'dezhwah'
fils, fēs

fine champagne, fē'nshANpah'nY
flair, flār̄
flânerie, flahnerē'
flâneur[s], flahnEUR'[z]
flèche[s], flāsh[ĭz]
force majeure, forR'smahzhEUR'
format, for'mah
foyer[s], fwah'yā[z]
franc[s] *tireur*[s], frANtērEUR'
frappant, frä'pant
friseur[s], frēzEUR'[z]
galimatias, gălĭmä'tĭah
gamin[s], gA'mIN[z]
garage[s], gä'rĭj[ĭz]
garçon[s], garRsAN'[ ]
gauche, gōsh
gaucherie, gōsherē'
gendarme[s], zhANdar'm[z]
gendarmerie, zhANdar'merē'
genre, zhAN're
glacé(e)[s], glA'sä
glacis, glā'sĭs
gobe-mouches [pl. same],
    gOb'mōōsh[ĭz]
gourmandise, goor'mandēz
gourmand[s], goor'mAN[z]
gourmet[s], goor'mä[z]
grande passion, graw'ndpAsyAN'
grande toilette, graw'ndtwahlĕ't
grand[s] *seigneur*[s],
    grAN'sänyEUR'[ ]
gratin, grA'tIN
grippe, grēp
grisaille, grĭzä'l
grisette[s], grēzĕ't[s]
gros de Naples, grōdenah'pl(e)
gruyère, grUyär̄R'
guerre de course, gär̄dekoor's
guilloche, gĭlō'sh
guipure, gēpoor'
habitué[s], Abē'tUä
hauteur, ōtEUR'
hors concours, orR'kANkoorR'
hors-d'œuvre, orRdEU'vr(e)
idée fixe, ēdä'fē'ks
impasse, INpA's
impayable, INpäyah'bl(e)
ingénue[s], INzhĕnU'[ ]
insouciance, INsōōsyAN's
insouciant, INsōōsyAN'
instantané, INstANtAnä'
internationale, INtär̄RnAsĭŏnah'l
intriguant[s], INtrēgAN'[ ]
intrigante[s], INtrēgANt'
jabot[s], zhAbō'[z]

jacquerie[s], zhAkerē'
jalousie[s], zhA'lōōzē[z]
jardinière[s], zhar'dĭnyār̄[z]
je ne sais quoi, zhensäkwah'
jeu[x] *de mots*, zhEUdemō'[ ]
jeu[x] *d'esprit*, zhEUdĕsprē'[ ]
jeunesse dorée, zhEUnĕ'sdOrā'
jongleur[s], zhANglEUR'[ ]
julienne, zhUlyĕ'n
jupe[s], zhUp[ ]
képi[s], kĕ'pē[z]
lacrosse, lahkrō's
laissez aller, lĕ'sā A'lā
laissez faire, lĕ'sāfār̄'
lansquenet, lä'nskenĕt
layette[s], lāĕ't[s]
lèse-majesté, lä'zmAzhĕstā'
lever de rideau, levā'derēdō'
liaison[s], lĭā'zn[z]
lingerie, lINzhrē'
liqueur, lĭkūr̄'
littérateur[s], lĭtĕ'rahtEUR'
livre[s], lĕ'vr(e)
longue haleine, lOnggAlā'n
lorgnette[s], lornyĕ't[s]
louis[ ], lōō'ĭ[z]
luge[s], lUzh[ĭz]
luxe, lUks
lycée[s], lēsā'[z]
macabre, makah'br(e)
macédoine[s], mäsĭdwah'n[z]
madame, mAdA'm
mademoiselle, mA'dmwahzĕ'l
malaise, malā'z
mal à propos, mA'lahpropō'
manège, manä'zh
mange-tout, mANzhtōō'
manqué(e)[s], mAN'kā
marguerite[s], margerē't[s]
mariage de convenance,
    mAryah'zhdekANvenAN's
marquise[s], marRkē'z[ ]
marron[s] *glacé*[s], mä'rANglA'sä[ ]
Marseillaise, marselä'z
massage, masah'zh
massé, mä'sā
masseur[s], mAsEUR[ ]
masseuse[s], mAsEU'z
matériel, matĕrĭĕ'l
matinée[s], mä'tĭnā[z]
mauvais quart-d'heure,
    mōvā'sUzhā'[ ]
mauvais sujet[s], mōvā'sUzhā'[ ]
mauvaise honte, mōvā'zaw'nt
mayonnaise, māonā'z

mélange, mĕlAN'zh
mêlée[s], mĕ'lā[z]
ménage[s], mĕ'nahzh[ ]
menu[s], mĕ'nōō[z]
meringue[s], merä'ng[z]
mésalliance[s], mĕzălĕAN's
mesdames, mädA'm
messieurs, mĕsyEU'
métayage, mĕ'tāahzh
métayer, mĭtā'er
métier, mĕ'tyā
mignon, mē'nyAN
migraine[s], mē'grän[z]
milor(d)[s], mēlorR'
mise-en-scène, mē'zANsä'n
mistral[s], mĭ'strahl[z]
mitrailleuse[s], mētrahyEU'z[ ]
modiste[s], mOdē'st[s]
moire, mwarR
moiré, mwah'rā
moire antique, mwarANtē'k
monde, mawnd
monseigneur, mANsänyEUR'
monsieur, mesyEU'
moral, morah'l
morceau[x], morsō'[z]
morgue, morg
morgue anglaise, morRgANglä'z
motif[s], mōtē'f[s]
moulin[s], mōō'lIN[z]
mousseline, mōōslē'n
musette[s], mUzĕ't[s]
naïf, nah-ē'f
naïve, nah-ē'v
naïveté, nah-ē'vtā
née, nā
négligé[s], nĕ'glĭzhā[z]
névé, nĕ'vā
noblesse, nōblĕ's
noblesse oblige, nOblĕ's Oblē'zh
noisette[s], nwahzĕ't[s]
nom de guerre, nANdegārR'
nom de plume, nANdeplU'm
non avenu, nOnAvenU'
nonchalant, nŏ'nshalant
nonpareil, nŏnparĕ'l
Notre-Dame, nOtredah'm
noyau, nwahyō'
nuance[s], nU'ANs[ ]
numéro, nū'merō
ogive[s], ojĭ'v[z]
on dit, ANdē'
opéra comique, ŏ'perakomē'k
opéra bouffe, ŏ'perabōō'f
outré, ōō'trā

paillasse, pălĭă's	*plateau*[*x*], plAtō'[z]
paletot[*s*], pA'ltō[z]	*point d'appui*, pwĬN'dApwē'
panache, panah'sh	*poisson*[*s*], pwah'sAN[ ]
papier mâché, păpyāmă'shā	*pompon*[*s*], pAN'pAN
par excellence, parĕkselAN's	*ponceau*, pANsō'
par exemple, parĕkzAN'pl(*e*)	*porte-cochère*, porR'tkŏshāṝR'
pari mutuel, par'ēmUtUĕ'l	*porte-crayon*, portkrā'on
parole[*s*], parō'l[z]	*portière*[*s*], por'tyāṝ[z]
parterre[*s*], partāṝ'[z]	*poseur*[*s*], pOzEUR'[ ]
parti[*s*], parRtē'[ ]	*poste restante*, pŏ'strĕstAN't
parvenu[*s*], par'venU[z]	*potage*, pOtah'zh
pas de deux, pah'dedEU'	*pot-pourri*, pōpōōrē'
pas seul, pahsEU'l	*pouf*, pōōf
passé(*e*)[*s*], pA'sā	*poult-de-soie*, pōō'deswah'
passementerie, pAsmANtrē'	*pourboire*, poorRbwarR'
passe-partout, pAsparRtōō'	*pourparler*[*s*], poorRparRlā'
pastiche, păstē'sh	*pour rire*, poor rēṝR
pastille[*s*], păstē'l[z]	*poussette*[*s*], pōōsĕ't[ ]
pâté de foie gras, pă'tādefwahgrah'	*pratique*, pră'tĭk
patois, pă'twah	*précis*[ ], prĕ'sē[z]
pavé[*s*], pAvā'[ ]	*première*[*s*], premyāṝ'[z]
paysage[*s*], pāēzah'zh	*prestige*, prĕstē'zh
peignoir[*s*], pānwar'[z]	*preux chevalier*[*s*], prEUshevA'lyā
peine forte et dure, pān forRt ā dUR	*prie-dieu*[ ], prēdyEU'[z]
pèlerine[*s*], pĕ'lerēn[z]	*primeur*[*s*], prēmEUR'
penchant[*s*], pAN'shAN	*procès-verbal*, prO'sāvāṝRbA'l
pension[*s*], pAN'syAN[z]	*prolétaire*[*s*], prOlĕtāṝR'
perdu(*e*)[*s*], perdū'[ ]	*protégé*(*e*)[*s*], prO'tĕzhā[z]
père, pāṝ	*provenance*, prŏ'vĭnans
perron[*s*], pĕ'rAN[z]	*prud'homme*, prUdO'm
persiennes, persĭĕ'nz	*purée*[*s*], pU'rā[z]
persiflage, pāṝ'sĭflahzh	*pur sang*, pURsAN'
personnel, personĕ'l	*Quai d'Orsay*, kādorsā'
petite, petē't	*quand même*, kANmā'm
petits chevaux, petē'shevō'	*quantité négligeable*,
petit[*s*] *maître*[*s*], petē'mā'tr(*e*)[ ]	kAN'tētā nĕglēzhA'bl(*e*)
petit[*s*] *souper*[*s*], petē'sōōpā'	*quenelle*[*s*], kenē'l[z]
petits soins, petēswIN'	*quinte*, kĬNt
petit[*s*] *verre*[*s*], petē'vāṝR'	*qui vive*, kēvē'v
pétroleur[*s*], pĕtrŏlEUR'[ ]	*raconteur*[*s*], rAkANtEUR'
pétroleuse[*s*], pĕtrŏlEU'z[ ]	*ragoût*[*s*], ragōō'[z]
picot[*s*], pĕ'kō[z]	*raison d'être*, rā'zANdā'tr(*e*)
pièce de résistance,pyā'sderĕzēstAN's	*râle*, rahl
pied à terre, pyā'dahtāṝR'	*ramequin*[*s*], rä'mĭkĭn[z]
pierrette[*s*], pyāṝĕ't[s]	*ranz des vaches*, rANzdävA'sh
pierrot[*s*], pyāṝ'ō[z]	*rapport*, rAporR'
pince-nez, pĬN'snā	*rapprochement*, rAprO'shmAN
piolet[*s*], pĕ'olā[z]	*razzia*[*s*], ră'zya[z]
piquant, pē'kant	*Réaumur*, rā'ōmUR
piqué, pē'kā	*réchauffé*[*s*], rĕ'shōfā'[z]
pis aller, pēzAlā'	*recherché*, reshāṝ'shā
plafond, plA'fAN	*réclame*, rĕ'klahm
planchette, plANshĕ't	*reconnaissance*, rĭkŏ'nĭsans
plaque[*s*], plahk[s]	*rédaction*[*s*], rĕdA'ksēAN
plat[*s*], plah[ ]	*redingote*[*s*], rĕ'dĭnggōt[s]

réduit[s], rĕ′dwē[z]
reflet[s], reflā′[z]
régie, rĕ′zhē
régime, rĕzhē′m
relevé, re′lvä
renaissance, rĭnä′sans
rencontre, rĕngkŏ′nter
rendezvous[ ], rAN′dävōō[z]
rente[s], rAN′t[z]
rentier[s], rAN′tyä[ ]
répertoire[s], rĕ′pertwar[z]
répondez s'il vous plait,
   rĕpAN′dä sēl vōō plä
repoussé, repōō′sä
restaurant[s], rĕ′storant[s]
restaurateur[s], restŏ′rAtEUR′[ ]
résumé[s], rĕ′zUmä[z]
retenue, retenU′
retroussé, rĭtrōō′sä
reveille, rĭvĕ′lĭ
revenant[s], revnAN′[ ]
revers, revär̄R′
revue[s], rĭvū′[z]
riant, rĭ′ant
ricochet[s], rĭ′koshä[z]
riposte[s], rĭpŏ′st[s]
risqué, rĕ′skä
rissole[s], rĭ′sŏl[z]
rivière[s], rĭ′vlär̄[z]
robe-de-chambre, rŎ′bdeshAN′br(e)
rocambole[s], rŏ′kambŏl[z]
rococo, rokŏ′kŏ
roi fainéant, rwahfä′näAN′
rôle[s], rŏl[z]
rondeau[x], rŏndŏ′[z]
rondel[s], rŏndĕ′l[z]
roquefort, rŎ′kforR
rôti, rŏ′tē
roturier[s], rŎtU′rēä
roué[s], rōō′ä[z]
Rouge Croix, rōōzhkrwah′
Rouge Dragon, rōōzhdrä′gon
Rouge et Noir, rōōzhänwahR′
roulade[s], rōōlah′d[z]
rouleau[x], rōōlŏ′[z]
roulette, rōōlĕ′t
ruche, rUsh
ruse[s], rōōz[ĭz]
rusé(e)[s], rU′zä
sabot[s], sA′bŏ[z]
sabotage, sä′botlj
sabretache[s], sä′bertäsh[ĭz]
sabreur[s], sAbrEUR′[ ]
sachet[s], sA′shä[z]
sacque[s], säk[s]

sacré, sAkrä′
salle-à-manger, sA′lahmAN′zhä
salle-d'attente, sA′ldAtAN′t
salmi[s], sä′lmē[z]
salon[s], sA′lAN[z]
sang-de-bœuf, sANdebEUF
sang-froid, sANfrwah′
sans cérémonie, sANsĕrĕ′mOnē′
sans-culotte[s], sANkUlO′t[s]
sans-culotterie, sANkUlŏterē′
sans doute, sANdōō′t
sans façon, sANfAsAN′
sans-gêne, sANzhä′n
sans peur et sans reproche,
   sANpEUR′äsANreprO′sh
sans phrase, sANfrah′z
sans-souci, sANsōōsē′
sauce piquante, sŏspĕkAN′t
sauté, -ée, -és, -ées, sŏ′tä
sauve-qui-peut, sŏvkĕpEU′
savant[s], sä′vAN[z]
savate, sAvah′t
savoir-faire, sAvwarfär̄′
savoir-vivre, sAvwarvē′vr(e)
scrutin d'arrondissement,
   skrU′tINdArAN′dēsmAN′
scrutin de liste, skrUtIN′delē′st
séance[s], sä′ANs[ ]
sec, sĕk
secrétaire[s], sĕkrĭtär̄′[z]
seigneur[s], sänyEUR′[z]
semé, sĕ′mä
sérac[s], sĕrä′k[s]
serviette[s], servĭĕ′t[s]
Sèvres, sä′vr(e)
silhouette[s], sĭlōōĕ′t[s]
sobriquet[s], sŏ′brĭkä[z]
soi-disant, swahdē′zAN
soirée[s], swar′ä [z]
sortie[s], sorRtē′[z]
sou[s], sōō[z]
soubrette[s], sōōbrĕ′t[s]
soufflé[s], sōō′flä[ᴢ]
soupçon, sōō′psAN
sourdine, soordē′n
soutache, sōō′tahsh
soutane[s], sōōtah′n[z]
souteneur[s], sōōtenEUR′[z]
souvenir[s], sōōvener̄′[z]
spirituelle, spĭrĭtŭĕ′l
succès d'estime, sUksä′dĕstē′m
succès fou, sU′ksäfōō′
suède, swäd
suivez, swē′vä
surtout[s], ser′tōō[z]

surveillance, servā'lans
svelte, svĕlt
tableau[x], tĂblō'[z]
tableau[x] *vivant*[s], tA'blō vē'vAN
table d'hôte, tahblđō't
tablier[s], tA'blĭä[z]
tache, tĂsh
tant soit peu, tAN'swahpEU'
tapis, tA'pē
tapotement, tApO'tmAN
Tartuffe, tarRtU'f
terrain, terä'n
terre-plein, tār'plān
terrine, tĕrē'n
tête-à-tête[ ], tātahtä't[s]
tic douloureux, tĭ'kdŏlorōō'
tiers état, tyār̄zĕtah'
tige, tēzh
timbale[s], tIN'bAl[ ]
timbre[s], tă'mber
tirailleur[s], tērahyEUR'[ ]
toilette, twahlĕ't
toison d'or, twah'zANdorR'
ton, tAN
tonneau[x], tŏ'nō[z]
tontine[s], tŏntē'n[z]
toque[s], tōk[s]
torchon, tor'shAN
tour de force, toordefor's
tournure, toornUR'
tous-les-mois, tōōlämwah'
tout court, tōōkoorR'
tout ensemble, tōōtANsAN'bl(e)
tracasseries, trAkA'serē'
trait[s], trä[z]
trente-et-quarante, trAN'tākArAN't
trois-temps, trwah'tAN
trottoir, trŏ'twarR
troubadour[s], trōō'badoor[z]
trou[s]*-de-loup*, trōōdelōō'
trousseau[x], trōōsō'[z]
trouvaille[s], trōōvah'Y
trouvère[s], trōō'vār[z]
tulle, tŬl
Turco[s], tUR'kŏ[z]
turquoise[s], ter'koiz[ĭz]
tuyère[s], twēr[z]
valenciennes, vAlANsyĕ'n
valse, vAls
vaudeville[s], vō'dvēl[z]
vedette[s], vĭdĕ't[s]
veilleuse[s], vālyEU'z
velours, veloor'
ventre-à-terre, vAN'trahtār̄R'
venue, vĕ'nū

verve, vār̄Rv
vieux jeu, vyEUzhEU'
vignette[s], vēnyĕ't[s]
villanelle[s], vĭlanĕ'l[z]
vinaigrette[s], vĭnāgrĕ't[s]
vingt-et-un, vIN'tāUN'
vingt-un, vINtUN'
vin ordinaire, vIN ordĭnār'
vis-à-vis, vēzahvē'
visé, vē'zā
vivandière[s], vē'vANdyār̄R'[ ]
vive, vēv
voix céleste, vwahsĕlĕ'st
vol-au-vent[s], vŏ'lōvAN
volte-face, vŎltfA's
voussoir[s], vōōswar'[z]
vraisemblable, vrāsANblA'bl(e)
vraisemblance, vrāsANblAN's
wagon-lit, vA'gANlē'
zouave[s], zōō'ahv[z]

frenum. See FRAENUM.
frequence, -cy. See -CE, -CY.
frequentative. See TECHNICAL TERMS.
frequently, as compared with *often*, is a FORMAL WORD.
fresco. Pl. *-oes* ; see -O(E)S 1.
friable. Confusion between the common word meaning crumbly & the *-able* adjective from *to fry* is not likely enough to justify the irregular spelling *fryable* for the latter, though oddly enough the OED's first quotation for *friability* illustrates the possibility : *Codfish for . . . friability of substance is commended.*

friar, monk. By the word *f.* is meant a member of one of the mendicant orders, i. e. those living entirely on alms, especially ' the four orders ' of Franciscans, Dominicans, Carmelites, & Augustinian Hermits. *M.* is used sometimes of all male members of religious orders including friars, but properly excludes the mendicants. In the latter case the general distinction is that while the monk belongs essentially to his particular monastery, & his object is to make a good man of himself, the friar's sphere of work is outside, & his object is to do a good work among the people.

fricandeau. Pronounce frĭ'kandō ; pl. *-eaux*, pron. -ōz, or *-eaus* (see -x).

fricative. See TECHNICAL TERMS.

Friday &c.) (on Friday &c.) *The Puritan way of eating fish is, to eat it Saturday instead of Friday./Can you dine with us Tuesday at 8.0 ?* The OED says : ' The adverbial use of the names of the days of the week is now chiefly *U. S.* except in collocations like " next Saturday ", " last Saturday " '.

friendlily. See -LILY.

frier, fryer. The first is better ; see DRY, 2, & VERBS IN -IE &c., 6.

frightful(ness). The words ought to revert in due time to their true English meaning. They have properly no implication of terrorism, & owe that sense merely to ignorance of English on the part of the journalists who seized on them as the handiest translation of German words that had that implication. The felt unnaturalness of the words had a certain value while war lasted, as suggesting the unnatural state of mind of a people that confused honest fighting with brutal cruelty ; but we do not want our language permanently corrupted by such accidents.

The mistranslation represented by *ruthless*, the original of which means regardless of consequences, or reckless, or unrestrained, though it garbles the German phrases, does not injure the English language, & is of temporary interest only ; but *culture* is, like *frightfulness*, in danger of a change of meaning that is to be deprecated.

friseur. See FRENCH WORDS.

frith. See FIRTH.

fritillary. The OED accents the second i ; but the M. Arnold line (*I know what white, what purple fritillaries*) seems likely to fix the stress on the first, for the flower at least.

frivol. See BACK-FORMATION.

friz(z). The double letter is preferred in general use & in the OED,

for the simple words as well as for inflected forms ; but see -Z-, -ZZ-.

frock. The use of *frock* for a dress, & especially for a dress regarded from the decorative point of view (' But in the language of fashionable society the use of *frock* for " dress " has within the last few years been revived ', said the OED in 1901), is in origin a nurseryism of the same kind as *nighty* & *shimmy* ; see VOGUE-WORDS.

frontage, frontal, frontier, frontispiece. It seems best to make the o in all these conform to that in *front* (ŭ, not ŏ), but the OED separates *frontier*, in which it prefers ŏ, from the rest.

frontispiece. For the use = face, see POLYSYLLABIC HUMOUR.

froth. See FOAM.

fructify. For inflexions see VERBS IN -IE &c., 6.

fruition. Pronounce frōōĭ'shn.

frustrate. See PARTICIPLES 5 A, & -ATABLE.

frustum. Pl. *-ta*, *-tums* ; the first is recommended.

fryable, fryer. See FRIABLE, FRIER.

fuchsia. So spelt.

fucus. Pl. *-ci*, pronounced -sī.

fuel, vb, makes *-lled*, *-lling* ; see -LL-, -L-.

fugacious. Chiefly in PEDANTIC HUMOUR.

fugue makes *fugal, fuguist.*

-FUL. The right plural for such nouns as *handful, spoonful, cupful, basketful*, is *handfuls* &c., not *handsful* &c.

fulcrum. Pronounce fŭl-, not fōōl- ; pl. *-cra*.

fulfil, fulfilled. So spelt ; see -LL-, -L-, 3.

fulgent. A poetical variant for the ordinary *refulgent*.

fuliginous. Chiefly in POLYSYLLABIC HUMOUR. *At present it is a f., not to say mysterious, matter.*

full for *fully* in such phrases as *f. twenty, f. as good as*, where it means quite, & such as *f. sweet, f. early*, where it means quite sufficiently or rather too, is idiomatic but colloquial. In the sense *very*, as in *f. fain, f. many a, f. weary*, where *fully* cannot be substituted, it is poetical.

ful(l)ness. Use *-ll-* ; see DULLNESS, & -LL-, -L-, 4.

FULL STOP. See STOPS ; & PERIOD IN ABBREVIATIONS.

fulsome. The OED recognizes only the pronunciation fŭl- (not fŏŏl-).

fumigate makes *-gable, -tor*; see -ABLE 1, -OR.

function. That such & such a thing ' is a function of ' such another or such others is a POPULARIZED TECHNICALITY :—*A man's fortitude under given painful conditions is a function of two variables.* As not everyone can cope unaided with mathematical technicalities, the following may be useful : ' When one quantity depends upon another or upon a system of others, so that it assumes a definite value when a system of definite values is given to the others, it is called a function of those others '.

fundamental is the established word in literary use for which writers with a taste for new fangled scientific-sounding terms substitute *basic* or *basal*.

funebrial, funeral (adj.), **funerary, funereal.** The continued existence of the first & third words, which no-one uses if he can help it, is due to what has happened to the other two. *Funeral*, though originally an adjective, has so far passed into a noun that it can no longer be used as an adjective except in the attributive position, as in *funeral customs, the funeral procession* ; *funereal* has become so tied to the meaning *as of a funeral, gloomy enough for a funeral*, that it can no longer mean simply of or for a funeral. In such a sentence as *The origin of the custom is* ——, it only remains to choose between *funebrial & funerary*.

fungus. Pl. *funguses* or *fungi* (pronounced -jī).

funicular. *Cable railway* is, when possible, preferable to *f. railway*.

funnel makes *-lled* ; see -LL-, -L-.

funniment. See HYBRID DERIVATIVES, FACETIOUS FORMATIONS, & -MENT.

funny. For ' too f. for words ' see HACKNEYED PHRASES.

furcate. See PARTICIPLES 5 A.

furiously. The British journalist finds it so amusing that the Frenchman should say *penser furieusement* where we say *think hard*, & *donner furieusement à penser* for *puzzle*, that he bores us intolerably with his discovery. *Ça donne furieusement à penser* is quoted, translated, paraphrased, & alluded to, till we are all heartily sick of it ; see GALLICISMS. *Making every allowance for special circumstances, the manner in which these amateur soldiers of seven weeks acquitted themselves compels one ' furiously to think '.*/*That word 'although' caused us furiously to think, but when we come to read the leading article in the* Times *we fancy that we get a clue to what may be meant.*/*That sentence of Professor Dicey's makes one think furiously.*/*The reduction in the majority from 6,000 to 1,400 has given many Coalition members f. to think.*

furore. Three syllables (fūror'ĭ).

furry. See PRONUNCIATION s.f.

further, adj. & adv. See FARTHER.

furze, gorse, whin. The first two would appear to be that very great rarity, a pair of exact synonyms, meaning the same thing & used indifferently in all localities & all contexts. The third differs not in sense, but in being chiefly a Scotch & northern word.

fuse. 1. The verb makes *fusible* ; see -ABLE 2.

2. It is worth while to remember that a fuse is not so called because it fuses, being named solely from its shape (L *fusus* spindle, while the verb is from L *fundo* pour) ; see TRUE & FALSE ETYMOLOGY.

FUSED PARTICIPLE is a name given to the construction exemplified in its simplest form by ' I like *you pleading* poverty ', & in its higher development by ' The collision was owing to *the signalling instructions* laid down by the international regulations for use by ships at anchor in a fog *not having been properly followed* '. The name was invented a dozen years ago for the purpose of labelling & so making recognizable & avoidable a usage considered by the inventor to be rapidly corrupting modern English style. A comparison of three sentences will show the meaning of the term.

1. Women having the vote share political power with men.

2. Women's having the vote reduces men's political power.

3. Women having the vote reduces men's political power.

In the first, the subject of the sentence is *women*, & *having* (*the vote*) is a true participle attached to women. In the second, the subject is the verbal noun or gerund *having* (*the vote*), & *women's* is a possessive case (i. e. an adjective) attached to that noun. The grammar in these two is normal. In the third, the subject is neither *women* (since *reduces* is singular), nor *having* (for if so, *women* would be left in the air without grammatical construction), but a compound notion formed by fusion of the noun *women* with the participle *having*. Participles so constructed, then, are called fused participles, as opposed to the true participle of Nº 1 & the gerund of Nº 2.

We are given to ridiculing the cumbrousness of German style, & the particular element in this that attracts most attention is the device by which a long expression is placed between a noun & its article & so, as it were, bracketed & held together. Where we might allow ourselves to say *This never to be forgotten occasion*, the German will not crane at *The since 1914 owing to the world-war befallen destruction of capital* ; only a German, we assure ourselves, could be guilty of such ponderous-

ness. But the fused participle is having exactly the same effect on English as the article-&-noun sandwich on German, the only difference being that the German device is grammatically sound, while the English is indefensible. The half-dozen examples that follow, in which the two members of each fused participle are in roman type, all exhibit both the bracketing capacity that makes this construction fatally tempting to the lazy writer, & its repulsiveness to a reader who likes clean sentences. In the last three may be observed a special fault often attending the fused participle —that the reader is trapped into supposing the construction complete when the noun is reached, & afterwards has to go back & get things straight.

Mr Fred Hall asked the Home Secretary if, in order to avoid the necessity of men *who desired to work & were wantonly attacked by strikers* being compelled *to arm themselves with fire-arms, he would* . . ./*No one is better qualified than Mr Charles Whibley to write the biography of* W. E. Henley ; *& there is some likelihood of* the life-story *of that influential & strenuous littérateur from his hand* appearing *before the close of the year./The machinery which enables one man to do the work of six results only in the others losing their job, & in* skill men *have spent a lifetime acquiring* becoming *suddenly useless./New subsections giving the Board of Trade power to make regulations for permitting* workmen *who are employed under the same employer, partly in an insured trade & partly not in an insured trade,* being treated, *with the consent of the employer, as if they were wholly employed in an insured trade./A dangerous operation, in which every-thing depends upon* the General Election, *which is an essential part of the operation,* being won./*The amazing resolution ' to take steps to prevent '* the Liberal demonstration *in Belfast to be addressed by Mr*

Churchill & Mr Redmond being held should surely open the eyes of the people of Great Britain to . . ./We have to account for the collision of two great fleets, so equal in material strength that the issue was thought doubtful by many careful statisticians, ending *in the total destruction of one of them & in the immunity of the other from damage greater than might well be incurred in a mere skirmish.*

It need hardly be said that writers with any sense of style do not, even if they allow themselves the fused participle, make so bad a use of the bad thing as is shown above to be possible. But the tendency of the construction is towards that sort of cumbrousness, & the rapidity with which it is gaining ground is portentous. A dozen years ago, it was reasonable, & possible without much fear of offending reputable writers, to describe as an 'ignorant vulgarism' the most elementary form of the fused participle, i.e. that in which the noun part is a single word, & that a pronoun or proper name ; it was not very easy to collect instances of it. Today, no-one who wishes to keep a whole skin will venture on so frank a description. Here are a dozen examples, culled without any difficulty whatever from the columns of a single newspaper, which would be very justly indignant if it were hinted that it had more vulgarisms than its contemporaries. Each, it will be seen, has a different pronoun or name, a sufficient proof in itself of abundant material. *We need fear nothing from* China *developing her resources* (China's)./*Which will result in* many *having to go into lodgings* (many's)./*It should result in* us *securing the best aeroplane for military purposes* (our)./*Germany pledges herself to put no obstacles in the way of* France *assuming a Protectorate* (France's)./*It is no longer thought to be the proper scientific attitude to deny the possibility of* anything *happening* (anything's)./*I quite fail to see what relevance there is in* Mr Lloyd George *dragging in the mis-*

deeds of . . . (George's)./*They wish to achieve this result without it being necessary to draw up a new naval programme* (its)./*I insisted on* him *at once taking the bill down* (his)./*We shall look forward with confidence to* Mr Buxton *adding to his reputation* (Buxton's)./*The reasons which have led to* them *being given appointments in these departments* (their)./*He is prepared to waive this prohibition upon* you *giving him a written undertaking as follows* (your).

It is perhaps beyond hope for a generation that regards *upon you giving* as normal English to recover its hold upon the truth that grammar matters. Yet every just man who will abstain from the fused participle (as most good writers in fact do, though negative evidence is naturally hard to procure) retards the progress of corruption ; & it may therefore be worth while to take up again the statement made above, that the construction is grammatically indefensible. At the first blush everyone probably grants this ; it is obvious, in any sentence so made as to afford a test (e. g., *Women having the vote reduces men's power*), that the words defy grammatical analysis. But second thoughts bring the comforting notion that the fusion must after all be legitimate ; it is only our old friend *occisus Caesar effecit ut*, which means not *Caesar when killed*, but *The killing of Caesar, had such & such results* ; why should not *Women having* mean *The possession by women of*, if *occisus Caesar* can mean *The killing of Caesar* ? The answer is that the Romans did resort to sensefusion, but did not combine it with grammar-confusion ; *The deaths of the Caesars had such effects* is *occisi Caesares effecerunt* (not *effecit*) ; but the fused-participlists say *Women having the vote reduces* (not *reduce*), & *You saying you are sorry alters* (not *alter*) *the case*. The Latin parallel is therefore of no value, & with it goes the only palliation of the bad grammar.

And now, in order that the reader may leave this disquisition sick to death, as he should be, of the fused participle, a few miscellaneous specimens are offered :—*We cannot reckon on* the unrest ceasing *with the end of one strike, or on* its not being renewed *in the case of other trades* (Compare *unrest* with *its*)./*It may be that this is part of the meaning & instinctive motive of* fish, *such as the perch,* going *in shoals at all.*/*The* ' *elastic defence* ', which *the Germans have prided themselves on* being *their speciality.*/*The Mullah's influence* (*as a result of* him having been denounced *at Mecca as an impostor*) *was declining.*/*Developments have occurred in consequence of the action of* one *of the accused, a man 31 years of age, & an ex-student of several colleges,* having turned *approver.*/*It was only after* Mr Buckmaster, Lord Wodehouse, & Mr Freake, finding *that they were unable to go, that the England team as now constituted was decided on.*/*The holiday habit is growing upon us, possibly owing partly to the persistent & recurrent habit of* Christmas Day falling *at the week-end.*/*We welcome* Tariff Reform being discussed *as often as possible.*/*This habit of* Ministers putting forth *their ideas through newspaper articles sometimes produced curious results.*/A place having bored & depressed *one is not a reason for regretting it.*/*But he objects to the cutting down of imports in war time, &* the fact *that we have to do without things* being taken *as an argument for our continuing to shut goods out after the war.*/*Some similar scheme can be introduced without* the school *doing so* suffering *pecuniary loss.*/*Good criticism combines the subtle pleasure in* a thing being well done *with the simple pleasure in* it being done at all./*The existence of these long term contracts is a large part of the case for* the coalowners refusing *to give increased wages to the men* (ambiguous : those who refuse ? or the refusal of them all ?)./*There is a big enough area for the speed men even in the narrow limits of these isles,*

without them making *the exquisite little corner of English lakeland the special field for their trials.*/*Conservatives proper neither want nor would willingly submit to* a question *of such gravity as the continued existence of the House of Lords as at present constituted* being again left to . . ./*One of the jurymen absented himself from the rest of the jury without* he, or the rest of the jury, being given *in charge of the proper officer* (after all, if it is not to be *his*, it may as well be *he* as *him*)./*Nor does it call for any great acumen to prophesy a torrent of specious sophistries on every single one of the* ' *Fourteen Points* ', which *the enemy relies on* being duly reprinted *in the Allied Press.*/*The truth of the old saw about* being a better thing *to wear out than to rust out.*/*Surely* the force of injustice *cannot be conceived of* going *any further.*/*The same objections apply to* the patient telling *the head attendant as to his telling the medical officer* (compare *patient* with *his*).

fuselage. So spelt : pronounce -z-.
fustigate, fustigation, are PEDANTIC-HUMOUR words.
futurism. A dictionary definition is : A recent movement in (esp. Italian) art, literature, &c., marked by violent departure from traditional methods & by the use of arbitrary symbols in the expression of emotion—*Concise Oxf. Dict.*

G

gabelle. For synonymy see TAX.
gaberdine. So spelt.
Gaelic, Gadhelic, Goidelic. The two longer forms are used chiefly by writers on philology & ethnology ; the two mean the same thing, but are distinguished from the usual meaning of *Gaelic*, i.e. Scotch-Celtic, by including also Irish-Celtic & Manx-Celtic. When precision is not required, *Gaelic* is the word chiefly used both in the narrow & the wide senses. Pronounce gā-, not gă-. The corresponding term to *Gadhelic*,

including Welsh-Celtic, Cornish-Celtic, & Breton-Celtic, is *Brythonic*.

gag. See CLOSURE for the Parliamentary sense.

gainsay is a LITERARY WORD, & now little used except in negative contexts such as *There is no gainsaying it*, *Without fear of being gainsaid*, *That can scarcely be gainsaid*.

gala. Pronounce gä-.

galaxy. Pronounce gă′laksĭ.

galimatias. See FRENCH WORDS.

gallant. The ordinary pronunciation is gă′lant. Certain senses, ' politely attentive to women ', ' amorous ', ' amatory ', are traditionally distinguished by the pronunciation gală′nt ; but these senses, & still more the special accent, are perhaps moribund.

gallery. *Que diable allait-il faire dans cette galère ?* is a famous line, & so often applicable that it is often applied. It is not possible for anyone who has seen it in its original place to be unaware that *galère* means galley ; & therefore to put it, or an allusion to it, into English with *gallery* betrays infallibly the jackdaw with borrowed plumes. To write galerie (*Mr McKenna, who has at least escaped being mixed up in that galerie*) is to say ' Yes, I know the French ', & so to add the sin of lying to the peccadillo of pretension. But then, whether one is caught out with *gallery* or *galerie*, one can always explain ' It was the printer ; I wrote *galley*, or *galère* '. See GALLICISMS, & FOREIGN DANGER.

galley. Pl. *-eys*.

Gallic, Gallican, Gaulish, French. *Gallican* is a purely ecclesiastical word, corresponding to *Anglican*. *Gaulish* means only ' of the (ancient) Gauls ', & is, even in that sense, less usual than *Gallic*. The normal meaning of *Gallic* is the same as that of *Gaulish*, but it is also much used as a synonym in some contexts for *French*. It means not simply ' French ', but ' characteristically ', ' delightfully ', ' distressingly ', or ' amusingly ', ' French ', ' so French,

you know ', &c. ; or again not ' of France ', but ' of the typical Frenchman '. We do not, or should not, speak of Gallic wines or trade or law or climate, but we do of Gallic wit, morals, politeness, & shrugs ; & the symbolic bird is invariably the Gallic cock. So far as *Gallic* is used for *French* without any implication of the kind suggested, it is merely a bad piece of ELEGANT VARIATION or AVOIDANCE OF THE OBVIOUS.

gallice, -cè. See LATINE.

GALLICISMS. By *Gallicisms* are here meant borrowings of various kinds from French in which the borrower stops short of using French words without disguise.

1. One form consists in taking a French word & giving it an English termination or dropping an accent or the like, as in *actuality, banality, & redaction*.

2. Another in giving to an existent English word a sense that belongs to it only in French or to its French form only, as in *intrigue* (v.t.,= interest, perplex, &c.), *impayable* (= priceless for absurdity, impudence, &c.), *arrive* (=attain success &c.), *exposition* (=exhibition), & *actual* (=concerned with the present, as in *The most actual & instructive article is on broadcasting*).

3. Another in giving vogue to a word that has had little currency in English but is common in French, such as *veritable* & *envisage*.

4. Another in substituting a French form or word that happens to be English also, but in another sense, for the really corresponding English, as when *brave* is used for *honest* or *worthy*, or *ascension* for *ascent*.

5. Another in translating a French word or phrase, as in *jump* or *leap to the eyes*, *to the foot of the letter*, *give furiously to think*, *knight of industry*, *daughter of joy*, *gilded youth*, *living pictures* (=tableaux vivants), *the half-world*, *rose-colour*, *curtain-raiser*, *do* one's *possible*, *castle in Spain*, *goes without saying*, *suspicion* (= soupçon), *dean* (=doyen)*, marriage* *of convenience, on the carpet,* & *success of esteem.*

To advise the abandonment of all Gallicisms indiscriminately would be absurd ; there are thousands of English words & phrases that were once Gallicisms, but, having prospered, are no longer recognizable as such ; & of the number now on trial some will doubtless prosper in like manner. What the wise man does is to recognize that the conversational usage of educated people in general, not his predilections or a literary fashion of the moment, is the naturalizing authority, & therefore to adopt a Gallicism only when he is of opinion that it is a Gallicism no more. To use Gallicisms for the worst of all reasons—that they *are* Gallicisms—, to affect them as giving one's writing a literary air, to enliven one's dull stuff with their accidental oddities, above all to choose Gallicisms that presuppose the reader's acquaintance with the French original, these are confessions of weakness or incompetence. If writers knew how ' leap to the eye ' does leap to the eye of the reader who, in dread of meeting it, casts a precautionary glance down the column, or how furious is the thinking that ' give furiously to think ' stirs in the average Englishman, they would leave such paltry borrowings alone for ever.

Some of the Gallicisms here mentioned, as well as others, are commented upon in their dictionary places. Words for which the reader is simply referred without comment to this article are to be regarded as undesirable Gallicisms.

Gallio. Pl. *-os*, see -O(E)S 8.

gallivant. See FACETIOUS FORMATIONS.

gallop makes *-oped, -oping* ; see -P-, -PP-.

gallows, though originally a plural form, is now singular (*set up a g.* &c.) ; the plural is usually avoided, but when unavoidable is *gallowses.*

galop, the dance, is so spelt ; **used**

as a verb, it does not double the p in inflexions, see -P-, -PP-.

galore, an Irish or Gaelic word, & no part of the Englishman's natural vocabulary, is chiefly resorted to by those who are reduced to relieving dullness of matter by oddity of expression. Like *anent,* it is a favourite with the writers of letters to the press.

galosh, golosh. The OED gives precedence to the first spelling.

galumph. See FACETIOUS FORMATIONS.

gambado. Pl. *-os* ; see -O(E)S 6.

gamboge. Pronounce -bōōzh.

gamin. See FRENCH WORDS.

gammon)(ham. The ordinary modern meaning of *g.* is the hinder end of a side of bacon including the ham ; in the sense of a cured h. alone it is now rare & old-fashioned.

gamp. See SOBRIQUETS.

gamut. For synonyms, in the extended sense, see FIELD.

gamy, not *gamey* ; see -EY & -Y.

gang agley is a BATTERED ORNAMENT.

ganglion. Pl. *-lia.*

gangway. *Below the g.,* as a parliamentary phrase, is applied to members whose customary seat does not imply close association with the official policy of the party on whose side of the House they sit.

gantry, gaun-. In the modern engineering sense the first spelling is usual.

Ganymede. See SOBRIQUETS.

gaol, gaoler, jail, jailor, &c. ' In British official use the forms with G are still current ; in literary & journalistic use both the G & the J forms are now admitted as correct, but all recent Dictionaries give the preference to the latter.'—OED. It may be added that the very anomalous pronunciation of g soft before other vowels than e, i, & y (only in *mortgagor* & in the popular mispronunciation of *margarine* ?) is a strong argument for writing *jail.* The spellings of the agent-nouns to which the OED gives precedence are *jailer* & *jaileress*.

garage, like many other French words in constant necessary use (e.g. *billet-doux, bulletin, cadre, chaperon, commissionaire, cordon, coupon, employé, liqueur, restaurant, valet*), should be completely anglicized in pronunciation (gă'rĭj).

garble. The original meaning is to sift, to sort into sizes with a view to using the best or rejecting the worst. The modern transferred sense is to subject a set of facts, evidence, a report, a speech, &c., to such a process of sifting as results in presenting all of it that supports the impression one wishes to give of it & deliberately omitting all that makes against or qualifies this. Garbling stops short of falsification & misquotation, but not of misrepresentation ; a garbled account is partial in both senses.

garçon. See FRENCH WORDS.
garden. For *the G.* in philosophy, see ACADEMY.
gargoyle, gur-. The first is the right form.
garret, attic. The two words mean the same thing, but the former is usually chosen when poverty, squalor, &c., are to be suggested.
gar(r)otte. The right spelling is *garrotte.*
gas. See FLUID.
gaseous. 1. The pronunciations recognized by the OED are gă'sĭus, gā'sĭus, in that order of preference. 2. *gaseous*)(*gassy.* The first prevails in scientific use ; the further the substitution of *gassy* for it can be carried, the better.
gasogene)(**gazogene.** The original is the French *gazogène* ; when the accent is dropped, it seems better to go the whole hog, assimilate to the established *gasometer*, & write s for z.
gauche(rie). See FRENCH WORDS.
gauge. So spelt, not *guage*. The verb makes *gaugeable* ; see MUTE E.
Gaul means ancient Gaul or one of its inhabitants ; the use of it for

France or Frenchman is poetic or facetious. See SOBRIQUETS.

Gaulish. See GALLIC.
gauntry. See GANTRY.
gay makes *gayer, gayest, gaily, gaiety.*
gazogene. See GASOGENE.
geezer, i.e. queer old character, orig. *guiser* or mummer, is spelt *geezer* in the OED.
gelatin(e). The form without final -e is in scientific (or pseudo-scientific) use only ; see -IN & -INE.
gemma. Pl. *-ae.*
gemmate. See PARTICIPLES 5 A.
gendarme, gendarmerie. See FRENCH WORDS.
gender, n., is a grammatical term only. To talk of *persons* or *creatures of the masculine* or *feminine g.*, meaning *of the male* or *female sex*, is either a jocularity (permissible or not according to context) or a blunder.

generalissimo. Pl. *-os* ; see -O(E)S 7.
generalize has *-zable* ; see MUTE E.
generate makes *-rable, -tor* ; see -ABLE 1, -OR.

GENERIC NAMES AND OTHER ALLUSIVE COMMONPLACES. When Shylock hailed Portia as *A Daniel come to judgement*, he was using a generic name in the sense here intended ; the History of Susanna was in his mind. When we talk of *the Mecca of Free Trade*, of *the Huns*, of *Ithuriel's spear*, of *a Naboth's vineyard*, of *shooting Niagara*, of *Procrustean regulations*, *draconic severity*, or *tantalizing opportunities*, we are using allusive commonplaces. Some writers revel in such expressions, some eschew them of set purpose, some are ill provided with them from lack of reading or imagination ; some esteem them as decorations, others as aids to brevity. They are in fact an immense addition to the resources of speech, but they ask to be employed with discretion ; this article is not intended either to encourage or to deprecate their use ; they are often in place, & often out of place ;

fitness is all. An allusion that strikes a light in one company will only darken counsel in another; most audiences are acquainted with the qualities of *a Samson,* fewer with those of *a Dominie Sampson,* fewer still with those of *the Laputans,* & yet fewer again with those of *Ithuriel's spear.* Nevertheless, to some audience or other each of these may well be, apart from any decorative value attaching to it, the most succinct & intelligible name for what is meant. It is for the writer to see that he does not try Ithuriel's spear on those whose knowledge stops short at Samson; for if the test reveals them as ignoramuses they will not like it, nor him.

It is perhaps worth while to call attention to a practical difference between the useful & the decorative allusions: when an allusive term is chosen because it best or most briefly conveys the meaning, triteness is no objection to it, intelligibility being the main point; but the choice for decorative purposes is a much more delicate matter; you must still be intelligible, but you must not be trite, & the margin in any audience between what it has never heard of & what it is tired of hearing of is rather narrow; it is necessary to hit it between wind & water.

These few remarks may suffice on the unanswerable question whether allusive terms should be sought or avoided. The purpose of this article is not to answer it, but to point out that if they are used it is inexcusable & suicidal to use them incorrectly; the reader who detects his writer in a blunder instantly passes from the respect that beseems him to contempt for this fellow who after all knows no more than himself. It is obvious that the domain of allusion is full of traps, particularly for the decorative allusionist, who is apt to take the unknown for the fine, & to think that what has just impressed him because he knows little about

it may be trusted to impress his readers. For an example or two see the articles BENEDICK, CUI BONO ?, DEVIL'S ADVOCATE, EXIT, GALLERY, FRANKENSTEIN, ILK.

genie. Pronounce jē'nĭ; pl. *genii,* pron. jē'nĭī; see LATIN PLURALS. Another form is *jinnee,* pl. *jinn.*

genitive(ly), genitival(ly). See ABLATIVELY.

genius. Pl. *-uses*; the form *genii* is now used only as pl. of *genie* (or of *genius* in the sense of *genie*); see LATIN PLURALS. For g. & talent, see TALENT.

genre. See FRENCH WORDS.

gens. Pl. *gentes,* pron. -ēz.

gent (= gentleman) is used only in uneducated speech or in jocular imitations of it.

genteel is now used, except by the ignorant, only in mockery.

genteelly. So spelt.

GENTEELISM. By *genteelism* is here to be understood the substituting, for the ordinary natural word that first suggests itself to the mind, of a synonym that is thought to be less soiled by the lips of the common herd, less familiar, less plebeian, less vulgar, less improper, less apt to come unhandsomely betwixt the wind & our nobility. The truly genteel do not offer *beer,* but *ale*; invite one to *step,* not *come,* this way; take in not *lodgers,* but *paying guests*; send their boys not to *school,* but to *college*; never *help,* but *assist,* each other to potatoes; keep *stomachs & domestics* instead of *bellies & servants*; & have quite forgotten that they could ever have been guilty of *toothpowder & napkins & underclothing,* of *before & except & about,* where nothing now will do for them but *dentifrice, serviette, lingerie, ere, save, anent.*

The reader need hardly be warned that the inclusion of any particular word in the small selection of genteelisms offered below does not imply that that word should never be used. All or most of these, & of the hundreds that might be classed with them, have their proper uses, in which they are not genteel, but natural. *Ale* is at home in historical novels, *ere* & *save* in poetry, *mirrors* in marble halls, *the military* in riots, *dentifrices* in druggists' lists, & so forth ; but out of such contexts, & in the conditions explained above, the taint of gentility is on them. To illustrate a little more :n detail, ' He went out without shutting the door ' is plain English ; with *closing* substituted for *shutting* it becomes genteel ; nevertheless, to *close* the door is justified if more is implied than the mere not leaving it open :— ' Before beginning his story, he crossed the room & closed the door ', i. e. placed it so as to obviate over-hearing ; ' Six people sleeping in a small room with closed windows ', i. e. excluding air. Or again, ' The schoolroom roof fell in, & two of the boys (*or* girls, *or* children) were badly injured ' ; *scholars* for boys &c. would be a genteelism, & a much more flagrant one than *closing* in the previous example ; yet *scholar* is not an obsolete or archaic word ; it is no longer the natural English for a schoolboy or schoolgirl, that is all.

The reader may now be left to the specimen list of genteelisms, which he will easily increase for himself. The point is that, when the word in the second column is the word of one's thought, one should not con-sent to displace it by the word in the first column unless an improve-ment in the meaning would result.

Genteelisms	Normal words
ale	beer
anent	about
assist	help
carafe	water-bottle
cease	stop
chiropodist	corn-cutter
close	shut
coal-vase	coal-scuttle
college	school
couch	sofa
dentifrice	toothpowder
distingué	striking
domestic	servant

Genteelisms	Normal words
edifice	building
endeavour	try
ere	before
exclusive	select
expectorate	spit
hither	here
inquire	ask
kinema	cinema
lady-dog	bitch
lady help	servant
lingerie	underclothing
military, the	soldiers
mirror	looking-glass
odour	smell
paying guest	boarder
perspire, -ration	sweat
peruse	read
place	put
preserve	jam
proceed	go
recreation	amusement
save	except
scholar	boy &c.
serviette	napkin
step	come, go
stomach	belly
sufficient	enough
woolly	sweater
tipsy	drunk

gentle. *The gentle art.* This phrase, long a favourite with anglers as an affectionate description of their pur-suit, was cleverly used by Whistler in his title *The Gentle Art of Making Enemies.* The oxymoron was what made it effective ; but the journal-ist, aware that Whistler made a hit with *the gentle art,* & failing to see how he did it, has now, by rough handling on inappropriate occasions, reduced it to a BATTERED ORNAMENT (cf. IRRELEVANT ALLUSION). Thus : *We have not the smallest doubt that this is what will actually happen, & without any undue exercise in* the gentle art of intelligent anticipation, *we may discuss the situation./In a Committee the gentle art of pro-crastinating may prove very deadly to progress.*

gentlemanly, gentlemanlike. If the ugly *-like* form were understood to suggest, while the other did not, a warning that all is not gold that glitters, there would be sufficient justification for their coexistence; but the OED quotations do not bear out, nor does the OED emphasize, such a distinction. It seems a pity, then, that *-like* should be kept in being; see SUPERFLUOUS WORDS.

gentlewoman)(lady. The first has no sense that does not belong to the second also, but *l*. has half a dozen for which *g*. will not serve—the Virgin, pl. of *madam*, titled woman, wife, beloved, woman politely described. It follows that in the one sense common to both (fem. of *gentleman*, i.e. woman of good birth & breeding, or woman of honourable instincts) *g*. is sometimes preferred as free of ambiguity or as more significant. It is, however, an old-fashioned if not quite archaic word, & as such tends to be degraded by facetious use, & to have associated with it constant epithets, of which some are derisive (*ancient, decayed, innocent*) & others are resorted to as protests against such derision (*true, Nature's*, &c.); it is therefore to be used with caution.

genuine. Compare AUTHENTIC.
genus. Pronounce jē-; pl. *genera*, pron. jĕn-; see LATIN PLURALS.
geographic(al). The short form 'now somewhat rare except in *Geographic latitude*'—OED. See -IC(AL).
geometric(al). 1. The long form prevails, & there is no difference in meaning; see -IC(AL). 2. *G. progression.* For the misuse of this, see PROGRESSION.

Georgy, -ie. See -EY, -IE, -Y.
germ. For synonymy see SCHIZOMYCETES.
German. *High & Low G. High G.* is the language known ordinarily as *German*; *Low G.* is a comprehensive name for English, Dutch, Frisian, Flemish, & some G. dialects. The words *High & Low* are merely geographical, referring to the Southern or mountainous, & the Northern or low-lying, regions in which the two varieties developed.

gerontocracy. See GREEK G.
gerrymander. The g is hard.

GERUND. 1. G. & gerundive. 2. G. & participle. 3. G. & infinitive. 4. G. & possessive.
1. Gerund)(gerundive. The second word is of importance only with regard to the languages that possess the thing, of which English does not happen to be one; but, as its being occasionally used for the other word *gerund*, which *is* of importance in English grammar, may cause confusion, the difference between the Latin gerund & gerundive should be explained. The gerund is a noun supplying a verb's infinitive or noun-form with cases; thus *amare* to love has the gerund *amandi* of loving, *amando* by loving, *amandum* the act of loving; correspondingly the word *loving* as a noun (but not as an adjective) is the gerund in English, though it is of the same form as the participle. From the same stem as *amandi* &c. is formed in Latin an adjective *amandus* lovable, & this in Latin grammar is named the gerundive as being formed from the gerund. The English adjectives formed in *-ble* from verbs, like *lovable*, might well enough be called gerundives from their similarity in sense to the Latin gerundive; but they are not in practice so called, & the word *gerundive* has accordingly no proper function in English grammar.
2. Gerund & participle. The English gerund is identical in form, but only in form, with the active participle; *loving* is a gerund in 'cannot help loving him', but a participle in 'a loving husband'. A grammarian quoted by the OED says 'Gerundives' [by which he means gerunds] 'are participles governed by prepositions; but, there being little or no occasion to distinguish them from other participles, we seldom use this name'. The distinction is, on the contrary,

of great importance, & the occasion for making it constantly occurs. In the article FUSED PARTICIPLE an attempt is made to show the fatal effects on style of disregarding it.

3. Gerund & infinitive. Among the lapses that are concerned not with particular words but with a whole class of phrases, & that without being describable as grammatical blunders reveal a writer's ignorance of idiom, few are more insidious than failure to recognize when the gerund with a preposition is required rather than an infinitive. *I look forward to meet*, or *to meeting, him* ? *I aim to remove*, or *at removing, the cause* ? *The duty is laid on us to do*, or *of doing*, our best ?

The variety of cases in which the question arises is so vast, & the rules that should answer it would be so many & need so many exceptions, that it is better not to state them. Three general remarks may suffice instead, to be followed by some specimens. A. There is very little danger of using the gerund, but much of using the infinitive, where the other would be better. B. Lapses are usually due not to deliberate choice of the worse, but to failure to think of the better. C. The use of the infinitive is often accounted for, but not justified, by the influence of analogy ; because *able*, or *sufficient*, or *adequate, to perform* is English, we assume that *equal to perform*, which is to bear the same meaning, must be English too. In the specimens, where analogy seems to have been at work, the analogous word is suggested in the correction bracket.

Specimens after nouns

But they have been blocked by the objections *of farmers & landlords* to provide *suitable land, & by the reluctance of local authorities to use their powers of compulsion* (to providing. Observe that the infinitive after *reluctance* is quite idiomatic. Analogues for *objection*, hesitation, refusal)./*I refer to the growing* habit

of a few hooligans to annoy & assault *those who* . . . (of annoying. Tendency)./*Germany's* plan to keep *to the present tariff flatly conflicts with* . . . (of keeping. Determination)./ *The Government can in no circumstances neglect its elementary* duty to protect *the worker* (of protecting. Obligation)./*They have been selected with a* view to illustrate *both the thought & action of the writer's life* (illustrating. Analogue for *with a view*, so as)./*Then Humperdinck had the happy* idea *one day* to write *a little fairy opera* (of writing. Inspiration)./*Russia assures us that she has no* intention to encroach *upon it* (of encroaching. But idiom after *intention* is less fixed than after most such nouns)./*You have likened the* resistance *of Ulster Unionists* to be driven *out of the Constitution of Great Britain to the economic opposition of a number of scattered citizens to a reform of the tariff* (to being driven. Refusal, reluctance).

Specimens after adjectives

A simplicity that seems quite unequal to treat *the large questions involved* (to treating. Incompetent)./ *The navy is not* equal *in numbers or in strength* to perform *the task* (performing. Sufficient).

Specimens after verbs

Since the Ulstermen have committed themselves to line *actual & visible trenches if a settlement is not arrived at* (lining. Threaten)./*He* confesses to have seen *little of the great poets of his time* (having. Profess)./*The cab-drivers* object to pay *their proportion of the increase* (paying. Refuse)./*France rightly* objects to allow *Germany to assume a position in Morocco which would* . . . (allowing. Hesitate)./*All the traditions in which she has been brought up* have not succeeded to keep *her back* (in keeping. Avail).

4. Gerund & possessive. The gerund is variously describable as an -*ing* noun, or a verbal noun, or

a verb equipped for noun-work, or the name of an action. Being the name of an action, it involves the notion of an agent just as the verb itself does ; *He went* is equipped for noun-work by being changed to *his going*, in which *his* does for *going* the same service as *he* for *goes*, i. e. specifies the agent. With the verb, the agent is usually specified, but not always ; it is seldom, e. g., used with the imperative (*go*, not *go you* or *you go*) because to specify the agent would be waste of words. With the gerund it is the other way ; the agent is usually not specified, but sometimes must be, i.e. a possessive must sometimes be inserted ; & failure to distinguish when this is required & when it is superfluous leads to some ugly or unidiomatic writing. Scylla is omission of the possessive when the sense is not clear without it ; Charybdis is the insertion of it when it is obvious waste of words ; but these are only the extremes, rarely run into. *Jones won by Smith's missing a chance* ; if you omit *Smith's*, & say *Jones won by missing a chance* (as in fact he did, only the missing was not his), Scylla has you. If you say *He suffers somewhat, like the proverbial dog*, from his having received *a bad name*, you & your *his* are in Charybdis. The second is a real extract ; of Scylla it was necessary to invent an illustration ; but even Charybdis is rare. What is not rare is something between the two. It will be noticed that the reason why that *his* (with *having received*) was felt to be so intrusive is that the receiver is the same person as the subject of the sentence ; compare Smith's missing, where *Smith's* was indispensable just because the misser was *not* the subject of the sentence. Hence has come a subconscious assumption that the possessive will be omitted if, & only if, the agent it would have specified is the same as the agent in the action denoted by the main verb, i.e. either the subject, or, if the verb is passive,

an agent following *by* or perhaps not even expressed. The following sentences are bad because they flout this assumption ; &, though they escape both Scylla & Charybdis, neither leaving out an essential possessive nor using a superfluous one, they offend against idiom by jumping from one agent to another without giving notice :—*By conniving at it, it will take too deep root ever to be eradicated* (*By our conniving* would give the necessary notice. *We shall root it too deeply* would avoid the jump. But better abandon the gerund & write *If connived at*)./*Why should not the punishment for his death be confined to those guilty of it, instead of* launching *expeditions against three tribes ?* (*Why should we not confine*, or *instead of our launching* or *instead of expeditions' being launched*. The first is best)./By allowing *month after month to pass without attempting to defend our trade, von Tirpitz had some excuse for supposing that we recognized it to be indefensible* (*By our allowing*—clumsy—, or—better—*we gave von Tirpitz some excuse*).

' The agent in the action denoted by the verb ' was spoken of above, & not simply ' the subject ' ; this complication was necessary because there is a common type of sentence in which the possessive is regularly omitted, & which would have seemed to contradict the rule if ' the subject ' had been allowed to pass as sufficient ; that type is seen in *This danger may be avoided by whitewashing the glass* ; the agent of the whitewashing is not the same as the subject i. e. *danger*, but is the same as the agent in avoiding, i. e. the owner of the plants that are not to be scorched ; consequently the possessive is not required.

A few wrong forms are added without comment :—*Sure as she was of her never losing her filial hold of the beloved.*/*Mr Chamberlain has no warrant for his limiting the phrase to . . ./I cultivated a cold & passionless exterior, for I discovered that* by assuming *such a character certain persons would talk more readily before me.*/After following *a country Church of England clergyman for a period of half a century, a newly appointed, youthful vicar, totally unacquainted with rural life, comes into the parish.*

gesticulation)(gesture. The usual relation between the two is that of abstract to concrete : gesticulation is the using of gestures, & a gesture is an act of gesticulation. On the other hand, *gesture* also is sometimes used as an abstract, & then differs from *gesticulation* in implying less of the excited or emotional or theatrical or conspicuous. Similarly, if *a gesticulation* is preferred to *a gesture*, it is in order to imply those characteristics. The use of *gesture* in political & diplomatic contexts, = advance, manifestation of willingness to treat or compromise or make concessions, exhibition of magnanimity or friendliness, &c., is so recent that the OED (1901) has no example of it. It dates from the war, & is apparently a GALLIC-ISM, having been substituted for the French *beau geste* ; that, after having a great vogue in the newspapers for a year or two, has now ceased to puzzle us, & bequeathed its vogue to *gesture* ; see VOGUE-WORDS.

get. 1. *Have got* for *possess* or *have* is good colloquial but not good literary English.
2. *Gotten* still holds its ground in American English. In British English it is in verbal uses (i.e. in composition with *have, am*, &c.) archaic & affected ; but as a mere participle or adjective it occurs in poetical diction (*On gotten goods to live contented*) & in mining technicalities (*The hewer is paid only for the large coal gotten* ; *There is no current wage rate per ton gotten*).
3. *Get-at-able.* See COME-AT-ABLE.

geyser. The pronunciation gā'ser is given precedence in the OED.

-G-, -GG-. Words ending in g preceded by a single vowel (a, e, i, o, u,

or y) double the g before a suffix beginning with a vowel : *waggery, priggish, froggy, sluggard, sandbagged, zigzagging, nutmeggy, periwigged, leapfrogging, humbugged.*

ghastlily. See -LILY.
ghaut, ghat, ghât. The first has precedence in the OED. Pronounce gawt.
ghetto. Pl. *-os* ; see -O(E)S 6.
ghoul. Pronounce gōōl.
giaour. Pronounce jowr.
gibber, gibberish. The first is usually pronounced with soft g, & occasionally spelt *ji-* ; the second is pronounced with hard g, & was sometimes spelt gui- or ghi- to mark the fact. It is doubtful whether one is derived from the other. For *gibberish, lingo*, &c., see JARGON.
gibbous. Pronounce with hard g.
gibe, jibe. The OED gives precedence to *g-*.
gibus. Pronounce ji-.
gild, n. See GUILD.
gild, vb. For *Gilded Chamber* see SOBRIQUETS. *Gild the lily* is a MIS-QUOTATION.
gill, ravine, has g hard ; *gill*, the measure, & *Gill*, lass, have g soft. In *Jack & Gill, Gill* (for *Gillian*) is the right form.
gillie has g hard ; *gilly*-flower has g soft.
gimbal has g soft ; the OED gives that only, & older spellings (often *ji-*) & the etymology (*gimmal, gemellus*) confirm it ; but in modern use the hard g is common.
gimp, gymp, guimp. *gi-* is best.
gingerly. The word, which is at least four centuries old, has probably no connexion with *ginger* ; see TRUE & FALSE ETYMOLOGY.
Giotto, Giovanni. See ITALIAN SOUNDS.
gipsy. See GYPSY.
gird, encircle, has past & p.p. *girded* or *girt.*
girl rhymes with *curl, whirl*, & *pearl*, with the first syllable of *early*, not of *fairly*. But a pronunciation gairl (gārl), not very easily dis-

tinguished from gal (găl), is much affected by persons who aim at peculiar refinement. Novelists who write *gurl* as a representation of coarse speech are presumably of this refined class.

girlie, -ly. See -EY, -IE, -Y.

gist has soft g.

give. 1. *Give* one *right*, in the sense justify him or allow that he is in the right, is both French (*donner droit à quelqu'un*) & German (*einem Recht geben*) ; but it is not English, & the OED appears to quote no example of it. In the first passage below it has been resorted to under the ELEGANT-VARIATION impulse, *justify* having been already used up :—*The local Liberals & the Chief Whip who supported them from headquarters are abundantly* justified *in their belief that a radical candidate had a better chance of winning this particular constituency than a Labour one, & the working-class voters have themselves given them right./M. Millerand is much praised in France for having resisted Mr Lloyd George's efforts, & M. Clemenceau apparently gives him right.*

2. *Give to think.* The phrase is commented on in the article GALLICISM as one of the two or three that surpass all other Gallicisms for ineptitude. It has, however, had a lamentable vogue, & a few examples follow ; others will be found under FURIOUSLY. *This is a powerful impressionistic sketch, true to life, which* gives to think./*In every chapter the author has that to say which arrests attention &* gives to think./*The Labour Party has made a clean sweep of the Transvaal Provincial elections, & the result is certainly one calculated to give furiously to think./But what we are told as to coal & cotton gives furiously to think, as they say in France.* This last gentleman seems to think he has got hold of a striking novelty ; he is mistaken.

glacé. See FRENCH WORDS.

glacial, glacier, glacis. The pro-

nunciations preferred by the OED are glā′shĭal, glā′sĭer, glā′sĭs.

glad(den). See -EN VERBS for the distinction.

gladiolus. The pronunciation recommended is glā′dyolus, or, if that is too difficult, gladĭ′olus ; for further discussion see FALSE QUANTITY. Pl. *-luses* or *-lī* ; see LATIN PLURALS.

gladsome. See -SOME.

glamour makes *glamorous* ; see -OUR- & -OR-.

glass. 1. *Glass-case*)(*glass case* ; the latter is better ; see HYPHENS. 2. *Glass eye*)(*glass-eye* ; a person has a g. e. ; a horse has g.-e. (a disease) ; see HYPHENS. 3. *Glassfuls*)(*glassesful* ; see -FUL.

glimpse. *Glance* & *g.* are synonyms only in a very loose sense ; the *g.* is what is seen by the glance, & not the glance itself ; you *take* or *give* a glance at something, but *get* a glimpse of it ; the following sentences are not English :—*Was there a member of either House who* gave a glimpse at *this schedule to see for himself whether all these documents deserved to be destroyed ?/A* glimpse at *the map will show why Turkey was not receiving munitions from Germany or Austria at that time.*

glissade. Pronounce glĭsah′d.

globe. In their primary sense *sphere, globe, orb,* & *ball,* do not differ, except with regard to the contexts they suit. And their particular applications (*a sphere of action, circumnavigate the globe, his sightless orbs, a ball of wool,* &c.) are too familiar to need setting forth.

glorify, glory vb. For inflexions see VERBS IN -IE, -Y, -YE, 6.

gloss. The two nouns (a, = comment ; b, = lustre) are of different origins, the first Greek, the other Teutonic ; but the meaning of the first, & of its derived verb *gloze*, has no doubt been considerably affected (see TRUE & FALSE ETYMOLOGY) by ignorance of this fact. Greek *glōssa* tongue had as secondary senses :

word or locution ; word needing explanation ; marginal word serving as explanation ; comment. The notions of falsity or misrepresentation or imputation or explaining away by which it (& still more *gloze*) is now so often coloured are not essential to it ; & though the development of explanation into misrepresentation is not unnatural without assistance, the confusion of the two nouns has had the effect that in popular as opposed to learned speech the first *gloss* is seldom without the suggestion of something sophistical.

glossary)(vocabulary. Both are partial dictionaries, & so far synonymous ; but the g. is a list to which a reader may go for explanation of unfamiliar terms (see GLOSS), while the v. is a stock in which he may hope to find words to express his meaning. The g. selects what is obscure, & the v. what is serviceable. *V.* has also the meaning of the whole stock of words used by a nation, by any set of persons, or by an individual. For *lexicon* &c. see DICTIONARY.

gloze. The original sense of simply commenting (see GLOSS) is obsolete.

gluey. So spelt ; see -EY & -Y.

glycerin(e). In pharmacy, manuals of chemistry, &c., -*in* is preferred ; in everyday use -*ine* is much commoner, & -*in* something of an affectation ; see -IN & -INE.

gnaw has p.p. *gnawed* or *gnawn*. The OED examples from the 17th & later centuries show -*ed* eleven times, & -*n* six ; half the six are 19th-c. (Jefferies, Southey, Browning), but the -*n* form may nevertheless be regarded as an archaism.

gnomic. See TECHNICAL TERMS.

go, n. Pl. *goes* ; see -O(E)S 2.

go, v. 1. *Goes without saying* is a gallicism (see GALLICISMS 5), but perhaps one of those that are nearing naturalization, ceasing to serve as meretricious ornaments, & tending to present themselves as first & not second thoughts. Still, the English

stalwart has ' needless to say ', ' need hardly be said ' or ' stated ', ' of course ', & other varieties to choose from.

2. *Go phut, fut*(*t*), or *foot*. The first spelling seems best, as suggesting by its obvious want of connexion with any English word that the point lies in the mere sound (that of a collapsing bladder).

gobe-mouches. The word is not common enough in English to be regarded as naturalized or subject to such liberties as we have legitimately taken with the spelling of *morale, locale, commissionaire*, & others. It should be treated as real French, printed in italics, & allowed its final -*s* in the singular (*a gobe-mouches* ; the literal sense is *a gorge-flies*) as well as in the plural.

godlily. See -LILY.

God's acre, as a name for churchyard or cemetery, though its beauty may be admitted, has not succeeded in establishing itself in English. It is not a phrase of home growth, but a translation from German ; & it is interesting that of four quotations for it in the OED only one shows it used simply without a reference to its alien nationality ; such a preponderance may be accidental, but remains significant.

Goidelic. See GAELIC.

golden. See -EN ADJECTIVES.

golden syrup. At table, as a synonym for treacle, this is a GENTEELISM ; at the grocer's, as denoting a particular quality of treacle, it is a good business name.

golf. The OED gives precedence to the natural pronunciation (gŏlf), & remarks :—' The Scotch pronunciation is (gŏf) ; the pronunciation (gŏf), somewhat fashionable in England, is an attempt to imitate this '.

golosh. See GALOSH.

goloptious, golup-. See FACETIOUS FORMATIONS.

G.O.M. See SOBRIQUETS.

goodness knows has two curiously divergent senses. In *Goodness knows* *who it can have been* it means God only knows, & I do not ; in *Goodness knows it wasn't I* it means God knows & could confirm my statement. Ambiguity is unlikely, but not impossible.

goodwill, good will, good-will. Except in the attributive use, which happens to be rare (*as a good-will token*, that is, as a token of good will), the choice should be between the unhyphened forms, since the accent falls on the second syllable ; see HYPHENS. *Good will* is required when the notion is virtuous intent &c., & *goodwill* is better when it is benevolence &c.

goody, -ie. The first is better ; see -EY, -IE, -Y.

goosy, -ey, -ie. See -EY, -IE, -Y.

gormandize, gourmandise. The first is the English verb, the second the French noun, for which see FRENCH WORDS.

gorse. Compare FURZE.

gossip makes *gossiped, gossiping* ; see -P-, -PP-.

gotten. See GET.

gouge. Pronounce gowj.

gourd. The OED gives precedence to the sound gōrd over goord.

gourmand)(gourmet. The first ranges in sense from greedy feeder to lover & judge of good fare ; the second from judge of wine to connoisseur of delicacies. The first usually implies some contempt, the other not. See FRENCH WORDS.

gourmandise. See GORMANDIZE.

governance has now the dignity of incipient archaism, its work being done, except in rhetorical or solemn contexts, by *government & control.*

governor, -nour. The second is almost obsolete ; see -OUR & -OR.

grace. For pronouns after *your g.* &c., see MAJESTY.

graduate makes *graduable* (see -ABLE 1), *graduator* (see -OR).

graece, -cè. See LATINE.

Gr(a)ecism, gr(a)ecize, gr(a)eco-, &c. The spelling *grec-* is recommended ; see Æ, Œ.

graffito. Pronounce grafē'tō ; pl. -*ti*, pronounce -tē.

grammar, syntax, &c. *G.* is the general term for the science of language. The following list gives the chief parts of it, in their logical (not actual) order of development :—

Phonology—How sounds are made & depicted.

Morphology—How words are made.

Accidence—How words are inflected.

Orthoepy—How words are said.

Orthography—How words are written.

Composition—How words are fused into compounds.

Semantics—How words are to be understood.

Syntax—How words are arranged in sentences.

Etymology—How words are tested by reference to their source.

Of these, *orthography, accidence, & syntax*, as the bare essentials for writing & reading, represent for most of us the whole of grammar ; & *morphology, orthoepy, phonology, & semantics*, are meaningless terms to the average person.

gram(me). There seems to be no possible objection to adopting the more convenient shorter form, except that the *-me* records the unimportant fact that the word came to us through French.

gramophone. A bad formation ; but incurable, & established.

GRAND COMPOUNDS. The separating, hyphening, or fusing, of the chief compounds is as follows in the OED :—

grandam(e) ; grand-aunt ; grandchild ; grand-dad ; grand-daughter ; Grand Duke ; Grand Duchess ; grandfather ; grandfatherly ; grandmamma ; Grand Master ; grandmother ; grandmotherly ; grand-nephew ; grand-niece ; grandpapa ; grandparent ; Grand Signior ; grandsire ; grandson ; grand-uncle.

grande passion, toilette. See FRENCH WORDS.

grangerize. Pronounce -ănj-.

granite. For *the g. city* see SOBRIQUETS.

granny. So spelt; see -EY, -IE, -Y.

granulate makes *-lable, -tor*; see -ABLE 1, -OR.

grapnel makes *-lled*; see -LL-, -L-.

gratify. For forms see VERBS IN -IE, -Y, -YE, 6.

gratin. See FRENCH WORDS.

gravamen. Pl. *-mina.*

grave, v. (carve &c.). P.p. *graven* or *graved*, the second much the commoner; but the whole verb is archaic except in particular phrases, esp. *graven image, graven on one's heart.*

gravel makes *-lled, -lly,* &c.; see -LL-, -L-.

gray. See GREY.

greasy. Pronounce -zĭ.

great. For the differences between *g., big,* & *large,* see BIG. For *the g. Commoner, the g. unwashed,* see SOBRIQUETS.

greatcoat, not *great-coat*; see HYPHENS.

greaten. See -EN VERBS; but it is now little used, though formerly common.

Grecian)(Greek. The first is now curiously restricted by idiom to architecture, facial outline, the Grecian bend & knot, & Grecian slippers. We seldom talk of *Grecian,* but usually of *Greek, history, fire, calends, lyrics, tyrants, Church, dialects, aspirations,* though *Grecian noses & brows, colonnades & pediments,* may still be heard of.

Grecism, grecize, Greco-, &c. For spelling see Æ, Œ.

GREEK G. There is something to be said for retaining the hard sound of g even before e, i, & y, in such Greek-derived words as are not in popular but only in learned, technical, or literary use. To those who know some Greek the sound of g in pĕ′dagŏjĭ (*paedagogy*) or jĕrontŏ′krasĭ (*gerontocracy*) or făjĭdē′na (*phage-*

daena) or sĭ′zĭjĭ (*syzygy*) or jĭnĭkŏ′lojĭ (*gynaecology*) either obscures the meaning, which they would catch with the aid of the hard g, or, if they happen to be prepared for it & so do not miss the meaning, is still repulsive. To those who do not know Greek, the sound of the words is indifferent, & they might allow the other party the indulgence of a harmless pedantry that affects after all but a few words. A list of deserving cases is given below with the pronunciations reminiscent of the Greek origin; in it are inserted some others in which the same principle is involved, but concerns instead of the sound of g some different point of pronunciation or spelling. In support of the proposed hard g it may be pleaded that the ch representing Greek chi is often or usually hard in similar cases (*diptych, trochee, trichinosis, tracheotomy, synecdoche, pachyderm, hemistich, catechism, polychaetan,* &c.).

Specimen words:—*anagoge* (-gō′gĭ); *anthropophagi* (-gī); *antiphlogistic* (-gĭs-); *antiphlogistine* (-gĭs-); *demagogical* (-gŏg-); *demagogy* (-gŏgĭ); *dialogist* (-gĭst); *epid(e)ictic* (-dĭk-); *gerontocracy* (gĕ-); *gynaeceum* (gĭnēkē′um); *gynaecocracy* (gī-); *hegemony* (hēgĕ-); *hemiplegia* (-lēg-); *isagogic* (-gŏg-); *laryngitis* (-gī-); *meningitis* (-gī-); *misogynist* (-ŏg-); *monogynist* (-ŏg-); *monologist* (-og-); *mystagogic* (-gŏg-); *osteomalacia* (-ăk-); *paedagogical* (pĕdagŏg-); *paedagogy* (pĕdagŏg-); *paragoge* (-gō′gē); *paral(e)ipsis* (-lĭp-); *paralogism* (-log-); *paranoia* (rather than *-noea*); *paraplegia* (-plēg-); *phagedaena* (făg-); *pharmaceutical* (-kŭt-); *pharyngitis* (-gī-); *philogynist* (-lŏg-); *phlogiston* (-log-); *polygynous* (-lĭg-); *proceleusmatic* (-ŏk-); *sceptic* &c. (sk-); *sciamachy* (sk-); *syringitis* (-gī-); *syzygy* (-ĭg-); *theodicy* (-kĭ).

greenness. So spelt.

greenth. See -TH NOUNS.

grey, gray. 'In Great Britain the form *grey* is the more frequent in use, notwithstanding the authority of

Johnson & later English lexico-graphers, who have all given the preference to *gray*'—OED.

greyhound is known to be uncon-nected with *grey*, though the mean-ing of its first part is doubtful ; see TRUE & FALSE ETYMOLOGY.

gridiron, griddle, grid. What the light of nature would suggest as to their relations would be that *grid* was the original word, *griddle* its diminutive, & *gridiron* a compound of it with *iron*. Inquiry seems to reveal, on the contrary, that *grid* is a mere curtailment of *gridiron*, which in turn has nothing to do with the word *iron*, but is a corruption of the earlier form *gredire*, a variant of *gredil* the source of *griddle*. The particular question is of no practical importance, but is here mentioned as illustrating well the kind of mis-take, sometimes dangerous, against which a knowledge of etymology may be a protection ; see TRUE & FALSE ETYMOLOGY.

griffin, griffon, gryphon. *Griffon* is the regular zoological form, i.e. as the name of a kind of vulture ; it is also the French dog name. For the monster *griffin* is the ordinary, & *gryphon* an ornamental spelling.

grimy. So spelt ; see -EY & -Y.
grippe, grisaille, grisette. See FRENCH WORDS.
grosbeak. Pronounce grōs-.
gros de Naples. See FRENCH WORDS.
grotto makes *grottoes*, see -O(E)S 1 ; & *grotto'd*, see -ED & 'D.
grouse, bird. See COLLECTIVES, 1.
grovel makes *-lling, -lled*, &c. ; see -LL-, -L-.
grow. For *a grown man* &c. see INTRANSITIVE P.P.
groyne. It appears that the word usually so spelt, & meaning beach-barrier, is of different origin from *groin* the part of the body or of a vault ; the separate spelling is there-fore useful.

gruel makes *-lling* &c. ; see -LL-, -L-.

Gruyère. See FRENCH WORDS.
gryphon. See GRIFFIN.
guano. Pronounce gwah- ; pl. *-os*, see -O(E)S 3.
guarantee, guaranty. Fears of choosing the wrong one of these two forms are natural, but needless. As things now are, *-ee* is never wrong where either is possible. As a verb, *-y* is called by the OED ' now rare, superseded by *-ee* ', & *-ee* should therefore always be used. As a noun, *-y* is correct in some senses, but *-ee* is established in all. Those who wish to avoid mistakes have in fact only to use *-ee* always.

For those who either wish to use words more accurately than their neighbours, or are curious about the history of the two forms, some further remarks are offered. The contexts in which *-y* may still be reasonably preferred are those in which the sense desired is rather the act or fact of giving security than the security given or its giver ; con-sequently, ' willing to enter into a *-y* ', ' contracts of *-y* ', ' a league of *-y* ', ' an act of *-y* ', ' treaties of *-y* ', ' be true to one's *-y* ', in all of which *-y* is a verbal noun & means guar-anteeing.

The history (if the OED suggestion is right) is as follows. French *garant* (person or thing that gives or serves as security) appears directly in Eng-lish as *warrant* ; *warranty* & *guar-anty* (the giving of or acting as warrant) are its derived verbal nouns. *Garant* also came indirectly (through Spanish *garante*) into Eng-lish as *garanté*, which having the *-e* pronounced came to be spelt *guarantee* ; the result was two differ-ent confusions : first with *guaranty* (the concrete with the abstract), which led to *guarantee*'s taking to itself the senses of *-y* as well as its own ; these it still keeps. Secondly with passive participles like *lessee*, by which *guarantee* is opposed to *guarantor* (though it is in one of its senses synonymous with it) & gets the sense, not much used, of person to whom security is given.

Guebre. The OED gives precedence to the pronunciation gē'ber.

guer(r)illa. The true spelling is with -rr-, not -r- ; & the true meaning is not a person, but a kind of fighting, *guerrillero* being the word for the person. But the -r- is four times as common as the -rr- in the OED quotations, & we should assert our right to spell foreign words as we choose when we have adopted them (cf. MORALE). And as to the meaning, the phrase *g. warfare* is now so firmly established in place of *g.* itself that the use of *g.* as a personal noun may be considered almost an inevitable BACK-FORMATION from it. The best course is to accept the spelling *guerilla*, & the sense (as old as Wellington's dispatches) irregular fighter.

guest. For *paying g.*, see GENTEELISMS.

guide makes *guidable*; see MUTE E.

guidon. Pronounce gī'dn.

g(u)ild. Though the form *guild* dates back only to 1600, it became so vastly predominant in the 17th & 18th cc. that the REVIVAL *gild* usually puzzles the reader for a moment, & should be abandoned as an affectation.

guillemot. Pronounce gǐ'lǐmŏt.

guilloche. Pronounce gǐlō'sh.

guillotine. For the parliamentary sense, see CLOSURE.

guimp. See GIMP.

guipure. See FRENCH WORDS.

gulden. Pronounce gōol-.

gulf, bay. Apart from the fact that each has some senses entirely foreign to the other, there are the differences (1) that *g.* implies a deeper recess & narrower width of entrance, while *b.* may be used of the shallowest inward curve of the sea-line & excludes a landlocked expanse approached by a strait ; & (2) that *b.* is the ordinary word, while *g.* is chiefly reserved as a name for large or notable instances.

gullible. For the form, which should have had -*able*, see -ABLE 2.

gulosity. A bad ANTI-SAXONISM.

gumma. Pl. -*as* or -*ata*.

gunwale, gunnel. The pronunciation is always, & the spelling not infrequently, that of the second.

gurgoyle. See GARGOYLE.

Gurkha. So spelt.

gusset makes *gusseted* &c. ; see -T-, -TT-.

gutta-percha. Pronounce -cha.

guttural. See TECHNICAL TERMS. Pronounce -ter-.

guy, vb. For inflexions see VERBS IN -IE, -Y, -YE, 5.

gybe. The nautical term is usually spelt thus.

gymnasium. Pl. -*ums* or -*a*; as the name of a German place of education, pl. *Gymnasien*.

gymp. See GIMP.

gynaeceum, gynaecocracy. See GREEK G.

gyp, as name of a college servant, belongs to Cambridge & Durham, not Oxford (cf. SCOUT).

gypsy, gipsy. In contrast with the words into which y has been introduced instead of the correct i, apparently from some notion that it has a decorative effect (*sylvan, syphon, syren, tyre, tyro,* &c.), there are a few from which it has been expelled for no better reason than that the display of two *y*s is thought an excessive indulgence in ornament. In *gypsy* & *pygmy* the first y is highly significant, reminding us that *gypsy* means Egyptian, & *pygmy* foot-high (Gk *pugmē* elbow to knuckles). It is a pity that they should be thus cut away from their roots, & the maintenance of the y is desirable. The OED's statement is :—' The prevalent spelling of late years appears to have been *gipsy.* The plural *gypsies* is not uncommon, but the corresponding form in the singular seems to have been generally avoided, probably because of the awkward appearance of the repetition of y '. See Y & I.

gyves. The old pronunciation was with the g hard, as indicated by a former spelling *gui-* ; but the g is now soft.

H

habergeon. Pronounce hă′berjn.

habiliments. See POLYSYLLABIC HUMOUR.

habilitate makes *habilitable* ; see -ABLE 1.

habit, v., has *-ited* ; see -T-, -TT-.

habitude. In some of its obsolete senses (relation *to*, intimacy or familiarity) the word was not exchangeable with *habit*. But in the senses that have survived it is difficult to find or frame a sentence in which *habit* would not do as well or better, the only difference being a slight flavour of archaism attaching to *habitude*. The following examples from the OED are chosen as those in which, more than in the rest, *habit* may be thought inferior to *habitude* ; *In the new land the fetters of habitude fall off./All the great habitudes of every species of animals have repeatedly been proved to be independent of imitation./They can be learned only by habitude & conversation.* The sense constitution or temperament, though not called obsolete in the OED, is so rare as to be negligible, & *habitude* may fairly be classed as a SUPERFLUOUS WORD.

habitué. See FRENCH WORDS.

hackneyed. So spelt.

HACKNEYED PHRASES. When *Punch* set down a heading that might be, & very likely has been, the title of a whole book, ' Advice to those about to marry ', & boiled down the whole contents into a single word, & that a surprise, the thinker of the happy thought deserved congratulations for a week ; he hardly deserved immortality, but he has—anonymously, indeed—got it ; a large percentage of the great British people cannot think of the dissuasive ' don't ' without remembering, &, alas ! reminding others, of him. There are thousands to whose minds the cat cannot effect an entrance unaccompanied by ' harmless necessary ' ; nay, in the absence of the cat, ' harmless ' still brings ' necessary ' in its train ; & all would be well if the thing stopped at the mind, but it issues by way of the tongue, which is bad, or of the pen, which is worse. King David must surely writhe as often as he hears it told in Sheol what is the latest insignificance that may not be told in Gath. How many a time has Galileo longed to recant the recanting of his recantation, as ' e pur si muove ' was once more applied or misapplied ! And the witty gentleman who equipped coincidence with her long arm has doubtless suffered even in this life at seeing that arm so mercilessly overworked.

The hackneyed phrases are counted by the hundred, & those registered below are a mere selection. Each of them comes to each of us at some moment in life with, for him, the freshness of novelty upon it ; on that occasion it is a delight, & the wish to pass on that delight is amiable ; but we forget that of any hundred persons for whom we attempt this good office, though there may be one to whom our phrase is new & bright, it is a stale offence to the ninety & nine.

The purpose with which these phrases are introduced is for the most part that of giving a fillip to a passage that might be humdrum without them ; they do serve this purpose with some readers—the less discerning—, though with the other kind they more effectually disserve it ; but their true use when they come into the writer's mind is as danger-signals ; he should take warning that when they suggest themselves it is because what he is writing is bad stuff, or it would not need such help ; let him see to the substance of his cake instead of decorating with sugarplums. In considering the following selection, the reader will bear in mind that he & all of us have our likes & our dislikes in this kind ; he may find pet phrases of his own in the list, or miss his pet abominations ; he should not on that account decline to accept a caution against the danger of the hackneyed phrase. Suffer a sea-change./Sleep the sleep of the just./The cups that cheer but not inebriate./Conspicuous by his absence./The feast of reason./The flow of soul./A chartered libertine./ A consummation devoutly to be wished./All that was mortal of ——./Which would be laughable if it were not tragic./But that is another story./Had few equals & no superior./But it was not to be./ Come into one's life./Has the defects of his qualities./Leave severely alone./Take in each other's washing./In her great sorrow./Metal more attractive./More sinned against than sinning./There is balm in Gilead./Fit audience though few./ My prophetic soul !/The scenes he loved so well./A work of supererogation./The irony of fate./The pity of it !/The psychological moment./ Curses not loud but deep./More in sorrow than in anger./Heir of all the ages./There's the rub./The curate's egg./To be or not to be./ Hinc illae lacrimae./Filthy lucre./ The outer man./The inner man./ Of the —— persuasion./Too funny for words./Get no forrader./My better half./Eagle eye./Young hopeful./Seriously incline./Snapper-up of unconsidered trifles./The logic of facts, events./The tender mercies of./Olive branches./Pity 'tis, 'tis true./Have one's quiver full./In durance vile./At the parting of the ways./Not wisely, but too well.

had. 1. *had*)(*had have*. There are two dangers—that of writing *had* . . . *have* where *had* is required, & that of writing *had* where *had* . . . *have* is required. The first has proved fatal in ' *Had she have done it for the Catholic Church, she would doubtless have been canonized as St Angela* ' ; & in ' *Had I have been in England on Monday, I should certainly have been present at the first performance* '. This is not uncommon, but is no better than an illiterate blunder, &

easily shown to be absurd. *Had she, had I*, are the inverted equivalents of *if she had, if I had* ; no-one would defend *if she had have done*, nor *if I had have been*, & it follows that *Had she done, Had I been*, are the only correct inverted conditionals.

The other wrong form is seen in ' *The country finds itself faced with arrears of legislation which for its peace & comfort had far better been spread over the previous years* '. It ought to be *had far better have been spread* ; but the demonstration is not here so simple. At the first blush one says : This *had* is the subjunctive equivalent of the modern *would have*, as in *If the bowl had been stronger My tale had been longer* ; i.e., *had far better been spread* is equivalent to *would far better have been spread*. Unluckily, this would involve the consequence that *You had far better done what I told you* must be legitimate, whereas we all know that *You had far better have done* is necessary. The solution of the mystery lies in the peculiar nature of the phrase *had better*. *You had better do it* ; *It had better be done* ; *You had better have done it* ; *It had better have been done* ; it will be granted at once that these are correct, & that *have* cannot be omitted in the last two ; but why ? Because the word *had* in this phrase is not the mere auxiliary of mood or tense, but a true verb meaning find ; *You had better do it* = You would find to-do-it better ; *You had better have done it* = You would find to-have-done-it better. The sense is a little strained with transfer to passives (*It had better have been done* = It would find to-have-been-done better), since it is in strictness the doer, & not the doing, that would find the result better ; but the transition is eased by such forms as *You had better have never been chosen*, & it must be remembered that in the evolution of an idiom the precise force of all the words concerned is seldom present to those who are evolving it. To return to the *arrears* sentence, those arrears would find to-have-been-spread-over-the-previous-years far better, i.e. would have been in a better state if they had been so spread. This reminds us that there is another possible way of arriving at the same sense : *The arrears would have been better if they had been spread* is compressible into *The arrears had been better spread* ; *better* then agrees with *arrears*, not with *to-have-been-spread* ; but that the writer did not mean to take that way is proved by the impossible order ' had better been ' instead of ' had been better ' (cf., in *Othello, Thou hadst been better have been born a dog*) ; he has perhaps combined the two possible forms, one idiomatic, & the other at least grammatical, into a third that is neither idiomatic, grammatical, nor possible. Another example like the ' arrears ' one is : *The object of his resistance was to force Great Britain to expend men & material in dealing with him which* had better been *utilized elsewhere.*

2. *Had* in parallel inverted clauses. *Had we desired twenty-seven amendments, got seven accepted, & were in anticipation of favourable decisions in the other twenty cases, we should think* . . . To write *Had we desired & were in anticipation* is wrong (see ELLIPSIS 6) ; to write *Had we desired & were we in anticipation*, though legitimate, is not only heavily formal, but also slightly misleading, because it suggests two separate conditions whereas there is only a single compound one. This common difficulty is best met by avoiding the inversion when there are parallel clauses ; write here *If we had desired & were in anticipation.*

haem-, hæm-, hem-. See Æ, Œ.

h(a)emorrhage, h(a)emorrhoids. Best spelt *hem-*, see Æ, Œ ; the *-rrh-* should be observed.

hagiarchy, hagiolatry, &c., have **hard g** ; see GREEK G.

hail, vb. *H. fellow well met* is now chiefly used as an adj., & should be, in that use, *hail-fellow-well-met.*

hair. *Hair shirt*, having the accent on *shirt*, should not be hyphened ; see HYPHENS.

half. **1.** *A foot & a h.*)(*One & a h. feet.* In all such mixed statements of integers & fractions (7¼ mill., 3¾ doz., 27¼ lb., &c.), the older & better form of speech is the first— *a foot & a h., seven millions & a quarter*, &c. In writing & printing, the obvious convenience of the second form, with figures instead of words, & all figures naturally placed together, has made it almost universal. It is a pity that speech should have followed suit ; the *1½ ft* of writing should be translated in reading aloud into *a foot & a half* ; & when, as in literary contexts, words & not figures are to be used, the old-fashioned *seven millions & a quarter* should not be changed into the *seven & a quarter millions* that is only due to figure-writing. But perhaps the cause is already lost ; we certainly cannot say *a time & a half as large* instead of *one & a half times.* For sing. or pl. after *one & a half*, use pl. noun & sing. vb.

2. *H. as much again* is a phrase liable to misunderstanding or misuse. *The train fares in France were raised this year 25%, & have again been increased by half as much again.* That should mean by a further 37½%, making altogether 62½% ; the reader is justified, though possibly mistaken, in suspecting that 12½ (half as much, not half as much again) was meant, making altogether 37½% instead of 62½. The phrase is better avoided in favour of explicit figures when such doubts can arise.

3. *Half-world = demi-monde.* See GALLICISMS. *The endless intrigues of the ' half-world '.*

4 *Better half* = wife. See HACKNEYED PHRASES.

5. *Half-weekly, -yearly*, &c. For the superiority of these to *bi-weekly, bi-annual*, &c., see BI-.

6. *Halfpennyworth* is best spelt & pronounced *ha'p'orth*, *hā'path*.

7. *H. of it is*, *h. of them are*, rotten. See NUMBER.

8. For *half-breed*, *half-caste*, see MULATTO 1 4.

hallelujah, halleluiah, alleluia. ' Now more commonly written as in the A.V. of the O.T. *hallelujah*'— OED. The mispronunciation -lōōlya should be avoided.

halliard. See HALYARD.

hallmark. For synonymy see SIGN.

halloo &c. The multiplicity of forms is bewildering ; there are a round dozen at the least—*hallo, halloa, halloo, hello, hillo, hilloa, holla, holler, hollo, holloa, hollow, hullo*. *Hello* may perhaps be put aside as American, *hillo* & *hilloa* as archaic, & *hollow* as confusable with another word. Then, with interjection, noun, & verb, to provide for, the best selection & arrangement from the remainder is perhaps: *Hullo* for the interjection & for the noun as the name of the interjection ; *halloo* for the noun as the name of a shout, & for the verb in dignified contexts ; *holla* (with past *holla'd*) for the verb in colloquial contexts. We thus get :—*Hullo ! is that you ?* ; *He stopped short with a Hullo* ; *The minstrel heard the far halloo* ; *Do not halloo until you are out of the wood* ; *He holla'd out something that I could not catch.* The forms *hallo(a), holler*, & *hollo(a)*, would thus be got rid of as well as *hello, hillo(a)*, & *hollow*.

halm. See HAULM.

halo. Pl. *-oes*, see -O(E)S 1 ; adj. *halo'd*, see -ED & 'D.

halyard, halliard, haulyard. The first spelling is best, not on etymological grounds, but as established by usage. It is true that the original form is *hallier* or *halyer*=thing one hales with, & that *-yard* is no better than a popular-etymology corruption (cf. AMUCK, & see DIDACTICISM) is vanity in more than one sense.

hamstringed, hamstrung. See the discussion of FORECAST(ED). With *h.*, no doubt of the right form is possible ; in *to hamstring*, *-string* is not the verb *string* ; we do not string the ham, but do something to the tendon called the hamstring ; the verb, that is, is made not from the two words *ham* & *string*, but from the noun *hamstring* ; it must therefore make *hamstringed*. On *bowstring* vb, where the notion that *-string* is verbal is not quite so obviously wrong, the OED says ' The past tense & p.p. ought to be *bowstringed*, but *bowstrung* is also found ' ; the case for *hamstringed* is still clearer.

hand. 1. *Hand & glove)(h. in glove*. Both forms are common ; the OED describes the second as ' later ', & *h. & glove* gives best the original notion, as familiar as a man's h. & glove are, while *h. in glove* suggests, by confusion with *h. in h.* (which is perhaps responsible for the *in*), that the h. & the glove belong to different persons. *H. & glove* is therefore perhaps better.

2. *At close h.* Those who follow the intricacies of German internal policy at close h. are able to . . . seems to be a mixture of *close at h.* & *at close quarters*.

3. *Get the better h.* If the Imperial troops got the better h., the foreigners would be in far greater danger similarly mixes *get the better of* with *get the upper h.*

4. *Handful* makes *-ls* ; see -FUL.

handicap makes *-pped* &c. ; see -P-, -PP-.

handsel, hansel. The OED gives precedence to the first ; *h.* makes *-lled* &c., see -LL-, -L-.

handy. For *h. man* see SOBRIQUETS.

hang. Past & p.p. *hanged* of the capital punishment & in the imprecation ; otherwise *hung*.

hangar. The aeroplane shed is so spelt, & pronounced -ngg-.

HANGING-UP. The indicating of your grammatical subject & leaving it to hang up & await your return from an excursion is not common in modern writing ; it belongs rather to the old days of the formal period. When a journalist of today does try his hand at it, he is apt, being a novice in the period style, to overdo things ; the subject & verb are here italicized for the reader's assistance :—' A stockbroker friend of the Z—s & of the Y—s, & then Lord Z— himself, passed through the box before the *interest* of the audience, which had languished as Lady Z— resumed her place at the Solicitors' table, & " Babs ", in her demure grey hat, with the bright cherries, & her deep white fichu, struggled through the crowd from the body of the Court in answer to the call of " Miss Z— X— ", *revived.*'

haply. See WARDOUR STREET.

happening(s). As all those whose reading days go back to the last century are probably aware, it is only in the last ten years or so that the word has set up for itself—i.e., has passed from a mere verbal noun that anyone could make for the occasion if he chose, but very few did choose, into a current noun requiring a separate entry in the dictionaries. To younger readers, who do not know how well we got on without ' happenings ' till about 1905, this may be (such is its vogue nowadays) a surprise. It is a VOGUE-WORD, which has had a startlingly rapid success, & which many of us hope to see wither away as quickly as it has grown. There is nothing to be said against it on the score of correctness ; but it is a child of art & not of nature ; may it prove sickly, & die young ! It comes to us not from living speech, but from books ; the writers have invented it, how far in SAXONISM (*event* is the English for it), & how far in NOVEL-TY-HUNTING, is uncertain. We cannot help laughing to see that, while the plain Englishman is content that *events* should *happen*, the Saxonist on one side requires that there should be *happenings*, & the anti-

Saxonist on the other that things should *eventuate*. The purpose of the long string of quotations appended is to suggest that the use of the word (still not common in talk) is an unworthy literary or journalistic affectation :—*The coal happenings of the last few hours are not without their significance./There was, first of all, one little happening which I think began the new life./The evening newspapers turn their backs & stop their ears upon the incessant march & clang of happenings./Mr William Moore (who has up to now played singularly little part in recent happenings) said . . ./So clear & vivid are his descriptions that we can almost see the happenings as he relates them./The silence from Tripoli continues, but we may be thankful that another day has passed without any serious happening elsewhere./There have been fears expressed of terrible happenings to crowded liners./Clearly there is strong resentment in the electorate at recent happenings./In his well written summary of happenings in the art world for the past year Mr . . ./From 1908 onwards we have lived in a chronic anxiety about the next happening.*

hara-kiri. Pronounce -kǐ'rǐ.

harass. So spelt ; cf. *embarrass.*

harassedly. A bad form ; see -EDLY.

harbour. See PORT.

hardly. 1. *Hardly*)(*hard*. 2. *Hardly* . . . *than*. 3. *Without h., no* — *hardly.*

1. *Hardly*)(*hard*. Except in the sense *scarcely*, the idiomatic adverb of *hard* is *hard*, not *hardly* : ' We worked hard, lodged hard, & fared hard '—DeFoe. It is true that in special cases *hardly* may or must be substituted, as in *What is made is slowly, hardly, & honestly earned*— Macaulay ; if Macaulay had not wanted a match for his two other adverbs in -*ly*, he would doubtless have written *hard* ; but there is now a tendency, among those who are not conversant enough with gram-

mar to know whether they may venture to print what they would certainly say, to amend *hard* into *hardly* & make the latter the normal wording; see UNIDIOMATIC -LY. It is even more advisable with *hard* than with other such adverbs to avoid the *-ly* alternative, since, as the following quotations show, a misunderstood *hardly* will reverse the sense :—*For attendance on the workhouse he receives £105 a year, which, under the circumstances, is hardly earned./It must be remembered that Switzerland is not a rich country, & that she is hardly hit by the war./ Upon Saturday the 25th there was another fluctuation of the line in this hardly contested & essential point./ The history, methods, & hardly won success of the anti-submarine campaign.*

2. *Hardly . . . than.* This, & *scarcely . . . than*, are among the corruptions for which ANALOGY is responsible; *hardly . . . when* means the same as *no sooner . . . than*, & the *than* that fits *no sooner* ousts the *when* that fits *hardly*. The OED marks the phrases (under *than*) with the ¶ of condemnation; but the mistake is so obvious that it should not need pointing out; it is, however, surprisingly common :—*The crocuses had hardly come into bloom in the London parks than they were swooped upon by London children./Hardly was the Marne salient obliterated, at such an expense to the enemy, than the Amiens salient followed./Hardly has Midsummer passed than municipal rulers all over the country have to face the task of choosing new mayors./ Scarcely had they arrived at their quarters on Ruhleben racecourse than their relations came to visit them.*

3. For *without hardly*, see WITHOUT
4. Equally bad is *no — h.*, as in *There is no industry h. which cannot be regarded as a key industry. There is h. any* is the English.

harem, -am, -um, -im. The established spelling & pronunciation are *harem, hār′em*; *haram, harram*, are antiquated; *hareem & harim*, pronounced harē′m, may still fairly be called DIDACTICISMS.

haricot. Pronounce -kō.

harmattan. See WIND, n.

harmony)(melody. When the words are used not in the general sense, which either can bear, of musical sound, but as the names of distinct elements in music, *h.* means 'the combination of simultaneous notes so as to form chords'—OED, & *m.* 'a series of single notes arranged in musically expressive succession' —OED.

harness. *Him that putteth on his h.* is a MISQUOTATION.

harquebus, arquebus. The OED gives precedence to the *h-* form. The word is the same as *hackbut* (= hook-gun), corrupted in passing through Italian by confusion with Latin *arcus* bow.

harry. For inflexions see VERBS IN -IE, -Y, -YE, 6.

hart, stag, buck, hind, doe. The following extracts from OED definitions will make the distinctions clear :—

Hart—The male of the deer, esp. of the red deer; a stag; *spec.* a male deer after its fifth year.

Stag—The male of a deer, esp. of the red deer; *spec.* a hart or male deer of the fifth year.

Buck—The he-goat, *obs.* . . . The male of the fallow-deer. (In early use perh. the male of any kind of deer.) . . . The male of certain other animals resembling deer or goats, as the reindeer, chamois. In S. Africa (after Du. *bok*) any animal of the antelope kind. Also, the male of the hare & the rabbit.

Hind—The female of the deer, esp. of the red deer; *spec.* a female deer in & after its third year.

Doe—The female of the fallow deer; applied also to the female of allied animals, as the reindeer . . . The female of the hare or rabbit.

hashish, -eesh. The OED gives precedence to the first spelling, with the stress on the first syllable.

hasten. The *t* should not be sounded ; see PRONUNCIATION, Silent t.

hate, v., makes *hatable* ; see MUTE E.

ha(u)lm, haunch, haunt. The OED gives precedence in all to the -aw- over the -ah- sound, & in the first to the spelling *haulm*.

hautboy, oboe. Pronounce hŏ′boi, ō′boi ; *oboe* is now the usual form.

hauteur. See FRENCH WORDS.

Havana. So spelt.

have. 1. *No legislation ever has or ever* will affect *their conduct.* For this common mistake see ELLIPSIS.

2. *Some Liberals would have preferred to have wound up the Session before rising.* For this mistake see PERFECT INFINITIVE 2.

3. *For if the Turks had reason to believe that they were meditating the forcible seizure of Tripoli, it was not to be expected that facilities for extending Italian influence* would readily have been *accorded. Would have been,* as often happens, is wrongly substituted for *would be.*

4. *What would have Beaconsfield thought ?* We need only substitute *he* for *Beaconsfield* to see that the right place for the subject in this type of question is between *would & have.*

5. For *does not have* &c. instead of *has not* &c., see DO 2.

haven. See PORT.

havoc, v., makes *-cking, -cked.*

hay. 1. *Look for a needle in a bottle of h.* This is the correct form of the phrase, *bottle* being a different word from the familiar one, & meaning truss ; but having become unintelligible it is usually changed into *bundle.*

2. *Hay fever*)(*hay-fever.* The first is better ; see HYPHENS.

HAZINESS. What is meant by this is a writer's failure to make a clear line between different members of a sentence or clause, so that they run into one another ; if he does not know the exact content of what he has set down or is about to set down, the word or words that he is now writing will naturally not fit without overlapping, or a gap will be left between them. This sounds so obvious that it may seem hardly worth while to devote an article to the matter & find a heading for it ; but even the more flagrant transgressions of the principle are so numerous as to make it plain that a warning is called for. Those more flagrant transgressions are illustrated first.

The effect of the tax is not likely to be productive of much real damage (overlapping ; part of *be productive of* has been anticipated in *effect* ; omit either *the effect of* or *productive of*)./*It is a pity that an account of American activities in aircraft production cannot yet be described* (overlapping ; *account* is contained in *described* ; omit *an account of,* or change *described* to *given*)./*A full account of this explosion & how it was brought about was narrated in* LAND & WATER *of April 11th* (like the last, but not quite so indefensible)./*The need of some effort, a joint effort if possible, is an urgent necessity for all the interests concerned* (*need & necessity* overlap)./ *A taste for arboriculture has always attracted a wealthy & cultured class* (*taste & attracted* overlap)./*It has not come up to the expectations which Grand Admiral von Tirpitz & von Holtzendorff himself had so confidently predicted* (they predicted results, only cherished or encouraged expectations)./*It is almost incomprehensible to believe at present that such works as his Five Orchestral Pieces can ever undergo such a total change of character as to . . .* (*to believe* is part of the content of *incomprehensible*)./*They have accounted for three times as many enemy casualties as they themselves have suffered* (cause enemy casualties ; account for enemies)./*The welfare of the poor & needy was a duty that devolved especially on those who had a seat in that House* (gap ; it is not the welfare, but the securing of the welfare, that is a duty)./*The Tories are not yet reconciled to the loss of power & privilege of which they were deprived by the last General Election* (*loss* & *deprived* overlap ; that *power & privilege* is not the antecedent of *which* is proved by the absence of the before *power*)./*The rather heavy expense of founding it could have been more usefully spent in other ways* (spend money ; incur expense)./*Hitherto the only way of tackling the evil was by means of prohibiting the exportation from certain places* (*way & means* overlap ; the only way of tackling was to prohibit ; it could only be tackled by means of)./*With the one exception of Sir Alfred Lyall, who chequers praise with somewhat tentative criticism, all these tributes are naturally eulogistic* (gap ; Sir Alfred is not a tribute).

Certain words seem to lend themselves especially to this sort of haziness, as AGO (*It is five years ago since I saw him*) ; REASON (*The only reason his wages have not been higher is because*—i.e. that—*the profits of the industry have been miserably low*), or with *due* (*The reasons of his success were due not only to . . .*) ; the illogical TOO (*We need not attach too much importance to . . .*) ; PREFERABLE with *more* (*the former alternative being, in our view, on every ground the more preferable*) ; BUT with superfluous negatives (*Who knows but what this memorial exhibition may not prove the starting point ?*) ; THAT conj. with questions or commands (*Crises arise so rapidly in these days that who can say what a few years may bring forth ?*/*Your correspondent suggests that if we lend money let us send it to . . .*) ; REMAIN with *continue* (*And yet through it all I continue to remain cheerful*) ; SEEM with *appear* (*These conclusions, it seems to me, appear to be reached naturally*).

Additional examples will be found under the words referred to by being printed in small capitals.

he. In spite of the frequency with which we all claim, by quoting *The Jackdaw of Rheims*, to know the grammar of *he* & *him*, an illegitimate *him* occasionally appears even in less colloquial placings than ' That 's him ' ; thus : *It might have been* him *& not President Wilson who said the other day that . . .* The tendency to use *he* where *him* is required is, however, much commoner in print. The mistake occurs when the pronoun is to stand in some out-of-the-way or emphatic position ; it looks as if writers, pulled up for a moment by the unusual, hastily muttered to themselves ' Regardless of grammar, they all cried " That 's him ! " ', & thanked God they had remembered to put ' he ' :—*The bell will be always rung by* he *who has the longest purse & the strongest arm.*/*The distinction between the man who gives with conviction &* he *who is simply buying a title.*/*And the severance then was followed four years later by the creation of yet another Secretary of State, &* he *for India.*/*One of its most notable achievements was the virtual ' warning off ' Newmarket Heath, though not in so many words, of a Prince of Wales,* he *who was afterwards George the Fourth.*/*The character of Bismarck is of an intrinsic greatness & completeness, which enables the spectator, even* he *who is most repelled by the results of Bismarck's appearance in the world, to . . .*

headmaster, headmistress, headquarters. Write each as a single unhyphened word, the accent being on the second element ; see HYPHENS, p. 246b.

heap. There are *heaps more to say, but I must not tax your space further. Are,* or *is* ? see NUMBER.

hearths. For pronunciation see TH & DH.

heave. Past & p.p. *heaved* or *hove*.

Hebe. See SOBRIQUETS.

hebraism, hebraist, hebraize, are the usual forms, not *hebrewism* &c.

Hebrew, Israelite, Jew, Semite. Persons to whom all these words are applicable are thought of by the modern Englishman as *Jews* ; if he uses in speech one of the other words instead of *Jew*, it is for some reason, known or possibly unknown to himself. He may be deliberately avoiding *Jew* for whichever of the others he first thinks of, & that either at the bidding of ELEGANT VARIATION or NOVELTY-HUNTING or facetiousness, or for the better reason that *Jew* has certain traditional implications (as usury, anti-Christianity) that are unsuited to the context. Or on the other hand he may be not avoiding *Jew*, but choosing one rather than another of the alternatives for itself : *Hebrew* suggests the pastoral & patriarchal, or again the possession of a language & a literature ; *Israelite*, the Chosen People & the theocracy, & him in whom was no guile ; *Semite*, the failure of most modern nations to assimilate their Jews. The fact remains that *Jew* is the current word, & that if we mean to substitute another for it, it is well to know why we do so. A remark or two of the OED bearing on the distinctions may be added :—(On *Hebrew*) ' Historically, the term is usually applied to the early Israelites ; in modern use it avoids the religious & other associations often attaching to Jew ' ; (on *Jew*) ' Applied comparatively rarely to the ancient nation before the Exile, but the commonest name for contemporary or modern representatives of the race ; almost always connoting their religion & other characteristics which distinguish them from the people among whom they live, & thus often opposed to *Christian*, & (esp. in early use) expressing a more or less opprobrious sense '.

hecatomb. Pronounce -ŏm.

hectic. *For a h. moment./M. Coué was taken up by some of our* h. *papers, & then dropped because he did not do what he never professed to do./ They have got pretty well used to the* h. *undulations of the mark.* The sudden blossoming of *h.* into a VOGUE-WORD, meaning excited, rap-

turous, intense, impassioned, wild, uncontrolled, & the like, is very singular. The OED (1901) shows hardly a trace of it, & explains its one quotation of the kind (' vehement & h. feeling ') as an allusion to the h. flush—no doubt rightly. Now a h. flush is one that is accounted for not, like other flushes, by exceptional & temporary vigour or emotion, but by the *habit* (Greek ἕξις) *of body* called consumption. The nearest parallel to this queer development seems to be the use of CHRONIC for severe, the only difference being that while that is confined to the entirely uneducated this has had the luck to capture the journalists.

hecto-. See CENTI-.

hedonist, Cyrenaic, epicurean, utilitarian. The first (literally, adherent of pleasure) is a general name for the follower of any philosophy, or any system of ethics, in which the end or the *summum bonum* or highest good is stated as (in whatever sense) pleasure.

The Cyrenaic (i.e. follower of Aristippus of Cyrene) is the hedonist in its natural acceptation—the pleasure-seeker who only differs from the ordinary voluptuary by being aware, as a philosopher, that the mental & moral pleasures are pleasanter than those of the body.

The epicurean (or follower of Epicurus), bad as his popular reputation is, rises above the Cyrenaic by identifying pleasure, which remains nominally his *summum bonum*, with the practice of virtue.

The utilitarian, by a still more surprising development, while he remains faithful to pleasure, understands by it not his own, but that of mankind—the greatest happiness of the greatest number.

It will be seen that the hedonist umbrella is a broad one, covering very different persons. Both the epicurean & the utilitarian have suffered some wrong in popular usage ; it has been generally ignored that for Epicurus pleasure consisted in the practice of virtue, & the utilitarian is unjustly supposed (on the foolish ground that what is useful is not beautiful & that beauty is of no use) to rate the steamroller higher than *Paradise Lost*. It may be worth while to quote the OED's statement of 'the distinctive doctrines of Epicurus :—1. That the highest good is pleasure, which he identified with the practice of virtue. 2. That the gods do not concern themselves at all with men's affairs. 3. That the external world resulted from a fortuitous concourse of atoms'.

hegemony. The pronunciation hēgĕ′monĭ is recommended ; see GREEK G.

hegira. Pronounce hĕ′jĭra (not ĭr′a).

heir. 1. For *h. of all the ages* see HACKNEYED PHRASES.

2. *H. apparent*)(*h. presumptive*. These phrases are often used, when there is no occasion for either & *heir* alone would suffice, merely because they sound imposing & seem to imply familiarity with legal terms. And those who use them for such reasons sometimes give themselves away as either supposing them to be equivalent or not knowing which is which. Thus : *By the tragedy of the death of the Crown Prince Rudolph in 1889 the Archduke Ferdinand became the Heir Apparent to the throne.* Rudolph, it is true, was heir apparent ; but by his death no-one could become h. a. except his child or younger brother (whereas Ferdinand was his cousin), since the Emperor might yet conceivably have a son who would displace anyone else. An h. a. is one whose title is indefeasible by any possible birth ; an h. p. is one who will lose his position if an h. a. is born. Mistakes are no doubt due to the double sense of the word *apparent*. Its old sense, retained in *h. a.*, & still possible elsewhere in literary use, but avoided for fear of confusion with the other & prevailing sense, is manifest or

unquestionable. But the current sense is almost the same as that of *seeming*, though with slightly less implication that the appearance & the reality are different ; *apparent* in this sense means much the same as *presumptive*, but in the other something very different ; hence the error.

heliotrope. Pronounce hē-.

helix. Pl. *helices*, pronounce -sēz.

hellebore. Pronounce hĕ′lĭbōr.

Hellene, Hellenic. The function of these words in English, beside *Greek*, is not easy to define ; but the use of them is certainly increasing. They were formerly scholars' words, little used except by historians, & by persons concerned not so much with Greeks in themselves as with the effects of Greek culture on the development of civilization in the world. With the modern spread of education, the words have been popularized in such connexions ; at the same time the national aspirations of Greek irredentists have called newspaper attention to pan-Hellenism & to the name by which the Greeks & their king call themselves ; so that the proportion of people to whom *Greek* means something, & *Hellene* & *Hellenic* nothing, is smaller than it was. Nevertheless, *Greek* remains the English word, into whose place the Greek words should not be thrust without special justification.

hello. See HALLOO.

helmet makes *-eted* ; see -T-, -TT-.

help, n. For *lady h.*, see GENTEELISMS.

help, v. *Than, & as,* one *can help, Don't sneeze more than you can help, Sneeze as little as you can h.*, are perhaps to be classed as STURDY INDEFENSIBLES. Those who refrain from the indefensible however sturdy it may be have no difficulty in correcting : *Don't sneeze more than you must, Sneeze as little as you can* or *may*. Out of *Don't sneeze if you can help it* is illogically developed *Don't sneeze more than you can help*, which would be logical, though not attractive, if *cannot* were written for *can*. And out of *Don't sneeze more than you can help* by a further blunder comes *Sneeze as little as you can help* ; a further blunder, because there is not a mere omission of a negative—' you can*not* help ' does not mend the matter—, but a failure to see that *can* without *help* is exactly what is wanted : the full form would be *Sneeze as little as you can sneeze little*, not *as you* either *can*, or *cannot*, *keep from sneezing*. The OED, which stigmatizes the idiom as ' erroneous ', quotes Newman for it :—*Your name shall occur again as little as I can help, in the course of these pages* (where *as little as may be* would have done, or, more clumsily, if the *I* is wanted, *as little as I can let it*).

helpmate)(helpmeet. The OED's remark on the latter is :—A compound absurdly formed by taking the two words *help meet* in Gen. ii. 18, 20 (' an help meet for him ', i. e. a help suitable for him) as one word.

hem-. See HAEM-, HAEMORRHAGE, & Æ, Œ.
hemiplegia. For pronunciation see GREEK G.
hemistich. Pronounce -k.
hempen. See -EN ADJECTIVES.
hendecasyllable, hendiadys, hephthemimeral. See TECHNICAL TERMS.
her. 1. Case. For questions of *her* & *she*, see SHE, & cf. HE.
2. For questions of *her* & *hers* (e. g. *Her & his tasks differ*), see ABSOLUTE POSSESSIVES.
3. For *her* & *she* in irresolute or illegitimate personifications (e.g. *The United States has given another proof of its determination to uphold* her *neutrality./Danish sympathy is writ large over all* her *newspapers*), see PERSONIFICATION.

Herculean. Pronounce herkū'lĭan. The normal sound of words in -*ean* is with the -e- accented & long ; so Periclē'an, Cytherē'an, Sophoclē'an, Medicē'an, Tacitē'an, pygmē'an, &

scores of others. Of words that vacillate between this sound & that given by shifting the accent back & making the -e- equivalent to ĭ, as in *Herculean,* most develop a second spelling to suit ; so *Caesarean* or *Caesarian, cyclopean* or *-pian, Aristotelean* or *-lian. Herculean,* like *protean,* changes its sound without a change of spelling ; & many people in consequence doubt how the words should be said. The sound herkū'lĭan is not a modern blunder to be avoided, but is established by long use. In the only three verse quotations given by the OED, -ē'an is twice impossible, & once unlikely :—

Robust but not Herculean—to the sight
No giant frame sets forth his common height.—*Byron*
Let mine out-woe me ; mine 's Hurculean woe.—*Marston*
    So rose the Danite strong,
Herculean Samson, from the harlotlap
Of Philistean Dalilah.—*Milton*

heredity. The word is now used, by good writers, only in the biological sense, i. e. the tendency of like to beget like. The extract below, where it has been substituted for *descent* solely because *descendant* is to follow, illustrates well what happens when zeal for ELEGANT VARIATION is not tempered by discretion :—*The Agha Khan . . . is unique because of his* heredity—*he is a lineal descendant of the Prophet Mohammed—though he is more noteworthy because of his being the leader of the neo-Moslems.*

heriot. For synonymy see TAX.
heritrix. For pl. see -TRIX.
hermit. For *the Hermit Kingdom* see SOBRIQUETS.
hero. Pl. -*oes* ; see -O(E)S 1.
heroic (of metres). See TECHNICAL TERMS.
herr. See MYNHEER.
herring. For *the h.-pond*, see WORN-OUT HUMOUR.
hers. See ABSOLUTE POSSESSIVES.

hesitance, hesitancy, hesitation.
The last has almost driven out the
others ; *-ce* may be regarded as
obsolete ; but *-cy* is still occasionally convenient when what is to be
expressed is not the act or fact of
hesitating, but the tendency to do
so. Two examples from the OED
will illustrate :—*She rejected it without hesitation./That perpetual hesitancy which belongs to people whose
intelligence & temperament are at
variance.*

heteroclite. See TECHNICAL TERMS.
hew. P.p. usu. *hewn*, sometimes
hewed.
hexameter. See TECHNICAL TERMS.
hiatus. See TECHNICAL TERMS.
Pl. *-uses*, see -US, & LATIN PLURALS.
Hibernian differs from *Irish(man)*
as GALLIC from *French*, & is of the
nature of POLYSYLLABIC HUMOUR.
hibernice, -cè. See LATINE.
hiccup makes *-uping, -uped*; see
-P-, -PP-. The spelling *-ough* is a
perversion of popular etymology,
& ' should be abandoned as a mere
error '—OED.

hide, vb. P.p. *hidden* or *hid*, the
latter still not uncommon.
hie makes *hieing* ; see MUTE E.
hierarchic(al). The long form is
the commoner.
highbrow. See MUGWUMP.
highly. 1. It should be remembered that *high* is an adv. as well as
highly, & better in many contexts ;
e.g., *It is best to pay your men high* ;
High-placed officials ; see UNIDIOM-
ATIC -LY. 2. Though *highly* in the
sense *to a high degree* is often unobjectionable (*a highly contentious
question* ; *highly farmed land*), it has
acquired, when used with adjectives
of commendation, a patronizing
taint (*a highly entertaining performance*) like *distinctly*, & is best avoided
in such connexions.

Highness. For pronouns after
Your H. &c., see MAJESTY.
hight. See WORN-OUT HUMOUR.
hillo(a). See HALLOO.
him. See HE.

hinc illae lacrimae. See HACK-
NEYED PHRASES.
hind, deer. For synonyms see HART.
hindermost. See -MOST.
Hindu, Hindoo. The OED gives
precedence to the former ; but it is
perhaps still permissible for the
old-fashioned to regard it as a
DIDACTICISM & keep to the anglicized
Hindoo.

hinge v. makes *hinging* ; see
MUTE E.
hippocampus. Pl. *-pi*, pron. -pī.
hippogriff, -gryph. The first spelling is recommended ; cf. GRIFFIN.
hippopotamus. Pl. *-muses* better
than *-mi*.
hire, v., makes *hirable* ; see MUTE E.
his. 1. *A graceful raising of* one's
hand to his *hat*. For the question
between *his* & *one's* in such positions, see ONE.
2. *The member for Morpeth has long
been held in the highest respect by all
who value sterling character & whole-
hearted service in the cause of* his
fellows. For this type of mistake
see PRONOUNS.

historic (in syntax). See TECH-
NICAL TERMS.
historic(al). The DIFFERENTIATION
between the two forms has reached
the stage at which it may fairly be
said that the use of one in a sense
now generally expressed by the
other is a definite backsliding. The
ordinary word is *historical* ; *historic*
means memorable, or assured of
a place in history ; *historical* should
not be substituted for it in that
sense ; the only other function
retained by *historic* is in the grammarians' technical terms *historic
tenses, moods, sequence, present*, &c.,
in which it preserves the notion
appropriate to narration of the past
of which it has been in general use
robbed by *historical*.

historicity. The earliest OED example of this ugly word is dated
1880 ; but, being effective in impart-
ing a learned air to statements that
are to impress the unlearned, it has
had a rapid success, & is now com-

mon. It has, however, a real use as a single word for the phrase *historical existence*, i.e. the having really existed or taken place in history as opposed to mere legend or literature. To this sense, in which it makes for brevity, it should be confined. *The historicity of St Paul* should mean the fact that, or the question whether, St Paul was a real person; the following quotation shows the word in a quite different sense; in that sense it would not have been worth inventing (why not *accuracy*?); & as soon as it has two or more senses liable to be confused, it has lost the only merit it ever had—that of expressing a definite compound notion unmistakably in a single word :—*He is compelled to speak chiefly of what he considers to be exceptions to St Paul's strict historicity & fairness ; & he tells us that he is far from intending to imply that the Apostle is usually unhistorical or unfair.*

hither, described by the OED as ' now only literary ', is even in literature, outside of verse, almost disused. It is still tolerable, perhaps, in one position, i.e. as the first word in an inverted sentence following a description of the place referred to —*Hither flocked all the . . .* Elsewhere, it produces the effect of a FORMAL WORD, being used mainly by the unpractised writers who bring out their best English when they write to the newspapers. The same is true of *thither* ; but, as often happens with stereotyped phrases, *hither & thither* retains the currency that its separate elements have lost.

hoarhound. See HOREHOUND.
hobbledehoy, hobbadehoy. The elements of the word being quite uncertain the best spelling is whichever is most used; that is *hobble-dehoy,*& the OED gives it precedence.

hob-nob makes *-bbed, -bbing* ; see -B-, -BB-.
hock, hough. *Hough,* the older spelling, is now pronounced like *hock,* which ' has largely superseded '

it (OED) in spelling also ; it is better to abandon the old spelling.

hocus. For inflexions see -SS-, -S-.
hodge-podge. See HOTCHPOT(CH).
hoe, v., makes *hoeable, hoeing* ; exceptionally, see MUTE E.
hoi polloi. These Greek words for the majority, ordinary people, the man in the street, the common herd, &c., meaning literally ' the many ', are equally uncomfortable in English whether *the* (= *hoi*) is prefixed to them or not. The best solution is to eschew the phrase altogether.

holey, holy. See -EY & -Y.
holily. See -LILY.
holla, holler, hollo(a), hollow. See HALLOO.
holy. Write *holy day* or *holy-day* according to an accent is or is not desired on *day* ; this depends on context.

home, n., makes *homy,* not *homey* ; see -EY & -Y.
home, vb, makes *homing* ; see MUTE E.
homelily. See -LILY.
homely. For ' to use a h. phrase ' see SUPERIORITY.
homoeopathic. Spell thus ; see Æ, Œ. For the use of the word as a substitute for *tiny, small, diminutive,* &c., see PEDANTIC HUMOUR, WORN-OUT HUMOUR.

Homeric. For *H. laughter,* see LAUGHTER.
homonym, synonym. Any confusion between the two is due to the fact that *s.* is a word of rather loose meaning. Broadly speaking, homonyms are separate words that happen to be identical in form, & synonyms are separate words that happen to mean the same thing. *Pole,* a shaft or stake, is a native English word ; *pole,* the terminal point of an axis, is borrowed from Greek ; the words, then, are two & not one, but being identical in form are called homonyms ; on the other hand *cat,* the animal, & *cat,* the flogging instrument, though they are identical in form & mean different things, are

not separate words, but one word used in two senses ; they are therefore not homonyms. An example of true synonyms, i. e. of separate words exactly equivalent in meaning & use, is seen in *furze* & *gorse* ; such synonyms are rare, & the word is applied more frequently to pairs or sets in which the equivalence is partial only ; see SYNONYMS.

homophone. See SYNONYMS.

hon. In the use of this prefix (*Hon.* or *the Hon.*), which requires the person's Christian name or initial, not his surname alone (*the Hon. James* or *J. Brown*, not *the Hon. Brown*), a common mistake is to suppose that the Christian name is unnecessary before a double-barrelled surname, as in *The Court, composed of Mr Justice A. T. Lawrence, the Hon. Gathorne-Hardy, & . . .* The same remarks apply to the prefixes *Rev.* & *Sir.* With *Hon.*, & *Rev.*, if the Christian name or initial is unknown, *Mr* at least should be inserted (*the Rev. R. Jones* or *the Rev. Mr Jones*, not *the Rev. Jones*, nor *the Rev. Pryce-Jones*).

honest. For *the honest broker* see SOBRIQUETS.

honeyed, honied. The first is best.

honorarium. Pl. *-iums* or *-ia.* The OED gives precedence to the pronunciation with a sounded h ; this, & the pl. *-ia*, seem proper tributes to the word as a distinguished foreigner.

hono(u)r. 1. Keep the -u- ; but see -OUR & -OR. 2. *A custom more honoured in the breach than the observance.* Whoever will look up the passage (*Hamlet* I. iv. 16) will see that it means, beyond a doubt, a custom that one deserves more honour for breaking than for keeping ; but it is often quoted in the wrong & very different sense of a dead letter or rule more often broken than kept. So : *The Act forbids entirely the employment of boys . . . ' by way of trade or for the purpose of gain '. Therefore, unless the Act be honoured more in its*

breach than in its observance, the cherubic choirboy . . . is likely . . . to be missing from his accustomed place in cathedral & church. For similar mistakes, see MISAPPREHENSIONS.

hoof. Pl. *-fs*, sometimes *-ves* ; see -VE(D).

hope. In the OED, the examples illustrating the use of the verb are nearly 60 in number ; of all these not a single one bears the slightest resemblance or gives any hint of support to any of the sentences here to be quoted. This seems worth mention as showing how very modern these misuses are ; in 1901, the date of H in the OED, they could apparently be ignored ; that they were not quite non-existent even then is shown by the fact that one of the offenders quoted below is Emerson, but it may be safely assumed that they were rare ; nowadays, the newspapers are full of them.

First, three examples of the monstrosity sufficiently discussed in the article DOUBLE PASSIVES : — *No greater thrill can* be hoped to be enjoyed *by the most persistent playgoer of today than . . ./What is* hoped to be gained *by the repetition of these tirades against Liberalism just now I cannot conceive./There was a full flavour about the Attorney-General's speech against him in the Assize Court at Launceston which cannot* be hoped to be revived *in these indifferent times.*

Secondly, ANALOGY has been at work, &, as *hope* & *expect* are roughly similar in sense, the construction proper to one (*I expect them to succeed*) is transferred to the other (*I hope them to succeed*, whence *They are hoped to succeed*) with which it is far from proper ; so :—*I need not say, how wide the same law ranges, & how much it* can be hoped to *effect./ In the form of a bonus intended to cover the rise,* hoped to be *temporary, in the cost of living./A luncheon at which the King* is hoped to be *present.* But the notion that, because *hope* means hopefully expect, therefore it can have the construction that that phrase might have is utterly at variance with the facts of language.

Thirdly, writers have taken a fancy to playing tricks with ' it is hoped ', & working it into the sentence as an essential part of its grammar instead of as a parenthesis ; the impersonal *it* is omitted, & *is* (or *are*) *hoped* is forced into connexion with the subject of the sentence, with deplorable results. See also IT. In the first two examples, *it* should be reinstated ; in the third, read *are not even yet, it may be hoped, at an end* :—*The actual crest of the Villeneuve hill was not reached, as was hoped might be possible./The final arrangements for what is hoped will prove a ' monster demonstration'./Who has held two of the most distinguished positions under the Crown, & whose self-sacrificing services for the Empire may be hoped even yet not to be at an end./Which ended in what is hoped is only a temporary breakdown./The chief actors in what is hoped will prove the final act./During what is hoped will prove to be a more active autumn.*

hopeful. For *young h.* see HACK-NEYED PHRASES.

horehound, hoarhound. Though ' the analogical spelling is hoar- ' (i.e. the word is connected with *hoary*), ' this is much less usual in England than hore- '—OED.

horrible)(horrid. The distinctions between the two are (1) that *horrid* is still capable in poetical & literary use of its original sense of bristling or shaggy ; & (2) that while both are much used in the trivial sense of disagreeable, *horrible* is still quite common in the graver sense inspiring horror, which *horrid* tends to lose, being now ' especially frequent as a feminine form of strong aversion '—OED.

horrify. For inflexions see VERBS IN -IE, -Y, -YE, 6.

hors concours, hors de combat, hors-d'œuvre. See FRENCH WORDS.

horse makes *horsy*, not *horsey* ; see -EY & -Y.

hose (stockings) is archaic, or a shop name, or rarely a GENTEELISM.

hospitable. The stress should be on *hos-*, not on *-pit-* ; for doubtful cases of such stress see RECESSIVE ACCENT ; but the stress on *hos-* is as old as Shakspere & Drayton (lines quoted in OED).

hospitaller, not *-aler* ; see -LL-, -L-.

hostler. See OSTLER.

hotchpot, hotchpotch, hodgepodge, hotpot. The first is nearest to the original form (Fr. *hochepot* = shakepot) ; 2, 8, & perhaps 4, are successive corruptions dictated by desire for expressiveness or meaning when the real sense was forgotten. *Hotchpotch* being the prevailing form, it would be best if the two later ones might perish ; *hotchpot*, being a technical legal term, would naturally resist absorption in *hotchpotch*, but might be restricted to its special use.

hotel. The old-fashioned pronunciation with the *h* silent (cf. *humble, humour, humorous, honorarium*) is certainly doomed, & is not worth fighting for.

hough. See HOCK.

houri. Pronounce hoor'ĭ or howr'ĭ.

houseful. Pl. *-ls* ; see -FUL.

housewife. The shortened pronunciation (hŭ'zĭf or hŭ'zwĭf), which is almost invariable for the sewing-case, is still fairly common also for the mistress or domestic manager ; displacement of the traditional hŭ'zĭf or hŭ'zwĭf by how'swĭf was in part brought about in the 16th c., when *housewife* & *hussy* were still realized to be the same word, by the feeling that a distinction between the two was due to the reputable matron.

housewifery. Pronounce hŭ'zĭfrĭ, hŭ'zwĭ'frĭ, or how'swĭfrĭ ; see HOUSE-WIFE.

hover. The OED gives precedence to the pronunciation hŭ'ver.

howbeit, according to the OED, is archaic in one of its senses (nevertheless) & obsolete in the other (although). The archaic has its place in modern writing, the obsolete has not ; see ARCHAISM. Those who, without much knowledge of the kind of literature in which archaism is in place, are tempted to use this word should carefully note the distinction. It is often a delicate matter to draw it aright ; but there is little doubt that the OED has done so here.

however. Several small points require mention. 1. *however, how ever, how . . . ever.* In everyday talk, *how ever* is common as an emphatic form of the interrogative *how* (*How ever can it have happened ?*) ; it should not appear in print except when dialogue is to be reproduced, being purely colloquial ; this does not apply to cases where *ever* has its full separate sense of at any time or under any circumstances, but it is then parted from *how* by some other word or words. *We believe that before many years have passed employers & employed alike will wonder* however *they got on without it* ; this should have been *how they ever got on* ; the other order is an illiteracy in itself, & the offence is aggravated by the printing of *however* as one word. See EVER.

2. *But however*)(*but . . . however.* *But it must be remembered, however, that the Government had no guarantee.*/ *But these schemes, however, cannot be carried out without money.* And for other examples of this disagreeable but common redundancy see BUT 5 ; either *but* or *however* suffices ; one should be taken, & the other left ; sitting on two stools is little better than falling between them. It is noteworthy that *But however* with nothing intervening, which would seem the most flagrant case, is on the contrary better than the form illustrated above ; the juxtaposition suggests that there is more in it than mere carelessness, & that *however* has the definite sense in spite of all—is in fact a full adverb & not a conjunction, & therefore strictly defensible as not trespassing on *but*'s

ground. The usage is colloquial only.

3. *However too late.* *These extravagant German counter-attacks in mass on the Cambrai front,* however, *materially helped the French operations in Champagne.* The excuse for such late placing of the conjunction —that *these . . . front* is in effect a single word—is sound only against a suggestion that it should be placed after *attacks* ; it, or *Nevertheless*, or *All the same*, could have stood at the head of the sentence. The undue deferring of *however* usually comes from the same cause as here, i.e. the difficulty of slipping it in where it interrupts a phrase, & should be recognized as a danger to be avoided.

4. *However too early.* It should be borne in mind that the placing of *however* second in the sentence has the effect, if the first word is one whose meaning is complete (e.g. *He* as compared with *When*), of throwing a strong emphasis on that word. Such emphasis may be intended, or short of that may be harmless ; but again it may be misleading ; emphasis on *he* implies contrast with other people ; if no others are in question, the reader is thrown out. *The Action Commission wished to get permission for meetings & had telephonic communication with Wallraff, who declared that he would not negotiate with the workmen.* He, however, *would receive the Socialist members of Parliament.* The only right place for *however* there is after *would*, the contrast being not between him & anyone else, but between *would not* & *would*. The mistake is made with other conjunctions of the kind usually cut off by commas, but is especially common with *however* & *therefore*.

hue. For synonymy see TINT.

hugeous. Those who use the form perhaps do so chiefly under the impression that they are satirizing the ignorant with a non-existent word, as others of their kind do with *mischevious* or *underconstumble* or *high-strikes* for *mischievous, understand, & hysterics*. It is in fact a good old word, & corresponds rather to *vasty & stilly* by the side of *vast & still*; but it is practically obsolete, &, as its correctness robs it of its facetious capabilities, it might be allowed to rest in peace.

huguenot. Pronounce hū′genŏt.
hullo. See HALLOO.
human makes *humanness*.
humanist. The word is apt to puzzle or mislead, first, because it is applied to different things & a doubt of which is in question is often possible, & secondly because in two of these senses its relation to its parent word *human* is clear only to those who are acquainted with a long-past chapter of history. The newspaper reader sometimes gets the impression that *humanist* means a great classical scholar; Why? he wonders, & passes on. Another time he gathers that a humanist is a sceptic or an agnostic or a freethinker or something of that sort, you know; again he wonders why, & passes on. Another time he feels sure that a humanist is a Positivist or Comtist, & here at last, since he knows that Comte founded the Religion of Humanity, there seems to be some reason in the name. And lastly he occasionally realizes that his writer is using the word in the sense in which he might have invented it for himself—one for whom the proper study of mankind is man, the student, & especially the kindly or humane student, of human nature.
The original humanists were those who in the Dark Ages, when all learning was theology, & all the learned were priests or monks, rediscovered pre-Christian literature, turned their attention to the merely human achievements of Greek & Roman poets & philosophers & historians & orators, & so were named *humanists* as opposed to the divines; hence the meaning classical scholar. But this new-old learning

had, or was credited with, a tendency to loosen the hold of the Church upon men's beliefs; hence the meaning free-thinker. The third meaning—Comtist—was a new departure, unconnected in origin with the first two, though accidentally near one of them in effect, but intelligible enough on the face of it. As to the fourth, it requires no comment.

humanity. For *the Humanities*, or *Litterae humaniores*, as an old-fashioned name for the study of classical literature, see HUMANIST.

humanize has *-zable*; see MUTE E.
humble-bee. See BUMBLE-BEE.
humbug. The verb makes *-gged, -gging*, &c.; see -G-, -GG-.
humerus. Pl. *-ri* (-rī).
humiliate makes *humiliable*; see -ABLE 1.
humour, n., makes *humorous*, but *humourist*; see -OUR- & -OR-. *Humour* is still often or usually pronounced without the h sound; the derivatives now being rarely without it, *humour* itself will probably follow suit. The spelling *-our* is better than *-or*; but see -OUR & -OR.

humour, wit, satire, sarcasm, invective, irony, cynicism, the sardonic. So much has been written upon the nature of some of these words, & upon the distinctions between pairs or trios among them (wit & humour, sarcasm & irony & satire), that it would be both presumptuous & unnecessary to attempt a further disquisition. But a sort of tabular statement may be of service against some popular misconceptions. No definition of the words is offered, but for each its motive or aim, its province, its method or means, & its proper audience, are specified. The constant confusion between sarcasm, satire, & irony, as well as that now less common between wit & humour, seems to justify this mechanical device of parallel classification; but it will be of use only to those who wish for help in determining which is the word that they really want.

	MOTIVE or AIM	PROVINCE	METHOD or MEANS	AUDIENCE
humour	Discovery	Human nature	Observation	The sympathetic
wit	Throwing light	Words & ideas	Surprise	The intelligent
satire	Amendment	Morals & manners	Accentuation	The self-satisfied
sarcasm	Inflicting pain	Faults & foibles	Inversion	Victim & bystander
invective	Discredit	Misconduct	Direct statement	The public
irony	Exclusiveness	Statement of facts	Mystification	An inner circle
cynicism	Self-justification	Morals	Exposure of nakedness	The respectable
The sardonic	Self-relief	Adversity	Pessimism	Self

hundred. See COLLECTIVES 3.

huntress. See FEMININE DESIGNATIONS.

hurricane. See WIND, n.

hurry, vb. For inflexions see VERBS IN -IE, -Y, -YE, 6.

hussy, huzzy. In the OED examples, the spelling with -*ss*- occurs nearly five times as often as that with -*zz*-. The traditional pronunciation (hŭ′zĭ, cf. HOUSEWIFE) is giving way before hŭ′sĭ, which, with the assistance of the spelling, will no doubt prevail.

hyaena. See HYENA.

hybrid. See MULATTO 1.

HYBRID DERIVATIVES are words formed from a stem or word belonging to one language by applying to it a suffix or prefix belonging to another. It will be convenient to class with these the words, abortions rather than hybrids, in which all the elements belong indeed to one language, but are so put together as to outrage that language's principles of formation. English contains thousands of hybrid words, of which the vast majority are unobjectionable. All such words as *plainness* or *paganish* or *sympathizer*, in which a Greek or Latin word has become English & has afterwards had an English suffix attached to it, are hybrids technically, but not for practical purposes. The same is true of those like *readable, breakage, fishery, disbelieve*, in which an English word has received one of the foreign elements that have become living prefixes or suffixes ; -*able*, -*age*, -*ery*,

dis-, though of Latin-French origin, are all freely used in making new forms out of English words.

At this point it may be well to clear the ground by collecting a small number of the words that may be accused of being hybrids in either of the senses explained above—i.e. as made of heterogeneous elements, or as having their homogeneous elements put together in an alien fashion :—*amoral, amusive, backwardation, bi-daily, bureaucracy, cablegram, climactic, coastal, colouration, dandiacal, floatation, funniment, gullible, impedance, pacifist, racial, sendee, speedometer*. An ill-favoured list, of which all readers will condemn some, & some all. It will not be possible here to lay down rules for word-formation, which is a complicated business ; but a few remarks on some of the above words may perhaps instil caution, & a conviction that word-making, like other manufactures, should be done by those who know how to do it; others should neither attempt it for themselves, nor assist the deplorable activities of amateurs by giving currency to fresh coinages before there has been time to test them.

A great difficulty is to distinguish, among the classical suffixes & prefixes, between those that are, though originally foreign, now living English, & those that are not. Of the former class -*able* & *dis*- have already been mentioned as examples ; to the latter -*ation*, -*ous*, -*ic*, & *a*- (not), may be confidently assigned. But others are not so easy to class; how about -*nce* (-*ance* & -*ence*)? An electrician, in need of a technical term, made the word *impedance*. ' I want a special word ' we may fancy him saying ' to mean much the same as *hindrance*, but be sacred to electricity; I will make it from *impede*; hinder, hindrance; impede, impedance '. If he knew nothing about word-formation, that was natural; but also he might easily know something of it, without knowing enough. 1. ' *Impede* & -*nce* are both from Latin; then it cannot be wrong to combine them '; so he would say; the defect in it is that they must be *rightly* put together; he ought to have written *impedience* (cf. *expedient*). 2. ' If -*ance* is a living suffix, it can be put straight on to a verb that is now, even if not by origin, English; & *hindrance*, *forbearance*, *furtherance*, & *riddance*, all from English verbs, are enough to prove -*ance* a living suffix.' The fallacy lies in the last sentence; it is true that -*ance* was, but not true that it is, a living suffix; suffixes, like dogs, have their day, & to find whether -*ance*'s day is now we need only try how we like it with a few English verbs of suitable sense, say *stoppance* (cf.*quittance*), *hurriance* (cf. *dalliance*), *dwellance* (cf. *abidance*), *keepance* (cf. *observance*).

Another suffix that is not a living one, but is sometimes treated as if it was, is -*al*; & it will serve to illustrate a special point. Among recent regrettable formations are *coastal*, *creedal*, *racial*, & TIDAL. Now, if -*al* were to be regarded as a living suffix, it would be legitimate to say that *coast* & *creed* are now English words, & could have the suffix added straight to them; but if it is tried with analogous English words (*shore*, *hill*, *belief*, *trust*), the resulting adjectives *shoral*, *hillal*, *beliefal*, & *trustal*, show that it is not so. The defence, then, would be different—that *coast* & *creed* are of Latin origin, & so fit for the Latin suffix. But then comes in the other requirement—that if both elements

are Latin, they should be properly put together; *coastal(is)* & *creedal(is)* are disqualified at sight for Latin by the -*oa*- & -*ee*-; *costal* & *credal* would have been free from that objection at least. The fault in *racial* is not that the Latin word is made unrecognizable by the spelling, but that there is no Latin word from which *race* is known to come. Words like *coastal* may be described as not hybrids but spurious hybrids; & whether the qualification aggravates or lessens the iniquity is a question too hard for a mere grammarian; at any rate, the making of words that proclaim themselves truly or falsely as hybrids by showing a classical suffix tagged on to some purely English vowel combination is a proof of either ignorance or shamelessness. The best collection of such curiosities is perhaps the words ending in -*meter*, among which are *creamometer*, *floodometer*, & *speedometer*, all with impossible English vowels. The wordmakers have missed an opportunity with *meter*; there is the English *meter* (from *to mete*) as in *gas-meter* & *water-meter*, as well as the unconnected Greek *metron*; why could they not have given us *flood-meter*, *cream-meter*, & *speedmeter*, instead of our present monstrosities? The classical connecting vowel -*o*- is quite out of place at the end of an English word; *gasometer* gave the analogy, but *gas*, being a word native in no language, might fairly be treated as common to all, including Greek, whereas *flood* & *speed*, with their double vowels, were stamped as English.

It will not be worth while to pursue the matter further, nor to explain in detail why each word in the above list is a correct or incorrect formation, since complete rules cannot be given. The object of the article is merely to suggest caution. When any word in its dictionary place is referred here without comment (*see Hybrid derivatives*), it is to be understood that it is, in the author's opinion, improperly formed for a reason connected with the making of words from different languages, but not necessarily specified in so slight a sketch as this. The words in the list that have not been already referred to are now repeated with the briefest possible indication of the objections that are rightly or wrongly made to them : Cl., E, F, Gk, L, = classical, English, French, Greek, Latin ; h. = hybrid ; w. f. = wrongly formed. *Amoral*, Gk+L h. ; *amusive*, non-L+L h. ; *backwardation*, E+L h. ; *bi-daily*, L+E h. ; *bureaucracy*, spurious h. ; *cablegram*, E+Gk h. ; *climactic*, w. f. ; *colouration*, spurious h. ; *dandiacal*, E+Cl. h. ; *floatation & funniment*, E+L h. ; *gullible*, E+L h. ; *pacifist*, w. f. ; *sendee*, E+F h.

hybridize makes *-zable*; see MUTE E.

hyena, -aena. The OED gives precedence to the first ; see also Æ, Œ.

hygiene, hygienic. Pronounce hī'-jīĕn, hījīĕ'nĭk. As the form of *hygiene* often puzzles even those who know Greek, it is worth while to mention that it is the French transliteration of Gk *hugieinē (tekhnē)* (art) of health.

hypallage. See TECHNICAL TERMS ; pronounce *-ajĭ.*

hyperbaton. See TECHNICAL TERMS. Pl. *-ta, -ns.*

hyperbole. See TECHNICAL TERMS. Pronounce hĭper'bolĭ.

hypermetre. See TECHNICAL TERMS.

HYPHENS. The chaos prevailing among writers or printers or both regarding the use of hyphens is discreditable to English education. Since it sufficiently proves by its existence that neither the importance of proper hyphening nor the way to set about it is commonly known, this article may well begin with a dozen examples, all taken faithfully from newspapers, in which the wrong use or wrong non-use of hyphens makes the words, if strictly interpreted, mean something different from what the writers intended. It is no adequate answer to such

criticism to say that actual misunderstanding is unlikely ; to have to depend on one's employer's readiness to take the will for the deed is surely a humiliation that no decent craftsman should be willing to put up with :—

(In a List of Beauty Recipes) 5. *An infallible wrinkle-remover.* 6. *A superfluous hair-remover* (i.e. a hair-remover that no-one wants)./*The financial record of the Lloyd George-Winston Churchill Government* (i.e. of the Government composed of Lloyd, Churchill, & George Winston)./*Mr Scott Dickson, the ex-Tory Solicitor-General for Scotland* (i.e. the Solicitor-General who formerly was but no longer is a Tory)./*The Unionist Housing of the Working-Classes Bill was read a second time yesterday* (i.e. the way the Unionists house the Working-Classes Bill ; poor ill-housed Billy !)./*Grieving, as a Nonconformist, over the sins of his fellow-Free Churchmen* (i.e. of his Churchmen who are unhampered by companions)./(Heading) *PEACE MEETING RIOT* (i.e. the way peace deals with riot ; what is meant is riot at a peace-meeting)./ *Even the most bigoted anti-trade unionist* (i.e. the unionist who is most opposed to trade)./*The Chancello. plans to reconstruct the Bülow (Conservative-National-Liberal) Block* (i.e. that of Conservatives, Nationals, & Liberals ; what is meant is that of the Conservatives & the National Liberals)./*Last April the Acting-British Consul at Shiraz was attacked* (i.e. the Consul who was pretending to be British)./*And Sir Henniker-Heaton is more fortunate than many of those who cry in the wilderness* (If *Henniker* is Christian name, nɔ hyphen ; if it is surname, a Christian name is wanted ; see HON.)./*If lay-writers can publish what they please, are naval officers to remain compulsorily silent?* (i.e. writers of lays)./(A Reichstag party) *intent on introducing an anti-English & strong Navy agitation into the elections* (i.e. a strong agitation about the Navy ; but what is meant is an agitation for a strong Navy).

Let us next put down a few specimens with corrections. It should first be observed that the most frequent cause of wrong hyphening is the treating of two or more normally spaced words as though they were one word & could be, though so spaced, a single item in a hyphen-compound ; the least that can be done to double-barrelled adjectives, even when they stand alone, is to hyphen them ; Mr Lloyd George (without a hyphen) forms the Lloyd-George Government (with one) ; the need is still greater when further complications come, but the result is then unsatisfactory— the Lloyd-George-Winston-Churchill Government. Obviously connexions of different power are needed; a short & a long hyphen (-, —), or a single & a double one (-, =), would do (the Lloyd-George—Winston-Churchill Government, the Lloyd-George = Winston-Churchill G.) ; but this is an innovation that would hardly find acceptance ; & is better than — or = (the Lloyd-George & Winston-Churchill G.) ; better than either is some evasion, the George-Churchill G., or the G. of Messrs Lloyd George & Churchill. Specimens :— *The mid-nineteenth century politicians* (politicians of the mid - nineteenth century)./*British Columbia peaches* (British - Columbia peaches). / *The Sidney Webb-Bernard Shaw-Fabian Society type of State interference* (State interference according to the ideas of Messrs Sidney Webb & Bernard Shaw & the Fabian Society)./ *The silk stocking-tax* (the silk-stocking tax)./*The Free Trade-Protectionist controversy* (the controversy between Free Trade & Protection ; or why not the Free-Trade controversy ?). / *The South African-born Indians* (Indians born in South Africa)./*Dean Stanley-street* (Dean-Stanley Street). / *Abingdon - street* (Abingdon Street). / *The Sambre Canal-Scheldt front* (the Sambre-canal & Scheldt front). / *Mr Cyril*

Maude was entertained at luncheon yesterday by his fellow-theatrical managers (fellow theatrical managers).

The object so far has been to enlist the reader's interest by setting before him cases in which no technicalities are necessary, in which common sense is all that is wanted, & that, when thus collected, will surprise him by the evidence they afford that common sense is in fact far from common. But there are questions about hyphens less easy of solution than those already glanced at, &, before coming to them, we must look for some principles.

1. A hyphen is a symbol conveying that two or more words are made into one ; the union may be for the occasion only (as in most of the examples above), or permanent (as in *fire-irons, committee-man*) ; the commonest form of temporary union is that in which a phrase (say *Home Rule*) is to be used attributively, i.e. as an adjective to another noun ; to this end it must be marked as one word by the hyphen (*the Home-Rule Bill*).

2. The hyphen is not an ornament ; it should never be placed between two words that do not require uniting & can do their work equally well separate ; & on the other hand the conversion of a hyphened word into an unhyphened single one is desirable as soon as the novelty of the combination has worn off, if there are no obstacles in the way of awkward spelling, obscurity, or the like.

3. The proper functions of the hyphen may be thus classified :—

A. To convert two or more separate words into a single one acting as one adjective or noun or other part of speech. Such unions of the temporary kind are *Housing-of-the-working-classes* as an epithet of *Bill*, & *strong-Navy* as epithet of *agitation* ; permanent ones are *ne'er-do-weel, stick-in-the-mud*, & *what's-his-name*, serving as noun, adjective, & pronoun.

B. To announce that a compound

expression consisting of a noun qualified adjectivally by the other element means something different from what its elements left separate would or might mean; in this function the hyphen is a recognition in print of what has already happened in speech, i. e. that the compound has kept only one accent, & that on the first element, whereas the elements had originally two, of which the stronger was usually on the second (compare the accentuation of *Thrushes are not black birds* with that of *Thrushes are not blackbirds* or *blackbirds*). If this modification of accent has not occurred, the hyphen is out of place & the words should be separate. The expressions coming under this head are chiefly those of which the second element is a noun & the first is an adjective (as in *black-bird, red-coat*) or an attributive noun (as in *water-rat*).

C. To render such compound expressions as a verb & its object or other appurtenances, or a noun & its adjective, amenable to some treatment to which it could not otherwise be subjected. Thus *Court Martial*, if it is to have a possessive case (*the Court-martial's decision was . . .*), must be one word; *long legs, storms beat, rend hearts, carry weight, come home, handle by means of men, proof against bombs, spits fire, go by*, can be converted into handy adjectives, nouns, or verbs, fit to receive suffixes or to play the part that may be required of them in a sentence, by being combined with the hyphen (often afterwards dropped out) into single words; so we get *longlegged, stormbeaten, heart-rending, weight-carrier, homecoming, man-handle, bomb-proof, spitfire*, & (*the*) *go-by*.

D. To show that two adjectives, each of which could be applied separately to a noun (*I saw a red hot face*, i. e. one both red & hot), are not to be so applied, but are to form one epithet conveying a compound idea (*holding a red-hot poker*); such

are *dark-blue, worldly-wise, mock-heroic, bitter-sweet, forcible-feeble*.

E. To attach closely to an active or passive participle an adverb or preposition preceding or following it that would not require hyphening to the parent verb (you *put up*, not *put-up*, a job, but the result is a *put-up* job). The question whether this hyphening is to be done or not is answered, as in B, by the accentuation; the hyphen is wrong unless the compound will have only one accent, & that on the first element; thus *oft-repeated* will usually be hyphened, & *ill served* usually not.

If the above statements & classification are adequate, we should now be able to pass judgement not only on the temporary combinations with which the article started, but on the more difficult questions of permanent compounds. The guiding principles will be : No hyphening of words that will do as well separate ; no hyphening of words in the B or E class if they retain the normal accentuation ; no hyphening together of double-barrelled expressions that themselves lack internal hyphens ; the difference between hyphening & full coalescence, in permanent compounds, a matter of expediency merely. It must be admitted on the one hand that the results will often differ from current usage, but on the other that that usage is so variable as to be better named caprice. Illustrative words will be roughly grouped, with occasional quotations to show that imaginary offences are not being set up in order to be knocked down, & the beginning of each group will be marked with an asterisk.

*Ex-, ante-, pre-, anti-, post-, &c., are often wrongly prefixed to unhyphened double expressions. The difficulty is real, but should always be circumvented ; e. g., the first quotation should be corrected to *opened the campaign against Home Rule*.

Quotations : *Mr Austen Chamber-*

lain opened the anti-Home Rule *campaign./The* anti-high tariff *Press in Germany./In comparison with the* pre-Boer war *figures./The* ex-Chief Whip's *association with the constituency. / ACTION BY AN* EX-LORD MAYOR./*The* ex-Navy League *President.*

The solution, however, described above as unsatisfactory, which would give *anti-high-tariff, pre-Boer-war, ex-Chief-Whip*, &c., would not be as bad in this Latin-preposition group as elsewhere.

*Blue - stocking, black - cap, red herring. Many wrong hyphenings occur of words that correspond in form to the simplest B variety (adjective+noun), but lack one or both of the qualifications : *ruling class, easy going* (as noun, = freedom from obstacles), *clean living* (as noun, = clean life), *wooden leg*, & *steel cap*, have not even the required specialization of sense, & *red herring, Holy Ghost, golden syrup, full back, full stop, full pitch*, though they can claim this, have not the single accent. Compare them with the legitimate *blackguard, black-cap, backwater*, & *blue-stocking*.

Quotations : *That touch of humanity which provides* easy-going *for whatever ship of venture he may be piloting./Charging the German* ruling-class *with the guilt of the war./Peter's* wooden-leg *had a bad habit of breaking down./To promote* clean-living *& laws of health.*

*Great coat, good will. These expressions, which have very definite specialized senses by the side of their general ones, are violations, if hyphened, of the accent rule for B words, which holds for the overwhelming majority ; they should therefore in the specialized senses always be made into single words without hyphens—*greatcoat, goodwill.*

*Court Martial, Governor General, Solicitor General, Princess Royal, time being. Expressions of this type (noun followed by its adjective) require no hyphen, except in the possessive case, the mark of which

cannot be affixed to the adjective until it is made one with the noun. It should be noticed that *Major-General* &c., when used as prefixes to names, are on a different footing & take the hyphen, not under B (when the accent would be anomalous) but under C. The needless hyphen in *Court-Martial* is partly due to reaction from the verb made from it, which has to be fused, under C, into one word with or without the hyphen.

Quotation: *A beaten enemy who must for the* time-being *accept everything.*

*Lord Mayor, Lady Superior, lady help, deputy Speaker, rogue elephant, cock robin, actor manager, trial heat, are examples of unqualified candidates for the B hyphen, differing from the previous groups in having the noun defined not by an actual adjective but by a noun synonym serving as one ; they all lack the accent qualification, & some of them the other as well, & should not be hyphened. Compare with them the words *bullcalf, turkey-poult*, & *object-lesson*, also composed of synonyms, but having the required accent. As before, there are cases of specialized meaning without change of accent, e.g. *fellow man, man child, head-master, headquarters* ; these should not be hyphened, but either kept separate or, if that seems impossible (as in *headquarters*), fully united. The difference should be noticed between *fellow man* &c., which cannot claim their hyphen under B, & *fellow-feeling* (from to feel like a fellow), which can claim it under C.

*Rule of thumb. In this the noun is defined not by an adjective but by a phrase (*of thumb*) ; the accentuation again forbids the hyphen ; the expression might be hyphened under C for use as an adjective (*rule-of-thumb procedure*), but not as a noun under B. Concessions, however, have to be made to longer expressions of similar type in which the orthodox accent becomes unmanageable, as *cat-o'-nine-tails, will-o'-the-wisp.*

Quotation : *Who warned us not to apply a* rule-of-thumb *to the delicate & responsible work of a judge.*

Business man, hay fever, summer time, winter garden, sea change, sea monster, glass case. In these unqualified candidates for B the place of the adjective is taken by an attributive noun ; they all fail to pass the accent test. As to *summer time,* the kind here meant is Mr Willett's, which is one thing, while God's summer-time or summertime is another ; the distinction is not only not useless, but not even arbitrary, corresponding as it does to the two different ways in which sensible people pronounce the words. Similarly, the glass case meant is a glazed case, while *glass-case* means or would mean a case to hold glass. Compare with the words in this list, besides the genuine *summer-time* & *glass-case, missel-thrush* (i.e. mistletothrush), *oak-apple, pew-rent, incometax, Stock-Exchange.*

Quotations : *The* business-men *who clamour that imports shall not be allowed./Is now a warm supporter of* summer-time*./If our clocks had remained at* summer-time*.*

Sub judice, ex officio, bona fide, bona fides, ex parte, ex postfacto, felo de se. These should never be hyphened except when the phrase happens to come under C & to require conversion in a particular sentence into an adjective ; that is never the case with *bona fides,* very seldom with *sub judice & felo de se,* often with *bona fide & ex postfacto & ex officio,* & nearly always with *ex parte. Sits on the Committee* ex officio, compared with *Is an* exofficio *member,* shows the difference. As these phrases, & others like them, are customarily printed in italics, the hyphen can really be dispensed with even where it is right, so that the safe course for the non-Latinist (see BONA FIDE for the dangers) is never to hyphen them.

Quotation : *Until the point, which is practically* sub-judice, *has been decided.*

From hand to mouth, in no wise, at any rate, above ground, up to date. Hyphening in such phrases is wrong, & most unsightly ; *in no-wise & in nowise, at anyrate, from hand-to-mouth,* are not unusual blunders ; & the fact that *up to date* is commonly turned into an adjective under C, & does then require hyphens, reacts upon the original phrase, which has no right to them, just as the verb *to court-martial* reacts upon the parent noun *Court Martial.*

Quotations : *The unburied past that still lay* above-ground*./Reforms which will bring the railways* up-to-date*./The Government, if it thinks only of these, will live from* hand-to-mouth.

Put-up, sought-after, ill-served, oft-repeated, well-done. Hyphenings of this type are resorted to oftener than they should be. The guiding principle is stated under E ; a few examples (a) of such compounds that should not be hyphened, (b) of some that should be either hyphened or fused, & (c) of some that may be hyphened if it is intended that the first element shall be overwhelmingly accented but not otherwise, will perhaps carry conviction about the truth of this rule :—(a) *Newspapers* ill served *with news ; Such badly contrived measures ; A* faithfully kept *promise ; Hilarity* put on *for the occasion ; A principle never* lived up to : (b) *Much* sought-after *opportunities ; The* above-mentioned *facts ; A* put-up *job ; His* oftrepeated *advice ; Such an* outstanding *personality* (to be hyphened by those who accent the *out,* & fully united by those who accent the *stand*) *; The* on-coming *flood ; The* outgoing *Ministry :* (c) *Well done* or *well-done beef ; Little needed* or *littleneeded economies ; A never to be forgotten* or *never-to-be-forgotten day.*

Quotation : *Indian newspapers are so* ill-served *with local news that . . .*

Any reader who has been interested by the various questions that have arisen in this lengthy article may like to glance over a list of the specimens of wrong hyphening contained in it ; the order is that in which they have occurred above, so that what was said about them may be referred to without much difficulty ; they are all printed in the wrong form, standing here in the pillory : Superfluous hair-remover ; The Lloyd George-Winston Churchill Government ; The Unionist Housing of the Working-Classes Bill ; His fellow-Free Churchmen ; Peace Meeting Riot ; The bigoted anti-trade unionist ; The Conservative-National-Liberal Block ; The Acting-British Consul ; Sir Henniker-Heaton ; Lay-writers ; A strong Navy agitation ; The mid-nineteenth century politicians ; British Columbia peaches ; The Sidney Webb-Bernard Shaw-Fabian Society type ; The silk stocking-tax ; The Free Trade-Protectionist controversy ; South African-born Indians ; Dean Stanley-street ; Abingdon-street ; The Sambre Canal-Scheldt front ; His fellow-theatrical managers ; The anti-Home Rule campaign ; the anti-high tariff Press ; The pre-Boer war figures ; The ex-Chief Whip ; An ex-Lord Mayor ; The ex-Navy League President ; Red-herring ; Holy-Ghost ; Golden-syrup ; Full-back ; Full-stop ; Full-pitch ; Easy-going (n.) ; The ruling-class ; A wooden-leg ; Clean-living (n.) ; Great-coat ; Good-will ; Court-Martial ; Governor-General ; Solicitor-General ; Princess-Royal ; The time-being ; Lord-Mayor ; Lady-Superior ; Lady-help ; Deputy-Speaker ; Rogue-elephant ; Cock-robin ; Actor-manager ; Trial-heat ; Fellow-man ; Man-child ; Head-master ; Head-quarters ; Rule-of-thumb ; Business-man ; Hay-fever ; Summer-time (Willett's) ; Winter-garden ; Sea-change ; Sea-monster ; Glass-case ; Sub-judice ; Ex-officio (adv.) ; Bona-fide (adv.) ; Ex-parte (adv.) ; Ex-post-facto ; Felo-de-se ; From hand-to-mouth ; In no-wise ; At anyrate ; Above-ground ; Up-to-date (adv.) ; Ill-served.

Finally, for readers who may like to play at addition & subtraction of hyphens, or who doubt whether so simple a matter is worth an intelligent person's attention, here are some unsorted specimens :—We shall place our orders with your good-selves./The price of fixed interest bearing securities./To declare martial-law in Constantinople./A small minority of mechanically propelled vehicle users./The middle-class began to find that . . ./The publication is an ill-service to the cause./One good arising from that ill-wind. / Language of this kind comes with specially ill-grace from . . ./We have not made use enough of labour economizing appliances./ With the dying off of the older non-English educated generation./He saw the prisoner in Oxford & Cambridge-terrace./With regard to the Chancellor of the Exchequership./ The Dardanelles-Sea of Marmora-Bosphorus line is more important./ The ill-effects of the kinema upon child-life.

hypocorisma. See TECHNICAL TERMS.
hypothecate. 1. *H.* makes *-cable*, *-tor* ; see -ABLE 1, -OR. 2. *H.* means only to mortgage or pledge. In the following extract—*The Nahua race, which, by tradition, served the Aztecs in much the same way as to origin as the hypothecated Aryans serve ourselves*—it is used as a verb corresponding to *hypothesis* ; if an allied verb is really necessary, *hypothesize* (or *-tize*) is the right form, though it is to be hoped that we may generally content ourselves with *assume.*

hypothesis. Pl. *-theses*, pron. -ēz.
hypothetic(al). The longer is much commoner ; otherwise there seems to be no distinction of meaning or usage ; see -IC(AL).

hysteric(al). The short form has almost gone out of use as an adjective, surviving, perhaps, only for reasons of euphony, as in *with a hysteric laugh* ; see -IC(AL).

hysteron proteron. See TECHNICAL TERMS.

I

I. 1. *Between you & I* is a piece of false grammar not sanctioned, like the contrary lapse *It is me*, even by colloquial usage ; a similar lapse is seen in *It was a tragedy of this kind which brought home to my partner & I the necessity for* . . .

2. *I*, like *we*, is liable to be used in successive sentences with different meanings. In the extract below, the first two *I*s mean the average moralist, while the third means the reviewer of Dr Westermarck's book. It is an insidious trap, but more often baited with *we*, which frequently means in one sentence the editor of his paper, & in the next the country . or the Party or any other of the many bodies of which he is a member : *In this respect Dr Westermarck has given a less adequate account of the moral sentiment than Adam Smith, who declares that our ideas of merit & demerit have a double origin, not only in sympathy with the resentment of the sufferer, but in want of sympathy with the motives of the doer.* I *condemn theft partly because* I *dislike thieving & sympathize with the sufferer's claim to keep his property.* I *cannot help thinking that, though every now & then he does justice to sympathy with the direct motives or impulses from which action arises, Dr Westermarck overlooks them in favour of retributive sympathy with the recipient.*

-i. The plurals with this ending need care in three points. See also LATIN PLURALS. 1. As plural of Italian words in -o or -e (*confetti, dilettanti, conoscenti*, &c.) -*i* is pronounced ē, but as plural of Latin & Greek words in -us or -os (*bacilli, syllabi*) it is pronounced ī ; those to whom Latin & Italian words are indistinguishable are apt to say basĭ'lē &c. ; safety lies in *-uses*, which is now permissible in nearly all words, & better in most. 2. Many classical words in -us are given impossible plurals in -i by those who

know little or no Latin. Such are *hiatus, meatus, afflatus, octopus, corpus, virus, & callus*, the Latin plurals of which end variously or do not exist ; safety for the non-Latinist again lies in *-uses*. 3. *Ignoramus, mandamus, & mittimus*, though now English nouns, are in Latin not nouns at all, but verbs, = we do not know, we command, we send ; having become nouns only in English, they can have only the English plurals *ignoramuses, mandamuses, mittimuses*.

iambics, iambus. See TECHNICAL TERMS.

iamb(us). The long form (pl. *-buses* or *-bi*) is recommended as both more usual & handier.

ibidem. Pronounce ĭbĭ'dĕm.

-IBLE. See -ABLE, -IBLE, &c.

-IC. For *-ic & -ics*, see -ICS.

-IC(AL). A great many adjectives appear with alternative forms in *-ic & -ical*. Often the choice between them on any particular occasion is indifferent, so far as the writer's immediate object is concerned. To those who can afford time to think also of the interests of the English language it may be suggested that there are two desirable tendencies to be assisted.

The first of these is DIFFERENTIATION. There are many pairs in *-ic & -ical*, each form well established & in constant use, but with a difference of meaning either complete or incipient. The final stage of differentiation is seen in *politic & political*, which are not even content, as usual, to share an adverb in *-ically*, but make *politicly* by the side of *politically*. Between *economic & economical* the distinction is nearly as clear, though the seal has not been set upon it by a double provision of adverbs ; most writers are now aware that the two words mean different things, & have no difficulty in choosing the one required. This can hardly be said of *comic(al)*, the short form of which is often made to do the other's work. And so the differentiations tail off into mere incipiency. Every well established differentiation adds to the precision & power of the language ; every observance of an incipient one helps it on the way to establishment, & every disregard of it checks it severely ; it is therefore clear that writers have a responsibility in the matter.

The second laudable tendency is that of clearing away the unnecessary. When two forms coexist, & there are not two senses for them to be assigned to, it is clear gain that one should be got rid of. The scrapping process goes on slowly by natural selection ; sometimes the determining cause is apparent, as when *hysteric, cynic,* & *fanatic,* give way to *hysterical, cynical,* & *fanatical,* because they have themselves acquired a new function as nouns ; sometimes the reasons are obscure, as when *electric* & *dynamic* supersede the longer forms while *hypothetic* & *botanic* are themselves superseded. But that one or other should prevail is a gain ; & it is a further gain if the process can be quickened. With this end in view, it is stated in this dictionary, about many *-ic(al)* words, which appears to be the winning side, that writers may be encouraged to espouse it.

Some words bearing on these points are (omitting *-ic, -ical*) :—botan-, casuist-, com-, con-, cub-, cyn-, diabol-, dynam-, econom-, electr-, fanat-, geograph-, geometr-, hypothet-, hyster-, mag-, philosoph-, polit-, ident-, lyr-, sto-, period-, trag-, typ-.

ice, n. *Ice cream, ice pudding,* should not be hyphened ; see HYPHENS.

ice, v., makes *iceable* ; see MUTE E.

-ics. 1. *-ics*) (*-ic.* Among the names of sciences, arts, or branches of study, are a few words in *-ic* that rank as real English ; the chief are *logic, magic, music,* & *rhetoric* ; but the normal form is *-ics,* as in *acoustics, classics, dynamics, ethics, mathematics, physics, politics, tactics.* The substitution of *-ic* for *-ics* (*dialectic, ethic, gymnastic, linguistic, metaphysic,* &c.) in compliance with French & German usage has the effect, whether it is intended or not, of a display of exotic learning, & repels the possibly insular reader who thinks that ' English is good enough for him '. It should be added, however, that the *-ic* & *-ics* forms can sometimes be usefully kept for separate senses ; thus, *dialectic* meaning the art of logical disputation, *dialectics* would mean rather a particular person's exhibition of skill in it ; but it is not with many words, nor on many occasions, that this need arises, & it is not usually with this end in view that the *-ic* words are made.

2. Grammatical number of *-ics.* This is not so simple a matter as it is sometimes thought. The natural tendency is to start with a fallacy : We say Mathematics *is* (& not *are*) a science ; therefore *mathematics* is singular. But the number of *is* there is at least influenced, if not (whether legitimately or otherwise) determined, by that of *a science.* The testing should be done with sentences in which there is not a noun complement to confuse the issue :—*Classics are,* or *is, now taking a back seat* ; *Comics is,* or *are, easier than I expected* ; *What are,* or *is, his mathematics like ?* ; *Politics are,* or *is, most fascinating* ; *Your heroics are,* or *is, wasted on me* ; *Athletics are,* or *is, rampant in the big schools* ; *Tactics are,* or *is, subordinate to strategy.* The rules that seem to emerge are : (1) Singular for the name of a science strictly so used ; *Metaphysics,* or *Acoustics,* deals *with abstractions,* or *sound.* (2) Plural for those same names more loosely used, e.g. for a manifestation of qualities ; often recognizable by the presence of *his, the,* &c. : *His mathematics are weak* ; *Such ethics are abominable* ; *The acoustics of the* *hall* are *faulty*. (3) Plural for names denoting courses of action or the like : *Heroics* are *out of place* ; *Hysterics* leave *me cold*. (4) The presence of a singular noun complement often makes the verb singular : *Mathematics*, or even *Athletics*, is *his strong point*.

ictus. See TECHNICAL TERMS.

idea. 1. *Humperdinck had the happy idea one day to write a little fairy opera*. The question between *to write* & *of writing* is discussed under GERUND 3.

2. *Idea'd* is preferable to *ideaed* ; see -ED & 'D.

idealogue, idealogy, idealogical, are 'erroneous forms' (OED) for IDEOLOGUE &c. ; cf. MINERALOGY.

idée fixe. See FRENCH WORDS.

identic(al). The short form has been so far ousted by the long as to be now a mere archaism except in the language of diplomacy (*identic note, declaration, action*, &c.). Cf. -IC(AL).

identify. For inflexions see VERBS IN -IE, -Y, -YE, 6.

id est. See I. E.

ideologue, -logist, -logy, &c. So spelt, not *ideal*-. The words are formed from Gk *idea*, & the Greek combining vowel is -*o*- for substantives of all declensions.

idiocy, -tcy. The -*t*- is wrong.

idiom. This dictionary being much concerned with idiom & the idiomatic, some slight explanation of the terms may perhaps be expected. For some synonyms, see JARGON. 'A manifestation of the peculiar' is the closest possible translation of the Greek word. In the realm of speech this may be applied to a whole language as peculiar to a people, to a dialect as peculiar to a district, to a technical vocabulary as peculiar to a profession, & so forth. In this book, 'an idiom' is any form of expression that, as compared with other forms in which the principles of abstract grammar, if there is such a thing, would have allowed the

idea in question to be clothed, has established itself as the particular way preferred by Englishmen & therefore presumably characteristic of them. 'Idiom' is the sum total of such forms of expression, & is consequently the same as natural or racy or unaffected English ; that is idiomatic which it is natural for a normal Englishman to say or write ; to suppose that grammatical English is either all idiomatic or all unidiomatic would be as far from the truth as that idiomatic English is either all grammatical or all ungrammatical ; grammar & idiom are independent categories ; being applicable to the same material, they sometimes agree & sometimes disagree about particular specimens of it ; the most that can be said is that what is idiomatic is far more often grammatical than ungrammatical ; but that is worth saying, because grammar & idiom are sometimes treated as incompatibles ; the fact is that they are distinct, but usually in alliance. To give a few illustrations : *You would not go for to do it* is neither grammatical nor idiomatic English ; *I doubt that they really mean it, The distinction leaps to the eyes, & A hardly earned income*, are all grammatical, but all for different reasons unidiomatic ; *It was not me, Who do you take me for ?, There is heaps of material*, are idiomatic but ungrammatical ; *He was promoted captain, She all but capsized, Were it true*, are both grammatical & idiomatic. For examples of special idioms see CAST-IRON IDIOM.

idiosyncrasy, -cratic. The right spelling (-*sy*, not -*cy*) is of some importance, since the wrong distorts the meaning, for all who have a tincture of Greek & so might otherwise grasp it, by suggesting a false connexion with *autocracy* & the many words in -*cracy*. Those words are from Greek *krātos* power ; this is from Greek *krāsis* mixture. Its meaning is peculiar mixture, & the point of it is best shown in the words that describe Brutus : His life was gentle, & the elements So mixed in him that Nature might stand up And say to all the world ' This was a man '. One's idiosyncrasy is the way one's elements are mixed, & the nearest synonyms for it are *individuality & character* ; both of these, however, having positive implications not present in *idiosyncrasy*, the continued existence of the latter in its proper sense is very desirable, & it should be kept to that sense. Thus it is reasonable to say that a person has no character or no individuality, but a person without an idiosyncrasy is inconceivable. Since *idiosyncrasy* means all the ingredients of which a unit is composed, & their proportions & reactions—a valuable compound notion that we may be thankful to find compressed into a single word—, it is a pity that it is often used as a polysyllabic substitute for various things that have good simple names of their own ; it is both pretentious & absurd to say that so-&-so is one of your idiosyncrasies when you mean one of your habits, ways, fads, whims, fancies, or peculiarities. See POPULARIZED TECHNICALITIES. In the quotations following (one with the mis-spelling), read *characteristic, fads, peculiarities, vagaries, antipathy* :— *It is an idiosyncrasy of this grumbler that he reads his own thoughts into the minds of others./For one reason or another—lack of money, lack of men, sometimes the idiosyncracies of committees—the library has been far less useful than it might have been to the serious student./I do not find him, though he is very quick in observing outward idiosyncrasies, a truthful or an interesting student of the characters, the minds & hearts, the daily actions & reactions, of men & women./Moreover, it* [a liturgy] *is desired as a protection against the idiosyncrasies of the minister, whether in his doctrine or its expression./ There are several kinds of food freaks ; some people have an idiosyncrasy to*

all fish, particularly shellfish & lobsters.

idiosyncratic is the adjective of *idiosyncrasy* — unfortunately, because it encourages by an accident the confusion between *-crasy* & *-cracy*. If *idiosyncrasy* is a word that has a real value, but should be much less used than it is, *idiosyncratic*, its hanger-on, should be kept still more severely in its place ; the quotations show that there is a danger of its getting more vogue than it deserves ; what the reader feels is not that his author has used the word in a wrong sense—he has not—, but that he would have done better to circumvent, somehow, the need of it :—*We continue to read for much the same reason as incites a Purple Emperor to feed on carrion, a cat on mice, a queen bee on nectar, the South Wind on a bank of violets ; we are in pursuit of the idiosyncratic (of what appeals to us)./What we cannot help learning of their maker, or discoverer —his philosophy, his idiosyncratic view of things—is there, not because he wittingly put it there, but because he could not keep it out* (personal. Here, at any rate, the writer could have kept *idiosyncratic* out)./*To be thinking & pondering, roving & exploring between the lines of a book is a less arduous & fussy, a quieter & more idiosyncratic enterprise* (eclectic ? self-pleasing ?)./*He never hesitates at any joke, however idiosyncratic* (however little amusing to anyone but himself ?).

idlesse. See WARDOUR STREET.
idola fori, idols of the market (place). This learned phrase, in Latin or English, is not seldom used by the unlearned, who guess at its meaning & guess wrong. It is a legitimate enough phrase in writing meant for the educated only, but hardly in the ordinary newspaper, where it is certain not to be understood by most readers, & where it therefore tends to be given, by SLIPSHOD EXTENSION, the false sense that those who have never been told

what it means may be expected to attach to it ; that false sense is vulgar errors or popular fallacies, one of which names should be used instead of it, since it in fact has a much more limited meaning than they, & one not obvious without explanation. See POPULARIZED TECHNICALITIES.

It is the third of Bacon's four divisions of fallacies, more often mentioned than the other three because its meaning seems, though it is not in fact, plainer. There are the idols (i.e. the fallacies) of the tribe, the cave, the market, & the theatre, which are picturesque names for (1) the errors men are exposed to by the limitations of the human understanding (as members of the *tribe* of man) ; (2) those a person is liable to owing to his idiosyncrasy (as enclosed in the *cave* of self) ; (3) those due to the unstable relation between words & their meanings (which fluctuate as the words are bandied to & fro in the conversational exchange or *word-market*) ; & (4) those due to false philosophical or logical systems (which hold the *stage* successively like plays). The tribe is the human mind, the cave is idiosyncrasy, the market is talk, & the theatre is philosophy ; who would guess all that unaided ? who, on the contrary, would not guess that an idol of the marketplace was just any belief to which the man in the street yields a mistaken deference ? The odd thing is that no better instance could be found of an idol of the market than the phrase itself, oscillating between its real meaning & the modern misuse, so that the very person who pours scorn on idola fori is often propagating one in the very act of ridiculing the rest ; well, 'tis sport to see the enginer hoist with his own petard. The mistake is common enough, but is not easily exhibited except in passages of some length, so that one must here suffice ; the tendency to exalt the man of action above the man of theory may be

ill-advised, but it has nothing to do with shifting acceptations of words, & is not an idolum fori :—*With us the active characters, the practical men, the individuals who, whether in public or in private affairs, ' get on with the job ', have always held the first place in esteem ; the theorists & philosophers a place very secondary by comparison. It is not easy to account for this common estimate. For one thing, as soon as inquiry is made into it, the belief proves to be without foundation—just one of the idols of the market place.*

idolatress. See FEMININE DESIGNATIONS.

idyl(l). The OED gives precedence to the form with -*ll*. It also recognizes only one pronunciation, ī-, not ĭ- ; on this, however, there is room for difference of opinion. (1) It is certain that many people say ĭ′dĭl ; (2) with *idol* & *idle*, both commoner words, ready to confuse the hearer, a separate pronunciation is all to the good, if there is nothing against it ; & (3) it has been pointed out in the article FALSE QUANTITY that the length of the first syllable in the Greek is nothing against its being shortened in the English word.

i.e., id est. 1. To write, or even to say, this in the full instead of in the abbreviated form is now so unusual as to convict one of affectation.

2. *i.e.* means that is to say, & introduces another way (more comprehensible to the hearer, driving home the speaker's point better, or otherwise preferable) of putting what has been already said ; it does not introduce an example, & when substituted for *e.g.* in that function, as in the following extract, is a blunder :—*Let your principal stops be the full stop & comma, with a judicious use of the semicolon & of the other stops where they are absolutely necessary* (i.e. *you could not dispense with the note of interrogation in asking questions*).

3. It is invariable in form ; the

changing of it to *ea sunt* &c.—*which deals with persons* (ea sunt, *all present & future members*)—is due to the same misconception (explained under FOLLOW) as the incorrect *as follow* ; cf. also INTER ALIA.

4. It is naturally preceded by a stop ; whether a comma stands first or not is indifferent, or rather is decided by the punctuation-pitch of the writer or the passage.

if & when. Any writer who uses this formula lays himself open to entirely reasonable suspicions on the part of his readers. There is the suspicion that he is a mere parrot, who cannot say part of what he has often heard without saying the rest also ; there is the suspicion that he likes verbiage for its own sake ; there is the suspicion that he is a timid swordsman who thinks he will be safer with a second sword in his left hand ; there is the suspicion that he has merely been too lazy to make up his mind between *if & when*. Only when the reader is sure enough of his author to know that in his writing none of these probabilities can be true does he turn to the extreme improbability that here at last is a sentence in which *if & when* is really better than *if* or *when* by itself.

This absurdity is so common that it seems worth while to quote a number of examples, bracketing in each either ' if & ' or ' & when ', & asking whether the omission would in any way change the meaning or diminish the force of the sentence :—*The Radicals do not know quite clearly what they will be at (if &) when the fight is renewed./The* Spectator's *Great Threat—that (if &) when Unionists get back to power & find an Irish Parliament in Dublin they will refuse to go on providing money for pensions./A clear warning to the electors that if they voted Liberal they could not afterwards complain (if &) when a Home Rule Bill was carried./ If (& when) we in this country depart from Free Trade India cannot fairly*

be deprived of the right of Protection./ For if (& when) Ulster fights Ulster will certainly be in rebellion./He endeavours to prove that the Government ' cannot be neutral ' if (& when) a Woman Suffrage Referendum is proposed in the House of Commons./ But if (& when) the notices are tendered it will be so arranged that they all terminate on the same day./We were under an honourable obligation to help France, if (& when) the time came for her to assert her claims./He told the Ilford Farmers' Association last year that if (& when) members of Parliament were paid that Association would benefit./In Morocco, what you profess to give us will only belong to us if (& when) we take it from the Moroccans./They must, of course, be certain that they are getting what they are bargaining for, but (if &) when they have made sure of that, they would be wisely advised to pay the price.

It was admitted above that cases were conceivable in which the *if* & the *when* might be genuinely & separately significant. Such cases arise when one desires to say that the result will or does or did not only follow, but follow without delay ; they are not in fact rare, & if a really good writer allows himself an *if & when*, one such must have presented itself ; but in practice he hardly ever does it even then, because any strong emphasis on the absence of delay is much better given by other means, by the insertion of *at once* or some equivalent in the result clause. So true is this that, when the devotees of *if & when* have had the luck to strike a real opportunity for their favourite, they cannot refrain from inserting some adverb to do over again the work that was the only true function of their *& when* ; in the quotations, these adverbs that make *& when* otiose are in roman type :—*The electors knew perfectly well that if & when the Parliament Bill was placed on the Statute-book it would* immediately *be used to pass Irish Home Rule./If*

& when the Unionist Party win a General Election we are to have at once a general tariff on foreign manufactured goods./It is true that if & when an amendment giving women the vote is carried this amendment is thenceforward *to become part & parcel of the Bill.*

When or if is not so purposeless as *if & when*; or *if* does serve to express that the writer, though he expects his condition to be realized, has his doubts:—*An official pronouncement as to what particular items of Lloyd George legislation it is proposed to repeal,* when, or if, *the opportunity arrives.*

Unless *& until* is open to the same objections as *if & when*, but is much less common.

ignite makes *ignitable*; see MUTE E.
ignoramus. Pl. *-uses*, not *-i*; see -I 3, & LATIN PLURALS.
ignoratio elenchi. See TECHNICAL TERMS.
ignore makes *ignorable*; see MUTE E.
ilex. Pl. *ilexes*; see -EX, -IX, 3.
ilk means same; it does not mean family or kind or set or name. *Of that ilk* is a form constructed for the case in which proprietor & property have the same name; *the Knockwinnocks of that ilk* means the Knockwinnocks of Knockwinnock. See POPULARIZED TECHNICALITIES. The common maltreatments of the phrase, some of which are illustrated below, are partly unconscious & due to ignorance of the meaning of *ilk*, & partly facetious; indulgence in such WORN-OUT HUMOUR is much less forgivable than for an Englishman not to know what a Scotch word means:—*The Walkers are a numerous race . . . one of the ilk has suggested that an ancestor probably walked to the Crusades./Printed the year after the death of Thomas Elzevir & in the reign of Daniel of that ilk.*/Robert Elsmere, *the forerunner of so many books ' of that ilk '.*/This publication was undertaken by John Murray, the first of that ilk./' Mystified ' & others of his

ilk do not seem to understand that the money that farmers & other producers make is . . .

illegible)(unreadable. The i. is not plain enough to be deciphered ; the u. is not interesting enough to be perused.

ILLITERACIES. There is a kind of offence against the literary idiom that is not easily named. The usual dictionary label for some specimens of it at least is *vulg.*; but the word *vulgar* is now so imbued on the one hand with social prejudices & on the other with moral condemnation as to be unsuitable ; the property common to these lapses seems to be that people accustomed to reading good literature do not commit them & are repelled by them, while those not so accustomed neither refrain from nor condemn them ; they may perhaps be more accurately as well as politely called illiteracies than vulgarisms ; their chief habitat is in the correspondence columns of the press. A few familiar types may be here collected for comparison, with just enough in the way of illustration to enable each usage to be recognized ; actual quotations will be found under many of the words mentioned in their dictionary places :—
Like as conjunction (*if I could think like you do*).
However, whatever, whoever, &c., interrogative (*However did you find out ?*; *Whatever can this mean ?*).
Same, such, & *various,* as pronouns (*Will submit same,* or *the same, for approval ;* *Have no dealings with such ; Various have stated*).
Frequent use of split infinitives (*Am ready to categorically affirm*).
Re in unsuitable contexts (*The author's arguments re predestination*).
Write with personal object only (*Though she had promised to write him soon*).
Think to = remember to (*I did not think to tell them when I was there*).
Negative after *should not wonder* (*I shouldn't wonder if it didn't come true yet*).

Present &c. after *as if* & *as though* (*It looks as if we are winning* or *shall win*).

Me &c. for *my* &c. in gerund construction (*Instead of me being dismissed*).

Between . . . or for *between . . . &* (*The choice is between glorious death or shameful life*).

Almost quite, rather unique, more preferable.

Aggravating for annoying.

Individual for person.

Any very bad hyphening (*the ruling-class, my wooden-leg*).

Rev. Jones ; *the hon. Smith*.

ILLOGICALITIES. The spread of education adds to the writer's burdens by multiplying that pestilent fellow the critical reader. No longer can we depend on an audience that will be satisfied with catching the general drift & obvious intention of a sentence & not trouble itself to pick holes in our wording ; the words used must nowadays actually yield on scrutiny the desired sense ; to plead that anyone could see what you meant, or so to write as to need that plea, is not now permissible ; all our pet illogicalities will have to be cleared away by degrees.

If Milton might be excused or even commended for calling Eve fairest of her daughters, the modern newspaper man must not expect pardon for similar conduct. *Sir Ernest Cassel's Christmas gift to the hospitals of £50,000 is only the latest of many acts of splendid munificence by which he has benefited his fellows before now*. If it is the latest of them, says the pestilent one, it is one of them ; if one of them, it was given before now ; but it is in fact given now, not before now ; which is absurd.

Take, again, the following comment on a quotation the commentator thinks unjustified : *Were ever finer lines perverted to a meaner use ?* We know well enough what he is trying to do—to emphasize the meanness of the use— ; it is in expressing the emphasis that he has gone wrong ;

it has escaped him that *Never were lines perverted to a meaner use* is made weaker, not stronger, if changed to *never were fine lines* &c., & that again is further weakened, not strengthened, by a change of *fine* to *finer* ; everything that narrows the field of rivals for the distinction of meanest perversion, as *fine* & *finer* do progressively, has an effect contrary to what was intended ; it may be worth while to insert *fine* in spite of that, since it adds a qualification of importance ; but the change to *finer* weakens the force without adding to the accuracy. Richard III says *Was ever woman in this humour won?* ; to have said *Princess*, or *prouder Princess*, instead of *woman* would have made the marvel less & not greater.

Another common, & more conspicuous, illogicality is the unintended anticlimax. *Masters, it is already proved that you are little better than false knaves, & it will go near to be thought so shortly*. Dogberry felt no uneasiness about putting it that way, & some writers seem to agree with him :—*A scepticism about the result of military operations which must have had & probably has had a damping effect upon the soldier* (If it must have had, it certainly, not probably, has had)./*It will, I think, delight the reader as if it were something told by Meadows Taylor ; indeed the mysterious ' sadhu ' who figures in it, & the account of the fight with the yellow leopard, are not unworthy of the suggested comparison* (Not unworthy, quotha ? but *indeed* led us to expect *more than worthy*, a climax instead of an anticlimax).

The abandonment of blind confidence in *much less* is another compliment that will have to be paid to the modern reader's logic. It is still usual to give no hearing to *much more* before deciding for its more popular rival ; sometimes a loose but illogical excuse is to be found in the general effect of the context, sometimes even that is wanting ; these two varieties appear in the quotations :—*The machine must be crushed before any real reforms can be initiated, much less carried./It is a full day's work even to open, much less to acknowledge, all the presents.* See MUCH 2.

A stray variety or two may now bring this subject, which might be treated at much greater length, to an end : *The Dukes of Grafton in the old days were almost invariably Lords-Lieutenant of Suffolk & Northamptonshire, but though the deceased held neither office his influence in Northamptonshire & West Suffolk was considerable* (i.e., previous Dukes were Lords Lieutenant, but this one had much influence ; have Lords Lieutenant, then, no influence ?)./ *The schedule we shall have to face will be a much longer one than it would have been if we had undertaken the work this year, & longer still than it would have been if we had been able to do the work last year.* We may deeply sympathize with a writer who has brought himself to the pass of having to choose between saying *still more longer* & being illogical, but we cannot let him off that *more./ That would quite easily & fairly redress what he admitted to be the only grievance he could see in Establishment.* The *he* is a supporter of the Established Church ; he would *maintain,* not *admit,* that it is the only grievance, & should have said ' what he admitted to be a grievance, though it was the only one he could see '.

Other examples or remarks will be found on BECAUSE, BUT 3, -ER '& -EST 7, 8, HAZINESS, REASON, THOUGH, TOO, YET, & passim.

illth. See -TH NOUNS.

illuminate makes -*nable,* -*ior* ; see -ABLE 1, -OR.

illumine &c. See LU.

illusion. See DELUSION for the differences between the two words.

illustrate should make *illustrable,* & though that form is called obs. by the OED it seems better than -*tratable* ; see -ABLE. Agent noun

-*trator.* The pronunciation ĭ'lŭstrāt (as opp. ĭlŭ'strāt) has been slowly arrived at, but is now general ; see RECESSIVE ACCENT. For *illustrative* the OED gives ĭlŭ'strătĭv only ; but the fixing of ĭ'lŭstrāt may before long produce ĭ'lŭstrătĭv.

im-. For spelling of words with variants in *em-,* see EM- & IM-. The following, not there mentioned, should have *im-,* & not the rarely used *em-* : *imbrue, imbrute, impale, imparadise, impark, impawn, imperil.*

image, vb., makes *imageable* ; see MUTE E.

imaginary)(imaginative. The meanings of the two are quite distinct, & never interchangeable. That is imaginary which exists only in someone's imagination ; he, or his powers or products, is imaginative who is able or apt to form mental pictures. Any confusion between the two is due to the fact that there are things to which either can be applied, though in different senses, & with some such things the distinction is not always apparent. The difference between an imaginary & an imaginative person is clear enough, but that between imaginary & imaginative distress is elusive ; the begging impostor exploits the former ; the latter is created & experienced (Such a price The Gods exact for song, To become what we sing) by the tragic or lyric poet. *The place is described with such wealth of detail as to lead one to the conclusion that it must have existed ; but, of course, on the other hand, it may have been purely imaginative* ; justifiable, or not ?

imagine makes *imaginable* ; see MUTE E.

imago. Pl. *imagos* or *imagines,* pronounce -ēz ; see LATIN PLURALS.

ima(u)m. The form without the u is recommended ; pron. ĭmah'm.

imbed, em-. *Em-* better ; see EM- & IM-.

imbibe makes -*bable,* see MUTE E. See also FORMAL WORDS.

imbroglio. Pronounce -ŏlyŏ ; pl. *-os*, see -O(E)S 4.

imbrue, imbrute, em-. The *im-* forms are better ; see IM-.

imbue makes *imbuable* ; see MUTE E. For construction, see INFUSE.

imitate makes *imitable, imitator* ; see -ABLE 1, -OR

immanent. The word is something of a stumbling-block ; the unlearned hearer or reader is not sure whether it & *imminent* are the same or different ; the Latin scholar feels that he does not recall *immaneo* in his Cicero, & wonders whether (*-ant* & *-ent* often playing hide-&-seek with each other) *māno* may be the source instead of *māneo.* Under these circumstances it is thought by some that the divines & philosophers who chiefly affect the word should be asked whether they would not gain in intelligibility what they might lose in precision by choosing according to context between *in-dwelling, pervading, pervasive, per-meating, inherent,* & other words that do not mystify us. ' All which though I most powerfully & potently believe, yet I hold it not honesty to have it thus set down ', & shall not venture to label *immanent* & *im-manence* SUPERFLUOUS WORDS. The OED's note on the use of *immanent* may be useful to those who, not reading philosophic & religious books, find it an enigma when it makes one of its occasional appear-ances in the newspaper : ' In recent philosophy applied to the Deity regarded as permanently pervading & sustaining the universe, as dis-tinguished from the notion of an external *transcendent* creator or ruler '. See POPULARIZED TECH-NICALITIES.

immense. Both the common slang use in the senses excellent or amus-ing, & the odd freak illustrated in the extract below, are instances of NOVELTY-HUNTING, though the first has lost its freshness & grown stale, as such perversions do whereas the second has not yet got beyond the circles in which the detection of generally unappreciated infinities makes one a luminary :—*These memoirs yield what is probably an immensely true account of Nelson's career.*

immerse makes *immersable* ; see MUTE E.

immesh. Use *en-* ; see EM- & IM-.

immobilize has *-zable* ; see MUTE E.

immortal, as a compliment to an author or one of his productions or personages, requires to be used with caution. Its real use is to make sure that a reader who may or may not be an ignoramus shall realize that the person or book referred to is well known in the literary world, & that without telling him the fact in too patronizing a manner. But, delicate as the device may originally have been, it is now too well known to escape notice ; & whether the reader will be offended or not de-pends on the exact depth of his ignorance. There are few who will not be angry if they are reckoned to require ' the immortal Shakspere ', or ' Don Quixote ', or ' Pickwick Papers ' ; those who can put up with ' the immortal Panurge ', or ' Dobbin ', or ' Mrs Poyser ', will be rather more numerous ; & so on in many gradations. The author of the following was probably ill in-spired in immortalizing Cervantes ; but not so ill as if he had done the same—& he might have—for Don Quixote :—*Lovers of Don Quixote will remember that the immortal Cervantes fought with great courage in this battle.*

immortalize makes *-zable* ; see MUTE E.

immovable, not *-veable* ; see MUTE E. Though the differentiation between *immov-* & *irremov-* is fully established, blunders sometimes oc-cur ; *The President, save for success-ful impeachment, is immovable by Congress./By suspending conscrip-tion & restoring the immovability of the judges.*

immunize has *-zable* ; see MUTE E.

impale, em-. *Im-* better; see IM-.
impanel, em-. *Em-* is better; see EM- & IM-. Past &c., *-lled, -lling*; see -LL-, -L-.
imparadise, impark, em-. *Im-* is better; see IM-.
imparisyllabic. See TECHNICAL TERMS.
impassable, impassible. The two are different in derivation, spelling, pronunciation, & meaning. The first is ultimately from Latin *pando* stretch, the second from Latin *patior* feel; in the first the second syllable is (at least in Southern use) pronounced pahs, while in the other it is always păs; the first means that cannot be passed, the second that cannot feel.

impasse. See FRENCH WORDS. The word is now becoming very common, but is still so little really at home with us that it is often printed *impassé* in newspapers.

impawn, em-. *Im-* better; see IM-.
impayable. There is perhaps no other word that is so indisputably an undesirable alien in English as this. It has a false air, since it is a not impossible English formation, of being intelligible at first hearing to an Englishman; but if we did make the word, we should certainly not mean by it what the French word means; & in point of fact the vast majority of people who hear it are completely puzzled by it. Incredible as, under these circumstances, it seems, we have the precise notion ready to our hands in plain current English; when someone does a thing absurd enough to enlarge our idea of what humanity is capable of in perverse or obstinate or capricious folly, we express our gratitude for this enlightenment by saying that he or his action is ' priceless '. The sentiment may be cynical, & the idiom may be, after all, a translation of *impayable*; the OED does not illustrate or give the sense, so that it is hard to tell whether it is native or not; but at any rate everyone has heard it, &

understands it without assistance from the French. It may be worth while to give the synonyms used in French dictionaries to convey the particular sense of *impayable* that is here referred to; Littré has *extraordinaire, très-plaisant, très-bizarre*, & Larousse *ridicule ou comique*. A newspaper example is :—*The results were discouraging in each case, but the Tariff-reformers are impayable, & have still a thousand arguments to prove that if the Tariff dose had only been stronger, disaster would have been turned into victory on either or each of these occasions.*

impeachment. For *own the soft i.*, see IRRELEVANT ALLUSION.
impedance. For the formation, see HYBRID DERIVATIVES. In the interests of both Electricity & English, the word should be strictly confined to the former.

impede makes *impedable*; see MUTE E.
impel makes *-lled, -llable, -lling*; see -LL-, -L-.
impenitence, -cy. There is no perceptible difference of meaning; *-ce* is recommended; see -CE, -CY.
imperil, not *em-*; see IM-. Past &c. *-lled, -lling*; see -LL-, -L-.
impersonate makes *-nable, -tor*; see -ABLE 1, -OR.
impetigo. Pronounce impĭtī'gō. Pl. *-gines*, pronounce -jĭnēz.
impetus. Pl. *-tuses*, not *-ti*; see -US.
impinge makes *-ging*; see MUTE E.
implement, n. & v. See NOUN & VERB ACCENT. The verb, meaning to carry out (a contract &c.), is chiefly Scotch. Newspaper uses like the following cannot be acquitted of the charge of pedantry : *But it comes after long & disastrous delays which have greatly lowered the prestige of the Allies & diminished their chance of getting their peace terms implemented by any authority that can speak for Russia./Increased taxation will be inevitable if Labour's promises to the electorate are to be implemented.*
A correspondent has favoured me with the following quotation : (David

Irving: *Elements of English Composition*, 11th Ed. 1841) To *impleme'nt*, signifying to fulfil, is likewise derived from the barbarous jargon of the Scotish (*sic*) bar.

implicate makes -*cable*; see -ABLE 1.

implicit. *I.*)(*explicit*; *i.*)(*implied*; *i. faith* &c. The human mind likes a good clear black & white contrast; when two words so definitely promise one of these contrasts as *explicit* & *implicit*, & then dash our hopes by figuring in phrases where the contrast ceases to be visible— say in 'explicit support' & 'implicit obedience', with *absolute* or *complete* or *full* as a substitute that might replace either or both—, we ask with some indignation whether after all black is white, & perhaps decide that *implicit* is a shifty word with which we will have no further dealings. It is in fact noteworthy in more than one respect.

First, it means for the most part the same as *implied*, &, as it is certainly not so instantly intelligible as that to the average man, it might have been expected to be so good as to die. That it has nevertheless survived by the side of *implied* is perhaps due to two causes: one is that *explicit* & *implicit* make a neater antithesis than even *expressed* & *implied* (*all the conditions whether explicit or implicit*; but *all the implied conditions*; *implied* is much commoner than *implicit* when the antithesis is not given in full); & the other is that the adverb, whether of *implicit* or of *implied*, is more often wanted than the adjective, & that *impliedly* is felt to be (see -EDLY 5) a bad form; *implicitly*, preferred to *impliedly*, helps to keep *implicit* alive.

Secondly, there is the historical accident by which *implicit*, with *faith*, *obedience*, *confidence*, & such words, has come to mean absolute or full, whereas its original sense was undeveloped or potential or in the germ. The starting-point of this usage is the ecclesiastical phrase *implicit faith*, i.e. a person's acceptance of any article of belief, not on its own merits, but as a part of, as 'wrapped up in', his general acceptance of the Church's authority; the steps from this sense to unquestioning, & thence to complete or absolute or exact, are easy; but not everyone who says that implicit obedience is the first duty of the soldier realizes that the obedience he is describing is not properly an exact one, but one that is based on acceptance of the soldier's status. See POPULARIZED TECHNICALITIES.

impliedly is a bad form; see -EDLY (5).

imply. For inflexions see VERBS IN -IE, -Y, -YE, 6.

impolitic makes the unusual adverbial form -*icly*, not -*ically*.

import. See NOUN & VERB ACCENT.

importune, v. The stress is variable, & the OED allows it on either the second or the third. Of the numerous verse quotations, there are twelve clear for impor'tune, & four for importu'ne; Shakspere, Spenser, Chapman, Gray, & Byron, all favour the former.

impose makes -*sable*; see MUTE E.

impost. For synonymy see TAX.

impost(h)ume. The *h*, which is not pronounced, & often not written, is better away, though the word is too well established to have its other corruptions removed & its sound altered. It should be, & was, *apostem*, from Greek *apostema* abscess; the *h* comes in by confusion with *posthumous*, in which it is due to a theory, though a false one, of the etymology.

impractical, un-. The second is better; see IN- & UN-, & PRACTICABLE. The constant confusion between *practicable* & *practical* is a special reason for making use of im- & un- to add to the difference in the negatives: *Its inability to address itself to the questions of the hour produces the impression that the Labour movement is all impracticable agitation* (read *unpractical*).

imprecate makes -*cable*; see -ABLE 1.

impregnate makes -*natable* (exceptionally, see -ATABLE), since *impregnable* would be inconvenient.

impresario. Pronounce -zar'ĭŏ, not -sār'ĭŏ; pl. -*os*, see -O(E)S 4.

imprescriptible is one of the words that are often used without a clear conception of their meaning. That right or property or grant is i. which is 'not subject to prescription'. What then is prescription? If we exclude doctors' prescriptions, most people take it to mean 'uninterrupted use or possession from time immemorial, or for a period fixed by law as giving a title or right; hence, title or right acquired by virtue of such use or possession: sometimes called positive prescription '—OED. But clearly 'not subject to prescription' in this sense does not give us the meaning we want, but something very like the opposite of it. The reading of the riddle requires a piece of legal knowledge that most of us have not, viz, that there is another kind of prescription 'now commonly called negative prescription', defined as 'Limitation or restriction of the time within which an action or claim can be raised'—OED. An imprescriptible right, then, is a right not subject to negative prescription, i.e., a right that is not invalidated by any lapse of time.

impress, n. For synonymy see SIGN.

impressible, impressionable. It is singular that the second form, adapted from the French, should have displaced the first, which might have done the work quite well, although the French verb *impressionner* has failed to produce a current English verb *to impression*. Whatever the reason, *impressionable* is undoubtedly the established form, & *impressible* rare.

imprint. See NOUN & VERB ACCENT.

impromptu, n. Pl. -*us*.

impropriate makes -*priable*; see -ABLE 1.

improve makes *improvable*; see MUTE E.

improvisator. Pronounce ĭmprŏ'-vizātor. Italian form -*vvisatore* pron. -ahtor'ĭ, fem. -*vvisatrice* pron. -ahtrē'chā, pl. -*ori* pron. -or'ē, -*ici* pron. -ē'chē.

improvise, not -*ize*, see -ISE; *i.* makes -*isable*, see MUTE E.

impuissant. For pronunciation see PUISSANT.

in. The combinations *inasmuch as*, *in order that* or *to*, *in so far*, *in that*, & *in toto*, are taken separately in their alphabetical places.

inacceptable. *Un-* is better; see IN- & UN-.

inadequate. *Since otherwise the number of troops available might be inadequate to those which might be brought into the field against her.* Though it is true that *adequate* & *inadequate* originally meant made & not made equal, & therefore might be & were followed by *to* with any suitable noun or infinitive, modern usage has restricted the words to the notion (un)equal to requirements, so effectually that it may now be regarded as unidiomatic to express the particular demand; vague additions like *to the need, to the occasion, to the task*, are still possible, though felt to be pleonastic; but specifications like that in the above extract, or like *His revenues were found inadequate to his expences* (Gibbon) or *Is language adequate to describe it?* (W. Collins) are abandonments of the differentiation that has taken place between *adequate & equal, inadequate & unequal.* *His resources were inadequate*, or *inadequate to the occasion,* but not *inadequate to those of his opponent,* nor *to take* or *taking the town.*

inadvertence, -cy. The first is recommended; see -CE, -CY.

inadvisable, inalterable. *Un-* is better; see IN- & UN-.

-IN & -INE. The distinction in Chemistry between the two terminations is outside the scope of this dictionary. But in certain words, e.g. *gelatine, glycerine, margarine*, the *-ine* of popular use violates that distinction. Nevertheless, the correct spellings *gelatin* &c. should be left to technical writers or kept for scientific moments, & the *-ine* forms used without hesitation when we are not thinking in terms of Chemistry—unless, indeed, the word *pedantry* has no terrors for us.

IN- & UN-. There is often a teasing *uncertainty*—or *incertitude*—whether the negative form of a word should be made with *in-* (including *il-, im-, ir-*), or with *un-*. The general principle that *un-* is English & belongs to English words, & *in-* is Latin & belongs to Latin words, does not take us far. The second part of it, indeed, forbids *inwholesome* (since *wholesome* has certainly no Latin about it) & thousands of similar offences ; but then no-one is tempted to go astray in this direction. And the first part, which is asked to solve real problems—whether, for instance, *unsanitary* or *insanitary* is right—seldom gives a clear answer ; it forbids *undubitable, uneffable, unevitable*, & other such words of which the positive form does not exist as an English word ; but about *sanitary* & the rest it says you may consider them English words & use *un-*, or Latin words & use *in-*. Fortunately the number of words about which doubts exist is not large ; for the great majority usage has by this time decided one way or the other. Fashion has varied : ' The practice in the 16th & 17th c.' says the OED ' was to prefer the form with *in-*, e.g. *inaidable, inarguable, inavailable*, but the modern tendency is to restrict *in-* to words obviously answering to Latin types, & to prefer *un-* in other cases, as in *unavailing, uncertain, undevout* '. A few extracts follow exhibiting the more common or important of the doubtful words, each in what is here considered the less desirable form ; the number

printed after some of these is that of the times that I happen to have seen the form in newspapers while attending to the point :—*The amount must be determined not by* impractical *discussions over restitution* (7)./*He has selected five of Gissing's novels for generous, but by no means* indiscriminating, *praise* (4)./*We agree with Mr Balfour in thinking it* inadvisable *to set up any form of Second Chamber which . . .* (2)./*Your modern diplomatist works this supposed* incontrollable *popular feeling for all it is worth* (2)./*Whose faded stare silenced his son-in-law by its* inexpressive *fixity.*/*Complaints that the present Finance Bills are* inacceptable./*We can only regret that his ideas are* indigested./*Every place at which war-ships, completed or* incompleted, *are lying.*/*Her letters, still* extant although inedited.

Before a fuller list of doubtful pairs, with recommendations, is attempted, some suggestive contrasts may serve to show the conflicting tendencies that are at work :—*unjust* but *injustice, unable* but *inability, unquiet* but *inquietude, uncivil* but *incivility*, show the influence of markedly Latin as opposed to nondescript endings in producing *in-*. *Undigested* but *indigestible, unanimated* but *inanimate, undistinguished* but *indistinguishable, unlettered* but *illiterate, unlimited* but *illimitable, unredeemed* but *irredeemable, unreconciled* but *irreconcilable*, illustrate the aversion of *-ed* to *in-* ; *unceasing* but *incessant, undiscriminating* but *indiscriminate*, do the same for *-ing*. *Unapproachable* but *inaccessible, undestroyable* but *indestructible, undissolvable* but *indissoluble, unbelievable* but *inconceivable, unprovable* but *improbable*, bring out well the tendency for *in-* to be restricted to the forms that are closest to Latin even in the very openminded *-ble* group (on which more will be found under -ABLE 3) ; & *uncertainty* but *incertitude* does the same for nouns. Lastly, *unaccountable* but *insurmountable*, &

unmelodious but *inharmonious*, are examples of apparent caprice fixed by usage.

A list is now given of the words about which doubt is most likely, with a statement of the prefix recommended for each ; the recommendations are sometimes supported by special reasons, but sometimes merely based on a general impression that one form is more likely than the other to prevail :—

acceptable	un-	*In-* form labelled rare in OED
advisable	un-	As *acceptable*
alterable	un-	
appeasable	un-	Delatinized by *-eas-*
apt	un-	*Inept* is the Latin
artificial	{ un-	in sense natural
	{ in-	in sense unskilful
communicative	un-	
completed	un-	The only indisputable *in——ed* word is *in-experienced*
consolable	in-	Established
controllable	un-	Much delatinized
decipherable	un-	
digested	un-	As *completed*
discriminating	un-	Words in *-ing* abhor *in-*
distinguishable	in-	Established
edited	un-	See *completed*; French *inédit* has kept the *in-* form in being
effaceable	in-	Established
escapable	un-	Much delatinized
essential	un-	
expressive	un-	Danger of confusion with *inexpressible*
frequent	in-	Most *-ent* words so
navigable	un-	
practical	un-	As *acceptable*; & confusion w. *impracticable*
recognizable	un-	
responsive	un-	Danger of confusion with *irresponsive*
retentive	ir-	Most words in *re-* so
substantial	un-	
supportable	in-	Established
susceptible	in-	Most *-ible* words so

inappeasable. *Un-* is better ; see IN- & UN-.

inapt(itude). *Unapt* is better (but *inaptitude*) ; see IN- & UN-.

inartificial, un-. See IN- & UN-.

inasmuch as has two meanings : one the original, now rarely met with, i. e. *to the same extent as* or *to*

whatever degree or *so far as* (*God is only God inasmuch as he is the Moral Governor of the world*) ; & the other worn down, with the notion of a correspondence between two scales gone, & nothing left but a four-syllable substitute for *since* (*I am unable to reply that I am much the better for seeing you, inasmuch as I see nothing of you*) ; this is the ordinary modern use, & its only recommendation as compared with *since* is its pomposity. On the other hand the old sense has been supplanted by *so far as* & *in so far as*, & is now unfamiliar enough to be misleading when a literary-minded person reverts to it. *At any rate, Mr Chamberlain's proposals, inasmuch as they were intended to secure continued loyalty & union amongst the Australian people, were considered altogether unnecessary.* Do we gather that the proposals were in fact rejected, & the reason for this was that their intention was so-&-so ? or that, whether rejected or accepted on other grounds, that intention was not held to justify them ? in other words, does *inasmuch as* mean since, or so far as ? we cannot tell, without extraneous information. A word that in one sense is pompous, & in another obscure or ambiguous, & in both has satisfactory substitutes, is better left alone.

inaugurate makes *-ator* ; see -OR.

incage, en-. The second is better ; see EM- & IM-.

incapacitate, incarcerate, make *-itable, -rable, -ator*; see -ABLE 1, -OR.

incarnate. Pronounce the verb ĭ'nkarnāt, & the adjective ĭnkar'nĭt. For adj. in *-able*, see -ATABLE.

incarnation. *This unfortunately is not the prisoner's first lapse from honesty, for when the Chief Constable of Peterborough said 'he was the very quintessence of cunning & the incarnation of a book-thief', he was not speaking without knowledge.* Either the C.C. has been misreported or he was playfully suggesting that a book-thief is not a human being, but a fiend or possibly a Platonic Idea ; for so eminent a person must be aware that incarnation of what is incarnate already is as idle as painting the lily, & much more difficult. Some of us, however, do need to be reminded that while a person may be an incarnation of folly, or Folly clothed in flesh, it is meaningless to call him the incarnation of a fool, because all fools are flesh to start with & cannot be fitted with a new suit of it. See POPULARIZED TECHNICALITIES.

incase. *En-* better ; see EM- & IM-.
incense makes *-sable* ; see MUTE E.
incensedly. A bad form ; see -EDLY.
inceptive, inchoative. See TECHNICAL TERMS.
incident adj.) (*incidental*. Two tendencies may be discerned ; one is for the shorter form with its less familiar termination to be displaced by the longer ; thus we should more usually, though not more correctly, now write *incidental* in such contexts as (shortened from OED examples): *All the powers incident to any government ; Those in the highest station have their incident cares & troubles ; The expedition & the incident aggressive steps taken ; The incident mistakes which he has run into ; A bank note, more than sufficient to defray any incident charges.* The other tendency, cutting across the first, is a differentiation of meaning, based on no real difference between the two forms, but not the less useful on that account ; while *incidental* is applied to side occurrences with stress on their independence of the main action, *incident* implies that, though not essential to it, they not merely happen to arise in connexion with it but may be expected to do so. A consequence of this distinction is that *incident* is mostly used in close combination with whatever word may represent the main action or subject, & especially with *to* as the link ; *Youth & its incident perturbations,* or *The enthusiasms incident to youth.* It would be well if the

swallowing up of *incident* by *incidental* could be checked, & a continued existence secured to it at least in the special uses indicated. *Half the money has gone in incidental expenses, & Our failure brought us an incidental advantage* ; but *Office & the incident worries,* & *The dangers incident to pigsticking.*

incidentally is now very common as a writer's apology for an irrelevance. Naturally, those who find it most useful are not the best writers.

incinerate makes *-rable, -ator* ; see -ABLE 1, -OR.
incise, not *-ize* ; see -ISE.
incise, incite, make *-sable, -table* ; see MUTE E.
incline. See NOUN & VERB ACCENT. For ' seriously incline ', see HACKNEYED PHRASES.
inclose. *En-* better ; see EM- & IM-.
include makes *-dable* ; see MUTE E.
include) (**comprise.** As used in the newspapers, these may be called a pair of WORKING & STYLISH WORDS. The one used in ordinary life is *include* ; the inferior kind of journalist therefore likes to impress his readers with *comprise.* The frequent confusion between *comprise & compose* (*comprised mainly of recruits*), is an indication that *include,* which writer & compositor alike know all about, would be in general a safer word. Given the two, however, it would be possible to turn our superfluity to much better purpose than as a chance for the stylish journalist. When two words have roughly the same meaning, examination will generally reveal a distinction ; & the distinction in meaning between the present two seems to be that *comprise* is appropriate when the content of the whole, & *include* when the admission or presence of an item, is in question ; good writers say *comprise* when looking at the matter from the point of view of the whole, *include* from that of the part. With *include,* there is no presumption (though it is often the fact) that all or even most of the components

are mentioned ; with *comprise*, the whole of them are understood to be in the list. The Guards, for instance, include the Coldstreams or the Life Guards, but comprise the Life Guards, Horse Guards, Dragoon Guards, & Foot Guards. *Comprise* is in fact, or would be if this partly recognized distinction were developed & maintained, whereas *include* is not, equivalent to *be composed of*. The following extracts show *comprise* in contexts where *include* would be the right word :—*The German forces . . . exceed twenty-three corps ; this number does not* comprise *the corps operating in the Masurian Lakes./The Commission points out that the ample crop of information it has gathered only* comprises *irrefragably established facts.*

incognito. The inflexions are of no great importance, being now little used, but should be done right if at all. Of the personal noun *incognito, incognita, incogniti*, are the masculine, feminine, & plural, = man, woman, people, of concealed identity. The abstract noun, = anonymity &c., is *incognito* only, with possible plural *incognitos* (never *dropping their incognitos*, or usually *incognito*). The adverb or predicative adjective (*travelling i.*) is usually *-to* irrespective of gender & number ; if declined, it is like the personal noun.

incognizable &c. For pronunciation see COGNIZANCE.

incommunicative. *Un-* is better ; see IN- & UN-.

INCOMPATIBLES. Under this heading are collected some phrases each consisting of ill-assorted elements. They differ greatly both in degree of badness & in kind ; neither point is here discussed, & each phrase is set down in as few words as will enable the usage to be identified. Discussion of any particular misuse will be found on reference to one or other of the terms composing the phrase. The object of this list is first to give the reader, when referred here, a

conspectus of mistakes similar to the one he was investigating, & secondly to give the mistakes themselves an extra advertisement. The reader confronted with these things baldly set down, stripped of the surroundings that would in many of them distract attention from the actual fault, will naturally doubt whether they really appear in print ; but the doubt will be set at rest by a few minutes devoted to looking up the words italicized :—almost quite ; without *scarcely* ; *scarcely . . .* than ; finally *scotched* ; *decimate* by 50% ; rather *unique* ; *somewhat* amazing ; *quite* all right ; more *preferable* ; *prefer* to die than yield ; *ago* since ; he *aims* to secure it ; *neither* of them were there ; ought to be *availed* of ; *between* death or disgrace ; methods honest or *otherwise* ; *both* complex as well as simple causation ; but that *however* is doubtful ; on a *conservative* estimate ; it *depends* whether we get rain ; *disagree* from ; did not *have* time ; I *doubt* that it ever happened ; six feet *between* each post ; a comparatively *few* ; *hardly*-earned wages ; with a *view* of deciding ; a line *worth* while pursuing ; people *seemed* to have been bolder in those days ; will *write* you soon ; shouldn't *wonder* if it wasn't true ; *lest* it will come true ; do *like* he does ; the *major* portion ; *mutual* friend ; *neither* good or bad ; *oblivious* to ; *onto* ; makes *one* forget his manners ; *in order* that the peace will be a lasting one ; was *promoted* to admiral ; the reason is *because* God willed it ; I *regard* it monstrous ; the *Hon.* Smith ; ₁ *Rev.* Smith ; I would *like* ; those *sort* of ; butter must be *substituted* by margarine ; were *issued* with two gas-masks each ; *superior* than ; *those* persons interested ; *tinker* with the constitution ; no reason for *undue* alarm ; *very* changed.

incompetence, -cy. The form recommended is *-ce*, cf. COMPETENCE ; in legal use, however, *-cy* seems to be preferred.

incompleted. *Un-* is the right form ; see IN- & UN-.

incondite. Pronounce ĭnkŏ'ndĭt. The word is of the learned kind, & should be avoided except in what is addressed to a definitely literary audience. It may not be out of place to mention that *condĭtus* composed, not *condĭtus* seasoned, is the Latin source, & that *artless, rude, rough, unpolished,* come near the sense.

INCONGRUOUS VOCABULARY. *Austria-Hungary was no longer in a position, an' she would, to shake off the German yoke.* Be in a position to is a phrase of the most pedestrian modernity ; *shake off the yoke,* though a metaphor, is one so well worn that no incongruity is felt between it & the pedestrianism ; but what is *an' she would* doing here ? why not the obvious *even if she had the desire* ? or, if *an' she would* is too dear to be let go, why not *Austria now could not, an' she would* ? The goldfish *an'* cannot live in this sentence-bowl unless we put some water in with it, & gasps pathetically at us from the mere dry air of *be in a position.* Only a child would expect a goldfish to keep his beauty out of his right element ; & only the writer who is either very inexperienced or singularly proof against experience will let the beauties of a word or phrase tempt him into displaying it where it is conspicuously out of place. Minor lapses from congruity are common enough, & a tendency to them mars the effect of what a man writes more fatally than occasional faults of a more palpable kind, such as grammatical blunders ; but they do not lend themselves to exhibition in the short form here necessary ; a few of the grosser & more recurrent incongruities, connected with particular words, must suffice by way of illustration ; the words out of their element are printed in roman type, & under most of them, in their dictionary places, will be found

further examples :—*M. de Bille has spent eighteen years in London as* Denmark's *Minister* (see 's INCONGRUOUS)./*Christmas books are put in hand long* ere *the season comes round./ It is really very difficult to imagine that the reply of the ballot can be* aught *but an answer in the affirmative./Having in mind the approaching General Election, it appears to me that the result of* same *is likely to be as much a farce as the last./There are, it may be noted, fewer marquises than any other section of the peerage* save *dukes./The Covenanted Civil Service with its old traditions & its hereditary hatred of interlopers,* be they *merchants, journalists, doctors, &c. (be* they *is nothing if not stiff, &c.* nothing if not slack).

inconsiderateness, -eration. For the distinction, see CONSIDERATENESS.

inconsolable, un-. *In-* is better ; see IN- & UN-.

incontinently,=straightway, is archaic & now literary only. Its connexion with *incontinent*=libidinous, which is apt to suggest wrong guesses, is not a close one ; the OED explains that it is from Latin *in continenti tempore* (in unbroken time), so that the *in-* of *incontinently* is the preposition meaning in, whereas that of *incontinent* is the prefix meaning not.

incontrollable. *Un-* is better ; see IN- & UN-.

incorporate makes *-rable, -tor* ; see -ABLE 1, -OR.

increase. See NOUN & VERB ACCENT.

incredible. See POSITIVE WORDS.

incrust, en-. *Encrust, encrustment,* but *incrustation* ; see EM- & IM-.

incubate makes *-tor,* see -OR ; for adj. in *-able,* see -ATABLE.

incubus. Pl. *-bi,* or *-buses.*

inculcate makes *-tor* (see -OR) ; for adj. in *-able,* see -ATABLE. A curious mistake often occurs, shown in the three quotations following :—*A passer-by saved him, formed a close friendship with him, &* inculcated him with *his own horrible ideas about murdering women.* / *An admirable training-place wherein to* inculcate the young mind with *the whys & wherefores of everything which concerns personal safety.*/*The Germans are chiefly busy in* inculcating *Americans with the idea that British Marinismus is more dangerous than German* Militarismus. Whether the explanation is that *inculcate* is one of the words liable to the maltreatment called OBJECT-SHUFFLING (*i.* *one with a doctrine* being substituted for *i. a doctrine upon one*), or whether the compositor has each time found *inoculate* & printed *inculcate*, is impossible to determine; if the latter, writers should take warning that *inoculate* is a word to keep an eye on (or inoculate in a new sense) in proofs. See MISPRINTS.

inculpate. See -ATABLE.

incur makes -*rred,* -*rring*; see -R-, -RR-. For *incurring* see PRONUNCIATION s.f.

indecipherable. *Un-* is better; see IN- & UN-.

indecorous. Accent the third syllable (ĭndĭkōr′ŭs).

indefeasible) (indefectible. The distinction between the two, not always very carefully observed, may perhaps best be kept in mind by associating them respectively with *defeat* & *deficit.* That is indefeasible which is not liable to defeat, i.e. to being impaired or annulled by attack from outside; the word is therefore applied to rights, titles, possessions, & the like. That is indefectible which is not liable to deficit, i.e. to failing for want of internal power; the word is therefore applied to qualities such as holiness, grace, vigour, resolution, affection, or abundance; the sense faultless, suggesting the noun *defect* rather than *deficit,* & not quoted for in the OED from before the 19th c., seems to be a modern change of meaning, & one not to be countenanced. Neither word lends itself to the sort of everyday use seen in:

And yet Mr. Barnstaple had the most subtle & indefeasible doubt whether indeed Serpentine was speaking.

indent. See NOUN & VERB ACCENT.
independence, -cy. The -*cy* form retains only some special senses—Congregationalism, an independent State, & an independent income—; & in these, though still preferred to -*ce,* is now usually displaced by *Congregationalism, sovereign* or *independent State,* & *competency.*

indescribable. So spelt; see MUTE E.
index. For pl. see -EX, -IX. 4. & LATIN PLURALS. For synonymy see SIGN.
Indian. For *the I. weed* see SOBRIQUETS.
indicate makes -*cable,* -*tor*; see -ABLE 1, -OR.
indication. For synonymy see SIGN.
indicative. The grammatical term is pronounced ĭndĭ′kătĭv; in other uses ĭ′ndĭkātĭv is not uncommon.
indict, -able, -ment. Pronounce -ĭt-. *Indict* means accuse, & *indite* compose or write.
indifference, -cy. Though the -*cy* form tends to disappear in all senses, its slower disappearance in one suggests a distinction that might usefully be maintained. That sense is the one corresponding to the objective sense of *indifferent*; a person is indifferent (subjectively) who feels no preference for either of a pair of things over the other; things are indifferent (objectively) for neither of which a preference is felt; the relation of the person to the things is indifference; the relation of the things to the person is still often, & might well be always, called indifferency. The following quotations from the OED show the word so used, & readers will perhaps agree that it is better in these contexts than *indifference* :—*You have arrived at an equivalence & indifferency of all actions.*/*Ceremonies . . . how indifferent soever they are in themselves, when they are once commanded, the indifferency ceases.*/*I still believe in the indiffer-*

*ency of customs, so long as they do
not make void the Divine word.* See
-CE, -CY, & DIFFERENTIATION.

indigested. *Un-* is the right form ;
see IN- & UN-.

indirect object. See TECHNICAL
TERMS.

INDIRECT QUESTION is the grammarian's name for a modification of
what was originally a question, such
that it does not stand by itself as
a sentence, but is treated as a noun,
serving for instance as subject or
object to a verb outside of it. Thus :
direct question, *Who are you ?* ;
indirect question, *I asked who he was,*
or *Tell me who you are,* or *Who you
are is quite irrelevant.* Two points
arise, one of grammar, & one of
style.
1. It must be remembered that
an indirect question is in grammar
equivalent to one noun in the
singular ; the number of its internal
subject has no influence on the
number of the external verb ; to
disregard this fact, as when *rest* is
written instead of *rests* in the following extract because *terms* happens to
be plural, is an elementary blunder—
*What terms Bulgaria may be ultimately given rest with the Peace
Conference.*
2. The point of style is of much
greater interest. How far is it
legitimate to substitute in an indirect question the order of words
that properly belongs to direct
questions ? The lamentable craze
for INVERSION among writers who
are fain to make up for dullness of
matter by verbal contortions is no
doubt responsible for the prevailing
disregard of the normal order in
indirect questions ; for inversion,
i.e. the placing of the subject later
than its verb, is a mark of the
direct, but not of the indirect question. Take these five types :—
A. How old are you ?
B. Tell me how old you are
   or Tell me how old are you ?
C. He wondered how old she was
   or He wondered how old was she?

D. He doesn't know how old I am
   or He doesn't know how old am I?
E. How old I am is my affair
   or How old am I is my affair.
A is the direct question ; in B, C,
D, & E, the first form contains the
normal, & the second the abnormal
form of the indirect question. It
will be seen that the abnormal form
is progressively disagreeable as we
recede from interrogative governing
verbs, until in E it might fairly be
thought impossible. To contortionists, however, all things are possible ;
readers possessed of the grammatical sense, or of literary taste,
will find the following examples of
the abnormal order repugnant in
the same degree as the types to
which the letters B, E, &c., assign
them ; it is only the encroachments
of inversion in general that palliate
this special abuse in indirect questions. *I have been asked by the
Editor to explain what are the duties
of the Army towards the civil power,
how* is it *constituted, to whom* does it
owe *allegiance, by whom* is it *paid,
& what* is the source *of its authority*
(B. The reason why the first & last
clauses here are less distasteful than
the others is explained later)./*It
shows inferentially how powerless* is
that body *to carry out any scheme
of its own* (D. Normal order—how
powerless that body is)./*Experience
has taught in what a restricted region*
can the State *as trader or owner act
to the general advantage* (D. Normal
order—the State can act to the
general advantage as trader)./*How
bold* is *this attack may be judged from
the fact that . . .* (E. Normal order—
How bold this attack is)./*Why*
should we *be so penalized must ever
remain a mystery* (E. Normal order
—Why we should).
The further remarks promised on
the first example are these : three
of the five indirect-question clauses
in that are clear cases of abnormal
order—*how is it* instead of *how it is,
to whom does it owe* instead of *to
whom it owes,* & *by whom is it paid*
instead of *by whom it is paid—* ;

but about the other two, which whether designedly or not act as advance-guard & rearguard covering those between & almost preventing us from discovering their character, it is not so easy to say whether they are abnormal or not. That is a characteristic of the special type of question consisting of subject, noun complement, & the verb *be* ; in the answer to such questions, subject & complement are transposable. Question, *What are the duties ?* ; answer, indifferently, *These are the duties*, or *The duties are these* ; to the first form corresponds in the indirect question *Explain what are the duties*, & to the second, *Explain what the duties are* ; & it can therefore hardly be said that one is more normal than the other. But to questions made of other elements than subject+*be* +noun complement, e.g. *How is it constituted ?*, the two answers (*It is constituted thus*, & *Thus is it constituted*) are far from indifferent ; one is plainly normal & the other abnormal. This minor point has been discussed only because sentences like *Explain what are the duties* might be hastily supposed to justify all other uses of direct-question order in indirect-question constructions.

indiscreet, indiscrete, should be distinguished in accent—ĭndĭskrē′t, ĭndĭ′skrĕt ; cf. DISCRETE.

indiscriminating. *Un-* is the right form ; ʳsee IN- & UN-.

indistinguishable, un-. The first is recommended ; see IN- & UN-.

indite. See INDICT ; *i-* makes *inditable*, see MUTE E.

individual, n. The remarks to be made concern the noun only, not the adjective. ' *Individual*, which almost made the fortune of many a Victorian novelist, is one of the modern editor's shibboleths for detecting the unfit ' ; so it has been said, but editors seem to relax their vigilance occasionally, & the word slips through on its sad old errand of soliciting a smile in vain ; here

are a couple of passages in which the choice of it can have been dictated by nothing but WORN-OUT HUMOUR :—*It is a most spirited episode, with a supernatural ending according to Tom Causey ; this wily individual is the hero of some highly diverting stories./Taking a leaf out of the book of the individual who some years ago put forth his recollections under the title ' Reminiscences of a Young Man '.*

The test for the right use of the word as opposed to the ' colloquial vulgarism ' (OED) is the question whether the writer means or not to contrast the person he calls an individual with society, the family, or some body of persons ; if he does, he may say *individual* with a clear conscience ; if not, he must expect us to like his evocation of this ghost of 19th-century jocularity as little as we enjoy the fragrance of a blown-out candle that just now gave us light, or of the smoking-room visited early next morning. A pair of examples will make the difference clear ; in the first, the individual is directly contrasted with, though a member of, the House of Commons, & is therefore rightly so called ; in the second it is true that there is a body of persons in question, but the individual is so far from being contrasted with this body that he is it ; the right way to have written the sentence is added in brackets, & the efficiency with which *his* does all the work of *of this longsuffering individual* (19th-century perfume excepted) reveals the writer's style as one not to be imitated :—*The House of Commons settled down very quietly to business yesterday afternoon ; all trace of the preceding sitting's violent protestation appeared to have been obliterated from the political mind ; the only individual who attempted to revive the spirit of animosity was Mr——./We are little inclined to consider the urgency of the case made out for the patient agriculturalist ; it would seem at first sight as if the needs of this long-suffering individual were such as could be supplied by . . .* (as if his needs could).

indorsation, but *endorse(ment)* ; see EM- & IM-.

induce makes *-cible* ; see -ABLE 2.

induct makes *-tor* ; see -OR.

induction) (deduction. The first is the drawing, from observed or known cases, of the conviction that something established of them is true either of all similar cases, or of any particular similar case, that may afterwards be met with. The child who, having observed that all the persons known to him have two legs, confidently expects two legs on the newborn brother he has not yet seen, has made an induction. Deduction is the drawing from a general principle, however derived, of the conviction that a particular fact is true because if it were not the general principle, which has been accepted as undeniable, would not be true. The child who, being told that if you take a seed & sow it you may expect thirtyfold or so of what you took it from to spring up, sows a caraway seed & awaits the thirty copies of the seedcake from which he saved it is acting on a deduction. Whether the conclusion reached by induction or deduction is true depends on many conditions, which it is the province of Logic to expound ; but the broad difference between the two is that induction starts from known instances & arrives at a generalization, or at the power of applying to new instances what it has gathered from the old, while deduction starts from the general principle, whether established by induction or assumed, & arrives at some less general principle, or some individual fact, that may be regarded as being wrapped up in it & therefore as having the same claim to belief as the general principle itself.

indue. *En-* better; see EM- & IM-.

indulge. 1. *I.* makes *indulgeable* ; see MUTE E. 2. *But here & there*

flashes out a phrase or a sentence that strikes the note of emotion & pride in the achievements of our armies which the most reticent of men may indulge. That passes the limit of what even this very elastic verb can be stretched to. You may i. your emotion, or i. in emotion, or i. yourself in emotion; further, you may i. in, or i. yourself in, a note of emotion ; but you cannot i. a note, whether of emotion or of anything else, but only strike or utter or blow it ; & no-one who knows any grammar would deny that *which* represents *note*, not *emotion & pride.* The object of *i.* as a transitive verb must be either a person or at least something that can be credited with a capacity for being pleased or gratified ; a passion, a fancy, an emotion, may be gratified, but not a note. The mistake is less a misunderstanding of the meaning of *i.* than an example of HAZINESS, *note of emotion* being confused with *emotion,* & the confusion escaping notice under cover of *which.*

industrialize makes *-izable, -ization* ; see MUTE E.

-ine. For *glycerin(e)* &c. see -IN & -INE.

inebriate makes *-riable* ; see -ABLE 1.

inedited, un-. The second is recommended ; see IN- & UN-.

ineffaceable, un-. The first is recommended ; see IN- & UN-.

ineffective, -fectual, -ficacious, -ficient. For distinctions see EFFECTIVE.

inescapable, inessential. *Un-* is better ; see IN- & UN-.

inevitable(ness), -bly. To those of us who read reviews of books & picture-shows & acting & music it has been apparent for some time that these words have been added to what may be called the *apparatus criticus,* making up, with *distinction, charm, meticulous, intrigue* v.t., *banal, sympathetic,* & a few other LITERARY CRITICS' WORDS, the reviewing outfit. A search through all the English & French dictionaries within reach shows them all ignorant of the specialized modern use ; the OED in particular, dated 1901 for the letter I, has no inkling of it. An example or two may therefore be welcome :—*And even when a song is introduced, such as Ariel's Where the bee sucks there suck I, its effect is so great because it seems dramatically inevitable./The mere matters of arrangement, of line therein, show how great was his power, how true his perception ; he has the inevitableness of the Japanese./Inevitably he led up to the unanswerable case for giving to all women the vote, & one felt he spoke, as he declared he did, with all sincerity, with all his heart, of what he believed in./Both themes are well, that is to say inevitably, worked out./Miss —— may not always sing inevitably & spontaneously, simply for the love of beauty.*

Better examples than these might be desired for the purpose of extracting the words' sense ; they are the ones that happen to be at hand, recorded possibly for the very reason that they were open to objection. What the literary critic does mean by *inevitable* is perhaps this : surveying a work of art, we feel sometimes that the whole & all the parts are sufficiently consistent & harmonious to produce on us the effect of truth ; we then call it, for short, *convincing* ; thus & thus, we mean, it surely may have been or may be ; nothing in it inclines us to doubt ; to be convincing is a step short of being inevitable ; when the whole & the parts are so far in a concatenation accordingly that instead of *Thus & thus it may have been* we find ourselves forced to *Thus & thus it must have been* or *was* or *is*, when the change of a jot or tittle would be plain desecration, when we know that we are looking at the Platonic idea itself & no mere copy, then the tale or the picture or the music attains to *inevitableness*. This is an outsider's guess at the meaning ; whether the guess is a good one or not, the meaning seems to be one

deserving expression in a single word—but only on the condition that that word shall be strictly confined to the works or parts of works that are worthy of it. Now it is, in fact, so often met with that one is compelled to infer the existence of a great deal more inevitability in twentieth-century art of all kinds than one at all suspected ; so many things seem inevitable to the reviewer in which the reader could contemplate extensive alterations without a pang. The question is whether *convincing* or *true to nature*, phrases for whose interpretation we should not search the dictionaries in vain, would not be nearer the critic's private meaning than *inevitable*, & indeed whether he does not choose *inevitable* just because the reader would understand the other words too easily & miss being impressed by his command of mysterious terms.

inexactitude. For *terminological i.* =lie, see POLYSYLLABIC HUMOUR

inexpressibles. See POLYSYLLABIC HUMOUR.

inexpressive, un-. The second is recommended ; see IN- & UN-.

infantile) (-ine. The OED does not lay down any distinction, giving as its sole definition of *-ine* ' =infantile'. But its quotations for the two words do on the whole bear out one that might well (see DIFFERENTIATION) be encouraged, something like that between CHILDISH & *childlike*, though less established : *-ile* means of or in infancy, & *-ine* infantlike or as of an infant. If this is accepted, each of the following quotations from the OED would be the worse if *-ile* & *-ine* were to change places :—*The interest which his story first impressed upon her* infantile *imagination./The countenance is so innocent &* infantine, *you would think this head belonged to a child of twelve.* It may be said roughly that *-ile* records a fact, & *-ine* an impression.

infatuate makes *-uable* ; see -ABLE 1.
infer makes *-rred* &c. ; see -R-, -RR-.

inferable, -rible, -rrable, -rrible.
The first (with stress on *in*-, not *-er-*)
is recommended, on the pattern of
preferable, referable, transferable ;
-rrible, the chief rival of *-rable,* is
described by the OED as a ' mon-
grel ' between *inferible* & *inferrable,*
neither of which has found favour.
See also CONFER(R)ABLE.

inferno. Pl. *-os* ; see -O(E)S 3.
inferrable. See INFERABLE.
infinite(ly). There are naughty
people who will say *i.* when they
only mean *great* or *much* or *far.*
Their offence is here dealt with by
a triple bench ; the first member
is a correspondent of a well-known
journal ; the second is its editor,
a meek man, it should seem ; the
third is he who should have shared
the writing of this book with me,
among whose papers I find the cutting with his comment appended :—
1. Sir,—May I appeal to your love
of accurate English against the
common use in writing, as in speaking, of the word 'infinitely' as
equivalent to ' considerably ' or
' indefinitely ' ?—you write that ' oil
is infinitely less bulky than coal in
proportion to the energy derived
from it '. You write that ' the
habitual loafer does infinite mischief '. In the first case you intend
' considerably ' & in the second case
you can only mean that the mischief
is indefinite, sometimes great, sometimes no worse than this letter from
your obedient servant, AN HABI-
TUAL LOAFER OF NECESSITY.
2. We stand corrected. Our use
was a vulgarism. And yet we must
not run into a taboo of this noble
word. Swinburne uses it finely,
accurately, & therefore without
vulgarity, in the line ' In the infinite
spirit is room for the pulse of an
infinite pain '. There the use is
exact, because it does not imply
mere magnitude.—Ed.
3. Rot. *Infinite* is no more a vulgarism than any other deliberate
exaggeration. And *indefinitely* is a
totally wrong substitute ; I have

known at least one person habitually
use it, with ludicrous effect.
It *was* naughty of that Editor,
though, to say *infinite* & then take
his punishment lying down.

INFINITIVE. 1. For unidiomatic infinitives after nouns that prefer the
gerund, as in the extract, see
GERUND. *The habit of mapmakers*
to place *lands & not seas in the fore-
front has obscured the oneness of the
Pacific.* **2.** See SPLIT INFINITIVE.

infinitude does not appear to be
now entitled to any higher rank than
that of a NEEDLESS VARIANT of
infinity. It might well have been,
but can hardly now be, differentiated
with the sense *quality of being infinite.* Milton & Sterne, however, will
keep it in being for poets to fly to
& stylists to play with when *infinity*
palls on them. An escape from *-ity*
is sometimes welcome : *It is just
this infinitude of possibilities that
necessitates unity & continuity of
command.*

infirmity. ' The last i. of noble
minds ' is a MISQUOTATION.
inflame. *Inflam(e)able,* formed
from the English verb, & used in
16th–17th centuries, has been displaced by *inflammable* adapted from
French or Latin. *Inflammable* &
inflammatory must not be confused
(see PAIRS & SNARES) as in *Sir
Edward Carson declares before an
inflammatory audience that in the
event of the Parliament of these realms
doing certain things that are distasteful
to him he will call out his Volunteers.*

inflate makes *-atable* ; see -ABLE 1.
inflection, -xion. The second is
better ; see -XION. See also TECH-
NICAL TERMS.
inflict is, owing especially to confusion with *afflict,* peculiarly liable to
the misuse explained in the article
OBJECT-SHUFFLING. The right constructions are : he inflicted plagues
on them, he afflicted them with
plagues, plagues were inflicted on
them, they were afflicted with
plagues. Examples of the blun-

der :—*At least the worst evils of the wage system would never have* inflicted *this or any other present-day community.*/*The misconception & discussion in respect of the portraits of Shakespeare with which the world is in such generous measure* inflicted *are largely due to* . . ./*Lively young girls are inflicted with stout leather hand-bags.*

infold. *En-* better; see EM- & IM-.
informedly. A bad form; see -EDLY.
infringe. 1. *I.* makes *infringeable*, but *infringing* ; see MUTE E. 2. *I.*) (*i. upon.* Many of those who have occasion for the word must ask themselves before using it what its right construction is : do you *i.* (or *i. upon*) a rule ? do you *i.* (or *i. upon*) a domain ? is the verb, that is, transitive, or intransitive, or sometimes one & sometimes the other ? Latin scholars, aware that both *frango* & *infringo* are transitive only, will probably start with a prejudice against *upon* ; but Latin is not English, as some of them know. A study of the OED examples leaves no doubt about which construction has predominated from the 16th to the 19th century ; there are 25 quotations for the transitive verb to four for *on* or *upon* ; but 20th-century newspaper columns give a very different impression, viz that *infringe* can no longer stand at all without *upon* :—*The Lords would have the choice of either a General Election or a Referendum for any Bill that even inadvertently* infringed *on their powers.*/*Is it wise to* i. upon *their rights & susceptibilities ?*/*You are* infringing on *our prerogative & trespassing on some of the ground that we intend taking up later.*/*It is suddenly desired to* i. upon & restrict *my Sovereign rights.*/*Terms which have unfortunately been* infringed on *by the Bolsheviks.*
The view here taken of what has been happening is that (1) an imperfect knowledge of Latin has suggested that *infringo* means break in =intrude, whereas it does mean break in = damage or violate or weaken ; (2) it has therefore been identified in sense with *trespass* & *encroach* & assimilated to them in construction, this being further helped by confusion with *impinge upon* ; (3) pretentious writers like to escape from *encroach* & *trespass*, familiar words, to *i.*, which will better impress readers with their mastery of the unfamiliar. And the advice tendered is (1) to conceive *i.* as a synonym rather of *violate* & *transgress* than of *encroach* & *trespass* ; (2) to abstain altogether from *i. upon* as an erroneous phrase ; (3) to use *i.* boldly with *right, rule, privilege, patent, sovereignty, boundary, restriction, constitution*, or the like, as object ; & (4) when the temptation to insert *on* or *upon* becomes overpowering, as it chiefly does before words like *domain* & *territory*, to be contented with *trespass* or *encroach* rather than say *i. upon*.

infuriate makes *-riable* ; see -ABLE 1.
infuse. 1. *Infusable*) (*infusible.* *Fusible* being the word for *that can be fused*, & *infusible* being therefore (see -ABLE 3 a) the word for *that cannot be fused*, it is convenient as well as allowable (see -ABLE 2 s.f.) to make from the verb *infuse* not *infusible* but *infusable*. *Infusable*, then, = that can be infused ; *infusible* = that cannot be fused.
2. *Infuse*) (*imbue.* *Infuse* is one of the verbs liable to the OBJECT-SHUFFLING mistake. You can i. courage into a person, or imbue or inspire him with courage, but not infuse him with courage. Examples proving the need of the caution :—*The work he did at one school has been repeated at others, until young Australia has been* infused with *the spirit of games.*/*One man, however, it has not affected ; say, rather, it has* infused him with *its own rage against itself.*/*He* infused *his pupils with a lively faith in the riches that were within.*

-ING. 1. *I would also suggest that,*

while admitting *the modernity, the proofs offered by him as to the recent date are not very convincing./We regret to announce that Mr —— died at —— today,* following *an operation for appendicitis.* For liberties of this kind taken with the participle, see UNATTACHED.

2. For the difference between participles in *-ing* & the gerund, see GERUND.

3. *On the Press Association's Oldham* representative informing *a leading Liberal of . . ., he replied . . .* For such mixtures of participle & gerund, see FUSED PARTICIPLE.

4. *In all probability he suffers somewhat, like the proverbial dog, from* his having *received a bad name.* For the need or no need of *his* & other possessives in such contexts, see GERUND 4.

5. *Dying at their posts rather than surrender(ing)./But America is doing more* than furnishing *us with loans./ We are bound to suspect that Italy is doing something more* than raise *a diplomatic question./The wearing down phase by phase has been an integral part of the plan, & it has enabled the attack to be kept up* as well as insuring *against hitches./*As well as closing *the railway, it should make the Danube impracticable for traffic.*

Tender grammatical consciences are apt to vex themselves, sometimes with reason & sometimes without, over the comparative correctness of the *-ing* form of a verb & some other part, especially the infinitive without *to*, in certain constructions; specimens are printed above. It is well, on the one hand, not to fly in the face of grammar, but eschew what is manifestly indefensible; &, on the other hand, not to give up what one feels is idiomatic in favour of an alternative that is more obviously defensible. We can surely all condemn the last two examples without a regret. *As well as* is not a preposition, but a conjunction; it therefore cannot govern the gerunds *insuring* & *closing*, as *besides* would have done; if *as well*

as is to be kept, *insuring* must become *insured* to match *enabled*, & *closing close* to match *make*; that the latter change is not possible with the sentence in its present order is irrelevant; so much the worse (unless *besides* is written) for the present order. The grammatical conscience was there asleep; in the *America & Italy* examples we see it awake once for certain, for *furnishing* represents second thoughts; *raise* may represent first thoughts, if conscience slept, or third thoughts if conscience let *raising* have its say & then went deliberately back to the idiomatic *raise.* Everyone's first idea in these sentences would be *raise, furnish*; 'But why infinitive?' says Conscience 'we must write out the sentence at length, clearing away doubts of the exact sense of *do*, the part of speech of *more*, &c.; & we get—*America is executing* (doing) *an achievement that is wider* (more) *than* furnish us *is wide*; obviously *furnish* is impossible; go to! write down *furnishing*, which works out '. So far second thoughts. Third thoughts succeed in constructing a defence for *raise* or *furnish*, thus: *I will raise the question; I will do-more-than-raise-the-question*; in this the hyphened group is one verb, & the part of it that takes inflexions (as *Court Martial* has pl. *Courts Martial*) is *do*: *I am-doing-more-than-raise-the-question.* The summing-up is: *raising* is easily defensible but unidiomatic; *raise* is less easily defensible, but idiomatic; & *raise* has it.

Some confirmation of the defence set up for *raise* may be extracted from the first specimen propounded above: *dying rather than surrender-(ing).* There are misguided persons who would actually write *surrendering* there; but they are few, the rest of us feeling that we must either find a justification for *surrender* or else write it without justification; this feeling is strengthened if we happen to remember that we should have no such repugnance to *rather than surrendering* after a participle if the relation to be expressed were a quite different one ; compare *acquiring rather than surrendering* with *dying rather than surrendering* ; one must have its *-ing*, & the other must not. Well, the justification is the same as with *raise* : *I will die rather than surrender* ; it is true that the form of *surrender* there is decided by *will*, like that of *die*, so that, when *will die* is changed to *dying*, *surrender* is left depending on air ; but meanwhile *die-rather-than-sur-render* has become a single verb of which *die* is the conjugable part : *they died rather than surrender* ; *dying rather than surrender*

ingeminate. The often used phrase *ingeminate peace* means to say Peace, peace ! again & again (Latin *geminus* double) ; the following sentence looks as if *i.* were in danger of confusion with *germinate* or *generate* or some such word :—*We have great hopes that the result* [of a discussion on a Royal Commission's report] *will be to i. peace & to avoid the threatened recurrence of hostilities.*

ingénue. See FRENCH WORDS.
ingraft. *En-* better ; see EM- & IM-.
ingrain(ed), not *en-* ; see EM- & IM-.
ingratiate has one sense & one construction only in modern English ; it is always reflexive & means only to make (one*self*) agreeable ; even in older English, the use shown below is, to judge from the OED, unexampled : *He set himself energetically to the art of ruling his island & ingratiating his new subjects./ Even if it does i. the men, it will only be by alienating the women.*

inhale makes *-lable* ; see MUTE E.
inherit makes *-tor*, with fem. *inheritress* or (in technical use) *-trix* (for pl. see -TRIX).
initiate. 1. *I.* makes *initiable*, *-ator* ; see -ABLE 1, -OR. 2. *I.* is liable to the OBJECT-SHUFFLING mistake ; you i. persons or minds in knowledge, not knowledge into persons or minds as in : *The Russian*

Review, a quarterly which is doing so much to i. into the minds of the British public what is requisite for them to know about the Russian Empire. Instil is perhaps the word meant.

initiative. 1. After *take the i.*, the construction is *in* doing, not *of* doing as in :—*The Diet should leave to the Tsar the i.* of taking *such measures as may be necessary./M. Delcassé took the i.* of turning *the conversation to Moroccan affairs.* 2. The sense of *i.* has been narrowed down by modern usage. Taking ' the first step ' as the simple-word equivalent, we might understand that of the first step as opposed to later ones, or of the lead as taken by one person & not another or others ; the latter is the only current sense, & it appears in all the special uses ; (a) the military, where the i. is the power of forcing the enemy to conform to *your* first step, so deciding the lines of a campaign or operation ; (b) the political, where the i., technically so called, is the right of some minimum number of citizens to demand a direct popular vote on any constitutional question ; (c) the two phrases in which *i.* is chiefly used, ' take the i.', i.e. act before someone else does so, & ' of (or on) one's own i.', i.e. without a lead from someone else.

inject makes *injector* ; see -OR.
injure makes *injurable* ; see MUTE E.
inlay. See NOUN & VERB ACCENT.
inmesh. *En-* better ; see EM- & IM-.
inmost. See -MOST.
innate & instinct (adj.) have complementary uses, e.g. *Courage is innate in the race,* & *A race instinct with courage.* To exchange the words (*The leisurely solidity, the leisurely beauty of the place, so innate with the genius of the Anglo-Saxon*) is the same sort of mistake as OBJECT-SHUFFLING.
innavigable, un-. The second is recommended   see IN- & UN-.
inner. For *the inner man*, see HACKNEYED PHRASES.

innermost. See -MOST.

innings. The pl. *inningses* is colloquial only, *innings* (originally plural) being used for either number —*an innings*, or *several innings*.

innocence, -cy. The latter is an archaism, chiefly kept alive by *Ps.* xxvi. 6.

innocent of, in the sense without (*windows innocent of glass*) is a specimen of WORN-OUT HUMOUR. ' She might profitably avoid such distortions as " windows i. of glass " & trays " guiltless of any cloth " '— says a *Times* review.

innovate makes *-tor* ; see -OR.

innuendo. For pl., *-os* is recommended. The OED gives precedence to *-oes*, & a count of the plurals in its quotations shows *-oes* 4, *-os* 2, *-o's* 2 ; but see -O(E)S 6 on the principle.

inobservance, but *unobservant,* are perhaps best ; see IN- & UN-.

inoculate makes *-lable, -lator* ; see -ABLE 1, -OR. For danger of misprints, see INCULCATE.

in order that is regularly followed by *may* & *might* ; *i. o. t. nothing may,* or *might, be forgotten.* In archaic writing, the subjunctive without a modal verb may be used instead ; *i. o. t. nothing be forgotten.* In some contexts, but not in most, *shall* & *should* may pass instead of *may* & *might* ; *i. o. t. nothing should be forgotten* ; but certainly the second, & perhaps the first also, of the *shall* examples below is unidiomatic. The other examples, containing *can* & *could, will* & *would,* are undoubtedly wrong :—*The effort must be organized & continuous* i. o. t. *Palestine* shall *attract more & more of the race./To influence her in her new adolescence* i. o. t. *we* shall *once more regain the respect & admiration we enjoyed under the old Russia./Those who have supported Mr Chamberlain's programme in its entirety are now prepared to waive a portion of it* i. o. t. *by so doing they* can *assist the complete union of the Unionist Party./Farmers object to*

portions of their farms being taken i. o. t. *small holdings* can *be created./ It will conclude before lunch-time* i. o. t. *delegates* can *attend a mass meeting in London./If the 2/- per quarter duty had been kept on wheat* i. o. t. *the farmers* could have *purchased the offals at a reasonable price* . . ./*To supplement the work of the doctors on the panel* i. o. t. *every insured person in London* will *be able to obtain the very best medical attention./Insisted on the need of a special method of representation* i. o. t. *the aviator* would *be able to grasp the correct measure of the obstacles to free progression.*
These solecisms are all due to ANALOGY, *in order that* being followed by what could properly have followed *so that.*

in petto. See FOREIGN DANGER.

inquire. See FORMAL WORDS.

inquire, -ry, en-. *In-* is better ; see EM- & IM-.

insanitary. The established form ; but see UNSANITARY.

inscribe makes *-bable* ; see MUTE E.

insinuate makes *-uable, -ator* ; see -ABLE 1, -OR.

in so far. He must have a long spoon that sups with the devil ; & the safest way of dealing with *in so far* is to keep clear of it. The dangers range from mere feebleness or wordiness, through pleonasm or confusion of forms, & inaccuracy of meaning, to false grammar. The examples are in that order, & the offence charged against each is stated in a word or two, & left undiscussed for the reader to decide upon ; if he is sufficiently interested to wish for fuller treatment, he should turn to FAR 4, 5, where different uses of *so far* are considered; the prefixing of *in* is for the most part not dictated by reasons either of grammar or of sense, so that much of what is there said applies to *in so far* also :—
He did not, with such views, do much to advance his object, save in so far that *his gracious ways everywhere*

won esteem & affection (Wordy. Read *though* for *save i. s. f. that*)./ *The question . . . is not in any way essentially British*, save i. s. f. as *the position of Great Britain in Egypt makes her primarily responsible* (Wordy. Read *except that* for *save i. s. f. as*)./ *Some of the defects are inevitable, at least* i. s. f. as that *no one can suggest an improvement* (Pleonastic. Omit *in & as*)./*The large majority would reply in the affirmative*, i. s. f. as to *admit that there is a God* (Confusion between *so far as to & i. s. f. as they would*)./ *No such department under present conditions is really requisite*, i. s. f. as *the action of the Commander-in-Chief is thwarted in cases where he should be the best judge* (Wrong sense. Read *since* for *i. s. f. as*)./ *The officials have done their utmost to enforce neutrality, & have* i. s. f. *succeeded* as *the Baltic fleet keeps outside the three-mile limit* (Wrong sense. Read *have so far succeeded that*)./*These resources have pulled him through* i. s. f. as *they have made his name popular, but an artist & a realist have been lost* (Wrong sense. Read *so far that* for *i. s. f. as*)./*It has the character of a classic* i. s. f. as the period *it covers* (Ungrammatical. *In so far as* is not a preposition, & cannot govern *period*).

insouciance, -ant. See FRENCH WORDS ; the adjective, however, is usually, & the noun often, anglicized in pronunciation to ĭnsŏō's-.

inspan makes *-nned* &c. ; see -N-, -NN-.

inspect makes *-tor, -tress* ; for the latter see FEMININE DESIGNATIONS.

inspire makes *-rable* ; see MUTE E.

instance. The abuse of this word in lazy periphrasis has gone far, though not so far as that of CASE. Here are two examples :—*The taxation of the unimproved values in any area, omitting altogether a tax on improvements, necessarily lightens the burden* in the instance of *improved properties./The stimulation to improve land, owing to the appreciable*

rating of the same, is more clearly established whenever the outgo is very direct & visible, such as in the instance of *highly priced city lands*. In the first, *in the instance of* should be simply *on* ; & in the second *such as in the instance of* should be *as on*. There is some danger that, as writers become aware of. the suspicions to which they lay themselves open by perpetually using *case*, they may take refuge with *instance*, not realizing that most instances in which *case* would have damned them are also cases in which *instance* will damn them. The crossing out of one & putting in of the other will not avail ; they must rend their heart & not their garments, & learn to write directly instead of in periphrasis. *Instance* has been called *case*'s understudy ; in the articles CASE, & ELEGANT VARIATION, will be found many examples of the substitution.

instance, v., makes *-ceable* ; see MUTE E.

instant, *proximo, & ultimo*, appended to numbers from 1st to 31st & meaning of this, next, last, month, are usually written & even said in the abbreviated forms *inst., prox.,* & *ult.* Why it should be laid down, as it is in some printing manuals, that the abbreviations should not be printed, but the full forms, is a mystery.

instigate makes *-gable, -tor* ; see -ABLE 1, -OR.

instil(l). The OED gives precedence to *-il.* In any case, *-lled, -lling* ; see -LL-, -L-. The word is liable to the OBJECT-SHUFFLING confusion. *The Tsar's words will undoubtedly instil the Christians of Macedonia with hope.* You can inspire men with hope, or hope in men ; but you can only instil it into them, not them with it. See ANALOGY.

instinct) (intuition. See INTUITION.
institute makes *-tutable, -tutor.*
institute) (institution. The two nouns have run awkwardly into &

out of one another. The neat arrangement would have been for *-ution* to mean instituting, & *-ute* a thing instituted ; but *-ution* has seized, as abstract words will, on so many concrete senses that neatness is past praying for. *Institution* is in fact the natural English word capable of general use, & *-ute* a special title restricted to, & preferred for, certain institutions. An *-ute* is deliberately founded ; an *-ution* may be so, or may have established itself or grown. A man leaves his fortune to institutions, but perhaps founds a parish or a mechanics' *-ute*, i.e. an *-ution* designed to give instruction or amusement to a special class of people. Whether a particular *-ution* founded for a definite purpose shall have *-ute* or *-ution* in its title is a matter of chance or fashion—*The Royal -ute of Painters in Water Colours*, but *The -ution of Civil Engineers* ; *The Royal -ution*, but *The Imperial -ute*. A child is to be got into some *-ution*, & is placed in the National *-ute* for the Blind or the Masonic *-ution* for Boys.

Cricket, five-o'clock tea, the House of Lords, Eton, the Workhouse, a hospital, the National Gallery, marriage, capital punishment, the Law Courts, are all *-utions* & not *-utes*.

instruct makes *-tor*, *-tress* ; see FEMININE DESIGNATIONS.

insubstantial. *Un-* is better ; see IN- & UN-.

insufficient. *But Austria also excludes altogether a food-product like meat,* of which *she produces* insufficient. This noun use (= not enough or too little) is worse than the corresponding use of SUFFICIENT.

insulate makes *-lable*, *-tor* ; see -ABLE 1, -OR.

insupportable, un-. The first is recommended ; see IN- & UN-.

insure. See ENSURE. *I.* makes *-rable* ; see MUTE E.

insusceptible, not *un-*. See IN- & UN-, & -ABLE 3 a.

intaglio. Pronounce -ă'lyŏ. Pl. *-os*, see -O(E)S 4. *Intaglio* is opposed to *relief* as a name for the kind of carving in which the design, instead of projecting from the surface, is sunk below it (*carved in i.*); & to ·*cameo* as the name for gems of the same kind but carved in i. instead of in relief.

integrate makes *-grable*, *-tor* ; see -ABLE 1, -OR.

intelligent) (intellectual. While an intelligent person is merely one who is not stupid or slow-witted, an intellectual person is one in whom the part played by the mind as distinguished from the emotions & perceptions is greater than in the average man. An intellectual person who was not intelligent would be, though not impossible, a rarity ; but an intelligent person who is not intellectual we most of us flatter ourselves that we can find in the looking-glass. *Intelligent* is usually a patronizing epithet, while *intellectual* is a respectful one, but seldom untinged by suspicion or dislike.

intelligentsia, -tzia. Both forms are current.

intended, n. It is curious that betrothed people should find it so difficult to hit upon a comfortable word to describe each other by. ' My intended ', ' my engaged ', ' my *fiancé(e)* ', ' my sweetheart ', ' my love(r) '—none of these is much to their taste, too emotional, or too French, or too vulgar, or too evasive. The last two objections are in fact one ; evasion of plain words is vulgarity, & ' my intended ' gives the impression that the poor things are shy of specifying the bond between them, an ill-bred shyness ; so too with ' my engaged ', & in *fiancé(e)* they resort to French instead of to vague English for their embarrassing though futile disguise. Is it too late to suggest that ' my betrothed ', which means just what it should, i.e. pledged to be married, & is not vulgarized but only out of fashion, & would be a dignified word for public use, should be given another chance ?

intensive. Just as *definitive* & *alternative* are ignorantly confused with *definite* & *alternate*, & apparently liked the better for their mere length, so *intensive* is becoming a fashionable word where the meaning wanted is simply *intense*. It must be admitted that there was a time before differentiation had taken place when Burton, e.g., could write *A very intensive pleasure follows the passion*; it there means intense, but the OED labels the use obsolete, & its latest quotation for it is from over two centuries ago ; the modern relapse had not come under its notice in 1901, when it issued letter I. *Intensive* perished as a mere variant of *intense*, but remained with a philosophic or scientific meaning, as an antithesis to *extensive* ; where *extensive* means with regard to extent, *intensive* means with regard to force or degree : *The record of an intensive as well as extensive development./Its intensive, like its extensive, magnitude is small.* This is the kind of word that we ordinary mortals do well to leave alone ; see POPULARIZED TECHNICALITIES. Unfortunately, a particular technical application of the philosophic use emerged into general notice, & was misinterpreted—intensive method especially of cultivation. To increase the supply of wheat you may sow two acres instead of one—increase the extent —, or you may use more fertilizers & care on your one acre—increase the intensity— ; the second plan is intensive cultivation, the essence of it being concentration on a limited area. Familiarized by the newspapers with *intensive cultivation*, which most of us took to be a fine name for very hard or intense work by the farmers, we all became eager to show off our new word, & took to saying *intensive* where *intense* used to be good enough for us. The war gave this a great fillip by finding

the correspondents another peg to hang *intensive* on—*bombardment*. There is a kind of bombardment that may be accurately called intensive ; it is what in earlier wars we called concentrated fire, a phrase that has the advantage of being open to no misunderstanding ; the fire converges upon a much narrower front than that from which it is discharged ; but as often as not the intensive bombardment of the newspapers was not concentrated, but was intense, as the context would sometimes prove ; a bombardment may be intense without being intensive, or intensive without being intense, or it may be both.

It may now interest the reader to decide in each of the following extracts whether *intensive* is the necessary word, or the barely defensible but ill chosen word, or the altogether wrong one :—*A work which in its historic unity, practical vision, & practical points of seamanship, recalls the immenseness of Hakluyt./The period would be one of* intensive *preparation, in which the energies of all the populations would be devoted to the one end of ensuring that when the day of trial came they should have the few hours' advantage that might decide the fate of the world./With the departure of Mr Lloyd George & President Wilson a period of* intensive *work will begin in Commissions with a view to having as much material as possible ready./ A small party rigidly selected from men who think furiously &* intensively *may have an effectiveness in propaganda out of all proportion to its direct influence./There are several allusions to ' dashing about in a car ' as an* intensive *form of domestic bliss./The audience joined in the chorus & sang it over & over again amid the most* intensive *excitement.*

intensive, gram. See TECHNICAL TERMS.

intent, a. *The case has its moral for librarians all over the country ; all hoods make not monks, nor are all* *visitors to libraries on serious studies intent.* When *i.* in its inverted construction (*on mischief i.*, instead of *i. upon mischief*) is mixed up with words so pedestrian & far from archaic as *visitors to libraries*, a tepid half-hearted jocularity results ; see INCONGRUOUS VOCABULARY.

intention. 1. Ordinary use. 2. *First, second, ii.* 1. A defining phrase is so often appended to *i.* that the question between gerund & infinitive, treated generally under GERUND 3, is worth raising specially here. Choice between the two is freer for *i.* than for most such nouns, & it can hardly be said with confidence that either construction is ever impossible for it. It will perhaps be agreed, on the evidence of the illustrations below, offered as idiomatic, that when *i.* is used in the singular & without *the, his, an, any*, or other such word, *to do* is better, but otherwise *of doing* :—Intention to kill is the essential point./You never open your mouth but with i. to give pain./He denied the i. of killing./He concealed his i. of escaping./Some i. of evading it there may have been./I have no i. of allowing it./Have you any i. of trying again ?/I have every i. of returning./He renounced all i. of retaliating./Not without ii. of finding a loophole.

2. *First, second, i.* These phrases have special senses in medicine & in logic, apt to puzzle the layman & to be confused with each other. In medicine, *first i.* denotes (OED) ' the healing of a lesion or fracture by the immediate re-union of the severed parts, without granulation '; & *second i.* ' the healing of a wound by granulation after suppuration '. In logic, *first ii.* are (OED) ' primary conceptions of things, formed by the first or direct application of the mind to the things themselves ; e.g. the concepts of *a tree, an oak* ' ; & *second ii.* ' secondary conceptions formed by the application of thought to first intentions in their relations

to each other ; e.g. the concepts of *genus, species, variety, property, accident, difference, identity* '.

inter, v., makes *-rred, -rring* ; see -R-, -RR-.

inter alia is Latin for amongst others when ' others ' are things. If the others are persons, *alia* must be changed to *alios* or rarely *alias* (the OED quotes, from 1670, *The Lords produce* inter alios *John Duke of Lancaster*) ; but when persons are meant, it is much better nowadays to use English. The writer of the following sentence was either ignorant both of *inter alia* & of Latin, or else pedantic enough to expect us to know that the Latin for *costs* is the masculine *sumptus* :—*She will pay twenty thousand million marks within two years* (*covering*, inter alios, *the costs of the armies of occupation & of food & raw material allowed by the Allies*).

intercalary. Pron. ĭnter′kalarĭ.
intercalate makes *-calable, -tor* ; see -ABLE 1, -OR.
intercept makes *-tor.*
interchange. See NOUN & VERB ACCENT. The verb makes *-geable* ; see MUTE E.
interdependence, -cy. No difference in sense ; *-ce* is recommended ; see -CE, -CY.
interdict. See NOUN & VERB ACCENT ; *i.* makes *-tor.*
interest, vb. On *interesting*, the OED, after giving the sound as ĭ′nterĭstĭng, adds ' formerly, & still dialectally, ĭnterĕ′stĭng '. All the longer inflexions—*interestedly, disinterested*, &c.—& even the simple verb, are often said by more or less illiterate speakers with the accent on -ĕst-.

interfuse makes *-sible.*
interior, internal, intrinsic. See EXTERIOR.
interlocutor. See COLLOCUTOR.
interlope(r). In the noun as well as the verb, the OED stresses -lo- & not in-. But in the noun at least, commoner than the verb, RECESSIVE ACCENT seems to have brought us to

ĭ'nterlōp*er* by this time ; this was the more likely to happen because *lope* is not a recognized verb.

interlude. See -LU-.

intermediary, n., is, even in its concrete sense of a go-between or middleman or mediator, a word that should be viewed with suspicion & resorted to only when it is clear that every more ordinary word comes short of the need. In its abstract sense of medium or agency or means, it is worthy only of the POLYSYL-LABIC HUMOURist ; & the OED's only two quotations for it (representing, alas ! a much larger body than would be guessed by anyone whose business it was not to observe such things) are clearly in that spirit :—*Mysteriously transmitting them through the intermediary of glib Jew boys with curly heads./We are the only European people who teach practical geometry through the recondite intermediary of Euclid's Elements.*

intermezzo. Pronounce -dzō. Pl. -*os* or -*i* ; see -O(E)S 6.

intermit makes -*tted*, -*tting*, -*ssible* ; see -T-, -TT-.

internal. See INTERIOR.

internecine has suffered an odd fate ; being mainly a literary or educated man's word, it is yet neither pronounced in the scholarly way nor allowed its Latin meaning. It should be called ĭnter'nĭsĭn, & is called ĭnternē'sĭn ; see FALSE QUAN-TITY. And the sense has had the Kilkenny-cat notion imported into it because mutuality is the idea conveyed by *inter-* in English ; the Latin word meant merely of or to extermination (cf. *intereo* perish, *intercido* slay, *interimo* destroy) without implying that of both parties. The imported notion, however, is what gives the word its only value, since there are plenty of substitutes for it in its true sense—*destructive, slaughterous, murderous, bloody, sanguinary, mortal,* & so forth. The scholar may therefore use or abstain from the word as he chooses, but it

will be vain for him to attempt correcting other people's conception of the meaning. See POPULARIZED TECHNICALITIES.

interpellate, -ation. The two words are little used now except in the technical sense proper to parliamentary proceedings, & especially those of the French Chamber. They are therefore felt to be half French words, & so the unnatural pronunciation given by the OED (ĭnterpĕ'lāt, ĭnterpĕlā'shn) is perhaps accounted for. Normal English would be ĭnter'pelāt, ĭnterpelā'shn. The OED renderings, whether really current or not, have the advantage of distinguishing the sound from that of *interpolate, -ation*—a need illustrated by : *M. Barthou intimated that, on the return of M. Millerand from London, he would* interpolate *him on the question.*

interpellate, interpolate, make -*lable*, -*tor* ; see -ABLE 1, -OR.

interpose makes -*sable* ; see -ABLE 1. For *interposal* see -AL NOUNS.

interpretative, not *interpretive*, is the right form, -*ive* adjectives being normally formed on the Latin p.p. stem, i.e. here *interpretat-* ; *coercive* is similarly irregular, but established. Read -*ative* in :—*They should be at the same time illustrative & interpretive./The literal & the interpretive are difficult to reconcile in a single statement.*

interregnum. Pl. -*ums* or -*a* ; see -UM. For the facetious use, = gap, see PEDANTIC HUMOUR.

interrogate makes -*gable*, -*tor* ; see -ABLE 1, -OR.

interstice. Pronounce ĭnter'stĭs.

intestinal. The OED pronounces ĭntĕ'stĭnal, not ĭntĕstĭ'nal ; the Latin i is long, but on this point see FALSE QUANTITY s.f.

in that is a conjunction that has gone a little out of fashion & does not slip from our tongues nowadays. It is still serviceable in writing of a formal cast, but, like other obsolescent idioms, is liable to ill treatment at the hands of persons who choose it not because it is the natural thing for them to say, but because, being unfamiliar, it strikes them as ornamental. So :—*This influence was so far indirect in that it was greatly furthered by Le Sage./ The legislative jury sat to try the indictment against Mr Justice Grantham* in that *during the Great Yarmouth election petition he displayed political bias.* In the first, two ways of saying the thing are mixed (*was so far indirect that, & was indirect in that*) ; & in the second *in that* is used in a quite suitable context, but wrongly led up to ; a man is guilty in that he has done so-&-so, but an indictment against him is not in that anything. After *the less, the more,* the clause that responds to *the* should not begin with *in that,* but with plain *that* ; omit the *in* in :—*Nor are they any* the less pleasing in that *the colourings are of the rich not gaudy type./Whose presence is none* the less welcome in that *he serves to provide the only element of humour.*

intimate, v., makes -*mable,* -*tor* ; see -ABLE 1, -OR.

intimidate. 1. *I.* makes -*dable,* -*tor* ; see -ABLE 1, -OR. 2. *Similar threats were uttered in the endeavour to* i. Parliament from *disestablishing the Irish Episcopal Church.* From is idiomatic after *deter* & *discourage,* but not after *i.* or *terrify* ; see ANALOGY.

into) (in to. The two words should be written separately when their sense is separate. *The doors of the great Opera-house let out the crowd ; when we went* into *the opera, the streets had been swept, but when we came out the snow was inches deep again.* Opera-house shows that *opera* means not the building, but the performance, & you do not *go into* that, but *go in to* it. Correct similarly :—*Lord Rosebery took her* into *dinner./All the outside news came* into *us immediately.*

intone makes -*nable* ; see MUTE E.

in toto means not on the whole, but wholly, utterly, entirely, absolutely, & that always or nearly always with verbs of negative sense—*condemn, decline, deny, reject, disagree, i. t.* The following is nonsense : *Nor do we produce as much in toto as we might if we organized.*

intoxicate makes -*cable,* -*tor* ; see -ABLE 1, -OR.

intransigent dates in England from about 1880 ; but, being now established, it should neither be pronounced as French nor spelt -*eant* any longer.

INTRANSITIVE P.P. This article is less severely practical than most in the book, & is addressed to those few enthusiasts only who find grammatical phenomena interesting apart from any rules of writing that may be drawn from them. As grammatical terminology is far from fixed in English, it must be premised that *p.p.* (past participle) is here taken as the popular name for the single-word participle that does not end in -*ing,* i.e., by the p.p. of *hear* is meant *heard,* not *hearing* nor *having heard* nor *being heard.* All verbs, with negligible exceptions such as *must* & *can,* have this p.p., though in many it is used only as an element in making compound parts like *has climbed* or *will have died.* That function of the p.p. is familiar to everyone & needs no comment. Further, the p.p. of all transitive verbs can be used as an adjective (*a broken jug*). What is not so fully realized is the part played by the adjectival p.p. in many intransitive verbs. It is in the first place much commoner than is supposed. Most of us, perhaps, would reply if asked that p.p. adjectives were all passive, i. e. were only made from transitive verbs. A moment's search is enough to correct that notion—*fallen angels, the risen sun, a vanished hand, past times, the newly arrived guest, a grown girl, a gone coon, absconded debtors, escaped prisoners, the deceased lady, the dear departed,* *coalesced stems, a collapsed lorry, we are agreed, a couched lion, an eloped pair, an expired lease.*

Secondly, when a verb is both transitive & intransitive, it is often difficult to say whether in some particular phrase the p.p. is active or passive, & the answer may affect the sense ; e.g., *a deserted sailor*, if *deserted* is passive, is one who has been marooned, but, if it is active, is one who has run from his ship ; *an angel dropped from heaven* has possibly been passive, but more likely active, in the descent ; *a capsized boat* may have capsized or have been capsized ; *my declared enemy* is more often one who has declared enmity than one I have declared an enemy ; *a flooded meadow* shows a passive p.p., *a flooded river* perhaps an active one ; *a well grown tree* means one thing in the virgin forest, & another in a nursery garden.

Thirdly, to realize the frequency of the intransitive p.p. will sometimes throw light on expressions whose origin is otherwise not quite obvious : *a determined* or *decided man* is perhaps one who *has* determined or decided, not been determined ; a person is *ill advised* who has advised, i.e. taken thought, badly, not one who has had bad advice given him ; he is *well-read* who *has* read well ; he is *drunk* who *has* drunk ; *-spoken* in *soft-spoken* &c. is more intelligible if it is regarded as active, & cf. *well-behaved* ; *mistaken clemency* seems to be clemency that *has* erred ; *an aged man* may be one who *has* aged, since the verb *age*, = grow old, dates from before 1400 ; *the dissipated* may be those who *have* wasted their substance, & *the experienced* those *having* experienced things rather than those possessed of experience.

intrench. *En-* is better ; see EM- & IM-.

intrigue, v. t. The meaning ' puzzle, perplex ' is given by the OED, but illustrated by only a single recent quotation, & labelled ' now.

rare '. Would that were still true ! the one quotation (19th-century) is from a newspaper from which I have before me sixteen 20th-century cuttings with the word & sense. The other chief dictionaries either ignore the sense or treat it contemptuously—English dictionaries, that is, for it is naturally well enough known to the French ; but it is one of the GALLICISMS, & LITERARY CRITICS' WORDS, that have no merit whatever except that of unfamiliarity to the English reader, & at the same time the great demerit of being identical with & therefore confusing the sense of a good English word. Besides *puzzle* & *perplex*, there are *fascinate, mystify, interest, & pique*, to choose from. Will the reader decide for himself whether the Gallicism is called for in any of the following places ?—*A cabal which has intrigued the imagination of the romanticists./ The problem, however, if it intrigues him at all, is hardly opened in the present work./Nor is this the only problem raised by this intriguing exhibition./Thus it is we read of Viper—that delightful dog—mouthing a hedgehog, much intrigued with his spines./Mr Phillpotts, besides imposing these negative discomforts upon minds content that he should be content with Dartmoor, intrigues them with speculations as to what will follow this conclusion./But her personality did not greatly intrigue our interest./When theologian, scientist, & philosopher have intrigued our minds with the subtlety of their arguments./The many whose imaginations have been intrigued by the fascinating personality of Borrow./ The latter appointment would have intrigued us more in normal times than at this moment./Roumania is not altogether intrigued with the conception of herself as the vassal of France.*

intrinsic. See EXTERIOR.

introduce makes *-cible* ; see -ABLE 2.

introit. Pronounce intrŏ'ĭt.

intromit makes *-tted, -tting, -missible* ; see -T-, -TT-.

introspect makes *-tor*.
introvert makes *-versible*; -ABLE 2.
intrude makes *intrusible*; -ABLE 2.
intrust. *En-* better; see EM- & IM-.
intuition & *instinct.* The word *intuition* being both in popular use & philosophically important, a slight statement of its meaning, adapted from the OED, may be welcome. The etymological but now obsolete sense is simply inspection (Latin *tueor* look): *A looking-glass becomes spotted & stained from their only intuition* (i.e., if they so much as look in it). With the schoolmen it was The spiritual perception or immediate knowledge ascribed to angelic & spiritual beings, with whom vision & knowledge are identical: *St Paul's faith did not come by hearing, but by intuition & revelation.* In modern philosophy it is The immediate apprehension of an object by the mind without the intervention of any reasoning process: *What we feel & what we do, we may be said to know by intuition*; or again (with exclusion of one or other part of the mind) it is Immediate apprehension by the intellect alone, as in *The intuition by which we know what is right & what is wrong*, or Immediate apprehension by sense, as in *All our intuition takes place by means of the senses alone.* Finally, in general use it means Direct or immediate insight: *Rashness if it fails is madness, & if it succeeds is the intuition of genius.* How closely this last sense borders on *instinct* is plain if we compare *A miraculous intuition of what ought to be done just at the time for action* with *It was by a sort of instinct that he guided this open boat through the channels.* One of the OED's definitions of *instinct*, indeed, is : 'intuition; unconscious dexterity or skill'; & whether one word or the other will be used is often no more than a matter of chance. Three points of difference, however, suggest themselves as worth keeping in mind : (1) an intuition is a judgement issuing in conviction, & an instinct an impulse issuing in action; (2) an intuition is conceived as something primary & uncaused, but an instinct as a quintessence of things experienced in the past whether by the individual or the race ; & (3) while both, as faculties, are contrasted with that of reason, intuition is the attribute by which gods & angels, saints & geniuses, are superior to the need of reasoning, & instinct is the gift by which animals are compensated for their inability to reason.

intwine, intwist. *En-* is better; see EM- & IM-.

inundate. See -ATABLE.

inure, enure. Both the connexion between the verb's different senses (*The poor, inured to drudgery & distress*; *The cessions of land enured to the benefit of Georgia*), & its derivation, are so little obvious that many of us, at any rate when minded to use the less common sense, feel some apprehension that we may be on the point of blundering, & that, again, there is a tendency to spell *in-* & *en-* for the two meanings as if they were different words. The origin is the obsolete noun *ure* (*We will never enact, put in ure, promulge, or execute, any new canons*), which is from French *œuvre*, which is from Latin *opera* work. To inure a person you set him at work or practise him ; a thing inures that comes into practice, or operates, in such & such a direction. Variant spellings are therefore unnecessary, & *in-* is preferred by the OED.

invade makes *-dable*; see MUTE E.
invalid. The word meaning not valid is pronounced ĭnvă'lĭd. For the noun & adjective meaning sick (person), & the verb made from these, the pronunciation recommended is ĭ'nvalēd, but neither the place of the stress nor the sound of the second *i* is yet fully fixed.

invalidate makes *-dable*, *-tor*; see -ABLE 1, -OR.
inveigle. The OED pronunciation

is ĭnvē'gl without the alternative of -vā'gl.

invent makes -*tor*.

inventory. Pronounce ĭ'nventorĭ.

INVERSION. By this is meant the abandonment of the usual English sentence order & the placing of the subject after the verb as in *Said he*, or after the auxiliary of the verb as in *What did he say?* & *Never shall we see his like again*. Inversion is the regular & almost invariable way of showing that a sentence is a question, so that it has an essential place in the language ; & there are other conditions under which it is usual, desirable, or permissible. But the abuse of it ranks with ELEGANT VARIATION as one of the most repellent vices of modern writing. Inversion & variation of the uncalled-for kinds are like the fashionable high heels placed somewhere below the middle of the foot—ugly things resorted to in the false belief that artificiality is more beautiful than nature— ; but as heels of the right kind are useful or indispensable, so too is inversion. Its conditions & motives are various, & cannot be set forth in a sentence ; it seems better to postpone analysis, & to try first to persuade the reader, by an exhibition of specimens, that inversion is often practised when it serves no useful purpose, that such inversion is ugly, & that resort to it is a mark of the unskilful writer. Here, then, are some bad inversions ; the uninverted form is indicated by a word or two in brackets, & the reader is invited to decide for himself whether it would not have been in all these instances clearly better:— *Then to the resident Medical Officer of the Brompton Hospital for Consumption for an authoritative opinion on the subject* went the inquirer (*The inquirer then went*, as the beginning of the sentence)./*Sufficient* is it *to terminate the brief introduction to this notice by stating* . . . (It is sufficient)./ *Appropriately* does the author prelude *his recollections with the story*

of . . . (The author appropriately preludes)./*Somewhat in the nature of a blow* is it, *therefore, to find that* . . . (It is therefore somewhat)./*Hard* would it *be to decide which of his many pursuits in literary study he found most absorbing* (It would be hard)./*By diligent search in sunny & sheltered places* could some short-stalked primroses *be gathered* (primroses could be gathered)./*Little by little* are these poor people *being hemmed in & ground down by their cruel masters* (people are being)./ *Gloomy though* is the precedent, *the only thing left for a War Lord to do is to follow the example of Ahab at Ramoth Gilead* (the precedent is)./ *These were persons to be envied, as* might be someone *who was clearly in possession of a sixth sense* (as someone might be)./*With good peripheral railways, such as* have our invaders, *the front can be strengthened at any point* (our invaders have)./ *A frigate could administer roughly half the punishment that* could a 74 (a 74 could)./*Carrying far more than* can the steam-driven vessel (vessel can)./*He looked forward, as* do we all, *with great hope & confidence to* . . . (we all do)./*He laid down four principles on which alone* could America *go further* (America could)./ '*I couldn't help liking the chap*' would shout Lingard *when telling the story* (Lingard would shout)./*Not only is it so necessarily bounded by that moving veil which ever hides the future, but also* is it *unable to penetrate more than a paltry hundred thousand years or so into the darkness that now enshrouds the past* (it is unable)./*An undefeated Prussia is ultimately the end of England, &, in particular*, is it *the end of fortune & security for* . . . (it is the end).

Whether all of these inversions are bad, as they were said to be, or not, they can hardly fail to convince anyone who reads them one after another that inversion is not an achievement to be aimed at for its own sake, as some of these writers evidently take it to be, but a means to be employed only when it is needed. Such a reader may now be willing to examine the occasions that demand it. The result will be something of this kind :—

Inversion is the deferring of the subject till after (especially in older English) the verb, or till after (especially in modern English) the verb's auxiliary only ; *What saith he ?*, *What does he say ?*, are both inversions, the uninverted forms being *he saith*, *he says*.

In questions & commands, as contrasted with the commoner form of sentence, the statement, inversion is the rule : *Doth Job fear God for nought ?/Hear thou from heaven thy dwelling-place.* The subject being usually omitted in commands, these do not much concern us ; but in questions the subject regularly follows the verb or its auxiliary except when, being itself the interrogative pronoun or adjective, it has to stand where that pronoun almost invariably stands (Browning's *Wanting is —what ?* supplies an exception) : *Who did it ? What caused it ?* In the other exceptional sentence-form, the exclamation, inversion is not indeed the rule as in questions, but is, & still more used to be, legitimate : *How dreadful is this place !/What a piece of work is a man !/O bonnie was the rosy brier !/Few & evil have the days of the years of my life been./Bitterly did he rue it.*

Inversion, then, is the natural though not universal order of words in sentences other than statements ; in exclamations particularly, when they do not contain a special exclamatory word such as *how* or *what*, the inversion is what announces their nature ; & one form of bad inversion arises from inability to distinguish between an exclamation & a mere statement, so that the latter is allowed the order that marks the former (*Hard is it to decide*, on the pattern of *Hard, very hard, is my fare !*). To these forms of sentence must be added the hypothetical clause in which the

work ordinarily done by *if* is done in its absence by inversion : *Were I Brutus./Had they known in time.*

Interrogative, Imperative, Exclamatory, & Hypothetical Inversions form a group in which inversion itself serves a purpose. With statements it is otherwise ; inversion is there not performed for its own significance, but comes about owing to the writer's wish to place at the beginning either the predicate or some word or phrase that belongs to it. He may have various reasons for this. The usual reason for putting the whole of the predicate at the beginning is the feeling that it is too insignificant to be noticed at all after the more conspicuous subject, & that it must be given what chance the early position can give it ; hence the *There is* idiom ; not *No God is*, but *There is no God.* That is Balance Inversion in its shortest form, & at greater length it is seen in : *Through a gap came a single level bar of glowing red sunlight peopled with myriads of gnats that gave it a quivering solidity* ; if *came through a gap* is experimentally returned to its place at the end of that, it becomes plain why the writer has put it out of its place at the beginning. Another familiar type is *Among the guests were A, B, C ... Z.*

Often, however, the object is not to transfer the predicate bodily to the beginning, but to give some word or words of it first place. Such a word may be meant to give hearer or reader the connexion with what precedes (Link Inversion), to put him early in possession of the theme (Signpost Inversion), or to warn him that the sentence is to be negative (Negative Inversion) :—*On this depends the whole course of the argument./By strategy is meant something wider./Never was a decision more abundantly justified.* On *this*, by *strategy*, *never*, are the causes of inversion here ; each belongs to the predicate, not to the subject ; & when it is placed first it tends to drag with it the verb or auxiliary, so that the subject has to wait ; tends, but with different degrees of force, that exercised by a negative being the strongest. We can if we like, instead of inverting, write *On this the whole course of the argument depends*, or *By strategy something wider is meant*, but not *Never a decision was more abundantly justified* ; & *Not a word he said* is a very out-of-the-way version of *Not a word did he say*.

If we now add Metrical Inversion, our catalogue of the various kinds may perhaps suffice. Where the Bible gives us *As the hart panteth after the water brooks*, & the Prayer Book *Like as the hart desireth the water-brooks*, both without inversion, the hymn-books have *As pants the hart for cooling streams*. That is metri gratiâ, & it must not be forgotten that inversion is far more often appropriate in verse than out of it for two reasons—one this of helping the versifier out of metrical difficulties, & the other that inversion off the beaten track is an archaic & therefore poetic habit. A very large class of bad inversions will be seen presently to be those in subordinate clauses beginning with *as* ; they arise from failure to realize that inversion is archaic & poetic under such circumstances, & non-inversion normal ; it is therefore worth while to stress this contrast between *As pants the hart* & both the prose versions of the same clause.

To summarize these results :

Interrogative Inversion : *What went ye out for to see ?/Doth Job fear God for nought ?*

Imperative Inversion : *Hear thou from heaven thy dwelling-place.*

Exclamatory Inversion : *How dreadful is this place !/What a piece of work is a man !/O bonnie was the rosy brier !/Few & evil have the days of the years of my life been./Bitterly did he rue it./Bang went saxpence !*

Hypothetical Inversion : *Were I Brutus, & Brutus Antony.*

Balance Inversion : *There is no God./Through a gap came* [an elaborately described ray]./*Among the guests were* [long list].

Link Inversion : *On this depends the whole argument./Next comes the question of pay.*

Signpost Inversion : *By strategy is meant something wider.*

Negative Inversion : *Never was a decision more abundantly justified./Not a word did he say.*

Metrical Inversion : *As pants the hart for cooling streams.*

We may now proceed to consider with the aid of grouped specimens some of the temptations to ill-advised inversion. It may conciliate anyone who suspects that the object of this article is to deprive him altogether of a favourite construction, if it is at once admitted that, though bad inversion is extremely common, non-inversion also can be bad. It is so rare as to call for little attention, but here are two examples:—*But in neither case* Mr Galsworthy tells *very much of the intervening years./Least of all* it is *to their interest to have a new Sick Man of Europe.* In negative sentences there is the choice whether the negative shall be brought to the beginning or not, but when it is so placed inversion is necessary ; read *does Mr G., & is it.*

INVERSION AFTER RELATIVES & COMPARATIVES

The problems offered are interesting, but most difficult to grapple with by way of argument. The line here taken is that the sort of inversion now being dealt with, however devoutly one may believe it to be mistaken, can hardly be proved illegitimate, at any rate without discussion of more tedious length than could be tolerated. On the other hand, it is hardly credible, after a look through the collection shortly to follow, that the writers can have chosen these inversions either as the natural way of expressing themselves or as graceful decoration ; so unnatural & so ungraceful are many of them. It follows that the motive must have been a severe sense of duty, a resolve to be correct, according to their lights, at any sacrifice. And from this again it follows that no demonstration that the inversions are incorrect is called for ; the task is only to show cause why non-inversion should be permitted, & these idolaters will be free of the superstitions that cramped their native taste. The quotations are arranged in batches, with a number attached to that one in each batch which is to be discussed below. The reader will perhaps be kind enough to translate each specimen into the uninverted order & pass a preliminary judgement upon it.

1. *A frigate could administer roughly half the punishment that* could a 74./ *With good peripheral railways, such as* have our invaders, *the front can be strengthened.*

2. *It costs less than* did administration *under the old companies./Ships without funnels, carrying far more than* can the steam-driven vessel.

3. *It is unlikely that a conflict can be localized, as* were the previous struggles *in* 1908 & 1909./*He looked forward, as* do we *all, with great hope & confidence to Monday's debate./It represents the business interests of Germany as* does no other organization./. . . *his fondness for the game, which he played as* should an Aberdonian./*These were persons to be envied, as* might be someone *who was clearly in possession of a sixth sense./The French tanks have had their vicissitudes, as* have had ours.

4. *Each has proven ably that the other's kind of Protection would be quite as ruinous as* would be Free Trade./*We are unable to . . . without getting as excited over the question of funds as* is a cat *on a hot iron./He was as far removed as* are the poles asunder *from the practices which made the other notorious./The lawn-tennis championships will be attracting as much attention as* has the golf championship. / *Thirteen divisions taken from reserve is now as serious as* would have been some fifty divisions *four months ago./Judge Parry's interest in ephemeral drama is known, of course, as well as* are his views *on the law of . . .*

5. *Bad as* has been our record *in the treatment of some of the military inventions of the past, it may be doubted whether the neglect of the obvious has ever been more conspicuously displayed than in . . ./And, hopeless as* seem the other divisions *of Belfast, progress is being made in them.*

6. *It is not all joy to be a War Lord in these days, & gloomy though* is the precedent, *the only thing left for a War Lord to do is to follow the example of Ahab at Ramoth Gilead.*

7. *The work stands still until* comes the convenient time *for arranging an amicable rupture of the old engagement & contracting of the new.*

Comments on these groups.

1. Compare some everyday sentence: *You earn twice the money that I do*, never *that do I*. The misconception is perhaps that the putting of the object first (here *that*) should draw the verb ; but this is not true of relative clauses ; *the people that I like*, not *that like I*.

2. A simple parallel is *I spend less than you do*, for which no-one in talk would substitute *than do you*. Many, however, would write, if not say, *I spend less than do nine out of ten people in my position*. The difference must lie in the length of the subject, & the misconception must be that it is a case for balance inversion, i.e. for saving the verb from going unnoticed ; but so little does that matter that if the verb is omitted no harm is done ; *did* in the quotation should in fact either be omitted or put in either of its natural places, after *administration*, or after *companies*.

3. *As*, in such sentences, is a relative adverb ; it & the unexpressed *so* to which it answers are equivalent to (*in the way*) *in which*, & what was

said above of relatives & inversion holds here also. *Try to pronounce it as I do*, not *as do I*; & when the subject is longer, e.g. *the native Frenchman*, though *as does the native Frenchman* becomes defensible, it does not become better than *as the native Frenchman does*, nor as good.

4. The *as* of this batch differs from that of batch 3 in that its fellow *as* of the main sentence belongs to an adjective (*ruinous, excited*, &c.) or adverb (*far, well*). This allows the inversionist a different defence, which he needs, since balance inversion is clearly not available for *as would be Free Trade* with its short subject. He might appeal here to exclamatory inversion. When the compound sentence is reduced to its elements, they are either (a) *Free Trade would be ruinous*; *Protection would be equally ruinous* (the first clause being a statement); or (b) *Ruinous would Free Trade be!* *Protection would be equally ruinous* (the first clause being an exclamation). He chooses, how reasonably let the reader judge, the (b) form, & retains its order in the compound sentence. The truth is that in three of these sentences the verb should have been omitted, & in the others kept in its ordinary place—*as the poles are asunder, as the golf championship has attracted, as 50 would have been.*

5. The meaning of this *as* idiom is clear; it is Though our record has been so bad, or However bad our record has been; but how it reached its present shape is less apparent. Some light is thrown by the presence in earlier English of another *as*, now dropped; Swift writes *The world, as censorious as it is, hath been so kind* . . .; this points to (*Be our record as*) *bad as our record has been* (*bad*) for the unabbreviated form. Omission of the bracketed words gives the uninverted order, which will only be changed if exclamatory inversion (*Bad has been our record!*) or balance inversion is needlessly applied.

6. *Gloomy is the precedent!* is a not

impossible exclamatory inversion; &, if the words were kept together with the effect of a quotation by having *though* before instead of in the middle of them, the exclamatory order might be tolerable, though hardly desirable, even in the subordinated form; but not with *though* where it is. This may be tested by trying a familiar phrase like *Bad is the best. Though bad is the best,* yes; but not *Bad though is the best*; instead of that we must write *Bad though the best is.*

7. There is no doubt about the motive. It is a balance inversion, & one that would be justified by the great length of the subject if the only place for the uninverted *comes* were at the end of the whole sentence. But what is too often forgotten in such cases is that there is usually a choice of places for the verb; here *comes* would be quite comfortable immediately after *time*. The conclusion suggested is that, so far as relative clauses, & especially those containing *as*, are concerned, the writer whose taste disposes him to use the natural uninverted order is at the very least free to indulge it.

INVERSIONS OF THE LITER-ARY PARAGRAPHIST

The gentlemen who provide newspapers with short accounts of newly published books have an inversion form all to themselves. The principle seems to be that the title of the book is to be got to a place where the reader shall be able to find it; at the same time the catalogue look is to be avoided that results if the title is printed at the head before the description; & a literary air is to be so given to the paragraph. The title is therefore worked to the end, by the use of odd inversions that editors would do well to prohibit. But, once broken in to inversion by this special use of it, the minor literary critics learn to love their chains, & it is among them that the false exclamatory inversions dealt with in the next section

are most rife. Here, meanwhile, are some of the characteristic form :—
Most racily written, with an easy conversational style about it, is Mr Frank Rutter's ' The Path to Paris './ Diplomatic & military are the letters that comprise the Correspondence of Lord Burghersh, edited by his daughter-in-law./From the point of view of the English reader timely is the appearance of M. Frédéric Masson's historical study [title]./*Lively & interesting are the pictures of bygone society in town & country presented in the two volumes, ' The Letter-bag of Lady Elizabeth Spencer-Stanhope './ Mainly concerned with the rural classes, who form something like two-thirds of the whole population, are the sketches & tales collected in ' The Silent India './Based on contemporary writers, her own love-letters, & ' anti-Napoleonic pamphleteers ', is* [title]./*Written in his most vivacious vein is Lieut. Colonel Haggard's latest historical study* [title].

FALSE EXCLAMATORY INVERSION

It has already been pointed out that a statement may be turned into an exclamation by inversion ; an adjective or adverb that conveys emotion is put first out of its place, & inversion follows. If Jacob had said *The days of the years of my life have been few & evil*, he would have been stating a bald fact ; by beginning *Few & evil have been*, he converts the statement into a groan, & gives it poignancy. Writers who observe the poignancy sometimes given by such inversion, but fail to observe that ' sometimes ' means ' when exclamation is appropriate ', adopt inversion as an infallible enlivener ; they aim at freshness & attain frigidity. In the following examples there is no emotional need of exclamation, & yet exclamatory inversion is the only class to which they can be assigned :—*Futile were the endeavor to trace back to Pheidias' varied originals, as we are tempted to do, many of the later statues./Finely*

conceived is this poem, & not less admirable in execution./Facile & musical, sincere & spontaneous, are these lyrics./Hard would it be to decide which of his many pursuits in literary study he found most absorbing./Fluctuating were the conditions under which the portage could be made./Sufficient is it to terminate the brief introduction to this notice by stating . . ./Irresistibly is the reader reminded, though direct analogy is absent, of Sheridan's reference to . . ./ Appropriately does the author prelude his recollections with . . ./Lately has been launched here the scare of an alleged Russian grain-export monopoly./By diligent search in sunny & sheltered places could some short-stalked primroses be gathered (This is perhaps, however, a negative inversion gone wrong by the omission of the necessary *only* at the beginning)./ *Little by little are these poor people being hemmed in & ground down by their cruel masters* (*Little by little* is quite the wrong expression to start an exclamatory inversion with, since its effect is not to enhance, but to diminish, the emotional effect).

YET, ESPECIALLY, RATHER, &c.

A curious habit has grown up of allowing these & similar words to dictate a link inversion when the stressing of the link is so little necessary as to give a noticeable formality or pomposity to the passage. It is a matter not for argument, but for taste ; will the reader compare the quoted forms with those suggested in the brackets ? *Especially & rather* usually change their place when inversion is given up, but *yet* remains first. The last example, in which the unusual *in particular* with this construction is felt to be intolerable, is strong evidence that the order to which custom has reconciled us with certain words only is not good on the merits :—*His works were burnt by the common hangman ; yet was the multitude still true to him* (yet the multitude was)./*Henry Fox, or no-*

body, could weather the storm which was about to burst ; yet was he a person to whom the court, even in that extremity, was unwilling to have recourse (yet he was)./*The set epistolary pieces, one might say, were discharged before the day of Elia ; yet is there certainly no general diminution of sparkle or interest* (yet there is)./. . . *springs of mineralized water, famous from Roman times onward for their curative properties ; especially did they come into renown during the nineteenth century* (they came into renown especially)./*Mr Campbell does not recognize a change of opinion, but admits a change of emphasis ; especially is he anxious at the present time to advance the cause of Liberal Evangelism* (he is especially anxious)./*It is to be hoped that some supervision will be exercised in the reproductions ; especially will care be needed in the painting process* (care will be needed especially in)./*His love of romantic literature was as far as possible from that of a mind which only feeds on romantic excitements ; rather was it that of one who was so moulded* . . . (it was rather that)./*There is nothing to show that the Asclepiads took any prominent share in the work of founding anatomy, physiology, zoology, & botany ; rather do these seem to have sprung from the early philosophers* (these seem rather)./*His book is not a biography in the ordinary sense ; rather is it a series of recollections culled from* . . . (it is rather)./*An undefeated Prussia is ultimately the end of England, &, in particular, is it the end of fortune & security for* . . . (& it is the end in particular).

INVERSION IN INDIRECT QUESTIONS

This point will be found fully discussed under INDIRECT QUESTION. Examples of the wrong use are : *How bold is this attack may be judged by* . . ./*Why should we be so penalized must ever remain a mystery. How bold this attack is,* & *Why we should be so penalized*, would be the right order.

SUBORDINATED INVERSIONS

Certain kinds of these have been discussed in the section on relatives & comparatives. A more general point is to be made here—that it is often well, when a sentence that standing by itself would properly be in the inverted form is subordinated as a clause to another, to cancel the inversion as no longer needed. The special effect that inversion is intended to secure is an emphasis of some sort, & naturally emphasis is more often suitable to a simple independent sentence than to a dependent clause. Examples are grouped under A, B, & C, according to the kind of inversion that has been subordinated, & comment on each group follows :—

A. Negative Inversion. *The amount involved is no less a sum than £300,000 per annum,* to not a penny of which have the drivers *a shadow of claim.*/*To give to all the scholars that firm grounding* upon which alone can we hope *to build an educated nation.*/*He laid down four principles* on which alone could America & Austria go *further in exchanging views.*/Now that not only are public executions *long extinct in this country, but the Press not admitted to the majority of private ones, the hangman has lost his vogue.*/*But it had only been established* that on eighteen of those days did he vote.

B. Exclamatory Inversion. *Suffice it to say* that in almost one half of the rural district areas is there *an admitted dearth of cottage homes.* / Though once, at any rate, does that benign mistily golden irony *of his weave itself in.*/While for the first time, he believed, did naval & military history *appear as a distinctive feature.*

C. Link Inversion. When, three years later, came the offer *of a nomination, it was doubtless a welcome solution.*/Whilst equally necessary is it *to press forward to that unity of thought without which* . . .

A. In the first three it will be admitted that, while *Upon this alone*

&c. (the independent forms) would require the inversion, *upon which alone* &c. (the subordinate forms) are at least as good, if not better, without it. The fourth example (executions) will on the other hand be upheld by many who have no inordinate liking for inversion ; *not only* is so little used except in main sentences, & therefore so associated with inversion, that *not only public executions are long extinct*, though legitimate, has an unfamiliar sound even after *Now that*. The subordinate inversion in the last A example is not quite what it seems, being due to irresolution between an inverted & an uninverted form ; the former would be, *But only on eighteen of those days had it been established that he voted* ; & the latter, *But it had only been established that he voted on 18 of those days*.

B. The subordination in two of these only makes more conspicuous the badly chosen pegs on which the inversion is hung. *In almost one half of the rural district areas, & once at any rate*, are not good exclamatory material ; *Many a time have I seen him!* shows the sort of phrase that will do. Even if main sentences had been used with these beginnings, they should have been put as statements, i.e. without inversion, & still more when they depend on *Though & Suffice it to say that*. In the third example *for the first time* is not incapable of beginning an exclamation ; it would pass in a sentence, but becomes frigid in a clause.

C. About these there can hardly be a difference of opinion. If the *when & whilst* constructions were absent, it would have been very natural to draw *Three years later, Equally necessary*, to the beginning to connect the sentences with what preceded, & inversion might or might not result. But with the interposition of *when & whilst* they lose their linking effect, & the natural order should be kept—*When the offer came three years later, Whilst it is equally necessary*.

INVERSION IN PARALLEL CLAUSES

As with combinations of a negative & a positive statement into one (see NEGATIVE & AFFIRMATIVE PARALLELS), so with inverted & uninverted members of a sentence care is very necessary.

Not only is it *so necessarily bounded by that moving veil which ever hides the future*, but also is it *unable to penetrate . . . into . . . the past (but also is it* is an impossible inversion, brought about by the correct one that precedes)./*Not only in equipment but in the personnel of the Air Battalion are we suffering from maladministration (Not only in equipment requires we are suffering ; in the personnel* requires *we are suffering*. To mix the two is slovenly ; the right form would be *We are suffering not only in* &c.)./*Even* were this tract *of country level plain &* the roads lent themselves *to the manœuvre, it would be so perilous to . . . (were this tract* is inverted ; *the roads lent themselves* is not, & yet, since there is no *if*, it absolutely requires it. Begin *Even if this tract were*; for the only ways to invert the second clause are the fantastic *& lent themselves the roads &* the clumsy *& did the roads lend*)./*Had we desired twenty-seven amendments, got seven accepted, &* were in anticipation *of favourable decisions in the other twenty cases we should think . . .* (Mend like the previous one. To read *& were we* would disguise the fact that the whole is one hypothetical clause & not several). For other examples see ELLIPSIS 6.

INVERSION IN DIALOGUE MACHINERY

Novelists & others who have to use dialogue as an ingredient in narrative are some of them unduly worried by the machinery problem. Tired of writing down *he said & said he & she replied* as often as they must, they mistakenly suppose the good old forms to be as tiring to their readers as to themselves, & seek relief in whimsical variations. The fact is that readers care what is said, but the frame into which a remark or a speech is fitted is indifferent to them ; or rather, the virtue of frames is not that they should be various, but that they should be inconspicuous. It is true that an absolutely unrelieved monotony will itself become conspicuous ; but the variety necessary to obviate that should be strictly limited to forms inconspicuous in themselves. Among those that are not inconspicuous, & are therefore bad, are many developments of the blameless & inconspicuous *said he*, especially the substitution of verbs that are only by much stretching qualified for verbs of saying, & again the use of those parts of verbs of saying that include auxiliaries. A few examples will make these points clear ; they are not of the more egregious kind, but most of them exhibit a writer trying not to bore his reader, & nothing bores so fatally as an open consciousness that one is in danger of boring :—' *Yes* ', *moodily consented John*, ' *I suppose we must* './ ' *Oh ?* ' *questioned he.*/' *Nossignore* ', *disavowed Don Ambrogio.*/' *Oh, what a sigh !* ', *marvelled Annunziata.*/ ' *But then* ', *puzzled John*, ' *what is it that people mean when they talk about death ?* '/' *The sordid sort of existence* ', *augmented John.*/' *You misunderstand your instructions* ', *murmured rapidly Mr Travers.*/' *I couldn't help liking the chap* ', *would shout Lingard when telling the story.*/ ' *I won't plot anything extra against Tom* ', *had said Isaac.*/' *At any rate, then* ', *may rejoin our critic*, ' *it is clearly useless . . .* '/' *I am the lover of a Queen* ', *had often sung the steward in his pantry below*.

The ordinary ' said he ' &c. (Thou art right, Trim, in both cases, said my uncle Toby) was described above as blameless & inconspicuous. Its place among inversions is in the ' signpost ' class. The reader is to be given the theme (i.e., here, the speech) at the earliest possible moment ; the speech, being grammatically the object of ' said ', yet placed first, draws ' said ' to it, & ' he ', or my uncle Toby, has to wait. But only such insignificant verbs as *said, replied, continued*, will submit to being dragged about like this ; verbs that introduce a more complicated notion, or that are weighted with auxiliaries or adverbs (compare ' went on my uncle Toby ' with ' continued my uncle Toby '), or that cannot rightly take a speech as object, stand on their dignity & insist on their proper place.

INVERTED COMMAS. See STOPS. For the use as apology for slang, see SUPERIORITY.

invest makes *investor*.

investigate, invigorate, make *-gable, -tor* ; see -ABLE 1, -OR.

invite, n. The OED compares *command* & *request* for the formation, but describes the noun use as colloquial ; & it has never, even as a colloquialism, attained to respectability ; after 250 years of life, it is less recognized as an English word than *bike*.

invite, v., makes *-table* ; see MUTE E.

invoke uses *invocable* (ĭ'nvokabl) rather than *invokable* (invō'kabl).

involution. See -LU-.

involve makes *-vable* ; see MUTE E.

involvedly. Four syllables, if used ; see -EDLY.

inwardness. *The i., the real i., the true i., of* something has a meaning that it would not occur to us to give it out of our own heads, but that we some time or other discover to be attached to it by other people, especially such as write books ; that meaning is, as defined by the OED, ' the inward or intrinsic character or quality of a thing ; the inner nature, essence, or meaning '. It is a literary phrase fit for a literary man to use when he is writing for or talking to literary people, but otherwise pretentious ; true wisdom is to abstain from it till it seems the really natural phrase ; & any inclination

INWEAVE   294   -ION & -NESS

to put inverted commas round it is a fair proof that one has not reached, or that one doubts whether one's readers have reached, that stage. There is a certain intrusiveness about the word in these quotations ; omission, or a simpler substitute, would have done no harm :—*When the First Lord gets to understand* (*the real i. of*) *the present situation, I have every confidence that he will do full justice to the Thames.*/*In this connexion I would warn readers who are unacquainted with* (*the i. of*) *South African affairs not to attach undue importance to a recent declaration.*/ *Will you allow me to send a few lines on the true i. of the situation ?* (realities)./*We have always contended that the true 'inwardness' of the Land Bill was not the wish to stop evictions, but the wish to stop the scandal of evictions* (motive).

inweave. Not *en-* ; see EM- & IM-.
inwrap. *En-* better ; see EM- & IM-.
iodine. For this, as well as for the three parallel element-names *bromine, chlorine, & fluorine,* the OED prefers the sound -ĭn, with -ĭn allowed as alternative. Popular use is almost universally for -ĭn in *iodine,* but varies in the other three.

-ION & -MENT. Many verbs have associated with them nouns of both forms, as *commit, commission & commitment* ; *require, requisition & requirement* ; *excite, excitement & excitation.* When both are well established, as in these cases, the two nouns usually co-exist because they have come by differentiation to divide the possible meanings between them & so tend to lucidity. How little the essential difference of meaning is may be seen by comparing *emendation* with *amendment* (where the first means rather correction made, & the second rather correcting), & *requisition* with *requirement* (where the first means rather requiring, & the second rather thing required), & then noticing that the two comparisons give more or less contrary results. Further,

when there is only one established form, it is not apparent to the layman, though the philologist sometimes knows, why one form exists & the other does not—why e.g. we say *infliction* & not *inflictment,* but *punishment* & not *punition.* The conclusion is that usage should be respected, & words that have been rarely used or may easily be coined, such as *abolishment, admonishment, pollutement, incitation,* & *punition,* should not be lightly resorted to when *abolition, admonition, pollution, incitement,* & *punishment,* are to hand. To illustrate what is meant by 'lightly' : if a writer suddenly realizes or suspects that he cannot say 'by chastisement of actual & admonition of prospective offenders', & changes to *admonishment* as fitter for the construction wanted, without taking the trouble to think either of *chastising & admonishing* or *chastisement & dissuasion,* he is treating the language with levity.

-ION & -NESS. The question between variants in *-ion & -ness* differs from that discussed in the previous article in several respects. First, *-ness* words can be made from any adjective or participle, whereas the formation of *-ment* words from verbs is by no means unrestricted ; by the side of *persuasion* you can make *persuasiveness,* but not *persuadement.* Secondly, there is more possibility of a clear distinction in meaning ; *-ion & -ment* are both attached to verbs, so that neither has any more claim than the other to represent the verbal idea of action ; but between *-ion & -ness* that line does exist ; though *-ion & -ness* are often appended to exactly the same form, as in *abjectness & abjection,* one is made from the English adjective *abject,* & the other from the Latin verbal stem *abject-,* with the consequence that *abjectness* necessarily represents a state or quality, & *abjection* naturally at least a process or action. Thirdly, while both *-ion & -ment* pass easily from the idea of a process or action into that of the product—*abstraction* e.g. being equivalent either to *abstracting* or to *abstract notion*—, to subject *-ness* to that treatment is to do it violence ; we can call virtue an abstraction, but not an abstractness ; in compensation for this disability, the *-ness* words should be secured as far as possible the exclusive right to the meaning of state or quality ; e.g. we should avoid talking of the *abstraction* or the *concision* of a writer's style, or of the *consideration* that marks someone's dealings, when we mean *abstractness*, *conciseness*, & *considerateness*. *Concision* means the process of cutting down, & *conciseness* the cut-down state ; the ordinary man, who when he means the latter says *conciseness*, shows more literary sense than the literary critic, who says *concision* just because the French, who have not the advantage of possessing *-ness*, have to say it, & he likes Gallicizing. It is not always easy to prove that writers do not mean the process rather than the quality, but appearances. are often against them ; in the following examples, if the epithet *short-winded*, & the parallel *pungency*, are taken into account, it is pretty clear that the quality of the style was meant, & *conciseness* would have been the right word :—*I really think any Muse (when she is neither resting nor flying) ought to tighten her girdle, tuck up her skirts, & step out. It is better than Tennyson's short-winded & artificial concision—but there is such a thing as swift & spontaneous style./But then as a writer of letters, diaries, & memoranda, Mr Gladstone did not shine by any habitual concision or pungency of style.* If it were not for this frequent uncertainty about what is really meant, it would be as bad to say *concision* for *conciseness* as to use *correction* (which also could be defended as a Gallicism) for *correctness*, or *indirection* (for which *Hamlet* II. i. 66 might be pleaded) for *indirectness*.

Simple reference of any word in *-ion* to this article may be taken to mean that there is a tendency for it to usurp the functions of the noun in *-ness*.

Irene. Three syllables (īrē′nĭ) ; as a Christian name it has now been largely adopted by those who take it for a disyllable & account to themselves for the third syllable when they hear others say it as an optional addition like those in *Johnny & Jeanie.*

irenicon. See EIRENICON.

Iricism. See IRISHISM.

iridescent. So spelt, not *irri-* ; the origin is Greek *iris* rainbow, not Latin *irrideo* laugh.

Irishism, Iricism. The first is the right ; see BRITICISM.

iron. For *the i. Chancellor, Duke, horse,* see SOBRIQUETS.

ironist. For the form, see -IST.

irony. For a tabular comparison of this & other words, see HUMOUR.

Irony is a form of utterance that postulates a double audience, consisting of one party that hearing shall hear & shall not understand, & another party that, when more is meant than meets the ear, is aware both of that more & of the outsiders' incomprehension. 1. *Socratic irony* was a profession of ignorance. What Socrates represented as an ignorance & a weakness in himself was in fact a non-committal attitude towards any dogma, however accepted or imposing, that had not been carried back to & shown to be based upon first principles. The two parties in his audience were, first, the dogmatists moved by pity or contempt to enlighten this ignorance, &, secondly, those who knew their Socrates & set themselves to watch the familiar game in which learning should be turned inside out by simplicity. 2. The double audience is essential too to what is called *dramatic irony*, i.e. the irony of the Greek drama. That drama had the peculiarity of providing the double audience—one party in the secret & the other not—in a special manner. The facts of most Greek plays were not a matter for invention, but were part of every Athenian child's store of legend ; all the spectators, that is, were in the secret beforehand of what would happen. But the characters, Pentheus & Oedipus & the rest, were in the dark ; one of them might utter words that to him & his companions on the stage were of trifling import, but to those who hearing could understand were pregnant with the coming doom. The surface meaning for the dramatis personae, & the underlying for the spectators ; the dramatist working his effect by irony. 3. And the double audience for *the irony of Fate*? Nature persuades most of us that the course of events is within wide limits foreseeable, that things will follow their usual course, that violent outrage on our sense of the probable or reasonable need not be looked for ; & these ' most of us ' are the uncomprehending outsiders ; the elect or inner circle with whom Fate shares her amusement at our consternation are the few to whom it is not an occasional maxim, but a living conviction, that what happens is the unexpected.

That is an attempt to link intelligibly together three special senses of the word *irony*, which in its more general sense may be defined as the use of words intended to convey one meaning to the uninitiated part of the audience & another to the initiated, the delight of it lying in the secret intimacy set up between the latter & the speaker ; it should be added, however, that there are dealers in irony for whom the initiated circle is not of outside hearers, but is an *alter ego* dwelling in their own breasts.

For practical purposes a protest is needed against the application of ' the irony of Fate ', or of ' irony ' as short for that, to every trivial oddity :—*But the pleasant note changed to something almost bitter as he declared his fear that before them lay a ' fight for everything we hold dear '*—*a sentence that the groundlings by a curious irony were the loudest in cheering* (oddly enough)./*It would be an irony of fate, according to many members, if Mr Chamberlain were elected to succeed Mr Balfour, for it was his father who dealt the first blow at Mr Balfour's ascendency* (interesting)./' *The irony of the thing* ' *said the dairyman who now owns the business ' lies in the fact that after I began to sell good wholesome butter in place of this adulterated mixture, my sales fell off 75 per cent.* ' (' It 's a rum thing that. . .' seems almost adequate). *The irony of fate* is, in fact, to be classed now as a HACKNEYED PHRASE.

irrecognizable, un-. The second is recommended ; see IN- & UN-.

irrefragable. Accent the second (irĕ'fragabl).

irrefutable. For pronunciation see REFUTABLE.

irrelevance, -cy. The first is recommended ; see -CE, -CY.

irrelevant. It is stated in the OED, which does not often volunteer such remarks, & which is sure to have documentary evidence, that ' a frequent blunder is *irrevalent* ' ; that form, however, does not get into print once for a hundred times that it is said ; but it is not difficult, with a little fishing, to extract it from ladies ; cf. ANEMONE. The word is one of those that we all know the meaning of, but seldom trouble to connect with their derivations—a state of mind commoner with Englishmen than with other people because so many of our words are borrowed that we are accustomed to apparently arbitrary senses. It is worth remembering that *relevant* & *relieving* are the same word ; that, presumably, is irrelevant which does not relieve or assist the problem in hand by throwing any light upon it.

IRRELEVANT ALLUSION. We all know the people—for they are the majority, & probably include our particular selves—who cannot carry on the ordinary business of everyday talk without the use of phrases containing a part that is appropriate & another that is pointless or worse ; the two parts have associated themselves together in their minds as making up what somebody has said, & what others as well as they will find familiar, & they have the sort of pleasure in producing the combination that a child has in airing a newly acquired word. There is indeed a certain charm in the grownup man's boyish ebullience, not to be restrained by thoughts of relevance from letting the exuberant phrase jet forth. And for that charm we put up with it when one draws our attention to the methodical by telling us there is *method in the madness*, though method & not madness is all there is to see, when another's every winter is *the winter of* his *discontent*, when a third cannot complain of the *light* without calling it *religious* as well as *dim*, when for a fourth nothing can be *rotten* except *in the state of Denmark*, or when a fifth, asked whether he does not owe you 1/6 for that cabfare, *owns the soft impeachment.* Other phrases of the kind will be found in the article HACKNEYED PHRASES. A slightly fuller examination of a single example may be useful. The phrase *to leave severely alone* has two reasonable uses—one in the original sense of to leave alone as a method of severe treatment, i.e. to send to Coventry or show contempt for ; & the other in contexts where *severely* is to be interpreted by contraries—to leave alone by way not of punishing the object, but of avoiding consequences for the subject. The straightforward meaning, & the ironical, are both good ; anything between them, in which the real meaning is merely to leave alone, & *severely* is no more than an echo, is pointless & vapid & in print intolerable. Examples follow : (1, straightforward) *You must show* him, *by leaving him severely alone, by putting him into a moral Coventry,* your *detestation of the crime* ; (2, ironical) *Fish of prey do not appear to relish the sharp spines of the stickleback, & usually seem to leave them severely alone* ; (3, pointless) *Austria forbids children to smoke in public places ; & in German schools & military colleges there are laws upon the subject ; France, Spain, Greece, & Portugal, leave the matter severely alone.* It is obvious at once how horrible the faded jocularity of N° 3 is in print ; &, though things like it come crowding upon one another in most conversation, they are not very easy to find in newspapers & books of any merit ; a small gleaning of them follows :— *The moral,* as Alice would say, *appeared to be that, despite its difference in degree, an obvious essential in the right kind of education had been equally lacking to both these girls* (as Alice, or indeed as you or I, might say)./*Resignation became* a virtue of necessity *for Sweden* (If you do what you must with a good grace, you make a virtue of necessity ; without *make, a virtue of necessity* is meaningless)./*I strongly advise the single working-man who would become a successful backyard poultry-keeper to ignore the advice of Punch, & to secure a useful helpmate.*/*The beloved* lustige Wien [merry Vienna] *of his youth had* suffered a sea-change. *The green glacis . . . was blocked by ranges of grand new buildings* (Ariel must chuckle at the odd places in which his *sea change* turns up)./*Many of the celebrities who in that most frivolous of watering-places do congregate.*/*When about to quote Sir Oliver Lodge's tribute to the late leader, Mr Law* drew, not a dial, *but what was obviously a penny memorandum book from his pocket* (You want to mention that Mr Bonar Law took a notebook out of his pocket ; but pockets are humdrum things ; how give a literary touch ? call it a *poke* ? no, we can better that ; who was it drew what from his poke ? why, Touchstone a dial, to be sure ! & there you are).

irremovable. So spelt, not -vea- ; see -ABLE.

irrespective(ly), adv. When *of* does not follow, the adverb still takes *-ly* : *Mercy that places the marks of its favour absolutely & irrespectively upon whom it pleases.* When *of* follows, the modern tendency is to drop *-ly* in the adverb (cf. *regardless*), as in *All were huddled together,* irrespective *of age & sex* ; see UN-IDIOMATIC -LY ; but good writers perhaps retain the *-ly* in sentences where *irrespective* might be taken for an adjective agreeing with the subject & meaning *not taking account,* whereas what is desired is an adverb meaning *without account taken* ; so *He values them,* irrespectively of *the practical conveniences which their triumph may obtain for him* (quoted from Matthew Arnold, who would doubtless have refused to drop the *-ly* here). This rather fine (if not imaginary) point of idiom does not practically affect the meaning of a passage, but does imply a view of the exact meaning & construction of the word *irrespective*—the view, namely, that it does not mean careless & does not agree with a person.

irresponsive, un-. The second is recommended ; see IN- & UN-.

irretentive, un-. The first is recommended ; see IN- & UN-.

irridescent. A wrong spelling for IRIDESCENT.

irrigate makes *-gable, -tor* ; see -ABLE 1, -OR.

is. 1. *Is* & *are* between variant numbers. 2. *Is* & *are* in multiplication table. 3. *Is* auxiliary & copulative. 4. *Is* after compound subject. 5. *Is,* or *has, nothing to do with.*

1. *Is* & *are* between subject & complement of different numbers. *What* are *wanted* are *not small cottages, but larger houses with modern conveniences.*/*The plausible suggestions to the contrary so frequently put forward* is *an endeavour to kill two birds with one stone.*/In the first

example the two *ares* should be *is* ; in the second, *is* should be *are* ; for discussion see ARE, IS. Mistakes are especially common with the word *what* : *What* is *really at issue* are *not questions of . . .*/*What* is *needed* are *a few recognized British corporations.* For these wrong forms, see WHAT.

2. *Is* & *are* in the multiplication table. *Five times six* is, or *are, thirty* ? The subject of the verb is not *times,* but *six,* the meaning of the subject being ' six reckoned five times '. Before we know whether *is* or *are* is required, then, we must decide whether *six* is a singular noun, the name of a quantity, or a plural adjective agreeing with a suppressed noun ; does it mean ' the quantity six ', or does it mean ' six things ' ? That question each of us can answer, perhaps, for himself, but no-one for other people ; it is therefore equally correct to say *twice two is four* & *twice two are four.* Moreover, as the two are equally correct, so they appear (OED, *s.v.* time) to be about equally old ; *four times six* was plural as long ago as 1380, & *ten times two* was singular in 1425.

3. Confusion between auxiliary & copulative uses. *The risk of cards being lost or mislaid under such circumstances is considerable, & great inconvenience ∧ experienced by any workman to whom this accident occurs.* This mistake of leaving the reader to supply an *is* of one kind out of a previous *is* of another kind is discussed under BE 5.

4. *Is* after compound subjects. *The Allies are prepared to retire if & when proper pledges & security is given.*/*Their lives, their liberties, & their religion* is *in danger.* In both these *is* should be *are* ; they seem to point to a mistaken theory that, when the parts of a compound subject differ in number, the verb follows the nearest ; that might reasonably, though it hardly does in fact, hold for *or*-groups (*whether we or she is right*) ; but it is entirely

wrong for *and*-groups, which always require a plural verb unless they are, like *bread & butter*, compound words rather than mere groups. See also NUMBER.

5. *Is*, or *has, nothing to do with*. *Sir,—Why do I see today, in a celebrated morning contemporary, the following sentence* : ' The trouble *is* nothing to do with education' (*Italics mine*) ? The facts are, first, that *has nothing to do with* requires no defence, secondly, that *is nothing to do with* is said by many to be indefensible, & thirdly, that *is nothing to do with* is nevertheless, if not far commoner than the other, yet very common. When a form of speech that one regards as a corruption gains wide currency, the question whether one should tilt at it is not quite simple. If it is an obvious outrage on grammar, yes ; if, on the other hand, its wrongness is of the kind that has to be pointed out before it is noticed, & its hold on the public strong enough to take a good deal of loosening, then perhaps it is better to buttress it up than to tilt at it. This, then, is an attempt to justify *is*.

Most of us, when we have occasion to repel an impertinent question, & are not in the mood for weighing words in the scales of grammar, feel that *That is nothing to do with you* expresses our feelings better than *That has* &c.; that is to say, the instinctive word is *is*, not *has*. But, says the champion of grammar, instinctive or not, it is a mere wrong mixture of two right ways of saying the thing : *That is nothing to you, & That has nothing to do with you.* He is very likely right, but it is not quite so certain as he thinks ; & the popular phrase that is on its trial for impropriety should always be given the benefit of the doubt if there is one. Now it does not seem impossible that *It is nothing to do with* may have arisen from sentences in which *to do* has acquired the status of an adjective meaning *concerned* or *connected* ; such sentences would

be : *There is nothing to do with prisons that he cannot tell you./' A Wife's Secret* ' (*nothing to do with the old play of that name*)./*Anything to do with spiritualism is interesting*. In the first of those *nothing to do* means not a single thing concerned, *nothing* being a noun ; & in the second it means not at all connected, *nothing* being an adverb. No doubt this use of *to do* is elliptical for *having to do* ; but the point is that it gives us a different construction for *nothing* or any corresponding word, which here is not the object of the omitted *having*, as it is of *has* in *It has nothing to do with*, but is either the noun with which the supposed *having* agrees or an adverb negativing it. On this theory, the two forms may be paraphrased thus : *It has nothing to do with you* = It has *no function* to perform with you ; & *It is nothing to do with you* = It is *not a matter* concerned with you ; the first is simpler to arrive at than the second, but the second is not impossible. The precisian who likes an easily analysable sentence, & the natural man who likes to say the thing that springs to his lips, had better agree to live & let live ; & that they will do the more readily if the first can believe that the two ways of putting the thing differ not only in the visible distinction between *has* & *is*, but also in the invisible one between two or more constructions of *nothing*. It may fairly be maintained that there are three right ways of saying the thing : *It is nothing to you* ; *It has nothing to do with you* ; *It is nothing to do with you* : instead of two right ways & a wrong.

isagogic. For pronunciation see GREEK G.

-ISE) (-IZE. On the general question of the spelling of verbs ending in the sound -īz, see -IZE. If *-ize* is accepted as the normal form, there are still a number of verbs in which the question between the two spellings does not arise, but *-ise* is for various reasons necessary. The more important of these are here given :—advertise, apprise, chastise, circumcise, comprise, compromise, demise, despise, devise, disfranchise, disguise, enfranchise, enterprise, excise, exercise, improvise, incise, premise, supervise, surmise, surprise.

island, isle. The two are etymologically unconnected, the first being native & having no right to its *-s-*, & the second being Latin by origin.

-ISM & -ITY. Many adjectives have each ending appended & give two words of different meaning. Occasionally choice between the two is doubtful. Roughly, the word in *-ity* usually means the quality of being what the adjective describes, or concretely an instance of the quality, or collectively all the instances ; & the word in *-ism* means the disposition to be what the adjective describes, or concretely an act resulting from that disposition, or collectively all those who feel it. A few of the more notable pairs follow, to enable the reader to judge how far this rough distinction will serve him in deciding where the difference is less established :— BARBARITY & *barbarism* ; *catholicity* & *catholicism* ; *deity* & *deism* ; *fatality* & *fatalism* ; FORMALITY & *formalism* ; *humanity* & HUMANISM ; *ideality* & *idealism* ; *latinity* & LATINISM ; *liberality* & *liberalism* ; *modernity* & *modernism* ; *reality* & *realism* ; *spirituality* & *spiritualism* ; *universality* & *universalism*.

isolate makes *-lable*, *-tor* ; see -ABLE 1, -OR.

Israelite. See HEBREW.

issue, v. 1. *I.* makes *issuable* ; see MUTE E. 2. The military construction, to i. a person with a thing (*The Company was issued with two gas-masks per man*), on the analogy of *supply* & *provide*, though much popularized by the war, is not to be recommended ; see ANALOGY.

-IST, -ALIST, -TIST, -YIST, &c. The use of the suffix *-ist* in English

is so wide & various that any full discussion of it is not here possible. But there are (A) some words whose exact form is still uncertain & should be fixed, & there are (B) others that are both established & badly formed, so that there is danger, unless their faultiness is pointed out, of their being used as precedents for new formations.

A

agricultur(al)ist, constitution(al)ist, conversation(al)ist, education(al)ist, & others of the kind. Either form is legitimate ; the shorter, besides being less cumbersome, usually corresponds more naturally to the sense ; expert in agriculture (*-turist*), for instance, is simpler than expert in the agricultural (*-turalist*) ; but in *constitution(al)ist*, perhaps, knowledge of or devotion to what is constitutional, rather than of or to the constitution, is required. Unless there is a definite advantage of this kind in the *-al-* form, the other should be preferred : *agriculturist, constitutionalist, conversationist, educationist.*

accompan(y)ist. Neither form is satisfactory ; the adding of *-ist* to verbs other than those in *-ize* is unusual (*conformist* is an example), & it is a pity that *accompanier* was not taken ; but of the two *-nyist* (cf. *copyist*) is better than *-nist* : *accompanyist.*

voluntar(y)ist. The *-y-* should be retained. The analogy of *militarist* is deceptive, because that has the Latin *militaris* to justify it ; there is no Latin *voluntaris*, & the Latin *voluntarius* objects to losing two syllables instead of one : *voluntaryist.*

pacif(ic)ist. It is perhaps oversanguine to class this among those still awaiting decision, the barbarous *pacifist* has taken so strong a hold ; but there are still a faithful few who resist it. It is formed on *pacific,* meaning believer in pacific methods ; the *-f-* in *pacifist*, with *-ic-* left out, has no meaning, & *pacist* would have been a better word. The omission of an essential syllable by what is called syncope (as in *idolatry*, syncopated from *idololatria*) belongs in English to the primitive stages of the language, & is not now practised; *symbology*, for *symbolology*, is an unprepossessing exception; to change *pacificist* to *pacifist* is no better than to change *deteriorate* & *authoritative*, as is often done by the uneducated, to *deteriate* & *authoritive*, & to acquiesce in such corruptions at a time when general education is equal to realizing their nature is to introduce a principle of swift decay into the language. *Pacifist* has been defended on the formula *pacifist* : *pacific* :: *philanthropist* : *philanthropic*; *philanthropist*, however, is formed not from *philanthropic*, but from *philanthropia*, the Greek for philanthropy; & actual or possible Greek & Latin nouns in -ĭa are among the commonest bases for -*ist* nouns; there is no possible Latin *pacifia* nor English noun pă'cĭfy̆ to account similarly for *pacifist*. Another plea, that *pacifist* is from French *pacifiste*, is equally unsound; the word, which is not in a popular French dictionary dated 1911, is one of the international kind to which each language gives its own normal form; the responsibility cannot be deported across the Channel.

ego(t)ist. The -*t*- is abnormal; but both forms are established, & a useful differentiation is possible if both are retained; see EGO(T)ISM.

B

analyst, ironist, separatist, & tobacconist, are open to objection, though they are all, except perhaps the least offending of them, *ironist*, firmly established.

analyst results from the mistaking of *analyse* for one of those -*ize* verbs from which so many nouns in -*ist* are formed; *analyse*, derived from *analysis*, should itself have been *analysize*, & then *analysist* would have been correct; given *analyse*,

analyser should have been the noun.

ironist supplies the need of a word to match *satirist* & *humourist*. The choice, if it was to end in -*ist*, lay between *ironicalist, ironicist, ironyist*, & *ironist*, of which the last is technically the least justifiable. If regarded as made on the English noun *irony*, the -*y* ought not to be omitted; if Greek is to be called in, the Greek verb & noun ought to have been *eironizo* & *eironia*, whereas they are *eironeuo* & *eironeia*; *philanthropist* & *telegraphist* do not obviate the objection, because they are made not on *philanthropy* & *telegraphy*, but on Greek *philanthropia* & English *telegraph*.

separatist, like all -*ist* words made on other verbs than those in -*ize* (*conformist, computist, controvertist, speculatist*, are the best of the few quoted by the OED), is at once felt to be an uncomfortable & questionable word; but it & (*non*)*conformist*, having attained to real currency, may unfortunately be imitated. *Separationist* would have been the right form.

tobacconist, like *egotist*, has no right to the consonant inserted before -*ist*.

isthmus. Pl. -*uses*; see -US.

it. 1. Omission of anticipatory *it* owing to confused analysis. 2. Other mistakes with anticipatory *it*. 3. Obscure or wrong pronoun reference. 4. *Its*) (*it's*.

The pronoun is so much used in various idiomatic constructions that considerable knowledge, instinctive or acquired, of the ins & outs of syntax is needed to secure one against lapses. The collecting of a few specimens, & comments on them, may put writers on their guard.

1. First, there is a present tendency to omit in relative clauses the anticipatory *it*, i.e. the *it* that heralds a deferred subject as in *It is useless to complain*. An example is : *The House of Commons is always ready to extend the indulgence which* ∧ *is a sort of precedent that the mover & seconder of the Address should ask for.*

If we build up this sentence from its elements, the necessity of *it* will appear, & the reader can then apply the method to the other examples. *That the mover should ask for indulgence is a precedent*; that, rearranged idiomatically, becomes *It is a precedent that the mover should ask for indulgence*; observe that *it* there does not mean *indulgence*, but means *that the mover should ask for indulgence*, *it* being placed before the predicate (*is a precedent*) as a harbinger announcing that the real subject, which it temporarily represents, is coming along later. *It is a precedent that the mover should ask for indulgence; the House extends the indulgence*; there are the two elements; to combine them we substitute *which* for *indulgence* in the clause that is to be subordinate, & place this *which* at the beginning instead of at the end of that clause : *the House extends the indulgence which . . .*; now, if *it* had meant indulgence, i.e. the same as *which* now means, it would have become superfluous ; but, as has been mentioned, it means something quite different, & is just as much wanted in the compound sentence as in the simple one. A parallel will make the point clear : *A meeting was held, & it was my duty to attend this*; whether *which* or *& this* is placed at the beginning of the second member instead of the present arrangement, no-one would dream of dropping *it* & writing *which was my duty to attend*, or *& this was my duty to attend*. After this rather laboured exposition it will suffice to add to the more or less similar examples that follow mere hints of the essential construction :—*The debate on the Bill produced a tangle of arguments which ∧ required all Mr Chamberlain's skill to untie*. *Which* means *tangle*; the missing *it* means *to untie which*. Here, however, if an *it* had been inserted after *untie*, *which* would have been subject to *required* instead of object to *untie*, so that the sentence as it stands is perhaps a

muddle between two possibilities./ *It has already cost the 100 millions which ∧ was originally estimated would be the whole cost.* The missing *it* means *that which would be the whole cost* (*that* the conjunction, not the pronoun)./*Faith in drugs has no longer any monetary motive such as ∧ has been asserted was formerly the case.* Without *it*, this implies as one of the elements *A monetary motive has been asserted was the case.*/*The great bulk of the work done in the world is work that ∧ is vital should be done.* Elements : (a) *That certain work should be done is vital*, or *It is vital that certain work should be done* ; (b) *Most work done is that work*. The missing *it* means not *work*, as *that* does, but *that whi'ch work should be done.*/*What ∧ was realized might happen has happened.* Elements : *It was realized that a thing might happen* ; *that thing has happened.*
At the end of the article HOPE the common omission of *it* with *is hoped* is illustrated.

2. Secondly, certain points have to be remembered about the anticipatory *it* besides the fact that it may be wrongly omitted :—*In connexion with the article by ——, it may be worth recalling the naïve explanation given to Dickens by one of his contributors.* Anticipatory *it* heralds a deferred subject ; it cannot be used when there is no subject to herald ; where is the subject here ? *explanation* is engaged as object of *recalling* ; *recalling* is governed by *worth* ; *worth* is complement to *may be* ; *it* neither has any meaning of its own nor represents anything else. The author might possibly claim that the construction was a true apposition like that in ' He 's a good fellow, that ', & that a comma after *recalling* would put all to rights ; but anyone who can read aloud can hear that that is not true. The real way to correct it is to write *worth while* instead of *worth*, which releases *recalling* to serve as the true subject ; see WORTH for other such mistakes./ *It is such wild statements as that Mr*

Sandlands has made that does harm to the Food Reform cause. By strict grammatical analysis *does* would be right; but idiom has decided that in the *it . . . that* construction, when *that* is the relative, it takes its number not from its actual antecedent *it*, but from the word represented by it—here *statements./He was a Norfolk man, & it was in a Norfolk village where I first ran across him.* There is no doubt that idiom requires *that* instead of *where*, & the sense of the idiomatic form is plain; *it that I ran across* means *my running across*; *my first running across him was in a village*; the use of *where*, besides being unidiomatic, is also less reasonable; *where* is equivalent to *in which*, & if *in which* or its equivalent is used we require *a Norfolk village* & not *in a Norfolk village*: *& it was a Norfolk village in which I* &c. The use of *in a village* together with *where* is analogous to the pleonasms discussed under HAZINESS./*It is impossible to enter on the political aspects of Mr* ——'s *book, but ∧ must suffice to say that he suggests with great skill the warring interests.* The reader of that at once thinks something is wrong, & on reflection asks whether the anticipatory *it*, which means *to enter* &c., can be 'understood' again before *must suffice* with the quite different meaning of *to say* &c. It cannot; but some more or less parallel types will show that doubts are natural. Here are (A) two in which the understanding of *it*, though the subjects are different, is clearly permissible : *It is dangerous to guess, but humiliating to confess ignorance./It must please him to succeed & pain him to fail.* And here are (B) two that will not do : *It is dishonest to keep silence, & may save us to speak./It cannot help us to guess, & is better to wait & see.* The distinction that emerges on examination is this : in the A examples *is*, & *must*, are common to both halves ; in the B examples it is otherwise, *is* being answered to

by *may*, & *cannot* by *is* ; it appears that *it* may be understood, even if the real subject is changed, when the verb or auxiliary is common to both parts, but not otherwise. If, in the sentence we are criticizing, *& sufficient* were substituted for *but must suffice*, all would be well.

3. Examples of *it & its* used when the reference of the pronoun is obscure or confused, or its use too previous or incorrect. These faults occur with *it* as with all pronouns, & are discussed generally under PRONOUNS ; a few examples are here printed without comment :—
This local option in the amount of outdoor relief given under the Poor Law has always operated inequitably & been one of the greatest blots on the system. To extend it to the first great benefit under the Insurance Act will greatly lessen its *usefulness./ Again, unconsciousness in the person himself of what he is about, or of what others think of him, is also a great heightener of the sense of absurdity.* It *makes* it *come the fuller home to us from his insensibility to* it.*/Viscount Wolverhampton has resigned the office of Lord President, & his Majesty the King has been pleased to accept* it./ *Where a settlement is effected a memorandum of the same, with a report of* its *proceedings, is sent by the Board to the Minister of Labour./ Both these lines of criticism are taken simultaneously in a message which* its *special correspondent sends from Laggan, in Alberta, to the Daily Mail this morning.*

4. The possessive of *it*, like that of *who*, & the absolute forms in *-s* of *her, their, our,* & *your,* has no apostrophe : *its, hers, theirs, ours, yours*, not *it's* &c.

itacism. See TECHNICAL TERMS.

ITALIAN SOUNDS. A rough notion of how Italian words should be said is sometimes needed. Certain consonant peculiarities are all that require notice ; for the vowels it suffices that they have the continental values, not the English.

The letters or letter-groups with which mistakes may be made are : c, cc, ch, ci ; g, gg, gh, gi, gli, gn, gu ; sc, sch, sci ; z, zz. If a few words, most of them to be met in English writing, are taken as types, the sounds may easily be remembered:—
cicerone (chĭche-) ; *c, & cc,* before *e & i,*=ch.
Chianti (kĭ-) ; *ch* always=k
cioccolata (chŏk-) ; *ci* before *a, o, u,* often=ch, the *i* merely showing that *c* is soft
Gesù (jä-) ; *g, & gg,* before *e* or *i*=j
ghetto (gĕ-) ; *gh* always=g
Giotto (jŏ-) ; *gi* before *a, o, u,* often= j, cf. *ci* above.
intaglio (-ahlyō) ; *gli* often=ly
bagni (bah′nyē) ; *gn*=ny
Guelfo (gwĕ-) ; *gu* always=gw
fascista (-shĭs-) ; *sc* before *e* or *i*=sh
scherzo (sk-) ; *sch* always=sk
sciolto (shŏl-) ; *sci* before *a, o, u,* often=sh, cf. *ci* above
scherzo (-tsō) ; *z*=ts
pizzicato (pĭtsĭ-) ; *zz* usually=ts
mezzo (mĕ′dzō) ; *zz* rarely=dz

ITALICS. During the war many persons less conversant with the art of writing than with strategy or artillery or surgery or aeronautics or blockade law or food supply have, to our great advantage, occupied much space, instructively, in the magazines & newspapers. But a regrettable by-product of their activities has been a relapse into primitive methods of soliciting attention. Newspaper columns filled with a mosaic of roman & italic type that would have horrified the pre-war editor have grown familiar. The practised writer is aware that his business is to secure prominence for what he regards as the essence of his communication by so marshalling his sentences that they shall lead up to a climax, or group themselves round a centre, or be worded with different degrees of impressiveness as the need of emphasis varies ; he knows too that it is an insult to the reader's intelligence to admonish him periodically by a change

of type, like a bad teacher imploring his boys to attend for a moment, that he cannot safely go to sleep just now. But to those who, however competent on their special subject, have not had enough experience of writing to have learnt these rudiments it comes as natural to italicize every tenth sentence or so as it comes to the letter-writing schoolgirl to underline whatever she enjoys recording. These mosaics have on discreet readers exactly the repellent effect that interjections had on Landor : ' I read warily ; & whenever I find the writings of a lady, the first thing I do is to cast my eyes along her pages to see whether I am likely to be annoyed by the traps & spring-guns of interjections, & if I happen to espy them I do not leap the paling '.

Space cannot be afforded for what would be the only adequate illustration, the reproduction of a whole mosaic article ; a few short extracts must suffice ; but it should be borne in mind that these are mostly taken from long articles that contain several other examples of the same trick. The right uses of italics will be afterwards classified & illustrated.

EXAMPLES OF ILL-ADVISED ITALICS

In comparison with this welding of valour with justice, the so-called ideal of total disarmament is shallow. *There is a way of peace that is at once manly & sure.* By far the deeper change lies in turning military institutions to nobler & saner ends./All human effort that creates values is Labour, & the highest values are *not* created by muscle. *The highest values are created, always have been created, & always will be, by Mind.* And working men as well as others recognize that fact./It is not merely that the Allied Powers are pledged to the reconstitution of Serbia because of her signal services to their cause & the sufferings of her intrepid people ; *their interest emphatically demands that past amor-*

celments by Turk & Austrian should be wiped out, & wiped out once & for all. And this is the Allies' interest because . . ./The change in the point of view is fundamental. The primary necessity is to recognize the change, & to realize that *the proposed function of a League of Nations, at once grand & simple, is something quite distinct from the function of a Power-group* formed under the conditions of the Old Order./It is not, however, the *length* of the road that matters so much as the rate at which the road is covered. And the rate depends mainly upon the impetus, & on the extent to which the impetus may become general. *An impetus of this kind does not spring from party programmes. It springs from change in underlying social philosophy.* Such a change has been initiated by the War./A great military menace cannot again rise in Central Europe so long as the inland seas are kept open. *Any steps, however insidious or gradual, again to close them must be vetoed.* In the past neglect of this precaution was a profound oversight in British naval policy.

RIGHT USES

The true uses of italics are very different from this of recommending to attention whole sentences whose importance, if they *are* important, ought to be plain without them. And these real uses are definite enough to admit of classification. Some of them may be merely mentioned as needing no remark : a whole piece may be in italics because italics are decorative ; text & notes may be distinguished by roman & italic type just as they may by different-sized types; quotations used as chapter-headings, prefaces, dedications, & other material having a special status, are entitled to italics. Apart from such decorative & distinctive functions, too obvious to need illustration, italics have definite work to do when a word or two are so printed in the body of a

roman-type passage. They pull up the reader & tell him not to read heedlessly on, or he will miss some peculiarity in the italicized word. The particular point he is to notice is left to his own discernment ; the italics may be saying to him :—

a. ' This word, & not the whole phrase of which it forms part, contains the point ': It is not only *little* learning that has been exposed to disparagement.

b. ' This word is in sharp contrast to the one you may be expecting ' : It would be an ultimate benefit to the cause of morality to prove that honesty was the *worst* policy.

c. ' These two words are in sharp contrast ': But, if the child never *can* have a dull moment, the man never *need* have one.

d. ' If the sentence were being spoken, there would be a stress on this word ' : The wrong man knows that if *he* loses there is no consolation prize of conscious virtue awaiting *him.*

e. ' This word wants thinking over to yield its full content ': Child-envy is only a form of the eternal yearning for something better than *this* (i.e., the adult's position with all its disillusionments).

f. ' This word is not playing its ordinary part, but is a word as such ': Here *will* is wrongly used instead of *shall.*

g. ' This is not an English word or phrase ' : The maxim that deludes us is the *progenies vitiosior* of one to which the Greeks allowed a safer credit.

h. ' This word is the title of a book or a newspaper, or the name of a fictitious character ': The Vienna correspondent of *The Times* reports that . . ./The man in *Job* who maketh collops of fat upon his flanks/A situation demanding *Mark Tapley.*

Such are the true uses of italics. To italicize whole sentences or large parts of them as a guarantee that some portion of what one has written is really worth attending to is a.

miserable confession that the rest is negligible.

italicize makes -*zable* ; see MUTE E.
its, not *it's* ; see IT 4.

-IZE, -ISE, IN VERBS. In the vast majority of the verbs that end in -*ize* or -*ise* & are pronounced -īz, the ultimate source of the ending is the Greek -*izo*, whether the particular verb was an actual Greek one or was a Latin or French or English imitation, & whether such imitation was made by adding the termination to a Greek or another stem. Most English printers follow the French practice of changing -*ize* to -*ise* ; but the *OED* of the Oxford University Press, the *Encyclopaedia Britannica* of the Cambridge University Press, *The Times*, & American usage, in all of which -*ize* is the accepted form, carry authority enough to outweigh superior numbers. The OED's judgement may be quoted :—' In modern French the suffix has become -*iser*, alike in words from Greek, as *baptiser*, *évangéliser, organiser*, & those formed after them from Latin, as *civiliser, cicatriser, humaniser*. Hence, some have used the spelling -*ise* in English, as in French, for all these words, & some prefer -*ise* in words formed in French or English from Latin elements, retaining -*ize* for those of Greek composition. But the suffix itself, whatever the element to which it is added, is in its origin the Greek -*izein*, Latin -*izare* ; &, as the pronunciation is also with z, there is no reason why in English the special French spelling should be followed, in opposition to that which is at once etymological & phonetic '.
It must be noticed, however, that a small number of verbs, some of them in very frequent use, like *advertise, devise, & surprise*, do not get their -*ise* even remotely from the Greek -*izo*, & must be spelt with -*s*- ; the more important of these are given in a list in the **article** -ISE. The difficulty of re-

membering which these -*ise* verbs are is in fact the only reason for making -*ise* universal, & the sacrifice of significance to ease does not seem justified.

J

jab, job, vv. & nn. = prod &c. The OED calls the first a variant, originally Scotch, of the second. *Jab* is usually preferred for a thrust with a weapon, & especially in army use for a particular bayonet thrust, & *job* for a rough jerk at a horse's bit ; of other blows the two are used indifferently. ' Forcible but abruptly arrested action ' (OED) is the characteristic of the blow or jerk or thrust to which the words apply.

jabber makes -*ering, -ered* ; see -R-, -RR-.
jabot. Pronounce zhǎ'bō.
jacket makes -*eted, -eting* ; see -T-, -TT-.
Jacky. So spelt ; see -EY, -IE, -Y.
jacquerie. See FRENCH WORDS.
jaggedly. Three syllables ; see -EDLY.
jail, jailer, jailor. See GAOL.
jail-like. For the hyphen, see -LIKE.
jalousie(s). For pronunciation see FRENCH WORDS.
jamb. Pronounce jăm.
Jamy, -ie. See -EY, -IE, -Y.
janizary, janissary. The OED gives precedence to -*zary* ; but in its 19th-c. quotations the -*ss*- occurs three times as often as the -*z*-.

Jansenism & *Erastianism* are liable to be confused under the general notion of resistance to ecclesiastical authority. It may be said roughly that those who hold that the State should be supreme in ecclesiastical affairs are Erastians, while Jansenists are (for the purpose of this comparison) those who hold that a national branch of the Church is entitled to a certain independence of, or share in, the authority of the Pope. Erastus was author of a treatise against the tyrannical use of excommunication by the Calvinistic Churches. Jansen was author of an exposition of St Augustine's doctrines, designed to reform the Church of Rome, condemned by the Pope, & long prominent in the struggle between Gallicanism & Ultramontanism.

jardinière. For pronunciation see FRENCH WORDS.

jargon is perhaps the most variously applied of a large number of words that are in different senses interchangeable, & under it the distinctions between them may be pointed out. The words are : *argot, cant, dialect, gibberish, idiom, jargon, lingo, parlance, patois, shop, slang, vernacular*. The etymologies, which are indeed several of them unknown, do not throw much light, but may be given for what they are worth : *dialect, idiom,* & *parlance,* are Greek (*dialegomai* I talk ; *idios* private or proper or peculiar ; *paraballo* compare) ; *cant* & *vernacular* are Latin (*cantus* song, chant, whine ; *verna* homeborn slave) ; *lingo* is Italian (*lingua franca* Frankish tongue) ; *argot, jargon,* & *patois,* are French, but otherwise of unknown origin ; *gibberish* & *shop* & *slang* are English, the first probably an imitation of the sound meant, the second a particular application of the common word, & the third of unknown origin.

argot is primarily the vocabulary of thieves & tramps serving to veil their meaning, & is applied secondarily to the special vocabulary of any set of persons. There is in these senses no justification for its use instead of whichever English word may be most appropriate, except in writing concerned with France ; for it is not a naturalized word.

cant in current English means the insincere or parrotlike appeal to principles, religious, moral, political, or scientific, that the speaker does not believe in or act upon, or does not understand. It is best to restrict it to this definite use ; but

its earlier sense—special vocabulary of the disreputable—is still used by philologists & in etymological discussions ; & it means sometimes what is now more often expressed by *jargon* or *slang,* the special vocabulary of an art, profession, &c.

dialect is essentially local ; *a d.* is the variety of a language that prevails in a district, with local peculiarities of vocabulary, pronunciation, & phrase.

gibberish is the name for unintelligible stuff : applied by exaggeration to a language unknown to the hearer (for which, as a familiar term, *lingo* is better), & to anything either too learnedly worded, or on the other hand too rudely expressed, for him to make out its meaning.

idiom is the method of expression characteristic of or peculiar to the native speakers of a language ; i.e., it is racy or unaffected or natural English (or French &c.), especially so far as that happens not to coincide with the method of expression prevalent in other languages ; & *an i.* is a particular example of such speech. An earlier sense, the same as that of *dialect,* still occurs sometimes. See also IDIOM.

jargon is talk that is considered both ugly-sounding & hard to understand : applied especially to (1) the sectional vocabulary of a science, art, class, sect, trade, or profession, full of technical terms (cf. *cant, slang*) ; (2) hybrid speech of different languages ; (3) the use of long words, circumlocution, & other clumsiness.

lingo is a contemptuous name for any foreign language. It is sometimes used instead of *jargon* (1) & (2).

parlance, which means manner of speaking, has the peculiarity of possessing no significance of its own & being never used by itself ; you can say That is dialect, That is slang, &c., but not That is parlance ; *parlance* is always accompanied by an adjective or defining word or phrase, & that adjective, not *parlance,* gives the point : *in golfing* or *nautical parlance, in the parlance of the literary critics,* &c.

patois, as used in English, means nothing different from *dialect,* & therefore, like *argot,* should not be used except about France. The French distinguish two stages ; dialects exist until a common literary language is evolved from them, after which, if they still linger, they become patois ; but in English we let them retain their title.

shop describes business talk indulged in out of business hours, or any unseasonable technical phraseology, & is thus distinct, in the special-vocabulary sense, from *jargon, cant,* & *slang.*

slang is the diction that results from the favourite game among the young & lively of playing with words & renaming things & actions ; some invent new words, or mutilate or misapply the old, for the pleasure of novelty, & others catch up such words for the pleasure of being in the fashion ; many slang words & phrases perish, a few establish themselves ; in either case, during probation they are accounted unfit for literary use. *S.* is also used in the sense of *jargon* (1), & with two distinctions : in general it expresses less dislike & imputation of ugliness than *jargon* ; & it is naturally commoner about sporting vocabularies (*golf s.* &c.) than *jargon,* because many of the terms used in sports are slang in the main sense also.

vernacular describes the words that have been familiar to us as long as we can remember, the homely part of the language, in contrast with the terms that we have consciously acquired. *The vernacular* was formerly common, & is still occasional, for English as opposed to any foreign language ; & by an unessential limitation, it is often applied specially to rustic speech & confused with *dialect.*

jarl. Pronounce y-.
jasmine, jessamine. The OED describes the 2nd as ' another form of *jasmine* '; *jasmine* is recommended.

jaundice, jaunt. Of the two pronunciations (jah-, jaw-), the OED gives precedence to the first in both words.

jaunty. The OED recognizes only jah-, & not jaw-, for the sound. French *gentil* is the source.

jawbation. See JOBATION.

Jeames. See SOBRIQUETS.

Jeanie. So spelt ; see -EY, -IE, -Y.

jehad. See JIHAD.

Jehu. See SOBRIQUETS.

jejune. Accented on the last by the OED, but often now jē'jōōn by RECESSIVE ACCENT.

Jemmy. So spelt ; see -EY, -IE, -Y.

je ne sais quoi. See FRENCH WORDS.

Jenny. So spelt ; see -EY, -IE, -Y.

jeopardy. Pronounce jĕ'pərdĭ.

Jerry. So spelt ; see -EY, -IE, -Y.

jessamine. See JASMINE.

Jessie. So spelt ; see -EY, -IE, -Y.

jetsam, jettison. See FLOTSAM. *Jetsam* is the goods, *jettison* is, as a noun, the action.

jeu &c. See FRENCH WORDS.

jeunesse dorée. See FRENCH WORDS.

Jew. For *J., Israelite,* &c., see HEBREW.

jewel makes *-lled, -lling, -ller* ; see -LL-, -L-.

jewel(le)ry. The longer is the commercial & popular form, the shorter the rhetorical & poetic. The pronunciation is always jōō'ĭlrĭ.

jibe. See GIBE.

jihad, je-. Until recently the second spelling was usual ; but the OED gives the first as the right.

Jill. See GILL.

JINGLES, or the unintended repetition of the same word or similar sounds, are dealt with in the article REPETITION OF WORDS & SOUNDS. A few examples of the sort of carelessness that, in common courtesy to his readers, a writer should remove before printing may be given here :—

The sport of the air is still far *from* free *from* danger./Mr Leon Dominian has a*massed* for us a valuable *mass* of statistics./The situation had *so far* developed *so* little that nothing useful can be said about it, save that *so far* the Commander-in-Chief was satisfied./We can now look *forward* hopefully to further steps *forward./* Market stability is a necessary *condition* of industry under modern *conditions./*The figures I have *obtain*ed put a very different complexion on the subject than that generally *obtain*ing./Most *of them* get rid *of them* more or less completely./The observation *of* the facts *of* the geological succession *of* the forms *of* life./He served his apprentice*ship* to statesman*ship.*/I *awaited* a be*lated* train./Their invalid*ity* was caused by a technical*ity.*/In such a union there is no prob*ability* of st*ability.*/The earliest lists, still so sad*ly* & probab*ly* irretrievab*ly* imperfect (for this commonest form of the jingle, see under -LY)./Hardworking folk should participate in the pl*easures* of l*eisure* in goodly m*easure.*

jingo. Pl. *-oes,* see -O(E)S 1.
jinn(ee). See GENIE.
jiu-jitsu. See JU-JUTSU.
job, v., = prod &c. See JAB.
jobation, jawb-. The first is the right form ; from *Job* came the verb *jobe* to reprove, common in the 17th & 18th centuries, & from that *jobation.*

jockey, n. Pl. *-eys.*
jockey, v. For inflexions see VERBS IN -IE, -Y, -YE, 2.
jocko, chimpanzee. Pl. *-os,* see -O(E)S.
jocose, jocular, &c. These & several other words—*arch, facetious, flippant, jesting, merry, pleasant* (in the archaic sense), & *waggish*—are difficult to separate from each other ; the dictionaries establish no very clear or serviceable distinctions, tending to explain each by a selection of the rest. They are marked off from *funny, droll,* & others, by the fact that in the latter the effect, but in these the intent, is the main point ; that is funny &c. which amuses, but that is jocular &c. which is meant (or, if a person, means) to amuse. In the following

remarks no definition of the whole meaning of any word is attempted ; attention is drawn merely to the points of difference between the one in question & some or all of the others. All of them are usable in contrast with *serious,* but for some an opposite may be found more appropriate than that for the present purpose, & that word is given in brackets.

arch (opp. *severe*) implies the imputation of roguery of some sort; the imputation is ironical, or the offence is to be condoned; the meaning is conveyed chiefly by look, tone, or expression. *An arch look, girl, insinuation.*

facetious (opp. *glum*) implies a desire to be amusing ; formerly a laudatory word, but now suggesting ill-timed levity or intrusiveness or the wish to shine. *A facetious remark, fellow, interruption.*

flippant (opp. *earnest*) implies mockery of what should be taken seriously, & want of consideration for others' feelings. *A flippant suggestion, young man ; f. treatment.*

jesting (opp. *serious*) differs from the rest in having perhaps no distinctive implication. *A jesting mood, parson, proposal.*

jocose (opp. *grave*) implies something ponderous, as of Adam & Eve's elephant wreathing his lithe proboscis to make them mirth. *A jocose manner, old boy, description.*

jocular (opp. *literal*) very commonly implies the evasion of an issue by a joke, or the flying of a kite to test the chances. *A jocular reply, writer, offer.*

merry (opp. *melancholy*) implies good spirits & the disposition to take things lightly. *A merry laugh, child, tale.*

pleasant (arch. ; opp. *stiff*) implies rallying, especially addressed by superiors to inferiors, as a means of establishing genial relations. Now rare, except in *pleasantry.*

waggish implies on the one hand willingness to make a fool of oneself & on the other fondness for making fools of others. *A waggish trick, schoolboy, disposition.*

Johnny. So spelt ; see -EY, -IE, -Y.
jollify. For inflexions see VERBS IN -IE, -Y, -YE, 6.
jollily, jolly adv. As a slang substitute for *very* (*a j. good hiding ; you know j. well*) the adverb is *jolly* ; in other uses (*he smiled j. enough*) it is *jollily.* See -LILY.

jongleur. See FRENCH WORDS.
jonquil. The OED gives precedence to the older pronunciation jŭ'ngkwĭl.
jostle has *t* silent ; see PRONUNCIATION, Silent t.
journal. Objections are often made to the extension of this to other periodicals than the daily papers. But ' Our weekly journals o'er the land abound ' (Crabbe, 1785) shows that it is much too late to object. Those who do so have presumably just learnt the connexion of *journal* with L. *dies* ; for, if it had been long familiar to them, they would surely have been aware also that language is full of such extensions. May a woman not be said to *cry* till she howls ? are there no *clerks* but those in Holy Orders ? is a milliner's box no longer to be a *band-box* ? And, to come back to *dies*, is it a blunder to call London to Moscow a *journey*, or a pedantry to call it anything else ?

journey, n. Pl. -*eys.*
journey, v. For inflexions see VERBS IN -IE, -Y, -YE, 2.
joust, just. Though *just* (jŭ-) is ' the historical English spelling ' (OED), *joust* (jōō-) was preferred by Johnson & used by Scott, & is consequently now more intelligible & to be preferred.

jubilate. Pronounce -lah'tĭ.
Judenhetze. Pronounce yōō'den-hĕtze (four syllables).
judgematical. See FACETIOUS FORMATIONS.
judg(e)ment. See MUTE E for the principle governing the retention &

omission of e in derivatives, viz, that it is dropped only before vowels. Modern usage, however, favours *judgment* ; but we are all familiar with *judgement* in the Bible (R.V. as well as A.V.), & the OED prefers the older & more reasonable spelling. *Judgement* is therefore here recommended, & the similar but slightly less important words *abridg(e)ment, acknowledg(e)ment, fledg(e)ling,* & *lodg(e)ment,* would naturally conform & keep the e. The question is complicated by the omission of the e in several proper names —Sedgwick, Hodgkin, Edgcumbe, &c.

judicial, judicious. The first has to do with judges & lawcourts & legal judgements, the second with the mental faculty of judgement. *Judicial murder* is murder perpetrated by means of a legal trial ; *judicious murder* is murder that is well calculated to serve the murderer's interests. The distinction is clear enough, except that *judicial* has one use that brings it near *judicious* ; this use is *impartial* or *such as might be expected of a judge or a lawcourt,* applied to such words as *view, conduct, care, investigation,* to which *judicious* is also applicable in the sense of wise or sagacious or prudent. In the following example, one may suspect, but cannot be sure, that the writer has meant one word & written the other : *The chapter on the relations between Holland & Belgium after the war in connexion with a suggested revision of the treaty of 1839 is fairly written in a* judicious *spirit.* Roughly, *judicial* = of a judge or lawcourt, *judicious* = exhibiting judgement. For other such pairs, see PAIRS & SNARES.

jugular. The large dictionaries (OED, *Century, Standard*) all want us to say jōōg- ; but for ordinary mortals, familiar from childhood with *the jŭgular vein,* it is as much out of the question as to make kō'kaĭn out of COCAINE.

ju-jutsu, jiu-jitsu. The first is preferred in the OED & the *Enc. Brit.*

jumbal, -ble. The name of the sweetmeat, an old word, is *-al*.

Jumbo. Pl. *-os*, see -O(E)S 3.

jump. *J. to the eye(s)* is a bad GALLICISM (5). Examples :—*The desperate discomfort of these places as living houses judged by our standards jumps to the eyes./How little there is essentially in common between Virgil & Isaiah jumps to the eye as we read the clever & tasteful paraphrase into Biblical language of the 4th Eclogue.*

Junker. Pronounce yŏŏ'ngker.

Juno. Pl. *-os*, see -O(E)S.

junta, junto. The first is the Spanish form, which is used in English also. *Junto*, pl. *-os*, see -O(E)S, is a corruption more used in English than *-ta*.

jupe. See FRENCH WORDS.

jurywoman. See FEMININE DESIGNATIONS.

just, v. & n. See JOUST.

just, adv. **1.** *Just exactly* is bad tautology. *Mr Gladstone's dearest friend in political life, who himself passed away* just exactly *half a century ago.*
2. *Just how many* & similar indirect-question forms are Americanisms. *Just what makes the best lodgement for oyster spawn has been greatly discussed.*
3. Frequent repetition of *just* is a danger. *A running hand was* just *what the name says, handwriting at a run, written in a hurry, as so many people write today. The letters were at first, we might say,* just *like those capital letters.*
4. Pronounce jŭst ; a warning against the vulgarism jĕst is not superfluous.

justiciable. The word not being very common, those who use it should take care it is not printed *justifiable*.

justify. For inflexions see VERBS IN -IE, -Y, -YE, 6.

juvenile makes *juvenilely*.

K

kadi. *C-* is the usual spelling.

Kaf(f)ir, Caffre. *Kaffir* is the now usual form, *Caffre* a more or less disused one, & *Kafir* (pron. kah-) is a more correct spelling.

Kaiser. Pronounce kīz-.

kale, kail. The first is treated by the OED as the standard form, & *kail* as a Scotch variant. The corresponding Southern-English word is *borecole*.

kalendar, kalends. See CALENDAR.

kangaroo. For the parliamentary sense, see CLOSURE.

kaolin. Pronounce kah'-olĭn.

kartell. See CARTEL.

Katy, -ie. See -EY, -IE, -Y.

kedgeree. This is now the usual spelling.

keenness. So spelt.

kelpie, -py. The *-ie* is usual.

kelson, keel-. Pronounce kĕl- ; *kel-* is the older, & *keel-* a recent, spelling.

Kelt(ic). See CELT(IC).

kennel makes *-lled* ; see -LL-, -L-.

kerb. See CURB.

kernel. As KENNEL.

kerosene, paraffin, petrol, petroleum. The popular use of the words is all that is here in question. *Petroleum* is the crude mineral oil ; *petrol*, or *petroleum spirit*, is refined petroleum as used in motors ; *kerosene & paraffin* (*oil*) are oils got by distillation from petroleum or coal or shale, *kerosene* being the usual name in America, & *paraffin* in England.

ketchup is the established spelling ; formerly also *catchup & catsup*, of which the second at least is due to popular etymology. A Chinese or Malay word is said to be the source.

key, v. For inflexions see VERBS IN -IE, -Y, -YE, 2.

Khedive. Pronounce kĭdē'v.

khilafat. ISLAM AND THE KHILAFAT (headline). These formidable learned newspapers have no regard for the things which belong to our peace ; can they not leave us our *caliphate* ? See DIDACTICISM.

kiddy. So spelt ; see -EY, -IE, -Y.

kidnap makes *-pped*, *-pping* ; see -P-, -PP-.

kidney. Pl. *-eys*.

kiln. The OED puts first the pronunciation without *-n*.

kilo-, milli-. In the metric system, *kilo-* means multiplied, & *milli-* divided, by 1000 ; *kilometer* 1000 metres, *millimeter* 1/1000 of a metre ; cf. DECA-, CENTI-.

kilty, Highlander. So spelt ; see -EY, -IE, -Y.

kind, n. The irregular uses—*Those k. of people, k. of startled, a k. of a shock*—are easy to avoid when they are worth avoiding, i.e. in print ; & nearly as easy to forgive when they deserve forgiveness, i.e. in hasty talk. *Those k. of* is a sort of inchoate compound, = *those-like* (cf. *such,* = *so-like*) ; *k. of startled* = *startled, like*, or *startled-like*. *A k. of a shock* is both the least criticized & the least excusable of the three.

kindly. *Authors are kindly requested to note that Messrs —— only accept MSS. on the understanding that* . . . Messrs —— may be kind in making the request, but did they really mean to boast of it ? This misplacement is very common ; for the ludicrous effect, compare the confusion between *It is our* PLEA-SURE & *We have the pleasure.*

kindly, -lily. See -LILY.

kinema(tograph). See CINEMA.

king. Under *King-of-Arms*, the OED says ' less correctly *King-at-Arms* ' ; but, as both phrases are shown by its quotations to have been in use at all periods, & as the *at* form is certainly the one familiar to people without special knowledge, insistence on the other seems pedantic. For *the King of Beasts, Terrors*, see SOBRIQUETS.

kinglily. See -LILY.

kinsfolk is plural without the addition of *-s* ; cf. FOLK.

kirsch(wasser). Pronounce kēr'sh-(vahser).

Kitty. So spelt ; see -EY, -IE, -Y.

knee. The adjective from *knock-knees, broken knees*, &c., is best written with an apostrophe— *knock-knee'd* &c. ; see -ED & 'D.

kneel. For *kneeled & knelt*, see -T & -ED.

knick-knack, nick-nack. The *k.* form is better, as preserving the connexion with *knack*, the parent word.

knife. For the verb &c., see -VE(D).

knight. For *k. of industry*, see GALLICISMS ; for *k. of the rueful countenance*, SOBRIQUETS.

knit(ted). Both forms are still in use for both the past tense & the past participle, but the short form is now unusual in the special sense of making with knitting-needles. *She knit(ted)*, or *had knit(ted)*, *her brows*, but *she knitted* or *had knitted a pair of socks* ; *a well-knit frame*, but *knitted goods* in ordinary use, though *knit goods* survives in the trade. *Knitten* is a pseudo-archaism.

knock-knee'd. See KNEE.

knoll. Pronounce nōl. The word being chiefly literary, so that most of us have to guess its sound from its spelling, & the sound of final *-oll* being so variable (dŏll, lŏll, Mŏll, Nŏll, Pŏll, against drŏll, rŏll, strŏll, tŏll, & trŏll, among clear cases), it is regrettable that the rival spelling *knole* has not prevailed, but *-ll* seems now established.

knout. The dictionaries give only nowt or nōōt ; but the k- is sometimes sounded.

knowledge. Pronounce nŏl-. The OED says that nōl- ' used by some, is merely a recent analytical pronunciation after *know* ' ; it is on the same level as *often* with the t sounded ; see PRONUNCIATION.

knowledgeable. So spelt.

kopje. Pronounce kŏ'pĭ.

koran. The OED gives korah'n precedence over kor'an, & has no doubt chosen the winner. It quotes from Byron, however, *And less to conquest than to Korans trust.*

kosher. Pronounce kŏ-.

kotow, ko-tow, kowtow. The dictionaries pronounce this kŏtow', & it is often printed *ko-tow* by way of showing that the first syllable is not to be weakened in the normal way, which would give kotow'. The real choice lies between both writing & pronouncing *kowtow*, & allowing the weakening to kotow'; for the word is now fairly common, & cannot possibly maintain under popular wear & tear the full vowel sound in the unaccented syllable; *kotow* (kotow') is recommended.

kraal. Pronounce krahl.

kukri. Pronounce kŏŏ'krĭ.

kyrie eleison. Of many competing pronunciations the OED prefers kĕr'ĭĭ ĭlā'ĭson (seven syllables).

L

laager. Pronounce lah'ger.

label makes *-lled* &c.; see -LL-, -L-.

labial. See TECHNICAL TERMS.

labium. Pl. *-bia.*

laboratory. The orthodox pronunciation is lă'boratŏrĭ; those who find four successive unaccented syllables trying do better to say labŏ'ratorĭ than to cut down the orthodox to lă'bratrĭ.

labo(u)r. Keep the -u- ; but see -OUR & -OR. *L.* makes *labourite*; see -OUR- & -OR-.

labouredly. Three syllables; see -EDLY.

lac, lakh. In its 15 quotations the OED shows 9 different spellings, but choice now lies between these two ; & of the two it treats *lac* as preferable.

lace. The noun makes *lacy*, the verb *laceable*, but *lacing*; see MUTE E.

lacerate makes *-rable*, *-tor*; see -ABLE 1, -OR.

laches is a singular noun, pronounced lă'chĭz, meaning negligence of certain kinds, rarely used with

a but often with *the* & *no*, & not requiring italics. Its formation is similar to that of *riches* (formerly *lachesse, richesse*), but not having become a popular word it has escaped being taken for a plural.

lachrym-. The true spelling for all the words would be *lacrim-*, & it would be at least allowable to adopt it ; but the *h* & the *y* are still usual.

lackey, lacquey. Pl. of noun, *-eys* ; for inflexions of verb, see VERBS IN -IE, -Y, -YE, 2. The *-key* form is recommended.

lacquer, lacker. The first is established.

lacrim-. See LACHRYM-.

lacteal. See POLYSYLLABIC HUMOUR.

lacuna. Pl. *-nae* ; see LATIN PLURALS.

laddie. So spelt ; see -EY, -IE, -Y.

lade, apart from the passive use of the p.p., is now almost restricted to the loading of ships. Even *laden*, though still in use, tends to be displaced by *loaded* & to sound archaic except in particular phrases & compound words : *heavy-laden buses*, but *loaded* rather than *laden buses* ; *sin-laden, sorrow-laden* ; *a hay-laden* rather than *a hay-loaded cart*, but *loaded*, rather than *laden, with hay* ; on the other hand *a soul laden*, rather than *loaded, with sin*, because the dignity attaching to slight archaism is in place.

ladleful. Pl. *ladlefuls* ; see -FUL.

lady. **1.** *L. Jones, L. Mary Jones, L. Henry Jones.* The first form is proper only for a peeress or a baronet's or knight's wife or widow ; the second for one called *L.* because she is a peer's daughter ; the third for a courtesy lord's wife or widow. **2.** *L.* by itself in the vocative is a wrong substitute, now common among the uneducated, for *madam*. **3.** *L.* prefixed to names indicating vocation as a mark of sex (*l. doctor, author, clerk*, &c.) is a cumbrous substitute for a FEMININE DESIGNATION, which should be preferred when it exists or can be made ; in default of that, *woman* or *female* would be better than *l.*, not confusing the essential point with irrelevant suggestions of social position, as in 4.

4. *L.* prefixed to vocation words to indicate social pretensions (*l. cook, nurse, companion, help,* &c.) is, it may be hoped, a GENTEELISM that will not last long.

5. For *l.* as undress substitute for *marchioness, countess, viscountess, baroness,* see TITLES.

ladyfied. So spelt ; see -FIED.

lager. Pronounce lah'ger.

lagoon, -gune. The first is now the established spelling.

laid, lain. See LAY & LIE.

laissez aller, laissez faire. See FRENCH WORDS.

lakh. See LAC.

lam, thrash &c. So spelt, not *lamb.*

lama, llama. *La-* for the Thibetan priest ; *lla-* for the animal.

lame. The adj. makes *lamish,* the verb *lamable ;* see MUTE E.

lamentable. Pronounce lă'm-.

lamia. Pronounce lā'mĭa ; pl. *-ae* or *-as.*

lamina. Pl. *-ae.*

lammergeyer. Pronounce -gīer.

lampoon, libel, pasquinade, skit, squib. There is often occasion to select the most appropriate of these words, & the essential point of each may be shortly given. A *lampoon* is a bitter published attack ; a *libel* is a defamatory statement made publicly or privately (see also LIBEL) ; a *pasquinade* is a published attack of unknown or unacknowledged authorship ; a *skit* is a making game of a person or his doings especially by parody ; a *squib* is a casual published attack of no elaboration.

lamprey. Pl. *-eys.*

lance makes *lanceable ;* see MUTE E.

lancet makes *lanceted ;* see -T-, -TT-.

land, n. *L. of the leal* means heaven, not Scotland. For *the L. of cakes* see SOBRIQUETS.

land, v. See INTRANSITIVE P.P.

landgrave. Fem. *-avine*, pron. -ēn.

languor, languorous, languid, languish. The pronunciation is anomalous : *languid* & *languish* have always the -gw- sound (-gwĭ-) ; for *languorous* the OED gives only that sound (-gwor-) ; but for *languor* it prefers the -g- sound (-gor-), though -gw- (-gwor-) is allowed as alternative ; & this probably represents general usage, except that perhaps most people would make *languorous* follow whichever sound they prefer for *languor.* On the merits, lă'nggor by the side of lă'nggwĭd & lă'nggwĭsh seems unreasonable, & is perhaps due to misapprehension ; either *-uor* is confused with the *-our* of *vigour, honour,* &c. ; or else the *-u-* is mistaken for one of the kind seen in *guest, guile, guess, guild,* where its function is to show that g is not as usual soft before e or i. *Liquor* & *liquid, conquer* & *conquest,* show similar inconsistencies, universal in the first & at least dominant in the second pair ; but in *languor* the omission of the -w- sound is hardly so general that its restoration, which would be reasonable, might not be brought about.

lank(y). The short form is almost only literary, the long chiefly colloquial.

lansquenet. See FRENCH WORDS.

lantern, -thorn. The second, now seldom seen, is a corruption due to the use of horn for the sides of old lanterns.

lapel. Pronounce lapĕ'l ; adj. *lapelled.*

lapis lazuli. Pronounce lă'pĭs lă'zūlī.

lappet makes *-eted ;* see -T-, -TT-.

lapsus. Pl. *lapsus* pronounce -ūs, not *-sĭ ;* see -US.

larboard. See PORT.

large. For a comparison of this with *great* & *big,* see BIG. *L.* makes *largish ;* see MUTE E.

large(ly). After the verbs *bulk* & *loom,* the idiomatic word is large, not largely ; cf. UNIDIOMATIC -LY. Examples of the wrong form are : *The Monroe doctrine of late years has* *loomed so largely in all discussions upon . . ./A phase of the Irish question which has bulked largely in the speeches of the Unionist leaders.*

largess(e). Pronounce lar'jĭs, & omit the final -*e*. If the word had remained in common use, it would doubtless have come to be spelt, as it often formerly was, *larges*; cf. *riches* & *laches*.

larva. Pl. -*vae*.

laryngitis. See GREEK G.

Lascar is very commonly accented on the second syllable; but the OED puts lă'skar first, & Longfellow rhymes it with *Madagascar*.

lassie. So spelt; see -EY, -IE, -Y.

lasso is pronounced lasoo' by those who use it; but the English pronunciation is lă'sō, & the OED gives that only. Pl. -*oes*, see -O(E)S 1.

last. 1. *The l. two* &c.) (*the two l.* &c. For this see FIRST 4.

2. *Last*) (*lastly.* In enumerations *lastly* is recommended on the same grounds as *firstly*, for which see FIRST 5.

3. *At* (*the*) *long l.* is an idiom labelled ' now rare ' by the OED; but it has experienced a revival, due more perhaps to its odd sound than to any superior significance over *at last*, & is now often heard & seen; ' in the end, long as it has taken or may take to reach it ' is the sense.

4. *Last*) (*latest.* In this now favourite antithesis (*Dr Marshall's latest, but we hope not his last, contribution*) we are reminded that *latest* means last up to now only, whereas *last* does not exclude the future. The distinction is a convenient one, & the use of *latest* for *last* is described by the OED as ' now archaic & poetical '. But no corresponding agreement has yet been reached for abstaining from *last* when *latest* would be the more precise word, & many idioms militate against it (*last Tuesday*; *last year*; *for the last fortnight*; *on the last occasion*; *as I said in my last*).

Latakia. Pronounce lătakē'a.

late makes *latish*; see MUTE E.

late, erstwhile, ex-, former(ly), quondam, sometime, whilom. With all these words to choose from, we are yet badly off: *erstwhile* & *whilom* smack of WARDOUR STREET; *ex-*, which tends to swallow up the rest, is ill fitted for use with compound words such as *Lord Mayor* (see HYPHENS), which nevertheless constantly need the qualification; *late* is avoided because of the doubt whether it means that the person's life, or his tenure of office, is over; *quondam* & *sometime* have become, partly owing to the encroachments of *ex-*, unusual enough to sound pedantic except in special contexts (*my quondam friend*; *sometime rector of this parish*). The best advice is to refrain from *ex-* except with single words (*ex-Mayor*, but not *ex-Lord-Mayor*, & still less *ex-Lord Mayor*), & from *late* except either in the sense of no longer living or when the person described is in fact dead, & to give *former(ly)*, & perhaps *quondam* & *sometime*, more work to do.

lath is pronounced in the sing. lahth, but in the pl. lahdhz. See -TH & -DH.

lathe. Pronounce lādh.

lather. The OED gives only lă-(rhyming with *gather*, not *father*); & an obsolete spelling *ladder* shows the old vowel sound. Though lah'dher is often heard, *l.* apparently does not belong to the class of words in which ah & ă are merely southern & northern variants (*pass* &c.).

latifundia is a plural.

latine, = in Latin, is a Latin adverb, pronounced in English latī'nē; similar adverbs are *anglice* (-sē) in English, *celtice* (-sē) in Celtic, *gallice* (-sē) in French, *graece* (-sē) in Greek, *hibernice* (-sē) in Irish, *scot(t)ice* (-sē) in Scots, *teutonice* (-sē) in Teutonic. All these are sometimes printed with -è to show that the -e is sounded.

latinism)(latinity. The first is a disposition to adopt Latin ways, especially of speech, or a particular idiom that imitates a Latin one ; the second is the quality of Latin (classical, debased, &c.) that characterizes a person's or a period's style. See -ISM & -ITY.

latinize makes -*zable* ; see MUTE E.

LATIN PLURALS (or latinized-Greek). Of most words in fairly common use that have a Latin as well as or instead of an English plural the correct Latin form is given in the word's alphabetical place. A few general remarks may be made here.
1. No rule can be given for preferring or avoiding the Latin form. Some words invariably use it ; nobody says *specieses, thesises, opuses*, or *basises*, instead of the Latin *species, theses, opera, & bases* (bā'sēz). Others nearly always have the Latin form, but occasionally the English ; *bacilluses, lacunas, & genuses*, are used at least by anti-Latin fanatics instead of *bacilli, lacunae, & genera*. More often the Latin & English forms are on fairly equal terms, context or individual taste deciding for one or the other ; *dogmas, formulas, indexes, hiatuses, & gladioluses*, are fitter for popular writing, while scientific treatises tend to *dogmata, formulae, indices, hiatus* (hīā'tūs), & *gladioli*. Sometimes the two forms are utilized for real differentiation, as when *genii* means spirits, & *geniuses* men. All that can safely be said is that there is a tendency to abandon the Latin plurals, & that when one is really in doubt which to use the English form should be given the preference.
2. Latin plurals in -*i* should be pronounced distinctly -ī, & not -ē or -ĭ like the Italian *dilettanti, pococuranti*, &c. ; the reformed pronunciation of Latin does not obtain in naturalized Latin words, & to say glă'dĭolē reveals that one is ignorant either that the word is Latin or how Latin words are pronounced. Latin plurals of words in -*is* (*theses, metamorphoses, neuroses*) should be plainly pronounced -ēz, not -ĭz like English plurals.

3. In Latin plurals there are naturally some traps for non-Latinists ; the termination of the singular is no sure guide to that of the plural. Most Latin words in -*us* have plural in -*i*, but not all, & so zeal not according to knowledge issues in such oddities as *hiati, octopi, omnibi, & ignorami* ; as a caution the following list of variations may be useful : *gladiolus, -li* ; *hiatus, -tūs* ; *Venus, -neres* ; *octopus, -podes* ; *corpus, -pora* ; *genus, -nera* ; *ignoramus*, no Latin plural. Similarly most Latin nouns in -*a* have plural in -*ae*, but not all : *lacuna, -nae* ; *dogma, -mata* ; *Saturnalia*, not singular but plural. And, though -*us* & -*a* are much the commonest Anglo-Latin endings, the same danger attends some others (-*ex, -er, -o*, &c.).
4. The treatment of a Latin noun as an English plural because it ends in -*s* is, when of modern introduction, surprising. The Latin plural of *forceps* is *forcipes*, & the English plural should be *forcepses* ; *a forceps, a set of forcipes or forcepses* ; & both these were formerly in use. But *shears & scissors & pincers & pliers* have so convinced us that no such word can have a singular that instead of *a forceps* we usually say *a pair of forceps*, & *forceps* has to serve for both singular & plural.

-**latry.** For words like *lordolatry* & *babyolatry*, see FACETIOUS FORMATIONS, & HYBRID DERIVATIVES.

latter survives almost solely in *the l.*, which provides with *the former* a pair of pronouns obviating disagreeable repetition of one or both of a pair of previously mentioned names or nouns. Such avoidance of repetition is often desirable ; for the principles, see ELEGANT VARIATION, and REPETITION. But *the l.* is liable to certain special misuses :—
(1) *The l.* should not be used when more than a pair are in question, as in : *The difficult problems involved in the early association of Thomas Girtin, Rooker, Dayes, & Turner are*

well illustrated by a set of drawings that . . . ; & what was undoubtedly the best period of the latter artist *is splendidly demonstrated by . . .* (2) Neither should it be used when less than two are in question ; the public & its shillings cannot be reasonably regarded as a pair of things on the same footing in : *The mass of the picture-loving public, however, may be assured of good value for the shillings—whatever be the ultimate destination of* the latter. (3) The true elegant-variationist, who of course works *the l.* very hard, should observe that a mere pronoun will not do for the antecedent of *the l.*, even though there may be a name in the background ; a writer who varies *Gordon* with *the hero of Khartoum & his relative* naturally does not shrink from picking up *him* with *the l.* ; it is all of a piece, & a bad piece : *Mr Hake was a cousin of the late General Gordon, of whom he entertained a most affectionate remembrance. On one occasion, when the hero of Khartoum was dining with* him, the latter *invited his relative to take wine with him, but Gordon imperiously declined.* (4) The true use of it is not to mystify, as in : *The only people to gain will be the Tories & the principal losers will be the working-class voters whose interests the Labour Party is supposed to have at heart. It is a very poor compliment to the intelligence of the latter* [which, in heaven's name ?] *to believe, as many Labour members seem to do, that their support of the Labour cause will be all the more ardent if their interests are thus disregarded.*

laudable means praiseworthy ; the quotation shows it confused with *laudatory* : see PAIRS & SNARES :— *He speaks in the most laudable terms of the work carried out by Captain Thompson in the Anglo-Egyptian Soudan.*

laudanum. Pronounce lŏ'dnum.
laugh. For *the laughing philosopher*, see SOBRIQUETS.
laughable. For the peculiar forma-

tion, see -ABLE 4. For '*would be laughable if it were not tragic*' &c., see HACKNEYED PHRASES.

laughter. *Homeric l.* is a now common phrase whose meaning must be vague to many readers. It is especially the laugh that runs round a circle of spectators when a ludicrous or otherwise pleasing incident surprises them. In Olympus, when Zeus & Hera have had words, the limping Hephaestus counsels his mother to deal in soft answers ; when he, in that former quarrel, had tried to protect her, had he not been flung forth & fallen nine days through air till he landed in Lemnos? & were not nectar & ambrosia in Olympian halls better than such doings ? And therewith he hastened round & filled the cups of all the gods ; ' & inextinguishable was the laughter of the blessed gods as they watched Hephaestus bustling about the hall '.
And again, when Penelope's suitors set the beggar-bully Irus to box with the seeming beggar Odysseus, ' then the twain put up their hands, & Irus struck at the right shoulder, but the other smote him on his neck beneath the ear, & crushed in the bones, & straightway the red blood gushed up through his mouth, & with a moan he fell in the dust, & drave together his teeth as he kicked the ground. But the proud wooers threw up their hands, & died outright for laughter '.
Such is Homeric l. ; but whether the frequent use of the phrase is justified by present-day familiarity with Homer is doubtful. See POPULARIZED TECHNICALITIES.

launch. The OED prefers the pronunciation law- to lah-.
laurel makes -*lled* ; see -LL-, -L-.
laurustinus. So spelt ; *tinus*, a Latin plant-name, not a suffix, was used in apposition to *laurus* ; *laures-* is a corruption.

lavabo. Pl. -*os* ; see -O(E)S 6.
lavatory. The euphemistic use,

which will end in driving the word out of currency, is to be deprecated.

laver, basin. Pronounce lā-.

law Latin, law-Latin. The first is best, except in attributive use (*law-Latin terms* &c.) ; see HYPHENS.

lawn tennis. No hyphen except in attributive use (*lawn-tennis court* &c.) ; see HYPHENS.

lay & lie. 1. Verbs. *To lay* is transitive only (=put to rest), & makes *laid* ; *to lie* is intransitive only (=be at or come to rest), & makes *lay, lain*, never *laid*. But confusion even between the words *lay & lie* themselves is very common in uneducated talk ; & still commoner, sometimes making its way into print, is the use of *laid*, which belongs to the verb *to lay* only, for *lay* the past tense, & *lain* the p.p., of *lie* (*we laid out on the grass, & could have laid there all day*). 2. Nouns. *Lie & lay* are both used in the senses configuration of ground, direction or position in which something lies. Neither has a long established history behind it ; the OED has only one quotation earlier than the nineteenth century, & that is for *lie* (*the proper lye of the land*, 1692) ; *lie* seems also the more reasonable form, *lay* having issued perhaps from sailors' & rustic talk, in which the verbs are not kept distinct.

layer makes *layered* ; see -R-, -RR-.

lay figure has no connexion with any of the English words *lay*, but is from Dutch *led* joint, & means literally jointed figure.

lazzarone. Pronounce lăzarō'ně (or lăts-) ; pl. *-ni* pronounce -nē.

leaded, & *double-leaded*, in printing, mean set with more than the ordinary space between the lines, as is done with matter in the newspapers for which special attention or a special status is desired ; the space is made by inserting strips of lead.

leaden. See -EN ADJECTIVES. *Leaden*, however, is less disused in the literal sense than most of the words among which it is there

placed ; *lead roof* or *pipe* is commoner than *leaden*, but *a leaden pipe* is not as unidiomatic as *a golden watch*.

leading question is often misused for a poser or a pointed question or one that goes to the heart of the matter (as though *leading* meant principal) ; its real meaning is quite different ; a l. q. is not hostile, but friendly, & is so phrased as to guide or lead the person questioned to the answer that it is desirable for him to make, but that he might not think of making or be able to make without help : used especially of counsel examining one of his own witnesses & unfairly prompting him. To object, as people do when they are challenged to deny or confirm an imputation, ' That is a leading question ' is meaningless. See PO-PULARIZED TECHNICALITIES.

(-) **leafed**, (-) **leaved.** See -VE(D).

lean. For *leant & leaned*, see -T & -ED.

leap. For *leapt & leaped*, see -T & -ED. Of *l. to the eyes*, as wearisome a GALLICISM as exists, some examples must be given to suggest its staleness ; others will be found under JUMP. *Bath, it may be admitted, does not* l. t. t. eyes *as an obvious or inevitable meeting-place for the Congress./This, however, does not* l. t. t. eye, *& for the moment I am concerned only with the impressions which strike a new-comer./I won't weary you with rehearsing all the possible consequences of the Bulgarian surrender ; they* l. t. t. eye./*We have not the smallest doubt that there is a perfectly satisfactory explanation of these widely differing totals, but certainly it does not* l. t. t. eyes.

learn. For *learnt & learned*, see -T & -ED. The existence of the disyllabic *learned* as an adjective is an additional reason for preferring *-nt* in the verb ; & so with *unlearned* & *-nt*.

learnedly. Three syllables ; see -EDLY.

leasing. The biblical word, = lying, is pronounced lē′zǐng.

least. The common confusion between *much less* & *much more* is mentioned & illustrated in the article ILLOGICALITIES ; *least of all* & *most of all* get mixed up in the same way : *If that is the case, what justification exists for the sentences, least of all for the way in which they were carried out ?*

leastwise, -ways. The OED labels the first ' somewhat rare ', & the second ' dialectal & vulgar ' ; see -WAYS & -WISE.

leather. 1. For *leather & leathern*, see -EN ADJECTIVES. 2. In *l. or prunella* (usually misquoted *l. and prunella*) the meaning is not two worthless things, but the contrast between the rough l. apron of a cobbler & the fine gown of a parson. It is true, however, that this difference is slighted in comparison with that between worth & the want of it : ' the rest is merely a question of whether you wear rough or fine raiment '. 3. For *the leather* see SOBRIQUETS.

lecher &c. Pronounce lĕch-.

lectureship, -turership. The first is of irregular formation, as a parallel for which the OED quotes *clergyship* (though a person can be clergy better than he can be a lecture) ; but it is long-established, & those who use the second instead perhaps make it in momentary forgetfulness that the irregular form exists.

leeward. Pronounce lū′ard.

left. 1. The l. bank of a river is that to its l. if it is imagined as a person walking downwards, & may therefore be north, south, east, or west, of it ; as this is often in conflict with the idea of l. (= westward) acquired from maps, some care is needed. 2. *L. hand* has no hyphen except when used attributively (*the l.-hand drawer*) ; see HYPHENS. 3. For *leftward(s)*, see -WARD(S).

legalism, legality. For the distinction, see -ISM & -ITY.

legalize makes -*zable* ; see MUTE E.

legend. Pronounce lĕ-.

LEGERDEMAIN WITH TWO SENSES, or the using of a word twice (or of a word & the pronoun that represents it, or of a word that has a double job to do) without observing that the sense required the second time is different from that already in possession. A plain example or two will show the point :—*The inhabitants of the independent lands greatly desire our direct government, which government has, however, for years refused to take any strong measures./ Although he was a very painstaking & industrious pupil, he never indicated any signs of developing into the great naval genius by which his name will in future be distinguished./ Mark had now got his first taste of print, & he liked it, & it was a taste that was to show many developments.* In the first of these, *government* means successively governance, & governing body—either of them a possible synonym for it, but not both to be represented by it in the same sentence. In the second, *genius* means a singularly able person, but *which*, its deputy, means singular ability. In the third, whereas the *taste* he got was an experience, the *taste* that showed developments was an inclination. Such shiftings from one sense to another naturally occur sometimes in reasoning, whether used by the disingenuous for the purpose of deceiving others, or by the over-ingenuous with the result of deceiving themselves ; but we are here concerned not with their material, but with their formal, aspect ; apart from any bad practical effects, they are faults of style.

The examples that follow presently are less flagrant than the typical specimens above ; what leads to them is a want of clear thinking on small points, & in this they resemble the contents of the article HAZINESS ;

other examples will be found under
I, and WE.

If the statements *made are true,*
they *constitute a crime against civilization.* Whereas *the statements*
means the things alleged, *they* means
the things done./*Even where it includes within its borders no important
differences of* nationality, which *has
no serious jealousies among* its *people,
a completely unitary organization is
becoming impossible.* Whereas *nationality* means an abstract property
(the belonging to one or another
nation), *which & its,* both representing it, mean a concrete nation./
The vital differences *of their respective
elders make* none *to their bosom
friendship.* Whereas *the differences*
are quarrels, *none* is (no) alteration./
Admission is by ticket, which *can be
obtained from Mr* . . . Whereas
ticket means a system, *which* means
a piece or pieces of paper./*It has the*
advantage, of *all mountain places
I have known, of being on a ridge
which gives you views in all directions.*
Whereas *advantage of* means the first
time superiority over, it means the
second time merit consisting in./
*Is he, however, correct in ascribing
this misnomer to confusion between
the English terms ' bend ', & ' bar ' ?
Is it not rather due to a mistake* in
spelling, which *should be the French
form ' barre sinistre ' ? Spelling* is
an art, but *which* is a correct word-
form.

legible, readable. See ILLEGIBLE.

legislation, legislature. By a long-
established & useful differentiation,
the first is the making of laws, & the
second only the body that makes
them ; there should be no going
back upon such distinctions, as in :
*It is physical science, & experience,
that man ought to consult in religion,
morals,* legislature, *as well as in
knowledge & the arts.*

legitimate, adj. *The l. drama* : the
OED's definition of the phrase is :
' the body of plays, Shaksperian or
other, that have a recognized theatrical & literary merit '.

legitimate vb., **legitimatize, legitimize.** The second & third are
mere substitutes without difference
of meaning for the first, which has
a longer history by two or three
centuries, & is neither obsolete nor
archaic ; it may be guessed that
they exist only because -*ize*, now so
common, saves a moment's thought
to those who want a word & forget
that there is one ready to hand ;
they might well be placed among
SUPERFLUOUS WORDS. The -*able*
adjective should be *legitimable* (-*atiz-
able, -izable*) ; see -ABLE 1, & MUTE E.

leisure. The OED puts the pronunciation lĕzh- (not lēzh-) first.
U.-S. dictionaries reverse the preference ; but in England the lē- is
now rare.

leit-motiv, -f. The right (German)
spelling is with -*v*. Pronounce
lītmōtē′f.

lengthways, -wise. See -WAYS,
-WISE.

lenience, -cy. The second is recommended ; see -CE, -CY.

lens. Pl. *lenses* ; see SINGULAR -S.

lèse-majesté. See FRENCH WORDS.
The English *lese-majesty* is not now
a legal term, *treason* having taken
its place ; the French form is often
used of treason in foreign countries,
& either is applied jocularly (cf.
PEDANTIC HUMOUR) to anything
that can be metaphorically considered treason.

less. 1. *Nothing l.* 2. *Much &
still l.* 3. *L., lesser, smaller, lower,
fewer.*
1. For the two meanings of *nothing
l. than,* a possible source of ambiguity, see NOTHING.
2. The illogical use of *much l.*
instead of *much more* is discussed
under ILLOGICALITIES, & MUCH.
Here are two examples of *still l.* for
still more, interesting in different
ways :—*Of course social considerations, still less considerations of mere
wealth, must not in any way be
allowed to outweigh purely military
efficiency.* Here, if *still . . . wealth*
had been placed later than *must not,*

it would have passed; coming before it, it is wrong; you can understand *must* out of a previous *must not*, but not out of a *must not* that is yet to come./*Perhaps Charles's most fatal move was the attempted arrest of the five members, undertaken on the Queen's advice, & without the knowledge, & still less without the consent of his three new advisers.* The writer of this has curiously chosen, by needlessly inserting that second *without*, to deprive himself of the usual excuse for using *less* instead of *more*, i.e. the fact that some ellipsis of a word prevents the illogicality from being instantly visible & permits a writer to lose sight of what the full phrase would require while he attends to the broad effect.

3. *L.*, *lesser, smaller, lower, fewer,* &c. *The letters & memoirs could have been published, we should imagine, at a less price./While Colonel Seely adheres to the determination to keep open the competition for the best aeroplane,* a lesser prize *will probably be offered which will be confined to British manufacturers.* These extracts suggest ignorance of, or indifference to, modern idiomatic restrictions on the use of *less* & *lesser.* The grammar of both is correct; but, when the context— unemotional statement of everyday facts—is taken into account, *at a less price* ought to be *at a lower price,* & *a lesser prize* ought to be *a smaller prize.* It is true that *less* & *lesser* were once ordinary comparatives of *little* (*lesser* differing from *less* in being used only as an adjective & only before a noun), & that therefore they were roughly equivalent in sense to our *smaller*; & further, this piece of archaism, like many others, is permissible in emotional passages or such as demand exceptionally dignified expression; but the extracts have no such qualification.

The modern tendency is so to restrict *less* that it means not *smaller,* but *a smaller amount of,* is

the comparative rather of *a little* than of *little,* & is consequently applied only to things that are measured by amount & not by size or quality or number, nouns with which *much* & *little,* not *great* & *small,* nor *high* & *low,* nor *many* & *few,* are the appropriate contrasted epithets : *less butter, courage*; but *a smaller army, table*; *a lower price, degree*; *fewer opportunities, people.* Plurals, & singulars with *a* or *an,* will naturally not take *less*; *less tonnage,* but *fewer ships*; *less manpower,* but *fewer men*; *less opportunity,* but *a worse opportunity,* & *inferior opportunities*; though a few plurals like *clothes* & *troops,* really equivalent to singulars of indefinite amount, are exceptions: *could do with less troops* or *clothes.* Of *less's* antipathy to *a,* examples are: *I want to pay less rent,* but *a lower rent is what I want./That is of less value,* but *a lower value attaches to this./Less noise, please,* but *a slighter noise would have waked me./Less size means less weight,* but *I want a smaller size.* Such is the general tendency: to substitute *smaller, lower, fewer,* or other appropriate word, for *less* except where it means ' a smaller amount of ', & for *lesser,* & to regard the now slightly archaic *less* in other senses as an affectation. There are no doubt special phrases keeping it alive even in quite natural speech, e.g. *in* or *to a less degree,* where *lower* is hardly yet as common as *less*; but the general tendency is unmistakable, & is moreover, since it makes for precision, one that should be complied with.

-LESS. Bare reference of any word in *-less* to this article means that the use of it in ordinary prose is deprecated.

The original & normal use of this suffix is to append it to nouns, producing adjectives meaning without the thing, e.g. *headless, tuneless*; to this use there are no limits whatever. Words made from verbs, with the sense not able to do or not liable to suffer the action or process, as *tireless, fadeless, & describeless,* are much fewer, are mostly of a poetical cast, & when new-minted strike the reader of prose at least as base metal. They have an undeniable advantage in their shortness ; compare *resistless, describeless, & weariless,* with *irresistible, indescribable, & unweariable* ; but this is outweighed for all except fully established ones by the uneasy feeling that there is something queer about them. Apart from a few so familiar that no thought of their elements & formation occurs to us, such as *dauntless, -less* words made from verbs are much better left to the poets ; this does not apply to the many in which, as in *numberless,* formation from the noun gives the sense as well, if not as obviously, as formation from the verb (without number ? or not able to be numbered ?) ; *dauntless* itself may perhaps have been made from the noun *daunt,* which in the 15th & 16th centuries was current in the sense discouragement.

To those who have any regard for the interests of the language as distinguished from its pliability to their immediate purposes, it will seem of some importance that it should not become necessary, with every word in which *-less* is appended to what can be either a noun or a verb, to decide which is this time intended. If the verb-compounds become much more frequent, we shall never know that *pitiless & harmless* may not mean ' that cannot be pitied ' & ' secure against being harmed ' as well as ' without the instinct of pity ' & ' without harmfulness ' ; we ought to be able to reckon that, with a few well-known exceptions, *-less* words mean simply without what is signified by the noun they contain ; & the way to keep that assumption valid is to abstain from reckless compounding of *-less* with verbs.

lessee, lessor. The lessee is the person who takes, the lessor the person who lets, on lease.

lesser. See LESS.

lest. The idiomatic construction after *l.* is *should,* or in exalted style the pure subjunctive (*l. we forget* ; *l. he be angry*). Instead of *should,* good writers rarely use *shall, may, & might.* The variations in the quotations below are entirely against modern idiom ; *will & would* after *l.* are merely a special form of the inability to distinguish between SHALL & *will.* Mistakes corresponding to those after *l.* are still more frequent after IN ORDER THAT. *We do not think Mr Lloyd George need be apprehensive lest the newspaper reader* will *interpret his little homily in Wales yesterday as . . ./There must be loyal cooperation, lest the last state of the party* becomes *worse than the first./The German force now lost no time in retreat, lest they* would *be cut off & surrounded by General Mackenzie.*

let. Mistakes in case are very rare in English ; forgetfulness of the construction, when *l.* is used in exhortations, is responsible for a wrong subjective now & then :—*And now, my dear,* let *you & I say a few words about this unfortunate affair./Our work is to inform & permeate the party, not to leave it ;* if anybody *must leave it,* let it not be we. Read *me, us.*

lethargy. *Mr ——, discussing the l. of the dental profession* to *the shocking condition of the teeth of the working classes, said . . . L. to* is unidiomatic, made on the ANALOGY of *indifference to,* but not justified by it.

let(t). For spelling cf. SET(T).

LETTER FORMS. Of the usual forms preceding the signature some are better suited than others to certain correspondents or occasions. The distinctions here offered are tentative, but may be useful. ' I am, Sir ' &c., or ' Believe me (to be) ', or ' I remain ', used to precede most of the following forms, but they are now more often omitted.

Your obedient servant, or *Yours obediently* : From or to officials ; letters to the Editor in newspapers.

Yours respectfully, or (old-fashioned) *Your obedient servant,* or (old-fashioned) *Yours to command* : Servant to master &c.

Faithfully : To newspaper (affected).

Yours &c. : To newspaper (now common).

Yours faithfully : To unknown person on business.

Yours truly : To slight acquaintance.

Yours very truly : Ceremonious but cordial.

Yours sincerely : In invitations & friendly but not intimate letters.

Yours ever, or *Ever yours,* or *Yours* : Unceremonious between intimates.

Yours affectionately : Between relations &c.

lettuce. Pronounce -tĭs.

levee. Write without an accent, & pronounce lĕ'vĭ.

level makes -*lled* &c. ; see -LL-, -L-. *Do* one's *l. best,* originally American, has lived long enough in England to be no longer slang.

lever makes *levered* &c. ; see -R-, -RR-.

lever de rideau. See FRENCH WORDS.

levigate, levitate, make -*gable,* -*itable* ; see -ABLE 1.

levy, n. For synonymy see TAX.

levy, v. For inflexions see VERBS IN -IE, -Y, -YE, 6.

lexicon. See DICTIONARY. Pl. -*ns,* -*ca* ; see -ON 2.

Leyden. Pronounce lī-, not lā-.

liable, possibly because it is a more or less isolated word lacking connexions to keep it steady, constantly has its meaning shifted. For its proper use, see APT, with which there is much excuse for confusing it. The first quotation illustrates that confusion ; in the second, *l. to assert* should be *capable of*

asserting ; in the third, *is l. to demand* should be *may demand* or *is likely* or *not unlikely to demand* ; & in the last the sporting reporter should have stuck to his last & said *in the running for* instead of *l. to win* :—*Political & religious bias are also* l. to operate./*The President having a Cabinet, & having to take note of the relics of the Tzu Cheng Yuan, still not officially made non-existent, & of the Nanking Assembly inferentially superseded, but still* l. to assert itself, *can hardly be held as invested with dictatorial power.*/*Walking through England must have been stripped of most of its charms, when at every inn you have to fill up forms about the colour of your wife's hair, & every policeman* is l. to demand *the production of a variety of tickets.*/ *Duncan has been for several years* l. to win *one of the big prizes of golf.*

liaison. Pronounce as English (lĭă'zn) ; the military use during the war has completed its naturalization.

liana. Pronounce lĭah'nă.

libel makes -*lled, -llous,* &c. ; see -LL-, -L-.

libel & some synonyms. The much-quoted saying ' The greater the truth the greater ' (or ' worse ') ' the libel ' makes us all occasionally curious about what a l. is. It & its synonyms, several of which have separate meanings in legal & in popular use, also differ from one another according as they imply or do not imply falsity, malice, & publication. The synonyms meant are *calumny, defamation, scandal,* & *slander.* The definitions that follow are taken verbatim from the OED ; distinctions between legal & popular use are shown ; & in the brackets are notes of the OED or, with inverted commas, illuminating sentences quoted by it. The presence or absence in the definitions of the words *false, malicious, published,* &c., should be carefully noticed.

Calumny : False & malicious misrepresentation of the words or actions of others, calculated to injure their reputation.

Defamation : The action of defaming, or attacking any one's good fame.

Libel : (Law) any published statement damaging to the reputation of a person (' The judge answered . . . that it was clearly possible to publish a libel for the public good ') ; (Pop.) any false & defamatory statement in conversation or otherwise.

Scandal : (Law) any injurious report published concerning another which may be the foundation of legal action ; (Pop.) the utterance of disgraceful imputations (The word differs from the etymologically identical slander in not implying the falsity of the imputations made).

Slander : The utterance or dissemination of false statements or reports concerning a person, or malicious misrepresentation of his actions, in order to defame or injure him (' Falsehood & malice, express or implied, are of the essence of the action for slander ').

liberal. In *l. education* the adjective retains a sense that is almost obsolete, & yet is near enough to some extant senses to make misunderstanding possible. A l. e. is neither one in which expense is not spared, nor one in which enlightened methods of teaching prevail, nor even one that instils broadmindedness ; or rather it is not so called because it is any of these. It is the education designed for a gentleman (Latin *liber* a free man), & is opposed on the one hand to technical or professional or any special training, & on the other to education that stops short before· manhood is reached.

liberate makes *-rable, -tor* ; see -ABLE 1, -OR.

libertine. For *chartered l.,* see HACKNEYED PHRASES.

libretto. Pl. *-etti* (pronounce -ē ; see -I) or *-os,* see -O(E)S 6.

Libyan. So spelt, not *Lybian.* See Y & I.

licence, -se. The first is better for

the noun, the second for the verb. Compare, for this convenient distinction, *advice, -se, device, -se, practice, -se, prophecy, -sy,* in all of which the c marks the noun.

lichen. Pronounce lī′kn ; Gk *leikhēn* is the source.

lich-gate, -house. So spelt ; the OED gives *lych-* only as a variant ; see Y & I.

lickerish, liquorish. The first is the right form, & the second, being wrongly associated with *liquor,* inevitably alters & narrows the meaning. The word means fond of dainties, sweet-toothed, greedy, lustful, & is connected with the verb *lick* & with *lecher,* not with *liquor.* See TRUE & FALSE ETYMOLOGY.

licorice. See LIQUORICE.

lie, be prostrate. See LAY & LIE.

lie, position. See LAY & LIE.

lie, speak falsely. For inflexions, see VERBS IN -IE, -Y, -YE, 3.

lien, n. ' The usual pronunciation in England is lē′en.'—OED.

-lier. For comparative-adverb forms, see -ER & -EST 3.

lieutenant. Pronounce left- or lĕft-, & in nautical & naval use letĕ′nant ; lūt- prevails in U.S. For hyphen in *l. general,* see MAJOR GENERAL.

life. 1. For *come into* one's *l.,* see HACKNEYED PHRASES. *We sense the tragedy of Anna Wolsky as she steps light-heartedly into Sylvia Bayley's life.* 2. For pl. &c., see -VE(D).

light, n. For *dim religious l.,* see IRRELEVANT ALLUSION. *In l. of* will not do for *in the l. of,* as in *That it should have been so,* in light of *all the facts, will always be a nine-days wonder to the student of history* ; see CAST-IRON IDIOM.

light, v. Both verbs (kindle. descend) make *lighted* or *lit* for past tense & p.p. ; but *lighted* is commoner for the p.p., especially that of the first verb used attributively : *Is the fire lighted* or *lit ?,* but *Holding a lighted candle.*

lightning. So spelt, not *-tening.*

like, adj. For *& the l.*, see FORTH 1.

like in questionable constructions.
1. It will be best to dispose first of what is, if it is a misuse at all, the most flagrant & easily recognizable misuse of *like*. A sentence from Darwin quoted in the OED contains it in a short & unmistakable form : *Unfortunately few have observed like you have done.* Every illiterate person uses this construction daily ; it is the established way of putting the thing among all who have not been taught to avoid it ; the substitution of *as* for *like* in their sentences would sound artificial. But in good writing this particular *like* is very rare, & even those writers with whom sound English is a matter of care & acquirement rather than of right instinct, & to whom *like* was once the natural word, deliberately weed it out. The OED's judgement is as follows : ' Used as conjunction, = " like as ", as. Now generally condemned as vulgar or slovenly, though examples may be found in many recent writers of standing '. Besides the Darwin quoted above, the OED gives indisputable examples from Shakspere, Southey, Newman, Morris, & other ' writers of standing '. The reader who has no instinctive objection to the construction can now decide for himself whether he shall consent to use it in talk, in print, in both, or in neither ; he knows that he will be able to defend himself if he is condemned for it, but also that, until he has done so, he will be condemned. It remains to give a few newspaper examples so that there may be no mistake about what the ' vulgar or slovenly ' use in its simplest form is :—*Or can these tickets be kept* (like the sugar cards were) *by the retailer ?/The retail price can never reach a prohibitive figure* like petrol has done./*Wasub's words sank into Lingard's heart* like lead sinks *into water./They studied the rules of a game* like a lawyer would study *an imperfectly-drawn-up will./Our great patron saint ' St George ' was a Greek,* like a good many of the saints are./ *The idea that you can learn the technique of an art* like you can learn *the multiplication table or the use of logarithms.*

2. The rest of this article is intended for those who decide against the conjunctional use that has been already discussed, & are prepared to avoid also some misuses of a less easily recognizable kind. All the examples in 1 were of the undisguised conjunctional use, & contained a subordinate clause with its verb ; most of those now to come have no subordinate verb, & in all of them *like* may be regarded as an adjective or adverb having the additional power (cf. *worth*) of directly governing nouns as if it were a preposition.

The first type is perhaps not really different from that discussed in 1. Examples are :—*Or should he have a palace some distance away,* like the Bishop of Winchester has *at Farnham ?/But in an industrialized county* like so great a part of Lancashire is, *the architecture can hardly fail to . . ./ The club doctor was the friend & adviser of its members,* something like the country parson has to be *to his labour parishioners in the present day.* The peculiarity of these is that in each there is a previous noun, *palace, county, something,* with which *like* may agree as an adjective, & an ellipsis of ' what ' or ' the one that ' may be supposed. Such a defence is neither plausible nor satisfactory, & the sentences are no better than others containing a verb.

Of sentences in which *like* is not followed by a verb, certain forms are unexceptionable, but are liable to extensions that are not so. The unquestioned forms are *He talks like an expert & You are treating me like a fool,* in which *like* is equivalent to a prepositional adverb = similarly to ; & *You, like me, are disappointed,* in which *like* is equivalent either to an adverb as before, or perhaps rather to a prepositional adjective

= resembling in this respect. The second, third, & fourth faulty types represent neglect of various limitations observed in the correct forms.

Second type :—*The Committee was today, like yesterday, composed of the following gentlemen.*/*The Turks would appreciate the change, as, unlike Koweit, their political title is here beyond dispute.*/*It is certain that now, unlike the closing years of last century, quotation from his poetry is singularly rare.*/*We may have 110, like last year, when Paignton . . . & Jersey all enjoyed a sun-bath of nearly 200 hours.* The limitation here disregarded is that the word governed by *like* must be a noun, not an adverb or an adverbial phrase. *Yesterday* & *last year* are not nouns, but an adverb & an adverbial phrase ; & *Koweit* & *the closing years*, meaning *at* Koweit & *in* the closing years, have also only a deceitful appearance of being nouns.

Third type :—*People get alarmed on each occasion* on which (like the present case) *dying children suddenly appear.*/*He has completed a new work* in which, like its author's recent books, *no failing in sparkle or vigour will be traceable.*/*And then came the war* ; like many another English village, *it filtered slowly, very slowly, through* to his. The limitation (suggested with diffidence) that has here been disregarded is that the preceding noun to which *like* is attached must be not one governed by a preposition, but subject or object of the main verb. The preceding nouns are *which* (i.e. occasion), *which* (i.e. work), & *his* (i.e. village), governed by *on, in,* & *to* ; instead of *like*, read *as in the present case, as in its author's recent books,* & *as to many another*.

Fourth type :—Like his Roman predecessor, *his private life was profligate* ; like Antony, *he was an insatiate gambler.*/*When the raging tearing propaganda was started, it was thought that,* like Mr Balfour, *his* convictions *on the fiscal question were unsettled.* The limitation is that the word governed by *like* must be *in pari materia* with the one to which it is compared. The *predecessor* & *Mr Balfour* are not so related to *life* & *convictions* ; but *Antony* is to *he,* & that sentence alone will pass muster. This mistake, however, of comparing unlike things is not, like the others, peculiar to *like*, but is a slovenly parsimony of words that may occur in many other constructions.

-like. ' In formations intended as nonce-words, or not generally current, the hyphen is ordinarily used ' —OED. To which it may be added that nouns in *-l* require the hyphen ; the OED prints, e. g., cowl-like, eel-like, flail-like, jail-like, owl-like, pearl-like, rebel-like, sentinel-like, veil-like.

like, v. 1. *L.* makes *likable* ; see MUTE E.

2. *I would l.* Even on those who use *should* & *would* idiomatically under all ordinary temptations the verb *l.* seems to exercise a corrupting influence ; a couple of examples follow *pro formâ*, but anyone can find as many as he pleases with very little search :—*We would l. to ask one or two questions on our own account.*/*There is one paragraph in it that I would l. to refer to.* There is indeed no mystery about why people go wrong ; it is because, if the thing had to be said without the use of the verb *like, would* & not *should* is the form to use : *We would ask, that I would refer to* ; but that has nothing to do with what is right when the verb *like* is used. Putting aside one idiom that with this particular verb is negligible (*When the post came I would like to be allowed to carry it in,* = I used to like), *I would l.* is no better than any of the *wills* & *woulds* that are well recognized as Scotch, Irish, American, & other kinds of English, but not English English. If the SHALL & WILL idiom is worth preserving at all, *I would l.* is wrong, & *I should l.* right.

likely, adv. *Yet it was not easy to divine the thought behind that intentness of gaze ; likely it was far from the actual scene apparently holding its attention.* In educated speech & writing the adverb is never used without *very, most,* or *more,* except by way of poetic archaism or, as presumably in the extract, of stylistic NOVELTY-HUNTING. American usage, however, may be different :—*The climate in America is so severe in winter that stocks will l. die out./It will l. be financed largely by capital raised in the United States.* For *likelily,* see -LILY ; for *likelier* adv., -ER & -EST 3.

likewise. The use as a conjunction (*Its tendency to wobble & its uniformity of tone colour, l. its restricted powers of execution*) is, like the similar use of ALSO, an ILLITERACY ; the OED quotes no example.

likin. Pronounce lēkē'n.

-LILY. Avoidance of the adverbs in *-lily,* i.e. adverbs made regularly from adjectives in *-ly,* is merely a matter of taste, but is very, & increasingly, general. Neither the difficulty of saying the words nor the sound of them when said is a serious objection so long as the three syllables are not passed ; *holily & statelily & lovelily* are not hard to say or harsh to hear ; but with *heavenlily & ruffianlily* hesitation is natural ; & the result has been that adverbs in *-lily,* however short, are now with a few special exceptions seldom heard & seldomer seen. Methods of avoidance are various :—

1. It is always possible to say *in a masterly manner, at a timely moment,* & the like, instead of *masterlily, timelily* ; or again to be content with *decorously* &c. instead of *mannerlily* ; the method of periphrasis or synonym.

2. A large number of adjectives in *-ly* are established as adverbs also. So *early, (most* or *very)* LIKELY, & the adjectives of periodical recurrence like *daily & hourly.* A single quotation will show the consequences of

making one's own adverbs of this kind : *External evidence, however, is rare ; & its rarity gives value to such work as Mr —— here masterly does.*

3. Before adjectives & adverbs the *-ly* adjective often stands instead of the *-lily* adverb, making a kind of informal compound. Though we should say *horribly pale* & not *horrible pale,* we allow ourselves *ghastly pale* rather than use *ghastlily* ; so *heavenly bright, beastly cold, jolly soon,* &c.—all without the hyphen that would mark regular compounds.

4. In sentences where it is just possible, though not natural, for a predicative adjective to stand instead of an adverb, that way is sometimes taken with an adjective in *-ly* though it would not be taken with another : *it happened timely enough,* though not *opportune enough* ; *she nodded queenly,* though not *she nodded significant.*

5. Perhaps any adjective formed by appending *-ly* either to an adjective (*kind, kindly* ; *dead, deadly*) or to a noun of the kind that is easily used in apposition like an adjectival epithet (*cowardly,* cf. *the coward king* ; *soldierly,* cf. *a soldier colonist*) is sometimes, though always consciously & noticeably, allowed to pass as an adverb : *it was ruffianly done* ; *a kindly thought, & kindly uttered.*

On the other hand, avoidance is not always called for ; some *-lily* words are current, though not many. Those that naturally present themselves (*he laughed jollily* ; *sillily complacent* ; *live holily* ; *dodged it wilily*) seem to be all from adjectives in which *-ly* is not the usual adjectival ending, but the *l* is part of the word-stem ; & though we are most of us not conscious of that fact nowadays, it may have had its effect in separating these from the others.

limb. When we first come across an eclipse in the newspapers & read of *the sun's lower limb,* we suspect the writer of making jokes or waxing poetical, so odd is the association of limbs with that globular form. It is a relief to learn that *limb* does mean edge without a metaphor; the *l.* in Astronomy &c. is from Latin *limbus* hem, & the *l.* of ordinary speech is a separate & native word. See TRUE & FALSE ETYMOLOGY.

limber, v., makes *-ered* &c.; see -R-, -RR-.

limbo. Pl. *-os*; see -O(E)S 3.

lime makes *limy*; see -EY & -Y.

limit, n. For some synonyms in sense *tether* &c., see FIELD.

limit, v., makes *-ited* &c.; see -T-, -TT-.

limited. *L. company* is an elliptical phrase for *l.-liability company,* & implies not that the number of members is l., but that their liability for its debts is so.

limn. In *l.* & *limned* n is silent, in *limner* sounded, & in *limning* either; cf. DAMNING.

limpid often has (*-er*) *-est*; see -ER & -EST, 2, 4.

linage, number of lines. Spell thus; the other spelling, *lineage,* though often seen in the newspapers, is, owing to the existence of *lineage* descent, still less desirable than other spellings with intrusive MUTE E. An example of the wrong form is: . . . *at the rate of 15s. per inch* (*set in display type*) *or 9d. per line* (*set in the lineage style*).

line, n. For some synonyms in sense *department* &c., see FIELD.

line, v., makes *-nable*; see MUTE E.

lin(e)age. See LINAGE.

lingerie. See FRENCH WORDS.

lingo. Pl. *-os*; see -O(E)S 6. For some synonyms, see JARGON.

links, golf-course. Sometimes used as a singular (*there is a good links here*); cf. *an ironworks*.

Linnaean, -nean. The first is usual, ' though the Linnean Society adopts the other form ' (OED). See Æ, Œ. Against *-nean* is the invariable spelling of *Linnaeus*.

lintel makes *-lled*; see -LL-, -L-.

liny, not *-ney*; see -EY & -Y.

lionize makes *-zable*; see MUTE E.

liquate makes *-atable*; see -ABLE 1.

liquefy. For inflexions see VERBS IN -IE, -Y, -YE, 6.

liqueur. Pronounce lĭkūr'; cf. AMATEUR.

liquid. See FLUID for fluid, gas, & l. For the phonetic sense, see TECHNICAL TERMS.

liquidize, liquidate, make *-dizable, -dable*; see MUTE E, -ABLE 1.

liquorice, lico-, The first is treated by the OED as the established form.

liquorish. See LICKERISH.

lira, Italian franc, has pl. *lire* (pronounce lēr'ā) or anglicized *liras*. To use *lira* as pl. (*A meal in a second-class restaurant costs from eight to ten lira*) is absurd.

lissom(e). The OED form is *-om*.

list, please. The third sing. pres. is *list* or *listeth,* the past tense *list* or *listed.* The verb being in any form archaic, it is of no great importance whether the more obviously archaic impersonal construction (*as him list* &c.) or the now commoner personal one (*as he list* &c.) is used.

listen(er). Pronounce lĭ'sn(*er*). See PRONUNCIATION, Silent t.

litany, liturgy. The two words have come so close to each other in use that it is a surprise when one first finds that the initial syllables are not the same in origin, nor even connected. For those who know the Greek words, a litany is a series of prayers, a liturgy is a canon of public service; the latter in practice includes prayer, but does not say so.

literally. We have come to such a pass with this emphasizer that where the truth would require us to insert with a strong expression ' not literally, of course, but in a manner of speaking ', we do not hesitate to insert the very word that we ought to be at pains to repudiate; cf. VERITABLE; such false coin makes honest traffic in words impossible. *If the Home Rule Bill is passed, the*

300,000 Unionists of the South & West of Ireland will be literally *thrown to the wolves.*/*The strong tête-de-pont fortifications were rushed by our troops, & a battalion crossed the bridge* literally *on the enemy's shoulders.* In both, *practically* or *virtually*, opposites of *literally*, would have stood. (At election time) *My telephone wires have been kept l. red-hot.*/*H. B. Stallard in the half-mile l. 'flew ' round the track.*/*Americans are l. fed up with these foreign conspirators.*/*He* [a climber] *came through safely, but he had l. to cling on with his eyebrows.*

LITERARY CRITICS' WORDS. The literary critics here meant are not the writers of books or treatises or essays of which the substance is criticism ; readers of that form of literature are a class apart, between which & its writers if a special lingo exists, the rest of us are not concerned to take exception to it. Anything said in this book about literary critics is aimed only at the newspaper reviewers of books & other works of art. Those reviewers, as anyone knows who examines them critically in their turn, give us work that ranges from the very highest literary skill (if the power of original creation is set aside as here irrelevant) to the merest hack-work ; but the point is that whether they are highly accomplished writers, or tiros employed on the theory that anyone is good enough to pass an opinion on a book, their audience is not the special class that buys critical works because its tastes are literary, but the general public, which buys its criticism as part of its newspaper, & does not know the critics' lingo. It follows that, the better the critic, the fewer literary critics' words he uses. The good critic is aware that his public wants to understand, & he has no need to convince it that he knows what he is talking about by parading words that it does not understand. With the inferior critic the establishment

of his status is the first consideration, & he effects it by so using, let us say, *actuality, inevitable, & sympathetic*, that the reader shall become aware of a mysterious difference between the sense attaching to the words in ordinary life & the sense now presented to him. He has taken *actuality* to mean actualness or reality ; the critic perplexes him by giving it another sense, which it has a right to in French, where *actuel* means present, but not in English, i. e. up-to-dateness, or resemblance not to truth in general but to present-day conditions ; & he does this without mentioning that he is gallicizing. And so with the other words ; the reader is to have it borne in upon him that a more instructed person than himself is talking to him. One mark of the good literary critic is that he is both able to explain his meaning without resort to these lingo words, & under no necessity to use them as advertisements.

Specimens of literary critics' words, under some of which (printed in capitals) further remarks will be found, are :—actuality, BANAL(ITY), CACHET, charm, CONCISION, DISTINCTION, IMMENSE, INEVITABLE, INTRIGUE, METICULOUS, MOT JUSTE, SYMPATHETIC.

LITERARY WORDS. A l. w., when the description is used in this book, is one that cannot be called archaic, inasmuch as it is perfectly comprehensible still to all who hear it, but that has dropped out of use & had its place taken by some other word except in writing of a poetical or a definitely literary cast. To use literary words instead of the current substitutes in an unsuitable context challenges attention & gives the impression that the writer is a foreigner who has learnt the language only from books. See also what is said of FORMAL WORDS. *Chill* for *chilly*, *eve* for *evening*, *gainsay* for *deny* &c., *loathly* for *loathsome*, *visage* for *face* &c., may be instanced ; but literary words are reckoned by thousands.

lithesome is, between *lithe* & *lissom*, a SUPERFLUOUS WORD.

lithontriptic. See BARBARISMS.

litotes. See TECHNICAL TERMS. Pronounce lī'totēz.

litre, -ter. See -RE & -ER.

litter, brood. See FARROW.

littérateur. See FRENCH WORDS.

little. See SMALL. Comparison *less(er)* (for limitations of sense see LESS 3), *least*, or more usually *smaller, -est*.

littoral, n., has a technical sense in which it is doubtless of value ; marine life being distributed into abyssal, pelagic, & littoral, *the l.* (sc. zone or region) is the shallow waters near the shore. But that is not the sense in which most of us know it ; it meets us as a name for the land region bordering & including the shore ; in that sense it may be important in treaties & the like to have a word that does not mean strictly the mere line of coast or shore ; but in ordinary contexts it should never be preferred to *coast*, & its present popularity is due to pretentiousness. Why not *coast* in *The towns along the Mediterranean littoral, The Russian settlements on the Eastern Caspian littoral ?* See FORMAL WORDS.

liturgy. See LITANY.

livable. So spelt ; see MUTE E.

-lived. In *long-l.* &c. the right pronunciation is līvd, the words being from *life* (cf. *-leaved* from *leaf* &c.) & not from *live* ; but līvd is often heard.

liven. See -EN VERBS.

llama. See LAMA.

-LL-, -L-. Final *l* is treated differently in British, but not American, usage from most final consonants, the rule being to double it, if single, in inflexions & in some derivatives irrespective of the position of the accent.

1. When verbs in *-l* (except those in which a compound vowel sound, as *ai, ea, ee, oi, ow, ur,* precedes the *-l*) make inflected or derived words in *-able, -ed, -en, -er,* or *-ing, -ll-* is written—*controllable, carolled, befallen, traveller, equalling* ; but *failed, boiling, curled,* &c., & before *-ment l* is not doubled ; see also PARALLELED, WOOL.

2. When nouns or adjectives in *-l* (with exceptions as in 1) make adjectives by addition of *-ed, -er,* or *-y*, the *l* is doubled : *flannelled, jeweller, gravelly* ; but see UNPARALLELED. Before *-ish* & *-ism* & *-ist, l* is not doubled : *devilish, liberalism, naturalist.* Irregular superlatives vary, most using one *l*, but words in *-ful* always two : *brutalest, loyalest, civil(l)est, joyfullest.*

3. The simple form of a good many verbs vacillates between *-l* & *-ll*, & no rule is possible that will secure the best form for all words & not conflict with strong usage for some ; but it is perhaps safe to say that where vacillation exists *-ll* is better if *a* precedes (*appall, befall, enthrall, install*), & *-l* if another vowel, especially *i* (*distil, instil, enrol, annul*) ; verbs in *-ll,* however, take single *l* before *-ment* (*enrolment, enthralment, instalment*).

4. Derivatives & compounds of words in *-ll* sometimes drop one *l* ; so *almighty, almost, already, altogether, always,* but not *alright* ; *chilblain* ; *fulfil* ; *skilful* ; *thraldom* ; *wilful.* This is perhaps helped by some apparent but not real examples such as *belfry, bulrush, bulwark,* & *walnut,* which are not from *bell, bull,* & *wall. Dul(l)ness* & *ful(l)ness* are debatable ; the older & much commoner spelling, but (according to the OED) the one less ' in accordance with general analogies ' has only one *l*.

Lloyd's, underwriters. So written, not *-ds* or *ds'*.

load, lode. In the compounds with *stone* & *star* it is usual to spell *loadstone*, but *lodestar.* The first element is the same, & is the ordinary *load*, of which the original sense was way, connected with the verb *lead* ; the spelling distinction is accidental, & both *lodestone* & *loadstar* are some times used.

loafed, -ved. See -VE(D).

loan. The verb has been expelled from idiomatic southern English by *lend*, but was formerly current, & survives in U.S. & locally in U.K.

lo(a)th. *Loth* is recommended. The OED gives precedence to *loath*, & it is true that that spelling avoids obscuring the connexion with the verb *loathe* ; but in its 19th-c. quotations the proportion is 7 : 1 for *loth*, a fair proof of establishment. The verb is always *loathe*, & *loathly* & *loathsome* have always the *a*.

lobby, v. For inflexions see VERBS IN -IE, -Y, -YE, 6.

lobular. See -ULAR.

local(e). 1. The ' erroneous form ' (OED) *locale* is recommended ; see MORALE, & À L'OUTRANCE. 2. Pronounce the noun lokah'l, whichever way it is spelt. 3. The word's right to exist depends on the question whether the two indispensable words *locality* & *scene* give all the shades of meaning required, or whether something intermediate is useful. The defence of *l.* would be on these lines : A locality is a place, with features of some sort, existing independently of anything that may happen there. If something happens in a locality, the locality becomes that something's locale, or place of happening. If the something that happens is seen or imagined or described in connexion with its locale, the locale becomes its scene or visible environment.

localize, locate, make *-zable, -atable* ; see MUTE E, -ABLE 1.

locative. See TECHNICAL TERMS.

loch. See LOUGH.

locomote. See BACK-FORMATION.

loculus. Pl. *-li* (-lī).

locum tenens, -ncy. Pronounce lō'kum tē'-. The *-ncy* word is usually *-ency*, not *-ancy*.

locus. Pl. *-ci* (-sī).

locution is a potentially convenient word as equivalent to *word* or *phrase* ; not more than potentially, because it so far smacks of pedantry that most people prefer to say *word* or *phrase* on the rare occasions when *expression* is not precise enough for the purpose, & *l.* gets left to the pedants. *His style is comparatively free from locutions calculated to baffle the English reader* ; does anyone really like that better than *expressions* ?

lode. See LOAD.

lodge makes *lodgeable* ; see MUTE E.

lodg(e)ment. Retention of the *-e-* is recommended ; see JUDGEMENT.

logan. Pronounce lō'gan(-berry), but lŏ'gan(-stone).

logaoedic. Pronounce lŏgaē'dĭk.

loggia. Pronounce lŏ'ja ; pl. *loggie*, pronounce lŏ'jā.

logic. For *the l. of facts* or *events*, see HACKNEYED PHRASES.

logion. Pron. lŏ'gĭŏn ; pl. *-ia*.

loiter has *-ered* &c. ; see -R-, -RR-.

lollop has *-oping* &c. ; see -P-, -PP-.

Lombard(y). The OED gives precedence to lŏm- over the probably more usual lŭm-.

lonelily. See -LILY.

long butt (billiards) should not be hyphened ; see HYPHENS on the relation of stress to hyphen.

long-lived. See -LIVED.

longue haleine. See FRENCH WORDS.

LONG VARIANTS. 'The better the writer, the shorter his words ' would be a statement needing many exceptions for individual persons & particular subjects ; but for all that it would, & especially about English writers, be broadly true. Those who run to long words are mainly the unskilful & tasteless ; they confuse pomposity with dignity, flaccidity with ease, & bulk with force ; see LOVE OF THE LONG WORD. A special form of long word is now to be illustrated ; when a word for the notion wanted exists, some people (1) forget or do not know that word, & make up another from the same stem with an extra suffix or two ; or (2) are not satisfied with a mere current word, & resolve to decorate it, also with an extra suffix ; or (3) have heard used a longer form that resembles it, & are not aware that this other form is appropriated to another sense. Cases of 1 & 2 are often indistinguishable ; the motive differs, but the result is the same ; & they will here be mixed together, those of 3 being kept apart.

1 & 2. Needless lengthenings of established words due to oversight or caprice : administrate (administer) ; assertative (assertive) ; contumacity (contumacy) ; cultivatable (cultivable) ; dampen (damp, v.) ; dubiety (doubt) ; epistolatory (epistolary) ; experimentalize (experiment, v.) ; extemporaneously (ex tempore) ; filtrate (filter, v.) ; fluviatile (fluvial) ; perfection, v. (perfect, v.) ; preventative (preventive) ; quieten (quiet, v.) ; wastage (waste).

Examples of 1 & 2

The capability of the Germans to administrate *districts with a mixed population./Still speaking in a very loud* assertative *voice, he declared that . . ./Mdlle St Pierre's affected interference provoked* contumacity./*If you add to the* cultivatable *lands of the immediate Rhine valley those of . . ./ His extreme sensitiveness to all the suggestions which* dampen *enthusiasm . . ./Lord Lansdowne has done the Liberal Party a good turn by putting Tariff Reform to the front ; about this there can be no* dubiety./ *Cowper's Letters . . . the best example of the* epistolatory *art our language possesses./A few old masters that have been* experimentalized *on./M. Delcassé, speaking* extemporaneously *but with notes, said . . ./A Christianity* filtrated *of all its sectional dogmas./The mud . . . is evidently* fluviatile *& not diluvian./The inner, religiously moral* perfectioning *of individuals./Jamaica ginger, which is a very good* preventative *of sea-*

sickness./*Whether that can be attributed to genuine American support or to a* quietening *down of the speculative position is a matter of some doubt./If we add to this number another 10,000 for normal* wastage, *we shall probably be fairly near the mark.*

3. Wrong use of longer forms due to confusion : advancement (advance) ; alternative (alternate) ; correctitude (correctness) ; creditable (credible) ; definitive (definite) ; distinctive (distinct) ; estimation (estimate) ; excepting (except) ; intensive (intense) ; partially (partly) ; prudential (prudent) ; reverential (reverent) ; transcendental (transcendent). The differences of meaning between the longer & shorter words are not here discussed, but will be found, unless too familiar to need mention, under the words in their dictionary place.

Examples of 3

It was only by advancement *of money to the tenant farmers that the calamity could be ended./When the army is not fully organized, when it is in process of* alternative *disintegration & rally, the problems are insoluble./Baron —— believes himself to be the oldest living Alsatian ; & there is small reason to doubt the* correctitude *of his belief./It is* creditably *stated that the length of line dug & wired in the time is near a record./But warning & suggestion are more in evidence than* definitive *guidance./Trade relations of an ordinary kind are quite* distinctive *from those having annexation as their aim./Since November 11 the Allies have been able to form a precise* estimation *of Germany's real intentions./The sojourn of belligerent ships in French waters has never been limited* excepting *by certain clearly defined rules./The covered flowers being less* intensively *coloured than the others./The two feet, branching out into ten toes, are* partially *of iron & partially of clay./It is often a very easy thing to act* prudentially, *but alas! too often only after we have toiled to our prudence through a forest of delusions./Their behaviour in church was anything but* reverential./ *The matter is of* transcendental *importance, especially in the present disastrous state of the world.*

It only remains to say that nothing in this article must be taken to countenance the shortening of such words as *pacificist* & *quantitative*. Examples of *pacifist* are needless ; but it is worth while to record *quantitive* & *authoritive* ; & see INTERPRE(TA)TIVE. *It is as if the* quantitive *theory of naval strategy held the field. / Her finely finished* authoritive *performance was of great value.*

longways, -wise. See -WAYS.

looby. So spelt ; see -EY, -IE, -Y.

loom, v. For *l. large(ly)* see LARGE(LY).

loony, lunatic. So spelt ; see -EY, -IE, -Y.

loose, loosen, vv. For the distinction, see -EN VERBS.

loquitur. Pronounce lŏ′kwĭter. *L.* is singular = speaks ; cf. EXIT for danger to non-latinists.

lord. Younger sons of Dukes & Marquises are spoken of by the title of *Lord* followed by Christian & family name, as *Lord Arthur Smith.* Omission of the Christian name is wrong ; the permissible shortening is not *Lord Smith,* but *Lord Arthur.* For *l.* as an undress substitute for *marquis, earl, viscount,* see TITLES.

Lord Bacon is a mixture ; the possible correct styles are *Bacon, Francis Bacon, Sir Francis Bacon, Lord Verulam, Lord* or *Viscount St Albans,* of which the first is usually the best.

Lord Justice. Pl. *Lords Justices.*

lordlily. See -LILY.

lordolatry. See -LATRY.

lorgnette. See FRENCH WORDS.

lose. *L. no time in* is a notoriously ambiguous phrase : *No time should be lost in exploring the question. L.* makes *losable* ; see MUTE E.

lot. *A lot of people* say *so, Lots of paper* is *wanted,* &c. · see NUMBER.

loth. See LOATH.

Lothario. Pl. *-os,* see -O(E)S 8.

lotto. Pl. *-os* ; see -O(E)S 3.

lotus. Pl. *-uses.*

louden. See -EN VERBS.

lough. The Irish *l.* & the Scotch *loch* are pronounced alike, i. e. either anglicized as lŏk, or with the breathed guttural instead of the -k. For *l* cf. HOUGH.

Louis, l-. See FRENCH WORDS.

lour, lower. The meaning is frown. Spell *lour* & pronounce lowr. The word is not connected with *low* & the other verb *lower* (lō′er), & it is a pity that it should be confused with that verb by the second spelling (the oldest forms are *lour* & *lure*) & so have its meaning narrowed & its pronunciation altered. The confusion is due chiefly to the word's being often applied to clouds.

louse, lousy. Pronounce lows, low′zĭ.

love. 1. *L.* makes *lovable* ; see MUTE E. 2. For *the scenes he loved so well* &c., see HACKNEYED PHRASES, & STOCK PATHOS.

lovelily. See -LILY.

LOVE OF THE LONG WORD. It need hardly be said that shortness is a merit in words ; there are often reasons why shortness is not possible ; much less often there are occasions when length, not shortness, is desirable ; but it is a general truth that the short words are not only handier to use, but more powerful in effect ; extra syllables reduce, not increase, vigour. This is particularly so in English, where the native words are short, & the long words are foreign. I open *Paradise Lost & The Idylls of the King,* & at each first opening there face me :—
' *Know ye not, then* ' *said Satan, fill'd with scorn ; ' Know ye not me ? ye knew me once no mate For you, there sitting where ye durst not soar.*'/ *And in those days she made a little song And call'd her song ' The Song of Love & Death ', And sang it ; sweetly could she make & sing.*
Fifty-six words, of which fifty-two

are monosyllables. Slightly selected passages, indeed, but such as occur on nearly every page ; & these are not exercises in one-syllable words for teaching children to read ; they are the natural as well as the best ways of saying what was to be said. Nor is it in verse only that good English runs to monosyllables ; I open a new religious book, & find at once this passage about the Kingdom of Heaven :—*His effort was, not to tell mankind about it, but to show it to them ; & He said that those who saw it would be convinced, not by Him, but by it. ' To this end was I born, & for this cause came I into the world, that I should bear witness unto the truth. Every one that is of the truth heareth my voice.' There for once he spoke in general & abstract terms. Those who are of the truth, those who seek truth for its own sake, will listen to Him & know that what he says is true.* Twelve words that are not monosyllables in 101 words ; and there is no taint whatever of affected simplicity in it. Good English does consist in the main of short words. There are many good reasons, however, against any attempt to avoid, because it is a polysyllable, the word that will give our meaning best ; what is here deprecated is the tendency among the ignorant to choose, because it is a polysyllable, the word that gives their meaning no better or even worse. In the article LONG VARI-ANTS, examples are given of long forms chosen in place of shorter ones of the same word or stem. Attention is here confined to certain words frequently used where unrelated shorter ones would be better ; they are doubtless chosen primarily not for their length, but because they are in vogue ; but their vogue is in turn due to the pompous effect conferred by length. They are : *mentality, meticulous, percentage, proportion, proposition, protagonist* ; there are many similar words, under which bare references to this article may be made ; but these will serve

as types. A quotation or two will be given under each, & a fitter word offered. Mentality :—*A twenty-foot putt by Herreshoff at the twenty-fourth hole did not help Hilton's golfing mentality* (nerve)./*As regards the present treatment of prisoners, although there has doubtless been an improvement in some of the German camps, the general mentality towards prisoners is ingrained* (mood)./*No one has so wide a knowledge of Afghan politics & of the mentality of the Pathan* (mind).

Meticulous :—*These meticulous calculations of votes which have not yet been given rather disgust us* (exact)./*Owing to a meticulous regard for the spirit of the party truce, their views have not been adequately voiced by their leaders* (strict)./*Most of the British & American proposals have been too vague & sentimental on the one hand & too elaborate & meticulous on the other* (detailed).

Percentage :—*Our tax revenue is now fully one hundred & sixty millions sterling, & the Single Land Tax would not yield more than a percentage of this* (part ; see also PERCENTAGE).

Proportion :—*The greater proportion of these old hands have by this time already dropped out* (part ; see also PROPORTION).

Proposition :—*F. Ouimet, who played so brilliantly yesterday, was the proposition the holder had to face* (opponent)./*The agriculturist asks that ' corn-growing shall become a paying proposition '* (job)./*The future of the taximeter-cab proposition in the Metropolis presents a very interesting problem* (trade).

Protagonist :—*The two great Western Powers who have acted as protagonists among the Allies in this war* (leaders)./*But most of the protagonists of this demand have since shifted their ground* (champions).

A few lines of the long-word style we know so well are added : *Vigorous condemnation is passed on the foreign policy of the Prime Minister, ' whose temperamental inaptitude for diplomacy & preoccupation with domestic issues have rendered his participation in external negotiations gravely detrimental to the public welfare '.* Vigorous indeed ; a charging hippopotamus hardly more so.

lovey. So spelt ; see -EY, -IE, -Y.
lower, adj. **1.** *L. case, upper case,* are printers' names for small letters, capitals.
2. *L. Empire* is a name for the Roman Empire from the time of Constantine (A.D. 323–337), when the seat of empire was shifted from Rome to Constantinople, & Christianity became the State religion. Also called *Later, Greek, Byzantine,* & *Eastern, Empire.*

lower, lour. See LOUR.
lowlily. See -LILY.
loyal. For *loyalest* see -ER & -EST 4, -LL-, -L- 2.

LU (pronunciation). There is clearly a movement going on in the pronunciation of this as lū (lyo͞o)) or lo͞o. It was formerly *de rigueur* to put in the *y* sound ; a lute, & even a flute, had to be called lūt (i.e. lyo͞ot) & flūt (i.e. flyo͞ot), not lo͞ot & flo͞ot, or the speaker was damned in polite circles. And great numbers of good people count the victorious progress of lo͞o one of the vulgarities of modern speech ; among these must be the OED, which goes so far as to prefer glū or glyo͞o to glo͞o for the pronunciation of *glue*, though it reverses this order for *blue* (blo͞o, blū) ; for most of us anything but blo͞o & glo͞o is surely now impossible, however refined we like to be where the trials of articulation are less severe.

On a question of this sort anyone who is not entirely illiterate is sure to think that the line he is accustomed to draw between pedantic refinement & acceptance of popular tendencies is the right line ; & the individual view here given is subject to that discount ; a view, however, must be given, for what it is worth ; & it is that lo͞o is slowly but surely

displacing lū. It forces its way especially into accented syllables, as may be seen by comparing *ludicrous, voluminous, lubricate, salute,* & *dilute* vb, in which lo͞o now prevails, with *interlude, volume, lubricity, salutation,* & *dilute* adj., in which lū is either the only possible sound (as in *volume, salutation*) or the usual one. And again into common words more than into less used ones ; compare *salute* (usually -o͞ot) with *volute* (usually -ūt), it is noticeable how the great currency of *absolutely* (& the emphasis on -ute-) due to its adoption as a colloquial counter has hastened the change to lo͞o. The corresponding fastnesses of lū are the unaccented syllable & the less used word. Points of a more special kind are : when a consonant precedes the *l*, lo͞o is almost universal (*blue, fluent,* &c.) ; when *r* follows, it helps to preserve lū (*lure, lurid*) ; a following syllable with a ū in it naturally produces lo͞o by dissimilation even in the unaccented syllable of a not very common word (*lugubrious, lucubration*).

Some specimen lists follow, going from undisputed lū to undisputed lo͞o. 1 (always lū). Volume, salutary, cellulose, pilule. 2 (usually lū). Lure, lurid, aluminium, interlude, lubricity, volute, dilute adj. 3 (usually lo͞o). Voluminous, lute, lupin, lunatic, illumine, lunar, Lucifer, collusion, delude, dissolute, evolution, lubricate, luminous, Lucy, absolute, salute, ludicrous, dilute vb, Lucian, Luke, lucre, lucubration, lugubrious, lukewarm, Lutheran. 4 (always lo͞o). Blue, clue, glue, fluent, Pluvius, exclude, sluice.

Readers will differ about the assignment of these to the various groups ; but, whether that is right or wrong, a glance at the words collected may help them to clear their minds on the point, & even possibly persuade some of them that the change to lo͞o has gone too far to be now stemmed. The advice offered is to accept lo͞o for all words in list 3 at least, & (these being merely specimens) for others on the same level.

lubricate, lubricity. See LU.
lucent. Pronounce lōō- ; see LU.
lucerne. Pronounce lū- or lōō- ; see LU.
lucid, Lucifer, lucrative, lucre. Pronounce lōō- ; see LU.
lucre. For *filthy l.*, see HACKNEYED PHRASES.
Lucretia. Pronounce lū- or lōō- ; see LU.
lucubrate, luculent. Pronounce lōō- ; see LU.
ludicrous, lugubrious, Luke, lukewarm. Pronounce lōō-; see LU.
lumbago. Pl. *-os* ; see -O(E)S 3.
luminary, luminous, lunacy, lunar, lunatic. Pronounce lōō-; see LU.
luncheon. See FORMAL WORDS.
lung(e)ing. See MUTE E ; omit the *e*.
lupin, lupine, lupus. Pronounce lōō- ; see LU.
lure, lurid. Pronounce lūr- ; see LU.
lustre, -ter. See -RE & -ER.
lustrum. Pl. *-tra*, sometimes *-trums* ; see -UM.
lusus naturae. Pronounce lōō'sus natūr'ē, see LU. Pl. *lusus n.*, pronounce -ūs, see -US.
lute, Lutheran. Pronounce lōō- ; see LU.
luxe. See FRENCH WORDS.
luxuriant, luxurious. *Luxurious* is the adjective that belongs in sense to *luxury* & conveys the ideas of comfort or delight or indulgence ; *luxuriant* has nothing to do with these, implying only rich growth, vigorous shooting forth, teeming ; as *luxurious* to *luxury*, so *luxuriant* to *exuberance*. *Luxurious houses, habits, life, people, climate, idleness, times, food, cushions, dreams, abandonment, desires* ; *luxuriant vegetation, crops, hair, imagination, invention, style.* The points at which they touch & become liable to confusion are, first, that abundance, essential to luxuriance or exuberance, also subserves luxury, though not essential to it ; &, secondly, their common property in the verb *luxuriate*,

which means both to enjoy luxury & to show luxuriance. A luxurious fancy is one that dwells on luxury ; a luxuriant fancy one that runs riot on any subject, agreeable or other.

-LY. 1. For the tendency among writers & speakers who are more conscientious than literary to suppose that all adverbs must end in *-ly*, & therefore to use *hardly, largely, strongly, &c.*, where idiom requires *hard, large, & strong*, see UNIDIOMATIC -LY.

2. For participial adverbs like *determinedly*, see -EDLY.

3. It was said in the article JINGLES that the commonest form of ugly repetition was that of the *-ly* adverbs. It is indeed extraordinary, when one remembers the feats of avoidance performed by the elegant-variationist, the don't-split-your-infinitivist, & the anti-preposition-at-ender, to find how many people have no ears to hear this most obvious of all outrages on euphony. Not indeed on euphony pure & simple, but on euphony & sense in combination ; for as many *-ly* adverbs as one chooses may be piled on each other if one condition of sense is fulfilled—that all these adverbs have the same relation to the same word or to parallel words. *We are utterly, hopelessly, irretrievably, ruined ; It is theoretically certain, but practically doubtful ; He may probably or possibly be in time.* These are all irreproachable ; in the first, each of the three adverbs expresses degree about *ruined* ; in the second, each limits the sense of an adjective, the two adjectives being contrasted ; in the third, the two give degrees of likelihood about the same thing ; that is to say, in all cases the *-ly* adverbs are strictly parallel. Euphony has nothing to say against repetition of *-ly* if there is point in it, which there is if the adverbs are parallel ; but, when parallelism is not there to comfort her, Euphony at once cries out in pain, though too often to deaf ears.

Russian industry is at present practically completely *crippled. Practically* is not marching alongside of *completely*, but riding on its back ; read *almost./He found himself* sharply, & apparently completely, *checked. Sharply & completely*, by all means ; but not *apparently completely* ; read *as it seemed./It is* probably generally *known that every individual plaice evolves from the original symmetrical form. Probably* qualifies not (like *generally*) *known*, but *generally known* ; read *perhaps./The earliest lists, still so* sadly & probably irretrievably *imperfect*. Whereas *irretrievably* qualifies *imperfect, probably* qualifies *irretrievably* ; read *perhaps*, or *it is to be feared./Maeterlinck* probably & wisely *shrank from comparison with 'Hérodias'*. Though *probably & wisely* both apply directly to the same word *shrank*, their relation to it is not the same, *probably* telling us how far the statement is reliable, & *wisely* how far the course was justified ; read *It is probable that Maeterlinck wisely shrank./It was* only relatively recently *that it had reached its present development*.

lycée. See FRENCH WORDS.

Lyceum. Pl. *-ms* ; see -UM. For the meaning in Greek Philosophy see ACADEMY.

lychgate &c. See LICHGATE.

lyric(al). *Lyric* is now the established adjective for most uses ; we speak of *lyric poets, poetry, verse, drama, muse, elements*, & not *lyrical. Lyrical* is in some sort a parasite upon *lyric*, meaning suggestive of lyric verse. *Lyric* classifies definitely, while *lyrical* describes vaguely. With some words either can be used, but with different effect ; a lyric rhapsody is one actually composed in lyric verse ; a lyrical rhapsody is talk full of expressions, or revealing a mood, fit for lyric poetry. *Lyrical emotion, praise, sorrow*, &c. ; or again, a person may *grow lyrical*. See also -IC(AL).

lyrics. See TECHNICAL TERMS.

M

macabre. Pronounce makah'ber.
macaco. Pronounce -ā'kō. Pl. *-os*, see -O(E)S 6.
macaroni. Pl. of the 18th-c. dandy, *-nies* ; pl. of the food-stuff, *-nis*.
macerate makes *-rable* ; see -ABLE1.
Machiavel(li(an(ism. The formerly current shortening *Machiavel* is now less common than *Machiavelli* not only as the personal but even as the generic name ; *a very Machiavel*, once much used, has become rare. The adjective is accordingly now spelt *Machiavellian*, not *-elian*. For the *-ism* noun, choice lies between *Machiavellianism* & *Machiavellism* ; in spite of greater length, the first is the better ; the clipping of the word to which *-ist* & *-ism* are to be added is always disagreeable, & yet *Machiavelliism* is clearly impossible ; see on *voluntar(y)ist* in -IST A.

machicolate. Pronounce machĭ'-kolăt, not mak-.
machination. Pronounce măk-.
mackerel, mackintosh. So spelt.
macula. Pl. *-lae*.
mad, v. For this & *madden*, & *the madding crowd*, see -EN VERBS.
Madagascar has adj. *Malagasy* (mălagă'si).
madam(e). In the English word, whether as appellation (*I will inquire, Madam ; Dear Madam ; What does Madam think about it ?*), as common noun (*the City madams*), or as prefix (*Madam Fortune, Madam Venus*), there should be no *-e*. As a prefix to a foreign lady's name instead of *Mrs, Madame* is right, with plural *Mesdames. Madam*, the appellation, suffers from having no plural, *Ladies* being the substitute, for which *Mesdames* is sometimes jocularly used. The shopgirls' odd pronunciation (mŏ'dam) is perhaps due to a notion that French *Madame* is more in keeping with haunts of fashion than English *Madam*.

Madeira. So spelt.
mademoiselle. See FRENCH WORDS.

madness. For *method in m.*, see IRRELEVANT ALLUSION.

maelstrom. Pronounce mā'lstrom.

maenad. See Æ, Œ.

maestoso, maestro. Pronounce mah-ĕstō'zō, maĕ'strō.

Magdalen(e). The spellings & pronunciations are tabulated at the end.

1. In the names of the Oxford (*-en*) & Cambridge (*-ene*) Colleges, pronounce mau'dlĭn.

2. In the use as a noun meaning reformed harlot &c., use *magdalen*.

3. When used with *the* instead of the name *Mary M.*, *the Magdalene* (*-ēn*) & *the Magdalen* (*-ĕn*) are equally correct.

4. In the full name *Mary Magdalene* the four-syllable pronunciation (măgdalē'nĭ) is the best, though if it were *Mary the Magdalene* -lēn would be right, as it is in *the Magdalene*, i.e. the famous person of Magdala. *Magdalene* may be regarded either as an English word = of Magdala, like *Lampsacene, Cyzicene, Tyrrhene,* &c., in which case *the* could not be omitted, or as the actual Greek feminine of *Magdalenos* become part of her name, in which case the final *-e* cannot be silent. *Mary Magdalen*, however, is also possible.

Magdalen (mau'dlĭn) *Coll., Oxford*
Magdalene (mau'dlĭn) *Coll., Cambridge*

A Home for magdalens (mă'gdalĕnz)
The Magdalene (-ēn) or *the Magdalen* (-ĕn)
Mary Magdalene (măgdalē'nĭ) or *Magdalen.*

maggoty. So spelt ; see -T-, -TT-.

magic(al), adjectives. See -IC(AL). *Magic* tends to lose those adjective uses that cannot be viewed as mere attributive uses of the noun. That is, first, it is very seldom used predicatively ; *the effect was magical* (never *magic*) ; *the ring must be magical* (not *magic*, though *must be a magic one* is better than *a magical one*). And, secondly, the chief non-predicative use is in assigning a thing to the domain of magic (*a magic ring, carpet, spell, crystal* ; *the*

magic art), or in distinguishing it from others & so helping its identification (*magic lantern, square*), rather than in giving its characteristics descriptively (*with magical speed* ; *what a magical transformation*) ; this second differentiation, however, is not yet strictly observed.

magma. Pl. *-mata.*

Magna C(h)arta. Authority seems to be for spelling *charta* & pronouncing kar'ta, which is hard on the plain man. But outside of histories & lecture-rooms the spelling & pronunciation *charta* will take a great deal of killing yet.

magnetize has *-zable* ; see MUTE E.

magneto is a CURTAILED WORD for *magneto-electric machine* ; pl. *-os*, see -O(E)S 5.

magnifical is one of the words that one should be pleased to look upon, embalmed in old books, but should not play the resurrectionist to.

magnifico. Pl. *-os* ; see -O(E)S 6.

magnify. For inflexions see VERBS IN -IE, -Y, -YE, 6.

magus. Pl. *-gi* (-jī).

Magyar. Pronounce mŏ'dyar.

maharaja(h). For the form see RAJAH.

mahlstick. See MAULSTICK.

Mahomet, Mohammedan, &c. Before making any statement on these words, I asked a middle-aged lady whom she understood by the Prophet of Allah ; she hesitated, suspecting some snare, but being adjured to reply said quite plainly that he was *Mahomet* (mā'omĕt), & further called his followers *Mahometans* (ma-hŏ'mĭtanz)—thus fulfilling expectations. The popular forms are *Mahomet(an)* (mā'omĕt *or* ma-hŏ'mĭt, ma-hŏ'mĭtn); the prevailing printed forms are *Mohammed(an).*

The worst of letting the learned gentry bully us out of our traditional *Mahometan & Mahomet* (who ever heard of *Mohammed & the mountain?*) is this : no sooner have we tried to be good & learnt to say, or at least write, *Mohammed* than they are fired with zeal to get us a step or two further on the path of truth, which at present seems likely to end in *Muhammad* with a dot under the h; see DIDACTICISM, PRIDE OF KNOWLEDGE. The literary, as distinguished from the learned, surely do good service when they side with tradition & the people against science & the dons. *Muḥammad* should be left to the pedants, *Mohammed* to historians & the like, while ordinary mortals should go on saying, & writing in newspapers & novels & poems & such general reader's matter, what their fathers said before them.

The fact is that we owe no thanks to those who discover, & cannot keep silence on the discovery, that *Mahomet* is further than *Mohammed*, & *Mohammed* further than *Muhammad*, from what his own people called him. The Romans had a hero whom they spoke of as *Aeneas* ; we call him that too, but for the French he has become *Énée* ; are the French any worse off than we on that account ? It is a matter of like indifference in itself whether the English for the Prophet's name is *Mahomet* or *Mohammed* ; in itself, yes ; but whereas the words *Aeneas* & *Énée* have the Channel between them to keep the peace, *Mahomet* & *Mohammed* are for ever at loggerheads ; we want one name for the one man ; & the one should have been that around which the ancient associations cling. It is too late to recover unity ; the learned, & their too docile disciples, have destroyed that, & given us nothing worth having in exchange.

mahout. Pronounce -owt.
maieutic. Pronounce mĭū′tĭk or (OED) māŭ′tĭk. The word means performing midwife's service (to thought or ideas) ; Socrates figured himself as a midwife (*maia*) bringing others' thoughts to birth with his questionings ; *educative* contains the same notion, but much overlaid with different ones, & the literary critic & the pedagogue consequently find *m.*

useful enough to pass in spite of its touch of pedantry.

Majesty, Highness, &c. When *your Majesty, her Grace,* &c., has been used, & need arises for a pronoun or possessive adjective to represent it, grammar would require *it, its* ; but instead of these either the full title is repeated (*Your Majesty can do as your Majesty will with your Majesty's ships*), or *you, your, she, her,* &c., is ungrammatically substituted for *it* or *its* (*Her Grace summoned her chef*). Stevenson indeed writes : *Your Highness interprets my meaning with his usual subtlety* ; but this is doubtless a mistaken imitation of the French *son* or *sa,* meaning its (i.e. highness's), not his. The English idiom, differing from & less correct than the French, requires either *your Highness's,* or *your, usual subtlety.*

major means greater, & those who like POMPOSITIES are within their rights, & remain intelligible, if they call the greater part the major portion ; they can moreover plead that *major part & portion* have been used by good writers in the times when pomposity was less noticeable than it now is. Those who do not like pomposities will call it *the greater part,* & deserve our gratitude, or at least escape our dislike. *I, who had described myself as ' sick of patriotism ' . . . found myself unable to read anything but a volume* the major portion of which *consisted of patriotic verse.*

major (in logic). See TECHNICAL TERMS.

majordomo. Pl. *-os* ; see -o(E)S 6.
major general. Hyphened when used as a prefix ; properly written as two words (cf. *court martial*) when used as an independent noun : *the Major General* ; *Major-General Jones.* See HYPHENS (C, & on *court martial* &c.) ; but the prefix use, being very frequent, naturally corrupts the rarer noun form, & the hyphen is used indiscriminately.

majority. 1. Distinctions of meaning. 2. Number after *m*. 3. *Great &c. m.*

1. Three allied senses, one abstract & two concrete, need to be distinguished if illogicalities are to be avoided : A, *m*. meaning a superiority in number, or, to revive an obsolete unambiguous word, a plurity (. . . *was passed by a bare, small, great, m.* ; *the m. was scanty but sufficient*) ; B, *m*. meaning the one of two or more sets that has a plurity, or the more numerous party (*The m. was*, or *were, determined to press its*, or *their, victory*) ; C, *m*. meaning most of a set of persons, or the greater part numerically (*The m. were fatally wounded* ; *A m. of my friends advise it*).

2. Number. After *m*. in sense A the verb will always be singular. After *m*. in sense B, as after other nouns of multitude, either a singular or a plural verb is possible, according as the body is, or its members are, chiefly in the speaker's thoughts. After *m*. in sense C, in which the thought is not of contrasted bodies at all, but merely of the numbers required to make up more than a half, the verb is almost necessarily plural, the sense being more people than not, out of those concerned. Correct *has* to *have* in : *The awful happenings at Riga, where the majority of all the bourgeois has been either shot or killed by exposure to cold & starvation, are due to* . . .

3. *Great &c. m.* With *m*. in sense A, *great, greater, greatest,* &c., are freely used, & cause no difficulty. With *m*. in sense B they are not often used, & then to give the special sense of party having a great, greater, plurity as compared with that enjoyed by some other (*This great m. is helpless* ; *having the greatest m. of modern times devoted to him*). With *m*. in sense C, *great* is possible & common, *the great m.* meaning most by far, much more than half ; but the use of *greater & greatest* with it, as if *m*. meant merely part or number, is, though frequent, an illiterate blunder ;

examples of it are :—*By far the greatest m. of American rails, apart from gambling counters, have gone across the Atlantic.*/*The club is representative of several hundreds,* the greater m. of whom *are repatriated Britishers from Russia.*/*By far the larger m. of the entries are not words.*

majuscule. See Technical terms.

make. *M. him repeat it,* very rarely *to repeat* ; *He must be made to repeat it,* very rarely *made repeat.*

make-believe is the true form of the noun as well as the verb, & *make-belief* a false correction ; to *make believe* has meant to pretend from the 14th c.

Malagasy. See Madagascar.

MALAPROPS. When Mrs Malaprop, in Sheridan's *Rivals,* is said to ' deck her dull chat with hard words which she don't understand ', she protests ' Sure, if I *reprehend* anything in this world, it is the use of my *oracular* tongue, & a nice *derangement* of *epitaphs* '—having vague memories of *apprehend, vernacular, arrangement,* & *epithets*. She is now the matron saint of all those who go wordfowling with a blunderbuss. Achievements so heroic as her own do not here concern us ; they pass the bounds of ordinary experience & of the credible. Her votaries are a feebler folk ; with them malaprops come single spies, not in battalions, one in an article, perhaps, instead of four in a sentence, & not marked by her bold originality, but monotonously following well beaten tracks. In the article Pairs & snares a number of words is given with which other words of not very different sound are commonly confused, & under most of the separate words contained in that list illustrations will be found ; *predict & predicate, reversal & reversion, masterful & masterly,* will suffice here as examples. Another kind of malaprop, in which two words are confused rather in construction than in meaning, is dealt with in Object-shuffling ; *sub-*

stitute & replace, instil & inspire, afflict & inflict, are specimens. And a long list might be made of words commonly so used as to show misapprehension of their meaning; a few, under which quotations will be found, are : *asset, comity, e.g., eke out, glimpse, oblivious, polity, proportion, proposition, protagonist, prototype, qua.*

But it is perhaps hardly decent to leave the subject without a single concrete illustration. Here are one or two less staled by frequent occurrence than those mentioned above : *He thought it* desirable *that the House of Lords should determine the tests to be applied./Mr —— has circulated what* portends *to be a reply to a letter which I had previously addressed to you./His capacity for continuous work is* incredulous.*/It was a great* humility *to be kept waiting about, after having been asked to come.*

malapropos. Pronounce măl̆ăpropō̆'.

male. 1. *M.) (masculine.* The distinction drawn between *female & feminine* is equally true for *m. & masculine* ; the reader will perhaps be good enough to look through the article FEMALE, FEMININE, & make the necessary substitutions ; the only modification needed is in the statement about the original part of speech of *female* ; *male* was not, like that, a noun before it was an adjective ; but this difference does not affect present usage.

2. *M.* &c. in prosody. *M. & masculine, female & feminine,* are used to distinguish rhymes & line-endings having a final accented syllable (m. or masculine : *Now is the winter of our disconte'nt)* from those in which an unaccented syllable follows the last accented one (female or feminine : *To be or not to be, that is the que'stion).*

malign. 1. For the difference between *m. & malignant,* see BENIGN. **2.** Pronounce the verb, as well as the adjective, măl̆i'n.

malignancy, -nity. These nouns

almost reverse the relation between the adjectives to which they belong. The general distinction between *malignant & malign* is that the first refers rather to intention & the second rather to effect (see BENIGN) ; it would therefore be expected that *malignancy* would be the word for spitefulness, & *malignity* for harmfulness ; but the medical use of *malignant* (see BENIGN 3) has so strongly affected *malignancy* that *malignity* has had to take over the sense of spite, & almost lost that of harm.

malinger. Pronounce mălĭ'ngger.
Mall. Pronounce măl ; *the Mall* (măl), but *Pall Mall* (pĕlmĕ'l).
malnutrition. A word to be avoided as often as *underfeeding* will do the work ; see ANTI-SAXONISM.
Mameluke. Three syllables (mă'-mĭlōōk).
mamilla. Pl. *-lae.*
mam(m)a, mother. Spell *mamma.*
mamma, breast. Pl. *mammae.*
man. For *the inner, outer, m.,* see HACKNEYED PHRASES.
manageable. So spelt ; see MUTE E.
manageress. See FEMININE DESIGNATIONS.
mandamus. Pl. *-uses* ; see -US. Pronounce măndā'mus.

mandatary, -tory. The *-ary* form is noun only, = one to whom a mandate is given ; the *-ory* form is primarily adjective, = of the nature of a mandate, & secondarily a noun, = mandatary. A distinction in spelling between the personal noun & the adjective is obviously convenient, & the form *mandatary* is therefore recommended for the holder of a mandate from the League of Nations. Similar personal nouns, some of them with associated forms in *-ory* of more or less different sense, are ACCESSARY, *adversary, commissary,* DEPOSITARY, *emissary, notary, registrary* (Cambridge form of *registrar), repositary* (person confided in, cf. *repository* storeplace), *secretary* (cf. the adjective *secretory), tributary.*

manducate makes *-cable* ; see -ABLE 1.

manes, spirit of dead person. Pronounce mā'nēz ; a plural noun, with plural construction though singular in sense.

mangel, mangold. The first is ' in English the now prevailing form ' (OED), &, as it is not less significant to the Englishman, & nearer the pronunciation, than the original German *mangold,* it is as well that it should continue to prevail.

mango. Pl. *-oes* ; see -O(E)S 1.

mangrove. Pronounce mă'nggrōv ; neither *man* nor *grove* is an element in the word.

mangy. So spelt ; see -EY & -Y.

Manichee. Pronounce -kē.

manifesto. Pl. *-os* ; see -O(E)S 7.

manifold. Pronounce măn-, not měn-. Owing to this difference in pronunciation between *m.* & *many,* the word is no longer felt to be a member of the series twofold, three-fold, thirtyfold, a hundredfold, & attempts to treat it as such result in unidiomatic English ; it is better to coin *many-fold* for the occasion (cf. BUSINESS, BUSYNESS) than to imitate the writers of the quotations below. Both the uses illustrated in them are called obsolete by the OED, & the revival of them after centuries of dormancy is perhaps accounted for by the adaptation of the ' now literary ' word to a commercial use in *manifold writing,* & its consequent popularization. *Such elimination would recoup that expense,* manifold, *by the saving which it would effect of food valuable to the nation—namely, salmon./This organization in capable hands should repay* in manifold *the actual funds raised on its behalf.*

manikin. So spelt by the OED.

Manil(l)a. ' The form *Manila* is correct, but rare except in geographical use '—OED. The established *-lla* is recommended.

manipulate has *-lable* ; see -ABLE 1.

mankind. Accent the second syllable for the ordinary sense of the human race, but the first for the special sense of the males of a family &c.

MANNERISMS. Mannerism consists in the allowing of a form of speech that has now & again served us well to master us.

Pater has a *so* :—*Ubiquitous, tyrannous, irresistible, as it may seem, motion, with the whole* so *dazzling world it covers, is—nothing./Himself* so *striking an instance of mobile humour in his exposure of the unreality of all movement, Zeno . . ./ Once for all, in harshest dualism, the only true* yet *so barren existence is opposed to the world of phenomena./ In the midst of that aesthetically* so *brilliant world of Greater Greece.*

Macaulay has an antithesis :—*In some points it has been fashioned to suit our feelings ; in others, it has gradually fashioned our feelings to suit itself./At first they were only robbers ; they soon rose to the dignity of conquerors./To enjoin honesty, & to insist on having what could not be honestly got, was then the constant practice of the Company./A system which was, perhaps, skilfully contrived for the purpose of facilitating & concealing a great revolution, but which, when that revolution was complete & irrevocable, could produce nothing but inconvenience.*

Carlyle has two superlatives :—A. *It is a sublime embodiment,* or sublimest, *of the soul of Christianity./ A mild pale splendour here & there, as of an April that were leading* to leafiest summer./*Sublime sorrow, sublime reconciliation ;* oldest *choral melody as of the heart of mankind./ B. Six hundred irresponsible senators would make of all tyrannies the insupportablest./I think it is* the mournfullest *face that ever was painted from reality. It is perhaps of all things* the usefullest *for us to do in these loud times.*

Bagehot has a repetition :—*He gave politics not an interesting aspect, but a new aspect./All these powers were States of some magnitude, &*

some were States of *great* magnitude./ A man like *Walpole,* or a man like *Louis Napoleon, is protected by an unsensitive nature.*

Meredith has a circumvention system for ' said so-&-so ' :—' *Now that is too bad,*' she pouted./' *I must see Richard tomorrow morning,*' Mrs Doria ended the colloquy by saying./ ' *She did all she could to persuade me to wait,*' emphasized Richard./' *Singular child!*' she mentally apostrophized the girl./' *At your age,*' Adrian relieved his embarrassment, ' *it is natural.*'/' *You breakfast with us,*' she freshened off again.

Mr Kipling has ' *But that is another story* '.

Mr Wells has a *Came*: *Came a familiar sound./Came the green flash again./Came that sense again of unendurable tension.*

And so on, & so on. Perhaps few of those who write much escape from the temptation to trade on tricks of which they have learnt the effectiveness ; & it is true that it is a delicate matter to discern where a peculiarity ceases to be an element in the individuality that readers associate pleasantly with the writer they like, & becomes a recurrent & looked-for & dreaded irritation. But at least it is well for every writer to realize that, for his as for other people's mannerisms, there is a point at which that transformation does take place.

mannikin. See MANIKIN.
manœuvre, vb, makes *-vred, -vring*; see MUTE E. For the n. & vb, see -RE & -ER.
manqué. See FRENCH WORDS.
mantel(piece, -shelf). So spelt.
mantle, vb. The common use in which the subject is *face, cheek, brow, flush, blush, colour, blood,* &c., appears to come not directly from the original sense to clothe as with a mantle, but from the special application of that to liquor that covers itself with foam &c. ; otherwise the natural construction would be (as idiom does not make it) *A*

blush mantled her cheek &c., & not (as idiom does make it) *A blush* or *The blood mantled in her cheek* or *Her cheek mantled with a blush.*

manumit makes *-tted, -tting* ; see -T-, -TT-.
manuscript. The abbreviation is MS. in singular, & MSS. in plural.
many. *While there have been m. a good-humoured smile about the Cody ' Cathedral ', we may yet shortly witness the advent of a flying-machine which . . . M. a* requires always a singular verb. For similar questions, see NUMBER.

Maori. Pronounce mowr'ĭ ; pl. *-is*.
maraschino. Pronounce mără-skē'no ; pl. *-os*, see -O(E)S 3.
margarin(e). The pronunciation marj- instead of marg- is clearly wrong, & is not even mentioned in the OED as an alternative. It was nevertheless prevalent before the war, when the educated had little occasion to use the word ; but now that we all know the substance, its g is coming to its own. Perhaps the only English words in which g is soft before a or o or u are *gaol* (with its derivatives) & *mortgagor*. See -IN & -INE for the termination.

marginalia is plural ; see LATIN PLURALS.
mariage de convenance. So spelt. See FRENCH WORDS.
Marie, Mary. See -EY, -IE, -Y.
marital. The OED gives mă'rĭtal, without even permitting marī'tal. This is no doubt a shock to those— & they are many—who know the sound of *marītus* in Latin better than that of *m.* in their own language ; see, however, FALSE QUANTITY for a batteryful of such shocks.

mark. For synonymy see SIGN.
markedly. Three syllables ; see -EDLY.
market, vb, makes *-eted, -eting, -etable* ; see -T-, -TT-.
marquetry, -eterie. Spell *-try,* & pronounce mar'kĭtrĭ.
marquis, -ess. The spelling recommended is *-is,* pl. *-ises.* The OED

note is : ' The prevailing spelling in literary use appears to be *marquis.* Some newspapers, however, use *marquess,* & several English nobles bearing the title always write it in this way '.

marquise (pronounce -kēz) is French for *marchioness,* not for *marquis.*

marquois. Pronounce mar′quoiz.

marriage. For *m. of convenience,* see GALLICISMS.

marriageable. So spelt ; see MUTE E.

marron glacé. See FRENCH WORDS.

marry. For inflexions see VERBS IN -IE, -Y, -YE, 6.

Marseillaise. Pronounce marselā′z.

marshal, vb, makes *-lled, -lling* ; see -LL-, -L-.

martello. Pl. *-os* ; see -O(E)S 6.

marten, -in. The beast has *-en,* the bird *-in.*

marvel, makes *-lled, -lling, -llous* ; see -LL-, -L-.

Mary, Marie. See -EY, -IE, -Y.

masculine. See MALE.

mashie, -y, golfclub. Usually *-ie.*

Masorah, Masorete, &c., **Mass-.** The OED gives the single *-s-* forms as the standard ones.

massacre, vb, makes *massacring.*

massage, -eur, -euse. Pronounce masah′zh, mäser′, mäser′z.

masterful) (masterly. Some centuries ago both were used indifferently in either of two very different senses : (A) imperious or commanding or strong-willed, & (B) skilful or expert or practised. The DIFFERENTIATION is now complete, *-ful* having the A & *-ly* the B meanings ; & disregard of it is so obviously inconvenient, since the senses, though distinct, are not so far apart but that it may sometimes be uncertain which is meant, that it can only be put down to ignorance. *Masterly* is not misused ; but *masterful* often appears, especially in the sporting reporter's productions, instead of *masterly.* A few examples follow, in all of which *masterly* should have been the word :—*The Australians did not collapse in the ordinary cricketing*

acceptance of the word ; they were simply the occasional victims of the always masterful attack./When he began to outplay the Englishman & picked up hole after hole the crowd was carried away by his masterful work & driven to applauding./The book is packed with characters masterfully managed, the most telling of whom are not the most virtuous but the most worldly./The influence of the engineering & mechanical triumphs of the staff of the canal zone has been dealt with by masterful writers./ Yates played a truly masterful game in defeating Reti.

masticate makes *-cable, -tor* ; see -ABLE 1, -OR.

mastodon. Pl. *-ns* ; see -ON 3.

mat, lustreless. So spelt ; it is a French adjective. The form *matt* is no doubt due to an instinct of differentiation ; cf. SET(T).

mate, checkmate. The full form is now chiefly in metaphorical use, while the shortened one is preferred in chess.

mate (match), vb, makes *matable* ; see MUTE E.

materfamilias. Pl. *matresfamilias* or *materfamiliases.*

material, adj. There are at least four current antitheses in aid of any of which *m.* may be called in when an adjective is required : there is matter & form (*m. & formal*) ; there is matter & spirit (*m. & spiritual*) ; there is matériel & personnel (*m. & personal*) ; & there is what matters & what does not matter (*m. & trifling*). Before using *m.,* therefore, with reference to any of these, the writer should make sure that there is no risk of confusion with another. *Agriculture, though the most m. of all our pursuits, is teaching us truths beyond its own direct province./The old bonds of relationship, & community of m. interests./A comparison between the French peasant-proprietor & the English small-holder as he might conceivably become under a freehold system, a comparison, be it* *said,* to the m. advantage *of the former.*

materialize. 1. *M.* makes *-zable* ; see MUTE E. 2. The word has uses enough of its own (*Those who would m. spirit. A soul materialized by gluttony. Virgil having materialized a scheme of abstracted notions. Ghosts or promises of ghosts which fail to m.*) without being forced to do the work of *happen* or *be fulfilled* or *form* :— *There would seem to be some ground for hope that the strike will not m. after all./Year after year passed & these promises failed to m./Out of the mist of notes & protocols a policy seems gradually to be materializing*). In these latter senses *m.* is on the level of *transpire* (happen), *proposition* (job), *eventuate* (happen), *negotiate* (pass), *unique* (notable), *individual* (man), & such abominations.

matériel. See FRENCH WORDS ; in antitheses with *personnel,* expressed or implied, the French spelling & pronunciation should be kept, & not replaced by those of the English *material.*

mathematics. For the grammatical number, see -ICS 2.

matinée. As *morning performance* has the double disadvantage of being very long & suggesting a wrong time of day, *m.* is likely to prevail.

matins, matt-. The OED treats *matins* as the standard form. For *m. & morning prayer,* see MORNING.

matriculate makes *-lable* ; see -ABLE 1.

matrix. For pl. see -EX, -IX, 4, & -TRIX.

matter. *The distribution shows that, as exceptional bravery is confined to no rank in the Army, so recognition is given to it* by no matter whom *it is displayed.* If elliptical phrases like *no matter who* are to be treated freely as units, care must be taken that the ellipsis can be filled in correctly. *By it is no matter whom it is displayed* is wrong, & *it is no matter by whom it is displayed* is right ; accordingly the order should

be *no matter by whom.* The principle is—by all means save your reader the trouble of reading more words than he need, but do not save yourself the trouble of rehearsing the full form by way of test. The real cause of the mistake here is the superstition against prepositions at the end ; *no matter whom it is displayed by* would have been correct ; but the writer was frightened at his final preposition, made a grab at it, & plumped it down in a wrong place ; see SUPERSTITIONS, & OUT OF THE FRYING-PAN. The offence is aggravated by the inevitable impulse to connect *by* with *is given.*

mattress. So spelt, not *-ass.*

matutinal. Chiefly in POLYSYLLABIC HUMOUR. *Here they were found by a m. gardener.*

maty, comrade. So spelt ; see -EY, -IE, -Y.

maudlin. So spelt, not *-ing* ; the origin is the name MAGDALEN.

maugre. See WARDOUR STREET.

maulstick. The OED gives this, not *mahl-,* as the standard form.

maunder, meander. Though the etymology of *maunder* is uncertain, it is clear that it is not a corruption of *meander,* its earlier sense being definitely to complain, growl, grouse. But it is also clear from the way some people use *meander* that they take the two words to be merely variant pronunciations. *Meander* means to follow a winding course, was originally used of rivers, is still often so used, describes frequent but not violent change of direction rather than aimlessness, & is applied more often to actual locomotion than to vagaries of the tongue, *Maunder* is best confined to speech. & suggests futility rather than digression, dull discontent rather than quiet enjoyment, & failure to reach an end rather than loitering on the way to it.

Mauser. Pronounce mow'zer.

mauvais sujet, quart d'heure, mauvaise honte. See FRENCH WORDS.

maxilla. Pl. *-llae.*

maximum. Pl. *-ma*, sometimes *-mums*.

maybe (=perhaps) has entered upon its third phase of existence. It was long ago normal English, as natural as *perhaps*, or more so. It then became a novelistic property, the recognized rustic or provincial substitute for *perhaps*. Having acquired, during this rustication, a certain unfamiliarity, it has now emerged stylishly archaic, so that *perhaps* & *m.* are a pair of WORKING & STYLISH WORDS. The following quotation shows this use or abuse : *But no-one imagines that we are not on the eve of an exciting* & maybe embittered *controversy.* The word has still however, a real function— to replace *perhaps* in a context whose tone demands a touch of primitive dignity ; so *Our Lord speaking quite simply to simple Syrian people, a child or two maybe at his knees.*

mazedly. Three syllables ; see -EDLY.

me is technically wrong in *It wasn't me* &c : but, the phrase being of its very nature colloquial, such a lapse is of no importance ; & this is perhaps the only temptation to use *me* instead of *I*. There is more danger of using *I* for *me*, especially when & *me* is required after another noun or pronoun that has taken responsibility for the grammar & has not a separate objective case ; *between you & I, let you & I try,* are not uncommon (see BETWEEN, LET), & : *Sir,—A rich friend of ours wrote & asked* my husband & I *to dine at the most expensive restaurant & go to the theatre on his birthday.*

meagre makes *meagrish* ; see MUTE E. See also -RE & -ER.

meal) (flour. See FLOUR.

mealies. The singular (chiefly in combinations as *m.-field, m. porridge*) is *mealie*, not *-ly*, the etymological connexion being not with *meal* & *mealy*, but with *millet*.

mean, adj., makes *meanness*.

meander. See MAUNDER.

means, n. (number). In the sense *income* &c., *m.* always takes a plural verb : *My means were* (never *was*) *much reduced.* In the sense *way to an end* &c. : *a means* takes singular verb ; *means, & the means,* can be treated as either singular or plural ; *all means* (pl.) & *every means* (sing.) are equally correct ; *the means do not,* or *does not, justify the end* ; *the end is good, but the means are,* or *is, bad* ; *such means are* (not *is*) *repugnant to me,* because *such* without *a* is necessarily plural ; cf. *such a means is not to be discovered* ; & similarly with other adjectives, as *secret means were found,* but *a secret means was found.*

measure. *Lord Curzon's policy has been overthrown by the present announcement, which* to a great measure *restores Bengal to her former greatness. To a great extent,* but *in great measure* ; see CAST-IRON IDIOM.

measure, v., makes *-rable* ; see MUTE E.

measuredly. Three syllables ; see -EDLY.

meatus. Pl. *meatus* (-ūs ; see -US), or *-uses.*

medal makes *-lled, -llist* ; see -LL-, -L-.

medi(a)eval. The shorter spelling is recommended ; see Æ, Œ.

mediatize. 1. To m. a ruler is to reduce him to dependence on another State, but without changing his titular dignity. The word originated in the Holy Roman Empire, & meant that the prince now owed *mediate* (i.e. indirect) allegiance instead of *immediate* to the Emperor. 2. *M.* makes *-zable* ; see MUTE E.

mediatrix. For pl. see -TRIX.

medicate makes *-cable* ; see -ABLE 1.

medicine. Two syllables (mĕ′dsn).

mediocre. Pronounce mē′dĭōker.

meditate makes *-itable, -tor* ; see -ABLE 1, -OR.

Mediterranean. So spelt.

medium. In the spiritualistic sense, the plural is always *-ums*. In all other senses—intervening or enveloping substance, element, liquid vehicle, means or agency, *-a* &

-ums are both in use, & *-a* seems to be the commoner. See -UM.

medlar (fruit). So spelt.

meerschaum. So spelt.

meet. For *we are met together* &c., see INTRANSITIVE P.P.

mein Herr. See MYNHEER.

meiosis. Pl. *-oses* (-ēz). For the meaning, see TECHNICAL TERMS.

mélange. See FRENCH WORDS.

mêlée (mě'lā). So spelt, accented, & pronounced.

meliorate, -ation, are common in American usage ; the British forms are *amel-.*

melodeon, -dion, -dium. The first appears to be the prevalent spelling.

melodrama is a term generally used with some contempt, because the appeal of such plays as are acknowledged to deserve the title is especially to the unsophisticated & illiterate whose acquaintance with human nature is superficial, but whose admiration for goodness & detestation of wickedness is ready & powerful. The melodramatist's task is to get his characters labelled good & wicked in his audience's minds, & to provide striking situations that shall provoke & relieve anxieties on behalf of poetic justice. Whether a play is or is not to be called a melodrama is therefore often a doubtful question, upon which different critics will hold different opinions. The origin of the name is in a form of play intermediate between opera, in which all is sung, & drama, in which music has no essential part ; the early m. was ' a form of dramatic musical composition in which music accompanied the spoken words & the action, but in which there was no singing. . . . This is the source of romantic dramas depending on sensational incident with exaggerated appeals to conventional sentiment rather than on play of character, & in which *dramatis personae* follow conventional types—the villain, the hero wrongfully charged with crime, the persecuted heroine,

the adventuress, &c.'—*Enc. Brit.* What the m. now so called inherits from the early form is the appeal to emotion ; the emotional effect of musical accompaniment is obvious, & it is on emotional sympathy that m. still depends for success.

melody) (harmony. See HARMONY.

melt. *Molten* as in the verbal use (*will be molten* &c.) is now confined to poetry ; as an adjective (*like molten glass* &c.) it can still be used without archaism, but only in literary contexts.

membership. The sense *number of members* (of a club &c.) is, though not a very desirable one, more or less established (*The necessity of adding to the m. of the House* ; *A large m. is necessary*). Much less desirable still is the extension from *number of members* to *members* (*the Committee being chosen from the m. of the two Houses of Parliament.*/*The employers' proposals may be distasteful to a large section of our m.*) ; needless substitution of the abstract for the concrete is one of the surest roads to flabby style.

membran(e)ous. There is no difference of meaning ; the *-nous* form is recommended.

memento. Pl. *-os* ; see -O(E)S 6. The word is sometimes sounded mōmě'n-tō by the ignorant.

memorandum. Pl. *-da* ; see -UM.

memorize has *-zable* ; see MUTE E.

ménage. See FRENCH WORDS.

menagerie. Pronounce mĭnă'jerĭ, & not as French.

mendacity, mendicity. The first is the conduct of a liar, the second that of a beggar.

meninx. Pl. usu. *meninges.*

meningitis. See GREEK G.

menstruum. Pl. *-ua.*

-ment. For differences between this & *-ion,* see -ION & -MENT. The stems to which *-ment* is normally appended are those of verbs ; freaks like *oddment* & *funniment* should not be made a precedent of ; they are themselves due to misconception of *merriment,* which is not from the adjective, but from an obsolete verb *merry* to rejoice.

mentality. *Sir,—The mentality of the politician is a constant source of amazement to the engineer.* Twenty years ago, no-one would have written that. The word would have been either *mind* or *idiosyncrasy*, according as the writer had a taste for short or for long words; in those days we had not discovered *m.*; in *Routledge's New English Dictionary* (first published in 1914, & equal to all ordinary demands up to that date) it was not even recorded as a word. But we all know the sound & the look of it now; the meaning we neither know nor are likely to know so long as it retains its present vogue; for it is thrust into the place of all the old familiar words—*mind, idiosyncrasy, disposition, character, nerve, mood, intellect,* & a dozen others—for which it can possibly be made to do duty. Examples of it will be found in LOVE OF THE LONG WORD. Some like it because it is longer than *mind*; some because it is a VOGUE-WORD; & some because it has a pseudo-scientific sound about it that may impress the reader; see POPULARIZED TECHNICALITIES. The best thing we can do with it is to let it lapse into its former obscurity; its meaning while it had one of its own instead of many borrowed ones was *purely intellectual power,* or more often the preponderance of that over the other faculties (*An insect's very limited m./Hudibras has the same hard m./Pope is too intellectual & has an excess of m.*); in which senses *intellect(uality)* was far more common, so that *m.* is a truly SUPERFLUOUS WORD.

menu. See FRENCH WORDS.

Mephistopheles. The adjective is *Mephistophelean* (mĕfĭstŏfĭlē′an) or *Mephistophelian* (mĭfĭ′stofē′lian), the latter perhaps more likely to last; see HERCULEAN.

mercy. For *the tender mercies of,* see HACKNEYED PHRASES.

merge makes -*geable*; see MUTE E.

meringue. Pronounce meră′ng.

merino. Pl. -*os*; see -O(E)S 3.

merit makes -*ited* &c.; see -T-, -TT-.

merriment. Not to be quoted in defence of bad formations like *funniment*; see -MENT.

merry. For *the m. monarch* see SOBRIQUETS.

mésalliance. See FRENCH WORDS.

mesembrianthemum should be so spelt. It is absurd not to correct, in a cumbrous word whose length can only be excused if it is at least significant to the learned, the misspelling *y* for *i*; the *y* at once puts the Greek scholar off the track by suggesting *embryo* or *bryony* (Greek *bruo* swell, burgeon), & forbids him to think of *mesembria* noon, which is what he ought to be thinking of. When a word like *rhyme* that is familiar to everyone has settled itself into our hearts & minds with a wrong spelling, there is much to be said for refraining from correction; but with the *y* of *m.* no-one has tender associations.

mesmerize has -*zable*; see MUTE E.

messuage. Pronounce mĕ′swĭj.

metal makes *metalled, metalliferous,* &c.; see -LL-, -L-. For *metal more attractive,* see HACKNEYED PHRASES.

metamorphosis. Generally accented on the middle syllable (-*mor-*); but the more regular accent on -*pho*- is still often heard; &, as *m.* seems to be the only word in -*osis* irregularly accented, as it retains the classical plural (-*oses,* pronounced with -ēz), & as the -*osis* ending is now familiar in *tuberculosis* & other medical terms, it may be expected to revert to mĕtamorfō′sĭs; cf. *metempsychosis,* which is stated by the OED to have formerly had the accent on the -*sy*-, & has now recovered.

METAPHOR. 1. Live & dead m. 2. Some pitfalls. 3. Self-consciousness & mixed m. 4. For m. & simile, see SIMILE & METAPHOR.

1. **Live & dead m.** In all discussion of m. it must be borne in mind that

some metaphors are living, i.e., are offered & accepted with a consciousness of their nature as substitutes for their literal equivalents, while others are dead, i.e., have been so often used that speaker & hearer have ceased to be aware that the words used are not literal ; but the line of distinction between the live & the dead is a shifting one, the dead being sometimes liable, under the stimulus of an affinity or a repulsion, to galvanic stirrings indistinguishable from life. Thus, in *The men were sifting meal* we have a literal use of *sift*; in *Satan hath desired to have you, that he may sift you as wheat, sift* is a live metaphor ; in *the sifting of evidence,* the m. is so familiar that it is about equal chances whether *sifting* or *examination* will be used, & that a sieve is not present to the thought—unless indeed someone conjures it up by saying *All the evidence must first be sifted with acid tests,* or *with the microscope—* ; under such a stimulus our m. turns out to have been not dead but dormant ; the other word, *examine,* will do well enough as an example of the real stone-dead m. ; the Latin *examino,* being from *examen* the tongue of a balance, meant originally to weigh; but, though weighing is not done with acid tests or microscopes any more than sifting, *examine* gives no convulsive twitches, like *sift,* at finding itself in their company ; *examine,* then, is dead m., & *sift* only half dead, or three-quarters.

2. Some pitfalls : A. Unsustained m. ; B. Overdone m. ; C. Spoilt m. ; D. Battles of the dead. E. Mixed m.

2. A. Unsustained m. *He was still in the middle of* those 20 years of neglect *which only began to* lift *in 1868.* The plunge into m. at *lift,* which presupposes a mist, is too sudden after the literal 20 years of neglect ; years, even gloomy years, do not lift./*The* means of education *at the disposal of the Protestants & Presbyterians of the North were stunted & sterilized. The means at*

disposal names something too little vegetable or animal to consort with the metaphorical verbs. Education (personified) may be stunted, but means may not./*The* measure *of Mr Asquith's shame does not* consist *in the mere* fact *that he has announced his intention to . . .* Metaphorical measuring, like literal, requires a more accommodating instrument than a stubborn fact.

2. B. Overdone m. The days are perhaps past when a figure was deliberately chosen that could be worked out with line upon line of relentless detail, & the following well known specimen is from Richardson :—*Tost to & fro by the high winds of passionate control, I behold the desired port, the single state, into which I would fain steer ; but am kept off by the foaming billows of a brother's & sister's envy, & by the raging winds of a supposed invaded authority ; while I see in Lovelace, the rocks on one hand, & in Solmes, the sands on the other ; & tremble, lest I should split upon the former or strike upon the latter.*

The present fashion is rather to develop a metaphor only by way of burlesque. All that need be asked of those who tend to this form of satire is to remember that, while some metaphors do seem to deserve such treatment, the number of times that the same joke can safely be made, even with variations, is limited ; the limit has surely been exceeded, for instance, with ' the long arm of coincidence ' ; what proportion may this triplet of quotations bear to the number of times the thing has been done ?—*The long arm of coincidence throws the Slifers into Mercedes's Cornish garden a little too heavily.*/*The author does not strain the muscles of coincidence's arm to bring them into relation.*/*Then the long arm of coincidence rolled up its sleeves & set to work with a rapidity & vigour which defy description.*

Modern overdoing, apart from burlesque, is chiefly accidental, &

results not from too much care, but from too little : *The most irreconcilable of Irish landlords are beginning to recognize that we are on the eve of the dawn of a new day in Ireland. On the eve of* is a dead m. for about to experience, & to complete it with *the dawn of a day* is as bad as to say *It cost one pound sterling, ten,* for *one pound ten.*

2. C. Spoilt m. The essential merit of real or live m. being to add vividness to what is to be conveyed, it need hardly be said that accuracy of detail is even more needed in metaphorical than in literal expressions ; the habit of m., however, & the habit of accuracy do not always go together :—*Yet Jaurès was the* Samson *who* upheld the pillars *of the Bloc.*/*Yet what more distinguished names does the Anglican Church of the last reign boast than those of F. D. Maurice, Kingsley, Stanley, Robertson of Brighton, & even, if we will* draw *our* net *a little* wider, *the great Arnold ?*/*He was the very essence of cunning, & the* incarnation *of a* book-thief. Samson's way with pillars was not to uphold them ; we draw nets closer, but cast them wider ; & what is the incarnation of a thief ? too, too solid flesh indeed !

2. D. Battles of dead metaphors. In *The Covenanters took up arms* there is no m. ; in *The Covenanters flew to arms* there is one only—*flew to* for quickly took up—; in *She flew to arms in defence of her darling* there are two, the arms being now metaphorical as well as the flying ; moreover, the two metaphors are separate ones ; but, being dead ones, & also not inconsistent with each other, they lie together quietly enough. But dead metaphors will not lie quietly together if there was repugnance between them in life ; e'en in their ashes live their wonted fires, & they get up & fight :—*It is impossible to* crush *the Government's* aim *to restore the means of living & working freely. Crush* for baffle, *aim* for purpose, are both dead metaphors so long as they are kept apart ;

but the juxtaposition forces on us the thought that you cannot crush an aim./*National military training is the* bedrock *on which alone we can hope to* carry through *the great struggles which the future may have in store for us. Bedrock & carry through* are both moribund or dormant, but not stone-dead./*The vogue of the motor-car seems destined to help forward the provision of good road communication, a feature which is sadly* in arrear. Good road communication may be a feature, & it may be in arrear, & yet a feature cannot be in arrear ; things that are equal to the same thing may be equal to each other in geometry, but language is not geometry./*They are* cyphers *living* under the shadow of *a great man.*

2. E. Mixed metaphors. For the examples given in D, tasteless word-selection is a fitter description than mixed m., since each of the words that conflict with others is not intended as a m. at all. *Mixed m.* is more appropriate when one or both of the terms can only be consciously metaphorical. Little warning is needed against it ; it is so conspicuous as seldom to get into speech or print undetected. *This is not the time to* throw up the sponge, *when the enemy, already weakened & divided, are* on the run to a new defensive position. A mixture of prize-ring & battle-field.

In the following extract from a speech it is difficult to be sure how many times metaphors are mixed ; readers versed in the mysteries of oscillation may be able to decide :—
No society, no community, can place its house in such a condition that it is always on a rock, oscillating *between solvency & insolvency. What I have to do is to see that our house is* built upon a solid foundation, *never allowing the possibility of the Society's* life-blood being sapped. *Just in proportion as you are careful in looking after the condition of your income, just in proportion as you deal with them carefully, will the solidarity*

of the Society's financial condition remain intact. Immediately you begin to play fast & loose *with your income* the first blow *at your financial stability* will have been struck.

3. Self-consciousness & mixed m. The gentlemen of the Press regularly devote a small percentage of their time to accusing each other of mixing metaphors or announcing that they are themselves about to do so (*What a mixture of metaphors ! If we may mix our metaphors,* or *change the m.*), the offence apparently being not to mix them, but to be unaware that you have done it. The odd thing is that, whether he is on the offensive or the defensive, the writer who ventures to talk of mixing metaphors often shows that he does not know what mixed m. is. Two typical examples of the offensive follow :—*The Scotsman says :* ' *The crowded benches of the Ministerialists contain the germs of disintegration. A more ill-assorted majority could hardly be conceived, & presently the Opposition must realize of what small account is the manœuvring of the Free-Fooders or of any other section of the party. If the sling be only properly handled, the new Parliamentary Goliath will be overthrown easily enough. The stone for the sling must, however, be found on the Ministerial side of the House, & not on the Opposition side'. Apparently the stone for the sling will be a germ. But doubtless mixed feelings lead to mixed metaphors./* ' *When the Chairman of Committees —a politician of their own hue— allowed Mr Maddison to move his amendment in favour of secular education, a decision which was not quite in accordance with precedent, the floodgates of sectarian controversy were opened, & the apple of discord— the endowment of the gospel of Cowper-Temple—was thrown into the midst of the House of Commons.' What a mixture of metaphor ! One pictures* this *gospel-apple battling with the stream released by the opened floodgates.*

In the first passage, we are well rid of the germs before we hear of the sling, & the mixture of metaphors is quite imaginary. Since literal benches often contain literal germs, but *crowded benches & germs of disintegration* are here separate metaphors for a numerous party & tendencies to disunion, our critic had ready to his hand in the first sentence, if he had but known it, something much more like a mixture of metaphors than what he mistakes for one. In the second passage, the floodgates & the apple are successive metaphors, unmixed ; the mixing of them is done by the critic himself, not by the criticized ; & as to *gospel-apple,* by which it is hinted that the mixture is triple, the original writer had merely mentioned in the *gospel* phrase the thing compared by the side of what it is compared to, as when one explains *the Athens of the North* by adding *Edinburgh.*

Writers who are on the defensive apologize for *change & mixture* of metaphors as though one was as bad as the other ; the two things are in fact entirely different ; a man may change his metaphors as often as he likes ; it is for him to judge whether the result will or will not be unpleasantly florid ; but he should not ask our leave to do it ; if the result is bad, his apology will not mend matters, & if it is not bad no apology was called for. On the other hand, to mix metaphors, if the mixture is real, is an offence that should not have been apologized for, but avoided. Whichever the phrase, the motive is the same—mortal fear of being accused of mixed m. :—

. . . *showed that Free Trade could provide the jam without recourse being had to Protective food-taxes ; next came a period in which (to mix our metaphors) the jam was a nice slice of tariff pie for everybody ; but then came the Edinburgh Compromise, by which the jam for the towns was that there were to be* . . . When *jam* is used in three successive sentences in its hackneyed sense of consolation, it need hardly be considered in the middle one of them a live m. at all ; however, the as-good-as-dead m. of jam *is* capable of being stimulated into life if anyone is so foolish as to bring into contact with it another half-dead m. of its own (i.e. the foodstuff) kind ; & it *was* after all mixing metaphors to say the jam was a slice of pie ; but then the way of escape was to withdraw either the jam or the pie, instead of forcing them together down our throats with a ramrod of apology./*Time sifts the richest granary, & posterity is a dainty feeder. But Lyall's words, at any rate—to mix the metaphor— will escape the blue pencil even of such drastic editors as they.* Since all three metaphors are live ones, & *they* are the sifter & the feeder, the working of these into grammatical connexion with the blue pencil does undoubtedly mix metaphors. But then our author gives us to understand that he knows he is doing it, & surely that is enough. Even so some liars reckon that a lie is no disgrace provided that they wink at a bystander as they tell it ; even so those who are addicted to the phrase ' to use a vulgarism ' expect to achieve the feat of being at once vulgar & superior to vulgarity./*Certainly we cannot detect the suggested lack of warmth in the speech as it is printed, for in his speech, as in the Prime Minister's, it seems to us that (if we may change the metaphor) exactly the right note was struck./We may, on the one hand, receive into our gill its precise content of the complex mixture that fills the puncheon of the whole world's literature ; on the other—to change the metaphor—our few small strings may thrill in sympathetic harmony to some lyrical zephyrs & remain practically unresponsive to the deep sea gale of Aeschylus or Dante.* Certainly, gentlemen, you may change your metaphors, if it seems good to you ; but you may also be pretty sure that, if you feel the necessity of proclaiming the change, you had

better have abstained from it./*Two of the trump cards played against the Bill are* (1) that ' it *makes every woman who pays a tax-collector in her own house* ', & (2) *that* ' *it will destroy happy domestic relations in hundreds of thousands of homes* ' ; *if we may at once change our metaphor, these are the notes which are most consistently struck in the stream of letters, now printed day by day for our edification in the* Mail. This writer need not have asked our leave to change from cards to music ; he is within his rights, anyhow, & the odds are, indeed, that if he had not reminded us of the cards we should have forgotten them in the three intervening lines ; but how did a person so sensitive to change of m. fail to reflect that it is ill playing the piano in the water ? a *stream of letters*, it is true, is only a picturesque way of saying many letters, & ordinarily a dead m. ; but once put your seemingly dead yet picturesque m. close to a piano that is being played, & its notes wake the dead—at any rate for readers who have just had the word *m*. called to their memories.

metaphysics & *metaphysical* are so often used as quasi-learned & vaguely depreciatory substitutes for various other terms, for *theory* & *theoretical*, *subtle*(*ty*), (*the*) *super-natural*, *occult*(*ism*), *obscure* & *obscurity*, *philosophy* & *philosophic*, *academic*(*s*), & so forth, that it is pardonable to forget that they have a real meaning of their own—the more that the usual resource of those who suddenly realize that their notion of a word's meaning is hazy, an appeal to its etymology, will not serve. It is agreed that *Metaphysics* owes its name to the accident that the part of Aristotle's works in which metaphysical questions were treated of stood after (*meta*) the part concerned with physics (*ta phusika*), & that the word's etymology is therefore devoid of significance. What is wanted, then, is a definition plain enough not to perplex, but precise enough not to mislead. Metaphysics is the branch of philosophy that deals with the ultimate nature of things, or considers the questions, What is the world of things we know ? &, How do we know it ? ' Three kinds of definite answers are returned. *Metaphysical materialism* is the view that everything known is body or matter. *Metaphysical idealism* is the view that everything known is mind, or some mental state or other. *Metaphysical realism* is the intermediate view that everything known is either body or soul, neither of which alone exhausts the universe of being '—Prof. T. Case in *Enc. Brit.* Such being the subject of Metaphysics, it is not wonderful, in view of the infinity of theories & subtlety of arguments evoked, that it should have come by some or all of the wrong acceptations mentioned above; but it is very desirable that the plain man, who at best finds the notion of it hard to grasp, should not have his difficulties increased by its being misapplied.

metathesis. See TECHNICAL TERMS. Pl. *-eses* (-ēz).

métayage, métayer. See FRENCH WORDS.

mete makes *-table* ; see MUTE E.

metempsychosis. Pl. *-oses* (-ēz). Pronounce mĭtĕmpsĭkō′sĭs.

-meter. For words like *speedometer*, see HYBRID DERIVATIVES. For verse-names, see *-meter* in TECHNICAL TERMS.

method. For *m. in madness*, see IRRELEVANT ALLUSION.

methodize has *-zable* ; see MUTE E.

meticulous. What is the strange charm that makes this wicked word irresistible to the British journalist ? does he like its length ? does he pity its isolation (for it has no kindred in England) ? can a Latin scholar like him not get *meticulosus* out of his head ? can so accomplished a Frenchman never be sure whether *méticuleux* or *m.* is the

1351

N

word he knows so well ? or what is it ? At any rate, he must have the word always with him, however unsuitable the surroundings. It is clear first that it is not a piece of latinity that cannot be forgotten ; ' ante- & post-classical ' say Lewis & Short ; that is, you may read your Cicero & Virgil & Horace & Livy through & never meet it ; & when it is unearthed in Plautus or somewhere it means not what the journalists make it mean, but just frightened ; it is the word for the timid hare, or the man who is gibbering with fear (*Nullust hoc meticulosus aeque . . . Perii, pruriunt dentes*— Was ever man in such a funk ? . . . Lord, how my teeth chatter !). That meaning, comprehensible enough through the Latin *metus* fear to all who have learnt any Latin, but not to others, since *metus* by some odd chance has given no common words to English, *meticulous* had some centuries ago ; but the word died out. When it was resuscitated in the nineteenth century, it was by the literary critics with a new sense for which it was not in the least needed, *scrupulous & punctilious* being amply sufficient ; but literary critics are given to gallicizing, & *méticuleux* appeared in the French-Academy dictionary in 1835, i.e., had lately become fashionable in France. The question is whether we are going to allow the word to be imposed upon us for general use, now that the journalist of the daily papers has caught it up from the literary critic. It is, for the uneducated, far less intelligible than *scrupulous & punctilious*, which have well-known nouns associated ; it is, for the educated, divorced from its etymological meaning ; it is, for the Englishman, a Gallicism. It might, indeed, have had a distinct shade of meaning that would have justified its existence, if it had been applied only to those that has its origin in terror of being caught breaking rules or mis-stating facts ; but how far it is from being so limited will be plain from the quotations below. It should have been a negative complement to *punctilious*, the two covering between them the positive accuracy that omits no detail & the negative accuracy that admits no error. The journalist enjoys a laugh at the man in the street with his ' chronic ' for serious ; but his own *m.* for exact lays him open to the same charge of leaving out the essential meaning of a word & using it promiscuously whether it is applicable or not ; had he not better consent to its being relegated to the list of SUPERFLUOUS WORDS ? In the long collection of examples, the first illustrates fairly the legitimate sense in which shrinking from any possible wrong element is the point ; the last is ludicrous in that it excludes not merely the idea of fear, but even that of care ; & the intermediate ones are arranged roughly in a descent from the less bad to the worse :—*It will be good for the New Englanders to contemplate Mr Joseph Southall's quiet & m. craftsmanship, as in ' Tadmarton ' (38)./That on the French artillery, with its plea for less m. care & more simplicity in our own batteries, should be read & digested by . . ./Japanese writers have not yet acquired either the methods of our art criticism or the m. attention to detail which our habits demand./Should any English reader think that the question of ' sources ' is somewhat too meticulously studied, let him turn to . . . /With the aid of the prodigious & m. survey being made under the famous, much-abused ' Finance (1909–10) Act, 1910 ', an entirely new method will be adopted of treating the soil./Gone is the wealth of m. detail with which he loved to elaborate his finely finished pictures./ More complete & satisfying, from their breadth & directness, their superb amplitude of handling, & from the absence of the m. detail with which the master might have overlaid them./ Who know how their output is affected by minor wage disputes, by the m. & indecisive criticism of Admiralty inspectors, by shortage of men & of material./We are told that in 1909–10 there were approximately 10300 (observe the m. 300) super-men./There was nothing to indicate that the actor did more than carry out admirably the very clever ideas of the author—an author, by the way, who happens to be very m. about having his ideas carried out./With method, with meticulousness, with machinery, . . . with the terrorism of bombs, poison gases, & outrages according to programme, decadent nations were to be taught the might of the Hohenzollern ' kultur './ Mr ——, who has succumbed to the wounds inflicted upon him ten days previously by a pet lion, had his fate foretold with m. accuracy more than 2000 years ago by the greatest Greek dramatist.

métier. See FRENCH WORDS.

metonymy. See TECHNICAL TERMS.

metope. The OED gives three syllables (mĕ′topĭ) ; disyllabic pronunciation (mĕ′tōp) as in French is perhaps equally common ; but cf. *epitome, strophe, systole, catastrophe,* as analogous Greek words.

metre, -ter. See -RE & -ER.

mews, originally a plural, but now used freely as singular with *a,* is best provided with a fresh plural *mewses.*

mezzanine. See FLOOR.

mezzo-rilievo. Pl. *-os,* see -O(E)S 6. The above is the Italian spelling, & the corresponding pronunciation is mĕ′dzō rĭlyā′vō ; if the spelling is, as often, corrupted to *rel-,* pronounce mĕ′dzō rĭlē′vō.

mezzotint. Pronounce mĕdz-.

miaow, miaul. It is better to be content with *mew* & *caterwaul* than to multiply phonetic approximations.

miasma. Pl. usually *-ata.*

mickle & **muckle** are merely variants of the same word, & the not uncommon version *Many a mickle makes a muckle* is a blunder ; the right forms are *Many a little* (or *Mony a pickle*) *makes a mickle* (or *muckle*), with other slight variations.

microbe, micro-organism. See SCHIZOMYCETES.

mid has superl. *midmost*; *mid air* should not be hyphened, see HYPHENS.

middle. *M. class* is hyphened as an adjective (*middle-class education*), but not as a noun (*belongs to the middle class*); see HYPHENS. For *middle* (*article*) & *middle voice* see TECHNICAL TERMS.

middling(ly). The *-ly* is unusual & undesirable : *a middling good crop*; *did middling well*; *it went only middling*. See UNIDIOMATIC *-LY*.

midwifery. Three syllables; mǐ´dwǐfrǐ is perhaps usual, but both mǐ´dwǐfrǐ & mǐ´dǐfrǐ are also heard; cf. HOUSEWIFE.

mighty. In the colloquialism *m. fine* &c., *mightily* should not be substituted ; see UNIDIOMATIC *-LY*.

mignon, migraine. See FRENCH WORDS.

mikado. Pl. *-os*; see *-O*(E)S 6.

milage. So spelt; see MUTE E.

milden. See *-EN* VERBS.

Milesian (Irish) is now chiefly a resource of the ELEGANT VARIATIONIST ; see also POLYSYLLABIC HUMOUR.

millenarian, of the, believer in the, millennium. The apparent inconsistency in spelling (*-n-*, *-nn-*) results from the fact that *millenarian*, like *millenary*, does not contain the stem of the Latin *annus* year, which is present in *millennium* ; if it were formed from *millennium*, the form would be *millenniarian*; *millenarian* strictly means thousander, not thousand-yearer. Cf. CENTENARY.

millenary. The OED pronounces mǐ´lǐnarǐ ; but see CENTENARY.

millennium. Pl. *-ms*, *-ia* ; see *-UM*.

milli-. See KILO-.

milliard means a thousand millions ; it is chiefly a French term, though perhaps advancing in general currency. In France it is the equivalent in ordinary use for the mathematical French (which differs from the English) BILLION.

million. 1. *A m. & a quarter, two millions & a half*, rather than *one & a quarter million*(*s*) & *two & a half millions* ; see HALF.
2. *It is safe to say, therefore* (*adds the ' Times '*), *that the total is considerably less than* 2½ millions, although *it must be well over* 1¼ million. This change from 2½ *millions* to 1¼ *million* is wrong (see ONE) unless 1¼ *million* is meant merely for the printed form that is to be said as ' a million & a half '.
3. *Forty-five million people* rather than *forty-five millions of people* (on the analogy of *dozen, score, hundred,* & *thousand*) ; but, with *a few & many, millions of* is perhaps the more usual form.
4. *Amongst the eight million are a few hundred to whom this does not apply* rather than *millions, hundreds*; but *He died worth three millions* rather than *million* ; this because ' a million ' is an established noun (as distinguished from a mere numeral) in the sense £1,000,000, but not in the sense a million people.

Milly. So spelt ; see *-EY*, *-IE*, *-Y*.

milor(d). See FRENCH WORDS.

mimic, vb, makes *-cked*, *-cking* ; see *-C-*, *-CK-*.

minacious, minatory. Both words smack of pedantry ; but while the first is serviceable only for POLYSYLLABIC HUMOUR, the second is not out of place in a formally rhetorical context.

mince, vb, makes *-ceable* ; see MUTE E.

mine. For (*my* or) *mine & your future depends upon it* &c., see ABSOLUTE POSSESSIVES.

mine, vb, has *-nable* ; see MUTE E.

mineralogy is a syncopated form (the syncopation done in French) for *mineralology*, & should not be quoted in defence of proposed wrong forms in *-alogy* ; cf. *pacifist*.

minify, minimize, diminish. *Minify* is a badly formed & little used word ; it owes its existence to the desire for a neat opposite to the correctly formed *magnify*, but is now chiefly used by people who, rightly enough offended by the extension of *minimize* to improper meanings, are too ready to catch at the first alternative ; a slight further search would bring them through *minish* (to which the only but fatal objection is that it is archaic) to *diminish*.

Minimize is both a rightly formed & a current word, but unfortunately current in more senses than it has any right to. It should be kept strictly to the limits imposed by its derivation from *minimus* (not less or little, but least), & therefore always mean either to reduce to the least possible amount (*We must minimize the friction*) or to put at the lowest possible estimate (*It is your interest to minimize his guilt*). The meanings given to *minimize* in the following quotations, i.e. reduce & underestimate, ignore the essential superlative element :—*The utility of our convoy would have been considerably minimized had it not included one of these.*/*The Shipping Federation has left little scope for unions of the men ; nobody who knows anything of that combination is likely to minimize its power.*/*An open window or door would greatly minimize risk.*

Minify should be given up as a SUPERFLUOUS WORD ; *minimize* should be kept to its proper senses ; *magnify* should have as its opposite, in one of its senses *diminish* (*the diminishing end of the telescope*), & in another *underestimate* (*neither magnify nor underestimate the difficulties*). See also BELITTLE.

minimum. Pl. usually *-ma*.

minister. The tendency to apply the word, in the sense m. of religion, to dissenters, & to avoid applying it to Anglicans, noteworthy seeing that m. is common in the Prayer-Book rubrics, is explained by historical circumstances ; it was adopted as an acceptable name ' at first chiefly by those who objected to the terms *priest & clergyman* as implying erroneous views of the nature of the sacred office '—OED.

Minnie. So spelt ; see -EY, -IE, -Y.

minor (in logic). See TECHNICAL TERMS.

minority is like MAJORITY, only more so, in its meanings, with which odd tricks can be played. Corresponding to the A, B, & C, of *majority*, m. has, A, inferiority of number or fewerness or pauciority, B, a party having a pauciority, & C, less than half of any set of people. ' More so ', because, if one presses one's rights, one may say that a small m. (sense B) is in a considerable m. (sense A) or is the vast m. (sense C), both of which statements happen to sound absurd ; & again, in a Board of 51 *a m. of one* may be either 25 persons (A) or one person (B). The point need not be laboured, but should be appreciated. There is a tacit convention, in the interests of lucidity, that adjectives naturally appropriate to magnitude shall not be used with m. to emphasize smallness of number, & another that *a m. of one* shall always mean one person. But the first is not always kept to :— *With* a considerable minority *of the votes polled, the Tory Party have obtained a clear & substantial majority over all other parties in the House.* Oddly enough, the newspaper whose own words are those has this paragraph about a fellow offender :— *Says a motoring writer in a Sunday paper :* ' *It is time that a period were put to the era of the trap on the open road, & that the interests of the public at large were considered by attacking the real evil—the dangerous & inconsiderate driver. Fortunately, he constitutes the* vast minority *of motor-car owners & drivers* '. *We know what is meant, but* ' *the vast minority* ' *is a very unfortunate way of saying it.* In the first passage m. is used in sense A, & in the second in sense C ; but the convention is applicable to both or neither.

Minotaur. Generally pronounced

mĭn-, though the i is long in Greek & Latin ; but see FALSE QUANTITY.

mint sauce should not be hyphened if the stress is on the second word, as it usually is ; see HYPHENS.

minuscule. See TECHNICAL TERMS.

miocene. A typical example of the monstrosities with which scientific men in want of a label for something, & indifferent to all beyond their own province, defile the language. The elements of the word are Greek, but not the way they are put together, nor the meaning demanded of the compound. See HYBRID DERIVATIVES (w.f.).

misalliance, though formed after the French *mésalliance*, is so natural an English word that it is free of the taint of gallicism, & should always be preferred to the French spelling.

MISAPPREHENSIONS of which many writers need to disabuse themselves. Discussion of each will be found under the word printed in small capitals.

That a DEVIL's advocate, or *advocatus diaboli*, is a tempter or the like.

That a PERCENTAGE is a small part.

That a LEADING QUESTION is a searching one.

That CUI BONO ? means What is the good or use ?

That *One* TOUCH *of nature makes the whole world kin* means much the same as *A fellow-feeling makes one wondrous kind.*

That POLITY is a scholarly word for *policy.*

That *more* HONOURed *in the breach than the observance* means more often broken than kept.

That ILK means clan or the like.

That *arithmetical,* & *geometrical,* PROGRESSION mean fast, & very fast, progress.

That *the* COMITY *of nations* means the members of a sort of league.

That any order of words that avoids a SPLIT INFINITIVE is better than any that involves it.

That PROPORTION is a sonorous improvement on *part.*

That SUBSTITUTE is an improve-

ment on *replace* in the sense take the place of.

That PROTAGONIST is an improvement on *champion* & *leader.*

That an EXCEPTION strengthens a rule.

That good writers do not end a sentence with a PREPOSITION.

That FRANKENSTEIN was a monster.

miscegenation. See HYBRID DERIVATIVES (w.f.).

miscellany. Pronounce mĭ′selănĭ or mĭsĕ′lănĭ ; the OED puts the former first, & RECESSIVE ACCENT is in its favour.

mise-en-scène. See FRENCH WORDS.

miserere, misericord, hinged seat. The first is labelled *an incorrect form* in the OED.

misogynist. See GREEK G.

MISPRINTS TO BE GUARDED AGAINST. *Adverse* & *averse, deprecate* & *depreciate, inculcate* & *inoculate, interpellate* & *interpolate, principal* & *principle, recourse* & *resource* & *resort, risible* & *visible, -tion* & *-tive* (e. g. *a corrective* & *a correction*), are common confusions worth providing against by care in writing & vigilance in proof-correcting. *Concensus* (non-existent) appears perhaps more often than the real word *consensus,* & *to signal out* (non-existent in the sense meant) more often than to *single out.*

MISQUOTATION. The correct words of a few familiar sayings that are more often wrongly than rightly quoted may be useful. The misquoting of phrases that have survived on their own merits out of little-read authors (e. g. of *Fine by degrees* &c. from *Prior*, usually changed to *Small* &c.) is a very venial offence ; & indeed it is almost a pedantry to use the true form instead of so established a wrong one ; it would be absurd to demand that no-one should ever use a trite quotation without testing its verbal accuracy. Again, the established change made in the *Leave-not-a-*

rack-behind quotation by shifting *the baseless fabric of a vision* from some lines earlier into the place of another phrase that does not suit general use so well, though most people no doubt make it without knowing what they are doing, might reasonably enough be made knowingly, & is no offence. Examples of these two kinds are placed at the end of the list. But when a quotation comes from such a source as a well-known play of Shakspere, or *Lycidas*, or the Bible or Prayer Book, to give it wrongly at least requires excuse, & any great prevalence of such misquotation would prove us discreditably ignorant of our own literature. Nevertheless, such words as *A poor thing, but my own*, are often so much more used than the true form that their accuracy is sure to be taken for granted unless occasional attempts like the present are made to draw attention to them.

In the sweat of thy *face* shalt thou eat bread (not *brow*).

To gild refined gold, to *paint* the lily (not *gild the lily*).

Pride goeth before *destruction*, & an haughty spirit before a fall (not *pride before a fall*).

Screw your courage to the sticking-*place* (not *point*).

I will a *round* unvarnished *tale* deliver.

An *ill-favoured* thing, sir, but mine own (not *poor*).

Let not him that *girdeth* on his harness boast himself as he that putteth it off (not *putteth on*).

That last infirmity of noble *mind* (not *minds*).

Make assurance *double* sure (not *doubly*).

Tomorrow to fresh *woods* & pastures new (not *fields*).

The devil can *cite* Scripture for his purpose (not *quote*).

A goodly apple rotten at the *heart* (not *core*).

Chewing the *food* of sweet & bitter fancy (not *cud*).

I am escaped *with* the skin of my teeth (not *by*).

And, like *this insubstantial pageant faded*, Leave not a rack behind.

Passing rich *with* forty pounds a year.

He that complies against his will Is of *his own* opinion still.

Fine by degrees & beautifully less.

When *Greeks joined Greeks*, then *was* the tug of war.

Miss. *The Misses Smith* &c. is the old-fashioned plural, still used when formality is required, e.g. in printed lists of guests present &c.; elsewhere *the Miss Smiths* is now usual.

mis-shapen &c. The hyphen is usual in compounds of *mis-* with words beginning with *s*.

missile. Usually pronounced -ĭl.

missis. See MISTRESS.

missy. So spelt; see -EY, -IE, -Y.

mistake makes -*kable*; see MUTE E. For the p.p. meanings *in error* &c., see INTRANSITIVE P.P.

mistaken makes -*nness*.

mistral. See WIND, *n*.

mistress. The title *Mrs* is pronounced mĭ'sĭz; the noun *missis* (joc. or illit. for *wife*) is pronounced mĭ'sĭs.

mite makes *mity*; see -EY & -Y.

mitigate makes -*gable*, -*tor*; see -ABLE 1, -OR.

mitrailleuse. See FRENCH WORDS.

mitre, -ter. See -RE & -ER.

mixed metaphor. See METAPHOR.

miz(z)en. The OED treats *mizen* as the standard form.

-M-, -MM-. Monosyllables ending in m double it before suffixes beginning with a vowel if it is preceded by a single vowel (a, e, i, o, u, or y), but not if it is preceded by a diphthong or a doubled vowel or a vowel & r: *hammy, gemmed, dimmest, drummer*; but *claimant, gloomy, worming*. Words of more than one syllable follow the rule for monosyllables if their last syllable is a word in composition, as *bedimmed, overcramming*, but otherwise do not double the m (*bemadamed, bedlamite, balsamic, diademed, emblematic, pilgrimage, victimize, seldomer, venom-*

ous, unbosomed, blossoming, bottomed, buxomest, harmoniumist, vellumy); but words in -gram double the m (compare *epigrammatic, diagrammatic,* with *systematic*).

mobilize makes *-zable* ; see MUTE E.

mobocracy. See HYBRID DERIVATIVES.

moccasin, which suggests the pronunciation better, is now preferred to the formerly current *mocassin.*

mocha, coffee. Pronounce mō′ka.

model makes *-lled, -lling,* &c. ; see -LL-, -L-.

moderate makes *-rable, -tor* ; see -ABLE 1, -OR.

modern makes *-nness.* For *the m. Athens, the m. Babylon,* see SOBRIQUETS.

modernize has *-zable* ; see MUTE E.

modest makes *-er, -est.*

modify. For inflexions see VERBS IN -IE, -Y, -YE, 6.

modish. So spelt ; see MUTE E.

modulate makes *-lable, -tor* ; see -ABLE 1, -OR.

modulus. Pl. *-li* (-ī).

modus vivendi (literally way of living) is any temporary compromise that enables parties to carry on pending settlement of a dispute that would otherwise paralyse their activities.

Mogul. Accent the second syllable. For the spelling *Mughal* see DIDACTICISM, MAHOMET.

Mohammed(an). See MAHOMET.

moiety, apart from uses as a legal term & a FORMAL WORD, exists merely for the delight of the ELEGANT-VARIATIONist in such triumphs as : *The Unionist candidate was returned by exactly* half *the number of votes polled, the other* moiety *being divided between a Labour & an Independent opponent.*

moire)(moiré. *Moire,* or *moire antique,* is the name of the watered silk material ; *moiré* is first an adjective meaning watered like moire (often of metal surfaces), & secondly a noun meaning watered surface or effect. *A moire dress* ; *velvets & moire antiques* ; *a moiré*

surface ; *the moiré has been improved by using the blowpipe.* Pronounce mwahr, mwar′ā.

moisten. The *t* is silent ; see PRONUNCIATION.

molasses is used as a singular.

molecule, atom, electron, corpuscle. To the mere literary man without scientific knowledge, the relations of these words to each other are puzzling, & not easy to learn, even in an elementary way, from consulting each by itself in dictionaries. Some sentences picked out from the *Enc. Brit.* article on *molecule* may throw light ; but here, first, are the etymological meanings : *molecule,* small mass ; *atom,* uncuttable (particle) ; *electron,* amber ; *corpuscle,* small body.

' The doctrine that matter can be divided into, or regarded as composed of, discrete particles (termed *atoms* by early writers, & *molecules* by modern ones) has at all times played an important part in metaphysics & natural science.'

' Democritus was the founder of the atomic theory, while Anaxagoras propounded that of continuity.'

' The atoms, they [the atomists] said, do not fill up the universe ; there are void spaces between them . . . The opposite school maintained then, as they have always done, that there is no vacuum—that every part of space is full of matter, that there is a universal plenum.'

' *Molecule,* the minutest particle of matter capable of separate existence. The word appears to have been invented during the 17th century, & remained synonymous with *atom* . . . until the middle of the 19th century, when a differentiation was established.'

' An enormous mass of experimental evidence now shows quite conclusively that matter cannot be regarded as having a continuous structure, but that it is ultimately composed of discrete parts. The smallest unit of matter with which physical phenomena are concerned is the *molecule*. When chemical phenomena occur the molecule may be divided into *atoms* ; & these atoms, in the presence of electrical phenomena, may themselves be further divided into *electrons* or *corpuscles*.'

mollify. For inflexions, see VERBS IN -IE, -Y, -YE, 6.

Molly. So spelt ; see -EY, -IE, -Y.

molten. See MELT.

momentarily, momently. The first means for a moment (*he was momentarily abashed*), the second from moment to moment or every moment (*am momently expecting a wire from him*). The differentiation is well worth more faithful observance than it gets ; & the substitution of either, which sometimes occurs, for *instantly* or *immediately* or *at once* is foolish NOVELTY-HUNTING.

momentary, momentous. The first means lasting only for a moment, or transitory ; the second means of moment, i. e. of great consequence.

momentum. Pl. usually *-ta*.

monachal, monastic, monkish. Each has its own abstract noun—*monachism, monasticism, monkery*. Of the three sets *monastic(ism)* is the one that suits all contexts ; it is useful that *monkish* & *monkery* should also exist, as serving the purpose of those who wish to adopt a certain tone. *Monachal* & *monachism*, though they would have passed well enough if *monastic(ism)* did not exist & were not much better known, seem as it is to have no recommendation unless it is a good thing that scholars writing for scholars should have other names for things than those generally current, even though the meaning is the same. If that is, on the contrary, a bad thing, *monachal* & *monachism* should be allowed to die.

monadism)(monism. Both terms owe their existence to the metaphysical problem of the relation between mind & matter. The view that regards mind & matter as two independent constituents of which the universe is composed is called *dualism*. In contrast with dualism, any view that makes the universe consist of mind with matter as a form of mind, or of matter with mind as a form of matter, or of a substance that in every part of it is neither mind nor matter but both, is called *monism* (see also META-PHYSICS). *Monadism* is the name given to a particular form of monism, corresponding to the molecular or atomic theory of matter (see MOLE-CULE), & holding that the universal substance (according to the third variety of monism described in the previous sentence) consists of units called *monads*.

monarchical, -chic, -chal, -chial. The first is the current form ; *-chic* is occasionally used for antithetic purposes (*the monarchic, the aristo-cratic, & the democratic branches of our constitution*) ; *-chal* with a slight rhetorical difference, where *kingly* might serve (*the royal harangue has a certain monarchal tone*) ; *-ial* seems superfluous.

monastic(ism). See MONACHAL.

Monday. For *He is coming M.*, &c., see FRIDAY.

monde. See FRENCH WORDS.

monetary, monetize. See PRO-NUNCIATION for the question be-tween mŏn & mŭn.

moneyed, moneys, not *monied, monies*.

mongoose. Pl. *-ooses*.

mongrel makes *-lly* ; see -LL-, -L-. See MULATTO 1 for synonyms.

monism. See MONADISM.

monitress. See FEMININE DESIG-NATIONS.

monk. For *m. & friar*, see FRIAR.

monkey, n. Pl. *-eys*.

monkey, vb. For inflexions see VERBS IN -IE, -Y, -YE, 2.

monoecious. Pronounce -nēsh- ; for *-noe-*, *-nœ-*, see Æ, Œ.

monocle. That this, a HYBRID DERIVATIVE, a GALLICISM, & a word with no obvious meaning to the Englishman who hears it for the first time, should be ousting the entirely satisfactory *eyeglass* is a melancholy illustration of the popular taste in language.

monologist. See GREEK G.

monologue, monometer. See TECH-NICAL TERMS.

monopolize makes *-zable* ; see MUTE E.

monotonic, -nous. The secondary sense of *monotonous* (same or tedious) has so nearly swallowed up its primary (of one pitch or tone) that it is well worth while to remember the existence of *monotonic*, which has the primary sense only.

Monroe doctrine. Its status is that of a manifesto addressed by the U.S.A. to all whom it may concern, not that of a treaty or a piece of international law.

Its contents are not definite, nor expressed as a legislative enactment, nor extractable from a single document, but are in course of development, having varied from the view that European Powers must not interpose with a view to securing control of independent American States, nor establish fresh colonies in America, to the principle that every portion of the American continent must be free from European control.

Its name is taken from President Monroe, who in 1823 made a declaration to Congress to the effect stated above in summary as the first view.

The original policy at least had the official approval of Great Britain.

monseigneur, monsieur. See FRENCH WORDS.

monsignor, -ore. Pron. -ēnyor'(ĕ). Pl. *-ori* (-ē).

monsoon. See WIND, n.

mood. It may save misconceptions to mention that the grammar word has nothing to do with the native word meaning frame of mind &c., & is merely a variant of *mode*.

moollah. See MULLAH.

mora. The Italian finger-flashing game is so spelt in Italian, not *morra*.

moral, adj. 1. For distinctions between *m.* & *ethical, morals* & *ethics*, see ETHICAL 5, 6. 2. *M. victory, m. certainty.* The first is often applied to an event that is from another point of view a defeat ; the second is always applied to what is in fact an uncertainty. It is so easy to see why *m. victory* should mean what it does, & so hard to see why *m. certainty* should, that anyone considering the point by the mere light of nature is tempted to guess that *m. certainty* is the illegitimate offspring of *m. victory*, & perhaps to abstain from using it as a solecism. The OED quotations show that, on the contrary, it is much the older of the two phrases ; &, though this peculiar sense of practical or virtual in combination with *certainty*, & of tantamount to demonstrative in combination with *evidence*, is hard to account for, it is established as idiomatic.

moral(e), n. Is a combination of pedantry & Gallicism to bully us into abandoning the English word *morale* ? For, until a few years ago, we all wrote that without thinking twice about it ; & to this day you will meet it in the local newspapers that have not time to keep up with the latest tricks of the London Press, & in those parts of the London Press itself that have to use a tongue understanded of the people.

The case for the spelling *moral* is that (1) the French use the word *moral* for what we used to call morale, & therefore we ought to do the same ; & that (2) the French use *morale* to mean something different from what we mean by it.

The case against *moral* is (1) that it is a new word, less comprehensible to ordinary people, even now after its wartime currency, than the old *morale* ; (2) that it must always be dressed in italics owing to the occasional danger of confusion with the English word *moral*, & that such artificial precautions are never kept up ; (3) that half of us do not know whether to call it mŏ'ral, moră'l, or morah'l, & that it is a recognized English custom to resolve such doubts by the addition of -*e* or other change of spelling.

The view here taken is that the case for *moral* is extraordinarily weak, & that against it decidedly strong, & in fact that the question is simply one between true pedantry & true English. A few remarks may be made on the points already summarized.

Here are two extracts from book-reviews in *The Times* : *He persistently spells* moral (*state of mind of the troops, not their morality*) *with a final* e, *a sign of ignorance of French./The purist in language might quarrel with Mr* ——'s *title for this book on the psychology of war, for he means by* morale *not ' ethics ' or ' moral philosophy ', but ' the temper of a people expressing itself in action'.* But no doubt there is authority for the perversion of the French word. Is it either ignorance of French or a perversion of the French word ? or would a truer account of the matter be that we have never had anything to do with the French word *morale* (ethics, morality, a moral, &c.), but that we found the French word *moral* (state of discipline & spirit in armies & the like) suited to our needs, & put an -*e* on to it to keep its sound distinct from that of our own word *moral*, just as we have done with the French *local* (English *locale*) & the German *Choral* (English *chorale*), & as, using contrary means for the same end of fixing a sound, we have turned French *diplomate* into English *diplomat* ? Our English *forte* (*geniality is not his forte*, &c.) is altered from the French *fort* without even the advantage of either keeping the French sound or distinguishing the spoken word from our *fort* ; but who proposes to sacrifice the reader's convenience by correcting its ' ignorant ' spelling ?

The French word *morale* has never had any currency in English, though it is no doubt used by misguided gallicizers from time to time, & it certainly need not be taken into account as an objection to spelling the French *moral* as suits our convenience.

If we reinstate the once almost universal *morale*, we need no italics, & there is no fear of confusion ; if we adopt *moral*, we need italics, & there is no hope of getting them ; it is at present printed oftener without than with them. The following five extracts, in some of which the English adjective *moral*, & in some the French noun *moral*, is meant, have all the same type for *moral* as for the rest. They are printed here, except for the italicizing of the whole, exactly as they appeared, & they are enough to suggest how easy it would be for real doubts to arise about which word is being used :— *An astounding decrease in the moral discipline & patriotism of German soldiers* (Has, or has not, a comma dropped out after *moral* ?)./*It is indeed a new proof of the failing moral & internal troubles of the German people* (Moral & internal ? Oh dear no !)./*A true arbitrator, a man really impartial between two contendants & even indifferent to their opposing morals./The Russian army will recover its moral & fighting power./The need of Poland, not only for moral, but for the material support of the Allies.*

The right course is to make the English word *morale*, use ordinary type, call it morah'l, & ignore or abstain from the French word *morale*, of which we have no need. See for other examples of pedantry with French words, À L'OUTRANCE & DOUBLE ENTENDRE ; cf. also GUERILLA.

moralize makes -*zable* ; see MUTE E.
morbid makes -*est* ; see -ER & -EST 4.
morbidezza. Pronounce -ĕtsa.
more. 1. For limitations on the

use of *he more*, see THE. 2. For the common confusion between *much m.* & *much less*, see ILLOGICALITIES, LESS, and MUCH. 3. *M. than one*, though its sense is necessarily plural, is treated as a sort of compound of *one*, following its construction, & agrees with a singular noun & takes a singular verb : *m. t. o. workman was killed, m. t. o. was killed*, not *workmen* or *were*. 4. For *m. in sorrow than in anger*, see HACKNEYED PHRASES. 5. *The new dock scheme affects the whole of the northern bank of the Thames in a more or less degree*. This is wrong because, though *a less degree* is English, *a m. degree* is not ; & the reason for that again is that while LESS still preserves to a certain extent its true adjectival use (=smaller) as well as its quasi-adjectival use (= a smaller amount of), the former use of *m.* (=larger) has long been obsolete, & it retains only the latter sense, a larger amount of. *Less butter, less courage, a less degree*, & even *a less price*, are possible ; but not *a m. degree* or *a m. price*, only *m. butter* or *courage*. *The m. part*, & *More 's the pity*, are mentioned by the OED as survivals of the otherwise obsolete sense.

morgue. See FRENCH WORDS.

morning. 1. *M. Service, M. Prayer, Matins*. The first is perhaps the usual unofficial term ; the other two are official, & the last is especially in High-Church & musical use. Similarly *Evening Service, Evening Prayer, Evensong*. 2. *M. performance*. See MATINÉE.

morocco. Pl. *-os* ; see -O(E)S 3.

morphia, morphine. The meaning is the same, the second being the scientific term, but the first surviving in ordinary use.

morra. See MORA.

mortal. For *all that was m. of*, & *the m. remains of*, see HACKNEYED PHRASES, & STOCK PATHOS.

mortgagee, -ger, -gor. 1. As the word *mortgager* is one that could be formed at will from the verb *mortgage* even if it were, as it is not, unrecorded, the maintenance of the form *-gor*, pronounced *-jor*, seems an absurdity ; the only other English words in which *g* is soft before *a* or *o* or *u* are perhaps *gaol* & its derivatives, & the debatable MARGARINE. 2. The mortgagee is the person who lends money on the security of an estate, the mortgager or *-or* the person who pledges his property in order to get the loan. But, as the owner of a mortgaged estate is often himself described as ' mortgaged up to the eyes ' &c., & as *-ee* suggests the passive, & *-or* & *-er* the active party, those who are not familiar with the terms are apt to have the meanings reversed in their minds.

mortifiedly. A bad form ; see -EDLY.

mortify. For inflexions see VERBS IN -IE, -Y, -YE, 6.

mortise, -ice. The first is better. In *m. & tenon*, the m. is the receiving cavity.

moslem, muslim. The OED treats the first as the ordinary English form, & there is no doubt that it is so. Correction into *muslim* is to be deprecated ; see DIDACTICISM. *M.* can be used as adjective or as noun, & the plural of the noun is preferably *-ms*, but sometimes the same as the singular ; the use of the plural *moslemin* or *muslimin* is bad didacticism. See also MUSSULMAN.

mosquito. Pl. *-os* ; see -O(E)S 6.

-most. The commoner words with this ending are best pronounced *-ost*, not *-ōst*, though mistaken effort is often expended on satisfying the supposed demands of the spelling. The origin was not the word *most*, but a double superlative suffix *-mest*, & it is not unlikely that the ordinary colloquial pronunciation records this fact. *Foremost, innermost, uppermost, topmost, inmost, utmost, hindermost*, are examples of the words in which the obscure *o* is better than the clear *ō*.

most(ly). *The internecine conflict*

has largely killed sentiment for any of the factions, & the Powers mostly concerned have simply looked on with a determination to localize the fighting. The only idiomatic sense of *mostly* is for the most part (*The goods are mostly sent abroad.*/*Twenty-seven millions, mostly fools*). But it is often wrongly used for *most*, as in the quotation; see UNIDIOMATIC -LY.

mot. See FRENCH WORDS. *The mot juste* is a pet LITERARY CRITICS' WORD, which readers would like to buy of them as one buys one's neighbour's bantam cock for the sake of hearing its voice no more. It has the disadvantage that you can find it, if you want to know more about it, neither in French dictionaries (at any rate, not in *Littré*) nor in English, & must be content to associate it vaguely with Flaubert. Yet, after meeting it in such a passage as the following, where the *m. j.* seems a trifle long, one does feel a curiosity about its meaning :— *The epitaph which she wrote for herself at an early age contains the* mot juste: ' *Here lies Sylvia Scarlett, who was always running away. If she has to live all over again & be the same girl, she accepts no responsibility for anything that may occur* '.

moth. The collective use of *moth* in the senses of moths or the moth or the ravages of moths (*furs harbour moth* ; *moth is the most destructive of these* ; *proof against moth* ; *to prevent moth*) is neither defined nor illustrated in the OED, but has at least a colloquial currency. The well-known Bible passages, however, on which this use is perhaps based, cannot in fact be quoted in defence of it, since in all of them the word may be taken in the ordinary sense, if one supposes the rhetorical omission of the article that is common enough in paired or contrasted phrases (*eye hath not seen, nor ear heard*), which has no resemblance to the examples of *moth* given above. The Bible words meant are : *where*

moth & rust doth corrupt ; where neither moth nor rust doth corrupt ; where no thief approacheth, neither moth corrupteth.

mother. For *the M. of Parliaments*, see SOBRIQUETS.

mother-of-pearl, -o'-pearl. The dictionaries favour the *of* form ; the other gives the usual pronunciation, & perhaps is what most people would print if the compositors would let them.

moths. For pronunciation see -TH & -DH.

motif. See FRENCH WORDS.

motive. *The victorious party has every motive in claiming that it is acting not against the Constitution, but in its defence. An* or *every interest in doing*, but *a* or *every motive for doing*. See ANALOGY, & CAST-IRON IDIOM.

motley, n. Pl. *-eys.*

motto. For synonymy, see SIGN. Pl. *-oes*, see -O(E)S 1 ; adj. *motto'd*, see -ED & 'D.

moujik, muzhik. Pronounce moō'-zhĭk. The first is the established form, & correction to the second does no-one any good & perplexes those who have just come to know what the old word means ; see DIDACTICISM.

mould. The three common words so spelt (shape n. & vb ; earth ; fungous growth) are probably all unconnected ; but the identity of form has no doubt caused the second to be tinged with the meaning of the third, & the original notion of powdery earth has had associated with it the extraneous one of rottenness. See TRUE & FALSE ETYMOLOGY.

mount, vb. For *mounted men* &c., see INTRANSITIVE P.P.

mouse. Pronounce the noun -s, the verb & its agent-noun -z(er). *M.* makes *mousy*, not *-sey* ; see -EY & -Y.

mousseline. See FRENCH WORDS.

mouth. Pronounce the verb, & the pl. of the noun, with -dh, *foul-*

mouthed &c. -dhd, & *mouthy* -dhǐ ;
see -TH & -DH.

mouthful. Pl. *-ls* ; see -FUL.

move makes *-vable*, not *-veable* ; see
MUTE E.

mow, stack or cock. Pron. mow.

mow, grimace. Pron. mow or mō.

mow, vb. The p.p., when used as
an adjective, should be *mown* (*the
mown*, not *mowed, grass* ; *new-
mown* &c.) ; when it is verbal, both
forms are current (*the lawn was
mown*, or *mowed, yesterday*).

M.P. Four forms are wanted :
ordinary singular, ordinary plural,
possessive singular, & possessive
plural. They are easily supplied :
M.P. (*He is an M.P.*) ; M.P.s (*M.P.s
now travel free*) ; M.P.'s (*What is
your M.P.'s name ?*) ; M.P.s' (*What
about income tax & M.P.s' salaries?*).
The following newspaper extract
contains two of the parts, but represents them both by the same form,
& that one belonging to another :

M.P.'S *PIGEON RACE*

A pigeon race, organized by M.P.'s,
took place on Saturday. Read (1)
M.P.S', (2) M.P.s.

Mr, Mrs. See PERIOD for the
question whether *Mr & Mrs* or *Mr.
& Mrs.* are better.

much. 1. For the use of *m.* rather
than *very* with participles (*m.
pleased* &c.), see VERY.

2. *M. more* & *m. less.* The adverbs
more, & *less*, are used in combination
with *m.* or *still* to convey that a
statement that is being or has been
made about something already
mentioned applies more forcibly yet
to the thing now to be mentioned :
*The abbreviating, m. more the garbling,
of documents does great harm./
Garbling was not permitted, m. less
encouraged.* The choice between
more & *less* is under some circumstances a matter of difficulty even
for those who are willing to be at
the pains of avoiding illogicality, &
a trap for the unwilling.

With sentences that are affirmative
both in effect & in expression it is

plain sailing ; *m. more* is invariable.
With sentences that are negative in
expression as well as in effect there
is as little doubt ; *m. less* is invariable : *I did not even see him,
m. less shake hands with him.* It is
when the effect is negative, but the
expression affirmative, even if technically affirmative only, that doubts
arise. The meaning of *technically,*
& the distinction between *effect* &
expression must be made clear. *It
will be a year before it is done* ; the
effect of that is negative, since it
means that the thing will *not* be
finished in less than twelve months ;
but its expression is simply affirmative, there being no negative word
in it. *It is not possible to do it under
a year* ; the effect & the expression
of that are obviously both negative.
It is impossible to do it under a year ;
the effect of that is negative, but the
expression is technically affirmative.
Though the difference in meaning
between the last two is undiscover-
able, the difference of expression
decides between *more & less* : *It is
not possible to do it under a year*,
m. less *in six months* ; *It is impossible to do it under a year*, m. more
in six months. What governs the
decision is the right words required
to fill up the ellipsis : *It is not
possible to do it under a year, much
——— ?* (*is it possible to do it*) *in six
months* ; *It is impossible to do it
under a year, much ——— ?* (*is it
impossible*) *to do it in six months.*

Careless writers make the mistake
of letting the general effect run away
with them instead of considering the
expression. In the example that has
just been worked out the fault is
a slight one, because the wrong
filling up of the ellipsis with changed
words (*is it possible* instead of *is it
impossible*) is so easy as to seem to
the reader not less natural than to
the writer. In less simple examples
the fault is much more glaring. In
all the following quotations *more*
should have been written instead of
less :—

It is a full day's work even to open,

m. less *to acknowledge, all the pre-sents, the letters, & the telegrams, which arrive on these occasions.* The (concealed) negative effect is : *You could not open them under a day* ; but the expression is, more than tech-nically, affirmative, & the words to be supplied are *is it a full day's work./The machine must be crushed before any real reforms can be initiated,* m. less *carried.* Negative effect : *You cannot initiate till the machine is crushed.* Expression, fully affirmative./*But of real inven-tion & spontaneity,* m. less *anything approaching what might be classed as inspiration, there is little enough.* Expression technically affirmative./*It would be impossible for any ruler in these circumstances,* m. less *a ruler who was convinced of his own in-fallibility, to guide the destinies of an empire.* Supply *would it be im-possible for* before choosing between *more & less./I confess myself altogether unable to formulate such a principle,* m. less *to prove it.* Supply *unable.*

M. less, where *m. more* is required, is in fact so common that it must be classed among the STURDY INDE-FENSIBLES.

muchly. See WORN-OUT HUMOUR.
mucilage, gum. See FORMAL WORDS.
mucous, -cus. The first is the adjective, the second the noun ; *mucous membrane.*
mud. *Mud pie* or *mudpie,* not *mud-pie* ; see HYPHENS.
mudir, muezzin. Pronounce mōō-dēr', mōōĕ'zĭn.
Mughal. See MOGUL.
mugwump, highbrow. As many of us are uncertain whether these American words mean the same or different things, the following de-finitions are extracted from the *Standard Dictionary* :—
Mugwump: A chief among the Algonkian Indians ; A conceited or self-consequential person ; A voter identified more particularly with one party but claiming the right to vote with another party.

Highbrow : A person observed or imagined to take a superior attitude toward the generality of mankind ; Any person of the intellectual classes.

Muhammad(an). See MAHOMET.
mulatto. Pl. *-os* ; see -O(E)S 6.
mulatto & other words of race mixture.
1. *M., halfbreed, halfcaste, Eurasian, hybrid,* & *mongrel,* all denote in-dividuals of mixed race, but each has a more special application from or to which it has been widened or narrowed. These are : *m.,* white & negro ; *halfbreed,* American-Indian & white or negro ; *halfcaste,* Euro-pean & East-Indian ; *Eurasian,* European & East-Indian ; *hybrid,* cross-bred plant or animal ; *mon-grel,* cross-bred dog.
2. *M., quadroon, octoroon.* The first is the offspring of a white & a negro (or other completely non-white person) ; the second that of a white & a mulatto, having a quar-ter negro (&c.) blood ; the third that of a white & a quadroon, having an eighth negro (&c.) blood.
3. *Creole* does not imply mixture of race, but denotes a person either of European or (now rarely) of negro descent born & naturalized in certain West-Indian & American countries.
4. *East-Indian, halfcaste, Eurasian, Anglo-Indian,* are all sometimes used of persons whose descent is partly European or British & partly Indian. That is the proper sense of *halfcaste* & *Eurasian,* the latter being a polite substitute for the former. *East-Indian* would more properly mean (as it was used in 1 above) a full native of India, in contrast with *American-Indian,* but is not common in that sense ; it was formerly what *Eurasian* is now, the escape from *halfcaste.* *Anglo-Indian,* again, would properly mean a halfcaste, & is now sometimes preferred in that sense to *Eurasian* as a further step in politeness ; but its traditional meaning, confusion

with which accounts for its being preferred, is an Englishman who has spent most of his life in India.

mule makes *mulish*.

muleteer. So spelt; three syllables.

mullah, moollah. The OED treats the first as the standard form.

multiply. For inflexions see VERBS IN -IE, -Y, -YE, 6.

Mumbo Jumbo. Pl. *Mumbo Jumbos* ; see -O(E)S 3.

mummify. For inflexions see VERBS IN -IE, -Y, -YE, 6.

mummy, mother. So spelt ; see -EY, -IE, -Y.

mumps. Usually treated as singular ; see PLURAL ANOMALIES.

Munchausen. The OED pronounces -chawzn.

murderess. See FEMININE DESIGNATIONS.

murex. For pl., see -EX, -IX.

MUSES. The nine were daughters of Zeus & Mnemosyne (-ŏ'zĭnē), Memory. Their names & provinces are :—*Clio*, history ; *Melpomene* (-ŏ'mĭnĭ), tragedy ; *Thalia* (-ĭ'a), comedy ; *Euterpe* (-pĭ), music ; *Terpsichore* (-ĭ'korĭ), dance ; *Erato* (ĕ'ra-), lyric ; *Calliope* (-ĭ'opĭ), epic ; *Urania*, astronomy ; *Polyhymnia*, rhetoric.

museum. Pl. *-ms* ; see -UM.

muslim. See MOSLEM.

muslin makes *-lined*; see -N-, -NN-.

mussel, bivalve. So spelt.

mussulman. Pl. *-ans*, not *-en*, the last syllable not being the English word *man*. It is perhaps to impartial dislike of the incorrect *-men* & the queer *-mans* that the comparative disuse of *m*. is due ; the plural is needed at least as often as the singular, & MAHOMETAN, *Mohammedan*, & MOSLEM, being resorted to for the plural, get the preference in the singular also.

must) (need. The following questions with their positive & negative answers illustrate a point of idiom — *Must it be so ? Yes, it must ; No, it need not./Need I do it ? No, you need not ; Yes, you must.*

mustachio. Pl. *-os*, see -O(E)S 4. *M.* is now archaic for *moustache*, but the adjective derived from it is often preferred to the other ; spell *mustachio'd*, see -ED & 'D.

muster. *Dental treatment was also kept very prominently before their consideration, so that, at the time of the Armistice, the general condition of these women's mouths would pass a very fair muster. M.* in the phrase *pass m.* means an inspection ; & to pass an inspection very fairly is quite a different thing from passing a very fair inspection. *Pass m.* is one of the many idioms that must be taken as they are or left alone.

mute. For the phonetic use, see TECHNICAL TERMS.

MUTE E. Needless uncertainty prevails about the spelling of inflexions & derivatives formed from words ending in mute e. Is this -e to be retained, or omitted ? It is a question that arises in thousands of words, & especially in many that are not separately recorded in the dictionaries, so that the timid speller cannot get it answered in a hurry. It is also one to which different answers are possible ; every dictionary-maker probably thinks that if he were recording all words with an internal-mute-e problem he would answer the question with paternal but arbitrary wisdom for each word ; but he also knows that it would be absurd for him to attempt to give even all those that are likely to be wanted. The need is not for such a gigantic undertaking, but for a rule of the simplest kind & with the fewest exceptions, to deliver us from the present chaos.

To get an idea of the number of words concerned, the reader should consider the following questions, & realize that some of the items stand for thousands, some for hundreds, & some for dozens, of similar cases. Does stale make *staleish* or *stalish* ? love, *loveing* or *loving* ? mile, *mileage* or *milage* ? live, *liveable* or *livable* ? strive, *striveing* or *striving* ? excite,

exciteable or *excitable* ? time, *timeous* or *timous* ? move, *moveable* or *movable* ? like, *likely* or *likly* ? dote, *doteard* or *dotard* ? judge, *judgement* or *judgment* ? hinge, *hingeing* or *hinging* ? singe, *singeing* or *singing* ? gauge, *gaugeable* or *gaugable* ? notice, *noticeable* or *noticable* ? mouse, *mousey* or *mousy* ? change, *changeing* or *changing, changeling* or *changling* ? hie, *hieing* or *hiing* ? glue, *gluey* or *gluy* ? due, *duely* or *duly* ? blue, *blueish* or *bluish* ? whole, *wholely* or *wholly* ? Whether such questions are idle was decided for me, as this article was being written, by the following in an evening paper :—
The almost ungaugable *Forces which make history & forge the destinies of the race will not be hurried.*

The only satisfactory rule, exceptions to which are very few, is this : If the suffix begins with a consonant, the mute e is retained ; if the suffix begins with a vowel, the mute e is dropped. Applying this to the list above, we get (with the wrong results in italics, as a basis for exceptions) : stalish ; loving ; milage ; livable ; striving ; excitable ; timous ; movable ; likely ; dotard ; judgement ; hinging ; *singing* ; *gaugable* ; *noticable* ; mousy ; changing ; *changeling* ; *hiing* ; *gluy* ; *duely* ; bluish ; *wholely*.

The chief exception (*gaugeable, noticeable, singeing*) is that e remains even before a vowel when the soft sound of c or g is to be made possible (as before -*able*) or to be insisted on (as in distinguishing the participles of *singe & sing*). There are no other general exceptions ; *duly, truly, & wholly,* are individual ones merely ; *hieing* is specially so spelt to avoid consecutive *is,* much as *clayey* has an e actually inserted to separate two *ys* ; & *gluey, bluey,* are due to fear that *gluy, bluy,* may be pronounced after *buy & guy.*

For practical purposes, then, a single rule, with a single exception, suffices—stated again below. The only sacrifice involved is that of the power (most arbitrarily & incon-sistently exercised at present) of indicating the sound of an earlier vowel by insertion or omission of the e (*mileage* for fear that *milage* may be pronounced mĭl-). The history of *dispiteous* is perhaps the best comment ; from *despite* came *despitous* (dĭspī'tŭs) ; when the spelling changed to *despiteous* (cf. the recent *lineage,* lĭ'nĭj), the pronunciation changed to dĭspĭ'tĭus (cf. the old-established *lineage,* lĭ'nĭ̆ëj), & out of this came a false association with *piteous,* cutting the word off from its etymology & attaching it to *pity* instead of to *spite.*

RULE

When a suffix is added to a word ending in mute e, the mute e is dropped before a vowel, but not before a consonant.

EXCEPTION

The e is kept even before a vowel if it is needed to preserve or em-phasize the soft sound of a preceding g or c.

EXAMPLES

change, *changeling, changing, changeable* ; singe, *singeing* ; hinge, *hinging* ; trace, *traceable* ; fake, *fakable* ; line, *linage* ; mite, *mity* ; strive, *striving* ; pale, *palish* ; judge, *judgement.*

mutilate makes -*lable,* -*tor* ; see -ABLE 1, -OR.

mutiny. For inflexions see VERBS IN -IE, -Y, -YE, 6.

mutism. So spelt ; see MUTE E.

mutual is a well-known trap. The essence of its meaning is that it involves the relation, *x* is or does to *y* as *y* to *x* ; & not the relation, *x* is or does to *z* as *y* to *z* ; from which it follows that *our mutual friend Jones* (meaning Jones who is your friend as well as mine), & all similar phrases, are misuses of *m.* An example of the mistake, which is very common, is : *On the other hand, if we* [i.e., the Western Powers] *merely sat with our arms folded there would be a peaceful penetration of*

Russia by the country [i.e., Germany] *which was the mutual enemy* [i.e., of both Russia & the Western Powers]. In such places *common* is the right word, & the use of *m.* betrays ignorance of its meaning. It should be added, however, that *m.* was formerly used much more loosely than it now is, & that the OED, giving examples of such looseness, goes no further in condemnation than ' Now regarded as incorrect ', ' Commonly censured as incorrect, but still often used in the collocations *m. friend, m. acquaintance*, on account of the ambiguity of *common*'. The Dickens title has no doubt much to do with the currency of *m. friend.*

Another fault is of a different kind, betraying not ignorance, but lack of the taste or care that should prevent one from saying twice over what it suffices to say once. This happens when *m.* is combined with some part of *each other*, as in : *It is this fraternity of Parliament-men serving a common cause,* mutually comprehending each other's problems & *difficulties, & respecting each other's rights & liberties, which is the foundation of the structure.* It may fairly be said that the sole function of *mutual(ly)* is to give the sense of some part of *each other* when it happens to be hard to get *each other* into one's sentence ; if *each other* not only can be, but is, got in, *m.* is superfluous ; in the quotation it adds nothing whatever, & is the merest tautology.

A few bad specimens follow :—*The ring was mutually chosen by the Duke & Lady Elisabeth last Wednesday./ They have affinities beyond a m. admiration for Mazzini./M. exchange of prisoners./A m. exchange of berthage accommodation at Southampton & Bremen./It involves . . . m. semibankruptcy of employers & employed./ M. quotation of each other.*

For the distinction between *m.* & *reciprocal,* see RECIPROCAL.

muzhik. See MOUJIK.

my. For *my & your work* &c. (not *mine*), see ABSOLUTE POSSESSIVES.

mynheer, mein Herr, Herr. The first is Dutch & can mean gentleman, sir, or Mr ; the second is German for sir ; the third is German for gentleman & Mr.

myriad is generally used of a great but indefinite number ; but it is well to remember that its original sense, still occasionally effective, is ten thousand.

mystic has been much slower than *mysterious* in becoming a popular word & thereby losing its definitely spiritual or occult or theological implications. Everything that puzzles one has long been called mysterious (who committed the latest murder, for instance), but not mystic. It is very desirable that *mystic* should be kept as long as possible from such extension. Unfortunately the NOVELTY-HUNTERS, tired of *mysterious,* have lately got hold of it : *But I don't want to be* mystic, *& you shall hear the facts & judge me afterwards.*

mystifiedly. A bad form ; see -EDLY.

mystify. For inflexions, see VERBS IN -IE, -Y, -YE, 6.

myth is a word introduced into English less than a century ago as a name for a form of story characteristic of primitive peoples & thus defined by the OED : *A purely fictitious narrative usually involving supernatural persons, actions, or events, & embodying some popular idea concerning natural or historical phenomena.* By those who wish to mark their adherence to this original sense the word is still often pronounced mīth. But the meaning popularly attached to the word is little more than a tale devoid of truth or a non-existent person or thing or event ; always in these senses, & usually even in the original one, the pronunciation is mĭth. See POPULARIZED TECHNICALITIES.

mythopoeic, -pœic. See Æ, Œ.

N

n. *To the* n*th*. As a mathematical symbol, *n* means an unspecified number ; it is a dummy occupying a place until its unknown principal comes along, or a masquerader who on throwing off the mask may turn out to be anything. It does not mean an infinite number, nor the greatest possible number, nor necessarily even a large number, but simply the particular number that we may find ourselves concerned with when we come to details ; it is short for ' one or two or three or whatever the number may be '. It follows that the common use of *to the* n*th* for to the utmost possible extent (*The Neapolitan is an Italian to the* n*th degree.*/*Minerva was starched to the* n*th*) is wrong. It is true that sentences can be constructed in which the popular & the mathematical senses are reconciled (*Though the force were increased to the* n*th, it would not avail*), & here, no doubt, the origin of the misuse is to be sought. Those who talk in mathematical language without knowing mathematics go out of their way to exhibit ignorance. See POPULARIZED TECHNICALITIES.

nacrous, nacreous. The first is better.

naiad. Pl. *-ds* or *-des* (pron. -dēz).

naïf. If we were now adopting the French word for the first time, & were proposing not to distinguish between masculine & feminine, but to choose either *-f* or *-ve* for all uses, something might be said for the masculine form (in spite of *pensive, effective*, &c.) as being the French word before inflexion. But both forms have been with us for centuries representing both genders, & it is undeniable that *naïve* is now the prevalent spelling, & the use of *naïf* (either in all contexts or whenever the gender is not conspicuously feminine) a conscious correction of other people's supposed errors. Such corrections are pe-dantic when they are needless ; on the needlessness of correcting established mis-spellings of foreign words, see MORALE.

nail. *Hit the* (*right*) n. *on the head.* It is clear from the OED quotations that *right*, which blunts the point by dividing it into two, is a modern insertion ; all the quotations up to 1700 are without it, & all after 1700 have it ; it is better omitted.

naïve, naïveté, naive, naivety. The slowness with which the naturalization of the words has proceeded is curious & regrettable. For it will hardly be denied that they deserve a warm welcome as supplying a shade of meaning not provided by the nearest single English words. The OED definition, for instance, ' Natural, unaffected, simple, artless ', clearly omits elements—the actor's unconsciousness & the observer's amusement—that are essential to the ordinary man's idea of naïveté. Unconsciously & amusingly simple ; *naïve* means not less than that, & is therefore a valuable word : but, as long as the majority of Englishmen are kept shy of it by what is to them queer spelling & pronunciation, its value will not be exploited. The difficulty is rather with the noun than with the adjective ; many by this time write *naïve*, & many call it nāv ; but *naivety*, though it was used by Hume & other 18th-century writers, has not yet made much headway against *naïveté* ; till it wins, these potentially useful words will be very much wasted.

name makes *namable* ; see MUTE E.

name-part. *Title-rôle* is the established word ; what is the matter with it ? See NOVELTY-HUNTING.

naphtha. So spelt. Pronounce năf-, not năp-.

napkin should be preferred to SERVIETTE.

narcissus. Pl. *-ssuses* or *-ssī*.

narcosis. Pl. *-oses* (-ōsēz).

narghile. Pron. -gĭlĭ.

narrate makes -table, -tor ; see -ABLE 1, -OR.

narratress. See FEMININE DESIGNATIONS.

nasal. For n. organ see PEDANTIC HUMOUR. For the phonetic sense see TECHNICAL TERMS.

nath(e)less. The OED puts first the spelling natheless & the pronunciation nă'thlĭs.

nationalize, naturalize, make -zable ; see MUTE E.

nature. 1. Periphrasis. The word is a favourite with the lazy writers who prefer glibness & length to conciseness & vigour. *The accident was caused through the dangerous nature of the spot, the hidden character of the by-road, & the utter absence of any warning or danger-signal.* The other way of putting this would be The accident happened because the spot was dangerous, the by-road hidden, & no warning given./ *It must not be supposed that when we speak of Mr Balfour as unwilling to snatch at office we are suggesting any feeling of a converse nature in Mr Asquith.* ‘Any feeling of a converse nature’ means the converse (or rather, perhaps, the opposite) feeling./It is true that *nature* slips readily off the tongue or pen in such contexts, but the temptation should be resisted ; see PERIPHRASIS.

2. *One touch of nature makes the whole world kin.* What Shakspere meant was : There is a certain tendency natural to us all, viz that specified in the following lines (*Troilus & Cressida*, III. iii. 176–9), which is, so far as one word may express it, fickleness. What is meant by those who quote him is : A thing that appeals to simple emotions evokes a wonderfully wide response ; this is both true & important ; but to choose for the expression of it words by which Shakspere meant nothing of the kind is unfair both to him & to it. That the first words of a cynicism appropriately put in the mouth of the Shaksperian Ulysses should be

the stock quotation for the power of sympathy is an odd reversal.

naught, nought. The variation of spelling is not a modern accident, but descends from Old English. The distinction, however, now usually observed between the senses borne by each form is a matter of convenience only, & by no means universally recognized. This distinction is that *nought* is simply the name of the cipher 0, while the archaic, poetic, & rhetorical uses in which the word is substituted for *nothing* in any other than the arithmetical sense now prefer *naught* :— *one, nought, nought, one* ; *noughts & crosses* ; *bring* or *come to*, or *set at*, *naught* ; *availeth naught* ; *give all for naught*.

nautilus. Pl. -lī.

navigate makes -gable ; see -ABLE.

navy. For n. & army, see ARMY.

near(ly). The use of *near* in the sense of *nearly* (*Not near so often* ; *near dead with fright* ; *near a century ago*) has been so far affected by the vague impression that adverbs must end in *ly* as to be obsolescent ; see UNIDIOMATIC -LY for other words in which the process has not gone so far. Those who still say *near* for *nearly* are suspected, if provincialism & ignorance are both out of the question, of pedantry ; it is a matter in which it is wise to bow to the majority.

nebula. Pl. -lae.

necessarian. See NECESSITARIAN.

necessary. For *essential*, *n.*, & *requisite*, see ESSENTIAL.

necess(it)arian. The existence of two forms of a word, unless they are utilized for differentiation, is inconvenient, putting those who are not thoroughly familiar with the matter to the needless pains of finding out whether the two do in fact stand for different things or for the same. It would therefore be well if one of this pair could be allowed to lapse. There is no valid objection to the formation of either ; but *neces-*

sitarian is the better word, (1) as having a less un-English or a somehow more acceptable sound, (2) because its obvious connexion with *necessity* rather than with *necessary* makes the meaning plainer, & (3) as being already the more usual word. *Necessarian* should be regarded as a NEEDLESS VARIANT.

nectar has kept the word-makers busy in search of its adjective ; *nectareal, nectarean, nectared, nectareous, nectarian, nectariferous, nectarine, nectarious, & nectarous*, have all been given a chance. Milton, with *nectared, nectarine, & nectarous*, keeps clear of the four-syllabled forms in which the accent is drawn away from the significant part ; & we might do worse than let him decide for us.

need. *He seems to think that the Peronne bridge-head was abandoned earlier than need have been./It was assumed that Marshal Foch's reserves & army of manœuvre had been used up and need no longer to be taken into account as a uniform, effective body.* These extracts suffice to show that lapses in grammar or idiom may occur with *need*. The first looks like some confusion between the verb & the noun *need* ; at least the two right ways of putting it would be (a) *earlier than it* (i.e. the bridge-head) *need have been* (sc. abandoned), where *need* is the verb, & (b) *earlier than need was* (sc. to abandon it), where *need* is the noun.

With uncertainties whether *need* is a noun or a verb, whether *needs* is a verb or a plural noun or an adverb, & what relation is borne to the verbal *needs & needed* by the abnormal *need* often substituted for them, there are certain difficulties. The writer of the second extract has missed the point of idiom that, while *needs & needed* are ordinary verbs followed by infinitive with *to*, the abnormal *need* is treated as a mere auxiliary, like *must*, requiring no *to* ; the reserves *needed no longer to be taken*, or *did not need any*

longer to be taken, but *need no longer be taken, into account.* The rules for the use of *need* instead of *needs & needed* are :—It is used only in interrogative & negative sentences ; in such sentences it is more idiomatic than the normal forms, which are however permissible ; if *need* is preferred, it is followed by infinitive without *to*, but *needs & needed* require *to* before their infinitive. Idiomatic form, *They need not be counted* ; normal form, *They did not need to be counted*, or *They needed not to be counted* ; wrong forms, *They need not to be counted, They needed not* (or *did not need*) *be counted*.

needle. *A n. in a bottle of hay* is the right wording, *bottle* being an old word, now dialectal only, for bundle ; it is often mistaken for a mistake, & changed to *bundle of hay* or *haystack*.

needleful. Pl. *needlefuls* ; see -FUL.

NEEDLESS VARIANTS. Though it savours of presumption for any individual to label words needless, it is certain that words deserving the label exist ; the question is which they are, & who is the censor that shall disfranchise them. Every dictionary-maker would be grateful to an Academy that should draw up an index expurgatorius & relieve him of the task of recording rubbish. There is no such body, & the dictionary-maker must content himself with recognizing, many many years after the event for fear he should be precipitate, that a word here & there is dead, aware the while that he is helping hundreds of others to linger on useless by advertising them once more. Natural selection does operate, in the worlds of talk & literature ; but the dictionaries inevitably lag behind. It is perhaps, then, rather a duty than a piece of presumption for those who have had experience in word-judging to take any opportunity, when they are not engaged in actual dictionary-making, of helping things on by irresponsible expressions of opinion. In this book, therefore, reference is made regarding many words that either are or ought to be dead, but have not yet been buried, to the present article or to that called SUPERFLUOUS WORDS. Those only belong here which can be considered by-forms differing merely in suffix or in some such minor point from other words of the same stem & meaning. Sometimes the mere reference has been thought sufficient ; more often short remarks are added qualifying or explaining the particular condemnation ; an incomplete list of these references is given below to enable the reader to examine details. Here the general principle may profitably be laid down that it is a source not of strength, but of weakness, that there should be two names for the same thing, because the reasonable assumption is that two words mean two things, & confusion results when they do not. On the other hand, it may be much too hastily assumed that two words do mean the same thing ; they may, for instance, denote the same object without meaning the same thing if they imply that the aspect from which it is regarded is different, or are appropriate in different mouths, or differ in rhythmic value or in some other matter that may escape a cursory examination. To take an example or two : it is hard to see why *necessarian* & *necessitarian*, or *hydrocephalic* & *hydrocephalous*, should coexist & puzzle us to no purpose by coexisting ; but *correctitude* by the side of *correctness* had once, if it has not now, a real value, since it was expressly made to suggest by its sound *conscious rectitude* & so present correctness in an invidious light ; again, it would be rash to decide that *dissimulate* was a needless variant for *dissemble* on the grounds that it means the same & is less used & less clearly English, without thinking long enough over it to remember that *simulate & dis-*

simulation have a right to be heard on the question.

Some of the words under which reference to this article is made (not always concerning the title-word itself) :—acquaintanceship, askant, blithesome, bumble - bee, burden, -cephalic, chivalry, cithern, competence, complacence, concernment, concomitance, corpulence, correctitude, covert *n.*, debark, depicture, diminishment, direful, disgustful, dismission, dissemble, infinitude, necessitarian, quieten.

ne'er-do-weel, ne'er-do-well. The Scotch spelling is recommended. The OED's remark is : ' The word being of northern & Sc. origin, the form *-weel* is freq. employed even by southern writers '.

negative. ' The answer is in the negative ' is Parliament language, but deserves much severer condemnation (as a pompous PERIPHRASIS for No, sir) than most of the expressions described as unparliamentary language.

NEGATIVE & AFFIRMATIVE IN PARALLEL CLAUSES. Of actual blunders, as distinguished from lapses of taste & style, perhaps the commonest, & those that afflict their author when he is detected with the least sense of proper shame, are various mishandlings of negatives. Writers who appear educated enough to know whether a sentence is right or wrong will put down the opposite of what they mean, or something different from what they mean, or what means nothing at all, apparently quite satisfied so long as the reader can be trusted to make a shrewd guess at what they ought to have said instead of taking them at their word ; to his possible grammatical sensibilities they pay no heed whatever, having none themselves. It is parallel clauses that especially provide opportunities for going wrong, the problem being to secure that if both are negative the negative force shall not be dammed up in one alone, & conversely that if one only is to be negative the negative force shall not be free to spill over into the other. Some classified specimens of failure to secure these essentials may put writers on their guard ; the corrections appended are designed rather as proofs of the error than as satisfactory, or at any rate as the best, emendations.

1. If you start with a negative subject you may forget on reaching the second clause to indicate that the subject is not negative there also :—No lots *will therefore be put on one side for another attempt to reach a better price*, but must *be sold on the day appointed* (but all must be sold)./No nation *which is given a tract of territory by the Conference will want the decision to be set aside*, or will consider *it an injustice if it is set aside* (any such nation will at least consider)./[During a Paris air-raid] Very few people *even got out of bed*, & went *through their ordeal by fire as an inescapable fate* (& the majority went)./*English mines were laid in the Cattegat*, but none were laid *at a depth of less than thirty-five feet*, & were *consequently not dangerous to commerce* (& they were)./Neither editor nor contributors *are paid*, but are moved *to give their services by an appreciation of the good work* (but all are).

2. You may use negative inversion in the first clause, & forget that the second clause will then require to be given a subject of its own because the inversion has imprisoned the original subject :—Nor does he refer *to Hubrecht's or Gaskell's theories*, & dismisses *the paleontological evidence in rather a cavalier fashion* (& he dismisses)./*Not only* was Lord Curzon's Partition detested *by the people concerned*, but was *administratively bad* (it was)./*In neither case* is this due *to the Labour Party*, but to *local Socialist aspirations* (This is due in neither case).

3. Intending two negative clauses, you may enclose your negative between an auxiliary & its verb in

the first & forget that it cannot then act outside its enclosure in the second :—*There is scarcely a big hotel, a brewery company, or a large manufactory, which* has not sunk *a well deep into the London chalk &* is drawing *its own supply of water from the vast store* (& succeeded in drawing ; if *has* continues, *not* does so with it)./*No scheme run by Civil Servants sitting in a London office is likely to succeed if these gentlemen* have not themselves lived *on the land*, & by experience are able *to appreciate actual conditions of agriculture* (& learnt to appreciate).

4. Conversely, intending a negative & an affirmative clause, you may so fuse your negative with a construction common to both clauses that it carries on to the second clause when not wanted :—*These statements* do not seem *well weighed*, & to savour *of the catchword* (& savour—cutting the connexion with *do not seem*)./*If the Colonial Secretary* is not going *to use his reserve powers when trial by jury breaks down*, & to acquiesce *in the view that no consequences need follow when a settler shoots a native for stealing a sheep, he may as well give up the business of governing altogether* (& acquiesces—cutting the connexion with *is not going*).

5. You may negative in your first clause a word that when supplied without the negative in the second fails to do the work you expect of it :—*To raise the standard of life of the many* it is not sufficient *to divide the riches of the few* but also to produce *in greater quantities the goods required by all* (it is also necessary to produce).

6. You may so misplace the negative that it applies to what is common to both clauses instead of, as was intended, to what is peculiar to one :—*It* is not expected *that to-morrow's speech will deal with peace*, but will be confined *to a general survey of* . . . (It is expected . . . will not deal).

7. You may treat a double negative expression as though it were formally as well as virtually a positive one :—*It would* not be difficult *to quarrel with Mr Rowley's views about art*, but not with *Charles Rowley himself* (It would be easy)./*He has cast about for &* neglected no *device chemical or mechanical that might add to his ability* (& tried every device).

NEGATIVES. It has been mentioned in the preceding article, which is directed against the most insidious form of the danger, that blunders with negatives are extraordinarily frequent. Such blunders require only care for their avoidance, to be conscious of the danger is enough to induce that care, & those who would realize the danger may easily do so. Abundant illustrations of it will be found in the articles on NEITHER, NO, NOR, NOT, NOTHING LESS THAN, & NEGATIVE & AFFIRMATIVE IN PARALLEL CLAUSES. For those who do not care for the trouble of turning up special articles, nor require detailed discussion, a few miscellaneous specimens are here collected without comment :—*Were it not for its liking for game eggs, the badger* could not but be considered other *than a harmless animal*./*Sir Willoughby is one of the staunchest of Liberals ; his defeat in North St Pancras at the General Election was* hardly less creditable *to the electors than his rejection at the L.C.C. election some years ago*./*When the boys come home the old club will start again ; in the meantime who* shall deny *that the ' Muddied Oafs '* have not *made good ?*/*Manifestly we can grant no armistice while they occupy French or Belgian territory*, or *delude ourselves into thinking that a League of Nations is possible while . . .*/*To consider & report whether the Council should not discontinue altogether the direct management of the service & should dispose of or lease the boats, piers, & plant.*/*No rival is* too small to be overlooked, *no device is* too infamous not to be practised, *if it will . . .*/*Not

a whit undeterred *by the disaster which overtook them last week*./*Is it* quite inconceivable *that if the smitten had always turned the other cheek the smiters* would not long since have *become so ashamed that . . ?*/*I do not think it is possible that the traditions & doctrines of these two institutions should* not fail to create *rival schools*./*But it would not be at all surprising if, by attempting too much*, Mr Sichel has not *to some extent defeated his own object*./*How can Mr Balfour tell* but that *two years hence* he may not be too tired *of official life to begin any new conflict ?*/*They could* hardly fail to regard it as anything but *an expression of want of confidence in our whole South-African policy*./*No age can see itself in a proper perspective*, & is *therefore incapable of giving its virtues & vices their relative places*.

négligé. So spelt & accented.

negligible, -geable. The first spelling is better ; cf. *incorrigible, dirigible*. The prevalence at one time of *-geable* is perhaps explained by the word's having been familiarized chiefly in the translated or untranslated French phrase *quantité négligeable*.

negotiate makes *-tiable, -tor* ; see -ABLE 1, -OR. The use of the verb in its improper sense of tackle successfully is comparable in faded jocularity with the similar use of *individual* (see also MATERIALIZE), & stamps a writer as literarily a barbarian. Novelty is what makes such misuses attractive, & when the novelty is gone people of sense discard them. See also POLYSYLLABIC HUMOUR.

negro, negrillo, negrito. Pl. *negroes*, but *negrillos & negritos* ; see -O(E)S 1, 6.

neighbourhood. *In the n. of* (e.g. £100) for *about* is a repulsive combination of POLYSYLLABIC HUMOUR & PERIPHRASIS.

neither. 1. Pronunciation. 2. Meaning. 3. Number of the pronoun & adjective. 4. Number & person of verb after *neither . . . nor.* 5. Position of *neither . . . nor.* 6. *Neither . . . or.* 7. *Neither* as conjunction. 8. *Neither* pleonastic.

1. The pronunciation recommended is nī′dher ; see EITHER.

2. The proper sense of the pronoun (or adjective) is ' not the one nor the other of the two '. Like *either*, it sometimes refers loosely to numbers greater than two (*Heat, light, electricity, magnetism, are all correlatives;* neither *can be said to be the essential cause of the others*) ; but *none* or *no* should be preferred ; cf. EITHER 3. This restriction to two does not hold for the adverb (*Neither fish nor flesh nor fowl*).

3. The number of the adjective & pronoun is properly singular, & disregard of this fact is a recognized grammatical mistake, though, with the pronoun at least, very common :—*The conception is faulty for two reasons, neither of which* are *noticed by Plato./What at present I believe neither of us know* ; grammar requires *is noticed,* & *knows.* The same mistake with the adjective is so obviously wrong as to be almost impossible ; not quite, however : *Both Sir Harry Verney & Mr Gladstone were very brief,* neither speeches *exceeding fifteen minutes.* An almost equally incredible freak with the pronoun is : *Lord Hothfield & Lord Reay were born the one in Paris & the other at The Hague, neither being British* subjects *at the time of his birth* (as indeed neither could be unless he were twins).

4. Number & person after *neither . . . nor.* If both subjects are singular & in the third person, the only need is to remember that the verb must be singular & not plural. This is often forgotten ; the OED quotes, from Johnson, *Neither search nor labour* are *necessary,* &, from Ruskin, *Neither painting nor fighting* feed *men,* where *is* & *feeds* are undoubtedly required. The right course is not to indulge in bad grammar ourselves & then plead that better men

like Johnson & Ruskin have done it before us, but to follow what is now the accepted as well as the logical rule. Complications occur when, owing to a difference in number or person between the subject of the *neither* member & that of the *nor* member, the same verbform or pronoun or possessive adjective does not fit both : Neither you nor I (was ?, were ?) chosen ; Neither you nor I (is ?, am ?, are ?) the right person ; Neither eyes nor nose (does its ?, do their ?) work ; Neither employer nor hands will say what (they want ?, he wants ?). The wise man, in writing, evades these problems by rejecting all the alternatives—any of which may set up friction between him & his reader—& putting the thing in some other shape ; & in speaking, which does not allow time for paraphrase, he takes risks with equanimity & says what instinct dictates. But, as instinct is directed largely by habit, it is well to eschew habitually the clearly wrong forms (such as *Neither chapter nor verse* are *given*) & the clearly provocative ones (such as *Neither husband nor wife is competent to act without* his *consort*). About the following, which are actual newspaper extracts, neither grammarians nor laymen will be unanimous in approving or disapproving the preference of *is* to *are* or of *has* to *have* ; but there will be a good majority for the opinion that both writers are grammatically more valorous than discreet :—*Neither apprenticeship* systems *nor technical education* is *likely to influence these occupations* (why not have omitted *systems ?*)./*Neither Captain C. nor I* has *ever thought it necessary to . . .* (Neither to Captain C. nor to me has it ever seemed . . .).

5. Position of *neither . . . nor. Which neither suits one purpose nor the other. Suits* being common to both members should not be inserted in the middle of the *neither* member. Such displacement has been discussed & illustrated under

EITHER 5, & need only be mentioned here as a mistake to be avoided.

6. *Neither . . . or.* When a negative has preceded, a question often arises between *nor* & *or* as the right continuation, & the answer to the question sometimes requires care; see NOR, OR. But when the preceding negative is *neither* (adv.), the matter is simple, *or* being always wrong. Examples of the mistake: *Diderot presented a bouquet which was neither well or ill received./Like the Persian noble of old, I ask 'that I may neither command or obey'.* Here again, to say that Morley & Emerson have sinned before us is a plea not worth entering.

7. *Neither* alone as conjunction. This use, in which *neither* means ' nor yet ', or ' & moreover . . . not ', & connects sentences instead of the ordinary *& not* or *nor* (*I have not asked for help, neither do I desire it*; *Defendant had agreed not to interfere, neither did he*) is much less common than it was, & is best reserved for contexts of formal tone.

8. *Neither* with the negative force pleonastic, as in *I don't know that neither* (instead of *either*), was formerly idiomatic though colloquial, but is now archaic & affected.

Nelly, or Nellie; see -EY, -IE, -Y.

nepenthe(s). Three syllables, whether with or without the -s. The -s is part of the Greek word, & should have been retained in English; but it has very commonly been dropped, probably from being mistaken for the plural sign as in *pea* for *pease* &c. The prevailing form (except in Botany, where the classical word is naturally used) is now *-the.*

Nereid. Pronounce nēr'ĭĭd.

Nero. Pl. *-os*, see -O(E)S 8.

nervy. So spelt; see -EY & -Y.

-ness. For the distinction between *conciseness* & *concision*, & similar pairs, see -ION & -NESS.

nestle, nestling. Pronounce without the -t-; see PRONUNCIATION, Silent t.

net. In the commercial sense (free from deduction, &c.) the spelling should, as elsewhere, be *net*, not *nett.* See SET(T).

nether. For *n. garments, n. man,* &c., see PEDANTIC HUMOUR.

neurasthenia. The OED gives -thē-, not -thĕ-. See FALSE QUANTITY.

neuroma. Pl. *-ata.*

neurosis. Pl. *-oses* (-ēz); see LATIN PLURALS 2.

neuter. See COMMON, & EPICENE, for some distinctions.

neutralize has *-zable*; see MUTE E.

névé. See FRENCH WORDS.

never so, ever so, in conditional clauses (*refuseth to hear the voice of the charmer, charm he never so wisely*). The original phrases, going back to Old English, are *never so*, & *never such.* The change to *ever*, ' substituted from a notion of logical propriety ' (OED), seems to date from the later seventeenth century only, & *never so* is very common in the Bible & Shakspere. *Ever so*, however, is the normal modern form, not *never so*, & it is in vain that attempts are occasionally made to put the clock back & restore *never* in ordinary speech. In poetry, & under circumstances that justify archaism, *never so* is unimpeachable; but in everyday style the purism that insists on it is futile. As to that ' notion of logical propriety ', it was perhaps that there was nothing negative in the sense; there was, however, if ' charm he never so wisely ' is a compressed form of ' charm he so wisely as never else '; we can at least see how the *never* idiom may have arisen; to account for *ever* (except as a mistaken correction of *never*) is a much harder problem. But the modern phrase, explicable or not, & logical or not, is *ever so.*

news. The number varied (*the n. is bad, are bad*) for more than two centuries, but has now settled down permanently as singular.

next. 1. *The n. three* &c. 2. *N. Friday, June,* &c. 3. *N.important* &c.

1. For the question between *the next three* &c. & *the three* &c. *next*, see FIRST 4.

2. *Next June, n. Friday,* &c., can be used as adverbs without a preposition (*Shall begin it next June*); but, if *next* is put after the noun, idiom requires a preposition (*may be expected* in *June next*, on *Monday next*). See FRIDAY.

3. The '*No Surrender*' *party had the rank & file at their back because they fought to the last ditch to save the grandest institution in the country; do they expect support now in wrecking the two* next *important institutions? The two* next *important institutions* is clearly used in the sense 'the two institutions next in importance'. The OED quotes no example of such a use, but it is perhaps not uncommon colloquially, & must be a conscious or unconscious experiment in extending the convenient *next best* idiom. That idiom requires a superlative, & such words as *oldest, worst, narrowest, weightiest*, suit it well; but it is ugly with adjectives having no superlative but that with *most*, & there is a temptation to try whether, for instance, *next important* will not pass for *next most important*. It should be resisted; the natural sense of *the two next important institutions* is 'the two next institutions that are of importance', which need by no means be the two that are next in importance.

nexus. The English plural *nexuses* is intolerably sibilant, & the Latin, *nexus* (-ūs), not *nexi* (see -US), sounds pedantic; the plural is consequently very rare.

nice. 1. *N.* makes *nicish*; see MUTE E.

2. *Nice & as* a sort of adverb = satisfactorily (*I hope it will be n. a. fine*; *Aren't we going n. a. fast?*) is an established colloquialism, but should be confined, in print, to dialogue.

3. Meaning. *N.* has been spoilt, like CLEVER, by its *bonnes fortunes*;

it has been too great a favourite with the ladies, who have charmed out of it all its individuality & converted it into a mere diffuser of vague & mild agreeableness. Everyone who uses it in its more proper senses, which fill most of the space given to it in any dictionary, & avoids the modern one that tends to oust them all, does a real if small service to the language.

Nicene. The name of the place from which the creed is so called is spelt *Nicaea* or *Nicea*, not *Nicoea*.

nic(e)y, sweetmeat. Omit the *e*; see -EY, -IE, -Y.

nickel makes *-lled*; see -LL-, -L-.

nick-nack. See KNICK-KNACK.

nict(it)ate, -ating, -ation. The forms with the extra syllable are the commoner, & those without it are NEEDLESS VARIANTS.

nidus. Pl. *-duses, -di* (-ī).

niello. Pl. *-li* (-ē), *-los*, see -O(E)s 3.

nigger, applied to others than full or partial negroes, is felt as an insult by the person described, & betrays in the speaker, if not deliberate insolence, at least a very arrogant inhumanity.

nighty (night-gown). So spelt; see -EY, -IE, -Y.

nihilism, -ist. Pronounce nī'ĭ-, with the h silent; see PRONUNCIATION.

nimbus. Pl. *-bi* (-ī). For *nimbus(s)ed* see -S-, -SS-.

nineties, 'nine-. See TWENTIES.

nitre, -ter. See -RE & -ER.

nitrify. For inflexions see VERBS IN -IE, -Y, -YE, 6.

-N-, -NN-. Monosyllables ending in n double it before suffixes beginning with vowels if the sound preceding it is a single vowel (a, e, i, o, u, y), but not if it is a diphthong or a double vowel or a vowel & r: *mannish*, but *darning*; *fenny*, but *keener*; *winning*, but *reined*; *conned*, but *coined*; *runner*, but *turned*. Words of more than one syllable follow the rule for monosyllables if their last syllable is accented, but otherwise do not double the n : *japanned* & *beginner*, but *dragoon-ed, womanish, turbaned, awakening, musliny.*

no. 1. Parts of speech. 2. Confusion of adjective & adverb. 3. *No* in negative confusions. 4. Negative parentheses. 5. Writing of compounds. 6. Plural.

1. *No* is (A) an adjective meaning in the singular not a (or not any), & in the plural not any ; it is a shortened form of *none*, which is still used as its pronoun form : *No German applied* ; *No Germans applied* ; *None of the applicants was,* or *were, German.* *No* is (B) an adverb meaning by no amount & used only with comparatives : *I am glad it is no worse.* *No* is (C) an adverb meaning not & used only after *or*, & chiefly in the phrase *whether or no* : *Pleasant or no, it is true* ; *He must do it whether he will or no.* *No* is (D) a particle representing a negative sentence of which the contents are clear from a preceding question or from the context :—*Is he there?—No* (i. e., he is not there). *No, it is too bad* (i. e., I shall not submit ; it is too bad). *No* is (E) a noun meaning the word *no*, a denial or refusal, a negative vote or voter : *Don't say no* ; *She will not take a no* ; *The Noes have it.*

2. Confusion of adjective & adverb. If the tabulation in 1 is correct, it is clear how the worse than superfluous *a, the,* & *her,* made their way into the following extracts. The writer of each thought his *no* was a B or a C adverb, against which the absence of the invariable accompaniments should have warned him, & did not see that it was the adjective, which contains *a* in itself & is therefore incompatible with another *a,* or *the,* or *her.* *We can hardly give the book higher praise than to say of it that it is* a no unworthy companion *of Moberly's ' Atonement '* (Omit *a,* or write *not* for *no*)./*The value of gas taken from the ground there & sold amounted to* the no insignificant

value of *54,000,000 dols* (the not)./ *Paintings by Maud Earl, who owes* her no small reputation *as an artist to the successes which . . .* (her reputation, no small one)./A fourth example is more excusable because the conditions are obscured by the accidental presence of a comparative : *We could ask for* no more cheerful a by-product *of our discontent than a second volume of this most patriotic of Christmas books.* Such a sentence as *The second volume will be no more cheerful a by-product than the first* would be right, *no* being there actually the adverb. But the phrase in its present setting means no by-product that shall be more cheerful, & *no* is the adjective & contains *a* & refuses to have another thrust upon it.

3. *No,* used in the first of two parallel clauses, ensnares many a brave unwary writer ; the modifications necessary for the second clause are forgotten, & bad grammar or bad sense results. See NEGATIVE & AFFIRMATIVE IN PARALLEL CLAUSES ; some specimens are :— *He sees in England* no attempt to *mould history according to academic plans,* but to *direct it from case to case according to necessity* (it is rather directed)./*There is* no reason to suppose *that the Government will accept any vital amendments,* & most certainly not *an amendment to exclude Home Rule* (& it will certainly not accept one)./*Although* no party *has been able to carry its own scheme out,* it *has been strong enough to prevent any other scheme being carried* (each has been)./No place *of any importance,* & a good many *of none at all, are now without their bowling greens* (All places of importance . . . now have).

4. Negative parentheses. The rule here to be insisted on concerns negative expressions in general, & is stated under *no* only because that word happens to be present in violations of it oftener perhaps than any other. The rule is that adverbial qualifications containing a

negative must not, like qualifications that, not being negative, do not so vitally affect the sense, be comma'd off from the words they belong to as though they were mere parentheses. The rule only needs stating to be accepted ; but the habit of providing adverbial phrases with commas often gets the better of common sense. It is clear, however, that there is the same essential absurdity in writing *He will, under no circumstances, consent* as in writing *He will, never, consent,* or *He will, not, consent.* It is worth while to add, for the reader's consideration while he glances at the examples, that it would often be better in these negative adverbial phrases to resolve *no* into *not* . . . *any* &c. *We are assured that the Prime Minister will, in no circumstances & on no consideration whatever, consent* (will not under any . . . or on any . . . Or omit the commas, at the least)./*And Paley & Butler, no more than Voltaire, could give Bagshot one thousandth part of the confidence that he drew from* . . . (could not, any more than . . . Or could no more than Voltaire give)./ *We are, of course, reminded that the doctors, no more than the friendly societies, are completely satisfied* (are not, any more than the societies . . . Or omit the commas)./*Proposals which, under no possible circumstances, would lead to any substantial, or indeed perceptible, protection for a home industry* (which would not lead under any . . . Or which would under no possible circumstances lead).

5. Writing of compounds. About *no ball* (noun) & *no-ball* (verb), *nobody,* & *nohow,* doubts are needless ; the forms given are the right ones. *No one,* on the principles explained in HYPHENS (3b, & 2), should be written either *noone* or *no-one,* since it both has a specialized meaning & has lost its second accent ; *noone* is disqualified by its monosyllabic look ; but there is no objection to *no-one,* & that form is

recommended, with the warning that printers are attached to *no one* ; for fuller discussion, see EVERYONE. The adverbs *noways & nowise* are best so written ; but *in nowise,* which is often used instead of the correct *in no wise,* is as absurd as *by nomeans* or *on no-account* would be ; cf. ANY 1.

6. Pl. *noes* ; see -O(E)S 2.

noblesse. See FRENCH WORDS.

nodus. Pl. -*di* (-ī).

nom-de-guerre, nom-de-plume, pen-name, pseudonym. *Nom-de-guerre* is current French, but, owing to the English currency of *nom-de-plume,* is far from universally intelligible to Englishmen, most of whom assume that, whatever else it may mean, it can surely not mean nom-de-plume. *Nom-de-plume* is open to the criticism that it is ridiculous for English writers to use a French phrase that does not come from France ; not perhaps as ridiculous as the critics think (see MORALE), but fear of them will at any rate deter some of us. Nobody perhaps uses *pen-name* without feeling either ' What a good boy am I to abstain from showing off my French & translate *nom-de-plume* into honest English ! ', or else ' I am not as those publicans who suppose there is such a phrase as *nom-de-plume* '. For everyone is instinctively aware that *pen-name,* however native or naturalized its elements, is no English-bred word, but a translation of *nom-de-plume.* *Pseudonym,* lastly, is a queer out-of-the-way term for an everyday thing. But it is perhaps the best of the bunch except for those who take the commonsense view of *nom-de-plume*—that it is the established word for the thing, & its antecedents do not concern us.

nomad makes -*adic* ; see -D-, -DD-.

nomenclature. The dictionaries that give a list of synonyms with each word do a very doubtful service to literature. One can hardly believe but that the authors of the extracts below have looked up *name* in search of some longer & more imposing word, some (shall we say ?) adequately grandiose vocable. That *nomenclature* does not mean a name, but a system of naming or of names, is to such writers what they would perhaps call a mere meticulosity ; see LOVE OF THE LONG WORD. *The forerunner of the present luxurious establishment was the well-known Gloucester Coffee House, the nomenclature of which was derived from that Duke of Gloucester who . . ./A small committee of City men has just launched a society, under the nomenclature of the ' League of Interpreters', with the object of . . ./The most important race of the season for three-year-old fillies ; the nomenclature was obtained from Lord Derby's seat, ' The Oaks ', in the little hamlet of . . .*

nominal. For this as the adjective of *noun*, see NOUN.

nominate makes *-nable, -tor* ; see -ABLE 1, -OR.

nominatival(ly), -tive(ly). See ABLATIVELY.

nominative. The grammatical word is always pronounced nŏ'mĭnătĭv ; the adjective connected in sense with *nominate* & *nomination* (e.g. in *partly elective & partly n.*) is often, & perhaps more conveniently, nŏ'mĭnātĭv.

nominativus pendens. See TECHNICAL TERMS.

non-. On *non-moral* & *amoral*, see A-, AN-.

non avenu. See FRENCH WORDS.

nonchalant, -ance. Pronounce nŏ'nshalant, *-ans* (i. e. as English words, but with -sh-).

none. 1. It is a mistake to suppose that the pronoun is sing. only & must at all costs be followed by sing. verbs &c. ; the OED explicitly states that pl. construction is commoner. 2. The forms *none so, none too*, are idiomatic (*It is none so pleasant to learn that you have only six months to live ; The look he gave me was none too amiable*), but are perhaps seldom used without a certain sense of condescending to

the vernacular as an aid to heartiness of manner or emphasis ; & condescension is always repellent.

nonentity, in the now rare abstract sense of non-existence, should have the *non* pronounced clearly nŏn, & perhaps be written with a hyphen (*non-entity*). In the current concrete sense of a person or thing of no account, it is written *nonentity* & said with the o obscured (nonĕ'ntĭtĭ).

nonesuch, nonsuch. The first is the original form, but the second the now usual one.

nonet(t)e. Spell *-et* ; see DUET.

nonpareil. Pronounce nŏnparĕ'l.

nonplus makes *-ssed, -ssing,* &c. ; see -S-, -SS-.

non sequitur. See TECHNICAL TERMS.

nonsuch. See NONESUCH.

nor is a word that should come into our minds as we repeat the General Confession. Most of us in our time have left undone those things which we ought to have done (i.e. failed to put in *nor* when it was wanted) & done those things which we ought not to have done (i.e. thrust it in when there was no room for it). The negative forms of *He moves & speaks, He both moves & speaks,* are *He moves not nor speaks, He neither moves nor speaks* ; or, with the verb resolved as usual in modern negative sentences, *He does not move* or *speak, He does not either move* or *speak.* The tendency to go wrong is probably due to confusion between the simple verbs (*moves* &c.) & the resolved ones (*does move* &c.) ; if the verb is resolved, there is often an auxiliary that serves both clauses, &, as the negative is attached to the auxiliary, its force is carried on together with that of the auxiliary & no fresh negative is wanted. Two cautions are necessary on this carrying on of the negative force & consequent preference of *or* to *nor.* The first is that it will not do to repeat the auxiliary & yet use *or* under the impression that the previous negative suffices ; that is what has been done in : *Sir Guy Granet was naturally & properly at pains to prove that his company had not acted negligently or carelessly* or had *been unduly influenced by reasons of economy* (There was a choice here between *or been* & *and had not been*; *or had been* makes nonsense).

The other caution, much more often required, is that if the negative is attached not to an auxiliary (or other word common to two clauses) that will carry it forward, but to some other part of the first clause, the negative force is cut off & has to be started afresh by *nor*. The following five examples illustrate the danger ; in each *or* must be corrected into *nor* if the rest of the sentence is to remain as it is, though some slight change of arrangement such as is indicated would make *or* possible :—*President Wilson has determined that* no troops shall *march*, or *anything resembling a military or naval demonstration be carried out* (that troops shall not march, or)./*In its six months of power it has offered* not one constructive measure or *done a single thing to relieve suffering* (it has not offered one)./*It is* with no unfriendly intention *to Germany* or *with any desire to question her right or her need to possess a powerful Navy* (it is not with any)./*Manifestly we can grant* no armistice *while they occupy French & Belgian territory*, or *delude ourselves into thinking that a League of Nations is possible* (we cannot grant an)./*He did* nothing *without consulting Lovel*, or *failed in anything without expecting & fearing his admonishing* (he did not do anything . . . or fail).

The above are the ordinary types of mistake with *nor*. Others that should hardly require mention are *either . . . nor*, & the poetical omission of the first negative. *Either . . . nor* is as bad as NEITHER . . . *or* ; but : *There was not*, either *in* 1796 *in Italy*, nor *on the Mediterranean coast of Spain in* 1808, *any British*

force at work which . . ./As we have not got the world's tonnage production for April, nor yet either *the British* nor *the world's losses for the same month, it is only possible to . . .*

Do nor undo is legitimate in poetry, but not in prose of so ordinary a kind as : *For her fingers had been so numbed that she* could do nor undo *anything.*

normalcy (= *normality*) is a HYBRID DERIVATIVE of the ' spurious hybrid ' class, & seems to have nothing to recommend it.

north-. Compounds (*n.-east* &c.) are pronounced with th. Of the derivatives, *northern* & *northerly* have dh, but *northward(s)*, *norther*, & *northing*, have th.

northerly. For the special uses & meanings of this set of words, see EASTERLY.

nostril makes (-)*nostrilled*; -LL-, -L-.

nostrum. Pl. *-ums*, not *-a*; -UM.

nosy, nosey. See -EY & -Y IN ADJECTIVES, & -EY, -IE, -Y.

not. 1. *Not all*)(*all . . . not*. 2. *Not* in meiosis & periphrasis. 3. *Not* in exclamations. 4. *Not* pleonastic. 5. *Not . . . but*. 6. *Not only*.

1. *Not all*)(*all . . . not*. *All is not gold that glisters* ; *Every land does not produce everything*. Precisians would rewrite these sentences as *Not all is gold that glisters* (or *Not all that glisters is gold*) & *Not every land produces everything*. The negative belongs logically to *all* & *every*, not to the verbs, & the strict sense of the first proverb would be that glistering proves a substance to be not gold. A valued correspondent writes—' Do not you think that the use of *all . . . not* ought to be restricted to propositions of the type *All A is not-B*, & where *Not all A is B* is meant, that should be the order ? Of course that never has been a rule, from " All of you have not the knowledge of God " onwards, but it would save a great deal of ambiguity if it could be made one. I notice that Somerville & Byrne, in their German Grammar,

with *Nicht alle Menschen sprechen Deutsch* before them, translate it " All men do not speak German ", neglecting the plain guidance of their original '. This gentleman has logic on his side, logic has time on its side, & probably the only thing needed for his gratification is that he should live long enough. The older a language grows, & the more consciously expert its users become, the shorter shrift it & they may be expected to grant to illogicalities & ambiguities. *All . . . not* for *Not all*, like *the two* FIRST for *the first two*, the displacements of BOTH & NEITHER & ONLY, the omission of *not* in *than you can* HELP, & the use of *much* LESS for *much more*, is already denounced by those who have time to spend on niceties ; but it is still, like many other inaccuracies, the natural & idiomatic English ; it will pass away in time, for *magna est veritas et praevalebit* ; in the meantime it is worth anyone's while to get on speaking terms with the new exactitudes (i. e., to write *Not all* himself), but worth nobody's while to fall foul of those who do not choose to abandon the comfortable old slovenries.

2. *Not* in meiosis & periphrasis. ' We say well & elegantly, not ungrateful, for very grateful '—OED quotation dated 1671. It is by this time a faded or jaded elegance, this replacing of a term by the negation of its opposite ; jaded by general over-use ; faded by the blight of WORN-OUT HUMOUR with its *not a hundred miles from*, *not unconnected with*, & other once fresh young phrases. But the very popularity of the idiom in English is proof enough that there is something in it congenial to the English temperament, & it is pleasant to believe that it owes its success with us to a stubborn national dislike of putting things too strongly. It is clear too that there are contexts to which e. g. *not inconsiderable* is more suitable than *considerable* ; by using it we seem to anticipate & put

aside, instead of not foreseeing or ignoring, the possible suggestion that so-&-so is inconsiderable. The right principle is to acknowledge that the idiom is allowable, & then to avoid it except when it is more than allowable. Examples in which their authors would hardly claim that elegance or point was gained by the double negative, & would admit that they used it only because they saw no reason why they should not, occur in every day's newspapers ; such are :—*The style of argument suitable for the election contest is, no doubt,* not infrequently *different from the style of argument suitable for use at Westminster* (often)./*One may imagine that Mr* —— *will* not be altogether unrelieved *when his brother actor returns tomorrow* (will be much relieved).

3. *Not* in exclamations. *But if you look at the story of that quadrilateral of land, what a complex of change & diversity do you* not *discover!* A jumble of question & exclamation. The right exclamation would be : *What a complex you discover !* The possible question would be : *What complexity do you* not *discover ? What* a *complex*, & the stop, are essentially exclamatory : *not* is essentially interrogative ; *do* is characteristically interrogative, but not impossible in exclamations. The forms in a simpler sentence are :—Exclamation : *What I have suffered !* ; Question : *What have I not suffered ?* ; Exclamation with inversion : *What have I suffered !* ; Confusion: *What have I not suffered!* See STOPS (question & exclamation marks).

4. *Not* pleonastic. The point discussed in 3 was the intrusion of a *not,* unnecessary indeed but explicable, into exclamations that are confused with rhetorical questions. Much less excusable, as needing no analysis to show that it is wrong & often destructive of the sense, is the *not* that is evoked in a subordinate clause as a mere unmeaning echo

of an actual or virtual negative in the main sentence. We all know people who habitually say *I shouldn't wonder if it* didn't *turn to snow soon* when they mean *if it turned*. But the same mistake in print is almost as common as it is absurd :—
Nobody can predict with confidence how much time may not *be employed on the concluding stages of the Bill./ Is it impossible to imagine that, in consequence of the growing friendship between the two great peoples on both sides of the Channel, an agreement might* not *one day be realized ?/I do* not *of course deny that in this, as in all moral principles, there may* not *be found, here & there, exceptional cases./He is unable to say how much of the portraiture of Christ may* not *be due to the idealization of His life & character./It would* not *be at all surprising if, by attempting too much, Mr —— has* not *to some extent defeated his own object./Who knows but what agreeing to differ may* not *be a form of agreement rather than a form of difference ?*

5. *Not . . . but.* Mrs Fraser's book, however, is not *confined to filling up the gaps in Livingstone's life in England & the after-history of his children*, but it *deals most interestingly with her father's own early adventures in Africa &* . . . See BUT 3 for more flagrant mishandlings of *not* followed by *but*. The difference between right & wrong often depends on the writer's seeing that the subject, for instance, of the *not* sentence must not be repeated (or taken up by a pronoun) in the *but* sentence, but allowed to carry on silently. The above double sentence, which is not idiomatic English as it stands, is at once cured by the omission of *it*. The relation between one form & the other is exactly that between *It is not black, but it is white* (which is impossible except in special conditions) & *It is not black, but white*.

6. *Not only* out of its place is like a tintack loose on the floor ; it might have been most serviceable somewhere else, & is capable of giving acute & undeserved pain where it is. To read the following extracts one after another, all of them requiring only a preference for order over chaos to have tidied them up, must surely call a blush to the Englishman's cheek for his journalists' slovenly ways :—*Ireland, unlike the other Western nations, preserved* n. o. *its pre-Christian literature, but when Christianity came, not direct from Rome but from Britain & Gaul*, that literature received *a fresh impulse from the new faith* (N. o. did Ireland . . . preserve)./*He referred his audience to a time when* n. o. was the Regular Army *in no difficulty of finding recruits*, but actually got them *as soon as compulsion for home defence had been introduced* (when the Army n. o. had no difficulty)./ *Professor Dicey's argument could be used most convincingly to prove that* n. o. *ought self-government never to have been granted to the Colonies* but ought also *immediately to be withdrawn from the English people itself* (to prove that self-government n. o. ought never)./*N. o. had she now a right to speak, but to speak with authority* (She had now a right n. o. to speak)./*Up to the last of them* it is assumed n. o. that the Allies *are not parties to the correspondence*, but are *even officially ignorant of its existence* (that the Allies n. o. are not parties)./*N. o. does the proportion of suicides vary with the season of the year, but with different races* (The proportion of suicides varies n. o. with)./N. o. would this scheme *help the poorer districts over their financial difficulties*, but would *remove from London the disgrace that in some parts of London the streets are* . . . (This scheme would n. o. help)./*N. o. was the audience drawn from central London ; those privileged to hear the speech came from all parts* (The audience was not drawn from central London only. The blunder is here double, & this tintack must be not merely picked up, but smashed up, before it can be harmless).

note, n. For synonymy see SIGN.

note, v., makes *-table* ; see MUTE E.

nothing less than. The OED remarks :—' The combination *nothing less than* has two quite contrary senses ', & gives as the first ' quite equal to, the same thing as ', with, for illustration, *But yet methinks my father's execution Was nothing less than bloody tyranny* ; & as the second ' far from being, any thing rather than ', with, for illustration, *Who, trusting to the laws, expected n. l. t. an attack.* To the second sense it adds the description ' Now rare '. As a matter of grammar, either sense is legitimate, *less* being different parts of speech in the two, as appears in the light of paraphrases :—my father's death was *no smaller thing than* tyranny (i. e., *less* is an adjective) ; they expected *nothing in a lower degree than they expected* an attack (i. e., *less* is an adverb) ; grammar, then, leaves the matter open. But the risks of ambiguity are very great. If the sense of *they expected n. l. t. an attack* did not happen to be fixed by *trusting to the laws,* who would dare decide whether they expected it very much or very little ? The sense called by the OED ' now rare ' should, in the interests of plain speaking, be made rarer by total abandonment. It is unfortunately less rare than the label would lead one to suppose ; passages like the two that follow are not uncommon, & are to many readers very puzzling :—*It recognizes also both the necessity of reform & liberation from dead dogmas & rubrics, & the impossibility of reform coming from a House of Commons desiring nothing less than to occupy its debates with discussions of the validity of the thirty-nine articles./Now we are introduced to inspired ' crowd-men ' or heroes who have a passion for making order out of the human chaos & finding expression for the real soul of the people ; these heroes or crowd-men* resemble n. l. t. *the demagogue as popularly conceived.*

1351

notice makes *-ceable* ; see MUTE E.

notify. For inflexions see VERBS IN -IE, -Y, -YE, 6.

nought. See NAUGHT.

noumenon. Pronounce now'mĭnŏn ; pl. *-ena,* see -ON 1.

noun has two adjectives—*nominal & nounal,* but is comfortable with neither. The objection to the first is that it is a word much used in other senses. This has induced grammarians to form the word from which they of all people should have shrunk—*nounal.* It is what is described in the article HYBRID DERIVATIVES as a *spurious hybrid* ; see that article for a discussion of *coastal* & similar words. The grammarian's right course is to work with the word *noun* as far as possible, &, when an adjective or adverb is indispensable, use *nominal(ly).*

NOUN & ADJECTIVE ACCENT. When a word of more than one syllable is in use both as a noun & as an adjective, there is a certain tendency, though much less marked than the corresponding one with nouns & verbs (see next article), to differentiate the sound by accenting the last syllable in the adjective, but not in the noun ; thus *He is an exper't golfer,* but *He is an e'xpert in handwriting.* A few examples are given, of which the first four are undisputed, & the rest questionable ; from these the reader will be able to form an opinion for application to similar cases :—compa'ct a., co'mpact n. ; exper't a., e'xpert n. ; insti'nct a., i'nstinct n. ; minu'te a., mi'nute n. ; conte'nt a., co'ntent(s) n. (sometimes) ; conver'se a. (sometimes ; & cf. the adv. *conver'sely*), co'nverse n. (= contrary &c.) ; supi'ne a. (usually ; & cf. the adv. *supi'nely*), su'pine n. ; suspe'ct a., su'spect n. (= suspect person ; sometimes) ; uprigh't a. (sometimes ; & cf. the n. *uprigh'tness*), u'pright n. (= post &c.).

NOUN & VERB ACCENT, PRONUNCIATION, & SPELLING. When there

O

is both noun & verb work to be done by a word, & the plan of forming a noun from the verb, or a verb from the noun, by adding a formative suffix (as in *stealth* from *steal*) is not followed, but the one word doubles the parts, there is a strong tendency to differentiate by pronunciation, as in *use* (n. ūs, vb ūz); such a distinction is sometimes, as in *use*, unrecorded in spelling, but sometimes recorded as in *calf* & *calve*. It is not possible to draw up a complete list of the words affected, because the impulse is still active, & the list would need constant additions, especially of words whose pronunciation can be modified without change of spelling. But, as the consequence is that the pronunciation of many words is for a time uncertain, a slight analysis of a fair number of examples may help those who are in doubt. It can be laid down, to start with, that DIFFERENTIATION is in itself an aid to lucidity, that this form of differentiation is making way, & therefore that, when one does not suspect oneself of being the innovator, & the only question is between accepting & rejecting a distinction initiated by others, acceptance is wisdom.

1. The largest class is that of words whose accent is shifted ; these, not being monosyllables, are mostly of foreign origin. A. Words in which the differentiation is established :— a′ccent n., acce′nt v. ; commu′ne v., co′mmune n. ; compou′nd v., co′mpound n. ; compre′ss v., co′mpress n. ; concer′t v., co′ncert n. ; condu′ct v., co′nduct n. ; confi′ne v., co′nfine(s) n. ; confli′ct v., co′nflict n. ; consor′t v., co′nsort n. ; co′ntest n., conte′st v. ; contra′ct v., co′ntract n. ; contra′st v., co′ntrast n. ; conver′se v., co′nverse n. (talk) ; conver′t v., co′nvert n. ; convi′ct v., co′nvict n. ; convoy′ v., co′nvoy n. ; decrea′se v., de′crease n. ; de′scant n., desca′nt v. ; dicta′te v., di′ctate(s) n. ; dige′st v., di′gest n. ; discor′d v., di′scord n. ; di′scount n., discou′nt v. ; di′scourse n.,

discour′se v. ; escor′t v., e′scort n. ; essay′ v., e′ssay n. ; e′xploit n., exploi′t v. ; extra′ct v., e′xtract n. ; ferme′nt v., fer′ment n. ; fore′taste n., foreta′ste v. ; foreto′ken v., fore′token n. ; impor′t v., i′mport n. ; impri′nt v., i′mprint n. ; increa′se v., i′ncrease n. ; insu′lt v., i′nsult n. ; interdi′ct v., i′nterdict n. ; pre′mise n., premi′se v. ; produ′ce v., pro′duce n. ; recor′d v., re′cord n. See also PARTICIPLES 5.
B. Words in which accent-shifting is tentative only :—construe′ v.(doubtful), co′nstrue n. ; co′stume n. (doubtful), costu′me v. ; defi′le (pass) v., de′file n. (doubtful) ; de′tail(s) n., detai′l v. (doubtful) ; entai′l v., e′ntail n. (doubtful) ; excer′pt v., e′xcerpt n. (doubtful) ; fina′ncier n. (doubtful), financier′ v. ; incli′ne v., i′ncline n. (doubtful) ; inde′nt v., i′ndent n. (doubtful) ; inlay′ v., i′nlay n. (doubtful) ; intercha′nge v., i′nterchange n. (doubtful) ; invi′te v., i′nvite n. (doubtful).
C. Words in which some speakers shift the accent, & others go half way by giving the last syllable of the verb with a clear instead of an obscure vowel ; so complement, compliment, experiment, implement, &c. ; *You pay me a co′mpliment* (-ent), but *You complime′nt* or *co′mplimĕnt me.*

2. Other words, especially but not only monosyllables, are differentiated not by accent but by a modification in noun or verb of the consonantal sound at the end, which is hard in the noun & soft in the verb. D. This difference is often for the ear only & does not affect spelling ; so abuse, close (hard s in *cathedral close*), excuse, grease, house, misuse, mouse, mouth. In this class, as in B & C, are words about which usage varies & material for comparison is therefore useful. E. More often the change of sound is recorded in the spelling ; about such words no doubts arise ; but examples are worth giving to confirm the fact that the distinguishing of the parts of speech by change of sound is very common, & that its extension to words whose spelling fails to show it is natural. If the soldier's now well-known *leaf* for *leave* (furlough) is an instinctive application of the principle, it provides a rare specimen still in the making to set beside the fully developed ones of which this class mainly consists. Examples are :— advice & advise, bath & bathe, belief & believe, brass & braze, breath & breathe, calf & calve, cloth & clothe, deaf & deave, device & devise, glass & glaze, grass & graze, grief & grieve, half & halve, life & live, loss & lose, proof & prove, relief & relieve, safe & save, sheath & sheathe, shelf & shelve, strife & strive, thief & thieve, teeth & teethe, troth & betrothe, wife & wive, wreath & wreathe.

NOVELESE. This heading is not to be taken as a suggestion that writers of novels are all alike in yielding to certain professional weaknesses. A single warning only is intended, & that on a point so elementary that it concerns only the beginner; but it is the novelist tiro rather than other sorts of tiro that needs it. What is here meant by *novelese* is the set phrases that the young writer remembers to have had his emotions stirred by in the days when he was reading novels instead of writing them, & relies upon to affect his own readers in turn. The phrases have had some wear & tear since he was first struck by them, & the emotional value of such things depreciates quickly. Influences that ' have come into ' somebody's ' life ', tempted ones who ' will not do this thing ', fallen ones ' more sinned against than sinning ', unfortunates ' hoping against hope ', strong silent men, living deaths, that supreme moment, demoniacal glee, demonic energy, diabolical malignity, & devilish ingenuity, magnetic personalities & sinister machinations, utter abandon & pathetic indifference, innocent

guile & serpentine charm, all these & hundreds of the like phrases, which thrilled our own youth, will not thrill but bore those on whom we sanguinely try the same experiment. The emotions may be sempiternal ; the stimuli to which they will react lose their power with use, & must be varied.

NOVELTY-HUNTING, or the casting about for words of which one can feel not that they give one's meaning more intelligibly or exactly than those the man in the street would have used in expressing the same thing, but that they are not the ones that would have occurred to him, is a confession of weakness. Anyone can say *improvement* & *complexity* & *conception* & *ancestors* & *title-rôle* ; I will say BETTERMENT & COMPLICACY & CONCEPT & FOREBEARS & *name-part.* Why ? Obviously because, there being nothing new in what I have to say, I must make up for its staleness by something new in the way I say it. And if that were all, if each novelty-hunter struck out a line for himself, we could be content to register noveltyhunting as a useful outward sign of inward dullness, & leave such writers carefully alone. Unluckily they hunt in packs, & when one of them has such a find as ASSET or HAPPENINGS or FORCEFUL or MENTALITY they are all in full cry after it, till it becomes a VOGUE-WORD, to the great detriment of the language. Further notes on the point will be found under most of the words already mentioned. Other specimens are *bookman* for author &c., CLAMANT for flagrant or crying, DEMESNE for domain, FEASIBLE for possible, MOMENTLY for instantly, LIKELY for probably, adverbs like *embarrassedly* (see -EDLY), & the comparatives & superlatives mentioned in -ER & -EST 5.

noyau, nuance. See FRENCH WORDS.
nth. For *to the* n*th*, see N. An example of the misuse is : *One marvels at the extraordinary French*

capacity & pertinacity in exploiting & exhausting a given motive, working it out to the nth power.

nucleus. Pl. *-lei* (-lï).
nugae. Pronounce nū′gē or nū′jē.
nullify. For inflexions see VERBS IN -IE, -Y, -YE, 6.

NUMBER. Several kinds of mistake are common, & various doubts arise, involving the question of number. With some of them pure grammar is competent to deal ; in others accommodations between grammar & sense are necessary or usual or debatable ; rarely a supposed concession to sense issues in nonsense. The following numbered sections are arranged accordingly, the purely grammatical points coming first. 1. Subject & complement of different numbers. 2. Subject of mixed numbers. 3. *Or.* 4. Red herrings. 5. Harking back with relatives. 6. Nouns of multitude. 7. Singular verb preceding plural subject, & vice versa. 8. *As follow(s)* &c. 9. *Other(s).* 10. *What.* 11. Pronouns & possessives after *everyone* &c. 12. Quantity words. 13. Nonsense.

1. If subject & complement are of different numbers, how is the number of the verb to be decided ? That is, to come to particulars in the simplest form, shall we use *are* in *Clouds are vaporized water, & was* in *The last crop was potatoes,* because the subject *clouds* is plural & the subject *crop* singular, or shall we prefer *is* & *were* to suit the number of the complements *water & potatoes*? The natural man, faced with these examples, has no doubt : ' Of course, *Clouds are, The crop was,* whatever may be going to follow '. The sophisticated man, who thinks of *The wages of sin is death,* hesitates, but probably admits that that is an exception accounted for by the really singular sense of *wages* (= guerdon). It may in fact be fairly assumed that when the subject is a straightforward singular without complications about nouns of multi-

tude (as in *party* &c.), or a straightforward plural without complications about a virtually singular sense (as in *wages*) or separate items (as in *he & she*), the verb follows the number of the subject, whatever that of the complement may be. That it is not as needless as it might seem to set this down will be plain from the following extracts, some of the simplest form, all violating the rule :—*Our only guide were the stars./Its strongest point are the diagrams./For Germany's great need are colonies./The plausible suggestions to the contrary so frequently put forward is an endeavour to kill two birds with one stone./Mr Shortt's quotations from seditious literature was, in the view of most members, poor evidence to support the new charges which he brought./Mr Coulton contests the idea that the pre-Reformation days was an age of religious instruction.* The only comment necessary on these is that when, as in the first three examples, it makes no difference to the meaning which of two words (*stars* or *guide, point* or *diagrams, need* or *colonies*) is made the subject & which the complement, the one that is placed first must (except in questions) be regarded as subject & have the verb suited to its number : *Our only guide was the stars,* or *The stars were our only guide.*

When the words *which* or *what* take the place of the subject, mistakes are more intelligible, but still mistakes ; *is* should be *are* in *The grass plots intersected with gravelled drives which* is *the ordinary achievement of the English gardener in India* ; but *which* does not bear its number on its face. The traps laid by WHAT are so many & various (*What puzzles us most are the references to* . . ., &c.) that it is better to refer the reader to that word.

2. Subject of mixed numbers. In *Mother & children were killed* we have a compound subject ; in *Mother or children are to die* we have not one compound subject, but two

alternative subjects ; the rules for the number of the verb differ in the two types. The compound subject is necessarily plural, whether its components are both plural, of different numbers, or both singular. To make the verb singular, as has been done in the extracts below, is accordingly wrong ; at least, it is ungrammatical, though grammar may sometimes, when there is a better justification than carelessness or ignorance, be overridden ; the reason why the rule is broken as often as it is is perhaps confusion between the two forms, compound & alternative, distinguished above, the latter admitting sometimes of a singular verb. Wrong examples :— *Those who have been encouraging one-half of these peoples to believe that their lives, their liberties, & their religion* is *in danger have assumed a great responsibility./The Allies are even prepared to retire troops & cease operations if & when proper pledges & security* is *given.*

If the verb in sentences of this type precedes the compound subject (*There were a table & some chairs in there*), it becomes legitimate to use a singular verb under some circumstances (see 7 below).

3. Or. *If the facts are as your correspondent (or your printer) state, Egypt must be an odd sort of country.* *State* should be *states* ; see 2 for the difference between a compound subject with *and* & two or more alternative subjects with *or*. When, as here, both alternatives are singular in grammar & in sense (*you* is plural in grammar even when singular in sense ; *army* may be plural in sense though singular in grammar, see 8), the verb can only be singular. So *Mother or child is* (not *are*) *to die.* But when the alternatives differ in number, as in *Mother or children are to die, Is the child or the parents to be blamed ?,* the methods in order of merit are : (a) Evade by finding a verb of common number : *Mother or children* must *die,* Shall *the child or the*

parents be blamed ? ; (b) Invoke ellipsis by changing the order : *The mother is to die, or the children, Is the child to be blamed, or the parents ?* (c) Give the verb the number of the alternative nearest it : *Mother or children are to die, Is the child or the parents to be blamed ?* What should not be said is *Mother or children is to die, Are the child or the parents to be blamed ?*

4. Red herrings. Some writers are as easily drawn off the scent as young hounds. They start with a singular subject ; before they reach the verb, a plural noun attached to an *of* or the like happens to cross, & off they go in the plural ; or vice versa. This is a matter of carelessness or inexperience only, & needs no discussion ; but it is so common as to call for a few illustrations :—*Further acquaintance with the memoirs of Prince Chlodwig zu Hohenlohe-Schillingsfürst enable us the better to appreciate . . ./The results of the recognition of this truth is . . ./The foundation of politics are in the letter only./An immense amount of confusion & indifference prevail./The partition which the two ministers made of the powers of government were singularly happy./ Those dangerous influences whose appearance were the chief cause of our action.*

5. Harking back with relatives. *Who, which, & that,* can in themselves be singular or plural, & there is a particular form of sentence in which this produces constant blunders. *He is one of the best men that have ever lived* (with which compare *He is one that has lived honestly*). In the first sentence there are two words capable of serving as antecedent to *that,* viz *one* (as in the bracketed sentence) & *men.* A moment's thought shows that *men* is the antecedent necessary to the sense : Of the best men that have ever lived (or of the best past & present men) he is one. But with *one & men* (or their equivalents) to attach the relative to, writers will hark back to *one* in spite of the nonsense it gives, & make their verbs singular :—*He is another of the numerous people who is quite competent in the art of turning what he has to say into rhyme & metre./ They have gone through one of those complete changes of occupation which does everybody good./One of the many well-known actresses who wears Sandow's corset./An account which, in our opinion, is one of the most suggestive contributions to animal & human psychology which has ever been published./It is quite one of the brightest productions that has been seen for a long time.* It will be observed that the critic of poets is no more proof against the temptation than the advertiser of underclothing.

An example or two offering peculiarities may be added :—*Mr Edwin Pugh is one of those intriguing people who can write well in any style, & does ; but who constantly leaves us with the impression that he is not quite serious* ; this writer wants to have it both ways ; *who* is to be plural with *can*, but singular with *does & leaves* ; read *& he does, but./ Describing him as one of those busy men who in some remarkable way* find *time for adding to* his *work* ; to have got safely as far as *find*, & then break away with *his*, is an odd freak./*Houdin was a wonderful conjurer, & is often reckoned the greatest of his craft who* have *ever lived* ; this reverses the usual mistake : Is the greatest who *has*, Is one of the greatest who *have*.

6. Nouns of multitude. Such words as *army, fleet, Government, company, party, pack, crowd, mess, number, majority*, may stand either for a single entity or for the individuals who compose it, & are called nouns of multitude. They are treated as singular or plural at discretion— & sometimes, naturally, without discretion. *The Cabinet* is *divided* is better, because in the order of thought a whole must precede division ; & *The Cabinet are agreed* is

better, because it takes two or more to agree. That is a delicate distinction, & few will be at the pains to make it. Broader ones that few will fail to make are that between *The army* is *on a voluntary basis* & *The army* are *above the average civilian height*, & that between *The party lost* their *hats* & *The party lost* its *way*. In general it may be said that while there is always a better & a worse in the matter, there is seldom a right & a wrong, & any attempt to elaborate rules would be waste labour. A single example will illustrate sufficiently :—*More money will be wanted if the number of teachers* are *to be adequate.* No-one will misinterpret that ; yet everyone will admit that the singular would have been what the plural is not, foolproof ; the writer meant if there are to be enough teachers ; he did not mean what his words ought to mean—if the numerous teachers are to be skilful enough.

But if the decision whether a noun of multitude is to be treated as a singular or as a plural is often a difficult business, & when ill made results at worst in a venial blemish, failure to abide by the choice when made, & plunging about between *it & they, have & has, is & their*, & the like, can only be called insults to the reader. A waiter might as well serve one on a dirty plate as a journalist offer one such untidy stuff as :—*The University of London Press* hopes *to have ready the following additions to* their *series of . . ./The latter Government* has *now attempted to link up with the Czechs & have published a programme./The village* is *at work now & ready to do* their *bit./The Tory party* has *never prospered when they* have *given over their policy into the keeping of the Ulster group./The Government, with the Clarke award before* them, is *yet unable to enforce it./The Haggin family* have *come down in the world, & consists first of . . .*

7. Singular verb preceding plural subject & vice versa. The excuse for this in speaking—often a sufficient one—is that one has started one's sentence before fixing the precise form of the subject, though its meaning may have been realized clearly enough. But the writer both can & ought to do what the speaker cannot, correct his first words before the wrong version has reached his audience. If he does not, he too, like the waiter with the dirty plate (see 6), is indecently & insultingly careless. Examples :—*For the first time there* is *introduced into the Shipyard Agreement* clauses *which hold the balance equally./A book entitled ' America's Day ', by Ignatius Phayre, in which* is *discussed the pressing* problems *of home & foreign policy that . . ./On these questions there* is *likely to be acute* differences *among the political groups & parties./ Instead, we had the Board of Trade figures upon which* was *reared successive* agitations *for increases in wages./ Where only three years ago was pasture land now* stands *vast engineering* shops, miles *of railway sidings, & the constant* hum *of machinery.*

The converse mistake is seldom made ; in the following, the influence of *these* no doubt accounts for *are* : *The Thames has certain natural disadvantages as a shipbuilding centre* ; *to these* are *added an artificial* disadvantage.

When the verb precedes a subject compounded of singular & plural, some questions of more interest than importance may arise. *There were a table & some chairs in there* ; *were* is better because the compound subject is compact. *There were a plain deal table in there & some wicker armchairs which Jorgenson had produced from somewhere in the depths of the ship.* The alteration of *were* to *was* would now be an improvement ; but why, if *were* was best in the bare framework given first ? How has the author elaborated it ? First & least, he has made table & chairs less homogeneous, less the equivalent of ' some articles of furniture ', by

describing one as plain deal & the others as wicker ; secondly, he has attached to *chairs* & not to *table* a long relative clause ; third & most important, he has had, in order to cut off the relative clause from *table*, to shift *in there* to an earlier place. But it results that the verbal phrase (*there were . . . in there*) is so arranged that it encloses one item of the compound subject (table) & leaves the other (chairs) out in the cold. The author would have done better to write *was* & let the second part be elliptical with *there were in there* to be understood out of *there was in there*.

8. *As follow(s), concern(s), regard(s),* &c. For higher incomes than £1,000 *the new rates will be as follow. As follow* is not English ; *as follows* is ; for discussion of the point see FOLLOW.

9. *Other(s). The wrecking policy is, like* other *of their adventures in recent times, a dangerous gamble. Other* should be *others* ; for discussion see OTHER.

10. *What. What* provoke *men's curiosity are mysteries.* See WHAT for the question whether it can be plural.

11. Pronouns & possessives after *each, every, anyone, no-one, one,* &c. *Everyone without further delay gave* themselves *up to rejoicing./But, as* anybody *can see for* themselves, *the quotation of the actually relevant portion of the argument in our columns would have destroyed . . . Each* & the rest are all singular ; that is undisputed ; in a perfect language there would exist pronouns & possessives that were of as doubtful gender as they & yet were, like them, singular ; i.e., it would have words meaning him-or-her, himself-or-herself, his-or-her. But, just as French lacks our power of distinguishing (without additional words) between his, her, & its, so we lack the French power of saying in one word his-or-her. There are three makeshifts :—A, *as anybody can see for himself or herself* ; B, *as anybody can see for themselves* ; & C, *as any-*

body can see for himself. No-one who can help it chooses A ; it is correct, & is sometimes necessary, but it is so clumsy as to be ridiculous except when explicitness is urgent, & it usually sounds like a bit of pedantic humour. B is the popular solution ; it sets the literary man's teeth on edge, & he exerts himself to give the same meaning in some entirely different way if he is not prepared, as he usually is, to risk C ; but it should be recorded that the OED, which quotes examples under *every, they, & themselves,* refrains from any word of condemnation. C is here recommended. It involves the convention that where the matter of sex is not conspicuous or important *he & his* shall be allowed to represent a person instead of a man, or say a man (homo) instead of a man (vir). Whether that, with A in the background for especial exactitudes, & paraphrase always possible in dubious cases, is an arrogant demand on the part of male England, everyone must decide for himself (or for himself or herself, or for themselves). Have the patrons of B made up their minds yet between *Everyone* was *blowing their noses* & *Everyone* were *blowing their noses* ?

12. Quantity words. *There* are *heaps more to say, but I must not tax your space further.* The plurals *heaps* & *lots* used colloquially for a great amount now always take a singular verb unless a plural noun with *of* is added : *There* is *heaps of ammunition,* but *There* are *heaps of cups* ; *There* is *lots to do,* but *Lots of people* think *so.* Compare the use of *half* in *Half of it* is *rotten,* but *Half of them* are *rotten.*

13. Nonsense. *He comes for the first time into the Navy at an age when naval officers—unless* they *are so meritorious or so fortunate as to be one of the three Admirals of the Fleet —are compelled by law to leave it.* Naval officers cannot be one admiral ; & what is wrong with *unless they are Admirals of the Fleet* ?

numerous is not, as the following extract makes it, a pronoun :— *These men have introduced no fewer than 107 amendments, which they know perfectly well cannot pass, & numerous of which are not meant to pass.* See VARIOUS, which is much more often misused in the same way.

nuncio. Pl. *-os* ; see -O(E)S 4.

nurse makes *-sable* ; see MUTE E.

nurs(e)ling. The form recommended, though rather less common hitherto than the other, is *nurseling* ; see MUTE E for the criterion.

nursy, not *-sey* ; see -EY, -IE, -Y.

O

-O- is a connecting vowel of Greek origin, its extended modern function being so to shape the end of a Greek or Latin word that when a suffix or another word is applied to it the two will coalesce recognizably into a single derivative or compound. Three points should be noticed :—
1. The thing ending in *-o-* is not a word, but essentially the beginning only of a word ; *We owe it to the genius of Hertz that we are now able to measure directly the velocity of* electro *& magnetic waves* ; *electro* is there used as an adjective instead of *electric,* & is indefensible. The use of CURTAILED WORDS such as *dynamo, photo, chromo, & electro* itself, for dynamo-electric machine, photograph, chromolithograph, & electro-plate, is another matter.
2. The words fit for the -o- treatment are, if not necessarily authentic ancient Greek or Latin, at least such as may pass for Greek or Latin. If the ancient Romans did not call the Russians *Russi* or talk of *America & Americani,* we can suppose that was only because they had not the chance, & are therefore entitled to make *Russo-, Americo-, & Americano-* ; but the Greeks & Romans knew what speed was, & yet no-one supposes they called it *speed,* whence it follows that *speedo-* & *speedometer* are barbarisms. 3. It

is not enough that the word to be treated should be actual or possible Latin or Greek ; the shaping must be done in the right way. *We must take account of* religio-*philosophic speculations with regard to the nature of Eternal Life* ; Latin, it is true, has both *religio* & *religiosus*, but only the second admits of the -o- treatment, & it gives *religioso- philosophic*. See also HYBRID DE- RIVATIVES.

oaf. Pl. *-fs*, rarely *-ves* ; see -VE(D).
oaken. See -EN ADJECTIVES.
O & oh. Usage has changed, *oh* having formerly been prevalent in many contexts now requiring *O*, & is still by no means fixed. The present tendency is to restrict *oh* to places where it has a certain independence, & prefer *O* where it is proclitic or leans forward upon what follows ; which means for practical purposes that as the sign of the vocative (*O God our help* ; *O mighty- mouthed inventor of harmonies*) *O* is invariable, & as an exclamation the word is *O* when no stop immediately follows it, but before any stop *oh* (*Oh, what a lie !* ; *Oh ! how do you know that ?* ; *O for the wings of a dove !* ; *O who will o'er the downs with me ?* ; *O worship the King !*).

oasis. Pl. *oases*, pron. -ēz.
oaten. See -EN ADJECTIVES.
oath. Pl. pron. ōdhz ; -TH & -DH.
obbligato. So spelt. Pl. *-os* ; see -O(E)S 3.
obdurate, adj. The OED quota- tions show Shakspere, Milton, & Barham, for obdūr′at, & Shelley for ŏ′bdūrat. The former is still some- times heard, but is old-fashioned. See PRONUNCIATION.

obedient. For *yours obediently* &c., see LETTER FORMS.
obeisance. Pronounce -ās-.
obelus. Pl. *-li* (-ī).
obfuscate makes *-cable, -tor* ; see -ABLE 1, -OR.
object, vb. 1. *O.* makes *objector* ; see -OR. 2. *France rightly objects to allow Germany to assume a position*

in Morocco which . . ./The cabdrivers object to pay *their proportion of the increase.* *To allow*, or *to allowing* ? to pay, or *to paying* ? The infinitive is deprecated & the gerund recom- mended ; for this see GERUND 3.

objectify. For inflexions see VERBS IN -IE, -Y, -YE, 6.
objection. *They have been blocked by the objections of farmers & land- lords* to provide *suitable land.* Or *to providing* ? see GERUND 3.

objective genitive. See TECHNICAL TERMS.

OBJECT-SHUFFLING. The confer- ring of a name on a type of mistake, making it recognizable & avoidable, is worth while if the mistake is common. *Object-shuffling* describes what unwary writers are apt to do with some of the many verbs that require, besides a direct object, another noun bearing to them a somewhat similar relation, but at- tached to them by a preposition. You can inspire courage in a person, or inspire a person with courage ; the change of construction is object- shuffling, which, with the verb *inspire*, is legitimate & does not offend against idiom ; but with *instil* the object-shuffling would be wrong ; you can instil courage into a person ; to instil a person with courage is contrary to idiom. Wher- ever reference is made under any word to this article, the meaning is that with that word object-shuffling is not permissible. Most of the verbs liable to this maltreatment are derived from Latin verbs com- pounded with prepositions & there- fore beginning with *in-, sub-, pre-,* &c. The Latin scholar, aware that the verbal parts of *substituo* & *instillo* & *praefigo* mean to put & to pour & to fasten, instinctively chooses for their direct objects the stopgap, the influence, & the ap- pendage, not the thing displaced, the person influenced, & the main body ; & in writing of the more educated kind his example is follow- ed. But the non-Latinist, if he is also unobservant, gives *substitute* the construction of *replace*, *instil* that of *fill*, & *prefix* that of *preface*. It is seldom that the mistake is made with native words; an example will be found under *foist*. Two or three specimens may be here given; the reader who wishes for more will find them under the words *substitute*, *prefix*, *inculcate*, *inflict*, *infuse*, *enforce*, *affix*, *ingratiate*, *enjoin*, & others. *The attempt to convict Mr Masterman yesterday of an indiscreet utterance in a public speech & to* affix the Government with *responsibility therefor utterly failed* (& to affix responsibility to the Government)./*A quarterly which is doing so much to* initiate into the minds *of the British Public what is requisite for them to know* (to initiate the B.P. in what is requisite)./*The ecclesiastical principle was* substituted by *the national* (the national principle was substituted for the ecclesiastical).

objurgate makes *-tor*; see -OR.

obligated as a synonym for *obliged* (having received a favour &c.) is now a mere solecism; but in the full sense of bound by law or duty *to* do something it is still used, esp. in legal language.

obligato. See OBBLIGATO.

obligatory. The pronunciation recommended is obli′gatori.

oblige makes *-ging*; see MUTE E. The derivatives of *o.* & *obligate* (see OBLIGATED above) are troublesome; there are two possible adjectives in *-able* (see -ABLE 1), viz, *obligable* from *obligate* (= that can be legally bound; pronounce ŏ′blĭgabl), & *obligeable* from *oblige* (= that can have a favour conferred; pron. obli′jabl). *Obligee* & *obligor* belong in sense to *obligate*, & have curious meanings: *obligor*, not one who confers an obligation, but one who binds or obligates himself to do something; *obligee*, not one who is obliged, but one to whom a service is due (towards whom a duty has been undertaken).

oblique complement. See TECHNICAL TERMS.

obliqueness)(obliquity. There is some tendency to confine the latter to the secondary or figurative senses; *obliquity of mind* or *judgement* or *outlook*, but *obliqueness of the ground*, *a Chinaman's eyes*, or *the alignment*; cf. OPACITY, & see -TY & -NESS. It is perhaps well to fall in with such DIFFERENTIATION.

obliterate makes *-rable*, *-tor*; see -ABLE 1, -OR.

oblivious. A word badly misused in two ways. 1. Its right sense is *no longer aware* or *no longer mindful*; it is not simply unaware or unconscious or insensible. The following examples all offend against this principle :—*A contempt to which the average Englishman in his happy self-sufficiency is generally oblivious.*/ *He may have driven off quite oblivious of the fact that any harm had been done.*/*And they are ingenuously oblivious to the ' howlers ' so constantly perpetrated.*/*General von Stein denied that the propaganda in the army was political, & he added, quite oblivious of the import of what he was saying :* ' *The soldier had to be instructed as to the reasons of the war* '.*/Singly or in groups, oblivious to the traffic in the streets, they pursued their eager quest.* 2. Even when the word might bear its true sense of forgetful (as opposed to unaware), it is often followed by the wrong preposition (*to*); this is an indirect result of the mistake explained in 1; it will be noticed that a majority of the quotations there given show *to* instead of *of*; that is on the analogy of *insensible to*. But in the following examples *to* has been used even where the meaning might otherwise be the correct one of forgetful :—*Each of them oblivious to the presence of anybody else, & intent on conversation.*/*A principle to which the romances of the eighteenth century were curiously oblivious.*/*Mr Humphreys is always oblivious to the fact that the minority in one part* *of the kingdom is represented by the majority in another part./In England the very completeness of the defeat of Roman Catholicism has rendered the people oblivious to the danger of its aggression.*

The making of these mistakes is part of the price paid by those who reject the homely word, avoid the obvious, & look about for the imposing ; *forgetful, unaware, unconscious, unmindful,* & *insensible,* while they usually give the meaning more precisely, lay no traps.

obnoxious has two very different senses, one of which (exposed or open or liable *to* attack or injury) requires notice because its currency is now so restricted that it is puzzling to the uninstructed. It is the word's rightful or *de-jure* meaning, & we may hope that scholarly writers will keep it alive, as they have hitherto succeeded in doing. Meanwhile the rest of us need not scruple to recognize the usurping or *de-facto* sense offensive or objectionable ; this has perhaps no right to exist (' apparently affected by association with noxious ' says the OED), but it does & will, &, unlike the other, it is comprehensible to everyone.

oboe. See HAUTBOY.

observance)(observation. The useful differentiation in virtue of which neither word can be substituted for the other, & each is appropriated to certain senses of *observe,* should not be neglected. *Observance* is the attending to & carrying out of a duty or rule or custom ; it has none of the senses of *observation* (watching, noticing, &c.), & *observation* in turn does not mean performing or complying. Though the distinction is modern, its prevalence in good writing may be judged from the OED's having only one 19th-c. & no 20th-c. example of *observance,* as against many of *observation,* in the sense consciously seeing or taking notice. Unfortunately, the journalists' perverted taste for out-of-the-

way forms is undoing this useful achievement, & in the last 20 years such uses as the following, almost unknown for two or three centuries, have again become common :—*To reinforce observance with imagination./That the Americans are & will remain interested in Europe, & that a close observance of European & Asiatic affairs is an essential & important part of the life of the citizen of the U.S./Emerson does not check his assumptions ; he scorns observance./Mr Abbott's verse, basing its claims to beauty on significant observance, is apt for that very reason to . . ./From him Mr Torr inherits both his gift for exact observance & lively humour./His early poetry, the product of exalted sensation rather than of careful observance./Whose powers of observance & memory have combined to make as varied a raconteur as . . .* In all these the word should be *observation* ; one quotation is added in which *observation* is wrongly used for *observance :* *The British Government has failed to secure* the observation of law *& has lost the confidence of all classes.*

obstacle. *Their apathy, fatalism, & resentment of interference constituted, & still constitute, a formidable obstacle of progress.* After *obstacle,* idiom requires *to,* not *of.*

obstetric(al). See -IC(AL). The short form is much commoner, & is recommended ; its formation is in fact faulty (a midwife is *obstetrix, -īcis,* so that *obstetricic* would be the true adjective), while that of *obstetrical* would pass ; but only pedantry would take exception to *obstetric* at this stage of its career.

obstruct makes *-tor* ; see -OR.

obtain. See FORMAL WORDS. *Customer*—Can you get me some ? *Shopman*—We can o. it for you, madam.

obturate makes *-tor* ; see -OR.

obviate makes *-iabïe, -tor ;* see -ABLE 1, -OR.

occiput. Pronounce ŏksĭ-.

occupy. For inflexions see VERBS
IN -IE, -Y, -YE, 6.

occur makes *-rred, -rring*, &c. ; see
-R-, -RR-. For *occurring* see PRO-
NUNCIATION S.f.

ocean. For *o. greyhound* see
SOBRIQUETS.

ocellus. Pl. *-lli* (-ī).

ochlocracy. Pronounce ŏk-.

ochre. For spelling see -RE & -ER ;
& for *ochr(e)ish* & *ochr(e)ous* see
SPELLING POINTS, 3 s.f.

octaroon. See OCTOROON.

octavo. See FOLIO. Pl. *-os* ; see
-O(E)S 6.

octet(te). Spell *-et* ; see DUET.

**octingentenary, octocentenary, octo-
centennial.** In preference to all
these *octingenary* is recommended ;
see CENTENARY.

octodecimo. See FOLIO. Pl. *-os* ;
see -O(E)S 6.

octonarius. See TECHNICAL TERMS.

octopus. Pl. *-uses* ; the Greek or
Latin pl., rarely used, is *-podes* (-ĕz),
not *-pi* ; see LATIN PLURALS, & cf.
POLYPUS.

octoroon, -taroon. Both are bad
forms, the -r- being imported from
quadroon, which has a right to it.
But the second is worse than the
first, since *octa-* is not (like *quadr-*)
Latin, but Greek. For meaning,
see MULATTO 2.

octosyllabics. See TECHNICAL
TERMS.

octroi. Pronounce ŏ'ktrwah. For
synonymy see TAX.

oddment. Though the word itself
is established & useful, its formation
is anomalous (see -MENT) & should
not be imitated.

ode. See TECHNICAL TERMS.

odo(u)r, odorous. Keep the -u- in
the noun ; see -OUR & -OR, -OUR- &
-OR-.

Odyssey. Pl. *-eys*.

OE, Œ, E. See Æ, Œ. The following
spellings of words beginning with *oe*
or its substitutes are recommended :
oecist ; oecology &c. ; ecumenical ;
oedema &c. ; Oedipus ; oesophagus ;

oestrum. The pronunciation in all
is simply ē.

-O(E)S. The Englishman has a
legitimate grievance against the
words in *-o*. No-one who is not
prepared to flout usage & say that
for him every word in *-o* shall make
-oes, or shall make *-os*, can possibly
escape doubts ; one kind of whole-
hogger will have to write *heros* &
nos & *potatos* & *gos* & *negros*, while
the other kind must face *embryoes,
photoes, cameoes, duodecimoes,* &
generalissimoes. In this book, most
words in *-o* have been entered with
the plurals that seem advisable ;
here, one or two guiding principles
may be indicated. Although there
are several hundred nouns in *-o*, the
ending is one that is generally felt
to be exotic, & the plural in *-oes,*
which is shown, by its being indispensable with the most familiar
words (*no, go, cargo, jingo, hero,
negro*, &c.) to be the normal form,
is allowed only to a small minority,
most words having *-os*. It must be
understood that the following rules
are not more than generally true,
& that sometimes they come to
blows with each other over a word.
1. Words used as freely in the
plural as in the singular usually have
-oes, though there are very few with
which it is invariable ; names of
animals & plants fall naturally into
this class. So *banjoes* ; *bravoes* ;
cargoes ; *dingoes* ; *dominoes* ; *heroes* ;
potatoes.
2. Monosyllables take *-oes* ; so
goes, noes.
3. Words of the kind whose plural
is seldom wanted or is restricted to
special uses have *-os* ; so *dos* (the
musical note) ; *bravados* ; *calicos* ;
crescendos ; *dittos* ; *guanos* ; *infernos* ;
lumbagos.
4. When a vowel precedes the *-o*,
-os is usual, perhaps because of
the bizarre look of *-ioes* &c. ; so
arpeggios ; *baboos* ; *bagnios* ; *cameos* ;
embryos ; *folios* ; *punctilios*.
5. The curtailed words made by
dropping the second element of a

compound or the later syllables have always *-os*; so *chromos*; *dynamos*; *magnetos*; *photos*; *stylos*.

6. Alien-looking or otherwise queer words have *-os*; so *albinos*; *alto-relievos*; *centos*; *commandos*; *duo-decimos*; *fiascos*; *ghettos*; *magnificos*; *negrillos*.

7. Long words tend to *-os*; so *archipelagos*; *armadillos*; *generalissimos*; *manifestos*.

8. Proper names have *-os*; so *Gallios*; *Lotharios*; *Neros*; *Romeos*.

of shares with another word of the same length, *as*, the evil glory of being accessory to more crimes against grammar than any other. But, in contrast with the syntax of *as*, which is so difficult that blunders are very excusable, that of *of* is so simple that only gross carelessness can lead anyone astray with it. Nevertheless, straying is perpetual, & the impression of amateurishness produced on an educated reader of the newspapers is discreditable to the English Press. Fortunately, the commonest type of blunder with *of* is very definite & recognizable, so that the setting of it forth with sufficient illustration has a real chance of working some improvement. That type is treated in the first of the following sections, the list of which is : (1) Wrong patching ; (2) Patching the unpatchable ; (3) Side-slip ; (4) Irresolution ; (5) Needless repetition ; (6) Misleading omission ; (7) Some freaks of idiom.

1. Wrong patching. In the ten examples to be given, the same thing has happened every time. The writer composes a sentence in which some other preposition than *of* occurs once but governs two nouns, one close after it & the other at some distance. Looking over his sentence, he feels that the second noun is out in the cold, & that he would make things clearer by expressing the preposition for the second time instead of leaving it to be understood. So far, so good ; care even when uncalled for is

meritorious ; but his stock of it runs short, & instead of ascertaining what the preposition really was he hurriedly assumes that it was the last in sight, which happens to be an *of* that he has had occasion to insert for some other purpose ; that *of* he now substitutes for the other preposition whose insertion or omission was a matter of indifference, & so ruins the whole structure. In the examples, the three prepositions concerned are in roman type ; the reader will notice that the later of the two *of*s can be either omitted or altered to the earlier preposition, & that one of these courses is necessary :—*An eloquent testimony* to *the limits* of *this kind of war,* & of *the efficiency of right defensive measures.*/ *Which clearly points the need* for *some measure* of *honesty* & of *at least an attempt at understanding of racial ambitions.*/*He will be in the best possible position* for *getting the most out* of *the land* & of *using it to the best possible advantage.*/*He would have recovered the power to manœuvre his armies in mass, a power absolutely necessary either* to *achieving a military decision, or in case* of *necessity* of *retiring in good order.*/ *The definite repudiation of militarism as the governing factor* in *the relation* of *States* & of *the future moulding of the European world.*/*The varying provisions in the different States* respecting *the length* & *nature* of *the voter's qualification, as well as* of *the kind of persons excluded from the suffrage.*/*A candidate who ventured to hint* at *the possible persistence* of *the laws of economics,* & *even* of *the revival of the normal common-sense instincts of trade.*/*The Ministry aims not merely* at *an equitable division* of *existing stocks, but* of *building up reserves against the lean months.*/ *It begins* with *the early enthusiasm of St Petersburg for the war,* & of *the anti-German feeling which transformed the city into Petrograd.*/*The magistrate commented* on *the nuisance* of *street-collections by means of boxes,* & of *the scandal of a system under* which a large proportion of the money given goes for the expenses of collection.

2. Patching the unpatchable. These resemble the previous set so far as the writers are concerned ; they have done the same thing as before ; but for the reader who wishes to correct them there is the difference that only one course is open ; *of* must be simply omitted, & *between* or *without* cannot be substituted. We can say *for you & for me* instead of *for you & me* if we choose, but not *between you & between me* for *between you & me* ; *with cries & with tears* means the same as *with cries & tears*, but *without cries or without tears* does not mean the same as *without cries or tears* ; on this point, see OVERZEAL. *It could be done without unduly raising the price of coal, or of jeopardizing new trade./ He will distinguish between the American habit of concentrating upon the absolute essentials, of 'getting there' by the shortest path, & of the elaboration in detail & the love of refinements in workmanship which mark the Latin mind./Without going into the vexed question of the precise geographical limitations, or of pronouncing any opinion upon the conflicting claims of Italy & of the Yugo-Slavs, what may be said is that* . . .

3. Side-slip. Besides the types given in the previous sections, so beautifully systematic in irregularity as almost to appear regular, there are more casual aberrations of which no more need be said than that the sentence is diverted from its track into an *of* construction by the presence somewhere of an *of*. Analogous mistakes are illustrated in the article SIDE-SLIP. *Sub-section 3 prohibits the Irish Parliament from making any law so as to directly or indirectly establish or endow any religion or prohibit the free exercise thereof or of giving a preference or imposing a disability on account of religious belief or ecclesiastical status./ The primary object was not the*

destruction of the mole forts, or of the aeroplane shed, or of whatever military equipment was there, or even of killing or capturing its garrison./ Lord Parmoor referred to the progress which had been made in the acceptance of the principle of a League of Nations, mentioning especially its inclusion in the Coalition programme, & of the appointment of Lord Robert Cecil to take charge of this question at the Peace Conference./ Its whole policy was, & is, simply to obstruct the improvement of the workingman's tavern, & of turning every house of refreshment & entertainment in the land into that sort of coffee tavern which* . . .

4. Irresolution. *Here again we have illustrated Germany's utter contempt for her pledged word & of her respect for nothing but brute force./His view would be more appropriate in reference to Hume's standpoint than of the best thought of our own day.* The results of having in mind two ways of putting a thing & deciding first for one & then for the other : *we have illustrated, & we have an illustration of ; to Hume's standpoint* (than to the thought), & *to the standpoint of Hume* (than of the thought).

5. Needless repetition of *of*. There is a classical tag about the pleasure of being on shore & of watching other folk in a big sea. A matter not of grammar, but of style & lucidity ; in style the second *of* is heavy, & in sense it obscures the fact that the pleasure lies not in two separate things but in their combination.

6. Misleading omission. *The prohibition of meetings & the printing & distribution of flysheets stopped the Radicals' agitation.* Unless an *of* is inserted before *the printing*, the instinct of symmetry compels us to start by assuming that *the printing* &c. *of flysheets* is parallel to *the prohibition of meetings* instead of, as it must be, to *meetings* alone.

7. Some freaks of idiom. *You are the man* of all others *that I did not suspect. He is the worst liar* of any man *I know. A child* of ten years

old. *That long nose* of *his*. The modern tendency is to rid speech of patent ILLOGICALITIES ; & all of the above either are, or seem to persons ignorant of any justification that might be found in the history of the constructions, plainly illogical : the man of all *men* ; the worst liar of *all liars* ; a child *of ten years*, or a child *ten years old* ; a *friend* of mine, i.e. among my friends, but surely not that *nose* of his, i.e. among his noses : so the logic-chopper is fain to correct or damn ; but even he is likely in unguarded moments to let the forbidden phrases slip out. They will perhaps be disused in time ; meanwhile they are recognized idioms—STURDY INDEFENSIBLES, possibly.

offer makes *-ered*, *-ering*, &c. ; see -R-, -RR-.

officer. Used absolutely, the word ordinarily means any member of Navy, Army, or Air Force, who holds the King's commission. The following rough distinctions between qualified uses may be serviceable :— *Flag officers* are all naval officers above & including rear-admirals ; *General officers* are all army officers above & including brigadier generals; *Field officers* are army officers between general & company officers, & include colonels, lieut.-colonels, & majors ; *Company officers* are regimental officers below & including captains ; *Regimental officers* are all from 2nd lieutenant to colonel whose duties are confined to the normal control of a regiment, battalion, battery, &c. ; *Staff officers* are officers of any commissioned rank in navy or army who have special duties not confined to a ship or regiment & a special relation to a commanding officer ; *Warrant officers* are petty or non-commissioned officers of the higher grades, such as boatswain & sergeant-major, who hold an Admiralty or War-Office certificate ; *Petty officers* in the navy, & *Non-commissioned officers* in the army, are men given authority by the commanders of their units, & not necessarily holding warrants.

officinal. Pronounced ofī'sĭnal, though the Latin noun is *officīna* ; compare *medicinal* (from *medicīna*), & see FALSE QUANTITY.

officious has a meaning in diplomacy so oddly different from its ordinary one that misunderstanding may arise from ignorance of it. A diplomatist means by *an o. communication* much what a lawyer means by one without prejudice ; it is to bind no-one, &, unless acted upon by common consent, is to be as if it had not been. The word is used as the antithesis of *official*, & the notion of meddlesomeness attaching to it in ordinary use is entirely absent.

offing, offish, &c. The pronunciation of *off* itself varies between ŏf & awf, the latter prevailing in Southern or standard English. It is probably true of compounds & derivatives that awf is usual in those whose connexion with *off* is naturally present to the mind, & ŏf in those where it is easily forgotten ; thus *offish, offscourings, offset, offshoot*, tend to awf, but *offing* & *offspring* to ŏf.

often. Pronounce aw'fn or ŏ'fn. The sounding of the *t*, which as the OED says is ' not recognized by the dictionaries ', is practised by two oddly consorted classes—the academic speakers who affect a more precise enunciation than their neighbours' & insist on dĕ'vĭl & pĭ'ktūr instead of dĕ'vl & pĭ'kch*er*, & the uneasy half-literates who like to prove that they can spell by calling *hour* & *medicine* howr & mĕ'dĭsĭn instead of owr & mĕ'dsn. See PRONUNCIATION.

ogee makes *ogee'd* ; see -ED & 'D.

ogre. For spelling see -RE & -ER ; for *ogr(e)ish*, SPELLING POINTS, 3 s.f.

Ogygian. Pronounce the first *g* hard ; see GREEK G.

oh. For *oh* & *O*, see o.

okapi. Pl. *-is.*

old. 1. For the distinction between *older, oldest,* & *elder, eldest,* see ELDER. 2. For the phrase *a boy* &c. *of ten* &c. *years old,* see OF 7. 3. For *the o. lady of Threadneedle Street* see SOBRIQUETS.

olden. 1. The adjective, which is of a strange formation & not to be reckoned among the numerous -EN ADJECTIVES, is also peculiar in use ; *the olden time(s)* is common, but outside that phrase the word is usually as ridiculous as *Ye* substituted for *the* in the sham-archaic advertisements of shopwindows. The combination of *olden* with *regime* in the following example is what one might expect the author to call very tasty ; see INCONGRUOUS VOCABULARY. *They form part of the olden railway regime, when every Great Western main-line train was deliberately halted for ten minutes at Swindon for refreshment.* 2. For the verb, = make or grow older, see -EN VERBS.

olfactory. For *o. organ,* see POLYSYLLABIC HUMOUR.

olio. Pl. *-os* ; see -O(E)S 4.

olive-branches. See HACKNEYED PHRASES, & SOBRIQUETS.

Olympian)(Olympic. The distinction, not as old as Shakspere & Milton, but now usually observed, is useful ; see DIFFERENTIATION. *Olympian* means of Olympus, of or as of the Greek gods whose abode was on it : *Olympian Zeus, splendour, indifference.* *Olympic* means of Olympia, of the athletic contests there held : *Olympic games, victors.*

omelet(te). The OED gives precedence to the shorter spelling.

omen. For synonymy see SIGN.

ominous. Pronounce ŏm-.

OMISSION OF IT. *As had been generally considered would be the case, the negotiations have been successful.* *As it had been* is necessary ; the rather difficult question of such omissions will be found discussed under IT 1.

omit makes *-tting* &c. (see -T-, -TT-), *omissible.*

omnibus. Pl. *-uses* ; see LATIN PLURALS.

omnium gatherum. See FACETIOUS FORMATIONS.

on. For *on all fours,* see FOUR. For *onto, on to,* & *on,* see ONTO.

-ON. Of words derived from Greek & having in English the termination *-on* : 1. Some may, & often or always do, form the plural in *-a* ; so *asyndeton, criterion, hyperbaton, noumenon, organon, oxymoron, phenomenon.* 2. Others seldom or never use that form, though it would not be incorrect, but prefer the ordinary English *-s* ; so *electron, lexicon, skeleton.* 3. In others again, the substitution of *-a* for *-on* to form the plural would be a blunder, their Greek plurals being, if they are actual Greek words, of some quite different form, & *-s* is the only plural used ; such are *anion, archon, canon, cation, cotyledon, demon, mastodon, pylon, siphon, tenon.* Words about which mistakes are possible are referred in the book to the above numbered classes.

onager. Pl. *-s,* or *onagri (-ī).*

once. 1. The use as a conjunction (i.e. = *if once* or *when once,* as in *Once you consent you are trapped*) is sound English enough, but it is sometimes forgotten that it is not for all contexts. There is a vigorous abruptness about it that makes it suitable on the one hand for highly literary expression, in poetry for instance, & on the other for the short sentences of actual conversation or dramatic dialogue. Between these extremes it is better to be content with *if* or *when,* supplemented or not by the adverb *once.* In the first quotation *if,* & in the second *when once,* would be better :— *It is to be explained perhaps by the fear that once foreign affairs become predominant, home affairs take a back place./But their aloofness might have quite the opposite result of that which they desire ; for once the crisis had* *arrived, home affairs would indeed be swamped.*

2. *Once & away*)(*once in a way*). The two phrases seem properly to have distinct meanings, the first *once & no more* (*It is not enough to harrow once & away*—1759 in OED), & the second not often ; but the present custom is to use both in the second sense, each person choosing the form that he considers fittest to convey that sense, & *in a way* being the favourite.

on dit. See FRENCH WORDS.

one. 1. Writing of *anyone, no-one,* &c. 2. *One & a half years* &c.)(*a year* &c. *& a half*). 3. *One of, if not the best book*(*s*). 4. *One of the men that does things.* 5. Kind of pronoun—numeral, indefinite or impersonal, or first-personal ? 6. Possessive of the numeral & the impersonal—*his* ? *one's* ? *their* ? 7. Mixtures of *one, you, we,* &c.

1. The forms recommended are *anyone, everyone, no-one, someone.* For discussion see NO 5 & EVERY-ONE 1.

2. *One & a half years*)(*a year & a half*). The second is recommended, when words & not figures are used ; for discussion, see MILLION 1, 2, & HALF 1. The wrong form is seen in *India has shown her loyalty by the fact that* one & a half millions *of her sons volunteered* ; *a million & a half of her sons* is obviously preferable.

3. *One of the, if not the, best book*(*s*). Grammar is a poor despised branch of learning ; if it were less despised, we should not have such frequent occasion to weep or laugh at the pitiful wrigglings of those who feel themselves in the toils of this phrase. That the victims know their plight is clear from the way they dart in different directions to find an outlet. Here are half a dozen attempts, all failures, but each distinguishable in some point of arrangement from the rest :—a. *Given in the Costume Hall—one of, if not the most, spacious of salons for dresses & costumes—the dancing has been . . .* b. *One of*

the finest, if not the finest, poem of an equal length produced of recent years. c. *I think the stage is one of, if not the best of all, professions open to women.* d. *Fur was one of the greatest—perhaps the greatest—export article: of Norway.* e. *The Japanese were one of the most, if not the most, enterprising nations in the East.* f. *One of, if not, the oldest Voortrek-kers of South Africa has just passed away.*

The nature of the problem is this : we have two expressions of the type ' one of the best books ' & ' the best book ' ; but we have been taught to avoid repetition of words, & therefore desire that part of one of these nearly similar expressions should be understood instead of said or written ; let us then enclose the partially expressed one inside the other, as a parenthesis. Can this be done ? It will be seen that a, b, & c, though they differ in minor points, all alike fail to pass the most obvious test—does the enclosing expression read rightly if the parenthesis is left out ?—*One of spacious of saloons, One of the finest poem, One of professions open to women* : the first & second nonsense, the third the wrong sense. In d, e, f, the enclosing expression taken alone does give sense ; the further test they have to pass is—if the words understood in the parenthesis are written in, does the whole read as sound, though perhaps inelegant, English ?—*One of the greatest* (*perhaps the greatest export article*) *export articles* ; *One of the most* (*if not the most enterprising nation*) *enterprising nations* ; *One of* (*if not the oldest Voortrekker*) *the oldest Voortrekkers.* Not sound English, but nonsense ; compare it with the expanding of a rightly compressed sentence : *He was, if not a perfect, a great orator,* which being filled up gives *if not a perfect orator, a great orator* ; that is not nonsense, but sound English. The rule that has been broken in the supposed compressions d, e, f, & not broken in the real one, is that you cannot understand out of a word that is yet to come another word (as *article* out of a coming *articles, nation* out of a coming *nations, Voortrekker* out of a coming *Voortrekkers*), but only the same word, as *orator* out of *orator*. When, as always happens in this idiom, there is a change of number, the only thing is to see that the place from which the understood word is omitted is after, not before, the word from which it is to be supplied ; for from a word that has already been expressed the taking of the other number is not forbidden. Accordingly, the right form for the words that concern us in the examples a–f will be :—*One of the most spacious, if not the most spacious, of salons* ; *One of the finest poems of an equal length produced of recent years, if not the finest* ; *One of the best professions open to women, if not the best of all* ; *One of the greatest export articles of Norway, perhaps the greatest* ; *One of the most enterprising nations in the East, if not the most* ; *One of the oldest Voortrekkers, if not the oldest.*

It may be thought that for a the best has not been done, & that *One of the, if not the, most spacious of salons* would have been less clumsy, & yet legitimate. It is an improvement on the original, & by inserting a *the* & correcting the stops makes a plausible attempt at compromise ; but it is not legitimate, because *most spacious* has to be taken as at the same time singular & plural ; English disguises that fact by its lack of inflexions, but does not annul it ; &, though most people are not quite sure what is the matter, they can feel that there is something the matter.

4. *One of the men who does things. Does* should be *do*. This blunder, easier to deal with than that in 3, but not less frequent, will be found discussed in Number, 5.

5. Kind of pronoun. To avoid confusion in this & the later sections between certain uses of the pronoun *one* that tend to run into each other. it will be necessary to ask the reader to accept, *pro hac vice* only, certain names. *One* is a pronoun of some sort whenever it stands not in agreement with a noun, but as a substitute for a noun preceded by *a* or *one* : in ' I took one apple ' *one* is not a pronoun, but an adjective ; in ' I want an apple ; may I take one ? ' *one* stands for *an apple* or *one apple*, & is a pronoun. But for the purpose of this article it is more important to notice that *one* is not always the same kind of pronoun ; it is of three different kinds in these three examples :—*One of them escaped* ; *One is often forced to confess failure* ; *One knew better than to swallow that.* In the first, *one* may be called a numeral pronoun, which description will cover also *I will take one, They saw one another, One is enough*, & so on. In the second, *one* has a special sense ; it stands for *a person*, i.e., the average person, or the sort of person we happen to be concerned with, or anyone of the class that includes the speaker ; it does not mean a particular person ; it might be called an indefinite, or an impersonal, pronoun ; for the sake of contrast with the third use, *impersonal pronoun* will here be the name. In the third, *one* is neither more nor less than a substitute for *I*, & the name that best describes it is the false first-personal pronoun. The distinction between the numeral & the impersonal, which is plain enough, is important because on it depend such differences as that between *One hates* his *enemies* & *One hates* one's *enemies* ; those differences will be treated in section 6. The distinction between the impersonal & the false first-personal, a rather fine one in practice, is still more important because it separates an established & legitimate use from one that ought not to exist at all. The false first-personal pronoun *one* is a new invention of the self-conscious journalist, & its suppression before it can develop further is very desirable. Outside this section, the rest of which will be devoted to illustrating the attempts to bring this novelty into being, it will be assumed that it does not exist except as a mere misuse of the impersonal *one*.

Let us take a fictitious example & pull it about, in order to make the point clear :—*He asked* me *to save his life, & I did not refuse* ; the true first-personal pronoun, twice. *He asked* me *to save his life ; could* one *refuse ?* ; true first-personal pronoun, followed by impersonal pronoun. *He asked* me *to save his life, & one did not refuse* ; true first-personal pronoun, followed by false first-personal pronoun. The *one did not refuse* cannot possibly mean anything different from *I* by itself, & is a fraud. But the self-conscious journalist has lately seen in this fraud a chance of eating his cake & having it ; it will enable him to be impersonal & personal at once ; he has repined at abstention from *I*, or has blushed over not abstaining ; here is what he has longed for, the cloak of generality that will make egotism respectable. The sad results of this discovery are shown in the following extracts ; in none of them is there any real doubt that *one & one's* mean I & my simply ; but in some more than in others the connexion with the legitimate impersonal use is traceable. The journalist should make up his mind that he will, or that he will not, talk in the first person, & go on the sound assumption that *one & one's* do not mean I & me & mine.

The false first-personal ONE.

But one *must conclude* one's *survey (at the risk,* I *am afraid, of tedious reiteration) by insisting that . . ./* I *have known in the small circle of* one's *personal friends quite a number of Jews who . . ./His accounts of Redan Ridge & the Schwaben Redoubt, too long to quote, are the best* one *has seen./To enjoy therein the pleasure & comfort for which the nation proposes to give it the means ;* one *here uses the word ' proposes ' advisedly, for there is as yet no Government which can promise./Here also, in England, the Peruvian Minister has reechoed these kind sentiments & shown in a practical manner his appreciation of* one's *efforts./On mildly suggesting that these sea-mists were probably quite local & that it might be quite clear inland,* one *received the crushing rejoinder . . ./This is not,* I *think, ecclesiastical prejudice, for* one *has tried to be perfectly fair./His later poems have their great limitation, as* one *will presently suggest, but they are extraordinarily powerful./A glossary of cricket terms, in which* one *was almost beside* oneself *with joy to find no reference to the ' cowshot './* I *take fresh hope, convinced that* one's *efforts will now be more fully & adequately supported./The book is bound in red & gold, & has the novelist's autograph in gold upon the front ;* one *mentions gold twice over, because . . .*

6. Possessive, & other belongings, of *one.* By other belongings are meant the reflexive, & the form to be used when the pronoun *one* has already been used & is wanted again either *in propria persona* or by deputy ; as, when Caesar has been named, he can be afterwards called either *Caesar* or *he,* so, when *one* has been used, is it indifferent whether it is repeated itself or represented by *he* &c. ?

In the first place, there is no doubt about the numeral pronoun *one* ; its possessive, reflexive, & deputy pronoun, are never *one's, oneself, & one,* but always the corresponding parts of *he, she,* or *it. I saw one drop* his stick ; *Certainly, if one offers* herself *as candidate ; One would not go off even when I hammered* it.

Secondly, the impersonal *one* always can, & now usually does, provide its own possessive &c.—*one's, oneself,* & *one* ; thus *One does not like to have* one's *word doubted* ; *If one fell,* one *would hurt* oneself *badly.*

But thirdly, in American, in older English, & in a small minority of modern British writers, the above sentences would run *One does not like to have* his *word doubted* ; *If one fell,* he *would hurt* himself *badly.*

The prevailing modern fashion (*one's, oneself,* &c.) should be made universal ; it gives a useful differentiation between the numeral & the impersonal, which however is not reliable till it is universal ; & it makes recourse to the horrible *their* &c. (*One does not like to have* their *word doubted*) needless. The following examples, all but one of them recent, will suffice to show that not all writers yet accept the modern idiom, though it is certainly in the interests of the language that they should :—*There are many passages which* one *is rather inclined to like than sure* he *would be right in liking* (19th-c. American)./*Assuredly, there is no form of* ' *social service* ' *comparable to that which* one *can render by doing* his *job to the very best of* his *ability.*/*Let* us*, in fact, substitute a* '*graceful raising of* one's *hand to* his *hat, with a nod* '.*/As* one *goes through the rooms,* he *is struck by the youth of most.*/*If seeing sixteenth-century Europe implied spending the nights in sixteenth-century inns,* one *imagines* he *would rather have stayed at home.*

The difference between *One hates* his *enemies* & *One hates* one's *enemies* is at once apparent if to each is added a natural continuation :—*One hates* his *enemies & another forgives them* ; *One hates* one's *enemies & loves* one's *friends.* The first *one* is numeral, the second impersonal, & to make *his* & *one's* exchange places, or to write either in both places, would be plain folly.

Let it be added, for anyone who may regard *one's* & *one(self)* in the use here concerned as fussy modernism, that they are after all not so modern : *I hope, cousin, one may speak to* one's *own relations*—Goldsmith.

7. Mixtures of *one* with *we, you, my,* &c. These are all bad, though the degrees of badness differ ; for instance, it is merely slipshod to pass from *one* in an earlier sentence to *you* in the next, but more heinous to bring two varieties into syntactical relations in a single sentence. *As* one *goes through the rooms,* he *is struck by the youth of most of those who toil* ; *the girls marry,* you *are told* ; *he* belongs to section 6, in which the sentence has been quoted ; *you* illustrates the more venial form of mixture./*As* one *who vainly warned* my *countrymen that Germany was preparing to attack her neighbours for many a long day before the declaration of war, I say that . . .* ; *My* should be *his, one* being the numeral pronoun ; but this kind of attraction in relative clauses (*my* taking the person of *I* instead of that of *one* & *who*) is very common./*To listen to his strong likes & dislikes* one *sometimes thought that* you *were in the presence of a Quaker of the eighteenth century* ; a bad case ; *you* were should be *one was.*/*Perhaps there are too many of them* ; we *might have enjoyed making their acquaintance still more had* one *been given pause* ; either *we* should be *one,* or *one* should be *we.*/*No* one *likes to see a woman who has shared* one's *home in distress* ; *no-one* contains the numeral, not the impersonal, *one,* & *one's* should be *his.*/*To be a good Imperialist* you *must assent to the impotence & decadence & backwardness of* one's *own motherland* ; *you* should be *one,* or *one's* should be *your.*

one-idea'd. So spelt ; see -ED & 'D.

ONE WORD OR TWO OR MORE. For ALL RIGHT, ALREADY, ALTOGETHER & *all together,* ANY *way* & *anyway,* at ANY *rate* & *at anyrate,* COMMON SENSE & *common-sense,* EVERYONE &

every one, INTO & *in to*, ONTO & *on to*, see the words in small capitals. For *blackbird* & *black bird*, see HYPHENS ; for *no-one* & *no one*, & for *in no wise* & *in nowise*, NO, 5 ; for *someone* & *some one*, EVERYONE.

only, adv. : its placing & misplacing. *I read the other day of a man who ' only died a week ago ', as if he could have done anything else more striking or final ; what was meant by the writer was that he ' died only a week ago '.* There speaks one of those friends from whom the English language may well pray to be saved, one of the modern precisians who have more zeal than discretion, & wish to restrain liberty as such, regardless of whether it is harmfully or harmlessly exercised. It is pointed out in several parts of this book that illogicalities & inaccuracies of expression tend to be eliminated as a language grows older & its users attain to a more conscious mastery of their materials. But this tendency has its bad as well as its good effects ; the pedants who try to forward it when the illogicality is only apparent or the inaccuracy of no importance are turning English into an exact science or an automatic machine ; if they are not quite botanizing upon their mother's grave, they are at least clapping a strait waistcoat upon their mother tongue, when wiser physicians would refuse to certify the patient.

The design is to force us all, whenever we use the adverb *only*, to spend time in considering which is the precise part of the sentence strictly qualified by it, & then put it there—this whether there is any danger or none of the meaning's being false or ambiguous because *only* is so placed as to belong grammatically to a whole expression instead of to a part of it, or to be separated from the part it specially qualifies by another part.

It may at once be admitted that there is an orthodox placing for *only*, but it does not follow that there are not often good reasons for departing from orthodoxy. For *He only died a week ago* no better defence is perhaps possible than that it is the order that most people have always used & still use, & that, the risk of misunderstanding being chimerical, it is not worth while to depart from the natural. Remember that in speech there is not even the possibility of misunderstanding, because the intonation of *died* is entirely different if it, & not *a week ago*, is qualified by *only* ; & it is fair that a reader should be supposed capable of supplying the decisive intonation where there is no temptation to go wrong about it. But take next an example in which, ambiguity being practically possible, the case against heterodox placing is much stronger :—*Mackenzie only seems to go wrong when he lets in yellow ; & yellow seems to be still the standing difficulty of the colour printer.* The orthodox place for *only* is immediately before *when*, & the antithesis between seeming to go & really going, which is apt to suggest itself though not intended, makes the displacement here ill advised ; its motive, however, is plain—to announce the limited nature of the wrong before the wrong itself, & so mitigate the censure : a quite sound rhetorical instinct, &, if *goes* had been used instead of *seems to go*, a sufficient defence of the heterodoxy. But there are many sentences in which, owing to greater length, it is much more urgent to get this announcement of purport made by an advanced *only*. E.g., the orthodox *It would be safe to prophesy success to this heroic enterprise only if reward & merit always corresponded* positively cries out to have its *only* put early after *would*, & unless that is done the hearer or reader is led astray ; yet the precisian is bound to insist on orthodoxy here as much as in *He died only a week ago.*

The advice offered is this : there

is an orthodox position for the adverb, easily determined in case of need ; to choose another position that may spoil or obscure the meaning is bad ; but a change of position that has no such effect except technically is both justified by historical & colloquial usage & often demanded by rhetorical needs.

The OED remarks on the point should be given : ' *Only* was formerly often placed away from the word or words which it limited ; this is still frequent in speech, where the stress & pauses prevent ambiguity, but is now avoided by perspicuous writers '. Which implies the corollary that when perspicuity is not in danger it is needless to submit to an inconvenient restriction.

A specimen or two of different kinds are added for the reader's unaided consideration :—*The address to be written on this side only./ Europe only has a truce before it, but a truce that can be profited by./Some of the Metropolitan crossings can only now be negotiated with considerable risk./If only the foundry trades had been concerned, probably the employers would not have greatly objected to conceding an advance./I only know nothing shall induce me to go again./ I only asked the question from habit./ We can only form a sound & trustworthy opinion if we first consider a large variety of instances.*

onomatopoeia. See Technical Terms.

onomatopoeic, -poetic. The first form (pronounce -pē′ĭk) is decidedly preferable, because the other inevitably suggests, at least to those who do not know Greek, irrelevant associations with poet. For writing of *-oeic*, see Æ, Œ.

onto, on to, on. *The logic of this electioneering leads straight to the abolition of the contributions & the placing of the whole burden on to the State. / The Pan-Germans are strong enough to depose a Foreign Secretary & force their own man* on to *the Government in his place.* Writers & printers should make up their minds whether there is such a preposition as *onto* or not ; if there is not, they should omit the *to* in such contexts as the above, which are good English without it ; if there is, & they like it better than the simple *on* or *to* (an odd taste, except under very rare conditions), they should make one word of it. Abstain from the preposition if you like ; use it & own up if you like ; but do not use it & pretend there is no such word ; those should be the regulations. The use of *on to* as separate words is, however, correct when *on* is a full adverb ; & very rarely doubts may arise whether this is so or not ; is *on* an adverb, or is *onto* a preposition, for instance, in *He played the ball on to his wicket ?* as *He played on* could stand by itself, it is hard to deny *on* its independent status. Occasions for *on to* : *We must walk on to Keswick* ; *Each passed it on to his neighbour* ; *Struggling on to victory.* Occasions for *on* or *to* or *onto*, but on no account *on to* : *Climbed up on*(to) *the roof* ; *Was invited* (*on*)*to the platform* ; *It struggles* (*on*)*to its legs again* ; *They fell 300 ft on*(to) *a glacier.*

onward(s). The shorter form is much commoner in all senses, except possibly in phrases of the type *from the tenth century onwards.*

oolite. Pronounce ō′olĭt.

opacity)(opaqueness. The figurative senses are avoided with the second, but the literal senses are not confined to it, though there is perhaps a tendency to complete differentiation : *The opacity of his understanding* ; *Owing to the opaqueness*, or *opacity, of the glass.*

operate makes *-rable, -tor* ; see -ABLE 1, -OR.

operculum. Pl. *-la*.

opinionated, -ative. Both have existed long enough in English to justify anyone in using either. But for those who do prefer a sound to a faulty formation it may be said that the first is unobjectionable, & the second not. A Latin *opinionatus* might have been correctly made from the noun *opinio*; cf. *dentatus* from *dens*, & many others; & the English representative of *opinionatus* would be indifferently *opinionate* or *opinionated*. But Latin *ativus* belongs to verb-derivatives only, & *opinativus* from the verb *opinor*, giving English *opinative* (which once existed), would have been the true source for a word in *-ative*.

opportunity. *He rapidly rose by the display of rare organizing ability to be superintendent over the affairs of the company in the Far East, with practically a free hand—a fact of which he took every opportunity.* You *take the o.*, or *an o.*, or *every o.*, of doing something. You *take advantage*, or *all possible advantage*, of a fact or event or state of affairs. The two sets of phrases must not be mixed; see CAST-IRON IDIOM, & ANALOGY.

oppose makes *-sable*; see MUTE E.
opposeless. See -LESS.
opposite tempts careless writers to the slovenly clipping seen in: *He can thwart him by applying it to the opposite purpose for which it was intended* (*he* is pupil, *him* teacher, & *it* the teaching). Insert *from* (or *to*) *that* after *purpose*; & for similar temptations cf. AS 3 (*the question as to whom it belongs*, &c.), REGARD (*I regard it my duty to . . .*, &c.), & DEPEND.

oppress makes *-ssible*, *-ssor*; see -ABLE 2, -OR.
optative. The natural pronunciation would have been ŏ′ptătĭv (' cf. *ablative, precative, relative* ' says the OED); but, as the word is very rare outside its technical use in grammar, & those who deal in grammar have somehow come to call it ŏptā′tĭv, it is not worth while to attempt to reform them; anyone who wishes to use it apart from grammar (*The will or optative power,*

choosing or rejecting among the objects presented to the mind) is justified in saying ŏ′ptătĭv. For the grammatical use see TECHNICAL TERMS.

optic. For the noun use, = eye, see PEDANTIC HUMOUR; ' Formerly the learned & elegant term '—OED.
optimism, -ist(ic). *Besides optimism, which affirms the definitive ascendency of good, & pessimism, which affirms the definitive ascendency of evil, a third hypothesis is possible.* / *The optimistic or sentimental hypothesis that wickedness always fares ill in the world.* / *The company had suffered severe losses, but at the last meeting the chairman spoke with a fair amount of optimism.* /*Mr Balfour, I learn, has rented his flat till October; but he is optimistic if he really thinks that he, or whoever represents the Foreign Office, can leave Paris by October.* The first two quotations show the words in their proper sense, the last two in their modern popular triviality. They have become VOGUE-WORDS, on much the same level as INDIVIDUAL & MENTALITY. They belong in time between those two, & are not yet discredited like the former, but have lost the charm of novelty that still lingers about the latter. Like both those, they owe their vogue to the delight of the ignorant in catching up a word that has puzzled them when they first heard it, & exhibiting their acquaintance with it as often as possible; & like both those they displace with what differs more or less from the idea intended the familiar words that would express it exactly. In the third & fourth quotations, *sanguine* & *hope* would have given the sense not less but more exactly than *optimistic* & *optimism*. See POPULARIZED TECHNICALITIES.

opus. Pl., seldom used, *opera*; see LATIN PLURALS.
opusculum. Pl. *-ula*.
or. 1. *Or*) (*nor.* 2. Number, pronouns, &c., after *or*. 3. *Or* in

enumerations. 4. Wrong repetition after *or*.

1. *Or*)(*nor*. There are sentences in which it is indifferent, & affects neither meaning nor correctness, whether *or* or *nor* is used. Compare with *I can neither read nor write* (in which *nor* is requisite), & with *I cannot either read or write* (in which *or* is requisite), *I cannot read nor* (or indifferently *or*) *write*. The alternatives in the last are differently arrived at, but are practically equivalent : *I cannot read, nor* (can I) *write* ; *I cannot read*(-)*or*(-) *write*, where the supposed hyphens mean that *write* may be substituted for *read* if desired. The use of *nor* in such cases was formerly in fashion, & that of *or* is now in fashion ; that is all. But the modern preference for *or* where it is equally legitimate with *nor* has led to its being preferred also where it is illegitimate ; so :— *It is of great importance that they should face them* in no academic spirit, or *trust too much to conclusions drawn from maps.*/*No Government Department or any other Authority has assisted.* The test of legitimacy has been explained in NOR ; & it suffices here to say that in the first extract it is the position of *no* (alter to *they should not face them in any*), & in the second the presence of *any* (precluding the carrying on of *no*), that forbid *or*.

2. Number, pronouns, &c., after *or*. When the subject is a set of alternatives each in the singular, however many the alternatives, & however long the sentence, the verb must be singular ; in the extract below, *account* should be *accounts* ; for discussion see NUMBER, 3 : *Either the call of patriotism & the opportunity of seeing new lands, or conscription, or the fact that tramping was discouraged even by old patrons when the call for men became urgent,* account *for it.* If alternative members differ in number &c., the nearest prevails (*Were you or he, was he or you, there ?* ; *either he or you were, either you or he was*), but some forms

(e. g. *Was I or you on duty ?*) are avoided by inserting a second verb (*Was I, or were you . . . ?*). Forms in which difference of gender causes difficulty with pronouns (*A landlord or landlady expects their, his or her, his, rent*) are usually avoided, *their rent* or *the rent due to them* being ungrammatical, *his or her rent* or *the rent due to him or her* clumsy, & *his rent* or *the rent due to him* slovenly ; some evasion, as *expects rent*, or *the rent*, is always possible.

3. *Or* in enumerations. *I never heard a sermon that was simpler, sounder, or dealt with more practical matters.* In the very numerous sentences made on this bad pattern there is a confusion between two correct ways of saying the thing, viz (a) *that was simpler, sounder, or more practical*, (b) *that was simpler or sounder or dealt with more practical matters.* See ENUMERATION, & for full discussion AND 2. The abundant illustration of the latter makes similar quotations here needless, & it will be enough to give a single sentence for the reader to apply the principle to—a sentence whose length slightly obscures the writer's mistake ; he should have inserted *and* in the place indicated : *A few years ago the natural instincts of the other Powers would have been to notify Italy that Tripoli was a Turkish possession,* ∧ *that if she wished to secure it she must do so by negotiation & purchase, or, failing that, put her case before a conference of the Powers.*

4. Wrong repetition after *or*. A misguided determination to be very explicit & leave no opening for doubt results in a type of mistake illustrated in the article OVERZEAL. It is peculiarly common with *or*, & to put writers on their guard a number of examples follow. False analogy from *and* explains it ; with *and*, it does not matter whether we say *without falsehood & deceit* or *without falsehood & without deceit*, except that the latter conveys a certain sledge-hammer emphasis ; but with *or* there is much difference between *without falsehood or deceit* (which implies that neither is present) & *without falsehood or without deceit* (which implies only that one of the two is not present). In all the examples except the last, either *or* must be changed to *and*, or the word or words repeated after *or* must be cut out ; in the last example, if *or* is to be retained, it will be necessary, besides omitting *no*, to change *one* to *person. No great economy or no high efficiency can be secured./All these principal causes were in operation before Mr Lloyd George came on the scene or before his budget was heard of./There would be nothing very surprising or nothing necessarily fraudulent in an unconscious conspiracy to borrow from each other./We need something more before we can conclude that Germany is going to be democratized in any effective way*, or before we can *be sure that this move also is not a weapon in the war./All this, we are told, can be done without any flirtation with Home Rule or without any sacrifice of the loyalists./. . . prevents the labourer from being a free agent or from having a free market for his labour./To no conference of pacifist tendencies or to no gatherings where representatives of the enemy people will be found, will American labour organizations send delegates./Every arrangement ends in a compromise, & no one or no party may ever be expected to carry its own views out in their entirety.*

-OR is the Latin agent-noun ending corresponding to the English *-er* ; compare *doer* & *perpetrator.* English verbs derived from the supine stem of Latin ones—i. e., especially most verbs in *-ate*, but also many others such as *oppress, protect, act, credit, possess, invent, prosecute*— usually prefer this Latin form to the English one in *-er.* Some other verbs, e. g. *govern, conquer*, & *purvey*, not corresponding to the above description have agent nouns in *-or*

owing to their passage through French or other circumstances that need not here be set forth. An attempt has been made to register the verbs whose agent nouns end in *-or*, with references to this article. A few odd differences may be of interest : *decanter* & *castor* ; *dispenser* & *distributor* ; *adapter* & *inventor* ; *digester* & *collector* ; *corrupter* & *corrector* ; *deserter* & *abductor* ; *eraser* & *ejector* ; *promoter* & *abettor.*

Orangism, -geism. The first is better ; see MUTE E.

orate. A BACK-FORMATION from *oration*, & marked by the slangy jocularity of its class.

oratio obliqua, recta. See TECHNICAL TERMS.

oratorio. Pl. *-os* ; see -O(E)S 4.

oratress. See FEMININE DESIGNATIONS.

orb. See GLOBE.

orchis, -chid. The first form is applied chiefly to the English wild kinds & is accordingly the poetic & the country word ; pl. *-ises* (see -S-, -SS-).

ordeal. All the verse quotations in the OED (Chaucer, Spenser, Cowley, Butler, Tennyson) show the accent on the first syllable. Whether -dēl or -dĭal is right is less clear.

order. For wrong constructions after *in order that* (*i. o. t. the complaint that colliery proprietors are diverting domestic coal for industrial purposes* can *be considered*), see IN ORDER THAT.

orderly. See -LILY.

oread. Pronounce or'ĭad.

oreography &c. See OROGRAPHY.

organize makes *-zable* ; see MUTE E.

organizedly. A bad form ; see -EDLY.

organon. Pl. *-ana, -ns* ; see -ON 1.

originate makes *-nable, -tor* ; see -ABLE 1, -OR.

orison. Pronounce ŏ'rĭzn.

Orleans. Pronounce or'lĭanz.

ornament. See NOUN & VERB ACCENT, 1 C.

ornithology, ornithorhyncus, &c.

The proper sound of the first element is orni'tho, not or'nītho, & it seems better to keep the ī except when the falling of the main accent on the next syllable (-o-) makes it unnatural ; see FALSE QUANTITY. This would give, among common words : ornitho-cepha'lic, ornitholo'gical, orni'tho-mancy, & ornithorhy'ncus ; but orni-tho'logist, ornitho'logy, & ornitho'-scopy.

orography, orolingual, &c. The identical representation of Greek *oros* mountain & Latin *os* mouth by *oro-* is regrettable. The most convenient arrangement consistent with correctness would have been to make *ori-* the combining form of Latin *os* mouth (*oricentral, ori-anal, ori-lingual,* &c.), & *oreo-* that of Greek *oros* mountain (*oreography, oreometric,* &c.). As *ori-* does exist in *orinasal* & other mouth-words, & *oreo-* has not been entirely superseded in the mountain-words, it is possibly not too late to suggest that this distinction should even now be established.

orotund. The odd thing about the word is that its only currency, at least in its non-technical sense, is among those who should most abhor it, the people of sufficient education to realize its bad formation ; it is at once a monstrosity in its form & a pedantry in its use. If the elocu-tionists & experts in voice-produc-tion like it as a technical term, they are welcome to it ; the rest of us should certainly leave it to them, & not regard it as a good substitute for *magniloquent, sounding, highflown, in-flated, pompous, imposing,* & the like.

oscillate makes *-llable, -tor* ; see -ABLE 1, -OR.

osculatory. A favourite POLY-SYLLABIC-HUMOUR word : *The two ladies went through the o. ceremony./ At the end of one letter were a number of dots which he (counsel) presumed were meant to represent an o. per-formance.*

ossify. For inflexions see VERBS IN -IE, -Y, -YE, 6.

ostler, h-. Pronounce ŏ'slẽr ; see PRONUNCIATION. The form without *h-* is the now established one, though etymologically wrong ; *hospital, hos-tel, hotel,* & *hostler,* belong together.

ostracize makes *-zable* ; see MUTE E.
other. 1. *Each o.)(one another.*
2. *On the other hand.* 3. *Of all others.*
4. *Other)(others* or *another.* 5. *Other than.*

1. *Each o.)(one another.* For the syntax of these, & for the distinction sometimes made between them, see EACH 2.
2. *On the o. hand.* For the difference between this & *on the contrary,* see CONTRARY 2.
3. *Of all others.* *You are the man of all others I wanted to see.* A mix-ture of *You are the man of all men* &c. & *You are the man I wanted to see beyond all others.* A still popular ILLOGICALITY, perhaps to be counted among the STURDY INDEFENSIBLES that are likely to survive their critics.
4. *Other)(others* or *another.* The writers of the following sentences may be supposed to have hesitated between *other* & *others* ; if they had decided for *others,* they would have been more in tune with modern usage ; to say they would have chosen more correctly is hardly possible :—*The Unionist Party will do well to remember that the wrecking policy is, like* other *of their adven-tures in recent times, a dangerous gamble./We find here, as in* other *of his novels, that he has no genius for . . ./Mrs —— will, we hope, incite* other *of her countrymen & countrywomen to similar studies./ We were quite prepared for the most rigid prohibition of trade with Ger-many ; so was France &* other *of our Allies./A Privy Councillorship, an honour which has but rarely been won by* other *than those who were British subjects from the moment of their birth.*
In four of these we have what the OED calls the absolute use of the adjective, the noun represented by *other* being present elsewhere in the

sentence, but not expressed with *other* (*like other adventures of the adventures* &c. would be the fully expressed forms) ; in the fifth we have the full pronoun use, *other* meaning *other persons, & persons* not being expressed either with *other* or elsewhere. But alike of the absolute & the pronoun use the OED describes the plural *other* as archaic, & the plural *others* as the regular modern form. In older English, however, *other* was normal in such contexts, so that those who like the archaic can justify themselves; *others* is here recommended.

If it is now contrary to usage to prefer *other* to *others*, it is much worse to prefer it to *another*, which is the modern absolute & pronominal form in the singular just as *others* is in the plural ; but that is what has been done in : *A number of writers on various subjects serve to give interest to the review on* other *than its political side*—unless indeed the meaning is *its other than political side*, which would stand or fall, as the equivalent of *its non-political side*, with the examples discussed at the end of 5 ; but, if so, the order of words has been dislocated.

5. Abuses of *other than*. The existence of an adverbial use of *other* is recognized by the OED, but supported by very few quotations, & those from no authors whose names carry weight ; its recent development may be heartily condemned as both ungrammatical & needless. A number of newspaper extracts will first be given in which the only correction necessary is to insert the real adverb *otherwise* instead of the false adverb *other* ; it will be seen that, every time, the phrase on the other side of *than* is adverbial like *otherwise*, & not adjectival like *other* ; in the article OTHERWISE the converse mistake is shown to be equally common ; both mistakes are as stupid as they are common ; &, though the substitution of *otherwise* for *other* or vice versa removes the blunder, it is usually true that it

would have been better to use neither *other than* nor *otherwise than*, but some different expression.

Other for *otherwise*

So that no new invention could come in o. t. through a specific company (except)./*A subordinate sprite will no more obey a conjuration addressed to him by a magician o. t. in the name of his proper superior than* . . . (in any other name than that)./*It could not possibly have been carried out o. t. by the mammoth vessels* (except)./ *Some via media whereby the influence of the community could be brought to bear o. t. through the Civil Service could probably be evolved* (otherwise)./ *Yet how many of the disputants would know where to look for them— o. t. by a tiresome search through the files of the daily Press—if they desired to consult them ?* (short of)./ *Although the world at large & for long refused to treat it o. t. humorously* (otherwise)./*There was never a moment when it could less become Englishmen to speak o. t. respectfully & courteously of the Russian nation* (otherwise).

But simple confusion between *other* & *otherwise* does not account for every bad *other than*. A notion seems to prevail that one exhibits refinement or verbal resource or some such accomplishment if one can contrive an *other-than* variant for what would naturally be expressed by some other negative form of speech : *with o. t. apprehension* is thought superior in literary tone to *without apprehension, could not leave o. t. restless* to *could not but leave restless, be other than flattered* to *help being flattered, o. t. when Parliament was sitting* to *when Parliament was not sitting* ; so :—*Up to the very end no German field company would look* with o. t. apprehension *to meeting the 25th on even terms./Four years of war could not leave a people* o. t. restless./*Mr Collier has some faults to find, but no Englishman* can be o. t. flattered *by the picture which he paints of British activities./The Premier sent telegrams to the various States suggesting that they should concur in the Governor-General residing in New South Wales* o. t. when Parliament was sitting. One or two of these are justifiable, while one is certainly not, from the grammarian's point of view ; regarded as ornaments, they are clearly of no great value ; on the whole, *other than* should be registered as a phrase to be avoided except where it is both the most natural way of putting the thing & grammatically defensible.

otherwise is now having very curious experiences—emphatically *is having* in the present tense, because, while the OED shows no trace whatever of the two uses to be illustrated below, both of them are so common at this moment that probably no-one ever reads his newspaper through without meeting them. Whether this popularity is a sign of lately developed indispensability, or merely a new example of the speed with which a trick of bad English can be spread by fashion (cf. ASSET, SUBSTITUTE, PROPOSITION, PROTAGONIST), it is hard to say with confidence ; but, as one use is a definite outrage on grammatical principles, & the other not very easy to reconcile with them, we may perhaps hope that they are freaks of fashion only, & that their future will be as short as their past.

The first is the ungrammatical use of the adverb *otherwise* when the adjective *other* would be correct ; cf. OTHER for the converse mistake. Comment will be better reserved till the reader has seen some examples :—*This reduction in total expenditure has been made concurrently with certain increases*—automatic & otherwise—*in particular items./There are large tracts of the country*, agricultural & otherwise, *in which the Labour writ does not run./No further threats*, economic or otherwise, *have been made./This is a common incident in all warfare*, industrial or otherwise./*No organi-*

zations, religious or otherwise, *had troubled to take the matter up./The United States is no longer under any obligation to preserve neutrality, whether* ' true ' or otherwise./*The author's line of demarcation between stamps* desirable & otherwise *is rather arbitrary./Place a fair share of taxation on the owners*, ducal & otherwise, *holding land & not developing it.*

An apology may fairly be expected for presenting so long a string of monotonous examples. The apology is that, before asking the journalist to give up a favourite habit, one should convince him that it is his habit. That the habit is a bad one needs no demonstration ; but it is worth while to consider how it has come into existence, & whether abstention from it is really a serious inconvenience. In all the above quotations, the structure is the same —an adjective deferred till after its noun & followed by an *and* or an *or* joining to it the adverb *otherwise*. Now, what should possess anyone, under those circumstances, to match the adjective with *otherwise* instead of *other* ? Is it not (far-fetched as the explanation may seem) that the old saying ' Some men are wise & some are otherwise ' has lately struck the popular consciousness as witty, & has incidentally inspired a belief that *otherwise*, & not *other*, is the natural parallel to an adjective ? The justification of the proverb's own wording is simple—that it is a pun, & that puns treat grammar as love treats locksmiths, with derision. A pun, however, & still more the faded memory of a pun, is a bad basis for a general idiom. But, next, there is no difficulty whatever in abstaining from this bit of bad grammar. It is true that things have now reached the stage when many people feel that to change the popular *otherwise* to the correct *other* is sometimes pedantic ; but it is only sometimes, & there are other resources. The above examples would none of them be less natural if the offending expression were rewritten thus: *certain automatic & other increases—some agricultural & some not—no further economic or other threats—industrial or not—religious or non-religious—whether ' true ' or not—desirable stamps & others—the ducal & other owners.* In correcting, the simple change of *otherwise* to *other* has been avoided, though in fact the critic who would say ' pedantry ' to it must be a little crazy on the subject.

In the second use now to be deprecated, the grammar admits of a rather elaborate defence, but the phrase is not worth the trouble of defending. It is this time not an adjective, but a noun, to which *otherwise* supplies the parallel. Take the three forms : *What concerns us is his solvency* ; *What concerns us is his solvency or insolvency* ; *What concerns us is his solvency or otherwise.* An enormous majority of the sentences in which *or otherwise* answers to a noun are of this type ; i.e., it makes no appreciable difference to the meaning & effect which of the three forms is chosen. The first & the second are as much & as little different in most contexts as *Are you ready ?* is different from *Are you ready or not ?* ; there is a possibility, which seldom passes into fact, that the expression of the alternative, which if not expressed would be implied, conveys a special emphasis. The third differs from the second (if grammar is put aside) only as a piece of ELEGANT VARIA-TION differs from the same meaning given without the variation ; *otherwise* is used to escape repeating, in *insolvency,* the previous *solvency.* Few readers who will compare without prejudice the three forms will refuse to admit that the best of the three, wherever it is possible, is the first & shortest—*What concerns us is his solvency*—, the additions *or insolvency* & *or otherwise* being mere waste of words. If writers in general put the question to themselves, made the admission,

& acted upon it, not one *or otherwise* in the long list that follows would have been written. *Or otherwise* after a noun is (a) nearly always superfluous, (b) when it is not superfluous, an inferior substitute for *or* with the negative form of the preceding noun or an equivalent, & (c) grammatically questionable. Examples of the ordinary foolish use now follow, & the reader is invited to agree that each would be improved by the simple omission of *or otherwise* :—*Crystalline character is acknowledged to be a safe test of identity o. o. in the realm of physiology./I do not think I made any assertion as to the mutability o. o. of nature./Its usefulness, o. o., to Germany depends entirely upon the material conditions of the wars to which it will be applied./The electorate may be consulted on the merits, o. o., of a single specific measure./A searching examination of the financial wisdom, o. o., of such undertakings./ This witness has been called as to the accuracy, o. o., of the statements of two other witnesses./A Royal Commission to consider & report on the need o. o. for State protection of this asset in our resources./To enable judgment to be passed upon the merits, o. o., of any fancy formula for winning wars./The success of our efforts depends on the success o. o. of the German submarine campaign./I am not concerned with the accuracy o. o. of the figures given./Without offering an opinion as to the desirability o. o. of the growth of a definite party./ Any inquiry as to the correctness o. o. of his assessment./It is entirely for the High Court to ascertain the truth o. o. of the statements./The provision of coal & the financing of raw materials for Austrian industry are not dependent on the solvency o. o. of the Austrian State.*

It has been allowed above that *o. o.* in this construction is not quite always superfluous. It is not superfluous in *With the view of showing the applicability (o. o.) to the practical affairs of government of the principles which* . . . That is due to the particular verb *showing*, which prevents *applicability* from including as usual its opposite. But, while such cases are rare (1 : 14 gives the proportion in which they have actually presented themselves to the collector), it is better even in these to give the sense in some other way, e.g. *to showing how far the principles which . . . are applicable.* Similarly, in *It has an area of under 100 square miles, & enjoys—o. o.—a very heavy rainfall* ' or does not enjoy ', ' or endures ', &c., would be better in grammar, as good in sense, &, considering the dimness with which *or otherwise* now sparkles, not inferior in brilliance.

The reader may perhaps be curious about the statement that such phrases as *applicability o. o.* are grammatically not quite indefensible. In *He never conveyed to me any intimation that he disapproved, strongly o. o., of my conduct*, we have an unquestionably legitimate use, *otherwise* being parallel to *strongly*, another adverb. In *Yesterday he was our hero, but today he is otherwise, otherwise* is parallel to·an adverb, but to the noun *hero* ; nevertheless grammar is not offended, because the complement of *to be* can be noun, adjective, or adverb, indifferently : *He is a hero, He is dead, He is abroad.* That is why *Governor Sulzer is the hero (o. o.) of a quaint election story* is excusable ; though not itself legitimate, it is a slight & natural extension of something that is legitimate ; yet it remains true that *or villain* (or other opposite of *hero*, according to the sense desired) would be better. The type of which so many examples were given, with *o. o.* answering to abstract nouns like *applicability* or *truth*, is similarly accounted for. *Is it applicable or is it otherwise ?* is sound enough English ; when we want to turn these questions into a noun, *its applicability o. o.* not unnaturally presents itself as a short form of *its being applicable or being*

otherwise ; it can claim a sort of secondhand soundness ; like an addled egg, it has in an earlier phase been good.

To sum up, *o. o.* is in grammar occasionally quite correct, often indefensible, but usually capable of a· rather far-fetched justification ; in meaning it is, except when strictly correct, nearly always superfluous, & always less exact than some equivalent ; & in style (again except when correct) it has the disadvantage of suggesting, even when the user is innocent of any such intent, a sort of insipid jocosity.

ottava rima. See TECHNICAL TERMS.

ought, n., is a wrong form for *nought.*

ought, v., is peculiarly liable to be carelessly combined with auxiliary verbs that differ from it in taking the plain infinitive without *to. Can & ought to go* is right, but *Ought & can go* is wrong. *We should be sorry to see English critics suggesting that they ought or could have acted otherwise* ; insert *to* after *ought*, or write *that they could or ought to have acted.* See ELLIPSIS 2.

our. 1. *Our*)(*ours.* 2. *Our* editorial & ordinary. 3. *Our*)(*his.*

1. *Our*)(*ours. Ours & the Italian troops are now across the Piave.* The right alternatives are : *The Italian troops · & ours, The Italian & our troops, Our & the Italian troops* ; the wrong one is that in the quotation ; see ABSOLUTE POSSESSIVES.

2. The editorial *our*, like *we & us* of that kind, should not be allowed to appear in the same sentence, or in close proximity, with any non-editorial use of *we* &c. In the following, *our* & the second *we* are editorial, while *us* & the first *we* are national : *For chaos it is now proposed to substitute law, law by which* we *must gain as neutrals, & which,* in our *view, inflicts no material sacrifice on* us *as belligerents. We do not propose to argue that question again from the beginning, but* . . .

3. *Our*)(*his. Which of us would wish to be ill in* our *kitchen, especially when it is also the family living-room ?* If a possessive adjective were necessary, *his* & not *our* would be the right one, or, at greater length, *his or her.* People of weak grammatical digestions, unable to stomach *his*, should find means of doing without the possessive ; why not simply *the* kitchen, here ? But many of them, who prefer even the repulsive THEIR to the right forms, are naturally delighted when *of us* gives them a chance of the less repulsive but at least slovenly *our.* It is undeniable that *which of us* is a phrase denoting a singular, & that the possessive required by it is one that refers to a singular.

-OUR & -OR. The American abolition of *-our* in such words as *honour* & *favour* has probably retarded rather than quickened English progress in the same direction. Our first notification that the book we are reading is not English but American is often, nowadays, the sight of an *-or.* 'Yankee' we say, & congratulate ourselves on spelling like gentlemen ; we wisely decline to regard it as a matter for argument ; the English way cannot but be better than the American way ; that is enough. Most of us, therefore, do not come to the question with an open mind. Those who are willing to put national prejudice aside & examine the facts quickly realize, first, that the British *-our* words are much fewer in proportion to the *-or* words than they supposed, &, secondly, that there seems to be no discoverable line between the two sets so based on principle as to serve any useful purpose. By the side of *favour* there is *horror*, beside *ardour pallor*, beside *odour tremor*, & so forth. Of agent-nouns *saviour* (with its echo *paviour*) is perhaps the only one that now retains *-our*, *governor* being the latest to shed its *-u-*. What is likely to happen is that either, when some general

reform of spelling is consented to, reduction of *-our* to *-or* will be one of the least disputed items, or, failing general reform, we shall see word after word in *-our* go the way of *governour.* It is not worth while either to resist such a gradual change or to fly in the face of national sentiment by trying to hurry it ; it would need a very open mind indeed in an Englishman to accept *armor* & *succor* with equanimity. Those who wish to satisfy themselves that the above denial of value to the *-our* spelling is borne out by facts should go to the article *-or* in the OED for fuller information than there is room for here.

-OUR- & -OR-. The contents of this article, with the exception of the next paragraph, are given as opinions only.

Even those nouns that in our usage still end in *-our* (see -OUR & -OR), as opposed to the American *-or*, e. g. *clamour, clangour, humour, odour, rigour, valour, vapour, vigour,* have adjectives ending in *-orous*, not *-ourous*—*humorous, vaporous,* &c.

Derivatives in *-ist, -ite,* & *-able,* are regarded as formed directly from the English words, & retain the *-u-* ; so *colourist* & *humourist, labourite* (cf. *favourite,* of different formation), *colourable* & *honourable.* But derivatives in *-ation* & *-ize* are best treated, like those in *-ous,* as formed first in Latin, & therefore spelt without the *-u-* ; so *coloration, invigoration, vaporize,* & *deodorize.*

ours)(**our.** See OUR 1.

ousel. See OUZEL.

outcome is one of the words specially liable to the slovenly use described in the article HAZINESS ; so : *The outcome of such nationalization would undoubtedly lead to the loss of incentive & initiative in that trade.* The o. of nationalization would *be* loss ; *nationalization* would lead to loss.

outermost. For pronunciation see -MOST.

out-herod. In view of the phrase's great popularity & many adaptations, two cautions are perhaps called for. The noun after *out-herod* should be *Herod* & nothing else (the OED quotes ' out-heroding the French cavaliers in compliment ' ; cf. *Ecclesiastical functionaries who out-heroded the Daughters of the Horse-leech*), &, after adaptations like *out-milton* & *out-nero*, *Milton* &c. should be repeated (*out-zola Zola*, not *out-zola the realists*). Secondly, the name used should be one at least that passes universally as typifying something ; to out-kautsch Kautsch (*The similar German compilation edited by Kautsch was good ; but Charles easily out-kautsches Kautsch*) is very frigid.

OUT OF THE FRYING-PAN. A very large proportion of the mistakes that are made in writing result neither from simple ignorance nor from carelessness, but from the attempt to avoid what are rightly or wrongly taken to be faults of grammar or style. The writer who produces an ungrammatical, an ugly, or even a noticeably awkward phrase, & lets us see that he has done it in trying to get rid of something else that he was afraid of, gives a worse impression of himself than if he had risked our catching him in his original misdemeanour ; he is out of the frying-pan into the fire. A few typical examples will be here collected, with references to other articles in which the tendency to mistaken correction is set forth more at large.

Recognition is given to it by no matter whom it is displayed. The frying-pan was ' no matter whom it is displayed by ', which the writer did not dare keep, with its preposition at end ; but in his hurry he jumped into nonsense ; see MATTER, & PREPOSITIONS./*When the record of this campaign comes dispassionately to be written, & in just perspective, it will be found that* . . . The writer took ' to be dispassionately written '

for a SPLIT INFINITIVE, & by his correction convinces us that he does not know a split infinitive when he sees it./*In the hymn & its setting there is something which, to use a word of Coleridge, ' finds ' men.* ' A word of Coleridge's ' is an idiom whose genesis may be doubtful, but it has the advantage over the correction of being English ; *a word of Coleridge* is no more English than *a friend of me.*/*The object is to bring before the public many ancient & modern aspects of the Theatre's Art which have too long been disregarded.* ' The theatre's art ' is a phrase that, apart from surroundings, no-one would prefer in prose to ' the art of the theatre '. What the writer has shied at is the repetition of *of* in *of the art of the theatre*, which is however much more tolerable than this 's INCONGRUOUS./*But the badly cut-up enemy troops were continually reinforced & substituted by fresh units.* The frying-pan was REPLACE in the sense ' take the place of ' ; the fire is the revelation that the writer has no idea what the verb SUBSTITUTE means./*Sir Starr Jameson has had one of the most varied & picturesque careers of any Colonial statesmen.* ' Of *any* statesman ', idiomatic but apparently illogical, has been corrected to what is neither logical (*of all* would have been nearer to sense) nor English./ *The claim yesterday was for the difference between the old rate, which was a rate by agreement, & between the new.* The writer feared, with some contempt for his readers' intelligence, that they would not be equal to carrying on the construction of *between* ; he has not mended matters by turning sense into nonsense ; see OVERZEAL./*The reception was held at the bride's aunt.* The reporter was right in disliking *bride's aunt's*, but should have found time to think of ' at the house of '.

The impression must not be left, however, that it is fatal to read over & correct what one has written. The moral is that correction requires as much care as the original writing, or more ; the slapdash corrector, who should not be in such a hurry, & the uneducated corrector, who should not be writing at all, are apt to make things worse than they found them.

outré. See FRENCH WORDS.

outworn. *There is, however, a little more in Mr Bonar Law's speech than these husks of a controversy outworn.* Allusions like this, shown to be such by the position of *outworn,* to *A pagan suckled in a creed outworn* betray mortal dread of being commonplace, & draw attention to the weakness they are meant to cloak.

ouzel, -sel. The OED calls the second obsolete.

overawe makes *-awing*; see MUTE E.

overflow has p.p. *-owed*, not *-own*.

overgrown. See INTRANSITIVE P.P.

overthrowal. *The drama lies in the development of a soul towards the knowledge of itself & of the significance of life, & the tragedy lies in the overthrowal of that soul.* See -AL NOUNS ; *overthrowal* is unknown to the OED.

overlay, -lie. It has been mentioned (see LAY & LIE) that the two simple verbs are sometimes confused even in print. It is still more common for *overlay & underlay* to be used where *-lie* is wanted, because the *-lie* verbs too are transitive, though in different meanings from those in *-lay*. *The talk about things in general which overlays the story is quite dull.* This should be *overlies* ; & it is worth special mention that a mother overlies, not overlays, her child : *Inquests on ' overlaid ' children have greatly diminished* (correct to *overlain*).

Overzeal. Readers should be credited with the ability to make their way from end to end of an ordinary sentence without being pulled & pushed & admonished into the right direction ; but some of their guides are so determined to prevent straying that they plant great signposts

in the middle of the road, often with the unfortunate result of making it no thoroughfare. In the examples the signpost word, always needless, often unsightly, & sometimes misleading, is enclosed in square brackets :—

He is aware that, while the science of boxing may be more exact than it was twenty or thirty years ago, & [*that*] *while many new tricks have been brought to the trade, the professional champion often forgets his science./But it does not at all follow that because Mr Long is 65* [*that*] *he will not be equal to . . .* See THAT, conj., for more./*We agree that the Second Chamber would be differently constituted according as we went forward to other schemes of devolution & federation,* [*& according as we*] *decided to make Home Rule for Ireland our one & only experiment.* Read *or decided* ; see ACCORDING for more./*The working-man has to keep his family on what would be considered a princely wage in England, but* [*which*], *in point of fact, is barely enough to keep body & soul together.* See WHAT for more./*The object for which troops were sent was* [*for*] *the protection of British property.* The object was not *for* protection ; it *was* protection./*But what no undergraduate or* [*no*] *professor in the art of writing verse could achieve is . . .* See OR 4 for more./ *There are others who talk of moving & debating a hostile amendment, & then* [*of*] *withdrawing it.* Moving, debating, & then withdrawing make up a single suggested course ; but the superfluous *of* implies that the talkers vacillate between two courses./*Had Bannockburn never been fought, or* [*had*] *seen another issue, Scotland would have become a second Ireland.* The motive is to exclude *never* from the second clause ; but either that ambiguity must be risked & *had* omitted, or *had it* must be inserted instead of *had*.

ovum. Pl. *ova*.

owing to is here inserted not because

it is misused, but in the hope of calling attention to it as a phrase that should be more used. Its rights are now perpetually infringed by DUE *to*. The difference is that, while *o. t.* can be either adjectival or adverbial (*The accident was not o. t. carelessness* ; *O. t. my carelessness he broke his leg*), *d. t.* can only be adjectival (*The accident was not d. t. carelessness*). In the following examples (& see DUE for others) *owing* must be substituted for *due* :— *Due to this omission he has unfortunately committed himself to views he finds it difficult to go back on.*/*But, due largely to the fact that the hall was situated a long distance from the Congress building, the visitors did not attend in such large numbers as previously.* See QUASI-ADVERBS.

owl-like. For hyphen see -LIKE.

own. For *own the soft impeachment,* see IRRELEVANT ALLUSION.

ox. Pl. *oxen*.

oxidize makes -*zable* ; see MUTE E.

oxymoron. Pl. -*s* or -*ra* ; see -ON. For meaning see TECHNICAL TERMS.

P

pacè. This latinism (*p. tuâ* by your leave, or if you will allow me to say so ; *p. Veneris* if Venus will not be offended by my saying so) is one that we could very well do without in English. Not only is it often unintelligible to many readers even when rightly used ; it is also by many writers wrongly used. In the two following pieces, which have unluckily to be long if the point is to be clear, the meaning is ' according to Mr Begbie ' or ' according to the Jungborn enthusiasts ' ; it ought to be just the opposite— ' though Mr B. (or the enthusiasts) will doubtless not agree ' :—*After the beauty of rural life in the South his picture of Belfast is a vision of horror. On the details of that picture we need not dwell ; but the moral which Mr Begbie appears to draw from his contrast is that a Conservative Irish Parliament will do little to*

better the conditions of town life, & that the industrial classes would find relief from those conditions more quickly under the rule of the English Parliament, which, pace *Mr Begbie, is advancing rapidly towards some form of Socialism.*/*For more than ten thousand years these things have been recognized in some part of the world ; during that lapse of time, at least, some men & women have been living according to their own lights rather than according to the light of nature. Now,* pace *the Jungborn enthusiasts, the time has come to change all this. If man would survive as a species, we learn in effect, he must begin the return journey to the place whence he came.*

Minor objections are that the construction is awkward in English (*p. Mr Smith* is the best we can do for *p. Caesaris* in the genitive), & that the Latinless naturally, but distastefully to those who know Latin, extend the meaning or application as they do those of VIDE, RE, & E.G. So : *But in the House of Lords there is no hilarity*—pace *Lord Salisbury's speech last night.* Pacè does not mean notwithstanding a fact or instance, but despite someone's opinion.

pacha. See PASHA.

pachydermatous. A favourite with the POLYSYLLABIC HUMOURISTS.

pacif(ic)ist. There is no doubt that the longer form is the better ; for full discussion see -IST A ; but its chances of ousting the wrong form are small.

pacify. For inflexions see VERBS IN -IE &c., 6.

Paddy. So spelt ; see -EY, -IE, -Y.

padrone. Three syllables (pad-rō′nĕ) ; pl. -*ni* (-ē).

paean. See Æ, Œ.

pageant. Pronounce pă′jant.

pailful. Pl. *pailfuls* ; see -FUL.

paillasse. See PALLIASSE.

painedly. A bad form ; see -EDLY.

paintress. See FEMININE DESIGNATIONS.

pair, n. See COLLECTIVES 3.

PAIRS & SNARES. Of the large number of words that are sometimes confused with others a small selection is here given. It will be noticed that nearly all are of Latin origin; the confusion depends on the Englishman's natural failure, if he has not learnt Latin, to realize instinctively the force of suffixes that are not native. Those who have any doubts of their infallibility may find it worth while to go through the list & make sure that these pairs have no terrors for them; under one of each pair in its dictionary place they will find remarks upon the difference & usually proofs that the confusion does occur. While the Englishman's vagueness about Latin suffixes or prefixes is the most frequent cause of mistakes, it is not the only one. Often the two words might legitimately have been, or actually were in older usage, equivalents, & the ignorance is not of Latin elements but of English idiom & the changes that DIFFERENTIATION has brought about. And again there are pairs in which the connexion between the two words is only a seeming one. To exemplify briefly, *contemptuous* & *contemptible* are a pair in which suffixes may be confused; *masterful* & *masterly* one in which differentiation may be wrongly ignored; & *deprecate* & *depreciate* one of the altogether false pairs. The list follows:—acceptance & acceptation; advance & advancement; affect & effect; alternate & alternative; antitype & prototype; ascendancy & ascendant; ceremonial & ceremonious; comity & company; complacent (-ency) & complaisant (-ance); compose & comprise; consequent & consequential; contemptible & contemptuous; contend & contest; continuance & continuation; definite & definitive; deprecate & depreciate; derisive & derisory; e.g. & i.e.; euphemism & euphuism; fatal & fateful; forceful & forcible; fortuitous & fortunate; glimpse & glance; hypo-

thecate & hypothesize; immovable & irremovable; inflammable & inflammatory; judicial & judicious; laudable & laudatory; legislation & legislature; luxuriant & luxurious; masterful & masterly; oblivious & unconscious; observance & observation; perspicacity (-acious) & perspicuity (-uous); policy & polity; precipitate & precipitous; predicate & predict; preface vb & prefix vb; proportion & portion; protagonist & champion; purport & purpose; regretful & regrettable; resource, recourse, & resort; reverend & reverent; reversal & reversion; transcendent & transcendental; triumphal & triumphant; unexceptionable & unexceptional.

pajamas. See PYJAMAS.
palace. Educated usage is exceptionally divided between the two pronunciations pă′las & pă′lĭs; the latter will probably win.

palaeo-, palæo-, paleo-. The first is recommended; see Æ, Œ.
palaestra. Best so spelt.
palankeen, -quin. The first is recommended.
palatable. So spelt; see MUTE E.
palatal. See TECHNICAL TERMS.
palaver. Pronounce palah′ver.
pale, adj., makes *palely, palish* (see MUTE E).
palen. See -EN VERBS.
paletot. Pronounce pă′ltō.
palisade, vb, makes *-dable*; see MUTE E.
palladium. Pl. *-ia*.
palliasse, paillasse. The first spelling is best; cf. MORALE.
palliate makes *-liable*; see -ABLE 1.
pallor, not *-our*; see -OUR & -OR.
palmetto. Pl. *-os*; see -O(E)S 6.
palpable. *The work that has yet to be done is palpable from the crowded paper of amendments with which the House is faced.* A good illustration of the need of caution in handling dead metaphors. *Palpable* means literally touchable, or perceptible by touch; that meaning is freely extended to perceptible by any of the senses, & even to appreciable by

the intelligence. The final extension is necessary here, & would pass but for the *from* phrase that is attached. *From the paper* &c. implies not sensuous perception, but intellectual inference ; the dead metaphor in *p.* is stimulated into angry life by the inconsistency ; see METAPHOR. *P.* is one of the words that are liable to clumsy treatment of this sort because they have never become vernacular English, & yet are occasionally borrowed by those who have no scholarly knowledge of them.

panache. See FRENCH WORDS.
pandemonium. Pl. -*ums.*
pander, n. & vb. Though -*ar* is the older & better form, it is waste of labour to try to restore it.
pandit. See PUNDIT.
panegyric, -rize, -rist. The pronunciations recommended are : pănĭjĭ'rĭk, panĕ'jĭrĭz, panĕ'jĭrĭst.
panel makes -*lled, -lling,* &c. ; see -LL-, -L-.
panful. Pl. -*ls* ; see -FUL.
panic makes *panicky*; see -C-, -CK-.
pannikin. So spelt by the OED.
pantaloons, pants. The British words for these, except in uneducated & shop use, are *trousers* (or colloq. *breeches*) & *drawers.* American idiom differs.

papier mâché. See FRENCH WORDS.
papilla, papula. Pl. -*ae.*
papyrus. Pl. -*ri* (-ī).
par (paragraph). See CURTAILED WORDS.
parabasis. Pl. -*ases* (-ēz) ; see LATIN PLURALS, 2.
parable. For p. & allegory, see SIMILE & METAPHOR.
parade, vb, makes -*dable* ; see MUTE E.
paradigm. See TECHNICAL TERMS. Pronounce pă'radīm.
paradise rivals NECTAR in the number of experiments that the desire for a satisfactory adjective has occasioned. But, whereas *nectar* is in the end well enough provided, no-one uses any adjective from *paradise* without feeling that surely

some other would have been less inadequate. The variants are *paradisaic*(al*), paradisal, paradisean, paradisiac(al), paradisial*, paradisian*, paradisic(al),* of which the asterisked ones are badly formed. *Paradisal* is perhaps the least intolerable, & that perhaps because it retains the sound of the last syllable of *paradise* ; but the wise man takes refuge with *heavenly, Edenlike,* or other substitute.

paraffin. See KEROSENE.
paragoge. See GREEK G.
Paraguay. The OED pronunciation is -gwā ; but -gwī is very widespread.
parakeet, paroquet. The OED gives precedence to the first.
parallel. 1. Exceptionally among verbs in -l (see -LL-, -L-), *p.* does not double the l : *paralleled* &c. ; the anomaly is due to the -ll- of the previous syllable. 2. The noun used, where *p.* itself will not serve, is *parallelism,* not *parallelity* ; the latter is not even recorded in the OED, but : *We have already had occasion to comment on the remarkable parallelity between . . . & . . .*

PARALLEL-SENTENCE DANGERS. 1. Negative & affirmative. 2. Inverted & uninverted. 3. Dependent & independent.

1. Negative & affirmative. A single example may be given here to show the kind of difficulty that occurs : *There is not a single town in the crowded district along the Rhine which* is not open *to these attacks, &* must be prepared *for defence with guns, troops, & aeroplanes.* But, for discussion & illustration of this & many other varieties, see NEGATIVE & AFFIRMATIVE.

2. Inverted & uninverted. *And not merely in schools & colleges, but as organizers of physical training,* are women readily finding *interesting & important employment.* The *not merely* part requires the inverted *are women finding* ; the *but* part requires the uninverted *women are* *finding.* The right solution is to start the sentence with *And women are finding employment not merely* &c. In INVERSION the section headed *inversion in parallel clauses* is devoted to this & similar types.

3. Dependent & independent. *The municipality charged itself with the purchase of these articles in wholesale quantities, & it was to the Town Hall that poor people applied for them, & were served by municipal employees.* The parallel sentences in question were, in their simple form, (a) *The poor people applied for them to the Town Hall,* & (b) *The poor people were served by municipal employees.* The writer has decided, for the sake of emphasizing *Town Hall,* to re-write *a* in the *it was . . . that* form ; but he has forgotten that he cannot make *a* dependent & leave *b* independent unless he supplies the latter with a subject (*& they were served*). The correct possibilities are : (i, both independent) *The people applied to the Town Hall for them, & were served by municipal employees* ; (ii, both dependent) *It was to the Town Hall that the people applied, & by municipal employees that they were served* ; (iii, dependent & independent) *It was to the Town Hall that the people applied, & they were served by municipal employees.*

parallelepiped. Pronounce pără-lĕlĕ′pĭpĕd.

paralogism. See GREEK G.

paralyse. So spelt ; for the curious form see ANALYSE.

paramo. Pl. -*os* ; see -O(E)S 6.

paranoea, -noia. The former would be the regular form, but the other, with unlatinized Greek spelling, is more used. For -noea, -nœa, see Æ, Œ.

parapeted. So spelt ; see -T-, -TT-.

paraphrase, vb, makes -*sable* ; see MUTE E.

paraplegia. See GREEK G.

paraselene. Five syllables (-ē′nĭ).

parasitic(al). The longer form has no special function, & is now little used. See -IC(AL).

parasitism. So spelt ; see MUTE E.

parcel makes -*lled* &c. ; -LL-, -L-.

parcimony. See PARSIMONY.

pardon makes -*oned, -onable,* &c. ; see -N-, -NN-.

parenchyma. Pron. parĕ′ngkĭma.

parenthesis. Pl. -*theses* (-ēz) ; see LATIN PLURALS, 2.

PARENTHESIS. 1. Relevance. 2. Identification. 3. Dashes as sign of p.

1. Relevance. A parenthesis may have or not have a grammatical relation to the sentence in which it is inserted. In *This is, as far as I know, the whole truth* there is such a relation, & in *This is, I swear, the whole truth* there is not ; but one is as legitimate as the other. It is not equally indifferent whether the parenthesis is relevant or not to its sentence ; parentheses like the following cannot possibly be justified : *In writing this straightforward & workmanlike biography of his grandfather (the book was finished before the war, & delayed in publication) Mr Walter Jerrold has aimed at doing justice to Douglas Jerrold as dramatist, as social reformer & as good-natured man.* The time of writing & the delay have no conceivable bearing on the straightforwardness, workmanlikeness, biographicality, grandfatherliness, justice, drama, reform, or good nature, with which the sentence is concerned. If it had been called a long-expected instead of a straightforward biography, it would have been quite another matter ; but, as it is, the parenthesis is as disconcerting as a pebble that jars one's teeth in a mouthful of plum pudding. The very worst way of introducing an additional fact is to thrust it as a parenthesis into the middle of a sentence with which it has nothing to do. A similar example is : *Napoleon's conversations with Bertrand & Moncholon (it is unfortunate that there are several misprints in the book) are a skilful blending of record & pastiche.*

2. Identification. Still more fatal than readiness to resort to parenthesis where it is irrelevant is inability to tell a parenthesis from a main sentence. *He attacked the Government, declaring that they cared more for votes than voters. A remarkable change had come over the Government,* he suggested, *since the Bill had left the Committee,* & expressed doubts *as to whether Mr Masterman altogether approved of the new turn of affairs.* In this, *he suggested* is as much a parenthesis as if it had been enclosed in brackets; if it were not parenthetic, the sentence would run *He suggested that a change had come.* But the writer, not knowing a parenthesis when he sees (or even when he makes) one, has treated it as parallel with *expressed,* & so fully parallel that its *he* may be expected to do duty with *expressed* as well as with *suggested.* Either the first part should be rewritten as above with *suggested* for its governing verb, or the second part should be cut off from the first & begin *He expressed doubts,* or else another parenthesis should be resorted to—*It was doubtful, he continued, whether Mr . . .*

3. For double dashes as a form of p., see STOPS.

parenthetic(al). In most uses the longer form is obsolescent; but it has still a special sense worth preserving, i.e. full of or addicted to parentheses (*a horribly -ical style*). See -IC(AL).

par excellence. See FRENCH WORDS.
parget. Pronounce -j-.
pariah. Pronounce pắr'ĭa or par'ĭa.
pari mutuel. See FRENCH WORDS.
pari passu. Pronounce pắr'ĭ pǎ'sū.
parisyllabic. See TECHNICAL TERMS.
parlance. See JARGON.
parley. Pl. of noun, *-eys.* For verb inflexion, see VERBS IN -IE &c., 2.
parliament. Pronounce par'lament.
parlo(u)r. Keep the u; but see -OUR & -OR.
parlous is a word that wise men leave alone. It is the same by

origin as *perilous*; but it had centuries ago the same fate that has befallen *awful* & *chronic* within living memory; it became a VOGUE-WORD applied to many things very remote from its proper sense; it consequently lost all significance, ' died of its own too much ', & was for a long time (for most of the 18th century) hardly heard of. In the 19th century it was exhumed by ARCHAISM & PEDANTIC HUMOUR, & the adepts in those arts should be allowed exclusive property in it. About the following curious example it is not very clear either why the writer selected or what he understood by the word: *Here & there, perhaps, human nature will out, & in Mr Lyttelton's introductory discourse on ' The Empire ' it is not surprising to find the speaker touching parlously on the controversy with which the name of Birmingham & the Chancellor of its University are inseparably connected. But with admirable restraint the right honourable gentleman soon waves that argument away & bows acknowledgment to Adam Smith.*

Parmesan. Pronounce -z-.
parody. See BURLESQUE for synonyms.
paronomasia. TECHNICAL TERMS.
paroquet. See PARAKEET.
parricide)(patricide. The first is the orthodox form. *Patricide* has no doubt been substituted by some deliberately, in order to narrow the meaning to murder(er) of a father, as *matricide* & *fratricide* are limited, & by others in ignorance of the right word. *Parricide* includes not only the murder of either parent or any near relative or anyone whose person is sacred, but also treason against one's country; & the making of *patricide* to correspond to *matricide* is therefore natural enough.

parry. For inflexions see VERBS IN -IE &c., 6.
parsimony, parci-. The variation dates back to Latin manuscripts; but ' Latin scholars appear to agree

that *parsimonia* was the actual spelling in classical Latin '—OED. As *pars-* is also the prevailing modern form, the *parc-* spelling should be abandoned.

partake makes *-kable* ; see MUTE E.
partially is often used where *partly* would be better. This is, no doubt, because it is formed normally, by way of the adjective *partial*, while *partly* formed direct from the noun *part* is abnormal. There is between the two words much the same difference as between *wholly* (opp. *partly*) & *completely* (opp. *partially*) ; in other words, *partly* is better in the sense ' as regards a part & not the whole ', & *partially* in the sense ' to a limited degree ' : *It is partly wood* ; *This was partly due to cowardice* ; *A partially drunken sailor* ; *His partially re-established health*. Often either will give the required sense equally well ; *partly* is then recommended, since it is *partially* that tends to be over-used ; see LONG VARIANTS for other such pairs. An example or two of the wrong *partially* are :—*The two feet are partially of iron & partially of clay.*/*Whether The Case is Altered may be wholly or partially or not at all assignable to the hand of Jonson.*
participate makes *-pable*, *-tor* ; see -ABLE 1, -OR.

PARTICIPLES. 1. Unattached p. 2. Absolute construction. 3. Fused p. 4. Initial p. &c. 5. Accent & pronunciation in p.p. (or adjective or noun) & verb.

1. Unattached p. For this danger, as insidious as notorious, see UN-ATTACHED PARTICIPLE.

2. Absolute construction. *The Municipal Council, having refused their assistant clerks' demand for a rise in salary, those in the Food Supply offices today declared a strike.* This false stopping (there should be no comma after *Council*) is an example of what is perhaps both the worst & the commonest of all mistakes in punctuation. See ABSO-LUTE CONSTRUCTION.

3. Fused p. *Jimmy Wilde's first fight in the United States resulted in him being beaten by Jack Sharkey.*/*They are so well chosen that there is little fear of the reader to whom the more familiar aspects of the subject have ceased to appeal being wearied by them.* ' Him being beaten ', ' the reader being wearied ', are examples of a construction regarded in this book as a corrupting influence in modern English, & fully discussed in the article FUSED PARTICIPLE.

4. Initial participle &c. If newspaper editors, in the interest of their readers, maintain any discipline over the gentlemen who provide inch-long paragraphs to stop gaps, they should take measures against a particular form that, by a survival of the unfittest, bids fair to swallow up all others. In these paragraphs, before we are allowed to enter, we are challenged by the sentry, being a participle or some equivalent posted in advance to secure that our interview with the C.O. (or subject of the sentence) shall not take place without due ceremony. The fussiness of this is probably entertaining while it is quite fresh ; one cannot tell, because it is no longer fresh to anyone. Examples :—*Described as ' disciples of Tolstoi ', two Frenchmen sentenced at Cheltenham to two months' imprisonment for false statements to the registration officer are not to be recommended for deportation.*/*Composed of the 3rd Royal Fusiliers, the Scottish Horse, & the 2nd Royal Dublin Fusiliers, the 149th Brigade, as General Jackson (50th Division) says in his foreword, represented ' the very best material, traditions, & qualities of England, Scotland, & Ireland '.*/*Winner of many rowing trophies, Mr Robert George Dugdale, aged seventy-five, died at Eton.*/*Appointed Inspector-General, West African Frontier Force, Brevet - Lieut. - Colonel A. H. W. Haywood, C.M.B., D.S.O., of the R.G.A., in 1910 spent six months' furlough by crossing the Sahara Desert.*/*Aged seventy-nine,* *the Rev. F. T. Wethered, vicar of Hurley, near Marlow, whose death is announced, bathed daily in the Thames, winter & summer, till a few months ago./Believed to be the youngest organist in the country, Master Herbert Woolverton, who officiates at Hutton Church, Essex, has passed the examination as Associate of . . ./ Thirty-four years in the choir of the Chapel Royal, Hampton Court Palace, Mr Francis P. Hill, of Milner Road, Kingston, has retired./Found standing in play astride the live rail of the electric line at Willesden & in danger of instant death, Walter Spentaford, twelve, was fined 12s. for trespass.*

5. Accent & pronunciation in p.p. (or participial adjective or noun) & verb. Beside many of the verbs formed from Latin supine stems (*animate, dilute, extract*, &c.) there are passive participles of the same spelling, now used as adjectives or nouns. They are often distinguished from the verbs by a difference of sound. This may be (A) a shifting of the accent, as in attri'bute n., a'ttribute n. ; co'nsummate v., consu'mmate a. ; convi'ct v., co'nvict n. ; dicta'te v., di'ctates n. ; dige'st v., di'gest n. ; dilu'te v., di'lute a. ; extra'ct v., e'xtract n. ; frustra'te v., fru'strate a. ; refu'se v., re'fuse n. ; (B) the obscuring of the vowel of *-ate*, as in advocāte v., advocate n. ; animāte v., animate a. ; articulāte v., articulate a. ; compassionāte v., compassionate a. ; degenerāte v., degenerate a. ; delegāte v., delegate n. ; deliberāte v., deliberate a. ; designāte v., designate a. ; desolāte v., desolate a. ; elaborāte v., elaborate a. ; estimāte v., estimate n. ; legitimāte v., legitimate a. ; moderāte v., moderate a. ; regenerāte v., regenerate a. ; reprobāte v., reprobate n. ; separāte v., separate a. ; subordināte v., subordinate a. & n. ; or (C) a change of consonant sound, as in diffuse (-z) v., diffuse (-s) a. ; refuse (-z) v., refuse (-s) n.

Words are referred to this article (PARTICIPLES 5 A or B or C) to draw

attention to a double pronunciation ; see also NOUN & VERB ACCENT.

parti-coloured, party-, partic-. The first is recommended.

particularize makes *-zable* ; see MUTE E.

parting. *The British Empire is at the p. of the ways.* Empires & men are now so familiar with that position that, when told they are there once more, they are not disquieted ; their only impulse is to feel in their breeches pockets for the penny with which they may toss up. See HACKNEYED PHRASES.

partisan, -zan. Whether the two nouns (adherent of a party, the weapon) are etymologically connected or not is doubtful. The weapon is accented on the first syllable, the adherent sometimes so & sometimes on the last. It would be well to make *partisa'n* (or *-za'n*) invariable for the latter ; & perhaps the -s- might be appropriated to it, & the -z- to the weapon : *partisa'n* adherent ; *par'tizan* weapon. But, as the distinction would be at least partly arbitrary, & as the weapon word is now seldom wanted, this suggestion is not very likely to be acted upon.

partitive. See TECHNICAL TERMS.

party. For this in the sense *person*, see POPULARIZED TECHNICALITIES.

parvenu, pas. See FRENCH WORDS.

pasha, pacha. Spell *pasha* & pronounce pah'sha.

pasquinade. See LAMPOON for synonyms.

pass makes *passed* for its past tense (*You passed me by*), & for its p.p. used verbally (*It has passed out of use*) ; but when the p.p. has become a mere adjective it is spelt *past* (*In past times*). The distinction between p.p. & adjective is rather fine in *Those times have passed away* (p.p.), *Those times are passed away* (INTRANSITIVE P.P.), *Those times are past* (adjective).

passable, passible. The first word (pronounced, usually, pah-) is the adjective from the verb *pass*; the second (pronounced păs-) is a separate word in learned & especially theological use, meaning capable of feeling. See also IMPASSABLE.

passé, passementerie, passe-partout. See FRENCH WORDS.

passer-by. Write the hyphen.

passible. See PASSABLE.

PASSIVE DISTURBANCES. 1. The double passive. 2. Passive of *avail oneself of*. 3. *Do* after passive. 4. *As*. The conversion of an active-verb sentence into a passive-verb one of the same meaning—e.g. of *You killed him* into *He was killed by you*—is a familiar process. But it sometimes leads to bad grammar, false idiom, or clumsiness.

1. The double passive. *People believed him to have been murdered* can be changed to *He was believed to have been murdered*; but *They attempted to carry out the order* cannot be changed to *The order was attempted to be carried out* without clumsiness or worse. For full discussion see DOUBLE PASSIVES.

2. Passive of *avail oneself of*. *We understand that the credit will be availed of by three months' bills, renewable three times, drawn by the Belgian group on the British syndicate.* A passive is not possible for *avail oneself of*; see AVAIL.

3. Active of *do* after passive verb. *Inferior defences could then, as now, be tackled, as Vernon did at Porto Bello, Exmouth at Algiers, & Seymour at Alexandria.* The active form would be *An admiral could then, as now, tackle inferior defences*; if *defences could be tackled* is substituted, the voice of *did* must be changed too—*as was done*, or *as they were, by Vernon* &c. This lapse is a common one; see DO 3 c.

4. *As*. *The great successes of the Co-operators hitherto have been won as middlemen.* Active form, sound enough—*The Co-operators have won their successes as middlemen.* Conversion to the passive has had the effect of so tying up *the co-operators*

with *of* that it is not available, as in the active form, for *as middlemen* to be attached to. A common lapse.

past. See PASS. *Past master*, two words unhyphened.

paste, vb, makes *-table*; see MUTE E.

pastel (pigment paste). Pronounce pă'stel.

Pasteurism, -ize. Accent the first syllables.

pastiche. See FRENCH WORDS.

pastil(le). The long form is now usual, though *pastil* was long ago established.

pastorale. Pronounce -ahlĕ; pl. *-li* (-ē).

pasty, n. Pronounce pah-.

pâté. See FRENCH WORDS.

patella. Pl. *-lae*.

paten, patten. The first spelling is now usual for the Eucharist platter, the second for the mud-shoe.

patent. Pā-, or pă-? Pā- predominates in England, pă- in America. But even in England some retain pă- for the sense connected with *letters p*., i.e. for the technical uses as opposed to the general or etymological senses open & plain. This distinction is based on the fact that *p*. in the general senses comes direct from Latin, & in the technical senses from French. The one pronunciation pā-, however, is recommended for British use in all senses. It should be remembered that the Latin quantity (pă-) is of no importance; see FALSE QUANTITY.

paterfamilias. In Roman history, or references to it, the plural should be *patresfamilias*; but as an adopted English word it makes *paterfamilias*. See LATIN PLURALS.

path. Pl. pronounced pahdhz; see -TH & -DH.

pathetic fallacy is a phrase made by Ruskin; the OED quotes from *Modern Painters*: *All violent feelings . . . produce . . . a falseness in . . . impressions of external things, which I would generally characterize as the ' Pathetic fallacy '*. In ordinary modern use *pathos* & *pathetic* are limited to the idea of painful emotion ; but in this phrase, now common though little recognized in dictionaries, the original wider sense of emotion in general is reverted to, & *the p. f.* means the tendency to credit nature with human emotions. *Sphinxlike, siren-sweet, sly, benign, impassive, vindictive, callously indifferent the sea may seem to a consciousness addicted to pathetic fallacies.*

pathos. For this & *bathos* the OED recognizes only the pronunciations pā-, bā-.

patois. For *p.*, *dialect*, &c., see JARGON.

patriot(ic). The sounds usually heard are perhaps ā in the noun & ă in the adjective. There is no objection to the difference, & the FALSE QUANTITY ā is of no importance.

patrol makes *-lling, -lled, -llable* ; see -LL-, -L-.

patron, -age, -ess, -ize. The OED gives the sound of the -a- as pātron, pătronage, pătroness, & pătronize.

patroness. See FEMININE DESIGNATIONS.

patten. See PATEN.

paulo-post future. See TECHNICAL TERMS.

pave makes the exceptional agent-noun *paviour.*

pavé. See FRENCH WORDS.

pawky. The Englishman is tempted to use the word merely as a synonym in certain contexts for *Scotch* ; any jest uttered by a Scot is pawky, & pawky humour is understood to be unattainable except by Scots. The underlying notions are those of craftiness, concealment of intention, apparent gravity, ironical detachment. The pawky person says his say, &, if the hearers choose to find more point in the words than a plain interpretation necessitates, that is their business ; more than other people's, his Jest's prosperity lies in the ear Of him that hears.

pay. For inflexions, see VERBS IN -IE &c., 1.

paysage. See FRENCH WORDS.

peasoup, not *pea-soup* ; for the principle, see HYPHENS 3 B.

pearl barley. No hyphen ; see HYPHENS 3 B.

peccadillo. Pl. *-os* ; see -O(E)S 7.

peccavi. Pronounce pĕkā′vī.

peculate makes *-lable, -tor* ; see -ABLE 1, -OR.

pedagogy, -gical. See GREEK G.

pedal makes *-lled, -lling* ; -LL-, -L-.

PEDANTIC HUMOUR. No essential distinction is intended between this & POLYSYLLABIC HUMOUR ; one or the other name is more appropriate to particular specimens, & the two headings are therefore useful for reference ; but they are manifestations of the same impulse, & the few remarks needed may be made here for both. A warning is necessary, because we have all of us, except the abnormally stupid, been pedantic humourists in our time. We spend much of our childhood picking up a vocabulary ; we like to air our latest finds ; we discover that our elders are tickled when we come out with a new name that they thought beyond us ; we devote some pains to tickling them further ; & there we are, pedants & polysyllabists all. The impulse is healthy for children, & nearly universal—which is just why warning is necessary ; for among so many there will always be some who fail to realize that the clever habit applauded at home will make them insufferable abroad. Most of those who are capable of writing well enough to find readers do learn with more or less of delay that playful use of long or learned words is a one-sided game boring the reader more than it pleases the writer, that the impulse to it is a danger-signal— for there must be something wrong with what they are saying if it needs recommending by such puerilities—, & that yielding to the impulse is a confession of failure. But now & then even an able writer will go on believing that the incongruity between simple things to be said &

out-of-the-way words to say them in has a perennial charm ; it has, for the reader who never outgrows hobbledehoyhood ; but for the rest of us it is dreary indeed. It is possible that acquaintance with such labels as *pedantic & polysyllabic humour* may help to shorten the time that it takes to cure a weakness incident to youth.

An elementary example or two should be given. The words *homoeopathic* (small or minute), *sartorial* (of clothes), *interregnum* (gap), are familiar ones :—*To introduce ' Lords of Parliament ' in such homoeopathic doses as to leave a preponderating power in the hands of those who enjoy a merely hereditary title./While we were motoring out to the station I took stock of his sartorial aspect, which had changed somewhat since we parted./ In his vehement action his breeches fall down & his waistcoat runs up, so that there is a great interregnum.*

These words are, like most that are much used in humour of either kind, both pedantic & polysyllabic. A few specimens that cannot be described as polysyllabic are added here, & for the larger class of long words the article POLYSYLLABIC HUMOUR should be consulted :— ablution ; aforesaid ; beverage ; bivalve (the succulent) ; caloric ; cuticle ; digit ; domestics ; eke (adv.) ; ergo ; erstwhile ; felicide ; nasal organ ; neighbourhood (*in the n. of,* = about) ; nether garments ; optic (eye) ; parlous ; vulpicide.

PEDANTRY may be defined, for the purpose of this book, as the saying of things in language so learned or so demonstratively accurate as to imply a slur upon the generality, who are not capable or not desirous of such displays. The term, then, is obviously a relative one ; my pedantry is your scholarship, his reasonable accuracy, her irreducible minimum of education, & someone else's ignorance. It is therefore not very profitable to dogmatize here on the subject ; an essay would

establish not what pedantry is, but only the place in the scale occupied by the author ; & that, so far as it is worth inquiring into, can be better ascertained from the treatment of details, to some of which accordingly, with a slight classification, reference is now made. The entries under each heading are the names of articles ; & by referring to a few of these the reader who has views of his own will be able to place the book in the pedantry scale & judge what may be expected of it. There are certainly many accuracies that are not pedantries, as well as some that are ; there are certainly some pedantries that are not accuracies, as well as many that are ; & no book that attempts, as this one does, to give hundreds of decisions on the matter will find many readers who will accept them all.

Spelling Niceties : See Didacticism ; -in & -ine ; Mute e ; amuck ; gypsy ; Mahomet ; morale.

Pronunciation : See False quantity ; French words ; Greek g ; Christmas ; diphtheria ; margarine.

Long or learned words : See dual-(istic) ; Love of the long word ; fuliginous ; intermediary ; meticulous ; thrasonical.

Synonyms : See apt ; authentic ; broad ; classic(al) ; exceedingly.

Variants & differentiation : See acceptance ; act(ion) ; alternative ; ascendancy ; complacent ; masterful.

Symmetry : See between ; both ; either ; nor.

Logic & pleonasm : See ago ; because ; equally as ; Haziness.

Rules of style : See and, 2 ; Elegant variation ; Fused participle ; only ; Preposition at end ; Split infinitive.

Reversion to etymological senses : See dastardly ; decimate ; egregious ; enormous ; infinite ; internecine ; journal.

Objections to particular words or constructions : See aggravate ; cablegram ; case ; coastal ; conservative ; different ; doubt(ful) ; feasible ; ilk ; Inversion ; like ; oblivious ; quieten.

pedestal makes *-lled* ; see -LL-, -L-.

pedigree. Adj. *pedigree'd* ; see -ED & 'D.

pedlar. So spelt.

peewit. See PEWIT.

peignoir. See FRENCH WORDS.

pekoe. Pronounce pē'kō.

Pelasgi, -gic. See GREEK G.

pellucid. See TRANSPARENT.

pelta. Pl. *-ae*.

pelvis. Pl. *-ves* (*-ēz*).

penalize makes *-zable* ; see MUTE E.

Penates. Pronounce pĭnā'tēz.

penchant. See FRENCH WORDS.

pencil. Pronounce *-sl*. *P.* makes *-lled, -lling*, &c. ; see -LL-, -L-.

pendant, pendent, pennant, pennon. There is much confusion between these ; the reasonable distribution of meanings to forms would be as follows : *pendent*, the adjective, hanging ; *pendant*, a noun, a hanging ornament or appurtenance ; *pennant*, a noun in nautical use for certain pieces of rigging & certain flags ; *pennon*, a noun in heraldic & military use for a lance-streamer or the like. *Pendent* should not be used as a noun ; *pendant* should be neither an adjective nor the nautical noun ; *pennon* should not be the nautical noun ; see DIFFERENTIATION.

pendente lite. Pron. pĕndē'ntĭ lī'tĭ.

pendulum. Pl. *-ms* ; see -UM.

penetralia. A plural noun.

penetrate makes *-trable, -tor* ; see -ABLE 1, -OR.

penful. Pl. *-ls* ; see -FUL.

peninsula(r). Uses of the noun (*-la*) instead of the adjective (*-lar*), as *the Peninsula War*, or vice versa, as *the Spanish Peninsular*, are wrong, but not uncommon. The former is indeed defensible, on the ground that nouns can be used attributively, but at least ill advised.

penman should be used with reference to handwriting only, not to the writing of books or articles ; in the sense writer or author it is an affectation—not indeed a new invention, but a REVIVAL.

pen-name. See NOM DE GUERRE.

pennant. See PENDANT.

pennon. See PENDANT. *P.* makes *-oned* ; see -N-, -NN-.

penny. Pl. usually *pence*, but *pennies* of the separate coins as such (*pennies only will work the machine*) or as objects (*buttons the size of pennies*).

pension makes *-oned, -onable* ; see -N-, -NN-. In the sense boarding-house, pronounce as French (see FRENCH WORDS).

pentameter is so much appropriated to the short line of the classical elegiac couplet that it is better to avoid it as a name for the English blank-verse or heroic-couplet line. See TECHNICAL TERMS.

penthemimeral, penult. See TECHNICAL TERMS.

peradventure. See ARCHAISM.

per capita. *The consumption of tobacco & alcohol has increased during the year as follows : spirits, 1·112 gallons per capita, compared with 1·030 in 1911./The entire production of opium in India is two grammes per capita yearly.* This use is a modern blunder, encouraged in some recent dictionaries. ' (So much) a head ', or ' per man ', which is the meaning here, would not be *per capita* (any more than it would be ' per men '), but *per caput*. *Per capita* describes the method of sharing property in which persons, & not families, are the units, & its opposite is *per stirpes* ; *Patrimonial estates are divided per capita* ; *purchased estates, per stirpes* ; it is out of place, & something of a barbarism, however lately popular, except in such a context.

percentage. See LOVE OF THE LONG WORD, & MISAPPREHENSIONS. The notion has gone abroad that a percentage is a small part. Far from that, while a part is always less than the whole, a percentage may be the whole or more than the whole ; there is little comfort to be had in 1925 from reflecting that our cost of living can be expressed as a percentage of 1914's. The un-educated public prefers a word that sounds scientific, even if it gives the sense less well, to another that it can understand ; see POPULARIZED TECHNICALITIES. In all the following examples but the last, the word *percentage* has no meaning at all without the addition of *small* or of something else to define it ; & in the last *the greater part* would be the English for *the larger percentage* :— *But in London there is no civic consciousness ; the London-born provides only a percentage of its inhabitants./ The wealthy employers do not really count when you consider the position of domestic service, because they are only few in number & employ only a percentage of the total of domestic servants./It is none the less true that the trade unions only represent a percentage of the whole body of railway workers./Our tax revenue is now fully one hundred & sixty millions sterling, & the Single Land Tax would not yield more than a percentage of this./The largest percentage of heat generated is utilizable, but the rest escapes & is lost.* For an exact parallel, see PROPORTION.

perchance is very much out of place in pedestrian prose, as, for instance, in *There is nothing, perchance, which so readily links the ages together as a small store of jewels & trinkets.* See ARCHAISM, INCONGRUOUS VOCABULARY, & POETICISMS.

percolate makes *-lable, -tor* ; see -ABLE 1, -OR.

perdu, formerly naturalized & common, has become comparatively rare, but can still be at least pronounced as English (perdū′ or per′dū), though now usually printed in italics as French.

père. See FRENCH WORDS.

peregrinate. A POLYSYLLABIC-HUMOUR word.

peremptory. Pronounce pĕ′rĭm-torĭ, not perĕ′mtorĭ.

PERFECT INFINITIVE, i.e. *to have done* &c. These are forms that often push their way in where they are not wanted, & sometimes, but less often, are themselves displaced by wrong presents.

1. After past tenses of *hope, fear, expect,* & the like, the perfect infinitive is used, incorrectly indeed & unnecessarily, but so often & with so useful an implication that it may well be counted idiomatic. That implication is that the thing hoped &c. did not in fact come to pass, & the economy of conveying this without a separate sentence compensates for lack of logical precision. So :—*Philosophy began to congratulate herself upon such a proselyte from the world of business,* & hoped to have extended *her power under the auspices of such a leader./It was the duty of that publisher to have rebutted a statement which he knew to be a calumny./ I was going to have asked, when . . .*

2. After past conditionals such as *should have liked, would have been possible, would have been the first to,* the present infinitive is (almost invariably) the right form, but the perfect often intrudes, & this time without the compensation noted in 1, the implication of non-fulfilment being inherent in the governing verb itself. So :—*If my point had not been this, I should not have endeavoured* to have shown *the connexion./Jim Scudamore would have been the first man* to have acknowledged *the anomaly./ Peggy would have liked* to have shown *her turban & bird of paradise at the ball./The Labour members opened their eyes wide, & except for a capital levy it is doubtful whether they would have dared* to have gone *further.* Sometimes a writer, dimly aware that ' would have liked to have done ' is usually wrong, is yet so fascinated by the perfect infinitive that he clings to that at all costs, & alters instead the part of his sentence that was right : *On the point of church James was obdurate ; he* would like to have insisted *on the other grudging items* (would have liked to insist).

3. With *seem, appear,* & the like, people get puzzled over the combinations of the present & past of *seem* &c. with the present & perfect of the infinitive. The possible combinations are : He seems to know, He seems to have known, He seemed to know, He seemed to have known. The first admits of no confusion, & may be left aside ; the last is very rarely wanted in fact, but is constantly resorted to as an *en-tout-cas* by those who cannot decide whether the umbrella of *He seems to have known* or the parasol of *He seemed to know* is more likely to suit the weather. The *en-tout-cas* has been taken in :—*I warned him when he spoke to me that I could not speak to him at all if I was to be quoted as an authority;* he seemed to have taken *this as applying only to the first question he asked me* (seems to have)./*It was no infrequent occurrence for people going to the theatre in the dark to fall into the marshes after crossing the bridge ; people* seemed to have been *much more willing to run risks in those days.*

perfect, vb. Accent the last syllable ; see PARTICIPLES 5 A. For the adj., *-able* is better than *-ible* ; see -ABLE 2.

perfection, vb, should not be substituted for *perfect* ; see LONG VARIANTS.

perforate makes *-rable, -tor* ; see -ABLE 1, -OR.

perfume. NOUN & VERB ACCENT.

perhaps. Of the pronunciations, that with the r & the h both sounded is obsolescent ; that with the r silent & the h sounded is orthodox ; that in two syllables with r sounded but h silent is rare among the educated ; that in one syllable (präps) is used by many more than would plead guilty, & does not deserve the scorn heaped on it by those who parody mispronunciations in print.

pericranium. Chiefly in POLY-SYLLABIC HUMOUR.

peril makes *-lling* &c. (see -LL-, -L-), but *perilous.*

period. For synonyms see TIME. For the full stop, see STOPS. For the use in rhetoric, TECHNICAL TERMS.

PERIOD IN ABBREVIATIONS. The practice of ending every abbreviation with a period (*Wm.* for William as well as *Gen.* for General, VIZ. for videlicet as well as *sc.* for scilicet, *qr.* for quarter as well as *lb.* for libra) is ill advised. Abbreviations are puzzling, but to puzzle is not their purpose, & everything that helps the reader to guess their meaning is a gain. One such help is to let him know when the first & last letters of the abbreviation are also those of the full word, which can be done by not using the period, but writing *wt* (not *wt.*) for weight, *Bp* (not *Bp.*) for bishop, *Mr* (not *Mr.*) for Mister, *Bart* (not *Bart.*) for baronet, *bot.* for botany but *bot* for bought, *Capt.* for captain but *Cpl* for corporal, *doz.* for dozen but *cwt* for hundredweight, *Feb.* for February but *fcp* for foolscap, *Frl.* for Fräulein but *Mlle* for Mademoiselle, *in.* for inches but *ft* for feet, *Geo.* for George but *Thos* for Thomas, *Lat.* for Latin but *Gk* for Greek, *h.w.,* but *ht wt,* for hit wicket.

periodic(al). The -ic form is not used of publications (*periodical literature, periodicals*) ; the -ical form is not used of literary composition (*Johnson's periodic style*) ; otherwise the two words do not differ in meaning, but the longer tends to oust the shorter.

peripeteia. See TECHNICAL TERMS

PERIPHRASIS is the putting of things in a round-about way. *In Paris there reigns a complete absence of really reliable news* is a periphrasis for *There is no reliable news in Paris* ; *Rarely does the ' Little Summer' linger until November, but at times its stay has been prolonged until quite late in the year's penultimate month* contains a p. for

November, & another for *lingers* ; *The answer is in the negative* is a p. for *No* ; *Was made the recipient of* is a p. for *Was presented with.* The periphrastic style is hardly possible on any considerable scale without much use of abstract nouns such as *case, character, connexion, dearth, nature, reference, regard, respect* ; the existence of abstract nouns is a proof that abstract thought has occurred ; abstract thought is a mark of civilized man ; & so it has come about that p. & civilization are by many held to be inseparable ; these good people feel that there is an almost indecent nakedness, a reversion to barbarism, in saying *No news is good news* instead of *The absence of intelligence is an indication of satisfactory developments.* Nevertheless, *The year's penultimate month* is not in truth a good way of saying *November.*

Strings of nouns depending on one another, & the use of compound prepositions, are the most conspicuous symptoms of the periphrastic malady, & writers should be on the watch for these in their own composition. An example or two may be illuminating :—A, nouns : *M. Witte is taking active measures for the prompt preparation of material for the study of the question of the execution of the Imperial Ukase dealing with reforms./One of the most important reforms mentioned in the rescript is the unification of the organization of the judicial institutions & the guarantee for all the tribunals of the independence necessary for securing to all classes of the community equality before the law./ I merely desired to point out the principal reason which I believe exists for the great exaggeration which is occasionally to be observed in the estimate of the importance of the contradiction between current Religion & current Science put forward by thinkers of reputation.* B, compound prepositions : *A Resolution was moved & carried* in favour of *giving facilities to the public vaccination*

officers of the Metropolis to enter the schools of the Board for the purpose of *examining the arms of the children* with a view to *advising the parents to allow their children to be vaccinated./ What harbours or territory were offered to this country in exchange for Walfisch Bay & Zanzibar* in connexion with *the proposed arrangement* with reference to *the exchange of these British ports ?*

Other examples will be found under some of the words that lend themselves especially to periphrasis— *case, character, connexion, dearth, eventuality, ilk, instance, nature, neighbourhood, not 2, reference, regard.*

perishable. For the formation, from an intrans. verb, see -ABLE 4.

perispomenon. Pl. -*ena.*

periwig makes -*gged* ; see -G-, -GG-. It is not a compound of *wig* ; see TRUE & FALSE ETYMOLOGY.

permanence, -cy. One of the pairs (see -CE, -CY) in which the distinction is neither broad & generally recognized, nor yet quite non-existent or negligible. Writers whose feeling for distinctions is delicate will prefer -*ce* for the fact of abiding, & -*cy* for the quality or an embodiment of it : *We look forward to its permanence* ; *The permanency of the orthodox marriage bond* ; *His new post is not a permanency.*

permeate makes -*meable, -tor* ; see -ABLE 1, -OR.

permit makes -*tted* &c., -*ssible* ; see -T-, -TT-, -ABLE 2. The noun is accented on the first ; see NOUN & VERB ACCENT.

perorate is not in fact one of the modern BACK-FORMATIONS like *revolute, enthuse,* & *burgle,* but it suffers from being taken for one, & few perhaps use it without some fear that they are indulging in a bold bad word.

perpetrate, perpetuate, make -*rable, -uable,* & -*tor* ; see -ABLE 1, -OR.

perplexedly. Four syllables ; -EDLY.

per proc., per pro., p.p., are abbreviations of *per procurationem* by the agency of. The proxy's signature should therefore be the one immediately after *p.p.* &c., the principal's name standing either before *p.p.* &c. or after the agent's name.

persecute makes *-table*, *-tor*; see MUTE E, -OR.

persiflage. For pronunciation see FRENCH WORDS; for meaning, TECHNICAL TERMS.

persistence, -cy. The distinction is the same as with *permanence*, *-cy*, but is more generally appreciated : *the persistence of poverty* or *of matter* ; *courage & persistency are high gifts.* See -CE, -CY.

PERSON. 1. Verb forms. 2. P. of relative.

1. When a compound subject consists of two or more alternative parts differing in person, there is sometimes a doubt about the right verb form to use (*Are you or I next ?* &c.). See NEITHER 4, OR 2, for discussion.

2. P. of relative. Two questions arise, for which see WHO ; these are exemplified in (a) *To me, who has* [or *have* ?] *also a copy of it, it seems a somewhat trivial fragment,* & (b) *Most of us lost our* [or *their* ?] *heads*.

persona grata. Pronounce persō'na.

personal equation is a phrase of definite meaning ; it is the correction, quantitatively expressed, that an individual's observation of astronomical or other phenomena is known by experiment to require ; minutely accurate assessment is essential to the notion. The learned sound of *equation*, however, has commended it to those who want some expression or other with *personal* in it, & are all the better pleased if such commonplace words as *view* or *opinion* or *taste* or *judgement* can be replaced by something more imposing. So : *M. Poincaré likes Mr Bonar Law better than he liked Mr Lloyd George ; let us hope that the improved p. e. will count for something./If Lady Astor's entrance upon the Parliamentary scene is*

worthy of commemoration, the cost of it . . . should have been under the control of the House, which naturally resents the treatment of this matter as a family affair ; in general there is too much p. e. about Astorian politics. See POPULARIZED TECHNICALITIES.

personal(i)ty. Personal property in the legal sense is *-alty* ; the other noun work of *personal* is done by *-ality* ; cf. *real(i)ty*.

personate makes *-nable*, *-tor*; see -ABLE 1, -OR.

PERSONIFICATION, NOUNS OF MULTITUDE, METONYMY. When a country is spoken of as *She*, we have personification ; when we doubt whether to write *The Admiralty refuse* or *The Admiralty refuses*, we are pulled up by a noun of multitude ; when we call King George *the Crown*, we use metonymy. Some mistakes incident to these forms of speech run into one another, & are therefore grouped together here, under the headings : 1. Ill-advised personification. 2. Vacillation. 3. Unattached possessives.

1. Ill-advised personification. To figure ' the world ' as a female, a certain ' quarter ' as sentient, or ' Irish womanhood ' as a woman, is to be frigid—the epithet proper to those who make futile attempts at decoration. Such personifications are implied in *Just now* the world *wants all that America can give* her *in shipping* (read *it* for *her*), in *But on application to* the quarter *most likely to know I was assured that the paper in question was not written by Dickens* (The quarter is no doubt a person or persons, & capable of knowledge ; but it will surely never do to let that secret out), & in *The womanhood of Ireland stands for individualism as against co-operation, & presents the practical domestic arguments in* her *support* (Whether *her* implies the personification of *womanhood* or of *individualism* does not much matter ; it must be one or the other, & neither is suited for the treatment).

It is in places like these, where a writer hardly intends personification, but slips unconsciously or half-heartedly into implying it, that he reveals his want of literary instinct. Far the commonest form taken by the weakness is that of which many examples are given under 's INCONGRUOUS. To write *famine's* or *Austria's* instead of *of famine, of Austria,* is virtually to personify them ; & the modern newspaper is perpetually doing this in the most prosaic contexts. So :—*A particular character of a monsoon season may reduce to* famine's verge *millions of industrious ryots* (The writer was afraid of *verge of famine* before *millions of ryots* ; see OUT OF THE FRYING-PAN). / *The tariff is also causing no profit, but heavy loss, to about nine out of ten of* Austria's *farmers* (Again, fear of *of . . . of . . . of*).

2. Vacillation. *The Government, the Times, the Party,* & the like, are nouns of multitude, which can be treated as units & therefore referred to by the words *it, its,* & followed by singular verbs, or as bodies of people to which *they, them, their,* & plural verbs, are appropriate. *Britain, Paris,* & the like, are words naturally admitting of personification, & can be referred to in their literal sense by *it* & *its,* or in their personified sense by *she* & *her.* So much everyone knows ; what will perhaps surprise the reader is to find from the examples below how many writers are capable of absurdly mixing the two methods in a single phrase or staggering, in longer sentences, from one to the other & back again. The noun-of-multitude examples (for yet more of which see NUMBER, 6) are placed first, the personification ones afterwards ; & the words in which the vacillation is exhibited are in roman type :—*The Times also gives some interesting comments by their special correspondent./During their six years of office the Government has done great harm./That will gain ground*

or *not in proportion as the public* is *secure in* their *minds about the Navy./ It is the party to which Sir Henry Howorth belongs that* is *discredited by* their *support of this unprincipled violation./The Union & Progress Party does not seem to be living up to* their *patriotic resolutions./The Government* is *pledged to reduce taxation, & of course* they *cannot begin to look at old-age pensions until* it *has had sufficient time to reduce expenditure./ The excuse of the Admiralty,* which were *responsible for these proceedings, is . . .* (*which was,* or *who were*)./ *The population,* who *was driven away on the morrow of the surprise of May 27,* are *glad to come back only two months later./Japan* itself now *ceases to be an island Power, & for the first time accepts responsibilities on the continent which* it *cannot abandon ;* her *frontier is no longer the sea./When Poplar* no longer *maintains* its own *paupers* she *must no longer determine the standard on which* they *are to be maintained./ The United States has given another proof of* its *determination to uphold* her *neutrality.*

3. Unattached possessives. *Danish sympathy with Finland is writ large over all* her *newspapers, literature, & public speeches, as the most casual visitor to Copenhagen can see.* Her means ' of (the personified) Denmark ' ; we can all see that ; but we most of us also resent, nevertheless, a personification that is done not on the stage, but ' off ' ; a Denmark personified & not presented is a sort of shadow of a shade./*This is a timely tribute from a man who has spent a large part of his life in Friendly Society work, & who would be the last to sanction anything that imperilled* their *interests. Their* means ' of the Friendly Societies ' ; but where are they ? The adjective *Friendly Society* is as unavailing here as *Danish* in the previous example./*The true doctrine is that every public act of the Crown is an act for which* his *advisers are responsible.* It is in some contexts indifferent whether one says *the King*, *His Majesty*, or *the Crown*; but while the King has *his* advisers, the Crown can only have *its*; as to the possessive proper to *His Majesty*, see MAJESTY.

personify. For inflexions see VERBS IN -IE &c., 6.

personnel, not *-sonel*. Pronounce personĕ'l.

perspic-. *Perspicacious, -acity,* mean (having or showing) insight; *perspicuous, -uity,* mean (the being) easy to get a clear idea of; see PAIRS & SNARES. *Shrewd & shrewdness, clear & clearness,* or other short words, are used in preference by those who are neither learned nor pretentious. The learned, however, can safely venture on the *perspic-* pairs; when the unlearned pretender claims acquaintance with them, they are apt to punish the familiarity by showing that he is in fact a stranger to them. The usual mistake is to write *-uity* for *-acity,* as in :—*Sometimes, however, Dr Bell's perspicuity was at fault./He claims for it superiority to other alternatives, the defects of which he sees with that perspicuity which the advocates of each ideal system invariably display towards rival systems./The high-class West End & provincial tailors are displaying considerable perspicuity in buying checks.*

perspire, perspiration. See GENTEELISMS.

persuade makes *-dable* (see MUTE E) as well as *persuasible*; the former is recommended (see -ABLE 2).

persuasion. Parodies of the phrase 'of the Roman, Protestant, &c., p.', e.g. *Hats of the cartwheel p.,* are to be classed with WORN-OUT HUMOUR; see also HACKNEYED PHRASES.

pertinence, -cy. There is no useful distinction; the first will probably prevail. See -CE, -CY.

perturbedly. Four syllables if used; see -EDLY.

peruse. See FORMAL WORDS. *P.* makes *-sable*; see MUTE E.

pervade makes *-dable*; see MUTE E.

pervert. See NOUN & VERB ACCENT.

pessimism. See OPTIMISM for comments on the popular use, & POPULARIZED TECHNICALITIES.

pester makes *-ered*; see -R-, -RR-.

pestle. Pronounce without -t-; see PRONUNCIATION, Silent t.

petal makes *-lled*; see -LL-, -L-.

petit. For *p.* & compounds see FRENCH WORDS.

petitio principii. See TECHNICAL TERMS.

petition, vb, makes *-oned* &c.; see -N-, -NN-.

petrel. The OED recognizes only the pronunciation pĕt-.

petrify. For inflexions see verbs in -IE &c., 6.

petrol(eum). For synonyms see KEROSENE.

petty. For *p. officer* see OFFICER.

pewit, pee-. The OED puts first the form *pewit,* but the pronunciation pĕ'-wĭt (not pū'ĭt). This makes things difficult, & it would seem better to spell *peewit,* unless pū'it, which has Tennyson for it, rhyming *pewit* with *cruet* in *Will Waterproof,* is to be the sound.

phaeton. The three-syllable pronunciation (fā'ĭtn) is best.

phagedaena. See GREEK G.

phalanstery. Accent on the first (fă'lan-).

phalanx. Ordinary pl. *-xes,* but in Anatomy *phalanges* (fală'njēz). See LATIN PLURALS.

phallus. Pl. *-li* (-ī).

phantasmagoria is sing., not (as in the following) pl.:—*We shall then be able to reach some conclusion as to the meaning & effect of these bewildering phantasmagoria.* The word was designed to mean 'crowd of phantasms'.

phantasm)(phantom. The two are by origin merely spelling variants, differentiated, but so that the differences are elusive; the following tendencies are discernable, but sometimes conflict. 1. *Phantom* is the more popular form, *-asm* being chiefly in literary use. 2. Both meaning roughly an illusive apparition, *phantom* stresses the fact that the thing is illusive, & -*asm* the fact that it does appear, so that they give respectively the negative & the positive aspect. 3. A phantom presents itself to the eye bodily or mental, a phantasm to any sense or to the intellect. 4. *Phantasm* has an adjective (*phantasmal*) of its own ; *phantom* has not, but is used attributively (*phantom hopes* &c.) with much freedom, & where a true adjective is necessary borrows *phantasmal* ; the two nouns are no doubt kept from diverging more definitely than they do by this common property in *phantasmal*.

Pharaoh. So spelt. Pron. fār'ō.

Pharisee. The adj. *Pharisaic* is preferable to *Pharisaical* ; see -IC(AL). The -*ism* noun is *Pharisaism*, not -*seeism*.

pharmaceutical &c. For pronunciation see GREEK G.

pharmacopoeia. Pronounce -pē'a. For the spelling see Æ, Œ.

pharyngitis. See GREEK G.

phenomenal means ' of the kind apprehended by (any of) the senses ' ; that is, everything that is reported to the mind by sight, hearing, taste, smell, or touch—& that whether the report answers to reality or not— is p. If the report is correct, the thing reported is also real ; if not, it is ' merely phenomenal '. The question of real existence & its relation to perception & thought is the concern of Metaphysics, & *p.* is a metaphysical word, contrasted variously with *real, absolute,* & *noumenal*. But the object here is not to expound the metaphysical meaning of these terms ; it is only to point out that *p. is* a metaphysical term with a use of its own. To divert it from this proper use to a job for which it is not needed, by making it do duty for *remarkable, extraordinary,* or *prodigious*, is a sin against the English language. It has gone through the phases, Philosophic term, POPULARIZED TECHNICALITY, & VOGUE-WORD, & is now

in the state of discredit (cf. INDIVIDUAL) that follows upon unreasonable vogue. That is the moment when believers in sound English may deliver their attack upon such usages with hope of success.

phenomen(al)ism. The longer form is recommended ; see -IST, -ALIST.

phenomenon. Pl. -*ena* ; see -ON. *P.* in the sense ' notable occurrence ' or ' prodigy ' is open essentially to the same objections as PHENOMENAL used correspondingly ; but less practical inconvenience results, since there is little danger of misunderstanding.

philately, -ist. It is a pity that for one of the most popular scientific pursuits one of the least popularly intelligible names should have been found. The best remedy now is to avoid the official titles whenever *stamp-collecting* & -*collector* will do.

-**phil(e).** The -*e* originally taken on from French is now usually dropped, with the good result of bringing back the pronunciation from the queer -fīl to -fĭl.

philharmonic, philhellenic, &c. The -h- is better unsounded in these, but not in syllables on which the accent falls, as in *philhellenism, -ist.* See PRONUNCIATION.

philippine, philopoena, &c., the forfeit game. The first spelling is perhaps the commonest in England.

Philistine. The special modern meaning is thus given by the OED— A person deficient in liberal culture & enlightenment, whose interests are chiefly bounded by material & commonplace things (But often applied contemptuously by connoisseurs of any particular art or department of learning to one who has no knowledge or appreciation of it ; sometimes a mere term of dislike for those whom the speaker considers ' bourgeois ').

philogynist. See GREEK G.

Philomel(a). See SOBRIQUETS.

philosophic(al). Except where -*ical*

is stereotyped by forming part of a title (*Philosophical Transactions* &c.), the *-ic* form is now commoner in all the more specific senses ; *-ical* still prevails in the very general sense ' resembling ' or ' befitting a philosopher ', i.e. wise or unperturbed or well balanced ; & this gives a basis for differentiation; see -IC(AL).

philtre, -ter. The first is usual.
phiz. See CURTAILED WORDS.
phlegm &c. The g is silent in *p.* & *phlegmy*, but sounded in *phlegmatic*.
phlogiston. See GREEK G.
Phoenician, phoenix. Best so written ; see Æ, Œ.
phone, vb. See CURTAILED WORDS.

PHONETICS. It often happens that one who is perhaps himself unacquainted with complicated & complete phonetic systems, & at any rate writes for those to whom they are mysteries, has occasion to make the pronunciation of some word intelligible in print. A scheme that would enable this to be done would be of value ; but it would have to meet several requirements rather hard to reconcile. 1. It must use no special types, or it cannot be printed on demand. 2. It must be both simple & systematic, or those who learn it, but have to read it only now & then, will not remember it. 3. It must be to a great extent self-explaining, or it will mean nothing to those who have not learnt it. 4. It must be capable of rendering all English sounds, un-English ones being ruled out as beyond the compass of a scheme subject to requirements 1 & 2. The following is offered as a solution that may serve for want of a better.

A. VOWEL SOUNDS

Each of the five vowels a e i o u represents two clear sounds & an obscure one, according as it has the long mark over it (māte mēte mīte mōte mūte), or the short mark (răck rĕck rĭck rŏck rŭck), or no mark (a in about, e in cozen, i in cousin, o in proceed, u in Whitsun).

When two or more italic letters are used, they form a single symbol, as *aw, ow, oi, ah, oor, owr* (*cawl, cowl, coil, bah, boor, dowry*). The italic symbols consisting of one vowel & *r*, & *oo*, have always a long or short mark over the first letter thus : māre, mēre, mīre, mōre, mūre, părt, pĕrt, pŏrt, stōol, stŏod ; their r is usually not trilled before a consonant, but is or may be before a vowel sound. If two italic symbols (see B also) come together, a vertical line (as in Illustrations, *rouge, douche*) should part them.

B. CONSONANT SOUNDS

b, d, f, h, j, k, l, m, n, p, r, t, v, w, z, are unambiguous.

c, q, x, are not used.

g is reckoned hard (get) ; s is reckoned hard (set) ; y is reckoned consonantal (yet).

The italic combinations *ch, sh, zh, th, dh, ng, ngg, hw*, represent the italicized parts of wi*tch*, wi*sh*, vi*sion*, pi*th*, wi*th*, si*nger*, fi*nger*, *wh*it : thus, wĭ*ch*, wĭ*sh*, vĭ*zh*on, pĭ*th*, wĭ*dh*, sĭ*nger*, fĭ*ngg*er, *hw*ĭt.

C. ACCENT

This should be placed after the vowel sound of the syllable on which it falls (tĕ′nder, fē′nĭan).

ILLUSTRATIONS

father, fah′*dh*er
iniquitous, ĭnĭ′kwĭtus
pyjamas, pĭj*ah*′maz
laboratory, lă′boratorĭ
fascination, făsĭnā′*sh*on
magical, mă′jĭkal
consciousness, kŏ′n*sh*usnĭs
rouge, rōo|*zh*
mountaineer, mowntĭnē*r*′
douche, dōo|*sh*
Colquhoun, kohōo′n
agriculture, ă′grĭkŭl*ch*ur
whetstone, *hw*ĕ′tstōn
coyness, koi′nĭs
burglary, bĕr′glarĭ
burglarious, bugl*ār*′ĭus
dubiety, dūbī′ĭtĭ
business, bĭ′znĭs

PHOTO 437 **PICTURE**

SUMMARY OF SCHEME

māte mēte mīte mōte mūte
răck rĕck rĭck rŏck rŭck
cawl cowl coil bah boor dowry
māre mēre mīre mōre mūre
părt pĕrt pŏrt stōol stŏod
No c, q, or x
g, s, y, as in get, set, yet
ch, sh, zh, sounds in witch, wish,
vision
th, dh, sounds in pith, with
ng, ngg, sounds in singer, finger
hw, sound in whet
Accent after the vowel sound of
the stressed syllable.

photo. See CURTAILED WORDS.
Pl. -os ; see -O(E)S 5.

phrase, vb, has -sable ; see MUTE E.

phraseology. Pron. frāzĭŏ'lojĭ.

phthisis. The old pronunciation
dropped the ph-, but this will probably recover its sound now that
everyone can read. The Greek
word had short i, but fthī- is now
usual ; see FALSE QUANTITY.

phylloxera. Pronounce & accent
fĭlokzēr'a.

phylum. Pl. -la.

physic, n. See FORMAL WORDS.

physic makes -cked, -cking, -cky ;
see -C-, -CK-.

physician, doctor, surgeon, in ordinary parlance. ' The p.' & ' the d.'
may be used to denote the same
person, viz one whose vocation is to
heal physical troubles, p. being the
FORMAL WORD, & no particular relation to s. being implied by either. A
s. is always a doctor who undertakes
to perform manual operations, but
not necessarily one who confines himself to them. Physician is also used
in contrast with s. to denote one who
deals with medicines & treatment,
not with surgical instruments, & again
in contrast with general practitioner
to denote a specialist or consultant.
It must be remembered, however,
that ' In the United Kingdom, every
medical practitioner is now required
to have a qualification as Physician
& also as Surgeon ; so that a general
practitioner usually describes himself
as " Physician & Surgeon " '—OED.

physics)(physiology. The two words
had once the same wide meaning
of natural science or natural philosophy. They have now been narrowed & differentiated, physics retaining only the properties of matter
& energy in inorganic nature, &
physiology only the normal functions
& phenomena of living beings.

physiognomy, -nomical. The g is
silent.

physiology. See PHYSICS. For the
adjective, -ical is so much the
commoner that it should be accepted
as the only form. See -IC(AL).

pi (pious). See CURTAILED WORDS.

pianist. Pronounce pē'anĭst.

piano. The instrument is piă'nō ;
pl. -os, see -O(E)S 5. The musical
direction is pyah'nō.

pianola. Pronounce pēanō'la.

piazza. The OED gives piă'za ;
but the Italian pyah'tsa is perhaps
as often said ; see ITALIAN SOUNDS.

pibroch. Pronounce as Scotch
(pē-, & ch as in loch).

picaresque. The p. novel is defined
in the Enc. Brit. as :—' The prose
autobiography of a real or fictitious
personage who describes his experiences as a social parasite, & who
satirizes the society which he has
exploited '. The type is Spanish,
but the most widely known example
is the French Gil Blas. Pícaro is a
Spanish word meaning vagabond.

piccolo. Pl. -os ; see -O(E)S 6.

pickaxe. For spelling see AXE.

picket, vb, makes -eted, -eting, &c. ;
see -T-, -TT-.

picket, picquet, piquet. The second
form serves no purpose at all ; the
third should be reserved for the
card-game, & picket be used for all
other senses, including that of the
military outpost often spelt with
-qu- or -cqu-.

picnic makes -cking, -cked, -cker,
-cky ; see -C-, -CK-.

picture. Pĭ'ktūr is academic ;
pĭ'ktyer is impossible except with
a deliberate pause after the t
(though many people think they say

it who do not) ; **pi'kcher** is the only form practicable for ordinary mortals. See Pronunciation.

pidgin, pigeon. ' Business-English ' was the name given by the Chinese to the Anglo-Chinese lingua franca ; but they pronounced *business* pidgin, & we have confused the meaningless *pidgin* with the significant *pigeon* ; cf. amuck. *Pigeon*, however, is two centuries younger in print than *amuck*, so that there is not the same reason to protest against *pidgin* as against *amok*.

piebald)(skewbald. *P.* is properly of white & black, *s.* of white & some colour.

piece makes *-ceable* ; see -able 1.
pièce de résistance. See French words.
pierce makes *-ceable* ; see -able 1.
pierrot, -ette. See French words.
pietà. Pronounce pyā'tah.
pig. See Collectives 4.
pigeon)(dove. Used absolutely, the words are coextensive in application, every d. being a p., & vice versa ; but *p.* is the ordinary word, & *d.* is now the rarity, suited for poetical contexts, symbolism, &c. *D.* is also still used without special significance of particular kinds of pigeon, especially the turtle & other natives, but not of exotics ; & much more often the kind is specified, as in *stock, ring, turtle, -d.*

pigeon English. See Pidgin.
piggy, -ie. See -ey, -ie, -y.
pigmy. See Pygmy.
pigsty. Pl. *-ies.*
pilau, -aw, -aff. The OED gives precedence to the spelling *pilau* & the pronunciation pilow'.
pile, vb, makes *-lable* ; see Mute e.
pilfer makes *-ered, -ering,* &c. ; see -r-, -rr-.
pill. For *the pill* see Sobriquets.
pillar makes *-ared* ; see -r-, -rr-.
pillory, vb. For inflexions see Verbs in -ie &c., 6.
pilot, vb, makes *-oted, -oting,* &c. ; see -t-, -tt-.
pilule. So spelt, not *-ll-.*
pimento. Pl. *-os* ; see -o(e)s 6.

pince-nez. See French words.
Pindarics. See Technical terms.
pine. See fir, pine for the difference. *P.* makes *piny* ; see -ey & -y.
pinion makes *-oned* ; see -n-, -nn-.
pinky, not *-key.*
pinna. Pl. *-ae.*
pinny (pinafore). For spelling see -ey, -ie, -y.
pintado. Pl. *-os* ; see -o(e)s 6.
pipe makes *pipy* ; see -ey & -y.
piquant. Pronounce pē'kant.
pique, vb, makes *-quable* ; see Mute e.
piquedly. A bad form ; see -edly.
pis aller. See French words.
piscina. Either pronounce as Latin (pĭsī'na) & use Latin pl. *-nae,* or pronounce pĭsē'na & use English pl. *-nas.*

pistachio. Pl. *-os* ; see -o(e)s 4. The pronunciation put first in the OED is pĭstā'shĭo.
pistil makes *-lled* ; see -ll-, -l-.
pistol makes *-lled, -lling* ; -ll-, -l-.
piteous, pitiable, pitiful. There are three broadly different senses for the words : 1. Feeling pity ; 2. Exciting pity ; 3. Exciting contempt. It would have been easy, then, if the problem had been posed beforehand, to assign a word to a sense, *piteous* to Nº 1, *pitiable* to Nº 2, & *pitiful* to Nº 3. But language-making is no such simple affair as that, & spontaneous development has worked badly here ; *piteous* has senses 1 & 2, *pitiable* senses 2 & 3, & *pitiful* senses 1, 2, & 3—a very wasteful confusion, but too inveterate to be got into order at present. See also Plenteous.

pithecoid. Pron. pĭthē'koid.
pituitary. Pronounce pĭtū'ĭtarĭ. Latinists grieved by the accent & the short second *i* may find consolation in False quantity.

pity, n. *In the meantime, we can only muse upon the pity of it.* For *the p. of it,* & *p. 'tis 'tis true,* see Stock Pathos, & Hackneyed phrases.

pivotal is open to the same objections as *coastal* ; see Hybrid de-

RIVATIVES. *Pivot* used attributively will almost always serve the need.

pixy, -ie. The first is better.
pizzicato. Pronounce pĭtsĭkah'tō. Pl. *-os* ; see -O(E)S 6.
placable. The OED gives plā-precedence.
placard. The pronunciation recommended is plă'kard for the noun & plakar'd for the verb ; see NOUN & VERB ACCENT.

placate. The pronunciation recommended is plakā't, but both plā'kāt & plă'kăt are also heard. The word is much more in American than in British use, but is quoted from the 17th c. Beside the adjective *placable, placatable* can be made for the gerundive use ; see -ABLE 1.

place, vb, makes *-ceable;* see -ABLE 1.
placid makes *-dest;* see -ER & -EST 4.
plagiarize makes *-zable* ; see MUTE E.
plague makes *-guable, -guing, -guy* ; see MUTE E, -EY & -Y.
plaice (fish). So spelt.
plaid. Pronounced plăd in Scotland, but plăd in England.
plain makes *plainness. P. sailing* is ('probably'—OED) a popular use of the nautical term *plane sailing,* which means navigation by a plane chart, 'a simple & easy method, approximately correct for short distances'. The corruption, if it is one, is so little misleading, since *plain sailing* is as intelligible in itself as *clear going* or any such phrase, that any attempt to correct it is needless as well as vain.

plait. Pronounce plăt.
planchette. See FRENCH WORDS.
plane, vb, makes *-nable* ; MUTE E.
plane sailing, as a correction of the *plain sailing* of ordinary use, is a pedantry ; see PLAIN.
plangent. Pronounce -ănj-.
plantain. Pronounce plă'ntĭn.
plaster makes *-ered* &c. ; -R-, -RR-.
plat (food served). See FRENCH WORDS.
plateful. Pl. *-ls* ; see -FUL.
plate glass. Two words unhyphened ; see HYPHENS 3 B.

plateau. See FRENCH WORDS ; but the sound plă'tō, & the pl. *-s,* are now common ; see also -x.
platen, -tt-, pressing-plate in printing. The OED prefers *-t-* to *-tt-.* Pronounce -ăt-.
platform. The political sense of party programme is still rather American than English, but in England too is now not uncommon.

platinize makes *-zable* ; see MUTE E.
platitude, -dinous. The words are misused in the following extracts; for the differences between *p.,* *commonplace,* & *truism,* see COMMON-PLACE. *He would probably in his speech at Glasgow have avoided the use of certain phrases & arguments which, though he clearly means them to be innocuous & even platitudinous, have none the less been the subject of vehement controversy. / The miners acknowledge the force of this principle or platitude as freely as the rest of us.*

Platonic love. For the origin of the expression, see Plato's *Symposium.* For its meaning, the definition, & one or two quotations, from the OED here follow :—(Definition) Applied to love or affection for one of the opposite sex, of a purely spiritual character, & free from sensual desire. (Quotations) : (Howell) It is a love that consists in contemplation & idaeas of the mind, not in any carnall fruition. (Norris) Platonic Love is the Love of Beauty abstracted from all sensual Applications, & desire of Corporal Contact. (Lewes) Love is the longing of the Soul for Beauty ; the inextinguishable desire which like feels for like, which the divinity within us feels for the divinity revealed to us in Beauty. This is the celebrated Platonic Love, which, from having originally meant a communion of two souls, & that in a rigidly dialectical sense, has been degraded to the expression of maudlin sentiment between the sexes.

platypus. Pl. *-puses,* not *-pi* ; see LATIN PLURALS.

play. For inflexions see VERBS IN
-IE &c., 1.

pleading. For *special p.* see
SPECIAL.

pleasant has -*er*, -*est*, in comparison;
see -ER & -EST 2.

pleased. For *very p.*, see VERY.

pleasure. *I have the p. of doing
so-&-so* means I do it, & am glad
to do it—a courteous announcement
that one is conferring some favour.
It is my p. to do so-&-so, or *that
so-&-so should be done*, means I
choose to, & therefore of course
shall, do it or have it done—an
imperious statement of intention.
The second idiom is based on the
definite special sense of *p.* with
possessives (*my, his, the king's,* &c.),
viz one's will, desire, choice. *It is
a p. to do*, on the other hand, means
the same as *I have the p. of doing.*
But insensibility to idiom often
causes *It is my* or *our* (not *a*) *p.* to
be substituted for *I* or *We have the
p.*; see CAST-IRON IDIOM. Examples of the mistake are :—*Once
again* it is our p. *to notice the annual
issue of ' The Home Messenger '.*/
In the experiment which it was my
p. *to witness, M. Bachelet used only
two traction coils.*/*When* it was my
p. *to address a public meeting of
more than 2000 at the Royal Theatre
the organized opposition numbered
less than seven score.*

pleb. See CURTAILED WORDS.

plebeian makes -*nness* (abstract
noun).

plebiscite, -tary. Pronounce plĕ′bĭ-
sĭt, plĭbĭ′sĭtarĭ.

plectrum. Pl. -*tra.*

Pleiad. Pronounce plī′ad. Pl.
-*ds* or -*des* (-ēz). The use in the
sing. for a group of brilliant people
comes from the Pléiade of poets of
the French Renaissance.

pleistocene, pliocene, miocene, are
regrettable BARBARISMS. It is worth
while to mention this, not because
the words themselves can now be
either ended or mended, but on the
chance that the men of science may
some day wake up to their duties to

the language—duties much less
simple than they are apt to suppose.

plenteous, -iful. As with other
pairs in -*eous* & -*iful* (e. g. from
bounty, beauty, duty, pity), the meaning of the two is the same, but the
-*eous* word is the less common &
therefore the better suited to the
needs of poetry & exalted prose ;
for these it should be reserved.

plenty. *Excuses are plenty* (i. e.
plentiful), *There is p. wood* (i. e., p.
of), *That is p. hot enough* (i. e. quite),
are irregularities of which the first
is established in literature, the
second is still considered a solecism
(though the omission of *of* is easily
paralleled, as in *a little brandy, a
dozen apples, more courage, enough
food*), & the third is recognized
colloquial, but not literary, English.

PLEONASM is the using of more
words than are required to give the
sense intended.

1. It is often resorted to deliberately for rhetorical effect (*Lest at
any time they should see* with their
eyes & *hear* with their ears). The
writer who uses p. in that way must
be judged by whether he does
produce his effect & whether the
occasion is worthy of it.

2. There are many phrases originally put together for the sake of
such emphasis, but repeated with
less & less of impressiveness until
they end by boring instead of striking the hearer. Such are the pairs
of synonyms *if & when, unless &
until, save & except, in any shape or
form, of any sort or kind.* These &
many others have long worn out
their force, & what those who would
write vigorously have to do with
them is merely to unlearn them ;
see IF & WHEN, the apparently least
pleonastic of these stock phrases,
for fuller discussion. Those who
use this form of p. can hardly be
unconscious that they are saying
a thing twice over, the *and* or *or*
being there as a reminder.

3. In other phrases, the offender is

evidently unconscious, & expresses the same notion twice over in the belief that he is saying it once. Such are EQUALLY AS (2), *more* PREFERABLE, & *continue to* REMAIN, which mean neither more nor less than *equally* (or *as*) *preferable*, & *remain*, by themselves, but which can be defended, by those who care to defend them, as not worse than uselessly pleonastic. With these may be classed the queer use of *both*, repugnant to sense but not to grammar, where *they* or *the two* is replaced by it though the emphasis necessarily attaching to *both* is absurd ; so :—*Both men had something in common./Archer Bey telephoned to General Morris & both conferred at the Residency.* See BOTH 2 for more varieties of this very common ineptitude.

4. A further downward step brings us below the defensible level, & we come to the overlappings described in the article HAZINESS :—*It is singular how apparently slow some minds* seem *to learn the elementary truth./We have been enabled to make large economies* while at the same time *increasing the efficiency of the fleet.* See also AGO & BECAUSE.

5. Lastly, there are the pleonasms in which by wrongly repeating a negative or a conjunction the writer produces a piece of manifest nonsense or impossible grammar. So :—
' *You just come with me in a tub pair, & I should* not *wonder if I could* not *lick you into shape './It should be a very great thing* that *before guns, shells, mountings, rangefinders, &c., are adopted,* that *the opinion of real & not of soi-disant experts shall be taken./We can only* say that *if the business men who read the* Times *are really of opinion that this is a sensible procedure, &* that, *if they find any satisfaction whatever in the writing down of a huge sum, which everybody knows can never be recovered, they will have only themselves to thank if . . .* See also NEGATIVES, THAT conj., & OVERZEAL.

plesiosaurus. Pl. -*ri* (-ī).

plethora. Pronounce plĕ'thora.

pleura. Pl. -*rae*.

pleurisy. So spelt, not *plu-* ; the derivation is from *pleura* rib, not *plus pluris*.

plexus. Pl. -*uses* or *plexus* (-ūs), not -*xi* ; see -US.

plica. Pl. -*ae*.

pliers. So spelt.

pliocene. See PLEISTOCENE.

plumb-. The b is silent in *plumber*, *plumbery*, *plumbing*, & *plumbless*, but sounded in *plumbago*, *plumbeous*, *plumbic*, *plumbiferous*, & *plumbism*.

plume makes *plumy* ; see -EY & Y.

plump(en), vb. See -EN VERBS.

plumpy. Poetical only.

plunder makes -*ered* &c. ; -R-, -RR-.

PLURAL ANOMALIES. See -ICS 2 for the question whether words in -*ics* are singular or plural. Plural names of diseases, as *mumps*, *measles*, *glanders*, can be treated as singular or plural ; *chickenpox* & *smallpox*, originally plural, are now reckoned singular. *Innings, corps*, & some other words in -s, are singular or plural without change of spelling, but, while *corps* has -s silent in singular & sounded in plural, *an innings & several innings* show no distinction, whence arises the colloquial double plural *inningses*. For the plural of *Court Martial* & *Lord Justice*, the number of *porridge*, & the difference between *pence* & *pennies*, see the words.

plurality. With three-cornered contests as common as they now are, we may have occasion to find a convenient single word for what we now call *an absolute majority*, i. e. a majority comprising more than half the votes cast. In America the word *majority* itself has that meaning, while a poll greater than that of any other candidate, but less than half the votes cast, is called a *plurality*. It might be well to borrow this distinction, but to better it by changing *plurality* to *plurity*. The correct meaning of *plurality* is not moreness (which is the notion wanted, but which would be *plurity*), but plural-ness or severalness or more-than-one-ness. *Plurity* is an obsolete English word exactly suited to the need; cf. REVIVALS. See also MAJORITY.

ply, vb. For inflexions see VERBS IN -IE &c., 6.

pneumatic, pneumonia, &c. The OED gives nū- only for these particular words, but prefers pnū- for less familiar words from the same stems, such as *pneumatology, pneumonometer*. It is to be hoped that these silent letters may recover their voices now that everyone can read ; cf. PHTHISIS, PSYCHOLOGY.

pochard. The OED puts pōch-first, but pŏch-, pŏk-, & pŏk-, are also recognized.

pocket makes *-eted, -eting*, &c. ; see -T-, -TT-.

pocketful. Pl. *-ls* ; see -FUL.

pococurante. Pronounce pōko-kōŏrah'ntĕ. Pl. *-ti* (-ē).

podagra. The OED puts first the pronunciation pŏ'dagra.

podgy. So spelt ; see -EY & -Y.

podium. Pronounce pō- ; pl. *-ia*.

poetess. See FEMININE DESIGNATIONS.

poetic(al). See -IC(AL). The two forms are more or less peculiar in being both in constant use, while yet there is no clear division of functions between them. Certain tendencies, not always operative, there are :—*poetical* labels, while *-ic* admires (*The -ical works of —* ; *Conceived in a truly -ic spirit*) ; *-ical* is the form for ' written in verse ', & *-ic* for ' instinct with poetry ' (*Poetical composition* ; *The -ic impulse*) ; *-ical* is the commonplace, & *-ic* the rhetorical form (*In a poetical mood* ; but *In -ic mood*) ; *-ical* is sometimes used at the end of a sentence when in another position *-ic* would be more natural (*An idea more true than -ical*, cf. *A no less true than poetic idea*) ; & *-ic* is sometimes jocularly substituted for *-ical* (*The -ic effusions of an advertising soapboiler*).

POETICISMS. Simple reference of words to this article warns the reader that to use them in ordinary prose contexts is dangerous ; see also INCONGRUOUS VOCABULARY. A small haphazard collection of specimens is :—*an*, conj. ; *aught* ; *beauteous* ; *broidery* ; *canorous* ; *childly* ; *clamant* ; *delightsome* ; *direful* ; *duteous* ; *eke*, adv. ; *ere* ; *erst* ; *lorn* ; *magnifical* ; *plain*, vb ; *plangent* ; *whilom*.

poeticize makes *-zable* ; see MUTE E.

pogrom. Pronounce pogrŏ'm.

poignant. Pronounce poi'nant.

point. For synonyms in the sense province &c., see FIELD. *P. of view* is the native phrase now being ousted by *standpoint*. The latter is a translation of the German *Standpunkt*, & appears in the form *standpunct* in one of the earliest OED quotations. What is killing *p. o. v.* is no doubt the awkwardness of following it, as is constantly necessary, with another *of* (*from the p. o. v. of philosophy*) ; the process may be expected to continue, & there is no valid objection to *standpoint* ; *p. o. v.* will linger for a time where the *of* difficulty does not present itself (*from my*, or *Mill's, p. o. v.*). It is certainly better that *standpoint* should be accepted than another solution that is being tried on purpose to avoid it—that is, the using of *point* by itself as equivalent to *point of view* (*from the point of the Tory Party*) : *They agree that the demand of £3 a week by the men was unreasonable if it was meant to sustain ' a mere existence ', but* from the point of a living wage *it was not unreasonable*. *View-point*, an earlier product of the repugnance to *standpoint*, has the disadvantage of calling to mind what *standpoint* allows to be forgotten, that the idiomatic English is undoubtedly *p. of view*. The perplexed stylist is at present inclined to cut loose & experiment with *angle*. What is here recommended is to use *p. o. v.* as the normal expression, but not be afraid of *standpoint* on occasion.

poke makes -*kable* (see MUTE E), & *poky* (see -EY & -Y).

polarize makes -*zable* ; see MUTE E.

polemarch. Pronounce pŏ'lĭmark.

polemic(al). It would be convenient, & not be counter to any existing distinctions, if -*ic* were kept to the noun use & -*ical* to the adjectival ; see -IC(AL).

police, vb, makes -*ceable* ; see -ABLE 1.

policewoman. See FEMININE DESIGNATIONS.

policy. The word meaning ' course of action ' &c., & that meaning ' Insurance Company's guarantee ', are of different origins, the first having started in Greek as *politeia*, & the other as *apodeixis*.

politic(al). See -IC(AL).

polity is a word that has lately emerged from its retirement in the writings of philosophic historians or political philosophers, become a newspaper word, & suffered the maltreatment usual in such cases. It has been seized upon as a less familiar & therefore more impressive spelling of *policy* (with which it is indeed identical in origin), & the differences that have long existed between the two have been very vaguely grasped or else neglected. A useful indication that the two words are of widely different meanings is that *policy* is as often as not without *a* or *the* in the singular, whereas *polity* in its right senses is very rarely so. *Polity* is not (like *policy* or *principle*) a line of action, nor (like *politics*) a branch of activity, nor (like *statesmanship*) an art or quality. But in the following newspaper extracts it will be seen that one of those senses is required, & that one of those words, or at any rate some other word, would be the right one instead of *polity* :— *This Newspaper Trust has during the last two years increasingly assumed the right & the power to upset ministries, to nominate new ministers & discharge others, & to dictate & veto public polity./The main obstacles to advancement have always been social superstitions, political oppression, rash & misguided ambitions, & gross mistakes in polity./Habits of living from hand to mouth engendered by centuries of crude polity will not die out in a month./Because the law of social progress has not been very clearly understood, for bad theory means faulty practice, & no theory rule of thumb, polity, which is the practical side of the matter, has had no certain guidance./And now that by their feats in arms peace has been brought within sight, the work in the field has admittedly to be rounded off, completed, & made lastingly effective for the common good by a work of Polity.*

The true meanings of *polity* are : (1, now rare) a condition, viz the being organized as a State or system of States ; (2, & most frequent) some particular form of such organization, e. g. a republic, monarchy, empire, confederation, Concert of Europe, or League of Nations ; & (3, not uncommon) a people organized as a State. The first three of the following examples are newspaper extracts showing the correct & usual sense 2, the fourth & fifth being OED quotations from Gladstone & Huxley illustrating the now rare sense 1 & the not very common sense 3 :—*Dr Hazeltine's lecture is an interesting account of the influence of English political & legal ideas upon the American polity./If the terms are accepted the future polity of Europe must be more than ever based on force./Mr Keynes points out that the commercial & industrial system of Europe has grown up with the pre-war polity as its basis./*(Gladstone) *At a period antecedent to the formation of anything like polity in Greece./*(Huxley) *Those who should be kept, as certain to be serviceable members of the polity.*

poll. The Cambridge pass degree, & the woman's & parrot's name, are pronounced pŏl ; other words pōl.

polloi. See HOI POLLOI.

pollute makes *-table* ; see MUTE E.

polyglot makes *-ttal*, *-ttic*, *-ttism* ; exceptionally, see -T-, -TT-.

polypus. Pl. *-pi* (-ī) or *-puses*. The inconsistency between this & *octopus* is due to its having come to us through classical Latin, in which it was declined like the ordinary Latin nouns in *-us*.

POLYSYLLABIC HUMOUR. See PEDANTIC HUMOUR for a slight account of the impulse that suggests long or abstruse words as a means of entertaining the hearer. Of the long as distinguished from the abstruse, *terminological inexactitude* for lie or falsehood is a favourable example, but much less amusing at the hundredth than at the first time of hearing. *Oblivious to their pristine nudity* (forgetting they were stark naked) is a less familiar specimen. Nothing need here be added to what was said in the other article beyond a short specimen list of long words or phrases that sensible people avoid. *Batavian, Caledonian, Celestial, Hibernian & Milesian*, for Dutch, Scotch, Chinese, Irish. *Solution of continuity, femoral habiliments, refrain from lacteal addition*, & *olfactory organ*, for gap, breeches, take no milk, & nose. *Osculatory, pachydermatous, matutinal, diminutive, fuliginous, fugacious, esurient, culinary*, & *minacious*, for kissing, thick-skinned, morning, tiny, sooty, timid, hungry, kitchen, & threatening. *Frontispiece, individual, equitation, intermediary, cachinnation*, & *epidermis*, for face, person, riding, means, laughter, & skin. *Negotiate & peregrinate* for tackle & travel.

pomade. The OED gives -ād as the English pronunciation, & -ahd as a foreign one ; the latter, however, is probably almost universal.

pommel, pu-. The first spelling is usual for the noun, the second for the verb, though the verb is merely a use of the noun, & not of different origin. Both are pronounced pŭm-, & both make *-lled* (see -LL-, -L-).

POMPOSITIES. Such words as *beverage, catarrh, collation, comestibles, condiment, co'nsort, divagation, edifice, emporium, ere, evince, exacerbate, intermediary, the military, munificent, save* (except), *spouse, vituperate*, have all ' a certain use in the world, no doubt ' ; but they are seen in the newspapers very much more often than occasions for those certain uses occur, & may serve as specimens of hundreds that are habitually substituted for others merely as pompous ornaments.

ponceau. See FRENCH WORDS.

poncho. Pronounce with -ch-. Pl. *-os* ; see -O(E)s 6.

pongee. Pronounce ponjē'.

pontifex. Pl. *-fices* (-ēz).

pontify. For inflexions see VERBS IN -IE &c., 6.

poor. The unorthodox pronunciations pōr & por are heard often enough to necessitate a warning. For *poorness & poverty* see the latter. For ' a p. thing but mine own ', see MISQUOTATION.

pop, = popular concert. See CURTAILED WORDS.

popularize makes *-zable* ⁚ MUTE E.

POPULARIZED TECHNICALITIES. The term of this sort most in vogue at the moment of writing (1920) is undoubtedly *acid test* (*The measure, as our correspondent says, provides an acid test for every Free Trader*), which became familiar through a conspicuous use of it during the war by President Wilson. In contrast with this newest acquisition may be set *intoxicated*, so long popular as to be not now recognizable for a medical term at all ; it is just a ponderous GENTEELISM for *drunk*. Have we to fear something of the kind with *anaesthesia* ? the extract that follows raises apprehensions : *This appetite grows by what it feeds upon, & it is accompanied by a total anaesthesia towards* [i.e. carelessness of] *the public interest & the results upon those who are victimized by these proceedings.* A few examples of these popularized technicalities may be gathered together ; they will be only as one in a score or a hundred of those that exist, but will serve as specimens. Upon most of them some remarks will be found in their dictionary places. Two general warnings will suffice : first, that the popular use more often than not misrepresents, & sometimes very badly, the original meaning ; & secondly, that free indulgence in this sort of term results in a tawdry style. It does not follow that none of them should ever be used.

From Philosophy—*optimism & pessimism, category, concept, dualistic.*

From Mathematics — *progression arithmetical & geometrical, to the nth, to be a function of, percentage & proportion* (= part), *curve* (= tendency).

From Religion—*devil's advocate, immanent, implicit, incarnation.*

From Psychology—*personal equation, idiosyncrasy, mentality, psychological moment, complex.*

From Law—*special pleading, leading question, party* (= person), *aforesaid & such & same, re, ilk, ferae naturae, exception that proves the rule.*

From War—*decimate, internecine.*

From Logic—*dilemma, idols of the market.*

From Commerce—*asset.*

From Architecture—*flamboyant.*

From Agriculture—*intensive, hardy annual, common or garden.*

From Astrology—*ascendant.*

From Politics—*conservative* (= small).

From Chemistry—*eliminate.*

From Literature—*protagonist, euphuism, Homeric laughter, myth, pathetic fallacy.*

From Medicine—*chronic, expectorate, hectic.*

populate makes -*lable* ; see -ABLE 1.

porcelain is china, & china is p. ; there is no recondite difference between the two things, which indeed are not two, but one ; & the difference between the two words is merely that *china* is the homely term, while *porcelain* is exotic & literary. See WORKING & STYLISH WORDS.

Porch. For *the P.* in Philosophy see ACADEMY.

pork pie. No hyphen ; see HYPHENS 3 B.

porpoise. Pron. por'*pus* (not -oiz).

porridge is treated in Scotch use as plural (' & butter in *them* ').

porrigo. Pronounce porī'gō.

port, harbour, haven. The broad distinction is that a haven is thought of as a place where a ship may find shelter from a storm, a harbour as one offering accommodation (used or not) in which ships may remain in safety for any purpose, & a port as a town whose harbour is frequented by naval or merchant ships.

port, larboard. The two words mean the same, but *p.* has been substituted for *l.* (the earlier opposite of *starboard*) because of the confusion resulting when orders were shouted from the too great similarity between *l.* & *starboard* ; *l.*, however, has not yet perished.

portcullis makes -*ised* ; see -S-, -SS-.

porte-cochère. See FRENCH WORDS.

portfolio. Pl. -*os* ; see -O(E)S 4.

portico. Pl. -*os* ; see -O(E)S 6.

portière. See FRENCH WORDS.

portion. *The Prime Minister, at the Lord Mayor's banquet on Saturday, devoted* the major portion *of his speech to Russia.* See FORMAL WORDS for *major p.* as compared with *greater part.* A favourite piece of buckram. See also MAJOR.

portly. For the adverb see -LILY.

portmanteau. Pl. -*s* (or -*x* ; see -x). For *p. word* the OED quotes from *Through the Looking-glass* ' Well, " slithy " means " lithe & slimy " . . . You see it 's like a portmanteau—there are two meanings packed up into one word '.

portray. For inflexions see VERBS IN -IE &c., 1.

portress. FEMININE DESIGNATIONS.

Portuguese, n., is both singular & plural. ' In modern times a sing. *Portug(u)ee* has arisen in vulgar use '—OED.

pose makes -*sable* ; see MUTE E.

The verb meaning nonplus (with its noun *poser* unanswerable question) is a different word from that meaning to lay down or place, being shortened from *appose*.

poseur. See FRENCH WORDS.

POSITION OF ADVERBS. The word *adverb* is here to be taken as including adverbial phrases (e.g. *for a time*) & adverbial clauses (e.g. *if possible*), adjectives used predicatively (e.g. *alone*), & adverbial conjunctions (e.g. *then*), as well as simple adverbs such as *soon* & *undoubtedly*. To lay down & illustrate exhaustive rules would not be possible in reasonable compass ; nor is there any need to do so ; the mistakes that occur are almost always due to certain false principles, & these may be isolated for treatment. Many readers may justly feel that they do not require advice on so simple a matter as where their adverbs should go, &, to save them the trouble of reading this long article, here is a string of sentences exhibiting all the types of misplacement to be discussed. Those who perceive that the adverb in each is wrongly placed, & why, can safely neglect the rest ; the bracketed number after each refers to the section in which its type is discussed :—*The people are now returning & trying to* again *get together a home* (1)./*He came to study* personally *the situation* (2)./*He exercised an influence that is still potent & has yet* adequately *to be measured on the education of our younger artists* (3)./*It deals with matters as to which most persons* long ago *have made up their minds* (4)./*We still are of opinion that the only way of getting rid of ' abuses ' is a root-&-branch alteration of the thing itself* (5)./*The Food Ministry must either take action or defend* effectively *their inactivity* (6)./*To decry the infantry arm for the sake* unduly *of piling up artillery & what not, is the notion of persons who* . . . (7)./*As ' the Monroe doctrine ' of late years* has loomed so

largely *in all discussions upon the international policy of the United States, an attempt to trace its growth & development as a popular ' cry ' might prove of some service* (8).

There are certain verb groups about which the question is conceivable— Should they be allowed to be interrupted by adverbs ? Such are the infinitive e.g. *to try* (may we say *to earnestly try* ?), the compound verb e.g. *have thought* (may we say *I have never thought so* ?), the copula & complement e.g. *was a riddle* (may we say *He was in some ways a riddle* ?), the verb & its object e.g. *passed the time* (may we say *It passed pleasantly the time* ?), the gerund & its governing preposition e.g. *by going* (may we say *by often going* ?). The first of these questions is a very familiar one ; almost all who aspire to write English have had the split infinitive forced on their attention, & the avoidance of it has become a fetish ; the other questions are not familiar, but the points here to be made are that they also require consideration, that a universal yes or a universal no is not the right answer either to the split-infinitive question or to any of the others, that the various answers sometimes come into conflict, & that to concentrate on the split-infinitive question & let the others take care of themselves is absurd.

The misplacements to be considered will be taken under the heads :— 1. Split infinitive. 2. Fear of split infinitive. 3. Imaginary split infinitive passive. 4. Splitting of the compound verb. 5. Separation of copulative verb & complement. 6. Separation of transitive verb & object. 7. Separation of preposition & gerund. 8. Heedless misplacings.

1. Split infinitive. The heinousness of this offence is estimated in the article SPLIT INFINITIVE. Here the general result of that estimate is merely assumed, viz : (A) that *to love* is a definitely enough recognized verb-form to make the clinging

together of its parts the natural
& normal thing, (B) that there is,
however, no sacro-sanctity about
that arrangement, (C) that adverbs
should be kept outside if there is
neither anything gained by putting
them inside nor any difficulty in
finding them another place, but
(D) that such gain or difficulty will
often justify the confessedly abnormal splitting. One pair of examples will throw light on C &
D :—*The people are now returning
& trying* to again *get together
a home./With us outside the Treaty,
we must expect the Commission* to at
least neglect *our interests*. In the
first, it is easy to write *to get a home
together again, &,* as *again* does not
belong to the single word *get*, but to
get a home together, nothing is gained
by its abnormal placing. In the
second, *at least* cannot be put before
to because it would then go with
Commission (= the Commission,
even if not other people), nor after
neglect because it would then be
doubtful whether it referred back
to *neglect* or forward to *interests*, nor
after *interests* because it would then
belong either to *interests* or to
neglect our interests, neither being
what is meant ; where it stands, it
secures our realizing that the writer
has in mind some other verb such
as *injure* or *oppose* with which the
weaker *neglect* is to be contrasted.

In a split infinitive, however, we
have not so much a misplacing of
the adverb as a violence done to the
verb. It is by repulsion, not by
attraction, that the infinitive acts
in effecting the many misplacings,
to be shown below, for which it is
responsible.

2. Fear of split infinitive. The
order of words in the following
examples is bizarre enough to offend
the least cultivated ear ; the reason
why the writers, whose ears were
perhaps no worse than their neighbours', were not struck by it is
that they were obsessed by fear of
infinitive-splitting. It will be seen
that the natural (not necessarily

the best) place for the adverb in
each is where it would split an
infinitive. *Such gentlemen are powerless to analyse* correctly *agricultural
conditions./A body of Unionist employers which still has power to
influence* greatly *opinion among
those who work for them./Might I
kindly ask you to forward ?* The
place into which each adverb has
been shifted is such that one or
other of the faults explained in
later sections is committed, & the
writer is OUT OF THE FRYING-PAN
into the fire ; see especially 6.

But the terrorism exercised by the
split infinitive is most conspicuous
where there is in fact (see next
section) no danger.

3. Imaginary split infinitive passive. In the following examples it
is again clear that the natural place
for the adverb is not where it now
stands, but invariably after the
words *to be*. To insert an adverb
between *to & be* would be splitting
an infinitive ; to insert one between
to be & forgotten or *pained* is nothing
of the kind, but is a particular case
of the construction explained in 5.
The position after *to be* is not only
the natural one in these sentences,
but the best. The mistake—& that
it is a definite mistake there is no
doubt whatever—is so common that
many examples are called for :—
*The awkward necessity for getting to
work & working as hard as possible
& with hearty goodwill* altogether
*seems to be forgotten./Every citizen
worth the name ought* vitally *to be
concerned in today's election./All of
us who believe in Parliamentary
institutions cannot fail* deeply *to be
pained at reading the story./But if
the home trade were really in a bad
state, it would be impossible for the
workers* so fully *to be employed as
they have been & are./There were
those who thought the Turkish Government would not be willing to adopt
a policy of conciliation, but it looks
as if they were* agreeably *to be disappointed./The nuisance of allowing
visitors to cross the footlights had*

begun so much *to be felt by the London theatrical managers that they* . . ./*We think the public will not fail* unfavourably *to be impressed by the shifting nature of the arguments./ An Act has been passed enabling agricultural land* compulsorily *to be acquired at a fair market price./The right of the privately managed denominational school* wholly *to be maintained out of public money.*

4. Splitting of the compound verb. By *compound verb* is meant a verb made up of an auxiliary (or more than one) & an infinitive (without *to*) or participle. When an adverb is to be used with such a verb, its normal place is between the auxiliary (or sometimes the first auxiliary if there are two or more) & the rest. Not only is there no such objection to thus splitting a compound verb as there is to splitting an infinitive, but any other position for the adverb requires special justification : *I have never seen her*, not *I never have seen her*, is the ordinary idiom, though the rejected order becomes the right if emphasis is to be put on *have* (*I may have had chances of seeing Bernhardt, but I never have seen her*). But it is plain from the string of examples now to come that a prejudice has grown up against dividing compound verbs ; it is probably a supposed corollary of the accepted split-infinitive prohibition ; at any rate, it is entirely unfounded. In each of the first five extracts there is one auxiliary, & after that instead of before it the adverb should have been put ; the other six have two auxiliaries each, which raises a further question to be touched upon afterwards :—Single auxiliary: *If his counsel* still *is followed, ' the conflict ' is indeed inevitable. / Its very brief span of insect-eating activity* hardly *can redeem its general evil habit as a grain-devourer. / Politicians of all sorts in the United States* already *are girding up their loins for the next election./Yet one of the latest Customs rulings by the United States Board of Appraisers* assuredly, *to use the*

phrase its members best *would understand, is ' the limit './Two years later he went to Russia as British Ambassador, &* he *also was entrusted with the mission of carrying the Garter to* . . ./Double auxiliary : *Oxford* must heartily be *congratulated on their victory./If the desired end is ever* attained it earnestly *may be hoped that especial care will be taken with the translation./The importance which* quite rightly *has been given to reports of their meetings./The Maharaja made arrangements for her education, which* never since *has been permitted to languish./A German apologist anxious to prove that the war* had needlessly *been prolonged by the Entente./It is fortunate that a certain amendment which they desired* was not carried, *or it* would gravely *have imperilled the solvency of certain of the approved societies.*

Write *must be heartily congratulated, it may be earnestly hoped, which has quite rightly been given, which has never since been permitted, had been needlessly prolonged, would have gravely imperilled.* This minor point of whether the adverb is to follow the first auxiliary or the whole auxiliary depends on the answer to a not very simple riddle—Is it in intimate connexion with the verbal notion itself independently of the temporal or other limitations imposed by the auxiliaries ? Fortunately this riddle can be translated into simpler terms—Do the adverb & verb naturally suggest an adjective & noun ? if so, let them stand next each other, & if not, not. *Heartily congratulated, earnestly hoped, needlessly prolonged, gravely imperilled,* suggest hearty congratulations, earnest hope, needless prolongation, & grave peril ; but *rightly given* does not suggest right gift or right giving, & still less does *never since permitted* suggest no subsequent permission ; which means that the notions of giving & permitting are qualified by *rightly* & *never since* not absolutely, but under the particular limitations of the auxiliaries, & that the adverb is better placed between the auxiliaries than next to *given & permitted*. This, however, is a minor point, as was said above ; the main object of this section is to stress the certain fact that there is no objection whatever to dividing a compound verb by adverbs.

5. Separation of copulative verb & complement. This is on the same footing as the separation of the compound verb discussed in 4; that is, it is a delusion to suppose that the insertion of an adverb between the two parts is a solecism, or even, like the splitting of the infinitive, a practice to be regarded as abnormal. On the contrary, it is the natural arrangement, & in the following examples *fundamentally, also, & often,* have been mistakenly shifted from their right place owing to a superstition :—*It would be a different thing if the scheme had been found* fundamentally *to be faulty, but that is not the case./It is not always in these times that the First Lord of the Treasury* also *is Prime Minister./The immense improvement which they have wrought in the condition of the people, & which* often *is quite irrespective of the number of actual converts.*

6. Separation of transitive verb & its object. The mistakes discussed in sections 2 to 5 have this in common, that they spring from a desire, instinctive or inculcated, to keep the parts of a verb group together & allow no adverb to intrude into it. But there is one kind of group whose breaking up by adverbs that ought to have been placed not in the middle of it, but before or after the whole, is only too common. That is the group consisting of a transitive verb & its object. *I had to second by all the means in my power diplomatic action. To second diplomatic action* is the verb & object, separated by a seven-word adverb ; it is a crying case ; everyone will agree to deferring the adverb, & the writer had either no literary ear or some

grammatical or stylistic fad. The longer the adverb in proportion to the object, the more marked is the offence of interpolating it. But the same mistake is seen, though less glaringly, in the following ten examples ; the italicized adverb in each should be removed, sometimes to a place before the verb, sometimes to one after the object :—*Are they quite sure that they have interpreted* rightly *the situation ?/I should counsel,* then, *the schoolboy to take plenty of exercise in the open./A lull of the breeze kept* for a time *the small boat in the neighbourhood of the brig./ Russia is sweeping the Bukovina clean of Austrians, & north of the Pripet marshes holds* firmly *Hindenburg's forces./He spoke in a firm voice, marking* strongly *the syllables, but in tones rather harsh./The only conceivable exception is some great question affecting* vitally *human liberty & human conscience./The Prime Minister made a couple of speeches on Saturday, but he did not discuss* any further *the Irish question./The little finny warriors endeavouring to rip* up *each other with their sharp spines./It is thought that the Allies will regard* favourably *Belgium's request./Continuation with the university courses would* most certainly *elevate* further *the people.*

There are conditions that justify the separation, the most obvious being when a lengthy object would keep an adverb that is not suitable for the early position too remote from the verb. One of the extracts below may be adapted to illustrate ; if it had run ' would expose to ridicule an authority that, as it is, is not very imposing ', the shortness of ' to ridicule ' compared with the length of the object would have made that order the best & almost necessary one. But anyone who applies this principle must be careful not to reckon as part of the object words that either do not belong to it at all or are unessential to it; else he will offend the discerning reader's ear as cruelly as the authors now to be quoted :—*They are now busy issuing blue prints & instructions, & otherwise helping* in all sorts of ways *our firms to get an efficient grip of the business of tractor-making in a hurry.* The object is *our firms* alone, not that & the rest of the sentence ; put it next to *helping./ Who are risking* every day with intelligence·& with shrewdness *fortunes on what they believe. Fortunes* alone is the object ; put it after *risking./His make-up, which approached* too nearly *sheer caricature to be reckoned quite happy.* A very odd piece of tit for tat ; *too nearly* divides *approached* from *caricature*, & in revenge *caricature* divides *to be reckoned* from *too nearly* ; put *sheer caricature* next to *approached./Failure of the Powers to enforce their will as to the Albanian frontier would expose* to the ridicule of all the restless elements in East Europe *their authority, which, as it is, is not very imposing.* There are two differences from the adaptation made above—first that the adverb has eleven words instead of two, & secondly that the relative clause is not an essential part of the object ; *their . . . imposing* should be put directly after *expose.*

7. Separation of preposition & gerund. This hardly needs serious treatment. But here is amusingly shown somebody's terror of separating *of & piling* by an adverb—which is no more than an exaggeration of the superstitions dealt with in 3, 4, & 5. *To decry the infantry arm for the sake* unduly *of piling up artillery & what not, is the notion of persons who . . .*

8. Heedless misplacings. It would appear from the analysis attempted above that when adverbs are found in wrong positions it is usually due to mistaken ideas of correctness. But now & then it is otherwise, & an example or two of merely careless placing may be given :—*Dressings of cotton & linen are reserved only for the most serious cases* (for the most serious cases only)./*The terms upon which the British ' governing classes ' have obtained their influence are those upon which it alone may be retained* (upon which alone it may)./ *As the Monroe doctrine of late years has loomed so largely* (has of late years loomed ; otherwise it means the recent Monroe doctrine)./*Should, too, not our author be considered ?* (*too* might go after *not*, or *author*, or *considered*, according to the meaning wanted ; but no meaning can justify its present position)./*But a work of art that is all form & no emotion* (*& we doubt whether, in all deference to* M. *Saint-Saens, such an anomaly did ever or could ever exist) would seem to belong more properly to the sphere of mathematics* (the putting of the *deference* adverb after instead of before *whether* makes nonsense)./ *It has been implied that Germany is a collectivist State, or, if not, that it has at least far advanced in Socialism* (*is* far advanced, but *has* advanced far).

POSITIVE WORDS IN NEUTRAL PLACES. There are words whose essential function is to express the speaker's strong opinion ; specimens are *excellent, admirable, remarkable. incredible, disgraceful* ; to use these in a negative, conditional, or interrogative sense is an offence against idiom too obvious to be common. You cannot stipulate that a thing shall be excellent ; you can only pronounce it excellent on trial. To ask for a *most delicious* peach, a bottle of *admirable* claret, a *profoundly* interesting novel, is absurd (unless you are playfully quoting someone else's commendation ; Martin Chuzzlewit, for instance, with his experience of remarkable men, could legitimately ask whether Mr Choke was one of the most remarkable men in the country). Examples :—*Smoked after dinner, with one or two glasses of* excellent brandy, *they are equal to Havanas./If they heard of the pecuniary trouble of an* excellent scholar *or man of letters, they should communicate the fact to* *their secretary./An American soldier who was serving on the special staff for taking over the German engines told him that exceptional care is now being taken to secure German railway engines that are* in admirable condition./*The amphibious part of the operation, then, would be limited to what he could do in* an incredibly short time./*The statesmen of Tokio, for instance, will not renew the war unless intolerably provoked. Their desire now will be to consolidate their acquisitions, to devise* an admirably cheap method *of defending Manchuria for the future, & to reap, as they have already begun to do,* the economic advantages of the splendid position to which their country has been elevated by the war* (*admirably* is wrong, *splendid* right ; the position is already secured ; it will be time enough for enthusiasm about the method when the Japanese have devised it)./*You should have written to your cousin Morden, the moment they had begun to* treat you disgracefully (*so* before *disgracefully*, implying ' as I consider they have treated you ', would have cured this)./*All Governments who get into power by* a most violent & unscrupulous use of party tactics *try to prolong their advantage by . . .* (Omit *most*)./*When will the Church leaders realize that unity in action is* so much more important *than unity of belief?* (Omit *so*)./*Mr Thornely is fond of finding his theme in the world of science & treating it* with extraordinary aptness.

posse. Two syllables.

possess makes -*ssor* ; see -OR.

possession. *In p. of,* holding ; *in the p. of,* held by : *Prisoner was found in p. of a revolver* ; *The necklace was found in the p. of prisoner's wife.*

POSSESSIVE PUZZLES. 1. *Septimus's* (*Achilles'*. 2. *Whose*) (*of which.* 3. *Mr Smith* (*now Lord London*)'*s.* 4. ' *The Times' 's opinion.* 5. *Somebody's else.*

1. *Septimus's, Achilles'.* It was

formerly customary, when a word ended in -s, to write its possessive with an apostrophe but no additional s, e.g. *Mars' hill, Venus' Bath, Achilles' thews.* In verse, & in poetic or reverential contexts, this custom is retained, & the number of syllables is the same as in the subjective case, e.g. *Achilles'* has three, not four ; *Jesus'* or *of Jesus,* not *Jesus's.* But elsewhere we now add the s & the syllable, *Charles's Wain, St James's* not *St James', Jones's children, the Rev. Septimus's surplice, Pythagoras's doctrines.* For *goodness' sake, conscience' sake,* &c., see SAKE.

2. *Whose*) (*of which.* See WHOSE for the question whether the use of *whose* as the possessive of *which,* & not only of *who,* (*My thought, Whose murder yet is but fantastical*) is permissible.

3. (A) *Mr Smith* (*now Lord London*)'*s intervention was decisive ?* or (B) *Mr Smith's* (*now Lord London*) *intervention ?* or (C) *Mr Smith's* (*now Lord London's*) *intervention ?* or (D) *The intervention of Mr Smith* (*now Lord London*) ? C is clearly wrong because the intervention was not Lord London's ; B is intolerable because we cannot be happy without the '*s* close before *intervention,* just as we cannot endure *someone's else umbrella* though we can with an effort allow the umbrella to be *someone's else* ; A is the reasonable solution, but has no chance against the British horror of fussy correctness ; &, failing it, the only thing is to run away, i.e. to use D. An actual example of B is : *It was Lord Dunedin's* (*then Mr Graham Murray*) *aid that was invoked.*

4. *In ' The Times' 's opinion.* This also has to be run away from. To write *in ' The Times' ' opinion* is not running away, but merely blundering ; if the newspaper title is to have inverted commas & the possessive is to be used, the form at the top with two independent apostrophes jostling each other is the only correct possibility. But there

are two escapes ; one is to write the title in italics instead of inverted commas, but the possessive *s* in roman type (*The Times's*), & the other is to fly to *of* (*in the opinion of ' The Times '*).

5. For *somebody else's* or *somebody's else* see ELSE.

possible. 1. *Do* one's *p.* 2. Construction. 3. *P.*) (*probable.*

1. *Do* one's *possible* is a GALLICISM ; &, with *do what* one *can* in established existence, it is superfluous.

2. Construction. *But no such questions are* possible, *as it seems to me,* to arise *between your nation & ours.*/ *No breath of honest fresh air is suffered to enter, wherever it is* possible *to be excluded.* These are wrong. Unlike *able*, which ordinarily requires to be completed by an infinitive (*able to be done, to exist,* &c.), *p.* is complete in itself & means without addition *able to be done* or *occur.* The English for *are p. to arise* & *is p. to be excluded* is *can arise, can be excluded.* The mistakes are perhaps due to the frequency of such forms as *It is p. to find an explanation,* in which *it* is not an ordinary pronoun, but merely anticipatory ; that is, the sentence in its simpler form would not be *An explanation is p. to find,* but *To find an explanation is p.* When it is felt that *p.* does require to be amplified, it is done by *of* with a verbal noun— *Limits that are p. of exact ascertainment*; but *susceptible* or some other word is usually better.

3. *P.*) (*probable.* It would be too much to demand that *p.* should always be kept to its strict sense & never so far weakened that *impossible* (or *possible* in a negative context) means no more than very unlikely ; but, when *probable* & *p.* are in explicit contrast, the demand may fairly be made. *The Prohibition Amendment can only be revoked by the same methods as secured its adoption. I met no one in America who deemed this probable, few who thought it even possible.* As all

sensible people know it, whatever its improbability, to be possible, the picture of American intelligence is uncomplimentary ; but this absurdity is common enough, & ranks with the abuse of LITERALLY.

poste restante. See FRENCH WORDS.
post hoc, ergo propter hoc. See TECHNICAL TERMS.
posthumous. The *-h-* is silent, & also, though never omitted, etymologically incorrect.
posticous. Pronounce postĭ'kus.
postil(l)ion. The OED prefers the single *-l-*.
postmistress. See FEMININE DESIGNATIONS.
postpone. Pronounce pospō'n.
postprandial. Chiefly in PEDANTIC HUMOUR.
postscript. Pronounce pō'skrĭpt.
postulate makes *-lable, -tor* ; see -ABLE 1, -OR.
pot, not *pott*, of paper. See POT(T).
potage. See FRENCH WORDS.
potato. Pl. *-oes* ; see -O(E)S 1.
poteen, -th-. The OED treats *-teen* as the established spelling.
potency, -nce. In general senses *-cy* is much commoner ; &, as *-ce* has technical senses in engineering, watch-making, &c., it would be better to confine *-ce* to these, & make *-cy* universal in the general senses. See -CE, -CY.

potentate. Pronounce pō'-.
potential has no longer the meaning of *potent*, which should have been the word in : *The Labour Party . . . was exercising most potential influence on some social problems.* See LONG VARIANTS.

potful. Pl. *-ls* ; see -FUL.
pother is now, except in dialects, a LITERARY WORD. The more correct, but now less usual, pronunciation is pŭ'dher rhyming with *other brother mother.* There is no proof of connexion with either *bother* or *powder*, though it is thought that *bother* may be an Irish corruption of *pother.* Between *pother* & *bother* there is the difference in meaning that *p.* denotes ado or bustle or

eonfusion in itself, while *b.* emphasizes the annoyance or trouble caused.

pot-pourri. See FRENCH WORDS.

pot(t). The paper size is so named from the pot that it formerly bore as a watermark ; the right spelling is *pot*, the *-tt* being merely like that in *matt, nett*, & SET(T).

potter makes *-ering* &c. ; -R-, -RR-.

poult-de-soie. See FRENCH WORDS.

poultice makes *-ceable* ; see -ABLE 1.

pourboire, pourparler, pour rire, poussette. See FRENCH WORDS.

poverty) (poorness. The dominant sense of *poor* is having little money or property. The noun corresponding to this dominant sense is *poverty*, & *poorness* is never so used in modern English. The further the dominant sense is departed from, the more does *poverty* give way to *poorness*—*Poverty is no excuse for theft* ; *The poverty* (or *poorness*) *of the soil* ; *The poorness* (or *poverty*) *of the harvest* ; *The poorness of his performance.* See -TY & -NESS.

-P-, -PP-. Monosyllables ending in *-p* double it before suffixes beginning with vowels if the sound preceding it is a single vowel (a, e, i, o, u, y), but not if it is a diphthong or a double vowel or a vowel & r : *trapped, scrappy, uppish, popping, sleepy, carping, leaper.* Words of more than one syllable follow the rule for monosyllables if their last syllable is accented (*entrapped*, but *upheaped*) ; they also double the *p* if, like *handicap* & *kidnap, milksop* & *lollipop*, they have a clear ă or ŏ as opposed to the obscure sound in *jalap* & *gallop*, or if, like *horsewhip* & *sideslip*, they are compounded with a monosyllable ; but otherwise they do not double it except *worship* : *chirruped, enveloping, galoping, galloper, gossipy, filliped, equipped, trans-shipping, hiccuped, handicapper, kidnapped, walloping, milksoppish, jalaped, lollipoppery, horsewhipping, worshipper, sideslipped.*

practicable) (practical. 1. The negative forms are *impracticable*, but *unpractical*; *impractical* is often wrongly written (*The most impractical of all persons—the man who works by rule of thumb*) ; see IN- & UN-.

2. Meanings. Each word has senses in which there is no fear that the other will be substituted for it ; but in other senses they come very near each other, & confusion is both natural & common. Safety lies in remembering that *practicable* means capable of being effected or accomplished, & *practical* adapted to actual conditions ; it is true that the practicable is often practical, & that the practical is nearly always practicable ; but a very practical plan may prove owing to change of circumstances impracticable, & a practicable policy may be thoroughly unpractical. In the extracts, each word is used where the other was wanted :—*In the case of a club, if rules are passed obnoxious to a large section of the members, the latter can resign ; in our national relationships, secession is not practical nowadays.* The last sentence is in clear antithesis to *the latter can resign*, & means You cannot secede, or in other words Secession is not *practicable./ But to plunge into the military question without settling the Government question would not be good sense or practicable policy ; & no wise man would expect to get serviceable recruits for the Army from Ireland in this way.* The policy was certainly practicable, for it was carried out ; & the writer, though he had not the proof that we have of its practicability, probably did not mean to deny that, but only to say that it was not suited to the conditions, i.e. practical./*We live in a low-pressure belt where cyclone follows cyclone ; but the prediction of their arrival is at present not* practical.

practice, -se. Noun *-ce*, verb *-se* ; see LICENCE.

practitioner. See PHYSICIAN.

pragmatic(al). In the diplomatic, historical, & philosophical senses, the -*ic* form is usual. In the general sense of officious or opinionated, -*ical* is commoner. In the interests of differentiation these tendencies should be encouraged ; see -IC(AL).

praise makes -*sable* ; see MUTE E.

pram (perambulator). See CUR-TAILED WORDS.

pratique. Pronounce prăˈtĭk.

pray. 1. For inflexions see VERBS IN -IE &c., 1.

2. *Pray in aid.* One of the picturesque phrases that people catch up & use without understanding : *We are disturbed to find that this principle of* praying in aid *the domestic circumstances of the woman appears to have been sanctioned officially by the Committee on production.* This writer, & most of those who use the words, suppose that *in aid* is an adverb, & that *pray* is therefore free to take an object—here *circumstances.* The fact is that the object of *pray* is *aid,* & *in* is not a preposition but an adverb, *to pray in aid* being word for word *to call in help* ; if the helper or helping thing is to be specified, it must have an *of* before it, as in the following OED quotations :—*A city or corporation, holding a fee-farm of the King, may* pray in Aid *of him, if anything be demanded of them relating thereto./ An incumbent may* pray in aid *of the patron & ordinary.*

pre-. In compounds whose second part begins with *e* or *i* a hyphen is used : *pre-eminent, pre-issue.* In others the hyphen is not necessary, but is freely used if the compound is one made for the occasion, or if any peculiarity in its form might prevent its elements from being instantly recognized, or if recurrence from the sense now developed to a more primitive one is to be marked by especial stress on the elements : *predetermine, prenatal, prearranged ; pre-Coalition, pre-war, pre-position* (in contrast with *preposition* the part of speech).

preachify. For inflexions see VERBS IN -IE &c., 6.

precede makes -*dable* ; see MUTE E.

precedence, precedent. The pronunciation is tricky. The OED gives for the first prĭsēˈdns only (not prĕˈsĭdns), & for the second prĭsēˈdnt only in adjectival use, but prĕˈsĭdnt only in noun use. This, which is a very disputable account of present usage, is not likely to remain true ; prĕˈsĭd- is here recommended for all alike.

precedent. *The House of Commons is always ready to extend the indulgence which* [*it*] *is a sort of precedent that the mover & seconder of the Address should ask for.* A bad piece of SLIPSHOD EXTENSION ; a p. is not a custom or a tradition (though it may start one ; cf. HAZINESS), but a previous case.

preciosity & *preciousness* illustrate well the differentiation that should be encouraged whenever there is an opening for it between the two terminations ; see -TY & -NESS. The special sense of excessive fastidiousness in diction, pronunciation, & the like, is almost confined to -*ty*, & the more general senses are left to -*ness.* The opening here was provided by the fact that -*ty* represents the French form & so calls up the *Précieuses Ridicules* of Molière.

precipitance, -ancy, -ation. The most economical way of dealing with the words would have been to let -*ancy* perish, & make -*ance* mean rashness of action or suddenness of occurrence or speed of motion, & -*ation* the bringing or coming to pass with especial rashness or speed. But what is happening is that all three exist side by side, -*ance* & -*ancy* slowly giving way to -*ation* just as their parent *precipitant* has given way to *precipitate.* See also PRECIPITOUS.

precipitate. 1. The verb makes -*itable* ; see -ABLE 1. 2. The verb is pronounced -āt, the adjective & noun -at or -ĭt ; PARTICIPLES 5 B.

precipitous. *The position, then, is*

this : (1) *Are the workers justified in taking the precipitous action suggested in the resolution ?/The step seems a trifle rash & precipitous when one remembers the number of banking & commercial failures that* ... Those who write thus either are ignorant of the established difference between *p. & precipitate*, or must not be surprised if they are taken to be so. Formerly, *-ous* was freely used where we now always say *-ate* ; but that time has long passed away. See PAIRS & SNARES.

précis. See FRENCH WORDS.

preclude makes *-dable* ; see MUTE E.

predestinate. 1. The verb makes *-nable* ; see -ABLE 1. 2. The verb is pronounced *-āt*, the adjective *-at* or *-ĭt* ; see PARTICIPLES 5 B.

predetermine has *-nable* ; MUTE E.

predicate. 1. The verb makes *-cable* ; see -ABLE 1. 2. The OED pronounces *p.*, & its derivatives *predicable & predication*, with prĕd-, not prēd-. The verb is said with -āt, the noun with -ĭt ; see PARTICIPLES 5 B. 3. *P.*) (*predict.* The Latinless have great difficulty in realizing that the words are not interchangeable variants. *P.* is from Latin *praedĭcare* to cry forth or proclaim, but *predict* from Latin *praedĭcere* to say beforehand or foretell ; the Latin simple verbs are different, & *prae* has not the same meaning in the two compounds. *P.* makes *predicable & predication*, *predict* makes *predictable & prediction*. It is naturally *predicate* & its derivatives that are misused ; examples of the misuse are :—*The case for establishing compulsory & voluntary systems side by side in the same country is not only not proven, but involves a change in strategic theory that predicates nothing but disaster* (threatens ? foreshadows ? presages ? just possibly predicts ; certainly not predicates)./*A profound change in the balance of the Constitution predicable by anyone who had searched the political heavens during the last four years & observed the eccentric*

behaviour of certain bodies & their satellites is now upon us (predictable)./ *What she would say to him, how he would take it, even the vaguest predication of their discourse, was beyond him to guess* (anticipation ? outline ? prevision ? just possibly prediction ; certainly not predication).

P. & its derivatives mean to assert, & especially to assert the existence of some quality as an attribute of the person or thing that is spoken of (*Goodness or badness cannot with any propriety be predicated of motives./ To predicate mortality of Socrates*, i.e., to state that Socrates is mortal). The words (apart from *predicate* n., the grammatical term) are mainly used in Logic, & are best left alone by those who have no acquaintance with either Logic or Latin. See PAIRS & SNARES.

predict makes *-tor* ; see -OR.

predispose makes *-sable* ; MUTE E.

predominate makes *-tor* ; see -OR.

preface. 1. The verb makes *-ceable* ; see -ABLE 1. 2. For *p. & foreword*, see the latter. 3. For *p. & prefix*, vv., see PREFIX.

prefect. Pronounce prē-. The adjective is *prefectorial*, not *-toral*.

prefer(able). 1. *-r(r)-*. 2. *More preferable*. 3. *To, rather than, than*. 1. *Prefer* makes *-rring, -rred* (see -R-, -RR-), but *preferable* (prĕ′fĕrabl) ; the latter formation is anomalous but established ; see CONFER(R)ABLE for similar words.

2. *More preferable* is an inexcusable PLEONASM (3). *The cure for that is clearly the alternative vote or the second ballot, the former alternative being, in our view, on every ground the more preferable*.

3. *To, rather than, than*. If the rejected alternative is to be expressed, the normal construction for it is *to* : *I p. pears to apples, riding to walking*. The OED, defining the construction, gives nothing besides *to* except *before & above*, both of which it obelizes as archaic or disused. A difficulty arises, however, with *to* : the object of *prefer* is often

an infinitive, but the sound of *I p. to die to to pay blackmail*, or even of *I p. to die to paying*, is intolerable. It is easy sometimes to make the change corresponding to that of *to die* to *death*, but by no means always. When the infinitive is unavoidable, the way out is to use *rather than* instead of *to* : *I p. to die rather than pay blackmail*. To use simple *than* instead of *rather than* (*I p. to die than pay*) is clean against established idiom, as bad as saying *superior than* or *prior than* instead of *superior* or *prior to*. But this solecism, of which there is hardly a trace in the OED article (1908), has recently become common ; the array of quotations given below is in amusing contrast with the solitary specimen (dated 1778) that the OED could show. Even the *rather than* mentioned above is not much to be recommended ; but, if the writer is bent on using *prefer*, it will pass ; a better plan is to change the verb *prefer* to *choose rather* or *would rather* (*He chose to die rather than pay* ; *I would rather die than pay*) ; the main point is that *prefer than* without *rather* is not English :—*We should greatly p. to pay the doctors more than to limit the area of insurance* (We would much rather pay . . . than limit)./*We should p. to entrust ourselves without a solitary guarantee to the goodwill of our Nationalist fellow-countrymen than fetter the Irish Parliament with safeguards* (we would sooner entrust). / *One would p. to have Mistress Alys Wryght's own account of herself than be invited to picture her* (would rather have)./*They are preferably left, we think, to the enjoyment of the reader than torn from their context* (are better left)./*The majority of them, we rather think, would prefer to bear the ills they know than to fly to the untried remedy of the State regulation of wages* (Shakspere preferred *rather bear* to *preferred to bear* ; the other *rather* has caused him to be corrected, but not improved)./*Many p. to go bareheaded than to reassume the fez* (many go

bareheaded rather than reassume)./ *They have always preferred to speculate on the chance of winning a General Election than to settle with their opponents* (rather than settle)./ *Surely the public would prefer to arrive half an hour later than run the ghastly risks* (would choose . . . rather than run)./*The nine deportees would p. to go home than to undergo sentence after trial by Court-martial* (would sooner go . . . than undergo)./ *Ukrainian peasants even prefer to fire their crops than to see them seized by these bullies* (even fire their crops rather than see)./*Any man of ordinary pride would have preferred to accept any responsibility than attribute to himself the cowardly evasion which* . . . (would have accepted . . . rather than attribute)./*He would certainly p. that we should credit him with none at all than allow him a grain too much* (would certainly rather have us credit)./*He is persuasive rather than dogmatic, & prefers to suggest than to conclude* (suggesting to concluding).

prefigure. For pronunciation of this & its derivatives, see FIGURE.

prefix. 1. The noun is prē′fĭks, the verb prĭfĭ′ks ; see NOUN & VERB ACCENT, &, for meaning, TECHNICAL TERMS. 2. For derivative nouns it is better to rub along with *prefix* & *prefixing* than to resort to *prefixion* & *prefixture*. 3. *Prefix*, vb) (*preface*, vb. *P.* is one of the verbs liable to the OBJECT-SHUFFLING abuse. You can prefix a title to your name, but not prefix your name with a title. Several examples of the confusion follow ; in each the construction must be turned inside out if *p.* is to be kept, but in most of them the change of *prefix*(*ed*) to *preface*(*d*) would put things right :—*The speeches in the present volume are* prefixed by *a clear & connected account of the administration of India.*/*Many others are Austrian Barons of modern creation, these titles being very numerous, because every son is allowed to* prefix his name with *the title.*/*A* ' *Collection of Poems & Essays by Mary Queen of Scots* ', prefixed by *an essay on the character & writings of Mary Stuart.*/*Two notes dealing with recent cases on the subject of company directors are* prefixed by the catchwords *in very prominent type* : ' *Retirement & Remorse* './*The story* is prefixed by *an introductory sketch of Pope Alexander VI's Spanish ancestry.*/*Every paragraph* is prefixed with *a kind of title to it.*

The poor old word *preface*, with *foreword* assailing it on one front & *prefix* on another, is going through troubled times.

pregnant construction. See TECH-NICAL TERMS.

prejudg(e)ment. Keep the *-e-* ; see MUTE E.

prejudice, n. *The Committee's Report adds that without doubt a* marked prejudice *to the eating of eels exists in Scotland.* The prepositions after *p.* are *against & in favour of* ; this *to* is transferred from *objection* ; see ANALOGY.

preliminary, adv. See QUASI-ADVERBS.

prelude. The noun is prĕ′lūd ; the verb used to be prĭlū′d (' All the verse quotations & the dictionaries down to *c* 1830 '—OED), but is now pronounced like the noun—a remarkable exception to the tendency mentioned in NOUN & VERB ACCENT.

premature. The pronunciation prĕ′matŭr is recommended, but the sound of the *e* & the place of the accent are both variable ; in any case, the last syllable is fully pronounced & not weakened to *-cher.*

premier as an adjective is now suggestive of tawdry ornament, though it was formerly not avoided by good writers. The ELEGANT-VARIATIONist finds it useful (*There was a time when the School of Literae Humaniores stood first in point of number, but of late the History School has taken* premier *place*), but would do better to find some other way out. It is wise to confine it now to such traditional phrases as *p. Earl* or *Baronet* (*Bacon had no issue of his marriage, the present Sir Hickman Bacon, premier Baronet of England, being descended from his half-brother*).

première. See FRENCH WORDS.

premise(s), -ss(es). 1. The noun is prĕ′mĭs, the verb prĭmī′z ; see NOUN & VERB ACCENT. 2. The verb is spelt *premise*, not *-ize* ; see -ISE) (-IZE. 3. The two noun spellings (*-ises* & *-isses* in the plural) may perhaps be thought useful ; but ambiguity cannot often arise between the parts of a syllogism (*-isses* ; see, for meaning, TECH-NICAL TERMS) & of a public house (*-ises*) ; &, except practical utility, there is no reason for the variation. The two words are one, the parts of a syllogism being ' the previously stated ', & the parts of a public house &c. being ' the aforesaid ', (facts, places, &c.). The uniform spelling *premise* (pl. *premises*) is recommended. 4. The verb makes *-sable* ; see MUTE E.

premium. Pl. *-ms* only ; see -UM.

preoccupiedly. A bad form ; -EDLY.

prep. See CURTAILED WORDS.

preparatory. For the use in *They were weighing it preparatory to sending it to town*, see QUASI-ADVERBS.

prepare makes *-rable* ; see MUTE E.

preparedly. Four syllables if used ; see -EDLY.

prepay. For inflexions see VERBS IN -IE &c., 1.

PREPOSITION AT END. It is a cherished superstition that prepositions must, in spite of the incurable English instinct for putting them late (' They are the fittest timber to make great politics *of* ' said Bacon ; & ' What are you hitting me *for* ? ' says the modern schoolboy), be kept true to their name & placed before the word they govern. ' A sentence ending in a preposition is an inelegant sentence ' represents a very general belief. One of its chief supports is the fact that Dryden, an acknowledged master of

English prose, went through all his prefaces contriving away the final prepositions that he had been guilty of in his first editions. It is interesting to find Ruskin almost reversing this procedure. In the text of the *Seven Lamps* there is a solitary final preposition to be found, & no more ; but in the later footnotes they are not avoided (*Any more wasted words . . . I never heard of./Men whose occupation for the next fifty years would be the knocking down every beautiful building they could lay their hands on*). Dryden's earlier practice shows him following the English instinct ; his later shows him sophisticated with deliberate Latinism :—' I am often put to a stand in considering whether what I write be the idiom of the tongue, . . . & have no other way to clear my doubts but by translating my English into Latin ' ; the natural inference in this matter would be : you cannot put a preposition (roughly speaking) later than its word in Latin, & therefore you must not do so in English. Gibbon improved upon the doctrine, &, observing that prepositions & adverbs are not always easily distinguished, kept on the safe side by not ending sentences with *on, over, under,* or the like, even when they would have been adverbs.

The fact is that the remarkable freedom enjoyed by English in putting its prepositions late & omitting its relatives is an important element in the flexibility of the language. The power of saying *A state of dejection such as they are absolute strangers to* (Cowper) instead of *A state of dejection of an intensity to which they are absolute strangers,* or *People worth talking to* instead of *People with whom it is worth while to talk,* is not one to be lightly surrendered. But the Dryden-Gibbon tradition has remained in being, & even now immense pains are daily expended in changing spontaneous into artificial English. *That depends on what they are cut with* is not improved by conversion into *That*

depends on with what they are cut ; & too often the lust of sophistication, once blooded, becomes uncontrollable, & ends with, *That depends on the answer to the question as to with what they are cut.* Those who lay down the universal principle that final prepositions are ' inelegant ' are unconsciously trying to deprive the English language of a valuable idiomatic resource, which has been used freely by all our greatest writers except those whose instinct for English idiom has been overpowered by notions of correctness derived from Latin standards. The legitimacy of the prepositional ending in literary English must be uncompromisingly maintained ; in respect of elegance or inelegance, every example must be judged not by any arbitrary rule, but on its own merits, according to the impression it makes on the feeling of educated English readers.

In avoiding the forbidden order, unskilful handlers of words often fall into real blunders (see OUT OF THE FRYING-PAN). A few examples of bad grammar obviously due to this cause may fairly be offered without any suggestion that a rule is responsible for all blunders made in attempting to keep it ; the words in brackets indicate the avoided form, which is not necessarily the best, but is at least better than that substituted for it :—*The War Office does not care, the Disposal Board is indifferent, & there is no-one on whom to fix the blame or* to hang (no-one to fix the blame on or to hang)./*The day begins with a ride with the wife & as many others as want to ride &* for whom *there is horseflesh available* (& as there are horses for)./*The question of an equal repartition of the cost of reparation, as well as of the interest & reimbursement of capital invested,* is on what *the whole matter hinges* (is what the whole matter hinges on)./*It is like the art* of which *Huysmans dreamed but* never executed (the art that Huysmans dreamed of)./*Recognition is given to it* by no matter whom *it is displayed* (no matter whom it is displayed by)./*That promised land* for which *he was to prepare, but scarcely* to enter (that he was to prepare for).

It was said above that almost all our great writers have allowed themselves to end a sentence or a clause with a preposition. A score of specimens follow ranging over six centuries, to which may be added the Bacon, Cowper, & Ruskin examples already given :—(Chaucer) But yit to this thing ther is yit another thing y-ioigned, more to ben wondred upon. (Spenser) Yet childe ne kinsman living had he none To leave them to. (Shakspere) Such bitter business as the day Would quake to look on. (Jonson) Prepositions follow sometimes the nouns they are coupled with. (Bible) I will not leave thee, until I have done that which I have spoken to thee of. (Milton) What a fine conformity would it starch us all into. (Burton) Fit for Calphurnius & Democritus to laugh at. (Pepys) There is good ground for what he goes about. (Congreve) And where those qualities are, 'tis pity they should want objects to shine upon. (Swift) The present argument is the most abstracted that ever I engaged in. (Defoe) Avenge the injuries . . . by giving them up to the confusions their madness leads them to. (Burke) The less convincing on account of the party it came from. (Lamb) Enforcing his negation with all the might . . . he is master of. (De Quincey) The average, the prevailing tendency, is what we look at. (Landor) The vigorous mind has mountains to climb, & valleys to repose in. (Hazlitt) It does for something to talk about. (Peacock) Which they would not otherwise have dreamed of. (Mill) We have done the best that the existing state of human reason admits of. (Kinglake) More formidable than any . . . that Ibrahim Pasha had to contend with. (M. Arnold) Let us see what

it amounts to. (Lowell) Make them show what they are made of. (Thackeray) So little do we know what we really are after. (Kipling) Too horrible to be trifled with.

If it were not presumptuous, after that, to offer advice, the advice would be : Follow no arbitrary rule, but remember that there are often two or more possible arrangements between which a choice should be consciously made ; if the abnormal, or at least unorthodox, final preposition that has naturally presented itself sounds comfortable, keep it ; if it does not sound comfortable, still keep it if it has compensating vigour, or when among awkward possibilities it is the least awkward.

presage. The noun is prĕ'sĭj, the verb prĭsā'j ; see NOUN & VERB ACCENT. The verb makes *-geable* ; see -ABLE 1.

prescience, -nt. The OED gives prēshyens, -nt, only ; but prĕ- is as often heard.

prescribe makes *-bable* ; see MUTE E.

prescription. For the meaning, & its relation to *imprescriptible*, see that word.

present, a. *The p. writer* is a periphrasis for *I* & *me* that is not entirely avoidable under existing journalistic conditions, & is at any rate preferable to the false first-personal *one* (see ONE 5) that is being tried as a substitute ; but it is very irritating to the reader ; personality, however veiled, should be introduced into impersonal articles only when the necessity is quite indisputable. The worst absurdity occurs when a contributor or correspondent whose name appears above or below his article or letter puts on this *Coa vestis* of a veil ; but they often do it.

present, n. & v. The verb is prĭzĕ'nt, the noun prĕ'znt ; see NOUN & VERB ACCENT.

presentiment, presentment, presentient. Nine people out of ten, challenged to pronounce the first, will do it with z. On the other hand the OED gives only the pronunciation with s ; that is undoubtedly the correct one, as in *sentiment* ; but the sound has been assimilated to that of *present*, with which *presentment* is, but *presentiment* is not, connected ; & with *presentient*, which is not in popular use, no-one would make the same mistake. Mistake or not, however, even the OED's authority is hardly likely to cure *presentiment* of its z, & the pronunciations here recommended are prīzĕ'ntĭment, prĭzĕ'ntment, prĕsĕ'nshent.

preserve, n. For *p.*=jam, see FORMAL WORDS.

preserve, vb, has *-vable* ; MUTE E.

presidentess. See FEMININE DESIGNATIONS.

prestidigitator, -tion. Now chiefly in POLYSYLLABIC HUMOUR.

prestige. The anglicized pronunciation prĕ'stĭj is given by the OED as well as the usual prĕstē'zh, but is perhaps seldom heard.

prestissimo, presto. Pl. *-os* ; *-o*(E)S 3.

presume makes *-mable* ; see MUTE E.

presumedly. Four syllables if used ; see *-EDLY* ; it is better to use *presumably* or other synonym.

presumptive. For *heir p.*, see HEIR 2.

PRESUMPTUOUS WORD-FORMATION. A selection of words follows that for one reason or another should not have been brought into existence. Some, as *basal*, were not wanted ; some, as *bureaucrat*, were bad formations ; some, as *intensive*, were essentially liable to confusion with others ; & against some, as *dandiacal*, more than one of these objections can be brought. They are not here sorted into classes, the particular faults of each being stated in its dictionary place, but are merely put together as a general warning to those who are given either to reckless wordmaking for themselves or to catching up of new vogue-words started by others. *Amoral, amusive, basal, bureaucrat, calmative, coastal, concision, dandiacal, declinal, demean* (lower),

devolute, duologue, epistolatory, eventuate, feature vb, *femininity, forceful, foreword, funniment, happenings, historicity, idiosyncratic, intensive, interpretive, lectureship, locution, mentality, mineralogy, minify, monachal, monarchial, opinionative, pacifist, pleistocene, purposive, speedometer.*

presuppose makes *-sable* ; MUTE E.

preterite. In dealing with English grammar, it is better to say *past.*

pretermit makes *-tted, -tting* (see *-T-, -TT-*), & *-ssible* or *-ttable* (see *-ABLE* 1, 2.

prettify. For inflexions see VERBS IN *-IE* &c., 6.

preux chevalier. FRENCH WORDS.

prevaricate makes *-tor* ; see *-OR*.

preventable, -ible. The first is recommended ; see *-ABLE* 2.

prevent(at)ive. The short form is better ; see LONG VARIANTS.

previous. 1. For the construction in *will consult you previous to acting*, see QUASI-ADVERBS. 2. *Too previous*, originally amusing both because the sense of *p.* was a specially made one, & because *too* was with that sense deliberately redundant, has passed into the realm of WORN-OUT HUMOUR. 3. *The previous question* is a phrase that does not explain itself. We all know that moving the p. q. is somehow a way of attempting to shelve the matter under debate, but the light of nature would suggest only, & wrongly, that the proposal was to go back to what the House had been engaged upon before this present matter. The p. q. is in fact a proposal that the matter under debate should not now (formerly, should now) be divided upon. Those who wish to shelve the matter move this p. q., to which they now vote ay (formerly no).

pre-war. The only justification for saying *p.* instead of *before the war* is that *before the war* makes a very unhandy adjective, & we are now constantly in need of a handy one ; *before-the-war conditions, politics, prices*, as phrases for everyday use, will never do, & the only justification is also sufficient. But it fails to cover the use of *pre-war* as an adverb, now making its way into the newspapers. There is nothing unhandy in that use of *before the war*, which should be restored in all contexts of the kind here shown— *The suggestion is utterly untrue, as a comparison of present prices with those* prevailing pre-war *will show./ The difference is made up, though not, of course,* to the same extent as pre-war, *by interest on our foreign investments./The season-ticket holder, too, is to pay about 75 per cent. more than* he did pre-war./*The number of houses* demolished annually pre-war *is again not accurately known.*

prey, vb. For inflexions, see VERBS IN -IE &c., 2.

price, vb, makes *-ceable*; -ABLE 1.

prickly. For the adverb, see -LILY.

pride. For *P. goeth before a fall*, see MISQUOTATION.

PRIDE OF KNOWLEDGE is a very unamiable characteristic, & the display of it should be sedulously avoided. Some of the ways in which it is displayed, often by people who do not realize how disagreeable they are making themselves, are illustrated in the following among many articles: à l'outrance, amuck, Army & Navy, averse, baluster, bedouin, course, different, double entendre, egregious, flautist, Hindu, implement, ingeminate, journal, Mahomet, moral(e), moslem, naïf, nom-de-guerre, shamefaced, taboo.

prie-dieu. See FRENCH WORDS.

priestess. See FEMININE DESIGNATIONS.

priestly. For the adv., see -LILY.

prig is a word of variable & indefinite meaning; the following, from an anonymous volume of essays, may be useful:—' The best thing I can do, perhaps, is to give you the various descriptions that would come into my head at different times if I were asked for one suddenly. A prig is a believer in red tape; that is, he exalts the method above

the work done. A prig, like the Pharisee, says: " God, I thank thee that I am not as other men are "— except that he often substitutes *Self* for *God*. A prig is one who works out his paltry accounts to the last farthing, while his millionaire neighbour lets accounts take care of themselves. A prig expects others to square themselves to his very inadequate measuring-rod, & condemns them with confidence if they do not. A p. is wise beyond his years in all the things that do not matter. A p. cracks nuts with a steam hammer : that is, calls in the first principles of morality to decide whether he may, or must, do something of as little importance as drinking a glass of beer. On the whole, one may, perhaps, say that all his different characteristics come from the combination, in varying proportions, of three things—the desire to do his duty, the belief that he knows better than other people, & blindness to the difference in value between different things '.

prima donna. Pronounce prē-. Pl. *prime donne* (-ēmā, -nā) or *prima donnas.*

prima facie. Pron. prī′ma fā′shĭē.

primary colours. As the phrase is used in different senses, the OED definition is here given :—Formerly, the seven colours of the spectrum, viz. red, orange, yellow, green, blue, indigo, violet; now, the three colours red, green, & violet (or, with painters, red, yellow, & blue), out of different combinations of which all the others are produced.

primates. Pronounce prīmā′tēz.

prime, vb, has *-mable*; MUTE E.

primer. The traditional pronunciation is prī′mer, & the word was very commonly spelt with *-mm-*. This pronunciation is still used in the names of types; but in the names of modern school manuals prī′mer is now more usual.

primeur. See FRENCH WORDS.

primeval, -aeval. The first is recommended : see Æ, Œ.

princely. For the adv., see -LILY.

princess. As a prefix (*P. Edith, P. Victoria, P. Royal,* &c.) pronounced prĭ′nsĭs ; as an independent noun, prĭ′nsĕs or prĭnsĕ′s.

principal, principle. Misprints of one for the other are very frequent, & should be guarded against.

prior. For the adverbial use (*p. to* = before) see QUASI-ADVERBS. But the phrase is incongruous, & ranks merely with FORMAL WORDS, except in contexts involving a connexion between the two events more essential than the simple time relation, as in *Candidates must deposit security prior to the ballot.* The use deprecated is seen in : *Prior to going to Wiltshire, Mr —— very successfully hunted the —— Hounds.*

prise. This spelling is sometimes used to differentiate the verb meaning to force up by leverage from the other verb or verbs spelt *prize* ; it is also the old spelling of the nautical verb meaning to capture. But the pronunciation (always -z) is against the success of this distinction, & the ordinary form *prize* is recommended.

privacy. The OED recognizes only prĭv-, not prīv-.

privative. See TECHNICAL TERMS.

privilege, vb. *He was generally believed to be an exceptionally taciturn man, but those who were* privileged *with his friendship say that this was a habit assumed against the inquisitive.* An unidiomatic use, on the ANALOGY of *honoured with.*

prize, vb, makes -*zable* ; see MUTE E. For the spelling in various senses, see PRISE.

pro (professional). See CURTAILED WORDS. Pl. *pros* ; see -O(E)S 5.

pro & con. Pl., as noun, *pros & cons.*

probable. Two temptations call for notice. The first is that of attaching an infinitive to *p.* ; cf. POSSIBLE ; a thing may be *likely to happen,* but not *p. to happen* ; ANALOGY is the corrupter : *Should Germany meditate anything of the* kind it would look uncommonly like a deliberate provocation of France, & for that reason it seems scarcely probable to be borne out by events. / Military cooperation against Russia is scarcely probable to be *more than a* dream. The second is the wrong use of the future after *p.* The *result will probably be* is right ; but *The probable result will be* is a mixture between that & *The probable result is* ; correct accordingly to *is* in : *It is believed that Said Pasha will be forced to resign, & that his most probable successor* will be *Kiamil Pasha.*

probe, if an -*able* adjective from it is required, must make *probeable* for fear of confusion with the ordinary *probable*—one of the extremely rare necessary exceptions to the rule given under MUTE E.

problematic(al). The longer form is slightly more common ; there is no clear difference in usage ; -IC(AL).

proboscis. The pl. recommended is -*scises* ; the Latin form is -*scides* (-ēz), & *probosces* is wrong. For *p.* = nose, see POLYSYLLABIC HUMOUR.

proceleusmatic. See GREEK G.

process. The OED gives prō′sĕs as the better pronunciation ; but prō′-sĕs or prō′sĭs seems more likely to prevail.

process (go in procession) is a BACK-FORMATION ; pronounce prosĕ′s.

procès-verbal. See FRENCH WORDS.

proclitic. See TECHNICAL TERMS.

procrastinate makes -*nable, -tor* ; see -ABLE 1, -OR.

proctorize makes -*zable* ; MUTE E.

procure makes -*rable* ; see MUTE E.

procuress. See FEMININE DESIGNATIONS.

produce. Verb prodŭ′s, noun prō′-dūs ; see NOUN & VERB ACCENT. The verb makes -*cible* ; see -ABLE 2.

proem, proemial. Pronounce prō′-ĕm, prōĕ′mĭal. But the words, not having made their way like *poem* & *poetic* into common use, remain puzzling to the unlearned & are better avoided in general writing.

profane, vb, has *-nable*; MUTE E.

professedly. Four syllables; -EDLY.

professorate, -riate. The differentiation that makes *-rate* the office of professor, & *-riate* the body of professors, deserves recognition.

professoress. See FEMININE DESIGNATIONS.

proffer makes *-ering, -ered*; -R-,-RR-.

profile. Pronounce prō'fēl.

profound makes *-er, -est*; see -ER & -EST 1 c.

profoundly. See POSITIVE WORDS.

profuse makes *-er, -est*; see -ER & -EST 1 c.

progenitress. See FEMININE DESIGNATIONS.

prognosis. Pl. *-oses* (-ēz); see LATIN PLURALS.

prognosticate makes *-cable, -tor*; see -ABLE 1, -OR.

prognostic. For synonymy see SIGN.

program(me). It appears from the OED quotations that *-am* was the regular spelling until the 19th c., & the OED's judgement is : ' The earlier *program* was retained by Scott, Carlyle, Hamilton, & others, & is preferable, as conforming to the usual English representation of Greek *gramma*, in *anagram, cryptogram, diagram, telegram,* &c.'.

progress. The OED gives prō- as preferable to prŏ-. Noun prō'grĭs, verb progrĕ's; see NOUN & VERB ACCENT.

progression. *Arithmetical p.* & *geometrical p.* These are in constant demand to express a rapid rate of increase, which is not involved in either of them, & is not even suggested by *a. p.* Those who use the expressions should bear in mind (1) that you cannot determine the nature of the progression from two terms whose relative place in the series is unknown, (2) that every rate of increase that could be named is slower than some rates of a. p. & of g. p., & faster than some others, & consequently (3) that the phrases ' better than a. p., than g. p.', ' almost in a. p., g. p.', are wholly meaningless.

In 1903 there were ten thousand

' *paying guests* ', *last year* [1906] *fifty thousand. The rate of increase,* is better, *it will be observed,* than *arithmetical progression.* Better, certainly, than a. p. with increment 1, of which the fourth annual term would have been 10,003 ; but as certainly worse than a. p. with increment a million, of which the fourth term would have been 3,010,000 ; & neither better nor worse than, but a case of, a. p. with increment 13333⅓. The writer meant a. p. with annual increment 10,000 ; but as soon as we see what he meant to say we see also that it was not worth saying, since it tells us no more than that, as we knew before, fifty thousand is greater than forty thousand.

Even g. p. may be so slow that to raise 10,000 in three years to as little as the 10,003 mentioned above is merely a matter of fixing the increment ratio low enough. Neither a. p. nor g. p. necessarily implies rapid progress. The point of contrast between them is that one involves growth or decline at a constant pace, & the other at an increasing pace. Hence the famous sentence in Malthus about population & subsistence, the first increasing in a g. & the second in an a. ratio, which perhaps started the phrases on their career as POPULARIZED TECHNICALITIES. Of the following extracts, the first is a copy of Malthus, the second a possibly legitimate use, according to what it is meant to convey, & the third the usual absurdity :—*The healthy portion of the population is increasing by a. p., & the feeble-minded by g. p./ Scientific discovery is likely to proceed by g. p./As the crude prejudice against the soldier's uniform vanished, & as ex-Regular officers joined the Volunteers, & Volunteers passed on to the Army, the idea that every man owes willing service to his country began to spread* in an almost geometrical *ratio.*

progressionist, progressist, progressive, nn. The last is recommended.

prohibit. The modern construction, apart from that with an object noun as in *an Act prohibiting export*, is *from doing*, not *to do* ; the OED marks the latter as archaic, but it is less archaism than ignorance of idiom & the analogy of *forbid* that accounts for it in such contexts as :— *Marshal Oyama prohibited his troops to take quarter within the walls./The German Government has decided to issue a decree prohibiting all Government officials to strike.* P. makes *-tor* ; see -OR.

prohibition. Pronounce prŏĭ- ; the *h* is sounded, however, where the *i* following it bears the accent, as in *prohibit* itself. See PRONUNCIATION.

project. Verb projĕ'kt, noun prŏ'-jĭkt ; see NOUN & VERB ACCENT. The verb makes *-tor* ; see -OR.

prolate, -lative. See TECHNICAL TERMS.

prolegomena. A plural, of which the sing., rarely used, is *-menon*.

prolepsis. See TECHNICAL TERMS.

prolific is in common use, but to make a satisfactory noun from it has passed the wit of man. *Prolificacy, prolificalness, prolificity, & prolificness,* have been tried & found wanting ; substitutes such as *fertility, productiveness, fruitfulness,* are the best solution.

prologue, -logize, -loguize. The prevalent modern pronunciation is prŏ'lŏg, but the OED gives preference to prŏ'lŏg. In the verb it seems best to spell *-gize*, the Greeks having the verb *-gizo*, but with licence at least (see GREEK G) to pronounce it prŏ'logīz.

promenade. Pronounce -ahd.
Promethean. See HERCULEAN.
prominence, -cy. The second is a NEEDLESS VARIANT. See -CE, -CY.

promiscuous. The colloquial use for *random, chance, casual,* &c., springs from POLYSYLLABIC HUMOUR.

promise makes *-sable* ; see MUTE E. The noun *promisor* is confined to legal use, & *-er* is the ordinary word. *P.,* vb, is liable to the abuse dis-cussed in DOUBLE PASSIVES : *If it had been taken down, even though promised to be re-erected, it might have shared the fate of Temple Bar.*

promissory. So spelt, not *-isory*.
promote. 1. *P.* makes *-table* ; see MUTE E. 2. Construction. You can *p.* a person *to an archbishopric*, or *p.* him *to be archbishop*, or *p.* him *archbishop*, but not mix two of these & *p.* him *to archbishop*. The unidiomatic construction, however, is now commoner in the newspapers than it should be :—*The crowning glory of an executive naval officer's career is to be promoted to Admiral of the Fleet./Major-General —— has been appointed to succeed Lieutenant-General —— as Director-General (temp.) of the Army Medical Service, & has been promoted to Lieutenant-General (temp.)./Over 1150 cadets of the Military Colleges were promoted to officers.*

promulgate makes *-atable, -tor* ; see -ATABLE, -OR.

pronounce makes *-ceable* ; see -ABLE 1. *Pronouncedly* has four syllables ; see -EDLY. *Pronouncement* is kept in being by the side of *pronunciation* owing to complete differentiation ; it means only declaration or decision, which the other never does.

PRONOUNS & pronominal adjectives are rather tricky than difficult. Those who go wrong over them do so from heedlessness, & will mostly plead guilty when they are charged. It is enough to state the dangers very shortly, & prove their existence by sufficient citations. 1. There must be a principal in existence for the pronoun or proxy to act for. 2. The principal should not be very far off. 3. There should not be two parties justifying even a momentary doubt about which the pronoun represents. 4. One pronoun should not represent two principals on one occasion. 5. The pronoun should seldom precede its principal.

1. No pronoun without a principal in being. *Viscount Wolverhampton,*

acting under medical advice, has resigned the office of Lord President, & His Majesty the King has been pleased to accept it (it is resignation; but as that word has not been used we can only suppose H.M. to have accepted the office)./The member for Morpeth has long been held in the highest respect by all who value sterling character & whole-hearted service in the cause of his *fellows; it was Earl Grey who once declared that Mr Burt was ' the finest gentleman ' he ever knew (His means a man's, & not, as grammar requires since ' a man ' has not been mentioned, Mr Burt's)./Now, the public interest is that coal should be cheap & abundant, & that it should be got without the dangerous friction which has attended the disputes between masters & men in this trade. And, if nationalization is to be the policy, it looks to an assured peace in the coal-trade as its main advantage. For this it will pay a fair price & be willing that a considerable experiment should be made, but without the sure prospect of such a peace it will see no benefit to itself & a very doubtful benefit to the miners in the change from private to State ownership (Each* of these *its* means the public, not the public interest)./The number of these abstainers is certainly greater than can be attributed to merely local or personal causes, & those who have watched the election agree that a portion of* them *are due to doubts & uncertainties about the Insurance Act* (A portion, that is, of the abstentions, not of the abstainers)./An *American Navy League Branch has even been established in London, & is influentially supported by* their *countrymen in this city* (Whose countrymen ?).

2. The principal should not be very far off. We have to go further back than the beginning of the following extracts to learn who *he & she* are :—
And yet, as we read the pages of the book, we feel that a work written when the story is only as yet half told, amid the turmoil of the events which

he *is describing, can only be taken as a provisional impression./It is always a shock to find that there are still writers who regard the war from the standpoint of the sentimentalist. It is true that this story comes from America & bears the traces of its distance from the field of action. But even distance cannot wholly excuse such an exterior view as* she *permits herself.*
3. There should not be two parties justifying even a moment's doubt about which the pronoun represents. *Mr Harcourt, who presided at a large public meeting, declared that it was* his *experience as Home Secretary which changed Sir William Harcourt's earlier views & convinced him that drastic legislation was necessary* (Mr H.'s experience, or Sir W.'s ? See also 5)./In the December previous to his raid on the Tower he was chief of a gang who, overpowering *his attendants, seized the Duke of Ormonde in St-James Street when returning from a dinner-party* (His refers not to the preceding *he,* but to the following *Duke;* see 5, & FALSE SCENT)./Four years, the years that followed *her marriage, suffice Lady Younghusband for her somewhat elaborate study, ' Marie Antoinette :* Her Early Youth, 1770–1774 ' (Not Lady Y.'s marriage; see FALSE SCENT)./Professor Geddes's fine example of sociology applied to Civics, *his plea for a comprehensive & exact survey of* his *own city as a branch of natural history required for the culture of every instructed citizen* (The professor's own city ? Ah, no; here comes, perhaps better late than never, the true principal)./As it is, *the shortsighted obstinacy of the bureaucracy has given its overwhelming strength to the revolution* (Not bureaucracy's, but revolution's, strength; see also 5)./Coriolanus *is the embodiment of a great noble; & the reiterated taunts which* he *hurls in play after play at the rabble only echo the general temper of the Renascence* (Not Coriolanus, but Shakspere, is the hurler; the interloping of Coriolanus between Shakspere &

his proxy makes things difficult for the reader)./*On the Lord Mayor's left was Queen Elena, as calm & placid as her husband, who had come into the Guildhall in Parma violet silk, with a large violet-coloured hat & a bouquet of orchids of the same hue.*

4. One pronoun, one job. ... *which opens up the bewildering question as to how far the Duma really represents the nation. The answer to this is far from solving the Russian riddle, but without answering it it is idle even to discuss it* (*It* represents, first, the bewildering question, secondly, the discussion of that riddle, & last, the riddle itself—which is not the same as the question)./*This local option in the amount of outdoor relief given under the Poor Law has always operated inequitably & been one of the greatest blots on the system ; to extend it to the first great benefit under the Insurance Act will greatly lessen its usefulness* (*It* is the blot, but *its* is the Act's)./*Again, unconsciousness in the person himself of what he is about, or of what others think of him, is also a great heightener of the sense of absurdity ;* it *makes* it *come the fuller home to us from his insensibility to* it (*It* is first the unconsciousness, secondly the sense of absurdity, & thirdly absurdity).

5. The pronoun should seldom precede its principal. *For Plato, being then about twenty-eight years old, had listened to the ' Apology ' of Socrates ; had heard from* them *all that* others *had heard or seen of his last hours* (had heard from others all that they had heard &c.)./*The old Liberal idea of cutting expenditure down to the bone, so that his money might fructify in the pocket of the* taxpayer, *had given place to the idea of* . . . (the taxpayer's money might fructify in his pocket)./*Both these lines of criticism are taken simultaneously in a message which its special correspondent sends from Laggan, in Alberta, to the* Daily Mail *this morning* (which the D. M. prints this morning from its correspondent &c.).

pronunciam(i)ento. The Spanish spelling is with the *i*, but the OED gives the English word without it. Pl. -*os* ; see -O(E)S 6.

PRONUNCIATION. The ambition to do better than our neighbours is in many departments of life a virtue; in pronunciation it is a vice ; there the only right ambition is to do as our neighbours. It is true this at once raises the question who our neighbours are. To reply that some people's neighbours are the educated, others' the uneducated, & others' again a mixture, is not very helpful in itself, suggesting social shibboleths ; but there is truth in it, for all that, which may serve us if we divide words also into classes, viz that of the words that everybody knows & uses, & that of the words that only the educated, or any other section of us, know & use. As regards the first of these classes, our neighbour is the average Englishman ; as regards the second, our neighbour is our fellow member of the educated or any other section. The moral of which is that, while we are entitled to display a certain fastidious precision in our saying of words that only the educated use, we deserve not praise but censure if we decline to accept the popular pronunciation of popular words. To make six syllables of *extraordinary*, or end *level* & *picture* with a clear -ĕl & -tūr, or maintain the old accent on the middle syllable of *contemplate*, all everyday words— these feats establish one's culture at the cost of one's modesty, & perhaps of one's hearer's patience. But if, with some word that most of us pass their lives without uttering—*comminatory*, for instance, or *intercalary*—, a scholar likes to exhibit his deftness in saying many successive syllables after a single accent where the vulgar would help themselves out with a second one (kŏ'mĭnā'torĭ, kŏ'mĭnā'torĭ ; ĭnter'kalarĭ, ĭ'nterkă'larĭ), why, no-one need mind. The broad principles are : Pronounce as your neighbours do, not better ; For words in general use, your neighbour is the general public. A few particular points may be touched upon :—

Silent t. No effort should be made to sound the t in the large classes of words ending in *-sten* (*chasten, fasten, listen*) & *-stle* (*castle, wrestle, epistle, jostle, bustle*), nor in *often, soften, ostler, nestling, waistcoat, postpone*. But some good people, afraid they may be suspected of not knowing how to spell, say the t in self-defence.

Silent h. In *Hunt has hurt his head*, it is nearly as bad to sound the h of *has* & *his* as not to sound that of *Hunt* & *hurt* & *head*. In many compounds whose second element begins with h, the h is silent unless the accent falls on the syllable that it begins ; so *philhe'llenism* sounds the h, but *philhelle'nic* does not ; similarly *Phi'lharmo'nic* has fi'lar-. In *nihilism* the h should be silent, though *nihil*, if there is occasion to say the word, sounds it.

Demonetize & *decolo(u)rize* raise the question whether the peculiar vowel sound of money & colour (-ŭ-) is to be extended to derivatives involving recurrence to the Latin nouns ; -mŏn- is recommended, &, if *decolorize* is spelt, as it should be, without *u*, then -cŏl-.

Clothes, forehead, fortune, fossil, knowledge, are samples of the many words whose spelling & ordinary pronunciation do not correspond, but with which mistaken attempts are made to restore the supposed true sound. They should be called klōz, fŏ'rĭd, for'chōon, fŏ'sl, nŏ'lĭj, in accordance with the principles laid down above.

The variations ah & ă for *a*, aw & ŏ for *o*, lōō & lū for *lu*, are widely prevalent in large classes of words (*pass, telegraph, ask* ; *gone, soft, loss* ; *lucid, absolute, illumine*) ; it need only be said that the first two are roughly local distinctions, ah & aw being southern & ă & ŏ northern, while lōō is displacing lū, especially

in certain positions (see LU), irrespective of locality.

Obdurate & *recondite*, formerly accented on the middle syllable, but now more often on the first, represent many more whose accent has shifted or is shifting towards the beginning ; but they are not in very common use, so obdu'rate & reco'ndite are more often heard than conte'mplate & illu'strate ; see RECESSIVE ACCENT.

For a particular affectedly refined pronunciation, see GIRL.

Participles &c. of verbs &c. in -er(r), -ur(r). Is *erring* to follow *err* (er'ĭng) or *errant* (ĕ'rĭng) ? are *furry* & *currish* to be fer'ĭ & ker'ĭsh, or fŭ'rĭ & kŭ'rĭsh ? The OED is nearly but not quite consistent ; in the words *concurring, currish, demurring, deterring, erring, furry, purring, slurring*, & *spurring*, the full er sound is given ; *recurring*, however, is given as rĭkŭ'ring, & *incurring* & *occurring* are not marked. It may be taken that -erĭng &c. (not -ĕrĭng, -ŭrĭ, &c). are the orthodox sounds.

Readers to whom the pronunciation of English words derived from Latin (very slightly touched upon in FALSE QUANTITY) is bewildering will find some clues in an interesting article by the late John Sargeaunt in S.P.E. Tract iv.

For an easily intelligible yet fairly complete system of showing pronunciation in print, see PHONETICS.

propaganda is singular, not plural : *a p., this p.*, &c. ; & the plural, if required, is *-as* (*The difference between these propagandas is obvious enough*). But it is not unnaturally mistaken for a Latin neuter plural = things to be propagated ; it is in fact a curtailed phrase *Congregatio de Propagandâ Fide* = Board for Propagating the Faith.

propagate makes -*gable*, -*tor* ; see -ABLE 1, -OR.

propel makes -*lled*, -*lling*, -*llable* ; see -LL-, -L-.

propensity. *That propensity of lifting every problem from the plane* of the understandable by means of some sort of mystic expression is very Russian. P. to do or for doing, not of doing; the ANALOGY of practice, habit, &c., is responsible.

proper makes -est ; see -ER & -EST 2.
prophecy, -sy. The noun prophecȳ. the verb prophesȳ ; see LICENCE.
prophetess. See FEMININE DE-SIGNATIONS.
prophetic. For my p. soul see HACKNEYED PHRASES.
prophetic(al). The -al form perhaps lingers only in such phrases as the -al books, in which the meaning is definitely ' of the Prophets ' ; -IC(AL).
propitiate makes -tiable, -tor ; see -ABLE 1, -OR.
propitiation. See -CIATION.

proportion. It has been recorded as a common MISAPPREHENSION that p. is a sonorous improvement upon part. What was meant will be plain from the following examples, in all of which the word has been wrongly used because the writers, or others whom they admire & imitate, cannot resist the imposing trisyllable ; the greater part, most, &c., should be substituted ; see POMPOSITIES for other such temptations. The greater proportion of these old hands have by this time already dropped out ; it is estimated that only 25,000 of them remain now (Most of)./A few years ago the largest proportion of the meat coming through Smithfield had its origin in the United States (the greater part)./ The total number of all classes & all nationalities carried outward & inward on board British & foreign ships was 6,053,382, of which the great proportion were carried in British ships (the great majority)./There was a large & fashionable audience, &, as might be expected, the greater proportion of them were natives of India (most of them)./By far the largest proportion of applications for using the machinery of the Act came from the employees (the most applications)./The larger proportion of the children received are those of un-married mothers (Most of)./Eighty-six estates worth over a quarter of a million paid death duties, & the total amount on which estate duty was levied was nearly 273 millions sterling; the largest proportion of this came from estates ranging between £1,000 & £25,000 (The greater part).

' The word has been wrongly used '. It is not merely that here are two words, each of which would give the sense equally well, & that the writer has unwisely allowed length to decide the choice for him ; p. does not give the sense so well as part. Where p. does so far agree in sense with part that the question of an exchange between them is possible, i.e. where it means not a ratio but a quota or amount, there is nevertheless a clear difference between them ; a p. is indeed a part, but a part viewed in a special light, viz as having a quantitative relation to its whole comparable with the same relation between some analogous whole & part. Thus a man who out of an income of £500 spends £200 upon house-rent is rightly said to spend a large p. of his income in rent, if it is known that most people's rent is about 1/5 of their income ; p. is a more precise & better word than part, just because other ratios exist for comparison. But to say ' A large p. [instead of a large part] of these statements is unverified ', where there is no standard of what ratio the verified facts bear to the unverified in most stories, is to use a worse long one instead of a better short one.

The case is much stronger against p. in the extracts, all of which, it will be noticed, show a comparative or superlative (greater, largest, &c.) accompanying p. & showing that the comparison is not between two ratios, that of the part & whole in question & that of another part & whole, e. g. the standard ones, but simply between the two parts into which one whole is divided ; of these two parts of course one is greater or less than or equal to the other, but that relation is adequately given by *greater* &c. *part*, & only confused by the dragging in of the comparison of ratios expressed by *p*. It is a clumsy blunder to use words like *greater* & *largest* with *p*. when the comparison is between the parts of one whole & not between the ratios borne by parts of different wholes to their respective wholes. To give contrasted examples of the wrong & the right : *We passed the greater proportion of our candidates* is wrong ; read *part* ; *We hope to pass a greater proportion of our candidates next year* is right. For a parallel, see PERCENTAGE.

proportionable, -nal, -nate. All three adjectives have existed since the 14th c., & it is presumptuous to advise the superannuation of any of them. The statement may be ventured that the latest OED quotation for *-nable* is dated 1832, & that far from needing three words we can hardly provide two with separate functions ; the *-al* word is better suited to the most general sense of all, ' concerned with proportion ', & the *-ate* word to the particular sense ' analogous in quantity *to* ', but *-al* & *-ate* are both so fully in possession of the most usual sense ' in proportion ' or ' in due proportion ' that it is useless to think of confining it to either.

proposal. See PROPOSITION.

propose. 1. *P*. makes *-sable* ; see MUTE E. 2. *The Insurance Commissioners proposed to be appointed will give their whole time to the work of the Commission. P*. is one of the verbs liable to be used in this ungainly construction, for which see DOUBLE PASSIVES.

proposition. The modern use as a VOGUE-WORD, in senses of which the OED, in a section published so recently as 1909, shows no trace, is an Americanism. It runs riot in 20th-c. newspapers, but is so slightly recognized in British dictionaries that probably few people realize its triumphant progress. Those who will look through the instances collected below may perhaps be surprised to see the injury that is being done by this single word to the language, & resolve to eschew it. Like MENTALITY, it is resorted to partly because it combines the charms of novelty & length, & partly because it ministers to laziness ; there is less trouble in using it than in choosing among the dozen or so of words, one or other of them more suitable, for any of which it will pass.

It may be granted that there is nothing unsound in principle about the development of sense. *Proposition* does or did mean propounding, &, like other *-tion* words, may naturally develop from that the sense of thing propounded, from which again is readily evolved the sense thing to deal with, & that sufficiently accounts for all or nearly all the uses to be quoted. And, on another line, there is no objection to *proposition*'s having the sense proposal, except one—that idiomatic usage is clean against it, & that confusion between the two words has been, until the Americanism reached us, very rare.

It is much to be desired that *p*. should be brought back to its former well defined functions in Logic & Mathematics, & relieved of its new status as Jack-of-all-trades.

Used for *proposal* : ' *Let us pull down everything* ' *seems to be his proposition./Newman said to Mr Hastings* ' *You must share my room & bed* '. *This (says Mr Hastings) was to me a curious proposition, but one I had to accept./He prefaced his speech by observing that he intended to put Home Rule before them as a business proposition.*

Used for *task, job, problem, objective* : *Servia certainly is up against a tough proposition./England has now to meet France, which is a different proposition./With Mr Holbrooke's* ' *Ulalume* ', *after Edgar Allan Poe, came a much stiffer proposition, unless one was prepared to . . ./Never let it be said again that the unlettered British public are a hopeless proposition in the matter of grand opera.*

Used for *undertaking, occupation, trade* : *He has got a foothold mainly because the English maker has been occupied with propositions that give a larger proportion of profit./Establishing floating supply depots at frequent intervals across the ocean, a proposition which only a multimillionaire could have undertaken./ The old spirit of common brotherhood amongst the members dies day by day, & insurance is becoming ' a business proposition './For good or evil, railway nationalization is a vast business proposition./Colonial Preference became the ' sentimental side ', merely appealing to the Colonies, of what had become a business proposition./The agriculturist asks that ' corn-growing shall become a paying proposition './ Agriculture in England can never again become a paying proposition./ The future of the taximeter-cab proposition in the Metropolis presents a very interesting problem.*

Used for *opponent* : *F. Ouimet, who played so brilliantly yesterday, was the proposition the holder had to face./The former is a very tough proposition as an opponent in singles./This Sixth Army now standing opposite us was not a very fearsome proposition./The Roumanian army has proved a peculiarly tough proposition.*

Used for *possibility, prospect* : *Petrol at 6¼d. or 7½d. a gallon was hardly a commercial proposition./The only way to increase the recruiting standard of the Territorial Force is to make the service a more attractive proposition to the man & the employer.*

Used for *area, field* : *The mining district, according to the best information obtainable, is a placer proposition, & placer mining ruins the land./ Lancashire is vitally interested to secure a sufficient supply of cotton on the Gezira plains in the Soudan, this locality being what one speaker described as ' the very finest cotton-growing proposition in the whole world '.*

Used for *method, experiment* : *The territories will certainly require many novel propositions for their development.*

proprietress. See FEMININE DESIGNATIONS.

propylaeum. Pl. *-laea.* For spelling see Æ, Œ.

prorogue makes *-gable, -gation.*

proscenium. Pl. *-ia.*

proscribe makes *-bable* ; see MUTE E.

prosecute makes *-table* (see MUTE E), *-tor* (see -OR), *-trix* (see FEMININE DESIGNATIONS, & -TRIX).

proselyte makes *-tism* ; see MUTE E.

prosify. For inflexions see VERBS IN -IE &c., 6.

prosody. See TECHNICAL TERMS. The adjective recommended is *prosodic,* & the *-ist* noun *prosodist,* for which see -IST B on *philanthropist.*

prosopopoeia. Pronounce prosōpopē'a ; for spelling see Æ, Œ, & for meaning TECHNICAL TERMS.

prospect, vb, makes *-tor* ; see -OR. The OED accents *pro'spect,* not *prospe'ct,* in the only current verb senses ; but the analogy of similar NOUN & VERB ACCENTS is almost sure to prevail before long.

prospectus. Pl. *-tuses,* not *-ti* ; -US.

prosper makes *-ered* &c. ; -R-, -RR-.

prostitute, vb, makes *-utable, -tor* ; see MUTE E, -OR.

prostrate. The adjective *pro'strate,* the verb *prostra'te* ; see PARTICIPLES 5 A.

prosy, not *-sey* ; see -EY & -Y.

protagonist. 1. Pronunciation. 2. Meaning & use.

1. Pronunciation. The popular rendering is protă'gonĭst ; but, if any weight is allowed to the considerations advanced in 2, prŏtagŏ'nĭst would be better, (a) as being the scholar's natural way of saying what should never have been anything but a scholar's word, & (b) as at least discouraging the mistaken notion that *p.* & *antagonist* are a pair of words showing the common contrast between *pro-* for & *anti-* against.

2. Meaning & use. The word that

has so suddenly become a prime favourite with journalists, who more often than not make it mean champion or advocate or defender, has no right whatever to any of those meanings, & almost certainly owes them to the mistaking of the first syllable (representing Greek *prōtos* first) for *prŏ* on behalf of—a mistake made easy by the accidental resemblance to *antagonist*. ' Accidental ', since the Greek *agonistes* has different meanings in the two words, in one combatant, but in the other play-actor. The Greek *protagonistes* means the actor who takes the chief part in a play—a sense readily admitting of figurative application to the most conspicuous personage in any affair. The deuteragonist & tritagonist take parts of second & third importance, & to talk of several protagonists, or of a chief p. or the like, is an absurdity as great, to anyone who knows Greek, as to call a man the p. of a cause or of a person, instead of the p. of a drama or of an affair. In the newspapers it is a rarity to meet *p.* in a legitimate sense ; but two examples of it are put first in the following collection. All the others are (for Greek scholars, who perhaps do not matter) outrages on this learned-sounding word, because some of them distinguish between chief pp. & others who are not chief, some state or imply that there are more pp. than one in an affair, & the rest use *p.* as a mere synonym for *advocate*.

Legitimate uses : *In* Jeppë *the subsidiary personages do little more than give the p. his cues./Marco Landi, the p. & narrator of a story which is skilfully contrived & excellently told, is a fairly familiar type of soldier of fortune.*

Pro- and *ant-* : *Protagonists & antagonists make a point of ignoring evils which militate against their ideals.*

Absurd uses with *chief* &c. : *The chief p. is a young Nonconformist minister./Unlike a number of the leading pp. in the Home Rule fight,* *Sir Edward Carson was not in Parliament when . . ./It presents a spiritual conflict, centred about its two chief pp., but shared in by all its characters./*

Absurd plural uses : *One of the pp. of that glorious fight for Parliamentary Reform in 1866 is still actively among us./One of these immense pp. must fall, &, as we have already foreshadowed, it is the Duke./By a tragic but rapid process of elimination most of the pp. have now been removed./As on a stage where all the pp. of a drama assemble at the end of the last act./That letter is essential to a true understanding of the relations of the three great pp. at this period./ The pp. in the drama, which has the motion & structure of a Greek tragedy, are . . .* (Fy ! fy ! a Greek tragedy & pp. ?).

Confusions with *advocate* &c. : *The new Warden is a strenuous p. of that party in Convocation./Mr* —— *, an enthusiastic p. of militant Protestantism./The chief p. on the company's side in the latest railway strike, Mr* ——*./It was a happy thought that placed in the hands of the son of one of the great pp. of Evolution the materials for the biography of another./ But most of the pp. of this demand have since shifted their ground./As for what the medium himself or his pp. may think of them—for etymological purposes that is neither here nor there.*

It was admitted above that we need perhaps not consider the Greek scholar's feelings ; he has many advantages over the rest of us, & cannot expect that in addition he shall be allowed to forbid us a word that we find useful. Is it useful ? or is it merely a pretentious blundering substitute for words that are useful ? *Pro-* in *protagonist* is not the opposite of *anti-* ; *-agonist* is not the same as in *antagonist* ; *advocate & champion & defender & combatant* are better words for the wrong senses given to *p.*, & *p.* in its right sense of *the* (not *a*) chief actor in an affair has still work to do if it could only be allowed to mind its own business.

protasis. Pl. -*ases* (-ēz) ; see LATIN PLURALS 2 ; &, for meaning, TECHNICAL TERMS.

protean. Pronounce prō'tǐan ; see HERCULEAN.

protect makes -*tor* (see -OR), -*tress* (see FEMININE DESIGNATIONS).

protégé. See FRENCH WORDS. A female p. is spelt -*ée*, pl. -*ées*.

protest. Verb protĕ'st, noun prō'-tĕst ; see NOUN & VERB ACCENT. The verb makes -*tor*, but it is less used than -*ter*.

protestant, when used as adjective or noun without reference to the specialized sense in religion, is often pronounced protĕ'stant for distinction.

Proteus. Pronounce prō'tūs.

protocol, vb, has -*lled,-lling*; -LL-,-L-.

prot(h)onotary. The spelling without h, & the pronunciation with -nō- as the accented syllable, are recommended ; but prot(h)ŏ'notarǐ is also permissible. 'Both pronunciations, with the variants *proto*- & *protho*-, are now in official use in different quarters '—OED.

prototype. *William Hickey, gay young man about town, . . . would be amazed if he could see his prototype of today drinking barley-water at luncheon./The book is ' A Guide to Modern Cookery ', & the author is no less an authority than M. Escoffier, the ruler of the Carlton roast, the modern prototype of the immortal Brillat-Savarin, & . . ./It is perplexing to find the American Expeditionary Force described as ' the immortal prototype of Britain's gallant " First Seven Divisions " ', until you find that for Mr —— the word ' prototype ' has exactly the opposite meaning of that which is given in the dictionary.* And by no means for Mr —— alone ; for *type, antitype, & prototype,* see TYPE.

protract makes -*tor* ; see -OR.

protrude makes -*dable* (see MUTE E),

recommended in preference to *pro-trusible* ; see -ABLE 2.

protyle (original undifferentiated matter). A BARBARISM ; *prothyl* would be better.

prove makes -*vable* ; see MUTE E. *Proved*, not *proven*, is the regular p.p., the latter being properly from the verb *preve* used in Scotland after it had given way to *prove* in England ; cf. *weave woven, cleave cloven.* Except in the phrase *not proven* as a quotation from Scotch law, *proven* is better left alone.

provenance, provenience. The word is, & will doubtless continue to be, in literary use only. It is therefore needless to take exception to the first much better known form on the ground that it is French & try to convert the literary to the second, even if it is better in itself.

provide makes -*dable* ; see MUTE E.

provided (that). The following examples show that care is needed in substituting this for *if* :—*Ganganelli would never have been poisoned provided he had had nephews about to take care of his life./The kicks & blows which my husband Launcelot was in the habit of giving me every night, provided I came home with less than five shillings./She & I agreed to stand by each other, & be true to old Church of England, & to give our governors warning, provided they tried to make us renegades./A society has just been founded at Saratoff, the object being, as the members declare in a manifesto to the Liberals, to use violent methods & even bombs provided the latter do so themselves./The chances are that the direction to proceed to Vladivostok at all costs, provided such instruction were ever given, may have been reconsidered./When will the War Council at the capital decide provided the war is to continue ?*

It will be agreed that *if* should have been written in all, & the object-lesson is perhaps enough. Those who wish for an abstract statement in addition may find that the following test, applied to each of the examples, will compel their rejection : A clause introduced by *provided* must express a stipulation (i.e. a demand for the prior fulfilment of a condition) made by the person who in the main sentence gives a conditional undertaking or vouches conditionally for a fact.

province. For synonyms, see FIELD.

proviso. Pl. *-os* ; see -O(E)S 6.

provoke. For the adjective *provocable* (prŏ'vokabl) is recommended in preference to *provokable* (provō'kabl).

provost. In the names of military-police officials, pronounce provŏ', elsewhere prŏ'vost.

proxime accessit. Pl., used in naming more than one, *proxime accesserunt* (ăksĕsēr'ŭnt).

prox(imo). See INSTANT.

prude makes *-dish* ; see MUTE E.

prudent makes *-est* ; -ER & -EST 4.

prudent(ial). While *-ent* means having or showing prudence, *-ial* means pertaining to, or considered from the point of view of, or dictated by, prudence. To call an act *-ent* is normally to commend it ; to call it *-ial* is more often than not to disparage it. A prisoner's refusal to go into the witness-box is prudential but not prudent if he refuses for fear of giving himself away but actually creates prejudice against himself, prudent but not prudential if it deprives the prosecution of a necessary link in the evidence but is dictated merely by bravado, & both or neither in conditions as easy to invent. But the difference is sometimes neglected, & *-ial* preferred merely as a LONG VARIANT.

prud'homme. See FRENCH WORDS.

prune, vb, makes *-nable* ; MUTE E.

prunella. For the meaning of *leather or* (usually misquoted &) *p.,* see LEATHER 2.

prunello. Pl. *-os* ; see -O(E)S 6.

prurience, -cy. There is no differentiation ; *-ence* is recommended ; see -CE, -CY.

prurigo. Pronounce proorī'gō ; pl. *-os* ; see -O(E)S 6.

pry. For inflexions, see VERBS IN -IE &c., 6.

PS-. With the advance of literacy the pronunciation of the p in words beginning thus is likely to be restored except in *psalm* & its family, e.g. in the compounds of *pseud(o)-* & such important words as *psychical* & *psychology*. The OED describes the dropping of the p sound as ' an unscholarly practice often leading to ambiguity or to a disguising of the composition of the word '.

pseud(o)-. For the sound, see PS-.

pseudonym. See NOM-DE-GUERRE, PS-.

Psyche. Pronounce psī'kĭ ; see PS-.

psychic(al). Both forms have been & are in common use in all senses, & differentiation has not yet started ; but *-al* is, partly perhaps as corresponding in form to the frequent antithesis *physical*, tending to prevail ; see -IC(AL). The spiritualists have indeed taken possession of *-ic* as a noun (=medium ?), & the rest of us might without much loss let them have it to themselves. Pronounce psī'kĭk- ; see PS-.

psychological moment. The original German phrase, misinterpreted by the French & imported together with its false sense into English, meant the psychic factor, the mental effect, the influence exerted by a state of mind, & not a point of time at all, *das Moment* in German corresponding to our *momentum*, not our *moment*. Mistake & all, however, it did for a time express a useful notion, that of the moment at which a person is in a favourable state of mind (such as a skilled psychologist could choose) for one's dealings with him to produce the effect one desires. But, like other POPULARIZED TECHNICALITIES, it has lost its special sense & been widened till it means nothing more definite than *the nick of time*, to which as an expression of the same notion it is plainly inferior. It should be avoided in the extended sense as a

Hackneyed phrase, & at least restricted to contexts in which *psychological* is appropriate; see also Irrelevant Allusion. Three examples follow, going from bad to worse :—*It is difficult to believe that grievances which have been spread over many years have suddenly reached the breaking-point at the precise p. m. when the Franco-German settlement was reaching its conclusion./There is a feeling that the p. m. has come to fight with some hope of success against la vie chère./Everything goes right, no sleeping calf or loud-crowing cock grouse is disturbed at the p. m., the wind holds fair.*

psychosis. Pl. *-oses* (-ēz); see Latin plurals 2.

PT-. In *ptarmigan*, & in *Ptolemy* & its derivatives, the p is always silent. In other words the OED favours its being sounded; cf. PS-. But *ptomaine* is perhaps the only one sufficiently common in talk for the pronunciation to matter.

ptomaine. The OED stigmatizes tomā'n as an illiterate pronunciation; but, as with *cocaine*, it is impracticable to maintain the three-syllable (p)tō'maĭn.

pub. See Curtailed words.

pucka, pakka, pucca, pukka, &c. The OED gives precedence to the first spelling.

pucker makes *-ered* &c.; -R-, -RR-.

pudenda, -dum, are used indifferently with the same sense, but the first with plural, the second with singular, construction.

puggree, puggaree. The OED treats the first as the standard form.

puisne. Pronounce pū'nĭ.

puissant. The disyllabic pwĭ'sant, the older pronunciation, is recommended, the word itself being archaic. *P.* makes *-est*; -ER & -EST 4.

pulley. Pl. *-eys*; for verb inflexions see Verbs in -IE &c., 2.

pullulate. Pronounce pŭ'lūlāt.

pulpify. For inflexions see Verbs in -IE &c., 6.

pulque. Pronounce pŏŏ'lkĭ.

pulsate makes *-atable, -tor*; see -ABLE 1, -OR.

pulse (heart-beat). The OED says ' Formerly sometimes construed erroneously as a plural '. The mistake is still made.

pulverize makes *-zable*; see Mute e.

pummel. See Pommel.

pun. The assumption that puns are *per se* contemptible betrayed by the habit of describing every pun not as *a pun*, but as *a bad pun* or *a feeble pun*, is a sign at once of sheepish docility & desire to seem superior. Puns are good, bad, & indifferent, & only those who lack the wit to make them are unaware of the fact.

Punchinello. Plural *-os*; -O(E)S 3.

punctilio. Pl. *-os*; see -O(E)S 4.

punctuate makes *-uable, -tor*; see -ABLE 1, -OR.

punctum. Pl. *-ta*.

puncture, vb, makes *-rable*; see Mute e.

pundit. For the correction of this into *pandit*, see Didacticism.

pupa. Pl. *-ae*.

pupil. For the derivatives *pupil(l)age, pupil(l)ary, pupil(l)ate, pupil(l)ed, pupil(l)ize,* &c., the double l is recommended; see -LL-, -L-.

purchase, vb, makes *-sable*; see Mute e. As a substitute for *buy* (goods for money), *p.* is to be classed among Formal words; but in figurative use (*p. victory by sacrifice* &c.) it is not open to the same objection.

purée. See French words.

purge makes *-geable*; see -ABLE 1.

purify. For inflexions see Verbs in -IE &c., 6.

PURISM. Now & then a person may be heard to ' confess ', in the pride that apes humility, to being ' a bit of a purist '; but *purist & purism* are for the most part missile words, which we all of us fling at anyone who insults us by finding not good enough for him some manner of speech that is good

enough for us. It is in that dis-
paraging sense that the words are
used in this book; by *purism* is to
be understood a needless & irritating
insistence on purity or correctness
of speech. Pure English, however,
even apart from the great number
of elements (vocabulary, grammar,
idiom, pronunciation, & so forth)
that go to make it up, is so relative
a term that almost every man is
potentially a purist & a sloven at
once to persons looking at him from
a lower & a higher position in the
scale than his own. The words have
therefore not been very freely used;
that they should be renounced altogether would be too much to expect
considering the subject of the book.
But readers who find a usage
stigmatized as purism have a right
to know the stigmatizer's place in
the purist scale, if his stigma is not
to be valueless. Accordingly, under
headings of various matters with
which purism is concerned, a few
articles are now mentioned illustrating the kind of view that may
be expected in other articles of a
similar nature :—

Word-formation : amoral, coastal,
funniment, Hybrid derivatives,
pleistocene.

New words : happenings, mentality, protagonist.

Old words : howbeit.

Foreign words : French words,
Gallicisms.

Foreign senses : intrigue, meticulous.

Distinctions of sense : apt, definitive, masterful, one.

Precision of sense : ago, because,
England, Haziness, only, Pleonasm.

Popular misuses : aggravate, asset,
dastard, idiosyncrasy, journal, optimism, otherwise, percentage, Popularized technicalities.

Corrections : bar sinister, Mahomet,
morale, naïf, plain sailing.

Bad constructions : avail, different,
Double passive, due, Fused participle, infringe, Object-shuffling,
oblivious.

Idiom : first, follow, Idiom, like.

Framework : and, between, neither,
of, or, Position of adverbs, Preposition at end.

Pronunciation : apophthegm, False
quantity, often, philharmonic, Pronunciation, Ps-.

Spelling : gypsy, Mute e.

Sound : Jingles.

puritanic(al). The long form is
commoner, & there is no perceptible
difference in meaning. The existence of a third adjective *puritan*,
which suffices for the mere labelling
function (= of the puritans), makes
the *-ic* form even less useful than it
might otherwise be, & it will probably be squeezed out; see -IC(AL).

purple makes *-lish*, *-ly*; see MUTE E.

purport. 1. Noun per′port, verb
perpor′t; see NOUN & VERB ACCENT.
2. Meaning. The word is one that,
whether as noun or as verb, requires
cautious handling. The noun may
be said to mean ' what appears to
be the significance ' (*of* a document,
an action, &c.) ; its special value is
that it is non-committal, & abstains
from either endorsing or denying,
but lightly questions, the truth of
the appearance. When such an
implication is not useful, the word
is out of place, & *tenor, substance,
pith, gist,* or other synonym, should
be preferred. But NOVELTY-HUNT-
ING discovers *p.* sometimes in place
of *scope* or *purview,* & even of
purpose. Read *purview* or *scope* in :
*In ' A Note on Robert Fergusson ' he
touches a theme outside the general
purport of the book.*

As to the verb, there are certain
well-defined idiomatic limitations
on its use, one of which, in an ugly
recent development, is beginning to
be neglected. This development is
the use of the passive, as in :—*Professor Henslow compiles from published works the information as to the
other world, Christian life & doctrines, the nature of man, &c.,* purported to be conveyed *in communications from ' the other side '.*/*Many
extracts from speeches* purported to
have been made *by Mr Redmond*

are pure fabrications./An alternative, briefer, & much more probable account of the Controversial Parts of the Dialogue Purported to be Recorded *in the Republic of Plato./He had no information of a Treaty between Japan & Germany* purported *to have been made during the war.* Though the verb is an old one, there is in the OED quotations only one passive use, & that dated 1894. The above extracts are doubtless due to the corrupting influence of the DOUBLE PASSIVE ; that construction is especially gratuitous with *p.*, the sense of which fits it to serve, in the active, as a passive to *suppose, represent*, &c. In all the extracts *supposed* would stand ; pretentiousness has suggested *purport* as a less familiar & therefore more imposing verb, & ignorance has chosen the wrong part of it (*purported*) instead of the right (*purporting*).

The first idiomatic limitation, then, is that the verb, though not strictly intransitive only (*It purports*, i. e. it is to the effect, *that someone from Oxfordshire applied*), should never be used in the passive. The second is that the subject, which is seldom a person at all, should at any rate not be a person as such—only a person viewed as a phenomenon of which the nature is indicated by speech, actions, &c., as the nature of a document is indicated by its wording. Normal subject : *The story purports to be an autobiography.* Legitimate personal subject : *The Gibeonites sent men to Joshua purporting to be ambassadors from a far country.* Illegitimate personal subject : *She purports to find a close parallel between the Aeschylean Trilogy & The Ring, but she does it by leaving out Siegfried altogether./Sir Henry is purported to have said 'The F.A. are responsible for everything inside the Stadium'./Its genuineness is denied by Rakovsky & by both Zinoviev & McManus, who are purported to have signed it.*

purpose, n. *It serves very little*

purpose to ask the Chancellor of the Exchequer to give a little more in this direction or in that. There are three idioms : Be *to the*, *to* (*very*) *little*, *to no, p.* ; Do something *to some, to much, to no, to* (*very*) *little, p.* ; Serve *the, my* &c., *no, p.* These should not (see CAST-IRON IDIOM) be confused. *Serve very little purpose* is a mixture of the third with one of the others.

purpose, vb., has *-sable* ; MUTE E.

purposive (' an anomalous form '— OED) is one of the HYBRID DERIVATIVES described in the article of that name as *spurious* ; the Latin suffix *-ive* is unsuited to the delatinized & anglogallicized *pur-*, which represents but conceals the Latin *pro. Purposeful* in some contexts, & *purposed* in others, will meet most needs, & there are *deliberate, designed, adaptive, teleological*, & many more synonyms. In the first of the following extracts *purposeful*, & in the second *adaptive*, would enable *p.* to be dispensed with :— *The tendency is all in the direction of what Mr Masterman calls national self-consciousness ; progress, steady & purposive, by the means of social science./The material origin of all purposive reactions would be adequately explained by the theory of natural selection.*

purr. For *purring* see PRONUNCIATION s.f.

pur sang. See FRENCH WORDS. *The men who direct it are* pur-sang *mandarins, trained in all the traditions of a bureaucracy which lives not for, but on, the people.* If one is brave enough to use the French words, one should be brave enough to place them as such—*are mandarins pur sang.*

purse, vb, makes *-sable* ; MUTE E.
purseful. Pl. *-ls* ; see -FUL.
pursuant(ly). See QUASI-ADVERBS.
pursue makes *-uable* ; see MUTE E.
pursuivant. Pron. per'swivant.
pursy, not *-sey* ; see -EY & -Y.
purulent. Pronounce pūr'ŏolent.

purvey makes -*or*. For inflexions see VERBS IN -IE &c., 2.

purview. For synonyms see FIELD.

Pushtoo. Pronounce pŭ-, not pŏŏ-.

pussy. So spelt ; see -EY, -IE, -Y.

put(t). According to the OED the pronunciation pŭt, with or without the additional -*t*, & with verbal forms *putted* instead of *put*, is universal in golf, but only Scotch in weight-putting.

putrefy. For inflexions see VERBS IN -IE &c., 6.

putrid makes -*est* ; see -ER & -EST 4.

puttee. Pronounce pŭ'tĭ, not pŭtē'.

putty. For verb inflexions see VERBS IN -IE &c., 6.

pyaemia. See Æ, Œ.

pygmean, -aean. The first is recommended ; see Æ, Œ. Pron. pĭgmē'an.

pygmy, pi-. For the reason why *py*- is the better, see GYPSY.

pyjamas, pa-. Spell *py*-, & pronounce pĭjah'maz. The adjective should be *pyjama'd* ; see -ED & 'D.

pylon. Pl. -*s* ; see -ON 3.

pyorrhoea. Write so ; see Æ, Œ.

pyramidal. Pronounce pĭrǎ'mĭdl, not pĭrǎmī'dl.

pyrites. Pronounce pĭrī'tēz.

pyrrhic. See TECHNICAL TERMS.

Q

qua is sometimes misused like other Latin words ; see E. G., I. E., PACÈ, RE, VIDE. The real occasion for the use of *q*. occurs when a person or thing spoken of can be regarded from more than one point of view or as the holder of various coexistent functions, & a statement about him (or it) is to be limited to him in one of these aspects : *Qua lover he must be condemned for doing what qua citizen he would be condemned for not doing* ; the lover aspect is distinguished from another aspect in which *he* may be regarded. The two nouns (or pronouns) must be present, one denoting the person or thing in all aspects (*he*), & the other singling out one of his or its aspects (*lover*, or *citizen*). In the first ex-

tract below, a gross misuse, Great Britain, & Ireland, are not aspects of the conviction, but things as different from a conviction as an hour from a walking-stick. In the second, a much less definite offence, financier &c. do not give aspects of the man to be distinguished from other coexistent aspects, but merely successive occupations ; the fault is that the occasion does not justify the substitution of the very precise *qua* for the here quite sufficient *as*. *The root of this conviction*, qua Great Britain, *is the preposterous fiction of the military value of the Ulster volunteers ; & the root of this conviction*, qua Ireland, *is the shameful & cruel bamboozling of a section of my unfortunate fellow-Provincials into the delusion that few soldiers & no artillery will be available against them.*/*The familiar gentleman burglar who, having played wolf to his fellows* qua *financier, journalist, & barrister, undertakes to raise burglary from being a trade at least to the lupine level of those professions.*

quad. See CURTAILED WORDS.

quadrate. The verb kwadrā't, the adjective & noun kwŏ'drat ; see PARTICIPLES 5 A.

quadr(i)ennium, -ial. *Quadriennium* is true Latin, & the -i- should not be, but usually is, dropped in the English words.

quadriga. Pron. kwadrī'ga ; pl. -*gae*.

quadrille. Pronounce ka- or kwa-.

quadrillion. See BILLION.

quadroon. See MULATTO 2.

quadruplicate. Verb -āt, adj. & n. -*at* ; see PARTICIPLES 5 B.

quaere, the original of *query*, is now little used, & nothing is gained by keeping it in being.

quaestor. See Æ, Œ.

qualify. For inflexions see VERBS IN -IE &c., 6.

quality. 1. For ' has the defects of his qq.' see HACKNEYED PHRASES. 2. The adj. is -*itative*, not -*itive* ; see QUANTITATIVE.

qualm. The OED puts first the pronunciation kwahm.

quandary. The pronunciation kwŏndār'ĭ ('the original stressing'—OED) is recommended, the word being hardly a popular colloquial one. But RECESSIVE ACCENT, giving kwŏ'ndarĭ, has been at work with it.

quand même. See FRENCH WORDS.

quantify. For inflexions see VERBS IN -IE &c., 6.

quantit(at)ive. The long form is the right ; but the use of the shortened one is more frequent, & perhaps less of a mere inadvertence, than that of *qualitive* for *qualitative*, & *authoritive* : *And what is true of railway traffic is true, so far as this* quantitive *economy of labour is concerned, of all industry in which mechanical power & labour-saving appliances are employed*; & see LONG VARIANTS s.f. In the light of the Latin words *tempestivus, primitivus,* & *adoptivus,* anomalous in different ways, it would be rash to say that *quantitive, qualitive,* & *authoritive,* were not defensible forms ; but at any rate good English usage is against them.

quantity. *A negligible q.* is a POPULARIZED TECHNICALITY, often used where *negligible* by itself gives all that is wanted, in the way noted in IRRELEVANT ALLUSION.

quarenden, -der, quarantine, the apple. The OED treats the first as the standard form.

quarrel makes *-lled* &c. ; -LL-, -L-.

quarry, vb. For inflexions see VERBS IN -IE &c., 6.

quart (fencing). See CARTE.

quarter, n. 1. Hyphening. 2. Constructions. 1. Hyphening. *Quarter mile*, not *quarter-mile* ; but *quarter-day*, not *quarter day* ; the difference depends upon the accent, & is explained in HYPHENS 3 B ; *winter quarters*, similarly, should be two separate words. 2. Constructions. *For a q. of the price, for q. of the price, for a q. the price, for q. the price,* are all blameless English. *After three & a q. centuries*, or *three centuries & a q.?* See HALF.

quarter, vb, makes *-ering, -ered,* &c. ; see -R-, -RR-.

quartet(te). Spell *-et* ; see DUET.

quarto. See FOLIO. Pl. *-os* ; -O(E)S 6.

Quasi-adverbs. *He was rolling up his sleeves* preparatory *to punching my head.* From a narrowly grammatical point of view, the word should be *preparatorily* ; but it never is, except in the mouths of those who know just enough grammar to be timid about it. The adjective is loosely attached to the action described in ' rolling up his sleeves '. Most of those who would correct, or be tempted to correct, *preparatory* to *preparatorily* feel no temptation to write *accordingly,* instead of *according, as* or *to,* because the latter is so familiar as not to draw their attention. See also UNIDIOMATIC -LY, in which words of a slightly different kind are considered. It should be observed that it is only certain adjectives with which the use is idiomatic ; for instance, *He did it contrary to my wishes,* but neither *opposite to* nor *different from* them. A few of the adjectives concerned are : *according & pursuant* ; *contrary* ; *preliminary, preparatory, previous,* & *prior* ; *irrespective & regardless.* Another pair of adjectives exhibiting the same arbitrary distinction of idiom as that between *contrary & opposite* is DUE & OWING.

quassia. The pronunciation likely to prevail is kwŏ'sha.

quater-centenary. The form recommended is *quadringenary* ; see CENTENARY.

quaternarius. See TECHNICAL TERMS.

quatorzain. See -STICH. Pronounce kă'terzān.

quatrain. See -STICH. Pronounce kwŏ'trān.

quatrefoil. Pron. kă'ter- or kă'tre-.

quattrocento. Pronounce -chĕ'ntō ; see ITALIAN SOUNDS, & TRECENTO.

quaver makes *-ered* &c. ; -R-, -RR-.

queen. For *the Q. of the Adriatic* see SOBRIQUETS.

queenly. For the adverb, see -LILY.

quenelle. See FRENCH WORDS.

querist. The form *queryist* would

be better (see -IST, & cf. *accompany-ist*), but *q.* seems established.

querulous. Pronounce -rōō-.

query, vb. For inflexions see VERBS IN -IE &c., 6.

question. 1. For LEADING QUESTION, see that article. 2. For *previous q.*, see PREVIOUS 3. 3. For order of words in indirect questions (*He asked what was he to do &c.*), see INDIRECT QUESTION. 4. For the question mark wrongly & rightly used, see STOPS. 5. For *beg the question*, see TECHNICAL TERMS. 6. *Question as to.* This ugly & needless but now common formula is discussed & illustrated under AS 3 ; but it is worth while to repeat here that it is at its worst when *question* has *the*, as in :—*When the nation repudiated Papal authority, the question naturally arose as to who were to have the endowments./From time to time there appears in the weekly Revenue Statement an item on the expenditure side of ' War Loans & Exchequer Bonds ', & the question has cropped up as to its meaning.* The reason is that you do not say *the* instead of *a* question unless either it is already known what q. is meant or you are about to supply that information at once ; the function of the *as to* phrase is to fulfil expectation of the latter procedure ; that is, you explain in it what the q. *is*, not what it concerns ; & to do that you must use an interrogative clause in simple apposition with q. (*the q. who was to have*), or, if a noun is to be used instead of such a clause, attach that noun to *q.* by *of* (*the q. of its meaning*) ; *of* is the preposition that expresses identity, as in *the city of Exeter, the crime of murder.*

question, vb, makes *-oned* &c. ; see -N-, -NN-.

question(n)aire is too recent an importation to be in the OED (1904). It should be treated like *commissionaire*, lose an *n*, & be called kwĕschŏnār', not kĕstĭŏnār'. But is the noun *questionary* ſ' rare '

—OED, but quoted from 16th & 19th cc.) too far gone to be resuscitated ? *Commentary, glossary, dictionary, & vocabulary,* with many less common words would keep it well in countenance, & the success of *closure* (see REVIVALS) lends hope to the attempt. Cf. also, under INTENDED, the case Betrothed *v.* Fiancé(e).

queue. Pronounce kū.

quid (sovereign). With plural numbers, use *quid*, not *quids*.

quiescence, -cy. The former is best ; see -CE, -CY.

quiet, adj., makes *-er, -est.*

quiet, n., *quietness, quietude.* The first is much more used than the others ; it is possible to distinguish roughly the senses to which each is more appropriate, but often there is a legitimate choice between two points of view. *Quiet* is a state of things or an atmosphere : *A period of quiet followed* ; *Seeking quiet & rest.* *Quietness* is a quality exhibited by something : *The quietness of his manner, of rubber tires.* *Quietude* is a habit or practice : *Quietude is out of fashion in these days.* An example of each follows in which (if what has been said above is true) one of the others would have been preferable :—*How becomingly that self-respecting quiet sat upon their high-bred figures* (quietude) ; *Enjoying the fruit of his victory, peace & quietness* (quiet) ; *The quietude of the meadows made them his favourite resorts* (quietness or quiet).

quieten, whether as transitive or as intransitive, is a SUPERFLUOUS WORD. *Whether that can be attributed to genuine American support or to a quietening down of the speculative position is a matter of some doubt./ GERMAN OPINION EXCITED: War Correspondents' Attempts to Quieten It./Real Prussianism would soon quieten Ireland.* It is perhaps used chiefly not in preference to *quiet*, but by writers who are hardly aware that there is such a verb as *quiet* ; at any rate, while good writers seem to avoid it, it is common in uneducated talk. See LONG VARIANTS, & -EN VERBS.

quinarius. See TECHNICAL TERMS.
quinte. See FRENCH WORDS.
quintet(t)e. Spell -*et* ; see DUET.
quintillion. See BILLION.
quire, choir. See CHOIR.
quite. 1. Excessive use of *q*. often amounts to a MANNERISM, & many writers would do well to convict & cure themselves of it by looking over a few pages or columns of their work. 2. The now favourite colloquial formula ' quite all right ' is a foolish PLEONASM, *quite & all* being identical in sense ; ' quite right ' is all right, & ' all right ' is quite right, but ' quite all right ' is all quite wrong. 3. *Quite* (*so*). Many people are in the habit of conveying their assent to a statement that has just been made to them in talk by the single word *quite*, where the rest of us say *quite so*. Oddly enough, they are mostly of a class that should know better, the class that attaches some importance to the way things are said ; *quite* sounds to them neater, conciser, than *quite so*. What they do not realize is that choice between the two is sometimes open to them, but by no means always ; used in wrong places, *quite* is an example of SLIPSHOD EXTENSION. Three specimen exchanges will make the matter clear :—(a) He seems to be mad.— Quite. (b) To demand that Englishmen should act on logic is absurd.— Quite (so), but . . . (c) Well, anyhow, he did it.—Quite so, but the question is . . . In a, *quite so* would be out of place, because what is to be qualified by *quite* is simply the word *mad*, understood directly from what precedes. In b, choice is open ; *quite* will amount to *quite absurd* (as in a) ; *quite so* will amount to *it is quite as you say* ; & the general effect of each is the same. In c, *quite* would be wrong, because the other speaker's words do not supply anything, as in a & b, for *quite* to

qualify ; the sense is clearly not *he quite did it*, but, as in the second alternative of b, *it is quite as you say*=so. The bad modern use, in actual life, is well shown in this scrap of lawcourt examination : *There was no power in anyone to bring the child back ?—Quite.*

quiver. For *have* one's *quiver full*, see HACKNEYED PHRASES.
qui vive. See FRENCH WORDS.
quoin, quoit. Pronounce koi-.
quondam. See LATE &c.
quorum. Pl. -*ums*, not -*a* ; see -UM, & LATIN PLURALS.
quota. Pl. -*as*.

QUOTATION. Didactic & polemical writers quote passages from others to support themselves by authority or to provide themselves with something to controvert; critics quote from the books they examine in illustration of their estimates. These are matters of business on which no general advice need be offered. But the literary or decorative quotation is another thing. A writer expresses himself in words that have been used before because they give his meaning better than he can give it himself, or because they are beautiful or witty, or because he expects them to touch a chord of association in his reader, or because he wishes to show that he is learned or well read. Quotations due to the last motive are invariably ill advised ; the discerning reader detects it & is contemptuous ; the undiscerning is perhaps impressed, but even then is at the same time repelled, pretentious quotations being the surest road to tedium ; the less experienced a writer is, & therefore on the whole the less well-read he is also, the more is he tempted to this error ; the experienced knows he had better avoid it ; & the well-read, aware that he could quote if he would, is not afraid that readers will think he cannot. Quoting for association's sake has more chance of success, or less certainty of failure ; but it needs a homogeneous audience; if a jest's prosperity lies in the ear of him that hears it, so too does a quotation's; to each reader those quotations are agreeable that neither strike him as hackneyed nor rebuke his ignorance by their complete novelty, but rouse dormant memories; quotation, then, should be adapted to the probable reader's degree of cultivation; which presents a very pretty problem to those who have a mixed audience to face; the less mixed the audience, the safer is it to quote for association. Lastly, the sayings wise or witty or beautiful with which it may occur to us to adorn our own inferior matter, not for business, not for benefit of clergy, not for charm of association, but as carvings on a cathedral façade, or pictures on the wall, or shells in a bowerbird's run, have we the skill to choose & place them? are we architects, or bric-à-brac dealers, or what?

Enough has perhaps been said to indicate generally the dangers of quoting. A few examples follow of oddities that may serve as particular warnings; see also MISQUOTATION.

PRETENTIOUSNESS

In the summer of 1867 England received with strange welcome a strange visitor. ' Quis novus hic nostris successit sedibus hospes?' *Looking forward into the future we may indeed apply yet other words of Dido, & say of the new comer to these shores* 'Quibus ille jactatus fatis!' *It was the Sultan of Turkey who came to visit England.*

MANGLINGS

It may seem somewhat unfair to quote the saying of the old Latin poet, ' Montes parturiunt, ridiculus mus est ', *in relation to the Government's achievements in matters of domestic legislation.* Something seems to have happened to the old Latin poet's metre./*His treatment of the old, old story of the Belgian franctireur is typical.* ' L'animal est très méchant, il se défend quand on l'at-

taque.' Something has happened to the French poet's rhyme, as well as his metre./*Here again, however, there was a fly in the amber—the incoming of the Italians.* A fly in amber, or a fly in the ointment—what can it matter?/*The happy phrase that an Ambassador is an honest man sent abroad to lie for his country.* There are lyings abroad & lyings abroad, but only one kind of lying for one's country.

QUOTATION SANDWICH

Yet if we take stock of our situation today, even those of us who are 'fearful saints' can afford 'fresh courage' to ' take './The ' pigmy body ' seemed ' fretted to decay' by the 'fiery soul' within it. Original: A fiery soul which, working out its way, Fretted the pygmy-body to decay.

FOREIGN OIL & ENGLISH WATER

Who will be pleased to send details to all who are interested in strengthening l'entente cordiale. Read *the* entente cordiale./*Even if a change were desirable with Kitchener duce et auspice./ Salmasius alone was not unworthy sublimi flagello./The feeling that one is an antecedentem scelestum./The clergy in rochet, alb, & other best pontificalibus.*

CLUMSY ADAPTATION

But the problem of inducing a refractory camel to squeeze himself through the eye of an inconvenient needle is & remains insoluble./ Modern fashions do not presuppose an uncorseted figure; that way would modish disaster lie./Gossip on a subject which is still on the knees of the future.

QUOTATION MARKS. See STOPS.

quote. 1. Q. makes -*table*; see MUTE E. 2. *The devil can q.* &c.; *q.* should be *cite*; see MISQUOTATION.

quotes, n. pl., may be regarded as a CURTAILED WORD, & left to those whose occupation makes a shortening of ' quotation marks ' indispensable.

quoth, quotha. See ARCHAISM.

R

rabbit makes *-iting*, *-ity*; see -T-, -TT-. For *Welsh r.*, see TRUE & FALSE ETYMOLOGY.

Rabelaisian, -aesian. The former is usual; those who write *-ae-* do so to avoid combining the unLatin vowel *ai* with the Latin termination; see HYBRID DERIVATIVES.

rabid makes *-est*; see -ER & -EST 4.

rabies. Three syllables—rā'bĭēz.

raceme, racemose. Pronounce rasē'm, ră'sĭmōs.

rachitis. Pronounce rakī'tĭs.

racial. See HYBRID DERIVATIVES for this & other questionable adjectives in *-al*.

rack & ruin. The OED, though it calls *rack* a variant of *wrack*, recognizes this spelling; it is no doubt helped by the visible alliteration.

racket (bustle &c.) makes *-eting*, *-ety*, &c.; see -T-, -TT-.

racket, racquet, (bat &c.). The OED treats *-ket* as the standard form.

raconteur. See FRENCH WORDS.

racoon, -cc-. The first is usual.

rad. See CURTAILED WORDS.

raddle. See RUDDLE.

radiance, -cy. The second is rare, but kept in being as metrically useful or rhetorically effective; see -CE, -CY.

radiate. The verb -āt, the adjective -at; see PARTICIPLES 5 B. The verb makes *-iable*, *-tor*; see -ABLE 1, -OR.

radius. Pl. *-ii* (-ĭī). For synonyms in sense *reach* &c., see FIELD.

radix. Pl. *-ices* (-ĭsēz; cf. -TRIX for the quantity).

Raffaelesque. See RAPHAELESQUE.

rage makes *-ging*; see MUTE E.

ragout. See FRENCH WORDS.

railroad. ' Now chiefly U.S., the usual term in Great Britain being railway '—OED.

rain or shine, as a phrase for ' whatever the weather ', is mentioned in very few dictionaries, & has an American sound. It is quoted, however, from Dryden—*Be it fair or foul, or rain or shine*—in the Century Dictionary.

raise makes *-sable*; see MUTE E. For *r.* one's *hat*, as compared with *take off* one's *hat*, & *bow*, see FORMAL WORDS.

raison d'être. See FRENCH WORDS. How not to use it can hardly be better shown than in : *It has been proposed by the Liberal Nonconformist M.P.s that it shall be sufficient for the Sovereign to affirm a belief in the Protestant Faith without pledging himself to be a member of the Church of England ; the raison d'être is obvious ; but . . .*

raj. Pronounce rahj.

raja(h) & *maharaja(h)* have the *-h*, an English addition, much more often than not, & it is better to abstain from the DIDACTICISM of omitting it.

Rajpoot, -ut. Spell *-oot*, & pronounce rah'jpŏot.

rake makes *-kable*, *-kish*, &c.; see MUTE E.

râle. See FRENCH WORDS.

rallentando. Pl. *-os*; see -O(E)S 6.

rally. For inflexions see VERBS IN -IE &c., 6.

ramekin, -quin. Pron. ră'mĭkĭn.

ramify. For inflexions see VERBS IN -IE &c., 6.

rancid makes *-est*; see -ER & -EST 4.

rancour, -corous. See -OUR & -OR, -OUR- & -OR-.

ranee. Pronounce rah'nĭ.

range, n. For synonyms in the sense *scope*, see FIELD.

range, vb. 1. *R.* makes *-ging*, *-geable*; see MUTE E. **2.** *Gratuities ranging from 10 lire for each of the singers in the Sixtine Chapel choir up to much larger sums for higher officials.* If one has not provided oneself with figures for both extremes, one should not raise expectations by using *r. from . . . to.* It is as bad as saying ' Among those present were A, B, & others '.

3. *Range* one*self* (*He had no intention of marrying & ranging himself just yet*) is a bad GALLICISM 2.

ranunculus. Pl. *-luses* or *-li* (-ī) ; see LATIN PLURALS 1.

ranz-des-vaches. FRENCH WORDS.

rape, vb, makes *-pable* ; see MUTE E.

Raphaelesque, Raffael(l)esque. For the change from the established English *Raphael* &c. to unfamiliar forms with *-f-* or *-ff-*, see DIDACTIC-ISM, MAHOMET.

rapid makes *-est* ; see -ER & -EST 4.

rapport, formerly common enough to be regarded & pronounced as English (rapor't), may now perhaps be called again a FRENCH WORD, & will not be missed in English.

rapprochement. See FRENCH WORDS.

rapt, meaning originally carried off, raped, snatched away, but now usually absorbed or intensely concentrated, has perhaps been affected by the identical sound of *wrapped* or *wrapt*, though *ravish* is enough to show that such an explanation is not necessary. The best known passage (*Thy rapt soul sitting in thine eyes*) has doubtless helped. A concordance to Milton supplies also :—*Wrapped in a pleasing fit of melancholy*/*Thus wrapped in mist of midnight*/*Rapt in a balmy cloud.*

rapture. For pronunciation see PICTURE.

rara avis is seldom an improvement on *rarity* ; IRRELEVANT ALLUSION.

rarebit. See *Welsh* RABBIT.

rarefaction, not *-fication,* is the correct as well as the usual form, the Latin verb being *rarefacere* (not *-ficare*)

rarefaction, rarefy. So spelt (in contrast with *rarity*), but pronounced rārĭ- (in contrast with *rarely*).

rase. See RAZE.

raspberry. Pron. with -z- for -sp-.

rate, n. For some synonyms in the sense *impost*, see TAX.

rate, vb, makes *ratable* ; see MUTE E.

rather. 1. *R. is it* &c. 2. *R. superb* &c. 3. *I had r.* 4. *Dying r. than surrender.*

1. *R. is it* &c. Towards the end of the long article INVERSION will be found a section headed *Yet, especi-*

ally, *rather.* The following examples should be rid of inversion as indicated :—*Mr Dooley seldom makes you laugh aloud ;* rather does he keep his readers continually in a state of the ' dry grins ' (r. he keeps, *or* he keeps his readers, r.,)./*I do not feel like one who after a day of storm & rain is glad to creep indoors, & crouch hopelessly over the fast-dying embers on the hearth ;* rather do I *feel like one who . . .* (r. I feel)./*The responsible leaders of the Opposition have abandoned the view that another General Election would ' probably but stereotype the last verdict '* ; rather is it *felt that . . .* (r. it is felt, *or* it is felt, r.,). It should be remembered, however, with r., that care is needed, in mending or avoiding the inversion, not to put r. where it might be interpreted as somewhat ; to write *I r. feel* or *it is r. felt* in the second & third examples would be worse than the inversion itself.

2. *R. superb* &c. *There is something* rather delicious *in the way in which some of these inventors ignore previous achievements.*/*This was* rather *a revelation.*/*While exercising generosity & kindliness more than most the* doctor rather loved *a quarrel.* What is the use of fine warm words like *delicious* & *revelation* & *love* if the cold water of r. is to be thrown over them ? ' R. agreeable ' if you will ; ' r. surprising ' by all means ; ' r. enjoyed ' certainly ; but away with r. *delicious*, r. *a revelation*, & r. *loved*! Cf. SOMEWHAT.

3. *I had r.* is as idiomatic as *I would r. ; had* is the old subjunctive, = I should hold or find, & is used with r. on the analogy of *I had liefer* = I should hold it dearer ; see HAD 1.

4. *Dying r. than surrender, He resigned r. than stifle his conscience,* &c. The use of the infinitive after r. *than* in such contexts is discussed in -ING 5.

ratify. For inflexions see VERBS IN -IE &c., 6.

ratio. Pl. *-os* ; see -O(E)S 4.

ratiocinate & its derivatives, as

exclusively learned words, may fairly be pronounced răti- rather than răshi- ; cf. GREEK G ; the OED, however, gives only răshi-.

ration. Pronounce ră- or rā-. But the army says ră-, & the military use is the prevalent one.

rationale is the neuter of the Latin adjective *rationalis*, & should therefore be pronounced răshonā'lĭ ; but confusion with such French words as *morale & locale* (there is no French *rationale*) naturally leads to its being sometimes mispronounced.

rationalize makes -*zable* ; MUTE E.

ratlin, ratline, ratling. The derivation is uncertain ; but the last syllable probably contains neither the word *line* nor the participle termination -*ing*. The spelling *ratlin* is perhaps, therefore, the best.

rat(t)an. The double *t* is usual.

ravage makes -*geable* ; see -ABLE 1.

ravel makes -*lled*, -*lling*, &c. ; see -LL-, -L-. The verb is curiously applied both to the tangling & the disentangling process. The verbs that can mean either to deprive of or to provide with what is expressed by the noun of the same spelling (compare *will but skin & film the ulcerous place* with *skin 'em alive*) are not parallel, because with them the noun is the starting-point.

ray, vb. For inflexions see VERBS IN -IE &c., 1.

Rayah. Pronounce rī'a.

raze, rase. *Rase* is the older spelling, but *raze* now prevails. There is some tendency to use *rase* still for senses, such as erase or scrape off, that are now archaic ; but the distinction corresponds to no difference of etymology, & *raze* should be the only form.

razzia. See FRENCH WORDS.

re. For the use of this telltale little word see ILLITERACIES, & POPULARIZED TECHNICALITIES. A quotation or two follow :—*Dear Sir,—I am glad to see that you have taken a strong line re the Irish railway situation./Why not agree to submit*

the decision of the Conference re the proposed readjustment to the people so that they alone can decide ?/Sir,— I have had sent me a cutting from your issue of the 14th inst., from which I gather that reference had been made in a former issue to some alleged statements of mine re the use of the military during the recent railway dispute./Sir,—There is another fact re above. Twice with, & twice without, italics.

re(-). In *re*(-) compounds, the hyphen is usual before e (*re-entrant, re-examine,* &c.); not uncommon before other vowels (*re-armament* or *rearmament, reiterate* or *re-iterate, reorganize* or *re-organize, re-urge* or *reurge*), especially when the look of the word, as in the first & fourth examples, is deceptive or puzzling without it ; common when the compound is used after the simple word (*make & re-make, discussion & re-discussion*) ; & necessary when a modern compound such as *re-cover* = put a new cover upon, *re-pair* = pair afresh, or *re-count* = count again, is to be distinguished from a better known & differently pronounced old word (*recover* get back, *repair* mend, *recount* narrate).

reaction. *Mr Darwin's observations upon the breeds of pigeons have had a reaction on the structure of European Society./Any apparent divisions in this country, even the threat of a vote of censure, might have had its reaction on public opinion in Italy. R.,* owing to its use in Chemistry, has become a POPULARIZED TECHNICALITY liable like other such terms to be used by SLIPSHOD EXTENSION where it is not wanted, e. g. where nothing more is meant than *effect* or *influence* or the simple *action*. This misuse is betrayed in the quotations by the word *on*, which suits *action* &c., but does not suit *r.* except in senses in which it means more than any of those three. The senses of *r.* may be distinguished thus : 1. The process of reversing what has been done or going back to the status quo ante : *progress & r.* ; *the forces of r.* 2. The recoil from unusual activity or inactivity, producing an equally unusual degree of the reverse : *extremes & r.* ; *the r. from passion, despair, a cold bath.* 3. The second half of interaction, B's retaliation upon the first agent A, making up with action the vicissitudes of a struggle &c. : *after all this action & r.* 4. The reflex effect upon A of his own actions : *the r. of cruelty upon the cruel.* 5. The action called forth from B by A's treatment : *stimulus & r.* ; *the r. of copper to sulphuric acid.* N° 5 is the sense that covers the chemical use, & the one also that is often interchangeable with *effect* &c.; but *on* or *upon* is out of place with it ; not *the r. of sulphuric acid on copper,* but either *the r. of copper to sulphuric acid* or *the action of sulphuric acid on copper.* Similarly, not *the r.,* but *the action* or *effect* or *influence,* of Darwinism *on* Europe & of English votes of censure *on* Italian public opinion.

read. For *a well read man, deeply read in the ancients,* &c., see INTRANSITIVE P.P.

readable)(**legible.** See ILLEGIBLE.

readily has *readier, -est,* as well as *more & most readily,* at least in talk ; *those who promise readiest* ; see -ER & -EST 3.

real. *The so-called* décadence *& the symbolist movement—strange dreaming & the search for consolation in irreality.* The negatives from *r.* are *unreal & unreality,* though it is true that there are analogies for nouns using *in-* or *ir-* when the adjectives have *un-* ; see IN- & UN-.

realize. 1. *R.* makes *-zable* ; see MUTE E. 2. *What was realized might happen has happened.* The insertion of *it* between *what & was* is, however, ugly, indispensable unless the sentence is to be recast. For discussion & parallels see IT 1.

realm. For synonymy see FIELD.

-RE & -ER. Many words usually spelt *-re* are pronounced as if the spelling were *-er* ; so *centre, fibre, acre, manœuvre.* In American usage the spelling of these is now *-er,* except when, as in *acre & lucre,* a preceding *c* would have its sound changed from k to s. In English usage the *-re* is preferred in the words in which it has not (as in diameter, number, & many others) completely disappeared. The American usage is, as the above statements are enough to show, more consistent ; but it does not follow (cf. -OUR & -OR) that we should do well to adopt it. The prophecy may be hazarded that we shall conform in time, one word in *-re* after another changing to *-er* ; but we prefer in England to break with our illogicalities slowly ; &, after all, while *acre & lucre & involucre &* other *-cre* words remain, with the words in *-chre & -gre* (*sepulchre, ochre, euchre, ogre, meagre,* &c.) halfway between them & those in which a consonant sound is not imperilled (as *accoutre, antre, bistre, calibre, centre, fibre, litre, lustre, manœuvre, metre, mitre, nitre, rencontre, sabre, sceptre, sombre, spectre, theatre*), logic & consistency are not all on one side.

rearmost. Pron. rēr'most ; -MOST.

reason. 1. *Have r.* = be in the right, *& give one r.* = admit that he is in the right, are GALLICISMS.
2. *It stands to r.* is a formula that gives its user the unfair advantage of at once invoking r. & refusing to listen to it ; or rather, he expects it to do that for him, but is disappointed, few of us being ignorant nowadays that it is the prelude to an arbitrary judgement that we are not permitted to question.
3. *The r. is because* &c. *The only* reason *his wages have not been higher* is because *the profits of the industry have been miserably low.* ' The r. is *that . . .*' is the English for this ; for further examples see BECAUSE, & for analogous mistakes HAZINESS. Wrong forms nearly as common as

this are *the r. is due to,* & *the r. is on account of,* as in :—*The* r. *of our success is largely due to unselfishness, power to combine, power to weather adversity & superhuman bravery.*/ *My only* r. *for asking your permission to comment upon his remarks* is due to *the fact that many of your readers will not have seen my previous replies.*/ *The* reasons *of his success* were due *not only to wide political knowledge & sincere conviction, but to a speed of work which . . .*/*The* r. why *I put such a poem as ' Marooned' so very high* is on account of *its tremendous imaginative power.*/*The* r. *for the past neglect has been* not on account of *fish being any less interesting than birds or mammals, but merely* because of *the difficulty of observing & photographing them.*

Réaumur. For pronunciation see FRENCH WORDS.

reave(r), reive(r). The normal English spelling is with *rea-* ; but, the words, especially -*r*, being commoner in Scotch use, the Scotch *rei-* has become familiar.

rebate (carpentry) is pronounced ră′bĭt & often spelt *rabbet.*

rebeck. Accent the first (rē′bĕk).

rebel. Noun rĕ′bl, verb rĭbĕ′l ; see NOUN & VERB ACCENT. The verb makes -*lled, -lling* ; see -LL-, -L-.

rebuke makes -*kable* ; see MUTE E.

rebus. Pl. -*uses* ; see -S-, -SS-.

rebut makes -*tted* &c., see -T-, -TT-.

recal(l). Write -*ll* ; see -LL-, -L-, 3.

recapitulate makes -*lable, -tor* ; see -ABLE 1, -OR.

receipt, recipe. In the sense ' formula for the making of a food or medicine ', with its transferred applications ' remedy ', ' cure ', ' expedient ', ' device ', &c., either word is as good as the other, except that, while *prescription* has almost displaced both as a name for a doctor's formula, *receipt* is in that special sense still more nearly disused than *recipe.* These facts are worth mention because it is sometimes debated, idly for the most part, which of the two is the right word. *Recipe* is

pronounced rĕ′sĭpĭ, being a Latin imperative = take, originally the first word of prescriptions written in Latin.

receive makes -*vable* ; see MUTE E.

RECESSIVE ACCENT. The accentuation of English words is finally settled by the action of three forces on the material presented to them in each word. First, the habit of concentrating on one syllable, or in long words sometimes on two, & letting the others take care of themselves ; this habit is in marked contrast to the French equality of syllables, is especially strong in Scotch as compared with southern English, & is responsible for that obscuring of the English vowel sounds which unnecessarily saddens some of our purists ; English words of three & four syllables are common in which there is only one clear vowel (*corruption, enlightenment,* &c.) ; it is a main characteristic of the language, to be recognized & not fought against or lamented over.

Secondly, recessive accent, or the drift of this usually single stress towards the beginning of the word. The most obvious illustration is what happens to the French words we borrow ; *château, plateau, tableau, garage, menu, charlatan, souvenir, nonchalant,* & hundreds of others, come to us with their last syllables at least as clear & fully stressed as any, but we soon turn them into shă′tŏ & shar′latan & the like. Again, other words that were long pronounced in English with stress on the middle syllable have it shifted to the first : *aggra′ndize, reco′ndite, obdur′ate, contrar′y, eque′rry, demo′nstrate,* become ă′grandĭz, ĕ′kwerĭ, &c.

These first & second forces work well enough together, &, as they are always extending their influence & gradually assuming control of new words, account for a large proportion of the variant pronunciations so much more numerous in English than in most languages. In deciding which of two renderings should be preferred, it may be remembered that when recessive accent has once opened an attack it will probably effect the capture, & that it is well to be on the winning side.

But, thirdly, there comes into conflict with both these tendencies a repugnance to strings of obscure syllables ; with the uneducated this is rather inability than mere dislike ; their tongues cannot frame a rapid succession of light syllables hardly differing from each other ; & the educated, who can manage it if they will, have the English objection to fussy precision & often do not choose to, except where academic surroundings constrain them to academic elocution. Hence reactions with many words whose surrender to recessive accent is on record in the dictionaries. *Deuteronomy & laboratory & disciplinary* are not easy to say with a single first-syllable accent each, & the attempt is apt to result in omission of syllables—dū'tronmĭ & lă'bratrĭ & dĭ'splĭnrĭ ; such dangers are shirked by the use of two stresses (dū'ter-ŏ'nomĭ, dĭ'sĭplĭ'narĭ) or by shifting the stress forward again (labŏ'ratorĭ) ; & *ho'spitable, de'spicable, a'pplicable, ca'pitalist, gla'diolus, su'lphuretted, co'ntumacy*, are a few examples of the many quadrisyllables from whose orthodox accent many speakers seek relief (dĭspĭ'kabl &c., gladĭ'olus or even glă'dĭō'lus, sŭ'lfŭrĕ'tĭd, kontū'-masĭ). In a large class, of which *recriminatory* (OED rĭkrĭ'mĭnatorĭ) may be taken as the type, there are regularly two pronunciations, one academic as above, & the other with a secondary accent or clearly pronounced ā (rĭkrĭ'mĭnātorĭ) used by ordinary people. The unsatisfactory clipping of words like *voluntar(y)ism* & *accompan(y)ist* (see -IST) is perhaps due to this dislike of many syllables unrelieved by an accent. The word CONTUMELY, with its five pronunciations, is an interesting case, discussed separately.

Rechabite. Pronounce rĕ'k-.

réchauffé, recherché. See FRENCH WORDS.

recidivist. Pronounce rĭsĭ'dĭvĭst.

recipe. See RECEIPT.

recipient. *The Serjeant-at-Arms & Lady Horatia Erskine were yesterday the recipients of presentations from members of the Press Gallery./ Sir Wilfrid Laurier, who was seventy years of age yesterday, was the r. of congratulations from Mr Asquith./Mr Albert Visetti, who has just been the r. of a pleasant presentation from his pupils./Mr John D. Clancy, K.C., M.P., who enjoys the unique distinction of having represented continuously an Irish constituency for a quarter of a century, has just been made the r. of a presentation to mark the event.* Can any man say that sort of thing & retain a shred of self-respect ?

reciprocal (in grammar). See TECHNICAL TERMS.

reciprocal)(mutual. To the difficulties presented by *m.* itself must be added that of the difference between it & *r.* *M.* regards the relation from both sides at once : *the m. hatred of A & B* ; never from one side only : not *B's m. hatred of A.* Where *m.* is correct, *r.* would be so too : *the r. hatred of A & B* ; but *m.* is usually preferred when it is possible. *R.* can also be applied to the second party's share alone : *B's r. hatred of A* ; *r.* is therefore often useful to supply the deficiencies of *m.* ; A, having served B, can say ' Now may I ask for a r. [but not *for a m.*] service ? '. Two parties can take m. or r. action, & the meaning is the same ; one party can take r., but not m., action. In the following passage, *m.* could not be substituted for the correct *r.* ; if the words had been not ' of the British people ', but ' of the two peoples ', *m.* would have been as good as *r.*, or indeed better ; it must be added, however, that since it takes two to make a friendship, which is essentially a m. or r. relation, to use either adjective is waste :—*Mr Wilson said : ' I trust* *your Government saw in the warmth of the greetings accorded to his Royal Highness the manifestation of friendly goodwill which the people of the United States hold for those of Britain. Believing in* the reciprocal friendship of the British people *it will be my aim in the future to . . .'.*

reciprocate has *-cable* ; *-ABLE* 1.

recitative. Pronounce rĕsĭtatē'v.

recite makes *-table* ; see MUTE E.

reckon makes *-oned &c.* ; *-N-, -NN-.*

reclaim. Noun spelt *reclamation.*

réclame. See FRENCH WORDS.

recline makes *-nable* ; see MUTE E.

recognizance. Pronounce rĭkŏ'n-.

recognize makes *-zable* ; see MUTE E.

re-collect, recollect, remember. To re-collect is to collect or rally what has been dissipated (*but he soon re-collected his courage* or *himself*) ; the distinction between this & the ordinary sense of *recollect* is usually though not always kept up in pronunciation, & should be marked by the hyphen ; see RE(-). Between *recollect* & *remember* there is a distinction often obscured by the use of *recollect* as a FORMAL WORD for the 'dominant term' *remember.* *Recollect* follows *I can't* as naturally as *remember* follows *I don't* ; i.e., *recollect* means not remember, but succeed in remembering, & implies a search in the memory. *Peter remembered* (not *recollected*) *the word of Jesus, which said unto him, Before the cock crow, thou shalt deny me thrice.*

recompense has *-sable* ; MUTE E.

reconcile makes *-lable* ; see MUTE E. Of the nouns *reconcilement* & *reconciliation*, the first is comparatively little used, but has the special function (perhaps as being more closely dependent on the verb ; but see -ION & -MENT) of representing the act of reconciling rather than the act or state of being reconciled, which means in practice that it is more fitly followed than *reconciliation* by an objective genitive, as in *The reconcilement of duty with pleasure is no easy problem.*

recondite. The old pronunciation rĭkŏ'ndĭt is maintained by some scholarly persons, but rĕ'kondĭt is now usual ; see RECESSIVE ACCENT.

reconnaissance. Pronounce as an English word—rĭkŏ'nĭsans.

reconnoitre makes *-tring.*

record. Verb rĭkor'd, noun rĕ'kord ; see NOUN & VERB ACCENT. For noun synonyms in the sense relevant facts, see FIELD.

recount. For *re-count* see RE(-). For the noun *recountal* (*When the very interesting stories of crime have been unfolded, we can follow the recountal of detection without any bewilderment*), see -AL NOUNS ; ' Frequent in recent journalistic use ' says the OED, perhaps not designing to commend it.

recourse. There is much confusion, writer's or printer's (see MISPRINTS), between this, RESORT, & *resource.*

recover, re-cover, recreation, re-creation, &c. See RE(-).

recriminate. *Idle people who pass their time in recriminating France.* For this transitive use, ' now rare ', the OED has only a single quotation later than the 18th c.

recriminatory. For the rival pronunciations (-ātorĭ, -atorĭ) see RECESSIVE ACCENT.

recrudescence. *Hong Kong, Friday.—There is an alarming r. of piracy in the West River./A literary tour de force, a r., two or three generations later, of the very respectable William Lamb (afterwards Lord Melbourne), his unhappy wife, Lady Caroline Lamb, & Lord Byron./ First, we have the unfortunate circumstances which caused England to be weakly represented in the second test match ; secondly, we have the r. of Mr Laver.* To recrudesce is to become raw again or renew morbid activity, as a wound or ulcer may, or metaphorically a pestilence or vice or other noxious manifestation. That being so, the first example above is proper enough ; but what have Mr Laver & Lord Melbourne done that their reappearance should be a r. ? Nothing, except fall into the hands of journalists who like POPU-LARIZED TECHNICALITIES & SLIPSHOD EXTENSION. This disgusting use is apparently of the twentieth century only; the recrudescences in the OED quotations are of ' abuses ', ' calumny & malignity ', ' Paganism ', ' the epidemic ', ' the wound ', ' a varicose ulcer ', & that is all.

recruital. See -AL NOUNS.

rectify. For inflexions see VERBS IN -IE &c., 6.

rectilinear, -neal. There is no objection to either in itself ; but -ar is so much commoner that, as there is no difference of meaning, -al should be abandoned as a NEEDLESS VARIANT.

recto. Pl. -os ; see -O(E)S 3.

rector. See VICAR.

recuperate makes -rable ; -ABLE 1.

recur. Pronounce the participle rĭker'ĭng ; see PRONUNCIATION, S.f.

recurve makes -vable ; see MUTE E.

recusancy, -ce. The second is much less common, & should be dropped as a NEEDLESS VARIANT.

red. Red heat & red tape ; HYPHENS 3 B. Red-hot ; HYPHENS 3 D.

redact, -or, -ion. See GALLICISMS.

reddle. See RUDDLE.

reddy is often preferred to reddish in compound colour words (reddy-brown &c.), but is now rare as a separate word.

rede. See WARDOUR STREET, & REVIVALS.

redingote. See FRENCH WORDS.

redintegrate makes -rable ; -ABLE 1.

reduce makes -cible ; see -ABLE 2. After r. to & be reduced to the gerund, not the infinitive, is idiomatic : He was reduced to retracting (not to retract) his statement ; see GERUND 3.

reductio ad absurdum. See TECH-NICAL TERMS.

reduit. See FRENCH WORDS.

redundancy, -ce. As RECUSANCY ; & see -CE, -CY.

reduplicate makes -cable ; -ABLE 1.

reduplication. TECHNICAL TERMS.

re-enforce. See REINFORCE.

reeve makes rove or reeved both in past & in p.p.

refection (meal). A FORMAL WORD.

refectory. The pronunciation rĕ'-fĭktorĭ is less common now than formerly, & RECESSIVE ACCENT is not likely to prevail.

refer makes -rred, -rring ; -R-, -RR-.

referable. Pronounce rĕ'ferabl. For the irregular form (cf. -R-, -RR-), see CONFER(R)ABLE.

reference. For synonyms in the sense scope or purview, see FIELD. By SLIPSHOD EXTENSION, the word is often now made to mean a person to whom r. is permitted as a witness to character, & even a written testimonial.

referendum, properly meaning a question to be referred (to the people), has been appropriated as a name for the system of so referring questions & for any particular occasion of its exercise ; the normal form would have been reference, but referendum has the advantage over that of not bearing several other senses. The plural -da is better avoided as too suggestive (cf. memoranda, agenda, &c.) of the correct sense—questions to be referred—; use -ms.

refill. Verb rēfĭl'l, noun rē'fĭl ; see NOUN & VERB ACCENT.

refine makes -nable ; see MUTE E. Refinedly is a bad form ; see -EDLY.

reflect makes -tor.

reflectable, -exible. The first, from reflect, is preferable to the second, from the obs. verb to reflex ; -ABLE 2.

reflection, reflexion. Though the second is 'the etymological spelling ' (OED), the first is in general senses (thought, remark, censure, &c.) almost invariable, & even in the physical senses (casting back of light &c.) at least as common as -xion. A clear differentiation being out of the question, & the variation of form being without essential significance, the best thing to do is to use the commoner spelling, reflection, in all senses. For the change from older reflexion see -XION.

reflective)(reflexive. The case is simpler with these than with *reflection & reflexion*. *Reflexive* has now lost all its senses except the grammatical one (see TECHNICAL TERMS), & *reflective* has resigned that & kept the rest ; the differentiation wanting with the nouns has been accomplished for the adjectives. But *reflective*, though it can at need have any of the adjective senses corresponding to *reflection*, is current chiefly as synonymous with *meditative*, & *reflecting* or *reflected* is substituted for it as often as possible in referring to the reflection of light &c. —*reflecting surface, reflected colour*, rather than *reflective*.

reflet. See FRENCH WORDS.

reflexion, reflexive. See REFLECTION, REFLECTIVE.

reform, re-form. See RE(-).

refract makes -*tor*. For *refractable & refrangible*, of which the first is recommended, see -ABLE 2.

refrigerate makes -*rable, -tor* ; see -ABLE 1, -OR. *Refrigeratory* is pronounced by the OED rǐfrǐ'jĕratŏrǐ, not -ātŏrǐ—a hard nut for some jaws ; see RECESSIVE ACCENT.

refuse. Verb rǐfū'z, noun rĕ'fūs ; see NOUN & VERB ACCENT. The verb makes -*sable* ; see MUTE E.

re-fuse. See RE(-).

refutable, irrefutable. The OED prefers the accent on -*fu-* in both, but allows the other also. The RECESSIVE-ACCENT force, & the analogy of words so familiar as *(dis)reputable & (in)disputable*, seem likely to result in the pronunciation here advised—(ǐ)rĕ'fūtabl.

refutal. For this SUPERFLUOUS WORD, see -AL NOUNS.

regalia. The word meaning royal emblems &c. is a plural ; that meaning a kind of cigar is a singular, with plural -*as*.

regard. 1. *R.* in periphrasis. 2. *Take r.* 3. *R.)(consider.*
1. *R.* in periphrasis. The noun is much used in COMPOUND PREPOSITIONS ; see that article for excesses

of the kind. The two examples that follow, in which *about* would have served for *with r. to*, & *in* for *in r. to*, are mere everyday specimens of a practice that is not strikingly bad on each occasion, but cumulatively spoils a writer's style & injures the language :—*It is well said, in every sense, that a man's religion is the chief fact with r. to him./In r. to three other seats there will be a divided Unionist vote.*

The verb is also much over-used periphrastically in *as regards* : *Turkish rule cannot be tolerated in future over any country the population of which is Christian as regards the majority of its inhabitants*. This should run—any country (a) whose population is chiefly Christian, or (b) with a predominantly Christian population, or (c) in which the majority of the population is Christian, or (d) in which the majority are Christians, or (e) where Christians are in a majority. See AS 3 for the disfigurements to which the very similar *as to* leads those who indulge in such phrases.

2. *Take r.* The vast majority, it would be safe to say, have patients over a field which takes no regard to *borough or other boundaries*. A mixture of the two phrases *take account of & have regard to* ; see CAST-IRON IDIOM.

3. *R.)(consider.* *I consider it monstrous* or *a shame* is English ; *I regard it monstrous* or *a shame* is not, but requires *as* : *I r. it as monstrous, as a shame*. This statement is offered, though as an opinion only, yet with confidence ; but since the OED, always chary of condemnation, does not expressly condemn, an opinion must not be passed off as authoritative. The OED's definition of the use in question runs : ' To consider, look on, *as* being something. Also occasionally with other constructions '. Its quotations consist of four with the normal *as* (Shakspere, Addison, Cowper, Froude), one of the type *I r. it a shame* (J. Gilbert), one of the type *I r. it to be* (or do so-&-so),

& one that is here irrelevant (*to r. his position under another aspect*). A strong preponderance, at any rate, against the modern journalist's trick of treating *regard* as the exact equivalent of *consider*—a trick that the OED, if the *regard* articles had been dated 1920 instead of 1905, would have had either to recognize more fully or to condemn.

A large number of examples will be given, in the hope that when they are seen in the mass their badness will be glaring enough to repel. *R. to be* (or do) is as unidiomatic as *r. it monstrous* &c., but far less common & therefore less in need of attention. First will come examples of it, secondly ordinary ones in which *as* should have been inserted, & thirdly some in which, since an *as* serving another purpose makes *r. as* undesirable, *consider* should be substituted.

A. *R. to be* (or do), & *r. that.* In all *consider*, or *think*, & in the second & third *r. as*, would do.

Dr Leonard Schmitz regards it to indicate the looseness of popular opinion./Some County Associations r. it to be *their first duty to accumulate large invested funds./Montenegro* regards this treaty to be *worthless because she was not previously informed of its existence./He* regards *Spiritism as practised today to be full of the gravest dangers./But for a long time* it seemed to be regarded that *the heads of important trade departments could be relegated to any gentleman of influence who happened to want a billet.*

B. Unprovoked omission of *as.* Insert *as*, or use *consider* or *think.*

Nations who may r. *the ex-Kaiser's nearness to his former dominions* a menace *to them./The present rulers of Germany will* r. themselves free *to pile up armaments./He* regards it beyond question that *Moses wrote practically the whole of the Pentateuch./But the Generals present* regarded the remedy worse *than the evil.*

C. Omission of *as* not excused, but

perhaps caused, by proximity of another *as*, or by abnormal order of words. *Consider* is the remedy in all.

It had regarded itself as certainly out of the war as a great city could be./ We in Ireland regard no insult so supreme as the insult that we are intolerant./Mr Maxse, so far from regarding the Hedging & Ditching controversy as remote as the authorship of the Letters of Junius, put down a motion saying . . ./The man who regards the postal system as stable as the solar system./We r. this attempt to create enthusiasm for the Union Jack by statutory enactment as ill-advised as the policy of ' Say Suzerain './Most people would r. Butler's ingenious theories about the connexion between memory & heredity quite as much contribution to literature as to science./Pufendorf went so far as to r. ratification superfluous./ Showing how fundamental they regarded the need of establishing the independence of the judiciary./So serious is the position regarded in some parts of Natal that . . ./Both these mansions were designed by the same architect, the late Louis Vulliamy, whose masterpieces they are generally regarded. To block a side-issue, let it be said that two or three of the pieces might be technically defended on the ground that *sound as a bell* means the same as *as sound as a bell*, & that the *as* before *remote, stable*, & *ill-advised*, may therefore be the one that belongs to the phrase *regard as*, & not correlative to the later *as.* It is obviously not so, & anyone who takes that line & omits those examples has still the others on his hands.

regardless. See QUASI-ADVERBS.

regenerate. Verb -āt, adjective -*at* or -ĭt ; see PARTICIPLES 5 B. The verb makes -*rable, -tor* ; -ABLE 1, -OR.

Reggy, -ie. See -EY, -IE, -Y.

régie, régime. See FRENCH WORDS.

regiment. Pronounce the noun in the current sense rĕ'jment ; but in derivatives (*regimental* &c.), & perhaps in the verb & archaic uses of the noun, the *-i-* is sounded.

region. For some synonyms in the sense *sphere* &c., see FIELD. *In the r. of* for *about* or *nearly* is a bad COMPOUND PREPOSITION.

register, vb, makes *-trable* ; the agent-noun is *-trar,* & in Camb. Univ. *-trary.*

regnal, regnant. The *-gn-* as in *magnify* &c., not as French, nor as in *poignant.*

regorge makes *-geable* ; see MUTE E.

regress. The verb rĭgrĕ's, the noun rĕ'grĕs ; see NOUN & VERB ACCENT.

regret makes *-tted, -ttable,* &c. ; see -T-, -TT-.

regretful means feeling or manifesting regret, not causing it ; the latter sense belongs to *regrettable.* In the extracts below the wrong word has been chosen ; see PAIRS & SNARES. *The possession of those churches was unfortunately the reason of the* regretful *racial struggles in Macedonia./Sir Newton Moore's resignation of the Premiership of Western Australia was a* regretful *surprise to Australians in London./ It was not surprising, however* regretful*, that Scotland had lagged behind.*

regular. *The r. clergy* (opp. *secular,* i. e. of the world) means those who are subject to one of the religious or monastic ' rules ' (Latin *regula* a rule) or special codes of discipline—monks as distinguished from parish priests & the like.

regularize makes *-zable* ; MUTE E.

regulate makes *-lable* ; see -ABLE 1.

regulus. Pl. *-li* (-ī).

regurgitate, rehabilitate, make *-itable* ; see -ABLE 1.

rehearse, reimburse, make *-sable* ; see MUTE E.

reindeer. For pl. see COLLECTIVES,1.

reinforce, re-enforce. The ordinary form (*rein-*) has been so far divorced from the simple verb (formerly *inforce* or *enforce,* now always the latter) that it seldom or never means to enforce again, as when a lapsed regulation is revived. For that

sense *re-enforce* should be used ; see RE(-). Both make *-ceable* ; -ABLE 1.

reiterant. *But the booing & reiterant cries of ' No ' grew louder, & at length he sat down.* This AVOIDANCE OF THE OBVIOUS, as often, has resulted in a blunder ; *r.* means repeating, not repeated ; but, at any rate, what are *booing* & *r.* doing in one sentence ?

reiterate makes *-rable* ; see -ABLE 1.

reive(r). See REAVE(R).

reject makes *-tor* ; see -OR.

rejoin, re-join. See RE(-). The hyphened form should be restricted to actual reuniting (*The parts will re-join if laid close end to end,* or *should be re-joined with care*).

rejuvenate, -nize, make *-nable, -nizable* ; see -ABLE 1, MUTE E.

relation, relationship, relative, as terms of kindred, have seen some changes. *Relative* started as an adjective meaning what we call *related,* but, being used as short for *related person,* became a noun denoting a person. *Relation* started as an abstract noun meaning our *relationship* (in its only right sense ; see next article) ; but, being transferred from the abstract to the concrete, came also to denote a person. We have had to take to *related* & *relationship* because the others in their original senses have failed us, & now find ourselves with *relation* & *relative* as two names for the same thing, only so far different as *-ive* is something of a Formal word, & *-ion* the dominant term.

relation(ship). The word *relation* has many senses, most of which are abstract. It approaches the concrete in the rather rare sense a story or narrative, & it is fully concrete in the very common sense a related person, i.e. a son or mother or cousin or aunt or the like. Now, *sonship, cousinship,* &c., being words for which there is a use, it is entirely natural that -ship should be affixed also to the word that summarizes them ; *sonship* the being a son, *relationship* the being a relation—with the extension (due to the generalizing sense of *relation*) into ' the being this, that, or the other relation,' or ' degree of relatedness '. To that use of relationship, then, there is no objection. But to affix -*ship* to *relation* in any of its other, or abstract, senses is against all analogy ; the use of -ship is to provide concretes (*friend, horseman, clerk, lord*) with corresponding abstracts ; but *relation*, except when it means related person, is already abstract, & one might as well make *connexionship, correspondenceship*, or *associationship*, as *relationship* from *relation* in abstract senses. Of the following extracts the first shows how *relationship*, when it is justifiable, may lend precision to the meaning ; the second suggests, by the writer's shifting from one to the other, that *relationship* in the improper sense has no superiority whatever to *relation* or *relations* ; & the rest show how needlessly the LONG VARIANT is often resorted to:—*The king was therefore not necessarily of royal blood, though usually he was the son of the previous Pharaoh ;* the relation of *Tut-ankh-Amen to his predecessor is not known./Why not leave the* relations *of landlord & farmers, as well as those of farmers & labourers, to the beneficial effects of the policy ? Why is a tribunal necessary in the one case & not in the other if mutual frankness will adjust all* relationships *?/A state of things may be created which is altogether inconsistent with the relationship which should properly exist between police & public./A step which must have great effect on the commercial relationship between America & Europe./By creating, if such be possible, a relationship of mutual amity between Britain & Russia./The most probable result of persistence in the present ambiguous relationship with Russia is that . . ./She declared that she & her husband had no business relationships./His attacks upon the Napoleonic tradition are well known, but* we are not aware that his relationship to it has ever been so carefully traced./Already a wholesome change has begun to operate in the relationship between this country & France.*

relatival(ly). Grammar words only ; see ADJECTIVALLY.

relative. For the use in *I wrote to him* r. *to renewing the lease*, see QUASI-ADVERBS.

RELATIVE PRONOUNS. See the separate words—*who, which, what, that, such as, as.*

release makes -*sable* ; see MUTE E.

relegate makes -*gable* ; see -ABLE 1. *The large terrace, usually a dining-room, has also been* relegated *to the King's use, & will be adorned with groups of Alpine plants.* Devoted ? *relegated* is not very polite to His Majesty ; has the writer looked up *assign* in a synonym dictionary & decided that *r.* is the least familiar of the list ? familiar to him it does not seem to be ; see NOVELTY-HUNTING.

relevance, -cy. The OED treats -*cy* as the standard form ; -CE, -CY.

relevé. See FRENCH WORDS.

reliable, -bility. *Another essential of successful aerial transport Mr Thomas describes by the term ' reliability ', or the not less doubtful word ' dependability '.* As this extract is from *The Times* in 1920, it is clear that the purists have not yet reconciled themselves to the inevitable. The OED quotes 16th, 17th, 18th, & 19th century passages for *reliable*, but states that it first became common 70 years ago. The objection common to it & several other words is obvious, & the kind of understanding that finds *different to* indefensible will listen to nothing in favour of *reliable*. Those who have an open mind on the point will find a full discussion in -ABLE 4.

relict. The OED pronounces rĕ'-lĭkt. Now that the word is hardly used except as a semi-legal term, or a FORMAL WORD, for *widow*, & is more often seen than heard, it may be questioned whether most people do not think of it as rĭlĭ'kt, & whether the avoidance of confusion between it & *relic* is not worth securing by that pronunciation.

relieve makes *-vable* ; see MUTE E. *Relievedly* is a bad form ; see -EDLY.

relievo. Pl. *-os* ; see -O(E)S 6. But the form might well be dropped as a needless mixture between the Italian *rilievo* (rēlyä'vō) & the English *relief* ; cf. ALTO-RELIEVO, BAS-RELIEF, MEZZO-RILIEVO.

religious. For *dim r. light,* see IRRELEVANT ALLUSION.

relume. For pronunciation, see LU.

rely. For inflexions see VERBS IN -IE &c., 6.

remain. 1. *There remain(s).* 2. *Continue to r.* 3. *I r.*

1. *There* remains *to be said* a few words *on the excellence of M. Vallery Radot's book.* The use of a singular verb before a plural subject is discussed in NUMBER, 7. The present example is perhaps due to confusion between *It remains to say* & *There remain to be said.*

2. *Continue to r. R.* (in the sense that concerns us) means in itself ' continue to be ' ; *to continue to continue to be* is, except in some hardly imaginable context, a ridiculous tautology, & would not call for mention if it were not surprisingly common ; see HAZINESS, PLEONASM. *The counsellors of the Sultan continue to remain sceptical./And yet through it all I c. t. r. cheerful./It is expected that very soon order will be restored, although the people c. t. r. restive.*

3. *I r.* For this see LETTER FORMS.

remark, vb, has as one of its senses ' to say by way of comment ' or ' say incidentally '. It would be absurd pedantry to insist that it should never be used for *say* except when ' by way of comment ' is clearly justified, & often very difficult to decide whether it is justified or not. Nevertheless, it is well to remember the qualification, & be thereby saved from two bad uses of *r.,* (1) as a mere FORMAL WORD, & (2) as a word relied on to give by its

incongruity a mildly facetious touch —one of the forms of WORN-OUT HUMOUR : *You may drive out Nature with a pitchfork but she will always return,* as Horace remarked *in a language no longer quoted in the House of Commons.*

remarkable. See POSITIVE WORDS.

remedy. For inflexions see VERBS IN -IE &c., 6. *Remediable & remedial* are pronounced rĭmē'-, but *remediless* either rĭmĕ'dĭlĭs (' the original stressing '—OED) or rĕ'mĭdĭlĭs.

remember. See RECOLLECT for the distinction. *R.* makes *-berable* or (now rarely) *-brable.*

remise (stabling, fencing). Pronounce rĭmē'z.

remise (law vb). Pronounce rĭmī'z. *R.* makes *-sable* ; see MUTE E.

remit makes *-tted, -tting,* &c. ; see -T-, -TT- ; but *remissible* ; see -ABLE 2. Of the nouns *remission & remittal,* the first is better in all senses but one, viz ' the act of referring a case from one court to another ' ; see -AL NOUNS.

remonetize. For -ŏn- or -ŭn-, see PRONUNCIATION.

remonstrate is pronounced (in contrast with *demonstrate*) rĭmŏ'nstrāt, perhaps because the current noun is *remonstrance.* The other noun, *-ation,* is now rare, & should not be used : *Although every attempt is made at this office to save people from being misled, our remonstrations have not hitherto met with success.*

remote makes *-er, -est* ; see -ER & -EST 1. *R.* is not one of the adjectives that can be used as QUASI-ADVERBS ; it must have a noun with which it can be more reasonably conceived to agree than it can with *knowledge* in the following extract ; read *Even some distance from . . . Even somewhat remote from the main tourist routes the knowledge of English in shops is remarkable.*

remove makes *-vable* ; see MUTE E. For *r.* one's *hat, the cloth,* &c., see FORMAL WORDS.

remunerate makes *-rable* ; see

-ABLE 1. *R.*, *-ation*, & *-ative*, are, as compared with *pay(ing)*, FORMAL WORDS, & should not be preferred, as often, without good reason.

renaissance. See FRENCH WORDS. *R.* was so far established as the English word for the thing before it was latinized or anglicized into *renascence* that it is still the more intelligible of the two, & may well be left in possession. Pronounce as English—rĭnā'sns.

rencontre, rencounter. The verb is now rare, & for the noun, also much less used than formerly, the first or French spelling is more usual, pronounced rĕngkŏ'nter.

rendezvous. Pronounce rŏ'ndĭvoo, but in the plural of the noun -ooz. The verb makes *-vouses* (pron. -vooz), *-voused* (pron. -vood), *-vousing* (pron. -vooing).

renegade, -ado. The latter, of which the plural when it was current was *-oes*, is archaic.

renounce makes *-ceable*; see -ABLE 1. Between *renouncement* & *renunciation* there is no such differentiation as that which preserves the two nouns of *pronounce*, & *renouncement* is accordingly passing out of use.

renovate makes *-vable*; see -ABLE 1.
rente, rentier. See FRENCH WORDS.
renunciation. For pronunciation see -CIATION. *Renunciative, renunciatory*, pron. -shatĭv, -shatorĭ.

rep. The OED treats this, not *repp* or *reps*, as the right form of the textile name.

repa(i)rable. *Reparable* (rĕ'pa-) is used almost only of abstracts such as *loss, injury, mistake*, which are to be made up for or to have their effects neutralized; *repairable* sometimes in that way also, but chiefly of material things that need mending. The negatives are *irreparable*, but *unrepairable*; see -ABLE 3.

repatriate makes *-riable*; -ABLE 1.
repel makes *-lled* &c.; see -LL-, -L-.
repellent, repulsive. That is repellent which keeps one at arm's length;

that is repulsive from which one recoils; that is, the second is a much stronger word.

repertoire. See FRENCH WORDS.

REPETITION OF WORDS OR SOUNDS. The first thing to be said is that a dozen sentences are spoilt by ill-advised avoidance of repetition for every one that is spoilt by ill-advised repetition. Faulty repetition results from want of care; faulty avoidance results from incapacity to tell good from bad, or servile submission to a rule of thumb—far graver defects than carelessness. This article is accordingly of slight importance compared with that in which the other side of the matter is presented; see ELEGANT VARIATION, where the rule of thumb against repetition is shown to have the most disastrous consequences.

The fact remains, however, that repetition of certain kinds is bad; &, though the bad repetitions are almost always unintentional, & due to nothing worse than carelessness, & such as their authors would not for a moment defend, yet it is well that writers should realize how common this particular form of carelessness is; the moral of the many examples that will be given is the extremely simple one—read what you have written before printing it. The examples are divided into batches under headings, & little comment need be added.

DEPENDENT SEQUENCES, i.e., several *of* phrases, or two or more *which* clauses or *that* clauses or *-ly* words, each of which is not parallel or opposed, but has a dependent relation, to the one before or after it. For the point of the distinction between dependent & parallel sequences, see -LY 3.

The founders of *the study* of *the origin* of *human nature./The atmosphere of mutuality must be created* which *will make it possible to discuss proposals* which *would have seemed impracticable./Taken up with war-*

fare with *an enemy./I do not forget* that *some writers have held* that *a system is to be inferred./He lived* practically exclusively *on milk.*

TWO ACCIDENTALLY SIMILAR BUT NOT PARALLEL USES OF A WORD. Some other examples may be found in JINGLES.

Space forbids us to give a translation of the entire article, which would run to several *columns ; but there are* several *points which, if quoted from* the rest of the article, would give the impression that . . ./In these days American revolutionary upsets appear small* enough *beside the other afflictions of the world ; yet the situation is interesting* enough./It was entitled ' Le Comité de Lecture ', & it resented, in language which our feminists would strongly resent, the presence of ladies on that committee.* Doubtful specimens of this kind sometimes occur in which the repetition may have been intended, but the parallel or contrast is so little significant or so untidily expressed that it was probably accidental ; so :—*The Japanese democracy are affronted at what they regard as an affront to their national dignity./They can, no doubt, do each other enormous injury, but the Bulgarians could only carry the trenches at enormous cost, & an offensive movement on the part of the Turks seems out of the question./The deputation asked Colonel Seely yesterday to give substantial encouragement to the British industry, pointing out the desirability of having adequate means of producing aeroplanes in this country in case of war, but at the same time pointing out that the League desired that the Government should acquire the very best machine that the world could produce./. . . spitting out its fangs when anyone entered the room ; this is quite an abnormal proceeding on the part of a snake built in the ordinary way, but possibly it is suffering from the prevailing epidemic of desiring to record a protest in some novel way.*

HAPHAZARD REPETITION, IN A DIFFERENT SENSE, OF A WORD (or

such use of one of its inflexions or derivatives or other belongings).

The cure for that is clearly the alternative *vote or the second ballot, the former* alternative *being the more preferable./This may have been* due *to undue power placed in his hands by the Constitution./To this* last unsuccessful *attempt* succeeded *the boredom of the trenches./We cannot believe that the Bill will be shipwrecked on this point, for that would be not only disastrous to itself, but disastrous to the reputation of the House of Lords itself./These years of his zenith were big with a bigger fate than Scotland's./Such a misfortune would give the impression that the English do not treat their religion* seriously—*an impression which would have a serious effect politically as well as morally. / The vacancy should by ordinary calculation* occasion *no anxiety to the Liberal Party ; the seat has consistently returned representatives of that faith ; on this* occasion, *however, it is probable that there will be a three-sided contest./ They dug their own clay, often in* front *of their own front doors./There is no good* putter *whose wrists do not move out after the ball ; indeed, the formation of the putter renders it necessary that they should do so if he intends to follow it through naturally./ If we could get the awards announced in the course of next week, it would probably help more than anything else to get to the end of this struggle./Sir William White has now received the crowning distinction of the Presidency of the Royal* Association ; *his* association *with the Navy may be said to date almost from his birth./They are kept in vigour for a time by the automatic generation of enthusiasm, but after a while the ebb begins ; a movement generally grows & dies with a* generation. Here again it is sometimes possible to suspect a writer of what is worse than carelessness, a pointless but intended repetition that is to have the effect of a play on words or the mildest of puns :—*The triple bill of Bills which are down for the autumn sitting, the Mines Bill, the Shops Bill, & the Insurance Bill./Of the octogenarians twenty-three died in the first, & thirty-three in the second half of the century; while if we add the nonagenarians twenty-five ancients died in the more ancient, & thirty-eight in the modern time./Anonymity seems to be a peculiar delight to writers on naval matters, though perhaps necessity has something to do with the matter./ I* agreed *with Mr Rawlinson's statement that the evidence at the inquest* disagreed *with the account of the riots as given by Mr Keir Hardie.*

ASSONANCE, RHYME, &c.

'*Worser & worser*' *grows the plight of the Globe* over *the* oversea *trade figures./If no such Council existed, the Secretary of State would have to* form *an* informal *one if not a* formal *one./The features which the* present *Government in this country* presents *in common with* representative *& responsible government are few & formal./. . . by committing* embezzlement—*an action too* imbecile *in the circumstances to deserve censure.*

REPETITION OF A NAME INSTEAD OF HE &c. For this see the *Lord Dudley* example near the beginning of ELEGANT VARIATION.

repetitional, repetitionary, repetitious, repetitive. With all these on record, *repetition* would seem to have a good stock of adjectives at need ; but few writers have the hardihood to use any of them. *Repetitious* is said to be ' common in recent American use ' ; *repetitive* is perhaps the least avoided in England.

replace makes *-ceable* ; see -ABLE 1. There is the literal sense of put (thing or person) back in the same place as before ; & there are, broadly different from this, various uses in which substitution is the idea—return an equivalent for, fill or take the place of, find a substitute for, supersede, & so forth. All the dictionaries, or certainly most of them, give the substitute uses without comment, & they are estab-lished in the language ; but some wise men of Gotham have lately discovered that, if one is perversely ingenious enough, one can so use *r.* that it shall not be clear whether literal putting back or substitution is meant. This is true ; here is an example in which a little thought is required : *We do not regard the situation as a simple one; a large proportion of the men on strike have* been replaced, *& as* complete *reinstatement is one of the demands of the union, there are obvious difficulties to be overcome.* To use *r.* there was foolish ; ' have had their places filled ' was the way to put it. But the wise men of Gotham are so proud of a discovery that ordinary people have made about hundreds of other words that they have issued a decree against using *r.* at all in the substitute senses. The consequences, in over-use & misuse of the verb SUBSTITUTE & the noun *substitution*, have been lamentable, but need not be set forth here ; it is enough to state that the objections to the secondary senses of *replace* & *replacement* are idle, & that only the same kind of care is required that is taken not to use *trip* in the special sense stumble, or *mistress* in the special sense female paramour, where the context makes confusion likely with the unspecialized senses.

replenishment)(repletion. The first is the process of filling something up or the amount of matter that effects the process ; the second is the filled-up condition. See -ION & -MENT.

replete. *No teacher's bookcase is replete without it.* Everyone at once rightly corrects to *complete* ; but why not *r.* ? you can say ' a bookcase r. with works of genius '. Because quite full (*r.*) is not the same as adequately filled (*complete*).

replica. *The* ' *Devil* ' *over the gateway,* a copy *of the grotesque on Lincoln cathedral, which gave rise to the proverb* ' *As sure as the Devil looks over Lincoln* '. *The present*

' *Devil* ' *is a mere modern replica of the original imp erected by the founder.* ' Properly one made by the original artist ' says the OED, after defining *r.* as a copy or duplicate of a work of art. *Properly*, therefore, there is no such thing as a modern *r.* of an ancient original ; & it is this *proper* sense that alone makes the foreign word *r.* worth maintaining in English by the side of the abundant English synonyms. ELEGANT VARIATION & NOVELTY-HUNTING account between them for much destruction of what is valuable in words.

reply. For inflexions see VERBS IN -IE &c., 6.

répondez s'il vous plaît. See FRENCH WORDS.

repose makes -*sable* ; see MUTE E.

repoussé. See FRENCH WORDS.

repp. See REP.

reprehend makes -*hensible* ; -ABLE 2.

repress makes -*ssible* ; see -ABLE 2.

reprieve makes -*vable* ; see MUTE E.

reprimand. Noun rĕ′prĭmahnd, verb rĕprĭmah′nd ; see NOUN & VERB ACCENT.

reprobate. Verb -āt, noun -ĭt or -*at* ; see PARTICIPLES 5 B.

reproduce makes -*cible* ; see -ABLE 2.

reprove makes -*vable* ; see MUTE E.

reps. See REP.

republicanize has -*zable* ; MUTE E.

repudiate makes -*diable* ; -ABLE 1.

repugn(ant). Pronounce rĭpū′n, but rĭpŭ′gnant.

repulse makes -*sable* ; see MUTE E.

repulsive. See REPELLENT.

request. *The German Commission* requested the Allied Commission for *information as to whether an extension of the Armistice could be relied upon.* R. information from the A. C., r. to be informed by the A. C., r. that the A. C. would inform ; any of these will do, but the form in the text is unidiomatic, & due to the ANALOGY of *ask*.

require makes -*rable* ; see MUTE E.

requirement)(requisite n. The two are so far synonyms that in some contexts either will do : *The require-*

ments, or *The requisites, are courage & callousness.* But *requirement* means properly a need, & *requisite* a needed thing : *That sum will meet my requirements,* never *my requisites* ; but, just as the abstract *need* is often used for the concrete *needed thing,* so *requirement* may perhaps always be substituted for *requisite* : *Sponge, toothbrush, & other requirements* will pass, though *requisites* is better & more usual.

requisite, adj. For *essential, necessary,* & r., see ESSENTIAL.

requisition, vb, has -*oned* &c. ; -N-, -NN-.

requite makes -*table* ; see MUTE E.

reredos. Two syllables (rēr′dŏs).

res judicata. Pl. *res judicatae.*

rescind has *rescission,* pron. rĭsĭ′zhn.

rescue makes -*uable* ; see MUTE E.

resentment. *May I, as one in complete sympathy with the general policy of the Government, give expression to the strong resentment I feel to the proposed Bill.* R. *of, at, against,* never *to. Repugnance* ? see ANALOGY, & CAST-IRON IDIOM.

reserve makes -*vable* ; see MUTE E.

reservedly. Four syllables ; -EDLY.

re-set, reset. The verb meaning set again is perhaps better with the hyphen (see RE-), though the other *reset* (receive stolen goods &c.) is not now common enough to make confusion likely.

residence, -cy. See -CE, -CY.

residue, -uum, -ual, -uary. There are two special uses, to each of which one noun & one adjective are appropriated—the legal sense concerned with what remains of an estate after payment of charges, debts, & bequests ; & the mathematical, chemical, & physical sense of what remains after subtraction, combustion, evaporation, &c. The legal noun & adjective are *residue* & *residuary,* the chemical &c. are *residuum* & *residual,* though the differentiation is occasionally infringed in both directions. In more general use, *residuum* implies depreciation, differing from *residue* as

leavings or *sweepings* from *remainder.*
Residuum has plural *-dua.*

resignedly. Four syllables ; -EDLY.
resilience, -cy. Pronounce with
-zĭl-. The very slight difference of
sense—that *-ce* can & *-cy* cannot
mean an *act* of rebounding—does
not, since there is no chance of *-ce's*
being confined to that special sense,
make the existence of the two anything better than an inconvenience ;
it is therefore best to use *-ce* always ;
see -CE, -CY.

resist makes *-tible* ; see -ABLE 2.
For *resistless* see -LESS.
resistance. *You have likened the r.
of Ulster Unionists* to be driven *out
of the Constitution . . . to the opposition . . .* Read *to being driven* ; see
GERUND 3.

resoluble, resolvable. Both are in
use without distinction of meaning,
the first being more a literary, & the
other more a colloquial word. The
negatives should be *irresoluble,* but
unresolvable ; see -ABLE 3 ; in *The
number of irresolvable difficulties is
relatively small,* correct either the
prefix or the suffix.

resolute, -tion, -ble. For pronunciation see LU.
resolution (in prosody). See TECH-
NICAL TERMS.
resolution)(motion. As names for
a proposition that is passed or to be
passed by the votes of an assembly,
the two differ in that the passing of
a motion results in action, & a m.
is that something be done ; while
a resolution is not necessarily more
than an expression of the opinion
that something is true or desirable.
Since, however, opinion often becomes operative, & since also resolutions as well as motions are moved,
i.e. are at least in one sense motions,
the distinction is elusive ; it is
nevertheless, if not too rigidly
applied, of some value.

resolvedly. Four syllables, if used ;
see -EDLY, & use *resolutely* or other
synonym.

resort)(re-sort. See RE(-).
resort, resource, recourse. Confusion between these three is very
frequent, &, since in some senses
each is really synonymous with each,
the confusion is, if not excusable, at
least natural. The usual mistake
is to say *resource* when one of the
others is required. Of the following
examples, the first four are unquestionably wrong ; in the other two,
the most idiomatic expression has
not been chosen :—*Such ships of the
German Navy as remain in the
Southern Seas must now have resource
to the many sparsely-inhabited islands*
(recourse)./*She will not be able to
do so, in Dr Dillon's opinion, without
resource to the sword* (recourse, resorting, resort)./*Surely he was better
employed in plying the trades of
tinker & smith than in having resource
to vice* (recourse)./. . . *should an
autonomous régime for Macedonia
have been agreed to by Turkey without
resource to war* (recourse, resort)./
. . . *binding all Powers to apply an
economic boycott, or, in the last
resource, international force, against
any Power which . . .* (resort)./*The
question of having to send troops to
Teheran is only considered as a last
resort* (resource).
The words are chiefly used in certain established phrases, given below ; when alternatives appear in
brackets, they are to be taken as
less idiomatic. *To resort to ; to have
recourse (resort) to ; without recourse
(resort, resorting) to. Without resources ; at the end of his resources ;
had no other resource left ; the only
resource (resort) ; as a last resource ;
in the last resort. His usual resource
was lying ; his usual recourse (resort)
was to lying ; his usual resort was
Brighton. A man of great or no
resource ; a man of many or no
resources. Golf is a great resource ;
Hoylake is a great resort.*
Without resource in the sense
' irreparably ', though it has been
used by good writers, is rather
a GALLICISM than an English
idiom.

respect. The compound prepositions *with* r. *to, in* r. *of,* should be
used not as often, but as seldom,
as possible ; see REGARD, & PERI-
PHRASIS.

respectfully. See LETTER FORMS.

respective(ly). Delight in these
words is a wide-spread but depraved
taste ; like soldiers & policemen,
they have work to do, but, when
the work is not there, the less we
see of them the better ; of ten
sentences in which they occur, nine
would be improved by their removal.
The evil is considerable enough to
justify an examination at some
length ; examples may be sorted
into five groups : A, in which the
words give information needed by
sensible readers ; B, in which they
give information that may be
needed by fools ; C, in which they
say again what is said elsewhere ;
D, in which they say nothing
intelligible ; E, in which they are
used wrongly for some other word ;
& F, in which they give a positively
wrong sense.

A. RIGHT USES

*There are two other chapters in
which Strauss & Debussy take
respectively a higher & a lower place
than popular opinion accords them.*
But for r., the reader might suppose
that both composers were rated
higher on some points & lower in
others ; r. shows that *higher* goes
with Strauss, & *lower* with Debussy./
*That training colleges for men &
women respectively be provided on
sites at Hammersmith & St Pancras.*
But for r. he might take both
colleges to be for both sexes ; r.
shows that one is for men & the
other for women./*This makes it
quite possible for the apparently
contradictory messages received from
Sofia & Constantinople respectively
to be equally true.* R. shows that the
contradiction is not, e. g., between
earlier & later news from the Near
East, but between news from one
& news from the other town.

B. FOOLPROOF USES

The particular fool for whose benefit each r. is inserted will be defined
in brackets. *Final statements are
expected to be made today by Mr
Bonar Law & M. Millerand in the
House of Commons & the Chamber
of Deputies respectively (r.* takes care
of the reader who does not know
which gentleman or which Parliament is British, or who may imagine
both gentlemen talking in both
Parliaments)./*The Socialist aim in
forcing a debate was to compel the
different groups to define their r.
attitudes* (the reader who may expect
a group to define another group's
attitude)./*It is very far from certain
that any of the names now canvassed
in Wall Street will secure the nomination at the r. Republican & Democratic Conventions* (the reader who
may think Republicans & Democrats hold several united conventions)./*We have not the smallest doubt
that this is what will actually happen,
& we may discuss the situation on
the footing that the respective fates of
these two Bills will be as predicted*
(the reader who has read the prediction without sufficient attention
to remember that it is double).

C. TAUTOLOGICAL USES

After each is given in brackets the
expression or the fact that makes r.
superfluous. *Having collected the
total amount, the collector disburses to
each proper authority its r. quota* (each
. . . its)./*He wants the Secretary for
War to tell the House in what countries they are at present stationed, &
the numbers in each country respectively* (each)./*Madame Sarah Bernhardt & Mrs Bernard Beere respectively made enormous hits in ' As in
a Looking Glass '* (*hits,* plural)./*The
October number of the* Rassegna *is
chiefly remarkable for the r. articles
of the Marchese Crispolto Crispolti
on Pope Benedict V & the War & by
the Marchese Colonna di Cesarò on
Zionism & the Entente* (the mention
of each article immediately after

its author's name)./*In the* Preussische Jahrbücher *for May the most noteworthy articles are those respectively by Werner Weisbach, who writes on Germany in modern Italian political criticism, & by Professor Hans Delbrück, who contributes an extremely interesting comparison between* . . . (as in the last).

D. UNINTELLIGIBLE *r.*

The writing-room, silence-room, & recreation-room, have respectively blue & red arm-chairs./A certain estate is for sale; its grounds border three main roads, namely, Queen's, Belmont, & King's respectively.

E. *r.* FOR ANOTHER WORD

The writers of these mean no more than *both* (to be placed in the second after *Fellow*). *The two nurses' associations respectively organized in Scotland make no secret of their membership./He was a Fellow of Balliol College, Oxford, & of the University of London respectively.*

F. REVERSAL OF SENSE

It is recognized that far too little is known by Englishmen & Americans about their r. countries; in this country there is only one lectureship on American history, & that is at King's College, Strand. This can only mean that Englishmen know too little of England, & Americans know too little of America—which is no doubt true, but is not the truth that the writer wished to convey; ' about each other's countries' would have served both writer & reader.

The simple fact is that *respective*(*ly*) are words seldom needed, but that pretentious writers drag them in at every opportunity for the air of thoroughness & precision they are supposed to give to a sentence.

respire makes *respirable* (rĭspīr´abl is the pronunciation preferred by the OED) ; see MUTE E.

respite, vb, makes -*table* (rĕ'spĭtabl) ; see MUTE E.

resplendence, -cy. The first is recommended ; see -CE, -CY.

restaurant, restaurateur. See FRENCH WORDS.

restore makes -*rable* ; see MUTE E.

restrain)(**re-strain.** See RE(-).

restrainedly. Four syllables; -EDLY.

resume makes -*mable* ; see MUTE E.

résumé. See FRENCH WORDS.

resurrect. See BACK-FORMATION.

resuscitate makes -*itable* ; -ABLE 1.

retable (eccl. n.). Pronounce rĭtā'bl.

retail. Verb rĭtā'l, noun rē'tāl ; see NOUN & VERB ACCENT.

retaliate makes -*iable* ; see -ABLE 1.

retenue. See FRENCH WORDS.

retina. Pl. -*as* or -*ae* ; see LATIN PLURALS, 1.

retire makes -*rable* ; see MUTE E. For *retired admiral* &c., see INTRANSITIVE P.P.

retrace makes -*ceable* ; see -ABLE 1.

retract makes -*tor*; see -OR. Of the two nouns *retrac*(*ta*)*tion*, the shorter is used in all senses, the longer only in the secondary or non-literal ones, i. e., where the meaning is not ' pulling backwards ', but ' apologizing for ' or ' cancelling ' or ' revoking '. *Protrusion & retraction of the tongue*; *Offer & retrac*(*ta*)*tion of terms*; *Publication & retrac*(*ta*)*tion of a libel.*

retrieve makes -*vable* ; see MUTE E. Of the nouns *retrieve & retrieval*, the first is used in particular phrases (*beyond, past, retrieve*), & the other elsewhere (*for the retrieval of his fortunes* &c.).

retro-. In most words the usual pronunciation is rētro ; but in the commonest of all, *retrospect & retrograde*, it is rĕtro ; in words derived from or allied with these two (*retrospective, retrospection, retrogression, retrogressive, retrogradation*) it varies, the tendency being to say rētro if the stress is shifted, as it is by most speakers in all these words, & by all in *retrogradation*, to the third or fourth syllable.

retrograd-, retrogress(-). There are two series : (1) adj. & vb *retrograde*, n. *retrogradation* ; (2) vb *retrogress*, n. *retrogression*, adj. *retrogressive.*

But, as most of us have a preference for *retrograde* as the adj. & *retrogression* as the noun, & no great liking for either verb, there is unfortunately little prospect that one series will oust the other.

retroussé. See FRENCH WORDS.
return. For *the returned exile* &c. see INTRANSITIVE P.P.
rev. See REVEREND.
reveille. See FRENCH WORDS.
revel: *-lled, -lling, -ller*; see -LL-, -L-.
Revelation(s). Though the Bible title is *The Revelation of St John the Divine*, the plural *Revelations* is quite established in ordinary speech, & to take exception to it is PEDANTRY; but *The Revelations* is a confusion of the correct *The Revelation* with the popular *Revelations*.

revenant. See FRENCH WORDS. *The book is thronged, too, with revenants & echoes; old familiar faces reappear, on whom years ago the reader closed the cover with a sigh.* One of the literary critics' needless GALLICISMS.

revenge. For *r.* vb & *avenge, r.* n. & *vengeance,* see AVENGE. *R.* makes *-geable*; see -ABLE 1.
revenue. Pronounce rĕ'vĭnū. ' The stressing *reve'nue,* common or usual during the 17th & 18th centuries & until recently in legal & parliamentary usage, is now obsolescent ' —OED.

reverberate makes *-rable, -tor*; see -ABLE 1, -OR.
revere. The adjective, if used, should be *-rable*; see MUTE E.
reverend, rev., reverent(ial). *Reverend* means deserving reverence, & *reverent* feeling or showing it.
Reverend is abbreviated *Revd* or now usually *Rev.* For ILLITERACIES like *Rev. Smith,* instead of *Rev. J. Smith* or *the Rev. Mr* or *Dr Smith,* see HON. Reporters giving lists of clergy have difficulties with the plural of the abbreviation; but, since *reverend* is an adjective (& not, like *parson* in the now disused ' Parsons Jones & Smith ', a noun), there is neither occasion for nor correctness

in such forms as *Revs & Revds*; *the Rev. J. Smith, W. H. Jones, P. Brown, & others* is the way to put it; if the initials, or some of them, are not known, it should run *The Rev. J. Smith, Messrs Jones & Brown, Dr Robinson, & other clergy.*
Between *reverent & reverential* the difference is much the same as that between PRUDENT & *prudential, reverential* being as applicable to what apes reverence as to what is truly instinct with it, while *reverent* has only the laudatory sense; but *reverential* is often wrongly chosen merely as a LONG VARIANT; when *reverent* would not be out of place, *reverential* is a substitute as much weaker as it is longer.

revers. See FRENCH WORDS.
reverse, n. Such phrases as ' remarks the r. of complimentary ', meaning uncomplimentary remarks, are cumbrous specimens of WORN-OUT HUMOUR.

reverse, vb. For the adjective, *-sable* is recommended rather than *-sible* on general principles; see *-ABLE 2*; negative *unreversable,* or *irreversible*; see -ABLE 3. But *-sible* is the prevalent form.

reversion has various senses, chiefly legal or biological, to be found in any dictionary, & not needing to be set forth here. It suffices to say that they all correspond to the verb *revert,* & not to the verb *reverse,* whose noun is *reversal.* In the following extracts it has been wrongly given the meaning of *reversal*:—*The reversion of our Free Trade policy would, we are convinced, be a great reverse for the working class./But to undertake a complete reversion of the Bolshevik policy is beyond their powers.*

revert makes *-tible*; see -ABLE 2.
revet makes *-tting, -tted*; -T-, -TT-.
reviewal. See -AL NOUNS, & use *review* n.
revile makes *-lable*; see MUTE E.
revisal. See -AL NOUNS. *The Union demands a ' thorough revisal*

of the whole tariff'; why not the established *revision*?

revise makes *-sable*; see MUTE E

REVIVALS. When some half-century ago a method of curtailing debate in the House of Commons was found necessary, there was much talk of the French *clôture*, & it seemed for some years as if the French name would have to be taken over with the French thing; the old English word *closure* had become so unfamiliar that it did not suggest itself readily, & when proposed was not cordially received. ' Moving the closure ' is now familiar enough; but, though the word had not become strictly obsolete, it was so rare as to strike most of us as either a new formation or a revival, & it is at once a good specimen of the kind of revival that justifies the reviver & a good proof of how effectually a more or less disused word may come to life again. To anyone below fifty years of age it would hardly occur that *closure* was on a different footing from *budget* or *motion* or *dissolution* or *division* or any other parliamentary term; &, as to ' the kind of revival ', the occasion may be defined as one on which a name has to be found for a new thing, & a question arises between a foreign word & a disused English one that might well have served if the thing & the word had been alive together.

It is by no means uncommon for very ordinary words to remain latent for long periods. To take only some notable cases in the letter B, the OED records such disappearances of *balsam* (600 years), *bloom* (the iron-foundry word; 600 years), *bosk* (500 years), *braze* (to make of brass; 550 years); but the reappearance of these, except perhaps of *bosk*, was not so much a deliberate revival as a re-emergence out of the obscurity of talk into the light of literature. It is only with deliberate revivals, however, that it is worth while to concern ourselves here—

words like *carven* (carved), *childly*, *dispiteous*, & *dole* (grief), or uses of words in obsolete senses such as *egregious* meaning excellent or *enormity* meaning hugeness. *Carven* seems to have been disused for 300 years, *childly* for 250; *dispiteous* (formerly *despīte/ous* full of despite, now *dis/piteous* unpitying; see MUTE E) for 200; *dole* for a long time in England at least. Revivals like these, & those of obsolete senses, not to fill gaps in a deficient vocabulary as *closure* did, but to impart the charm of quaintness to matter that perhaps needs adornment, are of doubtful benefit either to the language or to those who experiment in them. Is it absurdly optimistic to suppose that what the stream of language leaves stranded as it flows along consists mainly of what can well be done without, & that going back to rake among the debris, except for very special needs, is unprofitable? At any rate, the simple referring of any word to this article is intended to dissuade the reader from using it.

revive makes *-vable*; see MUTE E.

revivify. For inflexions see VERBS IN -IE &c., 6.

revoke makes *revocable* (rĕ'vokabl), *revocation*.

revolt. For *revolted*=insurgent, see INTRANSITIVE P.P.

revolute. See BACK-FORMATION.

revolve makes *-vable*; see MUTE E.

revue. See TECHNICAL TERMS.

Reynard, Rhadamanthus. See SOBRIQUETS.

rhapsodic(al). The short form is now usually limited to the original sense ' of the Greek rhapsodes ', while *-ical* has usually & might well have only the secondary sense of ecstatically expressed or highflown; see -IC(AL).

Rhenish. Pronounce rĕn-.

rhetorical question. See TECHNICAL TERMS.

rhino=rhinoceros. Pl. *-os*, see -O(E)S 5, or (see COLLECTIVES 4) *-o*. See also CURTAILED WORDS.

rhombus. Pl. *-buses* or *-bi*; see LATIN PLURALS.

rhotacism. See TECHNICAL TERMS.

rhyme. 1. For meaning of *r.*, & of *r. royal, feminine r.*, &c., see under TECHNICAL TERMS.

2. **rhyme, rime.** Nothing seems to be gained, except indeed a poor chance of the best of three reputes (learning, pedantry, & error), by changing the established spelling. The OED states that *rhyme* 'finally established itself as the standard form ', & that the revival of *rime* ' was to some extent due to the belief that the word was of native origin & represented OE *rím* ' (=number). *Rhyme* is in fact the same word as *rhythm*, & ultimately from Greek *rhuthmos*, though it came into English from French in the altered form *rime*, & was only later restored, like many other words, to a spelling more suggestive of its origin. It is highly convenient to have for the thing meant a name differently spelt from *rhythm*, but that convenience *rhyme* gives us as fully as *rime*, while it has the other advantage of being familiar to everyone.

RHYTHM. Rhythmless speech or writing is like the flow of liquid from a pipe or tap; it runs with smooth monotony from when it is turned on to when it is turned off, provided it is clear stuff; if it is turbid, the smooth flow is queerly & abruptly checked from time to time, & then resumed. Rhythmic speech or writing is like waves of the sea, moving onward with alternating rise & fall, connected yet separate, like but different, suggestive of some law, too complex for analysis or statement, controlling the relations between wave & wave, waves & sea, phrase & phrase, phrases & speech. In other words, live speech, said or written, is rhythmic, & rhythmless speech is at the best dead. The rhythm of verse is outside the scope of this book, & that of prose cannot be considered in its endless detail; but a few words upon it may commend the subject as worth attention

to some of those who are stirred by the mere name to ribald laughter at fads & aesthetes.

A sentence or a passage is rhythmical if, when said aloud, it falls naturally into groups of words each well fitted by its length & intonation for its place in the whole & its relation to its neighbours. Rhythm is not a matter of counting syllables & measuring the distance between accents; to that misconception is due the ridicule sometimes cast upon it by sensible people conscious of producing satisfactory English but wrongly thinking they do it without the aid of rhythm. They will tell you that they see to it, of course, that their sentences sound right, & that is enough for them; but, if their seeing to it is successfully done, it is because they are, though they do not realize it, masters of rhythm. For, while rhythm does not mean counting syllables & measuring accent-intervals, it does mean so arranging the parts of your whole that each shall enhance, or at the least not detract from, the general effect upon the ear; & what is that but seeing to it that your sentences sound right? Metre is measurement, rhythm is flow, a flow with pulsations as infinitely various as the shape & size & speed of the waves; & infinite variety is not amenable to tabulation such as can be applied to metre; so it is that the prose writer's best guide to rhythm is not his own experiments in, or other people's rules for, particular cadences & stress-schemes, but an instinct for the difference between what sounds right & what sounds wrong. It is an instinct cultivable by those on whom nature has not bestowed it, but on one condition only—that they will make a practice of reading aloud. That test soon divides matter, even for a far from sensitive ear, into what reads well & what reads tamely, haltingly, jerkily, lopsidedly, top-heavily, or otherwise badly; the first is the rhythmical, the other the rhythmless. By the time the reader aloud has discovered that in a really good writer every sentence is rhythmical, while bad writers perpetually offend or puzzle his ear—a discovery, it is true, not very quickly made—, he is capable of passing judgement on each of his own sentences if he will be at the pains to read them, too, aloud. In all this, reading aloud need not be taken quite literally ; there is an art of tacit reading aloud (' My own voice pleased me, & still more the mind's Internal echo of the imperfect sound '), reading with the eye & not the mouth, that is, but being as fully aware of the unuttered sound as of the sense.

Here are, to conclude, a few examples of unrhythmical prose, followed by a single masterpiece of rhythm. If these are read through several times, it will perhaps be found that the splendour of the last, & the meanness of the others, become more conspicuous at each repetition :—*Mr Davies does not let his learning cause him to treat the paintings as material only to be studied by the Egyptologist with a critical & scientific eye.* Never a chance of pausing, or an upward or downward slope, in the four lines./ *But, so far as I could see, nobody carried away burning candles to rekindle with holy fire the lamp in front of the ikon at home, which should burn throughout the year except for the short time it is extinguished in order to receive anew the light that is relit every year throughout the Christian world by Christ's victory over death.* Inordinate length of the last & subordinate member beginning at *except*, which throws the whole sentence off its balance./*But some two or three months ago I asked the hospitality & assistance of your columns to draw public & civic attention to the above position of affairs, & to the fact that the use of the Embankment, as a thoroughfare, was limited, &, in fact, almost prohibited, by the very bad & deterrent condition of the roadway at both ends of the portion from Chelsea to Westminster, the rest of the road being fairly good, of fine proportions, & easily capable of being made into a most splendid boulevard, for all ordinary traffic, as a motor road, in which respect it was dangerously impossible at parts, & as a typical drive or walk.* This writer has produced a single sentence seventeen lines long without a single slip in grammar. That so expert a syntactician should be rhythm-deaf is amazing./*Some simple eloquence distinctly heard, though only uttered in her eyes, unconscious that he read them, as, ' By the death-beds I have tended, by the childhood I have suffered, by our meeting in this dreary house at midnight, by the cry wrung from me in the anguish of my heart, O father, turn to me & seek a refuge in my love before it is too late ! ' may have arrested them.* Of what use to talk of simple eloquence in a sentence contorted & disproportioned like that ?/*Let anyone ask some respectable casuist (the Bishop of London, for instance) whether Lavengro was not far better employed, when in the country, at tinkering & smithery than he would have been in running after all the milkmaids in Cheshire/, though tinkering is in general considered a very ungenteel employment/, & smithery little better/, notwithstanding that an Orcadian poet, who wrote in Norse about 800 years ago, reckons the latter among nine noble arts which he possessed/, naming it along with playing at chess, on the harp, & ravelling runes/, or as the original has it, ' treading runes '/— that is, compressing them into small compass by mingling one letter with another/, even as the Turkish caligraphists ravel the Arabic letters/, more especially those who write talismans.* One of the decapitable sentences from which if piece after piece is chopped off at the end the remainder after each chop is one degree less ill-balanced than before.

And the king was much moved, & went up to the chamber over the gate

*& wept : & as he went, thus he said :
O my son Absalom, my son, my son
Absalom ! would God I had died for
thee, O Absalom, my son, my son !*

rhythmic(al). Both forms are too
common to justify any expectation
of either's disappearance ; yet there
is no marked differentiation ; what
there is perhaps amounts to this,
that *-al* is the more ordinary
pedestrian term, & therefore better
suited for the merely classifying use
(*& other rhythmical devices* : cf. *so
rhythmic a style*). See -IC(AL).

riant. See FRENCH WORDS.

ribbon, riband. The second is ' now
archaic '—OED.

ribes. Pronounce rī'bēz.

riches. *But the promoters will certainly not need to go back to ancient
history for it ; they will have an*
embarrassment of riches *from the
immediate past.* See GALLICISMS.

rick (twist, sprain). See WRICK.

rickety, not *-tty* ; see -T-, -TT-.

ricochet. The spelling, accent, &
pronunciation recommended are :
ricochet (rĭ'koshā) ; *ricocheted* (rĭ'ko-
shād) ; *ricocheting* (rĭkoshā'ĭng). Cf.
CROCHET, CROQUET.

rictus. Pl. *-uses* or *-ūs*, not *-i* ; see
LATIN PLURALS.

rid. There is no clear line between
rid & *ridded* in past inflexions, but
the prevailing usage is : past tense,
ridded (*When he ridded*, sometimes
rid, the world of his presence) ; p.p.
as active, *ridded* (*We have ridded*, or
rid, the land of robbers) ; p.p. as
passive, *rid* (*I thought myself well rid,*
rarely *ridded, of him*).

ride makes *-dable* ; see MUTE E.

rider (corollary). TECHNICAL TERMS.

ridge makes *-gy* ; see -EY & -Y.

ridicule, vb, has *-lable* ; MUTE E.

rifacimento. Pronounce -fahchĭ-.
Pl. *-os*, see -O(E)S 6, or *-ti* (-ē).

right. 1. *R. away* in the sense ' at
once ', ' without delay ', comes from
America, & is still far from comfortable in England. 2. *Right* (*right-
en*, vv. See -EN VERBS. 3. *Right-
(ly).* advv. The adverb *right*, in the

senses ' properly ', ' correctly ', is
being squeezed out by the tendency to UNIDIOMATIC -LY. It is
well, before using *rightly* in these
senses, to consider whether *right* is
not better, though usage is much less
decided than with many alternative
adverbs of the kind. In all the
following types *rightly* is possible,
but *right* is better :—*He guessed* or
answered right (cf. *He rightly guessed
that it was safe* or *answered twenty-
seven*) ; *You did right in apologizing*
or *to apologize* (cf. *You rightly
apologized*) ; *If I remember right*
(cf. *I cannot rightly recollect*) ; *I hope
we are going right* ; *If it was tied
right, it will hold* ; *Teach him to hold
his pen right.* Correct accordingly :
*Mr Lloyd George does rightly in
calling them to the aid of a larger
conception.*

righteous. Pron. rī'chus (or rī'tyus).

rigid makes *-est* ; see -ER & -EST 4.

rigour, but *rigorous* ; see -OUR &
-OR, -OUR- & -OR-.

rile makes *-lable* ; see MUTE E.

rilievo. See RELIEVO.

rime. See RHYME.

rinderpest. Pronounce rĭn-.

ring, vb. Both *rang* & *rung* are
still used for the past tense, but
rang is much commoner, & likely to
become universal.

ringlet makes *-eted, -ety* ; -T-, -TT-.

rinse makes *-sable* ; see MUTE E.

riot makes *-oted, -oting* ; -T-, -TT-.

riposte. See FRENCH WORDS.

ripply, not *-ley* ; see -EY & -Y.

rise. 1. For *the risen sun* &c. see
INTRANSITIVE P.P. 2. *It is hoped
that the Joint Committee will r. equal
to the occasion, & give India a constitution which . . .* Either *r. to* or *be
equal to* ; CAST-IRON IDIOM.

risible. 1. Pronounce rĭz'ĭbl. 2.
R. is very liable to MISPRINTING as
visible. 3. *Were I to send my library
of sixty specimens to auction I really
expect some risible bid of, say, ten or
fifteen pounds would be offered.* The
word has nearly perished except in
the special sense ' of laughter '
(*r. faculty, nerves, muscles*, &c.). To

use it in the sense ' ridiculous ', correct enough, but now unfamiliar, is a REVIVAL not to be recommended; the word that has taken its place is DERISORY.

risky, for French *risqué,* is an undesirable GALLICISM.

risqué, rissole. See FRENCH WORDS.

ritardando. Pl. *-os* ; see -O(E)S 6.

rival, vb, has *-lled, -lling* ; -LL-, -L-.

rive. Past tense *rived* ; p.p. *riven,* rarely *rived.*

rivel makes *-lled, -lling* ; -LL-, -L-.

rivet has *-eted, -eting, -eter* ; -T-, -TT-.

rivière. See FRENCH WORDS.

roast. 1. The use of the p.p. *roast* is very narrowly limited : *roast beef* or *hare,* but *roasted coffee-berries* or *cheeks* ; *a roast joint,* but *a well roasted joint* ; *is better roast(ed) than boiled,* but *should certainly be roasted.* 2. For *rule the r.,* see RULE.

Robby, -ie. See -EY, -IE, -Y.

robe, vb, makes *-bable* ; see MUTE E.

robe-de-chambre. FRENCH WORDS.

robust makes *-er, -est* ; -ER & -EST.

robustious. One of the words whose continued existence depends upon a quotation (*Hamlet* III. ii. 10).

rococo. See TECHNICAL TERMS.

rodomontade, not *rho-.*

role, rôle. Though the word is etymologically the same as *roll,* meaning the roll of MS. that contained an actor's part, the differentiation is too useful to be sacrificed by spelling always *roll.* But, there being no other word *role* from which it has to be kept distinct, both the italics & the accent might well be abandoned. As to the sanctity of the French form, see MORALE.

Roman-Catholic, Roman Catholic. *He is a Roman Catholic* ; *the Roman-Catholic faith* ; *in Roman-Catholic countries.* In the noun there is no need of or justification for the hyphen (see HYPHENS 3 B) ; in the compound adjective it is necessary or desirable (see HYPHENS 3 D).

Romanes, Romany, (gypsy language). Pronounce rŏ'mănĕz, -nĭ.

Romansh, Roumansh, Rumans(c)h.

The OED treats the first as the standard form.

Rome makes *Romish* ; see MUTE E.

rondeau, rondel. See TECHNICAL TERMS ; &, for pl. of *rondeau,* -X.

rondo. Pl. *-os* ; see -O(E)S 6.

Röntgen. Pronounce rŭ'ntyen.

roof. Pl. *-fs* ; see -VE(D).

roomful. Pl. *-ls* ; see -FUL.

root (philol.). See TECHNICAL TERMS.

root, rout, (poke about). The second form is called by the OED an ' irregular variant of ' the first. The two, with the other verb *root* directly connected with the noun, naturally cause some difficulty. It would be a convenient differentiation if the spelling *root* could be confined to contexts in which the notion of roots is essential, & *rout* were adopted where search or bringing to light is the point. So we should get rooting up trees, rooting out weeds or sedition, but routing about in a lumber-room or among papers, routing out secrets, routing a person out of bed, routing up a recluse or a reference. Pigs, being equally intent on roots & search, may root or rout indifferently.

rope makes *-pable, -py* ; see MUTE E.

roquefort. See FRENCH WORDS.

roquet. For spelling & pronunciation of inflexions see CROCHET.

rosary, -ery, (rose-garden). The first is the old word (from 15th c. in OED), direct from Latin *rosarium.* The second is a 19th-c. formation made presumably, from *rose* & *-ery,* by someone not aware that *rosary* has this sense. *Rose-garden* or *-bed* is recommended for ordinary use, & *rosary* for verse.

Rosicrucians, or *Brethren of the Rosy Cross,* much talked of in the 17th c., paid homage by their name not to anything symbolized by cross or rose, but to an alleged 15th-c. founder named *Rosenkreuz* (= cross of roses). ' The writers who posed as Rosicrucians were moral & religious reformers, & utilized the technicalities of chemistry (alchemy),

& the sciences generally, to make known their opinions, there being a flavour of mysticism or occultism promotive of inquiry & suggestive of hidden meanings discernible or discoverable only by adepts '— Enc. Brit.

rosin is by origin merely a form of *resin* changed in sound & spelling ; but the two are now so far differentiated that *resin* is usual for the liquid in or taken from the tree, & as the general chemical term for substances having certain qualities, while *rosin* denotes the distilled solid. *R.* makes *rosined, -iny* ; -N-, -NN-.

roster. Though the dictionaries are almost unanimous for rŏ′ster only, the army, which is the chief user of the word, says rō′ster ; & Skeat remarks : ' The *o* is properly long : pron. *roaster* '.

rŏstrum. Pl. : in the original sense (ship's beak), usually *-ra* ; in the secondary sense (pulpit or platform), *-rums* or *-ra*. See -UM, & LATIN PLURALS.

rotate makes *rotatable* (see -ABLE 1), *-tor* (see -OR).

rota(to)ry. *Rotary* is not, like *authoritive, deteriate,* & *pacifist,* a shortening of a more correct form, but is a separate word : *rota* wheel gives *rotarius* (English *rotary*) wheel-like ; *roto* revolve gives *rotatorius* (English *rotatory*) revolving &c. On the other hand there is no important difference in meaning either essential or customary, & therefore the short *rotary* should be preferred & *rotatory* avoided as a SUPERFLUOUS WORD.

rôti. See FRENCH WORDS.

rotten makes *-nness*. For *something r. in the state of Denmark*, see IRRELEVANT ALLUSION.

rotund makes *-er, -est* ; -ER & -EST.

roturier, roué, rouge et noir. See FRENCH WORDS.

rough(en), vv. See -EN VERBS ; but the relation between this pair demands some further treatment, 1. The intransitive verb (=become rough) is always *roughen*, except

that the addition of *up* occasionally enables *rough* to serve (*the sea, his bristles, its scales, their tempers, began to rough up*). 2. In the simple transitive senses also (=make rough), *roughen* is usual, but if *up* is added *rough* is preferred, & *rough* by itself is the word for arming horseshoes against slipping (*rough the shoes* or *the horse*). 3. In the other transitive senses of to treat roughly or shape roughly (the latter usually with adverbs, *in, off, out*), the verb is *rough* : *rough a horse,* break it in ; *rough a calf,* harden it by exposure ; *rough a person,* abuse or maltreat him ; *rough in the outlines* ; *rough off timber* ; *rough out a scheme* ; *rough a lens,* shape without polishing it. 4. To take things in the rough is to *rough it.*

roulade, rouleau. See FRENCH WORDS. *Rouleau* has pl. *-s* (or -x).

roundel, roundelay. Not, like *rondeau* & *rondel,* precise terms. *Roundel* is sometimes used loosely for *rondeau-or-rondel,* & see TECHNICAL TERMS ; *roundelay* is defined in the OED as ' A short simple song with a refrain '.

rouse makes *-sable* ; see MUTE E.

rout (poke about). See ROOT.

route is pronounced, in military phrases such as *route-march, column of r.,* rowt.

routine makes *routinism, -ist* (rōōtē′n-) ; see MUTE E.

rowan. The OED pronunciation is rō′an, Scotch row′an.

rowel makes *-lled, -lling* ; -LL-, -L-.

rowlock. Pronounce rŭ′lok.

-R-, -RR-. Monosyllables ending in -r double it before suffixes beginning with vowels if the sound preceding it is a single vowel (a, e, i, o, u, y), but not if it is a diphthong or a double vowel : *barring* but *nearing, stirred* but *chaired, currish* but *boorish*. Words of more than one syllable follow the rule for monosyllables if their last syllable is accented (with the exception noted below), but otherwise do not double the r ; *preferred* but *proffered, inter-*

ring but *entering*, *abhorrent* but *motoring*. Exception : *confer, infer, prefer, refer, & transfer*, though accented on the last, give adjectives in *-erable*, & shift the accent to the first syllable : *prĕ'ferable* &c. ; see CONFER(R)ABLE.

rubefy, -bify. The first is better, on the analogy of *liquefy, putrefy, stupefy*, than the second on the analogy of *horrify, terrify*, especially in view of *rubefacient & rubefaction* always so spelt.

rubricate makes *-cable, -tor* ; see -ABLE 1, -OR.

ruche. See FRENCH WORDS.

rucksack. Pronounce rŏŏ'ksăk.

ruddle (red ochre, &, as verb, colour with this) has the two variants *raddle & reddle*, of which *raddle* is the form usually preferred as a contemptuous synonym for rouge & rouging, & *reddle* is occasional instead of *ruddle*. *Ruddle* itself is applied chiefly to sheep-marking.

rude makes *rudish* ; see MUTE E.

ruff (bird) has fem. *reeve*.

ruination is not, like *flirtation, floatation, & botheration*, a HYBRID DERIVATIVE, being regularly formed from *ruinate* ; but it now has the effect of a slangy emphatic lengthening of the noun *ruin* ; this is only because the parent verb *ruinate*, which was common in serious use 1550–1700, is no longer heard ; but the result is that *ruination* is better avoided except in facetious contexts.

rule. 1. The verb makes *-lable* ; see MUTE E. 2. *R. of three & r. of thumb* should not be hyphened except when used as compound adjectives ; see HYPHENS (*Rule of thumb). 3. *Rule the roast (roost)*. The OED gives no countenance to *roost*, & does not even recognize that the phrase ever takes that form ; but most unliterary persons say *roost & not roast* ; I have just inquired of three such, & been informed that they never heard of *rule the roast*, & that the reference is to a cock keeping his hens in order.

Against this tempting piece of popular etymology the OED offers us nothing more succulent than ' None of the early examples throw any light on the precise origin of the expression '. In seven out of the eight pre-18th-c. examples quoted the spelling is not *roast* but *rost* or *roste* ; but the OED philologists would doubtless tell us that *rost(e)* could represent Old-French *rost* (roast), & could not represent Old-English *hrŏst* (roost). Writers should take warning, at any rate, that *rule the roast* is the orthodox spelling, & that when they have written it the compositor must be watched.

rumbustious. See FACETIOUS FORMATIONS.

ruminate makes *-nable, -tor* ; see -ABLE 1, -OR.

rumour. See -OUR & -OR.

run. For *fresh-run salmon* &c., see INTRANSITIVE P.P.

rune. See TECHNICAL TERMS.

rung (past tense). See RING.

rupture makes *-rable* ; see MUTE E.

ruridecanal. Pron. rooridikā'nal.

ruse, rusé. See FRENCH WORDS.

rush ring (*I'll marry thee with a* &c.). No hyphen ; HYPHENS 3 B.

russety, not *-tty* ; see -T-, -TT-.

rusticate makes *-cable, -tor* ; see -ABLE 1, -OR.

ruthless. For the war-time use as translation of German *rücksichtslos* (regardless or reckless, not r.), see FRIGHTFULNESS.

S

'S. 1. For *for conscience' sake* &c., see SAKE.

2. For *Achilles', Jones's*, &c., see POSSESSIVE PUZZLES.

3. For *England's* &c. & *of England* &c., see 'S INCONGRUOUS, & PERSONIFICATION 1. *In no part of the world, says* Ontario's Prime Minister, *will the returned soldier find a more appreciative public than in this province.*

4. For such corrections as *to use a word of Coleridge* instead of *of Coleridge's*, see OUT OF THE FRYING-PAN.

Sabbath day. No hyphen ; see HYPHENS 3 B.

Sabbatic(al). The long form is now rare ; see -IC(AL).

sabot makes -*oted*, pron. -ōd.

sabotage. See FRENCH WORDS.

sabre, -ber. See -RE & -ER.

sabretache, sabreur. See FRENCH WORDS.

sac is a medical & biological word, not a dressmaker's or tailor's ; see SAC(QUE).

saccharin(e). See -IN & -INE ; there is, however, some convenience in using *saccharin* for the noun & *saccharine* for the adjective.

sacerdotage. See FACETIOUS FORMATIONS.

sachem. The OED puts first the pronunciation sā'chĭm.

sachet. See FRENCH WORDS.

sack, dismiss(al), having been on record for a hundred years, may claim promotion from the slang to the colloquial class.

sac(que). For the garment, *sack* is the right form. The other spellings are pseudo-French, wrong in different degrees : there is no French word *sacque* ; there is a French word *sac*, but it is not, as the English *sack* is or has been, the name for a particular garment.

sacrarium. Pl. -*ia*.

sacred makes -*est* ; see -ER & -EST 4.

sacrifice makes -*ceable* ; see -ABLE 1. For *the supreme &c. s.*, see STOCK PATHOS.

sacrilegious. So spelt, & pronounced -ē'jus. It is often both mis-spelt & mispronounced from confusion with *religious*.

saga. See TECHNICAL TERMS.

sage. For *the s. of Chelsea*, see SOBRIQUETS.

sago. Pl. -*os* ; see -O(E)S 3.

Sahib. Pronounce sah'-ĭb. Fem. (European lady), *Memsahib*.

said. 1. *S.*=aforesaid. 2. *S. he & had s. he.* 3. Substitutes for *s. he.*

1. (*The*) *said.* In legal documents, phrases like ' the s. Robinson ', ' s. dwelling-house ', are traditional.

Jocose imitation of this use (*regaling themselves on half-pints at the s. village hostelries*), still not uncommon, though no longer indulged in by writers not desperately anxious to relieve conscious dullness, is to be classed with WORN-OUT HUMOUR.

2. *S. he, s. N.* or *M.*, placed after the words spoken, is entirely unobjectionable ; the ingenuity displayed by some writers (see 3) in avoiding what they needlessly fear will bore their readers is superfluous. But two points should be noticed : the sprightliness of *Said N.* or *M.* placed before instead of after the words said, & the ponderousness of *had said &c.* instead of plain *said*, are alike intolerable. *Said a Minister :*—' *American interests are not large enough in Morocco to induce us to . . .*'/' *I won't plot anything extra against Tom* ', *had said Isaac.* And see INVERSION s.f.

3. Substitutes for *s. he.* Many verbs, such as *whispered, cried, shouted, asked, answered, continued, groaned*, imply or suggest the use of words, & are naturally used after what is uttered, as equivalents of *said* with an adverb. With these (*asked Jones &c.*) to relieve the monotony of *said he*, no writer need be afraid of boring ; he may safely abstain from the very tiresome MANNERISM initiated perhaps by Meredith (' Ah ', fluted Fenellan), & now staled by imitation :—'*Hand on heart ?* ' *she doubted.*/'*Need any help ?* ' *husked A.*/'*They're our best revenue* ', *defended B.*/'*I know his kind* ', *fondly remembered C.*/'*Why shouldn't he ?* ' *scorned D.*/'*It's a lie* ', *perfunctorily denied E.*/'*He can win her love* ', *she faintly surrendered.*/'*Does it never occur to you* ' *I probed,* ' *that all your labour may be in vain ?* '.

sail. For *plain sailing*, see PLAIN. By the side of the usual but abnormal *sailor*, the normal agent-noun *sailer* exists for use in such contexts as *She* (ship) *is a slow sailer.*

Saint. *St* is better than *St.* for the

abbreviation (see PERIOD IN ABBR.) ; Pl. *Sts* or *SS.*

St Stephen's. See SOBRIQUETS.

sake. *For God's s., for mercy's s., for Jones's s., for Phyllis's s.* ; but when the enclosed word is both a common noun & one whose possessive is a syllable longer than its subjective, the s of the possessive is not used ; an apostrophe is often, but not always, written ; *for conscience s., for goodness' s., for their office s., for peace' s.*

salable. So spelt ; see MUTE E.

salad days (one's raw youth) is one of the phrases whose existence depends on single passages (see *Ant. & Cleop.* I. v. 73). Whether the point is that youth, like salad, is raw, or that salad is highly flavoured & youth loves high flavours, or that innocent herbs are youth's food as milk is babes' & meat is men's, few of those who use the phrase could perhaps tell us ; if so, it is fitter for parrots' than for human speech.

salamander. This, *gnome, sylph, & nymph,* are spirits of fire, earth, air, & water, in Paracelsus's system.

salary makes *salaried.*

Salic, Salique. In the most frequent use, i.e. in the name of the law excluding females from dynastic succession, 'still often spelt *Salique* & pronounced salē'k '—OED.

salicylic. So spelt.

saline. Pronounce sā'līn, & see FALSE QUANTITY.

salivary. Pronounce să'lĭvarĭ, & see FALSE QUANTITY (on *doctrinal*).

salle-à-manger, d'attente. See FRENCH WORDS.

sallow makes *-er, -est* ; *-ER & -EST* 2.

Sally. So spelt ; see *-EY, -IE, -Y.*

sally, vb. For inflexions see VERBS IN *-IE* &c., 6.

salmi. See FRENCH WORDS.

salmon. See COLLECTIVES 1, 4.

Salomonic has not, like *Salomon,* passed out of use ; but *Solomonic* is now the usual form.

salon. See FRENCH WORDS.

Salonica. Pronounce săloni'ka (or -ē'ka), not salŏ'nĭka.

saloon. *S. deck, s. pistol, s. rifle.* No hyphen ; see HYPHENS 3 B.

salt. *A bath of salt water* (no hyphen), but *a salt-water bath* ; see HYPHENS 3 B, 3 A.

saltus. Pl. *saltūs* ; see -US.

salubrious, salutation, salute. For pronunciation see LU.

salve. The noun & verb meaning remedy are pronounced sahv. The verb meaning save or rescue is an entirely separate one, a BACK-FORMATION from *salvage,* pronounced sălv. Both verbs make *-vable* ; see MUTE E. The Latin word meaning Hail !, & used chiefly as the name of a R.-C. antiphon, is pronounced să'lvē.

salvo (both nouns, reservation & volley). Pl. *-os* ; see -O(E)S 6.

sal volatile. Pronounce săl volă'tĭlĭ.

sambo (half-breed). Pl. *-os*; -O(E)s 6.

same. *S.* or *the s.,* in the sense the aforesaid thing(s) or person(s), as a substitute for a pronoun (*it, him, her, them, they*) is one of the usages whose effect is discussed in ILLITER-ACIES. It has the peculiarity that it occurs chiefly in writing, not often in speech, & yet is avoided by all who have any skill in writing. As the working man puts on his Sunday clothes to be photographed, so the unliterary adorns himself with ' (the) same ' when he is to appear in print ; each seems bent on giving the worst possible impression of himself. In all the extracts below, the writers would have shown themselves much more at their ease if they had been content with *it, them,* or other pronoun. *Shops filled to the doors with all kinds of merchandise & people eager to acquire* t. s./*Are the purveyors of ' bowlers ' able to meet the sudden requirements for s. likely to arise immediately on the signing of peace ?*/*Again, the doctors declaim against patients by contract, while they largely themselves set up the machinery for carrying on* t. s. (the system ?)./*If not directly, at least through the official presence of their representatives, or by a chosen delega-*

tion of t. s./*The atmospheric engine, by which work was done by the heating & expanding of atmospheric pressure air by the combustion of hydrocarbons in* s./*Sir,—Having in mind the approaching General Election, it appears to me that the result of* s. *is likely to be as much a farce as the last.*/*I again withdraw the statements, & express my regret for having made* t. s./*Sir,—Mr Asquith, in his speech at the West Indian Club dinner, & you in your comments on* s., *make reference to the Parliamentary grants.*/ *Mr Lloyd George has, by this time, considered almost every valid objection or grievance, & has promised amendments or favourable consideration touching* t. s./*I consider this question as already settled, & consequently any further discussion on* s. *is pure waste of time.*/*When is a majority a Coalition majority ?—When the parties composing* s. *refuse to unite with the Opposition.*/ *I can only confirm the statement of the transfer, but* t. s. *will be made slowly.*

samiel. See WIND, n.

samite. Pronounce să'mīt.

Samson. So spelt in *Judges*, and as a generic name.

samurai. Pron. să'mōŏrī. Pl. same.

sanat-, sanit-. The chief words, as they should be spelt, are :—*sanatorium* a healing-place ; *sanative & sanatory* curative ; *sanitary* conducive to wholesomeness ; *sanitation* securing of wholesomeness ; *sanitarian* a believer in sanitation. *Sanitarium* is a possible but now undesirable equivalent of *sanatorium* ; *sanitorium, sanatarium, & sanitory*, are wrong.

sanbenito. Pronounce -ē'tō. Pl. *-os* ; see -O(E)S 6.

sanctify. For inflexions see VERBS IN -IE &c., 6.

sanction, n. The popular sense (permission, authorization, countenance, consent) has so far prevailed over the more original senses still current especially in Law & Ethics that it is worth while to draw attention to these. The s. of a rule

or a system is the consideration that operates to enforce or induce compliance with it ; the death penalty is the s. of the law against murder. The OED quotes from T. Fowler : ' Physical ss. are the pleasures & pains which follow naturally on the observance or violation of physical laws, the ss. employed by society are praise & blame, the moral ss. . . . are . . . the approval & disapproval of conscience ; lastly, the religious ss. are either the fear of future punishment, & the hope of future reward, or, to the higher religious sense, simply the love of God, & the dread of displeasing Him '.

sanction, vb, makes *-oned* &c. ; see -N-, -NN-.

sandal makes *-lled* ; see -LL-, -L-.

sand-blind is neither (like, say, *purblind*) a current word, nor (like, say, *bat-blind*) intelligible at sight. Its modern existence depends on one passage (*M. of V.* II. ii. 35-80), & it can rank only as an ARCHAISM.

Sandy. So spelt ; see -EY, -IE, -Y.

sang-de-bœuf, sang-froid. See FRENCH WORDS.

sanguine is in danger of being superseded by the very inferior OPTIMISTIC. Candour, however, compels the admission that *optimistic, optimism, & optimist*, have the advantage in mechanical convenience over *sanguine, sanguineness, & sanguine person*.

Sanhedrim, -in. ' The incorrect form *sanhedrin* . . . has always been in England (from the 17th c.) the only form in popular use '—OED.

sans. As an English word, pronounce sănz ; but it is at best WARDOUR - STREET English : *The poet whom he met* sans *hat & coat one four-o'clock-in-the-morning*. For s. *cérémonie, sansculotte(rie), s. doute, façon, gêne, peur* &c., *phrase, -souci*, see FRENCH WORDS.

Sanskrit. So spelt.

Santa Claus. Pronounce -awz ; not a feminine name, but from a Dutch-dialect form of *Saint (Ni)cholas*.

sapid, unlike its negative *insipid*, is a merely LITERARY WORD.

sapient. Chiefly a LITERARY WORD, & usually ironical.

saponaceous, apart from its use in chemistry, is a favourite POLY-SYLLABIC HUMOUR word.

sapor. A merely LITERARY WORD ; for the spelling *-or*, see -OUR & -OR.

Sapphic, Sappho. Pronounce săf-.

Sapphics. See TECHNICAL TERMS.

sarcasm does not necessarily involve irony, & irony has often no touch of sarcasm. But irony, or the use of expressions conveying different things according as they are interpreted, is so often made the vehicle of sarcasm, or the utterance of things designed to hurt the feelings, that in popular use the two are much confused. The essence of sarcasm is the intention of giving pain by (ironical or other) bitter words. See also IRONY, & HUMOUR.

sarcoma. Pl. *-ata*.

sarcophagus. Pl. *-ī* ; for pronunciation see GREEK G.

sardine (stone ; *Rev.* iv. 3). Pronounce sar′dīn.

sardonic. See HUMOUR for some rough distinction between this, *cynical, sarcastic*, &c. The word is perhaps over-used in NOVELESE :— *The hollow laugh or at least the sardonic grin that is a sine qua non of every self-respecting poisoner.*

sargasso. Pl. *-os* ; see -O(E)S 3.

sarissa. Pl. *-ae*.

sartorial. See PEDANTIC HUMOUR.

Sassenach. Pronounce with -ch as in *loch*.

Satanic(al). The *-al* form ' now rare '—OED ; see -IC(AL).

satchel makes *-lled* ; see -LL-, -L-.

sate makes *-table* ; see MUTE E. For *sateless*, see -LESS.

sati. For this improvement on *suttee*, see PRIDE OF KNOWLEDGE.

satiate. Adj. *-at*, vb *-āt* ; see PARTICIPLES 5 B. The verb makes *-tiable* ; see -ABLE 1.

satiety. Pronounce satī′ĭtĭ.

satire. For rough distinction from some synonyms, see HUMOUR.

satiric(al). The senses addicted to, intending, good at, marked by, satire are peculiar to the long form (*a -al rogue* ; *you are pleased to be -al* ; *with -al comments* ; *a -al glance*). In the merely classifying sense of or belonging to satire (*the —— poems of Pope* ; *the Latin —— writers*), either form may be used, but *-ic* is commoner. This differentiation might well be hastened by deliberate support ; but the line of demarcation between the two groups is not always clear. See -IC(AL).

satiric)(satyric. The two spellings represent two different & unconnected words ; *satyric*, which is in learned or literary use only, means of satyrs, & especially, in *s. drama* (a form of Greek play), having a satyr chorus.

satirize makes *-zable* ; see MUTE E.

satisfy. For inflexions see VERBS IN -IE &c., 6.

satrap. Pronounce sā′trăp.

saturate makes *-rable* ; see -ABLE 1.

Saturday. For the adverbial use (*shall see you S.*), see FRIDAY.

Saturnalia. See LATIN PLURALS 3. The word is originally plural, but, as being the name of a festival, comes to be construed, both in literal & metaphorical use, more often as singular (*the S. was*, or *were, at hand* ; *now follows a s. of crime*). When a real plural is required (*the sack of Magdeburg, the French Revolution, & other such s. of slaughter*), the form is *-ia*, not *-ias*.

Saturnian verse. TECHNICAL TERMS.

satyr. See FAUN for distinctions.

satyric. See SATIRIC.

sauce. Combinations such as *mint s.* should be two words unhyphened if, as is usual, the accent remains on *sauce* ; see HYPHENS 3 B. The verb makes *-ceable* ; see -ABLE 1.

sauce piquante. See FRENCH WORDS.

sausage roll. Accent the *roll*, & use no hyphen ; see HYPHENS 3 B.

sauté, sauve-qui-peut. See FRENCH WORDS.

savannah. So spelt.

savant, savate. See FRENCH WORDS.

save (except). 1. For *s. & except*, see PLEONASM 2. 2. Trench (*English Synonyms*, 4th ed., 1858), writing on 'except, excepting, but, save', has no more to say of the last than that ' " Save " is almost exclusively limited to poetry '. He would have a surprise if he were to see a newspaper of 1920 ; we can still say that it ought to be, but no longer that it is, almost limited to poetry. Though nearly everyone uses *except* or *but*, not *s.*, in speaking, & perhaps everyone in thinking, & though the natural or ' dominant ' word *except* is neither undignified nor inferior in clearness, journalists have made up their minds that it is not good enough for print, & very mistakenly prefer to translate it, irrespective of context, into *s.* ; *s.* is becoming a FORMAL WORD, like the reporter's invariable *proceed* for *go*. Does anyone not a writer—& does any good writer—think that the substitution of the formal *s.* for the natural *except* or *but* in the following sentences has improved them ?—*The handful of ship's officers could do nothing s. summon the aid of a detachment of the Civic Guard./ One marked trait of Dr Griffith John has been displayed in his refusal to leave China s. at long intervals./ The spur proved to be so admirably adapted to its purpose that it has existed unaltered, s. in detail, to the present day./ So completely surrounded by other buildings as to be absolutely invisible—s. from a balloon or an aeroplane./ There can be no question, s. in the minds possibly of the Tariff Reform fanatics, that Mr Balfour's retirement is a heavy blow to the Unionist Party./ The baby takes no special harm, s. that it is allowed to do as it likes, & begins to walk too soon./ The increased rates will take effect on the Underground lines, s. on one stretch between Bow & Barking.*

save, vb, makes *-vable* ; see MUTE E. *S. the mark* (with variants *God s.*, *bless, God bless, the mark*) is a stylistic toy, of which no-one can be said to know, though different people make different guesses at, the original meaning. The OED's description of it, as it now survives, is : ' In modern literary use (after some of the examples in Shakspere), an expression of indignant scorn appended to a quoted expression or to a statement of fact '.

savoir faire, savoir vivre. See FRENCH WORDS.

savour(y). So spelt ; -OUR & -OR.

saw has p.p. *sawn*, rarely *sawed*.

Sawney, s-. So spelt ; -EY, -IE, -Y.

SAXONISM is a name for the attempt to raise the proportion borne by the originally & etymologically English words in our speech to those that come from alien sources. The Saxonist forms new dèrivatives from English words to displace established words of similar meaning but Latin descent ; revives obsolete or archaic English words for the same purpose ; allows the genealogy of words to decide for him which is the better of two synonyms. Examples of the first kind are FOREWORD (earliest OED quotation, 1842) for *preface, folklore* (1846) & *birdlore* (1830) for *tradition & ornithology*, BODEFUL (1813) for *ominous* ; of the second, BETTERMENT for improvement, HAPPENINGS for events, *english* for translate (into English), FOLK for people, & FOREBEAR for ancestor ; of the third, BELITTLE & *depreciate, wheelman & cyclist, love & charity* (1 *Corinthians* xiii, A. V. & R. V.), *burgess* or *burgher & citizen*. The wisdom of this nationalism in language—at least in so thoroughly composite a language as English— is very questionable ; we may well doubt whether it benefits the language, & that it does not benefit the style of the individual, who may or may not be prepared to sacrifice himself for the public good, is pretty clear. Here is the opinion of the *Dictionary of National Biography* on Freeman's English : ' His desire to use so far as possible only words which are purely English limited his vocabulary & was some drawback to his sentences '. The truth is perhaps that conscious deliberate Saxonism is folly, that the choice or rejection of particular words should depend not on their descent but on considerations of expressiveness, intelligibility, brevity, euphony, or ease of handling, & yet that any writer who becomes aware that the Saxon or native English element in what he writes is small will do well to take the fact as a danger signal. But the way to act on that signal is not to translate his Romance words into Saxon ones ; it is to avoid abstract & roundabout & bookish phrasing whenever the nature of the thing to be said does not require it. We can almost see the writer of the following sentence striking out *improvement* (which did not clash with *better* a few words later) & inserting his Saxon *betterment* in its place : *Instead of breaking heads over a* betterment *of Anglo-German relations, it would be* better *to study British finance*. But *betterment* has no single advantage over *improvement* except its Saxonism. It was once, indeed, a current English word, but that was as long ago as the 17th century. In recent times it has come back to us from America as a technicality in the tenant-&-landlord business, & now the Saxonists are making their readers uncomfortable by thrusting it into sentences like the one quoted.

saying. ' As the s. is ', or ' goes ', is often used by simple people, speaking or writing, who would fain assure us that the phrase they have allowed to proceed from their lips or pen is by no means typical of their taste in language ; no ; it only happens to be ' so expressive ' that one may surely condescend to it for once. Well, *qui s'excuse s'accuse* ; if the rest of their behaviour does not secure them from insulting suspicions, certainly the apology will not. See SUPERIORITY.

sbirro. Pl. *-ri* (-ē).

scabies. Three syllables (skā'bĭēz).

scalawag. See SCALLYWAG.

scald (poet). See SKALD.

scaldino. Pronounce skahldē'nō. Pl. *-ni* (-ē).

scale. The verbs make *-lable* ; see MUTE E. The adjective from one of the nouns is *scaly* ; see -EY & -Y.

scallawag. See SCALLYWAG.

scallop, sco-. The spelling is usually with *-a-*, but the pronunciation with *-ŏ-*. The verb makes *-oping, -oped* ; see -P-, -PP-.

scallywag, -ala-, -alla-. The first spelling is that preferred by the OED.

scandal. For distinctions between this, *libel, slander,* & other synonyms, see LIBEL.

scandalize makes *-zable* ; MUTE E.

scandalum magnatum. The second word is the genitive plural of Latin *magnas* a magnate, not a p.p. agreeing with *scandalum*. The phrase means the offence of uttering a malicious report against some high official, & the use of it in such senses as ' a crying scandal ' is a blunder.

scant, adj., is a LITERARY WORD, preferred in ordinary contexts to *scanty, small, few, short,* &c. (*The attendance was so scant as to suggest that many members must have anticipated the holiday*) only by those who have no sense of incongruity. It survives as a current word, however, in some isolated phrases, as *s. courtesy, s. of breath*.

scarce, adv., used instead of *scarcely,* is a LITERARY WORD. It is true that the OED says : ' Before adverbs in *-ly* the form *scarce* is often adopted instead of *scarcely,* to avoid the iteration of the suffix '. On that iteration, see -LY ; but such avoidance is a case of OUT OF THE FRYING-PAN.

scarcely. 1. *S. . . . than.* 2. *Not* &c. *. . . s.*

1. *S. . . . than.* S. *was the nice new drain finished than several of the children sickened with diphtheria.* For this construction, condemned

in OED s.v. *than* as erroneous, see
HARDLY 2. *Before* or *when* is what
should be used instead of *than*.

2. *Not* &c. . . . *s.* We most of us
feel safe against even saying ' I
don't s. know ', with *not* & *s.* in
hand-to-hand conflict ; but, if a
little space intervenes, & the negative is disguised, the same absurdity
is not very rare in print :—*The
services of the men who have worked
the railway revolution* without *the
travelling public being* scarcely *aware
that we are at war should not be
forgotten./It has been* impossible *to
tell the public* s. *anything about
American naval co-operation with
the British.* The English for *without
s. realizing* is either *s. realizing*, or
without quite realizing, or *not fully
realizing.*

scare makes *-rable* ; see MUTE E.
Scaredly is a bad form ; see -EDLY.
scarf. Pl. *-fs* or *-ves* ; see -VE(D).
scarify. For inflexions see VERBS
IN -IE &c., 6.
Scarlet Woman. See SOBRIQUETS.
scatteredly. Three syllables; see
-EDLY (4).
scavenge(r), vbs. *Scavenger*, n., is
the origin, in English, from which
to scavenge is a BACK-FORMATION,
the normal verb being *to scavenger* ;
cf. to soldier, to filibuster, to buc-
caneer, to privateer, to mountaineer,
to volunteer, to solder, to bicycle,
& hundreds of other verbs that are
in fact verbal uses of nouns. *Scavenge*, however, is much commoner
than the verb *scavenger*.

scazon. See TECHNICAL TERMS.
scena (mus.). Pronounce shā'nah.
scene. For synonyms in the sense
locale, see FIELD.
sceptic &c. The OED gives skě-
only, not sě-, as the pronunciation ;
see also GREEK G, & SKEPTIC.

sceptre, -ter. See -RE & -ER.
schedule. Pronounce shě'dūl.
schema. Pron. skē'm*a*. Pl. *-mata*.
scherzando, scherzo. Pronounced
skǟrtsă'ndŏ, skǟr'tsŏ (pl. *-os* ; see
-OES 6); ITALIAN SOUNDS.
Schiedam. Pronounce skĭdă'm.

schipperke. Pronounce skĭ'perkĭ.
schism(atic). Pronounce sĭ-.
schismatic(al). See -IC(AL). The
desirable consummation is that the
short form should be the noun, &
the long one the adjective.

schist. Pronounce sh-. The oddities of English treatment of Greek
words are well illustrated by *schism*
(sĭ-), *schist* (shĭ-), & *schizomycete*
(skĭ-), all three being from the same
Greek word.

schizomycetes (lit. split-funguses ;
pronounce skĭzomĭsē'tēz). Under
this as the most comprehensive
term are here collected for comparison the OED definitions of the
word itself & several others, about
whose inter-relations curiosity is
natural :—*s., bacterium, microbe,
bacillus, micro-organism, germ.*

Schizomycetes : a group of microscopic, rodlike, unicellular organisms, multiplying by fission, variously known as Bacteria, Microbes,
&c.
Bacterium : A genus of schizomycetae, microscopic unicellular rod-
shaped vegetable organisms, various species of which are found in
all decomposing animal & vegetable
liquids.
Microbe : An extremely minute
living being, whether plant or
animal ; chiefly applied to the
bacteria concerned in causing diseases & fermentation.
Bacillus : A genus of schizomycetae,
microscopic vegetable organisms of
the lowest grade among what were
once called *infusoria*. Separated from
bacterium, with which it agrees in its
rodlike form, & characterized by its
larger size & mode of reproduction.
Micro-organism : A microscopic
animal or plant ; a microbe.
Germ : A micro-organism or microbe ; often one of the microbes
which are believed to cause disease.

schnapps. So spelt.
scholar. Though there is no apparent reason why *s.* & *ss.* should
not mean pupil(s) at a school, schoolboy, schoolgirl, school-children, &c.,

it is not so used by those who are or have been at the great schools. A s. at schools is one who holds a scholarship, & the use of it in the other sense implies that the user is unacquainted with school idiom. *While he was a s. at Marlborough Grammar School he took part in a riot which broke out in consequence of the prohibition of a firework display one ' Guy Fawkes day './It is the sincere hope of the council that its endeavour to promote the ' sport ' in the schools will be recognized by the masters, & that they will bring the proposed championships to the notice of their scholars.* See also GENTEELISM.

scholium. Pl. *-ia*; see *-UM*.

schoolhouse, school-house, school house. The name of the building in which a school is carried on is one word, with or without hyphen. The name of the headmaster's as distinguished from the other boarding-houses of a large school should be two words unhyphened, since *house* bears the accent. See HY- PHENS 3 B.

school (of fish &c.), **shoal.** The two words are etymologically one, & equally unconnected with the ordinary word *school*; both are also current, & without difference of sense. The form *school* has the disadvantage of being liable to be taken for a figurative use of the other school.

sciagraphy &c., **ski-.** The regular representative in English of Greek *sk-* (here *skia* shadow) is *sc-*; but it is legitimate (see GREEK G) to pronounce c as k, cf. *sceptic.* This particular set of words has been taken into English twice—in the 16th c. as terms in perspective, usually with the spelling *sc-*, & in the 19th as equivalent to radio- graphy (production of Röntgen-ray pictures) &c., usually with the spelling *sk-*. To maintain both the *sc-* & the *sk-* forms is very unsatis- factory, &, with *radiography* in existence, also needless. It is best to abandon the Röntgen-ray sense, restrict the words to their older use in perspective, spell only *sc-*, & pronounce *sk-*.

sciamachy, sciametry. See GREEK G.

science & art. S. knows, a. does; a s. is a body of connected facts, an a. is a set of directions; the facts of s. (errors not being such) are the same for all people, circumstances, & occasions; the directions of a. vary with the artist & the task. But, as there is much traffic between s. & a., &, especially, a. is often based on s., the distinction is not always clear; the a. of self-defence, & the boxer's s.—are they the same or different? The OED, on s. ' contradistinguished from art ', says: ' The distinction as commonly appre- hended is that a s. is concerned with theoretic truth, & an a. with methods for effecting certain results. Sometimes, however, the term *s.* is extended to denote a department of practical work which depends on the knowledge & conscious applica- tion of principles; an a., on the other hand, being understood to require merely knowledge of tradi- tional rules & skill acquired by habit '.

scilicet, usually shortened to *scil.* or *sc.*, is Latin (*scire licet* you may know) for ' to wit '. It is not so often misused as *e.g.* & *i.e.*, not having been popularized to the same extent. Its function is to introduce : (a) a more intelligible or definite substitute, sometimes the English, for an expression already used : *The policy of the I.W.W.* (sc. *Independent Workers of the World*) ; *The Holy Ghost as Paraclete* (scil. *advocate*) : (b) a word &c. that was omitted in the original as unnecessary, but is thought to re- quire specifying for the present audience : *Eye hath not seen, nor ear heard* (sc. *the intent of God*).

scimitar, -etar. The OED gives the first as the standard form.

scintilla. Pl. *-lae.*

sciolto. Pronounce shŏ-; ITALIAN SOUNDS.

scirocco. See SIROCCO.
scission. Pron. sĭ'shn, not sĭ'zhn.
Sclav(onic) &c. See SLAV.
scleroma, sclerosis. Pl. *-ō'mata,*
-ō'ses (-ēz) ; see LATIN PLURALS 2.
sconce, vb, makes *-ceable* ; -ABLE 1.
scon(e). The spelling *scone,* & the
pronunciation skŏn, are given preference by the OED ; but the sound
skŏn is perhaps oftener heard.

scope. For synonyms see FIELD.
score n. (=20). See COLLECTIVES 3.
score, vb, makes *-rable* ; see MUTE E.
scoria is a singular noun, pl. *-iae* ;
but, as the meaning of the singular
& of the plural is much the same
(cf. *ash* & *ashes, clinker* & *clinkers*),
it is no wonder that the singular
is sometimes wrongly followed by
a plural verb (*The scoria were still
hot* &c.), or that a false singular
scorium is on record.

scot. See TAX.
scotch. This verb owes its currency entirely to the sentence in
Macbeth—' We have scotch'd the
snake, not kill'd it '. The contrast
between scotching (or disabling) &
killing is expressly drawn in five
quotations given in the OED for
the correct use, & is understood to
be implied even when it is not
expressed. *S.,* then, can say in six
letters & in one syllable ' put temporarily out of action but not
destroy '—a treasure, surely, that
will be jealously guarded by the
custodians of the language, viz
those who write. But no ; ' it is the
nature of extreme self-lovers as
they will set a house on fire and it
were but to roast their eggs ' ; & the
journalist self-lover is too much
delighted as finding in *s.* an uncommon substitute for such poor common words as *kill* or *destroy* to
remember that, if he & his like have
their way, the value of a precious
word will be not merely scotched,
but killed & destroyed, or, as he
would put it, ' finally scotched '.
Finally or *entirely* with *s.* should be,
in view of the history of *s.,* an
impossibility ; but it is now to be

met with daily in the newspapers ;
&, after all, a writer who, like the
author of the first extract below,
does not know the difference between a rumour & the contradiction
of a rumour, can hardly be expected
to recognize so supersubtle a distinction as that between wounding
& killing :—*The contradiction of a
rumour affecting any particular company, although it may have a certain
effect upon the price of shares at the
time, is seldom entirely scotched by
directorial statements./It is well that
this legend should be finally scotched./
The idea is so preposterous that by
the time this is in print it may be
definitely scotched./We hope the
proposal for a Government news
service for the Colonies is finally
scotched by the debate.*

Scotch, Scots, Scottish. 1 (as adjj.).
The third represents most closely the
original form, the first and second
being the contractions of it usual in
England & Scotland respectively.
Scottish is still both good English
(especially in formal contexts) &
good Scotch. The English form
Scotch had (OED) ' before the end
of the 18th c. been adopted into the
northern vernacular ; it is used
regularly by Burns, & subsequently
by Scott. . . . Within the last half
century there has been in Scotland
a growing tendency to discard this
form altogether, *Scottish,* or less
frequently *Scots,* being substituted '.
2 (as nn.). For the name of the
Scotch dialect, the noun *Scottish* is
little used; *Scotch* is the English
noun, & *Scots* the usual Scotch
noun.

**Scot, Scots(wo)man, Scotch(wo)-
man.** Englishmen use the third
forms by nature, the first sometimes
for brevity or for poetical or rhetorical or jocular effect, & the second
occasionally in compliment to a
Scotch hearer, *Scots-* being (OED)
' the prevalent form now used by
Scotch people '.

scot(t)icè, -cism, -cize. The OED
gives preference to *-tt-* in all. For

scotticè see LATINE. *Scotticize* makes *-zable* ; see MUTE E.

Scottish. See SCOTCH, SCOTS.

scoundrel has *-elism, -elly* ; -LL-, -L-.

scout, gyp, skip. College servants at Oxford, Cambridge, & T.C.D., respectively.

scrannel. One of the words depending on a single passage (*Lycidas* 124).

scream, screech, shriek. The first is the ' dominant word ' for a cry uttered, under emotion, at a higher pitch than that which is normal with the utterer. Those who wish to intensify the pitch & the emotion substitute *shriek* ; those who wish either to add the notion of uncanny effect, or to make fun of the matter, substitute *screech*.

screw *your courage to the sticking-place* (not *point*) ; MISQUOTATION.

scrimmage, scru-. The form with *-u-* is preferred in Rugby football, that with *-i-* in more general uses.

scrinium, scriptorium. Pl. *-ia*.

scrummage. See SCRIMMAGE.

scrumptious. See FACETIOUS FORMATIONS.

scrupulous should have its claims considered before the gallicism METICULOUS is substituted for it.

scrutin d'arrondissement, de liste. See FRENCH WORDS.

scrutinize makes *-zable* ; see MUTE E.

scudo. Pl. *-di* (-ē).

scull, skull. The single-handed oar has *sc-*, the cranium *sk-*. The notion that the words are ultimately the same is discountenanced by the OED.

sculptress. See FEMININE DESIGNATIONS.

scurry. For inflexions see VERBS IN -IE &c., 6.

scutum. Pl. *-ta*.

scyphus. Pl. *-phi* (-ī).

scythe, vb, makes *-thable* ; MUTE E.

sea. 1. *S. change.* 2. Hyphen in compounds.

1. *S. change.* *Suffer a s. c.* is one of the most importunate & intrusive of IRRELEVANT ALLUSIONS, & HACKNEYED PHRASES. *We hope that the Prime Minister will on this occasion stick to his guns, & see that his policy*

does not for the third or fourth time suffer a sea change when its execution falls into the hands of his colleagues.

2. Hyphened compounds. Owing to the vast number of phrases or compounds of which *sea* forms the first part, the word provides a good test of the rules laid down in HYPHENS 3 B. Whether a phrase beginning with *sea* used attributively should be hyphened or not depends on whether *sea* or the second word bears the accent ; in the latter case no hyphen should be used. Everyone says *sea' fight, sea' god, sea' gull. sea' horse, sea' mark, sea' nymph, sea' piece, sea' room, sea' serpent* ; & these words should therefore (if they are not made into single words —*seafight* &c.) be given the hyphen :—*sea-fight, sea-god, sea-gull, sea-horse, sea-mark, sea-nymph, sea-piece, sea-room, sea-serpent*. On the other hand, nearly everyone says *sea air', sea ane'mone, sea ba'thing, sea cha'nge, sea coa'st, sea fro'nt, sea law'yer, sea le'vel, sea mi'le, sea mo'nster, sea pay', sea ro'ver, sea shore', sea si'de* ; these, then, should either be made into single words (as *seaside*) or kept separate & unhyphened. It is true that not all compounds of *sea* are thus provided for ; there are many in which the accent is not undisputed, but variable, as *sea breeze, sea captain, sea kale, sea legs, sea pink, sea salt* ; & there are others in which *sea* is not used attributively, but is in some other relation to the second word, as *sea-born, sea-borne, seafaring, sea-girt, sea-going, seasick, seaworthy*. But the object of this article is merely to point out that many *sea* phrases are given hyphens to which they have no right.

seagreen incorruptible. See SOBRIQUETS.

seal. For some synonyms, see SIGN.

seamstress, semps-. The OED treats the first as the word, & the second as the variant.

séance. See FRENCH WORDS.

sear, sere. *Sear* for the nouns (part

of gunlock, mark of burn), & for the verb (burn) ; *sere* for the adjective (withered).

seasonable. See -ABLE 4.

seasonal belongs to the class of words discussed in HYBRID DERIVATIVES under the name of spurious hybrids. But it does differ from some specimens (see COASTAL) in being less easily done without.

seclude makes *-dable* ; see MUTE E.

second. 1. *S. chamber.* 2. *S. floor.* 3. *S.* (-)*hand.* 4. *S. intention.* 5. *S. sight.* 6. *S.,* vb (mil.).

1. *S. chamber,* in a Parliament, is the upper house, as concerned chiefly with rejection, confirmation, & revision.

2. For *s. floor* & *s. storey,* see FLOOR.

3. *S.* (-)*hand.* The second-hand of a watch is so written. The adjective meaning not new or original, & the adverb meaning not for or in first use, are best written as one word (*secondhand clothing* or *information* ; *always buys secondhand*) ; & the phrase (*heard only at second hand*) should be two words unhyphened.

4. For *s. intention,* see INTENTION.

5. *Second sight.* Two words unhyphened ; see HYPHENS 3 B.

6. The verb *s.* in its technical military sense, is pronounced sĭkŏ'nd or sĭgoō'nd.

secondary education is that which comes after the primary or elementary but before that of the universities (ages 14–19).

secundum quid. See SIMPLICITER.

secrete makes *-table* ; see MUTE E.

secretive (pronunciation). The OED gives only sĭkrē'tĭv ; but sē'krĭtĭv is often heard, & for *expletive,* perhaps the closest parallel, the OED gives ĕ'ksplĭtĭv before ĭksplē'tĭv. Probably those who conceive the meaning as fond of secrets say sē'krĭtĭv, & those who conceive it as given to secreting say sĭkrē'tĭv.

sect is a word whose sense is to some extent affected by its user's notion of its etymology. The OED favours Latin *sequor* (follow) as the

origin, so that *s.* would mean a following, i. e. a company of followers ; but the more generally known derivation is from Latin *seco* (cut). & this is naturally interpreted as giving ' a part cut away ' from a Church &c., & so a company of schismatics. According to the first, & probably correct, derivation, the Church of England, or the Roman-Catholic Church, may be called a s. without offence to its members ; according to the second it will not.

secular. For *s. clergy,* see REGULAR.

secure. The adjective makes *-er, -est* ; see -ER & -EST 1 c. The verb makes *-rable* ; see MUTE E.

sedate makes *-er, -est* ; see -ER & -EST 1 c.

sedge makes *sedgy* ; see -EY & -Y.

sedilia. Pron. sĭdĭ'lya. A plural noun, rarely used in singular (*sedile,* pr. sĭdĭ'lĭ).

seduce makes *-cible* ; see -ABLE 2.

see, bishopric, diocese. A bishopric is the rank belonging to a bishop ; a diocese is the district administered by a bishop ; a see is (the chair that symbolizes) a bishop's authority over a particular diocese. A b. is conferred on, a d. is committed to, a s. is filled by, such & such a man. *My predecessors in the see* ; *All the clergy of the diocese* ; *Scheming for a bishopric.*

seek. For two abuses to which the word is liable, see FORMAL WORDS, & DOUBLE PASSIVES.

seem. 1. Pleonasms with *s.* 2. *Seem(ed) to (have) be(en).* 3. *To my &c. seeming.* 4. *As seem(s) to be the case.*

1. Pleonasms. *These conclusions,* it seems to me, appear *to be reached naturally.* Such absurdities are not uncommon with *s.* ; see PLEONASM 4, & HAZINESS.

2. For confusion between *seem(s) to have been* & *seemed to be,* very common, see PERFECT INFINITIVE 3. An example is : *Lady Austen's fashionable friends occasioned no embarrassment ; they* seemed to have preferred *some more fashionable*

place for summering in, for they are not again spoken of; here *are* shows that *seemed* is wrong.

3. *To my &c. seeming. From wherever he may start, he is sure to bring us out very presently into the road along which,* to his seeming, *our primitive ancestors must have travelled.* To my &c. *seeming* has been good English in its time; its modern representative is *to my &c. thinking,* & *to his seeming* will pass only in archaic writing. That the author of the extract is an archaizer is plain independently, from the phrase 'very presently'; but he has no business to be archaizing in a sentence made unsuitable for it by the essentially unarchaic 'primitive ancestors'.

4. *As seem(s) to be the case. How can the Labour Ministry acquire proper authority if it has powers so limited as seem to be the case?* As seem to be the case is always impossible, because the relative pronoun *as,* for which see AS 5, never represents an expressed plural noun (such as *powers* here), but always a singular notion like fact or state of affairs, & that not expressed, but extracted out of other words. *As seems to be the case* is, then, the only right form of the phrase; but even that will not do here, because it involves the doubling of two parts by *as,* that of relative adverb, indispensable after the preceding *so,* & that of the relative pronoun required by the otherwise subjectless verb *seems.* What has happened is this. The writer wanted to say *if it has powers so limited as its powers seem to be.* He shied at the repetition of *powers,* & felt about for *as seems to be the case* as a substitute, though he forgot to alter *seem* to *seems.* But, since *so* makes the relative pronoun *as* impossible, the true solution was to let the *as* be a relative adverb, writing *if its powers are so limited as they seem to be.*

seemly. For the adverb, see -LILY.
seer has double pronunciation &

meaning: sē′er beholder, & sēr prophet &c.

segregate. Verb -āt, adj. -ĭt or -*at*; see PARTICIPLES 5 C.

Seidlitz. Pronounce sĕd-.

seigneur &c. Spellings recognized in the OED as current: seigneur, seignior; seigneuress; seigneury, seigneurie, seign(i)orage, seign(i)ory; seigneurial, seign(i)or(i)al. The pronunciation in all begins with sān followed by the y sound. Differences in meaning or use between alternative forms (as *seigneur* & *seignior,* *seigneury* & *seigniorage*) cannot be detailed here, but exist & are sometimes of importance.

seise, seisin. Pronounce sēz, sē′zĭn. The words are sometimes but less often spelt *-ze, -zin,* & belong etymologically to the ordinary verb *seize*; but in the legal phrases *to s. a person of,* i.e. put him in possession of, & *to be -ed of,* i.e. to possess, the -s- spelling is usual.

seize makes *-zable*; see MUTE E. For the spelling *seise,* see above.

seldom can be compared with *-er, -est*; see -ER & -EST 3.

select, vb, makes *-tor*; see -OR.

Seleucid. Pl. *-ids* or *-idae.*

self. *As both* self & wife *were fond of seeing life, we decided that . . ./* He ruined himself & family *by his continued experiments.* Correct the first to *both I & my wife,* & the second to *himself & his family.* Such uses of *s.* are said by the OED to be 'jocular or colloquial' extensions of a 'commercial' idiom; &, unless the jocular intent is unmistakable, they are best avoided.

self-. *Self-* compounds are sometimes used when the *self-* adds nothing to the meaning. *Agricultural depression & the rural exodus had made village life* self-despondent *& anaemic./Hence it is* self-evident *that economic changes in the agricultural system must greatly affect the general well-being.* There is perhaps never any difference of meaning between *despondent* & *self-despondent. Self-evident,* on the other hand, sometimes means evident without proof, or intuitively certain, which is a valuable sense, & sometimes no more than evident, not implying that proof is needless or has not been given (cf. *hence* in the extract), & therefore tending to confusion. Other words resembling *self-despondent* in being never preferable to the simple form without *self* are *self-collected* (calm &c.), *self-conceit(ed)*, *self-consistent*, *self-diffidence*, *self-opinionated*. And others resembling *self-evident* in having a real sense of their own but being often used when that sense is not in place are *self-assurance*, *self-complacent*, *self-confidence*, *self-consequence*. But these are samples only; there are scores that a writer should not use without first asking himself whether the *self-* is pulling its weight. It is not to be supposed that the otiose use of *self-* is a modern trick; on the contrary, the modern tendency is to abandon many such compounds formerly prevalent, & the object of this article is merely to help on that sensible tendency.

self-possessedly. A bad form; -EDLY.

selvedge, -vage. As the derivation is (OED) ' apparently f. *self*+*edge* ', it is a pity that the significant first form is not universal, & it is here recommended, though the OED 19th & 20th century examples show a slight majority for -*age*.

semaphore. Pronounce sĕ-, regardless of FALSE QUANTITY.

semé(e). See FRENCH WORDS.

semi-. Compounds are innumerable, & restrictions little called for : but the claims of *half-*, which is often better, should at least be considered : *This would be an immense gain over the existing fashion of a multitude of churches ill-manned & semi-filled.*

semicolon. See STOPS.

Semite. See HEBREW.

semivowel. See TECHNICAL TERMS.

semplice, sempre. Pronounce sĕ'm-plĕchă, sĕ'mprä ; ITALIAN SOUNDS.

sempstress. See SEAMSTRESS.

senarius. See TECHNICAL TERMS.

senatus. Pl., if required, -*tuses* or -*tūs*, not -*ti* ; see -US.

senhor (Portuguese title). Pronounce sănyor'.

senior. For *the s. service*, see SOBRIQUETS.

sennight. So written ; but the word is now almost out of use. It might have been, but will now hardly be, utilized as a substitute for *week* in the formula *on Monday* &c. *week* when the reckoning was to be backwards : *We start tomorrow week*, but *It happened yesterday sennight*.

señor, señora, señorita, Spanish titles. Pronounce sĕnyor', sĕnyor'a, sĕnyorĕ'ta.

sense, n. *S. of humour*, properly the power of finding entertainment in people's doings, more especially in such of them as are not designed to entertain. But the phrase has in the last half-century received an extension, or perhaps rather a limitation, that bids fair to supersede the original meaning. When we say nowadays that a person ' has no s. o. h.', or ' lacks humour ', we mean less that he is not alive to the entertainment provided by others' doings than that he is unaware of elements in his own conduct or character likely to stir the s. o. h. in others—has not, in fact, the power of seeing himself as others see him even in the degree in which it is possessed by the average man.

sense, vb. *We sense the tragedy of Anna Wolsky as she steps lightheartedly into Sylvia Bailey's life./ The water rail . . . is somewhat unwieldy in flight, & senses so much, for it seems to prefer to run.* The verb has been used for some three centuries in philosophic writing as a comprehensive form of ' see or/& hear or/& smell or/& taste or/& feel by touch ', i. e. of ' have sense-perception of '. From that the use illustrated above is distinct, meaning according to the OED definition ' to perceive, become aware of,

" feel " (something present, a fact, state of things, etc.) not by direct perception but more or less vaguely or instinctively '. The OED's earliest example is dated 1872, & the meaning is not yet part of ordinary English. It has, no doubt, the advantage of brevity as compared with *become conscious of, get an inkling of,* & other possibilities ; but whether that brevity is sufficient compensation for the irritation or suspicion of preciosity that most readers feel when confronted with it is not so certain.

sensibility. Just as *ingenuity* is not ingenuousness, but ingeniousness, so *sensibility* is not sensibleness, but sensitiveness ; to the familiar contrasted pair *sense & sensibility* correspond the adjectives *sensible & sensitive*—an absurd arrangement, & doubtless puzzling to foreigners, but beyond mending ; -TY & -NESS.

sensible, sensitive, susceptible. In certain uses, in which the point is the effect produced or producible on the person &c. qualified, the three words are near, though not identical, in meaning. *I am sensible of your kindness, sensitive to ridicule, susceptible to beauty.* Formerly *sensible* could be used in all three types of sentence ; but its popular meaning as the opposite of *foolish* has become so predominant that we are no longer intelligible if we say *a sensible person* as the equivalent of *a sensitive* or *a susceptible person,* & even *sensible of* is counted among LITERARY WORDS. The difference between *sensible of, sensitive to,* & *susceptible to* or *of,* is roughly that *sensible of* expresses emotional consciousness, *sensitive to* acute feeling, & *susceptible to* or *of* quick reaction to stimulus : *profoundly, gratefully, painfully, regretfully, sensible of; acutely, delicately, excessively, absurdly, sensitive to ; readily, often, scarcely, susceptible to* or *of.*

sensitize is a word made for the needs of photography, & made badly. It should have been *sensi-*tivize ; one might as well omit the adjective ending of *immortal, signal, fertile, human, & liberal,* & say *immortize, signize, fertize, humize, & liberize,* as leave out the -*ive.* The photographers, however, have made their bed, & must lie in it ; the longer the rest of us can keep clear, the better ; & extra-photographic use has not yet gone very far ; but the OED quotes : *Education, while it sensitizes a man's fibre, is incapable of turning weakness into strength.* Just as, failing *pacificist, pacist* would have been better than *pacifist* (see -IST), so, failing *sensitivize, sensize* would have been better than *sensitize.*

sensorium. Pl. (rare), -*ia.*

sensuous is thought to have been expressly formed by Milton to convey what had originally been conveyed by the older *sensual* (connexion with the senses as opposed to the intellect) but had become associated in that word with the notion of undue indulgence in the grosser pleasures of sense. At any rate Milton's own phrase ' simple, sensuous, & passionate ' in describing great poetry as compared with logic & rhetoric has had much to do with ensuring that *sensuous* shall remain free from the condemnation now inseparable from *sensual.*

sentence, in grammar, means a set of words complete in itself, having either expressed or understood in it a subject & a predicate, & conveying a statement or question or command or exclamation. If it contains one or more CLAUSES, it is a *complex s.* ; if its subject consists of more than one parallel noun &c., or its predicate of more than one verb &c., it is a *compound s.* ; if its subject or predicate or verb (or more) is understood, it is an *elliptical sentence.* One sentence does not contain two or more subjects each with its separate predicate unless all but one of such subjects & predicates are clauses subordinate to the other. Simple sentences : *I went* (state-

ment) ; *Where is he ?* (question) ;
Hear thou from heaven (command) ;
How they run ! (exclamation).

Complex sentence : *Where he bowed
there he fell down dead.*

Compound sentences : *You & I
would rather see that angel* ; *They
hum'd & ha'd.*

Elliptical sentences : *Listen* ; *Well
played* ; *What ?*

Two sentences (not one) : *You
commanded & I obeyed.*

sentinel, sentry. The first is the
wider & literary word, & the fitter
for metaphorical use ; the second is
the modern military term. *Sentinel*
makes *-lled* &c. ; see -LL-, -L-.

senza. Pronounce sĕ′ntsa; ITALIAN
SOUNDS.

separate. Verb -āt, adj. -ĭt ; see
PARTICIPLES 5 B. The verb makes
-rable, -tor ; see -ABLE 1, -OR. For
separat(ion)ist, see -IST B.

sepsis. Pl. (rare), *sepses* (-ēz) ; see
LATIN PLURALS 2.

septenarius. See TECHNICAL TERMS.
septet(te). Spell *-et* ; see DUET.
septillion. See BILLION.
septum. Pl. *-ta.*
sepulchre, -cher. See -RE & -ER.
sequelae. A plural word with rare
singular *sequela.*

SEQUENCE OF TENSES. 1. A certain assimilation normally takes
place in many forms of sentence,
by which the tense of their verbs is
changed to the past when they are
made into clauses dependent on
another sentence whose verb is past,
even though no notion of past time
needs to be introduced into the
clause. Thus, *Two will do* is a
sentence ; turn it into a clause
depending on *I think*, & the tense
remains unaltered : *I think that two
will do.* Next, into one depending
on *I thought* or *I should think* ; it
becomes *two would do* ; after *I
thought* there is a real change in the
clause to past time, & therefore
would do is not only normal, but
invariable ; after *I should think,
would do* is also normal, though there

is no change to past time ; but it is
not invariable, sequence of tenses
being often neglected. *Two will do* ;
I think that two will do ; *I thought
that two would do* ; *I should think
that two* (normal sequence) *would do*,
or (vivid sequence) *will do.* In these
examples, the usually omitted *that*
has been inserted merely to make
it clear that a real clause is meant,
& not a quotation such as *I thought
' two will do '*. The point to be
noticed is that the change to the
past tense is normal sequence, & the
keeping of the present (called *vivid
sequence* above) is, though common
& often preferable, abnormal. Some
further examples are :—*I wish I
knew what relativity* (normal) *meant,*
or (vivid) *means* ; *I should not
wonder if he* (normal) *came*, or
(vivid) *comes* ; *Would God it* (normal) *might*, or (vivid) *may, be so !*
Abnormal sequence was said to be
often preferable ; it is sometimes
so much so as to be practically the
only thing possible. Asking the
time, I do not say *Could you tell me
what the time was ?*—which nevertheless is strictly correct—, but
what the time is.

2. S. out of place. *One would
imagine that these prices* (normal)
were, or (vivid) *are, beyond the reach
of the poor* ; *These prices, one would
imagine, are beyond* &c. The base is
These prices are ; if made dependent
on *One would imagine, are* may be
changed, or may not, to *were* ; but
if *one would imagine* is a parenthesis
instead of being the main verb, the
change is impossible ; nevertheless
it happens : *The shops have never
had such a display of Christmas
presents, but here again the prices,
one would imagine, were beyond the
reach of any but the richest persons ;
one hundred francs is asked for a
common rag doll.* The mistake, a
common one, results from not knowing a parenthesis when one sees it ;
see PARENTHESIS 2.

seq., seqq., et seq(q)., are short for
Latin *et sequentes* (*versus*) & the

subsequent lines, or *et sequentia* & the words &c. following. Except in writing directed to scholars, it is kinder to the reader to use foll., of which he is sure to know the meaning.

sequestrate makes *-trable, -tor* ; see -ABLE 1, -OR.

sérac. See FRENCH WORDS.

seraglio. Pronounce sĭrah'lyō. Pl. *-os* ; see -O(E)S 4.

serai. Pronounce sĭri'.

seraph. Pl. *-phim* or *-phs.*

sere. See SEAR.

serene makes *-er, -est* ; -ER & -EST 2.

sergeant, -j-. For the military & police rank, *-g-* ; in legal titles (*Common S.* &c.), *-j-*. In *S. at arms*, the OED gives *-g-* (or *-j-*). *S. major* (hyphen ?). *The Sergeant major*, but *Sergeant-major Jones*, & *the Sergeant-major's wife* ; see HYPHENS (**Court martial* group).

seri(ci)culture. The full form is the right ; cf. *pacif(ic)ist* in -IST.

serif, ceriph, seriph. The first is now the accepted spelling.

serjeant. See SERGEANT.

serum. Pl. *-rums, -ra.*

servant. For the use in signatures, see LETTER FORMS.

serve makes *-vable* ; see MUTE E.

serviceable. See -ABLE 4, 1.

serviette. NAPKIN, & GENTEELISM.

servile. Adv. *servilely.*

session. ' The term *autumn session* (instead of ' autumn sitting ') is sometimes used to designate the exceptional resumption of the sittings of the Houses, after an adjournment in what is normally the autumn recess ; but this use is condemned by parliamentary authorities as incorrect '—OED. There is normally, whether an autumn sitting takes place or not, only one session in the year.

sestet(te), sex-. Spell *sestet* ; DUET.

sestina. See TECHNICAL TERMS.

set(t). The extra *t* is an arbitrary addition in various technical senses, from a lawn-tennis to a granite set. Each class of persons has doubtless added it to distinguish the special

sense that means most to it from all others ; but so many are the special senses that the distinction is now no more distinctive than an Esq. after a man's name, & all would do well to discard it. Cf. the less futile *matt* for MAT.

seventies, 'seventies. See TWENTIES.

sever makes *-ered* &c. ; -R-, -RR-.

severe has *-er, -est* ; -ER & -EST 1 c.

severely. For *leave s. alone*, see HACKNEYED PHRASES, & IRRELEVANT ALLUSION. There are degrees of badness ; in the first of the two following extracts, for instance, *s.* is less pointless than in the other :—
That immortal classic which almost all other pianists are content to l. s. a. on the topmost shelf./If our imports & exports balance, exchanges will be normal, whatever the price, & I am glad that Mr Mason agrees that exchanges should be left s. a.

Sèvres. See FRENCH WORDS.

sew. P.p. *sewed* or *sewn*. The first is, perhaps contrary to general belief, both the older form & (to judge by the OED 19th-20th c. examples) slightly the commoner in modern English.

sew(er)age. It is best to use *sewage* for the refuse, & *sewerage* for the sewers or the sewer system. *Sewage* is defensible as a derivative of the formerly recognized but now dialectal verb *sew* to ooze out.

sexcentenary. See CENTENARY.

sexillion. See BILLION.

sextet is (OED) ' an alteration of *sestet* '.

sexto, sexto-decimo,(book formats). See FOLIO. Pl. *-os* ; see -O(E)S 6.

sforzando. Pronounce sfortsah'ndō. Pl. *-os* ; see -O(E)S 6.

shade, n. For colour synonymy see TINT.

shade, vb, makes *-dable* ; see MUTE E.

shade, shadow, nn. It seems that the difference in form is fairly to be called an accidental one, the first representing the nominative & the second the oblique cases of the same word. The meanings are as closely parallel or intertwined as might be expected from this original identity, the wonder being that, with a differentiation so vague, each form should have maintained its existence by the side of the other. The OED's main heads of meaning are three for each, one set hardly distinguishable from the other. For *shade* : I. Comparative darkness ; II. A dark figure ' cast ' upon a surface by a body intercepting light, a shadow ; III. Protection from glare & heat. For *shadow* : I. Comparative darkness ; II. Image cast by a body intercepting light ; III. Shelter from light & heat. The most significant point is that, in II of *shade, shadow* is offered as a definition of *shade*, without reciprocity in II of *shadow*, the inference from which is that in division II *shadow* is the normal word, & *shade* exceptional. This almost identity of meaning, however, branches out into a considerable diversity of idiom, one word or the other being more appropriate, or sometimes the only possibility, in certain contexts. The details of this diversity are too many to be catalogued here, but it is a sort of clue to remember that shadow is a piece of shade, related to it as, e. g., pool to water. So it is that shade is a state—viz partial absence of light—, & not thought of as having a shape, nor usually as an appendage of some opaque object, both which notions do attach themselves to shadow. So too we say *light & shade* but *lights & shadows*, *in the shade* but *under a shadow* ; & so too *shady* means full of shade, but *shadowy* like a shadow.

shake makes *-kable* ; see MUTE E.
shako. Pronounce shă′kō. Pl. *-os* ; see -O(E)S 6.
Shakspere, Shakespear(e), -erian, -earian, -ean, &c. The forms preferred by the OED are *Shakspere, Shaksperian.* It is a matter on which unanimity is desirable, & on which, in view of the conflicting arguments, it will never be reached

unless an authoritative decision is accepted as such. *Shakspere, Shaksperian,* are therefore recommended.

shaky, shaly. So spelt ; -EY & -Y.
shall & will, should & would. 1. Plain future & conditional. 2. *I would like.* 3. Indefinite future & relative. 4. Elegant variation. 5. *That*-clauses. 6. Decorative & prophetic *shall.*
' To use *will* in these cases is now a mark of Scottish, Irish, provincial, or extra-British idiom '—Dr Henry Bradley in the OED. ' These cases ' are of the type most fully illustrated below (see 1), & the words of so high an authority are here quoted because there is an inclination, among those who are not to the manner born, to question the existence, besides denying the need, of distinctions between *sh.* & *w.* The distinctions are elaborate ; they are fully set forth in the OED ; & no formal grammar or dictionary can be held to have done its duty if it has not laid down the necessary rules. It will therefore be assumed here that the reader is aware of the normal usage so far as abstract statement can bring it home to him ; & the object will be to make the dry bones live by exhibiting groups of sentences, all from newspapers of the better sort, in which one or other principle of idiom has been outraged. The ' Scotch, Irish, provincial, or extra-British ' writer will thus have before him a conspectus of the pitfalls that are most to be feared.

1. Plain future or conditional statements & questions in the first person should have *shall, should* ; the roman-type *wills* & *woulds* in the following examples are wrong :— *It is impossible to exaggerate the terrible consequences of this proposed act; in Egypt, in India, in every country from the Mediterranean to the frontiers of China, we* will *teach the lesson that no reliance can be placed on the word of England./This is pleasant reading; but we won't*

get our £2,000 this year./Perhaps we will soon be surfeited by the unending stream of ' new ' literature, & will turn with relief to . . ./We might not be able to get all the oil we wanted from our coal, but we would always get enough to prevent . . ./What exactly was the original total of the Turkish forces in this area we do not know—& probably never will./He was plain to read from the beginning, & could hardly, we would have supposed, have made an appeal to a girl of this character./But the late King Edward brushed aside all such nonsense; & where would we be today without the French ' entente ' ?/If we traced it back far enough we would find that the origin was . . ./If we permit our contribution to be substituted for a part of the building programme, we will be casting our vote with the ' little navy ' people./If we compare these two statements, we will see that so far as this point goes they agree./I would not be doing right if I were to anticipate that communication./If it were true the Germans would be right, & we would be wrong./ If British trade interests are to be revived, we will stand in need of these men who know Russia./But if the re-shuffling of the world goes on producing new ' issues ', I will, I fear, catch the fever again./To the average citizen it would appear that in forestalling this plot we would in fact be rendering the German people no less service than . . ./I think I would be a knave if I announced my intention of handing over my salary to . . ./ It is quite clear that when Home Rule is being fought in the Commons I will have to devote all my time to it./ Reports of fighting in China are as conflicting as we would expect./I am confident that within three years we employers will be reaping benefit from it./We have collected more in consequence of that valuation than we would have done without it./We never know when we take up the morning paper, some of us, which side we will be on next./The whole story of the rescue of the men from

Kerrig Island is a heroism of the sea which we will do well to realize./ Mr J. H. Thomas's vision of the Utopia in which we will live ' When Labour Rules '. In all these the idea of intention, volition, choice, &c., which goes with will or would in the first person, is plainly out of the question. Two examples follow in which such an idea is precluded not by the actual words quoted, but by the unquoted context ; in such cases the offence against idiom is aggravated by the possibility of misinterpretation :—We would thus get at once the thing wanted ; an opera open practically all the year round (idiomatic sense, We aim at getting thus : intended sense, This, if it were not unfortunately impossible, would give us)./' Who 's Who ' is entirely without a competitor ; & there is perhaps no book on our reference shelves that we would miss sooner (idiomatic sense, There is no book we should be so glad to be rid of : intended sense, There is no book we should so quickly feel the want of). Two other examples will provide for a common exception to the rule as given absolutely above. In sentences that are, actually or virtually, reported, a verb that as reported is in the first person but was originally in the second or third often keeps will or would :—People have underrated us, some even going so far as to say that we would not win a single test match (the people said You, or They, will not, which justifies, though it by no means necessitates, We would not in the report)./ He need not fear that we will be ' sated ' by narratives like his (his fear was They, or You, will be sated, which makes we will not indeed advisable, but defensible).

2. The verbs like, prefer, care, be glad, be inclined, &c., are very common in first-person conditional statements (I should like to know &c.). In these should, not would, is the right form. ' I would like to say ' is no more idiomatic English than ' I would find it hard to say ' ;

but hundreds of people who would be horrified by the latter are ready to write the former. The explanation is to be found in confusion between two possible ways of speaking, the modern ' I should like to say ', & the archaic ' I would say ' ; in the modern form the desire is expressed in the verb *like* & requires no other expression ; in the archaic form the desire had to be given in *would* because otherwise it was not expressed at all. The roman-type *woulds* & *wills*, then, are all wrong :— *In regard to the general question, I* would like *to speak today with a certain amount of reserve.*/*The other argument upon which I* would like *to comment is as follows.*/*We must shut our ears to the tales of some of the lame dogs we* would like *to help over a stile.*/*We cannot go into details, &* would prefer *to postpone criticism until* . . .*/Nor has he furnished me with one thing with which I* would care *to sit down in my little room & think.*/*I, as Chief Liberal Whip,* will *be very glad to place them in touch with the local secretary.*/*If we should take a wider view, I* would *be inclined to say that* . . .*/In this month of ' grey rain & silver mist '* we will *be glad to keep within our average rainfall of a little over 2 in.* An example less patently wrong is : *We* would *be the last to argue that publication in this form commits our contemporary to agreement with the views expressed.* This is defensible if the writer will assure us that his meaning was We should wish to be the last, instead of, as it doubtless was, We should be the last.

3. In clauses of indefinite future time, & indefinite relative clauses in future time, *will* is entirely unidiomatic ; either *shall* is used, chiefly in formal contexts, or, much more often, futurity is allowed to be inferred from context & a present is used :—*Whatever sum & whatever goods* will *be received from Germany* will *be shared among the Allies* (shall be received).*/Germany will have to*

give back all kinds of property which have been taken from the invaded countries, & which will *be traced in German territory* (shall be traced).*/* . . . *has now had to go clean out of the county to find employment, leaving his wife with her mother until he* will *be able to make another home for her* (until he can make).*/So long as this* will *not be made clear, the discussion will go on bearing lateral issues* (is not made).*/When this* will *be perceived by public opinion the solution will immediately become obvious* (is perceived).*/When the Irish vote has been reduced by Home Rule, & the remaining Irish members* will *no longer have any reason to oppose a Suffrage Bill, Votes for Women will once more have a chance* (members have no longer any reason) . . .*/The farmers were expecting to get increased prices, & they will naturally be ' considerably annoyed ' if they do not get them, especially when they* will *be called upon to pay increased prices for all that they have to buy* (when they are called upon). Here also a less undeniably wrong example may be of service : *We have strong faith that a rally to the defence of the Act will be a feature of next year's politics, if the Tory Party will have the courage to come into the open & declare war upon it.* An assurance from the writer that by *will have the courage* he meant *chooses to have the courage* would be received, indeed, with incredulity, but would secure him a grudging acquittal ; *has the courage* is what he should have written.

4. The time-honoured ' I will be drowned, no-one shall save me ', so much too good to be true, is less convincing as a proof that there are people to whom the English distinctions mean nothing than the discovery that *shall* & *will*, *should* & *would*, are sometimes regarded as good raw material for elegant variation ; I said *should* in the last clause ; the one now to come is sadly similar to it ; go to ! I will write down *would* :—*If we found the*

instances invariably in mutual support we would *be content with but a few, but if we found even one in contradiction we* should *require a large body of evidence./We* should *have been exposed to the full power of his guns, &, while adding to our own losses,* would *have forgone the advantage of inflaming his./The control of Bessarabia, until such time as Russia* shall *be restored & the people* will *be free to pronounce for their return to Russia, by the League of Nations./You* shall *not find two leaves of a tree exactly alike, nor* will *you be able to examine two hands that are exactly similar./Words requiring the local authority to see that when vacancies occurred the appointments* should *be consistent with the terms of the trust & the teachers chosen* would *be qualified to give the special religious instruction.* But the follies to which ELEGANT VARIATION gives rise are without number.

5. *That*-clauses after *intend* or *intention, desire, demand, be anxious,* &c., have *shall* & *should* for all persons. Among the *&c.* are not included *hope, anticipate,* & the like; but the drawing of the line is not easy; roughly, *shall* & *should* are used when the word on which the *that*-clause depends expresses an influence that affects the result, as a demand does, but a hope or a fear does not; a serviceable illustration is *expect;* mistresses expect (i.e. demand) that their maids *shall* wear caps; but we expect (i.e. are of opinion) that tomorrow *will* be fine. Examples of the wrong *will* are :— *I am anxious that, when permanently erected, the right site* will *be selected./ And it is intended that this* will *be extended to every division & important branch./The strong desire that the relations of the English-speaking peoples* will *be so consolidated that they may act as one people./One of the conditions of improvement is that the help given to the deserving poor* will *be removed from the taint of Poor Law associations.*

6. The decorative second or third

person *shall* as in the quotation following is an archaism, before using which, as before using other archaisms, a writer should be very sure that his style in general will stand comparison with that of the few who have archaized to good purpose :—*You* shall *have watched, it may be, the ways of birds & beasts in a garden or wood for half a lifetime ; & your friend, the first time that you show him your preserves,* shall *straightway walk up the leverets, or point out the gold crest's nest which you have always wanted to find.* No-one will suggest that that is a maliciously chosen specimen ; it is better than nine out of ten that one comes upon in the newspapers ; but one who has a real right to this *shall* would have put otherwise ' the first time that you show him your preserves ' & the ' nest which you have always wanted to find '. Distinguished from this, far less conscious & artificial, but also better avoided. is the use of second or third person *shall* that may be called the oracular-prophetic :—*It has already found an honoured place in our national collections ; there will come a time when collectors* shall *fight for it.*

shallow has *-er, -est*; -ER & -EST 1.
sham. *S. fight* should not be hyphened ; see HYPHENS 3 B.
shame, vb, makes *-mable*; MUTE E.
shamefaced, -fast. It is true that the second is the original form, that *-faced* is due to a mistake, & that the notion attached to the word is necessarily affected in some slight degree by the change. But those who, in the flush of this discovery, would revert to *-fast* in ordinary use are rightly rewarded with the name of pedants ; see PRIDE OF KNOWLEDGE. To use *shamefast* as an acknowledged archaism in verse is another matter.
shamefacedly. Four syllables ; see -EDLY.
shampoo. Past *-poo'd* or *-pooed* ; see -ED & 'D.

shanghai. Pronounce -hī; for past & p.p. -*aied* or -*ai'd*, see -ED & 'D.

shanty, sailors' song. See CHANTY.

shape. For *in any s. or form* see PLEONASM 2; *Lord A— states that 'he is absolutely unconnected i. a. s. o. f. with the matter*'. The verb makes -*pable*; see MUTE E. The p.p. is -*ed*, & -*en* is archaic.

shapely. For the adv., see -LILY.

shard. In the sense fragment of pottery, the OED treats *shard* as the normal form & *sherd* as the variant; on the other hand, the greater familiarity of *potsherd* tends to keep *sherd* in being. In the well-known phrase 'the shard-borne beetle', the interpretation 'borne through the air on shards' (i. e. the wing-cases), which has so far prevailed as to set up *shard* as an entomological term for wingcase, appears to be an error; the real meaning was 'born in shard', there being another word *shard*, now obsolete except in dialects, meaning cowdung.

share makes -*rable*; see MUTE E.

sharp, adv. In such phrases as *pull up s., turn s. round, at eight o'clock s., sharp* is preferable to *sharply*; see UNIDIOMATIC -LY.

shave makes -*vable*; see MUTE E.

she. 1. For *she & her* in bad personifications (e. g. *The world wants all that America can give* her), see PERSONIFICATION 1, 2.

2. Case. A few violations of ordinary grammar rules may be given; cf. HE. *I want no angel, only she* (read *her*)./ *When such as her die* (read *she*)./*She found everyone's attention directed to Mary, & she herself entirely overlooked* (omit *she*)./*But to behold her mother— she to whom she owed her being* (read *her*)./*It is himself that he cheers rather than her* (doubtful; see THAN 6)./*I saw a young girl whom I guessed to be she whom I had come to meet* (read *her*)./ *Nothing must remain that will remind us of that hated siren, the visible world, she who by her allurements is always tempting the artist away* (read *her*).

sheaf. The noun has pl. -*ves*. For the verb, -*ve* or -*f*, see -VE(D).

shear, vb, has past *sheared* in ordinary current senses (*We sheared our sheep yesterday*; *A machine sheared the bar into foot-lengths, the nap quite short*; *This pressure sheared the rivets*), *shore* in archaic & poetical use (*shore through the cuirass, his plume away*, &c.). For the p.p., *shorn* remains commoner in most senses than *sheared*, but is not used in the technical sense of distorted by mechanical shear, nor usually in that of divided with metal-cutting shears.

shear-hulk, shearlegs, sheer-. The spelling *sheer* is due to & perpetuates a mistake. Shears or shearlegs are two (or more) poles with tops joined & feet straddled (& so resembling shear-blades), used in hoisting great weights. A shear-hulk is an old ship utilized for hoisting & provided with shearlegs. The spelling *sheer hulk* results from confusion with the adjective *sheer* (i. e. mere), & the omission of the hyphen & shifting of the accent from *shear* to *hulk* naturally follows, assisted by the rhythm of the line in *Tom Bowling*. It would be well to restore *shear-hulk* & make *shearlegs* (already often so spelt) invariable.

sheath(e). The noun (-*th*) is pronounced in sing. -th, but in pl. -dhz; see -TH & -DH. For noun (-*th*, so pronounced) & verb (-*the*, pron. -dh) see NOUN & VERB 2 E.

sheave, vb. See SHEAF.

sheep. Pl. same; see COLLECTIVES.

sheer hulk. See SHEAR-HULK.

sheer(ly). *They would say the money has, to the present, been sheerly wasted*./*A collection of brief pieces in which the sheerly poetical quality is seldom looked for & seldom occurs*./ *The economic condition of the people in Germany is sheerly desperate*. Perhaps owing to the adverbial use of *sheer* (*fell sheer down* &c.), the adverb *sheerly* is usually avoided, & always gives the reader a shock; though the OED quotes it from Burns, Scott, & Stevenson, it may fairly be called unidiomatic; possibly it is current in Scotland; at any rate the OED quotations include no well-known English writer.

sheet lightning. No hyphen ; see HYPHENS 3 B.

sheikh is the OED's spelling, & its preferred pronunciation shāk.

shekarry. See SHIKAREE.

shekinah, -chi-. Pronounce shĭkī'na. The OED's preferred spelling is the first.

shelf. There are two separate nouns, one meaning ledge, board, &c., & the other sand-bank &c. Each has pl. -ves, verb -ve, adjectives -ved, -fy, & -vy ; see -VE(D). Shelf-ful (of books &c.), n., is best written with hyphen ; pl. -ls (unless the two words shelves full are suitable & preferred).

shell-less. So written.

shellac, vb, makes -cked, -cking.

shelty, -ie. The word meaning Shetland pony is usually -ie ; see -EY, -IE, -Y. That meaning a hut (which the OED perhaps makes out to be rarer than it is, & condemns as ' prob. some error ') is usually -y.

shereef, sherif, sheriff. The Mohammedan & the English titles are not etymologically connected. For the former the spelling -eef is preferable to -if both as indicating the accent (shere'f) of an unfamiliar word, & as avoiding assimilation to the English -iff.

sheriffalty, sheriffdom, shrievalty. All three are four or more centuries old, & all are still current. The -dom termination is declining into one of contempt as in bumbledom, flunkeydom ; shrievalty has the disadvantage of not instantly announcing its connexion with sheriff ; & it is therefore likely that sheriffalty will prevail.

shew, show. ' The spelling shew, prevalent in the 18th c. & not uncommon in the first half of the 19th c., is now obs. exc. in legal documents '—OED. In shewbread the old spelling naturally persists.

shibboleth. For synonyms, see SIGN.

shikaree, -i, shekarry. The first is the OED's preferred form. Pronounce shĭkah'rĭ.

shillelagh. So spelt. Pron. -ā'la.

shilly-shally, vb. For inflexions see VERBS IN -IE &c., 6.

shingly, shiny. Not -ey ; -EY & -Y.

shire. The Ss. as the name of a hunting country means Leics., Northants., & Rutland ; it is also ' applied to other parts of England by the inhabitants of East Anglia, Kent, Sussex, Essex, & Surrey '—OED.

shockedly. A bad form ; see -EDLY.

shoe, vb, makes shoeing (exceptionally ; see MUTE E).

shogun. See TYCOON. Pr. shō'gōōn.

shoot, chute, shute. The last is ' app. in part a dial. form of shoot sb. & partly a variant spelling of chute '—OED. Between the English shoot & the French chute (lit. fall) there has been much confusion, & there seems to be no good reason against making shoot the only spelling & allowing it to retain such senses as it has annexed from chute.

shop. For the talk called s., as compared with cant, slang, &c., see JARGON.

shore, vb, makes -rable ; see MUTE E.

short circuit as a noun should not, & as a verb should, be hyphened ; see HYPHENS 3 B, C.

shorthand. So written.

short leg (cricket). No hyphen ; see HYPHENS 3 B.

shortlived. Pron. -īvd ; see -LIVED.

short sight. No hyphen ; but short-sighted ; see HYPHENS 3 B, C.

short slip. No hyphen ; see HYPHENS 3 B.

shot, n. For pl. shot see COLLECTIVES, 2.

should. For s. & would, see SHALL. For s. in inverted conditionals (s. it happen for if it s. happen), see SUBJUNCTIVE.

shoulder. 1. The cold shoulder (no hyphen, see HYPHENS 3 B), but to cold-shoulder. 2. S. arms. The military sense is not to put the rifle across the s. ; that is to slope arms.

shove makes *-vable* ; see MUTE E.

shovel. 1. The verb makes *-lled*, *-lling* ; see -LL-, -L-. 2. *Shovel hat*, not *shovel-hat* ; see HYPHENS 3 B.

show. For spelling see SHEW. The p.p. is usu. *shown*, rarely *showed*.

shred, vb. In the p.p. *shredded* & *shred* are both old & both extant ; the longer is recommended.

shriek. See SCREAM.

shrievalty. See SHERIFFALTY.

shrilly. Pronounce the adjective (poetic by-form of *shrill*) shrĭ'lĭ, the adverb shrĭ'l-lĭ.

shrink has past *shrank* (arch. *shrunk*), p.p. usu. *shrunk* as verb or pred. adj., & *shrunken* as attrib. adj. : *has shrunk*, *is shrunk* or *shrunken*, *her shrunken* or *shrunk cheeks.*

shrivel makes *-lled* &c. ; -LL-, -L-.

shy. The adj. makes *shyer*, *shyest*, *shyly*, *shyness*, *shyish.* The vb makes *shier* (shying horse). See DRY, & VERBS IN -IE &c., 6.

sibilant. See TECHNICAL TERMS.

sibyl(line). The spelling (not *sybi-*) should be noted ; see Y & I.

(sic), Latin for *so*, is inserted after a quoted word or phrase to confirm its accuracy as a quotation, or occasionally after the writer's own word to emphasize it as giving his deliberate meaning ; it amounts to Yes, he did say that, or Yes, I do mean that, in spite of your natural doubts. It should be used only when doubt *is* natural ; but reviewers & controversialists are tempted to pretend that it is, because (*sic*) provides them with a neat & compendious form of sneer. *The industrialist organ is inclined to regret that the league did not fix some definite date such as the year 1910* (sic) *or the year 1912.* (*sic*), because the reader might naturally wonder whether 1910 was meant & not rather 1911 ; a right use./*The* Boersen Courier *maintains that '* nothing remains for *M. Delcassé but to cry Pater peccavi to Germany & to retrieve as quickly as possible his diplomatic mistake* (sic) *'.　Mistake* is the natural term

for the quoted newspaper to have used ; the quoting one very superfluously repudiates it with (*sic*)./ *An Irish peer has issued a circular to members in the House, with an appeal for funds to carry on the work of enlightening* (sic) *the people of this country as to the condition of Ireland.* What impudence ! says (*sic*) ; but, as no-one would doubt the authenticity of *enlightening*, the proper appeal to attention was not (*sic*), but inverted commas./'*A junior subaltern, with pronounced military & political views, with no false modesty in expressing them, & who* (sic) *possesses the ear of the public* . . .' The quoter means ' Observe by the way this fellow's ignorance of grammar ; & *who* without a preceding *who* ! ' ; as the sentence is one of those in which the *&-who* rule of thumb is a blind guide (see WHICH), & is in fact blameless, the (*sic*) recoils, as often, & convicts its user of error.

sice, size, syce. For the six at dice &c., *sice* is better than *size* ; for the Indian groom, *syce* is better than *sice.*

sick. *The S. Man* ; see SOBRIQUETS.

sick, ill. The original & more general sense of *sick*, which has now been transferred for the most part to *ill*, was suffering from any bodily disorder. That sense remains to it in attributive use (*s. people, a s. child*, &c.), but is now uncommon in predicative use (*be, feel, s.*), in which it means vomiting or ready to vomit. In U.S. & Scotch use the wider sense is still common, & cf. *go sick* as the army phrase for declaring oneself ill. Instead of either *iller* or *sicker, more ill* or *more s., worse* is the comparative wherever it would not be ambiguous.

sick headache. No hyphen ; see HYPHENS 3 B.

sickly. For adverb see -LILY.

SIDE-SLIP. The grammatical accident to which a name is here given is most often brought about by the

word *of*, & in the article OF its
nature has been so fully explained
that nothing more is now required
than some examples of the same
accident not caused by *of*. In the
first half-dozen quotations, other prepositions play the part of *of* ; in the
later ones the mistakes, though due
also to the disturbing influence of
what has been said on what is to be
said, are not of quite the same pattern, & will need slightly more comment :— ... *possessing full initiative
after its success, & able at will to
expend a minimum force in defending
itself* against *one half of the defeated
body, & a maximum effort against
destroying the other half* (*in*, for the
second *against*)./*But there is one that
deserves special mention because it lies
at the root of the nation's confidence
in the Navy & in the Navy's own
cohesion as a loyal & united service*
(read *of* for the second *in*)./*Their
interest lies in getting through as
quickly as possible in order* to *put
in an extra journey, & consequently
to avoid waiting for passengers* (read
in avoiding for *to avoid*)./*In a plea*
for *the setting aside of this accord,
or at least* for *certain parts of the
accord, by the Conference, the 'Temps'
intimates that* . . . (read *of* for the
second *for*)./*The Independents would
then be in the position in which the
pledged Liberals now are of being
unable* to *appear on a platform or*
helping *any Liberal movements in
any of the 330 Tory constituencies*
(read *to help* for *helping*)./*When will
Englishmen allow Ireland to govern
herself, rather than* to *persist in the
hopeless task of perpetually conquering
or trying to conquer her?* (omit *to*
before *persist*).

Miscellaneous

Today we can but be thankful that
*the nerve of Fisher proved cool at the
crisis, & that to him we mainly owe
it that we have not to record a disaster
of almost historical importance in the
history of the railway.* Who is
Fisher, that we should prefer him as
saviour to other signalmen ? The

second *that* is there only because
the first has sent the writer off at
a tangent. To mend, *a*, omit the
second *that* ; or, *b*, insert *feel* before
it ; or, *c*, omit ' to him we mainly
owe it that './*It would not be surprising if this limit* were *reduced to
£125, the German limit, while voluntary insurance* were still *allowed for
persons with incomes up to £160
a year.* The legitimate & normal
(but not necessary) subjunctive *were
reduced* draws the writer into the
abnormal & almost illegitimate *were*
(instead of *was*) *allowed* ; for the
perils of subjunctive-using, see SUB-
JUNCTIVE./*If it can be done, &* only
if it can be done, shall we be *in the
position to re-establish civilization.*
The intervention of the parenthesis
with its *only* is allowed to upset the
order of words, viz *we shall be*, required by the start of the sentence ;
this variety of side-slip is further
illustrated in INVERSION *in parallel
clauses.*/*Whether* the cessation of
*rioting, looting, & burning which has
been secured largely by the declaration
of martial law & rigorous shooting of
leaders of the rabble is merely temporary or* has been put an end to for
good *remains to be seen.* If the
cessation of rioting *has been put an
end to for good*, a lively time is coming. To mend, read *permanent* instead of the words just italicized ;
& for this variety see HAZINESS./
*He therefore came round to the view
that simple Bible-teaching* were *better
abolished altogether & that the open
door for all religions* were *established
in its place.* The deadly subjunctive
again ; if the writer had been content with *would be* in place of the
first *were*, he would certainly not
have been trapped into thinking
that *would be* gave the right sense
where the second *were* stands ; but
venturing on dangerous ground,
which the subjunctive always is
except to skilled performers, he side-
slips. See SUBJUNCTIVE.

sidle makes *-dling* ; see MUTE E.
sidy (swaggering), not *-dey*; -EY & -Y.

sien(n)a, Sien(n)a, Sien(n)ese. The old-established -*nn*-is recommended; see MAHOMET.

sieve. Pronounce sĭv.

sign (indication) & some synonyms. The synonyms are so many that it seems worth while to collect some of them & add sentences showing each of them in a context to which it is better suited than any, or than most, of the others. The selected words are : badge, cachet, character, characteristic, cognizance, criterion, device, differentia, emblem, hallmark, impress, index, indication, mark, motto, note, omen, prognostic, seal, shibboleth, sign, slogan, stamp, symbol, symptom, test, token, touch, trace, trait, type, watchword.

Sufferance is the badge *of all our tribe. All his works have a grand* cachet. *These attributes of structure, size, shape, & colour, are what are called its ' specific* characters '. *Super-stition is not the* characteristic *of this age. Geoffrey assumed as his* cogniz-ance *the Sprig of Broom. Success is no* criterion *of ability. Shields painted with such* devices *as they pleased. To arrive at the true* differ-entiae *of Christian morals. The* spindle *was the* emblem *of woman. Lacking the* hall-mark *of a university degree. Lucerne bears most strongly the* impress *of the Middle Ages. The proverbs of a nation furnish the best* index *to its spirit. There is no* indication *that they had any knowledge of agriculture. Suspiciousness is a* mark *of ignorance. ' Strike while the iron's hot ' was his* motto. *Catho-licity is a* note *of the true Church. Birds of evil* omen *fly to & fro. From sure* prognostics *learn to know the skies. Has the* seal *of death in his face. Emancipation from the fetters of party* shibboleths. *An outward & visible* sign *of an inward & spiritual grace. Our* slogan *is Small Profits & Quick Returns. Bears the* stamp *of genius. The Cross is the* symbol *of Christianity. Is already showing* symptoms *of decay. Calamity is the true* test *of friendship. By what* token *could it manifest its presence ?*

One touch *of nature makes the whole world kin. Traces of Italian influence may be detected. They have no national* trait *about them but their language. The paschal lamb is a* type *of Christ. The old Liberal* watchword *of Peace, Retrenchment, & Reform.*

signal, vb, makes -*lled* &c. ; -LL-, -L-.

signal, single, vv. *But there is intense resentment that Japan should be signalled out for special legisla-tion./There was one figure more sinister than the rest, whom Mr Lloyd George signalled out for his wrath in true revivalist style./The German Emperor has been spared an inglorious end in obscurity ; but why has he been signalled out for the dignity of a special trial ?* Three specimens of a very common MIS-PRINT or blunder ; *singled* should be the word. Unfortunately, there is just nearness enough in meaning between the verb *single* on the one hand &, on the other, the adjective *signal* & the verb *signalize* to make it easy for the uncharitable to suspect writer rather than printer ; & therefore especial care is called for, as with *deprecate* & *depreciate*.

signatary, -ory. The established adjective is -*ory* (*the signatory* Powers) ; the OED quotations for the noun are evenly balanced be-tween -*ary* & -*ory* ; & it therefore seems wise to distinguish between noun & adjective by adopting -*ary* for the former (*the signataries*) ; see further on MANDATARY.

signify. For inflexions see VERBS IN -IE &c., 6.

Signor(a), -rina, Italian titles. Pro-nounce sēnyor'(*a*), sēnyorē'na.

Sikh. Usu. pronounced sēk ; sĭk, however, is more, not less, correct.

silex. For pl., see -EX, -IX.

silhouette. Pronounce sĭlŏŏĕ't.

siliceous, -cious. The first is better.

silk(en). See -EN ADJECTIVES.

sillabub, syl-. The OED attributes the -*y*- to ' the influence of *syllable* '. See Y & I for the intrusions of *y*.

sillily. One of the few current -*lily* adverbs ; see -LILY s.f.

silo. The noun has pl. -*os* ; see -O(E)S 6. The verb makes -*o'd* or -*oed* ; see -ED & 'D.

silvan, sylvan. There is no doubt that *si-* is the true spelling etymologically (Latin *silva* or *silua* a wood, changed in MSS. to *syl-* under the influence of Greek *hulē*) ; there is as little doubt that *sy-* now preponderates, & the OED does the word under that spelling, giving *silvan* as a variant. *Silvan* is here recommended, just as in Y & I restoration of the right letter is recommended in other words. Though the false form does prevail nowadays, it is by no means universal ; & it is worth notice that, out of seven Scott quotations in the OED, four show *sy-* & three *si-*. It is often too late to mend mis-spellings, but hardly so in this case.

silvern. See -EN ADJECTIVES.

silver paper. No hyphen ; see HYPHENS 3 B.

silver streak. See SOBRIQUETS.

simian. Pronounce si- ; the Latin noun is *si-*, but see FALSE QUANTITY.

similar is apt to bring disaster to certain writers, those namely to whom it is a FORMAL WORD to be substituted in writing for the *like* or *the same* with which they have constructed a sentence in thought. In the first quotation, *like* would stand, being both adjective & adverb, but *similar*, being adjective only, must be changed to *similarly*. In the second, *the same considerations that* would have been English, but *similar considerations that* must be corrected to *s. c. to those that. It is claimed that the machine can be made to turn on its own centres,* similar *to the motor-boats which the inventor demonstrated at Richmond in 1912./ Nevertheless, although adjoining New York all along its northern border & in its farming, manufacturing, & general industrial development swayed by* similar *business considerations that govern the Empire State, its people went* as strongly for Roosevelt as their neighbours in New York went against him.*

simile. To let this specialized & literary word thrust itself, as in the following quotation, into the place of the *comparison* or *parallel* that we all expect & understand is to betray that one has & uses a synonym dictionary, which is to some journalists what the rhyming dictionary is to some poets :—*The advent of Kossovo Day cannot but suggest a* simile between *the conflict then raging & that in which we are engaged today.* A simile is always a comparison ; but a comparison is by no means always, & still less often deserves to be called, a simile.

SIMILE & METAPHOR, *allegory & parable. Allegory* (uttering things otherwise) & *parable* (putting side by side) are almost exchangeable terms. The object of each is, at least ostensibly, to enlighten the hearer by submitting to him a case in which he has apparently no direct concern, & upon which therefore a disinterested judgement may be elicited from him. Such judgement given, it is to be borne in upon him, whether or not a Thou art the man is needed, that the conclusion to which the dry light of disinterestedness has helped him holds also for his own concerns. Every parable is an allegory, & every allegory a parable. Usage, however, has decided that *parable* is the fitter name for the illustrative story designed to answer a single question or suggest a single principle, & offering a definite moral, while *allegory* is to be preferred when the application is less restricted, the purpose less exclusively didactic, & the story of greater length. The object of a parable is to persuade or convince ; that of an allegory is often rather to please. But the difference is not inherent in the words themselves ; it is a result of their history, the most important factor being the use of *parable* to denote the allegorical stories told by Christ.

It is of *allegory* that the OED gives as one of the definitions ' an extended or continued metaphor '. But the comment may be hazarded that there is some analogy between the relation of allegory to parable & that of simile to metaphor, & that the OED definition would, if that is true, have been still better suited to *parable* than to *allegory*. For between simile & metaphor the differences are (1) that a simile is a comparison proclaimed as such, whereas a metaphor is a tacit comparison made by the substitution of the compared notion for the one to be illustrated (*the ungodly flourishing* ' *like* ' *a green bay-tree* is a confessed comparison or simile ; *if ye had not plowed with my heifer*, meaning dealt with my wife, is a tacit comparison or metaphor) ; (2) that the simile is usually worked out at some length & often includes many points of resemblance, whereas a metaphor is as often as not expressed in a single word ; & (3) that in nine out of ten metaphors the purpose is the practical one of presenting the notion in the most intelligible or convincing or arresting way, but nine out of ten similes are to be classed not as means of explanation or persuasion, but as ends in themselves, things of real or supposed beauty for which a suitable place is to be found.

It cannot be said (as it was of allegory & parable) that every simile is a metaphor, & vice versa ; it is rather that every metaphor presupposes a simile, & every simile is compressible or convertible into a metaphor ; there is a formal line of demarcation, implied in 1 above ; the simile is known by its *as* or *like* or other announcement of conscious comparison. There is no such line between allegory & parable, but in view of distinctions 2 & 3 it may fairly be said that parable is extended metaphor & allegory extended simile. To which may be added this contrast : having read a tale, & concluded that under its surface

meaning another is discernible as the true intent, we say This is an allegory ; having a lesson to teach, & finding direct exposition ineffective, we say Let us try a parable ; to reverse the terms is possible, but not idiomatic.

simony. Pronounce sī′monĭ.

simoom. See WIND, n.

simple. Adv. *simply*. *Fee simple* (not hyphened ; see HYPHENS, *Court Martial).

simpleness)(simplicity. -TY & -NESS.

simpliciter)(secundum quid. These convey, the first that the statement &c. referred to need not, the second that it must, be restricted to certain cases or conditions.

simplify. For inflexions see VERBS IN -IE &c., 6.

simulacrum. Pl. -cra.

simulate makes -lable, -tor ; see -ABLE 1, -OR.

sin. ' To sin one's mercies ', which puzzles everyone to whom it has not been familiar from childhood, is paraphrased by the OED, but without explanation, as ' to be ungrateful for one's blessings or good fortune '. ' More sinned against than sinning ' (*King Lear* III. ii. 60) has become a HACKNEYED PHRASE ; descent from the height of Lear to the latest triviality of ' tempted & fell ' lands us, naturally, in bathos, & STOCK PATHOS.

sī′napism. So pronounced.

since. For the very common mistake of using *s.* after *ago*, see AGO. For ' P.S. Since writing this your issue of today has come to hand ', see UNATTACHED. The following example of a mistake as uncommon as the others are common is offered merely as a curiosity to anyone who may wish to show cause why *s.* should be *after* :—*A little more than a century since the death of William Windham the suggestion made by a reviewer in 1831 that his Life might be ' written by his Letters ' is made good.*

sincerely. For ' yours *s.* ' &c. see LETTER FORMS.

'S INCONGRUOUS (*drink's victims* &c.). It will be a surprise, & to some an agreeable one, if at this late stage in our change from an inflexional to an analytic language we revert to a free use of the case that we formerly tended more & more to restrict. It begins to seem likely that *drink's victims* will before long be the natural & no longer the affected or rhetorical version of *the victims of drink*. The devotees of inflexion may do well to rejoice ; the change may improve rather than injure the language ; & if that is so let due praise be bestowed on the newspaper press, which is bringing it about ; but to the present (or perhaps already past) generation, which has been instinctively aware of differences between *drink's victims* & *the victims of drink*, & now finds them scornfully disregarded, there will be an unhappy interim.

It is the headline that is doing it. The fewer words to the headline, the larger can the type be, & CHINA'S INTEGRITY is two words less than THE INTEGRITY OF CHINA ; BEATTY & HAIG'S REPLY (i. e. that of Beatty & Haig), UGANDA'S POSSIBILITIES, NAVY & ARMY'S THANKS, are others ; but illustration is superfluous.

We who are old saw no such possessives when we were young ; but we could be content, if only the modern possessive kept to its own territory, the modern headline ; even ONTARIO'S PRIME MINISTER (so are we chastened !) we can bow down before while he is in capitals ; but when he comes amongst us in the ordinary garb of lower-case text, we pluck up heart again & want to kick him :—' *In no part of the world* ' says Ontario's Prime Minister ' *will* . . . '. / *It is barely four years since Bulgaria's ruler assumed the title of Czar.* / *The object is to bring before the public many ancient & modern aspects of the Theatre's Art which have* . . . / *And the narrative's charm, which is that of* . . . *is due to* . . . / *Although not returned to Westminster*

as Hanley's representative till . . . / *M. de Bille has spent eighteen years in London as Denmark's Minister.*

The time has perhaps not yet come when it is necessary to explain the old-fashioned restrictions on the use of possessives that are here defied ; those who allow the headline style to overflow into the text are doubtless aware of what they are doing & pleased with its effect as a novelty.

sinecure. The OED pronounces sī'nĭkūr, adding that ' in Scotland & America the first vowel is freq. pronounced short '.

sing. For the past tense ' recent usage has mainly been in favour of *sang* '—OED. *Sung* was formerly usual, & still lingers.

Singalese. See SINHALESE.

sing(e)ing. See MUTE E, & use the -e- in the part. of *singe*.

singeress. See FEMININE DESIGNATIONS.

Singhalese. See SINHALESE.

SINGULAR -S (or sibilant ending). The feeling that the z sound at the end of a noun proves it plural has played many tricks in the past ; *pea, caper* (the herb), & *Chinee*, have been docked under its influence of their endings, *riches* is usually treated as a plural, & many other examples might be collected, philologically interesting rather than of practical importance. On the other hand it may be worth while to notice that the glasses of spectacles are *lenses* & not *lens*, that *His pulse are good* is a by no means extinct blunder, & that the plural of *a forceps* should certainly be, & probably will be again, what it unfortunately is not at present, *forcepses*. Cf. GALLOWS.

Sinhalese, Sing(h)alese, Cingalese. The first, & the last, are recognized as the standard forms in the OED.

sinister in heraldry means left (& *dexter* right), but with the contrary sense to what would naturally suggest itself, the left (& right) being that of the person bearing, not of an observer facing, the shield. For *bar*, *baton*, *bend*, *s.*, see BAR.

sink, vb. 1. Past tense *sank* or *sunk*, the former now prevailing, especially in intransitive senses. 2. *Sunk(en)*. The longer form is no longer used as part of a compound passive verb : *the ship would have been, will be, was, sunk*, not *sunken*. But *sunken* has not a corresponding monopoly of the adjectival uses : *sunken eyes* ; *a sunken* (or *sunk*) *rock* ; *a sunk* or *sunken ship* ; *a sunk* (or *sunken*) *fence* ; *sunk carving* ; *a sunk panel, shelf, storey*. Roughly, *sunken* is used of what has *sunk* or is (without reference to the agency) in the position that results from sinking, i. e. it is an INTRANSITIVE P.P. ; & *sunk* is used of what has been sunk esp. by human agency.

sinus. Pl. *-uses*, or (see LATIN PLURALS) *sinus* (-ūs).

Sioux. Pronounce sōō or sū. Pl. spelt *Sioux* & pronounced like sing., or with final z sound.

sipahee, -hi. For the use of these instead of the established *sepoy* see MAHOMET, DIDACTICISM.

siphon, not *sy-*. See Y & I.

sir (as prefix). To say *Sir Jones* is, more than to say *Hon.* or *Rev. Jones*, a mistake peculiar to foreigners. But newspaper writers often (1) forget, as with HON., that a double-barrelled surname will not do instead of Christian name & surname, & (2) play foolish games of elegant variation when a knight or baronet has two Christian names, ringing the changes between Sir William Jones, Sir Henry Jones, Sir William Henry Jones, Sir William, & Sir Henry ; Sir William Jones, Sir W. Jones, & Sir William, are surely enough to provide relief.

siren, not *sy-*. See Y & I.

Sirius. The OED pronounces sĭ-, not sī- ; for neglect of classical quantities see FALSE QUANTITY.

sirloin. The knighting of the loin attributed to various kings seems to have been suggested by, & not to

have suggested, the compound word ; it has, however, so far affected the spelling (which should have shown French *sur*=upper) that *sir-* may now be taken as fixed.

sirocco, sci-. Both forms exist in Italian. The OED gives the first for the standard English spelling.

sirup. See SYRUP.

sirvente. See TECHNICAL TERMS.

sister, in hospital use, is applied properly to one in charge of a ward &c., or in authority over other nurses—matron, sisters, nurses, wardmaids, being the hierarchy. But *s.* is often substituted, especially by soldiers in hospital, as a courtesy title, for *nurse*.

sisterly. For the adv., see -LILY.

situate(d). The short form is still common in house-agents' advertisements, but elsewhere out of favour.

sixain. For these words see -STICH.

sixteenmo. See FOLIO. Pl. *-os* ; see -O(E)S 6.

sixth. Often mispronounced sĭkth.

sixties, 'sixties. See TWENTIES.

sixtyfourmo, 64mo. See FOLIO, Pl. *-os* ; see -O(E)S 6.

sizable. So spelt ; see MUTE E.

sizy (stiff with size). So spelt ; see MUTE E.

sjambok. The OED pronounces shăm-.

skald, sc-, Scandinavian poet. The OED preferred form is *sk-*.

skate makes *-table* ; see MUTE E.

skedaddle. FACETIOUS FORMATIONS.

skee. See SKI.

skene, skean, skian, skain. The OED preferred form is *skene*.

skeptic(al), skepsis, &c. The established pronunciation (see SCEPTIC) is sk-, whatever the spelling ; &, with the frequent modern use of *septic* & *sepsis* (the latter a 19th-c. word only), it is well that it should be so for fear of confusion ; but to spell *sc-* & pronounce sk- is to put a needless difficulty in the way of the unlearned. America spells *sk-* ; we might pocket our pride & copy.

skew, adj., though still current technically, e. g. in architecture, engineering, & carpentry, has so far gone out of general use as to seem, in other applications, either archaic or provincial.

skewbald. See PIEBALD.

ski, n. Pron. shē; pl. *ski*, or *skis*.

ski, vb. *Ski'd* (shēd) is preferable to *skied*; see -ED & 'D. Agent n., *skier* (shē'er).

skiagraphy &c. See SCIAGRAPHY.

skier, skyer. The user of ski is a *skier* (shē'er), obviously. The skied cricket-ball is spelt sometimes with y & sometimes with i; the OED prefers *skyer*, which has also the advantage of saving confusion; &, as it is more reasonable to derive it from *sky* n. (cf. *sixer* &c.) than from *sky* vb, there is no need to make it conform to *crier* & *flier* & *pliers*, for which see DRY &c.

skilful. So spelt; see -LL-, -L-, 4. For *skilfullest*, -LL-, -L-, 2.

skilled. The *skilled* & the *unskilled* are sheep & goats, distinguished by having or not having had the requisite training or practice; the two words exist chiefly as each other's opposites, or terms of a dichotomy. The point of the limitation is best seen by comparison with *skilful* : *skilled* classifies, whereas *skilful* describes; you are skilled or not in virtue of your past history, but not very or most or fairly skilled (in idiomatic speech, at least); you are skilful according to your present capacity, & in various degrees.

skill-less is better than *skilless*. Among the OED 19th-c. quotations are *skilless* (6), *skillless* (1), & *skill-less* (2); but that the help to pronunciation given by the hyphen is desirable is plain enough if a few other words with short vowel to which -*less* may naturally be appended are thought of :—*belless* or *bell-less, shelless* or *shell-less, willess* or *will-less, hilless* or *hill-less, dolless* or *doll-less, canalless* or *canal-less*? The first two of these, the only ones given in the OED (1922, with *will-less* not reached), are allowed the

hyphen. The reason for excluding from consideration words with long vowel, which yield *keelless, soulless,* &c., is that it is only after short vowels that -ll- is normally equivalent in sound to -l- & therefore deceptive.

skin. *With the s. of my teeth*; see MISQUOTATION.

skip (servant). See SCOUT.

skull. See SCULL.

Skupshtina. So spelt; pronounce skŏo'pshtĭna.

sky blue. The name of the colour is *sky blue*; the adjective *blue* qualified by *sky* becomes *sky-blue* : *sky blue will be best*; *a sky-blue tie*; *her eyes are sky-blue*. See HYPHENS.

skyer. For spelling see SKIER.

skyey. For spelling see -EY & -Y.

slack(en), vv. In the article -EN VERBS it is implied that the relation between the adjective & verb *slack* & the verb *slacken* is not simple enough to be there treated with the rest. One's first impression after a hasty look through the OED articles on the two verbs is that whatever either means the other can mean too—an experience familiar to the synonym-fancier. The following distinctions are therefore offered with the caution that they represent idiomatic usage only, & that quotations contravening them may be found in the OED & elsewhere. 1. *Slacken* is the ordinary word for to *become* slack, & for to make (or let become) slacker : *the tide, breeze, pace, demand, rope,* one's *energy, slackens*; *we slacken our efforts, grip, speed, opposition, the girth, the regulations.* 2. *To slack,* if it is to have such senses, is reinforced by *off, out, up,* &c. : *the train slacked up*; *had better slack off*; *slack out the rope.* 3. *Slack,* not *slacken,* trespasses on the territory of *slake* : *slack* one's *thirst, lime, the fire.* 4. *Slack,* not *slacken,* means to *be* slack or idle : *accused me of slacking.* 5. *Slack,* not *slacken,* means to come short of or neglect (one's duty &c.).

slake, slack, vv. Both are derived

from the adjective *slack*, & *slake* had formerly such senses as loosen & lessen, which have now passed to the newer verb *slack* owing to their more obvious sense-connexion with it ; *slake* tends more & more to be restricted to the senses assuage, satisfy, moisten, (thirst, desire, vengeance, lips, lime).

slakeless. See -LESS.

slander. For synonymy, see LIBEL.

slang. For comparison with the many synonyms, see JARGON.

slantendicular, -ingdicular. See FACETIOUS FORMATIONS.

slate, n., makes *slaty* ; see MUTE E.

slate, vb., makes -*table*; see MUTE E.

slatternly. For adv. see -LILY.

slave makes *slavish* ; see MUTE E ; but *slavey*, see -EY, -IE, -Y.

slaver, slobber, slubber, vv. The three words, as well as *slabber*, which is perhaps obsolete, may be assumed to be of the same ultimate origin, &, though they may have reached us by different routes & had more or less separate histories, they have so far acted & reacted upon one another that for people not deep in historical philology they are now variants of one word, partly but not completely differentiated. The base meaning is to run at the mouth (1), with kissing (2), licking (3), fulsome flattery (4), emotional gush (5), & superficial smoothing over or mere tinkering (6), as developments. All three have sometimes any of the first four senses, though *slubber*, which is now chiefly in archaic literary use, tends to be confined to sense 6 ; & in that sense *slobber* is exceptional & *slaver* not used. The difference between *slaver* & *slobber* is partly of status, the former being the more literary & dignified & the latter colloquial & vivid, & partly of extent, *slaver* not going beyond sense 4, while *slobber* covers sense 5 & even 6.

sled(ge), sleigh. Though all three are interchangeable, they tend to be distinguished in use as follows : *sled*, drag for transporting loads ; *sledge* English, *sleigh* U.S. & Cana-

dian, for carriage on runners. ' Chiefly U.S. & Canada ' is the OED label on *sleigh* ; but the use of sledges in Great Britain is comparatively so rare that the Canadian idiom may be expected to prevail, if it has not already done so.

sleep. For *the s. of the just* see HACKNEYED PHRASES.

sleigh. See SLEDGE.

sleight. Pronounce slīt ; it is related to *sly* as *height* to *high*. *S. of hand* ; no hyphens, see HYPHENS (group **rule of thumb*).

slew, slue. The first is the now accepted spelling, though the earlier examples show *slue*.

slice, vb, makes -*ceable*; see -ABLE 1.

slide, vb, makes -*dable*; see MUTE E. *sliding door*, two words without hyphen, see HYPHENS 3 B ; similarly *sliding keel, sliding rule, sliding scale, sliding seat*.

slime makes *slimy* ; see MUTE E.

sling, slink. Past tenses & p.p. *slung, slunk* ; the OED records but does not countenance the pasts *slang, slank*.

slip. *Short s., long s.,* (cricket) ; no hyphen ; see HYPHENS 3 B.

SLIPSHOD EXTENSION. To this heading, which hardly requires explanation, reference has been made in the articles on many individual words. Slipshod extension is especially likely to occur when some accident gives currency among the uneducated to words of learned origin, & the more if they are isolated or have few relatives in the vernacular ; examples are *protagonist, recrudescence, optimism, meticulous, feasible, dilemma ;* the last two of these offer good typical illustrations. The original meaning of *feasible* is simply doable (L *facere* do) ; but to the unlearned it is a mere token, of which he has to infer the value from the contexts in which he hears it used, because such relatives as it has in English—*feat, feature, faction, fashion, malfeasance, beneficence,* &c.—either fail to show the obvious family likeness to which he is accustomed among families of indigenous words, or are (like *malfeasance*) outside his range. He arrives at its meaning by observing what is the word known to him with which it seems to be exchangeable ; that is *possible* ; & his next step is to show off his new acquisition by using it instead of *possible* as often as he can, without at all suspecting that the two are very imperfect synonyms ; for examples see FEASIBLE. He perhaps notices now & then that people look at him quizzically as if he were not quite intelligible, but this happens seldom enough to let him put it comfortably down to their ignorance of the best modern idiom.

The case of *dilemma* as a word liable to slipshod extension differs in some points from that of *feasible*, though a dilemma is confused with a difficulty just as *feasible* with *possible*. A person who has taken a taxi & finds on alighting that he has left his money at home is in a difficulty ; he is not in a dilemma, but he will very likely say afterwards that he found himself in one. The differences are (1) that the mere Englishman has still less chance than with *feasible* of inferring the true meaning from related words, it being an almost isolated importation from Greek ; (2) that the user need hardly be suspected of pretension, since *dilemma* is in too familiar use for him to doubt that he knows what it means. Nevertheless, he is injuring the language, however unconsciously, both by helping to break down a serviceable distinction, & by giving currency to a mere token word in the place of one that is alive.

Slipshod extension, however, though naturally more common with words of learned antecedents, is not confined to them, & in the following list will be found several that would seem too thoroughly part of the vernacular to be in danger of misuse. In many of the articles referred to, further illustration of slipshod ex-

tension is given :—asset ; balance ; calculate ; chronic ; commonplace (on truism) ; conservative ; dead letter ; decimate ; dilemma ; eke out ; evidence ; feasible ; forgather ; idola ; liable ; meticulous ; mutual ; optimism ; possible (3) ; probable ; precedent ; protagonist ; recrudescence ; reference ; relegate ; tribute ; verbal.

Of the above words, all or most are habitually ill treated, & should be noted as needing care. A stray example may be added of a word with which such abuse is exceptional & apparently unaccountable, that slipshod extension may not be taken for the sort of blunder against which one is safe if one attends to a limited list of dangerous words ; what is required is the habit of paying all words the compliment of respecting their peculiarities. *An excellent arrangement, for there are thus none of those smells which so often disfigure the otherwise sweet atmosphere of an English home.* What has no figure or shape cannot be disfigured ; not that the limitation need be closely pressed ; not only a face or a landscape can be disfigured ; so also can an action, a person's diction, or a man's career, (to take things of which the OED quotes instances) be disfigured, because each of them can be conceived, with the aid of metaphor, as a shapely whole ; but a shapely atmosphere ?

slobber. See SLAVER.

sloe-worm. See SLOW-WORM.

slogan. Though the great vogue of the word as a substitute for the older *motto*, *watchword*, *rule*, &c., is of the 20th c. only, & we old fogies regard it with patriotic dislike as a Scotch interloper, it was occasionally so used earlier ; the OED has a quotation from Macaulay. For some synonyms, see SIGN.

sloid. See SLOYD.

slosh. See SLUSH.

slouch hat. Two separate words ; see HYPHENS 3 B.

slough. The n. & vb meaning bog

are pronounced -ow ; the n. meaning cast skin &c. & the vb meaning cast or drop off are pronounced -ŭf.

slovenly. For the adv., see -LILY.

slow(ly), advv. In spite of the encroachments of -*ly* (see UNIDIO-MATIC -LY), *slow* maintains itself as at least an idiomatic possibility under some conditions even in the positive (*how slow he climbs !, please read very slow, my watch goes slow*), while in the comparative & superlative *slower* & *slowest* are usually preferable to *more* & *most slowly* ; see -ER & -EST 3. Of the ' conditions ', the chief is that the adverb, & not the verb &c., should contain the real point ; compare ' We forged slowly ahead ', where the slowness is an unessential item, with ' Sing as slow as you can ', where the slowness is all that matters.

slow-worm, sloe-, is not connected with either the noun *sloe* or the adj. *slow* ; *slow-* is now the established form, & the OED calls *sloe-* obsolete.

sloyd, sloid. The OED prefers -yd.

slubber. See SLAVER.

sludge. See SLUSH.

slue. See SLEW.

sluice, vb, makes -*ceable* ; -ABLE 1.

slumber. Apart from mere substitutions of *s.* for *sleep* dictated by desire for poetic diction or dislike of the words that common mortals use, *slumber* is equivalent to the noun *sleep* with some adjective or the verb *sleep* with some adverb. Slumber is easy or light or half or broken or daylight sleep, or again mental or stolen or virtual or lazy sleep. The implied epithet or adverb, that is, may be almost anything ; but the choice of *slumber* instead of *sleep*, if not due to mere stylishness (see WORKING & STYLISH WORDS), is meant to prevent the reader from passing lightly by without remembering that there is sleep & sleep.

slumb(e)rous. The shorter form is recommended ; cf. DEXT(E)ROUS. But analogies for either are plentiful : *cumbrous, wondrous, monstrous,* *leprous, idolatrous* ; but *thunderous, slanderous, murderous.*

slur. See PRONUNCIATION, s.f., for *slurring.*

slush, sludge, slosh. The differences are not very clear. There is the natural one, resulting from the stickier sound, that *sludge* is usually applied to something less liquid than *slush* or *slosh*, e. g. to slimy deposits or clinging mud, whereas thawing snow is typical slush ; & of *slush* & *slosh* the latter is perhaps more often used to describe what is metaphorically watery stuff—twaddle or sentimentality.

sly makes *slyer, slyest, slyly, slyness, slyish* ; for comparison with other such words, see DRY.

small. Relations with *little* are complicated, & the task of disentangling them might excusably be shirked, if not as difficult, then as unprofitable ; but examination of the differences between seeming equivalents does give an insight into the nature of idiom. Under BIG some attempt has been made at delimiting the territories of *great, large,* & *big* ; *small* & *little* have to divide between them the opposition to those three as well as *much*, & the distribution is by no means so simple & definite as the pedantic analyst might desire.

Of the possible pairs of opposites let some be called patent pairs, as being openly & comfortably used with both members expressed ; & the rest latent pairs. The patent pairs start with three that are pretty clearly distinguishable in meaning. Contrasts of size or extent are given by *large & small*, those of quantity or amount by *much & little*, & those of importance or quality by *great & small* : ' large & small rooms ', ' of large or small size ', ' large or small writing ', ' large & small appetites ', ' large & small dealings, dealers ' ; ' much or little butter, faith, exercise, damage, hesitation, study ' ; ' the Great & the Small Powers ', ' great & small occa-

sions ', ' a great or a small undertaking ', ' great & small authors '. To
these, the main divisions, are to be
added two minor patent pairs sometimes substituted for one or other of
them—*great & little, big & little. Great
& little* as a patent pair is preferred
to *large & small* in distinctive names
('the Great & the Little Bear ', ' Great
& Little Malvern ', ' the great & the
little toe ') ; it is also common (see
below) as a latent pair in two senses.
Big & little is a patent pair often
colloquially substituted for either
large & small (' big & little farms,
motor-cars ') or *great & small* (' big
& little wars, people ') or *great &
little* (' the big & the little toe ').
The patent pairs are sets of
opposites so far felt to correspond
that one does not hesitate to put
them together as in all the expressions given above ; or again either
member can be used when the other
is not expressed but only implied ;
e. g., ' the Great Powers ' is more
often used alone, but ' the Great
& the Small Powers ' is also an
ordinary expression ; & ' the Little
Entente ', ' the Big Four ', depend
for their meaning on a ' Great
Entente ' & a ' Little Thirty (or so) '
that are seldom mentioned. By
latent pairs are meant sets of
opposites in which one member has
the meaning opposite to that of
another with which nevertheless it
could not be expressly contrasted
without an evident violation of
idiom. For instance, no-one would
put *large & little* together ; ' large
& little lakes ' sounds absurd ; but
one speaks of ' a (or the) little lake '
without hesitation, though ' large
lakes ' (not ' great lakes ', which
ranks with the distinctive names
above referred to) is the implied
opposite. Another latent pair is
much & small ; though ' much or
small hope ' is impossible, & ' much
or little hope ' felt to be required
instead, yet ' small hope ', ' small
thanks ', ' small credit ', ' small
wonder ', are all idiomatic when the
irregular opposite *much* is not ex-

pressed. Similarly with *big & small* ;
we never contrast them openly, but
in ' the big battalions ', ' big game ',
' a big investment or undertaking ',
' a big grocer ', the opposite in
reserve is *small. Great & little* was
said above to rank both as a patent
& as a latent pair. In the latter
capacity it allows us to talk of
' great damage ', ' great doubt ',
' great hesitation ', & again of ' little
damage ' &c., but forbids us to put
the pair together ; it is ' much or
little (not ' great or little ') doubt '.
Again, when *great* is substituted for
large, or *little* for *small*, with a view
to charging either idea of size with
contempt or indignation or affection, as in ' you great fool ', ' you
little fool ', ' he hit me with a great
stick ', ' a sweet little cottage ', the
opposites naturally do not appear
together, & we have another variety
of latent pair.
Tabulating now, we get :—
Patent pairs
1. Large & small (of size or extent).
2. Much & little (of quantity or
amount).
3. Great & small (of importance or
quality).
4. Great & little (in distinctive
names).
5. Big & little (colloq. for 1, 3, or 4).
Latent pairs
Large, little (for 1).
Much, small (for 2).
Big, small (for 1).
Great, little (for 2 or 1).

small beer, small hours. No hyphens ; see HYPHENS (3 B, & group
*blue-stocking).

smell, vb. 1. For *smelt & smelled*
see -T & -ED. 2. The intransitive
sense to emit an odour of a specified
kind is idiomatically completed by
an adjective, not an adverb ; a
thing smells sweet, sour, rank, foul,
good, bad, &c., not sweetly, badly,
&c. But the tendency referred to in
UNIDIOMATIC -LY sometimes misleads the unwary into using the
adverbs. The mistake is the easier
because (a) when the character of

the smell is given by ' of so-&-so ' instead of by a single word, an adverb is often added ; compare *smells strong* or *delicious* (i. e. has a strong or delicious smell) with *smells strongly* or *suspiciously of whisky* or *deliciously of violets* ; & (b) when to *smell* is used, as it may be, for to *stink*, an adverb is the right addition—*this water smells outrageously* ; *smells disgusting* & *smells disgustingly* are both idiomatic, but are arrived at in slightly different ways, the first meaning ' has a disgusting smell ', & the second ' stinks so as to disgust one '.

smell-less. Write so ; & for discussion see SKILL-LESS.

smite. *Smit* for *smote* is obsolete ; *smit* for *smitten* is archaic, but still in poetic use.

smoke. The verb makes *smokable* ; see MUTE E. *Smoking-room, smoke-room* ; the first is the older & better form.

smooth(e(n). The adjective is now always *smooth*. For the verb, *smooth* is recommended in preference to *smoothe*, but the latter still exists ; OED 19th & 20th c. examples that show the difference give it half as often as *smooth* ; for *smoothen* see -EN VERBS.

smudge, smutch. The earlier noun is *smutch*, the earlier verb *smudge* ; but this has no apparent effect on present usage ; *-dge* now prevails in ordinary literal use, *-tch* being preferred in metaphor & (even when the sense is literal) in poetic or literary writing.

snail-like. For hyphen, see -LIKE.

snake makes *snaky* ; see MUTE E.

snake, serpent. *Snake* is the native, & *serpent* the alien word ; it is not a necessary consequence of this, but it is also true, that *snake* is the word ordinarily used, & *serpent* the exceptional one. The OED's remark on *serpent* is ' now, in ordinary use, applied chiefly to the larger & more venomous species ; otherwise only *rhetorical . . .* or with reference to

serpent-worship '. We perhaps conceive serpents as terrible & powerful & beautiful things, snakes as insidious & cold & contemptible.

snapshot, vb. The OED recognizes no verb to *snapshoot*, though it gives *snapshooter* & *snapshooting* (chiefly in the original sense, i. e. with gun, not camera) ; but the verb to *snapshot* (with camera) is established ; its past & p.p. (see FORECAST & HAMSTRING) are properly *snapshotted*, & similarly the nouns of agent & action should be *snapshotter* & *snapshotting*, while *snapshooter* & *snapshooting* should be retained in the fire-arm sense.

snare makes *snarable* ; see MUTE E.
snipe makes *-pable, -py* ; see MUTE E.
snivel makes *snivelling* ; -LL-, -L-.
so. 1. Phrases treated elsewhere. 2. *So long, & so to —, do so.* 3. Appealing *so.* 4. Paterine *so.* 5. Repeated *so* (& *such*). 6. *So* with p.p. 7. Explanatory *so.* 8. *So* with superlatives & absolutes.

1. For *so far from, so far as, so far that*, see FAR ; for *so far forth* (*as*) see FORTH 2 ; for *& so on, & so forth*, see FORTH 1 ; for *quite* (*so*) see QUITE ; for *so to speak* see SUPERIORITY ; for *ever, never, so* see NEVER.

2. *So long, & so to —, do so. So long* used colloquially for *goodbye* or *au revoir*. It perhaps matters little for practical purposes, but the OED gives no countenance to the derivation from *salaam*, & treats the phrase as a mere special combination of *so* & *long* ; those who are inclined to avoid it as some sort of slang may be mollified by its naturalness as a short equivalent for Good luck till we meet again. *And so to a division, & so to dinner,* &c. This formula for winding up the account of a debate or incident, borrowed directly or indirectly from Pepys, is apt to take such a hold upon those who once begin upon it that, like confirmed cigarette-smokers, they lose all count of their indulgences ; it is wise to abstain from it altogether. *Do so. It is*

a study of an elderly widower who, on approaching sixty, finds that he knows hardly anything of his three daughters, & sets out to do so. For similar absurdities, *which are too common, see DO 3 b, c.

3. The appealing *so*. The type is *Cricket is so uncertain*. The speaker has a conviction borne in upon him, & in stating it appeals, with his *so*, to general experience to confirm him; it means *as you*, or *as we all, know*. A natural use, but more suitable for conversation, where the responsive nod of confirmation can be awaited, than for most kinds of writing. In print, outside dialogue, it has a certain air of silliness, even when the context is favourable, i. e. when the sentence is of the shortest & simplest kind, & the experience appealed to is really general. Readers will probably agree that in all the following extracts the context is not favourable; & the only object of exhibiting so many of them is to give proof that the danger of yielding to this weakness (' feminine ' it would have been called before the ladies had learnt to write) is a real one. The principle underlying the restriction to short simple sentences is perhaps that this use of *so* is exclamatory. The examples are ranged from bad to worse :—*In the case of Ophthalmology in the tropics a work of authority is so sadly overdue./Mr Stephen Walsh is, like so many of the miners' leaders, a man who started life in the pit./Along with so many other well-wishers for the prosperity & independence of the Ottoman Empire, I have been deeply grieved by . . ./But he does combine them ingeniously, though in instancing this very real power we feel that it might have been so much more satisfactorily expended./May I venture to point out that it would be so much better to make them freely & willingly than to have them wrung from her ?/ Beyond what so many people regard as the consoling fact that it was not destined for the cabinets or shelves of an American millionaire, it was not*

1351

known until now who was the happy purchaser./The book is written in a simple style which is foreign to so many lawyers./He was always kind, considerate, & courteous to his witnesses, this being so contrary to what we are led to expect from his successors. / Constant betel-chewing, he thinks, may be ' the predisposing factor producing a condition of nervous irritability that so easily might degenerate into* lâtah *'./The periodical discussions incidentally serve to show how in Scotland as in England so many of those interested in matters of this kind are town-dwellers.*

4. The Paterine *so*. This is a special form of the appealing *so* : *In the midst of that aesthetically so brilliant world of Greater Greece* is an example. The *so* is deliberately inserted before a descriptive adjective, & is a way of saying, at once urbanely & concisely, Has it ever occurred to you how brilliant &c. it was ? ; it differs from the *sos* in 3, that is, in being not careless & natural, but didactic & highly artificial. Effective enough on occasion, it is among the idioms that should never be allowed to remind the reader, by being repeated, that he has already met them in the last hundred pages or so. See MANNERISMS for more examples from Pater himself; & here, from imitators, are others :—*Here an Englishman has set himself to follow in outline the very distinctive genius of Russia through the centuries of its difficult but always so attractive development./And still no one came to open that huge, contemptuous door with its so menacing, so hostile air.*

5. *So* (& *such*) in repetition. From the artificial to the entirely artless. *So* is a much used word, but not indispensable enough to justify such repetitions of it as the following :— *The pity is that for so many men who can so hardly keep pace with rising prices it should become so difficult to follow the sport./It would do away with any suggestion of State purchase of which the country is at the present*

time so *nervous, as it would necessitate* such *large borrowing of money, which, in the present financial condition of the country, is* so *inadvisable. / The situation was well in hand, but it had* so far *developed* so *little that nothing useful can be said about it, save that* so far *the Commander-in-Chief was satisfied.*

6. *So* with p.p. The distinction usually recognized with VERY between a truly verbal & an adjectival p.p. is not applicable to *so* ; but it is well worth while, before writing plain *so*, to decide between it & *so much, so well,* &c. The insertion of *much* in the first & *well* in the second quotation after *so* is certainly desirable :—*Admiral Faravelli reports that Tripoli batteries have been* so damaged *that Turkish soldiers have been forced to retire into town. / Ireland being mainly an agricultural country, & England industrial, the Bill is not* so suited *to Ireland as to this country.*

7. The explanatory *so.* Type : *He could not move, he was* so *cold.* The second member is equivalent to a sentence beginning with *for,* & the idiom is mainly, but not solely, colloquial. What requires notice is that, when it is used in formal writing, it is spoilt if *for,* whose work is being done for it by *so,* is allowed to remain as a supernumerary. Two examples follow, the first right, the second wrong :—*The dangers of the situation seem to us very real & menacing ; both sides, in maintaining a firm attitude, may* so *easily find themselves bluffing over the edge into the precipice. / It would seem particularly fitting that an American professor of literature should discuss the subject of Convention & Revolt,* for *in that country the two tendencies are at present* so *curiously & incongruously mingled.*

8. *So* with superlatives & absolutes. *So,* when it qualifies adjectives & adverbs, means to such a degree or extent ; it is therefore not to be applied to a superlative, as in *The difficult & anxious negotiations in which he has taken* so *foremost a part*

in Paris. Nor to words that are felt not to admit of degrees (' absolutes ', for convenience), including, besides essential positives like *unique,* such indefinites as *some, several.* Among the latter is *oft-times,* though *often* is not, & ' so oft-times ' is as wrong, though not as unlikely, as ' so sometimes ':—*And now, as it* so *oft-times happens, the pupil well may claim to have out-passed the master.*

sober makes *soberer, -est* ; see -ER & -EST 1 b.

sobriquet, sou-. The first is much longer established in English, besides being the only modern French form. Pron. sō′brĭkā.

SOBRIQUETS. Under this heading, for want of a better, are here collected a hundred or so out of the thousands of secondary names that have become so specially attached to particular persons, places, or things, as to be intelligible when used instead of the primary names, each of which is thus provided with a deputy or a private pronoun. The deputy use is seen in ' It was carried to the ears of that famous hero & warrior, the Philosopher of Sans Souci ', where ' t. P. o. S. S.' acts for Frederick the Great ; & the private-pronoun use in ' He employed his creative faculty for about twenty years, which is as much, I suppose, as Shakspere did ; the Bard of Avon is another example . . .', where ' t. B. o. A.' means Shakspere or the latter. Some names have a large retinue of sobriquets ; Rome, e.g., may be the Eternal City, the City of the Seven Hills, the Papal City, the Scarlet Woman, the Scarlet Whore, the Empress of the Ancient World, the Western Babylon ; Mr Warner may be Plum, or P. F., or the Middlesex Captain, or the Recoverer of the Ashes ; & neither's list of sobriquets is half told.

Now the sobriquet habit is not a thing to be acquired, but a thing to be avoided ; & the selection that follows is compiled for the purpose not of assisting but of discouraging it. The writers most of all addicted to it are the sporting reporters; games & contests are exciting to take part in, interesting or even exciting also to watch, but essentially (i.e. as bare facts) dull to read about, insomuch that most intelligent people abandon such reading; the reporter, conscious that his matter & his audience are both dull enough to require enlivening, thinks that the needful fillip may be given if he calls fishing the gentle craft, a ball the pill or the leather, a captain the skipper, or a saddle the pigskin, & so makes his description a series of momentary puzzles that shall pleasantly titillate inactive minds. Here is a *Times* reviewer, who sighs over ' One sad fault, which runs through this, &, alas ! a good many other excellent books—the habit of seldom calling a spade a spade. Does it really help, or is it really humorous, to call the fox "Charles James ", a hare " Madam", a nose a " proboscis ", & Wales " Taffyland " ? Of course, a sporting book will tend to use sporting expressions; but a good deal of this irritating circumlocution is unnecessary, & might well be left for colloquial use '.

It is by no means true, however, that the use of sobriquets is confined to this, or to any, class of writers; the Philosopher of Sans Souci & the Bard of Avon quoted above are from Thackeray & Conan Doyle, though they are unfavourable specimens of those authors' styles. And, moreover, the sobriquet deputy has its true uses; just as Bacon knows of ' things graceful in a friend's mouth, which are blushing in a man's own ', so the sobriquet may often in a particular context be more efficient than the proper name; though ' the Papal City ' means Rome, its substitution may be a serviceable reminder, when that is appropriate, that Rome in one of its aspects only is intended. Again, many sobriquets have succeeded, like mayors of the palace, in usurp-

ing all or some of their principals' functions; the Young Pretender is actually more intelligible, & therefore rightly more used, than Charles Edward, & to insist on ' came over with William I ' in preference to ' with the Conqueror ' would be absurd.

No universal condemnation of sobriquets, therefore, is possible; but even the better sort of journalist, seldom guilty of such excesses as the sporting reporter, is much tempted to use them without considering whether they tend to illuminate or to obscure; ' the exile of Ferney ', he feels, at once exhibits his own easy familiarity with Voltaire the man (*Voltaire* the word, by the way, is itself one of the mayor-of-the-palace sobriquets) & gratifies such of his readers as know who is meant; as for those who may not know, it will be good for them to realize that their newspaper is more cultured than they. The sobriquet style, developed on these lines, is very distasteful to all readers of discretion. Those who may become aware, in glancing through the following alphabetical selection, that these & similar substitutes are apt to occur frequently in their own writing should regard it as a very serious symptom of perverted taste for cheap ornament. In most of the expressions an initial *the* is to be supplied :—Abigail (lady's-maid); Albion (Great Britain); Alma Mater (university); Black Watch (Royal Highlanders); Bruin(bear); Chanticleer (cock); Cœur de Lion (Richard I); Conqueror (William I); Cousin Jack (Cornishman); dismal science (Political Economy); Emerald Isle (Ireland); Empire City (New York); Erin(Ireland); Eternal City (Rome); Eton of the North (any northern public school); Father of History (Herodotus); Father of Lies (Satan); First Gentleman of Europe (George IV); gamp (umbrella); Ganymede (waiter); Garden of England (Kent); Gaul (France); Gilded Chamber (House of Lords); G.O.M. (Gladstone) ; Granite City (Aberdeen) ; Great Commoner (Pitt) ; great unwashed (populace) ; handy man (sailor) ; Hebe (waitress) ; Hermit Kingdom (Corea) ; honest broker (Bismarck) ; Indian weed (tobacco) ; Iron Chancellor (Bismarck) ; Iron Duke (Wellington) ; iron horse (railway engine) ; Jeames (footman) ; Jehu (cabman) ; jolly Roger (black flag) ; Kingmaker (Warwick) ; king of beasts (lion) ; King of Terrors (death) ; Knight of the Rueful Countenance (Don Quixote) ; Land of Cakes (Scotland) ; laughing philosopher (Democritus) ; leather (cricket-ball) ; Lion of the North (Gustavus) ; maestro di color che sanno (Aristotle) ; Man of Destiny (Napoleon) ; Merry Monarch (Charles II) ; modern Athens (Edinburgh) ; modern Babylon (London) ; Mother of Parliaments (British Parliament) ; nation of shopkeepers (the English) ; Neptune (sea) ; N° 1 (oneself) ; ocean greyhound (liner) ; Old Gentleman (devil) ; Old Lady of Threadneedle Street (Bank of England) ; Old Pretender (James, son of James II) ; olive branches (children) ; petit caporal (Napoleon I) ; Philomel (nightingale) ; pill (ball) ; Pillars of Hercules (straits of Gibraltar) ; Queen of the Adriatic (Venice) ; ramshackle Empire (Austria-Hungary) ; redcoats (British soldiers) ; Reynard (fox) ; Rupert of debate (Lord Derby, P.M. 1851) ; Sage of Chelsea (Carlyle) ; Sailor King (William IV) ; St Stephen's (House of Commons) ; seagreen incorruptible (Robespierre) ; senior service (navy) ; Seraphic Doctor (St Bonaventura) ; Sick Man (Turkey) ; silver streak (English Channel) ; Sol (sun) ; sport of kings (hunting) ; staff of life (bread) ; Stagirite (Aristotle) ; strawberry leaves (ducal rank) ; Tiger (Clemenceau) ; tommies (British soldiers) ; Uncle Sam (U.S.A.) ; Ville Lumière (Paris) ; Virgin Queen (Elizabeth) ; Warrior Queen (Boadicea) ; Water Poet (John Taylor) ; weaker sex (women) ; well of English undefiled

(Chaucer) ; weary Titan (British Empire) ; Wen (London) ; Wizard of the North (Scott) ; Young Chevalier (Charles Edward Stuart).

soc(c)age. The OED spelling is *socage* (pron. sŏk-).

soccer. See SOCKER.

sociable) (social. For confusion between pairs of adjectives in *-able* & *-al*, see EXCEPTIONABLE, PRACTICABLE. No such patent misuses occur with the present pair as with those ; there is merely a tendency to use *social* not where it is indefensible, but where the other would be more appropriate. Roughly, *social* means of or in or for or used to or shown in or affording society ; & *sociable* seeking, or loving, or marked by the pleasures of, company. *Social* is rather a classifying, & *sociable* rather a descriptive adjective : man is a social being, Jones is a sociable person ; people are invited to a social evening, & say afterwards (or do not say) that they had a very sociable evening. Obviously, overlapping is likely. The OED, under a definition of *social* that includes ' sociable ' as an equivalent, gives two quotations in which *sociable* should have been preferred (*His own friendly & social disposition*—Jane Austen / *He was very happy & social*—Miss Braddon), as well as one that is just on the right side of the border (*Charles came forth from that school with social habits, with polite & engaging manners*—Macaulay).

socialism, communism, anarchism. The things are not mutually exclusive ; the words are not an exhaustive threefold division of anything ; each stands for a state of things, or a striving after it, that differs much from that which we know ; & for many of us, especially those who are comfortably at home in the world as it is, they have consequently come to be the positive, comparative, & superlative, distinguished not in kind but in degree only, of the terms of abuse applicable to those who would disturb our peace. Little can be done in the short space available in such a book as this to clear up vague notions; but it is something gained if we realize two facts, that we are dealing neither with three degrees of the same thing, nor with three independent parallel terms.

Whatever their relations to one another, all three have in common a dissatisfaction with society as it is, & the goal of equal opportunities for all. The socialist blames our organization into classes (especially those of capitalists & wage-earners), the communist blames private property, the anarchist blames government as such, for what they all alike find unsatisfactory. The anarchist remedy is to abolish the State & leave all relations between persons & groups to be established & maintained by free contract. The communist's, on the contrary, is, by abolishing all private property, to make the State absolute master of the individual. The socialist's is less simple; he may accept either of the apparently opposite methods of anarchist & communist as being the shortest way to his own end; that is, anarchism & communism are sometimes forms of socialism; or he may be content with something short of communism—not abolishing all property, but transferring the control of public services & the means of large industrial production to the State or the municipality. And further, it is not a case with him, as with the others, of all or nothing; abolition of the State or of private property is for them the condition precedent of improvement, & is not to be brought about except by revolution; but, for the socialist, every curtailment of privilege, every nationalization or municipalization of a particular service, is a step forward, worth taking for itself as well as for its contribution to the gradual progress; that is, the changes required by communism & anarchism are more abrupt & violent than

what socialism need, but not than what it may, be actually striving to effect.

It should perhaps be added that not the comparative merit of three more or less different principles, but only the meaning of three often confused terms, is here in question.

sock. For *the s.*, = the comic stage, see BATTERED ORNAMENTS.

socker, -ccer. The -k- is recommended; *accept, success, eccentricity, accident, flaccid, coccyx,* show the almost invariable sound of -cc- before e, i, y; perhaps the sole exception is *baccy,* which the -cc- in *tobacco* makes more excusable than *soccer.*

socketed, not *-tted*; see -T-, -TT-.

socle. Pronounce sŏ'kl.

Socrates. Pronounce sŏk-, & see FALSE QUANTITY.

soddenness. So spelt.

Sofi(sm). See SUFI(SM).

soft. 1. For 's. impeachment' see IRRELEVANT ILLUSION. 2. For *play, sleep, fall,* &c., *s.,* see UNIDIOMATIC -LY.

soften. Pronounce saw'fn; see PRONUNCIATION.

soi-disant. See FRENCH WORDS. English is well provided, with *self-styled, ostensible, would-be, professed, professing, supposed,* & other words, for all needs.

soilless. Hyphen unnecessary; see SKILL-LESS.

sojourn. Pronounce sŭ'jern; OED gives sŭ-, sŏ-, sō-, in that order.

Sol, = the sun. See SOBRIQUETS.

solatium. Pl. *-ia.*

solder. The only pronunciation I have ever heard, except from the half-educated to whom spelling is a final court of appeal, is sŏ'der, which is accordingly here recommended; but the OED gives it only as favoured by American dictionaries, & allows sō'lder & sŏ'der only.

soldier. *S. ant, s. beetle, s. crab, s. orchis*; no hyphens; see HYPHENS 3 B.

soldierly. For adv. see -LILY.

solemnness, not -mness.

solicitor general is better without hyphen; see HYPHENS, group *Court Martial.

solid has solider, -est; -ER & -EST 2.

solidify. For inflexions see VERBS IN -IE &c., 6.

soliloquy. See TECHNICAL TERMS.

solo. Pl. -os, see -O(E)S 6, or in technical use soli (-ē).

so long,=goodbye. See SO 2.

soluble, solvable, make insoluble, unsolvable; see IN- & -UN-. Substances are soluble (or dissolvable), not solvable; problems are soluble or solvable.

solus, sola. The stage-direction use is often transferred to descriptions in novels, where it is a harmless affectation. Applied to a woman it is awkward, because solus in stage directions was of either gender, & yet now offends the grammar-conscious, while sola is unfamiliar & odd. Affectation apart, what is wrong with alone?

solution. For s. of continuity see POLYSYLLABIC HUMOUR.

sombre, -ber. See -RE & -ER.

some. 1. S. in meiosis. 2. Some one) (someone. 3. Sometime) (some time. 4. Somewhat. 5. Somewhen.

1. Meiosis. 'This is some war', with strong emphasis on some, is modern colloquial for 'This is a vast war', 'This is indeed a war, if ever there was one'. It is still felt as slang, & it comes to us from America; but it results from that love of meiosis (see TECHNICAL TERMS) which is shared with the Americans by us. We say a place is some distance off, meaning a long way; we say 'It needs some faith to believe that', meaning a hardly possible credulity. So far the effect is exactly parallel to the emphatic use of rather in answer to a question —'Do you like it?' 'Rather!', meaning not somewhat, but exceedingly. The irregular development comes in when some, meiosis & all, is transferred from its proper region of quantity or number to that of

quality; some faith is a wonderful amount of faith; but some war is a wonderful kind or specimen of war, & some pumpkins (at least 70 years old, & said to be the original American phrase) were not a great number of pumpkins, but very superior pumpkins. It is this irregularity that makes the use both noticeable & popular; perhaps, when it has become so trite as no longer to sound humorous, it may perish. Compare with it our own equivalent, which lacks the piquant irregularity only, 'something like a war'.

2. For someone) (some one, see EVERYONE.

3. Some time, sometime, advv. Some time is often used elliptically for at some time or other. There is no essential objection to writing it some-time or sometime, but it is convenient to keep it in two separate words for distinction from the sometime that appears in such descriptions as 'sometime Fellow of ...', 'sometime Rector of this Parish', meaning formerly.

4. Somewhat has for the inferior journalist what he ought not, but would be likely, to describe as 'a somewhat amazing fascination'. Thus:—The evidence furnished in the somewhat extraordinary report of the Federation as to its waste of huge sums of money on .../His election experiences were somewhat unique./ The flocks of wild geese, to which the flamingo is somewhat more or less closely allied. / The Labour motion introduced the proviso, somewhat for the first time, that the process should be gradual. These are examples selected for their patent absurdity, & their authors are doubtless so addicted to the word that they are no longer conscious of using it. What moves people to experiment first in the somewhat style is partly timidity—they are frightened by the coming strong word & would fain take precautions against shock—, & partly the notion that an air of studious under-statement is superior

& impressive ; & so in our news-papers ' the intemperate orgy of moderation is renewed every morning '.

5. *Somewhen* should be regarded as the progeny of *somewhere* & *somehow*, & allowed to appear in public under the wing of either or both of its parents, but not by itself.

-some. The OED collects a number of adjectives in *-some*, grouping them according to their age. The most established words are here given in three sets for comparison.

A (older) : buxom, cumbersome, fulsome, gamesome, gladsome, handsome, lightsome, loathsome, noisome, wholesome, winsome.

B (medium) ; awesome, brightsome, darksome, gruesome, healthsome, heartsome, quarrelsome, tiresome.

C (younger) : blithesome, bothersome, cuddlesome, fearsome, lithesome, lonesome.

Reading through the lists, one can hardly fail to notice that, while most words in the first are such as one feels to be independent wholes & is not tempted to resolve into root & suffix, the other lists are made up, with individual exceptions as for *quarrelsome* & *lonesome*, of artificial-looking & more or less fanciful formations. The inference is that *-some* has lost its efficiency as a suffix, & that it is wise to avoid such *-some* words, even including one or two of the older ones, as are not of quite unquestionable standing.

somersault, *summersault, somerset, summerset.* The first spelling is recommended.

somnolence, -cy. See -CE, -CY.

sonant. See TECHNICAL TERMS.

songstress. See FEMININE DESIGNATIONS.

sonnet. See TECHNICAL TERMS.

sonor'ous. So accented.

sōot, not sŏŏt.

sophistic(al). *Sophistical* is now the usual form. It would be well if, in accordance with what is said in the article -IC(AL), *sophistic* could be confined to the merely defining sense ' of the (Greek) Sophists '.

Sophy, -ie. See -EY, -IE, -Y.

soprano. Pl. *-os,* see -O(E)S 6, or *-ni* (-ē).

sorceress. See FEMININE DESIGNATIONS.

sore, adv. For *s. afflicted, let & hindered,* &c., see UNIDIOMATIC -LY.

sorites(sorī'tēz). TECHNICAL TERMS.

sorrow. For ' more in s. than in anger ', & ' in her &c. great s.', see HACKNEYED PHRASES, & STOCK PATHOS.

sorry, sorrow. The two words do not, as it is natural to suppose, belong to each other, *sorry* being the adjective of the noun *sore.* Sore & sorrow, however, are so near in sense (especially in earlier & wider meanings of *sore*) that the mistake has perhaps no ill effects ; still, the knowledge has its practical value ; connexion between *sore* & *sorry* helps to account for the use of *sorry,* = scurvy, poor, inferior, seen in *sorry rascal, meal, luck, excuse.*

sort is, in the irregular but idiomatic uses touched upon under KIND, equally common, & subject to the same limitations : *sort of* & *kind of* preceding a verb (*I s. o. expected it*) differ from the others in being more generally confined in practice to the colloquial. It is worth mention that the OED, always chary in condemnation, records all these idioms without seriously questioning their legitimacy ; & the same with the now common depreciatory *of sorts ;* ' still common colloquially, though considered grammatically incorrect ', on *these kind of men,* is its severest censure. For *of any sort or kind,* see PLEONASM 2 ; *We can only repeat that there is no inconsistency of any sort or kind in our attitude.*

sotto voce. Pronounce sŏ'tō vō'chā; see ITALIAN SOUNDS.

soubrette. See FRENCH WORDS.

soubriquet. See SOBRIQUET.

Soudan(ese). Better than SUD-.

soufflé. See FRENCH WORDS.

sough. The pronunciation alternatives in the OED are sŭf, sow, & sōō followed by the breathed guttural (cf. LOUGH).

soulless. Hyphen unnecessary ; see SKILL-LESS.

sound, adv. For *sleep sound(ly)*, see UNIDIOMATIC -LY.

soupçon. See FRENCH WORDS.

south-. Compounds (*s.-east* &c.) are pronounced with th. Of the derivatives, *southerly, southern, southernwood, southron,* have sŭdh- ; *souther & southing* have sowth- ; *southward(s)* is sowthward(z) or sŭdhard(z).

southerly. For the special uses & meanings of this set of words, see EASTERLY.

sovereign, sovran. Though the latter spelling may accord better with the etymology (It. *sovrano,* L. *superanus*), the occasional attempts to introduce it come into conflict with the present pronunciation (sŏ'vrĭn or sŏ'verĭn, not sŏ'vran), & their success is not to be desired.

sow, vb. The p.p. *sown* is four times as frequent, in the OED 19th–20th-c. quotations, as *sowed.*

spa. This spelling, & the pronunciation spah, have now displaced the older spaw.

space, vb, makes *spaceable* ; -ABLE 1.
spade, vb, makes *spadable* ; MUTE E.
spadeful. Pl. *-ls* ; see -FUL.
spare makes *sparable* ; see MUTE E.
spats. For *spatterdashes* ; see CURTAILED WORDS.
spavined, not *-nned* ; see -N-, -NN-.
spec,=*speculation.* CURTAILED WDS.
special. 1. *Special*) (*especial.* 2. *S. pleading.*

1. For *special(ly)* as distinguished from *especial(ly)*, see ESPECIAL. The two following quotations show the adverbs used each where the other would have been better :—*Ample supplies of food & clothing for the prisoners are now available there, having been shipped from America especially for this purpose./The neighbourhood is not specially well provided with places where soldiers can get amusement & refreshments.*

2. *S. pleading* is a POPULARIZED TECHNICALITY. When we say that a person's argument is s. p., we mean that he has tried to convince us by calling our attention to whatever makes for, & diverting it from whatever makes against, the conclusion he desires. But this is, not indeed the highest, but at any rate the almost universal, argumentative procedure. That is, it is advocacy or (in the untechnical sense) pleading, & the word *special* adds nothing to the meaning ; why then call it special ? Pleadings, in law, are a series of formal written statements by the parties to a suit designed to establish clearly, before the case is tried, what is the issue or question to be decided. *S. p.* is adaptation, to the particular circumstances, of the typical formulae or pleadings that may be applicable to them & are ready to be used by either party—the filling in of the details. As one consequence of modern legal reforms, pleadings are now very commonly dispensed with ; but formerly the s. p. had to be done with extreme accuracy if cases were not to be lost on points of form that were of no real importance. S. p. accordingly became identified with legal quibbling, & suffered the same fate as casuistry, passing into a byword for dishonest evasion of real issues. This vague & inaccurate sense the name has retained now that the thing itself is no longer familiar outside the legal profession.

speciality, -alty. The two words, like many pairs in -IC(AL), while they seem to cry out for DIFFERENTIATION, have made little progress in that direction. Anyone who thinks he knows which of the chief senses belong to which, & tests his notions by looking through the OED quotations, is likely to have a surprise ; he will perhaps conclude that writers use either form for any of the senses according as they prefer its sound in general or find it suit the rhythm of a sentence. Where usage is so undecided, it would be presumptuous to offer a profitable differentiation, or to recommend either of two fully established forms for extinction. The most that can be ventured is to state two facts, first that *speciality* is in most senses the commoner, & secondly that *specialty* prevails in the legal sense, defined in OED as ' A special contract, obligation, or bond, expressed in an instrument under seal '.

specie(s). The OED gives precedence to the disyllabic spē'shĭ, spē'shēz, over the pronunciations retaining the -ĭ- as in *rabies* & *scabies*. It is a case to which the general principle laid down in PRONUNCIATION should be applied & those who are familiar with Latin allowed the three syllables in their communications with one another.

species. Pl. the same ; see LATIN PLURALS.

specific(ally). These words, like RESPECTIVE(LY), though their real value need not be questioned, are often resorted to by those who have no clear idea of their meaning for the air of educated precision that they are held to diffuse. A short table of the senses of *specific*, showing the relation of each to the central notion of species, follows ; it is in the last rather loose sense that it is wise to avoid the word & choose one of the more generally understood synonyms.

1. Characterizing a kind or species. *S. gravity* is that belonging to gold &c. as a kind or as such.
2. Constituting kind or species. *S. difference* is that which entitles courage, man, &c., to be called by those names rather than by more general ones such as fortitude, mammal.
3. Indicating species in classification. In *Pinus sylvestris maritima* (Scotch Fir), the three words are the generic, specific, & subspecific names.

4. Applicable to a kind only. *S. remedy* is one used for a particular disease or organ, not for ill health, or for the body, in general.
5. Not universal but limited, not general but particular, not vague but definite. *S. directions, accusation, cause,* &c.

specify. For inflexions, see VERBS IN -IE &c., 6.
specs, = spectacles. CURTAILED WDS.
spectre, -ter. See -RE & -ER.
spectrum. Pl. *-tra, -ms* ; see -UM, & LATIN PLURALS.
speculum. Pl. *-la, -lums* ; see LATIN PLURALS.
speechify. For inflexions, see VERBS IN -IE &c., 6.
speed. Past & p.p. *sped* ; but *s. up,* = increase the s. of, makes *speeded* (*must be speeded up* &c.).
spelicans. See SPILLIKIN.
spell, vb. 1. For *spelt, spelled,* see -T & -ED. 2. The sense amount to, mean, involve as inevitable result, seen in *Democracy spells corruption,* & esp. in So-&-so *spells ruin* (' common in recent use '—OED), had its merit, no doubt, when new, but now ranks with WORN-OUT HUMOUR.

SPELLING POINTS. 1. Spelling reform. 2. Double & single consonants. 3. Cross references. 4. Miscellaneous.

1. Spelling reform. The notorious difficulty of English spelling, & the growing impatience caused by it, make it almost imperative to declare one's general attitude towards reform before touching any details. The line here followed is, then : that the substitution for our present chaos of a phonetically consistent method that should not sacrifice the many merits of the old spelling would be of incalculable value ; that a phonetically consistent method is in English peculiarly hard to reconcile with the keeping together of word families, owing to the havoc played on syllable sounds by variations of stress (in *fraternity fraternize* three vowel sounds are metamorphosed by the shifting of stress) ;

that most reformers are so much more awake to the obvious advantages of change than to its less obvious evils that we cannot trust them with the disposal of so vastly important a matter ; & finally that English had better be treated in the English way, & its spelling not be revolutionized but amended in detail, here a little & there a little as absurdities become intolerable, till a result is attained that shall neither overburden schoolboys nor stultify intelligence nor outrage the scholar. In this book some modest attempts are made at cleaning up the more obtrusive untidinesses ; certain inconsistencies have been regarded as, in the present diffusion of literacy, no longer required of us. The well-known type theoretic-radical practical-conservative covers perhaps a majority of our population, & its influence is as sound & sane in the sphere of spelling as elsewhere.

2. **Double & single consonants.** If a list were made of the many thousands of words whose spelling cannot be safely inferred from their sound, the doubtful point in perhaps nine tenths of them would be whether some single consonantal sound was given by a single consonant, as m or t or c, a double consonant, as mm or tt, or two or more, as sc or cq or sch ; *committee* & *comity*, *science* & *silence*, *tic* & *tick*, *harass* & *embarrass* & *Paris*, *levelled* & *unparalleled*, *personify* & *personnel*, *Britain* & *Brittany*, *bivouac* & *bivouacking*, *acquiesce* & *aqueduct*, *schist* & *ship*, are examples enough. The use of double consonants (tt &c.) or two consonants (ck &c.) to give a single sound is due sometimes to the composition of a word, as when *in-* not & *nocens* harmful are combined to make *innocent*, sometimes to the convention by which the sound of a preceding vowel tends to be of one kind (ā ē ī ŏ ū) before one consonant & of another (ă ĕ ĭ ŏ ŭ) before two, & sometimes to factors in word-formation philologically explicable, or inexplicable, but less obvious

than in compounds like *innocent*. Of these causes the only one that has a meaning for anyone who knows no language but English is the convention of vowel sounds ; he is aware that much more often than not a distinction analogous to that between *holy* & *holly* exists ; but the interference of the other causes is so incalculable & so frequent that he soon finds it hopeless to rely upon the principle in doubtful cases. Hence a large proportion of the tears shed over spelling. Little relief can be given ; the words in which sound is no guide to whether there is one consonant or two are not a score or so of which a list could be made & learnt, but thousands ; nothing short of a complete spelling-book will serve the turn of a really weak speller, though it is true that a short list can be made of words in which mistakes are especially common, & that some classes of mistake can be guarded against by rules. Such a list is best made by each person who finds himself in need of it, out of his own experience & to suit his own requirements ; a few words that will usually be included are *harass, embarrass, disappoint, disappear, unparalleled, accommodate, Britain, Brittany, Britannia, committee, abbreviate, all right, banister, battalion, bilious, Boniface, Buddha, bulrush, bunion, camellia, canonical, chicory, clef, desiccated, moccasin, exaggerate, woollen, saddler, skilful* ; it is worth remark that words presenting two opportunities for mistake like *disappoint* (dissap-, disapp-, dissapp-, disap-), or three like *unparalleled*, are more than two or three times as dangerous as others, temptations to assimilate or dissimilate the two or more treatments being added to the doubled or trebled opportunity.

The rules referred to above are those that govern the doubling or not of a word's final consonant when suffixes are added in inflexion or word-formation. Directions are given for the various consonants

under the articles -B-, -BB-, & -LL-, -L-, &c., to be found in their alphabetical places ; but it may be useful to state the main principle here :—
Words ending in a single consonant preceded by a single vowel (which excludes such combinations as ee, ai, ea), when they have added to them a suffix beginning with a vowel (e. g. -ed, -er of the agent or of comparison, -able, -y of adjectives), double the final consonant if they either are monosyllables or bear their accent on the last syllable ; they keep it single if they have their last syllable unaccented ; but a final l is doubled irrespective of accent, & with a final s usage varies. Thus the addition of -ed to the verbs pot, regret, limit, travel, & bias, gives potted (monosyllable), regretted (accented final), limited (unaccented final), travelled (final l), & biassed or biased (final s) ; the verbs tar, demur, simper, level, focus, give similarly tarring, demurring, simpering, levelling, & focussing or focusing ; the adjectives thin, common, cruel, give thinnest, commonest, & cruellest ; the nouns gas, japan, syrup, gruel, give gassy, japanny, syrupy, & gruelly.

Two more questions of single & double consonants are of importance to weak spellers. In forming adverbs in -ly from adjectives in -l or -ll, neither a single nor a triple l is ever right ; full, purposeful, especial, & dull, have adverbs fully, purposefully, especially, & dully—no distinction being made between fully & dully though the two ls are sounded in fully as one letter & in dully as two. And in forming nouns in -ness from adjectives in -n both ns are retained—commonness, rottenness, condignness, &c. ; even solemn, with its mute n, need hardly be excepted, but the OED gives the orthodox solemnness only as a variant for solemness.

3. Cross references. Various points are discussed in short special articles throughout the book ; & most words whose spelling is disputed will be found spelt with or without discussion in their alphabetical places. The following collection of references may serve as a conspectus of likely mistakes & desirable minor reforms.

For such words as lik(e)able, mil(e)age, gaugeable, mous(e)y, pal(e)ish, judg(e)ment, wholly, see MUTE E.

For plural of words in -o see -O(E)S ; most individual words are also given.

For tire tyre, tiro tyro, silvan sylvan, siphon, cipher, siren, sillabub, sibyl, gypsy, pygmy, &c., see Y & I, & the words.

For Aeschylus, Æschylus, Oedipus Œdipus, oecumenical œc-, ec-, diarrhoea -œa, Caesar Cæs-, diaeresis -œr-, &c., see Æ, Œ.

For dyeing, flier, triable, paid, tying, &c., see VERBS IN -IE, -Y, -YE.

For one-ideaed -ea'd, umbrellaed -a'd, mustachioed -o'd, shanghaied, &c., see -ED & 'D.

For the question between -ize & -ise as the normal verb ending, see -IZE ; & for a list of verbs in which -ise only is correct see -ISE)(-IZE.

For plural of handful, spoonful, &c., see -FUL. Choice is not between handfuls & handsful, but between handfuls & hands full, either of which is sometimes the right expression.

For manageable, reducible, gullible, fusible, collapsable, debatable, demonstrable, &c., see -ABLE.

For black bird black-bird blackbird, bona fide bona-fide, court martial court-martial, up to date up-to-date, &c., see HYPHENS.

For alternatives like enquiry & inquiry, undiscriminating & indiscriminating, see EM- & IM-, & IN- & UN-.

For diminutives like slavey, doggie, Sally, see -EY, -IE, -Y.

For adjectives like gam(e)y, hors(e)y, clayey, hol(e)y, see -EY & -Y.

For for(e)bears, for(e)gather, for(e)go, &c., see FOR-, FORE-.

For cooperate co-op- coöp-, preeminent &c., recover & re-cover, re-enforce & reinforce, &c., see CO-, & PRE-, & RE-.

For formulae -las, hippopotamuses -mi, &c., see LATIN PLURALS.

For *burnt -ned, leapt -ped*, &c., see -T & -ED.

For *by & by, by the bye, by-election*, &c., see BY, BYE, BY-.

For *driest, slyer, shyly*, &c., see DRY.

For *no one no-one, someone*, &c., see EVERYONE.

For *countryfied, Frenchified*, &c., see -FIED.

For *glycerin(e), gelatin(e)*, &c., see -IN & -INE.

For *into in to, onto on to*, see INTO, & ONTO.

For *ex-Lord-Mayor* &c., see HY-PHENS.

For blunders with *laid*, see LAY & LIE.

For *prophecy -sy, device -se*, &c., see LICENCE.

For *sipahi sepoy, amok amuck, flautist flut-*, &c., see MAHOMET, & MORALE, & PRIDE OF KNOWLEDGE.

For *net(t), mat(t), pot(t)*, &c., see SET(T).

For *deserter, corrector*, &c., see -OR.

For *governo(u)r, labo(u)r*, &c., see -OUR & -OR.

For *humo(u)rous, colo(u)ration*, &c., see -OUR- & -OR-.

For *cwt. cwt, Mlle. Mlle, Dr. Dr*, &c., see PERIOD IN ABBREVIATIONS.

For *Jones's Jones', Venus' Venus's*, see POSSESSIVE PUZZLES.

For *referable, inferrible*, &c., see CONFER(R)ABLE.

For *the 'seventies* &c., see TWENTIES.

4. Miscellaneous. The rule ' i before e except after c ' is very useful ; it applies only to syllables with the vowel sound ē ; words in which that sound is not invariable, as *either, neither, inveigle*, do not come under it ; *seize* is an important exception ; & it is useless with proper names (*Leith, Leigh, Menteith*, &c.). The c exception covers the many derivatives of Latin *capio*, which are in such common use (*receive, deceit, inconceivable* ; cf. *relieve, belief, irretrievable*) that a simple rule of thumb is necessary.

The plural of all nouns in -ey should be in -eys, not -ies—*donkeys* (but *ponies*), *moneys* (but *bunnies*).

The writing of the very common

anti- against instead of the rarer *ante-* before (e. g. *antichamber, antidated*) is to be carefully avoided.

Verbs in *-cede, -ceed*, are so many & so much used, & the causes of the difference are so far from obvious, that mistakes are frequent & a list will be helpful : *cede, accede, antecede, concede, intercede, precede, recede, retrocede, secede*, to which may be added *supersede* ; but *exceed, proceed, succeed*. The curious thing is that a division so little reasonable should be so religiously observed ; there is no disagreement among good spellers, & the only mistake into which they occasionally slip is *preceeding* for *preceding*.

Adjectives & nouns in *-ble, -cle, -tle*, &c., make their adverbs & adjectives not by adding -ly or -y, but by changing -le to -ly : *humbly, subtly, singly, supply* (not *supplely*), *treacly, tangly*.

Adjectives in *-ale, -ile, -ole*, add -ly for their adverbs : *halely, vilely, docilely, solely* ; but *whole* makes *wholly*.

Verbs in -c like *picnic* & *bivouac* add k before -ed, -ing, -er, &c. ; *picnicker, bivouacking*.

For verbs ending in *-bre, -tre*, &c., the forms *sabring, sepulchring, accoutring, centring, mitring, manœuvring*, are recommended in preference to *sabreing, manœuvering*, &c. Similarly *ochrous* & *ogrish* seem better than *ochreous* or *ocherous* & *ogreish* or *ogerish* ; but impious hands can hardly be laid upon *acreage*.

Of adjectives in *-(e)rous* some never use the e, as *cumbrous, disastrous, idolatrous, leprous, lustrous, monstrous, wondrous* ; some have it always, as *boisterous, murderous, obstreperous, slanderous, thunderous* ; *dextrous* & *slumbrous* are perhaps better than *dexterous* & *slumberous*.

Spencerian, of Herbert Spencer, philosopher, d. 1903.
Spenserian, of Edmund Spenser, poet, d. 1599 ; for *Spenserian stanza* or *Spenserians*, see TECHNICAL TERMS.

spew, spue. The first spelling is the more frequent in the OED quotations.

sphere. For synonyms in the sense province &c., see FIELD.

spice makes *spiceable*, see -ABLE 1 ; & *spicy*, see -EY & -Y.

spit(f)licate. OED spells -*ifl-* ; see FACETIOUS FORMATIONS.

spike makes *spikable*, see MUTE E ; & *spiky*, see -EY & -Y.

spill. For *spilt -lled*, see -T & -ED.

spillikin, spel(l)ican. The OED takes it as a diminutive from *spill*, & spells in the first way.

spilth. See REVIVALS. There is a gap of 200 years between Shakspere (who uses it once only) & the earliest modern OED quotation.

spin. For the past tense the OED 19th-c. quotations give *span & spun* in exactly equal numbers ; *span* is likely to prevail.

spinach, -nage. The first is the recognized spelling, though the other is not uncommon.

spindlage is better than *spindleage* ; see MUTE E.

spindrift, spoon-. The first is the usual modern word, & is here recommended for preference, being now more intelligible. The original *spoondrift* is from an obsolete nautical verb *spoon* or *spoom* meaning (of ship or foam) to scud ; there is no profit in trying to restore the correct but now puzzling form.

spinel. The OED pronounces spi'nl only.

spinet. OED prefers spi'nĭt to spĭnĕ't ; among its verse quotations is one in favour of each.

spinney, -nny. OED prefers the first form ; pl. -*eys*.

Spinozism. So spelt; pron. -ĭnō'z-.

spiny, not -*ney* ; see MUTE E.

spiraea rather than -*rœa* ; see Æ, Œ.

spirant. See TECHNICAL TERMS.

spire makes *spiry*, not -*rey*; MUTE E.

spirit, vb, makes-*ited,-iting*; -T-,-TT-.

spiritism & *spiritistic* mean the same as *spiritualism* in its most frequent & *spiritualistic* in its only acceptation ; ' preferred by those specially interested in the subject, as being more distinctive than *spiritualism* ' is the OED comment on *spiritism*. To ordinary people the old noun with a new meaning comes much more natural than the recent invention, & it is to be hoped that they will not let themselves be dictated to by the specially interested with their craving for distinctiveness. What first occurs to the mind of anyone who nowadays hears the word *spiritualism* is not the general sense, i.e. ' tendency towards a spiritual view or estimate of things ' ; it is the special sense of ' belief that the spirits of the dead can hold communication with the living ' ; so true is this that the addition of ' modern ', at first thought necessary to distinguish the special from the general sense, is no longer made. This being so, the demand for a separate word seems to imply the extravagant theory that no word should have two meanings—a theory that would require us no longer to use ' vessel ' in its special sense of ship, & to manufacture thousands of new words.

spiritual, -ous. The differentiation (-*al* of soul, -*ous* of liquor) is now complete, & neglect of it more often due to inadvertence than to ignorance ; cf. LUXURIOUS -*ant*, MASTERFUL -*ly*.

spirituel(le). Spell always -*el*. The word's meaning is not quite clear to everyone, & is therefore here given in the OED terms :—Of a highly refined character or nature, esp. in conjunction with liveliness or quickness of mind. And on the spelling the OED remarks : The distinction between the masc. & fem. forms has not been always observed in English. That is undoubtedly so, & the spelling problem presented is an awkward one. On the one hand, the notion of m. & f. forms for adjectives is entirely alien to English, & if a French adjective is to make itself at home with us it must choose first whether it will go in male or female attire & discard its other garments ; on this point cf. NAIF & NAIVE. On the other hand, the choice is with this particular word a dilemma ; if we decide for *-el* we are sacrificing the much more familiar of the two forms—more familiar because the word has been chiefly applied to women & in this application purposely made feminine by those who recognize both genders ; but, if we decide for *-elle*, few of us can rid themselves of the feeling that the word is feminine & suitable only to what, for the English, is alone feminine, viz woman, so that we find ourselves debarred from describing qualities, faces, talk, & above all men, as spirituelle, & cannot give the word its proper extension.

The lesser evil is to spell always *spirituel* ; the objection to it is not, like that to *-elle*, one that will endure for ever, but one that, when the form is settled, will no longer be felt.

spirt, spurt. The spelling is now very much a matter of personal fancy, & whether more than one word is concerned is doubtful. There are, however, two distinguishable main senses—that of gush, jet, or flow (vb & n.), & that of sprint, burst, hustle (vb & n.) ; & for the second sense the form *spurt* is far the commoner. It would plainly be convenient if the DIFFERENTIATION thus indicated were made absolute ; *a spirt of blood* ; *works by spurts* ; *oil spirts up* ; *Jones spurted past.*

spite makes *spitable* ; see MUTE E.
splay. For inflexions see VERBS IN -IE &c., 1.
splendid makes *-idest* ; -ER & -EST 4.
splendiferous. See FACETIOUS FORMATIONS.
splendo(u)r. Keep the u ; but see -OUR & -OR.
splice makes *-ceable* ; see -ABLE 1.

SPLIT INFINITIVE. The English-speaking world may be divided into (1) those who neither know nor care what a split infinitive is ; (2) those who do not know, but care very much ; (3) those who know & condemn ; (4) those who know & approve ; & (5) those who know & distinguish.

1. Those who neither know nor care are the vast majority, & are a happy folk, to be envied by most of the minority classes ; ' to really understand ' comes readier to their lips & pens than ' really to understand ', they see no reason why they should not say it (small blame to them, seeing that reasons are not their critics' strong point), & they do say it, to the discomfort of some among us, but not to their own.

2. To the second class, those who do not know but do care, who would as soon be caught putting their knives in their mouths as splitting an infinitive but have hazy notions of what constitutes that deplorable breach of etiquette, this article is chiefly addressed. These people betray by their practice that their aversion to the split infinitive springs not from instinctive good taste, but from tame acceptance of the misinterpreted opinion of others ; for they will subject their sentences to the queerest distortions, all to escape imaginary split infinitives. ' To really understand ' is a s. i. ; ' to really be understood ' is a s. i. ; ' to be really understood ' is not one ; the havoc that is played with much well-intentioned writing by failure to grasp that distinction is incredible. Those upon whom the fear of infinitive-splitting sits heavy should remember that to give conclusive evidence, by distortions, of misconceiving the nature of the s. i. is far more damaging to their literary pretensions than an actual lapse could be ; for it exhibits them as deaf to the normal rhythm of English sentences. No sensitive ear can fail to be shocked, if the following examples are read aloud, by the strangeness of the indicated adverbs. Why on earth, the reader wonders, is that word out of its place ? He will find, on looking through again,

that each has been turned out of a similar position, viz between the word *be* & a passive participle. Reflection will assure him that the cause of dislocation is always the same—all these writers have sacrificed the run of their sentences to the delusion that ' to be really understood ' is a split infinitive. It is not ; & the straitest non-splitter of us all can with a clear conscience restore each of the adverbs to its rightful place :—He was proposed at the last moment as a candidate likely *generally* to be accepted./ When the record of this campaign comes *dispassionately* to be written, & in just perspective, it will be found that . . ./The leaders have given instructions that the lives & property of foreigners shall *scrupulously* be respected./New principles will have *boldly* to be adopted if the Scottish case is to be met./This is a very serious matter, which clearly ought *further* to be inquired into./ There are many points raised in the report which need *carefully* to be explored./Only two ways of escaping from the conflict without loss, by this time become too serious *squarely* to be faced, have ever offered themselves./The Headmaster of a public school possesses very great powers, which ought *most carefully & considerately* to be exercised./The time to get this revaluation put through is when the amount paid by the State to the localities is *very largely* to be increased./But the party whose Leader in the House of Commons acts in this way cannot fail *deeply* to be discredited by the way in which he flings out & about these false charges.

3. The above writers are bogy-haunted creatures who for fear of splitting an infinitive abstain from doing something quite different, i.e. dividing *be* from its complement by an adverb ; see further under POSI-TION OF ADVERBS. Those who presumably do know what split infinitives are, & condemn them, are not so easily identified, since they in-clude all who neither commit the sin nor flounder about in saving themselves from it, all who combine with acceptance of conventional rules a reasonable dexterity. But when the dexterity is lacking, disaster follows. It does not add to a writer's readableness if readers are pulled up now & again to wonder— Why this distortion ? Ah, to be sure, a non-split die-hard ! That is the mental dialogue occasioned by each of the adverbs in the examples below. It is of no avail merely to fling oneself desperately out of temptation ; one must so do it that no traces of the struggle remain ; that is, sentences must be thoroughly remodelled instead of having a word lifted from its original place & dumped elsewhere :—What alterna-tive can be found which the Pope has not condemned, & which will make it possible *to organize legally* public worship ?/If it is to do justice between the various parties & not *unduly to burden* the State, it will . . ./It will, when better understood, tend *firmly to establish* relations between Capital & Labour./Both Germany & England have done ill in not combining *to forbid flatly* hostil-ities./Nobody expects that the exec-utive of the Amalgamated Society is going to *assume publicly* sackcloth & ashes./Every effort must be made *to increase adequately* professional knowledge & attainments./We have had *to shorten somewhat* Lord Den-bigh's letter./The kind of sincerity which enables an author *to move powerfully* the heart would . . ./Safe-guards should be provided *to prevent effectually* cosmopolitan financiers from manipulating these reserves.

4. Just as those who know & con-demn the s. i. include many who are not recognizable, only the clumsier performers giving positive proof of resistance to temptation, so too those who know & approve are not distinguishable with certainty ; when a man splits an infinitive, he may be doing it unconsciously as a mem-ber of our class 1, or he may be

deliberately rejecting the trammels of convention & announcing that he means to do as he will with his own infinitives. But, as the following examples are from newspapers of high repute, & high newspaper tradition is strong against splitting, it is perhaps fair to assume that each specimen is a manifesto of independence :—It will be found possible *to considerably improve* the present wages of the miners without jeopardizing the interests of capital./ Always providing that the Imperialists do not feel strong enough *to decisively assert* their power in the revolted provinces./But even so, he seems *to still be allowed* to speak at Unionist demonstrations./It is the intention of the Minister of Transport *to substantially increase* all present rates by means of a general percentage./The men in many of the largest districts are declared *to strongly favour* a strike if the minimum wage is not conceded.

It should be noticed that in these the separating adverb could have been placed outside the infinitive with little or in most cases no damage to the sentence-rhythm (*considerably* after *miners*, *decisively* after *powers*, *still* with clear gain after *be*, *substantially* after *rates*, & *strongly* at some loss after *strike*), so that protest seems a safe diagnosis.

5. The attitude of those who know & distinguish is something like this : We admit that separation of *to* from its infinitive (viz *be*, *do*, *have*, *sit*, *doubt*, *kill*, or other verb inflexionally similar) is not in itself desirable, & we shall not gratuitously say either 'to mortally wound' or 'to mortally be wounded'; but we are not foolish enough to confuse the latter with 'to be mortally wounded', which is blameless English, nor 'to just have heard ' with 'to have just heard', which is also blameless. We maintain, however, that a real s. i., though not desirable in itself, is preferable to either of two things, to real ambiguity, & to patent artificiality. For the first, we will

rather write ' Our object is to further cement trade relations ' than, by correcting into ' Our object is further to cement . . .', leave it doubtful whether an additional object or additional cementing is the point. And for the second, we take it that such reminders of a tyrannous convention as 'in not combining to forbid flatly hostilities ' are far more abnormal than the abnormality they evade. We will split infinitives sooner than be ambiguous or artificial ; more than that, we will freely admit that sufficient recasting will get rid of any s. i. without involving either of those faults, & yet reserve to ourselves the right of deciding in each case whether recasting is worth while. Let us take an example : ' In these circumstances, the Commission, judging from the evidence taken in London, has been feeling its way to modifications intended to better equip successful candidates for careers in India & at the same time to meet reasonable Indian demands '. To better equip ? We refuse ' better to equip ' as a shouted reminder of the tyranny ; we refuse ' to equip better ' as ambiguous (*better* an adjective ?) ; we regard ' to equip successful candidates better ' as lacking compactness, as possibly tolerable from an anti-splitter, but not good enough for us. What then of recasting ? ' intended to make successful candidates fitter for ' is the best we can do if the exact sense is to be kept ; it takes some thought to arrive at the correction ; was the game worth the candle ?

After this inconclusive discussion, in which, however, the author's opinion has perhaps been allowed to appear with indecent plainness, readers may like to settle for themselves whether, in the following sentence, ' either to secure ' followed by ' to resign ', or 'to either secure ' followed by 'resign ', should have been preferred—an issue in which the meaning & the convention are pitted against each other :—The speech has drawn an interesting letter from Sir Antony MacDonnell, who states that his agreement with Mr Wyndham was never cancelled, & that Mr Long was too weak *either to secure* the dismissal of Sir Antony or himself to resign office.

It is perhaps hardly fair that this article should have quoted no split infinitives except such as, being reasonably supposed (as in 4) to be deliberate, are likely to be favourable specimens. Let it therefore conclude with one borrowed from a reviewer, to whose description of it no exception need be taken : ' A book . . . of which the purpose is thus—with a deafening split infinitive—stated by its author :—" Its main idea is *to* historically, even while events are maturing, & divinely—from the Divine point of view—*impeach* the European system of Church & States ".'.

SPLIT VERBS. *There can be little doubt that the position of his troops all the way from Berat northward will seriously be imperilled.* For questions such as that suggested by the last four words of this, see POSITION OF ADVERBS, 4.

splodge, splotch. The second is two centuries older ; the first perhaps now more usual & felt to be more descriptive ; cf. SLUSH, & SMUDGE.

splutter, sputter. Without any clear or constant difference of meaning, it may be said that in *sputter* the notion of spitting is more insistent, & that it tends on that account to be avoided when that notion is not essential.

spoil. For *spoiled, -lt*, see -T & -ED.

-spoken. For the curious use in *fair, free, soft, out*, &c., *-s* (where *soft-speeched* &c. might have been expected), see INTRANSITIVE P.P. It should be remembered that in these compounds *fair-* &c. are adverbial as much as *out-*, & that what is remarkable is not the adverbial use of the adjective, but the active use of the participle.

spondee. See TECHNICAL TERMS.

sponge makes *spongeable*, see -ABLE 1 ; but *sponging* & *spongy*, see MUTE E.

spontaneity,-ousness. -TY & -NESS.

spook. Pronounce -ōōk.

spoondrift. See SPINDRIFT.

spoon(e)y. The adjective should be *-ny*, see -EY & -Y ; for the noun, in which either is legitimate, & *-ey* probably more frequent, -EY, -IE, -Y.

spoonful. Pl. *spoonfuls* ; see -FUL.

spouse. For the use in ordinary writing in preference to *wife*, see FORMAL WORDS ; but *s.* is serviceable as short for husband-or-wife in some styles, e. g. in dictionaries or legal documents.

sprain)(strain. It is natural to wish for a clear line of distinction between two words that, as applied to bodily injuries, are so near in sense & both so well established ; but even in medical books they are often treated as equivalent. *Sprain*, perhaps, describes the result rather of a momentary wrench or twist, & *strain* that of an exertion of muscle too strong or too long for its capacity.

spray, nn., make *sprayey* ; see -EY & -Y, exception 1.

spray, vb. For inflexions see VERBS IN -IE &c., 1.

spring. The past *sprang* is considerably more frequent than *sprung*, both in trans. & in intrans. senses.

spring, n. The compounds, like those of SEA, are of interest to the hyphen-fancier. For the principle, see HYPHENS 3 B ; *spring-bed, spring-mattress, spring-gun*, are usually forbidden by the accent, & must be changed to two words each ; *spring-time* & *spring-board* are allowed by accent, unless *springtime* & *springboard* are preferred ; *springtide* or *springtide* can stand only for the season, & the tidal term must be *spring tide* in two words ; *spring(-) cart* will usually be two words, but may be hyphened when all the stress is on *spring* & a spring-cart is to be distinguished from other carts & not from vehicles in general.

springbok. So spelt.

springe (snare). Pronounce -j.

springed, sprung. *Carriages well cushioned & springed./Choice easy chair, with cane arms, well sprung. Springed* is more reasonable, as formed from the noun; cf. STRINGED.

springhalt. See STRINGHALT.

sprint, spurt. The words are to a considerable extent interchangeable; *sprint* is, at least apart from dialectal use, a 19th-c. word only, *spurt* going further back, but the newer word is displacing the older; a short race, or a run at high speed, is now a sprint, while for a quickening of pace, or a spasmodic effort bodily or mental, *spurt* is still the more usual term, but is tending to be displaced even in these senses; if that tendency could be checked, the DIFFERENTIATION would be useful.

spry makes *spryer, spryest, spryly, spryness, spryish*; see DRY.

spue. See SPEW.

spur. See PRONUNCIATION, s.f., for *spurring*.

spurt. For *s. & spirt*, see SPIRT; for *s. & sprint*, see SPRINT.

sputter. See SPLUTTER.

sputum. Pl. *-ta*.

spy. For inflexions see VERBS IN -IE &c., 6.

squalid makes *-dest*; *-ER & -EST*, 4.

squalor, not *-our*; see -OUR & -OR.

squandermania(c). A FACETIOUS FORMATION.

square makes *squarable & squarish*, see MUTE E; *square leg* should have no hyphen, see HYPHENS 3 B.

squeeze makes *-zable*; see -ABLE 1.

squib. For synonymy see LAMPOON.

squir(e)archy. Though 'the spelling with *e* has been by far the more usual' (OED), the spelling without it is preferable (see MUTE E), & Sydney Smith & FitzGerald appear among its patrons in the OED quotations.

-S-, -SS-. The general rules for the doubling or not doubling of final consonants before suffixes can be seen in the articles -N-, -NN-, & -P-, -PP-; so few monosyllables or words

accented on the last syllable end in a single -s that rules need not be here stated; it will suffice to say that: (1) The plural of *bus* is usually *buses*; this irregularity is explained by the fact that *buses* is still regarded as an abbreviation of the regular *omnibuses*; when that is forgotten (& *bus* is now more usual than *'bus*), doubtless *buses* will become, as it should, *busses*. (2) *Biases & focuses*, nn. or vv., *biased & focusing*, are said by the OED to be 'more regular' than the *-ss-* forms that are nevertheless common in England; similarly *canvas* (the fabric) gives *-ases* (pl. n.), *-ased*, & so too *orchises, nimbuses, portcullised, trellised, boluses, bonuses, incubuses, atlases, cutlases*, &c. (3) *Nonplus* makes *nonplussed*.

St. For the question between *St Peter & St. Peter* &c., see PERIOD IN ABBREVIATIONS.

stable, adj., makes *stably, stability, stabilize*, so spelt.

stadium. Pl. *-dia*.

staff. 1. Pl. in music & in archaic senses *staves*, see *-VE*(D); in modern senses *staffs*. 2. For *s. of life* see SOBRIQUETS.

stag. See HART.

stage makes *stageable* (see -ABLE 1), *stagy* (see -EY & -Y); of the chief compounds, *stage-craft & stage-struck* should be hyphened or coalesce, *s. coach & s. manager* should be hyphened or separated (usually the latter) according to the stress required, & most others should be two words each—stage direction, stage door, stage effect, stage fever, stage fright, stage whisper; for the principle see HYPHENS 3 B.

Stagirite. *The S.*; see SOBRIQUETS.

stake, vb, makes *stakable*; MUTE E.

stalactite, stalagmite. Stress on the first, not the second, syllables is recommended; RECESSIVE ACCENT.

stale makes *stalable, stalish, stalely*; see MUTE E.

stalk, stem, trunk. *Stalk* is the stem of a plant less than tree or shrub; *trunk* is the stem of a large tree ; *stem* is the general word applicable irrespective of size.

stamp, n. For synonymy, see SIGN.

stampede makes *-dable* ; see MUTE E.

stanch, staunch. The adjective is usually *staunch*, the verb *stanch*.

stand. For *stands to reason*, see REASON 2. For *standpoint, point of view, & point*, see POINT. For *wash-stand, washing-stand, & wash-hand-stand*, see WASH.

standard. *S. pound, s. size, s. yard, s. lamp*, &c. ; no hyphens ; see HYPHENS 3 B.

stanza. See TECHNICAL TERMS. *-stanza'd* is preferable to *-stanzaed* ; see -ED & 'D.

star. *Shooting s.* should have no hyphen ; see HYPHENS 3 B.

starchedly. Three syllables ; -EDLY.

staring, not *stareing* ; see MUTE E.

starlight, -lit, -litten, adjj. The first (in adj. use, e.g. *a starlight night*) may or may not be historically, but is certainly now to be regarded as, the noun used attributively. Attributive uses of nouns, like adverbial uses of apparent adjectives (see UNIDIOMATIC -LY), sometimes strike people whose zeal for grammar is greater than their knowledge of it as incorrect ; & *starlit* is perhaps often substituted for *starlight* owing to this notion ; no harm is done, *starlit* being a blameless word, & indeed better in some contexts ; if ' a starlight night ' & ' a starlit sea ' have their epithets exchanged, both suffer to the extent at least of sounding unnatural. The further step to *starlitten* is not so innocent, *litten* being not archaic but pseudo-archaic ; the writer who uses *star-litten* is on a level with the tradesman who relies on such attractions as Ye Olde Curyosytie Shoppe.

starve makes *starvable, starveling* ; see MUTE E.

state, n. It is a convenient distinction to write *State* for the political unit, at any rate when the full noun use is required (not the attributive, as in *State*, or *state, trading*), & *state* in other senses.

The following compound forms are recommended (see HYPHENS) :— statecraft, state-room, State socialism, State prisoner, State trial.

state, vb. *I may state* ' *Irish Nationality* ' *was recommended to me by the Vice-Reine, Lady Aberdeen.* ' State ' is one of the verbs that insist on proper ceremony & resent the omission of THAT, conj. *S.* makes *statable*, see MUTE E.

stately. For the adv., see -LILY.

static(al). See -IC(AL) ; there is no marked differentiation, but the *-ic* form seems likely to prevail.

station makes *-oned* ; see -N-, -NN-.

stationary, -ery. The adj. (not moving), *-ary* ; the noun (paper &c.), *-ery.*

statist, statistician. The pronunciation of the first (stā´tĭst) is very much against it, inevitably suggesting state, & not statistics ; & in fact its old sense was statesman, though now, as if it were a back-formation from *statistics*, it means only statistician. Either it should be abandoned & *statistician* always used, or it should be cut off from *state* by being pronounced stă´tĭst ; it is likely that one or other of these things will come about, but the odds are unfortunately in favour of the first, with the cumbersome *statistician* left in sole possession.

statistic(al), adjj. See -IC(AL) ; the short form is almost obsolete.

status. ' The *status quo* ' is the position in which things (1) are now or (2) have been till now or (3) were then or (4) had been till then ; in senses 2 & 4 *ante* (*t. s. q. ante*) is sometimes, but need not be, added. With *in* the phrase becomes *in statu quo* (*ante*), without *the*, & with *ante* similarly optional.

statutable, -tory. For the first, see -ABLE ; the two words are hardly distinguishable in meaning ; *-table* is considerably older, & *-tory* perhaps now more usual ; a natural DIFFERENTIATION would be that *-table* should take the sense permitted, & *-tory* the sense enjoined, by statute.

staunch. See STANCH.

stave, vb. The past & p.p. *stove* (instead of *staved*) is modern & (OED) ' chiefly *Naut.*'.

staves. For *s.* as pl. of *staff*, see STAFF.

stead, n. *The atmosphere of the home life was favourable to the growth of qualities which were presently to stand him in inestimable stead.* To stand one in good or better, much or more, little or less, s. ; those are perhaps the limits within which the phrase can now, without affectation, be used ; words like *inestimable* should not be substituted ; see CAST-IRON IDIOM.

steadfast is now the established spelling, preferable as exhibiting the connexion with *stead & steady* ; *sted-* was formerly much the commoner, & is still seen.

steam. The chief combinations beginning with *steam* are best written as below ; for the principle, see HYPHENS.

1. As one word (or hyphened) : steamboat, steambox, steampower, steamship, steamtight,

2. Hyphened : s.-boiler, s.-chest, s.-engine, s.-gauge, s.-jacket. All these have the accent on *steam*, except perhaps *s.-boiler*, for which see below.

3. As two words : s. brake, s. coal, s. crane, s. hammer, s. navvy, s. plough, s. roller, s. tug, s. whistle. All these have the accent on the second word except in special uses, as *the s.-coal trade, navvies & s.-navvies.*

S.-boiler is not formed in the same way as *s. plough* & the rest, i. e. from two nouns *s.* & *boiler* with the sense a boiler worked by steam, but from the phrase *to boil steam*, or create s. by boiling ; it is a thing that boils s., & does not come under HYPHENS 3 B, but under Hyphens 3 C (cf. *weight-carrier* & the like).

steepen. See -EN VERBS.

steer, n. The OED definition is : A young ox, esp. one which has been castrated (in the United States &

the Colonies applied to male beef-cattle of any age).

stele. Pronounce stē´lē ; pl. *-lae.*

stem, n. See STALK ; &, for the sense in grammar, TECHNICAL TERMS.

stemma. Pl. *-mata.*

stencil makes *-llable, -lled, -lling* ; see -LL-, -L-.

step. For *s. this way, s. in,* &c., see FORMAL WORDS.

stereo. A CURTAILED WORD for *stereotype* ; pl. *-os,* see -O(E)S 5.

stereotype has *-pable, -pist* ; MUTE E.

sterile. The older spellings (usu. *-il, -ill*) suggest that the pronunciation *-īl* is modern, & it is still probably less common than *-ĭl*. Superl. sometimes *-ilest*, see -ER & -EST 4 ; noun *sterility* (cf. *tranquillity, civility*).

sterilize makes *-zable* ; see MUTE E.

stern, adj. For *the sterner sex*, see BATTERED ORNAMENTS.

stern, n. *S. chase*, two words (HYPHENS 3 B) ; *s.-wheeler*, hyphened (3 C) ; *s. sheets* or *s.-sheets*, the accent being variable.

sternum. Pl. *-na* or *-nums* ; see LATIN PLURALS.

stethoscope. Pronounce stĕ- ; see FALSE QUANTITY.

stevedore. Three syllables (stē´vĭ-dōr).

(-)stich & equivalents. For names of verse groups based on the number of lines they contain, the *-stich* words are the set nearest completeness, but forms in *-ain* & *-et* exist for the groups more commonly mentioned, & are often preferred in limited senses. Half (or part of) line—*hemistich* ; one line—*(mono)-stich* ; two lines—*distich, couplet* ; three—*tristich, triplet, tercet, tern* ; four—*tetrastich, quatrain, quartet* ; five—*pentastich, cinquain* ; six—*hexastich, sixain, sextain, sestet, sextet* ; seven—*heptastich* ; eight—*octastich, huitain, octet, octave* ; nine—wanting ; ten—*decastich, dizain* ; fourteen—*quatorzain* ; fifteen—*quinzain.* Pronounce *-ĭk.*

stichomyth. See TECHNICAL TERMS.

sticked, stuck. When the meaning is provided with sticks (e. g. of pea plants), the first form is the right ; cf. HAMSTRING, SPRINGED.

sticking-place, -point. In the *Macbeth* passage, *-place* is the word ; see MISQUOTATION.

stickleback, tittlebat. The first is the orthodox & etymological form, the other being (OED) ' a variant, of childish origin '.

stigma. The plural is *stigmata* in the eccl., bot., med., &c., senses ; *stigmas* only in the fig. sense of imputation or disgrace, in which a plural is rare. See LATIN PLURALS.

stigmatize makes *-zable* ; see MUTE E. The mistake fully dealt with under REGARD 3 occurs rarely with *s.* : . . . *bravely suffering forfeiture & imprisonment rather than accept what in this same connexion Lord Morley stigmatized the ' bar sinister '* ; things are not stigmatized monstrous, but stigmatized *as* monstrous.

stile, style. *Stile* is the spelling for the means of passage, & for the carpentry term (*stiles & rails*) ; *style* for all other senses. This division is not historically correct, being due to the confusing of Latin *stilus* (writing-tool) with Greek *stulos* (column) ; but it is so generally accepted, & attempts to improve upon it so conflicting, that it is better to refrain, & leave the y in all the classically derived senses ; see also Y & I.

stiletto. Pl. *-os* ; see -O(E)S 6.

stilly. Pronounce the poetic adj. stǐ'lĭ, the adv. stǐ'l-lĭ.

stimulate makes *-lable*, see -ABLE 1 ; & *-ator*, see -OR.

stimulus. Pl. *-lī* ; LATIN PLURALS.

stimy, stymie. The first spelling is recommended. Although the OED makes the other the orthodox form, *sti-* occurs nine times in its quotations, & *sty-* not at all. See Y & I.

stink. Past *stank* or *stunk*, to which the remarks made under SPIN exactly apply.

stipulate makes *-lable*, see -ABLE 1 ; & *-ator*, see -OR.

stirring. Pronounce -er'ing rather than -ŭ'ring ; PRONUNCIATION s.f.

stī'ver. So pronounced.

STOCK PATHOS. Some words & phrases have become so associated with melancholy occasions that it seems hardly decent to let such an occasion pass unattended by any of them. It is true that such trappings & suits of woe save much trouble ; it is true that to mock at them lays one open to suspicion of hard-heartedness ; it is also true that the use of them suggests, if not quite insincerity, yet a factitious sort of emotion, & those are well advised who abstain from them. A small selection, which might be greatly enlarged, is :—In her great sorrow ; The land he loved so well ; The supreme sacrifice ; The pity of it ! ; The mortal remains of ; All that was mortal of ; The departed ; One more unfortunate ; More sinned against than sinning ; A lump in one's throat ; Tug at one's heart-strings ; Stricken ; Loved & lost ; But it was not to be.

stoep. Pronounce stoōp.

stoic(al). See -IC(AL). Both forms are used as adjectives, *-ic* being indeed the commoner ; but points of difference are discernable. In the predicative use *stoic* is rare : *his acceptance of the news was stoical, he was stoical in temper*, rather than *stoic*. In the attributive use, *stoic* naturally preserves the original sense more definitely, while *stoical* forgets it ; when we say *stoic indifference*, we mean such indifference as the Stoics taught or practised ; when we say *stoical indifference* we think of it merely as resolute or composed ; the *stoic virtues* are those actually taught by the Stoics, the *stoical virtues* simply those of the sterner kind. Lastly, while either epithet is applicable to abstracts, *stoical* is the word for persons : *with stoic* or *stoical composure* ; *stoic* or *stoical life* or *tone* or *temper* or *views* ;

he is a stoical fellow ; these stoical explorers ; a stoical sufferer ; my stoical young friend.

stokehold, -hole. The earliest OED quotation for the first is dated 1887 ; the *-hole* form goes back to 1660. The natural inference is that *-hole* is the true form, but is now thought undignified & has been altered. Though the OED defines the two differently, the impression produced by its quotations is not that there are two names for two different things, but rather that *stokehole* has had in its time, & perhaps still has, more than one meaning. To maintain a distinction between words at once so similar in form &, to the general public, so vague in sense, is clearly impossible. The form *stokehole* is recommended.

stolid makes *-er, -est* ; -ER & -EST 2.
stomach. For genteel use see BELLY.
stomacher, article of dress. The old pronunciation was with *-cher*, which should be kept to as long as the word is historical only, & not revived with the thing in modern use.

stone, n. *Rolling stone* should not be hyphened ; *rocking-stone* or *rocking stone* according as the accent is on the first or the second word ; see HYPHENS 3 B.

stone, vb, makes *-nable* ; MUTE E.
stop, n. For the phonetic sense, see TECHNICAL TERMS.
stop, vb. Those who use *stop* when others would use *stay* (*Where are you stopping ?* &c.) are many, & are frequently rebuked. The OED deals very gently with them : ' Cf. *stay*, which is often preferred as more correct ' ; & it is not a case for denunciation, but rather for waiting to see which word will win. Meanwhile, careful speakers do prefer *stay* ; & it is in its favour, & a sign of its being still in possession, that its noun, & not *stop*, is certainly the right one in the corresponding sense (*during our stay*, not *our stop*). It may also be suggested that, if *stop* is a solecism, there are degrees

of enormity in the offence : *Won't you stop to dinner ?, I shall stop in town till I hear, We have been stopping at the Deanery,* of which the last is the worst, point to a limitation— that *stop* is tolerable only when postponement of departure rather than place of sojourn is in question.

STOPS &c. (comma, semicolon, colon, full stop, exclamation, question, inverted commas, apostrophe, hyphen, italics, brackets, dashes). There is not room in this book for a treatise on punctuation, nor for discussion of principles even where the question is one between opposed views of correctness, & not between acknowledged correctness & careless or ignorant error. But, if it is assumed (1) that the reader need be warned only against mistakes that experience shows to be prevalent, & (2) that the views here taken on disputed points are sound, an article consisting almost entirely of ill stopped sentences with corrections may be of use.

COMMA

A. In enumerations. For full discussion, see AND 3, & OR 3. Of the examples below, the last four show the ambiguity that makes it necessary to insist on full stopping in all enumerations, including the more usual ones, like the first nine, in which no doubt of the meaning is possible.
This new novel describes a love affair formed, precipitated, & rendered tragic by the events of the Revolution (for *tragic* read *tragic,*)./ *The resulting inquiry involves the consideration of the claims of consciousness, instinct, memory, habit, & desire to be regarded as the determining factors of psychic life* (for *desire* read *desire,*)./*Among present-day authors & poets Messrs Yeats, Sturge Moore, Binyon, & Davies are most in evidence* (for *Davies* read *Davies,*)./*The total burden imposed upon the German consumer by the duties on rye, wheat, & oats alone was £46,731,761* (for *oats* read *oats,*)./

A Court which is orderly, high-minded, & decorous may be an immense influence for good (for *decorous* read *decorous,*)./*We shall find it necessary to deal pretty drastically with the parental rights of drunken criminal & wastrel parents* (for *drunken criminal* read *drunken, criminal,*)./. . . & *(4) the earlier publication of the results of the returns received, which, it may fairly be assumed, would follow if proposals (1), (2), & (3) were adopted* (for *(3)* read *(3),*)./. . . *or whether they are an earlier variety of man from whom the fierce, strong warrior races have developed* (for *strong* read *strong,*)./ *He seeks by tracing the influence which Christianity has exerted in the successive emancipation of slave, of serf, & of servant to convince his fellow-workers that* . . . (for *servant* read *servant,*)./*The debate opened with the consideration of the Report stage on Ways & Means, & concerning this many topics arose—tobacco, land, & liquor in particular* (for *liquor* perhaps read *liquor,*)./*Nothing had been allowed to be published except books, pamphlets, & papers which had secured the approval of the Communist party* (for *papers* surely read *papers,*)./*But the general purport is the same—the blindness, the degrading passions, the short-sighted greed by which the economic unity of Europe has been broken, & as a result of which the Continent is drifting into economic anarchy, with the prospect of fresh wars* (impossible to tell, as commas now go, whether *by which* or *of which* refers to *greed* alone, or also to *blindness & passions* ; probably for *greed* read *greed,*)./*He wants to give workmen more interest in their work & vulgarity, sloth & luxury less scope* (a triumph of perversity, for which the putting right of the enumeration with commas after *sloth & luxury* is no full cure).

B. In the absolute construction. For the cause, & the effect, of this common mistake, see ABSOLUTE CONSTRUCTION.

M. Maurice Colin, having called

attention to the conditions of naval warfare, M. Pichon said . . . (read *Colin having*)./*In sport man is matching himself against Nature ; & Nature, being unlimited, there is no limit to the skill which man can employ* (read *&, Nature being*)./*But these objections were overruled, & the accused, having pleaded not guilty, the hearing of evidence commenced* (read *&, the accused having*).

C. Separating inseparables, e. g. a verb from its subject or object or complement, a defining relative from its antecedent, or an essential modification from what cannot stand without it.

The charm in Nelson's history, is, the unselfish greatness (read *history is the*). One comma parts verb from subject, the other complement from verb./*He has been called the Portuguese Froissart, but he combines with Froissart's picturesqueness, moral philosophy, enthusiasm, & high principles* (read *picturesqueness moral*). The comma parts the object (*moral* . . . *principles*) from its verb *combines*./*A literature of Scotch Gaelic poetry & prose exists, though too little notice has been taken of it, even within the Scotch borders, for the Scot, who ignores such literature, does not deserve his name, which proves him to be a Gael* (read *Scot who ignores such literature does*). The *who* starts a defining relative clause ; see THAT, relative./*The right & wholesome atmosphere in this country, as in all others, where payment is the rule, is that it should be taken for granted as a normal incident of Parliamentary life* (read *others where*). The *where* clause is in the same relation to *others* as the *who* clause in the last example to *Scot.*/. . . *whether some disease other than tuberculosis may not account for the symptoms & signs observed. Only, if we do not succeed in our investigations, are we entitled to admit the diagnosis of tuberculosis* (read *Only if we do not succeed in our investigations are*). Without the clause from which the comma parts it, *only* is mere nonsense./*Situated, as we are, with our vast & varied overseas possessions, our gigantic foreign trade, & our unapproachable mercantile marine, we at any rate can gain nothing by war* (read *Situated as*). We should write not ' How, are we situated ? ', but ' How are we situated ? ' ; the *as* clause is exactly parallel to, & as essential as, *how./We are assured that the Prime Minister will, in no circumstances & on no consideration whatever, consent to* . . . (read *will in no circumstances* . . . *whatever consent*). The words that negative *will* must not be cut off from it. Similarly : *The principals were, neither of them, of a class that ordinarily appears in the dock of the Old Bailey* (read *were neither of them of*).

D. In confluences, i. e. when alternatives &c. finish their course together, the necessary comma after the second is apt to be forgotten.

As regards the form of the festival, many, if not most of the customs popularly associated with it may, perhaps, be traced to . . . (read *most, of*)./*His craftsmanship, again, was superb—more refined, more intellectual than that of Frith* (read *intellectual, than*).

E. In compound appendages to names. *Mr F. Haverfield has collected & edited a volume of ' Essays by Henry Francis Pelham, Late President of Trinity College, Oxford & Camden Professor of History* ' (read *Oxford, &*).

F. In ambiguous appositions. Insertion or omission of commas is seldom a sufficient remedy, & indeed is usually impossible. The thing is to remember that arrangements in which apposition commas & enumeration commas are mixed up are dangerous & should be avoided.

To the expanded ' Life of Shakespeare ', first published in 1915, & to be issued shortly in a third edition by Mr Murray, the author, Sir Sidney Lee, besides bringing the text up to date, has contributed a new preface. Which is the author ?/ Some high officials of the Headquarter Staff, including the officer who is primus inter pares, the Director of Military Operations, & the Director of Staff duties. . . . How many were there going to St Ives ?/*Lord Curzon, Sir Edmond Elles, the present Military Member, & the Civilian Members of Council traverse the most material of Lord Kitchener's statements.* Was Sir Edmond the Military Member ?

G. Omitted between connected but independent sentences, or used instead of semicolon between unconnected sentences.

When the Motor Cars Act was before the House it was suggested that these authorities should be given the right to make recommendations to the central authorities & that right was conceded (read *authorities, &*)./' *Will the mighty* Times *aid us in this historic struggle ?* ' *Dear to the heart of an editor must be such an appeal, we wish someone would seek for our aid in so flattering a formula* (read *appeal ; we*).

SEMICOLON

The use of semicolons to separate parallel expressions that would normally be separated by commas is not in itself illegitimate ; but it must not be done when the expressions so separated form a group that is to be separated by nothing more than a comma, or even not separated at all, from another part of the sentence ; to do it is to make the less include the greater, which is absurd.

And therein lies a guarantee of peace & ultimate security, such, perhaps, as none of the States of South America ; such as not even Mexico herself can boast (read *America, such as not even Mexico herself, can*)./*If you say with the enemy pinned upon the West, suffering passively blow upon blow, & never able to restore himself after each blow, or to recover what he has lost ; with his territory blockaded ; his youngest boys drawn into the struggle, that your victory is impossible ; if you say* . . . (read *lost, with his territory blockaded, his)./ If, as Mr Gibson Bowles contends, the Law of Nations is all plain sailing ; if it is a thing of certainties & plain definitions, it would be strange that a conference of jurists should have . . .* (read *sailing, if*).

COLON

As long as the Prayer-Book version of the Psalms continues to be read, the colon is not likely to pass quite out of use as a stop, chiefly as one preferred by individuals, or in impressive contexts, to the semicolon ; but the time when it was second member of the hierarchy, full stop, colon, semicolon, comma, is past ; in general usage, it is not now a stop of a certain power available in any situation demanding such a power, but has acquired a special function, that of delivering the goods that have been invoiced in the preceding words ; it is a substitute for such verbal harbingers as *viz, scil., that is to say, i. e.,* &c.

FULL STOP

In abbreviations. For the use as a symbol of abbreviation, as in *i.e.* for *id est, Capt.* for *Captain,* & less reasonably in *Mr.* for *Mister* or *Master, cwt.* for *hundredweight,* see PERIOD IN ABBREVIATIONS.

In the spot plague. The style that has been so labelled, the essence of which is that the matter should be divided into as short lengths as possible separated by full stops, with few commas & no semicolons or conjunctions, is tiring to the reader, on whom it imposes the task of supplying the connexion, & corrupting to the writer, whose craving for brevity persuades him that anything will pass for a sentence :— *It was now clear. The light was that of late evening. The air hardly more than cool./They demand long years of accurate study—even when the student has the necessary aptitude for such things. Which three students out of every four have not.*

EXCLAMATION

Not to use a mark of exclamation is sometimes wrong : *How they laughed.,* instead of *How they laughed !,* is not English. Excessive use of exclamation marks is, like that of ITALICS, one of the things that betray the uneducated or unpractised writer : *You surprise me, How dare you ?, Don't tell such lies,* are mere statement, question, & command, not converted into exclamations by the fact that those who say them are excited, nor to be decorated into *You surprise me !, How dare you !, Don't tell such lies !.* It is, indeed, stated in a well-known grammar that ' A note of exclamation is used after words or sentences which express emotion ', with, as example, *How are the mighty fallen in the midst of the battle ! I am distressed for thee, my brother Jonathan !.* The second half of this quotation clearly violates the rule laid down above, being, however full of emotion, a simple statement, & yet having an exclamation mark. But anyone who will refer to 2 *Sam.* i. 26 will find that mark to be not the Bible's, but the grammarian's ; the earlier one of verse 25 is right. So far, the inference seems obvious & simple—to confine the exclamation to what grammar recognizes as exclamations, & refuse it to statements, questions, & commands. Exclamations in grammar are (1) interjections, as *oh !* ; (2) words or phrases used as interjections, as *Heavens !, hell !, by Jove !, my God ! great Scott !* ; (3) sentences containing the exclamatory *what* or *how,* as *What a difference it makes !, What I suffered !, How I love you !, How pretty she is !* ; (4) wishes proper, as *Confound you !, May we live to see it !, God forbid !* ; (5) Ellipses & inversions due to emotion, as *Not another word !, If only I could !, That it should have come to this !, Much care you !, Pop goes the weasel !, A fine friend you have been !* ; (6) apostrophes, as *You miserable coward !, You little dear !.* It is true that the exclamation mark should be given to all expressions answering to the above types, & also that it should not be given to ordinary fully expressed statements, questions, or commands ; but the matter is not quite so simple as that. Though a sentence is not to be exclamation-marked to show that it has the excited tone that its contents imply, it may & sometimes must be so marked to convey that the tone is not merely what would be natural to the words themselves, but is that suitable to scornful quotation, to the unexpected, the amusing, the disgusting, or something that needs the comment of special intonation to secure that the words shall be taken as they are meant. So : *You thought it didn't matter !, He learnt at last that the enemy was—himself !, Each is as bad as the other, only more so !, He puts his knife in his mouth !.* But not : *That is a lie !, My heart was in my mouth !, Who cares !, I wish you would be quiet !, Beggars must not be choosers !* ; in all these the words themselves suffice to show the tone, & the exclamation mark shows only that the writer does not know his business.

QUESTION MARK

The chief danger is that of forgetting that whether a set of words is a question or not, & consequently requires or repudiates the question mark, is decided not by its practical effect or sense, but by its grammatical form & relations. Those who scorn grammar are apt to take *Ask him who said so* for a question, & *Will you please stand back* for a request, & to wrongly give the first the question mark that they wrongly fail to give the second. But the first is in fact a command containing an INDIRECT QUESTION, & the question mark belongs to direct questions only, while the second is in fact a direct question, though it happens to be equivalent in sense

to a request. When the natural confusion caused by the conveying, for instance, of what is in sense a statement in the grammatical form of a question is aggravated by the sentence's being of considerable length—e.g. when *Will it be believed that* is followed by several lines setting forth the incredible fact—, the question mark at the end is often, but should never be, omitted. Still more fatal is a type of sentence that may be put either as an exclamation or as a question, but must have its stop adapted to the exclamatory or interrogative nature of the *what* or *how* whose double possibilities cause the difficulty. *How seldom does it happen* can only be an exclamation, & must have *happen !* ; but *How often does it happen* may be either a question (answer, Once a month &c.) requiring *happen ?*, or an exclamation (meaning, Its frequency is surprising) requiring *happen !*. *In that interval what had I not lost !* (either *lost !* should be changed to *lost ?*, or *not* should be omitted)./*A streak of blue below the hanging alders is certainly a characteristic introduction to the kingfisher. How many people first see him so ?* (read either *so !* for *so ?*, or *otherwise* for *so*).

The archness of the question mark interpolated in brackets infallibly betrays the amateur writer : *Sir,— The following instance of the doubtful advantages (?) of the Labour Exchanges as media . . . seems to deserve some recognition.*

INVERTED COMMAS

There is no universally accepted distinction between the single form (' . . . ') & the double (" . . . "). The more sensible practice is to regard the single as the normal, & to resort to the double only when, as fairly often happens, an interior quotation is necessary in the middle of a passage that is itself quoted. To reverse this is clearly less reasonable ; but, as quotation within quotation is much less common than the simple kind, & conspicuousness is desired, the heavy double mark is the favourite. It may be hoped that *The man who says ' I shall write to " The Times " tonight '* will ultimately prevail over *The man who says " I shall write to ' The Times ' tonight "*.

Questions of order between inverted commas & stops are illustrated by the following pairs, the first form being usual, but the second right :—

The first genuine " Collected Poems " admitted his stately " Sonnet on the Nile " only on the inducement of " a partial friend," a few lines from " The Nymphs," that fair humanity of old religion, on that same ground alone. The first genuine ' Collected Poems ' admitted his stately ' Sonnet on the Nile ' only on the inducement of ' a partial friend ', a few lines from ' The Nymphs ', that fair humanity of old religion, on that same ground alone./*Do you say, " Am I my brother's keeper " ?* Do you say ' Am I my brother's keeper ? ' ?/*With him it was always, " Damn the consequences " !* With him it was always ' Damn the consequences ! '.

APOSTROPHE

For difficulties with this as sign of the possessive case, see POSSESSIVE PUZZLES. For its use in avoiding certain bizarre word-forms, see -ED & 'D.

HYPHENS, ITALICS

See those articles.

PARENTHESIS BRACKETS & DOUBLE DASHES

Of these no more need be said than that after the second bracket or dash any stop that would have been used if the brackets or dashes & their contents had not been there should still be used. This is sometimes, but not very often, forgotten after the second bracket ; after the second dash it is seldom remembered, or rather, perhaps, is deliberately neglected as fussy ; but, if it is fussy to put a stop after a dash, it is messy to pile two jobs at once upon the dash, & those to whom fussiness is repugnant should eschew the double-dash form of parenthesis except where no stop can be needed. *So far as it is true—& how far it is true does not count for much—it is an unexpected bit of truth* (read *much—, it*)./*If he abandons a pursuit it is not because he is conscious of having shot his last bolt—that is never shot— but because . . .* (read *never shot—, but*).

store, vb, makes -*rable*; see MUTE E.

storey. Pl. -*eys*, adj. -*storeyed*. For the curious difference in sense between *s.* & *floor*, see FLOOR.

storey, story. Whether these names for the floor & the tale are etymologically the same word or not—on which the doctors differ—, there is an obvious convenience in the two spellings. It is, for instance, well to know *storied windows* (illustrating biblical or other stories) from *storeyed windows* (divided by transoms into storeys). The DIFFERENTIATION, however, is still a probationer, & indeed lacks the support of the OED ; that is sadly against it, especially when the 19th-c. quotations are found to show -*ry* & -*ries* four times as often as -*rey* & -*reys* ; but there is yet a chance that it may win through ; so may it be !

storm. See WIND, n.

story. For *but that is another s.*, see HACKNEYED PHRASES. It is not mended by variations, such as : *Presently it returned. He hoped he was not to be assailed by birds. He had read a story—but never mind that now.*

stouten. See -EN VERBS.

stove, = *staved*. See STAVE.

Strad. See CURTAILED WORDS.

straight(ly). *Certain members of the Labour Party, like Mr Snowden, have spoken very honestly & straightly about the growth of this idea./For once, he did not mince his words on a labour question ; would that he had spoken as straightly on previous occa-*

sions! These two examples, of which the first shows a perhaps defensible *straightly*, & the second a certainly indefensible one, throw some light on the regrettable but progressive extinction of our old monosyllabic adverbs; it is the company of *honestly* that partly excuses the first *straightly*; see UNIDIOMATIC -LY.

strain)(sprain. For the not very clear distinction, see SPRAIN.

strait(en). The chief phrases in which these, & not *straight(en)*, must be used are: *the strait gate, the straitest sect, strait jacket, strait waistcoat, strait-laced, straitened circumstances, straitened (for)*.

strappado. Pl. *-os*; see -O(E)S 3.

strategic(al), pronunciation. In the penult of adjj. & nn. in *-ic* (& the antepenult of *-ical* words), if *-ic* is preceded by a single consonant, there is an overwhelming preponderance for the short sound of the previous vowel (except *u*); so *errătic, barbăric, mechănic, trăgic, poĕtic, acadĕmic, ĕthic, angĕlic, arthrĭtic, prolĭfic, chrŏnic, exŏtic, microscŏpic, histŏric, spasmŏdic, lўric, paralўtic,* & hundreds more; cf., with *u, scorbūtic, mūsic, cūbic.* Nevertheless, *strate'gic* is at least as often said as *strate'gic*; the most notable of other exceptions is *scenic*; the OED recognizes both pronunciations for *scenic & strategic*, but gives the preference to ē in the first, & to ĕ in the other.

strategy)(tactics. Etymologically, strategy is generalship, & tactics is array, & the modern antithesis retains as closely as could fairly be expected the original difference. The OED definition of strategy & note on the distinction follow, with three quotations, of which the first two are from the OED. *Strategy.* The art of a commander-in-chief; the art of projecting & directing the larger military movements & operations of a campaign. Usually distinguished from *tactics*, which is the art of handling forces in battle or in

the immediate presence of the enemy. (Quotations) Strategy differs materially from tactic; the latter belonging only to the mechanical movement of bodies set in motion by the former./Before hostile armies or fleets are brought into contact (a word which perhaps better than any other indicates the dividing line between tactics & strategy)./The study of strategy, which is the art of bringing forces into contact with the enemy, & of tactics, which is the art of using those forces when they are in contact with the enemy.

Readers should perhaps be warned against supposing that the *tact* of *contact* & of *tactics* is etymologically the same, since these writers have utilized the accidental likeness; *contact* (Latin) is touch, *tactics* (Greek) is array.

stratify. For inflexions see VERBS IN -IE &c., 6.

stratum. Pl. *-ta*; see -UM.

stratus. Pl. *-ti.*

strawberry. For *the s. leaves* see SOBRIQUETS.

strayed, adj. INTRANSITIVE P.P.

streak. *The silvers.*; see SOBRIQUETS.

stress)(strain, as technical terms in Physics. In defining the use of *stress* in Physics, the OED remarks that it is 'used variously by different writers', & this statement is borne out by its quotations. Any close examination of such matters is outside our scope; but the layman may be glad of a rough distinction. It is perhaps safe to say that strain is the result of stress; stress being mutual action exerted by bodies or parts, strain is the alteration of form or dimensions produced by it.

strew. P.p. indifferently *-ed* & *-n.*

stria. Pl. *-iae.*

stricken. This archaic p.p. of *strike* survives chiefly in particular phrases, & especially in senses divorced from those now usual with the verb—*stricken in years, a stricken field, the stricken deer, for a stricken hour, poverty-stricken, panic-stricken.*

The use of the word by itself as an adjective=afflicted, in distress, is sometimes justified, but more often comes under the description of STOCK PATHOS.

stride. Past *-ode*; p.p. (rare) *-idden*.

stringed)(strung. Accurately, a bow is *stringed* or *unstringed* according as it is provided with a string or not, & *strung* or *unstrung* according as it is bent to the string or not; cf. *stringed instruments* & *strung nerves*; so *a high-strung temperament* but *a gut-stringed racket*. *Overstrung piano*, which suggests a difficulty, is right because the notion is not that of providing it with overstrings as the racket is provided with gut strings (implying formation from the noun *string*), but that of stringing it transversely (from the verb *string* with the adverb *over*). See HAMSTRINGED for discussion of that word & of *bowstring*, vb.

stringhalt, spr-. Both forms are common, & they denote the same disease; *str-*, which the OED regards as probably the original, might well be made the only word.

strive. Past *strove*, p.p. *striven*; but the OED adds that ' many examples of *strived* ' for both ' occur in writers of every period from the 14th to the 19th c.'.

stroke, v., makes *-kable*; MUTE E.

stroma. Pl. *-ata*.

strophe. See TECHNICAL TERMS; pronounce strŏ'fĭ; pl. *-s* or *-phae*, see LATIN PLURALS.

strow, formerly common, is now only a by-form of *strew*.

struma. Pl. *-mae*.

strung. See STRINGED.

strychnia, -nine. See MORPHIA; but *strychnia* has not, like that, maintained itself in popular use.

stubbornness. So spelt.

stucco. The noun makes *-os*, see *-o(E)s* 3; the verb *-oes, -oed* or*-o'd*.

studding-sail. Pronounce stŭ'nsl.

studiedly. For the legitimacy of the form see -EDLY, rule (3).

studio. Pl. *-os*; see *-o(E)s* 4.

study, vb, **stultify, stupefy.** For inflexions see VERBS IN -IE &c., 6.

stupid makes *-er, -est*; -ER & -EST 2.

stupor, not *stupour*; -OUR & -OR.

STURDY INDEFENSIBLES. Many idioms are seen, if they are tested by grammar or logic, to express badly, even sometimes to express the reverse of, what they are nevertheless well understood to mean. Good people point out the sin, & bad people, who are more numerous, take little notice & go on committing it; then the good people, if they are foolish, get excited & talk of ignorance & solecisms, & are laughed at as purists; or, if they are wise, say no more about it & wait. The indefensibles, sturdy as they may be, prove one after another to be not immortal. There was a time when no-one was more ashamed to say ' You was there ' than most of us now are to say ' It 's me '; ' you was ' is dead; ' it 's me ' has a long life before it yet; it too will die, & there are much more profitable ways of spending time than baiting it. It is well, however, to realize that there are such things as foolish idioms; that a language should abound in them can be no credit to it or its users; & the drawing of attention to them is a step towards making them obsolete; a few types follow, with references to articles in which each question is touched upon:—

It 's ME.

Don't be longer *than you can* HELP.

So far from hating him, I like him (FAR 2).

The man *of all others* for the job (OF 7).

The worst liar *of any man* I know (OF 7).

A child *of ten years old* (OF 7).

That long nose *of his* (OF 7).

It is no USE complaining.

Better known than popular (-ER & -EST 7).

Were ever *finer* lines perverted to a *meaner* use? (ILLOGICALITIES).

It is a day's work even to open, *much less* to acknowledge, all the letters (MUCH 2).

For two reasons, *neither* of which *are* noticed by Plato (NEITHER 3).

All men do *not* speak German (NOT 1).

He ONLY died a week ago.

It should not be taken TOO literally.

I should not be SURPRISED if it didn't rain.

sty, nn. Pl. *sties.* The separate spelling *stye* (pl. *styes*), sometimes used for the pimple on the eyelid, has not the support of the OED, & the danger of confusion is too slight for artificial DIFFERENTIATION.

sty, vb. For inflexions, see VERBS IN -IE &c., 6.

style)(**stile.** See STILE.

stylo. See CURTAILED WORDS ; pl. *-os*, see -O(E)S 5.

stymie. See STIMY.

Suabian, Swa-. *Swa-* (nearer the original German) is preferred by OED to *Sua-* (fr. the intermediate Latin).

sub, n. Used slangily for *subaltern, subscription,* & *substitute,* & also with help of context for other words ; see CURTAILED WORDS.

subdual. See -AL NOUNS.

subduedly. A bad form ; see -EDLY. *Both Siegfried Sassoon & W. J. Turner speak subduedly as if in recollection of ancient bitterness, but it is poetry of a distinguished dis-illusionment.*

subject. For synonyms in sense *theme* &c., see FIELD.

subjective genitive. See TECHNICAL TERMS.

subjugate makes *-jugable*, see -ABLE 1 ; & *-ator*, see -OR.

SUBJUNCTIVES. The word is very variously used in grammar. The subjunctives here to be considered (1) exclude those, often so called, in which the modal effect is given by an auxiliary such as *may* (*that he may do it* ; cf. *that he do it*), *let* (*let it be so* ; cf. *be it so*), or *shall* (*until he shall be dead* ; cf. *until he be dead*) ;

& (2) include any verb that is understood to be modally different from the indicative but is either indistinguishable from it in form or distinguished otherwise than by an auxiliary ; in ' that he learn ' it is clear that *learn* is subjunctive ; in ' that we learn ' it is not ; in ' that we, he, may learn ' there is no subjunctive that concerns us in this article ; any verb of the kind that has now been loosely indicated is for our present purpose a subjunctive, whether or not it is more specifically known as imperative (*sing we merrily*), conditional of the apodosis (*it were more seemly*) or of the protasis (*if it please you*), optative (*had I but the power !*), indirect question (*When I ask her if she love me*), indefinite future clause (*till he die*), or by any other such name.

About the subjunctive, so delimited, the important general facts are : (1) that it is moribund except in a few easily specified uses ; (2) that, owing to the capricious influence of the much analysed classical upon the less studied native moods, it probably never would have been possible to draw up a satisfactory table of the English subjunctive uses ; (3) that assuredly no-one will ever find it either possible or worth while to do so now that the subjunctive is dying ; & (4) that subjunctives met with today, outside the few truly living uses, are either deliberate revivals by poets for legitimate enough archaic effect, or antiquated survivals as in pretentious journalism, infecting their context with dullness, or new arrivals possible only in an age to which the grammar of the subjunctive is not natural but artificial.

Revival : When I ask her if she *love* me (prose, *loves*).

Survival : If this analysis *be* correct (normal, *is*).

Arrival : If this *were* so, it was in self-defence (sense, *was*).

We may now proceed to illustrate the four classes to which we have been brought, Alives, Revivals,

Survivals, & Arrivals, in the senses already explained ; & no concealment need be made of the purpose in hand, which is to discourage the last two classes.

ALIVES

Those uses are alive which it occurs to no-one to suspect of pedantry or artificiality, & which come as natural in speech as other ways of saying the thing, or more so. The giving of a few specimens is all that will here be necessary.

Go away (& all 2nd-pers. imperatives).

Manners be hanged ! (& such 3rd-pers. curses).

Come what may, Be that as it may, Far be it from me to . . ., (& other such stereotyped formulae).

I shall be 70 come Tuesday.

If he were here now (& all *if* . . . *were* clauses expressing a hypothesis that is not a fact ; *were* & not *be*, & *not a fact*, are essential).

I wish it were over.

Though all care be exercised (the difference is still a practical one between *Though* . . . *is*, = In spite of the fact that, & *Though* . . . *be*, = Even on the supposition that).

REVIVALS

What care I how fair she be ?
Lose who may, I still can say . . .
If ladies be but young & fair.

But illustration is superfluous ; there are no uses of the subjunctive to which poets, & poetic writers, may not resort if it suits them ; the point to be made is merely that it is no defence for the ordinary writer who uses an antiquated subjunctive to plead that he can parallel it in a good poet.

SURVIVALS

In the examples that will be given there is nothing incorrect ; the objection to the subjunctives in them is that they diffuse an atmosphere of dullness & formalism over the writing in which they occur ; the motive underlying them, & the

effect they produce, are the same that attend the choosing of FORMAL WORDS, a reference to which article may save some repetition.

If it have [has] *a flaw, that flaw takes the shape of a slight incoherence./It is quite obvious to what grave results such instances as the above may lead, be they* [if they are] *only sufficiently numerous./The causes which would probably bring about a protracted civil war in Servia should King Peter die before the question of his successor be* [is, *or* has been] *more firmly decided./If these others be* [are] *all we can muster, it were* [would be] *better to leave the sculpture galleries empty./If Mr Hobhouse's analysis of the vices of popular government be* [is] *correct, much more would seem to be needed./It were* [would be] *futile to attempt to deprive it of its real meaning./Unless immediate action be* [is] *taken, the country will be so tied that* . . ./*That will depend a good deal on whether he be* [is] *shocked by the cynicism.*

ARRIVALS

The best proof that the subjunctive is, except in isolated uses, no longer alive, & one good reason for abstaining from it even where, as in the Survival examples, it is grammatical, are provided by a collection, such as anyone can gather for himself from any newspaper, of subjunctives that are wrong. A collection follows, slightly grouped.

Mixed moods : That two verbs whose relation to their surroundings is precisely the same should be one subjunctive, & one indicative, is an absurdity that could not happen until the distinction had lost its reality ; but it does happen every day :—*If that appeal be made & results in the return of the Government to power, then* . . ./*There are those who, if there be common security & they are all right, not only care nothing for, but would even oppose, the* . . ./*If the verdict goes against him his home may be sold up, or if an injunction be obtained against him*

& he defies *it he may be imprisoned./ If the history of Christianity* is, *as Höffding suggests, but a world-drama which mythologizes in a passing symbol the inner psychological drama, if it* be *but a precipitate of the tides or storms of the spiritual imagination, if it* be *a mere projection of man's agitated subjectivism, how can it give us . . .?/*These *bes* are not themselves wrong ; they are Survival subjunctives ; but the fact that the verbs associated with them, which have subjunctives ready for use just as much as *to be,* are allowed to remain indicative shows that the use of *be* too is mechanical & meaningless.

Were in conditionals : The correct type, a common enough ' Survival ', is *Were that true there were no more to say* ; the first *were,* of the protasis, is right only in combination with the other *were,* of the apodosis, or with its modern equivalent, *would (should) be* ; & neither of them is applicable to past time any more than *would be* itself ; their reference is to present or to undefined time, or more truly not to time at all (& especially not to a particular past time) but to utopia, the realm of non-fact. If it is a hard saying that *were* (singular) in conditionals does not refer to past time, consider some other verb of past form in like case. Such a verb may belong to past time, or it may belong to utopia : *If he heard, he gave no sign* (*heard & gave,* past time) ; *If he heard, how angry he would be !* (*heard & would be,* not past time, but utopia, the realm of non-fact or the imaginary) ; the first *heard* is indicative, the second is *subjunctive,* though the form happens to be the same ; in the verb *be,* conveniently enough, there happens to be still a distinguishable form for the subjunctive, & what corresponds for the verb *be* to the two *heard* sentences is *If it was* (never *were*) *so it did not appear, If it were* (or nowadays alternatively *was*) *so how angry we should be !. Were* (sing.) is, then, a recognizable subjunctive, & applicable not to

past facts, but to present or future non-facts ; it is entirely out of place in an *if*-clause concerned with past actualities & not answered by a *were* or *would be* in the apodosis. It has been necessary to labour this explanation because for the many readers who are not at home with grammatical technicalities the matter is puzzling. Examples :—*It is stated that, during the early part of the War of Independence* (1821), *the Greeks massacred Mussulmans ; if this* were *so, it was only in self-defence./If rent* were *cheap, clothes were dearer than today./If the attitude of the French Government* were *known to our own Government last week it* explains *the appeal to the Dominions./ We must not look for any particulars as to that lost work (if it* were *ever written),* " *The Life & Adventures of Joseph Sell* ". These four contain *if . . . were* (sing.) in protasis—an ' Alive ' form if the apodosis is *would be* or *were,* i. c. if the conditional is of the utopian kind, but wrong if the time of the *were* is a particular past. Read *was* in each. Examples in apodosis :—*It* were *just & fitting that on such an occasion a Prince of the Royal House & Heir-apparent to the Throne should himself have plied the fires of the record warship with coal.* The newspaper is patting the Prince on the back for what he actually did, viz stoke ; it means not that it would be right on an imaginary occasion, but that it was on that past occasion right for him to stoke ; read *was./The dull winter prospect appeared so quiet & peaceful, it* were difficult *to imagine the Boches over there—on sentry, in their dugouts, eating, drinking, sleeping, just like the men about me ; but, proving their presence, a miniewurfer shell passed overhead.* Paraphrasing so as to get rid of the glamour of the word *were,* we get not ' I should find it difficult ', but ' I found it difficult ', as is shown by ' a shell passed ' ; read *it was difficult.*

Sequence : To those who have had

to do with Latin & Greek Grammar, there will be a familiar sound in *Sequence of tenses & Sequence of moods* ; what is implied in the terms is that it may be necessary to use a tense or a mood not to convey the meaning peculiar to it as such, but for the sake of harmony with the tense or mood of another verb on which it depends. The principle has its place, though little is heard of it, in English grammar also (see SEQUENCE OF TENSES) ; it is mentioned here because the most likely explanation of the subjunctives now to be quoted, some clearly wrong, some at the best uncalled-for, seems to be a hazy memory of sequence of moods ; after each example the supposed reasoning is suggested, not as sound, but as conceivable :—
Why should ordinary shop assistants enjoy a half-holiday, as is proposed in Sir William Bull's Bill, while the staff behind the scenes, often working underground & before a scorching fire, be *denied this privilege ?* (*Why should assistants enjoy* is in the subjunctive ; therefore the subordinate clause requires *the staff be*, not *is*, *denied*)./*But if, during the intercourse occasioned by trade, he finds that a neighbour in possession of desirable property* be *weaker than himself, he is apt to take advantage* (*if he finds* is a conditional ; therefore the clause dependent on it must be in the subjunctive)./*By all means let us follow after those things which make for peace, so far as* be *possible* (*let us follow* is an exhortation ; therefore the clause dependent on it must &c.)./*We should be glad to know that every chairman of a Local Education Authority or Education Committee* were *likely to read this short biography* (*should* is subjunctive, therefore &c. ; or, perhaps more probably, *should be glad to know* is in one word *wish*, & *wish . . . were* is beyond cavil)./*And if exceptional action were needed to prove love, what would after all be proved, except that love* were *not the rule ?* (*would* is a subjunctive, therefore &c.)./*No*

doctor *would inject horse serum into a patient if he knew that he* were *liable to horse asthma* (as the last)./*If I made a political pronouncement I should feel that I* were *outraging the hospitality of the Brotherhood movement* (*should* is a subjunctive, therefore &c.)./*It would not be surprising if this limit were reduced to £125, the German limit, while voluntary insurance* were *still allowed for persons with incomes up to £160 a year* (the meaning of the *while* clause is the same as if it had begun with *&*, in which case *were allowed* would have been inevitable). It may be admitted that some of these are less bad than others, & that, while the group is characteristic of a time that is not at ease with its subjunctives, anyone who wished to parallel its details in writers who used the mood far more frequently than we as well as more naturally could doubtless do so ; nevertheless they are best classed with Arrivals.

Indirect question : Latin grammar is perhaps also responsible for the notion that indirect question requires the subjunctive. There is no such requirement in English ; *Ask him who he be* is enough to show that. *Sir Adam asked Sir Richard Redmayne if he* were *aware that one of the miners' secretaries in Scotland had been . . .* Read *was* ; but again such subjunctives may be found in older writers.

Miscellaneous : *He therefore came round to the view that simple Bible teaching* were *better abolished altogether & that the open door for all religions* were *established in its place. Were better abolished* is a correct Survival ; but dealing with the now unnatural has tempted the writer into an impossible continuation./*Be the ventilation of a gaseous mine as efficient as it can be made, nothing will prevent . . .* An unidiomatic extension of the ' Alive ' *Be that as it may*, made absurd by its length./*He replied gently, but firmly, that if his department* were *to be successful, he must accommodate himself to the people who employed him.* His words were not ' If my department be to succeed ', but ' is to '. The sequence change of *is* should be to *was*, & *were* instead ruins the sense ; ' were to be successful ' means ' succeeded ' or ' should succeed ', not ' was to have a chance '.

The conclusion is that writers who deal in Survival subjunctives run the risks, first, of making their matter dull, secondly, of being tempted into blunders themselves, thirdly, of injuring the language by encouraging others more ignorant than they to blunder habitually, & lastly, of having the proper dignity of style at which they aim mistaken by captious readers for pretentiousness.

submerge. Gerundive usu. *submersible* rather than *-gible*.

submissible, -ittable. The second form is unexceptionable ; but on the principle explained in -ABLE 2, *submissible* would have been expected to establish itself on the analogy of *ad, o, & per, -missible.* It is in fact, to judge from the OED, hardly existent, but may nevertheless be recommended as preferable.

suborn. See FORMAL WORDS.

subpoena. Best so written, see Æ, Œ ; p.p. *subpoena'd*, see -ED & 'D.

subscribe makes *-bable*; see MUTE E.

subsellium. Pl. *-ia.*

subservience, -cy. See -CE, -CY.

subsidence. The OED gives preference to subsi'dence over su'bsidence. But *residence, confidence, providence, & coincidence,* all associated with verbs in -ī'de, & all disregarding that fact & conforming to the RECESSIVE ACCENT tendency, are a very strong argument on the other side, against which perhaps no opposite instance of any weight can be brought. *Su'bsidence* is therefore recommended ; the Latin quantity (*sīdo* settle) is of no importance (see FALSE QUANTITY).

subsidize makes *-zable* ; see MUTE E.

substantiate makes *-tiable* ; see -ABLE 1. For pronunciation of *substantiation,* see -CIATION.

substantivally, -ively. See ADJECTIVALLY.

substitute vb, **substitution.** A very rapid change—according to the view here taken, a corruption—has been lately taking place in the meaning & use of these words ; so rapid, indeed, that what the OED stigmatized in 1915 as ' Now regarded as incorrect ' will soon, if nothing can be done to stop it, become normal usage & oust what is here held to be the words' only true sense. The definition to which the OED adds the above note is (for the verb) ' To take the place of, replace ', & an examination of what other dictionaries are at hand (Century, Standard, Webster, Cassell's Encyclopaedic, & some small fry) discovers that none of them records this sense at all, with the exception of the Standard, in which it is confined to Chemistry. They all agree that the verb means something entirely different, viz to put (a person or thing) in the place of another. It is clear, then, what the orthodox use of the verb is ; the use of the noun follows it ; & we can set down for comparison a sentence or two that are right & one or two that are wrong, choosing as nouns that will make the points clear *butter & margarine, Englishman & alien.*

CORRECT

A. We had to substitute margarine (for butter).

B. Aliens are being substituted (for Englishmen).

C. [Aliens are replacing Englishmen.]

D. The substitution of margarine (for butter) is having bad effects.

E. Let there be no more substitution of aliens (for Englishmen).

F. Its substitution (for butter) is lamentable.

INCORRECT

A. We had to substitute butter (by margarine).

B. Englishmen **are being** substituted (by aliens).

C. Aliens are substituting English-men.

D. The substitution of butter (by margarine) is having bad effects.

E. Let there be no more substitution of Englishmen (by aliens).

F. Its substitution (by margarine) is lamentable.

One can hardly read those parallels, with the risks of ambiguity that they suggest, without realizing that either the old or the new must go ; we surely cannot keep such a treacherously double-edged knife as *substitute* has become ; either its original edge, or the one into which its back has been converted, must be ground off ; which is it to be ? Another reflection, which may not occur unsuggested to all, is that in the incorrect set the words *replace* or *replacement* would have done, whereas in the correct set they would either have been impossible or have changed the meaning. And here, probably, is what accounts for the whole perversion of our words ; *substitute* & *substitution* have been seized upon by people who failed to apprehend with precision the dictionary definitions & fancied they had found equivalents in sense for the words *replace(ment)*, which they had been ignorantly taught to regard as solecisms in the required senses (see REPLACE) ; so they determined (in their lingo) to substitute *replace* by *substitute*, whereas they ought to have refused (in English) to substitute *substitute* for *replace* or to replace *replace* by *substitute*.

To sum up : The dictionary definitions are right ; the new popular use is wrong & confusing, & is based upon a superstition ; but it has hitherto, as the dictionaries show, almost escaped detection, & therefore it will be necessary to give a convincing array of recent quotations, to satisfy readers that this article is not an attack on the negligible. It is indeed high time that *replace* were reinstated & *substitute* reduced to its proper function. In going through the sentences, those who are new to the question may observe that nearly all can be mended in two ways, shown for verb & noun in the first two examples—one the change to *replace(ment)*, & the other the turning of the sentence upside down & changing of *by* to *for*. One or two exceptional types are placed at the end with special corrections.

The ecclesiastical principle was substituted by the national, the Empire & the Papacy by the Communes (Either *was replaced* ; or *The national principle was substituted for the ecclesiastical, the Communes for the Empire & the Papacy*)./*Chief among these innovations is the substitution of the large & unwieldy geographical unit by a small & compact local administrative unit* (Either *is the replacement of* ; or *is the substitution of a compact local unit for the unwieldy geographical unit*)./*M. Chicherin also requested that in article VI the word ' foment ' should be substituted by the word ' prepare ', saying that ' foment ' has too vast an acceptation.*/*Although only a temporary, & liable to be substituted by an ex-service man at any time, because I was physically unfit for the army, I am glad to . . .*/*If it proves successful it will be extended all along the border ; if it fails it will be substituted by an arbitrary line along the lakes & rivers.*/*Many words, such as aviation, airship, dirigible, aeroplane, aviator, &c., have been assailed & substituted by terms which lend themselves to finer expression.*/*The ' Stampa' hopes that a definite pledge will be obtained for Greek evacuation, & that regular troops will not be substituted by ' sacred battalions '.*/*If a good raw hide gear is substituted by a set of laminated gears, they will be found quite as silent.*/*Mr Asquith concluded on a note of high appeal for the substitution of the Supreme Council by the League of Nations.*/*The Greek administration should continue under the supervision of the Allies until the time comes for its substitution by a Turkish administration.*/*The substitution of the Council by a Com-*

mittee of Ambassadors is about to be realized./You appear to recommend the abolition of the Council of India & its substitution by a regular Committee of Parliament./Even the suppression of the provinces, & their substitution by larger spheres of Government, is being considered./The substitution of a voluntary censorship by a compulsory Government one would result in a more onerous authority./The Chancellor of the Exchequer looked forward to the abolition of the excess profits duty & its substitution by a tax on war fortunes./ The proposals will include the dismissal of all Prussian or non-Rhenan officials in the occupied areas, & their substitution by officials born in the country./And the very slow diminution is due to the substitution of these barbaric methods by others rational & decent./A budget Tax on all ' land values ' should be levied in substitution of the duties on tea, sugar, cocoa, & other articles of food (It is true that *in replacement of* would have an awkward sound here ; but only because the still simpler *instead*, or *in place*, or *in lieu*, *of* is the plain English for it)./If potatoes substitute bread, what is going to substitute potatoes ?* is a question every German *will have to ask himself* (In the comparatively rare active use, the upside-down method is not quite applicable. Either read *replace*, or *If we substitute potatoes for bread, what are we going to substitute for potatoes ?*)./Money & talent, often substituted by their counterfeits, speculation & trickery, have here broken down all barriers* (often *substituted by* means simply or *often*).

subtle, subtil(e), &c. The modern forms are *subtle, subtler, subtlest, subtly*, but *subtilize* ; b is silent in all. Spellings with the i retained are (except in *subtilize*) usually left to archaists of various kinds ; &, as Milton was content with *suttle*, there seems little reason for going back beyond *subtle* to *subtil*.

subtract(ion), substr-. Spell in the

first way ; but the forbidden -s- is called by the OED only ' now illiterate '; & in the long array of writers who have used it are Bentham, the Duke of Wellington, & Carlyle.

subversal. See -AL NOUNS. *Since his ' Trade & Tariffs ' appeared (in 1906) the subversal of the economic conditions demands a fresh investigation of the problem.*

succedaneum. Pl. *-ea* ; but an examination of quotations is so far from suggesting any difference of meaning between this pedantic term & its synonym *substitute* that it may surely be relegated to the SUPERFLUOUS WORDS.

succeed. *All the traditions in which she has been brought up have not succeeded to keep her back.* Read *in keeping*, & see GERUND 3.

succès. For *s. d'estime, s. fou*, see FRENCH WORDS.

success. For *s. of esteem*, see GALLICISMS 5.

succinct. Pronounce -ks-.

succour. Keep the -u- ; -OUR & -OR.

succuba, -bus. Pl. *-ae, -ĭ* ; the words mean the same, & are not respectively feminine & masculine.

such. 1. *S. which, s. who, s. that, s. where*, &c. 2. *S. that* rel.) (*s. that* conj. 3. *S.* exclamatory. 4. Illiterate *s.=that* &c. 5. *S.=so*. 6. *S. as* for *as*. 7. *Suchlike*.

1. *S. which, s. who, s. that* (rel. pron.), *s. where* (rel. adv.). *Such* is a demonstrative adjective & demonstrative pronoun, to which it was formerly common to make other relatives besides *as* correspond, especially *which, who, that*, & *where*. Modern idiom rejects all these, & confines itself to *as* ; the OED's remark on the use of *such . . . which* &c. is ' Now rare & regarded as incorrect '. It is not in fact so very rare ; but most modern examples of it are due either to writers' entire ignorance of idiom or to their finding themselves in a difficulty & not seeing how to get out of it. In the

following extracts, when a mere change of *which* &c. to *as* is not possible, the way out, or *a* way, is indicated :—*The Roumanian Government contends that it has only requisitioned* such *things of which there is abundance in the country* (such things as are abundant, *or* as there is abundance of)./*Prussia & the Kaiser were preparing for* such *a war which they believed would result in the German Empire (& Prussia) becoming the master of the Old World.*/*The third year should be reserved for* such *additional or special subjects (elocution, for instance) which need not be regarded as essential.*/*It was proposed to grant to* such *casual employees of the Council who had been continuously employed for three months, & whose employment was likely to extend over twelve months, the privilege of additional leave* (read *those,* or *any,* for *such*)./*How, then, can* such *of these men who trouble to think regard the results of Mr Lloyd George's budget ?*/*It is the bourgeois who thrive,* such *of them who have escaped molestation at the hands of the Bolsheviks.*/. . . *urging its adoption as a means of enabling* such *of those men who are trained in certain occupations to get to & from their work.*/*It is subject, of course, to* such *possible changes of plan that any unexpected turn of events may bring about.*/*I noticed two cars approaching in* such *a manner that seemed to indicate they would both arrive at the junction together.*/*The first zone, where the regulations are not so onerous, covers* such *tracts where there are no real signs of war* (read *the* or *those* for *such* ; or *as show* for *where there are*).

2. *Such that* rel.)(*such that* conj. Now & then a *s. that* for *s. as* is perhaps due to the writer's hesitating between two ways of putting a thing, one with the relative *as* & the other with the conjunction *that*, & finally achieving neither, but stumbling into the relative *that*. They *will never learn the truth from this system of military inquiries, be-*

cause they will only see the results if those are such *that the Government would like them to see* (such as the Government would like them to see ? *or* such that the Government would like them to be seen ?)./*I cannot think that there is* such *a different level of intelligence among Englishmen & Germans that would prevent similar papers from being a profitable property in Great Britain* (such . . . as would prevent ? *or* such . . . that it would prevent ?).

3. *Such* exclamatory or appealing. *The Earl of Derby was the titular King of Man—a piece of constitutional antiquarianism of which Scott made* such *splendid use in ' Peveril of the Peak '.* Such is liable to the same over-use of this kind as *so* ; reference to so 3 will make further illustration unnecessary here. Use & over-use of an idiom are different things, & there is no need to avoid this *such* altogether ; in the above quotation it may be noticed that if the writer had said *the* piece of antiquarianism instead of *a* piece the *such* would have passed well enough.

4. The illiterate *such* (= *that, those, it, them,* &c.). The significance of the epithet will be found explained in ILLITERACIES, & half a dozen examples with corrections will suffice :—*His seven propositions for non-partisan legislation must appeal to the common-sense of every man & woman in the realm ; is it too much to hope that* such *will combine to render them realities?* (that all will)./*As a Canadian, with, I trust, a fair knowledge of the causes which led to the defeat of Sir Wilfrid Laurier in the recent election, I have been somewhat amused at some of the editorial articles in portions of the British Press ; the claim that the result of* such *election is an Imperialistic victory is very far from the truth* (of that election)./*We have seen during the war how those persons in humble circumstances who came suddenly into possession of moneys spent* such—*i. e., in* . . . (spent them)./

That there is a void in a millionaire's life is not disproved by anyone showing that a number of millionaires do not recognize such void (recognize it, *or* the *or* that void)./*But when it comes to us following his life & example, in all its intricate details, all will, I think, agree* that such is *impossible* (that that is)./*An appeal to philanthropy is hardly necessary, the grounds* for such being *so self-evident* (for it being)./*If I am refused the Sacrament I do not believe that I shall have less chance of entering the Kingdom of God than if I* received such Sacrament (received it).

5. *Such = so.* Most people have no hesitation in saying *such a small matter, such big apples, with such little justice, such conflicting evidence* ; others object that it should be *so small a matter, apples so big, with so little justice, evidence so conflicting.* It must first be admitted that the objectors are (with allowances for phrases of special meaning) entitled to claim the support of grammar. In 'such a small matter' it is usually *small*, not *matter* or *small matter*, that is to be modified by *such* or *so*, &, *small* being an adjective, the adverb *so* is obviously the grammatical word to do the job ; at the same time, *such a small matter*, though it usually means so small a matter, may also mean a small matter of the kind that has been described ; but, speaking generally, the objectors have grammar on their side. Shall we then be meek & mend our ways at their bidding ? Why, no, not wholesale. We will try to say *so* wherever idiom does not protest or stiffness ensue ; for instance, we will give up 'with such little justice' without a murmur ; but they cannot expect of us 'I never saw apples so big' instead of 'such big apples'. And they must please to remark that the *such* idiom has so established itself that the other is often impossible without a change of order that suggests formality or rhetoric ; *so big apples* ? *so convincing evidence* ? no ; the adjective

has to be deferred (*apples so big*) in a clearly artificial way ; but we grant that ' so small a matter ' does strictly deserve preference over ' such a small matter ', &, if so partial a concession is worth their acceptance, let it be made. Other idioms that are no better than they should be, & yet need not be ruthlessly expelled from society, are NICE *& long* &c., TRY *& manage it* &c., & perhaps the misplaced ONLY.

6. *Such as* for *as. Even the effects of unfavourable weather can be partially counteracted by artificial treatment* such as by *the use of phosphates.* The repetition of *by* results in a *such as* not introducing as it should a noun (*use*), but a preposition (*by*)— a plain but not uncommon blunder. Omit either *such* or *by.*/*Some are able to help in one way, such* as for instance in *speaking; some in another, such as organization.* The second part is right ; the first should be either *in one way such as for instance speaking*, or *in one way as for instance in speaking* ; *such as* requires a noun (*speaking*), not an adverbial phrase (*in speaking*), as its completion.

7. *Suchlike.* That the word is a sort of pleonasm in itself, being ultimately = *solike-like*, is nothing to its discredit, such pleonasms being numerous (cf. *poulterer = pullet + -er + -er*) ; but, whether as adjective (*barley, oats, & suchlike cereals*) or as pronoun (*schoolmasters, plumbers, & suchlike*), it is now usually left to the uneducated, *such* being used as the adjective & *the like* as the pronoun. The OED, however, abstains from comment.

Sudan(ese), Soud-. The spelling that prevailed when the name first became familiar about 1875 was *Soud-* ; the ninth edition of the *Encycl. Brit.* gives its article under that name ; in the tenth & eleventh it has become *Sudan*, which the OED describes as a ' variant of Soudan '. The older form has the advantages (1) of being the same as the French, (2) of precluding the pronunciation sū-, & (3) of being probably still the more familiar to ordinary people; *Sudan* has the merit, if it is one, of having the same number of letters (without suggesting the same sound) as the Arabic word, & the other of showing that its user claims to know more than his neighbours. *Sou-* is recommended; see PRIDE OF KNOWLEDGE.

sudarium, sudatorium. Pl. *-ia.*

suddenness. So spelt.

sue makes *suable*; see MUTE E.

suède. So written.

suet makes *suety*; see -T-, -TT-.

sufficient(ly) & enough. The words are discussed under ENOUGH; for *sufficient* in the following extracts, see the first paragraph of that article :—*So far as the building trade is concerned the complaint we have made to the Government is that sufficient has not been done to get materials organized./And there should be sufficient of a historic conscience left in the Midland capital to evoke a large subscription.*

suffix. See TECHNICAL TERMS.

suffocate makes *-cable*; see -ABLE, 1.

suffrage. For the comparative merits of *female s.* & *woman s.*, see FEMALE)(WOMAN.

suffragette. A more regrettable formation than others such as *leaderette* & *flannelette*, in that it does not even mean a sort of suffrage as they mean a sort of leader & of flannel, & therefore tends to vitiate the popular conception of the termination's meaning. The word itself may now be expected to die, having lost its importance; may its influence on word-making die with it !

suffuse makes *-sable*; see -ABLE 1, 2.

Sufi(sm), So-. The *So-* forms are called by the OED obsolete variants.

sugar makes *sugared* & *sugary*, see -R-, -RR-; & *sugar candy* (unhyphened), see HYPHENS 3 B.

suggest. So spelt; gerundive *-tible*, see -ABLE 2.

suggestio falsi. See TECHNICAL TERMS. *Pronounce* -tĭŏ fă'lsī.

suit, suite, nn. *Suite* is pronounced swēt. The two words are the same, & the differences of usage accidental & variable; but where, the sense being a set, either form would seem admissible, we do say at present *a suit of clothes, a suit of armour, a suit of sails, the four suits at cards, follow suit*; & on the other hand *a suite (of attendants* &c.), *a suite of rooms* or *apartments, a suite of furniture* or *chairs.*

Sukey. So spelt; see -EY, -IE, -Y.

sullenness. So spelt.

sully. For inflexions see VERBS IN -IE &c., 6.

sulphureous, sulphuric, sulphurous. The last has differentiated pronunciations sŭ'lfūrus & sŭlfūr'us, so that there are four adjectives to divide the work. *Sulphuric* & *sulphurous* (-ūr'us) can for general purposes be ignored as technical terms in Chemistry like other *-ic* & *-ous* pairs. *Sulphureous* & *sulphurous* (sŭ'l-), which remain, have never been effectively differentiated, & the OED refers the reader for most senses of one to definitions given under the other. Differentiation may be expected to come, & perhaps the likeliest course for it to take & therefore the best to fall in with is that *sulphurous*, now the more popular word, should take to itself the secondary or extended senses, & *sulphureous* be restricted to the primary material ones meaning ' of or containing sulphur ' without the specific limitations of *sulphuric* & *sulphurous* (-ūr'us). This would give—though naturally the borderline is not quite sharp—*sulphureous gases, springs, smells, drugs, substances,* but *sulphurous yellow, light, torments, language, preachers.*

sumach, -ac. The OED gives precedence to the first spelling, & pronounces sū'măk or shōō'măk.

summer. 1. *St Luke's, St Martin's, S.* Each of these is often used when the other would be the right one ; St Luke's day is in October (18th), St Martin's in November (11th).

2. *Summer time, summer-time, sum-mertime.* The first is the daylight-saving term ; in other senses either of the others should be used ; see HYPHENS, group **business man.*

summersault,-set. See SOMERSAULT.
summon(s). 1. For *summon & send for,* see FORMAL WORDS. 2. *Summons,* n., has pl. *summonses.* 3. *Summon* is the verb in ordinary use ; *summons* should not be used as a verb except in the special sense *to serve with a legal summons* or *issue a summons against,* & even in that sense *summon* is equally good.

Sunday. For the adverbial use (*S.* for *on S.*) see FRIDAY.
sunk(en). For idiomatic use of the two forms, see SINK.
Sunna, -nah. The first is the received spelling.
super, = *supernumerary, superficial measure,* or *superfine.* See CUR-TAILED WORDS.
super-. The use of this as an abbreviation for ' of a superior kind ', as in *superman, super-Dreadnought, supercritic,* & scores or hundreds of other words, is so evidently convenient that it is vain to protest when others indulge in it, & so evidently barbarous that it is worth while to circumvent it oneself when one can do so without becoming unintelligible. *Super-cinema,* meaning merely a cinema of exceptional size or splendour, & not something that transcends & thereby ceases to be a cinema, may serve as a specimen of the worse applications.

superb. See POSITIVE WORDS for a caution on contexts to which the word is unsuitable.
supererogation. For *a work of s.,* see HACKNEYED PHRASES.
superficies. Five syllables (-ff'-shĭēz) ; pl. the same.

SUPERFLUOUS WORDS. That there are such things in the language is likely to be admitted, & perhaps it might be safe even to hazard the generality that they ought to be put

in a black list & cast out ; but woe to the miscreant who dares post up the first list of proscriptions ! Brevity & timidity will therefore be the marks of our specification ; the victims will be mainly such as have no friends, with just one or two of other kinds slipped in to redeem the experiment from utterly negligible insignificance. Indeed, it is more necessary to account for the tameness of the list than to defend its boldness ; & for this purpose it must be borne in mind that most of the words naturally thought of as conspicuously suitable for expulsion (say *meticulous, asset, protagonist, individual,* & the like), abominable as they are in their prevalent modern senses, are not superfluous, because each of them has somewhere in the background a sense or senses at least worth preserving, & often of importance ; the use of them needs to be mended, but not ended, & they are dealt with elsewhere. The list follows ; reasons for the condemnation should be looked for under the word concerned, unless a special article is indicated :—*dampen* (-EN VERBS) ; *elevator ; emotive ; epopee ; faience ; femineity & femininity* (FEMININENESS) ; *filtrate ; flamboyant ; gentlemanlike ; habitude ; legitimatize & legitimize ; lithesome ; mentality ; minify ; olden,* vb (-EN VERBS) ; *quieten ; righten* (-EN VERBS) ; *rotatory ; smoothen* (-EN VERBS) ; *succedaneum ; un-come-at-able ; viceregent ; viceroyal.*

superior. 1. For *has few equals & no s.,* see HACKNEYED PHRASES. 2. The patronizing use (*a most s. woman*), in which one expects it to be understood always that the person one calls s. is nevertheless one's inferior, resembles the corresponding uses of *honest, worthy,* & *good,* in producing on the hearer an unfavourable impression of the speaker. 3. *S. to,* not *s. than,* is required by idiom ; but such is the power of ANALOGY that even people who obviously cannot be described as uneducated are sometimes capable of treating *s.* as we all treat *better* or *greater* (cf. PREFER, with which the same mistake is much more frequent); the quotations are purposely given at sufficient length to show that the writers are not mere blunderers :—*Mr Ernle, on the other hand, as we gather from his preface, desired first to translate Homer, & in looking about for a metre decided on the hexameter as the most appropriate & superior for this style of the heroic* than *the blank or rhymed verse of the great English masters* (read *better . . . than,* or *s. . . . to*)./*Whatever the conditions in the provinces—the present inquiry has dealt only with the Metropolis—able & public-spirited men have refused to accept the dictation of the B.M.A., & are giving far* superior *attention to the insured persons* than *was possible under the cheap conditions of the old club practice* (read *greater . . . than,* or *s. . . . to what*).

SUPERIORITY. Surprise a person of the class that is supposed to keep servants cleaning his own boots, & either he will go on with the job while he talks to you, as if it were the most natural thing in the world, or else he will explain that the bootboy or scullery-maid is ill & give you to understand that he is, despite appearances, superior to boot-cleaning. If he takes the second course, you conclude that he is not superior to it; if the first, that perhaps he is. So it is with the various apologies (*to use an expressive colloquialism—if we may adopt the current slang—as the streetboys have it—in the vernacular phrase— the " push-bike ", if the word may be permitted—so to speak—in homely phrase—not to put too fine a point upon it—if the word be not too vulgar —saving the reader's reverence*) to which recourse is had by writers who wish to safeguard their dignity & yet be vivacious, to combine comfort with elegance, to touch pitch & not be defiled. They should make up their minds whether their

reputation or their style is such as to allow of their dismounting from the high horse now & again without compromising themselves ; if they can do that at all, they can dispense with apologies ; if the apology is needed, the thing apologized for would be better away. *A grievance once redressed ceases to be an electoral asset* (*if we may use a piece of terminology which we confess we dislike*)./*Turgenev had so quick an eye ; he is the master of the vignette—a tiresome word, but it still has to serve.*/*About one thing there is complete unanimity;* " *Coalition* " *must go ;* " *it is not a Party name, & in any case it will not do at the next election* "*; to put it vulgarly, that cock won't fight.*/*M.* Baron *the younger is amusing as the* " *bounder* " *Olivier.*/*When the madness motif was being treated on the stage, Shakespeare* (*as was the custom of his theatre*) *treated it* " *for all it was worth* "*./ With its primary postulate,* " *steep* " *as it is, we will not quarrel.*/*It is a play that hits you, as the children say,* " *bang in the eye* "*./The annual conflict between the income-tax demand note & the January sales has ended, it seems, in the more or less complete triumph of what the Upper Fifth would call the former.*/*These otherwise admirable paintings are not carried far enough in the* " *finish* " *which, to use an Irishism, should be done before the painting is begun.*/ *To make use of an overworked phrase, the wall painting requires a more severe application of* " *fundamental brainwork* "*./England had been compelled, in homely phrase, to ' knuckle down ' to America.*/*Its work was, if we may use a somewhat homely expression, ' done to time '.*/*Palmerston is to all appearance what would be vulgarly called ' out of the swim '.*

For another form of superiority, that of the famous ' of course ', as often exposed & as irrepressible as the three-card trick, see COURSE.

I add a note that I find scribbled by my brother in his copy of *The King's English* :—Some writers use a slang phrase because it suits them, & box the ears of people in general because it is slang ; a refinement on the institution of whipping-boys, by which they not only have the boy, but do the whipping.

SUPERLATIVES : the naked kind, stripped of its *the* or *a*. *The problem is not one of Germany alone ; many of the other States which were in the Central Alliance are* in worst plight *for food, so far as can be gathered./ . . . addressed the Senate, declaring that* widest diversity *of opinion exists regarding the formation of a League of Nations./An extraordinary announcement is made tonight, which is bound* to stir profoundest *interest among all civilized peoples, & to mark a really new epoch in the story of democracy./But Stoddard did not strike the local note, whereas Stedman could tell of Stuyvesant & the " Dutch Patrol "* in pleasantest fashion *& in accordance with the very tone of the Irving tradition./The League of Nations is furnished with a task that will call* for utmost watchfulness *& probably for the exercise of the full power it can wield./Mr Vanderlip is, therefore,* in closest touch *with the affairs of international finance.* If the reader will be good enough to examine these one by one, he will certainly admit this much—that such superlatives are, for better or worse, departures from custom, & that in each sentence a change from ' most ——— ' or ' ———est ' to ' (a) very ——— ' or ' the most ——— ' or ' the ———est ' would be a return to normal English. If he will next try to judge, from the whole of the specimens taken together, what effect is produced by this artifice, it may be hoped, though less confidently, that he will agree with the following view. The writers have no sense of congruity (see INCONGRUOUS VOCABULARY), & are barbarically adorning contexts of straightforward businesslike matter with detached scraps of poetry or exalted feeling ; the impression on sensitive readers

is merely that of a queer simulated emotionalism.

SUPERSTITIONS. ' It is wrong to start a sentence with " But ". I know Macaulay does it, but it is bad English. The word should either be dropped entirely or the sentence altered to contain the word " however ".'. That ungrammatical piece of nonsense was written by the editor of a scientific periodical to a contributor who had found his English polished up for him in proof, & protested ; both parties being men of determination, the article got no further than proof. It is wrong to start a sentence with ' but ' ! It is wrong to end a sentence with a preposition ! It is wrong to split an infinitive ! See the article FETISHES for these & other such rules of thumb & for references to articles in which it is shown how misleading their sweet simplicity is ; see also the article SUBSTITUTE for an illustration of the havoc that is wrought by unintelligent applications of an unintelligent dogma. The best known of such prohibitions is that of the SPLIT INFINITIVE, & the hold of that upon the journalistic mind is well shown in the following, which may be matched almost daily. The writer is reporting a theatre decree for hat-removal : ' . . . the Management relies on the cooperation of the public to strictly enforce this rule '. *Even a split infinitive* (he comments) *may be forgiven in so well-intentioned a notice.* Theatre-managers are not stylists ; the split this manager has perpetrated, is it not a little one ? & to put him, irrelevantly, in the pillory for it betrays the journalist's obsession.

Well, beginners may sometimes find that it is as much as their jobs are worth to resist, like the champion of ' But ', their editors' edicts. On the other hand, to let oneself be so far possessed by conventions whose grounds one has not examined as to take a hand in enforcing them on other people is to lose the independence of judgement that, if not so smothered, would enable one to solve the numerous problems for which there are no rules of thumb.

supervacaneous. A SUPERFLUOUS WORD.

supervise, not *-vize* ; see -ISE.

supine. The grammatical noun (see TECHNICAL TERMS) is pronounced sū'pĭn. For the literary adjective the orthodox pronunciation is sūpī'n, & of six verse quotations in the OED five require that accent ; Shelley provides one of the five, & also the sixth, in which sū'pĭn is natural, though not quite necessary. But RECESSIVE ACCENT is likely to prevail sooner or later, as in CANINE &c.

supple. *The fine mass of the head, solidly yet* supplely *modelled, is set in a particularly beautiful convention of the hair.* The adverb is *supply,* not *supplely* ; cf. SUBTLE. It is true that the OED has found more instances in print of *-plely* than of *-ply,* & therefore on its historical principles makes *supplely* the standard form. But the pronunciation is undoubtedly sŭ'plĭ, not sŭ'pul-lĭ, & the long spelling has been due to the wish to distinguish to the eye from *supply* (suplī') n. & vb ; such devices are not legitimate except in the last necessity, as with *singeing* & *singing* ; & it is to be observed that, whereas the -e- in *singeing* selects the right of two possible pronunciations, the -le- in *supplely* suggests a wrong one. It is unfortunate that adjectives in -bble, -ckle, -ddle, -ffle, -ggle, -pple, -ttle, are few & not provided with adverbs common enough to settle the question ; *subtly* is in fact the best analogue, & its spelling, though *subtlely* has been occasionally used, is now established.

supplement. Noun sŭ'plĭment ; verb sŭplĭmě'nt or sŭ'plĭměnt ; see NOUN & VERB ACCENT C.

supply, vb. For inflexions see VERBS IN -IE &c., 6.

supposal. See -AL NOUNS.

supposedly. Four syllables if used ; see -EDLY.

suppositious, supposititious. *The* supposititious *elector who imagined that the Parliament Bill was a weapon for show & not for use is, we venture to say, a mythical being.* It is often assumed that the first form is no more than an ignorant & wrong variant of the other, like *pacifist* by the side of *pacificist* (see -IST A). Ignorant it often is, no doubt, the user not knowing how to spell or pronounce *supposititious* ; but there is no reason to call it wrong ; *suppositious* & *supposititious* may as well coexist, if there is work for two words, as *factious* & *factitious* ; &, if the support of analogy for the shorter form is demanded, there are *ambitious, expeditious, seditious, nutritious, cautious, & oblivious,* to supply it. There are moreover two fairly distinct senses to be shared, viz spurious, & hypothetical. *Supposititious* is directly from the Latin p.p. *suppositus*=substituted or put in another's place, & therefore has properly the meanings foisted, counterfeit, spurious, pretended, ostensible. *Suppositious* is from the English *supposition*=hypothesis (cf. *suspicious* similarly formed at an earlier stage, in Latin), & therefore may properly mean supposed, hypothetical, assumed, postulated, imaginary. It does not follow that *suppositious* is wanted ; probably the work it might do is better done by the more familiar synonyms above given ; it does follow that *supposititious* should not be given, as in the quotation at the head, senses proper to the synonyms of *suppositious,* but should be confined to those implying intent to deceive.

suppress makes *suppressible,* see -ABLE 2 ; & *suppressor,* see -OR.

suppressedly. A bad form ; -EDLY.

suppressio veri. See TECHNICAL TERMS. Pronounce -ēr'-ī.

supreme. See POSITIVE WORDS, &, for *the s. sacrifice,* STOCK PATHOS.

surcease, n. & vb, is a good example of the archaic words that dull writers at uneasily conscious moments will revive in totally unsuitable contexts ; see INCONGRUOUS VOCABULARY. The fact is that in ordinary English the word is dead, though the pun in *Macbeth* (*& catch, with his surcease, success*) is a tombstone that keeps its memory alive ; there are contexts & styles in which the ghosts of dead words may be effectively evoked ; but in newspaper articles & pedestrian writing ghosts are as little in their element as in Fleet Street at midday. The following quotations are borrowed from the OED :—*It was carried on in all weathers . . . with no surcease of keenness./Private schools for boys give four days' surcease from lessons./There is no surcease in the torrent of Princes . . . who continue to pour into the capital./I . . . thereupon surceased from my labors./They could never surcease to feel the liveliest interest in those wonderful meteoric changes./Intrigues & practices . . . would of necessity surcease.* These are all from 19th or 20th c. writers ; but it should be added that at least two of the verb examples are American ; & if the verb is, as seems likely, still alive in the U.S., American writers are naturally exempt from criticism on the point.

surd For the phonetic sense see TECHNICAL TERMS.

surety. Pronounce shoor'tĭ ; many verse examples show that the disyllabic sound is no innovation.

surgeon. See PHYSICIAN.

surloin. See SIRLOIN.

surly. Adv. *surlily* ; see -LILY s.f. ; the change of spelling from *sirly* disguises the fact that *-ly* in *surly* is the ordinary suffix, & perhaps accounts for *surlily* on the analogy of *jollily, sillily, holily*.

surmise, not *-ize* ; see -ISE.

surmisedly. Four syllables if used ; see -EDLY, & use *conjecturally* &c.

surprisal. See -AL NOUNS.

surprise. 1. Not *-ize* ; see -ISE.

2. The verb makes *-sable* ; see MUTE E. 3. ' *I should not be surprised if the Chancellor of the Exchequer* does not agree *with me.*' *Mr Asquith added that . . .* If Mr Asquith really said what the reporter attributes to him, which may be doubted, he meant ' agreed ' or ' agrees ', not ' does not agree '. The mistake, for other examples of which see NEGATIVES, & NOT, is particularly common after *should not be surprised*.

surprisedly. Four syllables, if used ; see -EDLY.

surtout. OED pronounces sertōo't or sertōo' ; it may be thought that ser'tōo represents a later development ; but the word is now so little used that the question is of no importance.

surveillance. Pronounce servā'lans.

survey. Noun ser'vā, verb servā' ; see NOUN & VERB ACCENT. For verb inflexions see VERBS IN -IE &c., 2. Agent noun, *surveyor*, see -OR.

survive makes *-vable*, see MUTE E ; & *survivor*, see -OR.

suspenders, = braces, is ' Chiefly U.S.'—OED ; to use it for *braces* in England is to throw away the advantage of having two names for two things.

suspense, suspension. In the verbal sense, = suspending, the second is the right. *Suspense,* though it still retains that force in *suspense of judgement*, has become so identified with a state of mind that to revive its earlier use puzzles the hearer. In the following quotation it is clear that *suspense* compels one to read the sentence twice, whereas *suspension* or *suspending* would have been understood at first sight :—*The state of war is inevitably the suspense of Liberalism, & in all the nations at war there are some men who greatly hope that it may also be the death of Liberalism.*

suspensible exists, but is perhaps not better than the normal *suspendable* ; see -ABLE 2.

suspicion. For *s.*=soupçon, see GALLICISMS.

sustain. *Mr* ――, *Master of the* ―― *Hounds, has sustained a broken rib & other injuries through his horse falling.* The very common idiom here illustrated is described by the OED as 'in modern journalistic use'; but with such abstract objects as *injury, loss, leak, bruise,* &c., instead of *broken rib* it is as old as the 15th c., & the extension is not a violent one. Nevertheless, *sustain* as a synonym for *suffer* or *receive* or *get* belongs to the class of FORMAL WORDS, & is better avoided both for that reason & for a stronger one: if it is not made to do the work of those more suitable words, it calls up more clearly the other meaning in which it is valuable, viz to bear up against or stand or endure without yielding or perishing, as in 'capable of sustaining a siege'.

sustainedly. Four syllables, if used; see -EDLY.

Susy, -ie. See -EY, -IE, -Y.

suttee, sati. Use the first, & see DIDACTICISM, MAHOMET, PRIDE OF KNOWLEDGE.

svelte. See FRENCH WORDS.

Swabian. See SUABIAN.

Swan of Avon. See SOBRIQUETS.

swap, swop. The OED prefers *-ap*.

SWAPPING HORSES while crossing the stream, a notoriously hazardous operation, is paralleled in speech by changing a word's sense in the middle of a sentence, by vacillating between two constructions either of which might follow a word legitimately enough, by starting off with a subject that fits one verb but must have something tacitly substituted for it to fit another, & by other such performances. These lapses are difficult to formulate & to exemplify, & any exposition of their nature naturally incurs the charge of PEDANTRY; nevertheless, the air of slovenliness given by them is so fatal to effective writing that attention must be called to them when-

ever an opportunity can be made, as by this claptrap heading.

Changing of a word's sense; *interest* is peculiarly liable to maltreatment:—*Viscount Grey's promised speech in the House of Lords on Reparations & inter-Allied debts furnished all the interest naturally aroused. Interest* is here virtually, though not actually, used twice— the speech furnished interest, interest was aroused; but what was furnished was interesting matter, & what was aroused was eager curiosity; *interest* can bear either sense, but not both in one sentence./ *For while the Opposition beat their drums as loudly as ever, it was well known that there was very little behind all this fuss, & that* in the very interests *which they so furiously protected they were anxious to meet the Government half-way. Which* stands for *interests*; they furiously protected certain interests, i.e. certain persons or sets of persons or rights or privileges; they were inclined to compromise *in* some people's interests, i.e. in their behalf or favour or name; but *behalf* is not a person or a privilege or the like. The difficulty of expressing the inconsistency, however, explains why the word *interest* is often thus abused. For similar treatment of other words than *interest*, see LEGERDEMAIN.

Shifting from one to another construction. *But supposing nothing changed & this Pope, who is made incompetent by the weight at once of his virtues & his ignorances, enjoys a long life, we should look for a great decline in ... Supposing* is followed first by an object (*nothing*) & adjectival complement (*changed*), & secondly by a substantival clause (*this Pope enjoys*). Either is right by itself, but to swap one for the other means disaster.

Tacit modification of the subject &c. *This barbarism could be stopped in a very short time, if it were made a punishable offence to throw rubbish into the street, & would have the added value of reducing the army of scaven-*

gers. It is not the barbarism, but the stoppage of it, that would have the added value./*Fifty per cent of the weight could be knocked off practically every new petrol vehicle produced & yet be able to carry exactly the same load.* What would carry the same load is not the 50% knocked off, but either the vehicle without it or the other 50% that remained./*Mr A. C. Benson recalls a pleasant fiction, supposed to have happened to Matthew Arnold.* A fiction neither happens nor is supposed to happen to anyone ; a fiction can be recalled, but before it can be supposed to have happened it must be tacitly developed into a fictitious experience ; for it is itself a statement or narrative & not an event. See HAZINESS for other specimens of similar confusion.

swath(e). The agricultural noun is spelt either way & pronounced swawth or swŏth or swădh ; see -TH & -DH ; the noun & verb meaning wrap is *swathe* (swădh). The possible differentiation is easy to see but very unlikely to be accepted.

sweat, sweater. Victims of GEN-TEELISM.

sweet. *Sweet brier, sweet oil, sweet pea, sweet sultan, sweet william* (or *S.W.*) should have no hyphens ; see HYPHENS 3 B.

sweety. So spelt ; see -EY, -IE, -Y.

swell. *Swollen* is the usual form of the p.p., & that not less, but more, than formerly. The chief use of *swelled* as p.p. is now in *swelled head*, in which its supposed irregularity may have been a recommendation as lending a homely expressiveness.

swim. The past *swam* & p.p. *swum* are now almost invariable, though the OED has a Carlyle quotation for *swam* p.p., & a Tennyson for *swum* past.

swine. Sing. & pl. the same ; *s.* makes *swinish*, see MUTE E.

swing. Past usually *swung*, though OED quotes for *swang* Wordsworth, Tennyson, Gosse, & Belloc.

swing(e)ing. *At the bottom was tripe, in a swinging tureen*—Goldsmith. A capacious one ? or one hung on pivots ? See MUTE E, & use the -e- in the part. of *swinge.*

swivel has -*lled, -lling,* &c.; -LL-, -L-.

swop. See SWAP.

sybarite. So spelt.

sybil. See SIBYL. This wrong spelling (the Greek is *Sibulla*) is especially common in the modern use as a feminine name.

syce, groom. So spelt ; see SICE.

syllabize &c. A verb & a noun are clearly sometimes needed for the notion of dividing words into syllables. The possible pairs seem to be the following (the number after each word means—1, that it is in fairly common use ; 2, that it is on record ; 3, that it is not given in OED) :—

syllabate 3	syllabation 2
syllabicate 2	syllabication 1
syllabify 2	syllabification 1
syllabize 1	syllabization 2

One first-class verb, two first-class nouns, but neither of those nouns belonging to that verb. It is absurd enough, & any of several ways out would do ; that indeed is why none of them is taken. The best thing would be to accept the most recognized verb *syllabize*, give it the now non-existent noun *syllabization*, & relegate all the rest to the SUPER-FLUOUS WORDS ; but there is no authority both willing & able to issue such decrees.

syllabub. See SILLABUB.

syllabus. Pl. -*bī*.

syllepsis. See TECHNICAL TERMS. Pl. -*psēs*.

syllogism. See TECHNICAL TERMS.

sylph. See SALAMANDER.

sylvan. See SILVAN.

symbol. For synonyms see SIGN.

symbology. For the form, see -IST on *pacif(ic)ist*. But *symbolology* is not used.

sympathetic. *The play, in spite of sublime scenes & poetry, is an illustration & a warning to artists who deny, or forget, that no powers of*

*execution & no subordinate achieve-
ment can compensate for a central
figure who is " unsympathetic ", &
that it is better for a " hero " to provoke active fear or hate than indifference or half-contemptuous pity./
Macbeth is not made great by the mere
loan of a poet's imagery, & he is not
made sympathetic, however adequately
his crime may be explained & pal-
liated, by being the victim of a halluci-
nation./Let me first say that Elsie
Lindtner is by no means sympathetic
to the writer of this paper ; if she
were, the tragedy of the book would be
more than one could bear.* It will be
seen that in these passages the word
does not mean what the man in the
street understands by it, i.e. capable
of or prone to sympathy, but has an
esoteric sense peculiar to book-
reviewers & dramatic critics &
familiar only to their readers, i.e.
capable of evoking sympathy. In
the OED there is no vestige of such
a sense ; but in the French dictionaries it is easily found :—Il se dit de
personnes qui éprouvent de la sympathie, ou qui se concilient la sympathie (Littré) ; qui inspire la
sympathie (Larousse). It is a
LITERARY CRITICS' WORD, & a GAL-
LICISM, & the possibility of confusion
between the Gallic & the English
senses is so obvious that the literary
critic should deny himself the pleasure of showing it off.

sympathy. The exception sometimes taken to following *s.* with *for*
instead of *with* is groundless ; the
OED, under the sense compassion,
even puts *for* before *with* as the
normal construction. For the principle at issue, see DIFFERENT.

symposium. Pron.-ŏ′zĭum ; pl.-*ia*.
symptom. For synonyms see SIGN.
synaeresis, synaloepha, synaphea.
See TECHNICAL TERMS.
synchronize is not a word that we
need regret the existence of, since
there is useful work that it can do
better than another ; but it is a
word that we may fairly desire to
see as seldom as we may, one of the
learned terms that make a passage
in which they are not the best
possible words stodgy & repellent ;
it may be compared with the lists in
POPULARIZED TECHNICALITIES. The
extracts below, for instance, would
surely have been better without
it :—*The lock-out mania, therefore,
has synchronized* [coincided ?] *with
an increased willingness for sacrifice
on the part of the men./Founder's
Day, annually observed at the Charter-
house, synchronizes this year with*
[is also, this year,] *the tercentenary of
Sutton's Charity./A movement of
Russian troops to the Caucasus was
ordered . . . This movement synchronized with* [There were at the same
time] *reports of an extensive movement of Turkish troops near the Persian frontier./The winter solstice,
which north of the Equator synchronizes with* [determines] *the first day of
the winter quarter, occurs at six
minutes to eleven tonight.*

syncopation. See TECHNICAL TERMS.
syncope. For the sense in grammar, see TECHNICAL TERMS. Three
syllables (-pĭ).
synecdoche, synesis, synizesis. See
TECHNICAL TERMS.

SYNONYMS, in the narrowest sense,
are separate words whose meaning,
both denotation & connotation, is
so fully identical that one can always
be substituted for the other without
change in the effect of the sentence
in which it is done. Whether any
such perfect synonyms exist is
doubtful ; *gorse* & *furze* may perhaps
be a pair ; but if it is a fact that one
is much more often used than the
other, or prevails in a different
geographical or social region, none
of which distinctions is apparent
from the OED quotations, then
exchange between them does alter
the effect on competent hearers, &
the synonymy is not perfect. At
any rate, perfect synonyms are
extremely rare.
Synonyms in the widest sense are
words either of which in one or
other of its acceptations can some-

times be substituted for the other without affecting the meaning of a sentence ; thus it does not matter (to take the nearest possible example) whether I say a word has ' two senses ' or ' two meanings ', & *sense* & *meaning* are therefore loose synonyms ; but if ' He is a man of sense ' is rewritten as ' He is a man of meaning ', it becomes plain that *sense* & *meaning* are far from perfect synonyms ; see FIELD, & SIGN, for sets of this kind.

Synonyms, or words like in sense but unlike in look or sound, have as their converse homonyms & homophones, or words like in look or sound but unlike in sense. The *pole* of a tent or coach or punt, & the *pole* of the earth or the sky or a magnet, are in spite of their identical spelling separate words & homonyms. *Gauge* & *gage*, not spelt alike, but so sounded, are homophones.

Misapprehension of the degree in which words are synonymous is responsible for much bad writing of the less educated kind. From the notion that CONSERVATIVE is a synonym of *moderate*, as it is when compared with *radical* in politics, come the absurdities, illustrated under the word, of its use with *estimate* &c. ; so with PROTAGONIST (& *champion*), METICULOUS (& *scrupulous*), REGARD (& *consider*), OPTIMISTIC (& *hopeful*), SUBSTITUTION (& *replacement*), DILEMMA (& *difficulty*), ERE (& *before*), SAVE (& *except*), EXTENUATE (& *excuse*), FEASIBLE (& *possible*), ILK (& *name*), PERCENTAGE (& *part*), PROPORTION (& *portion*), RE (& *concerning*), as well as numberless others. To appreciate the differences between partial synonyms is therefore of the utmost importance. There are unluckily two obstacles to setting them out in this book. One is that nearly all words are partial synonyms, & the treatment of them all from this point of view alone would fill not one but many volumes ; the other is that synonym books in which

differences are analysed, engrossing as they may have been to the active party, the analyst, offer to the passive party, the reader, nothing but boredom. Everyone must, for the most part, be his own analyst ; & no-one who does not expend, whether expressly & systematically or as a half-conscious accompaniment of his reading & writing, a good deal of care upon points of synonymy is likely to write well. A writer's concern with synonyms is twofold. He requires first the power of calling up the various names under which the idea he has to express can go ; everyone has this in some degree ; everyone can develop his gift by exercise ; but copiousness in this direction varies, & to those who are deficient in it ready-made lists of synonyms are a blessed refuge, even if the ease they bring has as doubtful an effect on their style as the old *Gradus ad Parnassum* on the schoolboy's elegiacs. Such lists, to be of much use, must be voluminous, & those who need them should try Roget's *Thesaurus* or some other work devoted to that side of synonymy. Secondly, he requires the power of choosing rightly out of the group at his command, which depends on his realizing the differences between its items. As has been implied already, such differences cannot be expounded for a language in anything less than a vast dictionary devoted to them alone ; no attempt at it has been made in this book except in cases where experience shows warnings to be necessary. Still, a book concerned like the present with English idiom in general cannot but come into frequent touch with synonymy ; & those who wish to pursue that particular branch of idiom will find the following list of articles (in addition to those previously referred to) useful as a guide :—act (n.), admission, apt, asset, assure, authentic, behalf, benign, besides, big, bloom, broad, burlesque, category, cease, ceremonial, certitude, cheerful, classic, clime, commonplace, conciseness, connote, continual, continuance, contrary, countenance, credence, decided, defective, definite, deism, delusion, dower, due, duteous, effective, England, enough, enteric, entity, epistle, especially, essence, essential, exceedingly, explicit, exterior, facile, faience, falsehood, fatalism, faun, female (bis), festal, fir, floor, foam, forceful, foreword, Formal words, frantic, friar, furze, Gallic, garret, Genteelism, glossary, gourmand, Grecian, gulf, happening, harmony, Hebrew, horrible, idiosyncrasy, illegible, include, Incongruous vocabulary, innate, intensive, intuition, jargon, jocose, judicial, lampoon, legislation, libel, Literary words, littoral, Long variants, luxuriant, male, malignancy, masterful, maunder, mentality, minify, molecule, monachal, mutual, Needless variants, observance, physician, pigeon, piteous, plenteous, polity, porcelain, practicable, proposition, purport, receipt, requirement, resort, reversion, shall, that (rel. pr.), tint, transparent.

synonymity, synonymy. There is work for both words, the first meaning synonymousness, & the second the subject & supply of synonyms.

synopsis. Pl. *-psēs.*

syntax. See TECHNICAL TERMS.

synthesis. Pl. *-thesēs.* The scientific sound of the word often tempts the pretentious to use it instead of more appropriate words such as *combination, alliance,* or *union* : *A flickering gleam on the subject may be found in a pamphlet called ' The Case against Home Rule ', by Mr Amery, which also propounds the new idea of a synthesis between the tariff & the opposition to Home Rule.*

synthetize, not *synthesize,* is the right formation.

syphon, syren. See SIPHON, SIREN.

Syriac, Syrian. There is the same difference in application as between *Arabic* & ARAB(IAN).

syringe. Pron. sĭ'rĭnj, not sĭrĭ'nj.

syringitis. See GREEK G.

syrup, syrupy. So spelt, the first by usage in England ; for the second, see -P-, -PP-. *Golden syrup* is, outside the grocer's, a GENTEELISM for *treacle.*

systemic, as compared with the regular *systematic,* is excused by its usefulness in distinguishing a sense required in physiology &c. ' of the system or body as a whole ' ; other wrong formations, *systemist, systemize,* &c., have no such excuse, & *systematist* &c. should be invariable.

systole. Pronounce sĭ'stolĭ.

syzygy. Pronounce sĭ'zĭgĭ (see GREEK G) or sĭ'zĭjĭ.

T

tabes. Pronounce tā'bēz.

tableau (vivant), table-d'hôte, tablier. See FRENCH WORDS.

taboo. Accent on last syllable ; though this accent is English only, it is established English, & to correct it is pedantry ; to spell *tabu* (except in ethnological dissertations) is no better ; see PRONUNCIATION, & PRIDE OF KNOWLEDGE. Past & p.p. usu. *tabooed,* sometimes (see -ED & 'D) *taboo'd.*

tabula (rasa). Pl. *-lae (-sae).*

tabulate makes *-lable* ; see -ABLE 1.

tache. See FRENCH WORDS.

tack. Confusion between the nautical word used figuratively & *tact* (*I think we have been on the wrong tact*) is not unknown in speech, though it seldom gets into print.

tactics. See STRATEGY for the distinction.

tactile)(tactual. Why two words ? And, there being two, is any useful differentiation either established or possible ? The existence of *tactile* is sufficiently explained by the desire for a form corresponding to a large class of adjectives that mean having the power or quality of doing or suffering some action—contractile, ductile, erectile, fictile, fissile, flexile, pensile, prehensile, protrusile, retractile, sessile, tensile, & textile, to omit more familiar words such as agile, docile, fragile, & volatile. And the existence of *tactual* is sufficiently explained by a natural preference for *tactually* over *tactilely*. But, in contrast with the differentiation between *agile* & *actual*, *textile* & *textual*, our pair are used almost indiscriminately. Careful writers should confine *tactile* to the meaning capable of feeling or being felt by touch, & apply it to organs & qualities, while *tactual* should mean of or by touch & be more generally applied—*tactual tests, sensation, anaesthesia, union, values.* The point is that the *-ual* words belong to Latin abstract nouns in *-us, -ūs,* & the *-ile* words to Latin verbs, & that on the whole their meanings are true to that difference, however little we may know or remember it.

taenia. Pl. *-niae.*

Taffy. See SOBRIQUETS.

talloress. FEMININE DESIGNATIONS.

take makes *takable*; see MUTE E.

talc makes *talcky.*

talent)(genius. Dr Henry Bradley, in the OED, sums up the familiar contrast thus :—' It was by the German writers of the 18th c. that the distinction between " genius " & " talent ", which had some foundation in Fr. usage, was sharpened into the strong antithesis which is now universally current, so that the one term is hardly ever defined without reference to the other. The difference between *genius* & *talent* has been formulated very variously by different writers, but there is general agreement in regarding the former as the higher of the two, as " creative " & " original ", & as achieving its results by instinctive perception & spontaneous activity, rather than by processes which admit of being distinctly analysed '.

talkative. Though a HYBRID DERIVATIVE, the word is much too firmly established to be attacked ; but it is worth while, with a view to discouraging imitation, to point out

that among 150 known words in -ative (see Walker's *Rhyming Dictionary*) *t.* is the only one in which -ative has been appended to a non-Latin verb.

tally, vb. For inflexions see VERBS IN -IE &c., 6.

talus. Pl. of the word meaning ankle &c., *talī* ; pl. of the word meaning slope &c., *taluses*. The first comes to us from Latin, the second from French.

tame makes *-mable* ; see MUTE E.

tan,=tangent. CURTAILED WORDS.

-T & -ED. Typical words are bereaved & bereft, burned & burnt, dreamed & dreamt, kneeled & knelt, leaned & leant, leaped & leapt, learned & learnt, smelled & smelt, spelled & spelt, spilled & spilt, spoiled & spoilt, tossed & tost.
In the last of these the point is purely one of spelling, & the sound is the same either way ; there are many other verbs of which that is true (husht, kist, whipt, curst, cookt, &c.), & individual writers make a practice of using the short form as a piece of spelling reform, a timesaver, or an eccentricity ; whichever the motive, the effect is with most words eccentric ; but *tost*, esp. in p.p. compounds such as *storm-tost*, is current, by the side of *tossed*.
Of the rest the spelling may affect the sound in some, & does affect it in others. Thus, *burned* may be sounded with d, but perhaps most even of those who spell it so sound it as with t, whereas *leaped & leapt* are pronounced by everyone with different vowels—lēpt, & lĕpt. The advice here offered is to use the -t spelling in both classes, & that in the face of the surely surprising figures to be given below ; it will hardly be denied that most people say bernt & lĕpt, not bernd & lēpt, & conformity between the written & the spoken word is worth securing where, since both spellings are already in use, it costs nothing. At present, however, the -ed forms still prevail in print over those in -t in

most of our list ; & it should be added that, if the past tense were distinguished from the p.p., the preponderance of -ed for it would be slightly greater. The figures are arrived at by counting the occurrences in all OED quotations of the 19th & 20th cc. ; the first figure for each word is the number for -ed, the second for -t.

1. toss—23, 3
2. burn—7, 16 (see also BURN)
   learn—5, 0
   smell—2, 8
   spell—4, 4
   spill—8, 17
   spoil—9, 5 (see below)
3. bereave—3, 3 (see also BEREAVE)
   dream—5, 3 (see also DREAM)
   kneel—3, 2
   lean—12, 2
   leap—7, 5

The figures for *spoil* are exclusive of examples in which -ed alone is possible ; that is to say, in the older sense strip (as opp. damage). On class 3 it is worth while to remark that there are so many similar verbs in which the -t form is now the only one (*creep, deal, feel, keep, leave, mean, sleep, sweep, weep, &c.*) that the adoption of *dreamt &c.* in print need expose no-one to the charge of eccentricity.

tantalize. *To the British motor industry Free Trade has become as tantalizing as a red rag to a bull.* See SLIPSHOD EXTENSION. He who is tantalized is usually irritated, but he who is irritated is comparatively seldom tantalized ; & to apply *t.* to a wrong kind of irritation is to betray ignorance.

tant soit peu. See FRENCH WORDS.
Taoism. Pronounce tow'izm.
tapis. See FRENCH WORDS.
tar,=sailor. See SOBRIQUETS.
targeted. So spelt ; see -T-, -TT-.
targum. Pl. *-ms* ; see -UM.
tarry, vb. For inflexions see VERBS IN -IE &c., 6.
tarsus. Pl. *-sī.*
tart)(pie. The current distinction is that a tart contains fruit or sweet stuff, & a pie meat or savoury stuff ; but the earlier distinction was that a tart was not, & a pie was, closed in with pastry above ; & as relics of the old use we retain *mince pie* as the only possible form, & *apple pie* & *cherry pie* as names of a trap bed & a flower, though more or less superseded by —— *tart* in their primary senses.

Tartar, Tatar. The second spelling may well be left to the ethnologists ; see PRIDE OF KNOWLEDGE.
tassel makes *-lled* ; see -LL-, -L-.
taste, vb, makes *tastable* ; MUTE E.
tasty (so spelt, see MUTE E) has been displaced, except in uneducated or facetious use, in its primary sense by *savoury* & in its secondary by *tasteful.*

Tatar. See TARTAR.
tattler. Now so spelt ; formerly, & esp. in the name of the 18th-c. periodical, *tatler.*
tattoo makes *tattooed* or *tattoo'd* ; see -ED & 'D.

TAUTOLOGY (lit. ' saying the same thing ', i. e. as one has already said) is a term used in various senses. To repeat the words or the substance of a preceding sentence or passage may be impressive & a stroke of rhetoric, or wearisome & a sign of incompetence, mainly according as it is done deliberately or unconsciously ; in either case it may be called tautology (though the word is in fact seldom used except in reproach), but it is with neither of these kinds that we are here concerned. Another sense is the allowing of a word or phrase to recur without point while its previous occurrence is still unforgotten ; this kind of t. will be found fully discussed in the articles REPETITION & ELEGANT VARIATION ; it is of great importance as an element in style, but need not here be treated again. Yet another form of t. is that dealt with in PLEONASM 2, in which synonyms, either capable of serving the purpose by itself, are

conjoined, as in *save & except.*
Again, the word is sometimes applied to identical propositions such
as ' I don't like my tea too hot ' ;
for such statements see the *truism*
section of COMMONPLACE.

What remains to be illustrated here
is the way in which writers who are
careless of form & desirous of
emphasis often fail to notice that
they are wasting words by expressing twice over in a sentence some
part of it that is indeed essential but
needs only one expression. It is
true that words are cheap, &, if the
cost of them as such to the writer
were the end of the matter, it would
not be worth considering ; the
intelligent reader, however, is wont
to reason, perhaps unjustly, that if
his author writes loosely he probably
thinks loosely also, & is therefore
not worth attention. A few examples follow, & under BOTH 2 &
EQUALLY AS 2 will be found collections of the same kind of t. :—*The
motion on constitutional reforms aims
at placing women on the same
equality with men in the exercise of
the franchise* (As no other equality
has been in question, *same* &
equality are tautological ; *in the
same position as,* or *on an equality
with*)./*The wool profits were* again
made the subject of another *attack by
Mr Mackinder last night* (Omit
either *again* or *another*)./*May I be
permitted to state that the activities of
the Club are not* limited only *to
aeronautics ?* (*Limited & only* are
tautological ; *limited to,* or *directed
only to*)./*It is sheer pretence to suppose that speed* & speed alone *is the*
only *thing which counts* (Omit either
& speed alone, or *only*).

tax & some synonyms—*cess, customs, due, duty, excise, fee, gabelle,
heriot, impost, levy, octroi, rate, scot
& lot, toll, tribute.* With such sets of
words it is often convenient to have
a conspectus of the distinctions &
be saved the labour of turning them
up for comparison in separate dictionary articles. Such convenience

is all that is here aimed at, a rough
definition of each word being given
after the OED's definition of *tax*
itself & its note thereon.

OED on *tax* :—(Definition) A compulsory contribution to the support of
government, levied on persons, property, income, commodities, transactions, etc., now at fixed rates,
mostly proportional to the amount
on which the contribution is levied.
(Note) ' Tax ' is the most inclusive
term for these contributions, esp.
when spoken of as the matter of
taxation, & in such phrases as *direct
& indirect tax,* including also similar
levies for the support of the work of
such local or specific bodies as county
or municipal councils, poor law or
school boards, etc. But in British
practice few of the individual imposts
are called by the name, the most
notable being the *Income tax, Land
tax,* & *Property tax* (also *dog-tax,
match-tax, window-tax*), the rest being
mostly styled ' duties ', as *excise, import, export, estate, house, stamp, death
duties,* etc. The ' taxes ' levied by
local bodies are usually called ' rates ',
e. g. *borough, county, poor, school,
water rate,* etc.

cess, = rate or tax, but chiefly in
local use, esp. in Ireland, Scotland,
& India.

customs, payment levied upon imports from foreign countries ; cf.
excise.

due, any obligatory payment, the
nature being usually specified by an
attributive noun, as *harbour, market,
dues.*

duty, tax levied on specific articles
or transactions, not on persons ; see
also the note on *tax* above.

excise, duty charged on home goods
before they can be sold ; cf. *customs.*

fee, regulation sum payable to
public official or to professional man
for a particular service performed.

gabelle, a tax, but esp. the French
pre-Revolution salt-tax.

heriot, payment in money or kind
due to lord of manor on tenant's
decease.

impost, a tax in the more indefinite sense, i.e. when *tax* is not to be taken as contrasted with *rate*.

levy, exaction from every person concerned of an equal amount or an amount proportional to his property.

octroi, duty charged on articles before they are admitted into a town.

rate, amount of assessment on property for local purposes ; see also the note on *tax* above.

scot & lot, a tax levied by a municipal corporation in proportionate shares upon its members for the defraying of municipal expenses.

toll, fixed charge for access or passage or permission.

tribute, periodical payment made in token of submission or as price of protection by a State or person to another.

taxi. Pl. *taxis* better than *-ies* ; cf. -O(E)S 5 & 6.

teacheress. See FEMININE DESIGNATIONS.

teasel, teazle. The OED treats the first as the standard form.

tec. See CURTAILED WORDS.

TECHNICAL TERMS of rhetoric, grammar, logic, prosody, diplomacy, literature, &c., that a reader may be confronted with or a writer have need of. The list is very far from exhaustive ; & the principle of selection has been to omit at one extreme the words of which most people who are given to reading at all may be assumed to know the meaning, & at the other those so unfamiliar that no sensible writer would use them unless he were addressing experts or students. The design is to give the briefest serviceable definition, & an illustration, of each term ; & they are roughly classified as Rhet.(orical), Gram. (matical), Log.(ical), Pros.(odical), Dipl.(omatic), Lit.(erary), &c. Some terms are included of which no account is needed beyond what is given in their alphabetical place in the Dictionary ; these are printed in small capitals. Cross references in italics with *above* or *below* are to items in this article.

absolute (Gram.) ; ' freed '. An adj. or a trans. vb is a. when the adj. has no noun, or the vb no object. Fortune favours the *brave* ; If looks could *kill*. See also ABSOLUTE CONSTRUCTION.

acatalectic (Pros.) ; ' not stopping short '. A verse or metre is a. when its last foot is complete ; cf. *catalectic* below. ' Ma'ny/me'n &/ma'ny /wo'men is a trochaic dimeter a.

accidence (Gram.) ; ' the things that befall (words) '. The part of grammar concerned with inflexions, or the forms that words can take ; a book of paradigms. Cf. *syntax* below.

ad captandum (Rhet.) ; ' for catching (the common herd ', *vulgus*). Applied to unsound specious arguments. *An a. c. presentation of the facts.*

affix (Gram.) ; ' thing fastened on '. A term including both prefixes & suffixes. *What is the stem when all affixes are removed ?*

a fortiori (Log.) ; ' from yet firmer ground '. Introducing a fact that, if one already accepted is true, must also & still more obviously be true. *It could not have been finished in a week ; a. f. not in a day.*

alcaics (Pros.) ; ' verses of Alcaeus '. A four-line Greek & Latin stanza :

‒‒∪‒‒/‒∪∪‒∪⏑ bis

‒‒∪‒‒‒∪‒‒

‒∪∪‒∪∪‒∪‒⏑

Imitated by Tennyson in :

O mighty-mouthed inventor of harmonies,

O skilled to sing of time or eternity.
God-gifted organ-voice of England,
Milton, a name to resound for ages !

alexandrine (Pros.) ; origin doubtful. A six-foot iambic line, i.e. one foot longer than that of blank verse ; the normal line in French verse (but see also *senarius* below), & ending each stanza in Spenserians. (A needless Alexandrine ends the song)

That like/a wound/ed snake/drags its/slow length/along.

allegory (Rhet.) ; ' other wording '. A narrative of which the true meaning is to be got by translating its persons & events into others that they are understood to symbolize. *The Faerie Queen & The Pilgrim's Progress* are aa. For synonymy see SIMILE.

alliteration (Rhet.) ; ' letter-tagging '. The noticeable or effective use in a phrase or sentence of words beginning with or containing the same letter or sound. *After life's fitful fever* ; In a *summer season* when *soft* was the *sun*.

amphibol(og)y (Log.) ; ' aiming both ways '. A statement so expressed as to admit of two grammatical constructions each yielding a different sense. *Stuff a cold & starve a fever* appears to be two sentences containing separate directions for two maladies, but may also be a conditional sentence meaning If you are fool enough to stuff a cold you will produce & have to starve a fever.

anacoluthon (Gram.) ; ' inconsequent matter '. A sentence in which there is wrongly substituted for the completion of a construction something that presupposes a different beginning. *Can I not make you understand that if you don't get reconciled to your father what is to happen to you ?* (the *that* construction requires a statement, not a question, to complete it). Pliny speaks of divers engaged in the strategy of ancient warfare, carrying tubes in their mouths & so *drew* the necessary air down to their lungs.

anacrusis (Pros.) ; ' a recoil '. A syllable (or more), in some metres invariable & in some optional, before the point at which the reckoning of the normal feet begins. In the couplet following, each line is a trochaic dimeter catalectic, but the first has not & the second has a. :

Clearer/loves sound/other/ways ;
I/miss my/little/human/praise

anagram (Lit.) ; ' rewriting '. A shuffling of the letters of a word or phrase resulting in a significant combination. Bunyan tells his readers that *John Bunyan* anagram'd makes *nu hony in a B* (new honey in a bee).

analogy (Log., Gram.) ; ' accordance with proportion '. Inference or procedure based on the presumption that things whose likeness in certain respects is known will be found or should be treated as alike also in respects about which knowledge is limited to one of them. The conclusion that a State, because its development in some respects resembles that of a person, must by lapse of time grow feeble & die is analogical. Since *opera* resembles *drama* both in being the name of a play & in ending in *-a*, analogy provides *opera* with the (incorrect) adj. *operatic* to match the rightly formed *dramatic*. For other examples, see ANALOGY.

anapaest (Pros.) ; ' struck back '. A metrical foot, ∪∪–. *And his co/horts were gleam/ing with pur/ple & gold* is an anapaestic dimeter or four aa.

anaphora (Rhet.) ; ' bringing back '. Marked repetition of a word or phrase in successive clauses or sentences. *At her feet he bowed, he fell, he lay down : at her feet he bowed, he fell : where he bowed, there he fell down dead.*

anastrophe (Rhet.) ; ' reversal '. Upsetting, for effect, of such normal order as preposition before noun or object after verb. *No war or battle's sound Was heard the world around. Me he restored, & him he hanged.*

antepenult (Gram.) ; ' before the nearly last '. Last syllable but two of a word. In *laboratory* the a. is *-ra-*, penult *-to-*, & ultima *-ry*.

anticlimax (Rhet.) ; ' climax-spoiling '. Annulment of the impressive effect of a climax by a final item of inferior importance. *The rest of all the acts of Asa, & all his might, & the cities which he built, are they not written in the book of the chronicles of the kings of Judah ? Nevertheless in the time of his old age he was diseased in his feet.*

antistrophe (Pros.) ; ' counter-turn '. The part of a Greek chorus chanted in reply to the strophe & exactly reproducing its metre. A short specimen (Aesch. P. V. 414 foll., transl. Whitelaw) of strophe & a. is :

And dwellers by the Colchian shore,	And Aria's warlike flower of men,
Maidens, of battle unafraid,	All they, whose fortress-city frowns
And Scythian hordes that range	Near Caucasus, high-perched ;
At earth's remotest verge	Wild host, whose battle-cry
Round the Maeotic pool :	Shrills mid the charging spears.

antithesis (Rhct.) ; ' placing opposite '. Such choice or arrangement of words as emphasizes a contrast. *Crafty men contemn studies ; simple men admire them ; & wise men use them.*

aorist (Gram.) ; ' undefined '. The Greek past tense corresponding to English *chose* &c. ; so named as not being definitely perfect or imperfect (like *had chosen*, a perfect tense, or *was choosing*, an imperfect tense) ; applied also to any such undefined tense, e. g. to *I choose* in opposition to *I am choosing* & *I have chosen*.

aphaeresis (Gram.) ; ' taking away '. The loss of an initial letter, syllable, &c. *Special* was formerly *especial*, *adder naddre*, & *cute acute*. Cf. *syncope*, *apocope*, below.

aphetic (Gram.) ; ' letting go '. An adj. now often used instead of the rare *aphaeretic* & meaning ' resulting from aphaeresis or aphesis ' —the latter a lately coined word to express gradual & unintentional aphaeresis as in *squire* (esquire), '*shun* (attention).

apocope (Gram.) ; ' cutting off '. The loss of a final letter or syllable or more. *My, curio, cinema*, were formerly *mine, curiosity, cinematograph*. Cf. *syncope* below, & *aphaeresis* above.

apodosis (Gram.) ; ' paying back '.

The main clause in a conditional sentence, so called as satisfying the expectation raised by the preceding protasis, but retaining the name even when the protasis follows. *If he would he could ; He could if he would* ; in each form the a. is *he could*, & the rest the protasis.

aposiopesis (Rhet.) ; ' falling silent '. Significant breaking off so that the hearer must supply the unsaid words. *If we should fail—. Oh, go to —— !*

a posteriori (Log.) ; ' from the hinder end '. Working back from effects to causes, i. e. inductively. *God's in his heaven—all's right with the world* is an a posteriori inference if it means The world is so clearly good that there must be a god in heaven ; but an a priori inference if it means that since we know there is a god, the state of the world must be right.

apostrophe (Rhet.) ; ' a turning away '. Words addressed to a present or absent person or thing & breaking the thread of discourse.

There is not wind enough to twirl
The one red leaf, the last of its clan,
That dances as often as dance it can,
Hanging so light, & hanging so high,
On the topmost twig that looks up
    at the sky.
Hush, beating heart of Christabel !
Jesu, Maria, shield her well !
She folded her arms beneath her
    cloak,
And stole to the other side of the
    oak.

apposition (Gram.) ; ' putting to '. The placing of a second description side by side with that by which something has first been denoted, the second being treated as grammatically parallel with the first. Simon, *son of Jonas*, lovest thou me ?

a priori (Log.) ; ' from the earlier part '. Working forward from known or assumed causes to effects, i. e. deductively. For an example, see *a posteriori* above.

arguing in a circle (Log.). The basing of two conclusions each upon the other. That the world is good follows from the known goodness of God ; that God is good is known from the excellence of the world he has made.

argumentum ad —— (Log.) ; ' argument directed to —— '. *a. a. hominem,* one calculated to appeal to the individual addressed more than to impartial reason ; *a. a. crumenam* (purse), one touching the hearer's pocket ; *a. a. baculum* (stick) or *argumentum baculinum,* threat of force instead of argument ; *a. a. ignorantiam,* one depending for its effect on the hearer's not knowing something essential ; *a. a. populum,* one pandering to popular passion ; *a. a. verecundiam* (modesty), one to meet which requires the opponent to offend against decorum.

arsis (Pros.) ; ' raising '. The more emphatic part of a foot, e. g. the first syllable of a dactyl or trochee, & the last of an anapaest or iambus ; opp. *thesis.* This is the Latin & the prevailing modern use, reversed from the original Greek ; since the Greek meanings are still sometimes preferred, confusion is not unknown. The accented syllables are in arsis in *Fro'ggy wou'ld a woo'ing go' Whe'ther his mo'ther would le't him or no'* ; *And so' the poor do'g had no'ne.*

aspirate (Gram.) ; ' breathed '. Sound of the letter h when not fused with another as in *Philip* (ph=f) or *thin* or *this* or *shin* or *chin* or *loch,* but pure as in *hot* & *greenhouse.* Also used loosely of ph, th, & Scotch ch, & of other letters now usually called spirant or fricative.

assimilation (Gram.) ; ' making like '. The changing of a sound into another identical with or nearer to a neighbouring sound, as when the d of *godsibb* (related in God) becomes s in *gossip,* or when the dental of *in* not becomes the labial m before the labial p in *impius* impious.

asyndeton (Rhet.) ; ' not bound together '. The omission, for effect, of conjunctions by which words or sentences would in normal speech be connected.

The first sort by their own suggestion fell,
Self-tempted, ∧ self-depraved ; ∧ Man falls, deceived
By the other first : Man, therefore, shall find grace ;
∧ The other, none.

attraction (Gram.) ; A tendency less commonly operative in English (except in mere blunders) than in Latin & Greek, by which a word is changed from the correct case, number, or person, to that of an adjacent word. When *him* [whom] we serve 's away ; The wages of sin *is* death. And (as a blunder) The small amount of classics which *are* still held to be necessary.

ballad (Lit.) ; ' dancing-song '. Originally a song as accompaniment to dancing ; later any simple sentimental song esp. of two or more verses each to the same melody, e. g. Jonson's *Drink to me only*— ; a separate modern use is as the name of simple narrative poems in short stanzas, such as *Chevy Chase.*

ballade (Lit.) ; ' dancing-song '. An elaborate poem consisting of three eight (or ten) line stanzas & a four (or five) line envoy, all on three (or four) rhymes only in the same order in each stanza, & with the same line ending each stanza & the envoy. An old French form, revived in France & England in the 19th c.

The Pompadour's Fan (ballade, by Austin Dobson)

Chicken-skin, delicate, white,
   Painted by Carlo Vanloo,
Loves in a riot of light,
   Roses & vaporous blue ;
   Hark to the dainty *frou-frou !*
Picture above, if you can,
   Eyes that could melt as the dew,—
This was the Pompadour's fan !
See how they rise at the sight,
   Thronging the *Œil de Bœuf* through,
Courtiers as butterflies bright,
   Beauties that Fragonard drew,
   Talon-rouge, falbala, queue,
Cardinal, Duke, to a man,
   Eager to sigh or to sue,—
This was the Pompadour's fan !

Ah, but things more than polite
  Hung on this toy, *voyez-vous !*
Matters of state & of might,
  Things that great ministers do ;
  Things that, may be, overthrew
Those in whose brains they began ;
  Here was the sign & the cue,—
This was the Pompadour's fan !

ENVOY

Where are the secrets it knew ?
  Weavings of plot & of plan ?
—But where is the Pompadour, too ?
  This was the Pompadour's *fan !*

baroque (Art.) ; ' mis-shapen pearl '.
See *rococo* below.
begging the question (Log.). The
English version of *petitio principii*
(see below).
BELLES LETTRES (Lit.) ; ' fine
letters '.
blank verse (Pros.). Strictly, any
unrhymed verse ; but in ordinary
use confined to the five-foot iambic
unrhymed verse in which *Paradise
Lost*, & the greater part of Shakspere's plays, are written.
brachylogy (Gram.) ; ' short speech '.
Irregular shortening down of expression. *Less sugar, This is no use,*
& *A is as good or better than B*, are
brachylogies for Less *of* sugar, This
is *of* no use, & A is as good *as* or
better than B ; the first is established as idiomatic, the others are
still regarded by many as illegitimate. See also *pregnant construction*
below.
BURLESQUE (Lit.) ; ' ridicule '.
caesura (Pros.) ; ' cutting '. The
point at which a verse line falls into
two parts. In Latin hexameters, an
obligatory break between words in
the third foot (*penthemimeral c.*) or
in the fourth (*hephthemimeral c.*),
called *strong* if after a long & *weak*
if after a short syllable ; in Latin
pentameters, an invariable break
between words after two feet & a
half. In English verse chiefly
noticeable in long metres such as
that of *Locksley Hall* :—Till the
war-drum throbb'd no longer,//&
the battle-flags were furl'd In the

Parliament of man,//the federation
of the world.
CARICATURE (Lit.) ; ' loading '.
catachresis (adj. *-estic*) (Gram.) ;
' misuse '. Wrong application of a
term, use of words in senses that do
not belong to them. The popular
uses of *chronic*=severe, *asset*=ad-
vantage, *conservative*=low, *annex*=
win, & *mutual*=common, are examples.
catalectic (Pros.) ; ' stopping short '.
Some metres consist of a specified
number of feet with the last foot
truncated ; these are called c. ; thus
Many / women / many / men / has only
the first syllable of the last trochee ;
cf. *acatalectic* above.
causerie (Lit.) ; ' talk '. Informal
newspaper essay or article esp. on
literary subjects & appearing as one
of a series. Named after Sainte
Beuve's *Causeries du Lundi* (Monday
talks), a series of weekly criticisms in
the *Constitutionnel* & *Moniteur* newspapers.
chiasmus (adj. *-astic*) (Rhet.) ;
' cross-fashion '. When the terms in
the second of two parallel phrases
reverse the order of those in the
first to which they correspond. If
the two phrases are written one
below the other, & lines drawn between the corresponding terms,
those lines make the Greek letter
chi, a diagonal cross :

I cannot   dig

to beg   I am ashamed

choliambic (Pros.) ; ' lame iambic '.
A classical metre changed from the
ordinary *iambic* (see below) by
having always a spondee in the
sixth & an iambus in the fifth foot :
Ō quĭd/sŏlūt/ĭs ēst/bĕāt/ĭŭs/cūrĭs ?
Also called *scazon*.
CLAUSE (Gram.) ; ' close, end '.
cliché (Rhet.) ; ' stereotype block '.
A French name for such hackneyed
phrases as, not being the simple or
natural way of expressing what is
to be expressed, have served when
first used as real improvements on

that in some particular context, but have acquired an unfortunate popularity & come into general use even where they are not more but less suitable to the context than plain speech. Such are ' to be made the recipient of ' for to be given, ' the devouring element ' for fire, ' make the supreme sacrifice ' for die in battle, ' stand to reason ' for be obvious ; & see for other examples HACKNEYED PHRASES.

climax (Rhet.) ; ' ladder '. Arrangement of a series of notions in such an order that each is more impressive than the preceding. (1) *Eye hath not seen*, (2) *nor ear heard*, (3) *neither have entered into the heart of man*,/the things which God hath prepared ; three progressive stages of strangeness.

cognate (Gram.) ; ' akin '. A noun that expresses again, with or without some limitation, the action of a verb to which it is appended in a sentence is distinguished from the direct object of a transitive verb (expressing the external person or thing on which the action is exerted) as the *cognate*, or the *internal*, or the *adverbial*, *object* or *accusative* :
is playing *whist* (cognate) ;
I hate *whist* (direct) ;
lived a good *life* (internal or cognate);
spent his *life* well (direct) ;
looked *daggers* (adverbial or cognate).
In the last example *daggers* is a metaphor for a look of a certain kind, & therefore cognate with the verb.

collectives. Applied primarily (A) to nouns denoting a whole made up of similar parts, such as *crew, flock, firm, Cabinet*. These are also called nouns of multitude (see NUMBER, 6). But other nouns, or uses of them, are often described by the term, & confusion may be saved by separating these. (B) Nouns whose plural is in form not distinguishable from the singular, as *sheep, deer, salmon, grouse, counsel* (= advocate); (C) Nouns whose singular is sometimes used instead of their plural, as *duck, fish, shot, cannon* ; (D) Nouns denoting either a thing or

a material consisting of many of them, as *hair, straw* ; (E) Nouns denoting either a material or a collection of things made of it, as *linen, silver, china* ; (F) Nouns denoting either a thing or some or all of them, as *fruit, timber* ; (G) Abstract singulars used instead of concrete plurals, as *accommodation* (= rooms), *kindling* (= pieces of wood), *royalty* (= royal persons), *pottery* (= pots) ; & even (H) Nouns denoting substances of indefinite quantity, as *butter,water*.

COMEDY (Lit.) ; ' festival song '.

COMMON (Gram.).

complement (Gram.) ; ' filling up '. That which completes, or helps to complete, the verb, making with it the predicate. This (A) is the widest sense of the word, not excluding e. g. the direct object of a transitive verb, or adverbs ; it is possibly the most reasonable application of the term ; it is also the least useful, & the least used. (B) Often the direct object is excluded, but all other modifications or appendages of the verb are called complements ; a sense found convenient in schemes of sentence analysis, but too wide to be precise & too narrow to be logical. (C) A further restriction admits only such words or phrases as are so essential to the verb that they form one notion with it & its meaning would be incomplete without them ; thus in *He put his affairs in order* the verb *put* is essentially incomplete without its complement *in order*, whereas in *He replaced the volumes in order* a new detail merely is added by the adverb *in order* to the complete verb *replaced* ; some verbs are in their nature incomplete, e. g. the auxiliaries, &, in *must go*, *go* is the complement of *must*. A serviceable use, especially if it were established as the only one. (D) Lastly, in the narrowest sense, *c.* is applied only to the noun or adjective predicated by means of a copulative verb (*be, become*, &c.) or of a factitive verb (*make, call, think*, &c.) of the subject (*He is a fool* ; *He grew wiser* ; *He*

was made *king*) or of the object
(Call no man *happy*); in such
examples as the last, the complement is called an *objective* or an
oblique c. A sense frequent in Latin
grammars.

concessive (Gram.); 'granting'.
The name given to subordinate
clauses beginning with *though* or
although, to those or equivalent conjunctions, & to participles used with
the corresponding effect, as in ' *Accepting* your facts, I dispute your
inference '.

concords (Gram.); 'agreement'.
The rules that an adjective is of the
same number, case, & gender, as its
noun, a verb of the same number &
person as its subject, & a noun of
the same case as that to which it is
in apposition.

conjugation (Gram.); 'yoking together'. Inflexion of verbs, or any
class of verbs inflected in a particular way (*first* &c., *strong* &c., *c.*);
cf. *declension* below.

conjunction (Gram.); 'joining together'. A word whose function is
to join like things together, i. e. a
noun or its equivalent with another
noun or its equivalent, an adjective
&c. with another, adverb &c. with
adverb &c., verb with verb, or
sentence with sentence; cf. prepositions, which attach a noun to
something different, especially to
verbs. The relation between the
things joined is shown by the particular conjunction chosen (*but, and*,
or *nor*; *if, although*, or *because*;
that or *lest*; *since* or *until*). Some
conjunctions, in joining two sentences, convert one into a depen-
dency of the other, or clause in it,
& are called *subordinating* or *strong
cc.*, the others being *co-ordinating* or
weak (strong—I hate him *because* he
is a Judas: weak—I hate him; *for*
he is a Judas). Many words are
sometimes conjunctions & sometimes adverbs (*therefore, so, however,
since*, &c.); & such words as *when*
& *where*, though often in effect cc.,
are more strictly described as relative adverbs with expressed or im-

plied antecedent (*I remember the
time when*, i. e. at which, *it happened*;
I will do it when, i. e. at the time at
which, *I see fit*).

conjunctive (Gram.); 'joining
together'.

consecutive (Gram.); 'following'.
A c. clause is a subordinate clause
that expresses the consequence of
the fact &c. stated in the sentence
on which it depends; & a c. conjunction, in English *that* corresponding to a preceding *so* or *such*, is the
word joining such a clause to the
sentence (He was so angry *that* he
could not speak).

continuant (Gram.); Another name
for *fricative* (below).

copulative (Gram.); 'linking'.
Copulative verbs are such as, like
the chief of them, *be*, link a complement to the subject (He *is* king;
we *grow* wiser); among them are
included the passives of factitive
verbs (This *is considered* the best).
For copulative conjunctions, see
disjunctive below.

correlatives (Gram.); 'mutual reference'. Pairs or sets of words
such that each implies the existence,
though not necessarily the mention,
of the other: *cause & effect, parent
& child, either & or, then & when, so
& as*, &c.

couplet (Pros.); 'joining'. Two
lines of verse, especially when of
equal metre, rhyming, & forming
a whole. See -STICH.

crasis (Gram.); 'mixture'. The
running of two separate vowel
sounds into one, as when *cocaine* &
naïve, originally pronounced kō'kaïn
& nah-ē'v, become kokā'n & nāv.
Confined in Greek grammar to such
combinations between the last vowel
sound of one word & the first of the
next, as in *kàgo* for *kai ego*.

cretic (Pros.); 'of Crete'. The
foot —◡—, as in the words *o'tio'se* &
su'ppleme'nt when pronounced with
two equal accents.

cursive (Palaeogr.); 'running'.
See *uncial* below.

dactyl (Pros.); 'finger'. The foot
—◡◡, as in *pottery* or *Julia*.

declension (vb *decline*) (Gram.) ; ' down-falling '. Inflexion of nouns & adjectives, or the nouns inflected in a particular way (*first* &c., *i* &c., *strong* &c., *d.*). Cf. *conjugation* above.

deduction (Log.) ; ' down-drawing '. Reasoning from the general to the particular ; basing the truth of a statement upon its being a case of a wider statement known or admitted to be true. If I argue that I shall die because I have been credibly informed that all men do so, & I am a man, I am performing d. Cf. *induction* below.

deliberative (Gram.) ; ' weighing well '. A name given, especially in Greek & Latin grammar, to the subjunctive (& optative) used in what may be called an interrogative command, corresponding to the English *Shall we go ?*, *What was I to do ?*

dénouement (Lit.) ; ' untying '. The clearing up, at the end of a play or tale, of the complications of the plot. A term often preferred to the English *catastrophe* because that has lost in popular use its neutral sense.

dental (Gram.) ; ' of teeth '. Consonants produced by applying the tongue-tip to the upper teeth or to the gum close behind them (t, d, th, n).

deponent (Gram.) ; ' laying aside '. Verbs passive in form but active in sense are so called, especially in Latin grammar, as *utor* I use, *labor* I slip.

desiderative (Gram.) ; ' of desire '. From some Greek & Latin verbs secondary verbs are formed with special suffixes expressing the wish to do, or the being on the point of doing, the action. Thus the Latin for *be hungry*, *be in labour*, is *esurio* from *edo* I eat & *parturio* from *pario* I give birth to ; these are d. verbs, & -urio, & in Greek -iao, -seio, are d. terminations.

diaeresis (Gram.) ; ' taking asunder '. The pronouncing of two successive vowels as separate sounds & not as a single vowel or diphthong ;

or the mark (·· over the second) sometimes used to indicate such separation, as in *Chloë*, *aërated*. A peculiarity in the French use of the mark may be mentioned by way of warning ; in such words as *aiguë*, *ciguë*, the mark means not that the e is separate from the u, but that ue is not silent as in *fatigue* & *vogue*, but forms a distinct syllable.

dialogue (Lit.); ' cross-talking '. Conversation as opposed to monologue, to preaching, lecturing, speeches, narrative, or description ; neither confined to nor excluding talk between two persons ; see DUOLOGUE.

digraph (Gram.) ; ' two-writing '. Any two written consonants expressing a sound not analysable into two, as ph, dg, ch ; or any two written vowels expressing a vowel sound, whether simple or compound, that is pronounced in one syllable, as (simple) ea in *beat* or *head*, ee in *heed*, au, ui in *fruit*, (diphthong) oi, oa in *boat*, ow. Digraphs therefore include all diphthongs except those, common in English, that are written as single letters (e. g. the ā, ī, ō, heard in *ale*, *white*, *no*) & are consequently often supposed not to be diphthongs.

dimeter (Pros.). See -*meter* below.

disjunctive (Gram.) ; ' unjoining '. Conjunctions implying not combination but an alternative or a contrast (as *or*, *but*) are so called, the others (as *and*) being *copulative*. The distinction is of some importance in determining the number of verbs after compound subjects ; see NUMBER 2, 3.

dissimilation (Gram.) ; ' making unlike '. Change in sound due to dislike of the same sound in neighbouring syllables, as when the noun from *negotiate* (-shīāt) is pronounced with -slāshn, not -shīāshn, or when the Latin *cinnamomum* becomes in English not *cinnamom* but *cinnamon*.

distich (Pros.) ; ' two-line '. See -STICH.

distributive (Gram.) ; Those adjectives & pronouns are so called which expressly convey that what is said of a class is applicable to its individual members, not merely to it as a whole. *Either* (cf. *both*), *every* (cf. *all*), *each* (cf. *both & all*), *neither* (cf. *no, none*).

DUOLOGUE (Lit.) ; ' two-talk '.

elegiacs (Pros.) ; ' of dirges '. A Greek & Latin metre, in couplets each consisting of a *hexameter* (see below) & *pentameter* (see below). Sometimes imitated in English, but ill suited for accentual (as opp. quantitative) verse. Two specimens follow, both from Clough, the first written with, & the second without, regard to the English accents ; to truly represent elegiacs, the second couplet would have to be read with the accents shown.

Where, under/mulberry/branches, the/diligent/rivulet/sparkles, Or amid/cotton &/maize//peasants their/waterworks/ply. From' thy/far' sour/ces', 'mid/ moun'tains/air'ily/climb'ing, Pass' to the/rich' low/land'//thou' busy/sun'ny ri/ver'.

elegy (Lit.) ; ' lamentation '. In the strict sense a song or poem of mourning, & properly applied in English to such pieces as *Lycidas, Adonais, & Thyrsis*. But, the favourite ancient metre for such pieces being the elegiacs so named on that account, a natural reaction caused anything written in elegiacs to be called an elegy, whatever its subject, & the name was extended to cover all short poems, irrespective of metre, that were of the subjective kind, i. e., were concerned with expressing their authors' feelings. The present tendency is to restrict the word to its original sense.

ELLIPSIS (Gram.) ; ' deficiency '.

enclitic (Gram.) ; ' on-leaning '. A word so devoid of emphasis that it sounds like part of the word before, as *not* in *cannot, me* (usually) in *give me* (cf. vulg. *gimme*), *one* in *everyone*, &c. In Greek & Latin some words are always enclitic & incapable of standing first in a sentence (as Greek *te*, Latin *autem*),

while Greek enclitics often affect the preceding word's written accentuation. Cf. *proclitic* below.

enjambment (Pros.) ; ' in-treading '. In couplet metres, continuation of a sentence or phrase beyond the end of one couplet into the first line of the next. In the heroic couplet as used by Dryden & Pope one may read hundreds of lines without finding an e. ; three examples follow :—

Him therefore e'er his fortune slip her time The statesman plots t'engage in some bold crime Past pardon. That praise was his ; what therefore did remain For following chiefs, but boldly to maintain That crown restor'd ? What nothing earthly gives, or can destroy, The soul's calm sunshine, & the heartfelt joy, Is virtue's prize.

envoy (Pros.) ; ' (sending) on the way '. Parting words of a poem, especially in the form of a final stanza of fewer lines than the preceding, or otherwise distinguished. For an example see *ballade* above.

epexegetic (Gram.) ; ' additionally explanatory '. Applied especially to various uses of the infinitive appended without strict necessity to limit & define the application of what has preceded. A common English use is exemplified in *This is very sad to find*. Greek has many idioms classed under this head.

epicene (Gram.) ; ' in common '. See COMMON.

epigram (Lit.) ; ' on-writing '. Four distinct meanings, naturally enough developed. First, now obsolete, an inscription on a building, tomb, coin, &c. Secondly, (inscriptions being often in verse, & brief) a short poem, & especially one with a sting in the tail. Thirdly, any pungent saying. Fourthly, a style full of such sayings.

epigraphy (Lit.) ; ' study of inscriptions '. Inscriptions & the science of interpreting them &c. Cf. the original sense of *epigram* above.

epode (Lit.) ; ' additional song '. In Greek choruses, the epode is a concluding part, distinct in metre, chanted after the *antistrophe* (see above). In Horace's *Epodes*, the name is a loose one, given because the metre chiefly used in the book is one in which a full iambic line is followed by a shorter one regarded metrically as a mere appendage or ' added verse '.

EPOPEE (Lit.) ; ' epic-making '.

equivocation (Log.) ; ' calling alike '. A fallacy consisting in the use of a word in different senses at different stages of the reasoning. If we conclude from Jones's having a thick head (i. e. being a dullard) that he is proof against concussion, we take *thick head* to mean first dull brain & afterwards solid skull, which is an equivocation.

etacism (Gram.) ; ' saying eta '. Pronounce ā'tasīzm. The preserving of the original ā sound of eta ; cf. *itacism* below.

ethic dative (Gram.) ; ' dative of emotion '. In Latin & Greek a person indirectly or vaguely concerned in the matter stated &c. is sometimes introduced into the sentence in the dative ; thus, in *Quid mihi Celsus agit?*, the word *mihi* (lit., to or for me) amounts to a parenthetic ' I wonder '. *Me* in Elizabethan English was often so used, as

See how this river comes *me* cranking in
And cuts *me* from the best of all my land
A huge half-moon, a monstrous cantle out.

EUPHEMISM (Rhet.) ; ' decorous speech '.

EUPHUISM (Lit.) ; ' giftedness '.

explosive (Gram.) ; ' clapping off '. A name given to those consonant sounds (b, hard g, d, p, k, t) which are produced by a sudden parting of the lips or other organs, & can

therefore not be prolonged ; cf. *fricative* below.

factitive (Gram.) ; ' of making '. Verbs of making, calling, & thinking (i. e., of making by deed, word, or thought) are given this name for the grammarian's convenience ; their common attribute is the power of attaching a complement (see above) to the object if they are active (*many do call* me fool) or to any noun if they are passive (*the* people *made* rich *by him*).

fallacy (Log.) ; ' deception '. A fallacy in logic is ' an argument which violates the laws of correct demonstration. An argument may be fallacious in *matter* (i. e. misstatement of facts), in *wording* (i. e. wrong use of words), or in the *process of inference*. Fallacies have, therefore been classified as : I. Material, II. Verbal, III. Logical or Formal.' —*Encycl. Brit.* Some types of f. are of frequent enough occurrence to have earned names that have passed into ordinary speech, & serve as a short way of announcing to a false reasoner that his conscious or unconscious sophistry is detected. Such are *arguing in a circle, equivocation, begging the question, ignoratio elenchi, argumentum ad hominem* &c., *petitio principii, non sequitur, post hoc ergo propter hoc, false analogy, undistributed middle,* all of which will be found alphabetically placed in this article.

false analogy (Log.) ; ' erroneous correspondence '. The unfounded assumption that a thing that has certain attributes in common with another will resemble it also in some attribute in which it is not known to do so ; e. g., that of a pair of hawks the larger is the male, on the ground that other male animals are larger than female ; or that *idiosyncracy* is the right spelling because words ending in the sound -krasī are spelt with -*cy*.

farce (Lit.) ; ' stuffing '. See COMEDY. The connexion with the etymological sense lies in the meaning interpolation, the farce having originated in interludes of buffoonery in religious dramas.

feminine rhyme (Pros.). See MALE 2.

final (Gram.) ; ' of the end '. A f. clause is one expressing the purpose of the action stated &c. in the main sentence of which it is a part, & a f. conjunction (esp. *that, in order that, lest*) is one that subordinates such a clause. *Eat that you may live ; Be wise, lest sorrow lend me words.*

frequentative (Gram.). F. verbs are formed with certain suffixes to express repeated or continuous action of the kind denoted by the simple verb. The chief f. suffixes in English are -le, -er, as in *sparkle, chatter, dribble* (drip). Most of the nouns in *-sation, -tation*, come from Latin frequentatives in *-so, -to*, as *conversation* (L *verto* turn, *versor* move about), *hesitation* (L *haereo* stick, *haesito* keep sticking).

fricative (Gram.) ; ' rubbing '. An adjective & noun applied to the consonant sounds produced by passage of breath through a narrowed space between organs ; a general term, exchangeable with *continuant*, including the more special *sibilant, aspirate, spirant, liquid, trill*, &c., & distinguished from *explosives* or *mutes* or *stops*.

gerund, gerundive (Gram.) ; ' doing '. See the article GERUND ; right treatment of gerunds is idiomatically of much importance.

gnomic (Lit., Gram.) ; ' sententious '. Gnomic literature is writing that consists of or is packed with maxims or general truths pithily expressed. The gnomic aorist in Greek is the aorist used, though it refers normally to the past, to state a fact that is true of all times, e. g. in proverbs.

guttural (Gram.) ; ' of the throat '. The sounds of k, g, & ch, heard in *keep, get*, & (Scotch) *loch*. But see also *palatal* below ; gutturals, properly speaking, are made with the root of the tongue & the soft palate. The word is also applied to other sounds to indicate that they are

made far back in the mouth, e. g. to the German r as opp. the English.

hendecasyllable (Pros.) ; ' eleven-syllable '. Applicable, & occasionally applied, to any metre having lines of eleven syllables, e. g. to Dante's terza rima ; but so far appropriated to what is called in full *the Phalaecian h.* that to use it of other metres risks misunderstanding. The P. h. is the Greek & Latin metre best known from Catullus, having the scheme $-\smile/-\smile\smile/$ $-\smile/-\smile/-\smile$, & imitated by Tennyson :—

Look, I come to the test, a tiny poem All composed in a metre of Catullus.

hendiadys (Rhet.) ; ' one by means of two '. The expressing of a compound notion by giving its two constituents as though they were independent & connecting them with a conjunction instead of subordinating one to the other, as ' pour libation from bowls & from gold '= from bowls of gold. Chiefly a poetic ornament in Greek & Latin, & little used in English ; but ' nice & warm ', ' try & do better ', instead of ' nicely warm ', ' try to do better ', are true examples. It should be noticed that such combinations as *brandy & soda, assault & battery, might & main, toil & moil, spick & span, stand & deliver*, since their two parts are on an equal footing & not in sense subordinate one to the other, do not need the name, & should not be called by it.

hephthemimeral (Pros.) ; ' at the seventh half(foot)'. See *caesura* above.

heroic (Lit., Pros.). *H. poetry*,= epic. *H. verse* or *metre*, or *heroics*, the metre used in h. poetry, i. e. hexameters in Greek & Latin, & the five-foot iambic in English, whether blank as in *Paradise Lost* or in rhymed couplets (*the h. couplet*) as in Chaucer's *Prologue* & in Dryden & Pope, e. g.

Expatiate free o'er all this scene of man ;

A mighty maze ! but not without a plan.

heteroclite (Gram.); 'having a second declension'. Greek & Latin nouns having forms belonging to more than one declension, as Latin *domus* (gen. pl. *domuum* 4th, *domorum* 2nd), are called *h.*

hexameter (Pros.); 'six-measure'. The Greek & Latin heroic metre, in full *dactylic h. acatalectic*, on the scheme

$$-\cup\cup/-\cup\cup/-\cup\cup/-\cup\cup/-\cup\cup/-\cup$$
$$--/ \quad --/ \quad --/ \quad --/ \quad /--$$

with a *caesura* (see above). Also used in *elegiacs* (see above). Imitated in modern languages, e. g. by Goethe in *Hermann und Dorothea*, by Longfellow in *Evangeline* & *Miles Standish*, & by Clough in *The Bothie* & elsewhere.

Chanced it my/eye fell a/side on a/ capless/bonnetless/maiden
Bending with/three-pronged/fork in a/garden up/rooting po/tatoes.

hiatus (Pros.); 'yawning'. The allowing of a word ending with a vowel to be followed by one beginning with a vowel without elision of the first; avoided in Greek & Latin verse.

historic (Gram.). *H. infinitive* is a present infin. used in Latin as a vivid substitute for an imperfect or past indicative; *pars cedere, alii insequi*, some were giving way, others pressing on. *H. present* is, in any language, the present indicative used instead of a past to give vividness in describing a past event (*He says nothing, but ups with his fist & hits me in the eye*). *H. sequence* is, esp. in Greek & Latin, the use of the tense or mood that is required after a historic tense (opp. *primary*). *H. tenses* are those proper to narrating past events, i. e., in Greek the aorist & imperfect & pluperfect, in Latin the imperfect, the perfect when = I did, & the pluperfect, & in English the past tense (I did), the past imperfect (I was doing), & the pluperfect; opp. *primary*.

homonym (Gram.); 'same name'. See SYNONYM.

homophone (Gram.); 'same sound'. See SYNONYM.

HUMOUR (Lit.); 'moisture'.

hypallage (Rhet.); 'exchange'. The transferring of an epithet from the more to the less natural part of a group of nouns, as when Virgil speaks of 'the trumpet's Tuscan blare' instead of 'the Tuscan trumpet's blare', or Spenser of 'Sansfoy's dead dowry', i. e. dead Sansfoy's dowry.

hyperbaton (Gram.); 'stepping over'. Transposition of words out of normal order, as in Browning's title *Wanting Is—What?*, or in Shakspere's *That whiter skin of hers than snow*.

hyperbole (Rhet.); 'over-shooting'. Use of exaggerated terms for the sake not of deception, but of emphasis, as when *infinite* is used for *great*, or 'a thousand apologies' for an apology.

hypermetre (adj. *-trical*) (Pros.); 'over-measure'. In Latin verse, a syllable at the end of a line after the metre is complete, to be elided before a vowel beginning the next line; a rarity. Sometimes applied in English to lines having a feminine instead of the normal masculine ending; no rarity in blank verse.

hypocorisma (adj. *-ristic*) (Rhet.); 'child's prattle'. Use of pet names, nursery words, or diminutives, or a word of these kinds, either simply, as *Molly* for Mary, *patball* for lawn tennis, *hanky* for handkerchief, &c., or by way of euphemism, as *fancy man* for paramour, *story* for lie, *frillies* for under-linen.

hysteron proteron (Rhet.); 'later earlier'. Putting the cart before the horse in speech, as in Dogberry's *Masters, it is proved already that you are little better than false knaves, & it will go near to be thought so shortly*.

iambics (Pros.); 'of the iambus'. Any metre consisting either of iambuses alone or of them with other feet allowed as substitutes in certain places; but especially the *iambic trimeter acatalectic*, or *senarius*, in which the dialogue of

Greek plays is written. The scheme in Greek Tragedy (with further variations in Comedy) is :

◡–	◡–	◡–	◡–	◡–	◡–
––		––		––	
◡◡◡	◡◡◡	◡◡◡	◡◡◡	◡◡◡	◡◡
◡◡–					
–◡◡		–◡◡			

These six-foot iambics are in modern use called *alexandrines* (see above), & rhymed couplets of them are the French dramatic metre.

iambus (Pros.) ; ' invective '. The foot ◡–, named as employed in early Greek satires.

ictus (Pros.) ; ' beat '. The stress laid on particular syllables in marking the rhythm of verse ; the part of a foot on which the ictus falls is said to be *in arsis* (see above), & the other part *in thesis* (see below). In the line

Unrespited, unpitied, unreprieved, there is no ictus on the first or the second un- but ictus on the third.

idola tribus, specus, fori, theatri (Log.) ; ' phantoms of the tribe, cave, market, theatre '. Bacon's classification of fallacies ; see IDOLA FORI.

ignoratio elenchi (Log.) ; ' ignoring of the (required) disproof '. A fallacy consisting in disproving or proving something different from what is strictly in question ; called in English *the fallacy of irrelevant conclusion*. If the question is whether the law allows me to pollute water passing through my garden, & I show instead that it *ought to* allow me, since the loss to me by abstaining is a hundred times greater than my neighbour's from the pollution, I am guilty of i. e.

imparisyllabic (Gram.) ; ' unequal-syllabled '. A name given to those Greek & Latin nouns which have fewer syllables in the nominative than in other cases, as nom. *virtus*, gen. *virtutis*.

inceptive, inchoative, (Gram.) ; ' on-taking ', ' beginning '. Names given to verbs meaning ' to begin to do something ' ; in Greek *-skō* & in

Latin *-sco* are the i. terminations, as *gignōskō* learn (i. e. come to know), *calesco* grow warm. The many English words in *-esce, -escent*, as *recrudesce, iridescent*, are from Latin ii.

indirect object (Gram.). The person or thing secondarily affected by the action stated in the verb, if expressed by a noun alone (i.e. without *to, for*, &c.) is called the i. o. ; in Latin & Greek it is recognizable, as it once was in English, by being in the dative, while the (direct) object is in the accusative. The English dative now having no separate form, the i. o. must be otherwise identified, viz by the fact that it stands between the verb & the object (Hand *me* that book), &, if it is to follow the object, must be replaced by a preposition phrase (Hand that book *to me*). Variations are (1) when no direct object is expressed, as *You told me yourself*, (2) when the direct object is a mere pronoun & is allowed to precede, as *I told it you before* (but not *I told the story you before*), (3) when the i. o. is after a passive verb, as *It was told me in confidence*.

INDIRECT QUESTION. A question subordinated & serving as object, subject, &c., of a sentence. For some cautions on order of words, see the article ; & for punctuation, see *question mark* in STOPS.

induction (Log.) ; ' bringing in '. Reasoning from particular (' cited ') cases to general principles ; inferring of a law from observed occurrences. If I argue, from the fact that all the MacGregors I have known are Scotch, that MacGregor is a Scotch name, I make an i. Cf. *deduction* above.

inflexion (vb *inflect*) (Gram.) ; ' making curved '. The general name, including declension, conjugation, & comparison, for changes made in the form of words to show their grammatical relations to their context or to modify their meaning in certain ways. *Cats, him, greater, sued*, are formed by i. from, or are ii. of, *cat, he, great*, & *sue*.

intensive (Gram.) ; ' tightening up'. Said of words or word-elements that add emphasis ; in *vastly obliged, perdurable, vastly* & *per-* are ii. Often in contrast with *privative* (see below) ; the in- of *incisive* (& *intensive*) is intensive, & that of *incivility* privative.

IRONY (Lit.) ; ' dissimulation '.

itacism (Gram.) ; ' saying ita '. Pronounce ē′tasĭzm. The use in Greek of the sound ē instead of the original ā for the letter eta ; also the tendency in late & modern Greek to reduce many sounds once distinct to ē ; also the substitution by copyists in MSS. of eta for other letters in consequence of this change in pronunciation. Cf. *etacism* above.

labial (Gram.) ; ' of the lip '. Sounds made by complete or partial closure of the lips are called *l.*, including the consonants p, b, m, w, & (labiodental) f & v, & the vowels ŏ (in *no*), ōō (in *fool*), ŏŏ (in *full*), ow (in *how*).

legitimate drama (Lit.). A phrase denoting the plays of permanent value such as are included in repertories & revived from time to time, in contrast with melodrama, musical farce, revue, adaptations of foreign plays, & other fugitive pieces.

liquids (Gram.). The letters l & r, & sometimes also m & n, are so called.

litotes (Rhet.) ; ' frugality '. The same as, or a variety of, *meiosis* (see below). Sometimes confined to the particular kind of rhetorical understatement in which for the positive notion required is substituted its opposite with a negative. In 1 *Cor.* xi. 17, 22, *I praise you not* has the effect of an emphatic I blame ; *not a few* means a great number ; *Not bad, eh ?*, after an anecdote, means excellent. But often used, indifferently with *meiosis*, of other understatements meant to impress by moderation.

locative (Gram.) ; ' of place '. Nouns in Indo-European languages have a case so called, equivalent in sense to an adverb of place, e. g. Latin *domi* at home, *Romae* in Rome.

lyrics (Lit.) ; ' of the lyre '. The OED definition (as regards modern usage) is : ' Short poems (whether or not intended to be sung), usually divided into stanzas or strophes, & directly expressing the poet's own thoughts & sentiments '. The short pieces between the narrative parts of Tennyson's *Princess* (*Home they brought her warrior dead*, &c.), are typical examples. Wordsworth's *Daffodils*, Shelley's *Skylark*, Keats's *Grecian Urn*, Milton's *Penseroso*, Burns's *Field Mouse*, Herrick's *Rosebuds*, Lovelace's *Lucasta*, Shakspere's *It was a lover*, may serve to illustrate ; but attempts to distinguish lyric poetry clearly from other kinds (epic, dramatic, elegiac, didactic, &c.) have not been successful, the classes not being mutually exclusive.

major (Log.). See *syllogism* below.

majuscule (Palaeography) ; ' somewhat larger '. See *uncial* below.

masculine rhyme (Pros.). See MALE 2.

meiosis (Rhet.) ; ' lessening '. The use of understatement not to deceive, but to enhance the impression on the hearer. Often applied to the negative opposite illustrated under *litotes* above, but taking many other forms, & contrasted with *hyperbole*. Very common in colloquial & slang English ; the emphatic *rather* (Did you ever hear Caruso ?—Rather !), the American *some* (This is some war ; see SOME 1), the schoolboy *decent* (=firstrate &c.), the retort *I'll see you further* (i. e. in hell) *first*, & the strangely inverted hyperbole *didn't half swear* (=swore horribly), are familiar instances.

MELODRAMA (Lit.); ' music drama '.

metaphor (Rhet.) ; ' transferring '. See the article, & SIMILE.

metathesis (Gram.) ; ' change of position '. When successive sounds in a word change places, as the s & p in *hasp* (earlier *hæpse*) & *clasp* (earlier also *clapse*), the s & k in *ask* (vulg., & formerly in equally good use, *ax*), the r & i in *third* (earlier *thridde*) & *thrill* (earlier *thirle*), the u & r in *curly* (earlier *crulle* : With lokkes crulle as they were leyd in presse—Chaucer).

-meter (Pros.) ; ' measure '. A little used sense of the word *metre* is the unit (itself consisting sometimes of one foot, sometimes of two) that is repeated a certain number of times in a line of verse. But the compounds made from it—*monometer, dimeter, trimeter, tetrameter, pentameter, hexameter*—are in regular use as one part of the full technical ames of metres (e. g. *iambic trimeter acatalectic*) ; the feet of which two & not one make a metre in this sense are the iambus, trochee, & anapaest, so that six iambi (or equivalents) make a trimeter, but six dactyls (or equivalents) make a hexameter.

metonymy (Rhet.) ; ' name-change '. Substitution of an attributive or other suggestive word for the name of the thing meant, as when *the Crown, Homer, wealth*, stand for the sovereign, Homer's poems, & rich people.

middle (*article*) (Lit.). Newspaper article of a kind so called from having stood between the leading articles & the book reviews, & being a short essay usually of some literary pretensions on some subject of permanent & general rather than topical or political interest.

middle term (Log.). See *syllogism* below.

middle voice (Gram.). Greek verbs may have, besides or without the active & passive voices, another called the middle, in most tenses identical in form with the passive, but expressing ' reflexive or reciprocal action, action viewed as affecting the subject, or intransitive conditions ' (OED).

minor (Log.). See *syllogism* below.

minuscule (Palaeography) ; ' somewhat smaller '. See *uncial* below.

monologue (Lit.) ; ' sole speech '. This & *soliloquy* are precisely parallel terms of Greek, & Latin, origin ; but usage tends to restrict *soliloquy* to talking to oneself or thinking aloud without consciousness of an audience whether one is in fact overheard or not, while *monologue*, though not conversely restricted to a single person's discourse that *is* meant to be heard, has that sense much more often than not, & is especially used of a talker who monopolizes conversation, or of a dramatic performance or recitation in which there is one actor only.

monometer (Pros.). See *-meter* above.

mute (Gram.). The letters p, b, d, t, g, k, are variously called mutes, explosives, or stops ; see *explosive* & *fricative* above.

nasal (Gram.) ; ' of the nose '. Sounds requiring the nose passage to be open, as in English those of m, n, & ng, are so called.

nominativus pendens (Gram.) ; ' hanging nominative '. A form of anacoluthon in which a sentence is begun with what appears to be the subject, but before the verb is reached something else is substituted in word or in thought, & the supposed subject is left in the air. The most familiar & violent instance is *which* used in Sarah Gamp's manner (*which fiddle-strings is weakness to expredge my nerves this night*) ; but the irregularity is not uncommon even in writing, & is always apt to occur in speech. Cf., in Shakspere, ' *They* who brought me in my master's hate/I live to look upon their tragedy ' (*Rich. III,* III. ii. 57).

non sequitur (Log.) ; ' does not follow '. The fallacy of assuming an unproved cause. Thus : It will be a hard winter, for holly-berries (which are meant as provision for birds in hard weather) are abundant. The reasoning called *post hoc, ergo propter hoc* is a form of n. s.

objective genitive (Gram.). The genitive that stands to a verbal noun or noun of action in the same relation as the object to a verb. In *fear God, God* is the object of the verb, &, in *put the fear of God in them, God* is in the same relation to the noun *fear*, & is called the

objective genitive. In English the
' of ' genitive is usual, but the
inflected genitive or the possessive
adjective also occurs, as in *the Tsar's
murder, the deep damnation of his
taking-off.*

oblique complement (Gram.). See
complement (D) above.

octonarius (Pros.) ; ' eight each '.
An eight-foot iambic line ; see
senarius below.

octosyllabics (Pros.) ; ' eight-syl-
lable '. The usual name of the
8-syl. rhyming iambic metre used in
Hudibras, The Lady of the Lake, &c.
The way was long, the wind was cold;
The minstrel was infirm & old.

ode (Lit.) ; ' song '. The OED
definition of the word in its prevailing modern sense may be given :
' A rimed (rarely unrimed) lyric, often
in the form of an address ; generally
dignified or exalted in subject, feeling,
& style, but sometimes (in earlier use)
simple & familiar (though less so than
a *song*)'. But what with confusion
between this very comprehensive
modern sense & the more definite
Greek sense (as in *choric ode* & *Pin-
daric ode*), what with the obvious
vagueness of the modern sense itself,
& what with the fact that 'elaborate'
& 'irregular' are both epithets commonly applied to ode metres, the
only possible conception of the ode
seems to be that of a Shape

> If shape it might be called that shape
>   had none
> Distinguishable in member, joint, or
>   limb.

onomatopoeia (adj. *-poeic, -poetic*)
(Gram.) ; ' name-making '. Formation of names or words from sounds
that resemble those associated with
the object or action to be named, or
that seem suggestive of its qualities ;
babble, cuckoo, croak, puff-puff, are
probable examples.

optative (Gram.) ; ' of wish '. Greek
verbs have certain forms called the
o. mood, used in expressing wishes
(=English *would that I were* &c.),
& also to serve in historic sequence
as the Greek subjunctive serves in

primary sequence. In modern grammar the word is sometimes applied
to whatever verbal form is used in
expressing a wish, e. g. *So help me
God !* or *Oh that I were young again !*

oratio obliqua, oratio recta, (Gram.) ;
' bent speech, straight speech '.
Latin names, the second for the
actual words used by a speaker,
without modification, & the first for
the form taken by his words when
they are reported & fitted into the
reporter's framework. Thus *How
are you ? I am delighted to see you*
(recta) becomes in obliqua *He asked
how I was & said he was delighted to
see me* ; or, if the framework is
invisible, *How was I ? he was delighted to see me.* Most newspaper
reports of speeches, & all third-
person letters, are in oratio obliqua
or reported speech.

ottava rima (Pros.) ; ' octave verse '.
The stanza invented by Boccaccio,
adopted & made the regular Italian
heroic metre by Tasso & Ariosto, &
used by Byron in *Don Juan.* Eight
five-foot iambic lines rhyming abab-
abcc.

> When Newton saw an apple fall, he
>   found
>   In that slight startle from his
>   contemplation—
> 'Tis *said* (for I'll not answer above
>   ground
>   For any sage's creed or calcula-
>   tion)—
> A mode of proving that the earth
>   turn'd round
>   In a most natural whirl, called
>   ' gravitation ' ;
> And *this* is the sole mortal who
>   could grapple,
> Since Adam, with a fall, or with an
>   apple.

oxymoron (Rhet.) ; ' sharp-dull '.
The combining in one expression of
two terms that are ordinarily contradictory, & whose exceptional
coincidence is therefore arresting.
A cheerful pessimist ; *Harmonious
discord* ; *His honour rooted in dishonour stood, And faith unfaithful
kept him falsely true.*

palatal (Gram.) ; ' of the palate '. Sounds made by placing the middle of the tongue against or near the palate—intermediate between gutturals & dentals. The y in *yet* is palatal ; & in English the so-called gutturals (k, g) tend to become palatals by being made with the middle instead of with the root of the tongue.

paradigm (Gram.) ; ' showing side by side '. A table of inflexion forms, e.g. of a particular declension of nouns or conjugation of verbs.

PARENTHESIS (Gram.) ; ' side insertion '.

parisyllabic (Gram.) ; ' equal-syllabled '. A name given to those Greek & Latin nouns which have the same number of syllables in the other cases as in the nominative, as nom. *collis*, gen. *collis*.

parody (Lit.) ; ' side-song '. See BURLESQUE.

paronomasia (Rhet.) ; ' word-shunting '. Puns, plays on words, making jocular or suggestive use of similarity between different words or of a word's different senses. The best known of all (though concealed in English) is perhaps that of *Matt.* xvi. 18 : *Thou art Peter* (Greek *Petros*), *& upon this rock* (Greek *petra*) *I will build my church* ; & another is *non Angli sed angeli*, not Angles but angels.

partitive (Gram.) ; ' of division '. *P. words* are such nouns & pronouns as by their nature imply the separating or distinguishing of a part of some whole from the rest, such as *part, portion, half, much,* superlatives, *some, any, each* ; the *p. geni-tive* is that of the word denoting the whole, which is made to depend on a p. word by being put in the genitive in fully inflected languages, but in English attached to it by *of. But the greatest of these is charity* ; *greatest* is the p. word, & *of these* the p. genitive.

paulo-post future (Gram.) ; ' about to be a little later '. A name for the future perfect (I shall have died) especially in Greek grammar, in which a peculiar use of it justifies a peculiar name ; the Greek for *I shall have died, It will have been done,* is better represented by *I shall be a dead man, It will be a done thing* or *fait accompli,* i. e., a future state, resulting from a less distantly future event, is described. Except with reference to this Greek usage, there is no reason for preferring the name to the ordinary intelligible *future perfect* ; but it is often used, & often misused.

pentameter (Pros.) ; ' five-measure '. Sometimes applied to the English heroic metres, i. e. blank verse or heroic couplet ; but an iambic p. should mean (see *-meter* above) ten iambic feet. The line universally called *p.* is the second line in *elegiacs* (see above) ; it was used in these couplets only, not by itself. The scheme is :

$$-\smile\smile\,/-\smile\smile\,/-\,/\,/-\smile\smile\,/-\smile\smile\,/\underline{\smile}$$

with invariable caesura.

This line also is not in fact a dactylic p., but a pair of dactylic trimeters catalectic in succession. Two examples of English imitation are given under *elegiacs* above.

penthemimeral (Pros.) ; ' of five halves '. The p. caesura in Latin hexameters (& pentameters) is that after two & a half feet ; see *caesura.*

penult (Gram.) ; ' nearly last '. The last syllable but one of a word.

period (Rhet.) ; ' circuit '. Strictly, any complete sentence ; but applied usually to one consisting of a number of clauses in dependence on a principal sentence, & so, in the plural, to a style marked by elaborate arrangement.

peripeteia (Lit.) ; ' falling round '. A sudden change of fortune in a drama or tale, e. g., in *The Merchant of Venice,* the downfall of Shylock, with Gratiano repeating to him his own words ' O learned judge '.

PERIPHRASIS (adj. *-phrastic*) (Rhet.) ; ' roundabout speech '.

persiflage (Rhet.) ; ' whistle-talk '. Irresponsible talk, of which the hearer is to make what he can without the right to suppose that the speaker means what he seems to say ; the treating of serious things as trifles & of trifles as serious. ' Talking with one's tongue in one's cheek ' may serve as a parallel. Hannah More, quoted in the OED, describes French p. as ' the cold compound of irony, irreligion, selfishness, & sneer ' ; irony, paradox, & levity, are perhaps rather the ingredients of the compound as now conceived.

PERSONIFICATION (Rhet.) ; ' making into a person '.

petitio principii (Log.) ; ' assumption of the basis '. The fallacy of founding a conclusion on a basis that as much needs to be proved as the conclusion itself. *Arguing in a circle* (see above) is a common variety of p. p. That foxhunting is not cruel, since the fox enjoys the fun, & that one must keep servants, since all respectable people do so, are other examples of begging the question or p. p., in which the argument is not circular.

Pindarics (Lit.) ; ' of Pindar '. The form of English verse in which a poem consists of several stanzas often of unequal length, with the rhymes within the stanza irregularly disposed, & the number of feet in the lines arbitrarily varied. In Pindar's own odes, the structure is an elaborate one of strophe, *antistrophe* (see above), & epode, far removed from irregularity ; but the English imitators noted the variety of metre within his strophes & neglected the precise correspondence between them ; *P.* came consequently to be the name for verse in which regularity of metre was scorned under the supposed impulse of high emotion.

PLEONASM (Rhet., Gram.) ; ' exceeding '.

post hoc, ergo propter hoc (Log.) ; ' after it, therefore due to it '. The fallacy of confusing consequence with sequence. On Sunday we prayed for rain ; on Monday it rained ; therefore the prayers caused the rain.

prefix (Gram.) ; ' attached in front '. An *affix* (see above) attached to the beginning of a word or stem to make a compound word, as re-, ex-, be-, a-, in *reform, ex-officer, belabour, arise*.

pregnant construction (Gram.). ' But Philip was found *at* Azotus ' is in the Greek ' But Philip was found *to* Azotus ' ; i. e., the expressed sentence contains an implied one— Philip was conveyed to & Philip was found at Azotus. Though we cannot (except in the dialect of Devon &c.) say He was found to Azotus, we do habitually say Put it in your pocket, meaning Put it in(to & keep it in) your pocket.

premise (Log.) ; ' thing sent before '. See *syllogism* below.

privative (Gram.) ; ' taking away '. Prefixes that deny the presence of the quality denoted by the simple word are called *p.* or *negative*. The a- of *aseptic* & the in- of *innocent* are privative, whereas the a- of *arise* & the in- of *insist* are not.

proclitic (Gram.) ; ' forward-leaning '. In Greek, certain words that coalesce in speech with the following word to the extent of not having, like other words, a written accent of their own. Applied in English to words like *a* or *an*, *the*, & prepositions normally placed, i. e. before their nouns.

prolate, -lative (Gram.) ; ' carrying forward '. Many verbs have meanings that are not self-sufficient, but need to be carried forward by another verb in the infinitive ; such are the auxiliaries, & other verbs meaning be able or willing or wont or desirous, begin, cease, seem, be said, &c. This infinitive is called prolate or prolative.

prolepsis (adj. *-ptic*) (Gram.) ; ' anticipating '. Anticipatory use of an epithet, i. e. the applying of it as if already true to a thing of which it only becomes true by or after the action now being stated. A strong example is

So the two brothers & their *murder'd* man

Rode past fair Florence

i. e., the man who was afterwards their victim. More ordinary examples are He struck him dead, Fill full the cup, &c.

prosody (Lit.) ; 'to song'. The science of versification, including (1) the rules of quantity & accent governing the pronunciation of words in a language, & (2) tables of the various metres showing the number & kind & arrangement of feet, lines, stanzas, &c., in each.

prosopopoeia (Rhet.) ; 'personification'. The Greek word of which *personificatio(n)* are the Latin & the English translations, occasionally used instead of the more familiar term. See PERSONIFICATION.

protasis (Gram.) ; 'laying out before'. The subordinate clause or condition in a conditional sentence, normally standing before the apodosis or result, but often after it, as *If I can come I will*, or *I will come if I can*, the *if*-clause being in each the p. Applied also to other subordinate clauses ; but both terms are chiefly used in stating rules for the syntax of conditional sentences, especially in Latin & Greek.

pyrrhic (Pros.) ; 'of the Pyrrhic (dance)'. The foot ◡◡ ; in English represented chiefly by double *anacrusis* (see above), as *O my* in

O my/Mari/on's a/bonny/lass

(a trochaic dimeter catalectic with double anacrusis).

quaternarius (Pros.) ; 'by fours'. A four-foot line, esp. the iambic or trochaic dimeter acatalectic, as in The way was long, the wind was cold. Why so pale & wan, fond lover ? Cf. *senarius* below.

quatorzain, quatrain, (Pros.) ; 'fourteener', 'fourer'. See -STICH.

quinarius (Pros.) ; 'by fives'. A five-foot line, esp. of iambi as in blank verse ; cf. *senarius* below. Old John of Gaunt, time-honour'd Lancaster.

reciprocal (Gram.) ; 'back-forward'. R. pronouns are those used in expressing similar action of A

upon B & B upon A ; *r. verb* is a term sometimes applied to verbs that can be used with a plural subject to denote mutual action ; e. g., *we fought*, or *argued*, or *corresponded*, can imply an unexpressed *(with) each other*, whereas *we shaved*, or *composed*, or *dressed*, cannot. Cf. *reflexive* below.

reductio ad absurdum (Log.) ; 'reducing to absurdity'. The method of disproving a thesis by producing something that is both obviously deducible from it & obviously contrary to admitted truth, or of proving one by showing that its contrary involves a consequence similarly absurd. A r. a. a. of the theory that the less one eats the healthier one is would be 'Consequently, to eat nothing at all gives one the best possible health'. The proof, as opp. disproof, by r. a. a. is the form often used by Euclid, e. g. in I. vi, where the contrary of the thing to be proved is assumed, & shown to lead to an absurdity. An extreme case, such as the eating nothing of the instance above, is often called 'the r. a. a. of' a plan.

reduplication (Gram.) ; 'doubling'. Repetition of a sound as a way of changing a word's form for inflexional or other purposes ; especially the syllable prefixed to Greek verb-stems in forming the perfect (*luō*, perf. *leluka*). *Mamma*, *poohpooh*, *puffpuff*, &c., are reduplications.

reflexive (Gram.) ; 'back-bent'. R. verbs are those of which the object & the subject are the same person or thing. *Pride*, vb, is reflexive, since one prides oneself, not someone else ; & many verbs that are not solely r. can be used reflexively, e. g. *kill* one*self*. R. pronouns are those serving as object to r. verbs, *myself* &c. ; the personal pronouns *me*, *you*, &c., are still rarely used as reflexives, e. g. in *He sat him down, I bethought me*.

resolution (vb, *resolve*) (Pros.) ; 'loosen again'. The substitution in a metrical foot of two shorts for a normal long ; a spondee by resolution becomes a dactyl or anapaest ; a resolved iambus or trochee is a tribrach.

revue (Lit.) ; ' review '. A loosely constructed play or series of scenes or spectacles satirizing, exhibiting, or referring to, current fashions & events.

rhetorical question (Rhet.). A question is often put not to elicit information, but as a more striking substitute for a statement of contrary effect. The assumption is that only one answer is possible, & that if the hearer is compelled to make it mentally himself it will impress him more than the speaker's statement. So *Who does not know . . . ?* for *Everyone knows*, *Was ever such nonsense written ?* for *Never was* &c.

rhotacism (Gram.) ; ' saying r '. Used of two tendencies : (1) abnormal pronunciation of r, as in some English dialects especially in the north ; (2) reduction of other consonants to r, especially in Latin when s between two vowels becomes r (*corpus*, *vulnus*, genitive *corporis*, *vulneris*).

rhyme (Pros.) ; ' rhythm '. As now understood in English verse, r. is identity of sound between words or lines extending back from the end to the last fully accented vowel & not farther ; *greet* & *deceit*, *shepherd* & *leopard*, *quality* & *frivolity*, *stationery* & *probationary*, are rhymes ; *seat* & *deceit*, *station* & *crustacean*, *visible* & *invisible*, are not. Words that, to judge from spelling, might have been rhymes, but have not in fact the required identity of sound, as *phase* & *race*, *love* & *move* & *cove*, are often treated as rhyming, but are called imperfect rhymes. One-syllable rhymes are called *male* or *masculine* or *single*, two-syllable *female* or *feminine* or *double*, three-syllable & four-syllable *triple* & *quadruple*.

rhyme royal (Pros.). A metre in stanzas of seven five-foot iambic lines rhyming ababbcc. Chaucer's *Clerk's Tale* is a well-known example :

This sergeant cam unto his lord ageyn,
And of Grisildis wordes and hir chere
He tolde him point for point, in short and playn,
And him presenteth with his doghter dere.
Somwhat this lord hath rewthe in his manere ;
But natheless his purpos heeld he stille,
As lordes doon, whan they wol han hir wille.

RHYTHM (Rhet.) ; ' flow '.

rider (Lit.). A clause tacked on to a Bill at a late stage with some addition or restriction or other alteration ; a corollary naturally arising out of a more general principle ; a problem soluble by means of some principle & used to test a learner's grasp of it.

rococo (Art) ; ' rockwork '. This & *baroque* are epithets applied, sometimes indifferently, sometimes with the distinction noted below, to tendencies prevailing in the architecture & furniture of the early 18th century in France & imitated elsewhere. Departure from the normal or expected, incongruous combinations, bristling surfaces, profuse ornament, strange or broken curves or lines, are the characteristic features. The distinction referred to is that r. is regarded as a form taken by b. when it aimed no longer at astounding the spectator with the marvellous, but rather at amusing him with the ingenious.

rondeau, *rondeau of Villon*, *rondel*, *roundel*, (Pros.) ; ' round '. Poems of fixed form (named as ending where they began) with the common characteristics that the opening word, words, line, or two lines, recur at stated places, & that all rhymes are set by the first two different endings.

In a *rondeau*, which is of thirteen lines exclusive of refrain, the first half line or less recurs as refrain after the eighth & the last lines.

In a *rondeau of Villon*, which is of

ten lines, the similar refrain is after the sixth & the last.

In a *rondel*, which is of fourteen or thirteen lines according as it ends with a refrain of the first two or only the first, the first two lines recur after the sixth, & the first two or the first only at the end.

The word *roundel* is, as ordinarily used, the English for rondeau or rondel, either or both. But it is also applied to a metre of Swinburne's, of nine lines exclusive of refrain, with a refrain of the rondeau kind after the third & the last lines.

RONDEAU

On London stones I sometimes sigh
For wider green & bluer sky ;—
   Too oft the trembling note is drowned
   In this huge city's varied sound;—
' Pure song is country-born '—I cry.

Then comes the spring,—the months go by,
The last stray swallows seaward fly ;
   And I—I too !—no more am found
         On London stones !

In vain !—the woods, the fields deny
That clearer strain I fain would try ;
   Mine is an urban Muse, & bound
   By some strange law to paven ground ;
Abroad she pouts ;—she is not shy
         On London stones.

RONDEAU OF VILLON

We loved of yore, in warfare bold,
   Nor laurelless. Now all must go ;
   Let this left wall of Venus show
The arms, the tuneless lyre of old.

Here let them hang, the torches cold,
   The portal-bursting bar, the bow,
         We loved of yore.

But thou, who Cyprus sweet dost hold,
   And Memphis free from Thracian snow,
   Goddess & queen, with vengeful blow
Smite,—smite but once that pretty scold
         We loved of yore.

RONDEL

Love comes back to his vacant dwelling,—
   The old, old Love that we knew of yore !
   We see him stand by the open door,
With his great eyes sad, & his bosom swelling.

He makes as though in our arms repelling
   He fain would lie as he lay before ;—
Love comes back to his vacant dwelling,—
   The old, old Love that we knew of yore !

Ah, who shall help us from over-spelling
That sweet forgotten, forbidden lore !
E'en as we doubt in our hearts once more,
With a rush of tears to our eyelids welling,
Love comes back to his vacant dwelling.

ROUNDEL OF SWINBURNE

A roundel is wrought as a ring or a starbright sphere,
With craft of delight & with cunning of sound unsought,
That the heart of the hearer may smile if to pleasure his ear
A roundel is wrought.

Its jewel of music is carven of all or of aught—
Love, laughter, or mourning—remembrance of rapture or fear—
That fancy may fashion to hang in the ear of thought.

As a bird's quick song runs round, & the hearts in us hear
Pause answer to pause, & again the same strain caught,
So moves the device whence, round as a pearl or tear,
A roundel is wrought.

root (Gram.). Roots are the ultimate elements of language not admitting of analysis. In the word *unhistorically*, un-, -ly, -al, -ic, -tor, can all be set aside as successive affixes modifying in recognized ways the meaning of what each was added to. There remains HIS, which would be called the root if *unhistorically* were an isolated word ; investigation shows that the same element, with phonetic variations that are not arbitrary, is present in many other words, e. g. in English *wit*, in the Latin-derived *vision*, & in the Greek-derived *idea* ; & that the Indo-European or Aryan root is VID, with the sense sight or knowledge. Cf. *stem* below.

roundel. See *rondeau* above.

rune (Lit.) ; ' secret '. In the plural, the letters of the earliest Teutonic alphabet, used especially by Scandinavians & Anglo-Saxons, & developed perhaps in the 2nd or 3rd century by modifying Roman or Greek letters to facilitate the carving of inscriptions. In the singular, a name given to certain Finnish (& sometimes incorrectly to old Scandinavian) poems or their cantos.

saga (Lit.) ; ' story '. ' Any of the narrative compositions in prose that were written in Iceland or Norway during the middle ages ; in English use often applied *spec.* to those which embody the traditional history of Icelandic families or of the kings of Norway '—OED.

sapphics (Pros.) ; ' of Sappho '. A Greek & Latin stanza metre

$$-\cup--/\cup\cup-\cup-\underline{\cup} \; ter$$
$$-\cup\cup-\underline{\cup}$$

often imitated, but with grotesque misrepresentation of the rhythm, in English. Hookham Frere, joint author with Canning of the best-known example, ' Needy knife-grinder ', illustrates the departure from the Latin rhythm by printing an English sapphic with the impossible quantities required :

Cŏld wăs *thē* nīght wīnd ; drīftĭng fāst thĕ snŏws fĕll ;

Wīde wĕre *thē* dōwns, *ānd* shĕltĕr*lēss* ănd nākĕd ;

Whĕn ă pōōr wănd'*rēr* strŭgglĕd ŏn hĕr jŏurnĕy Wēarў ănd wāysŏre.

Real sapphics would require a strong accent on the italic syllables, & no accent on *drift-*, *shel-*, & *strug-*, besides minor differences.

SARCASM (Lit.) ; ' flesh-tearing '.

satire (Lit.) ; ' medley '. See HUMOUR.

Saturnian verse (Pros.) ; ' of Saturn '. The supposed native Roman metre previous to the adoption of Greek forms. Whether it was a single definite metre, &, if so, what its scansion was, are disputed points; but the usually quoted specimen, *Dabunt malum Metelli Naevio poetae*, resembles in rhythm our *The queen was in her parlour eating bread & honey.*

scazon (Pros.) ; ' limping '. See *choliambic* above.

semivowel (Gram.) ; In modern technical use, the letters w & y ; but often applied, as in earlier use, to f, l, m, n, r, s, & x.

senarius (Pros.) ; ' by sixes '. A six-foot iambic line (iambic trimeter acatalectic). The line used in Greek & Latin dramatic dialogue, &, under the name of *alexandrine*, in the rhyming couplets of French plays & other verse. The French metre, however, has the peculiarity that it falls naturally into four anapaestic divisions rather than into six iambi, so that the effect is utterly unlike that of Greek verse. Thus :

Et, quand même/on pourroit/se resoudre/à le faire,
Croiriez-vous/obliger/tout le monde /à se taire ?
Contre la/médisance/il n'est point /de rempart.
A tous les/sots caquets/n'ayons donc/nul égard ;
Efforçons/-nous de vivre/avec toute /innocence
Et laissons/aux causeurs/une plein/e licence.

septenarius (Pros.) ; ' by sevens '. A seven-foot line, especially the trochaic tetrameter catalectic, —∪—∪—∪—∪—∪—∪—, as in *Comrades, leave me here a little, while as yet 'tis early morn*, which, however, should more properly be called an octonarius.

SEQUENCE (Gram.) ; ' following '.

sestina (Pros.) ; ' sixth '. ' A poem of six six-line stanzas (with an envoy) in which the line-endings of the first stanza are repeated, but in different order, in the other five '—OED. Chiefly an old Provençal, Italian, & French form, but occasionally copied in English; the most generally accessible example (since the length forbids the giving of one here) is Kipling's *Sestina of the Tramp Royal* in *The Seven Seas*.

sibilant (Gram.) ; ' hissing '. A sound or letter of the nature of s, z, sh, &c. ; cf. *fricative* above.

SIMILE (Rhet.) ; ' like '.

sirvente (Lit.) ; ' serving ' (perhaps in sense *man at arms*). Troubadours' poems not of special metrical form, but chiefly of moral & political satire, & adapted for singing to known tunes.

soliloquy (Lit.) ; ' sole speech '. See *monologue* above.

sonant (Gram.) ; ' sounding '. Of the *explosive* sounds (see above). some (b, d, g) are accompanied by vibration of the vocal cords & are called *voiced* or *sonant* ; others (p, k, t) are without such vibration & are called *unvoiced, voiceless, mute*, or *surd* ; when whispered, the sonants are not clearly distinguishable from the corresponding surds. See also *voiced* below.

sonnet (Pros.) ; ' sound-piece '. A kind of short poem of which there are in English three recognized varieties, the features common to all being (1) use of rhyme, (2) the line-metre, of five iambi, (3) the number of lines, fourteen, & (4) division into an octave (first eight lines) & a sestet (last six). The three varieties are the Petrarchan, the Shaksperian, & the Miltonic, of which specimens will be given.

The *Petrarchan s.* has a break in sense between octave & sestet, two rhymes only in the octave, arranged abbaabba, & two, or three, other rhymes in the sestet variously arranged, but never so that the last two lines form a rhymed couplet unless they also rhyme with the first line of the sestet. The following Wordsworth s. observes these rules :—

The world is too much with us ; late & soon,
Getting & spending, we lay waste our powers :
Little we see in Nature that is ours ;
We have given our hearts away, a sordid boon !
This Sea that bares her bosom to the moon ;
The winds that will be howling at all hours,
And are up-gathered now like sleeping flowers ;
For this, for every thing, we are out of tune ; [octave]
It moves us not.—Great God ! I'd rather be
A pagan suckled in a creed outworn ;
So might I, standing on this pleasant lea,
Have glimpses that would make me less forlorn ;
Have sight of Proteus rising from the sea ;
Or hear old Triton blow his wreathèd horn.

In the *Shaksperian s.*, though the pause between octave & sestet is present, the structure consists less of those two parts than of three quatrains, each with two independent rhymes, followed by a couplet again independently rhymed—seven rhymes as compared with the Petrarchan four or five :—

Let me not to the marriage of true minds
Admit impediments. Love is not love
Which alters when it alteration finds,
Or bends with the remover to remove :
O, no ! it is an ever-fixed mark
That looks on tempests & is never shaken ;
It is the star to every wandering bark,
Whose worth 's unknown, although his height be taken. [octave]
Love 's not Time's fool, though rosy lips & cheeks
Within his bending sickle's compass come ;
Love alters not with his brief hours & weeks,
But bears it out even to the edge of doom.
  If this be error & upon me proved,
  I never writ, nor no man ever loved.

Of the *Miltonic s.*, which follows the Petrarchan in the arrangement of the octave, the peculiarity is that the octave & the sestet are worked into one whole without the break of sense elsewhere observed :—

When I consider how my light is spent
Ere half my days in this dark world & wide,
And that one talent which is death to hide
Lodged with me useless, though my soul more bent
To serve therewith my Maker, & present
My true account, lest He, returning, chide,
' Doth God exact day-labour, light denied ? '
I fondly ask. But Patience, to prevent [octave]
That murmur, soon replies ' God doth not need
Either man's work or his own gifts. Who best
Bear his mild yoke, they serve him best. His state
Is kingly ; thousands at his bidding speed,
And post o'er land & ocean without rest ;
They also serve who only stand & wait '.

sorites (Log.) ; ' heap '. Applied to two entirely different things. 1. A process by which a predicate is brought into the desired relation to a subject by a series of propositions in which the predicate of one becomes the subject of the next, & the conclusion has the first subject & the last predicate. Thus : Schoolmasters are teachers ; Teachers are benefactors ; Benefactors are praiseworthy ; Therefore schoolmasters are praiseworthy. A sorites may be a short way of exhibiting truth, or, as in the above example, may conceal fallacies at each or any step. 2. A logical trick named from the difficulty of deciding how many

grains of corn make a heap ; is a man bald who has 1000, 1001, 1002, &c., hairs on his head ? If the Almighty cannot undo the done, where is the line of almightiness to be drawn ?

Spenserians (Pros.). The metre of the *Faerie Queen*, often used by later poets, especially by Byron in *Childe Harold*; eight five-foot & a ninth six-foot iambic lines, rhyming ababbcbcc.

> A gentle Knight was pricking on the plaine,
> Ycladd in mightie armes & silver shielde,
> Wherein old dints of deepe wounds did remaine,
> The cruel markes of many a bloudy fielde ;
> Yet armes till that time did he never wield :
> His angry steede did chide his foming bitt,
> As much disdayning to the curbe to yield :
> Full jolly knight he seemd, & faire did sitt,
> As one for knightly giusts & fierce encounters fitt.

spirant (Gram.) ; ' breathing '. ' A consonant which admits of a continued emission of some amount of breath, so that the sound is capable of being prolonged '—OED. Sometimes confined to f, th, v, as developed from p, t or d, b, followed by h ; sometimes including also the sibilants, liquids, nasals, semivowels, & aspirate. Cf. also *fricative* & *aspirate* above.

spondee (Pros.) ; ' libation '. The foot — —, as in *gold cup* or *dry rot*.

stanza (Pros.) ; ' standing '. Many poems consist of a succession of metrically similar line-groups each of which has the same number & length of lines & the same rhyme-scheme as the rest. This pattern unit is called, especially when of more than two lines, a stanza. It may be of a generally accepted kind, as the alcaic or Spenserian or rhyme royal s., or one made for the occasion & observed throughout a single poem only.

stem (Gram.). A word's stem is the part from which its inflexions may be supposed to have been formed by the addition of affixes ; in the inflexions it may be found unchanged, or may have been affected by phonetic tendencies ; thus the s. of

man is *man*, giving *man's*, *men*, & *men's*. Cf. *root* above ; of the English verb *wit* the root is VID, but the stem, giving *wit*, *wot*, *wist*, *wottest*, &c., is *wit*. Different parts of a ' word ' may be formed from different stems ; there are e. g. several stems in what is called the verb *be*.

stichomyth (Lit.) ; ' line-talk '. In verse plays, interchange of short speeches consisting each of a single line. Common in Greek plays ; & modern examples may be found in *Les Femmes Savantes* iii. v & *Richard III*, iv. iv. 342 foll.

stop (Gram.). For punctuation, see STOPS. In phonetics, *stop* is a term equivalent to *explosive* (see above).

strophe (Pros.) ; ' turn '. Part of a Greek choric ode chanted while the chorus proceeded in one direction, to be followed by a metrically exact counterpart as it returned. Number & length & metre of the lines composing it unrestricted. For an example see *antistrophe* above.

subjective genitive (Gram.). See *objective genitive* above for the principle. If from the sentence *God created man* two nouns are taken, *God's creation* contains a subjective genitive, & *man's creation* (or usually *the creation of man*) an objective genitive.

suffix (Gram.) ; ' attached below '. An *affix* (see above) at the end of a word or stem to make a derivative, as -cy, -ship, -ful, in *tenan(t)cy, lordship,* & *fearful.*

suggestio falsi (Rhet.) ; ' suggestion of the untrue '. The making of a statement from which, though it is not actually false, the natural & intended inference is a false one. E.g., if A, asked whether B is honest, replies, though he in fact knows no harm of B, that his principle is to live & let live & he is not going to give away his old friend, the questioner infers that A knows B to be dishonest. Cf. *suppressio veri* below.

supine (Gram.) ; ' lying face up '. A Latin-grammar term for two verbal nouns (or adverbs) ending in -um, -u, of no importance in English grammar except as an occasional name for the infinitive with *to* (*to go*) as distinguished from the infinitive without *to* (*go*).

suppressio veri (Rhet.) ; ' suppression of the true '. Intentional withholding of a material fact with a view to affecting a decision &c. ; cf. *suggestio falsi* above.

surd (Gram.) ; ' deaf, dumb '. See *sonant* above.

syllepsis & *zeugma* (Gram., Rhet.) ; ' taking together ', ' yoking '. Two figures distinguished by scholars, but confused in popular use, the second more familiar word being applied to both. Examples of syllepsis are : Miss Bolo went home *in* a flood of tears & a sedan chair./ He *lost* his hat & his temper./The *flood* of enthusiasm & flowers was terrific./She was seen washing clothes *with* happiness & Pears' soap.

Examples of zeugma are : *Kill* the boys & the luggage !/The pineapple *was* eaten & the apples neglected./With *weeping* eyes & hearts./See Pan with flocks, with fruits Pomona *crowned.*

What is common to both figures is that a single word (that italicized in each example) is in relations that seem to be but are not the same with a pair of others. The difference is that syllepsis is grammatically correct, but requires the single word to be understood in a different sense with each of its pair (e.g., in the last *with* expresses first accompaniment, but secondly instrument), whereas in zeugma the single word actually fails to give sense with one of its pair, & from it the appropriate word has to be supplied—*destroy* or *plunder* the luggage, the apples *were* neglected, *bleeding* hearts, Pan *surrounded.*

syllogism (Log.) ; ' combined reasoning '. Deduction, from two propositions containing three terms of which one appears in both, of a conclusion that is necessarily true if they are true ; a s. of the simplest form is :

All men are mortal ;
All Germans are men ;
Therefore all Germans are mortal.

The predicate of the conclusion (here *mortal*) is called the *major term,* & the preliminary proposition containing it the *major premise* ; the subject of the conclusion (here *Germans*) is called the *minor term,* & the preliminary proposition containing it the *minor premise.* The term common to both premises (here *men*) is called the *middle term.*

synaeresis (Gram.) ; ' taking together '. The opposite of *diaeresis* (see above) ; i. e., the making of two separate vowel sounds into one, as when *aerial* is pronounced like *Ariel, naïve* like *nave, extraordinary* as -*trord-,* or *cocaine* (originally three syllables) as -*cane.*

synaloepha (Pros.) ; ' smearing together '. The non-sounding of a final vowel before an initial vowel, whether indicated by written elision as in Greek verse or left to the reader's perception as in Latin verse. Cf. *crasis* & *prodelision* above, & *synizesis* below.

synaphea (Pros.) ; ' joining together '. In most Latin & Greek verse, the last syllable of each line is exempt from the strict metrical requirements, i.e. it may be either long or short, & is not, if it ends in a vowel, subject to elision before a vowel beginning the next line. But regularly in some metres, & by exception in others, the end of a line is regarded as continuous with the next line, & e.g. a syllable more than is needed to complete the metre of the line may be used, & elided. The treatment of lines as continuous is called synaphea ; verse treated on the ordinary principle that each line is metrically detached from the next is said to have no s. English blank verse has no s., as is shown by the fact that the fifth foot may have one or even two extra (unaccented) syllables after the accented one that completes the metre. E.g., the line *Look, where he comes ! Not poppy nor mandragora* is not an alexandrine, but a five-foot line with *mandrag(ora)* as the fifth foot.

syncopation (Gram., Mus.) ; ' cutting together '. In grammar, the use of *syncope* (see below). In music (a use lately much popularized by the advent of ragtime songs, jazz dances, &c.) the OED definition is : The action of beginning a note on a normally unaccented part of the bar & sustaining it into the normally accented part, so as to produce the effect of shifting back or anticipating the accent ; the shifting of accent so produced.

syncope (Gram.) ; ' cutting together '. The shortening of a word by omission of a syllable or other part in the middle ; cf. *aphaeresis* & *apocope* above. *Symbology & pacifist & idolatry* for *symbolology, pacificist, & idololatry*, are examples.

synecdoche (Rhet.) ; ' inclusive extended acceptation '. The mention of a part when the whole is to be understood, as in *A fleet of fifty sail* (i.e. ships), or vice versâ as in *England* (i.e. the English cricket XI) *won*.

synesis (Gram.) ; ' meaning '. The

adapting of the number &c. of a word to the meaning instead of to the grammatical form of the word that should determine it, as in *A large number were* (instead of *was*) *killed.*

synizesis (Pros.) ; ' sitting together '. In Greek verse, the counting of two long vowels, the first ending & the second beginning a word, as one syllable, without written elision ; rare except in certain combinations, as ἐπεὶ οὐ.

SYNONYM (Rhet.) ; ' with-name '.

syntax (Gram.) ; ' combined order '. The part of grammar concerned not with the etymology, formation, & inflexion, of words, but with the arrangement of them in sentences. Cf. *accidence* above.

tercet (Pros.) ; ' third '. A three-line group, especially one of those composing *terza rima* (see below), or half the sestet of a *sonnet* (see above). Cf. -STICH.

term (Log.). For *major, minor, middle, t.* see *syllogism* above.

terza rima (Pros.) ; ' third rhyme '. Dante's metre in the *Divina Commedia*—lines of five iambic feet with an extra syllable, so rhymed that every rhyme occurs thrice in alternate lines, except the rhymes of the first & last lines of a canto, which occur twice only. In every *tercet* (see above) reckoned from the beginning, the first & third lines rhyme while the second introduces a new rhyme to be carried on by the first & third of the next tercet, giving an effect of unending continuity to the piece. The last tercet is converted by an extra line into a quartet, to avoid the leaving of a line unrhymed. Dante's t. r. has double or feminine rhyme throughout. English imitations, since English has no such abundance of trochaic endings as Italian, have mostly single or masculine rhymes & ten instead of the Italian eleven syllables. The following lines of Byron, being three tercets & a line, show the same rhyme scheme at beginning & end as if they were a whole canto :—

Oh ! more than these illustrious far shall be
The being—& even yet he may be born—
The mortal saviour who shall set thee free,
And see thy diadem, so changed & worn
By fresh barbarians, on thy brow replaced ;
And the sweet sun replenishing thy morn,
Thy moral morn, too long with clouds defaced,
And noxious vapours from Avernus risen,
Such as all they must breathe who are debased
By servitude, & have the mind in prison.

tetralogy (Lit.) ; ' four pieces '. In ancient Athens, a *trilogy* (see below) with the addition of a satyric drama or comic play with chorus of satyrs, forming the unit offered by each competitor for the tragic prize. Now, any set of four connected plays or tales.

tetrameter (Pros.). See *-meter* above.

tetrastich (Pros.). See -STICH.

thesis (Pros.) ; ' putting down '. The unaccented part of a foot. See *arsis* above ; syllables not marked with an accent in the examples there given are said to be *in thesis*.

tmesis (Gram.) ; ' cutting '. Separation of the parts of a compound word by another word inserted between them, as when ' toward us ' is written *to usward*, or ' whatsoever things ' *what things soever*.

tribrach (Pros.) ; ' three short '. The foot ∪∪∪, chiefly serving as the resolved equivalent of a trochee or iambus, in Greek & Latin verse. English scansion is so loose that any example is of doubtful validity ; but the following line may be said to begin with a t. :

Travel you/far on,/or are/you at/ the farthest ?

trill (Gram.). A letter pronounced with vibration of the tongue or uvula, especially r.

trilogy (Lit.) ; ' three pieces '. In ancient Athens, there were dramatic competitions at which each dramatist presented three plays, originally giving successive parts of the same legend ; the extant *Agamemnon, Choephoroe, & Eumenides*, of Aeschylus formed a trilogy, &, with the addition of the lost *Proteus*, a *tetralogy* (see above). Later trilogies were connected not necessarily by a common subject, but by being works of the same poet presented on the same occasion. In modern use the word is applied to a work such as Shakspere's *Henry IV*, comprising three separate plays, or to a novel &c. with two sequels.

trimeter (Pros.). See *-meter* above.

triolet (Pros.) ; ' three-piece '; An eight-line poem in which the first line occurs thrice (1, 4, 7) & the second twice (2, 8), & the other lines rhyme with these two. An example (Robert Bridges) is :

All women born are so perverse
No man need boast their love
 possessing.
If nought seem better, nothing 's
 worse :
All women born are so perverse.
From Adam's wife, that proved a
 curse
Though God had made her for a
 blessing,
All women born are so perverse
No man need boast their love
 possessing.

triplet (Pros.). See -STICH. Applied specially to the occasional use, in rhymed-couplet metres, of three lines instead of two to a rhyme ; common in heroic couplets, especially in Dryden ; the following example is from Scott :

The humble boon was soon obtained;
The aged minstrel audience gained.
But when he reached the room of
 state,
Where she, with all her ladies, sate,
Perchance he wished his boon
 denied :
For, when to tune his harp he tried,

His trembling hand had lost the ease,
Which marks security to please;
And scenes, long past, of joy & pain,
Came wildering o'er his aged brain—
He tried to tune his harp in vain !
The pitying duchess praised its chime,
And gave him heart, & gave him time,
Till every string's according glee
Was blended into harmony.

tristich (Pros.) ; ' three-line '. See -STICH.

trochee (Pros.) ; ' running '. The foot $-\cup$, as in *manner* or *body*.

tu quoque (Rhet.) ; ' thou also '. The meeting of a charge or argument not by disproof &c. but by retorting it upon its user. E. g., Why don't you go yourself ? to a civilian urging one to enlist.

turn-over (Lit.). A light newspaper article named from beginning near the end of the first page & continuing into the second, & resembling the *middle article* (see above), but usually of a more journalistic & less literary tone.

ultima (Gram.) ; ' last '. The last syllable of a word ; see *antepenult* above.

uncial (Palaeog.) ; ' inch '. The style of writing, consisting of large letters, some of them rounded from the angular capital forms, but not run together, found in early Greek & Latin MSS. The later & smaller writing in MSS., in which the letters are further rounded, slanted, & run together, is called *cursive*. The terms *majuscule* & *minuscule* are sometimes used as synonyms of *uncial* & *cursive*, but strictly *majuscule* includes both capital & uncial writing, whereas *minuscule* & *cursive*, applied to MSS., are coextensive.

undistributed middle (Log.). A *fallacy* (see above). The u. m. is the logical name for a middle term that is not made universal ; see *syllogism* above, where the middle term *men*

is made universal by the word *all*, or ' distributed '. Such distribution is necessary to the validity of the conclusion, & *the fallacy of the u. m.* consists in allowing a middle term that is not universalized to pass as universally true. Thus we know or believe that wet feet result in colds ; we catch cold, & say ' I must have got my feet wet ' ; i. e., in syllogistic form :

Colds are wet-feet products.
My trouble is a cold.
Therefore my trouble is a wet-feet product.
Which would be sound if colds meant all colds, but not if it merely means some colds.

unvoiced (Gram.). See *sonant* above.

velar (Gram.) ; ' of the curtain (i. e. the soft palate) '. Applied to gutturals made farther back than the hard palate, esp. in dealing with the original Indo-European language ; see guttural & palatal above.

vers libre (Lit.) ; ' free verse '. Versification or verses in which different metres are mingled, or prosodical restrictions disregarded, or variable rhythm substituted for definite metre. A number of short specimens follow, collected from notices in the *Times Literary Supplement* :—

1. Colour, thick as dust, lay
   Spattered about the highway—
   Colour so bright that one would think
   White, blue, cherry-pink
   Were made to clutch and drink.
   Colour that made one stop and say :—
   ' Earth, are you Heaven to-day ? '
   Colour that made one pray.
   Lumps of colour, liquid and cool,
   Cool and near,
   Clear and gay,
   Tumbled about my way.

2. Life—give me life until the end,
   That at the very top of being,
   The battle-spirit shouting in my blood,

Out of the reddest hell of the
fight
I may be snatched and flung
Into the everlasting lull,
The immortal incommunicable
dream.

8. Because I saw her pass
With the flickering candle-light
Across her bosom's curve,
A circle on the wall,
In which she moved,
Alone,
Up to her little room.

4. Within an office whose exterior
Resembles an ultra-conservative
mind
You battle with the avaricious
words
Of a meager, petrified man.
Your face is brown stagnation
Sometimes astounded by a thrust
Of chattering wistfulness.
Bravery is fear
Effectively sneering at itself,
And you are forever wavering
Upon the edge of this condition.
Yet your obscurity
Is an important atom
In the mysterious march of time.

[A sonnet, skeletonized to modern
formula—*Times*]

5.   With running laughter
Her cailins came out of the
grassy morning
Calling her, and fierce hawks
rose from the trees
Around them.   Rushing down
the rocky glenside
They sobbed among the grum-
bling kerns and pulled
Their tumbling hair about them,
moaning : ' Ochone.'

6. Messengers,
Of varied fate,
Of pitch and toss and gain,
Of life and driven time,
And the inane
Of jesters.

7. Out into a green backyard came
a woman in a blue apron
Carrying yellow meal in a bright
tin pail.

The chickens came running ;
And those little hungry sparrows
that are my thoughts
All day teasing and quarrelling,
Settled down on the grass among
the plump flock,
Greedy and pleased.

8. Phœnix, bird of terrible pride,
ruddy eye and iron beak !
Come, leave the incinerary nest ;
spread your red wings.

And soaring in the golden light
survey the world ;
hover against the highest sky ;
menace men with your strange
phenomena.

9. We stand in the crowd, craning
our necks,
To see in small cages linnets new
caught,
And a puppy of dubious descent
is waved in our faces, and
here
With the daylight dimming his
eyes is an owl, fluffy, solemn
and queer.

10. Jammy-mouth from the feasts
of the gods
From the far crystal cities
We come,
Where in talking trees
The old beast sings
To himself
And his voice
Is terrible to the kings of
cities.
From this globular grey hubble-
bubble
We come.

vicious circle. In logic, *circle* &
vicious circle mean the same—the
basing of a conclusion on a premise
that is itself based on this conclusion ; for an example see *arguing in
a circle* above.   The phrase *v. c.* is
also applied outside logic to the
reaction between two evils that
aggravate each other : The wrecked
sailor's thirst makes him drink salt
water ; the salt increases his thirst.
villanelle (Pros.) ; ' country-piece '.
A form of poem in five (or more)
tercets & a quatrain, all on two

rhymes, one that in the middle line of each tercet & the second line of the quatrain, the other everywhere else. The first line ends the second & the fourth tercet ; the third line ends the first, third, & fifth tercets ; & the quatrain ends with the first & third lines. Example, from Austin Dobson :

When I saw you last, Rose,
You were only so high ;—
How fast the time goes !

Like a bud ere it blows,
You just peeped at the sky,
When I saw you last, Rose !

Now your petals unclose,
Now your May-time is nigh ;—
How fast the time goes !

And a life,—how it grows !
You were scarcely so shy,
When I saw you last, Rose !

In your bosom it shows
There 's a guest on the sly ;
(How fast the time goes !)

Is it Cupid ? Who knows !
Yet you used not to sigh,
When I saw you last, Rose ;—
How fast the time goes !

voiced (Gram.). See *sonant* above.

weak ending (Pros.). Blank-verse lines whose last word is a proclitic (e.g. a preposition with its noun still to come, the *if* of a clause, the auxiliary *have*) are said to have weak endings. These are of importance in determining the sequence of Shakspere's plays, being more frequent in the later. Examples :

    You demi-puppets that
By moonshine do the green sour ring-
    lets make.
    That calflike they my lowing
    followed through
Tooth'd briers.
Not a relation for a breakfast, nor
Befitting this first meeting.
    But, howsoe'er you have
Been justled from your senses, know
    for certain.

zeugma. See *syllepsis* above.

techy. See TETCHY.

teens (*in* one's *t.* &c.). No apostrophe.

teethe, teething. For the dh sound, see TH & DH.

teetotaller, but *teetotalism* ; see -LL-, -L-.

telephone, vb, makes -*nable* ; see MUTE E.

temerarious. ' Now only literary ' —OED ; see LITERARY WORDS.

templet, -plate. The -*et* form is better, the other being due to false association with *plate* in *wall-plate* &c.

temptress. See FEMININE DESIGNATIONS.

tenant. *Tenant farmer,* & *tenant right,* should be so written without hyphens ; see HYPHENS (3 B for the second, & group *Lord Mayor* for the first).

tempest. See WIND, n.

tend (=*attend*). *Dr Hutton has written an interesting account of the Eskimos of Labrador, among whom he has lived for some years past* tending to *their needs in his hospital.* Since this verb *tend* (unlike the one connected with *tendency*) is said to be merely an aphetic form of *attend,* it is remarkable that its construction & that of *attend* should differ ; but they certainly do ; *tend* one's *needs,* but *attend to* one's *needs* ; see CAST-IRON IDIOM.

tender makes -*er,* -*est* ; -ER & -EST 2.

tendon of Achilles is the English, & *tendo Achillis* the Latin ; mixtures of these should be avoided, & the only other form should be ' the Achilles tendon ' colloquially.

tendril makes *tendrilled* ; -LL-, -L-.

tenet. Pronounce tĕ'nĭt.

tenor. The form *tenour* is called obsolete by the OED for all senses, though it appears in some of its 19th-c. quotations, esp. in the sense course or procedure or purport ; see -OUR & -OR.

TENSES &c. Certain points requiring care will be found under SEQUENCE OF TENSES, SUBJUNCTIVE,

PERFECT INFINITIVE, AS 4, HAD, LEST, SHALL, WILL.

tenuis. Pl. -*uĕs* (-z).

tepefy. For inflexions see VERBS IN -IE &c., 6.

tepid makes -*est*, see -ER & -EST 4.

tercentenary. See CENTENARY.

tercet. See TECHNICAL TERMS.

teredo. English pl., *teredos*, see -O(E)S 6 ; Latin pl. *terē'dĭnēs*, see LATIN PLURALS.

term. For *major, minor, middle, t.* in logic, see TECHNICAL TERMS (*syllogism*).

terminate makes -*nable*, see -ABLE 1 ; & -*tor*, see -OR.

terminological. For *t. inexactitude* see POLYSYLLABIC HUMOUR.

terminus. Pl., even in the commonest sense of railway t., usu. *terminī* ; see LATIN PLURALS.

termly, a. & adv. The word has been so far displaced by *terminal(ly)* that there is now a tinge of affectation in its use. The analogy of *daily, weekly, monthly, yearly*, fails because *term*, unlike *day* &c., is of Latin origin.

tern. See -STICH.

Terpsichore. Pronounce terpsĭ'korĭ ; & see MUSES.

terrain. The justification of the word is that it expresses a complex notion briefly. When it is used as a substitute for *ground, tract, region*, or *district*—good ordinary words—, it lacks the justification that an out-of-the-way word requires, & becomes pretentious. It means a piece of ground with all the peculiarities that fit or unfit it for military or other purposes ; & to speak of ' the peculiarities of the t.', ' the nature of the t.', &c., instead of simply ' the t.', is, though the readers' assumed ignorance may excuse it, a pleonasm.

terrify. For inflexions see VERBS IN -IE &c., 6.

terrorize makes -*zable* ; see MUTE E.

tertium quid. 'A third something'. Originally a mixture of two things, having properties not so well ascertained as those of its elements. In

this sense an alloy, or a chord (' not a fourth sound, but a star '), or ' Fair Trade ', or Anglocatholicism, might be called *t. q.* Now often in the changed sense (the notion of unknown qualities being lost) of another alternative, a middle course, or third member of a set ; so temperance as between drunkenness & teetotalism, suicide as an escape from the choice between poverty & dishonour, or the third person playing propriety for a pair of lovers, is in popular language a t. q.

terza rima. See TECHNICAL TERMS.

tessera. Pl. -*rae*.

test. For synonyms see SIGN.

testatrix. For pl. see -TRIX.

testify. For inflexions see VERBS IN -IE &c., 6.

te(t)chy, touchy. In the sense irritable, over-sensitive, the OED suggests that *touchy* is perhaps an alteration of *techy* ; *techy* (or *teachy*) is the oldest recorded form, but *tetchy* is the usual modern spelling of those who do not prefer *touchy*. As the etymology of *te(t)chy* is unknown, & the much commoner *touchy* gives the same meaning without being a puzzle, any attempt to keep *te(t)chy* alive seems due to a liking for curiosities.

tête-à-tête. See FRENCH WORDS.

tether. For synonyms in the fig. sense see FIELD.

tetralogy, tetrameter. See TECHNICAL TERMS.

tetrastich. See -STICH.

Teutonice, -cè. See LATINE.

thalamus. Pl. -*mī*.

Thalia. See MUSES.

than. 1. *T. & prefer(able)*. 2. *T. &* inversion. 3. Part of verb after *rather t.* 4. *Hardly & scarcely t.* 5. *T.* after *the more* &c. 6. *T.* as strong conjunction, as weak conjunction, & as preposition. 7. Double standard of comparison. 8. *T.* after non-comparatives. 9. *T.* & ellipsis. 10. Flounderings.

1. For *t.* after *prefer & preferable* without *rather*, a common solecism, see PREFER(ABLE) 3.

2. *T.* & inversion. *No tariff-armed nation has got better entry for its potatoes in the U.S.A. market* than has Ireland.*/The evidence could not now be given in the same sense, any more* than could Mr Chamberlain's *speeches of 1903 be now delivered./ The success of the offensive will depend upon its ability to compel the enemy to lose men in a far heavier proportion* than do his assailants.*/The visit will be much more direct in its effect upon the war* than could be any indiscriminate bombing *of open towns.* Such inversions are deprecated ; see INVERSION, esp. the section on inversion after relatives & comparatives, group 2 & comment 2.

3. Infinitive, or gerund &c., after *rather t. They were all in favour of ' dying in the last ditch '* rather than sign *their own death-warrant.* The justification of *sign* instead of *sign-ing* is discussed in -ING 5.

4. *Hardly t., scarcely t. But hardly had I landed at Liverpool* than *the Mikado's death recalled me to Japan.* Read *no sooner* for *hardly*, or *when* for *than* ; & see under HARDLY 2, SCARCELY 1.

5. *T.* after *the more, the less,* &c. *If we simply take the attitude of accepting her theory of naval policy, we make it so much the less probable that she will change her law* than *if we enter into violent contention.* See THE for the wrongness of this construction.

6. *T.* as strong conjunction, weak conjunction, & preposition. In *You treat her worse than I treat her, t.* is a strong or subordinating conjunction, attaching an adverbial clause to its owner *worse.* In *You treat her worse than I,* the same account may be given with the explanation that there is an ellipsis of *treat her ;* or *t.* may be called a weak or coordinating conjunction linking the two similarly constructed nouns *you* & *I.* In *You treat her worse than me,* the same two names for *t.* are possible, but the ellipsis is of *you treat* (not *treat her*), or the similarly constructed nouns are *her* & *me* (not *you*

& *me*) ; those are the possibilities if the sentence is said with the only sense that an educated person gives it. But an uneducated person may mean by it You treat her worse than I treat her ; &, if it is to be so taken, *t.* is not a conjunction of either kind, but a preposition governing *me.* Doubts whether a word is a preposition or a conjunction or both are not unknown ; see e.g. BUT 1 with regard to such phrases as *all but he* (conj.) & *all but him* (prep.) ; usage, also, changes in such matters with time. It is obvious, however, that recognition of *t.* as a preposition makes some sentences ambiguous that could otherwise have only one meaning, & is to that extent undesirable. The OED statement on the preposition use is that, with the special exception of *t. whom,* which is preferred to *t. who* unless both are avoided, ' it is now considered incorrect '. That incorrectness occurs in the four following examples, where *us, him,* & *them,* should be *we, he, they* :—*That international accord will finish by reaching the great mass of the Socialist proletariat of Germany ; no one wishes it more* than us. */On the other hand, the moment he should become weaker* than us . . ./*The butcher of the last few months has been a good deal more obliging* than him *of the war period./ Do not let us split up our energy by having more* than one *society ; the idea is more* than them all.

On the other hand, the subjective *hes* that follow had better have been *him* on the weak-conjunction principle, since the ellipsis required for the strong-conjunction explanation is in each piece awkward, esp. ' no other artist than he was ' :—*If ever Captain O'Connor gives us a second volume, we beg him to engage no other artist* than he *who illustrated the first./The Entente had no better friend* than he *on the other side of the Atlantic.*

7. Double standard of comparison ; *more & more t.* A ludicrous example of conflicting *thans*, which almost any reader would detect, is : ' I have *less* confidence *than* Mr Orr in the valuers being obliged to adopt his method of valuation *than* that we all shall be compelled to adopt theirs '. *Less* is clearly unequal to its two jobs ; it can put *Mr Orr* in his place with regard to *I*, or the valuers with regard to us, but not both. Such a freak sentence would not be worth quoting but for the light it throws on a less flagrant but more frequent absurdity of the same kind, the following of *more & more* with *than* :—*My eyes are more & more averse to light than ever.*/*The order has gradually found more & more room for educational & learned work than was possible in the early centuries.* Both sentences would be right if *& more* were omitted ; but the introduction of it implies the tacit introduction of other *thans* which conflict with those that are expressed. *More & more* means more yesterday than the day before, & more today than yesterday ; to combine that shifting date with the unshifting dates *ever* & *in early centuries* is impossible. *T.* should never be used after *more & more*.

8. *T.* after non-comparatives. *Else*, *other*, & their compounds, are the only words outside true comparatives whose right to be followed by *t.* is unquestioned ; & ' true comparatives ' is to be taken as excluding such Latin words as *superior* & *inferior*, *senior* & *junior*, all of which, as well as *prefer(able)*, require not *t.*, but *to* ; the use of *t.*, on the analogy of *other t.*, after *different*, *diverse*, *opposite*, &c., is ' now mostly avoided ' (OED). Two examples follow of irregularities that should not appear in print ; for *what . . . t.* read *what . . . but* or *what else . . . t.* ; & for *increased, greater* :—*What, then, remains if this measure of agreement still continues than to dispose of the Bill by fair discussion in reasonable time ?*/*There is obviously a vastly increased number of people who can & do follow reasoned arguments in* *books & newspapers than there was before educational methods were so efficient.*

9. *T.* with ellipsis or brachylogy. Some kinds of ellipsis are so customary in the member of a sentence beginning with *t.* that to write out the whole sense would be much more noticeable than the ellipsis. But hasty writers are encouraged by this to think that any slovenliness will pass muster :—*Many of them take tea & coffee to excess, & I am convinced myself the evil consequences of excess of these beverages is much greater than alcohol* (are much greater than those of alcohol)./*The proceedings were more humiliating to ourselves, to a great party, than I can recollect in the course of my political experience* (than anything I)./*The interpretations of the words are more uniformly admirable than could, perhaps, have been produced by any other person* (than any other person, perhaps, could have made them)./*This was due to the feeling that the Bill went further than public opinion warranted or was justified in the case of a private member's measure* (than what public opinion warranted or what was).

10. Flounderings. There is often a difficulty in getting the things to be compared into sufficient grammatical conformity to stand on either side of a *than* ; but writers who take so little trouble about it as the authors of the following sentences must not be surprised if their readers are indignant :—*In countries where a Referendum is a recognized part of the constitutional machinery, the House of Representatives is much more ready to pass, provisionally, constitutional reforms, & submit them to the electorate, than are Bills passed by the Houses of Parliament in a country like ours.*/*The Awkward Age, which was just published, was being received with a little more intelligence & sympathetic comprehension than had been the habit of greeting his productions.*

-TH & -DH. Monosyllabic nouns ending in *-th* after a vowel sound (including *-ar-* &c.) differ in the pronunciation of the plural. Those only need be considered whose plural is in regular use, which excludes *sloth, broth, ruth,* & many others. The common words *lath, mouth, oath, path, truth,* & *youth,* all sound the plural as -dhz, not -ths ; but the equally common words *berth, birth, breath, death, fourth, girth, growth, smith,* & *myth,* have -ths in sound as well as in spelling. Others again, chiefly words whose plural is less commonly used than those above, are doubtful ; such are *bath, cloth, sheath,* & *wreath* (-dhz recommended), & (with -ths usual) *heath, hearth, moth, swath,* & *wraith.* Cf. the article -VE(D). It may be added that the verbs or verbal nouns connected with *bath, breath, cloth, mouth, sheath, teeth,* & *wreath,* have the dh sound (*bathe, breathe, clothe, mouthing, sheathe, teething, wreathe*) ; cf. also *smithy, worthy, northern,* & *southern,* all with -dh-.

thank you, thanks, &c. *I thank you* is now reserved for formal occasions or tongues ; *thank you* is the ordinary phrase, but tends more & more to be lengthened with or without occasion into *thank you very much* ; *thanks* is a shade less ceremonious than *thank you,* & *many* & *best* & *a thousand thanks* are frequent elaborations of it ; *much thanks* is archaic, but not obsolete ; *thanks much* is a hybrid form, confusing the noun with the verb, & an affectation.

that adj. & adv. 1. *T.* = such a, so great a, to such an extent. 2. *T.* with noun & participle.

1. The adjectival use (*He has* that *confidence in his theory that he would act on it tomorrow*) was formerly normal English, & survives colloquially, but in literary use *such a, so great a,* &c., are substituted. The adverbial use (*when I was* that *high* ; *he was* that *angry*) is still more unliterary ; & in spoken English it now passes only where, as in the first example, actual demonstration with the hand is possible ; where it is impossible, as in the second example, *that* is held uneducated or vulgar.

2. *T.* with a noun & a participle or other equivalent of a defining relative clause. The type meant is shown in *that part affected, that land lying fallow, that theory now in question,* & the contention is that it is a bad type. In the OED there is a solitary example, & that justifiable for special reasons ; but in modern newspaper use it is growing very common. Four specimens are :—*It was essential that both these phases of his art should be adequately represented in* that *branch of the National Gallery devoted to native talent./*That *part relating to the freedom of the seas was given fairly fully in the ' Times './Aphorisms & maxims are treated with* that *respect usually reserved for religious dogma./ Shorter hours in all departments of labour prevent* that *expeditious handling of cargoes needed.*

The use of *that* (demonstrative adjective) with the sole function of pointing forward to a defining relative clause is established English, & ' that part which concerns us ' is as common as ' the part that concerns us ' ; but when for the relative clause is substituted a participle or phrase, it is an innovation to keep the *that* ; it may safely be said that most good writers take the trouble to clear away the now needless *that,* & write *the* instead. The full form should have been *that branch which is devoted* (or *the branch that is devoted*), & the short form *the branch devoted* ; & similarly for the rest.

It should be observed that sentences occur at first sight similar to those condemned, but with the difference that another purpose is served by *that* instead of or as well as that of heralding the participle &c. One such is the OED quotation already referred to : *On* that *peninsulated rock called La Spilla* ; here *that* is justified as meaning ' the well-known '. Compare also : *The world needs peace. You will always find us at your side to preserve* that peace bought *by so much blood.* Here the justification of *that* is its referring back to the *peace* of the previous sentence.

The misuse here objected to is still commoner in the plural ; see THOSE.

that conj. 1. Kinds of clause attached by *t.* conj. 2. Omission of *t.* in substantival clauses. 3. *T.* & *whether* with *doubt(ful).* 4. Interim *t.* 5. *T.* & *as* after (*in*) *so far.* 6. Non-parallel *t.*-clauses in combination.

1. Kinds of clause attached by *t.* conj. In adjectival or relative clauses that begin with *t.*, it is a relative pronoun, not a conjunction ; see for these the next article. *T.* conj. attaches a substantival clause to the verb, noun, &c., to which it is object (*I hear that he is dead*), subject (*T. pain exists is certain*), in apposition (*The fact t. pain exists*), &c. ; or else an adverbial clause to the word &c. modified (*The heat is such that it will boil water*). The only point needing to be insisted on is that in either case, whether the *t.*-clause is substantival or adverbial, the sentence out of which it is made by prefixing *t.* must be of the statement form, not a question, command, or exclamation. Sentences of those other kinds can be subordinated or turned into clauses, but not by prefixing *t.* The mistake is not made by good writers, but yet occurs often enough to need mention. One way of avoiding it is so to arrange that there is unsubordinated quotation of the question &c., & the other is, before subordinating, to convert the question &c. into a statement giving the same meaning. Of the following examples all but the third are of impossible substantival clauses, & that (*Crises. . .*) adverbial :—*I should like to point out to Reformer that, had the brave defender of Ladysmith known*

he could hold out for another $2\frac{1}{2}$ *months,* would he not have *informed General Buller of the fact?* (a. I should like to ask R. this : Had . . . b. he would surely have informed)./*Your correspondent suggests* that *if we lend money* let us send *it to Canada for railways there* (a. suggests : If . . . b. we should send)./*Crises, international or national, arise so rapidly in these days* that *who* can say *what a few years may bring forth?* (a. arise rapidly in these days ; who . . . b. that none can)./*One can only comment* that *if such a refuge was open to the Romans,* how much more available is it *to our own people, with their vast territories over the seas, comprising some of the suavest climes & most fertile soils on our planet!* (a. comment : If . . . b. Romans, it is much more available).

2. Omission of *t.* in substantival clauses. *I know that my Redeemer liveth* : *I know I can trust you.* These are equally good English ; if *that* were shifted from the first to the second, both would still be grammatically correct, but each less idiomatic than as it is. That is, the use or omission of the *t.* of a substantival clause depends partly on whether the tone is elevated or colloquial. But a glance at the following examples of obviously wrong omission will show that there is not free choice after all verbs or in all constructions :—*I assert the feeling in Canada today is such against annexation that . . ./Sir,—In reply to Mr Baker, may I point out in the circular entitled ' A Word to English Women ' the opposition of South Africa to the Plumage Bill is expressly proclaimed?/Sir,—I am abashed to see in my notice of Mr Bradley Birt's book ' " Sylhet " Thackeray ' I have credited the elder W. M. Thackeray with ' sixteen ' children./For instance, you state the exemption of incomes under £250 from income-tax would reduce tax-payers by six millions./The enormous rents which would be asked for new houses would naturally render owners*

of existing properties restless &
envious, with the result they would
continually strive to raise their own
rents to a similar level./There was
much cheering when Mr Balfour
blurted out that his own view was the
House of Lords was *not strong*
enough. It will be noticed that most
of these are from the correspondence
columns of newspapers, i. e. are by
writers who may be unpractised. It
at once occurs to the reader that
state, assert, & point out, are words
that stand on their dignity & will
not dispense with the attendance
of *t.* The same idea is not suggested
about *see* in the fourth example,
since a moment's thought assures us
that *I see, & I see that, Vesuvius is*
active again are equally good. The
reason why *t.* is there required is
that by omitting it the chance is lost
of making plain the arrangement of
the sentence & showing that *in . . .*
Thackeray belongs not to *see*, but to
have credited. The lesson of the last
two examples is that omission is
unadvisable when the substantival
clause is in apposition to a noun, as
here to *result, & view.*

It may be useful to give tentative
lists, to which everyone can make
additions for his own use, of verbs
that (1) prefer *t.* expressed, (2) prefer
t. omitted, & (3) vary according to
the tone of the context. (1) *T.* is
usual with *agree, assert, assume,*
aver, calculate, conceive, hold, learn,
maintain, reckon, state, suggest ; (2)
T. is unusual with *believe, presume,*
suppose, think ; (3) *T.* is used or
omitted with *be told, confess, con-*
sider, declare, grant, hear, know, per-
ceive, propose, say, see, understand.
The verbs with which the question
may arise are many more than these
few, which may however be enough
to assist observation.

3. *T. & whether* with *doubt(ful).*
It gave him cause for wonder that no
serviceable [petroleum] '*pool*' *had*
been revealed in England ; that *any*
existed, however, seemed doubtful, for
clearly . . . The choice allowed by
idiom is between *Whether any ex-*

isted seemed doubtful, & That any
existed seemed unlikely, according to
the shade of meaning required. See
DOUBT(FUL).

4. Interim *t.* It often happens to
a writer to embark upon a substantival *t.*-clause, to find that it is
carrying him further than he reckoned, & to feel that the reader & he
will be lost in a chartless sea unless
they can get back to port & make
a fresh start. His way of effecting
this is to repeat his initial *t.* This
relieves his own feeling of being lost ;
whether it helps the inattentive
reader is doubtful ; but it is not
doubtful that it exasperates the
attentive reader, who from the
moment he saw *t.* has been on the
watch for the verb that it tells him
to expect, & realizes suddenly, when
another *t.* appears, that his chart is
incorrect. These interim *thats* are
definite grammatical blunders,which
can often be mended by leaving out
the offending *t.* with or without
other superfluous words ; in the
examples below the omittenda are
bracketed. The first two show the
most venial form of the mistake, the
resumptive *t.* being inserted at the
point from which progress to the
expected verb is not to be again
interrupted by subordinate clauses ;
the others are worse :—*There can*
be no question that, had the Navy
from the very beginning been un-
hampered by the restrictions volun-
tarily put upon its activities by the
unratified Declaration of London, had
neutral traders not been permitted to
supply the enemy with things essential
to war—& in vast quantities—[that]
the end of the war would have come
much sooner./He must have astonished
the ' First Gentleman in Europe '
when he wrote to him that if he did not
adopt the new principles, as laid down
in his ' Grammar of the Six Senses ',
founded on Space, Time, & Eternity,
[that] *neither he nor his subjects could*
possibly hope to be saved./Is there any
man of sane judgement in the Unionist
Party who does not know in his heart
that, if the Unionist Party were free

from the Protectionist entanglement, & [that,] if it] had not committed the gigantic error of inciting the Lords to reject the Budget, its position & prospects at the present moment would be vastly improved ?/It should be borne in mind that, whilst many things have increased in cost, & [that] therefore the value of the £1 has decreased, there are many items of expenditure which have not increased in anything like the same proportion./It has been shown that if that inheritance be widening, as it is, & [that] if] the means of increasing it exist, as they do, then growth of numbers must add to the power./We can only say that if the business men who read the Times *are really of opinion that this is a sensible procedure, & [that,] if they] find any satisfaction whatever in the writing down of a huge sum which everybody knows can never be recovered, they will have only themselves to thank if the politicians continue to make game of them.*

Another sentence is appended as showing not indeed an interim *t.*, but mistakes curable by the same method of excision. If the writer wishes to keep his *thats*, he must correct *had authorized* into *had not authorized*, & *knew* into *did not know*; the repetition of *t.* has lulled him into the state in which *yes* & *no* mean the same thing :—*The Minister added that there was no need to say that the Government knew nothing about these statements, still less [that it] had authorized them, or [that it] knew what amount of truth there might be in them.*

  See also OVERZEAL.

5. *T.* & *as* after (*in*) *so far.* For the rather elusive distinction, & its importance, see FAR 4, 5, IN SO FAR, & COMPOUND PREPOSITIONS.

6. Non-parallel *t.*-clauses in combination. Parallel *t.*-clauses can be strung together *ad libitum*, & may be rhetorically effective. It is otherwise with interdependent or dissimilar *t.*-clauses ; for the principle see REPETITION. The unpleasantness of the construction deprecated

is sufficiently shown in : *It is thoroughly in accordance with this recognition that the people have rights superior to those of any individual* that *Mr Roosevelt is seeking legislation that will perpetuate the Government's title to the coal & oil lands in the public domain.*

that rel. pron. 1. Relation between *that* & *which.* 2. *That*-ism. 3. Elliptical *that* as relative adverb. 4. *That*-clause not close up. 5. One *that* in two cases. 6. Double government.

1. Relation between *that* & *which.* What grammarians say should be has perhaps less influence on what shall be than even the more modest of them realize ; usage evolves itself little disturbed by their likes & dislikes. And yet the temptation to show how better use might have been made of the material to hand is sometimes irresistible. The English relatives, more particularly as used by English rather than American writers, offer such a temptation. The relations between *that, who,* & *which*, have come to us from our forefathers as an odd jumble, & plainly show that the language has not been neatly constructed by a master-builder who could create each part to do the exact work required of it, neither overlapped nor overlapping ; far from that, its parts have had to grow as they could. Whereas it might seem orderly that, as *who* is appropriated to persons, so *that* should have been appropriated to things, or again that, as the relative *that* is substantival only, so the relative *which* should have been adjectival only, we find in fact that the antecedent of *that* is often personal, & that *which* more often represents than agrees with a noun. We find again that while *who* has two possessives (*whose* & *of whom*), & *which* one (*of which*), *that* has none of its own, though it often needs it, & has to borrow *of which* or *whose.* Such peculiarities are explicable, but not now curable ; they are inherent

in the relative apparatus that we have received & are bound to work with. It does not follow that the use we are now making of it is the best it is capable of ; & perhaps the line of improvement lies in clearer differentiation between *that* & *which*, & restoration of *that* to the place from which, in print, it tends to be ousted.

A supposed, & misleading, distinction is that *that* is the colloquial & *which* the literary relative. That is a false inference from an actual but misinterpreted fact ; it is a fact that the proportion of *that*s to *which*s is far higher in speech than in writing ; but the reason is not that the spoken *that*s are properly converted into written *which*s, but that the kind of clause properly begun with *which* is rare in speech with its short detached sentences, but very common in the more complex & continuous structure of writing, while the kind properly begun with *that* is equally necessary in both. This false inference, however, tends to verify itself by persuading the writers who follow rules of thumb actually to change the original *that* of their thoughts into a *which* for presentation in print.

The two kinds of relative clause, to one of which *that* & to the other of which *which* is appropriate, are the defining & the non-defining ; & if writers would agree to regard *that* as the defining relative pronoun, & *which* as the non-defining, there would be much gain both in lucidity & in ease. Some there are who follow this principle now ; but it would be idle to pretend that it is the practice either of most or of the best writers.

A defining relative clause is one that identifies the person or thing meant by limiting the denotation of the antecedent : *Each made a list of books that had influenced him* ; not books generally, but books as defined by the that-clause. Contrast with that : *I always buy his books, which have influenced me greatly* ; the clause does not limit *his books*,

which needs no limitation ; it gives a reason (=for they have), or adds a new fact (=& they have). There is no great difficulty, though often more than in this chosen pair, about deciding whether a relative clause is defining or not ; & the practice of using *that* if it is, & *which* if it is not, would also be easy but for certain peculiarities of *that*. The most important of these is its insistence on being the first word of its clause ; it cannot, like *whom* & *which*, endure that a preposition governing it should, by coming before it, part it from the antecedent or the main sentence ; such a preposition has to go, instead, at the end of the clause ; that is quite in harmony with the closer connexion between a defining, (or *that*-) clause & the antecedent than between a non-defining (or *which*-) clause & the antecedent ; but it forces the writer to choose between ending his sentence or clause with a preposition, & giving up *that* for *which*. In the article PREPOSITION AT END it is explained that to shrink with horror from ending with a preposition is no more than foolish superstition ; but there are often particular reasons for not choosing that alternative, & then the other must be taken, & the fact accepted that the preposition-governed case of *that* is borrowed from *which*, & its possessive from *who* ; its cases are, then : subj. *that* ; obj. *that* ; poss. *whose* ; prep.-preceded (*in, by, from, for*, &c.) *which*. Another peculiarity of *that* is that in the defining clauses to which it is proper it may, if it is not the subject, be omitted & yet operative (*The man you saw* means the same as *The man that you saw*), while *which* in the non-defining clauses to which it is proper must be expressed (*This fact, which you admit, condemns you* cannot be changed without altering the sense to *This fact, you admit, condemns you*).

The following sentences (or parts of sentences) are re-writings, in conformity with the account already given of the difference between *that*

& *which*, of verbatim extracts from newspapers ; the originals, correspondingly lettered, are reproduced below, & the reader is invited to compare the two versions & to say whether, even apart from the grammatical theory here maintained, the re-writings do not offer him a more natural & easy English than the others :—

a. It examines the rat that carries the flea that harbours the germ that infects the poor Indian.

b. The Bishop of Salisbury is the third bishop that his family has given to the world.

c. Even the greatest enemy that this country may possess at this hour cannot fail to admire . . .

d. Visualize the wonderful things the airman sees & all the feelings he has.

e. It seems that the Derna, which arrived safely, was sent in the ordinary way.

f. It is extremely unwise to try to reinforce a bond that is quite adequate with others that might only prove disruptive.

g. Among the distinguished visitors the Crawfords had at Rome was Longfellow.

h. The greater proportion of Consols are held by persons or corporations that never place them on the market.

i. Even in the cathedral organ-loft there are grievances that flourish & reforms that call for attention.

k. It is necessary to root out the autocratic principles that underlie German militarism, which threatens the peace of the world.

l. King George & Queen Mary have been welcomed with the pomp & circumstance that may well attend an event new in the experience of India.

m. A hatred of the rule that not only is unable to give them protection, but strikes at them blindly & without discrimination.

n. He provides a philosophy that disparages the intellect, & forms a handy background for all kinds of irrational beliefs.

o. She cannot easily regain control of the threads of culture that she has let drop, which now lie in muddled tangles at her feet.

p. President Wilson has been very prompt with his reply to the Note that Dr Solf sent to President Wilson, which was received in Washington yesterday morning.

q. The life-work that Acton collected innumerable materials for, but never wrote, was a History of Liberty.

r. You give currency to a subtle fallacy that one often comes across, but does not like to see in one's favourite paper.

s. After a search for several days, he found a firm that had a large quantity of them for which they had no use.

t. No-one can fail to be struck by the immense improvement they have wrought in the condition of the people, which often is quite irrespective of the number of actual converts.

v. There will be a split in the Lutheran Church comparable to the quarrel that has broken out in the Catholic Church on the question of modernism, which seems to have run its course.

w. The class that I belong to, which has made great sacrifices, will not be sufferers under the new plan.

x. The Pan-German papers are calling for the resignation of Herr von Kühlmann in consequence of the speeches he has just made in the Reichstag, in which he admitted that it was impossible for Germany to win by force of arms.

y. All honour to these men for the courage & wisdom they have shown, which are of infinitely greater value to the country than . . .

In the original extracts, which are given below in italics, the words that have been changed in the above versions are in roman type ; & where the reason for the change is not at once obvious, a note is added. But it will save repetition to state shortly here what is explained more fully under WHICH WITH AND OR BUT, that a defining & a non-defining clause, whether *that* is used in both or *which* in both, or *that* in one & *which* in the other, ought not to be coupled by *and* or *but* as if they were parallel things. The verbatim extracts are :—*It examines the rat* which *carries the flea* which *harbours the germ* which *infects the poor Indian.*

b. *The Bishop of Salisbury is the third bishop* which *his family has given to the world.*

c. *Even the greatest enemy* which *this country may possess at this hour cannot fail to admire . . .*

d. *Visualize the wonderful things the airman sees & all the feelings* which *he has.* Two *thats*, one *that*, or no expressed relative (= a suppressed *that*) will do equally well.

e. *It seems that the Derna that arrived safely was sent in the ordinary way.* The defining *that*-clause would be right only if there were several Dernas, of which only one arrived safely.

f. *It is extremely unwise to try to reinforce a bond,* which *is quite adequate, with others* which *might only prove disruptive.*

g. *Among other distinguished visitors* which *the Crawfords had at Rome was Longfellow.*

h. *The greater proportion of Consols are held by persons or corporations* which *never place them on the market.*

i. *Even in the cathedral organ-loft there are grievances* which *flourish & reforms that call for attention.* The change from *which* to *that* is mere ELEGANT VARIATION, to which even two *whichs* would be preferable.

k. *It is necessary to root out the autocratic principles* which *underlie German militarism, that threatens the peace of the world.* ELEGANT VARIATION again ; *which*, having been wrongly chosen the first time, is wrongly rejected the second time for variety's sake.

l. *King George & Queen Mary have been welcomed with the pomp & cir-*

cumstance *which may well attend an event* which *is new in the experience of India. That* is the right relative in both places ; but, though its repetition is no worse than that of *which*, it is as well to avoid it.

m. *A hatred of the rule that is not only unable to give them protection, but* which *strikes at them blindly & without discrimination.* What has caused the change from *that* to *which* here is the writer's realizing that *but that* is somehow undesirable ; it is so, because of the repugnance of *that*, mentioned above, to being parted from its antecedent ; but the way out is to let the previous *that* carry on for both clauses, a task it is quite equal to.

n. *He provides a philosophy* which *disparages the intellect &* that *forms a handy background for all kinds of irrational beliefs.*

o. *She cannot easily retain control of the threads of culture* which *she has let drop, & now lie in muddled tangles at her feet.* The first clause is defining, & should have *that* ; the second is defining or non-defining, being unessential to the identification & yet capable of being regarded as helping it. Against allowing the *that* to carry on, as in m, there is the objection, disregarded indeed by the writer, that the two relatives are in different cases ; it is therefore best to make the second clause non-defining, & use *which*, without *and*.

p. *President Wilson has been very prompt with his reply to the Note* which *Dr Solf sent to President Wilson, & was received in Washington yesterday morning.* Similar to o, except that this time the second clause is certainly non-defining.

q. *The life-work for which Acton collected innumerable materials but never wrote was a History of Liberty.* Restoration of the defining *that* often solves the difficulty seen here & in the next piece, that of a relative under double government, first by a preposition, & then by a verb ; the postponing of the preposition, abnormal though possible with *which,* is with *that* not only normal but necessary.

r. *You give currency to a subtle fallacy across which one often comes, but does not like to see in one's favourite paper.*

s. *After a search for several days he found a firm* which *had a large quantity of them* & which *they had no use for.* Both clauses are defining, & *that* is required ; but the relatives have not the same antecedent, & the *and* is therefore (see WHICH WITH AND OR BUT) wrong. But there is a legitimate choice between *that . . . for* & *for which*, & the latter gives an escape from one *that*-clause depending on another.

t. *No one can fail to be struck by the immense improvement* which *they have wrought in the condition of the people*, & *which often is quite irrespective of the number of actual converts.* Defining & non-defining clauses joined by *and* ; see above.

v. *There will be a split in the Lutheran Church comparable to the quarrel that has broken out in the Catholic Church on the question of modernism,* but which *seems to have run its course.* The second clause may be either defining or non-defining ; if defining, *that* (or rather nothing, cf. m) is required instead of *which* ; if non-defining, *but* must be omitted, & *which* kept.

w. *The class* to which *I belong* & which *has made great sacrifices will not be sufferers under the new plan.* Defining & non-defining wrongly coupled ; omit *and*, & naturally prefer (*that*) *I belong to* to the equally legitimate *to which I belong* as better both in clearness & in sound.

x. *The Pan-German papers are calling for the resignation of Herr von Kühlmann in consequence of the speeches* which *he has just made in the Reichstag,* & *in which he admitted that it was impossible for Germany to win by force of arms.*

y. *All honour to these men for the courage & wisdom they have shown,* & which *are of infinitely greater value to the country than . . .* The second

clause is clearly non-defining ; the *and* should go, whether or not the difference between *that* & *which* is accepted.

2. *That*-ism. As has been explained, the tendency in modern writing is for *which* to supersede *that* even in the functions for which *t.* is better fitted. On the other hand some writers seem deliberately, where most other people would use *which*, to choose *that* under the impression that its archaic sound adds the grace of unusualness to their style. A few examples will show *that* in non-defining clauses to be certainly noticeable, & the reader will perhaps conclude that its noticeability is not a grace :—*But her fate, that has lately been halting in its pursuit of her, overtakes her at last./This is clearly recognized by Mr Macfall in his eloquent & well illustrated monograph, that is more than a mere record of the fortunes of its titular subject./ Our policy in Mesopotamia, our suppression of Egyptian manifestations, & the Amritsar tragedy, have all earned severe criticism among Americans in Europe, that in turn has found an exaggerated reflection in the United States./At Lingard's shout for Jorgenson, that in the profound silence struck his ears ominously, he raised his eyes./Neither . . ., nor . . ., nor . . ., will save the country if the town, that has all the power in its hands, is content to let it die./His arguments on these points were heard by the great audience of business men in almost unbroken silence, that gave place to an outburst of applause when he . . .*

3. Elliptical *that* as relative adverb. The familiar yet remarkable fact that a preposition governing *that* does not precede it but follows it at a distance has been mentioned in 1. The idiom now to be noticed may be traceable to that fact. In the five following examples *that* serves as a sort of relative adverb, equivalent to *which* with a preposition :—*It cannot treat any section of Labour with the inconsequence & variability*

that *it has treated the miner, or any industry with the incompetence* that *it has treated the coal industry, & then expect peace* (=with which)./*We very much question whether the eventual historian will regard it as a period of Rationalism in the sense* that *we have apparently agreed to regard the eighteenth century as a period of Rationalism* (=in which)./*She found herself after Trafalgar in the same position* that *Rome found herself after the destruction of the Carthaginian fleet* (=in which)./*He took him for his model for the very reason* that *he ought to have shunned his example* (=for which)./*Others, watching the fluctuating rates of exchange with* all *the anxiety* that *a mariner consults his barometer in a storm-menaced sea, are buying securities that can* ... (= with which).

This is a freedom that should no more be allowed to lapse than the right of putting a preposition last or of omitting an objective *that*. But idiom requires that *which* should not be so treated ; it has been tried, with obviously bad results, in :—
It touched them in a way which *no book in the world could touch them.*/ *The man who cleaned the slate in the way* which *Sir E. Satow has done both in Morocco & Japan.* And further, *that* itself cannot be so treated unless the preposition to be supplied in the clause has been actually expressed with the antecedent ; in the following, *at which* must be substituted for *that* : *One of the greatest dangers in London is the pace* that *the corners in the main streets are turned.*

4. *That*-clause not close up. The clinging of the defining *that* to its antecedent has been noticed in 1. It is the gap between it & the antecedent that occasions a certain discomfort in reading the correct sentences below. Each *that*-clause is, or at the least may be meant as, defining ; but between each & the actual noun of the antecedent (*formulae, fight, thoroughfare, country*) intervenes a clause or phrase

that would suffice by itself for identification. In such circumstances a *that*-clause, though correct, is often felt to be queer, & it is usually possible, though by no means necessary, to regard it as non-defining & change *that* to *which*. The reader will probably agree that the change would be desirable in some of the four, & in others for special reasons undesirable :—
' *Petty France* ' *was the name anciently borne by the thoroughfare. now known as York-street,* that *runs from the Broadway, Westminster, to Buckingham Gate.*/*Dingwall,* which *has taken a very active part in the electoral fight for the Wick Burghs,* that *has resulted in so striking a Liberal triumph, has other claims upon* . . ./ *The foolish formulae for which the Coalition was responsible, & that the Conservatives have taken over, are not good enough.*/*When Mr Raleigh writes, as he does, as if America was a country of bounding megalomaniacs,* that *measured everything by size & wealth, he is talking nonsense.*

5. One *that* in two cases. Examples o & p of the first section contained two relative clauses each, the *which* of each second one being suppressed. It is quite in order to let a relative *which* or *that* carry on & serve a second clause as well, but only if three conditions are satisfied : the antecedent of the two must be the same ; both must be defining, or both non-defining ; & the case of the relative must be the same : this last condition is violated with *which* in o & p, & with *that* in the examples now to be given. If there is a change of case, *that* or *which* must be repeated ; or, more often, the repetition should be saved by some change of structure, as suggested in the brackets :—*The whole thing is a piece of hypocrisy of a kind* that *few associations would care to avow even in committee, but is here exhibited unblushingly in the light of day* (committee ; but here it is exhibited)./ *The art of war includes a technique* that *it is indispensable to acquire &*

can only be acquired by prolonged effort (that must be acquired, but can).

6. Double government. *A book that I heard of & bought* is a familiar & satisfactory form of speech ; *that* is governed first by *of* & again by *bought* ; but it is not good enough for those who consider that spoken *that* should become written *which,* & that a preposition should not end a clause ; they change it to *A book of which I heard & bought,* forgetting that if they do not repeat ' which I ' this commits them to ' A book of which I bought '. Examples have already been given in q & r of the first section ; but the efficacy of *that* in making the mistake impossible is so little appreciated as to deserve special treatment. The first example below shows the right form for such needs, with *that* ; the others illustrate the frequency of the mistake, which is naturally not made by those who recognize that in writing as well as in speech *that* is the true defining relative, & the place for a preposition governing it is later in the clause :—' *Command* ', *by William McFee, is one of those fine roomy books that one lives in with pleasure for a considerable time & leaves at the last page with regret./ A great international conference to which America is to be invited, or is to be asked to* convene *at Washington./We must not be faced by a peace* of which *we may disapprove & yet must* accept./*An ammunition dump* on which *he dropped his remaining bombs* & left *blazing merrily./It is incarcerated in prison-like places,* to which *it objects, & does all in its power to* avoid.

the. 1. *The Times correspondent* &c. 2. *By the hundred* &c. 3. *The good & (the ?) bad.* 4. *The* with two nouns & singular verb. 5. Single adverbial *the* with comparatives. 6. Double adverbial *the* with comparatives.

1. *The Times correspondent* &c. *It is agreed that* The Hague Conference *is to be a meeting of technical experts.* The capital T of *The* raises a question that, however trivial, is for ever presenting itself with newspaper names : in ' the Conference at The Hague ', or ' the correspondent of The Times ', we know where to use a capital & where a small letter ; but when one *the* is cut out by using (*The*) *Hague* & (*The*) *Times* attributively instead of as nouns, is the remaining *the* that which belonged to *Hague,* or that which belonged to *Conference* ? & is it consequently to be *The,* or *the* ? Though compositors or writers often choose the wrong alternative & print *The,* a moment's thought shows that it is *Conference* or *correspondent* that must have its *the,* while *Hague* & *Times* can do without it. We say ' a Times correspondent ', & ' the last Hague Conference ', stripping *Hague* & *Times* of their *The* without scruple ; it follows that the indispensable *the* belongs to the other word, & should not be *The* unless after a full stop. For a similar question with *Times's,* see POSSESSIVE PUZZLES 4.

2. *By the hundred* &c. The mild revelations of a gentle domestic existence which some royal personages have given us command readers by the hundreds *of thousands.* The idiomatic English is *by the hundred thousand* ; *by hundreds of thousands* will also pass, but with the plural *the* is not used. So also with *dozen, score,* &c.

3. *The good & (the ?) bad. Primitively splendid dresses, which appealed after the manner of barbaric magnificence to* the most complex & elementary *aesthetic instincts.* Is the omission of another *the most* or *the* between *and* & *elementary* tolerable ? The purist will condemn it on principle, & probably most of us will, for this particular case, endorse his condemnation. But he will add that neither must we say ' The French, German, & Russian figures are not yet to hand ', unless we are talking of their combined total ; the Germans & the Russians, he will say, must have their separating *the* ; & in these rigours sensible people will not follow him. What may fairly be expected of us is to realize that among expressions of several adjectives or nouns introduced by *the* some cannot have *the* repeated with each item (*the black & white penguins*), & some can logically claim the repetition (*the red & the yellow tomatoes*). A careful writer will have the distinction in mind, but he will not necessarily be a slave to logic ; ' the red & yellow tomatoes ' may be preferred for better reasons than ignorance or indolence. For other attempts to impose a needless rigidity, see ONLY, & NOT 1.

4. *The* with two nouns & singular verb. *It is* the single-handed courage & intrepidity *of these men which appeal to the imagination, & are even more marvellous than their adventures.* Two nouns of closely allied meaning are often felt to make no more than a single notion ; *courage & intrepidity is* almost a hendiadys for *intrepid courage*; that feeling is here strengthened by the writer's choosing to use only one *the* instead of two ; & to change *appeal & are* to *appeals & is* would be not only legitimate, but an idiomatic improvement.

5. Single adverbial *the* with comparatives. In ' the more the merrier ' we have double *the* ; in ' They are none the better ' we have single *the*, & that is the type here to be discussed ; but in both types *the* is not the ordinary adjective or ' article ', as in ' the table ' &c., but an adverb (or, in the double type, two adverbs) ; the original meanings were in the double type *by what* (i. e. *by how much*) & *by that* (i. e. *by so much*), & in the single type *by that* (i. e. *thereby* or *on that account*, or sometimes *by so much* or *by that amount*). These facts are familiar to all students of grammar, & are simple enough ; but the modern idiom based on them is less easy to be sure of. It will appear from the extracts presently to be quoted that

the usage here ascribed to the best writers is not universal, but often violated. What is here maintained is that good writers do not, & bad writers do, prefix *the* to comparatives when it conveys nothing at all ; & again that good writers do not, & bad writers do, allow themselves a *than* after a comparative that has *the* before it. The second & more limited question may be taken first : Is *the* with comparatives idiomatic if *than* follows ?

Starting with the position that I have taken pills & you have not, I may be imagined saying I took the pills, but

(without *the*)

Λ, I am no better

B, I am no better for taking them

C, I am no better than if I had not taken them

D, I am no better than you

(or, with *the*)

a, I am none the better

b, I am none the better for taking them

c, I am none the better than if I had not &c.

d, I am none the better than you

All eight mean the same, but the ' the ' forms *a*, *b*, *c*, & *d*, are idiomatically in order of merit. The *the* in *a* means ' thereby ', or more fully ' for taking them ', or more fully still ' than if I had not taken them '. So *a* is better than *b* & *c* because it does not say the same thing twice, as they do. And *b* is better, idiomatically, than *c* because, though both are tautological, *b* is at least as often said as *a*, & is sanctioned by usage, while *c* is very rare. Yet *c*, though it is rare, & though nearly everyone who wished to use *than* would prefer to it the C form without *the*, is felt to be not worse than clumsy, & less bad at any rate than *d*, which sounds illogical. It would be hard to prove its illogicality against a defender of it, but there is no difficulty in seeing how the impression comes : ' but I am none *the* better than you ' means when expanded ' but I am no better *than if I had not taken them* than you ' ; that is, the comparison indicated by *better* is measured by two separate standards, a than-clause implied in *the*, & a than-clause expressed. The upshot is that *the* should never be used with a comparative if *than* follows, but that where the than-clause introduces a standard of comparison different from that implicit in *the* (as in *d* above), the departure from idiom is much more glaring. In all the following extracts the *the* form should be got rid of by omission of *the*, with any consequential change ; but they are arranged in three sets, the first of the *c* type (tautological & unusual), the second of the *d* type (prima facie illogical), & the third of the type in which *the* is entirely meaningless.

c type

I do not believe that the New Royalty productions would have pleased people any the more than at present *by having money lavished upon scenery* (any the more=any more than if money had not been lavished)./*If we take the attitude of accepting her theory of naval policy, we make it* so much the less probable *that she will change her law* than *if we enter into violent contention* (the less probable=less probable than if we did not take the attitude of accepting)./ *A sentence in the courts of summary jurisdiction has not* any the less effect *upon the status & prospects of a prisoner* than *a sentence in the superior courts* (any the less effect= any less effect than if it were not in courts of summary jurisdiction).

d type

Variety theatre audiences, however, are well accustomed to foreign artists speaking in strange tongues, to whom, indeed, they often take surprisingly kindly, in view of the linguistic difficulties involved ; & Madame Réjane is not likely to be any the less heartily appreciated *during her present stay* than *on the occasion of any of her former performances in London on the ' legitimate ' stage* (any the less heartily=any less heartily than if she did not speak in a strange tongue)./*But does that make Sophocles more Greek than Aeschylus or Euripides ? Each of the latter may be more akin to other poets ; but he is* none the less Greek than *Sophocles* (none the less Greek=no less Greek than if he were not more akin to other poets).

Meaningless type

Meanwhile the intellectual release had been none the less marked than *the physical* (read *no less marked*)./ *I am* the more disposed *to rely on Mr Austen Chamberlain's silence* than *on Mr Anderson's attempt to resuscitate a quotation which less adventurous Tariff Reformers seemed disposed to let drop* (read *I am more disposed*)./ *Herr von Kühlmann, no doubt, is defiant about Alsace-Lorraine & silent about Belgium in the hope that the Allies will be* the less willing *to go on fighting for the one* than *for the other* (read *will be less willing*).

The more general question of when *the* is appropriate & when it is out of place before a comparative, without the complication of a following *than*, is simpler. What is here submitted is that a fashion has grown up of inserting *the* where it is indefensible, in the false belief that it is impressive or literary ; such fashions are deplorable ; it is wisdom either to abstain altogether from the adverbial *the* or to clear one's ideas upon what one means by it. The function of this *the* is to remind or acquaint the reader that by looking. about he may find indicated the cause (or sometimes the amount, when *the* means rather *by so much* than *thereby*) of the excess stated by the comparative. If no such indication is to be found earlier or later in the passage, *the* has no justification, & merely sets readers searching for what they will not find. Normal examples are : *I am the more interested in his exploit be-*

cause he is my cousin, where *the* anticipates *because* &c. ; *Though he is my cousin I am not the more likely to agree with him*, where *the* refers back to *though* &c. ; *As the hour approached I grew the more nervous*, where *the* means *by so much* & refers back to *as* &c. In the examples that follow it will be found impossible to point to such a cause or measure of excess anticipated or recalled by *the*, & moreover it will probably be admitted at once that removal of *the* does not weaken the sense, but improves it. First will come a batch of quotations each meant to convey something of this sort : ' A says so-&-so ; (that really does not much concern us ;) what concerns us more is so-&-so else ' ; but in each *the* has been gratuitously inserted, with nothing for it to anticipate or recall ; the bracketed sentence above is not usually expressed, but it or an equivalent is a necessary part of the sense :—*This reference to the Bonnet Rouge & Turmel cases is said to have been well received, but that, after all, is a matter for France herself, & we are* the more concerned *with M. Painlevé's definition of what he called France's ' noble war aims './But whilst the origin of words is a very fascinating study, we are at the moment* the more interested *in some of the language used at yesterday's demonstrations./That was the principle asserted in the resolution, but what* the more interests *us is the reasons given for this advertised resistance./It would not be difficult to preach a very effective sermon out of the fact that Professor Dicey uses the word ' England' when he clearly means, so far as we can see, the United Kingdom, but we are* the more concerned *to examine the Professor's thesis./That is all very nice & pleasant, but what* the more interests us *is what ' A Peer ' has to say as to the political functions & actual working of the House of Lords./The gentleman who pleads for a charitable construction of their action is Mr Richard Jebb, in a letter in today's*

Morning Post. We confess to being the more interested *in the plan which Mr Jebb for himself puts forward.*

These are simple affairs ; the reader is mystified for a moment by *the*, but soon sees that all he has to do is to neglect it. The next batch is not quite so simple, because each specimen contains some expression, of a kind commonly associated with this *the*, that nevertheless is not to be associated with it here &, if it is so taken, will spoil the sense :—*It is socially inexpedient that the diseased should languish unattended because of inability to provide skilled assistance, & it is* not the less inexpedient *that the prisoner should stand unaided before justice because his means cannot secure legal representation.* The *because* clause does not explain *the*, as one might guess, but belongs to *stand unaided./Signor Nitti, who kept the Fiume question out of the San Remo programme, is the object of the liveliest criticism by the Italian Press, & the British newspapers are also* none the less severe *in their reproaches of Mr Lloyd George* for *his alleged attitude towards France.* The *for* phrase is of a form often corresponding to *the*, but is in fact to be taken with *reproaches*, leaving *the* inexplicable./*It is gratifying to receive such clear testimony to a widespread interest in an intelligent study of the Bible ; & it is* not the less gratifying *that many recent books deal with the subject from a special point of view.* The *that* clause looks like the explanation of *the*, but is in fact the subject of ' is not less gratifying '. In these examples the use of *the* goes beyond mere ineptitude, & amounts to the serious offence of laying FALSE SCENT.

It still remains to show how common these superfluous *thes* are becoming in the newspapers ; some unsorted examples follow, all of which would be better without *the*, though in some a defence of it might be attempted :—*The shortest road to peace is the destruction of the German forces ; those forces are jammed, &*

day by day are being jammed the more *stringently./The British utility car, if ever we get it, won't come from any of the old-established houses ; it will* the more likely *come from people who are entirely new to the business./ Mr Chamberlain, in a letter, has said :* '*I think now on the Irish question exactly as I thought in 1886* '*; that would be* the more informing *if we knew to what month in 1886 the reference was./Here we have a whole series of workmen, all of them day by day rendering us service of inestimable value ; nor are we* any the less dependent *upon those whose work is like that of the miner./I said at the election before last that I was in favour of the railways being national-ized, but it would be* all the more true *to say that they would have to be kept running & that those employed on them could not exercise their full powers of collective bargaining if they were nationalized* than *it is at the present time./And for the calendar year to date upwards of 9 millions have been cancelled ; this would be* the more significant *had we not to bear in mind that the increase in the issue was considerably accelerated during the latter weeks of 1918./This praiseworthy humanity would move us* the more *if there were not an obvious way of meeting the case—viz by making a grant.*

It may even be thought that in the vogue of this *the more* &c., where *the* is an adverb, is to be found the explanation of the wrong adjectival *the* in :—*This was by far* the more heroic course than *that of the average Tories who took* the more obvious *party line to the last ditch./It is curiously entertaining to see how, in all essential things,* the actor-play-wright is invariably the better crafts-man than *the literary man who com-mences dramatist.* Read *a far more heroic & a better craftsman.* Choice in such sentences lies between *A is a better man than B & Of the two A is* the better man ; the wrong form *A is the better man than B* either confuses those two or apes the adverbial use.

6. Double adverbial *the* with com-paratives. It has been stated in 5 that in this construction one *the* means *by how much* & the other *by so much.* The most familiar ex-ample, ' the more the merrier ', is the short for ' by how much we are more, by so much we shall be merrier '. To keep this in mind is useful in settling a doubt that often arises & is illustrated in the three quotations below—whether a rela-tive (*that* or *which*) is in order in the ' by how much ' or measure clause. *The better education a girl can re-ceive, & the more time which can be spent on her training, the better./ Probably the less that is said by outsiders the better./On shore the slipper limpets can be sold for £1 a ton for use as manure, & the more* of them can be kept *out of the sea the better are the prospects of the oyster.* ' By how much better education *which* a girl can receive ' ? No, that would be patent nonsense, with two objects to the verb instead of one, & the writer has not written *which* ; but ' by how much more time *which* can be spent ' is as bad, & he has written *which.* It should be noted that if a *the* had been inserted before *time* the construction would have been different, = *& the more the time* (*is*) *which can* ; that would have been correct, if needlessly long ; but the extra *the,* which is indispensable to it, is not there. The *which* of the first quotation, & the *that* of the second, must be omitted, while the third, in which the writers of the others would almost certainly have used *that* or *which* again, is correct. Those who can read Latin, with *quo & eo,* or *quanto & tanto,* to take them right with *the & the,* can appreciate the point at once ; & the mistakes of the first two pieces are due to the acci-dent that in English the adverbial *the* is the same in form as the adjectival *the* ; adjectival *the* & its noun (*& more, less,* can be nouns) are very commonly followed by *that* or *which,* so that ' the more time which ' & ' the less that ' have a quite natural sound though they happen to be ungrammatical. This account of the mistake finds support in : *He remarked that the opposition to them* increased with the more territory that *they occupied*, where *the* really is the adjective (or ' article ') & *that* is therefore not ungrammatical, but where it is nevertheless plain that the writer had in his head the double *the* construction : the more territory we occupy, the greater is the opposition. Otherwise he would certainly not have said ' with the more territory ', but ' with the territory '.

It may perhaps, then, safely be laid down that when, in the measure clause of a *the . . . the* construction, the question arises whether a relative pronoun should be inserted, the answer is no. But the quotation last used in reaching that result, with its halting between the construction we are considering & another, suggests the need of paying proper respect to this exceedingly neat idiom, of not confusing it with other forms of expression, & of using it in its most effective shape & in the most suitable context. A pair of specimens, one good & one bad in various ways, may serve as text :—

A, good

The more the merrier.

B, bad

The economic welfare of a community is likely to be greater (1) the larger is the average volume of the national dividend, (2) the larger is the average share of the national dividend that accrues to the poor, & (3) the less variable are the annual volume of the national dividend & the annual share that accrues to the poor.

The idiom may be described as a sliding scale stating that one process of increase or decrease varies with the variation in another, & the two parts are the measure & the thing measured. Points of merit are : brevity ; close correspondence between the two parts ; occurrence of

the in both parts ; measure first & thing measured afterwards ; no inversion in measure clause ; no inversion in thing measured if it stands first, but inversion common if it has its normal later place. All these points are found in A, except that its elliptical brevity leaves the inversion question open ; but the completion could only give *The more we are* (not *are we*) *the merrier shall we* (or *we shall*) *be*. B fails in almost all of them ; it is long ; the compound nature of the measure prevents neat correspondence ; the thing measured lacks its *the* ; the thing measured stands first ; & there is inversion in all three parts of the measure. Most of these faults are curable by some such rewriting as this : The larger the average volume of the national dividend is, & the larger average share of this accrues to the poor, & the less this volume & this share vary from year to year, the greater is the economic welfare of the community likely to be. But the fact is that this idiom is suitable chiefly to short emphatic pointed sentences, & should not have been set to so elaborate a task.

A specimen or two may be added with comments :—*The wider was the League the greater it would be.* A suitable case ; but read *The wider the League was, the greater would it* (or *it would*) *be* ; for the rights & wrongs of inversion, see the article so named, especially the section *After relatives & comparatives.*/*The less distinct was the message which he felt impelled to deliver, the more beautiful is often the speech in which he proclaims it.* A particularly suitable case, in spite of its length, because of the detailed correspondence of the two parts ; but read *the message was* instead of *was the message.*/*The less likely is the satisfaction of France's claims—morally just, but practically impossible—the more frantic grow these appeals to force on the part of certain deputies.* An unsuitable case, because the parenthesis, & the last phrase (*on*

&c.), disturb the correspondence. If these two could be omitted, the sentence would be well enough, except that the inversion should be got rid of by either shifting *is* to after *claims* or omitting it—the latter for choice.

theatre, -ter. See -RE & -ER.

their, as the possessive of *they*, is liable to the same kinds of misuse, for discussion of which see THEY. A mere specimen or two will here suffice without further comment than that in each *their* is wrong :— *Dr Hollander has brought within 200 pages a vast amount of evidence from 'the medical literature of the entire civilized world' ; this is arranged in chapters according to their origin./ A Unionist journal, having discovered a mare's nest in its attempt to show . . ., is now trying to inflict a sort of revenge upon Mr Lloyd George for their own mistake by . . ./But each knew the situation of their own bosom, & could not but guess at that of the other./But does anyone in their heart really believe that Ireland is only that ?/No one can be easy in their minds about the present conditions of examination./But every one of them must be present at the Durbar to pledge their loyalty to their King-Emperor.*

theirs. See ABSOLUTE POSSESSIVES.

theism. See DEISM for the difference.

them. For misuses common to *them* & *they*, see THEY. The reflexive use of *them*=*themselves* is archaic, & as such usually to be avoided ; but the following quotation is enough to show that with an archaic verb it is not well to avoid the archaic reflexive : *Together the two—employee & director—hied themselves to the Great Central Company's loco. superintendent's office.* Read *hied them to.*

theoretic(al). Except that *-ic, -ics,* are the noun forms, & that *-ical* is probably more often used in all adjective senses than *-ic*, the two words are indifferent. See -IC(AL).

there. In the well-known special use of *there* before *be, exist,* & such verbs, two things call for notice. First, the use is anticipatory, i.e. *there* accompanies & announces inversion of verb & subject, standing in the place usually occupied before the verb by the subject ; consequently, when there is no inversion, this *there* is out of place, & should be struck out, e.g., in : *Bombay is without a doubt the headquarters of whatever cricket there exists in India today.* An exception must however be made for the verb *be* itself ; 'whatever cricket there is ', or 'who there was to see it ', is English, though 'whatever cricket there exists ' & 'who there witnessed it ' are not. The reason is easy to see : *there* has become, where there is inversion, so regular an attendant on *is, are, was,* &c., in their very frequent use as parts of the substantive verb or verb of existence that even when there is no inversion the need is felt of inserting it as a sign of the particular sense (i.e. as substantive verb) in which *is* &c. is to be taken ; but with other verbs, whose meaning is not obscured by the doubt whether they are here & now substantive or auxiliary or copulative, no such sign is wanted, & *there* is used only with inversion.

Secondly, since in the *there* idiom verb precedes subject, there is a danger of the verb's being hastily put into the wrong number ; for examples see NUMBER, 7.

thereafter, thereat, therein, thereof. See remark under THEREFOR.

thereanent is in the same kind of use as ANENT.

thereby. 1. The use of *t.* after a number &c. (*half a dozen or t.*) is Scotch, the English idiom being *or thereabouts* or *or so*. 2. *A special tribunal will be constituted to try the accused,* thereby assuring *him the guarantees essential to the right of defence.* For this use of *t.* with an UNATTACHED PARTICIPLE (*assuring*'s noun is not *tribunal*, but an inferred *constitution*), see that article & THUS, which is more frequently resorted to in similar difficulties. In the following example it is clear that *thereby* means by the salary &c. ; but whether *affording* agrees with salary &c., so that the salary affords encouragement by the salary, or with ' firm ' looming in the distance, the writer probably knows as little as we :—*The latter is usually the recipient of a liberal salary & expenses, with periodical increments, holidays, & security,* thereby affording *every encouragement to promote the interests of his firm.*

therefor, therefore. The two are now distinct in accent & meaning as well as in spelling. *Therefor* is accented on the second syllable, *therefore* on the first ; & *therefor* is to be used only where *for that, for it, for them,* &c., could stand equally well. In grammatical terms, *therefore* is an adverbial conjunction, & *therefor* an adverbial or adjectival phrase (adverbial in *He was punished therefor,* & adjectival in *The penalty therefor is death*). The essential function of *therefore* is to make clear the relation of its sentence to what has gone before ; that of *therefor* is the same as that of *thereafter, thereat, therein,* & *thereof,* to give a touch of formality or archaism to the sentence in which it is substituted for the *for it* &c. of natural speech.

therefore. Apart from the danger of meaning *therefor* & writing *therefore,* the only caution needed is that commas should be used or not used with discretion before & after the class of words to which *t.* belongs. Like *then, accordingly, nevertheless, consequently,* & many others, it is an adverb often (itself, indeed, almost always) used as a conjunction ; & it is a matter of taste whether such adverbial conjunctions shall or shall not be comma'd off from the rest of the sentence in which they stand. Light punc-

tuators usually omit the commas (or comma, if *t.* stands first), heavy punctuators usually give them, & both are within their rights. But it must be remembered that the putting of a comma before *t.* inevitably has the effect of throwing a strong accent on the preceding word, & that some preceding words are equal to that burden, & some are not. From the three following examples it will be at once apparent that *although* can bear the commas, & the *and*s cannot :—*Although, therefore, the element of surprise could not come into play on this occasion, the Germans were forced to withdraw./ It would be impossible for the State to pay such prices, and, therefore, we must content ourselves with . . ./ Malaria was the cause of a very large proportion of the sickness, and, therefore, the disease deserves especial study by . . .*

Again, the word *it* is one that can seldom be emphasized & consequently abhors a comma'd *therefore* such as follows it in :—*It, therefore, comes rather as a shock to find simultaneously in many papers this morning articles declaring . . ./It, therefore, behoves those who have made the passage of the Bill possible to attend once more.* But where emphasis can reasonably be laid on *it,* & it can mean ' it more than others ' or the like, the commas become at least tolerable ; so : *It is a concrete & definite idea, the embodiment of which in practicable shape is by far the most urgent constructive problem of international statesmanship* ; & it, therefore, *calls for the most careful examination.*

Many words, however, are neither naturally emphatic like *although* nor naturally unemphatic like *and* & *it* ; & after them care should be taken not to use the commas with *therefore* except when emphasis is intended. The personal pronouns are good examples ; in the following, we ought to be able to conclude from the commas that ' we ' are being deliberately contrasted with others who believe otherwise : *We, therefore, find great comfort in believing that Canadian loyalty depends not on . . ., nor on . . ., but on . . .* Probably that is the case, & the commas are justified ; but if the light punctuation were generally accepted as the rule with these adverbial conjunctions, & commas used only when emphasis on the preceding word was desired, one of the numberless small points that make for lucidity would be gained.

A curious specimen may be added : *We therefore are brought again to the study of symptoms.* Here it is obvious that *We* is unemphatic ; but the writer, though he has rightly abstained from commas, has been perverse enough to throw an accent on *We* by other means, viz by putting *therefore* before instead of after *are* ; see POSITION OF ADVERBS 4.

thesis. Pl. *thesēs*, see LATIN PLURALS. Pron. thē- or thĕ-. For the metrical sense, see TECHNICAL TERMS.

they, them, their. 1. *One, anyone, everybody, nobody*, &c., followed by *their* &c. 2. Confusions with nouns of multitude & personifications. 3. Unsatisfactory pronoun reference. 4. Case.

1. *One* &c. followed by *their* &c. The grammar of the recently issued appeal to the Unionists of Ireland, signed by Sir Edward Carson, the Duke of Abercorn, Lord Londonderry, & others, is as shaky as its arguments. The concluding sentence runs : ' *And we trust that everybody interested will send a contribution, however small, to this object, thereby demonstrating their* (sic) *personal interest in the anti-Home Rule campaign* '. Archbishop *Whately* used to say that women were more liable than men to fall into this error, as they objected to identifying ' *everybody* ' *with* ' *him* '. *But no such excuse is available in this case. Their* should be *his* ; & the origin of the mistake is clearly reluctance to recognize that the right shorten-

ing of the cumbersome *he or she, his or her*, &c., is *he* or *him* or *his* though the reference may be to both sexes. Whether that reluctance is less felt by the male is doubtful ; at any rate the OED quotes examples from Fielding (*Everyone in the house were in their beds*), Goldsmith, Sydney Smith, Thackeray (*A person can't help their birth*), Bagehot (*Nobody in their senses*), & Bernard Shaw. It also says nothing more severe of the use than that it is ' Not favoured by grammarians ' ; that the grammarians are likely, nevertheless, to have their way on the point is suggested by the old-fashioned sound of the Fielding & Thackeray sentences quoted ; few good modern writers would flout the grammarians so conspicuously. The question is discussed in NUMBER, 11 ; examples of the wrong *their*, in addition to those that follow, will be found under THEIR ; & the article ONE, 5, 6, 7, may be useful. *The lecturer said that everybody loved their ideals./Nobody in their senses would give sixpence on the strength of a promissory note of that kind./Elsie Lindtner belongs to the kind of person who suddenly discovers the beauty of the stars when they themselves are dull & have no one to talk with.* The last is amusing by the number of the emendations that hurry to the rescue : E. L. is one of the people who discover . . . ; . . . kind of people who discover . . . ; . . . when he himself is . . . ; . . . when she herself is . . . ; . . . the kind of woman who discovers . . . when she herself is . . . As to ' . . . when she herself is . . . ' without further change, it is needless to remark that *each, one, person*, &c., may be answered by *her* instead of *him* & *his* when the reference, though formally to both sexes, is especially, as here, to the female.

2. Confusions with nouns of multitude & personifications. What is meant appears from the quotations following, with *Government, is, & them*, in the first, & *journal, its, is, & their*, in the second :—*The Govern-*

ment, with the Clarke award before them, is yet unable to enforce it./*A widely circulated Unionist journal, having discovered a mare's nest in its attempt to show that an Englishwoman's Drawing-room was to be open to the Government Inspector,* is *now trying to inflict a sort of revenge upon Mr Lloyd George for their own mistake by* . . . Discussion, & other examples, will be found in PERSONIFICATION, 2.

3. Unsatisfactory reference. For the many possibilities in this kind, see PRONOUNS. A few flagrant examples follow, the bracketed numbers referring to sections in Pronouns :—*The Germans will argue that, whatever* they *may undertake to keep the French at bay,* they *will still have no guarantee that* they *will evacuate their territory or even refrain from further occupations when* they *prove unable to meet the enormous demands still hanging over* them *(4)./ It must not repeat this history with the Poles or fall into a sudden scepticism about the* Minsk negotiations, *because* they *have succeeded in keeping the enemy from the capital* (3)./ *If the* Paris Conference *have to fight* the Bolshevists, *it is because, by attacking* their *decisions in advance, by waging war against States which* they *propose to set up, & by* their *unscrupulous propaganda,* they *have begun to fight the* Conference (4)./ *That the error in date, & the deduction, are from Dr Garnett's preface, I am well aware ; but that does not make* them *either correct or accurate.* In this last, *error in date* is necessarily part of the reference of *them* ; but, since a fact cannot make an error correct or accurate, it should have been ' the date ' or ' the erroneous date '.

4. Case. Like *him* & HE (which see for comment), *them* & *they* occasionally go wrong, as in :—*The whole foundation of our constitution depends upon the* King *being faithfully served by* his *advisers, &* they *taking complete responsibility for every act which* he *does.*/*Several bodies of the tribesmen*

then undertook to help Kaid Maclean to escape to the sacred oasis, to which his *captors had been careful to draw near in the event of* they *themselves being in danger.* Observe that responsibility for these two blunders rests with the FUSED PARTICIPLE ; read, in the first piece, *upon the* King's *being* . . . *& their taking,* &, in the second, *in the event of their being in danger themselves.*

thimbleful. Pl. *-ls* ; see -FUL.

thin makes *thinness* ; see SPELLING POINTS, 2.

thine. See ABSOLUTE POSSESSIVES.

thing. *Things musical, things canine, things Japanese,* & the like, are phrases sometimes serviceable & businesslike, as at the head of a newspaper column, but suggestive of affectation where the only reason for using them is that they are a slightly out-of-the-way form of expression.

thingumajig, thingumbob, thingummy, are the chief survivors of a large number of variants.

think. **1.** After *t., that* is usually omitted ; see THAT, conj., 2.

2. *T. to do,*=t. of doing or remember to do, is at best colloquial, though the OED does, without producing any quotations, recognize its existence, thus : ' *Mod.* Did you think to ask him how his father is ? '.

3. *No thinking man.* One of the bluffing formulae, like *It stands to reason* (see REASON, 2), that put the reader's back up & incline him to reject the view that is being forced on him. In the following piece it will be noticed that the writer by implication rules out all Liberals from rational humanity : *No thinking man can believe that, without fairer conditions of internal competition, without a broader basis of revenue, without a league of commerce & defence between the Mother country & her colonies, the Imperial State can continue to exist.*

thinkable is a word of the same unfortunate ambiguity as its much more popular opposite UNTHINK-

ABLE. *Protection is only a thinkable expedient on the assumption that competition in the home market is to be made unprofitable.*

thirty. *The thirties, 'thirties.* See TWENTIES.

thirty-twomo, 32mo. See FOLIO. Pl. *-os* ; see -O(E)S 6.

this. 1. *This three weeks, this five years,* &c., are as good English as *these* &c., the numeral & the plural noun being taken as the singular name of a period ; but the modern grammatical conscience is sometimes needlessly uneasy about it.

2. For *I will not do* &c. *this thing,* see NOVELESE, & STOCK PATHOS.

thistle. The -t- is silent ; see PRONUNCIATION.

thither. See HITHER. An OED quotation shows how the word is still available, though rarely indeed, when real ambiguity would result from *there* ; it is from a guidebook : *The road thither leaves the main road at right angles.*

-TH NOUNS. The remarks made in the article -AL NOUNS apply also to the invention of new or revival of obsolete nouns in -TH. There are large numbers of well established words such as *truth, depth, growth* ; but the suffix is no longer a living one (on this point see HYBRID DERIVATIVES), & the use of new or revived *-th* nouns is chiefly a poetasters' trick. Some specimens are : *greenth, gloomth,* & *blueth,* all made by Horace Walpole ; *blowth* (blossom &c.), more or less obsolete ; *spilth,* a revival ; & *illth,* made by Ruskin as antithesis to *wealth* in its older & wider sense.

those. 1. For *those kind of, those sort of,* see KIND, SORT.

2. *Those* (adj.)+noun+adjective. (*The winner will be selected from) those persons named* ; *persons* is the noun, & *named* the adjective. This arrangement is now very common in newspaper writing of the inferior kind, but is so little warranted by good literary usage that the OED,

which illustrates the constructions of which this is a hybrid product, does not quote a single example of it ; cf. what is said of the same construction under THAT adj., 2. The word *adjective* in the formula above is to be taken as including participles active or passive, & adjectival phrases, as well as simple adjectives—whatever, in fact, is equivalent to a defining relative clause (*those persons following, those persons named, those persons in the list below, those persons present*—all equivalent to *the persons that* &c.). *Those named* is a proper substitute for (*the*) *persons named,* the pronoun (not adjective) *those* taking the place of the noun *persons* with or without *the* ; & (*the*) *persons named* is itself a shortening of *the persons that are named.* But *those persons named* is a mixture of the long form (*the*) *persons that are named* & the short form *those named,* in which mixture what was gained by using the pronoun *those* instead of *the persons* is thrown away by reinserting the noun & making *those* an adjective. It is true that there is another legitimate form in which *those* does appear as an adjective, viz *those persons who are named* ; but that is a form in which not lightness & brevity, but on the contrary formality & precision, are aimed at ; it is therefore not one that should be abbreviated.

All this is offered not as a proof that *those persons named* is impossible grammar, but as a reasonable explanation of what is believed to be the fact, that good writers do not say it, but say either (*the*) *persons named* or *those named.* The following quotation is useful as containing samples both of the right & of the wrong usage : *It depends upon the extent to which* those in authority *understand their responsibility, & are able so to make their influence felt as to enlist the active support of* those boys with most influence *in the school. Those in authority is right, whereas* those persons in authority would have been wrong ; & *those boys with most influence* is wrong, & should be either *the boys*, or *those, with* &c. Several examples follow with corrections :—*Moreover, the Valley of Kings lacks* those conveniences & facilities essential *to expeditious & efficient work* (read *lacks the*)./*On several of* those points concerned *with the practical application of the general principles there is room for discussion* (read *the points*)./*The best advice the Allies can give to* those peoples bordering *on Russia is to . . .* (read *the peoples*)./*For he possessed just* those qualities needed—*courage, energy, driving power, & . . .* (read *just the*)./*The fitting of such a contrivance must give to* those people employing it *a considerable advantage* (read *to people, to the people*, or *to those, employing*)./*The Bishop of Oxford combines a personal appreciation of Dr Driver with a reply to* those recent charges made *by Canon Rashdall & Professor Bethune-Baker of inconsistency in his own attitude towards Biblical criticism* (read *to the*)./*This simply expressed estimate will be endorsed by all* those friends on this side *of Mr Howells.* This means ' by all those friends of Mr Howells who are on this side (of the Atlantic) ' ; but this particular development of the newfangled *those* makes the sentence almost unintelligible ; *the friends* is at least better.

The following use of *those* is quite another matter, & of no importance, but worth giving as a curiosity : *It is impossible for the Ambassador to issue invitations to those other than Americans.*

though. 1. *Though*)(*although*. **2.** *As though.* **3.** (*Al*)*though* with participle or adjective. **4.** Illogical use.

1. *Though*)(*although*. The definite differences between the two hardly need stating ; they are : first, that *though* can & *although* cannot be used as an adverb, placed last (*He said he would come ; he didn't, though*) ; & secondly that *though* is alone possible

in the *as though* idiom. In the use common to both forms, i. e. as a complete conjunction, no definite line can be drawn between them, & either is always admissible ; but it is safe to say, in the first place, that *though* is much commoner, & secondly that the conditions in which *although* is likely to occur are (a) in the more formal style of writing, (b) in a clause that does not follow but precedes the main sentence, & (c) in stating an established fact rather than a mere hypothesis : *He wouldn't take an umbrella though it should rain cats & dogs ; Although he attained the highest office, he was of mediocre ability.*

2. *As though.* It is not as though there has *been cruelty & injustice. Had*, in place of *has*, is the only right English ; see AS, 4, for discussion & examples.

3. (*Al*)*though* with participle or adjective. Like other conjunctions (*if, when, while*, &c.), (*al*)*though* is often followed by the significant word only of its clause, the subject & the auxiliary or copulative verb being readily supplied ; so *Though annoyed, I consented.* The convenience of this is obvious, but care is needed, as appears from the two quotations that follow :—*Though new to mastership herself, a lady master is not new to the pack, for she follows Mrs Garvey in the position./ Though* sympathizing *as I do with Poland, I cannot resist the impression that it would be doing Poland an ill service to . . .* The point shown by the first is that the omission must not be made when it leaves the participle or adjective apparently attached to a wrong noun ; *new* in fact belongs to *she*, but seems to belong to *a lady master* ; if *she is* had not been omitted after *though*, all would have been in order. In the Poland sentence, the correction really required is to omit *though*, ' sympathizing as I do ' being self-sufficient ; but, even if we suppose *as I do* omitted, there is a wrong sound about *though sympathizing* itself that suggests a restriction: *though,* & other conjunctions, must not be constructed with a participle unless that participle would have been used in the unabridged clause; but that would not have been *though I am sympathizing,* but *though I sympathize*; contrast with this the perfectly satisfactory *Though living he is no longer conscious,* where the full form would be not *Though he lives,* but *Though he is living.*

4. Illogical use. The danger of using adversative conjunctions where two propositions are not strictly opposed, but in harmony, is explained & illustrated in BUT, 3. In the following example, *though* would be right if the words ' is the only country in Europe that ' were not there; as it stands, the sentence is nonsense: *Though it is only in recent times that in England the Jewish civil disabilities were repealed, Turkey is the only country in Europe that has throughout been free of any anti-Jewish propaganda.*

thral(l)dom. See -LL-, -L-, 4.

thrash, thresh. One word, with two pronunciations & spellings differentiated. To separate grain is almost always *-esh*; to flog is always *-ash*; in figurative & transferred use the spelling varies as the user thinks of one or of the other of the two simple senses.

thrasonical. See PEDANTIC HUMOUR.

Threadneedle Street, Old Lady of. See SOBRIQUETS.

threaten. *The Mass Vestments, now threatened to be authoritatively revived, have to be decided upon.* See DOUBLE PASSIVE.

three-quarter(s). The noun expressing a fraction has the -s, &, though usually hyphened, is better written as two separate words; see HYPHENS, 3 B. This noun is often used attributively with another noun, e. g. with *back* at football, or with *length* or *face* in portraiture; in those conditions a hyphen is required to show that the adjective +noun has become one word; but further, it is usual, when a plural

noun is used attributively or compounded, to take its singular for the purpose, even if that singular does not otherwise exist (*shear steel,* not *shears steel; scissor-shaped,* not *scissors-shaped; racket-court,* not *rackets-court*; cf., however, *fives-court, breeches-maker,* &c.); accordingly, *three-quarter back & three-quarter face* are the normal forms. But the nouns *back, length,* &c., are often dropped when context allows, & the attributive compound is allowed to represent them as well as itself; being then an elliptical noun, it has a tendency to resume its -s, & *a three-quarters* is perhaps more often seen than *a three-quarter*; either is legitimate.

threnody, threnode. The OED treats the first as the standard form.

thrive. The OED gives *throve, thriven,* as the past & p.p., but allows *thrived* for either.

throat. For *a lump in* one's *t.,* see STOCK PATHOS.

throstle. The -t- is silent; see PRONUNCIATION.

thunderer. For *the T.* = The Times, see SOBRIQUETS.

Thursday. For the adverbial use, see FRIDAY.

thus. There is a particular use of *thus* that should be carefully avoided; it is very common in the newspapers, & the fact that the OED nevertheless does not quote a single example of it probably indicates that it is very uncommon elsewhere. In this use *thus* is placed before a present participle (*thus enabling* &c.), & its function, when it is not purely otiose, seems to be that of apologizing for the writer's not being quite sure what noun the participle belongs to, or whether there is any noun to which it can properly be attached (cf. UNATTACHED PARTICIPLES); the exact content of *thus* itself is often as difficult to ascertain as the allegiance of the participle. To each quotation is appended (1) a guess at the noun to which the participle belongs, &

(2) a guess at the content of *thus*; the guesses are honestly aimed at making the best of a bad job, but readers may prefer other guesses of their own :—*Our object can only be successfully attained by the substantial contributions of wealthy sympathizers, thus enabling us to inaugurate an active policy* (contributions? by being substantial?)./*Letters on the constant stopping of omnibuses*, thus causing *considerable suffering to the horses* (stopping? by being constant?)./*But now a fresh anxiety has arisen owing to the rising of the Seine*, thus making *the river navigation more difficult & slow* (rising? by occurring?)./*The Prince was, by the special command of his Majesty the Emperor, made the guardian of H.I.H. the Crown Prince*, thus necessitating *the Prince's constant presence in the capital of Japan* (the appointment as guardian? by occurring?)./*This circumstance is due to the sail innovation introduced at the eleventh hour by Captain Burton*, thus necessitating *a remeasurement of some of Shamrock's sails* (innovation? by occurring?). It should be noticed that the resolution of the participle into a relative clause, & the omission of *thus*, gets rid of the difficulty every time (which would enable; which causes; which makes; which necessitated; which will necessitate).

thyme. Pronounce tīm; before the 17th c. the usual spelling was *tyme* or *time*.

tiara'd is preferable to *tiaraed*; see -ED & 'D.

tibia. Pl. *-ae*; see LATIN PLURALS.

tic douloureux. The best pronunciation (pacè OED, which says 'often mispronounced') is tĭk dŏlo-rōō'; see FRENCH WORDS, 2.

ticklish. So spelt; see MUTE E.

tidal is a word badly formed, according to the views expressed in HYBRID DERIVATIVES; yet the light-hearted suggestion of abandonment made about *coastal* cannot be repeated for it; it has not the same

barbaric appearance, & it is not so easily done without. Nevertheless, since it is perhaps the only respectable-looking & useful word in which the rule against appending the adjectival *-al* to a Teutonic noun has been disregarded, & since it is therefore more likely than any other word to be quoted in defence of new hybrids in its own image, a protest against its form, though not a proposal for its disuse, is called for. It is of no hoary antiquity, the earliest OED quotation being dated 1807; the objection to it need not be set out again here; see the article already referred to. In case it should occur to any reader that the adjective *bridal* is comparable with *t.*, it should be mentioned that that word is not a true adjective from *bride+-al*, but an attributive use of the noun *bridal*, which= *bride+ale*, = wedding feast; & *bridal*, unlike *t.*, *is* of hoary antiquity.

tidbit. See TITBIT.

tidy, v. For inflexions see VERBS IN -IE &c., 6.

tie, v. For inflexions see VERBS IN -IE &c., 3.

tiers état. See FRENCH WORDS.

tigerish, tigress. So spelt.

tike. See TYKE.

tilde (tĭ'ldĕ). The mark put over n (ñ) in Spanish when it is to be followed by a y sound, as in *señor* (sānyor').

tile(r), tyle(r). The words used in freemasonry are usually spelt with y, but are not of different origin. See Y & I.

till, until. The first is the usual form; for what difference of usage exists, see UNTIL; & cf. (un)to, (al)though, (up)on, in(to), (al)though, amid(st), among(st), while & whilst, toward(s), beside(s), (be)twixt, (with)-in, with(al), (or) ere, whoso(ever), th(o)rough.

tilth. A word not open to the remarks made in -TH NOUNS, being very far indeed from a recent formation. It differs, however, from the really common nouns in -th, such as *truth & wealth & filth*; though still a business word in certain technical senses, it has become archaic in its general meaning of tillage or tilled land ; &, being therefore a favourite with those who affect poetic diction, it has unfortunately begotten a progeny that has not its own claims to respect ; see -TH NOUNS.

timbale. See FRENCH WORDS.

timbre. See FRENCH WORDS ; it has been proposed to substitute the spelling & pronunciation *tämber*.

time. Under this, as the most general term, may be collected some synonyms. Of the five following words each is given a single definition with a view merely to suggesting the natural relation between them. Though each is often used in senses here assigned not to it but to another (or not mentioned at all), the words *date, epoch, era, period, cycle*, form a series when they are strictly interpreted, & to keep that series in mind is helpful in choosing the right word.

A *date* is the identifiable or intelligibly stated point of time at which something occurs.

An *epoch* is the date of an occurrence that starts things going under new conditions.

An *era* is the time during which the conditions started at an epoch continue.

A *period* is an era regarded as destined to run its course & be succeeded by another.

A *cycle* is a succession of periods itself succeeded by a similar succession.

A *time*, & an *age*, are words often exchangeable with all or most of the above, & less precise in meaning. Cf. also the words *term, span, spell, season, duration, juncture, moment, occasion*.

time, v., makes *-mable* ; see MUTE E.
timeous. See TIMOUS.
timid makes -EST ; see -ER & -EST, 4.
timous, timeous. Omit the -e- ; see MUTE E. Whereas its sole function is to preserve the ĭ sound, the OED states that it actually results

in the erroneous pronunciations tĭ′mĭus & tī′mĭus.

tinge makes *-geable*, see -ABLE 1 ; but *tinging*, see MUTE E.

tinker, v. *It was an undesirable thing to be always tinkering with this particular trade.* The idiomatic preposition is *at*, not *with* ; the latter is probably due to confusion with *tamper with* ; see ANALOGY.

tinsel makes *-lled, -lly* ; see -LL-, -L-.

tint, *shade, hue.* All are available as substitutes for the dominant word *colour*. Different *hues* are, so far as meaning goes, simply different colours, so called because for good or bad reasons the everyday word is held to be unworthy of the context. Different *tints & shades* are properly speaking not different colours but varieties of any particular colour, *tints* produced by its modification with various amounts of white, & *shades* by various admixtures of black. These distinctions, however little present to the mind, have a growing influence in determining the choice of a synonym for *colour*.

tintinnabulum. Pl. *-la*.

-tion & other *-ion* endings. Turgid flabby English of the kind common in inferior leading articles is full of abstract nouns ; the commonest ending of abstract nouns is *-tion* ; & to count the *-ion* words in what one has written, or, better, to cultivate an ear that without special orders challenges them as they come, is one of the simplest & most effective means of making oneself less unreadable. It is as an unfailing sign of a nouny abstract style that a cluster of *-ion* words is chiefly to be dreaded ; but some nouny writers are so far from being awake to that aspect of it that they fall into a still more obvious danger, & so stud their sentences with *-ions* that the mere sound becomes an offence. These points are so simple that quotations need not be multiplied :— *Speculation* on the subject of the *constitution* of the British *representation* at the Washington *inaug-*

uration of the League of *Nations* will, presumably, be satisfied when Parliament meets, but there is a certain nervousness at the *suggestion* that Mr Lloyd George will go over there as chief of the British *delegation*.

tipstaff. Pl. *-affs* or *-aves*.

tiptoe, v., is, like *hoe* & *shoe*, an exception to the MUTE E rule, & makes *tiptoeing*.

tipsy. See GENTEELISM.

tirailleur. See FRENCH WORDS.

tire, v., makes *tirable* ; see MUTE E. *Tiredly* is a bad form if the views expressed in -EDLY are sound.

tire, tyre. For other words in which the same spelling question has arisen, see Y & I. The OED regards the word as a shortening of *attire*— the wheel's attire, clothing, or accoutrement ; & it states the spelling facts thus : ' From 15th to 17th c. spelt *tire* & *tyre* indifferently. Before 1700 *tyre* became generally obsolete, & *tire* remained as the regular form, as it still does in America ; but in Great Britain *tyre* has been recently revived as the popular term for the rubber rim of . . .'. From this it appears that there is nothing to be said for *tyre*, which is etymologically wrong, as well as needlessly divergent from our own older & the present American usage.

tiro, ty-. Spell *ti-*, & see Y & I ; pl. *-os*, see -O(E)S 6.

tissue. The OED gives precedence to tĭ'shū over tĭ'sū ; but the latter is probably now regarded as the better pronunciation. It is clear, however, that the sh sound prevailed in the 16th c., since h, which can only be accounted for as marking sound, occurs in quotations from 1501 ; & this may be the reason for the OED's choice. Tĭ'sū is here recommended.

Titan. For *the weary T.*, see SOBRIQUETS.

titbit, tid-. The older spelling is *tid-* ; but it is now so much less usual, & the significance of *tid* is so

doubtful, that there is no case for reverting to it. To make the two parts of such words rhyme or jingle is a natural impulse that need not be resisted unless it involves real loss of meaning.

tithe makes *-thable* ; see MUTE E.

titillate makes *titillable*; see -ABLE 1.

TITLES. A curious & regrettable change has come about in the last twenty or thirty years. Whereas we used, except on formal occasions, to talk & write of Lord Salisbury, Lord Derby, Lord Palmerston, & to be very sparing of the prefixes Marquis, Earl, & Viscount, the newspapers are now full of Marquis Curzon, Earl Beatty, Viscount Rothermere, & similarly Marchioness this & Countess that have replaced the Lady that used to be good enough for ordinary wear. We have taken a leaf in this as in other matters from the Japanese book ; it was when Japan took to European titles that such combinations as *Marquis Ito* first became familiar to us, & our adoption of the fashion is more remarkable than pleasing.

tittupy. Not *-ppy* ; see -P-, -PP-.

tmesis. See TECHNICAL TERMS.

to. 1. Substitution for other prepositions. 2. Unidiomatic infinitive.

1. *After three years' experience of the official machine I am of opinion that the causes are to be found* in *the rottenness of the present system, to the absence of any system at all so far as Cabinet control is concerned, & to the system of bestowing honours on the recommendations of Ministers.* The *tos* result from indecision between *are to be found* & some loosely equivalent phrase such as *may be traced*, perhaps assisted by the writer's glancing back to recover his construction & having his eye caught by *to*. This sort of mistake occurs much more often with OF, under which it will be found fully illustrated.

2. Unidiomatic infinitive. *The impossibility* to assert *himself in any manner galled his very soul./The two* *factors are the obvious necessity to put an end once & for all to the Turkish misrule over alien races, & the . . . To assert & to put should clearly be of asserting & of putting.* Discussion will be found under GERUND 3 ; but it may be added here that it is not difficult to account for this very common lapse, sequences apparently similar being familiar enough. There is, for instance, nothing against saying It was an impossibility to assert himself, or It is an obvious necessity to put an end ; the difference is that *to assert* &c. & *to put* &c. are not there, as in the examples, adjectival appendages of *impossibility & necessity*, but the real subjects of the sentences, which might have run To assert himself was an impossibility, & To put an end to so-&-so is a necessity.

toady, v. For inflexions see VERBS IN -IE &c., 6.

tobacco. Pl. *-os* ; see -O(E)S 3.

tobacconist. For the form, see -IST.

toboggan makes *-aner, -aning* ; see -N-, -NN-.

toco, -ko. Usually spelt with c ; no plural.

today, tomorrow, tonight. The lingering of the hyphen, which is still usual after the *to* of these words, is a very singular piece of conservatism ; it helps no-one to pronounce, it distinguishes between no words that without it might be confused, &, as the *to* retains no vestige of its original meaning, a reminder that the words are compounds is useless. Moreover, it is probably true that few people in writing ever dream of inserting the hyphen, its omission being corrected every time by those who profess the mystery of printing.

toffee. The successive forms seem to have been *taffy, toffy, toffee* ; it may be guessed that the last is due to the influence of *coffee*, but it is now established.

together. *All t.* must be carefully distinguished from ALTOGETHER, often written instead of it.

toilet, -ette. The word should be completely anglicized in spelling & sound (not *-e'tte*, nor twahlĕ't). The verb, = to wash, dress, &c., is chiefly U.S. ; adj. & p.p. *-eted*, see -T-, -TT-.

toilless. So written, but pronounced with two separate *l*s ; see SKILLLESS s.f.

token. For synonyms see SIGN. *By the same t., more by t.,* are phrases that probably those who know most about their meaning are least likely to use ; the one thing clear is that, when they were part of everyday English, they did not mean what they are usually made to by those who now adorn their writings with them. See WARDOUR STREET.

toko. See TOCO.

Toledo. Pl. *-os* ; see -O(E)S 6.

toll. For synonyms see TAX.

tomato. Pl. *-oes* ; see -O(E)S 1.

Tommy. See SOBRIQUETS.

tomorrow, to-m-. See TODAY.

ton (fashion). See FRENCH WORDS.

ton (weight). *Ton,* the weight ; *tun,* the cask, vat, & wine-measure.

tondo. Pl. *tondos,* see -O(E)S 6 ; or *tondi* (-ē).

tone, v., makes *-nable* ; see MUTE E.

tonight, to-n-. See TODAY.

tonneau. See FRENCH WORDS.

tonsil makes *tonsillitis* ; -LL-, -L-.

tonsorial. A word used almost only in PEDANTIC HUMOUR.

tonsure, v., makes *-rable* ; MUTE E.

too. 1. With passive participle. 2. Illogical uses.

1. With passive participles *t.* is subject to the same limitations, though the point has been less noticed, as VERY ; the line, however, between the adjectival & the verbal p.p. is often hard to draw ; in the following two quotations the addition of *with* &c. & *in* &c. to the participles turns the scale, & *too much* should have been written instead of *too* :—*Belfast is* too occupied with *its own affairs,* too confident of itself, *to be readily stirred to any movement which would endanger its prosperity./But he was* too engrossed in *Northern Europe to realize his failure.*

2. Illogical uses. These are very

common, so common as to deserve a place among the STURDY INDEFENSIBLES & to be almost idiomatic. They result from confusing two logical ways of making a statement, one with & the other without *too*, & are better avoided. *Praise which perhaps was scarcely meant to be taken* too *literally* (a, which may easily be taken too literally ; b, which was not meant to be taken literally)./*We need not attach* too *much importance to the differences between Liberal & Labour* (a, We may easily attach too much ; b, We need not attach much)./*It is yet far too early to generalize* too *widely as to origins & influences* (a, If we generalize too early we may generalize too widely ; b, It is too early to generalize widely).

tool. Of the forms *edge-tool, edge tool*, & *edged tool*, it appears from the OED that the last is the least common, especially in the literal carpenters' use ; choice between the others depends on whether *tool* retains its accent (edge tool), or parts with it to *edge* (edge-tool) as it naturally would with technical wear & tear, but not in the proverb & other metaphors ; see HYPHENS 3 B.

toothful. Pl. -*ls* ; see -FUL.
top, writing of compounds. In *topboots, topcoat,* & *topsawyer*, the accent is on the second part, & they are therefore not qualified for the hyphen (see HYPHENS 3 B), but should be either as printed above, or each in two separate words. In *top hamper* & *top hat* the same is true of the accent, but the two-word solution is best, because p & h unseparated are apt to coalesce, as in *Tophet*. In *topmast* & *topsail* the loss of the definite vowel sound in the second part so disguises the fact of their being compounds that hyphens, though legitimate, are clearly superfluous. In *topgallant* accent again forbids the hyphen, & the silence of the p forbids separate words. In *top-heavy* (where the question of accent does not arise as in compounds of adjective followed by noun), the hyphen is required to separate p & h. See HYPHENS.

topmost. See -MOST.
torchon. See FRENCH WORDS.
tormentress. See FEMININE DESIGNATIONS.
tornado, torpedo. Pl. -*oes* ; see -O(E)S 1. For *tornado*, see also WIND, n.
torpid makes -*est* ; see -ER & -EST 4.
torpor. So spelt ; see -OUR & -OR.
torso. Pl. -*os* ; see -O(E)S 6.
tortoise. Pronounce tor'*tus* ; the pronunciation -oiz or -ois is not even given as an alternative by the OED.
torus. Pl. -*rī*.
toss. For *tossed* & *tost* see -T & -ED.
total. The adjective makes -*alest*, -*ally*, -*alize*(r), -*alizator*, -*ality* ; & the verb -*alled*, -*alling*. See -LL-, -L-.
tother, now only colloquial, was formerly in good literary use, & was then more often written *tother* than *t'other* ; there is therefore no need for the apostrophe.

toto caelo. Literally, ' by the whole sky ', i.e. by the greatest possible distance. Properly used only with *differ, different,* & words of similar meaning ; the writer of the following extract has guessed that it is a high-class variant of *totally* : *... had the effect of habitually repealing its own canon in part, during the life-time of parties ..., & of repealing it,* toto caelo, *after the death of either of them.* See FOREIGN DANGER.

touchy. See TETCHY.
toupee, toupet. The first is the form common in England in the 18th c., written without an accent & pronounced tōōpē' ; the second is the French word, now used in England & pronounced tōō'pā. Adjective *toupeted*, pronounced tōō'pād.

tour de force. See FRENCH WORDS.
tourniquet. Pronounce toor'nǐkět.
tournure. See FRENCH WORDS.
tousle, tousy. The OED puts these spellings first ; *touz-, tows-, towz-,* also occur.

tout court, tout ensemble. See FRENCH WORDS.

tow- & towing-. There is perhaps an impression that in the compounds (e. g. -boat, -line, -net, -path, -post, -rope) *towing-* is the correct form, & *tow-* a slovenly modern abbreviation. But it appears from the OED that *tow-boat* & *tow-line* are the only forms recorded for boat & line (the latter 1719), & *tow-rope* is about a century older than *towing-rope*; *towing-path*, however, is as much older than *tow-path*. There is in fact no reason for avoiding either form. Cf. *wash(ing)-stand*.

toward, towards, towardly. The adjectives *toward* (including the predicative use as in *a storm is toward*, i. e. coming) & *towardly* are pronounced tō′ard(lĭ). The prepositions are best pronounced tŏrd(z), but in recent use the influence of spelling is forcing tŏŏwor′d(z) on the half educated. The adjectives in all senses are obsolescent, or at any rate archaic. Of the prepositions the -s form is the prevailing one, & the other tends to become literary on the one hand & provincial on the other.

towel makes -*lled*, -*lling*; -LL-,.-L-.

town. *T. clerk, t. council, t. hall, t. house,* & *t. talk,* should all be written as two separate words without hyphens; see HYPHENS 3 B. For *town-councillor,* which should be hyphened, see TRADE-*unionist*.

toy, n. A *toyshop* or *toy-shop* is a shop where toys are sold; a child's mock shop, on the other hand, is a *toy shop*; see HYPHENS 3 B.

toy, v. For inflexions see VERBS IN -IE &c., 4.

trace, n. For synonyms see SIGN.

trace, v., makes -*ceable*; see MUTE E.

trachea. Pronounce trăkē′a; pl. *tracheae.* The derived word in -itis is *tracheitis* (4 syl.), not *trachitis.* But the reaction of the many derivatives, such as *tracheotomy* & *tracheoscopic,* in which the relative stress on the first two syllables is reversed, has made tră′kĭa a popular

pronunciation. See also FALSE QUANTITY.

trade. Writing of compounds. *Trade mark* & *trade union,* no hyphens, see HYPHENS 3 B. In *trades(-)union* (cf. *swordsman, townsfolk,* &c.) the question is not so simple, but, as that form is dying out, need not be answered. In *trade-unionist* the hyphen, which would be wrong in *trade union,* is right, since -ist belongs not to *union* alone, but to the compound; cf. such words as *bow-legged,* never *bow legged.* In *trade-wind* the hyphen, though not obligatory (& not used in several of the OED quotations), is right if the stress is put, as the OED marks it, on *trade.*

trade, v., makes -*dable*; see MUTE E.

trade-wind. See WIND, n.

tradition(al)ism, -ist. For the general question between such variants, see -IST. In this case the longer forms are usual, probably because the words are often opposed to *rationalism,* -*ist,* the form of which is fixed by *ration*'s not having the necessary meaning.

traduce makes -*cible*; see -ABLE 2.

traffic, v., makes -*icked, -icker, -icking*; see -C-, -CK-.

tragédienne. See COMEDIAN.

tragic(al). See -IC(AL). It may almost be said that the longer form is, in serious use, dead; though the OED quotes it once or twice from modern writers in senses that it does not mark obsolete, in each of them *tragic* would have been the natural word. It survives, however, in playful use, often with a memory of the ' very tragicall mirth ' of Pyramus & Thisbe in *Midsummer Night's Dream.* For *tragic* (or *dramatic*) *irony,* see IRONY, 2.

tragicomedy, tragicomic, &c. The forms are due to medieval Latin, & too old to be themselves corrected to *tragico-comic* &c. But such syncopations should be at least noted as irregular when opportunity offers, with a view to discouraging imitations. See *pacifist* in the article -IST.

TRAILERS. Under this name a few specimens are collected of the sort of sentence that tires the reader out by again & again disappointing his hope of coming to an end. It is noticeable that writers who produce trailers produce little else, & that where one fine example occurs there are sure to be more in the neighbourhood ; the explanation probably is that these gentlemen have on the one hand a copious pen, & on the other a dislike (most natural, their readers must agree) to reading over what it may have set down. Whatever its cause, the trailer style is perhaps of all styles the most exasperating. Anyone who was conscious of this weakness might do much to cure himself by taking a pledge to use no relative pronouns for a year ; but perhaps most of its victims are unconscious. ' This type of wicket is always trappy, one ball coming first on to the bat, with another hanging fire, which so frequently causes a catch to be given by the batsman playing too quickly, as Hallows appeared to do when caught & bowled by Macaulay, when he promised a good innings, in spite of being missed at fine leg from a ball which certainly should have been caught, since the ball was played & not hit off the legs.'/' For instance, we conquered the Zulus & by exercise of sovereign powers set up a lot of chieftains in place of Cetywayo ; then, under protest from the Treasury, withdrew our hand & let them stew until, in the midst of their anarchy, Boer emissaries & fillibusters found a fertile soil for intrigues, that ended in a cession to them of territory to be called the New Republic, recognition of which was first refused & then, after a long period of acrimonious contention, assented to ; but not before many fine Zulus had been unnecessarily killed nor without some of the best of their agricultural land being lost to the tribe.'/' It is true that part of the traffic here is heavy, but at least the surface might

be conditioned by modern methods, even if the form of paving cannot well be altered, though I think it ought to be—e.g., if Sydney Smith's suggestion as to the wood pavement problem perplexing an old vestry— " Gentlemen, put your heads together, & the thing 's done "—is impracticable, there are now improved means open to a modern City Council, both in surface dressing, in hard woods, & even in macadam, by the use of slag— locally called dross—from the iron furnaces in Yorkshire, which makes the hardest & smoothest surface.'/ ' He deals also with Pemba Island, infested by hereditary wizards who are addicted to anthropophagy & theriomorphosis in the intervals of selling charms to natives to keep off thieves & to thieves to enable them to become invisible that they may the better plunder the natives.'/ ' It may be that the modification of our Free Trade principles to a sufficient form of Fair Trade will be all that is necessary to prevent the final decline, which probably the pinch of the last few years has prevented from setting in from a previous run of prosperity, which, by causing the easy realization of fine old businesses under the seductive lines of Limited Liability, has resulted in the " Super man " being eliminated in favour of a joint control in which the divergence of opinion among Directors with little personal interest has prevented a uniformity & continuity of policy absolutely essential in the management of any business with widespread interests.'/' But, so far as I could see, nobody carried away burning candles to rekindle with holy fire the lamp in front of the ikon at home, which should burn throughout the year except for the short time it is extinguished in order to receive anew the light that is relit every year throughout the Christian world by Christ's victory over death.'

traipse. See TRAPES.

trait. The final t is sounded in America, but still usually silent in England. For synonyms, see SIGN.

traitress. FEMININE DESIGNATIONS.
trammel makes -*lled*, -*lling*; -LL-,-L-.
tranquil makes -*illest*, -*illity*, -*illize*, -*illy*; see -LL-, -L-, 2. Mis-spellings are very common, esp. *tranquility*, wrong even on U.-S. principles.

transact makes *transactor*; see -OR.
transcendence, -cy. See -CE, -CY.
transcendent(al). These words, with their many specialized applications in philosophy, are for the most part beyond the scope of this book; but there are popular uses in which the right form should be chosen. 1. The word that means surpassing, of supreme excellence or greatness, &c., is *transcendent*, & the following is wrong—*The matter is of transcendental importance, especially in the present disastrous state of the world.* See LONG VARIANTS for similar pairs. 2. The word applied to God in contrast with IMMANENT is *transcendent*. 3. The word that means visionary, idealistic, outside of experience, &c., is *transcendental*. 4. The word applied to Emerson & his ' religio-philosophical teaching ' is *transcendental*.

transcribe makes -*bable*; MUTE E.
transfer. Noun *tra'nsfer*, verb *transfer'*, see NOUN & VERB; *transferred, -erring, -error*, see -R-, -RR-; but *transferable*, see CONFER(R)ABLE; & *transference, transferee, & transferor*. Of *transferrer & transferor*, the first is the general agent-noun, a person or mechanism that passes something on, & the second a legal term for the person who conveys his property to another, the *transferee*.

transfuse makes -*sible*; see -ABLE 2.
transgress makes *transgressor*; -OR.
tranship, transship, trans-ship. To all who do not happen to have been reconciled by familiarity to the short form it presents itself as an odd sort of monster, which they start by pronouncing trä'nshĭp cf.) *transom*), & do not at once connect

with shipping. And they have at any rate the justification, however little they may be aware of it, that there are no other words in which *trans* is curtailed to *tran* when it is prefixed to a word of English & not Latin origin like *ship*. The full & indisputably better form *trans-ship* is accordingly here recommended; but the OED accepts *tranship*, saying only ' *less commonly* trans-ship '. Generations of clerks have saved themselves trouble & nearly made away with the s & the hyphen; of 28 OED quotations, including those for *tran(s-)shipment*, nine only show s-s or ss—nine & the right against nineteen & the wrong.

translate makes -*table*, see MUTE E; & -*tor*, see -OR.
transliterate makes -*rable*, see -ABLE 1; & -*tor*, see -OR.
translucence, -cy. See -CE, -CY.
translucent. See TRANSPARENT.
transmit makes -*itted, -itter, -itting*, see -T-, -TT-; & -*issible* or -*ittable*, see -ABLE 2.
transmogrify. For inflexions see VERBS IN -IE &c., 6.
transom makes *transomed*; -M-,-MM-.
transparence, -ency. The second is the usual form. The first is marked *rare* in the OED; & indeed, in its only two -*ence* quotations that are as late as 1800 euphony plainly accounts for the avoidance of -*cy*:—*Motive may be detected through the transparence of tendency./Adamantine solidity, transparence, & brilliancy.*

transparent, & the synonyms *diaphanous, pellucid, translucent. Transparent* is the general word for describing what is penetrable by sight (lit. or fig.) or by light, & it can be substituted for any of the others unless there is some point of precision or of rhetoric to be gained. All three synonyms have the rhetorical value of being less common than *transparent*, & therefore appear more often in poetical writing. As regards precision, the following definitions of the words' narrower senses are offered, & to each are appended some specially appropriate nouns, & the adjective or participle that seems most directly opposed.

That is *diaphanous* which does not preclude sight of what is behind it ; *garments, vapour, membrane* ; opp. *shrouding.*

That is *transparent* which does not even obscure sight of what is behind it ; *glass, candour, pretence* ; opp. *obscuring.*

That is *pellucid* which does not distort images seen through it ; *water, literary style* ; opp. *turbid.*

That is *translucent* which does not bar the passage of light ; *alabaster, tortoise-shell* ; opp. *opaque.*

transpire. The notorious misuse of this word consists in making it mean happen or turn out or go on ; & the legitimate meaning that has been misinterpreted into this is to emerge from secrecy into knowledge, to leak out, to become known by degrees. It is needless to do more than give a single example of the right use, followed by several of the wrong :— *The conditions of the contract were not allowed to t.* (right)./*That strike has caused a not inconsiderable increase in the cost of production, while nothing similar has transpired in Germany within the past few years to produce any such effect here./Abeken . . . has a pretty fair idea, although no very accurate information, of what was transpiring in the inner circles of Bismarck's mind./What they demand is that, after negotiations have been carried through, a statement should be made as to what has transpired./Both men opened in a subdued mood in what transpired to be the last game of this grand fight.* The last of these adds to the wrong meaning of *t.* an unidiomatic construction after it in the infinitive *to be.* That construction will not do even when *t.* has its true sense ; that sense is complete in itself, & *transpired to be* is as little English as *came to light to be* ; here is the right sense followed

by the wrong construction : *They must have been aware of the possibility that the facts might be as they ultimately transpired to be.*
In the literal sense, *t.* makes *-rable*, see MUTE E.

transport. Noun *tra'nsport*, verb *transpor't* ; see NOUN & VERB.

transposal. See -AL.

transpose makes *-sable*; see MUTE E.

trans-ship(ment). The better spellings ; see TRANSHIP.

transubstantiation. The pronunciation *-sïă'shn*, which is recognized as an alternative by the OED, is here recommended ; see -CIATION.

trapes, traipse. The first seems to be at present the orthodox spelling ; but the word in this form has so puzzling a look that it would surely be better to use the second, which is allowed by the OED as an alternative, is quoted from Swift & Pope, & can be pronounced only one way. The objection to it is that, if the supposed origin (= French *trapasser* = *trespass*) is correct, it is obscured rather more by *traipse* than by *trapes*; but then it may not be correct.

trapezium. Pl. *-ia, -ms* ; see -UM.

travail, travel. Distinguished in pronunciation, but rather slightly, as tră'vĭl & tră'vel ; in the parts with an extra syllable (-ing, -er, -eth) the difference is plainer, *travail* making trisyllables & *travel* disyllables (tră'vlĭng &c.). *Travel*, but not *travail*, makes *-ller, -lled, -lling* ; see -LL-, -L-. For *travelled* adj. see INTRANSITIVE P.P.

traverse, v., has *-sable* ; MUTE E.

travesty. See BURLESQUE ; &, for verb inflexion, VERBS IN -IE &c., 6.

trayful. Pl. *-ls* ; see -FUL.

treacle makes *-cly* ; see MUTE E.

treasonable, treasonous. The meanings are not distinguishable ; *treasonous* is now comparatively rare, & more likely to be met in verse.

treasure, v., makes *-rable* ; see MUTE E.

Treasury. *T. bench, T. note* ; no hyphens ; see HYPHENS 3 B.

treble. See TRIPLE.

trecento, -tist. Pronounce trä-chě'ntō, -tĭst. This & *quattrocento, -ist, cinquecento, -ist*, are words constantly used by writers on Italian art. Though their true meaning is 300, 400, 500, they are used as abbreviations for the centuries 1300-1399 (1301-1400 is with us the 14th c.), 1400-1499 (our 15th c.), & 1500-1599 (our 16th). There is therefore a double puzzle, Italian 300 for Italian 1300, & Italian 13th c. for English 14th c. The words in *-ist* mean painters &c. of the century.

tree'd is perhaps preferable to *treed*; cf. FEE'D & PEDIGREE'D, & see -ED & 'D.

trefoil. OED gives preference to trē- over trě-.

trellis makes *-ised*; see -S-, -SS-.

trembly, not *-ey*; see MUTE E.

tremolo. Pl. *-os*; see -O(E)S 6.

tremor. So spelt; see -OUR & -OR.

trend. A word that, whether as noun or as verb, should be used by no-one who is not sure of both its meaning & its idiomatic habits. *There has unquestionably been a trend of German policy to strengthen the Empire's naval position by making relations closer with Austria-Hungary, Italy, & Turkey./His chapter on . . ., although it has little to do with the rest of his volume, & trends very closely upon the forbidden theme of history, is interesting.* ' There is a t. of German policy to do ' is not English, though ' The t. of German policy is to do ' would be. *Trends very closely upon* is perhaps a confusion with *trenches* &c. ; the essential idea in *t.* is direction, not encroachment.

trente et quarante. FRENCH WORDS.

trepan. Both verbs, that meaning entrap, & the surgical, make *trepanned, -nning*; see -N-, -NN-.

trepan, trephine, nn. & vv. The first, the older term for the instrument & for operating with it, is probably still the prevailing one in lay use ; but in surgical books &c. *trephine*, which as a noun is properly the name of an improvement on the trepan, is now the regular term. Pronounce trĭfĭ'n or trĭfē'n.

trestle. Pronounce -sl ; see PRONUNCIATION, Silent t.

trial. *T. heat, t. trip* ; no hyphens ; see HYPHENS 3 B.

tribrach. See TECHNICAL TERMS. Pronounce trī'brăk.

tribunal. Pronounce trĭbū'nal or trĭbū'nal ; the i is short in Latin, but OED puts trī- first, & see FALSE QUANTITY.

tributary. So spelt ; cf. *contributory*, & see MANDATARY.

tribute. 1. For synonymy see TAX. 2. A SLIPSHOD EXTENSION of the less excusable kind—since the meaning of *t.* is surely no mystery—is that which nowadays sets ' a t. to ' to do the work of *a proof* (or *illustration* &c.) *of*, as in :—*The debate on the whole was a tribute to the good taste & good form of the House of Commons./All these & many other prominent English works have been fairly & critically analysed, & it is a tribute to the modesty of the American editors that the European works receive first place.*

tricentenary. See CENTENARY.

triceps. For plural, see BICEPS.

tricksy)(tricky. DIFFERENTIATION is proceeding, in the direction of restricting *tricksy* to contexts in which the quality is regarded not with condemnation or dislike or apprehension (=dishonest, cunning, difficult, &c.) but with amusement or interest (=playful, ingenious, &c.). It had formerly, to judge from the OED record, all the meanings to itself, being more than two centuries older than *tricky*.

triclinium. Pl. *-ia*.

tricolor, tricolore, 'tricolour. The first is a Latin adjective (trī'kolor) used in botanical names ; the second is the French adjective used in describing the French flag (*le drapeau tricolore*) ; the third is a badly formed English noun (see COLOUR, & HYBRID DERIVATIVES) used by itself as a name (*the tricolour*) for the French flag, & usually pronounced trĭ'kŭler. It would be better to use *tricolor* (trĭ'kolor) in this sense also, & drop the other two forms.

triforium. Pl. -*ia*.

trigger makes -*ered* ; see -R-, -RR-.

trill. For the phonetic sense see TECHNICAL TERMS.

trillion. See BILLION.

trilogy,trimeter. TECHNICAL TERMS.

trio. Pron. trē'ō. Pl.-*os*, see -O(E)S 4.

triolet. See TECHNICAL TERMS. Pronounce trī-.

triple)(treble. If the musical sense of *treble* is put aside, there are perhaps no senses in which one is possible & the other impossible ; but they do tend to diverge. First, though either can be adjective, verb, or noun, *treble* is the more usual verb & noun, & *triple* the more usual adjective. Secondly, in the adjectival use *treble* now refers rather to amount (three times as great &c.), & *triple* rather to plurality (of three kinds or parts). A few phrases, in each of which the word used is clearly preferable to the other, will illustrate :—Newspaper has trebled its circulation. / Treble the money would not buy it now. / This is quite treble what I expected. / Going at treble the pace. / He offered me treble wages. / The fight was resumed with treble fury. / Treble difficulty (=three times the difficulty) ; a triple difficulty (=a difficulty of three kinds). / Surrounded with a triple wall. / Triple-expansion engines. / The classification is triple. / Triple alliance, contest, birth.

triplet. See -STICH, & TECHNICAL TERMS.

tripod. OED pronounces trī'pŏd, with no alternative (but trĭ'podal, also without alternative). But trĭ'pod is now certainly often heard, & is not unlikely to prevail.

triptych. Pronounce -k.

tristich. See -STICH.

trisyllable. So spelt.

triturate makes -*rable*; see -ABLE 1.

triumphal, -phant. The meanings are quite distinct, but to use the first for the second is usually a worse mistake than the converse, because the idea it ought to convey is narrower & more definite. *Triumphal* means only of or in the celebration of a victory, & belongs to the original ' triumph ' or victorious general's ' procession ; *triumphant* belongs to triumph in any of its senses, especially those of brilliant success or exultation. In the following quotations each word is used where the other was required. The ' progress ' of the first was not almost, but quite, triumphant ; & the ' career ' of the second, if it lasted 66 years & was troubled, may have been triumphant, but hardly triumphal. . . . *through the streets of which he had almost a triumphant progress, with women clinging about his car, manifesting in every possible way their delight at his presence.*/ . . . *the story he told us of the sixty-six previous years of his troubled, triumphal career.* See also MALAPROPS, & PAIRS & SNARES.

triumvir. Pl. -*rs* or less usu. -*rī* ; see LATIN PLURALS.

-TRIX. As any Latin agent noun in -*tor* could form a feminine in -*trix*, some of these when taken into English continue to do so, especially such as are, like *testator & prosecutor*, in legal use. It is a serious inconvenience that the Latin plural is -*ices* (-ī'sēz) ; if the Latin quantity is preserved, the accent has to be shifted in the plural, which makes the word hardly recognizable. The result is that it is sometimes given up as a bad job ; OED gives e. g. *prosecu'trices & ra'dices* (radix like the -trix words, with Latin pl. *radī'ces*), & allows *matrix* a popular ma'trices by the side of a correct matrī'ces ; but for *cicatrix & mediatrix* it allows only -trī'ces, & for *directrix, executrix, heritrix,* states only that the pl. is -*ices* & leaves us to deal with quantity & accent as we please.

This sort of confusion would be

best cured by sinking the words' latinity & giving them all the ordinary English plural—*testa'trixes* &c. instead of testatrī'ces or testa'trīces. For some of them the further anglicizing of *-trix* into *-tress* would also be possible. For the other escape of using the masculine form & dropping the feminine, see FEMININE DESIGNATIONS.

The chief words concerned are : administratrix, cicatrix, directrix, executrix, heritrix, inheritrix, matrix, mediatrix, prosecutrix, radix, testatrix.

troche. A word that it requires some ingenuity to pronounce wrong, trōsh, trōch, & trōk, being all recognized ; but the OED draws the line at trō'kĭ, which is, it appears, ' commercial & vulgar '.

trochee. See TECHNICAL TERMS.
trois-temps. See FRENCH WORDS.
trolley. Usually so spelt ; pl. *-eys.*
troop. *Trooping the colour* is the orthodox modern phrase ; but in the older quotations in the OED it is *colours.*

trophy. OED pronounces trō- without alternative.
trottoir. See FRENCH WORDS.
troublous. ' Now only literary or archaic ' says the OED ; & one of its quotations shows well the bad effect of diversifying commonplace contexts with words of that sort ; the ordinary *troublesome* was the word wanted : *Mr Walpole took on himself the management of the Home Office, little knowing what a troublous business he had brought upon his shoulders.*

trounce makes *-ceable* ; see MUTE E.
trousers. So spelt. Adjective *trousered*, see -R-, -RR-. Compounds best made without the -s, e.g. *trouser-button, -pocket, -stretcher.*

trousseau. See FRENCH WORDS, &, for plural, -X.
trout. Pl. usually the same, see COLLECTIVES 1, 4.
trouvaille, trouvère. See FRENCH

WORDS. *From time to time the rector records the arrival in this bird sanctuary of redstarts, or still rarer trouvailles* (visitors ?).

trow, when still in ordinary use, was pronounced trō.
trowel makes *-lled, -lling* ; -LL-, -L-.
truculence, -cy. See -CE, -CY ; &, for pronunciation, foll.
truculent. OED gives preference to trōō'kŭ- over trŭ'kŭ- ; but the latter is gaining, chiefly, no doubt, owing to the much greater ease given by the wider dissimilation of the two vowels ; cf. the substitution of lōō for lū in the still more difficult *lugubrious & lucubration* (see LU).

TRUE & FALSE ETYMOLOGY. English being the one of all languages that has gathered its material from the most various sources, the study of its etymology is naturally of exceptional interest. It is a study, however, worth undertaking for that interest, & as an end in itself, rather than as a means to the acquiring either of a sound style or even of a correct vocabulary. What concerns a writer is much less a word's history than its present meaning & idiomatic habits. The etymologist is aware, & the person who has paid no attention to the subject is probably unaware, that a *fuse* is so called not because it *fuses* anything, but because it is spindle-shaped ; that a *belfry* is not named from its *bell* ; that a child's *cot* & a sheep-*cot* come from different languages ; that *Welsh rabbit* is amusing & right, & *Welsh rarebit* stupid & wrong ; that *isle & island* have nothing in common ; & that *pygmy* is a more significant spelling than *pigmy*. But to know when it is & when it is not well to call an island an isle is worth more than to know all these etymological facts. Still, etymology has its uses, even for those whose sole concern with it is as an aid to writing & a preventive of blunders ; it may save us from treating *protagonist* as the opposite of *antagonist*, or from supposing a *watershed* to be a river-basin, or from materializing the *comity of nations* into either a committee or a company of them, or from thinking that to *demean* oneself is to lower oneself or do a *mean* thing ; but it must be added that the etymology providing such stray scraps of useful knowledge is much more that which deals with the French & Latin elements in our language than that which deals with its native or Teutonic substratum. Those who start with a knowledge of Latin & French have in this way a very real if not very calculable advantage over writers who are without it ; but to advise the latter to acquire Latin & French at a late stage with a view to ridding themselves of the handicap, still more to incite them to a course of pure English etymology, would be foolish indeed.

After this much of warning, which amounts to a confession that etymological knowledge is of less importance to writers than might be supposed, a selection of words is offered exemplifying the small surprises that reward or disappoint the etymologist. They are arranged alphabetically, but are a very low percentage of what might have been collected ; with each word the barest indication only is given of the point, which to many readers will be already known, & by others may be easily verified in any good dictionary ; the object of the list is not to give etymologies, but to provide anyone who is curious about the value of such knowledge with the means of testing it. The words in small capitals are the few that happen to have been treated in their places in any way that at all bears upon the present subject.

AMUCK, not E *muck*
anthem, not Gk *anatithēmi* to offer
apparel, not L *paro* prepare
arbour, not L *arbor* tree
barberry, not E *berry*
bastard, not E *base*
beetle, several words
belfry, not E *bell*

blindfold, not E *fold*
bliss, not E *bless*
boon, a prayer, not its granting
bound (homeward &c.), not E *bind*
BOURN, separate words
boxing-day, not pugilistic
bridal, not an adjective in *-al*
BRIER (pipe), not E *brier*
buckwheat, not E *buck*
buttonhole, not *hole* but *hold*
card (comb wool &c.), not from *card* (paper)
carnival, not from L *vale* farewell
case, separate words
chevaux de frise, = Frisian cavalry
cinders, not L *cineres*
cockroach, not *cock* or *roach*
COCOA, COCONUT, unconnected
COMITY, not L *comes* companion
convey, not L *veho* carry
cookie (bun &c.), not E *cook*
cope, several words
core, not L *cor* heart
COT(E), separate words
COUNTRY DANCE, not F *contre-danse*
COURT CARD, a corruption
crayfish, not E *fish*
CURARE, not L *curo*
curtail, not E *tail*
cutlet, not E *cut*
DEMEAN, not E *mean*
dispatch, not F *dépêcher*
egg on, not *egg* but *edge*
EQUERRY, not L *equus* horse
ERRAND, not L *erro* wander
FAROUCHE, not L *ferox* fierce
FETISH, not of barbarian but L origin
FINGERING (wool), not E *finger*
FORBEARS, = fore-beërs
FUSE, FUSEE, from L *fusus* spindle
GINGERLY, not E *ginger*
GIPSY, source disguised by spelling
GLOSS, one word coloured by another
GREYHOUND, not E *grey*
incentive, not L *incendo* to fire
ingenuity, stolen by *ingenious* from *ingenuous*
ISLAND, mis-spelt from confusion with *isle*
Jerusalem artichoke, not *Jerusalem*
LITANY, LITURGY, first syllables unconnected
lutestring, not *lute* or *string*
MESEMBRYANTHEMUM, deceptive -y- for -i-

MOOD (gram.), = *mode*, not *mood* (temper)

MOULD, several words

pen, pencil, unconnected

PIGMY, deceptive -i- for -y-

PROTAGONIST, Gk *prŏtos* first, not *prŏ* for

recover, not E *cover*

repair, two separate verbs

river, not L *rivus* river

scale, several words

scarify, not E *scare*

scissors, not L *scindo sciss-* cleave

SORRY, SORROW, unconnected

TUBEROSE, not *tube* or *rose*

tureen, not *Turin*

vile, villain, unconnected

WATERSHED, neither a store of water nor a place that sheds water

WELSH RABBIT, not *rare bit*.

truffle. OED gives precedence to the pronunciation trŭ'fl, which is the natural English ; but association with French cookery leads many people to partly assimilate the sound to that of the differently spelt French word, & say trōō'fl.

truism. The word's two meanings have been compared both with each other & with some synonyms under COMMONPLACE. *It is not permissible to be too sanguine of the outcome of the Conference, & A leading personage at the Conference declares that there is no cause for* undue *alarm,* are examples of the sort of t. that writers should not allow themselves ; mend them by changing *too* into *very* & *undue* into *much,* & see TOO 2. As to the use of the word itself, the temptation to say that a thing is a truism when no more is meant than that it is true, because it has a smarter sound, should be resisted ; so : *It probably owes much to the dialect in which it is played ; but that is a truism of almost every Irish or Scotch play.*

truly. See LETTER FORMS.

trumpet makes *-eting, -eted, -eter* ; see -T-, -TT-. *T. major* ; no hyphen ; see HYPHENS (Group *Court Martial).

truncate. See -ATABLE.

trunk. *T. drawers, t. hose, t. road,* no hyphens, see HYPHENS 3 B.

trunkful. Pl. *-ls* ; see -FUL.

trunnion makes *-oned* ; -N-, -NN-.

trust. The OED's definition of the commercial sense is here given, for comparison with CARTEL : A body of producers or traders in some class of business, organized to reduce or defeat competition, lessen expenses, & control production & distribution for their common advantage ; *spec.,* such a combination of commercial or industrial companies, with a central governing body of trustees which holds a majority or the whole of the stock of each of the combining firms, thus having a controlling vote in the conduct & operation of each.

trustworthy, -ily. The generation is perhaps nearly extinct that held it a duty to thrust this good word into places where it was in obvious discomfort in order that the naughty *reliable* might be kept out. The OED quotes from the *Daily News* of 1870 'I am trustworthily informed that . . .', with other specimens. See RELIABLE.

truth. Pl. pron. -dhz ; -TH & -DH.

try. The idiom *t. & do* something is described as colloquial for *t. to do.* Its use is almost confined to exhortations & promises : *Do t. & stop coughing ; I will t. & have it ready for you.* And it is hardly applicable to past time ; *He tried & made the best of it* is not English in the sense required, though *He did t. & make the best of it* is conceivable. It is, therefore, colloquial, if that means specially appropriate to actual speech ; but not if *colloquial* means below the proper standard of literary dignity. Though *t. to do* can always be substituted for *t. & do,* the latter has a shade of meaning that justifies its existence ; in exhortations it implies encouragement—the effort will succeed— ; in promises it implies assurance—the effort shall succeed. It is an idiom that should be not discountenanced, but used when it comes natural. See PEDANTRY.

trysail. Pronounce trī'sl.

Tsar. ' The now prevalent spelling '
—OED.

tsetse. So spelt ; pron. tsĕ'tsĭ.

-T-, -TT-. Words ending in -t are
very numerous, & there seems to be
some hesitation about making them
conform to the rules that prevail for
most consonants : forms like *rivetter,
blanketty, docketted,* are often seen,
though good usage is against them.
Monosyllables ending in -t double
it before suffixes beginning with
vowels if the sound preceding it is
a single vowel (a, e, i, o, u), but not
if it is a diphthong or a doubled
vowel or a vowel & r : *pettish, potted,
cutter,* but *flouting, sooty, skirting.*
Words of more than one syllable
follow the rule for monosyllables if
their last syllable is accented (*co-
quettish,* but *repeater*) ; but otherwise they do not double it : *discomfited, riveter, combatant, wainscoting,
snippety, pilotage, balloted.*

tub. For *the Tub* in philosophic
slang, see ACADEMY.

tube makes *tubing* ; see MUTE E.

tuber is the darling of the lower
class of ELEGANT-VARIATIONists—
the class that indulges in the practice not as a troublesome duty but
for pleasure. A potato is a t., but
the fact should be left in the decent
obscurity of agricultural textbooks.
*There was no difficulty in getting
potatoes one day—the next, so to
speak, you could search Paris without
discovering a single* tuber. /*The* potato
crop *in South Lincolnshire is in grave
danger owing to the shortage of labour ;*
the tubers, *which by this time should
be nearly all lifted, are still in the
ground.* /*Sir Walter Raleigh popularized* them, *& in all probability
Sir Francis Drake was the first to
bring* the tuber *that is ' doing its bit '
in the war from the New World.*

tuberose. Pronounce tū'berōs (not
tū'brōz) ; not from *tube* or *rose,* but
from (*Polianthes*) *tuberosa* = tuber-
ous, or grown from tubers.

tubful. Pl. *-ls* ; see -FUL.

Tuesday. For (*on*) *T.,* see FRIDAY.

tug. For *t. at* one's *heartstrings,*
see STOCK PATHOS.

tulle. See FRENCH WORDS.

tumblerful. Pl. *-ls* ; see -FUL.

tumbrel, -bril. OED gives the two
spellings in this order.

tumefy. So spelt, not *tumi-* ; for
inflexions see VERBS IN -IE &c. 6.

tumidity, tumidness. -TY & -NESS.

tumultuary)(tumultuous. The distinction between the two is not very
definite, & sentences may easily be
made in which either might be used
& give the same sense. But it may
first be said that *-tuous* is now the
much commoner word, which should
be chosen unless there is good reason
to prefer the other ; &, secondly,
what is emphasized by *-tuous* is
rather the violence & impetus &
force, while *-tuary* emphasizes the
irregularity & unorganized nature,
of the thing described : *tumultuous
applause, seas, attack, joy, crowd* ;
tumultuary forces (hastily levied),
thoughts (thronging confusedly), *risings* (sporadic).

tumulus. Pl. *-lī.*

tun. See TON.

tune makes *tunable & tuny* ; see
MUTE E, & -EY & -Y.

tunnel makes *-lled, -lling* ; -LL-, -L-.

tu quoque. See TECHNICAL TERMS.

turban makes *-aned* ; see -N-, -NN-.

turbid makes *-est* ; see -ER & -EST 4.

turbidity, turbidness. -TY & -NESS.

turbine. OED recognizes only the
pronunciation with -ĭn ; & that
with -īn, now often heard, & due
only to misguided reverence for
spelling, will doubtless pass away.

Turc-. See TURK.

Turcoman (pl. *-ans*) is the form
accepted by the OED in preference
to *Turkoman & Turkman* ; cf. TURK.

tureen. The right pronunciation is
terē'n, in accordance with the derivation (*terra* earth) & the older
English spelling (*terrene* &c.) ; but
it is now more often said as tūrē'n, &
perhaps associated with *Turin.*

turf. Pl. ; *-fs & -ves* appear an
equal number of times in the post-

18th-c. quotations of the OED, which itself uses *-fs*. See -VE(D).

turgid makes *-est*; see -ER & -EST 4. For *turgidity*, *-idness*, see -TY & -NESS.

Turk makes *Turco*, & *Turco-* (in compounds, as *Turcophil*, *-phobe*, *-mania*), but *Turkery*, *Turkic*, *Turkism*, & *Turkize* (as well as *Turkey* & *Turkish*).

turkey. Pl. *-eys*.

Turk(o)man. See TURCOMAN.

turn, v. In the age idiom three constructions are recognized : *I have turned 20*, *I am turned of 20*, & *I am turned 20* ; the last (see for the construction INTRANSITIVE P.P.) is apparently of more recent origin than the second, but is said by the OED to be now more usual in England ; the 'of' has certainly an old-fashioned or provincial sound.

turnip makes *-ipy* ; see -P-, -PP-.

turn-over. See TECHNICAL TERMS.

turps. See CURTAILED WORDS.

turquoise. Pronunciation debatable. With Ben Jonson, Shakspere, Milton, & Tennyson, all for ter'kĭz (or something like it), it is a pity that we cannot return to that ; but the adoption of the later French spelling has corrupted us, & the OED labels ter'kĭz archaic ; it refuses, on the other hand, to recognize the kw sound for the *-qu-* & complete the triumph of spelling ; ter'koiz seems the best solution.

turret makes *-eted* ; see -T-, -TT-.

tusser, tussore. The first, though now the less used, is preferable not only as keeping the sound of the last syllable closer to the original, but also as preventing a shift of the accent from the *tus-*. *T.* is a sufficient name for the material without the addition of *silk*.

tutoress. FEMININE DESIGNATIONS.

tuyere. Pronounce twēr.

twelvemo, 12mo. See FOLIO. Pl. *-os* ; see -O(E)S, 6.

twenties, thirties, &c. These words do not require an apostrophe (*the 'twenties* &c.) when used for the years 20–29 &c. of a century, & still less for those of a person's life.

twentymo, twenty-fourmo, 20mo, 24mo. See FOLIO. Pl. *-os* ; see -O(E)s 6.

twilit. The earliest OED quotation for the word is 1869, so that it is, whatever its merits may be, not venerable. Its formation implies a verb *to twilight* made from the noun ; & that verb, though unknown to most of us, is recorded to have been used ; it also implies that *to twilight* has p.p. *twilit* rather than *twilighted*, which is not impossible. But, though *twilit* can therefore not be absolutely ruled out, it is better to use *twilight* attributively where, as usually, that does the work as well, & elsewhere to do without. In the two following quotations, *twilight* would have served at least as well :—
He found himself free of a fanciful world where things happened as he preferred—a twilit world in which substance melted into shadow./The years of the war were a clear & brilliantly lit passage between two periods of twilit entanglement.

twine, v., makes *-nable* ; see MUTE E.

TWOPENCE COLOURED. The insertion of irrelevant details, resort to needless rhetoric, & such devices for the heightening of effect, move the reader (as Mr Burchell ' at the conclusion of every sentence would cry out " *Fudge* " ') to exclaim in more modern phrase 'twopence coloured !'. A couple of specimens of what meets us every day must suffice ; it will be noticed that cantons & heights & plains have nothing to do with the matter ; & that the rhetoric of the second extract has a very factitious sound :—
Again, I look around & see in the Cantons of Switzerland, on the heights of Quebec, & in the plains of Hungary, Protestants & Roman Catholics living, as a rule, in harmony & peace together./The glib, thin-lipped Burian, the soulless hybrid product of Magyar arrogance & of the Vienna Ballplatz diplomacy, has already been swept away with the polished formulas on which he thought to ride the storm.

-TY & -NESS. The number of legitimate words in -ness is limited only by that of the adjectives that exist in English ; but, though any adjective may be formed into a noun on occasion by the addition of -ness, the nouns of that pattern actually current are much fewer, there being hundreds, usually preferred to the -ness forms, that are made from Latin adjectives with -ty, -ety, or -ity, as their ending. Thus from *one* & *loyal* & *various* we can make for special purposes *oneness, loyalness,* & *variousness* ; but ordinarily we prefer *unity, loyalty,* & *variety.* Of the -ty words that exist, a very large majority are for all purposes commoner & better than the corresponding -ness words, usage & not anti-Latinism being the right arbiter. Scores of words could be named, such as *ability, honesty, notoriety, prosperity, sanity, stupidity,* for which it is hard to imagine any good reason for substituting *ableness, notoriousness,* &c. On the other hand words in -ness that are better than existent forms in -ty are rare ; perhaps *acuteness* & *conspicuousness* have the advantage of *acuity* & *conspicuity* ; & if *perspicuousness* could be established in place of *perspicuity* it might help to obviate the common confusion with *perspicacity* ; but in general a -ty word that exists is to be preferred to its rival in -ness, unless total or partial differentiation has been established, or is designed for the occasion. Total differentiation has taken place between *ingenuity* & *ingenuousness, casualty* & *casualness, sensibility* & *sensibleness, enormity* & *enormousness* ; the use of either form instead of the other necessarily changes or destroys the meaning. Partial differentiation results from the more frequent use made of the -ty words ; both terminations have, to start with, the abstract sense of the quality for which the adjective stands ; but while most of the -ness words, being little used, remain abstract & still denote quality only, many of the -ty

words acquire by much use various concrete meanings in addition ; e.g., *humanity, curiosity, variety,* beside the senses ' being human, curious, various ', acquire those of ' all human beings ', ' a curious object ', & ' a sub-species '. Or again they are so habitually applied in a limited way that the full sense of the adjective is no longer naturally suggested by them ; *preciosity* is limited to literary or artistic style, *maturity* suggests the moment of reaching rather than the state of matureness, *purity* & *frailty* take a sexual tinge that *pureness* & *frailness* are without, *poverty* is more nearly confined to lack of money than *poorness.* It is when lucidity requires the excluding of some such meaning or implication attached only to the -ty form that a -ness word may reasonably be substituted.

One or two articles under which special remarks will be found are BARBARISM &c., ENORMOUS, OBLIQUENESS, OPACITY, POVERTY, PRECIOSITY, SENSIBILITY. For similar distinctions between other nearly equivalent terminations, see -CE, -CY, -IC(AL), -ION & -NESS, -ION & -MENT, -ISM & -ITY.

A few specimens may be added & classified that have not been cited above, but are notable in some way. A. Some words in -ty for which, the Latin adjective not having been taken into English, there is no companion in -ness : celerity, cupidity, debility, fidelity, integrity, lenity, utility. B. Some more in which the -ty word has a marked concrete or limited sense not shared by the other : capacity, commodity, fatality, festivity, monstrosity, nicety, novelty, speciality, subtlety. C. Some of the few in -ness that are as much used as those in -ty, or more, though the -ty words exist : clearness (clarity), crudeness, falseness, graciousness, inevitableness, jocoseness, literalness, litigiousness, morbidness, moroseness, passiveness, ponderousness, positiveness, punctiliousness, spaciousness, sublimeness, tenseness, unctuousness. D. Some -ness words that have no corresponding form in -ty, though the adjective is of Latin origin & might have been expected to produce one : crispness, facetiousness, firmness, largeness, massiveness, naturalness, obsequiousness, pensiveness, proneness, robustness, rudeness, seriousness, tardiness, tediousness, tenderness (tenerity), vastness, vileness.

tycoon, shogun. Two separate titles of different meanings, describing the same person ; *t.* = great prince, *s.* = army-leader. The official so named was the military ruler of Japan in the times (before 1867) when the Mikado's temporal power was usurped ; & the title *tycoon* was substituted in diplomatic dealings for that of *shogun*, used at home, in order to represent him to foreigners as the real sovereign.

tyke, tike. The earliest quotations show y, & in modern use (from 1800) it is, in the OED, six times as common as i ; see Y & I.

tyle(r). See TILE(R).

tympanum. Pl. -*na.*

type. 1. For some synonyms of the noun, see SIGN. 2. The verb makes -*pable* ; see MUTE E. 3 (below). Sizes of printing-type. 4. (below). *Type, prototype,* &c. 5. (below). *Type-writer*)(*typist.*

3. Sizes of printing-type. The following list of size-names, in order from small to large, may be useful : brilliant, diamond, pearl, ruby, nonpareil, emerald, minion, brevier (brĭvēr'), bourgeois (berjoi's), long prī'mer, small pī'ca, pī'ca, English, great prī'mer, canon.

4. *Type, prototype, antitype, antetype.* There is much confusion & other misuse of these words, as in all the following extracts & in some others given under PROTOTYPE :— *Foremost among them is the aged Wu Ting Fang, an Oriental prototype of the Vicar of Bray* (should be *antitype,* or better *parallel*)./*People may wonder whether he always knows the meaning of the words he uses*

when they find him calling a wooden copy of the Queen Elizabeth put up to deceive the Germans her ' prototype ' (*antitype,* if any type, but better *counterfeit*)./*The fees of the most successful barristers in France do not amount to more than a fraction of those earned by their* prototypes *in England* (should be *fellows* or *confrères* or *likes*)./*The type of mind which prompted that policy finds its* modern prototype *in Unionist Ulster* (should be *antitype* or *manifestation*)./' *I presume you bring this war figure into dramatic contrast with his* anti-type.'—' *Yes ; & with the other types of the . . .*' (should be *opposite*).

The word *antetype* may be set aside as one that should hardly ever be used, first because its similarity in sound & opposition in sense to the established *antitype* is inconvenient, secondly as being liable to confusion with *prototype* also from their closeness in meaning, & thirdly because *forerunner* & *anticipation* are ready to take its place when it really does not mean prototype. Even with that ruled out, the relations between the other three are such as to make mistakes likely, but not pardonable. *Prototype* & *antitype* both owe their existence to *type,* & have no meaning except with reference to it ; but *type* has many meanings besides that in which alone it has anything to do with *prototype* & *antitype* ; that meaning is symbol or emblem or presage or pattern or model considered with regard to the person or object or fact or event in the sphere of reality that answers to its specifications ; this answering reality, or thing symbolized &c., is called the antitype, *anti* (against) conveying the notion of match or answer or correspondence. *Type* & *antitype,* then, are a complementary pair, or correlatives & opposites. It is very different with *type* & *prototype* ; far from being opposed to *a type, a prototype* is a type, & serves as a synonym for it, though with limitations ; it is preferred to *type,* first when stress is to be laid on the priority in time of a particular type over its antitype, such priority not being essential to the notion of type & antitype ; secondly when *type*, which has other senses than that to which *antitype* is opposed, might be ambiguous ; & thirdly when typification itself is of no great consequence, & the sense wanted is no more than 'the earliest form' of something. For those who feel a temptation to use the word *prototype* without being sure that they know the difference between the three words, it is well to remember that *antitype* is much more likely to be safe than *prototype*, but that real safety lies in abstaining from so tricky a set of words altogether.

5. *Type-writer)(typist*. It is of practical importance that, as the two words exist, the first should be restricted to the machine & not extended, at the risk of ambiguity, to the operator.

typhoid. See ENTERIC.

typhoon. See WIND for synonymy.

typic(al). *Typic* survives only as a form occasionally useful to verse-writers in metrical straits, & as a (now rare) epithet of fevers,=*intermittent* &c., in which use *typical* would be ambiguous. See -IC(AL).

typify. For inflexions see VERBS IN -IE &c., 6.

typist. See TYPE 5.

typo,=*typographer*. Pl. *-os*, see -O(E)S 5. A CURTAILED WORD.

typographic(al). Both forms are in use, & no shade of difference seems discernible in the OED quotations, except that those for -al are more numerous. See -IC(AL).

tyrannic(al). *Tyrannic* is now not at home outside verse. See -IC(AL).

tyrannize. *This attempt to coerce & tyrannize us will produce results which the Government will have good reason to regret./They were 'the strong, rugged, God-fearing people' who were to be tyrannized & oppressed by a wicked Liberal Government.* Most readers of good modern writing will have the familiar slight shock

incident to meeting a solecism & want to insert 'over'. But the OED's comment on the transitive use is merely 'now rare', & it produces abundant examples from older writers ; still, the present idiom is to *tyrannize over*, not to *tyrannize*, one's subjects.

tyrant. The original Greek sense of the word is so far alive still that readers must be prepared for it. Neither cruel nor despotic conduct was essential to the Greek notion of a tyrant, who was merely one who, or whose ancestors, had seized a sovereignty that was not his or theirs by hereditary right. Despotic or tyrannical use of the usurped position was natural & common, but incidental only.

tyre, tyro. See TIRE, TIRO.

Tyrrhene, Tyrrhenian. So spelt.

Tzar, tzetze. See TSAR, TSETSE.

U

u. N.B. In this article the symbol ū stands for the sounds yōō or yŏŏ. The pronunciation of long u (as ū, or ōō) is a point that has been discussed at length for the special case in which practical doubts arise, i. e. when l precedes the u ; see LU. The same question presents itself, but the answers are less doubtful, when the preceding letter is not l. 1. When it is the other liquid, r, attempts at ū are difficult ; few people make them, & ōō (or ŏŏ) being generally accepted should be made universal (see PRONUNCIATION) ; so rōōl (*rule*), krōōd (*crude*), intrōō'zhn (*intrusion*), kwĕ'rōōlus & gă'rōōlus (*querulous, garrulous*), grōō (*grew*), frōōt (*fruit*). 2. When no letter precedes, ū is invariable (*unit, ubiquity*, &c.) except in foreign words such as *uhlan, Ural, unberufen, umlaut*. 3. After the sounds ch, j, sh, zh, attempts at ū are as ill advised as after r ; so chōō, jōōn, jōōt, jōōs, shōōt, shoor, ū'zhōōal, for *chew, June, jute, juice, chute, sure, usual* ; not chū, jūn, jūt, jūs, shūt, shūr, ū′zhūal. **4.** After s & z there is a tendency to convert the orthodox ū to ōō or ŏŏ, e.g. in *superior, Susan, supreme, suzerain, suicide, suet, suit, presume, Zulu* ; this class is comparable to the lu words, but the decline of ū is far less marked. **5.** Outside the positions stated, ū rarely changes to ōō ; dōōs (*deuce*), stōō′ard (*steward*), lōō′ard (*leeward*), are often heard, but these & others are generally regarded as carelessnesses or vulgarities.

uglily is less rare than most adverbs in -LILY.

uhlan. So spelt ; pronounce ōō′lan or ū′lan.

ukase. Pronounce ūkā′s.

-ULAR. Adjectives ending thus are something of a trap to those who like words to mean what they seem to say. They are made from diminutive nouns, but no diminutive sense can be reckoned upon in them ; a glandule is necessarily a small gland ; but *glandular* is as likely to mean ' of glands ' as ' of small glands '. The ending -ular has become a favourite with adjective-makers, & such an adjective is often preferred to one that is or might be made directly from the simple noun instead of from the diminutive. So *auricular* for *aural*, *glandular* for *glandal*, *globular* for *globose*, *granular* for *graneous* or *granose*, *tubular* for *tubal*, *valvular* for *valvar*.

Ulema. Pronounce ōō′līma or ōōlīmah′.

ulna. Pl. -*nae*.

ultima. See TECHNICAL TERMS.

ultimatum. Pl. -*ta*, -*tums* ; see LATIN PLURALS. Considering that -*tums* is about 200 years old (Swift is quoted in OED), it is strange that anglicization is still delayed, & that -*ta* is in a large enough majority to justify OED in presenting it alone as the plural ; -*tums* is here recommended.

ultimo, ult. See INSTANT.

ultra, originally a Latin preposition & adverb meaning beyond, is now used in English as a noun (pl. -*as*) meaning a person who goes beyond others in opinion or action of the kind in question. This is no doubt a development of the use as a prefix in such adjectives (& nouns) as *ultra-fashionable*(s), *ultra-revolutionary* (-*ries*). Such compounds were curtailed into *ultra* adj. & n. ; but it is no longer felt to be, like *sub* when used for *subaltern* or *subscription*, a CURTAILED WORD ; it has rather won independence of any second element, its own meaning being sufficient, & is a synonym for *extremist*.

ultramontane. With the full or exact meaning of ultramontanism as now understood we need not concern ourselves, beyond defining it roughly as the policy of raising the authority of the Pope in all matters to the highest possible level. But to those who are not content to accept words as arbitrary tokens, & do not see why a papal zealot should be an ' over-the-hills ' man, an explanation may be welcome. The mountains are the Alps, & beyond the mountains means, to an Italian, outside Italy, &, to others, in Italy. So, when there were differences in the Church about the right relation between the Italian bishops & the extra-Italian, each party could describe the other as the Ultramontanes, which makes the historical use of the word confusing ; in modern use it is applied, chiefly by opponents, to the party of Italian predominance, whose principle is the absolute supremacy of the Pope, & the denial of independence to national Churches.

ultra vires. Pronounce -ir′ēz.

ululate, -ation. OED gives precedence to ŭlū- over ūlū-, & it may know that it is stating the prevalent usage ; but the pronunciation of words seldom heard is hard to be sure of ; &, unless there are reasons against it, it seems plain that the imitative effect got by repeating the same sound should not be sacrificed ;

ūlūl- suggests howling much more vividly than ŭlūl-.

-UM. For general remarks on the plural of Latin nouns adopted in English, see LATIN PLURALS. Those in -um are numerous & demand special treatment. The Latin plural being -a, & the English -ums, three selections follow of nouns (1) that now always use -ums, either as having completed their naturalization (as it is to be hoped that the rest may do in time), or for special reasons ; (2) that show no signs at present of conversion, but always use -a ; (3) that vacillate, sometimes with a differentiation of meaning, sometimes in harmony with the style of writing, & sometimes unaccountably. In deciding between the two forms for words in the third list, it should be borne in mind that, while anglicization is to be desired, violent attempts to hurry the process actually retard it by provoking ridicule.

1. Plural in -ums only : albums ; antirrhinums (& plant names) ; asylums ; decorums ; delphiniums ; Elysiums ; factotums* ; forums ; harmoniums ; laburnums ; lyceums ; museums ; nasturtiums ; nostrums ; pendulums ; petroleums ; pomatums ; premiums ; quantums* ; quorums* ; targums* ; vellums* ; *The -a plural for these would violate grammar as well as usage ; they are included here not as Latin nouns, but as words that might be given wrong plurals by mistake.

2. Plurals in -a only : agenda† ; bacteria (& many scientific terms) ; corrigenda† ; curricula ; desiderata† ; errata† ; memoranda† ; scholia (& other such learned words) ; strata† ; succedanea. †Latin gerundives & passive participles often resist naturalization.

3. Words with either plural ; some notes are inserted as suggestions only : aquarium (usu. -ms) ; compendium ; cranium (-ums in joc. use for heads) ; emporium ; encomium (usu. -ms) ; exordium ; interregnum

(usu. -ms) ; medium (-ms in spiritualism) ; millennium (usu. -ms) ; rostrum (usu. -a) ; spectrum (usu. -a) ; trapezium (usu. -a) ; ultimatum (-ms better) ; vacuum (usu. -a) ; viaticum (-a in eccl. sense).

umbilicus, -ical. The OED recognizes only ŭmbĭ'lĭkal for the adjective, but for the noun gives precedence to ŭmbĭlĭ'kus over ŭmbĭ'lĭkus. See FALSE QUANTITY for the question involved.

umbo. Pl. -os or -ō'nēs ; see LATIN PLURALS.

umbra. Pl. -rae.

umbrella makes umbrella'd ; see -ED & -'D.

umlaut. Pronounce ōō'mlowt or ŏŏ'mlowt.

un, 'un, = one, as in that un, young un, old un, game un, & such phrases, needs no apostrophe or hyphen.

UN-. 1. Danger of ellipsis after unwords. 2. Un-)(in-.

1. Danger of ellipsis after un-. *Untouched* means not touched, but with the difference that it is one word & not two, a difference that in some circumstances is important. In *I was not touched, & you were* the word *touched* is understood to be repeated, & not to carry the *not* with it ; but *I was untouched, & you were* cannot be substituted with the same effect ; if it means anything, it means that both were untouched, the *un*- having to be understood as well as the *touched*. Needless as such a statement may sound in a simple case like the above, where there is nothing to distract attention from the wording, blunders essentially similar are frequent ; a couple of examples follow, & the state of mind that produces them is fully illustrated in the articles NEGATIVE & AFFIRMATIVE, & NEGATIVES :— *Dr Rashdall's scholarship is unquestioned ; most of his writings & opinions on ecclesiastical matters are.* What is meant is that most of them are questioned, not unquestioned./ *When I sat in the square of Oudenarde, opposite the old Hôtel de Ville, which* *happily has come through the war untouched by Vandal hands, methought, if it had been, who in Belgium could have built the like of it ?* That is, had been touched, not untouched; correct *untouched* into *without being touched*.

2. Un-)(in-. When positive adjectives, including participles, are to be converted into negative, it is usually done by prefixing one of these ; which of the two it should be is a question that most people can answer without difficulty for most words, & the laying down of exhaustive rules would be both tedious & useless ; some of the tendencies have been shown in the article IN- & UN-. One or two quotations are here given to prove that the wrong decision is sometimes made : *The Government let loose their ' Black & Tans ' to deal out summary &* indiscriminating *punishment./Olrig, of whose* incompleted *labours we spoke lately in these columns./It was inevitable that many men of* instable *nervous organization should be included.*/Read *undiscriminating, uncompleted, & unstable.* All three lapses result from the commonest cause of error, the existence of a familiar allied word beginning rightly with the prefix that, in the word used, is wrong—here *indiscriminate, incomplete, & instability.* One other point is perhaps worth stressing. It is a general truth that, while it is legitimate to prefix un-, but not in-, to any adjective of whatever form, those negative adjectives in in- that exist are normally preferred to the corresponding un- forms ; but when an in- (or il- or im- or ir-) adjective has developed a sense that is something more than the negation of the positive adjective, an un- form is often used to discharge that function without risk of ambiguity ; *immoral* having come to mean offending against morality or wicked, *unmoral* is called in to mean not moral or outside the sphere of morality ; others are *irre, & unre, -ligious* ;

in, & un, -human ; in, & un, -artistic ; in, & un, -artificial ; in, & un, -sanitary ; inept & unapt ; insoluble & unsolvable ; im, & un, -material.

unabashedly. Five syllables, if used ; see -EDLY.

unaccountable. *Occurrences that are for the time being, & to the spiritualist, unaccountable by natural causes. U.* itself belongs to the class of words, including *reliable,* whose legitimacy is upheld in -ABLE 4 ; but to use *by* after it, compelling the reader to resolve it into its elements (*not to be accounted for*), & so discover that *for* is missing, is very indiscreet.

unadornedly, unadvisedly. As UN-ABASHEDLY.

unapt, inapt, inept. *Inept* represents the normal Latin negative of *aptus,* &, like many such negatives in in-, has developed a special sense. We have therefore made in English, also normally, the new negative of *apt,* free of the special sense, *unapt* ; & this, not the hybrid *inapt,* should be used when *inept* is not meant.

unartificial, in-. The differentiation is now generally recognized by which the first means free from artifice or artless or natural, & the second lacking art or unskilful or rude ; see UN- 2.

unartistic, in-. The second is the usual word ; but since it has acquired a sort of positive sense, ' outraging the canons of art ' &c., the other has been introduced for contexts in which such condemnation is not desired ; the *unartistic* are those who are not concerned with art. See UN- 2.

unashamedly. As UNABASHEDLY.

UNATTACHED PARTICIPLES & adjectives (or wrongly attached). A firm sent in its bill with the following letter :—*Dear Sir,—We beg to enclose herewith statement of your account for goods supplied, & being desirous of clearing our Books to end*

May will you *kindly favour us with cheque in settlement per return, & much oblige.* The reply ran :—*Sirs,—You have been misinformed. I have no wish to clear your books.* It may be hoped that the desire on which they based their demand was ultimately (though not per return) satisfied, but they had certainly imputed it to the wrong person by attaching *being desirous* not to the noun it belonged to (*we*), but to another (*you*). The duty of so arranging one's sentences that they will stand grammatical analysis is much more generally recognized than it formerly was, & it is now not a sufficient defence for looseness of this kind to produce parallels, as can very easily be done, even from great writers of past generations ; on this see ILLOGICALITIES. On the other hand it is to be remembered that there is a continual change going on by which certain participles or adjectives acquire the character of prepositions or adverbs, no longer needing the prop of a noun to cling to ; we can say *Considering the circumstances you were justified*, or *Roughly speaking they are identical*, & need not correct into *I acquit you* & *I should call them identical* in order to regularize the participles. The difficulty is to know when this development is complete ; may I write *Referring to your letter, you do not state . . .*, or must it be *I find you do not state . . .* ? i.e., is *referring* still undeveloped ? In all such cases, it is best to put off recognition. A good example of what may prove to have been such a development is caught in the act is the phrase *due to.* Every illiterate in the land is now treating *due to* as though *due* had passed into an adverb not needing a noun to agree with, just as *owing*, in *owing to*, has actually done. The prepositional use of *owing to* is more than a century old ; but of a similar use of *due to* there is not a vestige in the OED (dated 1897 for D). It is now as common as can be, though only, if the view

taken in DUE is correct, among the illiterate ; that term is here to be taken as including all who are unfamiliar with good writers, & who consequently are unaware of any idiomatic difference between *Owing to his age he was unable to compete*, & *Due to his age he was* &c. Perhaps the illiterates will beat idiom ; perhaps idiom will beat the illiterates ; our grandsons will know.

The conscious or unconscious assumption that a participle or adjective has acquired the powers of preposition or adverb when it has in fact not done so perhaps accounts for most of the unattached & wrongly attached ; but there are many for which no such excuse is possible. Before proceeding to them, let us make a few sentences containing undoubtedly converted participles, sentences in which the seeming participle is not felt to need a noun :—*Talking of test matches, who won the last ?* ; *Coming to details, the spoilt ballot-papers were 17* ; *They are illiterate (using the word in its widest sense)*; *Granting his honesty, he may be mistaken* ; *Failing you, there is no chance left* ; *Twelve were saved, not counting the dog* ; *Allowing for exceptions, the rule may stand.* It is natural, & perhaps right, to explain this common type as originally not a participle at all, but a shortening of the gerund preceded by the old preposition *a* ; *talking of* = *a-talking of*, i.e. in talking or while there is talk of. However that may be, it is only fanatical purists who will condemn such sentences ; & a clear acknowledgement of their legitimacy should strengthen rather than weaken the necessary protest against the slovenly uses now to be illustrated. After each extract will be given in brackets first the noun, whether present or not, to which the participle or adjective ought to be attached, & secondly the noun, if any, to which careless grammar has in fact attached it :—*Unlike the other great European capitals which lay themselves out to cater for the tourist, Russian is the only language spoken* (the capital in question ; Russian)./*A belief that a Committee of Inquiry is merely an evasion, & that, if* accepted, *the men will be caught out* (Committee; men)./ *Experiments have shown that, while* affording *protection against shrapnel, the direct bullet at moderate range would carry fragments of the plate into the body* (plate ; bullet)./Based *on your figures of membership, you suggest that the Middle Classes Union has failed* (suggestion ; you)./*I would also suggest that, while* admitting *the modernity, the proofs offered by him as to the recent date of the loss of aspiration are not very convincing* (I ; proofs)./*A girl fell on a pen, which pierced her eye, &, causing meningitis, she died* (which ; she)./ Having muzzled *the House of Lords it is difficult to see at the moment any real obstacle to the successful passage of the Bill* (the Government ; ——)./ *Whilst* placing *little hope in the present dynasty, it is always possible in the East for some official to rise to power who may change the destinies of his people* (we ; official).

unavowedly. As UNABASHEDLY.

unbeknown(st). Both forms are now out of use except in dialect or uneducated speech or in imitations of these. The -st form is more exclusively adverbial ; cf. *unawares* as the adv. of *unaware*, & *whiles, whilst*.

unbending, as participle of *to unbend*, means throwing off stiffness, but as a compound of *un-* & *bending* it means never throwing off stiffness; contrasts, not usually so diametrical as this, often result from the prefixing of *un-* at different stages ; e. g., in 'lessons learnt & unlearnt', *unlearnt* may mean either of two very different things.

unberufen. Pronounce ōōnbĭrōō′fn. It means 'unchallenged', i. e. without defying Fate.

unbias(s)ed. The spelling varies ; see -s-, -ss-.

uncia. Pl. -*ae*.

uncial. See TECHNICAL TERMS.

Uncle Sam. See SOBRIQUETS.

un-come-at-able. The word had doubtless, two or three centuries ago, a jolly daredevil hang-the-grammarians air about it ; that has long evaporated ; it serves no purpose that *inaccessible* does not ; it requires a writer to choose between five forms (*uncomatable* is the other extreme) ; & it surely deserves a place among SUPERFLUOUS WORDS.

uncommon. The old slang use as an adverb=remarkably (*an u. fine girl* &c.) has nearly died out, & is no longer in place outside the dialogue of historical novels.

unconcernedly, unconstrainedly. As UNABASHEDLY.

uncontrollable. Better than *in-* ; see IN- & UN-.

uncontrolledly. As UNABASHEDLY.

undeceived. Two words of different meaning, like UNBENDING.

undependable. For the legitimacy of this & similar words, see -ABLE 4.

under, prep. See BELOW for distinctions ; & UNDERNEATH.

underlay, -lie, vbs. The confusion noticed in LAY & LIE is worse confounded for the compounds ; see the remarks on OVERLAY.

undermost. See -MOST.

underneath (prep.), compared with BELOW & *under*, is not, like BENEATH, a word that tends to become archaic ; on the contrary, it is still in full colloquial as well as literary use ; its range is much narrower than that of *under*, being almost confined to the physical relation of material things (cf. ' underneath the bed ' with ' under the stimulus of competition '), but within that range it is often preferred as expressing more emphatically the notion of being covered over, & carrying a step further the difference pointed out between *below* & *under*.

undeservedly, undesignedly. As UNABASHEDLY.

undigested, undisciplined, undiscriminating. All better than the informs; see IN- & UN-. The *in-*, which is at variance with the prevalent modern usage, owes its escape to the protection afforded by *indigestion*, *indiscipline*, & *indiscriminate*.

undisguisedly. As UNABASHEDLY.
undistinguishable. The in- form is better; see IN- & UN-.
undistributed middle. See TECH-NICAL TERMS.
undisturbedly. As UNABASHEDLY.
undue, -duly. *There is no need for undue alarm.* Well, no; that seems likely. See TRUISM; in the making of truisms *u.* is at present the favourite ingredient.

uneconomic(al). For the distinction see ECONOMIC(AL).
unedited. Better than the in- form, which those who are literary by profession seem to prefer; see IN- & UN-.

unequal. *She has been compelled to undertake an offensive for which, as events have proved, she was wholly unequal./A simplicity that seems quite unequal to treat the large questions involved.* The preposition after *u.* is *to*, not *for*; but if a verbal phrase with *to* is used it must be *to* with the gerund, not with the infinitive; see GERUND 3 C.

UNEQUAL YOKEFELLOWS. The phrase is here used in a comprehensive sense enabling a number of faults, most of them treated at length in other articles, to be exhibited side by side as varieties of one species. They are all such as not to obstruct seriously the understanding of the passage in which they occur, but to inflict a passing discomfort on fastidious readers; to a writer who is not fastidious it is an irksome task to keep in mind the readers who are, & he inclines to treat symmetry as troublesome or even obtrusive formalism; he too could be mechanically regular if he would, but he is not going to be at the pains of revising his first draft into conformity with niceties that are surely of no consequence. It is true that such revising is an un-grateful task; but there must be something wrong with a writer who is not free, by the time he is through his apprenticeship, of the need for this sort of revision; to shape one's sentences aright as one puts them down, instinctively avoiding lopsidedness & checking all details of the framework, is not the final crown of an accomplished writer, but part of the rudiments; if one has neglected to acquire that habit in early days, one has no right to grumble at the choice that later confronts one between slovenliness & revision.

Conspicuous among the slights commonly inflicted upon the minor symmetries are those illustrated below:—

Between demands *and*, but—*The nine employees whose record of service ranged* between *61* down to *50 years.* See BETWEEN.

Both demands *and*, but—*The enemy despairs both of victory on land or of such success as will give him a compromise peace.* See BOTH.

Neither demands *nor*, but—*Diderot presented a bouquet which was neither well or ill received.* See NEITHER 6.

Neither this nor that demands a singular verb, but—*Neither John nor Richard were English.* See NEITHER 4.

Scarcely (temporal) demands *when* or *before*, but—*Scarcely was the drain finished* than *several sickened with diphtheria.* See SCARCELY.

Each demands a singular verb, but—*The opportunities which each are capable of turning to account.* See EACH.

Has & does as auxiliaries demand different continuations, but—*The Government has never & does not now* close *the door to overtures.* See ELLIPSIS.

A subjunctive in one of two parallel clauses demands a subjunctive in the other, but—*If the appeal be made & results in . . .* See SUBJUNCTIVES (arrivals).

Similarly with inversion in parallel clauses, but—*Even were this tract of *country level plain & the roads lent themselves to the manœuvre . . .* See INVERSION.

Hermetic sealing up of a subject within its verb demands repetition of the subject if it is to serve again, but—*Does he dislike its methods, & will only mention . . . ?* See PARALLEL-SENTENCE DANGERS.

One or two other types may be added without quotations :—*Either he did not know or was lying* (read *He either*) ; *The old one was as good if not better than this* (read *as good as this if not better*) ; *One of the worst kings that* has *ever reigned* (read *have*) ; *It is all & more than* I expected (read *all I expected, & more*) ; *He was young, rich, handsome, & enjoyed life* (read *& handsome* ; see AND 2).

unescapable, unessential. Better than in- ; see IN- & UN-.

unexceptionable)(-al. See EXCEPTIONABLE.

unfeignedly. Four syllables ; -EDLY.

unfortunate. For ' one more u.', see STOCK PATHOS.

ungula. Pl. *-lae.*

unhuman. For the use of this by the side of *inhuman*, see UN- 2.

unidea'd. Best so written ; -ED & 'D.

UNIDIOMATIC -LY. As the lapses from idiom here to be illustrated probably owe their origin to the modern wider extension of grammatical knowledge, it may be prudent to start by conciliating the sticklers for grammar & admitting that a -ly is sometimes missing where it is wanted. So :—*The Carholme course, shaped very similar to the Doncaster Town Moor, is one of the best in England./Proceedings instituted by the local Education Committee against the mother for neglecting to send her girl to school regular./If the Government is going to nationalize the coal, we believe it would do wiser to leave its hands free to . . .* (more *wisely*)./*most teachers in the present day have learnt to read the Old Testament* (thanks to the higher critics) *different*

from the way I was taught to read it in my youth./Surely no peace-loving man or woman will deny that it would be advisable to prevent strikes & lock-outs consistent with the principles of liberty as set forth by John Stuart Mill.

But, if grammar is inexorable against *consistent & different* & the rest, it would in the following sentences allow *contrary & irrespective* without a frown, while idiom for its part would welcome them :—*The provision is quite inadequate & very grudgingly granted, & often,* contrarily *to the spirit of the Act, totally denied./Loyal obedience is due to the* ' *powers that be* ', *as such, irrespectively of their historical origin./His method is to whitewash them all vigorously with the same brush, irrespectively of differences in the careers & characters of his heroes. Contrary & irrespective* are among the adjectives that have, with others mentioned in UNATTACHED &c. & in QUASI-ADVERBS, developed adverbial force ; to ignore that development is bad literary judgement, but, among the mistakes made with -ly, one of the least.

A degree worse is the use of a -ly adverb where idiom requires not an adverb at all, but a predicative adjective. See LARGE(LY) for the phrases *bulk & loom large,* & substitute adjectives for adverbs in the four following quotations :—*But over the rival claims of the Marquess Curzon & Mr Baldwin controversy waxed* vigorously./*In neither direction can we fix our hopes very* highly./*This country was brought much more closely to disaster at sea than ever the Allies were on land* (much closer)./ *It is a gigantic labour before which the labours of Westphalia, of Utrecht, of Vienna, pale* insignificantly.

Yet a little worse is the officious bringing up to date of such time-honoured phrases as *mighty kind & sure enough* :—*Still, it is* mightily *kind of the* Morning Post *to be so anxious to shield the Labour Party from the wrath to come./We begin to remember the story of the detective who died murmuring to himself ' More clues ! ' & towards the end of the book, surely enough, more clues there are.*

But much more to be deprecated than all the particular departures from idiom already mentioned is the growing notion that every monosyllabic adjective, if an adverb is to be made of it, must have a -ly clapped on to it to proclaim the fact. Of very many that is not true ; see MOST, RIGHT, & STRAIGHT, for wrong or needless uses of *mostly, rightly, & straightly.* Two such words may here be taken for special treatment, *much(ly)* as the least, & *hard(ly)* as the most, important of all. We do all know that *much* can be an adverb, & probably most of us would guess that *muchly* was a modern facetious formation, perhaps meant to burlesque the ultra-grammatical, & at any rate always used jocosely. We should be wrong ; it is 300 years old, its earliest use was serious, & even now it may rarely be met in contexts where the point of the joke is not apparent : *Many players who were in the habit of relying muchly upon the advice of their caddies found themselves completely at sea.* Nevertheless, as it seems from the OED to have lain dormant for over 200 years, our guess is not so far out, & its revival in the 19th c. illustrates the belief that adverbs must end in -ly. *Muchly* does not often make its way into print, except in dialogue as a recognized symbol of the mildly jocose talker, & has been worth attention only in contrast with *hardly.* That, as will appear, is substituted in print for the idiomatic *hard* neither seldom nor with any burlesque intention, but seemingly in ignorance. Ignorance that *hard* can be an adverb seems incredible when one thinks of *It froze hard, Hit him hard, Work hard, Try hard,* & so forth ; the ignorance must be of idiom rather than of grammar. Neglect of idiom is, in this case, aggravated by the danger

that *hardly,* written as meaning hard, may be read as meaning scarcely ; for some proofs that that danger is real, see the article HARD-LY. The examples that here follow are free from such ambiguity, but in each of them idiom demands expulsion of the -ly :—*How hardly put to it the Tories are for argument is shown by . . ./Another sign of how hardly the great families are pressed in these times./The invasion of Henley by the fashionable world bears very hardly on those who go only for the sport./But what about the agriculturist, who is so hardly hit by our present system ?/They have been as hardly hit as any class in the community by the present state of trade./ If there is a man more hardly hit by existing conditions than the average holder of a season ticket he is hard to find* (harder hit).

Other such adverbs are *wide, late, deuced, high,* each spoilt in the appended extracts by an unidiomatic -ly :—*And then he'd know that betting & insurance were widely apart./ Several drawings in the new volume are dated as lately as August & September, 1922. / I bite it—it is deucedly big—I light it & inhale./ M. Millerand has played highly, but he has lost his stake. Middling, soft, & sharp,* are specimens of the many others that might be named.

unify. For inflexions see VERBS IN -IE &c., 6.

unimpassionedly. A bad form ; see -EDLY.

unique. A watertight definition or paraphrase of the word, securing it against confusion with all synonyms that might be suggested, is difficult to frame. In the first place, it is applicable only to what is in some respect the sole existing specimen, the precise like of which may be sought in vain. That gives a clean line of division between it & the many adjectives for which the illiterate tend to substitute it— *remarkable, exceptional, rare, marvellous,* & the like. In the qualities represented by those epithets there are degrees ; but uniqueness is a matter of yes or no only ; no unique thing is more or less unique than another unique thing, as it may be rarer or less rare ; the adverbs that *u.* can tolerate are e. g. *quite, almost, nearly, really, surely, perhaps, absolutely,* or *in some respects* ; & it is nonsense to call anything *more, most, very, somewhat, rather,* or *comparatively u.* Such nonsense, however, is often written :—*M. Georges Buisson, in recognition of his valuable services as shorthand writer to the Chamber of Deputies, has been made an Officer of the Legion of Honour ; this is* a rather unique *distinction./ I have just come across the production of a boy aged seven which is, in my experience,* somewhat unique./*Sir,— I venture to send you a copy of* a rather unique *inscription on a tombstone./A* very unique *child, thought I.* But, secondly, there is another set of synonyms—*sole, single, peculiar to,* &c.—from which *u.* is divided not by a clear difference of meaning, but by an idiomatic limitation of the contexts to which it is suited. It will be admitted that we improve the two following sentences if we change *u.* in the first into *sole,* & in the second into *peculiar* :—*In the always delicate & difficult domain of diplomatic relations the Foreign Minister must be* the unique *medium of communication with foreign Powers./ He relates Christianity to other religions, & notes what is* unique to the former *& what is common to all of them.* The emendations are easy to make or accept ; to explain the need of them is more difficult ; but the reason why *u.* is unsuitable is perhaps that it belongs to the class of epithets discussed in Positive words.

unity. *The unities,* or *dramatic unities,* are the u. of time, the u. of place, & the u. of action. The first has been observed if all that happens in a play can be conceived as sufficiently continuous to fill only something like the same time

(stretched by generous reckoning to a day) as the performance. The second is observed when changes of scene, if any, are slight enough to spare an audience the sensation of being transported from one place to another. The third is observed when nothing is introduced that has no bearing upon the central action of the play. The last only is universally recognized as among the essentials of good drama.

unlearned, -nt. See LEARN.

unless & until. See PLEONASM, 2, for other such duplications ; one of the conjunctions is always superfluous, as in the still commoner IF & WHEN, the discussion in which article may serve for this pair also ; but a few quotations will allow the reader to judge whether ' unless & ' might not in each be left out with advantage :—*Unless & until it is made possible for a builder or householder to obtain an economic rent, so long will building be at a standstill./ Speaking for himself he said that unless & until the Second Chamber was reformed & the constituencies were given some constitutional means of expressing their opinion, he treated every measure that proceeded from the House of Commons as at present constituted as coming from a tainted source./Provided further that any Bill shall not be presented to his Majesty nor receive the Royal Assent under the provisions of this section unless & until it has been submitted to & approved by the electors./Sir Albert Stanley assured some alarmed manufacturers that a certain embargo which he had temporarily removed should be speedily reimposed & not removed again* unless & until *they had been consulted.*

unlike, in its less simple uses, i. e. when we get beyond ' unlike things ', ' the two cases are u.', & ' this is u. that ', to ' unlike you, I feel the cold ' & further developments, is subject to the complications set out in LIKE, though occasions for it are much fewer. In addition to what is there said, two special warnings may be given. *I counted eighty-nine rows of men standing, & unlike in* London, *only occasionally could women be distinguished. U.* is there treated as though it had developed the adverbial power described in the article UNATTACHED &c. as acquired by *owing* (*to*) but not by *due* (*to*); it has not, & something adverbial (*in contrast with London ways?*) must be substituted.

M. Berger, however, does not appear to have—unlike his Russian masters—the gift of presenting female characters. As with many negatives, the placing of *u.* is important; standing where it does, it must be changed to *like*; *unlike* would be right if the phrase were shifted to before ' does not appear '.

unmaterial, if chosen instead of the ordinary *im-*, confines the meaning to ' not consisting of matter ', & excludes the other common meaning of *immaterial,* viz ' that does not matter ', ' not important or essential '; see UN- 2.

unmentionables. WORN-OUT HUMOUR.

unmoral. For this & *im-*, see UN- 2.
unnavigable. Better so; IN- & UN-.
unparalleled. Not *-lled*; see PARALLEL for the irregularity.
unperturbedly. As UNABASHEDLY.
unpractical. Better so; IN- & UN-.
unrecognizable. Better so; IN- & UN-.
unreligious, chosen instead of the usual *ir-*, excludes the latter's implications of sin &c., & means outside the sphere of religion; see UN- 2.

unreservedly. As UNABASHEDLY.
unresponsive. Better so; IN- & UN-.
unrestrainedly. As UNABASHEDLY.
unretentive. *Ir-* is better; IN- & UN-.
unsanitary, in-. *In-* is the established form; but it would not be used, as *un-* might, of a place &c. that neither had *nor needed* provisions for sanitation : *a primitive & unsanitary but entirely healthy life* or *village*; *insanitary* implies danger. See UN- 2.

unsolvable differs from *insoluble* in having its reference limited to the sense of the English verb *solve,* & not covering, as *insoluble* does, various senses (dissolve as well as solve) of the Latin verb *solvere*; it is therefore sometimes useful in avoiding ambiguity; see UN- 2.

unstable. Better than *in-*, in spite of *instability*; see UN- 2.
unstringed)(**unstrung.** See STRINGED.
unthinkable is now a sort of expletive. When we say *damn*, it relieves us because it is a strong word & yet means nothing; we do not intend the person or thing or event that we damn to be burnt in hell fire; far from it; but the faint aroma of brimstone that hangs for ever about the word is savoury in wrathful nostrils. So it is with *unthinkable,* ' that cannot be thought '. That a thing at once exists & does not exist, or ' the things which God hath prepared for them that love him ', are unthinkable, i. e., the constitution of the human mind bars us from conceiving or apprehending them; but we do not mean all that with our VOGUE-WORD *unthinkable* at present; anything is now unthinkable from what reason declares impossible or what imagination is helpless to conceive down to what seems against the odds (as that Oxford should win the boat-race), or what is slightly distasteful to the speaker (as that the Labour Party should ever form a Government). The word is so attractive because the uncompromising intensity of its proper sense in metaphysics & philosophy lingers around it, like the brimstone of *damn,* even when it is transferred to ordinary regions; & this recommends it to all who like to combine the most forcible sound with the haziest meaning. The haziness is easily accounted for; the *un-* & *-able* meaning ' that cannot be —ed ' are regarded as affixed to (1) *think* in the philosophic sense

' frame a conception of ', (2) *think* in the everyday sense ' believe ' or ' be of opinion ', (3) *think of*, in the sense ' consider advisable ' or ' contemplate doing ', (4) *think likely*. To attach to so protean a verb-notion the affixes that make it mean ' that cannot be which-you-please-of-four-different-things-ed ' does result & could not but result in haziness. Here is a quotation from yesterday's paper (*Westm. Gaz.*, 31/1/24) that comes pat to show it : *What Conservatives are trying to decide is whether they are Protectionists or not ; . . . to abandon Protection is unthinkable, because the majority of Conservatives have Protection in their bones.* To abandon Protection cannot be thought ? if that has a meaning, it is that the mind cannot form an idea of it, which is obviously untrue. Then, cannot be thought *of* ? that means that Conservatives cannot consider its advisability, which it is plain from the sentence before that some of them are doing. Then, cannot be thought *likely* ? to that we seem to be brought, & it amounts merely to saying that abandonment is unlikely (which may be true) & adding that no-one can think otherwise (which is false).

It is probable that even now no really clear thinker ever uses the word out of its severely limited philosophic sense, or applies it to anything but what the mind is incapable of conceiving ; & at any rate that is the only sense in which it is likely to live long ; its present vogue will last only till the necessity of confining it to one clear meaning has forced itself on the general consciousness. A few quotations, beginning with the philosophic use, but chiefly of the bad trivial kinds, are added, not because anyone cannot find such things for himself, but because their massed variety may have a chance of disgusting those who do not reckon shiftiness a virtue in the words they use :—' *Ultimate* ' *scientific ideas may be unthinkable without prejudice to the* ' *thinkable-*

ness ' *of* ' *proximate* ' *scientific ideas./ Yet we do not know how plastic the mind is ; we do not know what thoughts are thinkable by man./If the reformers of our time, generously impatient as they are, could count upon the wisdom, the devotion, & the caution of this older school, as near an ideal combination as is thinkable would be effected.* A cross between the philosophic sense, which the writer is aiming at, & the popular ; for an ideal combination of generous impatience & caution is itself not unthinkable, however unlikely./*It is unthinkable that we should continue a policy under which a given locality may be allowed to commit a crime against a friendly nation.* In this & the next, each with a *that*-clause as the unthinkable thing, the defence is possible that *think* has its ordinary meaning, the one numbered 2 above, & that *unthinkable* cannot be deprived of its right to embody this ; the answer is that the defence is, for the particular construction, sound, but that abstention would nevertheless be better. / *The Arbitration Treaty is going through ; about that I have no manner of doubt ; that it may be altered in some details is possible ; that it will be rejected altogether is unthinkable.* See the preceding ; & read *incredible./A tariff, having regard to its effects upon the textile industries of the country, is unthinkable.* Impracticable ?/*With all respect to the advocates of a third reading amendment, such a course appears to us to be simply unthinkable.* A course that has advocates unthinkable !/*A popular vote, entailing no adverse consequences to a Government on its chief constructive policies, is unthinkable under our system.* Yet the referendum has been thought of ; read *inconsistent with./He said that he would welcome any improvement in our relations with Germany, & described a war with Germany as unthinkable.* Out of the question ?/*It is unthinkable that hundreds upon hundreds of people should be getting their freedom on the ground of adultery, whilst thousands of innocent sufferers under desertion, drink, cruelty, & insanity, are left outside any relief.* He is plainly stating what he takes to be the existing position ; how can that be unthinkable ? read *flagrant injustice./He said we were apt to forget the lessons of the war ; some people he met said ' I want to forget ' ; that was, to his mind, a wrong & unthinkable attitude to adopt.* Unthinking ?

until. 1. *Until*)(*till.* 2. *U.* or *till*) (*before* or *when.* 3. *Unless & u.*

1. *Until* has very little of the archaic effect as compared with *till* that distinguishes *unto* from *to*, & substitution of it for *till* would seldom be noticeable, except in any such stereotyped phrase as *true till death.* Nevertheless, *till* is now the usual form, & *until* gives a certain leisurely or deliberate or pompous air ; when the clause or phrase precedes the main sentence, *until* is perhaps actually the commoner (*until his accession he had been unpopular*).

2. Neither *until* nor *till* is idiomatic in sentences of a certain type, which require *when* or *before* : *In one of the city parks he was seated at one end of a bench, & had not been there long until a sparrow alighted at the other end.* The reason is that *till & until,* strictly defined, mean (if there is no negative) ' throughout the interval between the starting-point (i.e., here, his sitting down) & the goal (here, the sparrow's arrival) ' ; or (if there is a negative) ' at any point in that interval ' ; & to say that it was not long at any point in that interval is meaningless. The OED calls the misuse dial. & U.S.

3. For *unless & until,* see UNLESS. The writer of the following has evidently a praiseworthy antipathy to *u. & u.,* which would have given, however verbosely, his meaning ; but in struggling to escape he has made nonsense, which is worse than verbosity : *He will still be able to*

supply his front & to be in touch with Jerusalem by two avenues of supply, the road & the railway, until, or if, *the critical point of Nablous is lost to him.*

untoward. Pronounce ŭntŏ′ard.
unvoiced. See TECHNICAL TERMS.
unwieldy. So spelt, not -*ldly.*
up. 1. The phrase *up to date* is three words unhyphened, except when it is used as an attributive adjective ; then, it is hyphened : *An up-to-date bungalow* ; but *You are not up to date, Bring the ledger up to date.* See HYPHENS, group *From hand to mouth.

2. *Up against* (faced or confronted with), & *up to* (incumbent upon), are good examples of the rapidity with which in modern English new slang phrases make their way through the newspapers into literary respectability.

upon. 1. For (*up*)*on all fours,* see FOUR.

2. *Upon*)(*on.* For a list of other such pairs, see TILL. The difference is much the same as between UNTIL & *till* ; but euphony plays a considerable part in the choice, *upon* being usually rejected when its position would cause it to be pronounced as two unaccented syllables instead of with a clear -ŏ- ; compare *upon my word* with *on no account,* & *that depends on who it was* with *depend upon it* ; at the end of a sentence, consequently, *upon* is often preferred : *There is very little to go upon.*

upper. For *u. case,* see LOWER 1.
uppermost. See -MOST.
upright, accent. Stand upri′ght ; u′pright people ; one of the u′prights gave way.
upstair(s). Come upstair′s ; an u′pstair room.
urinal. The natural pronunciation (see RECESSIVE ACCENT) is ūr′īnal ; ūri′nal accords better with the imaginary sanctity of Latin quantities ; but how little that comes to is shown in FALSE QUANTITY.

us. 1. Case mistakes. 2. *His, our,* &c., after *of us*.

1. Case. The roman-type *uses* & *we* in the following examples are ungrammatical :—*They are as competent as* us *as regards manufacture, & so why not serve them the same as they serve us ?/The Germans are involved like ourselves in a blind struggle of forces, & no more than* us *to be blamed or praised./Age & experience bestow the skill to recognize in a book only what we require ; that* we *not only read & mark, but inwardly digest ; it becomes* us.*/Let us be content*—we *Liberals, at any rate*—*to go on in the possession of our old principles.* In the first two, after *as* & *than,* there can be no objection to letting grammar have its rights, with the correct *we.* In the third, if *becomes we* is thought pedantic, *becomes ourself* or *ourselves* is an easy way out ; & in the last, if it is obtrusively formal to keep the required case in mind for the duration of a dash & repeat it on the other side, *Let us Liberals at any rate be content* would not have been unbearably ordinary.

2. *Our,* or *his* &c., after *of us. Types, it must be admitted, under which each of us can classify a good many of* his *acquaintances.* That is the logical arrangement, which, as the quotation shows, is free from any taint of over-precision ; but much more commonly *our acquaintances* is substituted owing to the attraction of *us.*

-US. The plurals of nouns in *-us* are troublesome. 1. Most are from Latin second-declension words, whose Latin plural is *-i* (pronounced ī) ; but when that should be used, & when the English plural *-uses* is better, has to be decided for each separately ; see LATIN PLURALS, -I, & the individual words. 2. Many are from Latin fourth-declension words, whose Latin plural is *-us* (pronounced ūs) ; but the English plural *-uses* is almost always preferred, as *prospectuses* ; *hiatus* (-ūs)

is occasionally seen as a plural ; words of this class, which must never have plural in *-i,* are *afflatus, apparatus, conspectus, hiatus, impetus, lusus, meatus, nexus, plexus, prospectus, saltus, senatus, status.* 3. Some are from Latin third-declension neuters, whose plurals are of various forms in *-a* ; so *corpus, genus, opus,* make *corpora, genera, opera,* which are almost always preferred in English to *-uses.* 4. *Callus, octopus, polypus,* & *virus,* nouns variously abnormal in Latin, can all have plural *-uses* ; for any alternatives see the words. 5. Some English nouns in *-us* are in Latin not nouns, but verbs &c. ; so *ignoramus, mandamus, mittimus, non possumus, omnibus* ; for these the only possible plural is the English *-uses.*

use, n. The forms *What is the use of complaining ?,* & *There is no use in complaining,* are current & uncriticized. The forms *It is no use complaining* (or *to complain*), & *Complaining* (or *To complain*) *is no use,* are still more current, but much criticized, & the critics would have us correct them by inserting *of* (*is of no use*). General adoption of their *of* is at this time of day past praying for ; we should all take refuge instead in *useless,* which would do well enough if we could remember to say it. Still, on the assumption that *use* in these idioms means utility or usefulness, they are justified in their objection, if not in their remedy ; & they will probably refuse to be pacified by the admittedly imperfect analogy of *It is no good, It is no harm.* Perhaps the OED, which has unfortunately not yet reached *use,* may find us a better defence ; at any rate most of us would like to be allowed our *It is no use,* if it is but on the footing of a STURDY INDEFENSIBLE ; we should welcome the rites of the church, but, if they are withheld, we mean, like Touchstone, to live in bawdry. In so full-dress a sentence as the following, however, the writer might have been wise to defer to strict etiquette : *If the Government yields to these counsels, it will simply take us back into the worst period of Anglo-Irish contention, & its voluntary recruiting campaign will be no more use than its threat of conscription.*

use, v., makes *-sable* ; see MUTE E. Pronounce ūz ; but *used*, which is ūzd in general senses, is ūst in the senses was accustomed, & (as adj.) accustomed.

useful. See -ER & -EST, 4.

user. The words meaning (1) person who uses, & (2) right or act of using, as a legal term, are not one, but two of distinct formation.

usual. Of the pronunciations, ū'zhl is slipshod, ū'zūal pedantic, & ū'zhŏŏal the inoffensive ; see U.

usufruct. Pronounce ū'zū-.

uterus. Pl. *-rī.*

utilize makes *-zable* ; see MUTE E.

uti possidetis. Pronounce ū'tĭ pŏsĭdē'tĭs.

utmost, uttermost. See -MOST.

uvula. Pronounce ū'vū-. Pl. *-lae.*

V

vacant. For *vacantest*, see -ER & -EST, 4.

vacate makes *-table* ; see -ATABLE.

vaccinate makes *-nable*, see -ABLE 1 ; & *-tor*, see -OR.

vacillate. So spelt, not *-cc-* ; pron. vă'sĭ-. *V.* makes *-tor*, see -OR.

vacuity,-uousness. The first is the usual word ; the second may reasonably be chosen when a noun is wanted for *vacuous* as applied to the face, eyes, expression, &c. ; see -TY & -NESS.

vacuum. Pl. *-ua* or *-ms* ; see -UM. *V.* brake & v. cleaner need no hyphens ; see HYPHENS 3 B.

vade-mecum. Four syllables.

vagary. Pronounce vagār'ĭ ; the OED gives this pronunciation only, & among its verse quotations requiring it are lines from Milton, Gay, & the *Ingoldsby Legends.*

vagina. Always pronounced vajī'na ; but the adjective either vajī'nal or vă'jĭnal ; see FALSE QUANTITY.

vainglory. Best written as one word without hyphen.

vainness. So spelt ; sometimes preferred to *vanity* when the notion of conceit is to be excluded.

valance, drapery. The OED gives this, not *-ence* or *-ll-*, the preference.

Valenciennes. The pronunciation vălensē'nz is recommended ; but OED gives only the French, for which see FRENCH WORDS.

valet. Pronounce both noun & verb vă'lĭt ; the verb makes *-eted, -eting*, see -T-, -TT-.

valiant. See FORMAL WORDS.

valid makes *-est* ; see -ER & -EST, 4.

validate makes *-dable* ; see -ABLE 1.

valise. Except in military use as the official term for a soldier's knapsack, the word is now archaic in England, but survives in America ; cf. BAGGAGE.

Valkyrie. This is the prevailing spelling in modern English ; pl. *-s*, or (after the Old Norse) *Valkyriur.* The pronunciation shown in verse, & suggested by the formerly common spelling *Valkery*, is vă'lkirĭ ; but vălkĭ'rĭ is often heard.

valley. Pl. *-eys.*

valour, valorous. For spelling see -OUR & -OR, & -OUR- & -OR-.

value, n. *What value will our Second Chamber be to us if it is not to exercise such control ?* An interesting specimen of ANALOGY. *What good will it be ?* is unexceptionable ; *What use will it be ?* is not, but a plea has been put in for it in USE, n. ; *What value will it be ?* is ruled out, because no instinct tells us, as about *Of what use*, that *Of what value* is a piece of pedantry. *Is no good* is both grammatical & idiomatic ; *is no use* is idiomatic but not grammatical ; & *is no value* is neither.

valve. For the preference of *valvular* as the adjective over *valval* & *valvar*, see -ULAR.

vandalish, vandalism. Not *-ll-* ; see -LL-, -L-, 2.

Van Dyck, Vandyke, vandyke. The painter's name, originally *Van Dyck*, was anglicized into (*Sir Anthony*) *Vandyke* ; the derived noun & verb should be, & usually is, *vandyke* ; the painter or a picture of his may properly be called by either the first or preferably the second form, each written as above.

vanity. The Catechism phrase is *The pomps & vanity of this wicked world* (not *vanities*) ; see MIS-QUOTATION.

vapid makes *-est* ; see -ER & -EST, 4. Of its nouns, *vapidness* is usually better than *vapidity* (in strong contrast with the nouns of *rapid*), except when the sense is a vapid remark ; then *-ity* prevails, & still more the plural *-ities* ; -TY & -NESS.

vapour & its belongings. For the word itself see -OUR & -OR. Allied words are best spelt : *vapourer*, *vapourish, vapourless, vapoury* ; but *vaporific, vaporize* (-*zation*, -*zer*), *vaporous* (-*osity*) ; for the principle see -OUR- & -OR-.

vapulation. PEDANTIC HUMOUR.

variability, -bleness. Both are in constant use, without any clear difference of sense or application. This is unusual (see -TY & -NESS) ; but, while -ity would be expected to prevail, -ness probably persists owing to the familiar 'with whom is no variableness, neither shadow of turning' (*James* i. 17).

varia lectio. Pl. *variae lectionēs*.

variant, n., as compared with *variation* & *variety*, is the least ambiguous name for a thing that varies or differs from others of its kind ; for it is concrete only, while the others are much more often abstract ; *variation* is seldom concrete except in the musical sense, & *variety* seldom except as the classifying name for a plant, animal, mineral, &c., that diverges from the characteristics of its species. It is worth while to help on the differen-

tiation by preferring *variant* in all suitable contexts.

VARIATION. *The friendship between France & ourselves is rooted deep in* mutual *sacrifice,* mutual *suffering, & a* common *victory.* There is no change of meaning in passing from *mutual* to *common* ; the latter should have been used three times. The superstition that leads to foolish variations of this sort is discussed fully in ELEGANT VARIATION.

varicose. Pronounce vă'rĭkōs.

variegated. Five syllables (-rĭĭg-).

variorum, when used as a noun, has pl. *-ms* ; see -UM.

various as a pronoun. ANALOGY has lately been playing tricks with the word & persuading many people that they can turn it at will, as *several, few, many, divers, certain, some,* & other words are turned, from an adjective into a pronoun. In the OED article, published in 1916, there is no hint of such a use, which was apparently thought too illiterate to be even worth condemnation ; but the following quotations will show that it cannot safely be passed by without a warning. To write *various of them* &c. is no better than to write *different of them, diverse of them,* or *numerous or innumerable of them. Mr William Watson is only the latest of many poets—various of them Poets Laureatc —who have . . ./A like series of conflagrations in various of our towns & villages./That is not so easy as at onc time appeared, because various of the subsidies which were to disappear may come again into the national accounts./The fearsome noise these instruments emit when set in motion in various of the rooms within the precincts of the House./Various of those who had been prominent in her at the outset suggested . . ./In various of the territories under the control of the Colonial Powers the minimum has been exceeded./The Queen has caused large hampers of the choicest blooms to be forwarded to various of the hospitals.* For subsidies, rooms, territories, & hospitals, mere omission of *of the*, without the trouble of finding substitutes for *v*. &c., suffices.

varlet. Now, outside the historical novel, a PEDANTIC-HUMOUR word.

varmint, besides its reputed use as a rustic variant of *vermin* in the sense of rascal &c., is an established SOBRIQUET for the fox that is being hunted.

varsity is perilous stuff for those who are not familiar with universities to deal in ; it plays them just the tricks that any English slang plays the foreigner ; thinking that to say the word shows intimacy with the undergraduate's (or the Englishman's) characteristic language, they naturally put it into places where it would never occur to him, & reveal themselves not as natives, but as foreigners. Naturally also, they sometimes use it in the right places ; but it is perilous, for all that ; such trifles as *Varsity Extension Lectures, Varsity College,* or *at Cambridge Varsity* (as a correction, perhaps, of *at Cambridge College*), will sooner or later tempt & betray.

vary. For inflexions see VERBS IN -IE &c., 6.

vasculum. Pl. *-la* ; see -UM.

vase. So spelt (not *vause*), & pron. vahz (not vawz).

vaseful. Pl. *-ls* ; see -FUL.

vastly. In contexts of measure or comparison, where it means by much, by a great deal, as *is vastly improved, a vastly larger audience, v.* is still in regular use. Where the notion of measure is wanting, & it means no more than much or to a great degree, as in *I should vastly like to know, is vastly popular,* it is an affectation ; see WARDOUR STREET.

vaticinate makes *-tor* ; see -OR. The verb, formerly equivalent to *prophesy,* now usually connotes contempt, & means rather to play the prophet, to be a Cassandra ; *vaticination* is similarly limited.

vaudeville. See FRENCH WORDS.

vedette, not *vi-*.

-ve(d), -ves, &c., from words in -f & -fe. Corresponding to the change of sound discussed in -TH & -DH that takes place in the plural &c. of words ending in -th, like *truth,* there is one both of sound & of spelling in many words ending in -f or -fe, which become -ves, -ved, -vish, &c. As the change is far from regular, & sometimes in doubt, an alphabetical list of the chief words concerned follows ; with each are given those parts in which *f is* changed to *v* ; if the verb is stated to be -ve, it is to be understood that all parts of the verb (including the agent noun in -er) have *v* & not *f* ; the statements (or omissions, implying retention of *f*) cover (a) the noun's plural, (b) the corresponding verb, (c) the adjective in -ed, & (d) miscellaneous derivatives. Where no *v* form is given, the change to *v* does not take place, but forms in *f* are not mentioned except in the (d) or miscellaneous place, unless there is an alternative form in *v*. When alternatives are given, the first, if either, is better.

beef. Pl. *beeves* oxen, *beefs* kinds of beef ; (d) *beefy*.

belief. Vb *believe*.

calf. Pl. *calves* ; vb *calve* ; -ed *plump-calved* (legs) &c. ; (d) *calfish, calves-foot* or *calfs-foot*.

elf. Pl. *elves* ; (d) *elvish, elfish*.

grief. Vb *grieve* ; (d) *grievous*.

half. Pl. *halves* ; vb *halve*.

hoof. Pl. *hoofs, hooves* ; vb *hoof* ; -ed *hoofed, hooved* ; (d) *hoofy*.

knife. Pl. *knives* ; vb *knife, knive* ; -ed *knived*.

leaf. Pl. *leaves* ; vb *leaf, leave* ; -ed *leaved, leafed* ; (d) *leafy, leavy*.

life. Pl. *lives* ; vb *live* ; -ed *-lived* ; (d) *liven, lifer*.

loaf. Pl. *loaves* ; vb *loaf, loave* ; -ed *loafed, loaved* ; (d) *loafy*.

mischief. (d) *mischievous*.

oaf. Pl. *oafs, oaves* ; (d) *oafish*.

proof. Vb *prove*.

relief. Vb *relieve* ; (d) *rilievo, relievo*.

roof. No *v* forms.

safe. Vb *save*.

scarf. Pl. *scarfs*, *scarves*; -ed *scarfed*, *scarved*.

scurf. (d) *scurfy* having scurf, *scurvy* contemptible &c.

self. Pl. *selves*; (d) *selfish*, *selvedge*.

sheaf. Pl. *sheaves*; vb *sheave*, *sheaf*; -ed *sheaved*; (d) *sheafage*, *sheafy*.

shelf. Pl. *shelves*; vb *shelve*; -ed *shelved*; (d) *shelfy*, *shelvy*.

staff. Pl. *staffs*, (arch. & mus.) *staves*.

strife. Vb *strive*.

thief. Pl. *thieves*; vb *thieve*; (d) *thievery*, *thievish*.

turf. Pl. *turfs*, *turves*; vb *turf*; (d) *turfen* (adj.), *turfite*, *turfy*.

wharf. Pl. *wharfs*, (U.S.) *wharves*; (d) *wharfage*, *wharfinger*.

wife. Pl. *wives*; vb *wive*; -ed *-wifed*, *-wived*; (d) *-wifery*.

vehement, vehicle. Pronounce vē′ĭ-, not vē′hĭ-, in both; but vĭhĭ′kūl*ar*.

veiledly. Three syllables, if used; see -EDLY.

veilleuse. See FRENCH WORDS.

velamen, velamentum. Plurals *-amina*, *-amenta*.

velar. See TECHNICAL TERMS.

velarium. Pl. *-aria*.

veld(t). The modern form is *veld*, but the -dt still prevails in English use, & has the advantage of not disguising the sound, which is vĕlt.

velleity)(volition. The first is chiefly used either in direct opposition to the second, or (when *volition* has its widest sense) as expressing a particular form of it that is sometimes described as 'mere volition'. *Volition* meaning in the wide sense will-power or the exercise of it, & in a narrower but more usual sense such an exercise of it as shall if not baffled take effect, a choice or resolution or determination, *velleity* is an abstract & passive preference. The man in Browning—'And I think I rather . . . woe is me!—Yes, rather should see him than not see, If lifting a hand would seat him there Before me in the empty chair To-night '—is expressing a velleity, but not in the ordinary sense a volition. And the OED quotes from Bentham:

'In your Lordship will is volition, clothed & armed with power—in me, it is bare inert velleity '.

vellum. Pl. *-ms*, see -UM; adj. *vellumy*, see -M-, -MM-.

velum. Pl. *-la*.

velvet makes *velvety*; see -T-, -TT-.

vend makes *vendible*; see -ABLE 2. *Vendor & vender* are both in frequent use, with a tendency to DIFFEREN-TIATION; *-or* is better when the contrast or relation between seller & buyer is prominent, & *-er* when purveyor or dealer is all that is meant.

venerate makes *-tor*; see -OR.

venery. The existence of homonyms, one synonymous with hunting, the other with sexual indulgence, makes it necessary to provide against ambiguity in using either—the more that neither of them is now an everyday expression.

vengeance. See AVENGE.

venison. Pronounce vĕ′nzn.

ventilate makes *-lable*, *-tor*; see -ABLE 1, -OR.

ventre à terre. See FRENCH WORDS.

venturesome, venturous. See AD-VENTUROUS.

venue. Pronounce vĕ′nū. A term formerly common in fencing (obs.—OED), still used in law as the place appointed for a jury trial (esp. *lay*, & *change, the v.*), & lately become something of a VOGUE-WORD for what used to be called a rendezvous or meeting-place, e.g. for races &c. The following quotation, in which it means merely place without the meeting- (or *stage* ?), shows it undergoing the loss of character to which vogue-words are liable : *One of our most distinguished actresses acquired one of these coastal landmarks* [a lighthouse] *a good many years ago, & I believe the quietude of the interior provided a much appreciated venue for her dramatic work.*

Venus. Pl. *Venuses*, see -S-, -SS-. For *Venus' & Venus's*, see 's.

veranda(h). OED gives the *-da* form first, & there is no reason for the -h ; the adjective is best written *veranda'd*, see -ED & 'D.

verbal. Misuse of the word in the sense proper to *oral*, as in the quotation, is very common, & is to be deprecated : *The Attorney General said it was really a point of no substance ; the object of the provision was to apply it to all contracts, whether in writing or verbal. Verbal* meaning of or in words, *oral* meaning of or with the mouth, & words being as much used in writing as in speaking, it is obviously foolish to say ' in words ' (*verbal*) when the sense wanted is ' in spoken words ' (*oral*) ; &, though ambiguity may not result in a particular case, & Mr Attorney may be acquitted of it, each use of the wrong word makes ambiguity more likely in the ordinary layman's talk.

VERBS IN -IE, -Y, & -YE, sometimes give trouble in the spelling of inflexions & derivatives. The following rules apply to the normally formed parts only, & are merely concerned with the question whether -y-, -ie-, or -ye-, is to be used in the part wanted ; they do not imply that a part of entirely different formation such as *flew, lay, applicable, liar,* may not exclude *flied, lied, appliable,* or *lier,* but merely that e. g. *paid* & not *payed, deniable* & not *denyable,* are right.

1. -ay : *plays, played, playing, player, playable,* is the form for all except *lay, pay,* & *say,* & their compounds (*inlay, repay, gainsay,* &c.), which use *-aid* instead of *-ayed. Allay, assay, belay, delay,* & *essay,* do not follow *lay* & *say,* but use *-ayed.*

2. -ey : *conveys, conveyed, conveying, conveyer, conveyable.* All follow this type, except that *purvey, survey,* have *purveyor, surveyor.*

3. -ie : *ties, tied, tying, tier, tiable ;* all follow the type, but *-er* & *-able* are hardly in use.

4. -oy : *destroys, destroyed, destroying, destroyer, destroyable ;* no exceptions.

5. -uy : *buys, guyed, buying, buyer, buyable.*

6. -y after consonant : *tries, tried,*

trying, trier, triable ; denies, denied, denying, denier, deniable ; copies, copied, copying, copier, copiable. Neither number of syllables, place of accent, nor difference between ȳ & y̆, affects the spelling.

7. -ye : *dyes, dyed, dyeing, dyer, dyable ; dyeing* is so spelt merely to avoid confusion with *dying* from *die* (cf. *singeing*) ; *abye* accordingly would make *abying,* & so *eying* (5 quotations in OED) rather than *eyeing* (2 in OED).

verbum sap. (scil. *sapienti sat est*). a word is enough to the wise. Also *verb. sap., verbum sat, sat verbum,* or at full length. Ostensibly an apology for not explaining at greater length, or a hint that the less said the better, but more often in fact a way of soliciting attention to what has been said as weightier than it seems.

verdigris. The orthodox pronunciation is -ĭs, the popular -ēs ; *-gris* is derived not from *grease,* though the notion that it is probably accounts for the prevalent -ēs, but from Greece (green of Greece) ; but as the true origin no more requires -ĭs than the false, there seems no reason why the -ēs of the majority should not be accepted by the minority.

veridical. Apart from a modern technical use in psychology, mostly a PEDANTIC-HUMOUR word.

verify. For inflexions, see VERBS IN -IE &c., 6.

verily. Apart from its occasional appearances as a stylistic ornament, & its legitimate use in the dialogue of historical novels, *v.* is now perhaps confined to one single phrase—*I verily believe,* which has the special meaning, It is almost incredible, yet facts surprise me into the belief.

veritable, in its modern use, is probably to be classed as a journalistic GALLICISM, & its function is, when one contemplates an exaggeration, to say compendiously, but seldom truthfully, ' I assure you I am not exaggerating ' : *a veritable hail of* *slates* &c. It is a pity that the early 19th c. could not leave well alone ; for the OED records that by about 1650 the word was dead, but the early 19th c. revived it. Would it had not ! its appearance in a description has always the effect of taking down the reader's interest a peg or two, both as being a FORMAL WORD, & as the now familiar herald of a strained top note. The adverb, which could equally well be spared, does the same service, or disservice, to adjectives as the adjective to nouns (*veritably portentous* &c.) ; it is also used with verbs as a supposed improvement on the various natural adverbs, as in : *If this is to be the last word, we shall find ourselves thrown back into a hopeless impasse, & there will veritably be no way of reforming our Parliamentary institutions* (actually? really? positively? absolutely? in very truth?).

vermeil. Pronounce ver'mĭl ; the verb makes *vermeiled*, see -LL-, -L-.

vermilion makes *-oned*; -N-, -NN-.

vermin. The plural form *-ns* is now hardly used ; the word is a collective (see *collectives* F in TECHNICAL TERMS) meaning either all the creatures entitled to the name, or any particular species or set of them, or some of them ; it is treated usually as a plural (*these v. ; the v. are an incessant torment* ; *v. infest everything*), but sometimes as singular (*this v.* = these rascals &c.), & occasionally has *a* both in the collective sense (*a v. that I hope to reduce the numbers of*) & as denoting an individual (*such a v. as you*).

vermouth. So spelt ; pronounce vār'mōōt.

vernacular. For v., idiom, slang, &c., see JARGON. For the use of the word in apologies, see SUPERIORITY.

verruca. Pl. *-cae* (-sē).

versatile. Adverb *versatilely*.

vers libre. For the nature of it, see *vers libre* in TECHNICAL TERMS. The French phrase is still in general use ; but there seems to be no good reason why 'free verse' should not be preferred. For the writers we have to choose between 'free-verse-writer' (since the handier 'free-verser' would probably be thought unduly familiar by the designated) & 'verslibrist' (as queer a fish for English waters as *bellettrist*) or its jocose anglicization here quoted : *Scholarly elaboration is, we are aware, out of fashion with the modern verse-librettists*. A 'verse-librettist' can only be one who writes librettos in verse ; as to the other forms, if the free-versers will let us call them so, we shall take it kindly of them, & if not, had better fall back on 'free-verse-writers'.

versify. For inflexions, see VERBS IN -IE &c., 6.

verso. Pl. *-os* ; see -O(E)S 3, 6.

vert. A CURTAILED WORD.

vertebra. Pl. *-brae.*

vertex. For plural, see -EX, -IX, 4.

vertigo. Pl. *-os*, see -O(E)S 3. The correct pronunciation in accordance with the Latin quantity is vertī'gō, but the OED gives ver'tĭgō precedence, & see FALSE QUANTITY. It is worth remark, however, that all the OED verse quotations (Jonson, Swift, Fletcher, Wither) show vertĭ'gō (or -ē'gō).

vertu. See VIRTU.

verve. See FRENCH WORDS.

very with passive participles. The legitimacy of this, or at least the line limiting its idiomatic use, is an old & not very easy puzzle. It will at once be admitted that *I was much tired* is improved by the substitution of *very* for *much*, whereas, in *I was very inconvenienced*, *much* has undoubtedly to be substituted for *very*. And it may be said generally that the critics of *very* have a way of going too far & damning the laudable ; they fail to recognize that *very* & *much* are complementary, each being suited to places in which the other is unnatural or wrong. Here is part of a newspaper letter : *Sir,—When the* Westminster Gazette *can write & publish ' the " Common Cause " is very affronted '*, *it seems* *time for some-one to raise a gentle protest. ' Very much affronted ', or ' highly affronted ', if you like, but surely not ' very affronted '. Try another tense : one cannot say ' your language very affronts me ' ; but I can say (with truth) ' your language very much affronts me '.* How reasonable it sounds : see *different* for a similar argument ; but it proves too much ; similarly I cannot say *This very tires me* ; & yet, dissimilarly, I can say *I am very tired* ; & with *affronted* itself I can say *He wore a very affronted look* ; & *His look was very affronted* is, if not a likely expression, at least better than *His look was much affronted.*

The points that have to be taken into account are : 1. Has the p.p. passed into a true adjective in common use, as *tired* & *celebrated* have, & *inconvenienced* has not ? 2. Is it used attributively (*a —— damaged reputation*), or predicatively (*the car is —— damaged*) ? 3. Is the noun to which the p.p. belongs the name of the person or thing on which the verbal action is exercised (*he was —— surprised at the question*), or that of something else (*his expression was —— surprised*) ? 4. Is its participial or verbal (as opp. adjectival) character unbetrayed by e. g. a telltale preposition such as *by* ?

A word that is in form a p.p., if it is to be qualified by *very* instead of *much* (or *very much*), must be able to say Yes to N° 1, *or* to the first part of N° 2, *or* to the second part of N° 3, *and* to N° 4. That is, *He is very celebrated* is right (1), but *Attic taste is very celebrated by the poets* is wrong (4) ; *A very worried official appeared* is right (2), but *The Government, very worried, withdrew the motion* is wrong (2), & still more *The Government, very worried with questions, withdrew* &c. (4) ; *His tone was very annoyed* is right (3), but *You seem very annoyed* is wrong (3), & still more *He was very annoyed by the interruption* (4).

All this amounts substantially to no more than that a participle (in -ed) that *is* a participle requires *much*, while a participle that is an adjective prefers *very* ; but the bare rule is not very intelligible without some such expansion as has been given. In the quotations that follow, which represent fairly the proportion in which idiom is offended one way & the other, it will be noticed that there is only one *much* where *very* would be better against a large number where *very* should have been *much* (or *very much*) :— *Opera & theatre engagements are also* much *limited & by no means easy to get./We shall be* very *surprised if a good many of the suggested amendments are not clear breaches of . . ./ We should be* very *surprised if the Liberal agents ever received the alleged ' warning './Sir Alfred said that the hostility of the Arabs was* very *exaggerated in this country./The latter had been* very *annoyed on learning that . . ./We are all* very *annoyed at those figures being published./A friend in Cornwall tells me that listeners-in there are* very *annoyed because . . ./The* Evening Standard *was* very *concerned last night to protest against ' Methods of Anarchy './We are not* very *concerned about these subtle distinctions./Both parties are* very *jealous, &* very *afraid of each other (afraid, & other purely predicative adjectives, rank with the p.p.)./He is* very *afraid that somebody will recognize him./Your mind seems* very *exercised just now as to whether . . ./The peasant deputies consider themselves* very *aggrieved./' Imperialist ' is* very *disgusted with Earl Grey for his statements./When the husband returned, he found her manner towards him* very *changed.*

In conclusion, the worst & the most venial misuses of *very* are represented by *I was very inconvenienced by it*, & *I shall be very pleased* (i. e. glad, happy) *to accept.*

-ves. See -VE(D).

vesica. Pronounce vĭsī′ka ; but

the derived words vĕ'sĭkl (*vesical* & *vesicle*), vĕ'sĭkāt, &c. ; cf. *doctrinal* in FALSE QUANTITY.

vessel. See FORMAL WORDS.

vest. The older meanings robe, tunic, or collectively clothes (= *vesture*), are still in poetic or archaic use ; as a synonym for a man's waistcoat it is chiefly a shop word, but is more generally applied to the corresponding partly visible feminine garment ; & it is now the usual name (*singlet* being another) for the woven piece of underlinen formerly called *jersey*.

vesta. Chiefly a shop word, but occasionally used elsewhere of the kinds of match carried in the pocket ; formerly wax, now of wood also.

vet. A CURTAILED WORD.

veto. Pl. *-os* ; see -O(E)S 3.

vexedly. A bad form ; see -EDLY.

vexillum. Pl. *-la*.

via, viâ. In *via media*, *via* is the Latin nominative, & must not have *-â*. In the use as a preposition meaning ' by way of ' or ' passing through ' it is the Latin ablative, the distinguishing of which by a circumflex accent is optional. As both forms are pronounced vī'a, & there is never any risk of confusion, it seems idle to retain the accent, but accent & italics are still usual.

viable (*-bility*). A word apt to puzzle an Englishman. Formed in French from *vie* life (see -ABLE 4), it means capable of living, & its special application is to newborn children (e. g. in contrast with *stillborn*), but there is some tendency to widen its use. The two words of the same form applied to a road, a pass, &c., & obviously associated with Latin *via* way, are of recent origin ; they mean ' that can be passed through ', ' passability ', & it may be conjectured that they owe their existence to a misconception of the older *viable* ; they are certainly better avoided.

viaticum. Pl. *-ms*, *-ca*, see -UM ; but the plural is rare, & e. g. in the

PEDANTIC-HUMOUR uses one's provisions &c. are one's *viaticum*.

vibrate makes *-table*, *-tor* ; see -ATABLE, -OR.

vibrato. Pronounce vēbrah'tō ; pl. *-os*, see -O(E)S 6.

vicar. Vicar & rector, as parish priests, are distinguished by the rector's retaining the tithes, which are lost to the vicar by having been appropriated to a monastery or other religious corporation or impropriated to a lay person or corporation.

vice, prep., prefix, & abbreviated noun. The preposition is pronounced vī'sĭ, & means in the place of (esp. in the sense succeeding to), being, like PACE, the ablative of a Latin noun followed by an English noun regarded as in the genitive (*appointed Secretary vice Mr Jones deceased*).

The prefix is the same word treated as an adverb compounded with English nouns such as *chancellor*, *president*, *chairman*, *admiral*, but meaning rather deputy, & pronounced vīs.

The noun is the prefix used without its second element, but with the aid of context, as a CURTAILED WORD for some of its compounds, e. g. for *vice-chairman* & *vice-chancellor*, but not for *vice-admiral*. Cf. SUB, SUPER, PRO.

vicegerent)(**viceregent.** The first is a word of very wide application, including anyone who exercises authority committed to or supposed to be committed to him by another, from the Pope as the Vicar of Christ on earth or the regent of a sovereign State to the clerk running an office during his employer's holiday. *Viceregent*, on the other hand, is defined in the OED as ' One who acts in the place of a regent ' ; but from the quotations given it would appear that that is rather what it ought to mean than what it does. A regent is a particular kind of vicegerent, viz a sovereign's. But *viceregent* is sometimes used in error for *vicegerent*, & sometimes used pleonastically for *regent* (which word includes the notion of vice-), so that it seems to have no right to exist, & may be classed among SUPER-FLUOUS WORDS.

vice-queen)(**vicereine**. The first is recorded from the 16th c., the second (in English) from the 19th only. *Vicereine* is now the regular word for viceroy's wife, & *vice-queen*, in much less frequent use, is now reserved for a woman ruling as a queen's representative—a useful DIFFERENTIATION.

viceregal)(**viceroyal**. There being no distinction of meaning, it would be better if there were one word only ; *viceregal* is the better, & *viceroyal* may fairly be called a SUPERFLUOUS WORD.

vicinage is now, compared with *neighbourhood*, a FORMAL WORD, &, compared with *vicinity*, a dying one.

vicious circle. See under TECH-NICAL TERMS. *There is a vicious circle in which starvation produces Bolshevism, & Bolshevism in its turn feeds on starvation.* What, then, produces starvation, & on what does starvation feed ? The writer can no doubt retort with truth that nothing (i.e. no food) produces starvation, & that starvation feeds on nothing ; but he will have proved his wit at the expense of his logic. Such blunders in stating the elements of a vicious circle are not uncommon.

victimize makes -*zable* ; see MUTE E.
victress. FEMININE DESIGNATIONS.
victual. The verb makes -*ller*, -*lling*, see -LL-, -L- ; pronounce vĭ′tl, vĭ′tler, vĭ′tling.

vide. Pronounce vī′dĭ ; literally ' see ' (imperative). It is properly used in referring readers to a passage in which they will find a proof or illustration of what has been stated, & should be followed by something in the nature of chapter & verse, or at least by the name of a book or author. But it has, like RE, been taken over by the illiterate, & is daily used by them in extended

senses with an incongruity of which the following is a comparatively mild specimen : *Numbers count for no-thing—vide the Coalition—it is the principles that tell.*

videlicet in its full form is now rare except in PEDANTIC HUMOUR, the abbreviation *viz* being used instead ; see VIZ for meaning.

vidimus. Pl. -*uses* ; see -US. Pronounce vī′dĭ-.
vie. For inflexions, see VERBS IN -IE &c., 3.
view forms part of three well established idioms each equivalent to a preposition, & each liable to be confused in meaning or in form with the others. These are *in v. of, with a v. to*, & *with the v. of. In view of* means taking into account, or not forgetting, or considering, & is followed by a noun expressing external circumstances that exist or must be expected : *In v. of these facts, we have no alternative* ; *In v. of his having promised amendment* ; *In v. of the Judgement to come. With a view to* means calculating upon or contemplating as a desired result, & is followed by a verbal noun or a gerund or less idiomatically an infinitive : *With a v. to diminution of waste*, or *to diminishing waste*, or (less well) *to diminish waste. With the view of* has the same meaning as *with a v. to*, but is both less usual & less flexible, being naturally followed only by a gerund : *With the v. of proving his sanity.* It will be observed that in the first phrase *v.* means sight, in the second eye, & in the third purpose. The forms of confusion are giving the first the meaning of the others or vice versa, & neglecting the correspondences *a* & *to*, the & *of*, in the second & third. After each of the following quotations a correction, or a statement that it is right, is bracketed :—
There was very little likelihood in the report of disaster to a Turkish destroyer in harbour at Preveza, in view of *the fact that no Turkish destroyer was stationed there* (right)./

This may be interesting in view of *the fact that the atmosphere has been reeking with pugilism for some time* (right)./*I will ask your readers to accept a few further criticisms on matters of detail*, in view of *ultimately finding a workable solution* (read *with a v. to*)./*The Sultan will seek to obtain money* in view of *beginning for himself the preliminary reforms* (read *with a v. to*)./*If Germany has anything to propose* in view of *the safeguarding of her own interests, it will certainly meet with courteous consideration* (read *with the v. of*, or *with a v. to*)./*My company has been approached by several firms* with a view of *overcoming the difficulty* (read *to* for *of*)./*Dr Keane was educated* with a view of *becoming a priest* (read *to* for *of*)./*The time has come when it ought to be tackled effectively* with a view of *giving some relief* (read *to* for *of*)./*They have been selected* with a view to illustrate *both the thought & action of the writer's life* (read *illustrating* for *illustrate*)./*The question of reducing the cost of bread production*, with the view *both to preventing the price of the loaf from rising & of arresting any increase in the subsidy, is under consideration* (ELEGANT VARIATION again? read *of* for *to*).

view-point. See POINT.
vignette. Pronounce vēnyĕ't.
vigour, -gorous. For spellings, see -OUR & -OR, -OUR- & -OR-.
viking. Pronounce vī-.
vilayet. Pronounce vĭlah'yĕt.
vilify. For inflexions see VERBS IN -IE &c., 6.
vilipend. A LITERARY WORD only.
villain &c. 1. *Villain*)(*villein*. 2. *Villain*-)(*villan*-. 1. *Villain*)(*villein*. The retention of the second form for the word meaning serf is a useful piece of DIFFERENTIATION, & the OED accordingly gives it in a separate article, though it states that ' the tendency to use the form *villain* [in this sense] has increased in recent years '. This tendency looks like PRIDE OF KNOWLEDGE,

the man in the street who is familiar with the two forms having to be shown that he has been under a delusion all this time.
2. *Villain*-)(*villan*-. The OED makes *villainous* & *villainy* the standard forms. *Villanous* & *villany* are & have been common also, & are not open to the objection that prevents *mountain* (perhaps the only analogous case) from forming *mountanous* instead of *mountainous*, i.e. that *moun*- precludes (see HYBRID DERIVATIVES) direct formation from Latin *montanus*; Latin *villanus* could fairly result in *villanous* & *villany*; but, while the *de jure* claims are equal, *-ainous* & *-ainy* seem to have established themselves *de facto* in the 19th c.

villanelle. See TECHNICAL TERMS.
villeggiatura. Pronounce vĭlĕ'ja-toor'a.
ville lumière. See SOBRIQUETS.
villus. Pl. *-lī.*
vinaigrette. See FRENCH WORDS.
vinculum. Pl. *-la.*
vindicate makes *-cable, -tor* ; see -ABLE 1, -OR.
vindicatress. See FEMININE DESIGNATIONS.
vindictive has become so generally restricted to the notion of personal thirst for revenge or desire to hurt that the phrases in which it means punitive & not revengeful or cruel are apt to mislead ; these are *v. damages* (designed to punish the offender & not, or not only, to indemnify the injured party), & *v.* (now more often *retributive*) *justice*.

vine makes *viny* ; see -EY & -Y.
vingt-et-un. See FRENCH WORDS.
vin ordinaire. See FRENCH WORDS.
viola. The flower is vī'ola, the instrument vēō'la.
violate makes *-lable, -tor* ; see -ABLE 1, -OR.
violet makes *-etish, -ety* ; -T-, -TT-.
violin. The victory of this over *fiddle*, to which it should have borne the same relation as, say, *gourmet* to *epicure*, or *savant* to *scientist*, or *belles lettres* to *literature*, or *porcelain*

to *china*, or *parasol* to *sunshade*, or *robe de chambre* to *dressing-gown*— the relation, that is, of refined journalese to ordinary plain language—, may be deplored, but hardly now reversed. Already to talk of *fiddles* & *fiddlers* & *fiddling*, unless with contempt or condescension, is to be suspected of eccentricity.

violoncello. So spelt (not *-lin-*); pl. *-os*, see -O(E)S 6. For pronunciation, vēolonchĕ'lō is the approximation to the Italian; vīolonsĕ'lō, which the OED puts first, is the complete anglicization; & vīolonchĕ'lō is the usual compromise, which, having in its favour both *violin* & *'cello* (chĕ'lō), is here recommended.

virago. Pl. *-os*; see -O(E)S 3.

Virgil & *Virgilian* gain or lose as much by being corrected into *Ver*- as MAHOMET by the change to *Muhammad*.

virgin. *V. Queen*; see SOBRIQUETS.

Virginia(n). The noun used attributively (*Virginia creeper*, *tobacco*, &c.) has maintained itself by the side of the adjective (*Virginian creeper* &c.) from the early 17th c. till now in spite of a modern tendency (like that noticed under UN-IDIOMATIC -LY) to insist on an adjectival form where one is available.

virile. The pronunciation of both *i*s varies between ī & ĭ; accent on first syllable; OED puts first vī'rĭl. The proper sense is ' having the qualities of a male adult ', but the emphasis is on *male*, &, though *vigorous* can often be substituted for *v*. without affecting the required meaning, *v*. must not be substituted for *vigorous* where the notion male is out of place, as in : VIRILE AT 93 : *Despite her great age, Mrs Jones is fairly virile, & performs all her own household work*. Probably the reporter associates *v*. with *viridis* green, not *vir* man, & was thinking of a green old age.

virtu. So spelt (not *ver-*); pronounce vertōō'.

virtue. *To make a v. of necessity* is one of the maltreated phrases illustrated in IRRELEVANT ALLUSION, being often applied to the simple doing of what one must, irrespective of the grace with which one does it.

virtuoso. Pl. *-si* (-sē).

virulent. The OED pronounces vī'ryŏŏlent ; in view of the difficulty of this, see U.

virus. Pl. *-uses*.

visa. See VISÉ.

visage. See COUNTENANCE.

vis-à-vis. See FRENCH WORDS. *The French situation viz-à-viz Mustapha Kemal is uncertain* is probably the result of spelling a foreign word by ear ; see FOREIGN DANGER ; *viz-à-viz* is, however, recorded as an obsolete form.

viscount. For *V. Smith* & *Lord Smith*, see TITLES. Of the two forms of the rank-name, *viscounty* & *viscountcy*, the first is both much older & of better formation.

visé (vē'zā), in French a p.p.= ' examined ' or ' endorsed ', is used in English with regard to passports (1) as a noun=endorsement, for which the French noun *visa* is sometimes preferred, (2) as a verb= endorse, with inflexions *visés*, *viséd*, *viséing*, & (3) as a p.p.=endorsed, sometimes preferred to *viséd*.

visibility)(visibleness. See -TY & -NESS. The second has always been in more frequent use than most -ness·words with predominant partners in -ty, & the special sense of *visibility* that became so familiar in the war may be expected to throw more general work on the other.

vision, in the sense of statesmanlike foresight or political sagacity, is enjoying a noticeable vogue ; ' . . . in those days : there was no open vision ' (*1 Sam.*, iii. 1) is perhaps what makes the word tempting to politicians who wish to be mysteriously impressive ; at any rate they are much given to imputing lack of v. to their opponents & implying possession of it by themselves when they are at a loss for more definite matter ; see VOGUE-WORDS.

visit, vb, makes -*tor* ; see -OR.

visor &c. *Visor & vizor* pronounced vĭz- ; *vizard & visard* pronounced vĭz-. The -ard forms are not etymologically significant, being merely corruptions, but they differ in meaning by being restricted to the sense mask (lit. & fig.), whereas the -or forms have also, & chiefly, the sense movable helmet-front.

vista'd is preferable to *vistaed* ; see -ED & 'D.

visual. For the pronunciation vĭ'zūal there is a much better case than for ū'zūal (see USUAL), because it is a word used chiefly by the educated ; for the principle, see PRONUNCIATION ; the OED, however, puts vĭ'zhūal first.

visualize, vitalize, make -*zable* ; see MUTE E.

vitellus. Pl. -*lī*.

vitiate makes *vitiable*, -*tor* ; see -ABLE 1, -OR.

vitrify. For inflexions, see VERBS IN -IE &c., 6.

vitriolize makes -*zable* ; see MUTE E.

vitta. Pl. -*tae*.

vituperate makes -*rable*, -*tor* ; see -ABLE 1, -OR.

viva¹. See VIVA VOCE.

viva², vivat, vive, (pronounce vē'-vah, vī'văt, vēv) are the Italian, Latin, & French, for ' long live —— ! ' ; they can all be used as nouns also, with plural -*s*. The verbs have, like EXIT, plurals (*vivano, vivant, vivent*) for use with plural subjects—a fact forgotten in :— *Cries of ' Vive les Anglais ' attended us till we were inside the hotel./ Triumphal arches were prepared ; ' Bienvenue à nos libérateurs '— ' Vive les Allies '—such were the words variously devised in illuminations & in posters.*

vivace. Pronounce vēvah'chā.

vivandier, -ère. See FRENCH WORDS.

vivarium. Pl. -*ia*.

vivat. See VIVA².

viva voce. Pronounce vīvavō'sĭ. Often shortened colloquially into the CURTAILED WORD *viva*, which is used both as noun & especially as v. t. (past & p.p. *viva'd*)=examine in viva voce.

vive. See VIVA².

vivid makes -*est* ; see -ER & -EST 4.

vividity. *A theme worthy of poetry . . . ; here it is handled with occasional vividity & general inconsequence.* V.'s ugliness is no doubt its misfortune rather than its fault ; but it is as natural to prefer *vividness* to it as to choose the one of two otherwise equal applicants who does not squint.

vivify. For inflexions, see VERBS IN -IE &c., 6.

vivisect makes -*tor* ; see -OR.

viz, sc(il)., **i. e.** Full forms *videlicet, scilicet, id est.* The meanings are so close to one another that a less instead of the most appropriate is often chosen. *Viz*, as is suggested by its usual spoken representative *namely*, introduces especially the items that compose what has been expressed as a whole (*For three good reasons, viz* 1 . . ., 2 . . ., 3 . . .) or a more particular statement of what has been vaguely described (*My only means of earning, viz my fiddle*). *Sc.* or *scil.* is in learned rather than popular use, is for instance commoner in notes on classical texts than elsewhere, & has as its most characteristic function the introducing of some word that has been not expressed, but left to be ' understood ' ; so *His performance failed to satisfy* (*sc.* himself),=not, as might be guessed, other people. What *i. e.* does is not so much to particularize like *viz*, or supply omissions like *scil.*, as to interpret by paraphrasing a previous expression that may mislead or be obscure : *Now you are for it*, i. e. punishment ; *The answer is in the negative*, i. e. is No ; *Than that he should offend* (i. e. harm) *one of these little ones.*

Even the above examples suffice to show that choice may sometimes be difficult ; it does not follow that it is not worth making rightly. The writing of *viz* rather than *viz.* depends partly on the principle stated in Period in abbreviations, but partly also on the fact that z is not the letter, but the old symbol of contraction for the -et of *videlicet* ; but *viz.* is the prevalent form.

vizard. See visor.

vizier, vizierate, are the established forms, variously pedanticized as *wazir-, vizir-, vezir-,* &c. ; see Mahomet.

vizor. See visor.

vocabulary. See glossary.

vocalize makes *-zable* ; see Mute e.

VOGUE-WORDS. Every now & then a word emerges from obscurity, or even from nothingness or a merely potential & not actual existence, into sudden popularity. It is often, but not necessarily, one that by no means explains itself to the average man, who has to find out its meaning as best he can ; his wrestlings with it have usually some effect upon it ; it does not mean quite what it ought to, but in compensation it means some things that it ought not to, before he has done with it. Ready acceptance of vogue-words seems to some people the sign of an alert mind ; to others it stands for the herd instinct & lack of individuality ; the title of this article is perhaps enough to show that the second view is here taken ; on the whole, the better the writer, or at any rate the sounder his style, the less will he be found to indulge in the vogue-word. It is unnecessary here to discuss in detail the specimens that will be given ; most of them are to be found in their dictionary places, & they will here be slightly classified only. The reason for collecting them under a common heading is that young writers may not even be aware, about some of them, that they are not part of the normal vocabulary, but still repulsive to

the old & the well-read. Many, it should be added, are vogue-words in particular senses only, & are unobjectionable, though liable now to ambiguity, in the senses that belonged to them before they attained their vogue.

1. Old vogue-words. *Individual* & *nice* may be instanced ; the first now past its vogue but lingering in its vogue sense as a nuisance ; the second established in a loose & general sense instead of its earlier & now infrequent precise one.

2. Words owing their vogue to the ease with which they can be substituted for any of several different & more precise words, saving the trouble of choosing the right : *annex* ; *asset* ; *intensive* ; *mentality* ; *optimism* ; *unthinkable.*

3. Words owing their vogue to the joy of showing that one has acquired them : *conservative* ; *feasible* ; *hectic* ; *idiosyncrasy* ; *meticulous* ; *percentage* ; *protagonist* ; *psychological moment* ; *slogan* ; *venue.*

4. Words taken up merely as novel variants on their predecessors : *forceful* for *forcible* ; *frock* for *dress* ; *happening* for *event* ; *intrigue* vb for *interest.*

5. Words made or revived to suit a literary theory : *foreword* ; *english* vb.

6. Words owing their vogue to some occasion : *acid test* ; *gesture*= *beau geste.*

7. Words of rhetorical appeal : *far-flung* ; *vision.*

volatilize makes *-zable* ; see Mute e.
vol-au-vent. See French words.
volcano. Pl. *-oes* ; see -o(e)s 1.
volition. See velleity.
Volkslied. Pronounce fō'kslēt.
volley. Pl. *-eys.* For verb inflexions, see Verbs in -ie &c., 2.
volte-face. See French words.
voluminous. See lu.
voluntar(y)ism, -ist. See -ist.
volute. See lu.
vomit makes *-ited, -iting* ; -t-, -tt-.
vortex. For plural see -ex, -ix, 4.
votaress. Feminine designations.

vote, vb, makes *-table* ; see MUTE E.
vouch. See AVOUCH.
voussoir, vraisemblable, -emblance.
See FRENCH WORDS.
vulcanize makes *-zable* ; see MUTE E.
vulgar(ity). For the use in apologies
for slang, see SUPERIORITY.

VULGARIZATION. Many words
depend for their legitimate effect
upon rarity ; when blundering
hands are laid upon them & they are
exhibited in unsuitable places, they
are vulgarized. *Save* (prep.) & *ere*
were in the days of our youth seldom
seen in prose, & they then consorted
well with any passage of definitely
elevated style, lending to it & receiving from it the dignity that was
proper to them. Things are now so
different that the elevated style
shuns them as tawdry ornament ; it
says what the man in the street says,
before & *except*, & leaves *ere* & *save*
to the journalists who have not yet
ceased to find them beautiful—
which is naturally confusing, & an
injury to the language. The fate
of *awful* is of rather earlier date,
but is still remembered, & *weird*
has, almost in our own century,
been robbed of all its weirdness.
One would like to represent to the
makers of fountain pens that the
word *fount*, which some of them are
desecrating, is sacrosanct ; but they
would probably be as indignant at
the notion that their touch pollutes
as the writer who should be told that
he was injuring *faerie* & *evanish* &
mystic & *optimistic* & *unthinkable* &
replica by selecting them in honourable preference to *fairy* & *vanish* &
mysterious & *hopeful* & *incredible*
& *copy*. Vulgarization of words that
should not be in common use robs
some of their aroma, others of their
substance, others again of their
precision ; but nobody likes to be
told that the best service he can do
to a favourite word is to leave it
alone, & perhaps the less said here
on this matter the better.
vulgarize makes *-zable* ; see MUTE E.
vulpicide. See PEDANTIC HUMOUR.

W

wabble. See WOBBLE.
wade makes *-dable* ; see MUTE E.
wadi, -dy. Pronounce wah'dī. The
-di form (pl. *-dis*) is recommended ;
but *-dy* & *-dies* are also common.
wafer has *-ery, -ered,* &c.; -R-, -RR-.
wag(g)on. The OED gives precedence to *wagon*, but concludes its
note on the two forms with : ' In
Great Britain *waggon* is still very
commonly used ; in the U.S. it is
rare '. Counting its post-18th-c.
quotations we find 35 *waggon* to
11 *wagon*, & it is clear that *waggon*
is the British form.

wagon-lit. See FRENCH WORDS.
wainscot has *-oted, -oting* ; -T-, -TT-.
waistcoat. The pronunciation wĕ's-
kut is recommended ; see PRO-
NUNCIATION.
wait. The transitive use, as in
w. one's *opportunity, w. the result,
w.* another's *convenience* or *arrival*,
is good English, but is described by
the OED as ' now rare ' & as being
' superseded ' by *await* & *wait for* ;
the assignment of the intransitive
uses to *wait* & of the transitive to
await is a natural DIFFERENTIATION,
& may be expected to continue ;
see also AWAIT.

waitress. FEMININE DESIGNATIONS.
waive. The broad distinction between *wave* & *waive*, viz that to
wave is, & to waive is not, proper to
physical motion, is now generally
observed ; but confusion, & especially the assumption that the two
forms are mere spelling variants,
still occurs, & is confirmed by the
fact that till recently senses certainly belonging to waive were at
least as often as not spelt *wave*.
The following example shows the
form often taken by this confusion :
*The problem of feeding the peoples of
the Central Empires is a very serious
& anxious one, & we cannot* waive
it aside *as though it were no concern
of ours.* To *waive* is not a derivative,
confined to certain senses, of to

wave, but a derivative of *waif*, meaning to make waif or abandon ; to wave aside or away is one method of waiving ; but to *waive aside* or *away* is no better than to *abandon aside* or to *relinquish away*.

wake. See A)WAKE(N.

Walach, Walachian, not *Wall-*, is the OED preferred spelling.

wale, weal, wheal. For the mark left on flesh by a cane &c., the right word appears to be *wale* ; this was confused with *wheal*, properly a pimple or pustule, & *weal* was a wrong correction of the mistake.

Walhalla. See VALHALLA.
Walkyrie. See VALKYRIE.
Wallach(ian). See WALACH.

WALLED-UP OBJECT. *I shut & locked him in* is permissible English ; *I scolded & sent him to bed* is not. In the first, *in* is common to *shut & locked* ; *him* is therefore not walled up between *locked* & a word that is the private property of *locked*. In the second, *to bed* is peculiar to *sent*, & therefore *him*, enclosed between *sent* & *sent*'s appurtenance *to bed*, is not available as object to *scolded* ; it is necessary to say *I scolded him & sent him to bed*, though *I scolded & punished him* requires only one *him*. If it is said that the agitated disciplinarian cannot be expected to decide when her boy is two *hims*, & when not, the plea may at once be admitted ; it is not in hasty colloquial use that such lapses are wicked, & the examples chosen were the simplest possible in order that the grammatical point might be unmistakable ; but in print it is another matter. The string of quotations following shows how common this slovenliness is, & no more need be said of them than that for nearly all the cure is to release the walled-up noun, place it as object to the unencumbered verb (which usually comes first), & fill its now empty place with a pronoun, *it*, *them*, &c. ; this is done in brackets after the first, & any change

not according to this simple formula is shown for later ones :—*An earnest agitation for increasing & rendering* that force *more efficient* (read *for increasing that force & rendering it . . .*)./*It is for its spirited reconstructions of various marches & battles that we counsel the reader to buy & make* the book *his own.*/*The Czar, who must ' truly conserve & keep* the peasantry *living simply & sweetly on the land '.*/*I hope the Ministry will also avail itself of the same effective machinery if not to reform, then to make* the Church of England *a free Church in a free country.*/*He had to count, trim, press, & pack* the furs *into bales* (read *& press the furs, & pack them* ; or, of course, the omission of *into bales* would put all right)./*It is not deterring, but is exasperating* women *to ever more dangerous acts of violence.*/ *The efforts which the French are now making to interest & attract* the Rhinelanders *to French civilization.*/ *He urged that Allenby should attack & drive* the Turks *out of Palestine.*/ *They had definitely beaten & knocked* one of their opponents *out of the war.*/*Ruby Ayres knows well how to spin out & yet keep* the story *thoroughly alive.*/*A season in Opposition will invigorate & restore* them *to health* (read *invigorate them & . . .*)./*There is no means of defence against submarines, & no means of fighting, attacking, or driving* them *from certain waters* (read *of fighting or attacking them, or of . . .*)./*The wish to hear a sermon which will soothe or ' buck* you *up '*, *according to the needs of the moment* (read *soothe you or . . .*).

The great majority of such mistakes are of that form ; one or two are added in which the principle infringed is the same, but some slight variation of detail occurs :— *We were not a little proud of the manner in which we transported* to *& maintained* our Army *in South Africa*. This is the old type, complicated by the well-meant but disastrous *to* ; read *in which we*

*transported our army to S.A. &
maintained it there.*

*I trust you will kindly grant me
a little space to express, in my own
& in the name of those elements in
Russia whom I have the honour to
represent, our indignation at . . .*
The walled-up noun here (*name*) is
governed not by a verb, but by
a preposition ; read *in my own name
& in that of the elements.* . . .

*The fourteen chapters explore the
belief in immortality in primitive &
in the various* civilizations *of antiquity taken in order.* Like the
preceding ; read *in primitive civilizations & in those of antiquity.*

wall-eye should be so written, not
as separate words ; its proper meaning is the state of being wall-eyed,
i.e. of having both eyes, or one,
abnormally light-coloured, whether
because the iris is very pale, or
because the whites are dispropor-
tionately large, or because a squint
exposes one white excessively. *Wall-
eye* is formed from *wall-eyed*, not
vice versa.

wall-less. Write so ; see SKILL-LESS.
wallop makes *-oped, -oping, -oper* ;
see -P-, -PP-.
walnut. So spelt ; unconnected
with *wall*.
waltz, valse. The first is the form
that has established itself as the
ordinary English, the other being
confined to programmes & the like.

wampum. Pronounce wŏ-.
want. *No man can say what is
wanted to be done in regard to the
military affairs of a nation till . . .*
For this ugly construction, see
DOUBLE PASSIVE.

wanton makes *-oned, -oning, -onest*
(adj.), see -N-, -NN- ; but *wantonness*.
wapiti. Pronounce wŏ'pĭtĭ.
wap(ping). *Whop(ping)* is now the
established spelling.
war. 1. *Wars & rumours of wars*
is the correct quotation (*Matt.*
xxiv. 6) ; see MISQUOTATION. 2.
*Secretary of War, Secretary at War,
Secretary for War.* The first two are

obsolete titles that belonged to
officials whose duties have been
rearranged ; *Secretary for War* (or
War Secretary) is the current abbreviation of the present Minister's
title—*The Secretary of State for War.*

WARDOUR STREET. ' The name
of a street in London mainly occupied by dealers in antique & imitation-antique furniture '—OED. As
Wardour Street itself offers to those
who live in modern houses the
opportunity of picking up an
antique or two that will be conspicuous for good or ill among their
surroundings, so this article offers
to those who write modern English
a selection of oddments calculated
to establish (in the eyes of some
readers) their claim to be persons
of taste & writers of beautiful
English. And even as it is said of
some dealers in the rare & exquisite
that they have a secret joy when
their treasures find no purchaser &
are left on their hands, so the present
collector, though he has himself no
practical use for his articles of *virtu*,
yet shows them without commendation for fear they should be carried
off & unworthily housed.

albeit* ; ANENT* ; AUGHT* ; *belike* ;
ERE ; ERST(WHILE) ; ETHIC dative
with *me* & *you* ; FOREBEARS, n. ;
haply ; HOWBEIT ; inverted protasis
with *had**, *should*, & *were* ; *maugre* ;
more by TOKEN ; *oft* ; PERCHANCE ;
p.p. in *-en*, as *knitten, litten*, PROVEN ;
rede ; SANS ; SAVE, prep. or conj. ;
SHALL (6) as in *You shall find* ; SUB-
JUNCTIVE as in *If it be* ; *there*-
compounds such as THEREFOR, *thereof, thereto* ; THITHER ; *to wit** ;
trow ; VARLET ; WELL-NIGH ; *where*-
compounds such as *wherein, whereof* ;
whit* ; *withal* ; *wot*.

**A book that in the main is bright,
chatty, & readable, albeit rather too
kindly in its lavish distribution of
praise./So much has been written
about the selfishness & stupidity of
women* anent *the servant clause of the
Insurance Bill that . . ./I have never
written* aught *conflicting with that*

theory of State function./Had *the eighteenth century bishops more vision there would have been no Wesleyan schism.*/*Like many other eminent scientific men—Huxley,* to wit—*Sir Ray Lankester has a cultivated taste.*/ *The platform, the golf club, the bridge table, in no* whit *less than the factory & the workshop, must relax their claims.*

The words in small capitals are further commented upon in their dictionary places.

wardress. FEMININE DESIGNATIONS.

-WARD(S). Words ending with *-ward(s)* may most of them be used as adverbs, adjectives, or nouns. The -s is usually present in the adverb, & absent in the adjective ; the noun, which is rather an absolute use of the adjective, tends to follow it in being without -s ; *moving eastwards ; the eastward position ; looking to the eastward(s).* This usage prevails especially with the words made of a noun+*-ward(s)*, but is also generally true of the older words in which the first part is adverbial, such as *downward.* Some words, however, have peculiarities ; see AFTERWARDS, FORWARD, ONWARD, TOWARDS.

ware, in the warning cry *w. wire !* &c., is usually pronounced wor.

warehouse. For the verb the pronunciation -z is recommended ; see NOUN & VERB 2.

warp, n. See WOOF.

warrant, vb, makes *-tor* ; see -OR.

wash. The rivals *wash-hand-stand, washing-stand,* & *wash-stand,* are all in themselves justifiable, but it would be well to be rid of two of them. The first is obviously cumbrous, & there is no reason for preferring the longer second to the shorter third, especially with (*Moab is my*) *wash-pot, wash-house,* & *washtub,* waiting to welcome *wash-stand,* which is recommended.

washing. For *take in one another's w.,* see WORN-OUT HUMOUR.

wassail. The pronunciation pre-

ferred by OED is wŏ′sl. *W.* makes *-ailing* ; see -LL-, -L-.

wast)(wert. See BE 7.

wastage. It is possible that sentences may be constructed in which this word is for some reason better than *waste* ; what is certain is that in nearly all the places in which it nowadays appears it is not better ; see LONG VARIANTS.

waste. 1. *W.* makes *-table* ; see MUTE E. 2. *Waste paper.* No hyphen ; see HYPHENS 3 B.

wastrel. The sense spendthrift (adj. & n.), now the most frequent one, is a recent development, the older senses being a piece of waste land, & a flawed or spoilt piece of workmanship ; but there is no need to object to the new sense.

watchword. For synonymy see SIGN.

watershed. The original meaning of the word, whether or not it is an anglicization of German *Wasserscheide* (lit. waterparting), was the line of high land dividing the waters that flow in one direction from those that flow in the other. The older of us were taught that that was its meaning, & that the senses riverbasin & area of collection & drainage-slope were mere ignorant guesses due to confusion with the familiar word *shed.* Such classics as Lyell & Darwin & Geikie are all quoted for the correct sense ; & that being so it is lamentable that the mistaken senses should have found acceptance with those who could appreciate the risks of ambiguity; yet Huxley proposed that *water-parting* should be introduced to do *watershed's* work, & *watershed* be allowed to mean what the ignorant thought it meant. The inevitable result is that now one has no idea, unless context happens to suffice without aid from the word itself, which meaning it has in any particular place. The old sense should be restored & rigidly maintained. OED quotations from Lyell & Geikie follow to make the old use clear, & an extract from a newspaper shows the modern misuse :—(Lyell) *The crests or water-sheds of the Alps & Jura are about eighty miles apart./ (Geikie)The watershed of a country or continent is thus a line which divides the flow of the brooks & rivers on two opposite slopes./ (Newspaper)The Seine, be-tween its source in the Côte d'Or & the capital, has many tributaries, & when there is bad weather in the watershed of each of these an excessive flow is bound to be the result.*

waterspout. See WIND, n.

wave makes *-vable, -vy*; see MUTE E.

wax. *Wax doll,* & *wax candle* ; no hyphen ; HYPHENS 3 B.

waxen. See -EN ADJECTIVES.

way. 1. For ' at the parting of the ways ' see PARTING. 2. *Under way* (not *weigh*) is the right phrase for in motion. 3. *See* one's *way to. We hope that the Government will see their way of giving effect to this suggestion.* What has happened ? The writer doubtless knows the idiomatic phrase as well as the rest of us, but finding himself saying ' will see their way *to* give effect *to* ' has shied at the two *tos* ; but he should have abandoned instead of mutilating his phrase ; see OUT OF THE FRYING-PAN, & CAST-IRON IDIOM.

waylay. For inflexions see VERBS IN -IE &c., 1.

-ways. See -WISE.

wazir. See VIZIER.

we. 1. Case. 2. National, editorial, generic, & personal uses.

1. Case. Use of *us* for *we* has been illustrated under US 1 ; the con-verse is seen in :—*The Turk in his harem, this man who was entitled to have four wives if he liked for chattels —which to we Western people, with our ideas about women, is almost unintelligible./Whether the Commit-tee's suggestions are dictated by Patriotism, Political expediency, or . . ., is not for we outside mortals to decide.*

2. National &c. uses : *We* may mean I & another or others, or the average man, or this newspaper, or

this nation, or several other things. The newspaper editor occasionally forgets that he must not mix up his editorial with his national *we*. *But still, we are distrusted by Germany, & we are loth, by explaining how our acts ought to be interpreted, to put her in a more invidious position.* The first *we* is certainly England, the second is probably the newspaper. See I 2, & OUR 2, for similar con-fusions of different senses that are legitimate apart, but not together.

weak. For *w. ending,* see TECH-NICAL TERMS. For *weaker sex,* see SOBRIQUETS.

weal. For the word meaning stripe, see WALE.

wear. For the word meaning dam, see WEIR.

weariless. See -LESS.

weasand. Pronounce wē′znd.

weather gage. So spelt (OED) in the nautical phrase *have the w. g. of,* though *gage* is the same word as that spelt *gauge* ; no hyphen, see HY-PHENS 3 B.

weave. Ordinary p.p. *woven* ; see also WOVE.

weazen. See WIZENED.

web. See WOOF.

wed is a poetic or rhetorical synonym for *marry* ; & the estab-lished past & p.p. is *wedded* ; but it is noticeable that the need of brevity in newspaper headings is bringing into trivial use both the verb instead of *marry* (DUKE WEDS ACTRESS), & the short instead of the long p.p. (SUICIDE OF WED PAIR) ; see INCONGRUOUS VOCABULARY ; here is a chance for sub-editors to do the language a service, if they will. For the effect of headlines, cf. WORKLESS.

wedge makes *wedgeable* ; MUTE E.

Wedgwood. So spelt.

Wednesday. For the adverbial use (*Can you come W. ?*), see FRIDAY.

weekly, adv. See -LILY 2.

ween. A WARDOUR-STREET word.

weevil makes *-lled, -lly* ; see -LL-, -L-, 2 ; pronounce wē′vĭld, wē′vĭl.

weft. See WOOF.

weigh. For *under w.*, see WAY.

weir, wear, n. The first form is recommended as obviating doubts both of identity & of pronunciation.

weird. A word ruined by becoming a VOGUE-WORD.

Welch. See WELSH.

well, adv. It is time for someone to come to the rescue of the phrase *as well as*, which is being cruelly treated. Grammatically, the point is that *as well as* is a conjunction & not a preposition; or, to put it in a less abstract way, its strict meaning is not *besides*, but *& not only*; or, to proceed by illustration, English requires not *You were there as well as me* (as it would if the phrase were a preposition & meant *besides*), but *You were there as well as I* (since the phrase is a conjunction & means *& not only*). The abuses occur, however, not in simple sentences like this with a common noun or pronoun following *as well as*; indeed, it is usually not possible in these to tell whether the construction intended is right or wrong; in *They killed women as well as men*, *men* may be rightly meant to be governed by *killed*, or wrongly meant to be governed by *as well as* = besides; only the writer, & very likely not he, can say. They occur in places where the part of a verb chosen reveals the grammar :—*The Territorial officer still has to put his hand in his pocket as well as giving his time.* Read *give* ; it depends on *has to* ; or else substitute *besides./ A German control of the Baltic must vitally affect the lives of all the Scandinavian Powers as well as influencing the interests of a maritime country like England.* Read *influence* ; it depends on *must* ; or else substitute *besides./His death leaves a gap as well as creating a by-election in Ross & Cromarty.* Read *creates* ; it is parallel to *leaves* ; or else substitute *besides./As well as closing the railway, it should make the Danube impracticable for traffic between Turkey & the Central Powers.* Read *besides* ; *as well as* should

never precede ; or else read *as well as close* & put this after *Powers./ What should be made into cheap meals is now being used by dog-biscuit & other animal food makers as a basis of their wares,* as well as converting it *into manure.* Read *converted* for *converting it,* continuing the construction of *being.* A more obviously illiterate sentence than the rest.

The process of first noticing that *as well as* means nearly the same as *besides,* & then giving it a wrong construction that would be right for *besides,* is illustrated in ANALOGY.

well & well-. In combinations of a participle & *well* there is often a doubt whether the two parts should be hyphened or left separate. The danger of wrong hyphens is greater than that of wrong separation ; e. g., to write *His courage is well-known* (where *well known* is the only tolerable form) is much worse than to write *His well known courage* (where *well-known* represents the accent more truly). Some help will be found under HYPHENS (E, & group **put-up*) ; & it may be here repeated that if a participle with *well* is attributive (*a well-aimed stroke*) the hyphen is desirable but not obligatory, but if the participle is predicative (*the stroke was well aimed*) the hyphen is wrong. Similarly in such phrases as *well off* : *They are not well off,* but *Well-off people cannot judge.*

well-nigh. See WARDOUR STREET. *Archaeology had strengthened its hold on art, &* went well-nigh *to strangling it.* The natural English would have been *& came near strangling it,* or *& nearly strangled it.* But if the writer was bent on displaying his antique, he should at least have said *& well-nigh strangled it* ; the use of *well-nigh* is purely adverbial ; i.e., it needs a following verb or adjective or noun to attach itself to ; *well nigh worn to pieces, & well nigh dead,* says Shakspere, & *well nigh half the angelic name,* says Milton. To say *come well-nigh to* is to put the antique in an incongruous frame. As the OED has not reached *well* when this is written, the idiomatic restriction may be proved false, & is to be taken only as a guess.

well-read. See INTRANSITIVE P.P.

Welsh, Welch. The established modern spelling is -sh, except in the official names of regiments, for which -ch is used. That distinction, being meaningless, is regrettable. A much more profitable one would be that -sh should be universal for the national adjective, while -ch was assigned to the verb *to welch* & to *welcher*—& that whether the verb is or is not etymologically connected (a disputed point) with *Welsh*. Which spelling is in itself preferable, apart from custom, depends merely on the prevalent pronunciation, which is -sh. The analogy of *French & Scotch & Dutch* is irrelevant because the preceding dentals account for the harder ch in them, & that of *English, Scottish, Irish, & British,* because the familiar -ish, to which *Welsh* has not surrendered, disqualifies them.

wen. For *the W.*, see SOBRIQUETS.

were. For the subjunctive uses in the singular, as *If I were you, Were he alive, It were futile,* some of which are more inconsistent than others with the writing of natural English, see SUBJUNCTIVES.

werewolf, werw-. The first is recommended ; it is the more familiar, it suggests the usual pronunciation, & it dates back to Old English.

wert. See BE 7.

westerly. See EASTERLY.

westernmost. See -MOST.

Westminster, = Parliament.   See SOBRIQUETS.

westward(s). See -WARD(S).

WH. The sounding of h in words containing wh (*what, whether, nowhere, &c.*) is a matter of locality or nationality, & comes under the general principle suggested in PRONUNCIATION.

wharf. For plural &c., see -VE(D).

wharfinger. Pronounce -jer.

what is a word of peculiar interest, because the small problems that it poses for writers are such as on the one hand yield pretty readily to analysis, & on the other hand demand a slightly more expert analysis than they are likely to get from those who think they can write well enough without stopping to learn grammar.

1. Wrong number attraction.   2. *What* singular & *what* plural. 3. One *what* in two cases. 4. *What* resumed by (*and, but*) *which.* 5. Miscellaneous.

1. Wrong number attraction. In each of the examples to be given it is beyond question that *what* starts as a singular pronoun (=that which, or a thing that), because a singular verb follows it ; but in each also the next verb, belonging to the *that* of *that which,* or to the *a thing* of *a thing that,* is not singular but plural ; this is due to the influence of a complement in the plural, & the grammatical name for such influence is *attraction* ; all the quotations are on the pattern *What is said are words,* instead of *What is said is words.* Whether attraction of verb to complement is idiomatic in English has already been discussed in NUMBER, 1 ; it is here assumed that it is not ; in all the quotations, which are multiplied to show how common the mistake is, the roman-type verb should have its number changed from plural to singular :—
What is of absorbing & permanent interest are *the strange metamorphoses which this fear underwent./What is required* are *houses at rents that the people can pay./What seems to be needed, & what, I believe, public opinion calls for,* are *stringent regulations to restrict the sale./What makes the omission still more amazing* are, *first, that the Allies . . .; secondly, that . . ./What is required* are *three bedrooms, a good large living-room . . ./What puzzles us very much* are *the constant references in the Observer's*

article to Mr Borden./What is really at issue in the present conflict are *not questions of territory, but the future of democracy./What is wanted to meet it* are *proposals which are practical./ What is wanted now* are *men who are Liberals today./What strikes the tourist most* are *the elegant Paris toilettes./What is needed* are *a few recognized British financial corporations./What is of more importance in the official statement of profits* are *the following figures.*

2. *What* singular & *what* plural. In each of the above quotations, the writer made it plain, by giving *what* a singular verb, that he conceived *what* there as a singular pronoun. But the word itself can equally well be plural : *I have few books, & what there* are do *not help me.* So arises another problem concerning the number of verbs after *what,* & this second one naturally gets mixed up with the first. It will here, however, be kept to itself, & the position will be that attraction has already been disposed of, & that the number of the verb has nothing whatever to do with the number of the complement, being merely the outward sign that *what* is singular or is plural. First comes a particular form of sentence in which plural *what* is better than singular, or in other words in which its verb should be plural. These are sentences in which *what,* if resolved, comes out as *the* ——*s that,* ——*s* standing for a plural noun actually present in the complement. After each quotation a correction is first given if it is desirable, & in any case the resolution that justifies the plural :—*We have been invited to abandon what* seems *to us to be the most valuable parts of our Constitution* (read *seem ;* abandon the parts of our Constitution that seem)./*The Manchester City Council, for what* was *doubtless good & sufficient reasons, decided not to take any part* (read *were ;* for reasons that were)./*Exception was taken to what* was *referred to as the* ' *secret & dictatorial methods* ' *of M.*

Poincaré in the Ruhr (read *were ;* to the methods that were)./*It is a diatribe against M. Loucheur & M. Clementel, but the personal aspect is of little importance to English readers ;* what are *important* are *the criticisms of the operation of protective duties in France* (The criticisms that ; but *What is important is* would have been better, *what is* standing for *the thing that is,* in contrast with aspect)./*They specially approved what to Liberals* was *the most reactionary & disastrous parts of it* (read *were ;* approved the parts of it that to Liberals were)./*Confidence being inspired by the production of what* appears *to be bars or bricks of solid gold* (read *appear ;* production of bars or bricks that appear)./*Mr Wheatley urged a curtailment of what* is *called luxury buildings* (read *are ;* of buildings that are called ; but probably the plural *buildings* is a misprint).

But resolution of *what* often presents us not with a noun found in the complement, but with some other noun of wider meaning, or again with the still vaguer *that which.* A writer should make the resolution & act on it without allowing the number of the complement to force a plural verb on him if the most natural representative of *what* is *that which* or *the thing that ;* in several of the following quotations the necessary courage has been lacking ; corrections & resolutions are given as before :—*I can well believe that Mr B. Russell's whip is heavy ; however, what I wish to point out* are *certain instances wherein philosophy has made serious error* (read *is ;* the thing that)./*No other speaker has his peculiar power of bringing imagination to play on what* seems, *until he speaks, to be familiar platitudes* (read *seem ;* on sayings that seem)./*Instead of the stupid agitation now going on in South Wales, what* are *needed* are *regular working & higher outputs* (read *what is needed is ;* the thing that is needed—rather than things, as opp.

agitation)./*What* are *wanted* are *not small cottages, but the larger houses with modern conveniences that are now demanded by the working classes* (read *what is wanted is* ; the thing that is wanted—rather than the buildings that are)./*What* provoke *men's curiosity* are *mysteries, mysteries of motive or stratagem ; astute or daring plots* (read *provokes . . . is* ; that which provokes—rather than the things that provoke)./*In order to reduce this material to utility & assimilate it, what* are *required* are *faith & confidence, & willingness to work* (read *what is required is* ; but the qualities that are required justifies the plurals, though it does not make them idiomatic).

It will be observed that there is more room for difference of opinion on this set of examples than on either those in 1 or the previous set in 2, & probably many readers will refuse to accept the decisions given ; but if it is realized that there are problems of number after *what*, & that solutions of them are possible, that is sufficient.

3. One *what* in two cases. For the general question whether in a language that like English has shed nearly all its case-forms the grammatical notion of case still deserves respect, see CASES ; it is here assumed that it does, to the extent that no word, even if it has not different forms such as *I & me* for the subjective & objective uses, ought to be so placed that it has, without being repeated, to be taken twice over first in one & then in the other case. The word *what* is peculiarly liable to such treatment. There are two chief ways of sparing grammatically-minded readers this outrage on their susceptibilities ; sometimes a second *what* should be inserted ; sometimes it is better to convert a verb to the other voice, so that *what* becomes either object, or subject, to both. Corrections are given in brackets ; to correct Pater, from whom the last example comes, is perhaps impudence, but grammar

is no respecter of persons :—*This is pure ignorance of what the House is & its work consists of* (& what its)./ *But it is not folly to give it what it had for centuries & was only artificially taken from it by force rather more than a hundred years ago* (what belonged to it for)./*Mr —— tells us not to worry about Relativity or anything so brain-tangling, but to concentrate on what surrounds us*, & we *can weigh & measure* (& can be weighed & measured)./*Impossible to separate later legend from original evidence as to what he was*, & said, *& how he said it* (& what he said).

4. *What* resumed by (*and, but*) *which. Francis Turner Palgrave, whose name is inseparably connected with what is probably the best*, & *which certainly has proved the most popular, of English anthologies* (what is probably the best, & has certainly proved)./*It is an instructive conspectus of views on what can hardly be described as a ' burning question '*, *but which certainly interests many Irishmen* (but certainly interests)./ *Mr Gladstone received a peculiarly warm welcome when he appeared clothed in what has been described as a Yeomanry uniform, but which was really the peaceful but picturesque scarlet & silver of a Lord Lieutenant* (but was really)./*We are merely remembering what happened to our arboreal ancestors*, & which *has been stamped by cerebral changes into the heredity of the race* (& has been stamped). A want of faith either in the lasting power of *what* (which has a good second wind & can do the two laps without turning a hair), or in the reader's possession of common sense, has led to this thrusting in of *which* as a sort of relay to take up the running. These sentences are not English ; nothing can represent *what*—except indeed *what*. That is, it would be English, though hardly idiomatic English, to insert a second *what* in the place of the impossible *which* in each. If the reader will try the effect, he will find that the second *what*, though permissible, sometimes makes ambiguous what without it is plain ; in the last example, for instance, ' what happened ' & ' what has been stamped ' might be different things, whereas ' what happened, & has been stamped ' is clearly one & the same thing. The reason why *which* has been called ' impossible ' is that *what* & *which* are of different grammatical values, *which* being a simple relative pronoun, while *what* (= that which, or a thing that) is a combination of antecedent & relative ; but the second verb needs the antecedent-relative just as much as the first, if *but* or *and* is inserted ; if neither *but* nor *and* is present, *which* will sometimes be possible, & so omission of *but* & *and* would be another cure for the last two examples.

Two specimens are added in which the remedy of simply omitting *which* or substituting for it a repeated *what* is not possible without further change. The difficulty is due to, & vanishes with, the superstition against PREPOSITION AT END. *I can never be certain that I am receiving what I want & for which I am paying.* Read *what I want & am paying for./ But now we have a Privy Councillor & an ex-Minister engaged daily in saying & doing what he frankly admits is illegal,* & for which *he could be severely punished.* Read *& what he could be severely punished for.* The repetition of *what* is required because the relative contained in the first *what* is subjective, & that in the second objective ; see 3.

5. Miscellaneous. The beautiful conciseness belonging to *what* as antecedent-relative seems to lure the unwary into experiments in further concision. They must remember that both parts of it, the antecedent (*that* or *those*) & the relative (*which*), demand their share of attention :— *What I am concerned in the present article is to show that not only theory but practice support the unrestricted exercise of the prerogative.* Read *concerned to do,* or the *which* in

what is without government./*What my friend paid less than a pound a day for last year he had to pay two guineas a day at a minor Brighton establishment last Easter.* Read *two guineas a day for,* or the *that* in *what* is without government./*Entering the church with feelings different from what he had ever entered a church before, he could with difficulty restrain his emotions.* Read *entered a church with,* or the *which* of *what* is without government.

The following shows a different *what. When one reflects what great importance it is to the success of the League of Nations that America should become a member of it.* Read *of what,* & see VALUE.

what ever, whatever. The various uses are complicated, & cannot be all set out, for readers who are not specialists in grammar, without elaborate explanations that would demand too much space. This article will avoid all technicalities except what are needed in dealing with two or three common mistakes.

1. The interrogative use. 2. The antecedent-relative use. 3. The concessive use.

1. The interrogative use. *What ever can it mean ? What ever shall we do ?* For the status of this, see EVER. It should never appear in print except when familiar dialogue is being reproduced, & should then be in two separate words, differing in this from all other uses. Three examples follow in which both these rules are disregarded ; in the second of them we have an indirect instead of a direct question, but the same rules hold :—*Which is pretty, but whatever can it mean ?/Whatever you mean by ' patriotic ' education I do not know, but Lord Roberts's use of the term is plain enough./And, considering that 180,000 actually arrived in the country, whatever was the cost ?*

2. The antecedent-relative use. *Whatever* in this use is an emphatic form of *what* as antecedent-relative (see WHAT 4, 5) ; i.e., while *what* means *that which* or *the* (*thing, things*) *that*, *whatever* means *all that* or *any*(*thing* &c.) *that*. The point ignored in the quotations below is that *whatever* contains in itself the relative (*that* or *which*) as well as the demonstrative or antecedent (*all, any,* &c), & that another relative cannot grammatically be inserted after it ; *whatever* (or *whatsoever*) means not *any*, but *any that*, & *whatever that* is as absurd as *any that that*. In the first two, omit the roman-type *that* ; in the third, which has gone wrong, as often happens, owing to the PREPOSITION-AT-END superstition, get rid of *which* by rewriting *in whatever component, big or small, their attention is concentrated upon* :—*His cynical advice shows that whatever concession to Democracy* that *may seem to be involved in his words, may not be of permanent inconvenience.*/*Keep close in touch with Him in whatsoever creed or form* that *brings you nearest to Him.*/*They see in the shell, the gun* —*in whatever component, big or small,* upon which *their attention is concentrated*—*the essence of all that matters.*

3. The concessive use. *Whatever one does, you are not satisfied* ; *I am safe now, whatever happens* ; *Whatever you do, don't lie.* These are concessive clauses, short for Though one does A or B or C, Though this or that or the other happens, Though you do anything else. They differ from the *whatever* clauses dealt with above in being adverbial, *whatever* meaning not *all* or *any that* (*that* beginning an adjectival clause), but *though all* or *any*. The difference is not a matter of hair-splitting ; *Whatever he has done he repents* may mean (*a*) He is one of the irresolute people who always wish they had done something different, or (*b*) Though he may be a great offender, repentance should count for something ; *whatever* antecedent-relative gives *a*, & *whatever* concessive gives *b*. In practice it should be noticed that proper punctuation distin-

guishes the two, the *a* meaning not having the two clauses parted by a comma, since *whatever* belongs to & is part of both, & the *b* meaning having them so parted, since *whatever* belongs wholly to one clause. In the following sentence, the reader is led by the wrong comma after *have* to mistake the *whatever* clause for a concessive & adverbial one : *Sir Edward Grey has no reason to be displeased with this sequel to his effort, and, whatever responsibility he may have, he will no doubt accept gladly.* The words concerned should run : and whatever responsibility he may have he will no doubt accept gladly.

wheal. See WALE.
wheaten. See -EN ADJECTIVES.
whence, whither. The value of these subordinates of *where* for lucidity & conciseness seems so obvious that no-one who appreciates those qualities can see such help being discarded without a pang of regret. Why is it that substitutes apparently so clumsy as *where . . . from*, & *where . . . to*, can be preferred ? It is surely because the genius of the language actually likes the PREPOSITION AT END that wiseacres have conspired to discourage, & thinks ' Where are you coming to ? ' more quickly comprehensible in moments of threatened collision than ' Whither are you coming ? '. We who incline to weep over *whence* & *whither* must console ourselves by reflecting that in the less literal or secondary senses the words are still with us for a time ; ' Whither are we tending ? ', & ' Whence comes it that . . . ? ', are as yet safe against *where . . . to* & *where . . . from* ; & the poets may be trusted to provide our old friends with a dignified retirement in which they may even exercise all their ancient rights. But we shall do well to shun all attempts at restoration, & in particular to eschew the notion (see FORMAL WORDS) that the writer's duty is to translate the *where . . .*

from or *where* . . . *to* of speeeh into *whence* & *whither* in print. On the other hand, let us not be ultra-modernists & assume that *whence* & *whither*, even in their primary senses, are dead & buried ; that must be the view of the journalist who writes : *The Irregulars have been compelled to withdraw their line from Clonmel, to* where *it is believed they transferred their headquarters when they had to flee from Limerick.* If *whither* was too antiquated, the alternative was ' to which place ', but occasions arise now & then, as in this sentence, to which *whence* & *whither* are, even for the practical purposes of plain speech, more appropriate than any equivalent.

whenever, the right form for the ordinary conjunction, should not be used instead of the colloquial *when ever* (*When ever will you be ready ?*), for which see EVER.

WHERE- COMPOUNDS. A small number of these are still in free general use, though chiefly in limited applications, with little or no taint of archaism ; these are *whereabouts* (as purely local adv. & n.), *whereas* (in contrasts), *wherever*, *wherefore* (as noun plural in *whys & wherefores*), *whereupon* (in narratives), & *wherewithal* (as noun). The many others—*whereabout, whereat, whereby, wherefore* (adv. & conj.), *wherefrom, wherein, whereof, whereon, wherethrough, whereto, wherewith,* & a few more—have given way in both the interrogative & the relative uses either to the preposition with *what* & *which* & *that* (*whereof*= of what ?, what . . . of ?, of which, that . . . of), or to some synonym (*wherefore*= why) ; resort to them generally suggests that the writer has a tendency either to FORMAL WORDS or to PEDANTIC HUMOUR.

wherever, *where ever.* As WHEN-EVER.

wherewithal. The noun, as was mentioned in WHERE- COMPOUNDS, has survived in common use (*but I haven't got the w.*), no doubt be-cause the quaintness of it has struck the popular fancy. But the noun should remember that it is after all only a courtesy noun, not a noun in its own right ; it means just ' with which ', but seems to have forgotten this in : *They* [France's purchases] *have been merely the* wherewithal *with which to start business again.*

whether. 1. For *w.* & *that* after *doubt(ful)*, see DOUBT(FUL). 2. *W.* or *no*(*t*). *Whether he was there or was not there* easily yields by ellipsis *Whether he was there or not,* & that by transposition *Whether or not he was there. Whether or no he was there* is not so easily accounted for, since *no* is not ordinarily, like *not,* an adverb (see NO) ; & in fact the origin of the idiom is uncertain ; but the fact remains that *whether or not* is (OED) ' less frequent ' than *whether or no*—especially, perhaps, when the *or* follows *whether* imme-diately : *Whether or no he did it* ; *whether he did it or not.* Whichever form is used, such a doubling of the alternative as the following should be carefully avoided : *But clearly, whether or not peers will* or will not *have to be made depends upon the number of the Die-Hards.* Omit either *or not* or *or will not.*

which. Relative pronouns are as troublesome to the inexpert but conscientious writer as they are useful to everyone, which is saying much. About *which*, in particular, problems are many, & some of them complicated ; that the reader may not be frightened by an article of too portentous length, the two that require most space are deferred, & will be found in the separate articles WHICH)(THAT)(WHO, & WHICH WITH AND OR BUT. The points to be treated here can be disposed of with more certainty & at less length, under the headings :—

1. Relative instead of demonstra-tive. 2. One relative in two cases. 3. One relative for main & sub-ordinate verbs. 4. Break-away from relative. 5. Confused construction.

6. Late position. 7. *One of the best which has.* 8. Commas. 9. *In which to.*

1. Relative instead of demonstrative. The type is : *He lost his temper, which proving fatal to him.* The essence of a relative is to do two things at once, to play the part of a noun in a sentence & to convert that sentence into, & attach it to another as, a subordinate clause. *He lost his temper ; this proved fatal ;* these can be made into one sentence (a) by changing the demonstrative *this* into the relative *which*, or (b) by changing the verb *proved* to the participle *proving ;* one or the other, not both as in the false type above. Actual examples of the blunder, with corrections in brackets, are :— *It was rumoured that Beaconsfield intended opening the Conference with a speech in French, his pronunciation* of which language leaving *everything to be desired* (read *of that language ;* or else *left* for *leaving*)./*Surely what applies to games should also apply to racing, the leaders* of which being *the very people from whom an example might well be looked for* (read *of this* or *of the latter ;* or else *are* for *being*)./*Persons who would prefer to live in a land flowing with milk & honey if such could be obtained without undue exertion,* but, failing which, *are content to live in squalor, filth, & misery* (read *failing that ;* or else *failing which they* for *but failing which*)./*The World Scout principle— namely, of bringing into an Order of the young the boys of different races,* by which means not only educating *the children in scouting, but* . . . (read *by this means ;* or else *we should not only educate* for *not only educating*).

2. One relative in two cases. See WHAT 3 for this question ; in all the following extracts, a single *which* is once objective & once subjective. The cure is either to insert a second *which* in the second clause, or to convert one of the two verbs into the same voice as the other, e. g. in the first example ' & others to study ' :—*Mr Roche is practising a* *definite system, which he is able to describe, & could be studied by others.*/*He went up to a pew in the gallery, which brought him under a coloured window which he loved & always quieted his spirit.*/*It gave a cachet of extreme clericalism to the Irish Party which it does not deserve, but must prejudice it not a little in the eyes of English Radicalism.*/*The queer piece, which a few find dull, but to most is irresistible in its appeal.*/*Shakespearian words & phrases which the author has heard, & believes can be heard still, along this part of the Avon valley.*

3. One relative for main & subordinate verbs (or verb & preposition). The following sentence is provided with three endings, A, B, C, with each of which it should be read successively : *This standard figure is called Bogey, which if you have beaten* (A) *you are a good player,* (B) *you are apt to mention,* (C) *is sometimes mentioned.* In A the grammar is unexceptionable, *which* being the object of *have beaten,* & having no second job as a pronoun (though as relative it attaches to *Bogey* the clause that is also attached by *if* to *you are* &c.). In modern use, however, this arrangement is rare, being usually changed to ' if you have beaten which '. In B we come to questionable grammar, *which* being object first to *have beaten* & then to *mention ;* English that is both easy & educated usually avoids this by making *which* object only to *mention,* & providing *have beaten* with another—*which, if you have beaten it, you are apt to mention.* Meeting the B form, we incline to ask whether the writer has used it because he knows no better, or because he knows better than we do & likes to show it. Grammatically, it must be regarded as an ellipsis, & to that extent irregular, but many ellipses are idiomatic ; this particular kind is perhaps less called for as idiomatic than noticeable as irregular. About C there are no such doubts ; it is indefensible, the *which* having not only to serve twice (with *have beaten*, & with *is mentioned*), but to change its case in transit ; see 2.

Illustrations follow of B & C ; A, being both legitimate & unusual, & having been introduced only for purposes of comparison, need not be quoted for.

B, doubtfully advisable

With a fire in her hold which he managed to keep in control, although unable to extinguish (add *it* ?)./*Mr Masterman was a little troubled by the spirit of his past, which, if he had not evoked, no one would have remembered* (*evoked it* ?)./*And it was doubtless from Weldon that he borrowed the phrase which his use of has made so famous* (*of it* ? or *his use of which has made it* ?). This last is no more ungrammatical, though certainly more repulsive, than the others.

C, undoubtedly wrong

The programme is divided up into a series of walks, which, if the industrious sightseer can undertake, will supply him with a good everyday knowledge of Paris (undertake them)./ *In general the wife manages to establish a status which needs no legal proviso or trade union rule to protect* (protect it ; *or* which it needs ; *or* to protect which needs no . . . rule).

4. Break-away from relative. *He shows himself extremely zealous against practices in some of which he had greatly indulged, & was himself an example of their ill effects./ It imposes a problem which we either solve or perish.* Both of these are strictly ungrammatical. In the first, which is the easier to deal with, it will be noticed that in sense the third part (*& was* to the end) is clearly coupled by *and* not to the first part or main sentence (*He shows* to *practices*), but to the second part or relative clause (*in some* to *indulged*). Nevertheless, by the use of *their* it has been definitely broken away from connexion with *which*, & become grammatically, but il-

logically, a second main sentence with, for subject, the *He* that begins the first. There are two possible correct versions of the second & third parts, (a) *some of which he had greatly indulged in & himself exemplified the ill effects of*, or (b) *in some of which he had greatly indulged, & of the ill effects of (some of) which he was himself an example* ; *a* will be repudiated, perhaps more justifiably than usual, by those who condemn final prepositions ; *b* fails to give the precise sense, whether the bracketed *some of* is inserted or not ; to both these the break-away, which is not an uncommon construction, will be preferred by some.

The other example (*It imposes a problem which we either solve or perish*) is, owing to Lord Grey's ' The nations must learn or perish ', of a now very popular pattern. The break-away depends on the nature of *either . . . or* alternatives, in which whatever stands before *either* must be common to both the *either* & the *or* groups. *Either we solve this or we perish* can therefore become *We either solve this or perish*, but cannot become *This we either solve or perish*, because *this* is peculiar to the *either* group—else the full form would be *Either we solve this or we perish this*. With *this* as object the escape is easy—to put *this* after *solve*— ; with *which* as object that is not tolerable (*we either solve which or perish*), & strict grammar requires us to introduce into the *or* group something that can take *which* as object—*a problem which we either solve or perish by not solving, either solve or are destroyed by*, &c. Even those who ordinarily are prepared to treat *either* with proper respect (see EITHER 5, & UNEQUAL YOKE-FELLOWS) may perhaps allow themselves the popular form ; if not, ' A problem which if we do not solve we perish ' (see 3 A) is worth considering.

5. Confused construction. *He may be expected to make a determined bid for the dual rôle* which *is his right &*

duty as Prime Minister to occupy. In that sentence, is *which* subject to *is*, or object to *occupy* ? It is in fact, of course, the latter, *occupy* having no other object, & not being able to do without one ; but the writer has effectually put us off the track by dropping the *it* that should have parted *which* from *is.* *To occupy which is his right* becomes, when *which* is given its normal place, *which it is his right to occupy.* This mistake is very common, & will be found fully discussed under IT 1.

6. Late position. In the examples, which are arranged as a climax, the distance between *which* & its antecedent is shown by the roman type. Grammar has nothing to say on the subject, but common sense protests against abuse of this freedom. The specimens given may easily be matched or surpassed by anyone who will search the newspapers. *She is wonderful in her brilliant* sketch *of that querulous, foolish little old lady* which *she does so well./ Lord Hemphill made his maiden speech from the Front Opposition* Bench *in the House of Commons, his place on* which *he had won by filling the position of* . . ./*The whole art of clinching is explained in this little* book *from the concentrated harvest of wisdom in* which *we present some specimens to our readers./Nothing has more contributed to dispelling this illusion than the* camera, *the remarkable & convincing evidence it has been possible to obtain with* which *has enormously added to the knowledge of the habits of animals.*

7. *One of the best which has.* In *which* case one *of the greatest & most serious strikes* which *has occurred in modern times will take place. Has* should be *have.* For this very common but inexcusably careless blunder see NUMBER, 5.

8. Commas. In the present article the distinctions between *which* & other relatives—see WHICH)(THAT) (WHO—have been left alone, & it has been assumed, as it seems to be in most matters by 99 out of 100

writers, that *which* is the relative & the relative is *which.* A consequence of this is that the defining & the non-defining kinds of relative clause alike begin with or contain *which*, & are not known apart by the difference between *that* & *which.* This being so—& it is not a mere hypothesis, but in most writers a patent fact—, it is important to have another means of distinguishing. A comma preceding *which* shows that the *which*-clause is nondefining, & the absence of such a comma shows that it is defining. *He declares that the men were treated like beasts throughout the voyage, & he gives the worst description of the general mismanagement* which *was most conspicuous.* There is no comma before *which*, & therefore the clause must be a defining one ; i. e., it limits the sense of *the general mismanagement* by excluding from it such parts as were less conspicuous ; the most conspicuous part of the mismanagement is described as very bad indeed—that is what we are told. Or is it not so, & are we to understand rather that the whole of the general mismanagement is described as very bad, & moreover that it was conspicuous ? Surely the latter is meant ; but the loss of the comma forbids us to take it so. The difference between the two senses (or the sense & the nonsense) is not here of great importance, but is at least perfectly clear, & the importance of not misinterpreting will vary infinitely elsewhere. That right interpretation should depend on a mere comma is a pity, but, until *that & which* are differentiated, so it must be, & writers must see their commas safely through the press.

9. *In &c. which to.* *England is, however, the last country in which to say so./I have no money with which to buy food.* The current English for the second is indisputably *I have no money to buy food with* ; & there can hardly be a doubt that this has been formalized into the other by

the influence of the PREPOSITION AT END superstition. No-one need hesitate about going back to nature & saying *to buy food with*. And even for the first ' the last country to say so in ' is here recommended, though the very light word *so* happens to make with the other very light word *in* an uncomfortably weak ending ; much more is ' a good land to live in ' superior to ' a good land in which to live '. A confessedly amateur guess at the genesis of these constructions may possibly throw light. The assumption underlying the *in which to* form is obviously that there is an elliptical relative clause—perhaps This is a good land in which (one is) to live. The amateur guess is that there is no relative clause in the case at all, & that the form *to live in* originated in an adverbial infinitive attached to the adjective *good*. He is a hard man to beat ; how hard ? why, to beat ; what Greek grammars call an epexegetic (or explanatory) infinitive. *It is a good land to in-habit* is precisely parallel, & *to live-in* is precisely the same as *to in-habit*. If this account should happen to be true, the unpleasant form ' in which to live ' might be dismissed as a grammarians' mistaken pedantry.

which)(that)(who. 1. General. 2. *Which* for *that*. 3. *Which* after superlative &c. 4. *Which* in *It is . . . that*. 5. *Which* as relative adverb. 6. Elegant variation. 7. *That* for *which*. 8. *Which, who*, & nouns of multitude. 9. *Who & that*.

1. General. If the evidence of a first-class writer who was no purist or pedant counts for anything, Lord Morley's opinion exhibited below should make it worth while to master the differences between *which* & the other relatives. The extracts are from an article in the *Westminster Gazette* of 3rd Oct. 1923 by Miss Hulda Friedrichs : ' In 1920 Messrs Macmillan published a new edition of Lord Morley's works . . . He was determined to make it a

carefully revised edition, & made one or two attempts at revising it himself . . . He then asked me whether I would care to help him, & explained what my part of the work would be. It sounded rather dull, for he was particularly keen on having the word *which*, wherever there was the possibility, exchanged for *that* . . . He was always ready & very willing to go with me through the notes I had jotted down while going through a book page by page, " which " hunting & looking out for other errors '.

Let it be stated broadly, before coming to particular dangers, that : (A) of *which & that, which* is appropriate to non-defining & *that* to defining clauses ; (B) of *which & who, which* belongs to things, & *who* to persons ; (C) of *who & that, who* suits particular persons, & *that* generic persons. (A) *The river, which here is tidal, is dangerous*, but *The river that flows through London is the Thames*. (B) *The crews, which consisted of Lascars, mutinied*, but *Six Welshmen, who formed the crew, were drowned*. (C) *You who are a walking dictionary*, but *He is a man that is never at a loss*. To substitute for the relative used in any of those six examples either of the others would be, if the principles maintained in this book are correct, a change for the worse ; &, roughly speaking, the erroneous uses (if they are so) illustrated below are traceable to neglect or rejection of A, B, & C.

2. *Which* for *that*. The importance & convenience of using *that* as the regular token of the defining clause has been fully illustrated under THAT REL. PRON., & no more need be done here on that general point than to give an example or two of *which*s that are misleading where *that*s would have been plain :—*Mr E. Robertson, who spoke for the Government, admitted that ships with nucleus crews were not so efficient as ships fully manned, but the Admiralty were satisfied with them. They were* *certainly a great improvement on the old plan of having ships in reserve without crews* . . . *But Mr Robertson does not mention the case of the* nucleus-crew ships, which *are a substitute, not for unmanned ships, but for fully manned ships.* It is startling to read that Mr R. does not mention nucleus-crew ships when we have just been told that he did ; we recover after a bewildered moment, but we should have been spared that moment if ' the nucleus-crew ships that ' had been written instead of ' the nucleus-crew ships, which './*Serious works on Russia from Polish sources, which are not intended as merely propagandist pamphlets, are a valuable contribution towards a better understanding of that country.* If the clause is non-defining, as ' , which ' suggests, none of these serious works are propagandist, & all are valuable. The real meaning is that some of them are free of propaganda, & are therefore valuable ; but this real meaning requires ' that ' instead of ', which './*The second statement which, taken as it stands in Mr Wedgwood's letter, is misleading is that which implies that* . . . Impossible to tell, since there are no commas after *statement* & *misleading*, whether the clause is defining (= the second misleading statement) or non-defining (= the second statement made—a misleading one) ; probably it is defining, & should have *that* instead of *which*.

Much more often there is no danger of misinterpretation, but *that* is desirable because its regular association with defining clauses helps to establish a workmanlike distribution of the relatives to the work that has to be done. Examples need not be multiplied ; *that* should be preferred to *which* in all such places as : *If the amending Bill is to serve the purpose which responsible men in all parties profess to desire.* Special circumstances that make *which* undesirable are set out in Nos 3–5.

3. *Which* after superlative &c. When the antecedent of a defining

clause includes a word of exclusive meaning, such as a superlative, an ordinal numeral, or ' the few ', the use of *which* instead of *that* (or *who* as second best) is bad enough to be almost a solecism even in the present undiscriminating practice. The question between *that* & *who* in such places will be touched upon in 9 ; but at least *which* should be expelled from the extracts ; by rule B *who* is better than *which*, & by rule C *that* is better than *who* :—*All three will always be ranked among the foremost physical theorists & experimenters which Great Britain has produced./ Lord Spencer came to be regarded as one of the best Viceroys which the country had ever had./Had the two men of greatest genius in the respective spheres, which the British Navy has ever produced, had their way* . . ./*He was a true musical poet—perhaps, with one exception, the most gifted which England has ever produced./ The Bishop of Salisbury, is the third bishop which his family has given to the world./One of the few composers of the first rank which England has produced.*

Besides the particular type here described there are others in which for various reasons *which* is wrong, but whether *who*, or *that*, should replace it is doubtful, e. g. *persons or corporations which, against an enemy which, the many friends which* ; these will be dealt with in No 9.

4. *Which* in *It is* . . . *that* . . . The constructions exemplified in simple forms by *It was the war that caused it, It was yesterday that we came*, are often difficult to analyse grammatically or account for ; the difficulty need not concern us here ; one thing can be confidently said about them, which is that they require *that* & not *which*—*that* the defining relative (*It was Jones that did it*, the clause defining *It* ; often tacit, as *It was Jones did it*), or *that* the conjunction (*It is with grief that I learn* . . .). In the three examples, *that* should replace *to which*, *in which*, & *which* :—*It is to the State,*

& to the State alone, to which *we must turn to acquire the transfer of freeholds compulsorily, expeditiously, & cheaply./It is in the relation between motive, action, & result in a given chain of historical causation,* in which *history consists./So once again East is West, & it is shown that it is not only the Japanese* which *have the imitative instinct strongly developed.*

5. *Which* as relative adverb. The curious & idiomatic use of *that* in this construction is explained in THAT REL. PRON. 3, where it is added that *which* is unsuitable for similar treatment. The clauses are defining, attached to such words, expressed or implied, as *way, extent, time, place. That* should be substituted in each example for *which.* It will be noticed that in the last of all *in which* has been used, which is in itself not irregular ; but see the comment there :—*In England the furthest north* which *I have heard the nightingale was near Doncaster./ Parliament will be dissolved not later than Monday week—the earliest moment, that is to say,* which *it has ever been seriously considered possible for the dissolution to take place./The curtain went up & down & up & down in a way* which *only the curtain at the New Theatre when Miss Julia Neilson is at home to worshippers can do./So long as the Unionist Party is conducted on the lines* which *Mr Locker-Lampson desires it to be./Before we can find a Government or a Parliamentary majority expressing itself in the way* which *Americans express themselves./ He made a good ' legend ' during his lifetime in a way* which *very few actors have done./Before railway working was ' sped up ' to the extent* which *it is at present, continuous work of this character was no great strain./The opportunity has been denied me of showing in the way* which *I am convinced a contest would have enabled me to do how small the real opposition is./The public will not be likely to misinterpret it in the way* in which *the party-capital*

makers would desire. In this last, singularly enough, the insertion of *in* makes matters worse ; *which,* or better *that,* might have been a pronoun, object to *desire* ; but with *in which* the clause needs to be completed with ' that they should ' or some equivalent.

6. Elegant variation. I was surprised many years ago when a very well known writer gave me his notion of the relation between *which & that* : When it struck him that there was too much *which* about, he resorted to *that* for a relief. So he said ; it was doubtless only a flippant evasion, not a truthful account of his own practice, but still a tacit confession that he followed instinct without bothering about principles. Of the unskilled writer's method it would be a true enough account ; here is a specimen : *Governments find themselves almost compelled by previous & ill-informed pledges to do things* which *are unwise & to refrain from doing things* that *are necessary.* The two relative clauses are exactly parallel, & the change from *which* to *that* is ELEGANT VARIATION at its worst. When two relative clauses are not parallel, but one of them depends on the other, it is not such a simple matter ; as is stated in REPETITION (dependent sequences), there is a reasonable objection to one *which*-clause, or one *that*-clause, depending on another. Two examples will show the effect (*a*) of scorning consequences & risking repetition, & (*b*) of trying elegant variation ; neither is satisfactory :— (*a*) *Surely the reductio ad absurdum of tariffs is found in a German treaty with Switzerland* which *contains a clause* which *deserves to remain famous* ; (*b*) *The task is to evolve an effective system* that *shall not imperil the self-governing principle* which *is the corner-stone of the Empire.* The repetition is easily avoided in *a* by the change of *which contains* to *containing* ; both *which*s ought to have been *that,* which is here irrelevant. In *b* the absence of a comma shows that the *which* is meant as a defining relative & should therefore be *that* ; but, as a non-defining clause would here give a hardly distinguishable sense, the escape is to use one & keep *which*, merely inserting the necessary comma. The reader may like another example to play with : *. . . was recalled to the passer-by in Pall-Mall by Foley's fine bronze statue of the War Minister who deeply cared for the private soldier*, which *stood in front of the now destroyed War Office*, that *has very recently given place to the palatial premises of the Royal Automobile Club.*

7. *That* for *which*. After all these intrusions of *which* into the place of *that*, it must be recorded that retaliation is not quite unknown ; but it is rare. *In the island of South Uist, that I have come from, there is not one single tree./A really happy party was the Chiverton family, that had a carriage to itself & almost filled it.* The justification of *that* in these would require that there should be several South Uists from one of which I have come, & several Chiverton families of which one only had a carriage to itself ; but even those suppositions are precluded by the commas. Other examples are given in THAT REL. PRON. 2.

8. *Which, who*, & nouns of multitude. Words like *section, union, world*, sometimes mean all the persons composing a section &c. ; idiom then allows us to regard them as grammatically singular or plural as we prefer, but not to pass from one to the other ; see PERSONIFICATION &c. 2. Now a section, if we elect to treat it as singular, is a thing ; but, if we make it plural, it is persons, & by rule B *which* belongs to things, whereas *who* belongs to persons. Three examples that accordingly need correction are :—*There was a strong section* which *were in favour of inserting the miners' 5s. & 2s., as the debate proved* (*which* is required by the preceding *was*, but in turn requires a second *was* instead of *were*)./All the world *who is directly*

interested in railway projects will have paid a visit to the Brussels Exhibition (*who* is possible, but only if *are* follows ; otherwise not indeed *which* since the clause is defining, but *that* is required)./The Canon is writing in justification of the Christian Social Union*, which, *he tells us*, are *tired of the present state of things* (*which is*, or *who are*, *tired*).

9. *Who* & *that*. It would be satisfactory if the same clear division of functions that can be confidently recommended for *that* & *which*, viz between defining & non-defining clauses, could be established also for *that* & *who* ; this would give us *that* for all defining clauses whether qualifying persons or things, & *who* for persons but *which* for things in all non-defining. But at present there is much more reluctance to apply *that* to a person than to a thing. Politeness plays a great part in idiom, & to write *The ladies that were present*, or *The general that most distinguished himself*, is perhaps felt to be a sort of slight, depriving them of their humanity as one deprives a man of his gentility by writing him Mr instead of Esq. At any rate the necessarily defining *that* is displaced by the not necessarily defining *who* especially where the personal noun to be defined denotes a particular person or persons, & holds its own better when the person is a type or generic. In *It was you that did it*, the *It* defined is the doer— a type, not an individual ; & such antecedents as *all, no-one, a man*, ask for nothing better than *that*. Expressions in which we may prefer *that* without being suspected of pedantry are : *The most impartial critic that could be found ; The only man that I know of ; Anyone that knows anything knows this ; It was you that said so ; Who is it that talks about moral geography ?.* To increase by degrees the range of *that* referring to persons is a worthy object for the reformer of idiom, but violent attempts are doomed to failure. Accordingly, in the following sentences, all exhibiting a wrong *which, that* should be sparingly preferred to *who*, though it is in all of them strictly legitimate :—*The greater proportion of Consols are held by* persons or corporations which *never place them on the market* (*that*, the only relative applicable to both persons & things, is here specially suitable)./*With the Allies moving forward against* an enemy which *has nowhere been able to make a successful stand* (who)./*They are harassing* an enemy which *is moving in the open* (who)./*Among other distinguished* visitors which *the Crawfords had at Rome was Longfellow* (that)./*A woman who is devoted to the many dear & noble* friends, *famous in art, science, & literature,* which *she possesses* (whom).

which with and or but. It is well known that *and which & but which* are kittle cattle, so well known that the more timid writers avoid the dangers associated with them by keeping clear of them altogether—a method that may be inglorious, but is effectual & usually not difficult. Others, less pusillanimous or more ignorant, put their trust in a rule of thumb & take the risks. That rule is that *and which* or *but which* should be used only if another *which* has preceded. It is not true ; *and-which* clauses may be legitimate without a preceding *which* ; & its natural if illogical corollary—that *and which* is always legitimate if another *which* has preceded—induces a false security that begets many blunders. On the other hand, it probably saves many more bad *and-whichs* than it produces. Anyone who asks no more of a rule of thumb than that it should save him the trouble of working out his problems separately, & take him right more often than it takes him wrong, should abandon the present article at this point.

Those for whom such a rule is not good enough may be encouraged to proceed by a few sentences in which it has not averted disaster :—*The*

defeat of M. Poincaré for the office for which *he has put himself forward—& for which, by the way, he has been much criticized—would be regarded as an Anti-R. P. triumph./A special measure of support & sympathy should be extended to the Navy & Admiralty,* which *have certainly never been more in need of it,* & to which *they have never been more entitled than today./After a search for several days he found a firm* which *had a large quantity of them* & which *they had no use for./A period in* which *at times the most ungenerous ideas & the most ignoble aims have strutted across the stage,* & which *have promptly been exploited by unscrupulous journalists & politicians.* True, it is easy to see the flaw in all these, viz that the two *whichs* have not the same antecedent, & to say that common sense is to be expected of those who apply rules ; but then rules of thumb are meant just for those who have not enough common sense to do without them, & ought to be made foolproof.

Here, on the other hand, are examples in which there is no preceding *which*, & yet *and which* is blameless :—*Mandates issued, which the member is bound blindly & implicitly to obey, to vote & to argue for, though contrary to the clearest conviction of his judgment & conscience—these are things* utterly unknown to the laws of this land, and which *arise from a fundamental mistake of the whole order & tenor of our Constitution* (BURKE)./*Another natural prejudice,* of most extensive prevalence, and which *had a great share in producing the errors fallen into by the ancients in their physical inquiries, was this* (J. S. MILL)./*In the case of calls* within the London area, but which *require more than three pennies, the same procedure is followed./The naked-eye comet* discovered by Mr Brooks in the summer, and which *was visible in the early evening a few weeks since,* has now reappeared.

The first of these is from Burke, the second from Mill, & the other two from the most ordinary modern writing. Supporters of the rule of thumb will find it more difficult to appeal here to common sense, & will perhaps say instead that, no matter who wrote them, they are wrong; it will be maintained below that they are right. The rule of thumb fails, as such rules are apt to do, for want of essential qualifications or exceptions. The first qualification needed is that the *which* that has preceded must belong to the same antecedent as the one that is to be attached by *and* or *but*; our set of wrong examples would have been written otherwise if that had been part of the rule. The next amendment is both more important &, to the lovers of simple easy rules, more discouraging: the ' another *which* ' that was to be the test must be changed to ' a clause or expression of the same grammatical value as the coming *which*-clause '. Now what is of the same grammatical value as *a which*-clause is either another *which*-clause or its equivalent, & its equivalent may be an adjective or participle with its belongings (*utterly unknown to the laws of this land*; *discovered by Mr B. in the summer*), or an adjectival phrase (*of most extensive prevalence*; *within the London area*); for before these there might be inserted *which are*, *which was*, &c., without any effect on the meaning. But, secondly, what is of the same grammatical value as *the which*-clause that is coming is an expression that agrees with it in being of the defining, or of the non-defining, kind; i.e., two defining expressions may be linked by *and* or *but*, & so may two non-defining, but a defining & a non-defining must not.

A defining expression is one that is inserted for the purpose of enabling the reader to identify the thing to which it is attached by answering about it such questions as which —— ?, what —— ?, what sort of —— ?. If the Burke quotation had stopped short at *things*

(*Mandates . . . are things.*), we should have said No doubt they are things, but what sort of things ? we cannot tell what sort of things Burke has in mind till the expressions meaning ' unknown to law ' & ' arising from mistake ' identify them for us; both expressions are therefore of the defining kind, & legitimately linked by *and*; whether *which* occurs in both, or only in one, is of no importance. In that example there can, owing to the vagueness of the antecedent *things*, be no sort of doubt that the expressions are defining. Often there is no such comfortable certainty; in the Mill sentence, for instance, ' another natural prejudice ' is not a vague description like *things*, demanding definition before we know where we are with it; if the sentence had run simply *Another natural prejudice was this*, we should not have suspected a lacuna; it cannot be said with confidence whether the two expressions were defining, so that the summary might be *Another natural, widespread, & fatal prejudice was this*, or non-defining, so that it would be *Another natural prejudice— & it was a widespread & fatal one— was this*. It is clear, however, that whichever ' of most extensive prevalence ' is the *which*-clause is also, & the *and which* is legitimate. It was because it is not always possible to say whether clauses & expressions of the kind we are considering are defining or non-defining that the phrase ' inserted for the purpose of enabling the reader to identify ' was so worded; the difference is often, though not usually, a matter of the writer's intention.

After these explanations the rule, as now amended, can be set down: *And which* or *but which* should not be used unless the coming *which*-clause has been preceded by a clause or expression of the same grammatical value as itself. And a reasonable addition to this is the warning that, though the linking of a relative clause to a really parallel expression that is not a relative clause is logically & grammatically permissible, it has often an ungainly effect & is not unlikely to convict the writer of carelessness ; if he had foreseen that a relative clause was to come (& not to foresee is carelessness), he could usually have paved the way for it by throwing his first expression into the same form.

It may possibly be noticed by persons who have read other parts of the book that so far *that* has not been mentioned in this article, though defining & non-defining clauses have been in question. That is so ; it has been assumed, to suit the large number of people for whom the relative *that* hardly exists in print, that *which* is the only relative. For the advantages of recognizing *that* & giving it its fair share of work, especially that of distinguishing the defining from the non-defining clause, see THAT REL. PRON. ; & in what follows, which will consist largely of bad *and-which* or *but-which* clauses with corrections, the assumption will be, on the contrary, that *which* & *that* are, with some special exceptions, respectively the non-defining & the defining relatives.

Quotations will be arranged, with a view to their serving a practical purpose, in groups for each of which a particular cure is the best or simplest, & not according to the fault that necessitates a change. But, that any doubts about the latter may be resolved, an index letter appended to each quotation will refer to the following table :

A. No preceding parallel clause or equivalent
B. Different antecedents
C. Defining & non-defining expressions linked
D. *Which* instead of *that*
E. *What* preceding (see WHAT 4)
F. Right but ungainly

There is often room for difference of opinion either about the fault found or about the remedy offered. In some of the quotations the relative pronoun *who*, or the relative

adverb *where* (= *at* or *in which*) plays a part instead of *which* or *that*, but need cause no difficulty.

USE DEMONSTRATIVE IN- STEAD OF RELATIVE

I have also much Russian literature on that subject, but from which, *out of respect to certain English prejudices, I forbear to quote* (C ; from this)./*Every male Kaffir must go to a Pass Office & obtain a form, which he presents to his employer immediately he enters his employ,* & who *keeps it as long as the Kaffir is with him* (A ; & the latter)./*The tunnel will be closed daily for several hours whilst the work is in progress,* & which *is expected to take two years* (A ; & this)./*At one time there was a drop of something over 35 per cent,* but *from which point there has been a recovery* (A ; from that)./*In the next act—Athens during the Trojan War—we meet Diogenes, & are entertained by many clever allusions to ancient Greek mythology,* & where *our millionaire tourist falls in love with Helen of Troy* (A ; & there)./*Motor-car accessories have been taxed in America, in the belief that the 5 per cent would be absorbed by the makers or dealers,* but *which in reality is being passed on to the consumer* (A ; but in reality it).

OMIT THE RELATIVE

A book the contributors to which come from many different countries, & who *are writing under conditions which necessarily impose some restrictions upon them* (A ; & are writing)./*How different from hers is Saint Augustine's, whose ' Confessions ' are the first autobiography,* & which *have this to distinguish them from all other autobiographies, that they are addressed directly to God* (A ; & have)./*An effort in this direction is, I believe, under consideration,* & which, *if given effect to, should be greatly in the interest of effectual unity* (A ; &, if)./*They are from a dossier placed in Lord Dufferin's hands in the autumn of*

1882, & which, *so far as I am aware, have not yet been published* (A ; &, so far)./*That is a speech that might have been delivered by one of the Labour leaders,* but which, *in spite of its emphatic language, ended in smoke* (D ; but, in)./*The first peer was Attorney General in the first Reform Government,* & who *developed into what Greville calls ' a Radical of considerable vehemence '* (A ; & developed).

USE A *THAT* IN THE FIRST EXPRESSION ONLY

This does not include the amount payable in respect of the buildings & improvements erected & provided during the past year, & which *were not the property of the company vendors* (D ; that were erected . . . & were not)./*I have carefully noted the earnest & sagacious advice* constantly given in your columns to the Ottoman Government, & which *may be summed up in the phrase ' Put your house in order '* (D ; that has constantly been given . . . & may)./*The ' Matin ' details the policy* agreed upon at yesterday's meeting of the Cabinet, & which *the French Government will pursue in dealing with the grave problem of Reparations* (D ; that was agreed upon . . . & will be pursued by). When both expressions are defining, if the first is not a clause, the unfortunate result follows that the second requires a *that* far removed from its antecedent, on which point see THAT REL. PRON. 4 ; correction may entail a change of voice or some other detail, as shown above.

OMIT THE *AND* OR *BUT*

Vastly the greater number of mistakes, whether they are of the worse or the more venial kinds, can be treated thus, but the number of examples need not be correspondingly greater :—*Again, take Pascal, the praise of whom in Sainte-Beuve never rings true,* & who *sees in the ' Pensées ' which Pascal crowded into his short life mainly attacks on Papal Catholicism* (B ; *whom* is Pascal, but *who* is Sainte-Beuve ; *who* without the *and* is bad enough ; it should really be *for he sees*)./*He has attempted to give an account of certain events of which, without doubt, the enemy knew the true version,* & which version *is utterly at variance with everything that fell from my hon. friend* (B ; the writer has tried to mend things by putting in the second *version,* but failed ; omit that as well as *and*)./*His Majesty then took up the case of the Dartmoor Shepherd, who had been three times in the Church Army,* & whose *officers had failed to produce any lasting results upon the shepherd* (B)./*Large crowds congregated in the vicinity of the Dublin Mansion House last night, where the James Connolly anniversary concert was to have been held,* & which *was proclaimed* (A)./*So he sent him what he spoke of to Forster as a ' severe rating ',* but which *was in reality the mildest of remonstrances* (E)./*Mr Asquith said he would be glad to go into the question later in order to justify every statement he had made, & every recommendation he had ever suggested to the House with regard to Iraq during the last four years,* and which *were absolutely consistent with the pledges given by the Governments of the past* (C).

USE (THAT) . . . WHICH

The class to which I belong & which *has made great sacrifices will not be sufferers under the new plan* (C ; class I belong to, which)./*No-one can fail to be struck by the immense improvement which they have wrought in the condition of the people,* & which *often is quite irrespective of the number of actual converts* (C ; improvement they have . . ., which is)./*The Pan-German papers are calling for the resignation of Herr von Kühlmann in consequence of the speeches which he has just made in the Reichstag,* & in which *he admitted that it was impossible for Germany to win by force of arms* (D ; speeches that he . . ., in which).

ADVANCE THE *WHICH* INTO THE FIRST EXPRESSION

If this is done the *which* after *and* &c. may be omitted or retained as seems best :—*The enormous wire nets, marked by long lines of floating barrels & buoys*, & which *reach to the bottom of the sea, were pointed out to me* (F ; which are marked . . ., & reach)./*Mr Corbett's Nelson is a very great commander, bountifully endowed with that indispensable gift, a sound ' imagination '*, but who *scorned to rely upon mere uncorroborated insight* (F ; who was bountifully . . ., but scorned)./*Hallam, that most impassive of writers*, & whose *Liberalism would at the present day be regarded as tepid, tells us that* . . . (A ; who was the most . . ., & whose)./*A Byzantine cross, reported to be valued at £250,000*, & which *belonged to a church in the province of Aquila, has to be returned to the parish priest* (F ; which is reported . . ., & which).

Anyone who has lasted out to this point may like to finish up with a few specimens of exceptional interest or difficulty, to be dealt with according to taste :—

With what difficulty had any of these men to contend, save that eternal & mechanical one of want of means & lack of capital, *& of which* thousands of young lawyers, young doctors, young soldiers & sailors, of inventors, manufacturers, shopkeepers, have to complain ?—*Thackeray*./Nothing would gratify, or serve the purpose of, our enemies so much as would a panic in the capital of the Empire, as a result of their murderous aircraft attacks, *& which* might involve serious national consequences./An amendment setting forth that the Government's action is in accordance with the strict Constitutional practice of the country & is *the only method by which* the will of the people as expressed by the majority of the elected representatives of the House of Commons can be made effective, *and among*

the good consequences of which will be that the absolute veto of an unrepresentative & hereditary Chamber will for ever cease to exist./But the review contains several criticisms which are uncalled-for, incorrect, *and to which* I wish to take exception./Dealings are allowed in securities in such cases as those *where* negotiations between buyer & seller had been in course before the close of the House, *but which* were not completed by three o'clock./Mr De Haviland made a preliminary test with consummate success, *and which* was all the more impressive as the craft went through it in a casual way./Bulgaria announces a Servian repulse with severe losses at Kochana, *where* the fourth & fifth Bulgar armies are uniting, *and which* is only some twenty miles distant from Ishtib./It is precisely in those trades *in which* unionism is the strongest *that* we have the most stability *and in which* we have made the greatest advance./I got him to play in one of the charity matches at Lord's, many of which were held during the war, *and by which means* we raised a good deal of money.

whichever, which ever. See EVER.

while (or whilst) is a conjunction of the kind called strong or subordinating, i. e. one that attaches a clause to a word or a sentence, not a weak or coordinating conjunction that joins two things of equal grammatical value ; it is comparable, that is, with *if* & *although*, not with *and* & *or*. The distinction is of some importance to what follows. Nothing, perhaps, is more characteristic of the flabbier kind of journalese than certain uses of *while*, especially that which is described by the OED as ' colourless '. The stages of degradation may be thus exhibited :—

1. Temporal strong conjunction, = during the time that : *While she spoke, the tears were running down.*

2. The same with inversion, a foolish variant of 1 : *And while is being noticed just now the advance Germany*

& other nations are making in aerial navigation, we see that . . .

3. Non-temporal strong conjunction in contrasts, = whereas : *While this is true of some, it is not true of all.*

4. Strong conjunction with correct ellipsis : *While walking in the road he was run over* (= while *he was* walking).

5. Strong conjunction with incorrect ellipsis of two kinds (a) disregard of the full form, (b) wrongly attached participle &c., see UNATTACHED : *But while being in agreement with Sir Max Waechter's main thesis, I am bound to confess my opinion that he* . . . (the full form is not *while I am being*, but *while I am*, which should be used without ellipsis)./*We abide by that generous gesture, & while being prepared to remit all that our Allies owe to us . . . we ask only that they should* . . . Omit *being.*/ *While willing to sincerely sympathize with those who would suffer by such an order, they can only console themselves with the thought how lucky they have been that the fortunes of war have not affected them sooner* (the full form would be not *while they are willing*, which could be got from what follows, but *while I am* or *we are willing*, which cannot, so that *willing* is wrongly attached ; read *while we are willing*)./*Whilst admitting that much could still be done to speed up the production, it is absurd to suggest that* . . . (this contains both faults, a & b ; read *whilst we admit*)./ *While battling savagely inside the northern ditch of the Fort to extend the footing he had gained, repeated attacks were made in force from Caillette wood* (what is to be understood between *while & battling* ?)./ *An action was brought on account of injuries received in an accident whilst being driven in one of the company's cars* (were the injuries or the accident or the action being driven ?).

6. Strong conjunction playing the part of weak, i. e. introducing what may be defended as a subordinate clause but is in sense a coordinate sentence ; the 'colourless' use, =

and, so common in bad newspaper writing that illustration is almost superfluous : *White outfought Ritchie in nearly every round, & the latter bled profusely, while both his eyes were nearly closed at the end.*

7. The same as 6, but with the defence prevented by the interrogative form of the *while* sentence ; = and : *There is surely in this record a plain hint to the twin-Protectionist members for the City, Mr Balfour & Sir Frederick Banbury ; while was it not Disraeli who in 1842 admiringly traced the close connexion of the Tory Party with Free Trade principles ?/We can only console ourselves with the thought that the German people are also ' slaves ' on this showing ; whilst what are we to think of a House of Lords which permitted this Slavery Act to become law ?*

8. Use as FORMAL WORD or ELEGANT VARIATION for *and*, with complete abandonment of the strong conjunction character : *Archbishops, bishops, & earls were allowed eight dishes ; lords, abbots, & deans six ; while mere burgesses, or other ' substantious ' men, whether spiritual or temporal, no more than three./The initial meridian to be that of Greenwich, while the descriptive text to be in the language of the nation concerned.*

whilom. For the adverbial use (*the wistful eyes that w. glanced down*), see WARDOUR STREET ; for the adjectival (*a w. medical man*), LATE.

whilst. See WHILE.

whin. See FURZE.

whine. Adj. -*ny* ; -EY & -Y.

whinny, vb. For inflexions see VERBS IN -IE &c., 6.

whip. *Whip hand,* not *whip-hand* ; see HYPHENS 3 B.

whirlwind. See WIND, n.

whir(r). The second r is now usual, in the noun as well as in the verb.

whisht, whist, int. The first is recommended.

whisky, -ey. The OED treats the first as the standard form.

whiskyfied. For spelling see -FIED.

whit. See WARDOUR STREET.

Whit. The forms recommended are *Whit Sunday, Whit Monday,* &c., *Whit-week, Whitsuntide.* The adjective is *Whit* (i. e. white), & the word *Whitsun* is a curtailment of *Whit Sunday,* used attributively in the forms *Whitsun Monday, Whitsun week.* It is true that *Whit* with other words than *Sunday* is merely a further curtailment of *Whit Sunday*; but, as *Whit Monday* is now established, it is better to prefer *Whit* to *Whitsun* wherever the latter is not, as in *Whitsuntide,* too firmly in possession to be evicted. It must be remembered, however, that *Whit-sun-Week* & *Whit-Sunday* are the Prayer-Book forms, & that the Oxford Almanack prints *Whitsun Day,* so that the advice given above can be neglected without danger. It was designed to suit modern convenience & pronunciation; the Oxford *Whitsun Day* implies two accents, neither of them on -sun-, & the Prayer-Book *Whit-Sunday* implies (see HYPHENS) at most a secondary accent on -sun-, whereas in modern speech -sun- bears the chief accent. The *Whitsun* forms owe their survival partly also to the mistaken derivation ('a specimen of English popular etymology'—Skeat) from German *Pfingsten*=pentecost.

white, adj., makes *whity*; -EY & -Y.
white(n), vb. See -EN VERBS. For the noun meaning prepared chalk the old word, still in use, is *whiting*; but it is being ousted by *whitening,* perhaps partly because the verb is now to *whiten* instead of to *white,* & partly for distinction from the fish whiting.

whither. See WHENCE.
whiting, Whitsun, whity. See WHITE(N), WHIT, WHITE adj.
whiz(z). The single z is recommended, except in the verb inflexions, to which the doubling of z elsewhere is doubtless due; -z-, -zz-.

who & whom. 1. Miscellaneous questions of case. 2. *Young Ferdinand, who(m) they suppose is drown'd.* 3. *Who(m)* defining & non-

defining. 4. *And* or *but who(m).* 5. Person & number of *who(m).* 6. Personification. 7. *Who(m)* & participle.

1. Miscellaneous questions of case. *Who* being subjective & *whom* objective, & English-speakers being very little conversant with case-forms, mistakes are sure to occur. One is of importance as being extraordinarily common, & is taken by itself in N⁰ 2; the others can be quickly disposed of here.

The interrogative *who* is often used in talk where grammar demands *whom,* as in *Who did you hear that from ?.* No further defence than 'colloquial' is needed for this, & in the sort of questions that occur in printed matter other than dialogue the liberty is seldom taken. The opposite mistake of a wrong *whom* is not uncommon in indirect questions. Examples are:—*Speculation is still rife as to* whom will captain *the English side to Australia./There is quite a keen rivalry between father & son as to* whom is to *secure the greater share of distinction as a cattle-breeder./There has been some speculation as to* whom *the fifth representative from South Africa* was./ *The French-Canadian, who had learned* whom *the visitors* were, *tried to apologize to Prince Albert.* The mistake is a bad one, but fortunately so elementary that it is nearly confined to sports-reporters & patrons of the *as-to* style (see AS 3), & needs no discussion.

The relative *who* now & then slips in for *whom,* giving the educated reader a shock; so:—. . . *on the charge of 'feloniously receiving, comforting, harbouring, assisting, & maintaining one Hawley Crippen,* who she then knew to have *committed the murder of his wife'./There is the Lord Chancellor, for example,* who *in other days we knew as Galloper Smith./As Mr Bevin reminds those* who *in other circumstances we should call his followers, the agreement provided for . . . That is a mistake that should not occur in print ; & at least as bad is the making of one *whom* serve two clauses of which the first requires it as the object, & the second as subject ; this practice is untidy enough with words that, like *which & that,* have only one form for both cases (see THAT REL. PRON. 5, WHICH 2), but is still worse with *who & whom* ; the correct form should invariably be inserted in the second clause when a different case is wanted :—*He ran upstairs & kissed two children* whom *he only faintly* recognized, *& yet were certainly his own./But there has emerged to the final a Spaniard, in Señor Alonso,* whom *few people* would have supposed to have *a good chance a fortnight ago but* is delighting *the advocates of the older style by the beauty & rhythm of his strokes.*

For the incorrect formula *whom failing,* see ABSOLUTE CONSTRUCTION ; & for *than whom* see THAN 6.

2. *Young Ferdinand, whom they suppose is drown'd.*—Tempest III. iii. 92. It was said in 1 that the question between *who & whom* illustrated by this Shakspere quotation is of importance. That is because the *whom* form, though probably no grammarian would have a word to say for it, is now so prevalent in the newspapers that there is real danger of its becoming one of those STURDY INDEFENSIBLES of which the fewer we have the better, & of good writers' taking to it under the hypnotism of repetition. We have not come to that pass yet ; good writers keep clear of it ; but it is high time for emphatic protests. What makes people write *whom* in such sentences ? In the Shakspere, the preceding words are ' while I visit ', so that *Ferdinand* is objective; the relative, which should be *who* as subject to *is drown'd,* may have become *whom* by attraction to the case of *Ferdinand* ; or by confusion with another way of putting the thing—*whom they suppose (to be) drown'd* ; or again a writer may have a general impression that with

who & whom to choose between it is usually safer to play *whom* except where an immediately following verb decides at once for *who.* Any of these influences may be at work, but none of them can avail as a defence against the plain fact that the relative is the subject of its clause ; nor can Shakspere's authority protect the modern solecist ; did not the Revisers, in an analogous case, correct the *whom* of a more familiar & sacred sentence (*But whom say ye that I am ?*—Matt. xvi. 15) into conformity with modern usage ? Of the newspaper extracts that follow, the earlier show easily intelligible *whoms,* because an active verb follows that could be supposed by a very careless person to be governing it, while in the later ones a passive verb or something equivalent puts that explanation out of court :—*Madame Vandervelde spoke for women,* whom, *she claimed, most* hated *war because they suffered most from it./Mr Austen Chamberlain,* whom *we are glad to see* has *returned to lead the House./Success depended entirely upon the attitude of the Prussians,* whom *Pitt believed* would *assist him, but* whom *Mr Fortescue knows well* could *never be depended upon./The witness was Admiral Birileff,* whom *the Kaiser well knew* was *a thoroughly improper person to witness a document of the kind./The letter gives the name of a man* whom *the writer alleges* was *responsible for the child's death./Arrangements were made to accommodate a few ladies* whom *it was certain* would *not be likely to raise any Suffragist interruption./Lord Justice Younger,* whom *it is rumoured* may *be nominated for the Lord-Chancellorship./Mr Asquith, a statesman* whom *we are convinced* will *be more honoured by posterity than by the present generation./A very modern Japanese, one* whom *it may be observed* spoke *English fluently./ Amongst others* whom *it is hoped* will *be among the guests are . . ./Mention was made of ' Ayesha ',* whom *it is alleged* meant *Mrs Bryce.*

After reading these we can perhaps fix upon the vague impression that *whom* is more likely beforehand to be right as probably the decisive influence ; but it need hardly be said that slapdash procedure of that kind deserves no mercy when it fails. That every *whom* in those quotations ought to be *who* is beyond question, & to prove it is waste of time since the offenders themselves would admit the offence ; they commit it because they prefer gambling on probabilities to working out a certainty.

As, however, an unsound proof is worse than no proof at all, discrediting the truth that depends on it when itself discredited, an argument sometimes used in this matter should be abandoned. It is that the necessity of the correct form (whether *who* or *whom*) is shown when it is realized that the words between *who*(*m*) & what decides its case are parenthetic—*Ferdinand who* (*they suppose*) *is drown'd*. It is true that that analysis is much more often possible than impossible, e. g. in all the above examples ; it is even sometimes, though rarely, probable, e. g. in the first (Vandervelde) example ; but it is often impossible, as in : *Jones, who I never thought was in the running, has won.* That sentence is built up thus. Jones has won ; I never thought that Jones was in the running : Jones, I never thought (that) who was in the running, has won : Jones, who I never thought was in the running, has won. No parenthesis there ; nor, surely, in most examples where it is logically possible. A single live example of the impossible parenthesis is : *Cambridge's Vice-Chancellor lumped all these interesting & inspiring folk together as ' foreigners & others '*, whom he did not intend should *desecrate Cambridge by their presence on a Sunday. Whom* should be *who*, not on the parenthesis argument, since ' he did not intend ' cannot be parenthetic, but because the object of *did not intend* is the

clause ' that who should desecrate '. The argument from parenthesis is unsound, unless indeed its champions are prepared to support it seriously by the analogy of ' You are a beauty, I don't think ', where the essential main statement is playfully dressed up as a parenthesis. But it is as true that *who* is the only right case in the quoted sentences as if the parenthesis argument were unassailable.

3. *Who*(*m*) defining & non-defining. As has been suggested in WHICH) (THAT)(WHO, 9, the thing to aim at is the establishment of *that* as the universal defining relative, with *which* & *who*(*m*) as the non-defining for things & persons respectively. That consummation will not be brought about just yet ; but we contribute our little towards it every time we write *The greatest poet* that *ever lived*, or *The man* that *I found confronting me*, instead of using *who* & *whom* ; see WHICH)(THAT)(WHO, 9 & 3. Failing the use of *that* as the only defining relative, it is particularly important to see that *who* defining shall not, & *who* non-defining shall, have a comma before it. *Readers of the* ' Westminster ', who *are also readers at the great Bloomsbury* institution, will *be able to admire the new decorations for themselves.* Those wrong commas (see STOPS, Commas C) make the sentence imply that all readers of the ' Westminster ' frequent the British Museum.

4. *And* or *but who*(*m*). The use of these is naturally attended by the same dangers as that of *and which*. These have been fully discussed under WHICH WITH AND, & nothing need here be added beyond a few specimens containing *who*(*m*) ; the letters appended refer to the table of faults in WHICH WITH AND (see p. 719) :—*Alfred Beasley was examined as to a meeting at which Mrs Pankhurst was present* & a note of whose *speech he had taken* (A)./*A letter speaks of the sorrows of children* which *their parents are powerless to* *assuage*, & who have *little experience of the joys of childhood* (B)./*They have noticed the apparent importance which these men seem to occupy in the councils of the nation*, and who are *granted passports to Russia, in order to assist our Ally in settling his domestic difficulties !* (A)./*The working classes*, for long in enjoyment of *all the blessings of ' Tariff Reform '*, & who are *therefore fully competent to appreciate their value, are moving with a startling rapidity towards Socialism* (F)./*We should be glad of further assistance to pay the cost of putting up relatives of men* who *live in the provinces*, & to whom *we like to extend invitations to come & stay near them for a few days at a time* (B). In this last, the antecedent of *who* is *men*, but that of *whom* is *relatives*.

5. Person & number of *who*(*m*). *To me*, *who* has *also a copy of it, it seems a somewhat trivial fragment.* Read *have* ; the relatives take the person of their antecedents ; the Lord's Prayer & the Collects, with *which art, who shewest*, & scores of other examples, are overwhelming evidence that *who* is not a third-person word, but a word of whichever person is appropriate.

The relatives take also the number of their antecedents—a rule broken in : *The death of Dr Clifford removes one of the few Free Churchmen whose work had given* him *a national reputation.* The antecedent of *whose* is not *one*, but *Churchmen*, whereas the use of *him* instead of *them* shows that the writer assigned *whose* to *one* ; read either *removes a Churchman whose work had given him*, or *removes one of the few Churchmen whose work has given them*.

A less simple point is raised by :—
I cannot help feeling that some of us who *feel as strongly as I do that the Lord Chamberlain's authority ought to be swept away are making* ourselves *a little ridiculous by protesting at the appointment of Mr Brookfield./* All of us who *have not the opportunities which Mr Jonescu has*

enjoyed wish to know all that we *can of the personality of the men who play a great part in the world.* In these the *ourselves* & the *we* show that *who* is to be taken as first-personal ; its antecedents, however, are *some*, & *all*, not *us*, & *ourselves* & *we* should in strict grammar be *themselves* & *they.* The writers have treated *some of us*, & *all of us*, as = *we people*, & *all we.* That will pass if the first writer means (which is a little doubtful) that he too is making himself ridiculous. The question sometimes arises in contexts where more turns on the person of *who*(*m*) than here.

6. Personification. *Who*(*m*) must be ventured on in personifications only with great caution. It will be admitted that in the following *who* is intolerable, & *which* the right word : *The joint operation for ' pinching out ' the little kingdom of Serbia*, who *had the audacity to play in the Balkan Peninsula a part analogous to that which the little kingdom of Piedmont had played in the old days in Italy.* Yet, if we had had *little Serbia* instead of *the little kingdom of Serbia*, *who* might have passed. Again, when we say that a ship has lost *her* rudder, we personify ; yet, though *She had lost her rudder* is good English, *The ship, who had lost her rudder* is not, nor even *The Arethusa, who* &c. ; both these can do with *her*, but not with *who* ; possibly *Arethusa, who* (& the naval writers drop the *the* with ships' names) is blameless ; if so, it is because the name standing alone emphasizes personification, which must not be half-hearted or dubious if *who* is to follow. See PERSONIFICATION.

7. *Who*(*m*) & participle. *I have been particularly struck by the unselfishness of the majority of sons & daughters*, many of whom even remaining *unmarried because they lacked the wherewithal to do more than help their parents.* The mistake has been treated under WHICH 1. Read *many of them remaining*, or *many of whom remain.*

whoever &c. 1. Forms. 2. *Who ever*)(*whoever*. 3. Case.

1. Forms. Subjective : *whoever, whosoever* (literary), *who-e'er* (poet.), *whoso* (arch.). Objective : *whomever* (rare), *whoever* (colloq.), *whomsoever* (literary), *whomsoe'er* (poet.), *whomso* (arch.). Possessive : *whoseever, whoever's* (colloq.), *whosesoever* (literary).

2. *Who ever*)(*whoever*. See EVER. *Whoever can it be ?* is illiterate, & *Who ever can it be ?* is colloquial only. In print, when an emphasizing *ever* is used, it should not come next to *who* ; correct the following to *But who could ever* &c. : *But whoever could have supposed that the business interests which are threatened would not have organized to resist ?*

3. Case. " For whoever was responsible for that deliberate lie there can be no forgiveness." The reviewer who quotes these words does so after saying ' His views on . . . are by an accident ungrammatical, but vigorous '. Obviously there is nothing ungrammatical in the sentence unless *whoever* is so, & we must conclude that the reviewer would have written *whom-ever* or *whomsoever*, & that the subjective case therefore requires defence. The defence is not difficult, & *whom-ever* would be wrong. This, the ordinary use of the pronoun, should be distinguished from (a) the incorrect interrogative use mentioned in 1 & (b) the concessive use as in *Whoever consents, I refuse* ; apart from these, *whoever* is a relative that resembles *what* in containing its antecedent in itself ; as *what*=that which, so *whoever*=any person who ; the *that* & the *which* of *what* may or may not be in the same case, & similarly the *any person* & the *who* of *whoever* are often in different cases ; but the case of *whoever* is that of the *who*, not that of the *any person*, that is, it is decided by the relative clause, not by the main sentence : *He asked* whom-ever *he met*, but *He asked* whoever *came near him* ; *For* whomever *he met he had a nod,*

but *For* whoever *met him he had a nod.*

wholly. So spelt, but pronounced as if it were *wholely* & normally formed like *palely, vilely,* & *solely* ; see MUTE E.

whom. See WHO.

whortleberry. Pronounce wer-.

whose. 1. General. 2. *Whose*=of which.

1. General. The word is naturally liable to some of the same misuses as *who*, which need not be here discussed separately ; see WHO & WHOM, 3–6. Even the making of *whose* serve in two clauses requiring different cases (cf. WHO & WHOM, 1) is not unexampled : *The whole scheme may be likened to the good intentions of the dear old lady whose concern for the goldfish led her to put hot water into their bowl one winter's day,* & *was grievously surprised when they died.*

2. *Whose*=of which. A literary critic observes of an author : ' His style is clear & flexible ; yet it still needs a little clarifying—weeding out " whose " as a relative pronoun of the inanimate, & the like '. If one knows neither who the author nor who the critic is, one cannot help suspecting that the flexibility commended may owe something to the condemned *whose* ; in the starch that stiffens English style one of the most effective ingredients is the rule that *whose* shall refer only to persons ; to ask a man to write flexible English, but forbid him whose ' as a relative pronoun of the inanimate ', is like sending a soldier on ' active ' service & insisting that his tunic collar shall be tight & high ; activity & stocks do not agree. If the reader will glance at the specimens of ' late position of *which* ' given in WHICH 6, he will see how cumbrous a late-placed relative is ; now insistence on *of which* instead of *whose* accounts for more late-placed relatives than anything else ; *whose* would often replace not only *of which*, but *in* &c. *which* ; even the specimens just referred to, though they were selected long before the present article was designed, supply illustrations of that ; ' This book, from the-concentrated-harvest-of-wisdom-in-which we' would become 'This book, from whose concentrated harvest of wisdom we'; 'The camera, the-remarkable-&-convincing-evidence-it-has-been-possible-to-obtain-with-which has' would become 'The camera, whose remarkable & convincing evidence has'. To take everyday samples instead of such monstrosities, would not ' Courts whose jurisdiction ', & ' a game of whose rules it is ignorant ' be clear improvements in the following ?—*The civilians managed to retain their practice in* Courts the jurisdiction of which *was not based on the Common Law./In Whistler* v. *Ruskin—the subject of a most entertaining paper—we have the law standing as umpire in* a game of the rules of which *it is quite ignorant.* Of course they would, & of the convenience of *whose*=*of* &c. *which* there can really be no question ; nor is the risk of ambiguity worth considering, so rare is it in comparison with that of artificial clumsiness. The tabooing of *whose* inanimate is on a level with that of the PREPOSITION AT END ; both are great aids to flexibility ; both are well established in older as well as in colloquial English ; *My thought, Whose murder yet is but fantastical* (Macbeth), & *The fruit Of that forbidden tree whose mortal taste Brought death into the world* (Paradise Lost), are merely the first instances that come to mind. The Milton happens to be a little out of the ordinary in that *whose* is not a mere possessive, but an objective genitive ; but that even such a use is not obsolete is shown by the following from a newspaper: *Sir William Harcourt thrice refused an earldom,* whose acceptance *he feared might be a barrier to his son's political career.*

Let us, in the name of common sense, prohibit the prohibition of *whose* inanimate ; good writing is surely difficult enough without the forbidding of things that have historical grammar, & present intelligibility, & obvious convenience, on their side, & lack only—starch.

why. Pl. *whys.*

wicker makes -*ered* ; see -R-, -RR-.

wide. 1. For the distinction between *w.* & *broad*, which is of considerable idiomatic importance, see BROAD. 2. *Wide(ly).* It should be remembered that there are many positions in which, though *widely* is grammatically possible, *wide* is the idiomatic form ; see UNIDIOMATIC -LY for other such adjectives ; *yawn wide, aim wide, wide apart, wide awake, open* one's *eyes wide, is widespread*, are all usually better than *widely apart* &c., & there are many more.

wide(-)awake. He is *wide awake* ; A very *wide-awake* person ; He was wearing a *wideawake* or *wide-awake.*
widely. See WIDE.
widish, not *wideish* ; see MUTE E.
wife. For the verb &c. see -VE(D). Diminutive *wifie*, see -EY, -IE, -Y. For *all the world & his wife* see WORN-OUT HUMOUR.

wight. A WARDOUR STREET word.
wild. 1. Hyphens &c. We saw *a wild boar* or *a wild duck*, but They were hunting *wild-boar* or *wildboar* or shooting *wild-duck* ; *a wild cat* is an untamed one of the domestic kind, *a wildcat* or *wild-cat* one of the species so named ; *wild oats,* not *wild-oats* ; see HYPHENS. 2. *Wild-(ly).* For *play, run, shoot, talk*, &c., *wild*, see UNIDIOMATIC -LY.

wilful. So spelt ; see -LL-, -L-, 4.
will, n. 1. Phrases like *the will to power*, in which a noun is tacked on to *will* by *to*, have come from Germany & been allowed to sojourn amongst us for a time ; but there is a stronger case for their deportation & repatriation than against many human aliens, & it may now be hoped that our philosophers, if they really do require the meaning

of them, will at least dress it in English clothes. Meanwhile, GROW-ING WILL TO RECONSTRUC-TION, says a newspaper headline. 2. *Will* makes *will-less*; see SKILL-LESS.

will, vb. 1. Forms. 2. *Will* & *shall*.

1. Forms. There is a verb *to will*, conjugated regularly throughout— *will, willest, wills, willed, willedst, willing*; it means to intend so far as one has power that so-&-so shall come about, the so-&-so being expressed by a noun or a *that*-clause or an infinitive with *to*: *You willed his death, that he should die, to kill him*. The much commoner auxiliary verb has none of the above forms except *will*, & on the other hand has *wilt* & *would* & *would(e)st*; it has also none of the above constructions, but is followed by an infinitive without *to*: *He will die, Would it be true?* The meaning of this auxiliary is curiously complicated by a partial exchange of functions with *shall*, the work of merely giving future & conditional forms to other verbs being divided between certain persons of *shall* & certain persons of *will*, while the parts of each not so employed retain something of the senses of ordering (*shall*) & intending (*will*) that originally belonged to the stems.

2. *Will* & *shall*. There is the English of the English, & there is the English of those who repudiate that national name; of the English of the English *shall* & *will* are the shibboleth, & the number of those who cannot ' frame to pronounce it right ', as they talk to us in the newspapers, best reveals to us the power in the English Press wielded by Scots & others who are not English. That power need not be grudged them, & it is perhaps presumption to take for granted that *shibboleth* is better than *sibboleth*; but the mere Englishman, if he reflects upon the matter at all, is convinced that his *shall* & *will* endows his speech with a delicate precision that could not be attained without it, & serves more important purposes than that of a race-label.

The idiom is a strange one, & under *shall* has been sufficiently illustrated to save those who may wish to acquire it some of the usual mistakes. The general statement will be enough here that nearly all misuses are of *will* for the idiomatic *shall*, not of *shall* for *will*; to which may be added a small selection of various common wrong forms, with references to the sections of *shall* :—

See SHALL, 1

If we add too much to these demands we *will* be in grave danger of getting nothing. / We are facing the consequences today, & *will* have to face them for many years to come in the affairs of Europe./We have no proper place at the Coronation of King George, & *would* lay ourselves open to the gravest misunderstanding by departing, on this occasion, from the settled policy of our party.

See SHALL, 2

We *would* like to bring together two extracts dealing with the effects of the Budget on land./But at any rate we *would* feel sorry to have missed anything that is told us of Edison in the biography.

See SHALL, 3

The Gold Medal of the Royal Astronomical Society will go to a foreign astronomer, when this evening the President of the Society *will* present it to Professor Max Wolf.

See SHALL, 4

The Greeks will now decide whether their country *shall* continue to be a Monarchy or *will* become a Republic./In a very few years we *shall* not remember, & *will* scarcely care to inquire, what companies were included.

See SHALL, 5

The King has expressed a desire that on Sunday all flags *will* be flown at the masthead./It is intended that the exterior scenes in no fewer than four different pictures *will* be taken before they return.

Willy, -ie. See -EY, -IE, -Y.
wily makes *wilily* ; see -LILY.
wind, n. Words for wind, & names of particular winds, are apt to be troublesome & to be confused with one another. The following words are in alphabetical order, & the definitions are those of the OED, except where (for *wind* itself only) the OED was not yet out :—
anti-trade wind. A wind that blows steadily in the opposite direction to the trade-wind, that is, in the northern hemisphere from S.W., & in southern hemisphere from N.W.
bise. A keen dry N. or NNE. wind prevalent in Switzerland & the neighbouring parts of France, Germany, & Italy.
blast. A strong gust of wind.
blizzard. A furious blast of frost-wind & blinding snow.
breath. A gentle blowing, a puff.
breeze. A gentle or light wind.
cloud-burst. A violent storm of rain, a ' waterspout '.
cyclone. a. A storm in which the wind has a circular course. b. A hurricane or tornado of limited diameter & destructive violence. c. A system of winds rotating around a centre of minimum barometric pressure.
draught. A current of air, esp. in a confined space, as a room or a chimney.
föhn. A warm dry south wind which blows down the valleys on the north side of the Alps.
gale. a. A wind of considerable strength. b. A gentle breeze.
gust. A sudden violent rush or blast of wind.
harmattan. A dry parching land-wind, which blows during December, January, & February, on the coast of Upper Guinea in Africa ; it obscures the air with a red dust-fog.
hurricane. A name given primarily to the violent wind-storms of the West Indies, which are cyclones of

diameter of from 50 to 1000 miles, wherein the air moves with a velocity of from 80 to 130 miles an hour round a central calm space, which with the whole system advances in a straight or curved track ; hence, any storm or tempest in which the wind blows with terrific violence.
mistral. A violent cold north-west wind experienced in the Mediterranean provinces of France & neighbouring districts.
monsoon. A seasonal wind prevailing in southern Asia & esp. in the Indian Ocean, which during the period from April to October blows approximately from the south-west, & from October to April from the north-east.
puff. A short impulsive blast of breath or wind ; a whiff.
samiel. The simoom.
simoom. A hot, dry, suffocating sand-wind which sweeps across the African & Asiatic deserts at intervals during the spring & summer.
squall. A sudden & violent gust, a blast or short sharp storm, of wind.
storm. A violent disturbance of the atmosphere, manifested by high winds, often accompanied by heavy falls of rain, hail, or snow, by thunder & lightning, & at sea by turbulence of the waves. Hence sometimes applied to a heavy fall of rain, hail, or snow, or to a violent outbreak of thunder & lightning, unaccompanied by strong wind.
tempest. A violent storm of wind, usually accompanied by a downfall of rain, hail, or snow, or by thunder.
tornado. a. A very violent storm, affecting a limited area, in which the wind is constantly changing its direction or rotating ; loosely, any very violent storm of wind, a hurricane. b. On the west coast of Africa, a rotatory storm in which the wind revolves violently under a moving arch of clouds. c. In the Mississippi region of U.S., a destructive rotatory storm under a funnel-shaped cloud like a waterspout, which advances in a narrow path over the land for many miles.

trade-wind. The wind that blows constantly towards the equator from about the thirtieth parallels, north & south ; its main direction in the northern hemisphere being from the north-east, & in the southern hemisphere from the south-east.

typhoon. a. A violent storm or tempest occurring in India. b. A violent cyclonic storm or hurricane occurring in the China seas & adjacent regions, chiefly during the period from July to October.

waterspout. a. A gyrating column of mist, spray, & water, produced by the action of a whirlwind on a portion of the sea & the clouds immediately above it. b. A sudden & violent fall of rain ; a cloudburst.

whiff. A slight puff or gust of wind, a breath.

whirlwind. A body of air moving rapidly in a circular or upward spiral course around a vertical or slightly inclined axis which has also a progressive motion over the surface of land or water.

wind. Air in more or less rapid natural motion, breeze or gale or blast (*Concise Oxf. Dict.*).

zephyr. A soft mild gentle wind or breeze.

wind, verbs. *Wīnd, wound,* to twist &c. *Wĭnd, wĭnded* (or *wound*), to blow (a horn). *Wīnd, wīnded,* to give breath to or exhaust the breath of. The two latter are from the noun *wind* (*wound* being a natural corruption), & unconnected with the first.

windward(s). See -WARD(S).

wine makes *winy* ; see MUTE E.

winning makes *-est* ; *-ER* & *-EST*, 4.

winter. *W. garden, w. quarters, w. solstice* ; each should be two words, unhyphened ; see HYPHENS 3 B. For *the w. of our discontent,* see IRRELEVANT ALLUSION.

wire makes *wirable, wiry* ; see MUTE E. *Wire rope* should be two words unhyphened ; see HYPHENS 3 B.

wise, n. In the phrases *in no wise, in any wise,* &c., *wise* should be a separate noun unhyphened ; see HYPHENS, Group **From hand to mouth* ; if *in* does not precede, there is no objection to any of the three forms *no wise, no-wise, nowise.*

-WISE,-WAYS. 1. The ending *-ways,* or occasionally *-way,* is often used indifferently with *-wise,* & is very seldom the only form without one in *-wise* by its side—perhaps only in *always.* 2. In a few established words, *-wise* is alone, esp. *clockwise, coastwise, likewise, otherwise, sunwise.* 3. In other established words both forms are used, as *breadth-, broad-, end-, least-, length-, long-, no-, side-, slant-.* 4. In words made for the occasion from nouns, as in *Use it clubwise* or *pokerwise, Go crabwise* or *frogwise, Worn cloakwise* or *broochwise* or *chainwise, Placed studwise* or *fencewise, -wise* is now much the commoner.

wishful is a word chiefly used by those who disapprove of the phrase ANXIOUS *to,* & it has consequently a certain taint of purism about it. If it should ever lose that, & come into general use, it would at once relieve *anxious* of a meaning that is open to exception, & provide *desirous* with a grammatically convenient synonym ; compare *desirous of doing* with *wishful to* do. In the mean time, *wishful* (with its ludicrous suggestion of *wistful*) gives the reader a slight shock as he comes to it : *We should recommend a perusal of the whole article to those wishful to understand the real nature of the conflict.*

wistaria. So spelt.

wit, n. See HUMOUR ; that the two are different names for the same thing is no doubt still a popular belief ; but literary critics at least should not allow themselves to identify the two, as in : *It is to be doubted whether the author's gifts really do include that of humour. Two jests do not make a wit.*

wit, vb. Pres., *wot, wottest* ; past *wist* ; infin., *to wit* ; part. *witting.* See WARDOUR STREET.

witch-. See **wych-**.

witenagemot. Pron. wĭ'tenagĭmō't.

with. Writers who have become conscious of the ill effect of AS *to* & *in the* CASE *of*, casting about for a substitute that shall enable them still to pull something forward to the beginning of a sentence (' The modern journalistic craving for immediate intelligibility ' said Dr Henry Bradley), have lately hit upon *with*, which is sometimes found displacing *of* or some really appropriate preposition—a trick that should be avoided :—*With pipes, as with tobacco, William Bragge was one of the most successful collectors.*/ [Collins, Blair, Parnell, Dyer, Green] *Collins has had his excellent editors, & we must suppose that the manuscript has finally disappeared ; but, with the others, we suspect that the poems are extant.*/Read *of pipes, of tobacco, the poems of the others.*

withal. See WARDOUR STREET.

withe, withy. Both spellings, & the monosyllabic as well as the disyllabic pronunciation, are in use. As against those who condemn the monosyllable as a novelty or an ignorance, there is the plural *withs* in the A. V. of *Judg.* xvi. 7. But probably *withy*, pl. *-ies*, is the best form for modern purposes, obviating uncertainty.

without. 1. *W.*=outside. 2. *W.*= unless. 3. *Without or without.* 4. *Without hardly.* 5. *Without him being.* 6. Negative confusion.

1. *W.*=outside. Both as adverb (*listening to the wind without* ; *clean within & without*), & as preposition (*is without the pale of civilization*), the word retains this meaning ; but it is no longer for all styles, having now a literary or archaic sound that may be very incongruous.

2. *W.*=unless. *No high efficiency can be secured* without *we first secure the hearty cooperation of the 30,000,000 or so workers.* The use is good old English, but bad modern English— one of the things that many people say, but few write ; it should be

left to conscious stylists who can rely on their revivals' not being taken for vulgarisms.

3. *Without . . . or without . . . It can be done without any fear of his knowing it,* or without *other evil consequences.* The well meant repetition of *without* is not merely needless, but wrong. See OR 4.

4. *Without hardly. The introduction of the vast new refineries has been brought about quickly, silently, & effectively, &* without *the surrounding community hardly being aware of what was happening.* Again, like 2, a common colloquialism, but, unlike it, one that should never appear outside spoken or printed talk ; the English for *without hardly* is *almost without.*

5. *Without him being.* The word is peculiarly apt to usher in a FUSED PARTICIPLE, e. g. *The formidable occasion had come & gone without anything dreadful happening.* The fused participle is no worse after *without* than elsewhere, but those who are prepared to eschew it altogether should take warning that *without* will sometimes try their virtue, so often does the temptation present itself ; it is, for instance, a pure accident that the sentence quoted in 4 for a different point contains the fused participle *without the community being aware.* Escapes are usually not hard to find ; here ' & nothing dreadful had happened ', or ' without any dreadful results ', would do, but particular suggestions for a particular case are of little value ; the great thing is general readiness to abandon & recast any of one's phrases that one finds faulty.

6. Negative confusion. Like all negative & virtually negative words, *without* often figures in such absurdities as :—*It is* not *safe for any young lady to walk along the Spaniards-road on a Sunday evening by herself* without *having unpleasant remarks spoken as she passes along.*/ *Rendering it possible for a Government to accept some at any rate of the recommendations of the Committee* without *any loss of face*, & least of all without *loss of office*.

witticism. A HYBRID DERIVATIVE.

wive. See -VE(D).

wizard. For *W. of the North*, see SOBRIQUETS.

wizened, wizen, weazen. All three forms are or have been used as adjectives, but the first is now usual. The -en of *wizen* & *weazen* is a p.p. termination, as well as the -ed of *wizened*.

wizier. See VIZIER.

wobble, wab-. The first is now the established spelling.

wolf. See -VE(D).

wolverene, -ine. The first appears to be accepted.

woman. For *woman suffrage*, as a phrase, see FEMALE)(WOMAN. For *chairwoman & chairman*, as applied to a woman, see FEMININE DESIGNATIONS. *Womankind*, not *womenkind*, for the whole sex or women in general ; but *womenkind* is common for one's female relatives &c.

womanly. See FEMALE, FEMININE.

wonder. For *I shouldn't w. if it didn't rain*, see NOT 4, & STURDY INDEFENSIBLES.

wood. *Wood anemone* is better as two separate words ; also, without question, *wood pavement* ; see HYPHENS 3 B. *Woodbine*, not *-bind*, is the established form, esp. with Shakspere & Milton to maintain it. *Tomorrow to fresh woods*, not *fields* ; a pasture, by the way, *is* a field ; see MISQUOTATION.

wooden makes *woodenness*.

woof, warp, web, weft. The *warp* is a set of parallel threads stretched out ; the threads woven across & between these are the *woof* or *weft* ; & the fabric that results is the *web*.

wool makes, in British spelling, *woollen, woolly*, & in American *woolen, wooly* ; *woollen* is perhaps anomalous even by British standards (see -LL-, -L-), but is certainly established ; &, on its analogy, *-woolled* should be better than *-wooled*.

woolly bear. No hyphen ; see HYPHENS 3 B.

WORD-PATRONAGE. Under SUPERIORITY, the tendency to take out one's words & look at them, to apologize for expressions that either need no apology or should be quietly refrained from, has been mentioned. To pat oneself on the back, instead of apologizing, for one's word is a contrary manifestation of the same weakness, viz self-consciousness ; but it is rare enough to deserve this little article all to itself : . . . *propose to use their powers to force a dissolution. That is a contingency which has been* adumbrated (to revive a word which has been rather neglected of late) *; but this is one more case in which we must be content to wait & see.*

work, vb. The disappearance of the form *wrought* is so manifest, yet so far from complete, that it is impossible to say from year to year where idiom still requires it & where it is already archaic. A few sentences with blanks for *wrought* or *worked* will illustrate. As the direction of progress is clear, prudence counsels falling in with it in good time. *A contemporary who —— in brass. These things have —— together for good. She —— upon his feelings. This —— infinite mischief. They have —— their will. Conscience —— within him. He —— his audience into fury. When they were sufficiently —— up.*

workaday is now displaced, wholly in the noun use, & for the most part as an adjective, by the normal *workday*, of which it is regarded as a slipshod pronunciation to be used only as a genial unbending ; ' this workaday world ' is still usual.

working. *W. capital, w. expenses,* &c., should have no hyphens ; see HYPHENS 3 B.

WORKING & STYLISH WORDS. Anyone who has not happened upon this article at a very early stage of his acquaintance with the book will not suppose that the word *stylish* is meant to be laudatory. Nor is it ; but neither is this selection of stylish words to be taken for a blacklist of out-&-out undesirables. Many of them are stylish only when they are used in certain senses, being themselves in other senses working words ; e. g., *antagonize* is a working word for ' to arouse antagonism in the mind of ' or ' make hostile ', though nothing if not stylish for ' to oppose ' ; *category* is a working word in the philosopher's sense, though stylish as a mere synonym for *class* ; *protagonist* a working word for the one person upon whom the interest centres, but aggressively stylish for an advocate ; *college* stylish for *school* but the working word for—*college*. Others again, such as *bodeful* & *deem* & *dwell* & *maybe*, lose their unhappy stylish air when they are in surroundings of their own kind, where they are not conspicuous like an escaped canary among the sparrows.

What is to be deprecated is the notion that one can improve one's style by using stylish words. Those in the list below, like hundreds of others, have, either in certain senses or generally, plain homely natural companions ; the writer who prefers to one of these the stylish word for no better reason than that he thinks it stylish, instead of improving his style, makes it stuffy, or pretentious, or incongruous. About the words in small capitals remarks bearing on the present subject will be found in their dictionary places :—

STYLISH	WORKING
ANGLE, vb	fish
ANTAGONIZE	oppose
assist	help
beverage	drink
BODEFUL	ominous
catarrh	cold
CATEGORY	class
COLLATION	repast, meal
COLLEGE	school
comestibles	eatables, food
COMMENCE	begin
comprise	INCLUDE

STYLISH	WORKING
CRYPTIC	obscure, mysterious
deem	think
DESCRIPTION	kind, sort
DWELL	live
ENVISAGE	face, confront
FEASIBLE	possible
FORENOON	morning
MAYBE	perhaps
PORCELAIN	china
PROTAGONIST	champion, advocate
sufficient	ENOUGH
VIOLIN	FIDDLE

workless. In the article 's INCON-GRUOUS some illustrations have been given of how the newspaper head-line is affecting the language ; see also WED. *Workless* gives another example. We have all known ' the unemployed ' as long as we can remember. But *unemployed* fills up a good deal of headline ; something shorter is wanted, & *workless* is invented for the need. But, second-ly, *workless* by itself is shorter than *the workless* ; so *workless* is turned from an adjective into an indeclin-able plural noun—all to make possible such gems as :

KENT WORKLESS WANT TO
SEE PREMIER

TO AID WORKLESS

world. *All the w. & his wife* is like the Psalmist ; it has been young & now is old ; see WORN-OUT HUMOUR.

worldly. So spelt, not *wordly* ; but the mistake is common ; cf. *un-wieldly* for *unwieldy*.

WORN-OUT HUMOUR. ' We are not amused ' ; so Queen Victoria baldly stated a fact that was discon-certing to someone ; yet the thing was very likely amusing in its nature ; it did not amuse the person whose amusement mattered, that was all. The writer's Queen Vic-toria is his public, & he would do well to keep a bust of the old Queen on his desk with the legend ' We are not amused ' hanging from it. His public will not be amused if he serves it up the small facetiae that it remembers long ago to have taken delight in. We recognize this about anecdotes, avoid putting on our friends the depressing duty of simulating surprise, & sort our stock into chestnuts & still possibles. Anecdotes are our pounds, & we take care of them; but of the phrases that are our pence we are more neglectful. Of the specimens of worn-out humour exhibited below nearly all have had point & liveliness in their time; but with every year that they remain current the proportion of readers who 'are not amused' to those who find them fresh & new inexorably rises.

Such grammatical oddities as *muchly*; such puns as *Bedfordshire & the Land of Nod*; such allusions as the Chapter on Snakes in Iceland; such parodies as *To —— or not to ——*; such quotations as *On —— intent*, or *single blessedness*, or *suffer a sea change*; such oxymorons as *The gentle art of* doing something ungentle; such polysyllabic uncouthness as calling a person an *individual* or an old maid an *unappropriated blessing*; such needless euphemisms as *unmentionables* or a table's *limbs*; such meioses as *the herringpond*, or *Epithets the reverse of complimentary*, or 'some' as a superlative; such playful archaisms as *hight* or *yclept*; such legalisms as *(the) said ——*, & *the same*, & *this deponent*; such shiftings of application as *innocent* or *guiltless of hs*, or *of the military persuasion*, or to *spell ruin* or *discuss a roast fowl* or *be too previous*; such metonymies as *the leather & the ribbons* for *ball & reins*; such metaphors as *timberyard & sky-pilot & priceless*; such zeugmas as *in topboots & a temper*; such happy thoughts as *taking in each other's washing*—with all these we, i. e. the average adult, not only are not amused; we feel a bitterness, possibly because they remind us of the lost youth in which we could be tickled with a straw, against the

scribbler who has reckoned on our having tastes so primitive.

worry. For inflexions see VERBS IN -IE &c., 6.
worsen. See -EN VERBS.
worship makes *-ipped*, *-ipper*, *-ipping*; see -P-, -PP-.
worsted. Pronounce wŏŏs-.
worth)(worth while. In certain uses great confusion prevails, which can be cleared up with the aid of grammar. The important fact is that the adjective *worth* requires what is most easily described as an object; it is meaningless to say *This is worth*, but sense to say *This is worth sixpence*, or *This is worth saying* (i. e. the necessary expenditure of words), or *This is worth while* (i. e. the necessary expenditure of time); but one such object satisfies its requirements, so that *This is worth while saying*, with the separate objects *while* & *saying*, is ungrammatical. A less essential point, which must nevertheless be realized if all is to be clear, is the doubtful nature of the *It* that is often present in sentences containing *worth*. Though *This is worth while saying* is wrong, *It is worth while saying this* is right, but again *It* (viz whatever has just been said) *is worth while saying* is wrong; the last *It* is the ordinary pronoun, & *this* or *that* might have stood instead of it, but the *It* of *It is worth while saying this* is what is called the anticipatory *it* (see IT, 1, 2) & means not *this* or *that*, but *saying this*. In the following table, this source of confusion will be avoided, every *it* used being of the anticipatory kind. A & B are two faultless forms, B usually appearing not in the direct order, but with *It*; C is another correct form, but slightly less idiomatic than A & B; it, like B, is usually not in direct order, but with *It*. Of the *a*, *b*, *c*, forms, *a* is A spoilt by having *worth while* instead of *worth*, which means that *worth* has two objects; *b* is B spoilt by the verb *say*'s having no object, the cause being, as will

appear when we come to examples, the mistaking of an anticipatory *it* for something else ; *c* is C spoilt by *worth*'s having no object.

A. This is worth saying.
B. To say this is worth while, *or* It is worth while to say this.
C. Saying this is worth while, *or* It is worth while saying this.
a. This is worth while saying.
b. To say is worth while, *or* It is worth while to say.
c. Saying this is worth, *or* It is worth saying this.

The faults are obvious enough in these naked specimens, stripped of disguising additions, except possibly in *b*, about which it must be remembered that the sentences are complete ones, & that there is nothing to be supplied as object to *say*.

The earlier examples will be simple, & it will suffice to give after each a small letter indicating the wrong type to which it belongs, & a capital for the right type to which it should be corrected :—*A spare captain, to take charge of any prize that might be worth while turning into a raider (a. A)./Was not that a line worth while pursuing ? (a. A)./A problem which should be quite manageable—if we make up our minds that it is worth while tackling (a. A)./An experience of weariness slashed with crowded hours of intensest life ; & it was worth while putting on record (a. A)./It is worth recalling Lord Salisbury's declaration in 1885 that, if she yielded to pressure, we should consider ourselves released from our obligations (c. B)./It is worth tabulating the more important of matters thus communicated to us (c. B).*

The next two are clear examples of C, & are given merely that the reader may try whether the conversion of them to B, by the change of *harking* & *remarking* to *to hark* & *to remark* does not produce more idiomatic English :—*It is not often worth while harking back to a single performance a fortnight old./It is worth while remarking on Signor Nitti's very curious attitude toward the question of responsibility for the war.*

But of many sentences that are defensible as C it is open to doubt whether they are really C, or A gone wrong ; these are sentences in which, while an anticipatory *It* is used, there are two possible views of what *It* stands for ; an example will first be examined, & some more on the same pattern will show how common the type is.

It is worth while remarking that the Greek National Anthem is really a very interesting & harmonious air. Does *It* represent ' remarking . . . air ', or ' that . . . air ' ? If the first, the direct form is (1) Remarking (2) that the Anthem is so-&-so (3) is worth while ; which is exactly C (1) Saying (2) this (3) is worth while. But if the second, the direct form is (1) That the Anthem is so-&-so (2) is worth while (3) remarking ; which spoils A (1) This (2) is worth (3) saying, by having *worth while* instead of *worth*.

The reader will easily apply this to the three next examples. Each is defensible as a C, yet it may be doubted whether it was so meant, & also whether B (*it may be worth while to recall* &c.) would not have been better. *It is worth while pointing out that out of an electorate of nearly fourteen & a half millions no fewer than four & a quarter million votes were recorded in 1912 for the Socialist candidates./It is worth while saying, if one thinks so, that Mr Kipling is a great writer, some of whose work will survive as long as anything contemporary with it./It may be worth while recalling that the most interesting account of the novelist's visit to the little German capital is contained in his letter to George Henry Lewes.*

It may be asked, however, why a conversion of A should not be recommended, & only B be offered ; ' A in the table is not provided with a conversion, which would be *It is worth saying this* ; was the omission an oversight ? ' No, it was not ;

that conversion is impossible because anticipatory *it* represents a deferred subject of *is*, whereas the *this* in the proposed conversion is object of *saying* & cannot be also subject of *is*.

The only further point that needs special discussion is the complication sometimes introduced by a relative clause. *The Chinese Labour Corps & its organization was one of the side issues of the war which is well worth while to hear about.* The skeleton of this, before subordination by the relative, is : *The Corps was a side issue ; to hear about this* (issue) *is worth while*, or *it is worth while to hear about this.* Subordination by the relative should give accordingly either *to hear about which is worth while*, or *which it is worth while to hear about.* But the writer has taken that anticipatory *it* (= to hear about which) for the ordinary pronoun *it* (= this issue), & has therefore left it out because he supposes it to mean only the same thing as the *which* that is to connect the clause ; the result is that his *which* is both subject to *is* (which he has deprived of its *it*) & object to *about.* Correct grammar would be A *which is well worth hearing about*, or B *which it is well worth while to hear about*, or C *which it is well worth while hearing about.*

Some mixed examples now follow, with references to the table as before, & with a note where it seems called for. In choosing between A & B or C, it is plain that A, being incapable of conversion, is disqualified for places where the *worth* part of the sentence cannot comfortably be deferred owing to the length of the other part or for other reasons :— *In your excellent account of the late Miss —— there is one omission, & it is worth filling it up* (*c.* A). Observe that the first *it* is *it* anticipatory (= filling it up), & the second is the ordinary pronoun (= the omission). When it is corrected to A, the first *it* becomes the pronoun = the omission, & the second disappears./*On*

that point it is worth quoting a passage from Mr Carroll's election address (*c.* B)./*It is worth adding its opinion upon the measures that Germany is taking* (*c.* B or A)./*It is worth dwelling on this method of approach to the characters* (*c.* B)./*It is worth quoting the ' Echo de Paris ', which was one of the journals which cried loudest for large reparations* (*c.* B).

worth-while. This attributive-adjective compound recently extracted from the phrase ' is worth while ' (*a worth-while experiment* from *the experiment was worth while*) is at the best of doubtful value ; &, having been seized upon as a Vogue-word, it is fast losing all precision of meaning : *That motherhood is a full-time job all worth-while mothers will readily admit./An attractive programme of w.-w. topics has been arranged for discussion.*

worthy. The construction in which *w.* was treated like *worth* & *like*, governing a noun (*in words worthy the occasion, a deed worthy remembrance*, without *of*), is now rare, & appropriate only in exalted contexts.

would. The very common misuses of *would* for *should* are dealt with under WILL vb, & more fully under SHALL. A few specimens, in all of which *would* is wrong, are here given to enable those who doubt their mastery of the idiom to test it : *If we were to go on borrowing money in this country we would keep the position of the unemployed better while borrowing, but we would have to pay for it./If we could but hear what post-Georgians will have to say on the matter we would be even less inclined to value Georgian criticism./ We would like to see a little less talk about Constantine./He might well have struck such a blow as we would have felt to the quick./I would feel safer in backing England had their batting not been so disappointing in the first Test.*

wove, p.p., instead of the usual

woven, is chiefly in commercial terms, as *wove paper, hard-wove fabrics, wire-wove*.

wraith. Pronounce the plural -ths ; see -TH & -DH.

wrapt, wrapped, rapt. See RAPT for the confusion between the English adjective made from Latin *raptus* & the p.p. of *wrap*. It might perhaps be well if the form *wrapt* could be abandoned, so that writers would have to make up their minds between *rapt* & *wrapped*.

wrath, wrathful, wroth. It is very desirable that differentiation should be clearly established. The OED has unfortunately not yet reached the words ; but it may safely be said (1) that many people ignore the existence of *wroth* & treat *wrath* as both noun & adjective, pronouncing it always rawth, & (2) that the useful arrangement would be for *wrath* to be noun only = anger & pronounced rawth, & for *wroth* to be the adjective = angry & pronounced rŏth. This does not put *wrathful* out of use ; it is the attributive adjective, & *wroth* is the predicative : *A wrathful god*, but *God was wroth*. For *wroth*, the pronunciation rŏth is better not only than rawth, but also than rŏth, because much more easily distinguishable from the rawth of *wrath*.

wreath. Pronounce the plural -dhz ; see -TH & -DH for this, & for *wreathe*, vb.

wrestle. PRONUNCIATION, silent t.

wrick. See CRICK.

wrinkle makes *wrinkly*; see MUTE E.

wristband. Pronounce rĭ'zband.

write. 1. *W.* with personal object. 2. *Writ large.*
1. *W.* with personal object. In *I will write you the result*, there are two objects, (direct object) *the result*, & (indirect object) *you*. In literary English, an indirect object is used after *write* only if there is also a direct object, but the direct

object may be used without an indirect ; that is, *I will write the result*, & *I will write you the result*, are idiomatic, but *I will write you soon*, or *about it*, is not ; if a direct object is wanting, the person written to must be introduced by *to* : *I will write to you about it. We wrote you yesterday, Please write us at your convenience*, &c., are established in commercial use, but avoided elsewhere. The following from a novel is to be condemned : *The Lady Henrietta, she who was to keep him out of Arcadia, & who believed him to be in Cannes or Mentone*, wrote him *regularly through his bankers, & once in a while he* wrote her.

2. *Writ large.* The famous line *New Presbyter is but old Priest writ large* (Milton, Sonnet On the New Forcers of Conscience . . .) owes its fame to its double sense ; *priest* & *presbyter* being derived alike from Greek *presbuteros*, the second word is literally a larger writing of the first ; &, metaphorically, a presbyter turns out to be a priest, only more so. Nowadays, whenever a reform disappoints, the new state is said to be the old writ large ; but, as circumstances seldom allow the literal sense as well as the other, some wrong is done to the inventor of the phrase by blunting its point.

wrong is one of the words whose adverbial use should be remembered ; *did his sum wrong* is better than with *wrongly*, but cf. *a wrongly done sum*. See UNIDIOMATIC -LY.

wroth. See WRATH.

wrought. See WORK.

wry makes *wryer, wryest, wryly, wryness, wryish* ; see DRY.

wych-, wich-, witch-, in *w.-elm* &c. The first & third forms are those usually seen, though the second best represents the earliest spelling *wice* (= drooping). Of the current forms *wych-* has the real advantage of not suggesting connexion with witches, & is recommended.

Wykehamist. So spelt.

X

-x, as French plural. It is still usual, in various degrees, to write -x instead of the English -s in the plurals of words in -eau & -eu borrowed from French, the pronunciation being -z, as in English plurals. It is to be hoped that some day all of these that are in familiar English use will be anglicized with -s ; but a list of the chief words, here given in the plural in order that the reader may judge of their looks, is admittedly forbidding : adieus ; beaus ; châteaus ; flambeaus ; plateaus ; portmanteaus ; rondeaus ; rouleaus ; trousseaus. The fact, however, that *purlieu,* which has all the air of a French word without being one, looks right with the plural -s (*purlieus*) because we are used to it suggests that courage with the others might soon be rewarded. Phrases such as *feux de joie* & *jeux d'esprit* would naturally keep their French -x, & so would any single words whose anglicization was so far from accomplished that the plural was still pronounced like the singular, without the sibilant ; that is hardly true of any of the list above ; we say not ' bŏ like Brummell ', but ' bŏz like Brummell ', & ' all portmantŏz will be opened ', not ' all portmantŏ . . .'.

xebec. Pronounce zē'bĕk or zĭbĕ'k.

-XION, -XIVE. About certain nouns, especially *connexion, deflection, inflexion, & reflection,* there is a doubt whether they should be spelt with -*xion* or -*ction,* & the adjectives in -*ive* are also concerned. The forms *connexion, deflexion, inflexion, & reflexion,* are all called by the OED the ' etymological spellings '. In the first place, each is derived from an actual Latin noun in -xio, the change to English -ction being due partly to the influence of the verbs *connect & de-, in-, re-, flect,* & partly to that of the multitude of English nouns in -tion ; & secondly, a vast majority of nouns in -ion were formed from

the p.p. stem & not from the present stem of Latin verbs, so that *flecto flex-,* & *necto nex-,* would be expected to use *flex-* & *nex-* as the basis of their -ion nouns. As a few Latin nouns in -io were nevertheless formed from present stems, e.g. *oblivio,* the philological lapse is of no great importance. It may be well to retain the x in *connexion* & *inflexion,* in which it has by no means gone out of use, though the earlier *connexive* has been displaced by *connective.* For *reflection* & *reflexion, reflective* & *reflexive,* with which attempts at differentiation have had unequal success, see the separate articles.

Y

-Y. For the suffix used in making adjectives from nouns (*slaty* &c.), as it affects spelling, see -EY & -Y in adjectives. For the diminutive suffix (*Johnny, doggie,* &c.), see -EY, -IE, -Y, in diminutives.

yacht. So spelt.

yager. The form now usual is the German word *Jäger* itself.

yahoo. See FAUN.

Y & I were in older English writing freely interchanged ; that general liberty has long been abandoned, but there are still a few words in which usage varies or mistakes are common ; they are, in the spelling here recommended : cipher ; GYPSY ; Libya(n) ; lichgate ; Mytilene ; PYGMY; sibyl & Sibyl ; SILLABUB ; SILVAN & Silvanus ; siphon ; siren ; STILE (in hedge) & style (manner) ; STIMY ; TILER (in free-masonry) ; TIRE (of wheel) ; tiro ; WYCH-elm. In *Libya, sibyl,* & *Mytilene,* the right spelling is indisputable, but with the same sound in successive syllables it is difficult to remember which is i & which y ; even those who have read Herodotus & Thucydides are often fain to visualize the Greek words before they feel safe. In *cypher, lychgate, syllabub, sylvan, syphon, syren,* & *tyro,* the intrusive y is probably due to a vague feeling that an unEnglish-looking word is all the better for a little aggravation of its unEnglishness. In *tyler* & *tyre* differentiation may have been at work, but without need ; & on *tyre* it may be added that in some people's opinion to say that *tire* is the American spelling is a sufficient reason for our using *tyre* ; on the contrary, agreement between English & American spelling is much to be desired wherever it is practicable. In *gipsy* & *pigmy*, we have dissimilation, again without need ; for if *invisibility* can carry five *i*s, these can surely do with two *y*s. But the fact that *stimy* & *stymie*, not *stymy*, are the usual forms illustrates the power of dissimilation ; & it may be guessed that the y starts in the oftener used *stymied*, in which the necessary i of the second syllable tends to produce y in the first ; with this compare the greater frequency of the correct y in *gypsies* & *pygmies* than in *gypsy* & *pygmy*. On the words in the list that are in small capitals, further remarks will be found in the separate articles.

yankeefied. See -FIED.

yclept. See WORN-OUT HUMOUR.

yᵉ. The pronunciation of this is the, not ye, the y being not our letter, but a representation of the obsolete single letter (þ, called *thorn*) now replaced by th.

year. Phrases such as *last year*, *next year*, may be either nouns or adverbs (*Next year may be warmer* ; *We may have warmer weather next year*) ; they should not be both at once, as in : *Disquiet will be caused in Tariff Reform circles by the announcement that in the quinquennium ending & including last year Canada has borrowed the enormous cum of over six hundred million dollars from this country.* The 'last year' that the quinquennium included was a noun ; the 'last year' that the quinquennium ended was an adverb ; indeed, far from the quinquennium's ending the year,

the year ended the quinquennium. It is the same kind of mistake as making one word serve twice in two different cases, for which see, e. g., THAT REL. PRON. 5.

yearly. See -LILY 2.

ye(a)sty. The spelling & pronunciation *yesty*, still alive up to the 19th c., are regarded by the OED as now obsolete.

yelk, yolk. 'The spelling *yelk* appears to have ceased to be frequent since the third quarter of the 19th century, but it is found in recent scientific & technical works ' —OED.

yellow. Y. *fever, y. jacket, y. jaundice, y. ochre,* all two words without hyphen ; see HYPHENS 3 B. In *yellow-(h)ammer*, it cannot be said with safety either that h is due to ignorant assimilation by popular etymology to *hammer*, or that the absence of h is mere h-dropping ; each form has an etymological theory on its side, & OED says that both forms 'are historically justifiable '. The only reason for resisting the prevalent h is thus removed.

yen. Pl. the same.

yeoman. *Yeoman service* & *yeoman's service* are both in use.

yes. Pl. *yeses*.

yester-. Other combinations than *yesterday* are incongruous except in verse or in designedly poetic prose. It is true that *yestereve* is shorter than *yesterday evening*, but the saving of space is paid for by the proof that one has no literary sense.

yet. 1. Inversion. 2. Illogical pregnant use.

1. Inversion. The tendency of *yet* to inspire foolish inversions has been specially treated in INVERSION under the heading *Yet, Especially, Rather.* The effect of ill-timed rhetoric that attends it is obvious in : *Mr Domville-Fife does not recommend South America to the Englishman with small capital desirous of settling on the land & living on his own labour.* Yet are there Englishmen

so settled—in the Argentine & in Chile, for instance.

2. Illogical pregnant use. When *yet* is used to point a contrast, the opposition between the fact it introduces & that which has gone before should be direct & clear. Examples of failure in this respect must necessarily be of some length ; some simpler specimens of a rather similar kind will be found under BUT 3. In each of those that follow it will be noticed that the particular fact with which the *Yet* sentence is in contrast is by no means the essential contents of the previous sentence, but has to be got out of it at the cost of some thought. *We confess to being surprised at the line taken by the railwaymen at Crewe with reference to Colonel Yorke's conclusion that the Shrewsbury disaster occurred through the engine-driver having momentarily fallen asleep. Yet at a meeting the Crewe railwaymen are very indignant at the suggestion, & denounce Colonel Yorke as an Army officer who does not understand the real working of railways.* Here the *Yet* fact is that the men are indignant. What is that in contrast with ? Apparently with the correctness of Colonel Yorke's conclusion ; but, though many other things not in contrast with their indignation can be got out of the sentence, the correctness of the conclusion is inferable only from the newspaper's surprise at the men's indignation at the conclusion. If *yet* were omitted, the second sentence would come in logically enough as an explanation of what the men's ' line ' referred to had actually been.
Sir,—I doubt if sufficient attention has been drawn to the injustice of throwing on the landlord in whose house they happen to be resident the cost of a large additional insurance benefit for those who are sick. Yet, under Clause 51, a sick tenant would be able to live rent free for a year at the expense of his or her landlord. This is a less glaring case. The

essence of the *Yet* sentence is that a tenant has power to injure a landlord. What is that in contrast with ? with the fact that justice would protect landlords ; that is, not with the main sentence preceding, which is a statement of why the writer is writing, but with a mere inference from a noun that occurs in it, viz *injustice.* As in the first example, the logical work of the second sentence is to explain the nature of a noun contained in the first, viz (again) *injustice,* but an explanation is presented in the guise of an opposition ; the sentence would do its work properly if *yet* were omitted.

Yiddish is not a kind of Hebrew, but a kind of German. As misconception is common, the OED definition follows : The language used by Jews in Europe & America, consisting mainly of German (orig. from the Middle Rhine area) with admixture (according to local or individual usage) of Balto-Slavic words, & printed in Hebrew characters.

yodel, vb, has *-lled, -lling* ; -LL-, -L-.
yoke, vb, makes *-kable* ; see MUTE E.
yokel makes *yokelish* ; -LL-, -L-, 2.
yon. See WARDOUR STREET.
Yorkshire pudding. No hyphen ; see HYPHENS 3 B.
young. For *Y. Chevalier, Y. Pretender,* see SOBRIQUETS.
yours. For misuses in place of *your,* see ABSOLUTE POSSESSIVES. For epistolary uses, LETTER FORMS.
youth. Plural pron.-dhz; -TH & -DH.

Z

Zarathustrian. See ZOROASTRIAN.
Zeitgeist. Pronounce tsī'tgĭst.
zemstvo. Pl. *-os* ; see -O(E)S 6.
zephyr. See WIND, n.
zero. Pl. *-os* ; see -O(E)S 3.

ZEUGMA. Pl. *-as* or *-ata.* The meaning of the word & its relation to *syllepsis* are explained under *syllepsis* in TECHNICAL TERMS. Intentional use of these figures has been so much overdone as to be now a peculiarly exasperating form of WORN-OUT HUMOUR. To judge from the few specimens below, it is unfortunately still in favour with dramatic critics. The first example is perhaps not of the intentional kind meant to amuse, & is, as an established formula, hardly realized to be a syllepsis. *Sir Charles Wilson (U.), the newly elected member for Central Leeds,* took *the* oath *& his* seat./*Mr Basil Sydney played the Duke quite ably; & the* flood *of* flowers *& enthusiasm was terrific./ Half-clad stokers toiled in an atmosphere consisting of one part air to ten parts mixed* perspiration, coal-dust, & profanity./*And the rest was Miss McCarthy playing parody with languor,* washing clothes with happiness & Pears' soap, *& playing the business man with energy./Impassively malignant Chinamen scramble after each other* in *hot* haste, *& three-line* paragraphs.

zigzag, vb, has *-gged, -gging*; -G-, -GG-.

zinc, n. & vb. Inflexions & derivatives give trouble with spelling & pronunciation. The forms *zinced* & *zincing* are obviously wrong; cf., from nouns in -c, *trafficking, mimicked, panicky, picnicker, bivouacked*; the c, clearly, is not allowed to come before the English suffixes -ing, -ed, -er, & -y, the change of sound to s being before them intolerable; *zinc* differs from *traffic* & the others in having a consonant before the c instead of i or a, & the natural result of that is that *zinked* & *zinking* are better than *zincked, zincking*. Before classical suffixes, as -ism, -ist, there is, on the other hand, no objection to the s sound,

for which compare *cynicism, criticism, classicist, rubricist*; & in *physicist* by the side of *physicked & physicking* we have a proof of this distinction between the English & the classical suffixes when attached to the same word. The forms should therefore be (with c pronounced as s before i, according to the regular custom) : *zinked; zinking; zinkish; zinky*; but *zincic; zinciferous; zincify; zinco-*; *zincoid*.

Zingaro. Fem. *-ara*; pl. *-arĭ.*
zithern. See CITHERN.
zodiac. A dictionary definition may be quoted as likely to be useful :—A belt of the heavens outside which the sun & moon & major planets do not pass divided crosswise into twelve equal areas called *signs of the z.* each named after a zodiacal constellation formerly but not now contained in it (signs of the z. : Aries or Ram, Taurus or Bull, Gemini or Twins, Cancer or Crab, Leo or Lion, Virgo or Virgin, Libra or Balance or Scales, Scorpio or Scorpion, Sagittarius or Archer, Capricornus or Capricorn or Goat, Aquarius or Water-carrier, Pisces or Fishes).

zollverein. Pronounce tsŏ'lferīn.
Zoo. See CURTAILED WORDS.
Zoroastrian, *Zarathustrian.* For the substitution of *Zarathustra* &c., see DIDACTICISM, & MAHOMET.
Zulu. For pronunciation see U, 4.
zwieback. Pronounce tswē'bahk.

-Z-, - ZZ-. In *buz(z), fiz(z), quiz,* & *whiz(z),* there is no need for a second z, & when it appears it is doubtless due to the influence of inflected forms like *buzzer, quizzed, & whizzing,* in which it serves to show that ĭ & ŭ, not ī & ū, are the sounds ; *buz, fiz, quiz, & whiz,* are recommended.

APPENDIX

FOWLER'S PRONUNCIATION PREFERENCES

One of the interesting uses of the *Dictionary* is to see it as a guide to the changes in the pronunciation of words which have taken place during the past century. The following list identifies the main items where the pronunciation Fowler observes or recommends is not the one we use today. Several more are listed at **NOUN & ADJECTIVE ACCENT**.

abdomen	conduit	leeward
accomplice	consistory	machination
acoustic	consols	-most
almoner	constable	offing
amateur	consummate (*adj.*)	often
amenity	costume	plethora
amour	coulomb	pogrom
anchovy	cretin	premature
angina	culinary	primates
baths	damning	privacy
caliph	decorous	rabies
camellia	despicable	rationale
catacomb	detour	refutable
caveat	disputable	regiment
caviar	enema	remonstrate
cervical	espionage	retro-
ceteris	expletive	salve
chagrin	fantasia	scabies
chaperone	fasten	seer
chloroform	forehead	ski
cicada	gibberish	soften
clandestine	gladiolus	species
clarify	hair shirt	strategic
clematis	hangar	tortoise
clientele	honorarium	untoward
cloth	ibidem	vagary
codify	indiscreet	vermouth
cognizance	kiln	vertigo
combat	kow-tow	waistcoat
commissionaire	laboratory	ware
concerto	largesse	wristband

NOTES ON THE ENTRIES

a, an: '*a historical* should be said & written'

In the late twentieth century the old use of *an* before an unaccented syllable beginning with *h* (e.g. *historic, habitual, horrific*) began to reassert itself in written English, especially in the UK. It also began to be used in speech, despite the at times awkward pronunciation.

aborigines: 'the adj. *aboriginal* used as a noun is the best singular'

The situation, especially in Australia, is more complex today. Usage is divided, with some people finding *Aborigine* (now always capitalized for Australian indigenous people) demeaning, and others (including the people themselves) having no problem with it. Official documents have vacillated over time, with usage in the early 2000s favouring *Aboriginal* for both noun and adjective. However, *Aborigine* remains the most common general usage.

accept of: 'We can still *accept of* a gift or favour, *of* a person's love . . . though even these phrases tend to become archaic.'

This usage is now obsolete, but still encountered in situations where older usage is privileged, such as some religious, legal, and literary writing.

accessary, accessory: 'The words . . . are often confused; but a fairly clear line of distinction can be made out.'

Not any longer. The latter spelling is now the norm, and the former is these days encountered only in occasional legal contexts.

acoustic: 'Pronunciation varies between -ow- & -ōō-. . . . If the word came into popular use, it would probably be with -ow-, which even now perhaps tends to prevail.'

This shows the dangers of trying to predict the future. Fowler could hardly have anticipated the huge developments in acoustic science, with acoustic guitars and a host of other devices all employing the *-oo-* pronunciation, and making *-ow-* obsolete.

advocate: 'is not idiomatically followed by a *that-* clause'

This construction is normal usage today, commoner than the more formal verbal-noun construction.

Æ, Œ: 'all words in common enough use to have begun to waver between the double letter & the simple e . . . should be written with the e alone'

It is odd that Fowler here makes no mention of the standard use of the *e* spelling in American English, which would greatly influence British spelling later in the century. It is also notable that there is no separate entry for *Americanism* (though there is one for *Briticism*), despite the many references in the entries to American usage. Perhaps this stemmed from the controversial reaction to the anti-Americanism expressed in *The King's English* twenty years before. He frequently referred to his lack of experience in dealing with American English.

aery, aerie, eyry, eyrie: 'The first two forms are preferable'
This is on etymological grounds—and illustrates the point that usage consensus pays no attention to etymology, for today's standard spelling is *eyrie* in the UK, with *aerie* more common in the USA.

agenda: 'If a singular is required (= one item on the agenda) it is now *agendum*'
Modern usage has totally dispensed with *agendum*. The expression 'an item on the agenda' is now the standard way of referring to an individual point.

aggravate, aggravation: 'a feminine or childish colloquialism'
The ferocity of this entry is a good example of the way Fowler's obsession with etymology knocks out his usual high regard for usage. The use of these words to mean 'vex, annoy' (as opposed to the etymological sense of 'make [an evil] worse') had been in English since the early seventeenth century, and is widely found in the novels of Dickens and Thackeray, to name but two. It was primarily Fowler's stance on the matter that kept antagonism to this usage alive in the twentieth century. The semantic history of these words is not over yet, as illustrated by the later development of *aggravation* to mean 'aggressive confrontation', shortened to *aggro* in the 1960s.

aim: 'The verb in the metaphorical sense of purpose . . . is idiomatically followed by *at* with the gerund & not by *to* with the infinitive.'
Not any more. Usage today is evenly split, with a slight bias for *to* in corpus counts. We can see the split in cases like this pair of examples from BBC News Online (1 August 2007). The headline reads 'Tories aim to end forced marriage', but the first paragraph has 'The Conservatives have outlined proposals aimed at cracking down on forced marriages'. Doubtless the American usage, which Fowler recognizes, has been influential.

-AL NOUNS: 'there is no work for them [i.e. *revisal, refutal, appraisal, accusal*] that cannot be adequately done by the more ordinary verbal nouns'
Fowler's evaluation of 'needless' *-al* nouns has proved accurate, on the whole—but he was wrong about *appraisal*, which has now largely replaced *appraisement* as standard usage.

alarm, alarum: 'This being a clear & useful differentiation, it is to be regretted that *alarm-clock* . . . should . . . be reviving.'
This is a good illustration of how subjective the criterion of 'usefulness' is. Plainly, people have not found the distinction useful, except perhaps in poetry. It is not a question of meanings being lost, for all that has happened is that *alarm* is now used for both meanings ('fear' and 'warning'), context evidently being enough to differentiate the two. The meanings are close enough, however, to allow people to make jokes when they see such notices as 'This door is alarmed'.

alien: '& the truth seems rather that *to* is getting the upper hand'
It was—and today *alien to* is the norm. Fowler's entry is illuminating in the light it throws on a usage change evidently taking place in the early 1900s.

align(ment), aline(ment): 'The OED pronounces for the spelling with ne & against that with gn.'

Here is Fowler daring to take on the prestigious *OED*—and winning, for usage today has voted for *alignment*. Google in 2008 had 86 million *gn*'s to 76,000 *ne*'s. Many dictionaries do still record the alternative form.

alleluia: 'The spelling now usual is *hallelujah*.'
It depends which denomination one is thinking of. It was certainly the dominant spelling in the dissenting Protestant tradition, and it can be seen in such usages as the Salvation Army *hallelujah-lass*. But in the Roman Catholic and mainstream Anglican tradition, the preferred usage was always *alleluia*, as it is today. Usage is therefore split. The famous chorus from Handel's *Messiah* is spelled with an *H* as opposed to an *A* in a ratio of about 10 : 1. (See also **hallelujah, halleluiah, alleluia**.)

all right: 'The words should always be written separate'
The controversy continues to rumble on today, despite the fact that dictionary usage, including the *OED*, has come down firmly in favour of recognizing both spellings. Sentence pairs such as *The answers are all right* (= 'all correct') vs *The answers are alright* (= 'satisfactory') show it is a useful distinction. The analogy of *altogether* from *all together*, *already* from *all ready*, and other such developments show that the merger of two words into one is an ancient process in English. The entry illustrates Fowler's powerful influence: nobody worried about it until he condemned it, here and in other writing. What is puzzling is why he sees the usefulness of the distinction in his entry on *altogether*, but refuses to allow it here. (Later pedants would take Fowler to task for not writing 'separately' instead of 'separate', in his opening sentence. See also **slow(ly)**.)

almoner: 'it is perhaps safe to prophesy that the pronunciation ah´moner . . . will prevail.'
The analogy with *alms* has not been enough to stop the increased use of the spelling-pronunciation with /l/. It is the dominant form in the USA, and is given as a regular alternative in UK dictionaries, such as the *OED*.

amateur: 'it is high time that vain attempts at giving the French -eur should cease'
They didn't. Despite the strong statement, this is the pronunciation which has prevailed. Fowler's 'amatoor' preference is now rarely heard.

amenity: 'the restoration of -mēn- (Latin *amoenus*) is pedantic'
The pronunciation with 'mean' is now normal in the UK; the sound of 'men' is preferred in American English.

among, amongst: 'It may be said with some confidence'
A nice example of Fowler the linguist at his best, looking carefully at usage patterns. Today his intuitions are confirmed: *among* is far more frequent than *amongst*. In British English it is the preferred form in nearly 80 per cent of cases, and in American English in well over 90 per cent. Larger samples show that there is no phonetic reason for the distinction, as Fowler thought might be the case. Which one you use seems to be a matter of personal taste, though regional background may have a role, as the *-st* ending on several words (e.g. *amidst, alongst*) is still widespread in parts of the UK. (See also **while (or whilst)**.)

amour: 'it is better pronounced with the normal English accent' (ă´moor)'

In fact the French accentuation has become the norm, despite it being, in Fowler's view, 'very undesirable'. A pronunciation with stress on the first syllable is no longer listed in the *English Pronouncing Dictionary*, in neither British nor American English.

amuck: 'the familiar spelling should . . . be maintained'

But in fact *amok* has become the norm, being used twelve times as often in British English and twenty-five times as often in American English. The reason for the change isn't clear: perhaps the association with *muck* weighed against it.

anchoret, anchorite: 'The OED states that the two forms are now equally common.'

Not any more. The latest edition states that anchorite 'is now usual'. Evidently the influence of the familiar *-ite* ending outweighed the etymological considerations which Fowler preferred.

and, 3: 'There is no agreement at present on the punctuation'

There is now, for one of Fowler's examples. The use of a comma between subject and verb, as in his example *Every man, woman, & child, was killed*, is now universally rejected in punctuation manuals. But there is still optional variation before *and* in an adjective sequence. Fowler preferred to keep the 'serial comma', as it later came to be called, following the practice of Oxford University Press (the usage is also called the 'Oxford comma'), and it is the dominant usage in the USA. Cambridge University Press, by contrast, avoids it.

appal(l): 'The double l is better'

But here, as in so many instances of this kind, Fowler does not say why. In fact, it is an unusual choice for him, for *appall* was becoming the spelling norm in American English (along with a few other words, such as *enthrall*), as opposed to *appal* in British English.

authoress: 'is a word regarded with dislike in literary circles'

It is interesting that objections to this word were already being voiced in the 1920s; they are not simply the consequences of modern feminism. Fowler, however, wanted the distinction to be maintained.

awake: 'rarely *woke* or *woken*'

Usage has opted for the *o*-forms in many cases today. Fowler's *I should like to be waked at 7.30* now sounds archaic.

barytone, -ritone: 'The first is the best spelling.'

Writers on music, Fowler says, 'are not yet irrevocably committed' to *baritone*. They are now.

basal, basic: '*fundamental* should be substituted in . . . *the basic idea*'

Fowler's sense that basic is 'unnecessary & incongruous' has long been overtaken by usage. *Basal* remains a specialized use, especially in science. *Basic* has become the norm for 'more important or necessary than anything else', and can be used in relation to quite everyday matters—we talk about *basic needs*, *ingredients* (in a recipe), and *words* (in learning a language). It has also developed the meaning 'first level' or 'ridiculously easy' (*that's basic*). As a result, *fundamental* has narrowed its meaning, referring to a deeper or more serious level, and is more widely used with reference to major issues and processes: we talk about *fundamental beliefs* or *changes* (in a political system). A *fundamental difference* suggests something more profound than a *basic difference*. But there is still an overlap: people talk *of basic principles* or *fundamental principles* with little if any difference in meaning. Most people would find *basic fundamental principles* tautologous.

bath: 'Pl. pron. bahdhz'
The voiced form, with *th* as in *seethe*, is still used; but it has now been supplemented by the voiceless form, with *th* as in *wreath*. If you pronounce *bath* with a short *a*, as is normal in the north of England, you would only use the voiceless form.

because: 'After such openings as . . . *The reason why . . . is*'
It is noteworthy that Fowler does not criticize this usage, though later commentators often did.

below, under: 'There is a fairly clear distinction between the prepositions'
The examples show that a simple distinction was not possible in Fowler's day. *Under* has continued to 'encroach', especially with certain types of phrase, such as numerical comparisons: *below the age of* has around a million hits on Google (in 2008), whereas *under the age of* has twice has many. *Under my breath* has now virtually replaced *below my breath*.

betterment: 'the English for *betterment*, which is *improvement*'
Etymologically, *better* is actually the more native form: it is from Old English, whereas *improve* is from Old French.

between: '1. *B you & I* '
From the brevity of the treatment, it would seem that concern over this usage was not as marked in Fowler's time as it is today. He is right in his comment: the usage has emerged as a 'hypercorrection'. People who had had their natural use of *It is me* corrected to the Latinate *It is I* in schools assumed that other cases where *me* was strongly stressed were equally suspect. The frequency and prominence of *between you and me* at the beginning of a sentence (it is often a discourse opener) made it particularly susceptible to change. Although the *I* usage can be traced back to Shakespeare and before, the issue has exasperated modern language pundits, even to the extent of appearing as part of a book title on proper usage. It is actually quite a rare construction in either form, especially in formal written English, where the meaning of confidentiality makes its use unlikely. (See also **I**.)

bi-: 'the *bi-* hybrids should . . . be allowed to perish'
People seem no happier today with the potential ambiguity of *bi-* in *biannually*, *bimonthly*, and *biweekly*, which context often does not resolve (as in *bimonthly magazine*). This is the only numeral prefix which allows two meanings—'two' and 'twice', and it is the latter which causes the confusion. (*Bi-* meaning 'two' is normal in many words, such as *bicycle* and *bifocals*.) Even if you know the meaning, there is no guarantee that your reader will

interpret your usage in the way you intend. As a result, there is a strong tendency to replace the 'twice' meaning with a phrase (*twice a month*), or to use an alternative (*semi-monthly*).

big, great, large: 'The differences in meaning & usage cannot be exhaustively set forth'

Not in this kind of book, certainly. The *OED* distinguishes ten main senses of *big*, fifteen of *large*, and twenty of *great*, along with various restricted or idiomatic uses. Fowler's is a brave effort to summarize the main differences, but there are too many exceptions to permit a clear picture to emerge.

billion, trillion, quadrillion, &c.: 'a billion is a thousand thousand thousands'

This American use (10^9) emerged in the nineteenth century, under the influence of French, and slowly became the dominant one throughout the English-speaking world during the second half of the twentieth century. However, the earlier meaning of 'a million millions' is still encountered, and the risk of ambiguity suggests that in critical contexts the values should be spelled out in numerals.

blond(e): 'The *-e* should be dropped'

Today *blonde* is twice as common as *blond*. An unusual natural gender distinction seems to have emerged, with people associating the *blonde* spelling with females. But usage varies: some people reserve *blonde* for the noun and *blond* for the adjective, regardless of sex.

bluebell: 'In the south'

This is an untypical entry for Fowler, introducing dialect differences and the kind of descriptive detail which would be more in place in an encyclopedia. Reference to some other encyclopedic entries is made in my Introduction.

brainy: 'is . . . an Americanism'

The usage has now become part of international standard English, adding a specific nuance of 'especially good at studying' to the more general notions of *intelligent* or *clever*. However, many people still feel *brainy* to be an informal word, and prefer the genteel Latinate *intelligent* to its Anglo-Saxon directness in formal speaking or writing.

bravo, brava, bravi

The distinction might appeal to some opera-goers, but is virtually unknown elsewhere. *Brava* has an entry in the *OED*, but there is no mention of *bravi*. (See also **viva, vivat, vive**.)

Briticism: 'should be either *Britannicism* or *Britishism*'

Britannicism is rare indeed—a mere thirty-one instances on Google (in 2008) and no mention in the *OED*. *Britishism* seems to have won, with 20,000 instances on Google, but Fowler's criticism has not stopped people using *Briticism*, which garners a healthy 14,000.

brochure, pamphlet: '*B*. has no right to exist in English, since it is not needed by the side of *p*.'

Later usage has proved Fowler wrong. There is a major difference today between the contexts in which we typically use *brochure* and *pamphlet*, though there is still some overlap. *Brochures* are leaflets which advertise something;

pamphlets present information or argument. We are more likely to encounter *political pamphlets* rather than *political brochures* and *travel brochures* rather than *travel pamphlets*. Fowler does not mention *flier* (or *flyer*)—despite its first recorded use being 1889—which has become popular since the 1960s.

burgle: 'it is to be hoped that *burgle* may . . . become generally current'
Indeed it has, especially in the passive (*our house was burgled*). The 'facetiousness' which Fowler sensed has now gone. This makes it unlikely that US *burglarize* will make much headway in British English.

cachet: 'should be expelled as an alien'
The first recorded use in the sense of 'distinguishing mark' is found in Thackeray, in 1840, so it was not particularly new even in Fowler's day. It has since developed a more abstract sense of 'prestigious quality'. But its unusual spelling and pronunciation has given it a foreign character which remains today. *Cachet* has a certain—cachet.

café: 'is naturalized in the sense coffee-house'
The accent, of course, is not a natural feature of the English alphabet. It is surprising that Fowler does not talk about it, for the practice of omitting it was known in the 1920s. Indeed, the writer of a Society for Pure English Tract in 1929 expresses his concern that, if the accent were dropped, people would soon pronounce the word to rhyme with *safe*.

camellia: 'the mispronunciation -mē- . . . will no doubt give way to -mĕ-'
Fowler is noting the double consonant, which would normally motivate the preceding vowel to be short in English (compare *fell* vs *feline*). Originally pronounced with a short vowel (the plant was named after a Moravian botanist named Kamel), the single -*l*- spelling in European languages began to influence the way the word was spelled in English, and the long vowel emerged as a natural consequence. It is now the dominant pronunciation, even among people who spell the word with -*ll*-.

caption: 'is rare in British use'
No longer. There are 37 million instances on Google (in 2008). Surprisingly, Fowler does not mention the verb use ('to provide with a caption'), which was coming into English around 1900.

carafe: 'a GENTEELISM'
Today the usage has become standard in such contexts as *a carafe of wine*.

carpet: '*on the c.* (under discussion)'
The phrase itself is now obsolete in this meaning: modern usage is *on the table*. However, the phrase is still common in the sense of 'receiving a reprimand'.

cartel: 'expected to accent the last syllable for some time at least'
This pronunciation has now become standard, for this meaning.

cease: 'the poets & the rhetoricians'
And the lawyers. The main modern use of the term is legal, in such phrases as *cease and desist*. Any letter from a lawyer asking you to stop doing something will probably say *cease* rather than *stop*. The word is also used in military

contexts (*cease fire*) and remains in colloquial use in the idiom *wonders never cease*.

chanty, sh-: 'Spell *c-*, but pronounce shă-'

This recommendation of an unusual pronunciation for *ch-* never stood much chance of catching on, and modern spelling is now normally *sh-*. Only clearly French words have retained the *sh-* pronunciation, such as *Chablis*, *chaconne*, and *charlatan*.

chaperon: 'a final e is wrong'

Not any more. The *-e* spelling is today the norm, and the associated pronunciation has stress on the first syllable and an ending rhyming with *tone*.

char-à-banc: 'if the spelling . . . *charabanc*, could be introduced'

Fowler would be happy to see that this is now the normal spelling. His other suggestion, *sharabang*, never caught on. There are no instances recorded in the *OED*.

childish: '*childish* is in some danger of being restricted to the deprecatory use'

The negative meaning is now the dominant one. It is unusual to see it used in a positive way, though this is still possible in a strongly affirming context, such as *childish delight*.

Chinaman: 'normal uses'

None of these uses are found today. The word (along with *Chinee*) is found only in derogatory contexts, and has generally been replaced by *Chinese*.

chiropodist: 'is a BARBARISM & a GENTEELISM'

The Institute of Chiropodists and Podiatrists would presumably disagree. Fowler is objecting to the curious etymology (apparently a combination of the Greek words for 'hand' and 'foot'), but the word had been in the language for over a century, by the time he was writing. The *OED* finds it first used in 1785.

clari(o)net: 'the *-onet* form is in more general use'

No longer. The *OED* examples are all from the nineteenth century.

clause: 'applied only to . . . a *subordinate c.*'

This was not normal practice in traditional grammar, and the restriction is never found in a modern grammar. It is a Fowlerian idiosyncrasy.

clerk: 'due to excessive respect for spelling'

Fowler omits to mention that the *er* pronunciation is standard in American English.

cliché

It is surprising, to modern readers, that Fowler does not devote more space to clichés. The issue seems not to have been as contentious then, probably because the term in its linguistic sense was so recent: the *OED* has a first recorded use of 1892.

close: 'instead of *shut*'

This is one of Fowler's more surprising objections. *Close* in its sense of 'shut an opening' has been in English since the thirteenth century. Fowler misses the sense distinction, well summarized by the entry in the *OED*: '*Close* is . . . a more general word, to *shut* being properly only a way of closing; hence the former is generally used when the notion is that of the resulting state, rather than the process.' There is nothing genteel about it at all.

co-: 'the spelling printed is to be taken as recommended'
Usage varies enormously in the use of the hyphen, and modern dictionaries recognize alternatives in most cases. For example, *cooperate* is now the norm (31 million instances on Google in 2008), but *co-operate* still has over 2 million instances. The general trend is for hyphens to be dropped, except in cases where it presents readers with a real reading difficulty (as in *co-workers*, *co-opt*). But preferences vary among publishers.

coastal: 'should be abandoned'
Quite the contrary has happened. *Coastal* is now the normal adjectival use in all kinds of contexts—*coastal erosion, coastal weather forecasts, coastal defences*, and so on.

codify: 'Pronounce kŏ-, not kō-.'
Notwithstanding the list of similar words with short vowels, *codify* has developed a pronunciation with a long vowel, probably because of a dislike of the association with *cod*. The short vowel is not even listed as an alternative in the 1997 (15th) edition of the *English Pronouncing Dictionary*.

cognizance, cognizant, cognizable, cognize: '*Cognize* alone has the *-g-* always sounded.'
Not any more. The *-g-* has spread through the whole paradigm, and is now the primary pronunciation given in dictionaries.

collocutor, colloquist, interlocutor: 'are rival candidates'
Fowler's preference for *collocutor* had no effect. *Interlocutor* became increasingly popular in the late nineteenth century and this carried over into the twentieth, ultimately becoming the standard form.

colossal: 'in the sense not of enormous . . . is . . . not deserving adoption'
This usage developed towards the end of the nineteenth century (the first recorded uses include Twain and Shaw), and became fashionable slang in the 1920s and 1930s, when Fowler was compiling his book. It has a dated feel today, and is probably on its way out.

come-at-able, get-at-able: 'the experiment has not been successfully repeated, & probably will not be'
Fowler was wrong. During the middle decades of the twentieth century several more such coinages emerged, such as *unputdownable, unswitchoffable*, and *unwearoutable*.

commiserate: 'the OED gives no quotation showing *with*'
It does now. Indeed, with uncharacteristic humour, the *OED* editors actually quote Fowler's words, then follow it up with three quotations using *with*, and comment: 'The only current usage.'

computable, -ative: 'the accent . . . will probably settle on the first syllables'
This shows how difficult it is to predict accent movement in English. It is the second syllable that usually has the accent in modern usage, British and American, though a first-syllable accentuation is sometimes heard.

concept: 'should be left to the philosophers'

And, these days, to the advertisers and designers, in such phrases as *a total furnishing concept*. Usage has grown, especially since the 1970s.

confer(r)able: 'accent . . . fixed'

The accent on *transferable* may have been fixed on the first syllable in Fowler's time, but it isn't now. The usual pronunciation today emphasizes the second syllable—a pattern which follows the natural rhythm of the language in such phrases as *trans<u>fer</u>able <u>vote</u>*, avoiding a sequence of three unstressed syllables. (See also **refutable, irrefutable**.)

confiscate . . . congratulate: 'makes *confiscable* . . . [*congratu*]*lable*'

Here, and with the many other *-ate* verbs listed in the book (*conjugate, coordinate, corroborate, decorate*, etc), the *-ate-* forms increased in frequency during the twentieth century, though not usually overtaking the shorter alternatives. Intuitions are divided because of the existence of some *-ate* verbs where the *-atable* ending is obligatory (such as *translatable*), and Fowler himself goes in the other direction, from time to time (e.g. recommending *designatable*). Some of his recommendations, such as *suffocable*, now seem archaic.

conservative: 'ridiculous . . . in the sense of moderate'

This sense originated in American English at the end of the nineteenth century, but *The Times* was using *conservative estimate* and other such phrases as early as 1915. The usage is now standard.

content(s): 'still almost always accented on the last [syllable]'

Not any more. The *OED* editors noted the change taking place as early as the 1890s, 'especially among young people', so that even by the 1920s 'almost always' was probably an overstatement.

contradictious, -tory: 'if either word is to be used, it must be *-tious*'

Fowler's preference was ignored. Standard usage is now *contradictory*. The *OED* has no instance of *contradictious* later than 1859.

criterion

It would seem, from the shortness of the note, that the use of *criteria* as a singular was not an issue in Fowler's day, but it has certainly become one since—dictionary examples date from the 1940s. Today, its use as a new collective singular noun is increasing in speech (along with a new plural *criterias* alongside older *criterions*) and is often seen in unmoderated written language (e.g. on the Internet), so it seems likely that the new forms will become standard in a generation or so, along with other similar formations (especially *data* and *media*). In the meantime, standard English as represented in dictionaries and style guides remains resolutely opposed to any change.

critique: 'some hope of its dying out'

In fact it became established, with a nuance (of greater sharpness or incisiveness in the criticism) that is lacking in the other words Fowler lists.

curb, kerb: 'The second is a variant merely'

Modern usage distinguishes *curb*, standard in American and Canadian English, from *kerb*, standard in British and Australian English. *Curb* in the latter is used only in the sense of 'restrain'.

data: 'is plural only'
  The controversy over the use of *data* as a singular is still very much alive, and many authors take pains to avoid using the word in contexts where the choice would be contentious. These contexts are not many, however: some 80 per cent of the uses of *data* are neutral with respect to grammatical agreement (*downloading the data, access to data*, etc.). What seems to have happened is that *data* has developed a use as a mass noun (*data is*), in addition to its traditional use as a count noun (*data are*), the two forms meeting different semantic needs—the former being used when one wants to talk about items of information as a whole, the latter when one wants to draw attention to their individuality or separability.

deal: 'in the sense of a piece of bargaining . . . is still slang'
  The word has since entered standard English, though retaining its colloquial character, not least because of its continued use in such informal phrases as *raw deal, square deal*, and *big deal*.

dean: 'unfamiliar GALLICISM'
  Hardly unfamiliar, in the 1920s. The usage is known from the seventeenth century, and in its university, monastic, and other uses in the sense of 'senior person' it dates from the 1200s.

decent: 'makes *-er, -est*'
  Not any more. The word has aligned with other polysyllabic adjectives, so that the norm today is *more decent* and *most decent*.

decimate: 'is naturally extended'
  Fowler's balanced view is noteworthy. He allows the extension of meaning in general contexts while noting that a juxtaposition of the verb with a numerical value other than 'tenth' would feel incongruous to those aware of the etymological meaning.

declinal, declination, declinature: 'attempts to provide *decline* with a noun'
  It is surprising that Fowler does not mention *declining*, which (in the sense of 'refusal') is known from the early seventeenth century. This is the word that has now filled the gap.

depend: 'The slovenly construction . . . is growing common'
  It is now standard informal English, a contrast still available with the more formal *depend upon*. The two usages have similar frequencies for many common locutions: for example, *depends on what you mean* and *depends what you mean* both turn up with around 15 million instances in Google in 2008.

dialectal, -ic, -ical: '*dialectal* has recently been formed & found acceptance'
  Indeed it has, and especially in linguistics, but in general use there is still uncertainty about it, for it will often be heard replaced by *dialectical*.

different: 'objections to *d. to* . . . are mere pedantries'
  Fowler's arguments in favour of the *to* usage were influential, but they have not displaced *from*, which is used about five times more frequently in British English. It is to be noted that he does not even mention the American use of *different than*, which is also used in British English in such sentences as *The answer was different —— we expected* and sometimes in other constructions too.

dike, dyke: 'The first is the right form.'

This is one of Fowler's less helpful entries. The forms in Old English were spelled with an *i*, but *y* is found from the fourteenth century, and as a result practice is split in the UK. The usual spelling of *Offa's Dyke* is with a *y*, for example, and *y* outnumbers *i* on Google by over 2 to 1 (in 2008). However, this is partly because of another application of the word (= 'lesbian') which has arisen since the 1940s. Here, US usage makes a distinction, with *dike* being used for the earlier sense, and *dyke* for the later.

diplomat(ist): 'The longer English formation is preferable'

Usage has gone the other way. *Diplomatist* was already dying out at the end of the nineteenth century, and is only sporadically used today.

discomfit: 'too weak or indefinite a sense'

It is surprising that Fowler is so against the less definite sense, which dates from the fourteenth century. Both senses are found in Shakespeare. 'The Earl of Douglas is discomfited', says King Henry to Westmorland in *Henry IV Part 1* (I. i. 67). 'Be not so discomfited', says Baptista to Hortensio in *The Taming of the Shrew* (II. i. 163). Today, it is the indefinite sense which is standard, and the sense of 'utterly defeat' is obsolete.

disgustful: 'unobjectionable'

The word is still listed in some dictionaries, but with only around 30,000 entries on Google (in 2008) against over 14 million for *disgusting* it seems destined for obsolescence.

disinterested

It is surprising that Fowler does not comment on the issue of this word vs *uninterested*, for the overlap of meaning was certainly present in his day. Indeed, it can be traced back to the seventeenth century. The first recorded use of *disinterested* meaning 'uninterested' is 1612; *disinterested* meaning 'impartial' is later, 1659. The earlier usage was never replaced, however, and today around a quarter of all instances of *disinterested* mean 'uninterested', and other senses of this word are emerging, such as 'losing interest' (as in *John and Mary have become disinterested in each other in recent weeks*). Context usually makes it clear which sense is intended; but there are enough cases of ambiguity to fuel the arguments of those who feel an important semantic distinction is being lost.

dream: 'in poetry & in impressive contexts'

The past-tense choice is more fundamental, and is now recognized to be one of aspect, a grammatical term Fowler does not include. *Dreamt* tends to be used for single, short, and determinate instances of dreaming, where the dreamer is asleep (*I dreamt last night I was in Italy*); *dreamed* tends to be used for a more continuous and indefinable dreaming, where the dreamer is awake (*I dreamed of meeting you all week*). There is some overlap, though not in contexts where the 'awake' sense is clear, such as day-dreaming, which gives rise to *I day-dreamed*, not *I day-dreamt*. (See also **-T & -ED**.)

due: 'is impossible'

The battle to preserve the obscure grammatical distinction between *due to* (adjectival only) and *owing to* (adverbial as well as adjectival) was already lost in Fowler's day: the entry **owing to** says that it is now 'perpetually infringed'. *Due to* has simply followed the path of becoming a compound preposition—a path that *owing to* had already travelled a century before (receiving the same kind of objection in the process). The controversy has left a hint of formality difference between the two usages (with *owing to* slightly more formal than *due to*), but both are now firmly established in standard English. (See also **UNATTACHED PARTICIPLES**.)

either: 'ī . . . is displacing ē . . . & will probably prevail.'
The *i* pronunciation (rhyming with *my*) has certainly become the commoner usage in the UK; but the *e* pronunciation (rhyming with *me*) is commoner in the US. However, usage remains divided on both sides of the Atlantic, being much affected by regional preferences.

elevator: 'a cumbrous & needless Americanism'
Its length compared with *lift* has not prevented the word from becoming standard US English; and through the influence of films and television the American usage has become increasingly used in British English.

enormous, enormity: 'suspicion of pedantry . . . of ignorance'
This is one of Fowler's more obscure entries, because of the juxtaposition of adjective and noun, but whatever the situation in the 1920s, the supposed difference between the words (*enormous* for physical size, *enormity* for moral intensity) is not maintained today. The reason is probably that people felt uncomfortable with the cumbersome noun *enormousness*, and *enormity* gradually took its place (the latter being used today around fifty times more often (in 2008), as a search on Google will quickly show).

entire: 'may as well become rarer'
Apart from in a few specialist areas, such as stamp-collecting, the noun use seems now to be obsolescent.

envisage: 'surely undesirable'
The word, first recorded in Keats's *Hyperion* in 1820, was already well established in the UK by the time Fowler was writing, so it is difficult to understand his objection to it. He might rather have been expected to turn his guns on *envision*, whose first recorded use (by Lytton Strachey) was contemporary (1921), and which is now the dominant use in American English.

epic: 'it is probably new'
Fowler was writing before the era of blockbuster films. Despite recommending *Homeric* here, in his entry **epopee** he seems to accept it has become established.

-ER & -EST, MORE & MOST: '2 . . . . awkward . . . can take *-er* & *-est*'
These last examples, common in Dickens and other nineteenth-century writers, illustrate the changeable nature of the comparative constructions in English, notable in the very different system used by (for example) Shakespeare (*more rarer, most unkindest*). Today they use the periphrastic construction. The same change has affected *seldom* and *often*, referred to under point 3. *More/most often/seldom* are today the norm, with the inflected forms encountered occasionally.

even: '1. . . . in the wrong place'

Fowler's solution does not work: *very* changes the meaning, and his suggestion to put *even* after *names* is not only 'uncomfortable' but positively misleading, as it would then modify *I*. The illustration he uses presents what is sometimes called a pseudo-problem: the general emphatic sense of *even* does not necessarily call for a semantic contrast, any more than it would if the modifying adverb had been *actually*.

ever: 'should be a separate word'

Fowler's influence here was long-lasting, but the predominant modern usage is to write these words solid—for example, *however* is a thousand times more common on Google (in 2008) than *how ever*. He was wrong to call the usage 'uneducated or ultra-colloquial': it certainly tends to be colloquial, reflecting its expressive function, but it is used by people regardless of their educational background. (See also **what ever, whatever**.)

every one: 'This dictionary's opinion'

Usage has on the whole followed Fowler's recommendations, though other language pundits (such as Ernest Gowers) later expressed the opposite preference. Today, *no-one* is commoner in British English and *no one* in American English, but there is considerable variation among publishing houses. The 'misleading' appearance of *noone* has kept its usage low.

exit: 'are apt to forget or not know'

One of the clearest examples of Fowler's persisting but inconsistent Latinate mindset. *Exit* is here an English verb, not a Latin one, and to suggest that writers are wrong not to use the Latin plural is absurd. The inconsistency is illustrated in the very next entry, where he advises that the Latin plural should not be used for words which are 'for the period of their lives English' (**-ex, -ix, 2**).

-ex, -ix: '4. . . . partly scientific & partly popular'

Fowler omits to mention that for many people *appendix* (in the anatomical sense) is different from *appendix* (in the bibliographical sense) in not allowing the irregular plural. Likewise, many give different endings to the bibliographical sense of *index* (*indexes*) as opposed to the mathematical sense (*indices*). But usage is divided, both in British and American English.

extend: 'the modernism does not extend direct from the native use'

This is an unusual piece of tortuous reasoning, in which Fowler acknowledges that the usage he dislikes is indeed 'native', but that the nativeness is somehow made irrelevant by a US period of use. He is in fact wrong in suggesting that the usage ended in Britain in the eighteenth century. The *OED* has two quotations from the nineteenth century (see sense 9a) from Maria Edgeworth and Benjamin Jowett—both impeccably British writers.

-EY & -Y IN ADJECTIVES: 'shaky -*y* adjectives'

Several of these remain shaky, a century on, but in some cases the -*ey* spellings have increased: a Google search will show that *whitey* and *horsey* are now (in 2008) ten times more common than *whity* and *horsy*, and *cakey* is five times more common than *caky*. On the other hand, such forms as *wavy*, *chancy*, and *nosy* have moved in the opposite direction. There is still a great deal of divided usage.

farther, further: 'it is less likely that [a differentiation] will be established'
Fowler was accurate in his prediction. It is still the case that 'the preference of the majority is for *further*', and has if anything increased—the ratio is 70 : 1 in British English (10 : 1 in American English). The superlative forms are more closely matched: *furthest* is commoner than *farthest* in British English, but only by 3 : 1, and this ratio is almost reversed in American English.

female) (woman: 'as impolite as to call a lady a woman'
A cross-reference to the entry on *lady* would have been helpful. As it is, Fowler does not make much of the usage issue between *lady* and *woman*—something which became more contentious in later decades. *Woman* is no longer 'reasonably resented', and indeed corpus studies of written English show that its use doubled during the later decades of the twentieth century.

FEMININE DESIGNATIONS: 'These ladies . . . object'
It is interesting that the *-ess* issue was contentious as early as the 1920s, well before the feminist movement focused attention upon it. Fowler saw the suffix as something women would want, and recommended its increased use: 'with the coming extension of women's vocations, feminines for vocation-words are a special need of the future'. In fact, as we now know, the mood went in the opposite direction: *-ess* was felt to demean the work of a woman by comparison with the corresponding male term, and words such as *author* and *manager* gradually became standard during the 1980s. Today, the only *-ess* forms which are uncontentious and frequently encountered are traditional titles (e.g. *duchess*) and literary fictions (e.g. *shepherdess*).

feminineness, feminism, &c.: 'It would be well if *feminity* could be appointed'
In fact *femininity* became standard, despite the extra syllable, along with *feminineness*. Although *feminity* is still to be found, it is used ten times less often than *femininity*.

filtrate: '*filter* . . . is a SUPERFLUOUS WORD'
Fowler backs the wrong horse: *filtrate* today has narrowed to a specialist use, and *filter* is the norm, in a wide range of special settings (e.g. acoustics, linguistics, astronomy) as well as in everyday use (e.g. road traffic control). The phrasal verb *filter out* is also a twentieth-century development.

first: '5. . . . the idiom-book of a century hence will probably not even mention *first, secondly*'
This shows the danger of making predictions about usage. Today the more succinct form has become standard, with the *-ly* forms felt to be pedantic. *First* is fifty times more frequent than *firstly*, and a common trend is to make the other ordinals follow suit—*second, third, fourth*, etc. The origins of the antagonism to *firstly* are obscure, but the preference for *first* was probably reinforced by its use in the marriage ceremony of the Book of Common Prayer ('First, it was ordained for the procreation of children . . . Secondly').

fivepenny, fivepence: 'The pronunciations . . . will no doubt become universal if decimal coinage is introduced.'
Fowler was probably thinking of the way *twopence* and *threepence* became 'tuppence' and 'thrupence'. As we now know, it didn't happen.

flair: 'means keen scent'
This is no longer the case. Even in Fowler's time, the more general senses ('sagacious perceptiveness, liking') had become standard. Indeed, the *OED* uses Fowler's example about homely accomplishments as an illustration of the word's use in this way.

floor, storey: 'The numbering . . . is peculiar'
Fowler does not refer to the distinction between British and American English, where the usage differs. In American English the *first floor* is what in British English would be the *ground floor*.

forrader: 'well-known anecdote'
Well known no longer, Fowler is presumably here referring to *Get no forrader*, listed among the 'Hackneyed phrases' later in the book.

fragile: 'a woman may be frail (i.e. weaker than others in moral strength)'
This sense of *frail* is now obsolete. The *OED* has no examples later than 1868.

FUSED PARTICIPLE: 'abstain'
Both constructions have been used for centuries, and continue to be, despite Fowler's lengthy attack. Usage has moved on, as we can readily sense when we see Fowler recommending such alternatives as *many's* and *anything's*. A distinction of formality is often present: *I worry about John eating soup* is more colloquial than *I worry about John's eating soup*. But there is also a subtle difference of meaning. In the first of these sentences, the focus of the worry is on John (perhaps soup is bad for him). In the second, the focus is on his way of eating (perhaps he slurps it).

gender: 'a grammatical term only'
Not any more. The word has now an established (non-jocular) use in social contexts, where it is used to express a specific contrast with *sex*—socially or culturally constructed identity as opposed to physical or biological identity.

GENTEELISM: 'an improvement in the meaning'
It should be noted that some of the pairings have since developed different contexts of use, such as *lingerie* and *underclothing*. Others might these days be added to the list, such as *utilize* for *use*. (See also **WORKING & STYLISH WORDS**.)

gill: '*Gill* . . . is the right form'
Gill is the earliest spelling, certainly; but the spelling alliteration of *J* has promoted the use of *Jill* since at least the seventeenth century.

governance: 'incipient archaism'
The term has received a new lease of life, and is now widely used in relation to national and international politics, business, and industry, especially in such phrases as *good governance, corporate governance, global governance*, and *governance indicators*.

grammar: 'the general term for the science of language'
Fowler anticipates the common use in linguistics, as used by Chomsky and many others. 'Orthoepy' has now been replaced by 'Phonology', and his definition of Phonology is today more appropriate to Phonetics.

had: 1. . . . . 'the peculiar nature of the phrase *had better*'
Indeed it is peculiar. Fowler's sense of the idiomaticity of *had better* has been reinforced by the analysis found in modern grammars, such as the *Comprehensive Grammar of the English Language* (1985), which labels it as one of the 'modal idioms', and relates it to *would rather, have got to*, and *be to*. They all begin with an auxiliary verb and are followed by an infinitive form; they do not have non-finite forms; and they do not follow other verbs in the verb phrase.
2. 'write here *If we had desired & were in anticipation*'
Fowler's recommendation does not really solve the problem, as the change of tense from *had* to *were* retains the anomaly. A change to *had been in anticipation* would avoid it.

hallelujah, halleluiah, alleluia: 'Now more commonly written as in the A.V.'
There are other variants too, such as *alleluya, alleluja*, and *halleluia*. Usage depends very much on religious tradition. *Hallelujah* is commoner among evangelical Protestant groups and *alleluia* among Catholics and mainstream Anglicans. In a hymn-book which represents all Christian traditions, both spellings will be found. (See also **alleluia**.)

halloo &c.: '*Hello* may perhaps be put aside'
This is now by far the dominant form. What Fowler doesn't mention is how recent *hello* (*hallo, hullo*) is—mid-nineteenth century.

happening(s): 'we got on without "happenings" till about 1905'
Fowler is wrong: the earliest recorded use of *happenings* in the plural is 1581. The much later use (*happenings* as spontaneous theatrical events, from 1959) would doubtless have given him apoplexy!

hay: '1. . . . *in a bottle of h.* . . . . the correct form of the phrase'
In fact it isn't the earliest recorded use, which is *looke a nedle in a medow* (1581). We then also find . . . *in a truss of hay* before the arrival of . . . *in a haystack* in the mid-nineteenth century. This last is now the only common form.

HAZINESS
From the examples, Fowler seems to be thinking of this phenomenon as a kind of tautology; but he gives no cross-reference at **TAUTOLOGY**.

HYPHENS: 'The chaos prevailing'
It is not surprising that this entry is one of the longest in the dictionary: hyphenation is the most volatile element in the English punctuation system. Fowler does not explore the reasons for the 'chaos', which are partly to do with compound words gradually losing their strangeness over time and partly to do with typographical fashion.
    In relation to strangeness: when two words first become a compound, they are typically spaced (e.g. *bumble bee*, 1530); then, with increasing familiarity, some begin to be hyphenated (*bumble-bee*, 1678); and eventually they may be written solid (*bumblebee*, as now recognized in the 6th edition of the *Shorter Oxford English Dictionary* (henceforth *SOED*), 2007). However, the earlier conventions do not always die out, so that alternative usage is routine—making this the largest type of exception to the concept of a 'standard' English orthography.

In relation to fashion: the late twentieth-century tendency to simplify punctuation (e.g. omitting full points after *Mr* or in acronyms such as *BBC*) in order to avoid typographical 'clutter' has led to a marked reduction in the use of hyphenated words in British English (they were already far less used in American English). The *SOED* sixth edition attracted considerable media interest when it appeared because of its hyphenation decisions: around 16,000 words lost their hyphens, either because previously hyphenated words were printed as spaced (*ice cream, pot belly*) or solid (*bumblebee, crybaby*).

Given the vagaries of language change (about to be hugely increased through the Internet), Fowler's description of the situation as one where 'usage is so variable as to be better named caprice' (p. 244) is as accurate a summary as one can hope to have. But trends do exist, and can be identified by studies of large corpora of usage, such as are carried out by lexicographers—so dictionary recommendations are the surest guide we have to contemporary practice(s) in hyphenation.

I: '1. . . . a piece of false grammar'
Fowler does not go into the reasons for this usage. Plainly it is the result of hypercorrection. Generations of prescriptive grammarians have instilled a sensitivity to the *I/me* distinction which people have generalized to such cases as this. This is the kind of thing that happens when a false rule is established, based on another language (in this case, Latin). Ordinary users cannot win, in such circumstances: condemned for failing to use the nominative in one context, they are then condemned for using it in another. (See also **between**.)

ILLITERACIES: 'accustomed to reading good literature'
This is one of Fowler's less-well-structured entries, with no clear relationship in the examples to his notion of 'good literature'. Some of the examples (e.g. the split infinitive, *me* for *my*, *like* for *as*) are simply prescriptive shibboleths.

impayable: 'an undesirable alien'
Fowler comments that 'the OED does not illustrate or give the sense'. It does now, with citations for the 'priceless' sense from 1818. The word has very little usage today, and most dictionaries do not record it.

importune: 'Shakspere . . . Chapman . . . favour the former'
The accentuation of words in Shakespeare's day was very different to what it was at the beginning of the twentieth century. Citing these authors is of no relevance to present-day usage, which displays the same variation as was around in Fowler's time.

IN- & UN-: 'the recommendations'
Usage has not always gone with Fowler's 'impressions'. A comparison of usage frequency using Google (in 2008) shows the following results:
Present-day usage agrees with Fowler:

    acceptable: *un*- 4,900,000; *in*- 271,000
    appeasable: *un*- 58,000; *in*- 8,000
    communicative: *un*- 180,000; *in*- 20,000
    consolable: *in*- 388,000; *un*- 16,000
    controllable: *un*- 708,000; *in*- 23,000

     digested: un- 551,000; *in*- 43,000
     discriminating: un- 84,000; *in*- 30,000
     distinguishable: *in*- 1,250,000; *un*- 126,000
     edited: un- 511,000; *in*- 44,000
     effaceable: *in*- 32,000; *un*- 818
     frequent: *in*- 1,120,000; *un*- 46,000
     navigable: un- 65,000; *in*- 18,000
     practical: un-216,000; *in*- 18,000
     recognizable: un- 217,000; *in*- 343
     responsive: un-598,000; *in*- 1,870

Present-day usage disagrees with Fowler:
     advisable: *in*- 591,000; *un*- 69,000
     alterable: *in*- 1,370,000; *un*- 467,000
     apt: un- 239,000; *in*- 31,000
     decipherable: *in*- 464,000; *un*- 147, 000
     escapable: *in*- 501,000; *un*- 64,000
     essential: *in*- 275,000; *un*- 133,000
     expressive: *in*- 90,000; *un*- 34,000
     retentive: un- 14,000; *ir*- 3,000

Present-day usage is divided:
     completed: un- 191,000; *in*- 142,000
     substantial: un- 201,000; *in*- 195,000
     supportable: *in*- 359,000; *un*- 280,000
     susceptible: *in*- 75,000; *un*- 58,000

INCOMPATIBLES: 'They differ greatly'
They do indeed. It is impossible to see any coherence in this list of items that Fowler finds objectionable—a mixture of tautologies (*finally scotched*), etymological clashes (*decimate*), prescriptive issues (*like*), and others.

inflame: '*Inflam(e)able* . . . has been displaced by *inflammable*'
The problems surrounding *inflammable* had not emerged when Fowler was writing. Safety instructions now avoid the word because of the ambiguity in the prefix, which can be both an intensifier (as in *inflame*) as well as a negator. An *OED* citation from 1959 recommends *flammable* vs *non-flammable* rather than *inflammable* vs *non-flammable*. The figurative usage remains, as in *inflammable comments*.

innings: 'being used for either number'
But not in present-day American English, where in baseball people talk about *an inning, in the sixth inning*, etc.

innuendo: 'a count'
Frequency of usage on Google (in 2008) is: *innuendos* 418,000; *innuendoes* 185,000 (and 17,000 *innuendo's*).

intelligentsia, -tzia: 'Both forms are current.'
The *-z-* spelling seems to have been used when the word first arrived in English, in the first decade of the twentieth century. *OED* citations show only *intelligentsia* after 1910.

-IST, . . . &c.: 'exact form is still uncertain & should be fixed'

Fowler's intuition frequently fails to anticipate usage, in this section—see for example his negative judgements on *accompanist* and *analyst*. His view that the omission of a syllable (as in *idolatry*) belongs to 'the primitive stages of the language' is unclear. Words have always been syncopated in spoken English, and still are today, as in *libr'y* or *febu'ry* (as he acknowledges in the entry on **laboratory**). What has happened is that these shortened forms are no longer spelled as such, since the establishment of standard written English. By 'primitive' he must mean 'pre-standard English'.

it: '2. . . . it cannot be used where there is no subject to herald'

In the example in question, the *it* is perfectly acceptable. This is not an example of anticipatory *it*, and Fowler's explanation is beside the point. Fowler comments: 'it neither has any meaning of its own nor represents anything else'. That is precisely one of the other uses of *it* in English, found in many sentences such as *What time is it?*, *How far is it to Brighton?*, *Isn't it a shame*, *I take it that you've heard*, *It's getting dark*, and *You're in for it*. Today, grammarians call it 'prop *it*' or 'empty *it*'.

judg(e)ment: 'Modern usage . . . favours *judgment*'

This is still true: Google (in 2008) has 8.7 million for *judgment*, as opposed to 3.7 million for *judgement*.

leading question: 'To object . . . is meaningless.'

On the contrary: this is simply a new meaning. The sense 'awkward or pointed question' is listed in the 6th edition of the *SOED*.

licence, -se: 'The first is better for the noun'

It is not obvious why Fowler considers the distinction 'convenient', for the distinction has long been dispensed with in American English, which he does not mention in this entry.

like, adj.: '1 . . . . vulgar or slovenly'

The antagonism to this use of *like*, despite its presence in many 'writers of standing', remains as strong today. Fowler does not however discuss the problem in its entirety. In particular he omits to mention the occasional ambiguity of *as*—with causative and temporal uses as well as manner (some of which are discussed in the **as** entry). To take just one of his examples: to write *Our great patron saint 'St George' was a Greek, as a good many of the saints are* leaves it unclear whether the *as* means 'like' or 'because'. There is some sign of a lessening of antipathy to *like* in many of the examples cited in section 2, so it may be that this shibboleth of usage will one day disappear.

like, v.: '2. . . . If the SHALL & WILL idiom is worth preserving'

The fact that all the examples in this entry are uncontentious today illustrates the extent to which this distinction has ceased to be relevant, in all but a few contexts of usage. English English is here simply following the worldwide trend. (See also **shall & will, should & would.**)

literally: 'We have come to such a pass'

It is interesting that this usage was already so strong in Fowler's day that it warranted comment. The intensifying meaning can be traced back to the eighteenth century, with the extension to 'false' contexts noted by the *OED* from the 1860s. If anything, the use of *literally* as a general intensifier has increased since Fowler's time, and the battle to retain the word only in its narrow sense has been lost. The 6th edition of the *SOED* calls the usage simply 'colloquial' and glosses it as 'emphatically', circumspectly adding 'with some exaggeration'. As a consequence, in contexts where there is likely to be ambiguity, alternative phrasing is needed, such as 'in a literal sense'.

lo(a)th: '7 : 1 for loth'
Usage preference has since gone in the other direction: all dictionaries now give pride of place to *loath*.

LU: 'clearly a movement going on'
This perceptive and thorough account of a sound shift is of considerable value to students of the history of pronunciation. For example, this is the only reference I know drawing attention to the popular currency of *absolutely* as an emphatic response in the early decades of the twentieth century. There is a present-day impression that this usage is very recent; Fowler is a corrective.

Magna C(h)arta: '*charta* will take a great deal of killing yet'
It did not take so long. Modern usage is now predominantly *Carta*.

Mahomet, Mohammedan, &c.: 'ordinary mortals should go on saying . . . what their fathers said before them'
Ordinary mortals did not follow Fowler's advice, notwithstanding the ferocity of his attack on *Mohammed* and other spellings. The *OED* now refers to the *Mahomet* spelling as having been 'superseded' by *Mohammed* and later *Muhammad*. For some people nowadays, the *Mahomet* spelling is felt to be demeaning.

majority: '2. . . . either a singular or a plural verb is possible'
Fowler clearly identifies the issue here—'according as the body is, or its members are, chiefly in the speaker's thoughts'. It is surprising how much this basic semantic distinction was ignored by later usage pedants, who would devote much space to arguing whether the 'correct' usage was *committee is* or *committee are*, and similarly for other collective nouns. They should have followed Fowler, in such cases.

Mall: 'but *Pall Mall*'
The transcription 'pelmel' is a nice reminder of the pronunciation of a bygone age.

malnutrition: 'A word to be avoided'
Underfeeding was never common, even in Fowler's day—it is not even listed in the *OED*—and his objection is curious. *Malnutrition* soon became the norm, with *malnourishment* also in use from the 1930s on.

Maori: 'pl. -*is*'
The plural without -*s* is now the preferred form in New Zealand English.

mentality: 'a truly SUPERFLUOUS WORD'
The mentality of the politician . . . Fowler suggests that 'Twenty years ago no-one would have written that'. *OED* records now show that this was not the case.

It was already in *Funk's Standard Dictionary* in 1895 with the meaning 'cast or habit of mind'. Today, it is the primary sense.

meticulous: 'this wicked word'

The modern meaning of 'punctilious, scrupulous' is now the dominant one. What is interesting is to note the way the sense has ameliorated. It is a positive remark to say today that someone is meticulous. In Fowler's day, the usage was typically negative, meaning 'over-scrupulous, over-careful'. Some usage pundits still regret this change, much as Fowler regretted the loss of the meaning of 'fear' from the word (which is how it was first used in English in the sixteenth century). It seems to have been the distance the word has travelled from its etymological past that made Fowler inveigh against it at such length.

momentarily: 'means for a moment'

Fowler does not include the sense of 'at any moment' in American English, which the *OED* cites from the 1920s. The usage can sometimes take aback those international air travellers who have been brought up on British English: *We shall be landing momentarily.*

moslem, muslim: 'Correction into *muslim* is to be deprecated'

Fowler's dislike has long been ignored. The spelling *muslim* is now twenty times more common.

-most: 'the obscure *o* is better'

All these forms are now commoner with the long vowel, and present-day pronouncing dictionaries often do not even mention the short vowel as an alternative.

mutual: 'are misuses of *m*'

The development of the sense of *mutual* to mean 'common' is now standard in all dictionaries, and gradually the criticism of 'improper' has been removed, in the light of everyday usages such as *mutual acquaintance*. The meaning is actually long-standing: the *OED*'s first recorded use is Shakespearean, 'one mutual happiness' (in *The Two Gentlemen of Verona*, v. iv. 173).

NEEDLESS VARIANTS: 'Every dictionary-maker would be grateful to an Academy'

Quite the opposite, in fact. Johnson was one of the first to point out, in his preface to Roscommon's works, the impracticality of an academy:

> In this country an academy could be expected to do but little. If an academician's place were profitable it would be given by interest; if attendance were gratuitous it would be rarely paid, and no man would endure the least disgust. Unanimity is impossible, and debate would separate the assembly.
>
> But suppose the philological decree made and promulgated, what would be its authority? In absolute governments there is sometimes a general reverence paid to all that has the sanction of power and the countenance of greatness. How little this is the state of our country needs not to be told. We live in an age in which it is a kind of publick sport to refuse all respect that cannot be enforced. The edicts of an English academy would probably be read by many, only that they might be sure to

    disobey them. (*Prefaces, Biographical and Critical to the Works of the English Poets*, 1779)

Fowler's comment about helping things on 'by irresponsible expressions of opinion' is a curious remark for him to make, and—unless it is a piece of self-effacing humour—suggests that a negative element has gone awry somewhere: 'experience in word-judging' leads us to expect 'responsible' rather than 'irresponsible'.

nigger: 'applied to others than full or partial negroes'

The use by non-blacks to blacks has also become proscribed since Fowler's time. Indeed, no racial term currently attracts so much opprobrium, with its own abbreviation, 'the N word', other than in the situation where black people use it about themselves.

nomenclature: 'The dictionaries that give a list of synonyms with each word do a very doubtful service to literature.'

Fowler is unfair here: a list of synonyms without explanation is of doubtful use, indeed, but 'synonym essays', in which subtle distinctions of meaning or style are pointed out, are an invaluable addition to a dictionary. And Fowler himself gives several lists of words with similar meaning: see Introduction, p. xix.

none: '1. It is a mistake to suppose that the pronoun is sing. only'

People who have been persuaded by later prescriptivists that *none* has to be followed by a singular will be surprised at Fowler's tolerance of divided usage here, and (given his reference to the *OED*) his apparent support for plural concord. The use of *none* with a plural verb can be traced back to Old English, with *OED* citations including Dryden, Goldsmith, and Southey. Judging by the short size of the entry, the issue was evidently not so contentious in Fowler's day.

noun: 'is comfortable with neither'

Nominal has since become widely used as an adjective in linguistics as an alternative to *noun*.

NOUN & ADJECTIVE ACCENT: 'the first four are undisputed'

The accentual alternation noted by Fowler is still an important feature of English, but not all of his examples are heard today—for example, nobody today pronounces *expert* and *instinct* with a stress on the second syllable.

NUMBER: '11. . . . There are three makeshifts'

It is interesting to see that this usage problem was already long-standing in Fowler's day. His analysis remains uncontentious, but his choice of solution is unpalatable today, where C is now indeed considered by many to be an 'arrogant demand on the part of male England'. The popular solution today is the same as it was then: B.

oblivious: 'A word badly misused'

The 'misuse' has now become standard, both with respect to the meaning of *oblivious* and the following preposition. It is a characteristic puzzle why Fowler considers this semantic shift a bad misuse, whereas the next entry *obnoxious*, showing a similar semantic shift, he finds acceptable.

-o(E)s: 'a legitimate grievance against the words in *-o*'

It is surprising that Fowler does not refer to the non-standard use of an apostrophe to mark a plural *-s* after words ending in *-o*—a usage that is found from the sixteenth century (such as in Shakespeare's First Folio and Johnson's *Dictionary*) and which was certainly common in Fowler's day.

offing, offish, &c.: 'awf . . . prevailing in Southern or standard English'

Pronouncing dictionaries today no longer recognize 'awf' as a pronunciation of *off*, though it is still occasionally heard in the speech of older people, especially those with an aristocratic background.

often: 'The sounding of the *t* . . . is "not recognized by the dictionaries" '

It is now. Although indeed a spelling pronunciation, as Fowler suggests, the usage has spread so that it is now a recognized alternative pronunciation (though with a short vowel: see the comment at **offing**).

only: 'the pedants . . . [are] clapping a strait waistcoat upon their mother tongue'

People who think of Fowler only as a linguistic pedant and purist have to think again when they read this entry. There have indeed been many twentieth-century pedants who have ignored Fowler's advice and tried to turn English into 'an automatic machine'. Fowler points out, correctly, that the risk of misunderstanding in the vast majority of cases is 'chimerical', and draws attention to the intonation which enables ambiguity to be avoided. His quotation from the *OED* describes the intonational feature involved: contrastive accentuation. The emphasis on *only* and *week* in *He only died a week ago* links the two words and makes the sentence unambiguous. '[W]hen perspicuity is not in danger it is needless to submit to an inconvenient restriction.' It is a wise principle, and one which Fowler might equally have followed in several of his own entries.

optative: 'those who deal in grammar have somehow come to call it ŏptā´tĭv'

Not always. The standard pronunciation is very common among grammarians today.

our: '3. . . . the repulsive THEIR'

Fowler repeats his dislike of this construction, as an alternative to *his or her*, at various places in the *Dictionary*. The usage however steadily grew during the twentieth century, and became particularly common in writing after indefinite words, such as *Anyone who arrives after midnight will find their key in the porter's lodge*. The next stage, with the usage extending to singular nouns (*Each applicant will find a form in their pack*), is also under way. The usage is not new: it dates from the sixteenth century, and survived the attacks of the eighteenth-century prescriptive grammarians, who (as Fowler) denied it any natural role in English. And yet all that is happening is a similar development to what has already taken place with the pronoun *you*, originally a plural pronoun, which began to be used with singular reference. Nobody objects now to *you/your* as a singular, and it will probably be the same with *they/their* one day.

-OUR & -OR: 'It is not worth while either to resist such a gradual change or to fly in the face of national sentiment by trying to hurry it'

Another sensible observation, and Fowler's initial analysis is perceptive: 'The American abolition of *-our* ... has probably retarded rather than quickened English progress in the same direction.' Even a century on, and despite a considerable influence of American spellings on British ones, there is very little sign of change with respect to *-or*.

PAIRS & SNARES: 'words that are sometimes confused'
Fowler's influence here was considerable. Many dictionaries and usage manuals subsequently began to include entries or mini-essays on 'confusibles', and whole books have been devoted to them, such as *Room's Dictionary of Confusibles* (1979).

parasitic(al): 'The longer form ... is now little used.'
This is true. *Parasitic* is used over twenty times as often as *parasitical*, in Google searches (in 2008), and the bias is found in both British and American English.

periodic(al): 'the two words do not differ in meaning'
This remains the case, in most contexts, but there has been a sharp difference in usage, with *periodic* being over ten times as common, both in British and (even more marked) in American English. Specialized usages have also helped to differentiate them, with *periodic* developing notably in science (*period table*, *periodic functions*) and *periodical* in publishing.

phenomenal: 'a sin against the English language'
The sense Fowler objected to so strongly ('extraordinary, exceptional') is now recognized as a standard sense in all dictionaries.

pleasure: 'the definite special sense of *p.* with possessives'
The 'insensibility to idiom' which Fowler bemoans would now be seen simply as a new idiomatic usage: *It's my pleasure* today invariably has the subjective sense. The only remaining use of the 'will' sense of the word is in such locutions as 'detained at the Queen's pleasure'. The *OED* has no citations after 1849.

POSITION OF ADVERBS: 'the avoidance of it [the split infinitive] has become a fetish'
Fowler is especially harsh in his attack on those who maintain a rigorous avoidance of the split infinitive, calling it (p. 447) 'terrorism'. It is surprising that his words had so little influence. Although it is almost de rigueur among pedants today to pour scorn on the practice of avoiding split infinitives, it is remarkable how this particular shibboleth has stayed in the popular mind.

Fowler also shows considerable linguistic awareness in his section 6, where he notes that '[t]he longer the adverb in proportion to the object, the more marked is the offence of interpolating it'. Modern linguists would replace 'offence' by such terms as 'unacceptable' or 'ungrammatical', but otherwise the point is well made.

practicable) (practical: '1. ... *impractical* is often wrongly written'
The twentieth century saw considerable vacillation between the possible alternatives: *impracticable/unpracticable, impractical/unpractical*. Today, usage has

come out overwhelmingly in favour of the *im-* versions, for both words: *impractical* is over twenty times more common than *unpractical* in Google searches (in 2008) and *impracticable* over 150 times more common than *unpracticable*. A few people still maintain a distinction, using *unpractical* for persons and *impractical* for inanimate objects and ideas, but they are in a decreasing minority.

precedence, precedent: 'prĕ ́sĭd- is here recommended'

Fowler does not mention the pronunciation with a long vowel, *pree*, which is common in US English and increasingly heard in the UK.

premature: 'the last syllable is fully pronounced & not weakened to -che*r*'

This pronunciation has now become standard. One of the variables Fowler probably had in mind was the use of a long vowel: *pree-* is standard in US English and often now heard in the UK.

PREPOSITION AT END: 'a cherished superstition'

This is another entry where Fowler expresses his opposition to unrealistic prescriptive rules that have captured the public imagination. His analysis of the origins of the situation (from Dryden onwards) is accurate, as is his placing the blame at the door of those who have been 'overpowered by notions of correctness derived from Latin standards'. After reading that 'immense pains are daily expended in changing spontaneous into artificial English' and that those who support the rule 'are unconsciously trying to deprive the English language of a valuable idiomatic resource', it is hard to believe that pedants persisted in attacking end-placed prepositions throughout the twentieth century. The point is of interest, for the historian of ideas, as it is often claimed that Fowler exercised a major influence on usage attitudes. 'Up to a point, Lord Copper', one might say. Few pundits, it seems, were prepared to follow Fowler's words: 'Follow no arbitrary rule'.

PRESUMPTUOUS WORD-FORMATION: 'words . . . that . . . should not have been brought into existence'

Looking at Fowler's list, we see several words that have since become standard, such as *bureaucrat*, *coastal*, *feature*, *forceful*, *lectureship*, and *speedometer*, and some that have not, such as *amusive*, *dandiacal*, *funniment*, and *minify*. Why some words take root and others do not is one of the great mysteries of language change. But the examples well illustrate the pointlessness of trying to compile such lists in the first place.

program(me): 'the regular spelling'

It comes as a surprise to many people to hear that *-am* was the normal spelling in Britain, when the word first arrived in the early seventeenth century (from Greek *programma*), with the meaning of a public notice. But in the early nineteenth century, the word came into English again, this time from French, in the now familiar sense relating to concerts and festivities, and the *-mme* spelling became fashionable in Britain (though such writers as Carlyle, Scott, and Shaw preferred *-am*). Fowler stands up for *-am*, and would doubtless be pleased to see the reappearance of this spelling in present-day British English (with two-thirds of instances being in computer contexts).

proposition: 'the injury that is being done by this single word to the language'
This is one of Fowler's more self-contradictory entries. On the one hand he grants 'that there is nothing unsound in principle about the development of sense'; but he doesn't like this particular development. His grounds, though, are extremely vague: 'idiomatic usage is clean against it'—though what else is idiomatic usage but the usage of the majority? The mention of 'Americanism' suggests a second agenda. In the event, *proposition* developed as a somewhat more formal alternative to *proposal*. Fowler did not live to see the emergence of the sexual sense of *proposition* as a verb, cited from the mid-1930s.

ps-: 'the pronunciation of the p . . . is likely to be restored'
We now know that this never happened, except in jocular pronunciations. Fowler seems to have overestimated the influence of literacy on pronunciation here. *OED* editor James Murray also supported it.

PURISM: 'every man is potentially a purist & a sloven at once'
It is often forgotten how strongly Fowler objected to purism, which he defines as 'a needless & irritating insistence on purity or correctness of speech'. Although critics have pointed out that many of Fowler's own entries would have to be considered purist by this definition, he was certainly right to emphasize the relativity inherent in the term, and it is a pity that his view did not exercise greater influence in the twentieth century.

pur sang: 'one should be brave enough to place them as such'
This is a curious recommendation—that when a word is borrowed from another language, it should follow the word-order preferences of that language. If taken literally, it would mean that all adjectives taken from French should appear in English after the nouns they qualify—which would go clean against Fowler's oft-stated predilection for natural English idiom. He does not assert this principle anywhere else in the book, and French adjectives are allowed to take up their English pre-noun position without comment.

question(n)aire: 'It should be treated like *commissionaire*'
And so it came to pass. The standard spelling today has just one *n*, and the usual pronunciation is with a [kw-] onset, though the [k-] onset is still heard.

quieten: 'it is common in uneducated talk'
And in educated talk, now. It can hardly be called a 'superfluous word' today. Indeed, the dominant uses of the two verbs seem to have reversed, with *quiet* becoming more restricted than *quieten*. The intransitive use, especially followed by *down* (as in *The crowd quieted down*) is labelled 'Now chiefly North American' by the 6th edition of the *SOED*.

quite: ' "quite all right" is all quite wrong'
Why was the locution so popular then, and why does it continue to be today? Because Fowler was wrong in his analysis: *quite* and *all* are not 'identical in sense'. *Quite* is here an emphasizer of the whole phrase *all right*, and has more the meaning of 'truly' or 'definitely'.

Fowler does not mention an important semantic difference between British and American usage. When British people say that something is *quite relevant*, they mean that it is 'somewhat relevant'; for Americans, however, the phrase means 'very relevant'.

rapport: 'will not be missed in English'
This is an example where Fowler's sense of usefulness let him down. Far from the word being allowed to disappear, it increased in usefulness. Most of the *OED* citations are from the twentieth century.

rationale: 'sometimes mispronounced'
Fowler's Latin influenced preference never caught on, and the French analogy became the norm. Pronouncing dictionaries do still mention the Latin version, but it is rarely heard today.

reason: '3. . . . Wrong forms nearly as common'
Fowler has *the reason why* in his list of examples, but pays it no special attention. This usage attracted greater criticism later in the century.

reference: '& even a written testimonial'
This is one of the best examples of a case where subsequent usage shows Fowler's notion of 'slipshod extension' to be seriously flawed. No one today would think of the 'testimonial' sense of *reference* as being anything other than a perfectly legitimate and useful lexical development, whether initiated by the 'uneducated' or not. In fact the earliest citations for reference in this sense in the *OED* are not by uneducated people at all: they include the novelist Galsworthy.

refutable, irrefutable: 'seem likely to result in the pronunciation here advised'
Fowler's sense of analogy let him down here: the pronunciation with stress on *ref* never caught on, probably because people wanted to avoid a sequence of three following unstressed syllables. (See also **confer(r)able**.)

regiment: 'Pronounce the noun'
The recommendation to omit the *i* was never taken up, apart perhaps from in military usage. Modern dictionaries give only a three-syllable pronunciation.

relation(ship): 'in the improper sense'
Fowler's argument seems plausible—that *relation* is already abstract, and therefore *relationship*, using the abstract suffix *-ship*, is unnecessary. But the fact of the matter is that *relationship* has settled down nicely in the language. So why has it proved to be useful? Partly because a whole new set of social circumstances evolved which the word *relation(s)* did not express: the emotional (and especially sexual) association between two people (*I'm in a relationship*). In the 1970s it became a more genteel way of expressing what would otherwise be called an *affair*.

remonstrate: 'is pronounced (in contrast with *demonstrate*) rĭmŏ´nstrāt'
This pronunciation hardly outlived Fowler. Most modern dictionaries give only the version with stress on the first syllable. A few allow Fowler's version as a minor alternative.

repetitional, repetitionary, repetitious, repetitive: 'few writers have the hardihood to use any of them'
Both *repetitious* and *repetitive* are now commonplace, the former having lost whatever American associations it may have had. Google statistics (in 2008)

speak for themselves about the way usage has diverged: *repetitional* (5,900), *repetitionary* (1,300), *repetitious* (1.1 million), *repetitive* (37 million).

respective(ly): 'The evil is considerable enough to justify an examination at some length'
This is one of those entries in Fowler where the length of the entry is well justified by the range of examples collected. The *respectively* construction is governed by very precise rules in English grammar, and requires careful control if it is not to be misleading, unclear, ambiguous, or unintelligible.

retro-: 'In most words the usual pronunciation is rētro'
This pronunciation has now disappeared. Only a short vowel is given in modern pronouncing dictionaries.

RHYTHM: 'is not a matter of counting syllables & measuring the distance between accents'
This is one of Fowler's most insightful essays, providing a valuable corrective to the mechanical approach to prosody which was common in the late nineteenth century. Rhythm is essentially our perception of regularity in the stream of speech, and is phonetically easy to define, for a given language. Rhythmicality—our sense of appropriateness or acceptability of rhythm in specific utterances—is a much more difficult matter to address; and Fowler provides some useful guidelines. He does not, however, say much more than that sentences must 'sound right', and that we must rely on 'instinct'. Analysis of his examples would show that the reason for the unrhythmicality is not just a phonetic matter, but is more to do with syntactic (and occasionally lexical) complexity, as indeed he suggests himself with his reference to reducing the length of one of the examples (the last on p. 505) by 'chopping off' piece after piece. His contrast with the 'masterpiece of rhythm' at the very end of his essay is not really fair, as that extract from the Bible illustrates a simple sequence of short coordinate clauses, which it would be difficult to read in anything other than a rhythmical way.

right: '*right* is better'
There has been a marked preference to use *rightly* in formal usage since Fowler's time, doubtless because of the increasing association of the dropped -*ly* ending with colloquial or regional speech, as in *the time went quick*. (See also **slow(ly)**.)

root, rout: 'It would be a convenient differentiation'
The senses involved militate against any clear differentiation. There is no clear semantic dividing line between the meanings 'attach by a root', 'search for roots', 'search around, rummage', and 'search someone out'. The trend is to use *root* for all, but *rout* is still common in the last instance.

salve: 'are pronounced sahv'
This pronunciation is still mentioned in dictionaries, but it has been largely replaced by the spelling-pronunciation in which the *l* is sounded.

sambo: '(half-breed)'
This word has now become taboo, along with other labels considered to be offensive when applied to non-white people.

seer: 'has double pronunciation'
This subtle phonetic difference is no longer recognized—if it ever was. Modern pronouncing dictionaries make no distinction.

sense (vb.): 'the meaning [of "perceive"] is not yet part of ordinary English'
It is now. Collocations such as *sense danger* and *sensing someone's presence* have become standard, especially with the meaning of 'become vaguely aware'. The word soon lost the 'irritation or suspicion of preciocity' which Fowler claimed 'most readers feel'—though it is open to question whether there was ever any basis for that claim. It is an occupational hazard for writers on usage to generalize their personal intuitions to an imaginary populace. One of the values of corpus studies and studies of acceptability is that they have repeatedly shown the unreliability of individual judgements, especially when usage is mixed or changing.

sensitize: 'extra-photographic use has not yet gone very far'
A century on, it is possible to see how this usage has become standard. The *OED* citation quoted by Fowler has now been supplemented by another from 1978, and it is regular dictionary practice to list the three main senses—photographic, physiological, and general—without comment.

sentence: 'If it contains'
Fowler's definitions are no longer the norm in descriptive grammars of English. His notion of *compound sentence* includes cases where 'a subject consists of more than one parallel noun' (or pronoun, as in his example *You & I...*). And because his notion of *clause* is restricted to subordinate clauses (see note on **clause** above), he is unable to deal with coordination (as in *John went by bus and Mary went by train*) other than by calling the two elements different sentences (as in his final example in the entry). This makes it impossible for him to use the traditional definition of a sentence as 'ending in a full stop'. By contrast, for example in the grammars by Randolph Quirk and his associates (such as *The Comprehensive Grammar of the English Language*), compound and complex are seen as two types of multiple sentence: compound sentences contain clauses in a coordinate relationship (*John went by bus and Mary went by train*), and complex sentences contain at least one clause in a subordinate relationship to another (*John went by bus because the train was cancelled*). In this approach, a sentence containing coordinate noun phrases (*the man and the woman*) remains simple.

Shakspere ... &c.: '*Shakspere, Shakspian*, are therefore recommended'
While Fowler was not the last to opt for the *Shakspere* spelling (there is an online Shakespeare forum called *Shaksper*), his choice now seems eccentric. More contentious is the distinction between *Shakespearian* and *Shakespearean*. The consensus in Shakespeare studies is for the latter, and this is reflected in a Google search (in 2008), with *-ean* being four times more common than *-ian*.

shall & will, should & would: 'the necessary rules'
This is a very strong statement by Fowler: 'no formal grammar or dictionary can be held to have done its duty if it has not laid down the necessary rules'. However, there is now abundant evidence to show that the distinction was

forced and artificial, even in the seventeenth century when the rules govern-ing the complementary use of *shall* and *will* were first introduced. Today, the situation is rapidly simplifying, as *shall* is common today only in British English; it has virtually disappeared from American English, and is rare in other global varieties. In British English, moreover, its functions are reducing, being associated with written rather than spoken English, and increasingly found only in more formal or polite styles (especially in legal and authorita-tive statements). The only context in which *shall* is now at all frequent is in the first person in questions: *Shall we go by car?*

Fowler returns to the subject in the entry on **will, 2**, where he addresses the regional issue: 'There is the English of the English, & there is the English of those who repudiate that national name'—thinking mainly of the Scots. It is probably the strongest statement from any defender of the *shall/will* distinction, that it 'endows his speech with a delicate precision that could not be attained without it, & serves more important purposes than that of a race-label'.

shoot, chute, shute: 'there seems to be no good reason against making *shoot* the only spelling'
This is a curious line for Fowler to be taking, as his usual stance is to maintain difference whenever sense distinctions are to be found (as in the case of **spirt, spurt**). In this case, his feelings about the matter were ignored. *Chute* and *shute* are both well-established spellings today.

silvan, sylvan: 'It is often too late to mend mis-spellings, but hardly so in this case.'
Fowler was wrong. A century on and we find *sylvan* the norm, with *silvan* an occasional alternative.

ski(n.): 'Pron. shē'
This pronunciation is no longer given in modern dictionaries.

slow(ly): '*slow* maintains itself as at least an idiomatic possibility'
The 'encroachments of *-ly*' have continued to make many people avoid the *-ly*-less form in formal speech and writing. Today, *-ly*-less forms can sound odd, as in Fowler's own usage: at the end of the entry on **try**, he writes, 'It is an idiom that should be not discountenanced, but used when it comes natural.' (See also **right**.)

small: 'patent pairs . . . latent pairs'
Fowler here anticipates one of the strategies used in linguistically inspired semantics, where words are related in meaning through such sense associ-ations as synonymy and antonymy, and where sequences of words are related through the notion of collocation. His set of examples is illuminating, and his judgement correct—'the distribution is by no means so simple & definite as the pedantic analyst might desire'.

spirt, spurt: 'It would plainly be convenient'
Later usage ignored his recommendation. The only spelling given by modern dictionaries is *spurt*.

SPLIT INFINITIVE: '2. . . . tame acceptance of the misinterpreted opinion of others'

It is surprising that Fowler's ferocious attack on those who defend split infinitives at all costs—'bogy-haunted creatures'—was not more influential, but the antagonism to this construction continued long after his death, and still rumbles on—though modern pedants race to distance themselves from it. John Humphrys, for example, calls it a 'bogus rule' in his *Lost for Words* (2004, p. 49). Fowler's arguments are exactly those which any linguist might make. He points out that these people are 'deaf to the normal rhythm of English sentences'. A typical modern linguist's observation is: '*To boldly go* has one big thing in its favour. It is following the natural rhythm of English' (myself, in *Who Cares about English Usage* (1984, p. 30). Fowler was well aware of his strong views on this matter. As he wryly remarks (p. 560): 'the author's opinion has perhaps been allowed to appear with indecent plainness'.

statist, statistician: 'with the cumbersome *statistician* left in sole possession'

It is puzzling why Fowler found this word 'cumbersome', given the frequency with which its accentual pattern (weak-weak-strong-weak) is used in English. And *statistic* as a noun is known in English from the end of the eighteenth century. (See his next entry.)

steam: '3. . . . All these have the accent on the second word'

This is no longer the case: words like *steam-roller* have all conformed to an initial-word pattern.

STOPS &c.: p. 566 'for *Davies* read *Davies*' (p. 566)

The insertion of a comma between the subject and the verb in such sentences is usually condemned in modern punctuation guides, notwithstanding the coordination.

'read *much—*,' (p. 571)

This kind of double punctuation mark is indeed considered 'fussy' these days, and would generally be avoided.

strategic(al): 'overwhelming preponderance for the short sound'

Fowler notes that the pronunciation with a long vowel 'is at least as often said', and this has proved to be the preferred version since.

STURDY INDEFENSIBLES: '"it's me" . . . it too will die'

Fowler was never more wrong than in his writing off this usage. On the contrary, if anything is near to death, it must be *it is I*. (See also **between**, I.)

SUBJUNCTIVES: 'ARRIVALS . . . one good reason for abstaining from it'

Given Fowler's inclination for traditional grammatical constructions, it comes as a surprise to see his general condemnation of the subjunctive. Modern approaches are not so severe, recognizing that a useful contrast of formality is involved, as illustrated by *If this was to happen* vs the more formal *If this were to happen*. American English also makes more use of the subjunctive than British English. Fowler makes no secret of his aim 'to discourage' what he calls survivals and arrivals; but a century on, the contrast expressed by the subjunctive continues to be used.

SUPERSTITIONS: 'That ungrammatical piece of nonsense'

This is Fowler at his best. The use of an introductory conjunction has been part of English since Anglo-Saxon times, and innumerable authors—not just Macaulay—have used it.

syllabize &c.: 'The best thing would be to accept the most recognized verb *syllabize*'

Usage eventually went in other directions. *Syllabify* and *syllabification* are now used far more than *syllabize* and *syllabization*, in a ratio of about 10 : 1.

-T & -ED: 'use the -t spelling in both classes'

Fowler sees this contrast as solely one of spelling and pronunciation. However, linguistic research has shown that there is a potential semantic contrast expressed by these forms. The difference is subtle, but is best explained in relation to the durational meaning of the verbs—part of what grammarians refer to as *aspect*. In such pairs of sentences as *The house burnt down*, the implication is that the event took place quite quickly, whereas *burned* is more likely in *The house burned for days*. Similarly, *I've dreamed all my life of living in Scotland* is more likely than *I dreamt all my life of living in Scotland*. It is not a hard-and-fast rule, but it does help to explain the point about frequency which Fowler mentions. *Spilt* is much more likely than *spilled* because the action of spilling is usually short. *Learned* is much more likely than *learnt* because the action of learning usually takes some time. (See also **dream**.)

tasty: 'has been displaced, except in uneducated or facetious use'

This observation surprises modern readers, for the word no longer has such restrictions, though in British English it is often informal and used in metaphorical ways (as in *tasty mortgage deals*). Corpus studies show that *tasty* is now about ten times more common than *tasteful*.

templet, -plate: 'The *-et* form is better'

Fowler is right to point to the 'false association' with *plate*, which emerged in the nineteenth century (the *OED*'s earliest reference is 1844), but false association of ideas has never stopped a usage developing, and today *templet* has dropped out of use and *template* is the norm.

that (conj.): '2. . . . the use or omission of the *t*. of a substantival clause depends partly on whether the tone is elevated or colloquial'

Fowler accurately captures the stylistic contrast in this use of *that*, anticipating such later linguistic descriptions of the contrast in terms of 'formal' vs 'informal'. The choice is not solely a stylistic one, however, for sometimes a question of intelligibility is involved. In such sentences as *I saw that the man in the brown overcoat was ready to leave*, the use of *that* helps to signal straight away that we are dealing with an object clause. If it is omitted, there is an expectation that the sentence is going in a different direction—*I saw the man in the brown overcoat*—and it is only after we get to *overcoat* that we realize what the true construction is. We then have to go back in our minds and reanalyse. Linguists sometimes call such potentially misleading constructions 'garden-path sentences', because of the way we have been led 'up the garden path'.

that (rel. pron.): '2. . . . it is a fact that the proportion of *thats* to *whichs* is far higher in speech than in writing' (p. 635)

This entry shows Fowler's sophisticated stylistic awareness. His observation is not only correct; so is his explanation, referring to the different kinds of syntactic construction found in speech compared with writing. The only point to be added, perhaps, is that considerations of euphony do sometimes promote the avoidance of one or the other, if a different use of these words is found nearby. Many writers dislike such sequences as seen in *I realize that the answer that was provided* . . . and would change the second *that* to *which*. Likewise, a change from *which* to *that* is more likely in *I don't know which of the answers which were given is the one to accept*. Fowler allows for this in his section on 'Elegant variation' under **which)(that)(who, 6**.

therefore: 'it is a matter of taste'

Fowler is right to refer this matter to the distinction between 'light punctuators' and 'heavy punctuators', but his subsequent observation is worth noting: 'the putting of a comma before *t*. inevitably has the effect of throwing a strong accent on the preceding word'. It is good advice to listen to the sound of a sentence while writing it, and to judge whether the intonational emphasis conveyed supports the intended semantic content.

-TH NOUNS: 'the suffix is no longer a living one'

But it is not completely dead either, as the facetious revival of *coolth* illustrates. First cited in 1547, it was revived in the late eighteenth century (the *OED* has a 1781 citation from Fanny Burney), and later used by such writers as Kipling, Tolkien, and Ezra Pound.

tidal: 'barbaric appearance'

It is unclear why Fowler should have so strongly objected to *tidal*. It had already developed a huge range of general and technical uses during the nineteenth century (*tidal alarm, tidal river, tidal wave, tidal boats*, and many more), and had been used by such writers as Charles Dickens, Wilkie Collins, George Eliot, and Mark Twain.

tire, tyre: 'there is nothing to be said for *tyre*'

Apart from the etymological issue, Fowler's observation that it is 'needlessly divergent' from American usage is surprising, given that in other places he is suspicious of Americanisms and at the same time willing to recognize the importance of regional differentiation (as in his entry on **synonyms**). The distinction is now standard, for American vs British English, with Canadian English showing mixed usage (*tire* predominating). Both spellings have long been present as alternates in English, but the modern British usage is a twentieth-century development, probably influenced by the use of the *tyre* spelling in the first British patent application for tyres on wheels in 1890.

tortoise: 'the pronunciation -oiz or -ois is not even given as an alternative by the OED'

It is now. The 6th edition of the *SOED* gives *-oiz* as an alternative.

transpire: 'The notorious misuse'

The meaning of 'happen' is now standard. This is another curious example where Fowler takes against a change in meaning, even though the kind of semantic shift involved (from a narrower to a broader meaning) is something that has often happened in the history of English. Perhaps he was influenced by Dr Johnson, who also disliked it. But the fact of the matter is that the word in this meaning has now established itself as a more formal alternative to *happen* or *occur*, both in British and American English (in the latter, being found in dictionaries over a hundred years ago).

tribute: '2. A SLIPSHOD EXTENSION'
Fowler's examples are indefensible. In each case, the primary sense of *tribute* ('act showing respect, admiration, etc') is perfectly possible.

try: 'It is an idiom that should not be discountenanced'
Fowler's analysis of *try and . . .* as a colloquial usage is accurate, and his drawing-out of its semantic nuances is worth noting, for these are always ignored in blanket pedantic condemnations.

turbine: 'will doubtless pass away'
Quite the opposite. 'Reverence for spelling' is a very powerful influencer of usage, and people today usually rhyme *turbine* with *mine*, though the short-vowel version is still mentioned in pronouncing dictionaries. Why Fowler feels this to be 'misguided' is unclear, given that in several other entries he fulsomely acknowledges the role of spelling in pronunciation change.

type: '5. . . . as the two words exist'
This is a nice illustration of a historical issue in the evolution of terminology. The issue was resolved very quickly, but it is interesting to learn that it was felt to be a worry in Fowler's time.

tyrannize: 'the present idiom is to *tyrannize over*, not to *tyrannize*, one's subjects'
Both forms are now used, with the latter predominant. The 6th edition of the *SOED* describes *tyrannize over* as being 'chiefly historical'.

u. '5. . . . rarely changes'
Fowler ignores the normal American usage in such words.

UNATTACHED PARTICIPLES: 'our grandsons will know' (p. 675)
They do indeed. *Due to* is now around fifty times more common than *owing to*. The example demonstrates the unreliability of Fowler's notion of 'idiom'. All dictionary definitions of *idiom* and *idiomatic* rely on a notion of wide-spread and conventional natural use among native speakers. No definition says 'among certain kinds of native speakers only'. Fowler's characterization of 'illiterates' as those 'who are unfamiliar with good writers' unduly restricts the notion of idiom, and gives it a subjective (and elitist) interpretation which is ultimately circular—for anyone who uses *due to* cannot, according to Fowler, be counted as a 'good writer'. (See also **due**.)

Despite Fowler's condemnation of 'fanatical purists' who condemn any sentence in which there is a seemingly unattached participle, he is himself open to criticism for not taking context sufficiently into account in determining whether a construction is ambiguous or not. From the opening example of this entry, it is clear that Fowler is concerned about cases where unattached participles cause ambiguity. But few of his quoted examples actually give rise to ambiguity at all. Because we know, for instance, that it has to be the pen which caused the meningitis (p. 676), and that it is impossible for the girl to have caused it, there is no conceivable ambiguity. The word order might be rhythmically inelegant, certainly—but that is a separate issue, which Fowler does not address. Nor, for that matter, do later language pundits, who inveigh against the unattached participle regardless of whether or not a semantic issue is involved.

unique: 'the adverbs that *u.* can tolerate'
Fowler is right to allow adverbs with *unique*, but his divide between the two groups is arbitrary and unsustainable. The arbitrariness can be seen in the contrast between *absolutely unique* (which he finds acceptable) and *very unique* (which he doesn't), even though both usages strongly affirm the uniqueness. And if it is possible to emphasize the uniqueness of something (as in *absolutely unique*), there is no reason why one should not de-emphasize it, by using a word which in effect says 'I think this is unique but I am not sure'. That is partly the motivation for people saying such things as *rather unique* and *somewhat unique*.

But there is another motivation, in that the meaning of the word *unique* has developed a secondary, non-absolute sense—not 'the only one of its kind' but 'a remarkable example of its kind'. This in turn allows such usages as *more unique* and *most unique* to develop. What seems to have happened, semantically, is that *unique* is now seen as part of a scale, at the top of which is the absolute ('the only one') sense. Points on this scale are selected by the use of an adverb: *absolutely unique* is equivalent to what was once simply called *unique*, and lower down we have *rather unique* and the others. The adverbs seem to be increasingly relied upon to resolve potential ambiguity. If I say, these days (e.g. referring to a stamp), *This is a unique example*, it is unclear whether I am using *unique* in the absolute or relative sense. Adverbs would clarify: *This is an absolutely unique example* vs *This is a somewhat unique example*.

us: '1. . . . if *becomes we* is thought pedantic'
It is surprising that Fowler's obsession with Latinate cases should lead him to even allow that *becomes we* is grammatical in English. His reluctance to accept the inevitable is perhaps seen in his tortuous circumlocutory negatives at the end: '*Let us Liberals at any rate be content* would not have been unbearably ordinary.'

-ve(d), -ves, &c.: 'roof. No *v* forms.'
Roof has certainly had a -*v* form—there are many examples in the Middle English period—and the analogy with *hoof/hooves* probably kept it alive. It is allowed as an alternative plural in the 6th edition of the *SOED*, for example, and a pronunciation with a /v/ is not unusual. There are 79,000 instances listed in Google (in 2008)—but nearly 10 million for *roofs*.

vend: 'a tendency to DIFFERENTIATION'
This does not seem to have taken place. The -*er* spelling is found only in American English, with perhaps a slight trend for it to be used for machines that sell things (whereas *vendor* is for people who sell things). But all varieties show the predominant use of -*or*, in any of its applications.

vertigo: 'The correct pronunciation'
The pronunciation with stress on the second syllable has now been entirely replaced by one with stress on the first. The older pronunciation receives no mention in modern dictionaries.

very: 'similarly I cannot say'
This testing of a usage in various syntactic contexts shows Fowler as close to modern linguistics as it is possible to get. The last few lines of his first paragraph could have been written by any descriptive linguist interested in grammatical acceptability, as could the criteria listed in the second paragraph. The examples of course show a gradient between the adjectival and participial constructions.

viva, vivat, vive: 'a fact forgotten'
The use of the plural would have been considered extreme pedantry even in Fowler's day. (See also **bravo, brava, bravi**.)

VOGUE-WORDS: '*nice*'
Fowler's criticism of this word reinforced the anxiety about its overuse which had been around since the late eighteenth century, and during the twentieth century it came to be virtually banned from children's school writing. It is difficult today to see the basis for Fowler's objections with reference to the other words in his list. Words evidently have a temporary vogue use and then either die out or settle down.

VULGARIZATION: 'when blundering hands are laid upon them'
Fowler perhaps realized the trap he was laying for himself, in this entry. He ends it: 'perhaps the less said here on this matter the better', and he was right. His problem is the contradiction which lies within his observation 'Vulgarization of words that should not be in common use'. For who is to decide which words should or should not be in common use? His examples do not support his fears: in a few cases, a word has died out, but *faerie* is still available to us, notwithstanding the use of *fairy*, as is *optimistic* and *hopeful* and most of the others. In all cases, it is the usage of the majority of people who have made it happen—all presumably 'blunderers', to Fowler.

WARDOUR STREET: 'mainly occupied by dealers in antique & imitation-antique furniture'
This is a fascinating insight into a past time. Today, Wardour Street reminds us primarily of film companies, leaving Fowler's interesting list of archaisms in need of a new heading.

wastage: 'not better [than *waste*]'
The two words have developed very different contexts of use, over the years. Chiefly, *waste* is countable and *wastage* uncountable. So we find *a waste of time* and *icy wastes* alongside *wastage of tissue* and *natural wastage*. In cases where both words can be used with the same collocation (*waste/wastage of natural resources*), the former tends to refer to a specific instance of the problem, whereas the latter gives more emphasis to the process taking place over time.

well (adv): 'English requires not *You were there as well as me* . . . but *You were there as well as I*'

How then can one explain the predominance of the former, then and now? Fowler misses the syntactic complexity of *as well as*. He assumes that it is a conjunction, not a preposition. However, it patterns along with *besides* and *in addition to* in most of its uses (*There were ten people in the room besides/in addition to/as well as the chairman*) so that its primary use has to be prepositional. A secondary use does indeed move *as well as* towards coordination: *The referees, as well as the players, were very tired.* But this usage is not like the usual conjunctions, as reflected in the label chosen for it by *The Comprehensive Grammar of the English Language*: 'quasi-coordinators'—a label also applied to such linking items as *rather than*, *as much as*, *if not*, and *not to say*. But even here the parallel with prepositions is strong: compare *John, as well as his friends, protested* and *John, with his friends, protested.* So if the usage is prepositional after all, the pronoun in Fowler's example is going to be *me*—which is what we find in general use today. Only people who have become oversensitized to the *I/me* distinction are likely to hypercorrect and use *I*.

well-nigh: 'only as a guess'

Fowler's guess was right. Later citations all have an associated word. But the usage seems to be dying out. The 6th edition of the *SOED* (2007) labels it as 'Now archaic and literary'.

what ever, whatever: 'should then be in two separate words'

Fowler was insistent that in interrogative or exclamatory cases there had to be a space (and also in *however* and *whichever*). But there were many examples in his day when the words were set solid, and this practice has increased since, both in British and American English. The 6th edition of the *SOED*, for example, gives pre-eminence to the solid variants, inserting 'also as two words' as an alternative. (See also **ever**.)

while (or whilst): 'is a conjunction'

Fowler treats the two forms as synonymous, which they usually are. But there are different patterns of usage depending on regional and stylistic factors. *Whilst* is very rare in American English, and in standard British English tends to be restricted to formal writing and speaking. It is hardly ever seen in the daily press or in everyday conversation. It will however be heard in some regional dialects, along with such words as *amidst*. (See also **among, amongst**.)

whisky: 'the first as the standard form'.

Today it is recognized that usage is split: whisky from Ireland and the USA is usually spelled *whiskey* (plural *whiskeys*); whisky from Scotland, Canada, and Australia is usually spelled *whisky* (plural *whiskies*). British English spelling on the whole favours *whisky*, as the generic term, regardless of where the spirit comes from, and American English favours *whiskey*.

whose: 'in the starch that stiffens English style'

One of Fowler's most memorable metaphors, used to castigate the view that '*whose* shall refer only to persons'. The prescriptive view, around since the eighteenth century, had insisted on *of which*, despite the awkwardness which often ensued (*I chose a book the cover of which was torn*). Fowler is in no doubt that *whose* is the right usage: 'good writing is surely difficult enough without the forbidding of things that have historical grammar, & present intelligibility, & obvious convenience, on their side, & lack only—starch'.

His entry does not deal with all uses of *whose*, however. In particular, he omits to point out that, when opening a question, *whose* retains its animate sense. *Whose book were you reading?* means 'Who did the book belong to?' not 'Which of the books were you reading?'

WORKING & STYLISH WORDS: 'stylish words'
Several of the words in Fowler's list have since changed their status. Some now express a sharper difference of meaning, as in the case of *catarrh/cold* and *antagonize/oppose*. Some have become associated with stylistically restricted varieties, such as *angle* (in the sport of angling). Some have simply become standard working usage, as with *violin*, where *fiddle* is now the stylistically special form. A number, however, do still retain the same kind of stylishness that Fowler disliked, such as *assist* and *dwell*. (See also **GENTEELISM**.)

workless: 'something shorter is wanted'
The brevity demanded by headlines has motivated several stylistic developments in English. Why Fowler should be opposed to this feature of newspaper language isn't clear.

WORN-OUT HUMOUR: 'we feel a bitterness'
There are signs of a Fowlerian sense of humour in several of his entries—but not in this one. Boredom rather than bitterness is the emotion more likely to be generated by humour when it is genuinely 'worn out'. Many of the examples he cites are now unintelligible, without special historical knowledge. However, some of them hardly fit his description. The *Hamlet* parody, for example, is still alive and well, and frequently to be seen in contemporary writing, showing that people still find new applications appealing.

worth)(worth while: '*This is worth while*'
The standard spelling today is to print the words solid, as *worthwhile*. This usage developed steadily during the twentieth century. Fowler's support for *worth while* and (in attributive position) *worth-while* influenced several later usage writers (such as Ernest Gowers), and this usage retains favour among those who follow the style manuals. But *worthwhile* is now by far the most common in both British and American English—eight times as frequent as *worth while* on Google (in 2008).

wrath, wrathful, wroth: 'It is very desirable that differentiation should be clearly established.'
Fowler's desire to use *wroth* as an adjectival form was already being ignored in his day, as he recognizes. It ceased to be used soon after. The *OED*'s latest quotation is 1883.

write: '*I will write you soon* . . . is not [idiomatic]'
Why 'must' the person being written to be introduced by *to*? Fowler gives no reason, other than to assert it is not 'idiomatic'. But if idiomaticness is a function of widespread usage, then this assertion will not stand. The omission of

to in adverbial contexts has long been a feature of formal and informal American English and has been increasing in British English.

-x: 'It is to be hoped that some day all of these . . . will be anglicized with -s'
There is little sign of this happening, a century on, apart from *portmanteaus*, as these Google searches (2008) suggest, though the totals under *plateaux* are interesting:

adieux	1.8 million	adieus	84,000
beaux	28 million	beaus	282,000
chateaux	7.6 million	chateaus	335,000
flambeaux	445,000	flambeaus	10,000
plateaux	3.9 million	plateaus	1.8 million
portmanteaux	21,000	portmanteaus	42,000
rondeaux	113,000	rondeaus	9,000
rouleaux	1.5 million	rouleaus	7,000
trousseaux	52,000	trousseaus	12,000

yᵉ: 'The pronunciation of this is the, not ye'
Historically, Fowler is correct; but he ignores the dominant usage, which is in fact 'ye'. Although largely facetious, the pronunciation illustrates the way that people are much more likely to follow the spelling of a word rather than its etymology.

zinc: 'The forms *zinced* & *zincing* are obviously wrong'
They certainly do not follow the usual spelling rules, so that Fowler's recommendation of *zincking* (perhaps, *pace* his view, better than *zinked*) has a certain appeal. But the meaning and pronunciation of the word *zinc* is so clear-cut that the problem seems to be purely a theoretical one. Dictionaries generally give *zinced*, etc. without comment.